P9-EEL-968

c. 485–c. 380 B.C.)
–399 B.C.)
———— Plato (c. 427–347 B.C.)
———————— Aristotle (384–322 B.C.)
———————————— Pyrrho (c. 360–270 B.C.)
of the fifth century B.C.)   Perictione II (c. 300–c. 100 B.C.)
                  • Diogenes Laertius (third century B.C.)
                                              Sextus Empiricus (second–third centuries A.D.) •   ———— Plotinus (c. 204–270)
c.)   ———— St. Augustine (354–430)
nocritus (460–370 B.C.)   Hypatia of Alexandria (370/75–415 A.D.) ——

–399 B.C.)   ———— Seneca the Elder (c. 60 B.C.–A.D. 37)
———— Aristippus (435–350 B.C.)   ———— Seneca the Younger (c. 4 B.C.–A.D. 65)
———— Plato (c. 427–347 B.C.)   ———— Epictetus (A.D. 60–117)
ogenes (fourth century B.C.)   ———— Marcus Aurelius (121–180)
———————— Aristotle (384–322 B.C.)   ———— St. Augustine (354–430)
——————————— Epicurus (341–270 B.C.)
——————————— Zeno of Citium (334–262 B.C.)
———————————— Cleanthes (331–232 B.C.)
•Aesara (c. 350 B.C.)

———— Plato (c. 427–347 B.C.)
———————— Aristotle (384–322 B.C.)
•Aesara (c. 350 B.C.)   ———— Cicero (106–43 B.C.)
                                                                              ———— St. Augustine (354–430)

ng Tzu (c. fourth century B.C.)
——————————— Mencius (371–289 B.C.)   Hui Neng (638–713) ————

(Continued on back endpaper)

PHILOSOPHY

The Power of Ideas

PHILOSOPHY

The Power of Ideas

THIRD EDITION

Brooke Noel Moore • Kenneth Bruder

California State University, Chico

with contributions by

Ellen Fox
Illinois Institute of Technology

Greg Tropea
California State University, Chico

Mary Ellen Waithe
Cleveland State University

Mayfield Publishing Company
Mountain View, California
London • Toronto

Library of Congress Cataloging-in-Publication Data

Moore, Brooke Noel.
    Philosophy : the power of ideas / Brooke Noel Moore, Kenneth
Bruder ; with contributions by Ellen Fox, Greg Tropea, Mary Ellen
Waithe. — 3rd ed.
        p.   cm.
    Includes index.
    ISBN 1-55934-519-5
    1. Philosophy—Introductions.   2. Philosophy—History.
I. Bruder, Kenneth.   II. Fox, Ellen.   III. Title.
BD21.M62   1995b
100—dc20   95-25338
                                                                 CIP

Manufactured in the United States of America

10 9 8 7 6 5 4 3 2 1

Mayfield Publishing Company
1280 Villa Street
Mountain View, CA 94041

Sponsoring editor, James Bull; production editor, April Wells-Hayes; manuscript
editor, Beverley J. DeWitt; text and cover designer, Nancy Benedict; art manager,
Robin Mouat; illustrator, Kevin Opstedal; art director, Jeanne M. Schreiber;
cover image, The Image Bank/Garry Gay; photo researcher, Brian Pecko; manufacturing manager, Amy Folden. The text was set in 9.5/12 Stone Serif by
Thompson Type and printed in black and PMS 286 on 45# Miami Satin Thin
by The Maple-Vail Book Manufacturing Group.

Acknowledgments and copyrights continue at the back of the book on pages
741–743, which constitute an extension of the copyright page.

To Linda Moore, Kathryn Dupier Bruder, and Albert Bruder

Preface

This edition of *The Power of Ideas* contains some marvelous new features, including, especially, significant contributions by Mary Ellen Waithe and Gregory Tropea. Professor Waithe, a leading authority on women in the history of philosophy, has integrated women philosophers into the text from the Pre-Socratics forward; Professor Tropea has added a splendid chapter on post-colonial philosophy with excerpts from Martin Luther King, Jr., Mahatma Gandhi, Kwasi Wiredu, bell hooks, Vine Deloria, Jr., and others. Both additions are fully in keeping with our basic theme: that philosophy is powerful stuff.

Also, Ellen Fox has updated her chapter on feminist philosophy, incorporating material (from the *Brief Second Edition*) on feminist epistemology. We've also included an excerpt from J. J. Thomson's classic, "A Defense of Abortion," as well as a fine piece by Nicholas Rescher on the status of American philosophy today. We've made a lot of little changes and done some fine-tuning, too, and added some fresh boxes. We've also included a fairly detailed chronology of important events to help readers locate philosophical developments in the broader context of human history.

Despite the alterations, this book is still a straightforward, ungimmicky historical introduction to philosophy. Unlike other historical texts, though, it is topically subdivided. You'll find it contains separate historical overviews of the major branches of philosophy—these topical subdivisions help readers keep similar concepts together and help instructors avoid leaving the impression that philosophy is a parade of unconnected speculations. Basically, the book represents something of a middle road between the two traditional approaches to philosophy, the historical approach and the "problems" approach.

Features

- A truly broad coverage of philosophy, including a topically subdivided history of Western philosophy, important philosophies-of-subject, the analytic and Continental traditions, Eastern philosophy, feminist philosophy, and post-colonial philosophy
- Recognition of specific contributions of women to philosophy throughout its history
- A generous supply of original readings that won't overwhelm beginning students with their difficulty

- Boxes that highlight important concepts and principles and distinctions or contain interesting anecdotes or historical asides
- Biographical profiles of many of the great philosophers
- End-of-chapter checklists of key philosophers and concepts, with mini-summaries of the philosophers' leading ideas
- End-of-chapter questions for review and reflection, and lists of additional sources
- A glossary that, with over two hundred entries, is a reasonably complete brief compendium of philosophical concepts, distinctions, and theories
- Appendixes on logic, truth, and knowledge, and a pronunciation guide to the names of philosophers
- A brief subsection on American Constitutional theory
- A detailed instructor's manual containing point-by-point chapter summaries, lists of boxes, lists of reading selections (with brief description of contents), names of philosophers' main works, lecture ideas relating to questions asked at ends of chapters, and a complete bank of objective test questions, as well as a chronology of important events in world history and the evolution of consciousness

Women in the History of Philosophy

Histories of philosophy make scant mention of women philosophers prior to the twentieth century. For a long time it was assumed that this lack was because there just weren't many women who were influential as philosophers. Recent scholarship, however, such as that by Mary Ellen Waithe (*A History of Women Philosophers*) suggests that women have been considerably more important in the history of philosophy than has been assumed. Their contributions, as Waithe has argued and as now seems clear, have for generations been edited by teachers and commentators who applied conscious and unconscious gender-based standards of merit.

For example, Diotima traditionally has been regarded as a fictional character devised by Plato for his dialogue *Symposium*. However, contemporary scholarship discloses strong (but not incontrovertible) evidence that Diotima was an actual philosopher. Waithe has argued that Diotima became fictional partially as a result of a fifteenth-century scholar's remark that it would be absurd to suppose a woman would have been a philosopher, and partially as result of such gender-based notions as that Socrates couldn't have learned anything from a woman and Plato would never have cast a woman in a central role in the *Symposium*.

To date we lack full-length translations and modern editions of the works of women philosophers. Until this situation changes, Waithe has argued, it is difficult accurately to reconstruct the history of the discipline.

We don't claim that this text fully acknowledges the contributions of women to the history of philosophy. We hope, though, that it represents at least a small step in the proper direction.

Philosophy: A Worldwide Search for Wisdom and Understanding

Until the middle of the twentieth century, few philosophers and historians of ideas in American and European universities accepted the proposition that philosophical reflection occurred outside that tradition of disciplined discourse which began with the ancient Greeks and has continued on into the present. This narrow conception of philosophy has been changing, however, first through the interest in Eastern thought, especially Zen Buddhism, in the fifties, then through the increasingly widespread publication of high-quality translations and commentaries of texts from outside the Western tradition in the following decades. But—and here is the crux of the matter for some thinkers—the availability of such texts does not mean that unfamiliar ideas will receive a careful hearing or that they will receive any hearing at all.

Among the most challenging threads of the worldwide philosophical conversation is what has come to be known in recent years as post-colonial thought. The lines defining this way of thinking are not always easy to draw—but the same could be said for existentialism, phenomenology, and a number of other schools of thought in philosophy. The point is that in many cultures and sub-cultures around the world, thinkers are asking searching questions about methodology and fundamental beliefs that are intended to have practical, political consequences. Because these thinkers frequently intend their work to be revolutionary, their ideas run a higher-than-usual risk of being lost to philosophy's traditional venues, either by intentional disregard or by unconsciously biased reading. In any case, we hope that our inclusion of the work of a range of post-colonial writers from around the world will give readers a taste of how these thinkers expand the horizons of consciousness by focusing on some very specific issues.

Philosophy—Powerful Stuff

We concluded many years ago that most people like philosophy if they understand it, and most understand it if it isn't presented to them in exhausting prose. In this text we strive above all else to make philosophy understandable while not over-simplifying.

But we also concluded many years ago that some people just aren't moved by the subject. Worse, we learned that among those who aren't are a few who are sane, intelligent, well informed, and reasonable and who have generally sound ideas about the world, vote for the right people, and are even worth having as friends. Philosophy, we learned, just isn't for everyone, and no text and no instructor can make it so.

So we don't expect that every student, or even every bright student, who comes in contact with philosophy will necessarily love the field.

But we do hope that every student who has had an introductory course in philosophy will learn that philosophy is more than so much inconsequential mental flexing. Philosophy contains powerful ideas, and it affects the lives of real people. Consequently it must be handled with due care. The text makes this point clear.

Acknowledgments

For their help and support in various forms we want to thank, first, friends and colleagues at California State University, Chico: Maryanne Bertram, Cathy Brooks, Judy Collins, Frank Ficarra, Esther Gallagher, Ron Hirschbein, David Hull, Alexandra Kiriakis, Scott Mahood, Greg Maxwell, Clifford Minor, Adrian Mirvish, Anne Morrissey, Richard Parker, Michael Rich, Dennis Rothermel, Robert Stewart, Greg Tropea, Alan Walworth, Eric Gampel, Tony Graybosch, Tom Imhoff, Jim Oates, and Marianne Larson.

Also, for their wise and helpful comments on the manuscript, we thank David Adams, California State Polytechnic, Pomona; Sue Armstrong-Buck, Humboldt State University; Edward Bloomfield, Cerritos College; David Boyer, St. Cloud State University; M. C. Bradley, Sam Houston State University; Frank Bruno, San Bernardino Valley College; M. Ange Cooksey, Ball State University; David Cope, Grand Rapids Junior College; Robert Ferrell, University of Texas, El Paso; James P. Friel, SUNY, Farmingdale; Ann Garry, California State University, Los Angeles; Raymond Herbenick, University of Dayton; Craig Ihara, California State University, Fullerton; Richard J. Jones, Jr., Romulus, Minnesota; Jacqueline Kegley, California State University, Bakersfield; Clysta Kinstler, American River College; Wesley Kobylak, Monroe Community College; Thomas Leddy, San Jose State University; John Marran, Delaware County Community College; Ed McCraby, Midlands Technical College, Columbia, South Carolina; Chet Meyers, Metropolitan State University, Minneapolis; Michael Morden, University of Michigan, Dearborn; Mary D. Morton, Gaston College; Thomas Nenon, Memphis State University; Don Porter, College of San Mateo; Joan Price, Mesa Community College; Leonard Riforgiato, Pennsylvania State University, Shenango Campus; Dennis Rohatyn, University of San Diego; John Sallstrom, Georgia College; Minerva San Juan, George Mason University; Tom Satre, Sam Houston State University; Martin Schonfeld, Indiana University; William Springer, University of Texas, El Paso; and Mark Williamson, Southwest Texas State University.

And we wish to express our gratitude to the Mayfield staff: April Wells-Hayes, Jim Bull, Pam Trainer, Uyen Phan, and Beverley DeWitt.

Very special thanks are due to the late Ralph J. Moore, the father of Brooke Moore, for his detailed and painstaking commentary on several chapters of the original text; to Betty Ames for her kind permission to use Van Meter Ames's metaphor of philosophy as explosive and dangerous material; to Dan Barnett for his work on the Instructor's Manual and for substantial contributions to the chapters on philosophy of religion and Continental philosophy; to Ellen Fox for her chapter on feminist philosophy; to Gregory Tropea for his chapter on post-colonial philosophy; to Mary Ellen Waithe, for helping us recognize at least some of the important women in the history of philosophy; and to Emerine Glowienka for helping us with Aquinas's metaphysics.

The next century glimmers with promises: space trips to Mars, world peace, cures for cancer and old age, fat-free strawberry Ho-Hos. If this text does not deliver on its promises, please blame Moore or Bruder and none of the individuals mentioned above.

Contents

PART 4

Philosophy of Religion: Reason and Faith   421

13   God in the Age of Science   458

Part 4   Summary and Conclusion   492

PART 7

Eastern and Post-Colonial Philosophy   585

16   The Path of Right Living   587

Dangerous Stuff

Beware when the great God lets loose a thinker on this planet. Then all things are at risk.

—Emerson

I do not know how to teach philosophy without becoming a disturber of the peace.

—Baruch Spinoza

There are two powers in the world, the sword and the mind. In the long run, the sword is always beaten by the mind.

—Napoleon

What I understand by "philosopher": a terrible explosive in the presence of which everything is in danger.

—Friedrich Nietzsche

Better to be on a runaway horse than to be a woman who does not reflect.

—Theano of Crotona

For a revolution you need more than economic problems and guns. You need a philosophy. Wars are founded on a philosophy, or on efforts to destroy one. Communism, capitalism, fascism, atheism, humanism, Marxism—all are philosophies. Philosophies give birth to civilizations. They also end them.

The philosophy department works with high explosives, Van Meter Ames liked to say. It handles dangerous stuff. This book is an introduction to philosophy. From it you will learn, among other things, why philosophy, as Ames said, is dynamite.

You will also see that philosophy is foundational to many other disciplines. What yesterday was called philosophy today is often called psychology or government or physics or some other subject, or even just plain common sense. Many of the basic concepts you have come from philosophy, maybe more so than from physics or psychology or biology or sociology or any other field. Whether it's a concept about the way the world is, or about the way people are or should be, or about what is and can be known, or about what's right and wrong and beautiful

Why Should You Want to Study Philosophy?

One answer, anyway, comes from the ancient philosopher Perictione II (lived c. 300–100 B.C.), who is classified as a Pythagorean philosopher. (You'll read about the Pythagoreans in Chapter 2.) Perictione II believed there is but one basic principle (*harmonia*) governing the universe. Philosophers, she believed, who are lovers of wisdom, try to understand all things in terms of this single principle. When you possess such wisdom, she maintained, you are close to catching sight of god. For lots of people, that's a good enough motive to learn philosophy.

Here is a brief quotation (edited slightly) from the surviving fragment of Perictione II's work, *Sophias,* or *On Wisdom:*

Humans came into being and exist in order to contemplate the principle of the nature of the whole. The function of wisdom is to possess this very thing, and to contemplate the purpose of the things that are . . . Wisdom is concerned with all that is, just as sight is concerned with all that is visible and hearing with all that is audible. . . .

It is appropriate to wisdom to be able to see and to contemplate those attributes which belong universally to all things . . . wisdom searches for the basic principle of all the things that are, natural science for the principles of natural things, while geometry and arithmetic and music are concerned with quantity and the harmonious.

Therefore, whoever is able to analyze all the kinds of being by reference to one basic principle, and, in turn, from this principle to synthesize and enumerate the different kinds, this person seems to be the wisest and most true and, moreover, to have discovered a noble height from which to see god and all the things separated from god in seried rank and order.

Incidentally, Perictione II shouldn't be confused with Perictione I, who was Plato's mother—and also a writer. "Perictione" was a common woman's name in ancient Greece.

and ugly—at bottom, it's in large part philosophy. Other fields fill in the details, but the basic conceptual framework is mostly pure philosophy. Even the Judaeo-Christian concept of God we are familiar with today owes much to philosophy—as you will see.

So the questions philosophers raise can strike right at the foundations of what we think and do and claim to know—and can send tremors through our entire edifice of beliefs.

Philosophy once encompassed nearly everything that counted as human knowledge. Among the ancient Greeks nearly every subject that is currently listed in college catalogues was or would have been considered philosophy. One by one, these intellectual enterprises gained sufficient maturity and stature to stand alone as separate subjects. Mathematics, rhetoric, physics, biology, government, politics, law—all once fell under the general heading of philosophy.

The word *philosophy,* as every introductory book on the subject tells us, comes from the two Greek words *philein,* which means "to love," and *sophia,* which means "knowledge" or "wisdom." Because knowledge can be discovered in many fields, the Greeks thought of any person who sought knowledge in any area as a philosopher.

Consider physics for a moment. One of the first known Greek philosophers, Thales, was actually doing what we might call speculative physics (in contrast to experimental physics) when he claimed that everything in the natural world was made of water. Two other ancient Greeks, Leucippus and Democritus, arrived at the conclusion that all matter was made from tiny particles—atoms—that were similar except for their size and shape, but that accounted for differences in larger bodies by means of their different arrangements.

Should we think of these early thinkers as physicists or philosophers? The Greeks had no difficulty answering this question, because they thought of physics as a part of philosophy. And this view of physics persisted for over two thousand years. The full title of Isaac Newton's *Principles,* in which Newton set forth his famous theories of mechanics, mathematics, and astronomy, is *Mathematical Principles of Natural Philosophy.* Physics, even by the seventeenth century, was still thought of as a variety of philosophy. By the twentieth century, however, physics had outgrown the nest and, though it still has important points of contact, is no longer considered a part of philosophy. Similar stories can be told for each of the disciplines listed a couple of paragraphs back.

If philosophy can no longer claim those subject areas that have grown up and moved out, what's left for it to claim? As you'll see by the end of this book, the current list of philosophical subjects is by no means short and discloses the deep and wide concern of philosophy for some very important questions about the universe, the earth, humankind and all life, and each of us. Just what is this concern? What is philosophy today?

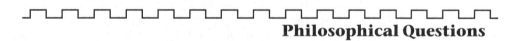

Philosophical Questions

Mathematics, the physical and biological sciences, economics and political science, and the full array of existing intellectual disciplines, including theology, leave unanswered in part some of the most important and fundamental questions a person can ask.

- What is truth?
- Is it possible to know anything with absolute certainty?   Consciousness
- Does the universe have a purpose? Does life have a purpose?
- Is there order in the cosmos independent of what is put there by the mind? Could the universe be radically different from how we conceive it?
- Is a person more than a physical body? What is the mind? What is thought?
- Do people really have free will?
- What is art? What is beauty?
- What is moral obligation? What is the extent of our moral obligation to other people and other living things?

- What kind of person should I be?
- What are the ethically legitimate functions and scope of the state? What is its proper organization?
- Is there a God?
- What difference does it make if there is or isn't a God?

Perhaps it's possible to go through life and never spend a minute wondering about such questions. But most of us have at least occasional moments of reflection about one or another of them. In fact, it's really pretty difficult *not* to think philosophically from time to time. For one thing, it's just plain *boring* always to be thinking and talking about everyday affairs and objects—say, shopping, for instance. (Do you like to shop? Fine. So do we, sometimes. But do you want to spend *all* your time thinking and talking about it?) And what's more, any time we think or talk about a topic long enough, if our thinking or discussion is the least bit organized, we may well become engaged in philosophy.

As an example, let's just take shopping. If, while shopping, you have ever taken a break for a soft drink or a cup of coffee, some conscientious person may have observed that the Styrofoam cup you are drinking from is manufactured by a process that contributes to the breakdown of the ozone layer and unnecessarily contributes to a rise in skin cancer. You, in return, may have said, or at least have thought, that what *you* as an individual do is not going to have much of an effect on the Styrofoam industry or the fast-food business or the ozone layer. But by this time you're no longer thinking or talking about a cup of Diet Pepsi; you're pondering a matter of moral obligation, one of ethical philosophy.

Unfortunately, when people get to this point in their thinking or conversation, they often just stop. They don't know what to think or say next in the matter.

Or, to take another example of philosophy lurking in a situation, if you've seen any science fiction movies, it may have occurred to you to wonder whether a robot really could feel emotions, as the robots in the movies seem to do. Could a robot feel an emotion as we do? It's just a machine—but is there anything about feelings that says they couldn't be experienced by the right kind of robot? Perhaps your opinion is that robots can't have feelings. Well, *why* couldn't they? Is it because robots are not made out of the right kind of *stuff,* the kind of organic stuff that you and we are made of? But intelligent beings from other galaxies might also not be made out of the same kind of stuff as you and we, and could still have feelings, we suppose. So why couldn't robots, if they were sufficiently complex? Is it because robots couldn't have a soul? Because they couldn't be alive? Well, *why couldn't* they? What, for that matter, is a *soul?* What is it to be *alive?*

Now, each of the questions posed in the last paragraph is a philosophical question, and each is the kind of question a thoughtful person might be inclined to ask after seeing a science fiction movie—or after listening to some enthusiast make predictions for computers. In later chapters we'll consider just such questions, for this process of analyzing and trying to answer such questions is the task of philosophers.

People scarcely ever want to philosophize. But whenever their thinking is at all organized, they may well be engaged in philosophy—though they are probably not aware of the fact.

You're wondering, maybe, just what makes these questions—or any other philosophical question—*philosophical?* Unfortunately, no very precise definition of *philosophical question,* or of *philosophy* itself, that is satisfactory to many philosophy teachers has ever been formulated. True, the definition of philosophy as the love or pursuit of wisdom is widely circulated, but this is altogether too vague and general to be particularly helpful. Do you know of any discipline that doesn't pursue wisdom in one way or another?

The problem is that what philosophy *is* is itself a philosophical issue, and the issue hasn't yet been settled. It's like asking, What is art?—another philosophical question that has not been answered to the satisfaction of very many philosophers.

One important feature of philosophical questions is that they can't be answered just by looking around—that is, by the discovery of some fact or collection of facts. Philosophy, in other words, is not an empirical science. That part of the wisdom business has now been turned over to physics, chemistry, and the rest of the sciences. Of course, facts are often *relevant* to a philosophical question, but they cannot by themselves provide us with an answer. What observable "fact" would settle whether a robot could feel pain? Clearly, no fact by itself will do: the problem must be approached in some other way.

Many philosophical questions concern norms. **Normative** questions ask about the value of something. The sciences are interested in finding out how things *are,* but they cannot tell us how things *ought* to be. When we decide that this or that is good or bad, right or wrong, beautiful or ugly, we are applying ethical or aesthetic norms, which are standards of one kind or another. How can we establish that doing one thing is morally acceptable whereas doing something else is morally wrong? Does it just *strike* us that way? Is it what the majority of people in one's society thinks that determines the issue? Is some *feature* of the action right or wrong, or is it the *consequences* of the action? What *is* morally right, anyway? All these are philosophical questions, and nearly any answer to each is based on a commitment to some kind of ethical theory or principle. To many people, indeed, philosophy *is* ethics, and even though that's not correct—many philosophical questions have nothing to do with ethics—there's no denying that ethics is important stuff. People may *kill* you if they think it's morally right to do so.

Often, too, philosophers ask questions about things that seem so obvious we might not wonder about them—for example, *the nature of change,* an issue within that branch of philosophy known as metaphysics. What is change? Perhaps that seems a strange thing to ask because in a way we all know what change is. If something changes, it becomes different. But then—and here's the problem—if we have a different thing after the change, then we are considering *two* things, the original thing and the new and different thing. If something changes, then it is different from the way it was, and if it is different, then is it the same thing?

Further, if after the change we have a new thing, then were we wrong to speak of the original thing as "changing"? Wasn't the original thing in fact "replaced" rather than changed? Isn't there only replacement of, rather than change in, things, and so only continuous replacements, rather than changes, of the universe, of the earth, and of each of us?

Here you may suspect that an easy solution is at hand. When something changes, it need not become *entirely* different. It may change only in this or that respect. Or it may retain many of its original constituents or features. Suppose a thing retains a lot of its original features or constituents. Then, if only a few other of its features or constituents change, it will still be the same thing. It will now have some different features or constituents, true, but it won't be a different thing.

Unfortunately, this solution is not wholly satisfactory, and, in addition, it leads to further mystery. It is not satisfactory because some things *do* change entirely—that is, in all respects. An old oak, for example, and the tiny seedling from which it grew are the same tree, yet the old oak is in no respect like the seedling, and none of the molecules that existed in the seedling needs to be present in the old oak. When he was a child, one of the authors found an ugly green sluglike little thing that, after a while, became a beautiful butterfly that in no way resembled the thing it had been originally.

Granted, the oak and the seedling (and the butterfly and the larva) are thought to be unfoldings of the same *genetic pattern:* the oak, as Aristotle would say, is the actualization of the potential in the seedling. But does this thought help us understand how it can be said of *two* things that are entirely different, both in features and even in constituents, that they are *one?*

That easy solution mentioned here also leads to a further mystery, for even if it explains how a thing can change, it leaves us puzzling about how a thing's *features* may change. If a thing's changing is to be understood in terms of some of its features becoming different, then how is a feature's changing to be understood?

The problem of change leads to other difficult philosophical questions. For example, is the man who committed a heinous deed, perhaps as a child, the same person as an adult and as such still to be looked upon with horror or censure? Of course, we think of him as still John Doe, or whatever his name is. But is this

Monday.

Contemporary American Philosophical Concerns

University of Pittsburgh philosophy professor Nicholas Rescher has compiled the following general list of contemporary American philosophical issues:

- ethical issues in the various professions (medicine, business, law, etc.)

- computer issues: artificial intelligence, can machines think?, the epistemology of information processing

- rationality and its ramifications

- social implications of medical technology (abortion, euthanasia, right to life, medical research issues, informed consent)

- feminist issues

- social and economic justice, distributive policies, equality of opportunity, human rights

- truth and meaning in mathematics and formalized languages

- the merits and demerits of skepticism and relativism regarding knowledge and morality

- the nature of personhood and the rights and obligations of persons

- issues in the history of philosophy

Two "Philosophical" Questions

What comes to mind for many people, when they think of philosophy and of philosophical questions, is either or both of these inquiries: "Which came first, the chicken or the egg?" and "If there's nobody around, does a tree falling in a forest make a sound?"

The first question is not particularly philosophical and, in the light of evolution, is not even especially difficult: the egg came first.

The second question is often supposedly resolved by distinguishing between sound viewed as the mental experience of certain waves contacting certain sensory organs and sound as the waves themselves. If sensory organs are absent, it is said, there can be no sound-as-experience, but there can still be sound-as-waves. Philosophy, however, asks not simply whether a tree falling in the forest makes a sound if no one is there, but rather, *If nobody is there, is there*

even a forest? Is there even a universe? In other words, the question, for philosophers, is whether things depend for their existence on being perceived, and if so, how we know that. A somewhat similar question (equally philosophical) is debated by contemporary astrophysicists, who wonder whether the universe and its laws require the presence of intelligent observers for their existence.

philosophically correct, in that the chemical and physical constituents of the child's body and brain may have been completely replaced by new material and his mind by new mental elements, whatever the "elements" of the mind really are? Has the child not indeed been replaced? And if so, can his guilt possibly pertain to his replacement?

These considerations suggest also that the problem of change, of whether what we call change is really replacement, is not merely an unimportant question of semantics. For what is at stake is whether the man did indeed do the awful deed. It's pretty hard to see how whether he did or did not is simply a matter of semantics.

Here again you can see why it might be said that philosophy lies right at the foundation of thought. Practically everything we think—and do—depends on our understanding of what it is for things to change.

Sometimes philosophical questions come to light when our beliefs seem to conflict with one another. Let's take a look at a question of this sort, this time considering the matter in a bit more detail.

We would be willing to wager a rather large sum of money that you believe people should be held accountable for what they do voluntarily. If you choose to drink and then you choose to drive and you end up killing someone, well, you are to blame because your actions were voluntary.

We'd bet you would also say that when someone chooses to do something, he or she chooses it because he or she wants to do it, or at least wants to do it more than he or she wants not to do it. True, we often choose to do what we think is right even though doing so sometimes isn't pleasant. But still, when we do this, it is because we want to do what is right.

We'd bet on something else, too. We'd bet that, after considering the matter, you will concede that a person is not responsible for having the wants he or she has. You do not yourself cause or create your wants. You do not yourself determine what you like or desire. We, for example, Moore and Bruder, wanted to write this book, but we didn't *cause* ourselves to want to write it. And you—do you like reading this book? If you do, would you say that you *caused* yourself to like to read it? Or, if you hate it, would you say that you *made* yourself hate it? We'd bet your answer to both questions is "no." Our wants, desires, preferences, likes, and so on all seem to be something *we just have*. They are not things we *made* ourselves have.

So it seems, then, that our wants are not our doing. And it also seems that we shouldn't be held responsible for what is not our doing. But it also seems that our wants determine what we choose to do. So how can we be held responsible for what we choose to do? Does this make sense? If, in other words, our voluntary acts are the result of what we want to do, but we can't be held responsible for what we want to do, how can we be held responsible for our voluntary acts?

"Interesting," you may be thinking, "but unconvincing, because we *are* responsible for what we want." After all, we can determine our wants, if we feel like it. Consider, for instance, someone who doesn't like vegetables. He may decide that it would be nice to like vegetables, and he may then set about acquiring this new want by telling himself how good vegetables are, by forcing himself to eat them, or by mixing them with something he does like, say, jelly. Ultimately he may succeed in acquiring a taste for the straight goods.

Notice, though, that when you examine a case like this carefully, it seems that what the person has done is only this: he has talked to himself about how good vegetables are and has made himself eat them. But whether those actions had the effect he hoped for—namely, instilling a fondness for vegetables—is something

Are Philosophical Questions Unanswerable?

Philosophical questions are unanswerable and philosophy never makes any progress. If you haven't heard someone say that already, you will sooner or later.

Therefore you should know this: though many philosophical questions have not been *answered,* that a question is truly *unanswerable* would be considered by many philosophers a reason for abandoning the question.

As for progress, you should remember that it is not easily defined. It is probably not true in any case that progress occurs only when questions are answered. Questions can also be clarified.

They can be subdivided or abandoned. They can be discovered to rest on confusions or to be unanswerable. All this is progress, according to most conceptions of progress. For that matter, if earlier answers to a question are seen to be inadequate, that constitutes progress even if the question has not been finally answered.

Finally, notice that it isn't entirely clear in the first place just what counts as progress or as an answer to a question. As a matter of fact, what does count is itself a question of philosophy.

Another idea some people have is that as soon as any head-

way is made in a philosophical inquiry, the matter is abandoned to (or becomes) another field of learning. True, as mentioned at the beginning of the chapter, many disciplines that are relatively independent of philosophy today had their origin within philosophy. But philosophy does not always relegate to some other discipline subjects in which clear progress has been made.

To take the most obvious example, *logic*—despite an enormous expansion in scope, complexity, and explanatory power, especially during the last hundred years—is still a branch of philosophy.

---

beyond his control. Those actions might have made him positively detest vegetables, too, and if they had, that wouldn't have been his doing, either.

Or, to take a different example, let's say that Harold likes wine a bit too much and gets counseling in hopes of ridding himself of this problem. Suppose, then, that Harold does what his counselor prescribes, and the therapy is successful: he no longer craves wine quite as much as he did earlier. But is this *Harold's* doing? He followed his counselor's advice, yes, but whether her advice *would actually work* is not something *Harold* could control.

So, when you look closely at cases in which we appear to cause ourselves to change our wants or desires, what happens is that we do certain things, perhaps hoping that the result will be an alteration of our likes and preferences. Whether the hoped-for alteration takes place, however, is arguably not our doing.

Let's apply these considerations to a concrete case. Do you smoke? If you do, you may well regret ever having started. And if you are like most of us, you may be inclined to suppose that it was *your fault* that you took up smoking. You may say, "I have only myself to blame, after all. No one forced me to keep lighting up those first times, and I knew very well I might get hooked."

But is this correct? Is it really *your fault*? Consider. You kept lighting up those first times because you wanted to, certainly. It's unlikely that it was the flavor or effect of cigarette smoke that made you keep smoking at first. More likely it was that you wanted to be like your friends. In any case, you wanted to smoke more than you wanted not to smoke, and it was because of this that you kept lighting up. And it was because you kept lighting up that you are now an addicted smoker.

Now because, apparently, it was due to your wants that you ultimately became a smoker, then, if you aren't responsible for having those wants, it doesn't seem that *you* are to blame for having gotten hooked. Are you responsible for having had those wants? Assuming that you kept smoking because you wanted to be like your friends, did you *cause* yourself to have this want? Did you *make* yourself have a desire to be like your friends? Did you *create* within yourself this fondness for being like them?

When the question is posed this way, it doesn't seem completely plausible to suppose that you did create your wants. *You* didn't make yourself desire to be like your friends, just as we, the authors, didn't make ourselves want to write philosophy texts. Having these wants just happened to us, and wanting to be like your friends just happened to you.

Still, it may occur to you that, when you kept lighting up there at first, you were *giving in* to your wants and *allowing* yourself to be governed by your desire to be like your friends (or whatever). And therefore you *are* to blame for having become hooked because it was you who gave in to your wants.

But notice that even if you did give in to your wants, then you did so because you wanted to more than you wanted not to. So again we trace your actions back to a set of wants that it seems implausible to suppose you created.

Perhaps by now it's clear that what's really at stake here is a profoundly important and basic question: *Are we ever really to blame for what we do?* This is a philosophical question, one that comes to light because some of our beliefs seem not to get along so well together. On the one hand, it seems that we are to blame for what we choose to do. On the other, if what we choose to do is the result of our wants, and if we aren't to blame for our wants, then how *can* we be to blame for what we choose to do?

Let's conclude this discussion by turning to something a bit more important than cigarettes or wine. Let's talk about one Ted Bundy, who was executed in 1989 in Florida for having committed several brutal rape-murders. Bundy was not found insane: presumably he knew the difference between right and wrong, and knew that what he was doing was wrong. Why did he do what he did? Ultimately, he did what he did because he wanted to do it more than he wanted not to. His actions resulted from what he wanted to do.

But now, *if* this wanting to do it more than wanting not to do it is not something Bundy could be blamed for, then can he really be blamed for what he did? And can he be blamed for wanting to do it more than wanting not to do it, if we do not create our wants?

The basic issues here—whether we are morally accountable for what we want and, if we are not, whether we are morally accountable for what we do—are fundamental to our judgment of individuals like Ted Bundy. In fact, whether it even

Some Comments on Philosophy

Wonder is a feeling of a philosopher, and philosophy begins in wonder.

Plato

All *definite* knowledge—so I should contend—belongs to science; all *dogma* as to what surpasses definite knowledge belongs to theology. But between theology and science there is a No Man's Land, exposed to attack from both sides; this No Man's Land is philosophy.

—Bertrand Russell

Without it [philosophy] no one can lead a life free of fear or worry.

—Seneca

Uncertainty, in the presence of vivid hopes and fears, is painful, but must be endured if we wish to live without the support of comforting fairy tales.... To teach how to live without certainty, and yet without being paralyzed by hesitation, is perhaps the chief thing that philosophy, in our age, can still do for those who study it.

—Bertrand Russell

The most important and interesting thing which philosophers have tried to do is no less than this; namely: To give a general description of the whole Universe, mentioning all of the most important kinds of things which we *know* to be in it, considering how far it is likely that there are in it important kinds of things which we do not absolutely *know* to be in it, and also considering the most important ways in which these various kinds of things are related to one another.

—G. E. Moore

The philosopher has to take into account the least philosophical things in the world.

—C. Chincholle

Life involves passions, faiths, doubts, and courage. The critical inquiry into what these things mean and imply is philosophy.

—Josiah Royce

What is philosophy but a continual battle against custom; an ever-renewed effort to transcend the sphere of blind custom?

—Thomas Carlyle

[Philosophy] consoles us for the small achievements in life, and the decline of strength and beauty; it arms us against poverty, old age, sickness and death, against fools and evil sneerers.

—Jean de la Bruyère

Not to care for philosophy is to be a true philosopher.

—Blaise Pascal

There is no statement so absurd that no philosopher will make it.

—Cicero

The most tragic problem of philosophy is to reconcile intellectual necessities with the necessities of the heart and the will.

—Miguel de Unamuno

Without philosophy we would be little above animals.

—Voltaire

Philosophy asks the simple question, What is it all about?

—Alfred North Whitehead

Philosophy limits the thinkable and therefore the unthinkable.

—Ludwig Wittgenstein

makes sense to make moral judgments about people depends on these issues. It should be clear that a general change in perspective on these issues might have shattering consequences for human thought and action, and this example of a philosophical question might help you understand why Spinoza despaired of teaching philosophy without disturbing the peace. It will also, we hope, suggest to you that studying philosophy can be both interesting and worthwhile.

Of course, we know that these few examples of philosophical questions won't make the nature of philosophy as clear as window glass. But that's what the rest of this book is for, to give you a reasonable understanding of some of the central philosophical questions and issues and how they have been treated over the years.

Philosophy Pies

Now, just how do the various philosophical questions and issues relate to one another? First, philosophy as an entire subject consists of seven interrelated branches or fields or main areas. These are:

- **Metaphysics,** which studies the nature of being. What *is* being? What are its fundamental features and properties? These are two basic questions of metaphysics.

     Metaphysics, by the way, as a branch of philosophy, has precious little to do with the occult, but we'll get to that later.

- **Epistemology,** the theory of knowledge. What is knowledge? Is knowledge possible? These are the basic questions of epistemology.

- **Ethics,** the philosophical study of moral judgments, which includes, most importantly, the question: Which moral judgments are correct?

- **Social philosophy,** the philosophical study of society and its institutions. This branch of philosophy is concerned especially with determining the features of the ideal or best society.

- **Political philosophy,** which focuses on one social institution, the state, and seeks to determine its justification and ethically proper organization. Political philosophy is so closely related to social philosophy that it is common to treat them as a single area, social-political philosophy.

- **Aesthetics,** the philosophical study of art and of value judgments about art, and of beauty in general.

- **Logic,** the theory of correct reasoning, which seeks to investigate and establish the criteria of valid inference and demonstration.

So philosophy as a big pie can be cut up in terms of its seven major fields. Needless to say, this is not a quantitative division of the pie. The pie slices in the diagram are equal in size, but we are not suggesting that each of the branches of philosophy contains an equal number of theories or concepts or words. Your library probably has more holdings under political philosophy than under any of the other areas, and fewest under epistemology or aesthetics.

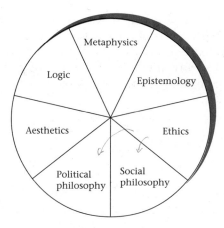

The Branches of Philosophy

In terms of historical periods, the same philosophy pie is divided into four pieces:

- **Ancient philosophy** (sixth century B.C. through, approximately, the third century A.D.)
- **Medieval philosophy** (fourth through sixteenth centuries, approximately)
- **Modern philosophy** (fifteenth through nineteenth centuries, approximately)
- **Contemporary philosophy** (twentieth century)

Thus:

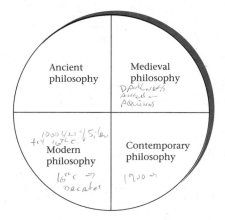

Historical Periods of Philosophy

There are other ways of dividing the philosophy pie. The fundamental assumptions and methods of many disciplines and areas of intellectual inquiry have been examined philosophically (which perhaps isn't too surprising because at one time or other nearly every intellectual endeavor counted as a part of philosophy). Thus, the philosophical pie can also be cut up in such slices as philosophy of science and philosophy of mathematics. Some of the most important of these "philosophy-of-discipline" areas are—in addition to those just listed, and in no particular order—philosophy of law, philosophy of education, philosophy of biology, and philosophy of psychology. So here's another way of dividing the pie:

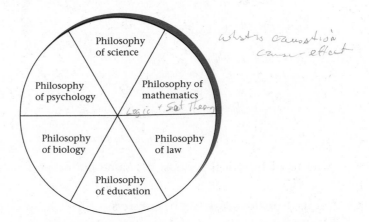

Philosophies-of-Discipline

Then the philosophy pie can be divided according to the philosophies-of-subject. To name a few, there are philosophy of mind, philosophy of religion, philosophy of history (sometimes classified as a philosophy-of-discipline), philosophy of sport, philosophy of love, philosophy of culture, and (very important of late) philosophy of feminism—feminist philosophy. Philosophies-of-subject and philosophies-of-discipline cut across the branches of philosophy and involve issues from more than one branch. For example, philosophy of religion and philosophy of science involve both metaphysical and epistemological issues, and philosophy of law involves questions of ethics, metaphysics, and epistemology.

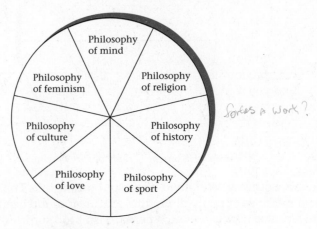

Philosophies-of-Subject

The pie can also be divided geographically, Eastern philosophy and Western philosophy being the main divisions, with further subdivisions of the obvious sort—American philosophy, Indian philosophy, Scandinavian philosophy, Continental philosophy (referring to the European continent), etc., etc.

In this century, the predominant interests and methods of philosophers in the West have tended to separate them into two fairly distinct "traditions."

- **Analytic philosophy:** Analytic philosophers believe (or are the intellectual descendents of those who did believe) that the proper method of philosophy is what is called analysis.

- **Continental philosophy:** There are several approaches to philosophy that fit under this heading, including principally the following (here we'll just name these approaches; we'll explain what they are about in Part 6): existentialism, phenomenology, hermeneutics, deconstruction, and critical theory.

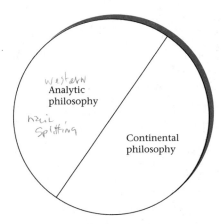

Twentieth-Century Traditions

In the twentieth century, as it so happens, generally (and with important exceptions) the predominant tradition in English-speaking countries is analytic philosophy, and you sometimes hear the expression *Anglo-American philosophy* used as a virtual synonym for analytic philosophy. And generally (and again with important exceptions) the predominant tradition in continental Europe is, as you would expect, Continental philosophy. As odd as it sounds, if an American or British philosopher happens to be most concerned with the issues discussed within Continental philosophy, it is acceptable to refer to the person as a Continental philosopher even if he or she never set foot on the European continent.

And by the way, many philosophers would list **Marxism** along with analytic philosophy and Continental philosophy as a third "tradition," but we'll treat Marxism as a species of political philosophy.

Philosophy and *a Philosophy*

There's a difference between *philosophy* and *a philosophy*. Philosophy is the discipline that comprises logic, metaphysics, ethics, epistemology, and so on, as explained in the text. A philosophy is a system of beliefs, concepts, or attitudes of an individual or group, or a theory about or underlying a sphere of activity or thought. Everybody, without ever having read a book in philosophy, has a philosophy of some sort or other—several of them, in fact.

Often, someone's or some group's philosophy becomes a subject for examination and discussion within the discipline of philosophy. In this way those philosophies listed at the beginning of the chapter as explosive forces in the world, such as atheism, communism, and so forth, are a part of the subject matter of philosophy, the discipline. Many such philosophies were originally expounded by individuals who were *philosophers*, that is, students of the discipline philosophy.

Studying philosophy, the discipline, will inevitably affect your own philosophy (or philosophies)—we certainly hope, for the better.

As is quite evident, a whole range of classification schemes applies to philosophy. As you read this book, you should refer back to these various diagrams when you need to get your bearings.

Preview

In this book, we want to give you some exposure to most of the divisions of philosophy. So we'll present material on some of the main branches of philosophy—namely, metaphysics, epistemology, ethics, and political philosophy. We'll also cover three important philosophies-of-subject, namely, philosophy of feminism, philosophy of religion, and philosophy of mind. In addition, we want to acquaint you with the Continental tradition in philosophy and with Eastern and other non-Western philosophy. What you will be getting is a historical overview of these various major components of philosophy.

Remember, if you forget how the various sections and topics relate to one another and to philosophy as a whole, refer back to the diagrams.

The Benefits of Philosophy

The importance of some philosophical questions—like, "Is there a God who is attentive, caring, and responsive to us?" and "Is abortion morally wrong?"—is obvious and great. A justification would have to be given for *not* contemplating them. But, quite honestly, some philosophical questions are of more or less ob-

The Side Benefits of Philosophy

Few employers actively seek philosophy students as such to fill openings. But many employers indeed seek people with the skills that philosophy students tend to have in abundance, such as the ability to think clearly and critically, reason carefully, and recognize subtle but important distinctions. Philosophy students tend to score above students in all other subjects on admissions tests for professional and graduate schools, too. This helps explain why, according to The Economist, philosophy PhDs are less likely to be unemployed than even chemists or biologists.

scure, and seemingly only academic or theoretical, consequence. Not everything philosophers consider is dynamite. The questions posed earlier about robots having feelings would be perceived by many as pretty academic and theoretical.

But then, every field has its theoretical and nonpractical questions. Why do astronomers wonder about the distance and recessional velocity of quasars? Why are paleontologists interested in 135-million-year-old mammalian fossil remains in northern Malawi? Why do musicologists care whether Bach used parallel fifths? The answer is that some questions are *inherently* interesting to those who pose them. An astronomer wonders about a quasar *just because it is there.* And some philosophical questions are like that, too: the philosopher wants to know the answer just simply to know the answer.

But there are side benefits in seeking answers to philosophical questions, even those that are difficult, abstruse, or seemingly remote from practical concerns. Seeing philosophical answers usually entails making careful distinctions in thought, words, and argument, and recognizing subtle distinctions among things and among facts. Philosophical solutions require logical and critical thinking, discussion, and exposition. So students of philosophy learn to look carefully for similarities and differences among things. They also develop an ability to spot logical difficulties in what others write or say and to avoid these pitfalls in their own thinking. In addition, they learn to recognize and critically assess the important unstated assumptions people make about the world and themselves and other people and life in general. These assumptions affect how people perceive the world and what they say and do, yet for the most part people are not aware of them and are disinclined to consider them at all critically. These abilities are of great value in any field that requires clear thinking.

It is not surprising, therefore, that according to The Economist, "philosophy students do better in examinations for business and management schools than anybody except mathematicians—better even than those who study economics, business or other vocational subjects." It's possible, of course, that philosophy attracts unusually capable students to begin with and that this accounts for results like these. But there is at least some reason to believe that the kind of training philosophy provides helps students to think, read and write, and possibly speak more critically, carefully, and cogently.

Finally, students who have learned their philosophical lessons well are not as likely as those who haven't to become trapped by dogmatism. Such students have learned the value of keeping an open mind and seeking solutions to problems that meet standards of coherence and reasonableness. These general attitudes, along with the critical skills that come with practice of philosophical argumentation, can stand a person in good stead when he or she is faced with many of the problems life generously provides for us.

Two Myths About Philosophy

We'll close this chapter by mentioning two misconceptions some people have about philosophy.

First, there's the notion that in philosophy one person's opinion is as valid as the next person's and that therefore anything you write or say goes and probably should get a good grade. Some people who have this idea may sign up for a philosophy course thinking that it's maybe an easy way to bolster the GPA.

We will jump all over this line of thought, but there is something in it that's not completely false. As you will see in Chapter 5, according to an old and respectable tradition in philosophy known as **skepticism,** there is no certain criterion for judging the truth of anything, and therefore all arguments are equally valid. Now, a good bit of hard and disciplined thinking has been done in support of these and other skeptical contentions. And, though some philosophers may well be skeptics of sorts, not many of them are likely to be much impressed with some half-baked form of skepticism that someone assumes *unthinkingly.*

Most philosophers make a distinction between philosophy and mere opinion, the difference being that philosophy at the very least involves opinion supported by good reasoning. Someone who expresses his or her own views without providing the supporting reasoning may be commended by a philosopher for having interesting *opinions,* but he or she is probably not going to receive high marks for having produced good *philosophy.* Philosophy requires you to support your claims with careful application of argument, and that is *hard work.* You should be aware of this.

A second wrong idea some people have is that philosophy is *light reading,* something you relax with in the evening, after all the serious work of the day is done.

In reality, philosophical writing is often complex and technical and almost always takes time and effort to understand. Philosophical prose often does not *seem* particularly complex or technical, because often it is written in familiar, everyday language. But that wrapping of familiar, everyday language is deceiving. Really, it is best to approach a work in philosophy with the kind of mental preparedness and alertness appropriate for a textbook in mathematics or science. As a general rule of thumb, you might expect to be able to read an *entire novel* in the time it takes you

Argument

What is the difference between just taking a position on an issue and *supporting* your position? The difference is that when you support your position, you give someone else *reasons for agreeing with you*. When you don't do this, you're just expressing an opinion, take it or leave it.

When you present a reason for accepting your position, you are setting forth an **argument**. Setting forth arguments is the most basic of philosophical activities and is what, among other things, distinguishes philosophy from the mere having of opinions.

When you study some subjects, you are expected only to remember what certain individuals believed or discovered or accomplished. When you study philosophy, you should try to remember not merely what the philosopher believed, but also the arguments he or she gave. (We concede that this is difficult in the case of some early philosophers about whose arguments we don't really have much information.)

Logic, which is concerned with the criteria of correct argument, is treated briefly in the first appendix at the back of this book. Have a look.

Personal Truth

Let's not be confused. The fact that people sometimes say "what's true for me isn't necessarily true for you" doesn't mean that truth is a personal thing. What is personal is *belief,* not truth.

Thinking that truth is "personal" is a mistake beginners in philosophy sometimes make. It is a mistake equivalent to thinking that statements are all basically just attempts to express *subjective feelings.* When we maintain that truth is personal, we fail to see the distinction between a statement that only attempts to express a subjective feeling, like "Baseball is boring," and a statement that attempts to assert an objective fact, like "Cincinnati has a major league baseball team." Baseball might be *boring* for one person and not for the next (and in *that* sense the statement might be "true" for one person and not for the next), but Cincinnati cannot both have and not have a major league baseball team.

If your physician tells you that you have high blood pressure, it would not seem reasonable for you to react by thinking that that's just *your doctor's* truth.

to get through just a chapter or two of good philosophy. To understand philosophy, you usually have to reread a passage several times and think about it a lot.

Of course, you don't *have* to read a philosophy book slowly and carefully. But if you don't, you may well find it dull and uninteresting, sort of like baseball is to someone who doesn't understand the game and doesn't get involved in what's going on.

Having been forewarned, you can turn your attention to Part 1, on metaphysics and epistemology. Thanks for joining us.

Suggested Further Readings

Here are some of the best reference books on philosophy in the English language:

Simon Blackburn, *The Oxford Dictionary of Philosophy* (New York: Oxford University Press, 1995). Concise and readable.

Diané Collinson, *Fifty Major Philosophers* (London: Routledge, 1988). A relatively accessible and short reference book.

F. C. Copleston, *History of Philosophy,* 9 vols. (New York: Doubleday, 1965). The most complete history of philosophy available to English-only readers.

Arthur C. Danto, *Connections to the World: The Basic Concepts of Philosophy* (New York: Harper & Row, 1989). An important contemporary analytic philosopher summarizes some of the main problems.

Paul Edwards, ed., *The Encyclopedia of Philosophy,* 8 vols. (New York: Macmillan, 1967). If you need to find out something about a philosopher or philosophical topic, begin here.

A. C. Ewing, *Fundamental Questions of Philosophy* (London: Routledge, 1985). Readable. Written from an analytic viewpoint.

Albert Hakim, *Historical Introduction to Philosophy* (New York: Macmillan, 1987). An extensive collection of short original writings.

W. T. Jones, *History of Western Philosophy,* 2nd ed., 5 vols. (New York: Harper & Row, 1976). Shorter than Copleston and a tad more difficult to read, in our view.

Anthony Kenny, ed. *The Oxford History of Western Philosophy* (New York: Oxford University Press, 1994). An authoritative and beautifully illustrated history of Western philosophy, with articles by important contemporary philosophers.

Thomas Nagel, *What Does It All Mean?: A Very Short Introduction to Philosophy* (New York: Oxford University Press, 1987). A very short introduction to philosophy. Nagel is an influential contemporary analytic philosopher.

G. H. R. Parkinson, *An Encyclopaedia of Philosophy* (London: Routledge, 1988). A nice one-volume set of essays on most of the important topics in analytic philosophy.

G. H. R. Parkinson and S. G. Shanker, gen. eds., *The Routledge History of Philosophy,* 10 vols. (London and New York: Routledge, various dates). A detailed chronological survey of the history of Western philosophy, together with chronologies and glossaries. Some volumes of the series are still in progress.

Bertrand Russell, *A History of Western Philosophy* (New York: Simon & Schuster, 1945). As readable as a novel, though some critics find Russell brash and opinionated.

J. O. Urmson and Jonathan Rée, *The Concise Encyclopedia of Western Philosophy and Philosophers* (London: Routledge, 1995). A fine, one-volume survey from an analytic viewpoint.

Mary Ellen Waithe, ed., *A History of Women Philosophers,* 4 vols. (Dordrecht: Martinus Nijhoff/Kluwer Press, 1987, 1989, 1991, 1995). The volumes cover: Vol. 1: *Ancient Women Philosophers* (through 500 A.D.), Vol. 2: *Medieval, Renaissance, and Enlightenment Women Philosophers* (500–1600), Vol. 3: *Modern Women Philosophers* (1600–1900), and Vol. 4: *Contemporary* (twentieth century) *Women Philosophers.*

PART 1

**Metaphysics
and
Epistemology:
Existence and
Knowledge**

The First Philosophers

2

ⅬⅬⅬⅬⅬⅬⅬⅬⅬⅬⅬⅬⅬⅬⅬⅬⅬⅬⅬⅬⅬⅬ

You cannot know what is not, nor can you express it. What can be thought of and what can be—they are the same.

    —Parmenides

It is wise to agree that all things are one.

    —Heraclitus

Metaphysics and epistemology are the dancing partners of philosophy. You usually don't find one very far from the other.

Metaphysics quite possibly you have heard of, epistemology maybe not. We'll say something about **metaphysics** and then after a bit explain what epistemology is.

In its popular usage, the word *metaphysics* has strange and forbidding associations. "Metaphysical bookstores," for example, specialize in all sorts of occult subjects, from channeling, harmonic convergence, and pyramid power to past-life hypnotic regression, psychic surgery, and spirit photography. If you know something about the history of metaphysics, you tend to be amused by this association with the occult, especially given the way in which the term was originally coined. Here is the true story.

Aristotle (384–322 B.C.) produced a series of works on a wide variety of subjects, from biology to poetry. One set of his writings is known as the *Physics,* from the Greek word *physika,* which means "the things of nature." Another set, to which Aristotle never gave an official title but which he referred to occasionally as "first philosophy" or "wisdom," was called simply "the books after the books on nature" (*ta meta ta physika biblia*) by later writers and particularly by Andronicus of Rhodes, who was the cataloguer of Aristotle's works in the first century B.C. The word *metaphysics,* then, translates loosely as "after the *Physics.*"

Being

When a philosopher asks, "What is the nature of being?"—and who besides philosophers would ask?—he or she may have in mind any number of things, including one or more of the following:

- Is being a *property* of things, or is it *some kind of thing* itself? Or is there some third alternative?

- Is being basically *one*, or are there *many* beings?

- Is being *fixed* and *changeless* or is it *constantly changing*? What is the relationship between *being* and *becoming*?

- Does everything have the *same kind* of being?

- What are the fundamental *categories* into which all existing things may be divided?

- What are the fundamental *features* of reality?

- Is there a fundamental *substance* out of which all else is composed? If so, does it have any properties? Must it have properties?

- What is the world like *in itself,* independent of our perception of it?

- What manner of existence do *particular things* have, as distinct from *properties, relations,* and *classes*? What manner of existence do *events* have? What manner do *numbers, minds, matter, space,* and *time* have? What manner do *facts* have?

- That a particular thing has a certain characteristic—is that a fact about the *thing*? Or is it a fact about the *characteristic*?

Several narrower questions may also properly be regarded as questions of metaphysics, such as: Does God exist? Is what happens determined? Is there life after death? and Must events occur in space and time?

We'll admit that some of these questions are none too clear, but they indicate some of the directions a person might take in coming to answer the question, "What is the nature of being?" or in studying metaphysics. Because they are so numerous, they also indicate that we'll have to make some choices about what topics to cover in the pages that follow. We cannot go on forever.

The subjects Aristotle discussed in these works are more abstract and difficult to understand than those he examined in the *Physics*. Hence later authorities determined that their proper place was indeed "after the *Physics,*" and thus *"Metaphysics"* has stuck as the official title of Aristotle's originally untitled work and, by extension, as the general name for the study of the topics treated there—and related subjects. As you will see, philosophers before Aristotle had also discussed some of these things. This means that, though Aristotle's works are the source of the term *metaphysics,* Aristotle was not the first metaphysician.

The fundamental question treated in Aristotle's *Metaphysics,* and thus the fundamental metaphysical question, can be put this way: *What is the nature of being?* But a number of different subjects might qualify as "related" to this question. So you should not be surprised that in contemporary philosophical usage metaphysics is rather a broad and inclusive field, though for most philosophers it doesn't include such subjects as astral projection, psychic surgery, or UFOs.

What is the nature of being? One of the authors used to ask his introductory classes to answer that question in a brief essay. The most common response, along with "Huh?" "What?" "Are you serious?" and "How do you drop this class?" was "What do you *mean,* 'What is the nature of being?'" People are troubled by what the question means and are uncertain what sort of thing is expected for an answer. It's this way, incidentally, with a lot of philosophical questions—you don't know exactly what is being asked or what an answer might look like.

In this chapter we'll see several different approaches that have been taken to this question through the history of philosophy.

Now, as to **epistemology**—it's the branch of philosophy concerned primarily with the nature and possibility of knowledge. *What is knowledge? Is knowledge possible?* These are the two most fundamental questions of epistemology, the questions to which most epistemological inquiries relate.

Despite widespread current interest in the first of these questions, historically most epistemologists have been more interested in issues related to the second question: *Is knowledge possible?* So we are going to concentrate on that second question.

Skepticism

Is knowledge possible? Well, you say, "Of *course* it's possible. *Are you kidding?* Lots of things are known."

But are they? We'll make a little wager: we'll bet that before you finish this chapter, you are not going to be so sure.

Now a person who questions or suspends judgment on the possibility of knowledge is a **skeptic.** This is a word you should remember. Generally, there are two kinds of skeptics, total skeptics and modified skeptics. **Total skeptics** maintain that nothing can be known or, alternatively, suspend judgment in all matters. Sounds preposterous? Well, we'll see.

A **modified skeptic** does not doubt that at least some things are known, but denies or suspends judgment on the possibility of:

1. Knowledge about some particular thing, such as God or the external world; or

2. Knowledge within some subject area, such as history or metaphysics; or

3. Knowledge from this or that source, such as reason or experience.

Thus, the question on which we are focusing—*Is knowledge possible?*—must be viewed as a summary in shorthand for several more specific questions that have concerned philosophers, such as these:

- Is knowledge of a world outside the self possible?
- Is it possible to have knowledge of future experience?
- Is there knowledge beyond what can be derived from experience?
- Can anything at all be known?

We'll see how philosophical interest in some of these issues developed historically.

⎍⎍⎍⎍⎍⎍⎍⎍⎍⎍⎍⎍⎍⎍⎍⎍⎍⎍

Early Philosophy: The Pre-Socratics

The first philosophers, or first Western philosophers, at any rate, lived in Ionia, on the coast of Asia Minor, during the sixth century B.C. These philosophers are known collectively as the **pre-Socratics,** a loose chronological term applied to the Greek philosophers who lived before Socrates (c. 470–399 B.C.). Most left little or nothing of their own writings, so scholars have had to reconstruct their views from what contemporaneous and later writers said about them.

Before we tell you something about these philosophers, let's just say one thing. Experience indicates that it is sometimes difficult to relate to people who lived so long ago. If you have this problem with what follows, then it may help if you remember this:

It was during this period in Western history—ancient Greece before Socrates—that the decisive change in perspective came about that ultimately made possible a deep understanding of the natural world. It wasn't *inevitable* that this change would occur, and there are societies that exist today whose members, for lack of this perspective, do not so much as understand why their seasons change. We are not arguing for the virtues of advanced technological civilization over primitive life in a state of nature, for advanced civilization is in some ways a mixed blessing. But advanced civilization is a fact, and that it is a fact is a direct consequence of two developments in thought. One of these, which we will not discuss, is the discovery by the Greeks of mathematics. The other, which we are about to discuss immediately, is the invention by the Greeks of philosophy, specifically metaphysics.

The Milesians

Tradition accords to **Thales** (c. 640–546 B.C.), a citizen of the wealthy Ionian Greek seaport town of Miletus, the honor of being the first philosopher. And philosophy began when it occurred to Thales to consider whether there might be some *fundamental kind of stuff* out of which everything else is made. Today we are so accustomed to thinking of the complex world we experience as made up of a few basic substances (like hydrogen, oxygen, carbon, and the other elements) that we are surprised there ever was a time when people did not think this. But before Thales, people did not think this. So Thales deserves credit for introducing a new and rather important idea into Western thought.

Thales also deserves credit for bringing forth a new way of looking at the world, for he introduced a perspective that is not mythological in character. At the time it was traditional to *personify* the components of the universe—to perceive the sea,

The Corner on Olives

Thales (c. 640–546 B.C.) was considered by many to be the wisest of the seven wise men of the ancient Greek world. But not by everyone. Once, when Thales was studying the stars, he stumbled into a well and was found by a Thracian maiden, who was inclined to think that Thales might know much about the heavens but was a bit dull when it came to what was right before his eyes.

But Thales was not dull. Aristotle called him the first philosopher, and he was also a valued political advisor. His prediction of an eclipse of the sun probably impressed even the Thracian maiden. Once, according to Bertrand Russell, when an Egyptian king asked Thales to determine the height of a pyramid, Thales simply measured the height of the pyramid's shadow at the time of day when his own shadow equaled his own height.

When Thales took time away from his higher pursuits, he could be extremely practical. To counter the criticism of his fellow Milesians concerning his poverty, he used his knowledge of the heavens to foresee a bumper crop of olives. Then he hired all the olive presses in Miletus and Chios. When the crop came and the olives were harvested, Thales was able to rent the presses at his own price.

Philosophers, naturally, have said that this was Thales's way of showing that a philosopher could easily be wealthy, if he had an interest in money.

the air, the sun, the earth, and so on, as gods. Although to a certain extent the pre-Socratics still viewed the cosmos from a mythological perspective, they began to de-personify it. Beginning with Thales, they began to see the world naturalistically, as consisting of substances and processes.

What is the basic substance, according to Thales? Unfortunately, his answer was that *all is water,* and this turns out to be wrong. But it was *not* an especially silly answer for him to have come up with. You can imagine him looking about at the complicated world of nature and reasoning: Well, if there is some underlying, more fundamental level than that of appearances, and some kind of substance exists at that level out of which everything else is made, then this basic substance would have to be something very flexible, something that could appear in many forms. And of the candidates Thales saw around him, the most flexible would have been water—something that can appear in three very different states. So we can imagine Thales thinking that if water can appear in these three very different forms that we know about, it may be that water can also appear in many others that we do not understand. For example, when a piece of wood burns, it goes up in smoke, which looks like a form of steam. Therefore, perhaps—Thales might have speculated—the original piece of wood was actually water in one of its more exotic forms.

We're guessing about Thales' reasoning, of course. And in any case Thales did come to the wrong conclusion with the water idea. But let's just be really clear that it wasn't Thales' *conclusion* that was important: it was what Thales was *up* to. Thales attempted to explain the complex world that we see in terms of a simpler underlying reality. This attempt marks the beginning of metaphysics and, for that matter, of science. Science is largely just an effort to finish off what Thales started.

Two other Milesians at about this time advanced alternatives to Thales' theory that the basic stuff is water. One, **Anaximenes** (c. 585–528 B.C.), pronounced the basic substance to be air and said that air becomes different things through the processes of condensation and rarefaction. The other, **Anaximander** (c. 611–547 B.C.), a pupil of Thales, argued that the basic substance out of which everything comes must be even more elementary than water and air and indeed every other substance of which we have knowledge. The basic substance, he thought, must be ageless, boundless, and indeterminate. Anaximander also proposed a theory of the origination of the universe. He held that from the basic stuff a nucleus of fire and dark mist formed; the mist solidified in its center, producing the world. The world is surrounded by fire, which we see (the stars and other heavenly bodies) through holes in the mist. Thus he produced a model of the universe.

Pythagoras

Quite a different alternative was proposed by the followers of **Pythagoras** (c. 582–c. 507 B.C.), who lived in the Greek city of Croton in southern Italy at the beginning of the sixth century B.C. The Pythagoreans kept their written doctrines pretty secret, so it's no surprise that by the time of Aristotle (384–322 B.C.) a few ideas had gotten a bit confused. For example, Aristotle reported in his *Metaphysics* that the Pythagoreans "construct natural bodies out of numbers, things that have lightness and weight out of things that have not weight or lightness." Apparently, Aristotle wasn't the only Greek who got Pythagoras's views wrong. The confusion about whether Pythagoras said that things were numbers dates back to Pythagoras. Now maybe he really did say that, and maybe his wife, Theano, is just trying to fix his mistake, but in this selection she sets the record straight.

SELECTION 2.1

On Piety   **From Theano of Crotona**

I have learned that many of the Greeks believe Pythagoras said all things are generated from number. The very assertion poses a difficulty: How can things which do not exist even be conceived to generate? But he did not say that all things come to be from number; rather, in accordance *with* number—on the grounds that order in the primary sense is in number and it is by participation in order that a first and a second and the rest sequentially are assigned to things which are counted.

Now this makes a lot more sense than what Aristotle *thought* Pythagoras said. How do we know that things are things? How do we know where one thing begins and another ends? Well, Theano says, we know because we can *enumerate*. When

Pythagoras and the Pythagoreans

Pythagoras (c. 582–c. 507 B.C.) was born on the Greek island of Samos. You may safely disregard the reports that he descended from the god Apollo because he was really the son of a prominent citizen named Mnesarchus.

Not much is known for certain about the life of Pythagoras, though it is known that eventually he traveled to southern Italy, where he founded a mystical-scientific school in the Greek-speaking city of Croton. The Pythagoreans be-lieved in the transmigration of the soul, shared their property, and followed a strict set of moral max-ims that, among other things, for-bade eating meat.

Unfortunately for the Pythag-orean community, it denied mem-bership to a rich and powerful citizen of Croton named Cylon. After Pythagoras retired to Meta-pontium to die, Cylon had his fel-low Cronians attack the Pythago-reans and burn their buildings to the ground. Worse still, from the Pythagorean point of view, he had all the Pythagoreans killed, except for two.

The Pythagorean school was eventually restarted at Rhegium, where it developed mathematical theorems, a theory of the struc-ture of sound, and a geometrical way of understanding astronomy and physics. To what degree these ideas actually stem from Pythag-oras is a matter of conjecture.

we count off things as first, second, and so on, what we're really doing is showing that we can distinguish one thing from another. A thing begins here and ends there, and between beginning and end is one thing.

On Theano's account, it wouldn't matter whether the thing is a physical object or an idea. If we can delineate it from another of its type, it's a thing. It exists. Simple, isn't it?

So, while we're getting back to Pythagoras, remember, according to Theano, Pythagoras meant to say that there is an analogy between things and numbers. Whether a thing is physical or not, it participates in the universe of order and harmony, it can be sequenced, it can be counted, it can be ordered. When you read about Pythagorean philosophy, remember that the idea of a universe characterized by orderliness and harmony is meant to apply to all things, not just to objects. These ideas apply to mathematics, to ethics, and (as *we* use the term *harmony*) to music.

It is important to notice, too, that the Pythagoreans in effect combined math-ematics and philosophy. This combination gave birth to a very important concept in metaphysics, one that we will encounter frequently. This is the idea that the fundamental reality, like the truths of mathematics, is ideal, perfect, eternal, un-changing, and accessible only to reason. Often this notion about fundamental reality is said to come from Plato, but it originated with the Pythagoreans.

Heraclitus and Parmenides

Another important pre-Socratic was **Heraclitus** (c. 535–c. 475 B.C.), a Greek noble-man from Ephesus, who proposed yet another candidate as the basic element. According to Heraclitus, *all is fire*. In fixing fire as the basic element, Heraclitus wasn't just listing an alternative to Thales's water and Anaximenes's air. For Heraclitus wished to call attention to what he thought was the essential feature of reality, namely, that it is *ceaselessly changing.* There is no reality, he maintained, save the reality of change: permanence is an illusion. Thus fire, whose nature it is to ceaselessly change, is the root substance of the universe, he said.

Heraclitus didn't believe that the process of change is random or haphazard. Instead, he saw all change as determined by a cosmic order that he called the *logos,* which is Greek for "word." He taught that each thing contains its opposite, just as, for example, we are simultaneously young and old, and coming into and going out of existence. Through the *logos* there is a harmonious union of opposites, he thought.

Change does seem to be an important feature of reality, as Heraclitus said. Or does it? A younger contemporary of Heraclitus, **Parmenides,** thought otherwise. Parmenides' exact dates are unknown, but he lived during the first quarter of the fifth century B.C.

Parmenides wasn't interested in discovering the fundamental *substance* or *things* that underlie or constitute everything or in determining what the most important *feature* of reality is, and his whole method of inquiry was really quite unlike that of his predecessors. In all probability the Milesians, Heraclitus, and the Pythagoreans reached their conclusions by looking around at the world and considering possible candidates for its primary substance or fundamental constituents. Parmenides, by contrast, mainly simply assumed some very basic principles and attempted to *deduce* from these what he thought *must be* the true nature of being. For Parmenides it would have been a complete waste of time to look to the world for information about how things really are.

Principles like those Parmenides assumed are said in contemporary jargon to be "principles of reason" or **a priori principles,** which just means that they are known "prior" to experience. It's not that we learn these principles first chronologically, but rather that our knowledge of them does not depend on our senses.

For example, consider the principle "You can't make something out of nothing." If you wished to defend this principle, would you proceed by conducting an experiment in which you tried to make something out of nothing? In fact, you would not. You would base your defense on our inability to *conceive* of ever making something out of nothing.

Parmenides based his philosophy on principles like that. One of these principles was that if something changes, it becomes something different. Thus, he reasoned, if being itself were to change, then it would become something different. But what is different from being is non-being, and non-being just plain *isn't.* Thus, he concluded, being *does not change.*

What is more, being is *unitary*—it is a single thing. For if there were anything else, it would not be being; hence, it would not be. (The principle assumed in this argument is something like: a second thing is different from a first thing.)

Further, being is an *undifferentiated whole:* it does not have any parts. For parts are different from the whole. And if something is different from being, it would not be being; hence, it would not be.

time is not a linear measurement when dissociated from motion y velocity

On Rabbits, Zeno, and Motion

Parmenides' most famous disciple was Zeno (c. 489–430 B.C.), who devised a series of ingenious arguments to support Parmenides' theory that reality is one. Zeno's basic approach was to demonstrate that motion is impossible. Here are two of his antimotion arguments:

1. For something, let's say a little rabbit, to move from its own hole to another hole, it must first reach the midway point between the two holes. But to reach that point, it must first reach the quarter point. Unfortunately, to reach the quarter point, it must reach the point that is one-eighth the distance. But first, it must reach the point one-sixteenth the distance. And so on and so on. In short, a rabbit, or any other thing, must pass through an infinite number of points to go anywhere. Because some sliver of time is required to reach each of these points, a thing would require an infinite amount of time to move anywhere, and that effectively rules out the possibility of motion.

2. For a rabbit to move from one hole to a second, it must at each moment of its travel occupy a space equal to its length. But when a thing occupies a space equal to its length, it is at rest. Thus, because the rabbit—or any other thing—must occupy a space equal to its length at each moment, it must be at rest at each moment. Thus, it cannot move.

Well, yes, it seems obvious that things move. But that just means either that there is a mistake in Zeno's logic or that rabbits, and just about every other thing, aren't really the way they seem. Zeno, of course, favored the second alternative. You, probably, will favor the first alternative. So what is the mistake in Zeno's logic?

Further, being is *eternal:* it cannot come into existence because, first, something cannot come from nothing (remember?) and, second, even if it could, there would be no explanation why it came from nothing at one time and not at another. And because change is impossible, as already demonstrated, being cannot go out of existence.

By similar arguments Parmenides attempted to show that motion, generation, and degrees of being are all equally impossible.

So, whereas for Heraclitus being is ceaselessly changing, according to Parmenides being is absolutely unchanging. Being is One, Parmenides maintained: it is permanent, unchanging, indivisible, and undifferentiated. Appearances to the contrary are just gross illusion.

Empedocles and Anaxagoras

The philosophies of Parmenides (being is unchanging) and Heraclitus (being is ceaselessly changing) seem to be irreconcilably opposed. The next major Greek philosopher, **Empedocles** (c. 495–c. 435 B.C.), however, thought that true reality is permanent and unchangeable; yet he *also* thought it absurd to dismiss the change we experience as mere illusion. Empedocles quite diplomatically sided in part with Parmenides and in part with Heraclitus. He was in fact the first philosopher to attempt to reconcile and combine the apparently conflicting metaphysics of those who came earlier.

Additionally, Empedocles' attempt at reconciliation resulted in an understanding of reality that in many ways is very much like our own.

According to Empedocles, the objects of experience *do* change, but these objects are composed of basic particles of matter that do *not* change. These basic material particles themselves, Empedocles held, are of four kinds: earth, air, fire, and water. These basic elements mingle together in different combinations to form the objects of experience as well as the apparent changes among these objects.

The idea that the objects of experience, and the apparent changes in their qualities, quantities, and relationships, are in reality changes in the positions of basic particles is very familiar to us and is a central idea of modern physics. Empedocles was the first to have this idea.

Empedocles also recognized that an account of reality must explain not merely *how* changes in the objects of experience occur, but *why* they occur. That is, he attempted to provide an explanation of the *forces* that cause change. Specifically, he taught that the basic elements enter new combinations under two forces, Love and Strife, which are essentially forces of attraction and decomposition.

Empedocles' portrayal of the universe as constituted by basic material particles moving under the action of impersonal forces seems very up-to-date and "scientific" to us today, and, yes, Empedocles was a competent scientist. He understood the mechanism of solar eclipses, for example, and determined experimentally that air and water are separate substances. He understood so much, in fact, that he proclaimed himself a god. Empedocles was not displeased when others said that he could foresee the future, control the winds, and perform other miracles.

A contemporary of Empedocles was **Anaxagoras** (c. 500–428 B.C.). Anaxagoras was not as convinced of his own importance as Empedocles was of his, but Anaxagoras was just as important historically. For one thing, it was Anaxagoras who introduced philosophy to Athens, where the discipline truly flourished. For another, he introduced into metaphysics an important distinction, that between *matter* and *mind*.

Anaxagoras accepted the principle that all changes in the objects of experience are in reality changes in the arrangements of underlying particles. But unlike Empedocles, he believed that everything is *infinitely* divisible. He also held that each different kind of substance has its own corresponding kind of particle and that each substance contains particles of every other kind. What distinguishes one substance from another is a preponderance of one kind of particle. Thus fire, for example, contains more "fire particles" than, say, water, which presumably contains very few.

Whereas Empedocles believed that motion is caused by the action of two forces, Anaxagoras postulated that the source of all motion is something called **nous.** The Greek word *nous* is sometimes translated as "reason," sometimes as "mind," and what Anaxagoras meant by *nous* is apparently pretty much an equation between mind and reason. Mind, according to Anaxagoras, is separate and distinct from matter in that it alone is unmixed. It is everywhere and animates all things but contains nothing material within it. It is "the finest of all things, and the purest, and it has all knowledge about everything, as well as the greatest power."

Before mind acted on matter, Anaxagoras believed, the universe was an infinite, undifferentiated mass. The formation of the world as we know it was the result of a rotary motion produced in this mass by mind. In this process gradually the sun and stars and moon and air were separated off, and then gradually too the configurations of particles that we recognize in the other objects of experience.

Notice that according to Anaxagoras, mind did not *create* matter but only acted on it. Notice also that Anaxagoras's mind did not act on matter for some *purpose* or *objective*. These are strong differences between Anaxagoras's mind and the Judaeo-Christian God, though in other respects the concepts are not dissimilar. And, although Anaxagoras was the first to find a place for mind in the universe, Aristotle and Plato both criticized him for conceiving of it, mind, as merely a mechanical cause of the existing order.

Notice finally that Anaxagoras's particles are not physical particles like modern-day atoms. This is because, if every particle is made of smaller particles, as Anaxagoras held, then there are no smallest particles, except as abstractions, as infinitesimals, as idealized "limits" on an infinite process. For the idea that the world is composed of actual physical atoms, we must turn to the last of the pre-Socratics we shall mention here, the Atomists.

The Atomists

The **Atomists** were **Leucippus** and **Democritus.** Not too much is known of Leucippus, although he is said to have lived in Miletus during the mid-fifth century B.C., and the basic idea of atomism is attributed to him. Democritus (460–370 B.C.) is better known today, and the detailed working out of atomism is considered to be the result of his efforts. Democritus is yet another philosopher who was also a brilliant mathematician.

The Atomists held that all things are composed of physical atoms—tiny imperceptible, indestructible, indivisible, eternal, and uncreated particles composed of exactly the same matter but different in size, shape, and (though there is controversy about this) weight. Atoms, they believed, are infinitely numerous and eternally in motion. By combining with one another in various ways, they comprise the objects of experience. They are continuously in motion, and thus the various combinations come and go. We, of course, experience their combining and disassembling and recombining as the generation, decay, erosion, or burning of everyday objects.

Some qualities of everyday objects, such as their color and taste, are not really "in" the objects, said the Atomists, though other qualities, like their weight and hardness, are. This is a distinction that to this day remains embodied in common sense—and yet, as you will see in Chapter 4, it is totally beset with philosophical difficulties.

Democritus

Democritus was the most widely traveled of the early philosophers. On the death of his father, he took his inheritance and left his home in Abdera, Thrace, to learn from the Chaldean Magi of Persia, the priest-geometers of Egypt, and the Gymnosophists of India. He may also have gone to Ethiopia. But he came to Athens as an unknown, for Democritus despised fame and glory.

Democritus thought that most humans waste their lives pursuing foolish desires and pleasures. He himself was far more interested in pursuing wisdom and truth than riches, and he spent his life in relative poverty. He found the cemetery a congenial place in which to cogitate.

Anyway, the Atomists, unlike Anaxagoras, believed that there is a smallest physical unit beyond which further division is impossible. And also unlike Anaxagoras, they saw no reason to suppose that the original motion of atoms resulted from the activity of mind; indeed, they did not believe it necessary in the first place to explain the origin of that motion. As far as we can tell, they said in effect that the atoms have been around forever, and they've been moving for as long as they've been around.

This Atomist depiction of the world is quite modern. It is not such an extravagant exaggeration to say that, until the convertibility of matter and energy was understood in our own century, the common scientific view of the universe was basically a version of atomism. But the Atomist theory did run up against one problem that is worth looking at briefly.

The Greek philosophers generally believed this: for motion of any sort to occur, there must be a void, or empty space, in which a moving thing may change position. But Parmenides had argued pretty convincingly that a void is not possible. For empty space would be nothingness, that is, non-being, and therefore does not exist.

The Atomists' way of circumventing this problem was essentially to ignore it (though this point, too, is controversial). That things move is apparent to sense perception and is just indisputable, they maintained. And because things move, they held, empty space must be real—for otherwise motion would be impossible.

One final point about the Atomist philosophy must be mentioned. The Atomists are sometimes accused of maintaining that chance collisions of atoms cause them to come together to form this or that set of objects and not some other. But even though the Atomists believed that the motion of the atoms fulfilled no purpose, they also believed the atoms operate in strict accordance with physical laws. Future motions would be completely predictable, they said, for anyone with sufficient information about the shapes, sizes, locations, direction, and velocities of the atoms. In this sense, then, the Atomists left nothing to chance; according to them, purely random events, in the sense of just "happening," did not occur.

The view that future states and events are completely determined by preceding states and events is called **determinism.**

catalyst intervention

Free Will vs. Determinism

Here are two beliefs that are both dear to common sense. Note that we hold the first belief thanks (in part) to the Atomists.

1. The behavior of atoms is governed entirely by physical law.
2. Humans have free will.

Do you accept both (1) and (2)? We are willing to wager a very large sum of money that you do.

Unfortunately, (1) and (2) do not get along comfortably with each other. Here's why. It seems to follow from (1) that, whatever an atom does, it had to do, given the existing circumstances. For phy-sical laws determine what each atom does in the existing circumstances. Thus, if the laws determine that an atom does X in circumstance C, then, given circumstance C, the atom has to do X.

But anything that happened as a result of free will presumably did not have to happen. For example, suppose that I, of my own free will, move my arm. Whatever the circumstances were in which I chose to move my arm, I could always have chosen otherwise and not moved my arm. Therefore, when I moved my arm of my own free will, my arm, and thus the atoms in my arm, did not have to move, even given the existing circumstances. Thus, if (2) holds, it is *not* true that an atom must have done what it did, given the existing circumstances. But if (1) holds, then it *is* true.

Now, (1) and (2) are equally basic postulates of common sense. But it seems difficult logically to accept them both. One or the other, therefore, has to be rejected, if they are logically incompatible.

Philosophy has a way of showing that basic beliefs are sometimes incompatible. It can be a troublemaker.

we have 2. only because 1.   1. is a precondition of 2.

Let's sum up to this point. Despite the alternative theories the pre-Socratics advanced, an important common thread runs through their speculation, and it is this:

All believed that *the world we experience is merely a manifestation of a more fundamental, underlying reality*.

That this thought occurred to people represents a turning point in the history of the species and may have been more important than the invention of the wheel. Had it not occurred, then any scientific understanding of the natural world would have proved to be quite impossible.

The desire to comprehend the reality that underlies appearances did not, however, lead the various pre-Socratic philosophers in the same direction. It led the Milesians to consider possible basic substances and the Pythagoreans to try to determine the fundamental principle on which all else depends. It led Heraclitus to try to determine the essential feature of reality, Parmenides to consider the true nature of being, and Empedocles to try to understand the basic principles of causation. Finally, it led Anaxagoras to consider the original source of motion and the Atomists to consider the construction of the natural world. Broadly speaking, these various paths of inquiry eventually came to define the scope of scientific inquiry. But that was not until science and metaphysics parted ways about two thousand years later.

What About Socrates?

If you have heard of only one philosopher, it is **Socrates** (470–399 B.C.). Despite having written nothing, Socrates was one of the most influential thinkers in the history of Western civilization, primarily because he gave the discipline its preeminent method. But we won't focus on Socrates in the main text in this chapter because he advanced no metaphysical theory.

To this day, over twenty centuries after his death, most philosophers equate proficiency within their own field with skill in the Socratic method. So let us take a brief look at it.

The Socratic method is intended to unlock the true nature of an abstract thing, such as justice or beauty or knowledge, through a search for its proper definition, a definition that won't permit refutation under Socratic questioning. Here's an example.

Suppose Bruder and Moore wish to find out what knowledge is. Bruder proposes, tentatively, that knowledge is strong belief. Moore asks if that means that people who believe strongly that fairies exist automatically know that fairies exist. Bruder, seeing that he has made a mistake, reconsiders and offers a revised thesis: Knowledge, he says, is not belief that is strong, but belief that is true.

Moore then says, "Well, suppose my true belief is just based on a guess. This is true belief, but is it knowledge?" Bruder then sees that knowledge isn't just true belief, and so he proposes a further revision or an alternative analysis. Eventually, Bruder and Moore may find a definition of knowledge that neither one can refute.

This method does not imply that the questioner knows the essential nature of the thing under consideration, but only that he or she be adept at detecting misconceptions of it and at revealing those misconceptions through appropriate questioning. Though in many cases the process may not actually disclose the essence of the thing (if Plato's dialogues are an indication, Socrates himself did not have at hand many final, satisfactory definitions), it will, presumably, bring those who practice it closer to this terminal understanding.

We can therefore understand why, when the Delphic oracle pronounced Socrates the wisest man alive, Socrates thought the pronouncement must have been a reference to the fact that he, unlike most men, was aware of his ignorance. For as one applies the Socratic method, one becomes skilled at discerning misconceptions of things, that is, one learns to recognize ignorance, including one's own.

Plato and Aristotle

Two very important philosophers of ancient Greece, and of all time, were **Plato** (c. 427–347 B.C.) and **Aristotle** (384–332 B.C.). Plato was the pupil of Socrates and the teacher of Aristotle. Plato and Aristotle were both interested in practically every subject, and both said something worth listening to about the great majority of philosophical topics and problems. But their metaphysical ideas were especially important for posterity. Platonic metaphysics, for example, formed the model for Christian theology for around fifteen centuries, and this model was superseded only because the translations of Aristotle's works were rediscovered by European philosophers and theologians in the thirteenth century A.D. After the rediscovery

The most detailed source of information about Socrates is Plato's dialogues, especially the early dialogues, in which Socrates is the star. There is controversy about how accurately these dialogues represent Socrates; the later dialogues almost certainly reflect Plato's own view, even though "Socrates" is doing the speaking in them. Socrates was primarily concerned with finding the essences of the particular virtues, and of virtue in general, and proceeded by using the Socratic method to critique proposed definitions. (We'll get into this in Chapter 7.) But it was doubtless Plato, and not Socrates, who invented the Theory of Forms.

Socrates was famous among his contemporaries not only for his philosophical ability but also for his virtue, courage, and stamina. He staunchly opposed transgressions of justice, at considerable risk to himself. His trial and subsequent death by drinking hemlock after his conviction (for "corrupting" young men and not believing in the city's gods) are reported by Plato in the gripping dialogues *Apology*, *Crito*, and *Phaedo*. These dialogues reveal that Socrates was an individual of towering character and true grit. Although it would have been easy for him to escape from prison, he did not do so because, by having chosen to live in Athens, he had implicitly promised to obey the laws of the city. J. O. Urmson and Jonathan Rée's *The Concise Encyclopedia of Western Philosophy and Philosophers* summarizes as follows:

> The greatest value of Plato's Socrates is his superb championship of the ideal of reason, and his high and clear conceptions of what reason demands. He impresses us, more than any other figure in literature, with the supreme importance of thinking as well as possible and making our actions conform to our thoughts. To this end he preaches the knowledge of one's own starting-points, the hypothetical entertainment of opinions, the exploration of their consequences and connections, the willingness to follow the argument wherever it leads, the public confession of one's thoughts, the invitation to others to criticize, the readiness to reconsider, and at the same time firm action in accordance with one's present beliefs. Plato's *Apology* has in fact made Socrates the chief martyr of reason as the gospels have made Jesus the chief martyr of faith.

of Aristotle, *his* metaphysics came to predominate in Christian thinking, though Christianity remained and is still Platonic in many, many ways.

What we shall do now is examine Plato's conception of reality, which is encapsulated in what is known as the Theory of Forms.

Plato and the Theory of Forms

The Theory of Forms is discussed in several of the some two dozen compositions that are known as Plato's dialogues. The best known account is given in Plato's most famous dialogue, the *Republic*. The *Republic* comes from the so-called middle period of Plato's writings, during which Plato is thought to have reached the peak of genius.

According to Plato's Theory of Forms, what is truly real is not the objects we encounter in sensory experience but rather **Forms,** and these can only be grasped intellectually. Therefore, once you know what Plato's Forms are, you will understand the Theory of Forms and the essentials of Platonic metaphysics.

An example or two will help to make clear what a Form is. The Greeks were excellent geometers, which isn't too surprising because they invented the subject. Now, when a Greek geometer demonstrated some property of, say, *circularity*, he was not demonstrating the property of something that could actually be found in the physical world. After all, you don't really find circularity in the physical world: what you find are *things*—various round objects—that approach perfect circularity but are not *perfectly* circular. Even if you are drawing circles with an excellent compass and are paying close attention to what you are drawing, your "circle" is not really perfectly circular. Thus, when a geometer discovered a property of circularity, for example, he was discovering something about an *ideal* thing. Circularity doesn't really exist in the physical world. Circularity, then, is an example of a Form.

Let's take another example. Consider two beautiful objects, let's say a beautiful statue and a beautiful house. These are two very different objects, clearly. But they have *something* in common, for they both qualify as beautiful. What they have in common is beauty. Beauty is another example of a Form. Notice that beauty, like circularity, is not something you encounter directly, in the physical world. What you encounter in the physical world is always some object or other, a house or a statue or whatever, which may or may not be beautiful. But beauty itself is not something you meet up with; rather, you meet up with *objects* that to varying degrees *possess* beauty, or, as Plato said, "participate" in the Form *beauty*. Beauty, like circularity, is an ideal thing, not a concrete thing.

You may be tempted to suppose that the Forms are just ideas or concepts in someone's mind. But this might be a mistake. Before any people were around, there were circular things, logs and round stones and so on—that is, things that came close in varying degrees to being perfectly circular. If there were circular things when there were no people around or people-heads to have people-ideas in, it would seem that circularity is not just an idea in people's heads. You may find it more difficult to suppose that there were beautiful things before there were people to think of things as beautiful, but your difficulty might only be due to your assuming that "beauty is in the eyes of the beholder." Whether that assumption truly is justified is actually an unsettled question (it's a question that belongs to the aesthetics branch of philosophy, by the way).

Unfortunately, sometimes Plato's Forms are referred to as **Ideas,** and the Theory of Forms is also said to be the Theory of Ideas. But *Idea* is misleading because, as you can see, Plato's Forms are not the sort of ideas that exist in people. So we will stick with the word *Forms*.

At this point let's consider two important features of Forms. We'll begin by asking: How *old* is circularity? Immediately on hearing the question, you will realize that circularity is not any age. Circular things, sand dollars and bridge abutments and so on, are some age or other. But circularity itself has no age. The same

PROFILE / Aristocles, a.k.a "Plato" (c. 427–347 B.C.)

"**P**lato" was the nickname of an Athenian whose true name was Aristocles. The nickname, which means "broad shoulders," stuck, and so did this man's philosophy. Few individuals, if any, have had more influence on Western thought than Plato.

Plato initially studied with Cratylus, who was a follower of Heraclitus, and then with Socrates. He was also influenced by the Pythagoreans, from whom he may have derived his great respect for mathematics. Plato thought that the study of mathematics was a necessary introduction to philosophy, and it is said that he expelled from his Academy students who had difficulty with mathematical concepts.

Plato founded his Academy in 387, and it was the first multisubject, multiteacher institution of higher learning in Western civilization. The Academy survived for nine centuries, until the emperor Justinian closed it to protect Christian truth.

Plato's dialogues are divided into three groups. According to recent respected scholarship, the earliest include most importantly the *Apology*, which depicts and philosophically examines Socrates' trial and execution; the *Meno*, which is concerned with whether virtue can be taught; the *Gorgias*, which concerns the nature of right and wrong; and the first book of the *Republic*. The dialogues from the middle period include the remaining books of the *Republic*, *Phaedo*, *Symposium*, *Phaedrus*, *Cratylus*, *Parmenides*, and *Theaetetus*. In the most famous of these, the *Republic*, Plato explains and interrelates his conceptions of justice, the ideal state, and the Theory of Forms. Plato's later dialogues include most notably the *Timaeus*, which is Plato's account of the creation of the universe; the *Sophist*, which examines the nature of nonbeing; and the *Laws*, which is concerned with what laws a good constitution should contain. The *Laws* is Plato's longest dialogue and the only dialogue in which Socrates is not present.

thing is true of beauty, the Form. So we can see that the Forms are ageless, that is, *eternal*.

They are also *unchanging*. Your beautiful house may change as you make alterations or it ages, but that couldn't happen to beauty itself. And you, having learned that the circumference of the circle is equal to π times twice the radius distance, aren't apt to worry that someday the circle may change and, when it does, the circumference will no longer equal $2\pi r$. Mathematics teachers didn't have to revise what they knew about circularity when New Math came in.

Finally, the Forms are *unmoving* and *indivisible*. Indeed, what sense would it make even to suppose that they might move or be physically divided?

Plato's Cave

In the *Republic,* Plato uses a vivid allegory to explain his two-realms philosophy. He invites us to imagine a cave in which some prisoners are bound so that they can look only at the wall in front of them. Behind them is a fire whose light casts shadows of various objects on the wall in front of the prisoners. Because the prisoners cannot see the objects themselves, they regard the shadows they see as the true reality. One of the prisoners eventually escapes from the cave and, in the light of the sun, sees real objects for the first time, becoming aware of the big difference between them and the shadow images he had always taken for reality.

The cave, obviously, represents the world we see and experience with our senses, and the world of sunlight represents the realm of Forms. The prisoners represent ordinary people, who, in taking the sensible world to be the real world, are condemned to darkness, error, ignorance, and illusion. The escaped prisoner represents the philosopher, who has seen light, truth, beauty, knowledge, and true reality.

Of course, if the philosopher returns to the cave to tell the prisoners how things really are, they will think his brain has been addled. This difficulty is sometimes faced by those who have seen the truth and decide to tell others about it.

When you think of these various characteristics of Forms and remember as well that Plato equated the Forms with true reality, you may begin to see why we stated that Plato's metaphysics formed the model for Christian theology. You may also be reminded, we hope, of what Parmenides said about true being (i.e., that it is eternal, unmoving, unchanging, and indivisible). Of course, you should also remember that for Parmenides there is only one being, but for Plato there are many Forms.

But why did Plato say that only the Forms are truly real? Stop and think: a thing is beautiful only to the extent it participates in the Form *beauty,* just as it is circular only if it participates in the Form *circularity*. Likewise a thing is large only if it participates in the Form *largeness,* and the same principle would hold for all of a thing's properties. Thus, a large, beautiful, round thing—a beautiful, large, round oak table, for instance—couldn't be beautiful, large, or round if the Forms *beauty, largeness,* and *circularity* did not exist. Indeed, if the Forms *oak* and *table* did not exist, "it" wouldn't even be an oak table. Sensible objects—that is, the things we encounter in sensory experience—are what they are only if they sufficiently participate in their corresponding Forms. They—sensible objects—owe their reality to the Forms. So the ultimate reality belongs to the Forms.

Many people tend to scold philosophers, mathematicians, and other thinkers for being concerned with abstractions and concepts. "That's all very interesting," they say about some philosophical or mathematical theory, "but I'm more interested in the *real* world." By "real world" they mean the world you experience with your senses. On the face of it, at least, Plato makes out a convincing case that that world is *not* the real world at all.

Of course, Plato was aware that there is a sense in which the objects we see and touch are real. Even appearances are *real* appearances. But Plato's position is that

In Plato's "Myth of the Cave," a group of prisoners is placed so they can see, on the wall of the cave, only reflections of objects carried back and forth in front of a fire behind them. Because the reflections are all they see, the prisoners assume the reflections to be reality.

the objects we see and touch have a _lesser_ reality. They have a lesser reality because they can only approximate their Form and thus are always to some extent flawed. Any particular beautiful thing will always be deficient in beauty compared with the Form _beauty_. And, as any particular beautiful thing owes whatever degree of beauty it has to the Form _beauty_, the Form is the source of what limited reality as a beautiful thing the thing has.

Thus, Plato introduced into Western thought a _two-realms_ concept. On one hand, there is the realm of particular, changing, sense-perceptible or "sensible" things. This realm Plato likened to a cave. It is the realm of flawed and lesser entities. Consequently it is also, for those who concern themselves with sensible things, a source of error, illusion, and ignorance. On the other hand, there is the realm of Forms—eternal, fixed, and perfect, the source of all reality and of all true knowledge. This Platonic dualism, you shall see, was incorporated into Christianity and transmitted through the ages to our thought today, where it lingers still and affects our views on virtually every subject.

Lesser reality

two-realms
particulars
forms

Now Plato believed that some forms, especially the Forms *truth, beauty,* and *goodness,* are of a higher order than other Forms. For example, you can say of the Form *circularity* that it is beautiful, but you cannot say of the Form *beauty* that it is circular. So the Form *beauty* is higher than the Form *circularity.* This fact will turn out to be very important when we consider Plato's ethics in the third part of this book. Also, as we shall see in Part 3, Plato connected his Theory of Forms with a theory of the ideal state.

Aristotle

Plato's most distinguished pupil was **Aristotle** (384–322 B.C.), on whom Plato had a tremendous influence. Aristotle was eventually hired to be a teacher of Alexander the Great, but if Aristotle in turn had a tremendous influence on Alexander, there is little evidence of it. It's a good bet that Alexander, who conquered the world, had other things on his mind besides philosophy.

We noted earlier that we owe the term *metaphysics* to Aristotle, or at least to those who catalogued his works. But metaphysics formed just a part of Aristotle's interests. Aristotle was interested in every subject that came along, and he had something reasonably intelligent to say about all of them, from poetry to physics, from biology to friendship.

Aristotle's books are more systematic than are Plato's, providing evidence of his more painstaking attention to nature. It should tell you something, however, that although Plato is a main staple of any decent literature program, Aristotle is not. Cicero did praise Aristotle for his "copious and golden eloquence," but many find Aristotle a bit tedious. Maybe that's because what we have from Aristotle is mainly lecture notes edited by some of his students.

Nevertheless, Aristotle was a careful observer and a brilliant theorizer, and his thought influenced philosophy in the future. Some fifteen centuries after his death, he was considered the definitive authority on all subjects outside religion, a fact that may have impeded more than it helped scientific progress. This is because science, to get anywhere, cannot assume that something is so solely because some authority says that it is so, even if that authority is Aristotle.

What we call metaphysics Aristotle called "first philosophy." First philosophy, in Aristotle's view, is in some sense more abstract and general than are the specific sciences, and it considers the most basic questions of existence. Therefore, since the most basic question of existence is, What is it to be? we'll begin there.

In Aristotle's opinion, to be is to be a particular thing. And each thing, he maintained, is a combination of *matter* and *form.* A statue, for example, is a chunk of marble with a certain form. It is the same with other things, too. There is some stuff out of which each thing is made, and there is the particular form this bit of stuff takes. Without the stuff, the thing wouldn't exist, because you can't have a thing made out of nothing. And without form, the thing wouldn't exist, either. Without form, the stuff would not be some *particular kind of thing;* it would just be *stuff.* So the form is what determines what the thing is. It is the essential nature of the thing.

PROFILE / Aristotle (384–322 B.C.)

Aristotle wasn't correct about everything. He thought that the brain is a minor organ compared with the heart and that eels are spontaneously generated from mud. He also thought that parsnips cause erections and that women are an inferior product.

But he did know a great deal. In fact, Aristotle systematized all that was then known and, as if that weren't sufficient, he extended the limits of knowledge in virtually every existing subject, including biology, psychology, zoology, physics, and astronomy as well as in those areas that today are deemed the province of philosophy, including ethics, politics, aesthetics, metaphysics, and logic. His work was of enormous and lasting significance.

Aristotle was born in Stagira, a Greek colony along the Macedonia coast. His father, Nicomachus, was the physician of the king of Macedonia, Amyntas II. When he was eighteen, Aristotle went to Athens, where he studied under Plato at Plato's Academy for some twenty years. Plato may ultimately have come to resent Aristotle, and Aristotle eventually discovered that he disagreed with important Platonic doctrines, but Aristotle always retained a great respect for his teacher.

In 342, Aristotle was hired by Philip of Macedonia to tutor his son, Alexander, who was thirteen at the time. Alexander, of course, went on to conquer most of the then civilized world, but we suspect that none of this was the result of anything Aristotle taught him. Whatever Alexander learned from Aristotle, he repaid by sending Aristotle zoological specimens from his many travels and by funding his studies.

In 335, Aristotle formed his own school at the Lyceum, in Athens, and some of the sharper members of the Academy joined up with Aristotle. Because of his practice of lecturing in the Lyceum's walking place, or *peripatos,* Aristotle's followers became known as the peripatetics, the "walkers."

Aristotle emphasized the importance of direct observation of nature and believed that you must obtain factual data before you can begin to theorize. He also maintained that knowledge of things requires description, classification, and causal explanation. This is, of course, the modern scientific view, though (as we explain in the text) Aristotle emphasized a different aspect of causation from that stressed in modern science.

Aristotle's works are often classified under five headings: the *Organum,* which consisted of six treatises on logic; the *Rhetoric* and the *Poetics;* his works on natural science, including most importantly the *Physics* and *De Anima* (on the soul); *Metaphysics;* and the works on ethics and politics, which include the *Nicomachean Ethics, Eudemian Ethics,* and *Politics.*

To illustrate this: the marble of the statue is the same marble as it was when it was cut into a block at the quarry. But now it has a new form, and that form is what distinguishes the marble now from the marble in the block in the quarry. Yes, the marble has always had *some* form or other, but its transformation to this particular form is what makes it a statue. Thus, the form is what determines what a thing is, and for this reason Aristotle equated a thing's form with its essence.

So you need both form and matter to have a thing, and, with the exception of god, discussed later, neither form nor matter is ever found in isolation from the other, according to Aristotle.

Things do change, of course: they become something new. Thus another basic question is: What produces a change? Now because in Aristotle's opinion each change must be directed toward some end, there are really just *four* basic questions that can be asked of anything:

1. *What is the thing?* In other words, what is its form? Aristotle called this the **formal cause** of the thing. We don't use the world *cause* that way, but Aristotle did, and we just have to accept that.

2. *What is it made of?* Aristotle called this the **material cause.**

3. *What made it?* This Aristotle called the **efficient cause**—and this is what today we often mean by "cause."

4. *What purpose does it serve?* That is, for what end was it made? This Aristotle called the **final cause.**

Consider again a statue, Michelangelo's *David,* for example. What it is, (1), is a statue. What it is made of, (2), is marble. What made it, (3), is Michelangelo (or Michelangelo's chisel on the marble). And (4), it was made for the purpose of creating a beautiful object. Of course, natural objects were not made by humans for their purposes, but they still do have "ends." The end of an acorn, for instance, is to be a tree.

But consider the acorn example more closely. The acorn is not actually a tree, only potentially so, correct? Change can therefore be viewed, according to Aristotle, as movement from potentiality to actuality. Therefore, because actuality is the source of change, *pure actuality* is the *ultimate* source of change. Pure actuality is thus the unchanged changer or unmoved mover or, in short, god. It should be noted that the pure actuality that Aristotle equated with god is not God, the personal deity of the Jewish or Christian religions.

It is an important fact that Aristotle took great issue with Plato's Theory of Forms. For Plato, two or more items, coins, let's say, can both be said to be circular if they participate in a third thing, the Form *circularity*. According to Plato, the Form *circularity* exists apart or separately from individual coins and other circular things, and they are dependent on it for their existence as circular things, as explained earlier. But according to Aristotle, this talk of participating is metaphorical and meaningless. Further, he thought that Plato was mistaken in holding that, although individual circular things depend for their existence as circular things on the Form *circularity,* the reverse does not hold true. For in fact (believed Aristotle), the reverse does hold true: if there weren't individual circular things, there would be no such thing as the Form *circularity*.

One of Aristotle's most compelling arguments against the Theory of Forms is known as the **Third Man argument.** It goes like this.

Consider a couple of circular coins. Plato said that what ties the coins together, what they have in common, is the Form *circularity.* But what, Aristotle asked, ties the coins together *with* the Form *circularity?* Some *further* form? Well, what ties this further Form together with the first Form, yet *another* Form? You can see the problem.

Aristotle's own view is that the Forms are **universals**—something that more than one individual can be. Many different individual things can be beautiful or circular or large or green; so beauty, circularity, largeness, and greenness are universals. But only one thing can be you, and only one thing can be Aristotle; so you and Aristotle are not universals, but particulars. Universals, Aristotle insisted, do not exist separately or apart from particulars. Circularity and greenness, for example, have no independent existence apart from particular round things and particular green things.

Aristotle is fairly convincing when he tells us what is wrong with Plato's Theory of Forms, but he is less helpful in explaining just what universals are. The apparent failure of Aristotle (or Plato or their contemporaries) to produce a satisfactory theory of universals and their relationship to particulars resulted in an obsession with the problem through many centuries, and we will elaborate on the problem in a later box.

Now, a summary statement of the differences between Plato's and Aristotle's metaphysics in a few sentences is bound to be a grotesque oversimplification, unless the sentences were to be very complicated. Nevertheless, the overly simplified difference comes to this: according to Plato, there are two realms. One is the realm of particular, changing, sensible things, and the other is a separate and superior realm of eternal, fixed, and unchanging Forms to which the particular things owe their reality. According to Aristotle, forms are found only within particular things, which are an embodiment of both form and matter. Aristotle did not disdain having knowledge of particular, sensible things, and therefore, because these things are always changing, Aristotle was much concerned with change itself. This concern led him to his theory of the four causes that underlie change.

Checklist

To help you review, here is a checklist of the key philosophers and concepts of this chapter. The brief descriptive sentences summarize leading ideas. Keep in mind that some of these summary statements represent terrific oversimplifications of complex positions.

Philosophers

- **Thales** Held that the basic stuff out of which all else is composed is water.

- **Anaximenes** Said that the underlying principle of all things is air.
- **Anaximander** Held that the original source of all things is a boundless, indeterminate element.
- **The Pythagoreans** Maintained that enumerability constitutes the true nature of things.
- **Heraclitus** Held that the only reality is ceaseless change and that the underlying substance of the universe is fire.
- **Parmenides** Said that the only reality is permanent, unchanging, indivisible, and undifferentiated being and that change and motion are illusions of the senses.
- **Zeno** Devised clever paradoxes seeming to show that motion is impossible.
- **Empedocles** Held that apparent changes in things are in fact changes in the positions of basic particles, of which there are four types: earth, air, fire, and water. Said that two forces cause the basic changes: Love and Strife.
- **Anaxagoras** Maintained that all things are composed of infinitely divisible particles; said that the universe was caused by mind (*nous*) acting on matter.
- **The Atomists** (especially **Leucippus** and **Democritus**) Said that all things are composed of imperceptible, indestructible, indivisible, eternal, and uncreated atoms. Held that motion needs no explanation.
- **Socrates** Not primarily a metaphysician. Practitioner of the Socratic method.
- **Plato** Most influential in metaphysics for his doctrine of two separate worlds and his Theory of Forms.
- **Aristotle** Held that particular things embody both form and matter (no separate realms); proposed a four-cause explanation of change.

Concepts

metaphysics

the question "What is the nature of being?" in all its aspects

epistemology

total vs. modified skepticism

basic substance/element/stuff

a priori principle

nous

determinism

free will vs. determinism

Theory of Forms (Ideas)

allegory of the cave

Platonic dualism

peripatetics

formal, efficient, material, and final causes

Third Man argument

universal

Questions for Discussion and Review

1. Explain the derivation of the word *metaphysics*. *[handwritten: 25; After the Physics; ARistotle after the books on physics or nature]*

2. Provide some possible interpretations of the question "What is the nature of being?" *[handwritten: 26]* *[margin notes: Property - Thing; one - many; fixed - changing; one kind, many kinds; degrees of reality; fundamental substance]*

3. Explain the difference between total and modified skepticism. *[handwritten: 27; Nothing can be known   Knowledge might be possible]*

4. What are some of the questions that philosophers have been concerned with under the heading: Is knowledge possible? *[handwritten: 27; External, internal, senses, future, skeptic]* *[margin notes: Things, events, numbers, minds, matter, space, time, facts]*

5. Compare and contrast the metaphysics of the three Milesians. Whose metaphysics seems most plausible to you, and why? *[handwritten: 28-; Thales water; Anaximenes Air; Anaximander ageless indeterminate]* *[margin notes: Thing - characteristic ie red, green]*

6. The Pythagoreans theorized that all things come to be in accordance with number. What does this theory mean? *[handwritten: Things, Ideas exist as separate entities if they can be enumerated; order, sequence, fundamental reality is like numbers - unchanging]* *[margin: ideal, perfect, eternal]*

7. Compare and contrast the metaphysics of Heraclitus and Parmenides, *[handwritten: fire - reality is ceaseless change vs unchanging - change & motion are illusions]*

8. Explain and critically evaluate Parmenides' arguments that being is unitary, undifferentiated, and eternal. *[handwritten: motion imp.; reasoning founded on assumed principles - misleading false concept; being is unitary assumes that a second thing is different from the 1st, does not have parts, beginning or end - motion impossible]*

9. Compare and contrast the metaphysics of Empedocles, Anaxagoras, and the Atomists. Whose views are the most plausible, and why?

10. Plato's metaphysics incorporates ideas from some of the other, earlier philosophers mentioned in this chapter. Identify as many of those philosophers and ideas as possible.

11. "The behavior of atoms is governed entirely by physical law." "Humans have free will." Are these statements incompatible? Explain. *[handwritten: yes + No   29 37]*

12. Give an example of a Platonic Form other than one mentioned in the text. Now explain whether it really exists, and why. *[handwritten: The perfect time keeper vs clocks]*

13. What are some reasons for believing that a world of Forms exists separately from the world of concrete, individual things? *[handwritten: O, checks, Abstracts ie can constitution, Justice, freedom, time]*

14. Are appearances real for Plato? Are they real in fact? *[handwritten: degrees of reality, temporary reality, contradiction]*

15. What are the four Aristotelian causes of a baseball? *[handwritten: form, mat. efficient, final purpose]*

16. Aristotle believed that if individual horses didn't exist, then there would be no such thing as the Form *horse*. Is this correct?

Suggested Further Readings

Aristotle, *Metaphysics,* in J. Barnes, ed., *The Complete Works of Aristotle,* vol. 2 (Princeton: Princeton University Press, 1984). Aristotle's *Metaphysics* is not always easy to read and understand, but it is entertaining. Don't hesitate to have a look. It contains useful information on Aristotle's predecessors, too.

[handwritten at bottom: 1, 2 - 12 10 pgs]

John Burnet, *Early Greek Philosophy,* 4th ed. (London: Macmillan, originally published in 1930). This is generally considered the standard work on the subject.

E. Hamilton and H. Cairns, eds., *The Collected Dialogues of Plato* (New York: Bollingen Foundation, 1961). This is what you need to acquaint yourself firsthand with Plato's dialogues. Be sure to read the *Republic,* if you haven't already.

G. S. Kirk, J. E. Raven, and M. Schofield, *The Presocratic Philosophers: A Critical History with a Selection of Texts,* 2nd ed. (Cambridge: Cambridge University Press, 1983). This is a comprehensive recent treatment of the pre-Socratics.

Merrill Ring, *Beginning with the Pre-Socratics* (Mountain View, Calif.: Mayfield Publishing Company, 1987). An introductory-level text about the beginnings of philosophy in ancient Greece.

A. E. Taylor, *Aristotle* (New York: Dover Publications, 1955). A popularly written introduction to Aristotle's ideas.

A. E. Taylor, *Plato: The Man and His Works* (New York: Methuen, 1960). A standard introduction to Plato's philosophy.

Gregory Vlastos, *Socrates: Ironist and Moral Philosopher* (Ithaca, N.Y.: Cornell University Press, 1991).

Mary Ellen Waithe, ed., *A History of Women Philosophers,* vol. 1 (Dordrecht, Boston and London: Kluwer Academic Press, 1991). The first of a four-volume series on the history of women philosophers.

The Philosophers of the Hellenistic and Christian Eras

3

Though philosophers disagree on the <u>nature of things</u>, and <u>the mode of investigating truth</u>, and of the <u>good to which all our actions ought to tend</u>, yet on these three great general questions, all their intellectual energy is spent.

—St. Augustine

Before he died in 323 B.C. at age thirty-two, Aristotle's student Alexander the Great, son of the Macedonian king Philip II, had conquered the entire civilized Western world, pulverizing all opposition and naming a score of cities after himself to ensure that everyone got the message. This period of Macedonian domination of the Greek-speaking world, known as the **Hellenistic age** (_Hellene_ means "Greek"), was a period of major achievements in mathematics and science.

Having started with Alexander around 335 B.C., Macedonian hegemony was carried forth by the families of three of Alexander's generals and lasted about a century and a half, until Philip V of Macedon and Antiochus III of Syria were each defeated (around 190 B.C.) by a new ascending power: Rome. From that time on for approximately the next seven hundred years, the Western world _was_ the Roman Empire, built on plunder and the power of the sword.

For two centuries, beginning in 27 B.C. with the reign of Julius Caesar's grand-nephew Octavian, who was known as "Augustus, the first Roman emperor and savior of the world," the Roman Empire enjoyed peace, security, and political stability. But eventually, after the reign of Marcus Aurelius (A.D. 161–180), conditions deteriorated into chaos. Nevertheless, the ultimate fall of the empire was postponed by Diocletian, who divided the empire into eastern (Byzantine) and western (Roman) halves, and by Constantine I, who granted universal religious tolerance, thus in effect recognizing Christianity. Finally, however, internal anarchy opened the Roman frontiers to the barbarians. Although the Eastern empire survived until the fifteenth century, in 476 the last emperor of the West was deposed by the Goths. The Dark Ages followed.

If the Romans were anything, they were practical. They built aqueducts and underground sewers and had glass windows. Wealthy Romans lived in lavish town houses equipped with central heating and running water. Roman highways were built on road base four feet thick and were paved with concrete and squared stone. Roman roads and bridges are still used today, and some may outlive the interstates.

But although they were masters of the applied arts and of practical disciplines such as military science and law (Roman law provided the basis for modern civil law), the Romans had little use for art for art's sake or for literature or science. From the Roman perspective, no form of entertainment was quite so satisfying as watching men fight other men to the death, although seeing humans fight animals came in a close second. Witnessing public torture was a popular amusement.

Metaphysics in the Roman Empire

In philosophy the contributions of the Romans were minimal and almost entirely unoriginal. During Hellenistic and Roman periods there were four main traditions or "schools" of philosophy; three of these arose around the time of Alexander and were in fact products of Greek culture, not Roman. Two of these—known as **Stoicism** and **Epicureanism**—were concerned mainly with the question of how individuals should best conduct their affairs. If there had been supermarkets at the time, then Stoic and Epicurean advice would have been available in paperbacks for sale at the checkout counters. But these schools of philosophy are a subject for our section on ethics. The third school—**Skepticism**—was concerned with the possibility of knowledge. In just a second we will say something about it. The remaining school, unlike these other three, did arise during Roman times, but this school was for all intents and purposes a revision of Plato's philosophy. It is known as **Neoplatonism.** Because it had considerable influence on the metaphysics of Christianity, we should say something about Neoplatonism now.

Plotinus

The great philosopher of Neoplatonism was **Plotinus** (c. A.D. 204–270). During Plotinus's lifetime, the Roman Empire was in a most dismal state, suffering plague, marauding barbarian hordes, and an army incompetent to do anything but assassinate its own leaders. Civilization was in fact tottering dangerously near the abyss. Plotinus, however, was inclined to ignore these earthly trifles, for he had discovered that by turning his attention inward, he could achieve union with god.

Now think back for a moment to Plato. According to Plato's metaphysics, there are two worlds. On one hand, there is the cave, that is, the world of changing appearances: the world of sensation, ignorance, error, illusion, and darkness. On

Plotinus

Plotinus's interest in philosophy began when he was twenty-eight in Alexandria (the most famous Alexandria, the one in Egypt). His first teacher was Ammonius, the "Sack Carrier," who was so called because he earned his living as a gardener.

About 244, Plotinus traveled to Rome and founded what came to be a renowned school of Neoplatonic philosophy. Even the Emperor Gallienus and his wife, Salonina, patronized the school. Plotinus tried to get his students to ask questions for themselves; consequently the discussions were lively and sometimes almost violent. On one occasion Plotinus had to stop a particularly ugly confrontation between a senator and a rich man; he urged both parties to calm themselves and think rather only of the One (about which see the text).

Plotinus himself was a quiet, modest, and selfless human being. He was thought to possess an uncanny ability to penetrate into the human character and its motives, and so he was sought out for all manner of practical advice.

He would not, however, acknowledge his birthday. This is because, at least according to Porphyry, who wrote a biography of Plotinus, Plotinus was ashamed that his immortal soul was contained in a mortal body, and the event of his soul entering his body was therefore something to be regretted. He also would not allow his face to be painted or his body to be sculpted. In fact, his long disregard of his body eventually caused him to lose his voice, and his hands and feet festered with abscesses and pus. Because Plotinus greeted his students with an embrace, the net result was a falling off in enrollment.

Plotinus's philosophy had a great influence on St. Augustine and other doctors and fathers of the Church. Christian theology is unthinkable without the mystical depth that comes from him.

the other hand, there is the light, that is, the world of Forms: the world of intellect, knowledge, truth, reality, and brightness whose ultimate source of existence and essence is the Form *the Good*. Plotinus further specified this ultimate source or reality as god or the One. For Plotinus, god is above and beyond everything else— utterly transcendent.

But Plotinus's god, like Plato's Good, and unlike the Christian God, is not a *personal* god. God, according to Plotinus, is indefinable and indescribable, because to define or describe god would be to place limitations on what has no limits. About god it can only be said that god is. And god can be apprehended only through a coming together of the soul and god in a mystical experience. This mystical "touching" of god, this moment in which we have the "vision," is the highest moment of life.

Plotinus's thought was very influential on the last of the great ancient philosophers, Augustine, who also happens to be one of the two or three most important Christian theologians of all time. We might just say a word here about the spread of Christianity because its eventual predominance in Europe came to define the framework within which most Western philosophizing took place. Not long after Plotinus, the great philosophers of the western part of the Roman Empire, or what became of the western part, were almost without exception Christians.

The original Christians, including the rabbi Jesus and his followers, were Jews, though Christianity gradually evolved from a Jewish sect to a separate religion. Now, the Romans were generally pretty tolerant of the religious ideas and practices of the various peoples under their subjugation, but the Jews, including members of the Christian splinter sect, were not willing to pay even token homage to the Roman emperor-deities. The Christians, moreover, were unusually active in trying to make converts. Thus, to Roman thinking, the Christians not only were atheists who ridiculed the Roman deities, but they also, unlike more orthodox Jews, were fanatical rabble-rousers who attempted to impose on others what to the Romans counted as gross superstition. So for a couple of centuries or so, the Christians were persecuted from time to time by assorted Roman emperors, sometimes rather vigorously.

Nevertheless, of the numerous cults that existed during the first couple of centuries A.D., Christianity eventually became the most popular. Its followers became so numerous and, thanks to the administrative efforts of Paul of Tarsus (later St. Paul), so well organized that by the early part of the fourth century, the emperor Constantine announced its official toleration.

Specifics of Christian doctrine need not concern us, though its central beliefs are well known: Jesus is the son of God, and Jesus's life, crucifixion, and resurrection are proof of God's love for humans and forgiveness of human sin; in addition, those who have faith in Christ will be saved and have life everlasting. The God of Christianity is thought (by Christians) to be the creator of all; and he is also thought to be distinct from his creation.

St. Augustine (A.D. 354–430), who came from the town of Tagaste, near what is today the Algerian city of Annaba, transferred Platonic and Neoplatonic themes to Christianity. Transported down through the ages to us today, these themes affect the thought of both Christian and non-Christian.

St. Augustine

"Whenever Augustine," Thomas Aquinas later wrote, "who was saturated with the teachings of the Platonists, found in their writings anything consistent with the faith, he adopted it; and whatever he found contrary to the faith, he amended." Through Augustine, Christianity became so permanently interwoven with elements of Platonic thought that today, as William Inge said, it is impossible to remove Platonism from Christianity "without tearing Christianity to pieces."

St. Augustine regarded Plotinus and Plato as having *prepared* him for Christianity by exposing him to important Christian principles before he encountered them in Scripture. (Neither Plato nor Plotinus was Christian, it should be clear.) Augustine had a very strong inclination toward skepticism and was tempted to believe that "nothing can be known." Plato and Plotinus enabled Augustine to overcome this inclination.

We should be more specific, however. Today we take for granted the concept of a separate, immaterial reality known as the transcendent God. Even those who do not believe in God are familiar with this concept of an immateriality and are not

PROFILE / Saint Augustine (354–430)

Augustine grew up in northern Africa. His father was a successful man of the world, and Augustine was expected to follow a similar path. Accordingly, he studied rhetoric in Carthage. While there, however, he fell in with a group of students known as the "rebels," who found amusement in such pasttimes as attacking innocent passersby at night. Augustine, to his credit, did not participate in these episodes, though he did steal fruit from a neighbor's tree for the sheer perversity of doing so.

As a young man Augustine also indulged in many love affairs. He took a concubine, and the union produced a son. He came to have doubts about his lifestyle, however, and eventually these doubts began to take the upper hand. With the encouragement of his family, he became engaged to a young woman of a prominent family. But Augustine grew impatient and took a new lover.

In the meanwhile, Augustine's studies had taken him to Rome and to Milan, where he became a professor of rhetoric. His mother, Monica, had already become a Christian. Through her encouragement and through Augustine's exposure to St. Ambrose, the celebrated preacher, Augustine was baptized into Christianity at the age of thirty-three. He returned to northern Africa and soon thereafter was called on to serve as Bishop of Hippo.

As bishop, Augustine used his rhetorical abilities to the full in fiercely attacking what he perceived to be the many heresies of the time. His thinking was dominated by two themes, the sinfulness of human beings and the inscrutability of God. At the age of seventy-two, he withdrew from the world and died in self-chosen solitude.

inclined to dismiss it as blatant nonsense (though some, of course, do). But careful reflection reveals that there isn't much within experience that gives rise to this concept, for we seem to experience only concrete, physical things. Through the influence of Plato and Plotinus, St. Augustine perceived that belief in a distinct immaterial reality was not the blindly superstitious thing that it might seem. And through Augustine's thought, the Christian belief in a nonmaterial God received a philosophical justification, a justification without which (it is arguable) this religion would not have sustained the belief of thoughtful people through the ages. (Other explanations of the durability of the Christian belief in God are, of course, possible.)

Augustine accepted the Platonic view that "there are two realms, an intelligible realm where truth itself dwells, and this sensible world which we perceive by sight and touch." Like Plato before him, St. Augustine thought that the capacity of the

Augustine, God, and Time

The *ex nihilo* theory (God created it all out of nothing) invites a troublesome question for Christian theology: Why did God choose to create the world at the time he did and not at some other? Thanks to Plato and Plotinus, Augustine was able to provide a potentially reasonable answer to this question.

According to Augustine, the question rests on a false assumption, that God (and his actions) exist *within* time. On the contrary, Augustine maintained, God does not exist in time; instead, time began with the creation by God of the world. God is *beyond* time. In this way the timeless attribute of Plato's Good and Plotinus's One was transferred by Augustine to the Christian God.

But what exactly, Augustine wondered, is time? Here Augustine broke new philosophical ground by coming forth with a very tempting answer to this question.

"What, then, is time?" he asked. "If no one asks of me, I know; if I wish to explain to him who asks, I know not." On one hand only the present exists, for the past is no more, and the future is not yet. But on the other hand certain things did happen in the past, and other things will happen in the future, and thus past and future are quite real. How can the past and the future be both real and nonexistent?

Augustine's answer to this almost hopelessly baffling question is that past and future exist only in the human mind. "The present of things past is memory; the present of things present is sight; and the present of things future is expectation."

Thus, Augustine's analysis of time is that it is a subjective phenomenon. It exists "only in the mind." (Thus, before God created us, there was no time.) The idea that time is subjective was later developed by Kant into the theory that time, space, causation, and other basic "categories" of being are all subjective impositions of the mind on the world. The same idea was then carried to its ultimate conclusion by the Absolute Idealists, who said that the world *is* mind. We will turn to all this in due course.

Augustine's views on time can be found in the eleventh book of his *Confessions*.

human mind to grasp eternal truths implies the existence of something infinite and eternal apart from the world of sensible objects, an essence that in some sense represents the source or ground of all reality and of all truth. This ultimate ground and highest being Augustine identified with God, rather than Platonic Forms.

Augustine, however, accepted the Old Testament idea that God created the world out of nothing. This idea of creation ***ex nihilo,*** creation out of nothing, is really quite a startling concept when you think about it, and Greek thinkers had had trouble with it. Their view had been that getting something from nothing is impossible.

Augustine also accepted, of course, the Gospel story of the life, death, and resurrection of Jesus Christ and believed that God took on human form in the person of Jesus. Thus the Augustinian theology gives God a human aspect that would have been unthinkable for Neoplatonists, who thought that the immaterial realm could not be tainted with the imperfection of mere gross matter.

It is sometimes said that St. Augustine is the founder of Christian *theology*. Certainly his influence on Christian thought was second to none, with the exception of St. Paul, who formulated a great deal of Christian doctrine. One very important aspect of his thought was his concept of evil, in which the influence of Plato and Plotinus is again evident. We will say something about this in Part 2 on ethics.

Hypatia ♀

Another significant figure of this period was **Hypatia** (370/75–415). A traditional platonist, Hypatia was sympathetic to Plotinus's metaphysics, and to stoicism (Chapter 7). All good Plotinians knew that the solution to the mystery of the *One,* the ultimate source of reality, would explain everything. It would explain the nature of God, the nature of the universe, and our place in it.

Today, for most people, philosophical views about metaphysics have nothing to do with how they act. But you can't really understand and appreciate philosophers like Hypatia (or Plotinus) without understanding that, for Hypatia, the philosophical *is* the personal. Holding certain philosophical views about metaphysics implies seeing the world in a particular way. Hypatia was a philosopher who introduced beginning students to Plato's metaphysics. She addressed moral and cosmological concerns that were fleshed out in Plotinus's mysteries. Plotinus's teachings were tinged with deep religious awe and quasimystical contemplation of the One. For Hypatia and for her students, Plotinus's interpretation of Plato's metaphysics implied a way of life. Teaching philosophy was not just a job, and the activity of teaching was not merely an entertaining academic exercise that had nothing to do with daily life. Philosophy *was* life.

You should also know that mathematics and astronomy, for Hypatia, are sciences that apply particular metaphysical views to the physical universe. They are the key to achieving personal ethical and religious knowledge. But the truths of mathematics—especially "divine geometry," as Hypatia's students called it (and probably she did, too)—prepare you to study Plato's metaphysics and its subdivision, cosmology (theories about the shape and composition of the universe).

For Hypatia and her students, developing technical expertise in mathematics and astronomy was a prerequisite to testing cosmological theories. Testing theories in mathematics and astronomy involved filling in significant gaps in the logic of the prevailing theories. In mathematics, those theories were by Diophantus, Euclid, Apollonius, and Pappus. In astronomy, the theories were by Aristarchus and Ptolemy.

Mathematics and geometry were practical tools with which to calculate astronomical truths. And what was astronomy but the study of the great mystery of the physical universe? And what was the universe? Why, it was God's mysterious creation. And what was God? Well, that was what religion and philosophy were to study, using two different but related approaches.

Religious worship, which included everything from pagan necromancy (check it out) and astrology to Christian communion, was a way of coming to know God through experiencing God's presence or God's messages. We don't know anything about the content of Hypatia's paganism, nor even whether she herself practiced

PROFILE / Hypatia of Alexandria (c. 370/75–415)

Hypatia taught in Alexandria, Egypt, at what was called the Museum. Her father, Theon, was a famous mathematician and astronomer there. Back then, philosophy was still a pretty wide field, and philosophers like Plotinus and Hypatia were not about to impose distinctions (as we now do) between such subjects as religion mathematics, astronomy, and the slice of philosophy known as metaphysics.

Hypatia became famous when she was very young. By 390, students were coming to her from throughout northern Africa. (Europe was still an uncivilized place, but Alexandria was late antiquity's equivalent of Silicon Valley.) Every decent scientist and philosopher passed through Alexandria.

Hypatia was a pagan, but she had lots of students who were Christians, and maybe even a few Jewish students. Considering that by 410 relationships among different religious groups were so bad that there were constant riots, Hypatia must have made sense to lots of people with very different orientations. Synesius came from Cyrene (in Libya) to become her student and went on to convert to Christianity, becoming first a priest and then a bishop.

Over the past thousand or so years, when anybody has bothered to write about Hypatia, the chronicler has invariably told the story of how she dealt with sexual harassment by one of her male students. She supposedly threw the fifth-century equivalent of a used sanitary napkin at him—and never heard from him again. (Apparently, the Museum didn't have procedures for dealing with sexual harassment. Does your college?)

Until this century, it was thought that Hypatia wrote only three books and that all of them were lost. Can you imagine your copy of this book being found *fifteen centuries* from now, and its being discovered to contain the last surviving fragment of Descartes's *Meditations?* That's what happened to all of Hypatia's works! From what we know now, it looks as if Hypatia prepared about half a dozen scholarly writings of various lengths. Some of those writings have only recently been identified by scholars as being by her. Her works were copied, edited, translated, retranslated, incorporated into other people's writings, bought, sold, and traded by scholars from Rome to Baghdad to Britain for more than a thousand years. Versions of her different works exist in Greek, Latin, Hebrew, and Arabic—but not in English. Sorry. Here's a list of writings by Hypatia: an edition of Diophantus's *Arithmetica,* a work based on Archimedes' *Sphere and Cylinder;* an anonymous work on one-sided figures; a commentary edition of Archimedes' *Dimension of the Circle;* a commentary edition of Apollonius Pergaeus's *Conics* that formed the basis for later commentary editions, including one by the astronomer Edmund Halley (of Halley's Comet fame); and a commentary edition of part of Ptolemy's *Syntaxis Mathematica.*

In 415, Hypatia was savagely murdered, allegedly by a gang of monks. Her corpse was then hacked into pieces and burned.

Philosophy professors are glad things have changed.

pagan rites. People were called "pagan" philosophers when they taught non-Christian—i.e., Greek—philosophy.

Hypatia was a dedicated teacher who prepared for her students careful, symmetrical expositions of elements of mathematical and astronomical proofs. She tried to demonstrate the completeness of Ptolemy's astronomy, and Diophantus's theory of algebra (then called arithmetic). Now, the philosophical problem of showing that a scientific theory was complete (explained everything within its scope) was a problem that philosophers pretty much ignored until the twentieth century. Nobody, not even Hypatia, had a clue how to show that a theory was complete.

But she gave it her best shot. Hypatia tried to show that scientific and mathematical theories were complete by introducing as many analogous cases and counterexamples as she could think up. She also tried to stick with extremely precise terminology so that a term's meaning wouldn't subtly shift from one appearance to another. Her efforts were philosophically motivated: she took her students along on a quest for completeness, instilling in them a desire to consider all the possible ways that a problem could be conceptualized.

For Hypatia, mathematics and astronomy were ways of checking metaphysical and epistemological features of Plato's, Aristotle's, and Plotinus's philosophies against the physical universe. Was Aristotle right, that the circle is the most perfect shape? Is it the most perfect because its periphery requires only one line, a line that has no beginning and no end? Or, is it the most perfect because, of all geometric shapes (as any mathematician worth her salary knew), it contains more area than any shape having a perimeter of an identical length? Mmm.

If a circle is the most perfect shape, then its ideal Form (in Plato's sense of Form) must be that which is reflected by God's most perfect and most mysterious creation, the universe. Is the universe circular? Inquiring astronomers wanted to know (they still do). Now, although pagans tended to think that the universe was God's most perfect creation, Christians and Jews tended to think that humans were. If God's most perfect creation is us, then we must be at the center of everything. The sun must revolve around us. This geocentric theory of the universe had been proven by the great second-century scholar Ptolemy Claudius.

Both Hypatia and her father, Theon (a mathematician and astronomer), taught Ptolemaic astronomy. They prepared an updated edition of Ptolemy, one that included thousands of astronomical observations that had been recorded in the centuries after Ptolemy's death. Now, one of the interesting problems with Ptolemy's theory (and this is true of any astronomical theory) was that the further away in time an observer was from Ptolemy, the less accurately Ptolemy's theory predicted the exact position of a particular star in the sky.

Unlike her father, Theon, Hypatia was not satisfied with approximate calculations, nor with rounded-off results. Sometimes she played with the theories, extending computations to many additional place values. This improved accuracy, which, in turn, improved the predictability of astronomical calculations. (Can you imagine doing astronomical calculations without a calculator? Hypatia did them in base 6 on an abacus!)

Hypatia tinkered with Ptolemy's theory, using more sophisticated algebra and geometry than he had, to make the astronomical facts a better fit with his theory and with theories of mathematics and geometry that he had relied on to develop his theory of astronomy. Sometimes she connected geometrical theorems to their astronomical applications and to Plato's metaphysics and cosmology. What she was seeking was something that theories should have, a feature called congruence. Sometimes she improved the rigor of theorems by finding and filling in gaps to achieve greater completeness. (When you study philosophy of science, you learn about congruence and completeness.) Sometimes Hypatia improved the soundness of proofs by devising direct proofs where only indirect proofs existed before. (You can learn the difference when you study logic.) Often, she came up with two seemingly competing hypotheses, and then worked the proof twice, as if to show that no matter how you reasonably might approach the problem, you would get the correct result. She saw the larger picture, the greater metaphysical ideas that ultimately may be confirmed by science.

Hypatia was the last major commentator on Ptolemy. Now, as we said, Ptolemy's astronomical theory fit nicely with Christian theology. After all, it seems only right that if we were created in God's image and likeness, that we, and our planet, should be the center of the universe. Ptolemy's work was then, and would remain for a thousand years (until Copernicus in the sixteenth century), the most influential work on astronomy. Hypatia found some errors in the part of Ptolemy's theory that showed how the sun revolved around the earth. She was concerned that Ptolemy's theory didn't always accurately predict the position of the sun.

We aren't sure which later astronomers noticed her work, because only two copies of her commentary on Ptolemy survived. Both of them were bought at a Byzantine garage sale by Lorenzo di Medici's library. Her work could have been seen by a young graduate student named Nicholas Copernicus, who was traveling around Italy trying to read all the Ptolemy he could find. But we don't know whether Copernicus actually saw it or whether it influenced him to rethink the geocentric model of the universe.

The Skeptical Challenge

Now recall that after Aristotle there emerged four main traditions or schools of philosophy, the Stoics and Epicureans (whose story belongs to Part 2 on ethics), the Neoplatonists (remember Plotinus?), and the Skeptics. To discuss the famous Skeptic tradition that emerged after Aristotle, we'll backtrack a bit to the beginning of epistemological philosophy, for although the Neoplatonists were mainly metaphysicians, the Skeptics were epistemologists. Epistemology, remember, is the branch of philosophy concerned with the nature and possibility of knowledge.

The roots of Skepticism—and the beginnings of epistemology—may be traced back to certain pre-Socratic philosophers. **Xenophanes** (c. 570–c. 480 B.C.), for example, declared that even if truth were stated, it would not be known. Xenophanes, to fix dates, was born about two hundred years after the first Olympic games were held and alphabetic writing began in Greece and about two hundred years before Alexander the Great demonstrated that it is possible to conquer the world, or what then passed for it in Alexander's circles. **Heraclitus** (c. 535–c. 475 B.C.), a contemporary of Xenophanes, had the theory that, just as you cannot step into the same river twice, everything is in flux, and this theory suggests that it is impossible to discover any fixed truth beyond what is expressed in the theory itself. (Heraclitus, however, did not himself deduce skeptical conclusions from his theory.) **Cratylus,** a younger contemporary of Socrates (469–399 B.C.), carried this view concerning flux even further and said that you cannot step even once into the same river, because both you and the river are continually changing. Because everything is changing, our words themselves change in their meaning as we speak them, and therefore communication, Cratylus maintained, is impossible.

Cratylus, by the way, is said to have refrained from conversation and merely to have wiggled his finger when someone spoke to him, figuring that his understanding of the words he heard must necessarily be different from the meaning intended by the speaker.

Skeptic themes may also be found in the pronouncements of the Sophists, those itinerent Greek teachers of the fifth century B.C. discussed in Chapter 7. At this time, if you were a citizen of Athens and wanted to be influential or, say, able to defend yourself in a court of law, you needed to be trained by a Sophist. The Sophists were essentially skilled debaters and speechwriters who could devise an argument to support any claim and were glad to try to teach you how to do the same—for a fee. Because they often argued against the accepted views, they are said to have produced a breakdown in traditional morals. And because they apparently could advance a plausible argument for any position, they seemed to show that any position is as valid as the next.

Gorgias (c. 485–c. 380 B.C.), one particularly famous Sophist, said this: There is no reality, and if there were, we could not know of it, and even if we could, we couldn't communicate our knowledge. This statement, obviously enough, parallels that of Xenophanes, just mentioned.

And the remark of perhaps the best-known Sophist philosopher of all, **Protagoras** (c. 490–c. 421 B.C.), that "man is the measure of all things," can be interpreted (and was so interpreted by Plato) as meaning that there is no absolute knowledge—that one person's beliefs about the world are as valid as the next person's. **Plato** (c. 427–347 B.C.) employed several arguments in his dialogue *Theaetetus,* in an effort to refute this view.

The greatest skeptic of ancient times, however, and perhaps of all time, was **Sextus Empiricus** (second–third centuries A.D.), about whose life very little is known (which seems fitting enough). So far, you've heard several skeptical pronouncements, but with Sextus, we get something more than bald pronouncements. We get some very interesting explicit *reasons* for *accepting* skepticism, and we're talking here about *total* skepticism. So let's bring Sextus into clearer focus.

Plato's *Theaetetus*

Plato (c. 427–347 B.C.) played an important role in the history of epistemology, but we won't dwell on him in this chapter. That is because he was less interested in our question about the possibility of knowledge than in the nature of knowledge and its proper objects, and we just don't have the space to cover everything.

You should, however, be aware that in the *Republic*, Plato argued that true knowledge must concern itself with what is truly real, and therefore the proper objects of true knowledge, he said, are the Forms. (Plato's Theory of Forms is explained in Chapter 2 of this book.) And you should be aware that Plato's most extensive treatment of knowledge was in his dialogue *Theaetetus*, in which Plato imagines Socrates discussing knowledge with a young mathematician after whom the dialogue is named. In this dialogue Socrates and Theaetetus examine and reject some possible answers to the question What is knowledge?

First, the notion that knowledge may be equated with sense perception is rejected, principally on the grounds that if you come to know about something, you can retain your knowledge even after you are no longer in sensory contact with the thing. Then the theory that knowledge is "correct thinking" or true belief is discarded: your true belief might be based on nothing better than hearsay evidence, for example. Knowledge, Theaetetus and Socrates finally conclude, must consist of "correct belief together with an account." This means, essentially, that correct belief, to qualify as knowledge, must be based on something solid; it must be more than a lucky guess. Nevertheless, Socrates and Theaetetus find themselves unable to clarify to their own satisfaction this concept of an "account." The dialogue leaves off on this unsatisfactory note. (For a closer look at the question What is knowledge? see Appendix 3.)

Plato is also important because he is one of the first rationalists, but this is a theme we will pick up later.

Sextus Empiricus and Total Skepticism

Again, as we mentioned before, in the Hellenistic and Roman periods after Plato, four principal philosophical schools developed: the Stoics, the Epicureans, the Neoplatonists, and the Skeptics. There were two kinds of Skeptics, and they were something like rivals: the **Academics** (who flourished during the third and second centuries B.C. in what had earlier been Plato's Academy) and the **Pyrrhonists** (stemming from Pyrrho of Elis, c. 360–270 B.C.). Sextus Empiricus, with whom we are concerned in this section, was the last great Pyrrhonist. He is also the principal source of information we have about classical skepticism.

Now the Academics, at least according to Sextus, maintained that "all things are inapprehensible," whereas the Pyrrhonists, he said—and he counted himself as a Pyrrhonist—suspend judgment on all issues.

All things are inapprehensible, said the Academics. If that means that nothing can be known, then it certainly sounds pretty totally skeptical. Actually, there is some controversy among recent scholars about whether the Academic Skeptics really held this view, but this has been their reputation through the centuries (thanks to Sextus).

Aristotle and the Deaf

We don't emphasize Aristotle in this chapter because he wasn't as central to the history of skepticism as some other thinkers were. But let us note in passing that Aristotle had the idea that hearing is more important than sight in acquiring knowledge, and he believed that the blind are more intelligent than the deaf. Probably at least in part because of Aristotle's authority, it was not generally believed that the deaf were educable until after the Middle Ages. In fact, during the Middle Ages, priests barred the deaf from churches on the ground that they could not have faith. Schools for the deaf are only a relatively recent phenomenon.

Pyrrho

Not a great deal is known about **Pyrrho,** after whom the Pyrrhonist tradition is named, for he left no writings. **Diogenes Laertius,** a third-century Greek biographer (whose tales about the ancient philosophers, despite their gossipy and sometimes unreliable nature, are an invaluable source of history) reported that Pyrrho was totally indifferent to and unaware of things going on around him. A well-known story told by Diogenes Laertius is that once, when Pyrrho's dear old teacher was stuck in a ditch, Pyrrho passed him by without a word. (On the other hand, maybe this story indicates that Pyrrho was quite aware of things around him.) According to other reports, however, Pyrrho was a moderate, sensible, and quite level-headed person.

It is at any rate true that Pyrrho held that nothing can be known about the hidden essence or true nature of things. He held this because he thought every theory can be opposed by an equally sound contradictory theory. Hence we must neither accept nor reject any of these theories, but rather must suspend judgment on all issues. The suspension of judgment, **epoche,** was said by Pyrrho to lead to **ataraxia,** tranquility or unperturbedness. Pyrrho's fame was apparently primarily a result of his exemplary **agoge** (way of living), though there are differences of opinion about what that way of life actually was.

agōgē   epoché

Is it true that nothing can be known? This is one of those philosophical questions that must be handled with a certain amount of care, for if it is true that nothing can be known, or if people came to believe that it is, then we might expect to see some fairly spectacular changes in lifestyles.

Fortunately, there seems to be an obvious and conclusive objection to this notion that nothing can be known. First of all, the claim that nothing can be known appears to be a knowledge-claim. Thus the claim that nothing can be known seems to be self-canceling.

Second, if it is true that nothing can be known, then any argument used to establish that fact cannot be known, either. Apparently, the idea that nothing can be known is thus not only self-cancelingly unknowable but also cannot be established on any grounds that are themselves claimed to be known.

Sextus Empiricus

Pyrrho was the first of the great Pyrrhonist Skeptics, and **Sextus Empiricus** was the last. (Note that the tradition endured fully five or six centuries.) Although Sextus's writings are extensive and constitute the definitive firsthand report on Greek skepticism, little is known about Sextus himself. We don't know where he was born or died or even where he lived. We do know, however, that he was a physician.

In Sextus's writings may be found virtually every skeptical argument that has ever been devised. He too, like Pyrrho, emphasized suspension of judgment (*epoche*) as the way to attain unperturbedness (*ataraxia*).

It is little wonder, then, that Sextus differentiated his own position from that of the Academics. Sextus, unlike the Academics, did not proclaim that nothing can be known. Instead, he said, in effect: "I suspend judgment in the matter. Also, I suspend judgment on all other issues that I have examined, too." His position was, in short, that *he did not know whether knowledge is possible.*

Sextus's version of total skepticism does not seem nearly so easy to refute as that attributed by him to the Academics. And even today (as we'll see later) Sextus's version of total skepticism has its adherents. Sextus did not affirm the possibility of knowledge of any sort, so it's fair to call him a skeptic. But by not making any judgments—that is, by not committing himself to any claims whatsoever, including the claim that knowledge is impossible—he did not place himself in the self-defeating position of claiming to know that he could not know.

You're not totally convinced by Sextus? Perhaps, then, you have noticed that Sextus certainly *appears* to make judgments despite the fact that he says that he does not make them. For example, doesn't he make a judgment when he explains the position of the Academics? Doesn't he commit himself to a claim when he says that Pyrrhonists suspend judgment in all matters?

But Sextus said that none of the *apparent* judgments that came from his mouth were genuine claims of knowledge. He said, in effect, that when it appeared that he was making a knowledge-claim, he was merely expressing his momentary impressions of the way things seem. He wrote:

> It must be understood in advance that we make no assertions to the effect that they are absolutely true. We even say that they can be used to cancel themselves, since they are themselves included in those things to which they refer, just as purgative medicines not only remove the humors from the body but expel themselves together with the humors.

Think about that for a moment.

Sextus's Rationale

Now what was Sextus's rationale for suspending judgment on every issue? In his *Outlines of Pyrrhonism,* Sextus set forth the infamous "**Ten Tropes**," a collection of

ten arguments by the ancient skeptics against the possibility of knowledge. The idea behind the Ten Tropes is this. Knowledge is possible only if we have good grounds for believing that the world is exactly as we think it is or perceive it to be. But we do not have good grounds for believing that the world is exactly as we think it is or perceive it to be. For one thing, we never are aware of any object as it is independent of us but only as it stands in its relationship to us. Therefore we cannot know how any object really is in itself. For another thing, the thoughts and perceptions of one person are different from those of the next and depend on the person's own circumstances. So who is to say that one person's thoughts and perceptions are more accurate than those of the next?

Sextus's main reason for thinking that one must suspend judgment on every issue, however, was that "to every argument an equal argument is opposed." If this is true, then wouldn't it indeed be rational to suspend judgment on every issue? (Thus the balance scale, which represents the equally compelling force of two contradictory views, is the symbol of skepticism—as well as of justice.)

Before you complain that Sextus was in no position to say what is true of *every* argument, you should remember that he restricted his remarks to arguments "I have examined."

Selection 3.1 is the "Third Trope" from Sextus's *Outlines of Pyrrhonism.* (In this translation, "mode" is used for "trope.") Here we find Sextus arguing that we cannot know what the true nature of any object is. Think of an apple. The qualities we think it has are those we perceive by sense. But—not so fast! We have a slight problem here. Does the apple have *only* those qualities that it appears to us to have? Or does it have some *additional* qualities that are unknown to us (and which might be known to us, for example, if we had additional sense organs)? Or does it have *fewer* qualities than appear to us (perhaps some of its apparent qualities are its *real* qualities and the other apparent qualities are just the by-products of our sense organs). Well, which of these three options is the correct one? The senses them-

Sextus's Asterisk

In a play by the great French comic playwright Molière called *The Forced Marriage*, a skeptic is beaten in one scene. While he is being beaten, the skeptic is reminded that skeptics can't be sure that they are being beaten or feel pain. Molière, evidently, did not view skepticism as a serious philosophy.

In defense of Sextus, we might mention that Sextus placed a small asterisk beside his skepticism. He said that he did not "deny those things which, in accordance with the passivity of our sense impressions, lead us involuntarily to give our assent to them." That I am in pain is an *involuntary* judgment on my part and therefore doesn't count, Sextus would say.

We'll leave it up to you and your instructor to determine if this tactic enables Sextus to escape Molière's criticism.

selves cannot tell us, Sextus says; and because the senses cannot tell us, the mind cannot either, he argues, because the mind, he implies, gets its information from the senses.

This actually is quite a difficult little problem, and it has occupied the attention of some philosophers to the present day.

SELECTION 3.1

Outlines of Pyrrhonism   **From Sextus Empiricus**

Chapter 14—Concerning the Ten Modes

The *Third Mode* is, we say, based on differences in the senses. That the senses differ from one another is obvious. Thus, to the eye paintings seem to have recesses and projections, but not so to the touch. Honey, too, seems to some pleasant to the tongue but unpleasant to the eyes; so that it is impossible to say whether it is absolutely pleasant or unpleasant. The same is true of sweet oil, for it pleases the sense of smell but displeases the taste. So too with spurge: since it pains the eyes but causes no pain to any other part of the body, we cannot say whether, in its real nature, it is absolutely painful or painless to bodies. Rainwater, too, is beneficial to the eyes but roughens the wind-pipe and the lungs; as also does olive-oil, though it mollifies the epidermis. The crampfish, also, when applied to the extremities produces cramp, but it can be applied to the rest of the body without hurt. Consequently we are unable to say what is the real nature of each of these things, although it is possible to say what each thing at the moment appears to be.

A longer list of examples might be given, but to avoid prolixity, in view of the plan of our treatise, we will say just this. Each of the phenomena perceived by the senses seems to be a complex; the apple, for example, seems smooth, odorous, sweet and yellow. But it is nonevident whether it really possesses these qualities only; or whether it has but one quality but appears varied owing to the varying structure of the sense-organs; or whether, again, it has more qualities than are apparent, some of which elude our perception. That the apple has but one quality might be argued from what we said above regarding the food absorbed by bodies, and the water sucked up by trees, and the breath in flutes and pipes and similar instruments; for the apple likewise may be all of one sort but appear different owing to differences in the sense-organs in which perception takes place. And that the apple may possibly possess more qualities than those apparent to us we argue in this way. Let us imagine a man who possesses from birth the senses of touch, taste and smell, but can neither hear nor see. This man, then, will assume that nothing visible or audible has any existence, but only those three kinds of qualities which he is able to apprehend. Possibly, then, we also, having only our five senses, perceive only such of the apple's qualities as we are capable of apprehending; and possibly it may possess other underlying qualities which affect other sense-organs, though we, not being endowed with those organs, fail to apprehend the sense-objects which come through them.

"But," it may be objected, "Nature made the senses commensurate with the objects of sense." What kind of "Nature"? we ask, seeing that there exists so much unresolved controversy amongst the Dogmatists concerning the reality which belongs to Nature. For he who decides the question as to the existence of Nature will be discredited by them if he is an ordinary person, while if he is a philosopher he will be a party to the controversy and therefore himself subject to judgement and not a judge. If, however, it is possible that only those qualities which we seem to perceive subsist in the apple, or that a greater number subsist, or, again, that not even the qualities which affect us subsist, then it will be nonevident to us what the nature of the apple really is. And the same argument applies to all the other objects of sense. But if the senses do not apprehend external objects, neither can the mind apprehend them; hence, because of this argument also, we shall be driven, it seems, to suspend judgement regarding the external underlying objects.

Augustine and Skepticism

So much, then, for the Academics and Pyrrhonists. As mentioned earlier, total skepticism has its adherents even today, so we shall have an opportunity to return to these issues later. For the most part, however, until recently, skepticism after Sextus was of the "modified" variety, as we will now see.

During the Christianization of the Roman Empire, skepticism waned. St. Augustine (A.D. 354–430) discussed Academic Skepticism, as it has been described by the Roman historian Cicero, and concluded that skepticism is refuted by the **principle of noncontradiction.** This principle is stated in various ways, but the basic concept is that a proposition and its contradictory cannot *both* be true, and one or the other *must* be true. The statements "The world now exists" and "The world now doesn't exist" cannot both be true, and one must be true. Thus we know, presumably, that the world can't both exist and not exist.

Skepticism is also refuted by the very act of doubting, Augustine held, for the act of doubting discloses your existence as something that is absolutely certain: from the fact that *I am doubting,* it follows automatically that *I am.* (Later we'll find that another important philosopher, René Descartes, elaborated on a similar refutation of skepticism.)

What Is Truth?

To understand what knowledge is and whether it is possible to have knowledge, mustn't I understand what truth is? After all, we can know something only if it is true.

It would take a chapter in its own right to tell the philosophical story of truth. For a summary version of that story, see Appendix 2. And don't forget there are appendixes on the related topics of knowledge and logic!

Furthermore, according to Augustine, even in sense perception there is a rudimentary kind of knowledge. Deception in sense perception occurs, he said, only when we "give assent to more than the fact of appearance." For example, an oar appears bent at the point it enters the water. And if we assent only to the appearance of the oar and say merely that it looks bent, we make no mistake. It is only if we judge that the oar actually is bent that we fall into error.

But Augustine did not particularly develop these three insights. He saw in them a refutation of skepticism and regarded this refutation as highly important. But he did not try to derive anything else of great importance from them. The most important truths, for Augustine, are received by revelation and held on faith, and this doctrine was (of course) assumed throughout the Christian Middle Ages.

The Middle Ages

Augustine died in 430, some forty-six years before the date usually assigned as the end of the (Western) Roman Empire. The final centuries of the empire had witnessed the spread of Christianity through all classes of society and eventually an alliance between the Church and the state. They also had seen a growing belief in demons, magic, astrology, and other dark superstitions. After the abdication of the last Roman emperor in 476, the light of reason was all but extinguished in Europe, and only a few candles flickered in the night. These Dark Ages lasted to about 1000. Compared with the shining cultures of the East at the same time, Europe barely qualified as a civilization.

Precipitating the fall of the empire were the barbarian incursions, and after the fall the invading hordes arrived in waves. In the first wave, a group of Germanic kingdoms replaced the empire. In the next century (i.e., the sixth), Justinian, the Byzantine emperor, partially reconquered the Western empire; but shortly after his death Italy was invaded by the ferocious Lombards, and Syria, Egypt, and Spain were conquered by the Muslims. The Carolingian Franks under Charlemagne restored stability for a brief time, bringing into existence (on Christmas Day, 800) what later was called the Holy Roman Empire, though subsequent invasions by the Vikings and Muslims again spread chaos and destruction. During this period Slavic conquests of the Balkans separated Greek and Latin cultures, and the Greek and Latin churches also gradually drew apart.

Original philosophy was virtually nonexistent during the Dark Ages, though the two most capable and learned thinkers of this grim and lightless period, Boethius in the sixth century (who was executed for treason) and John Scotus in the ninth (whose work was posthumously condemned), were both philosophers of remarkable ability. The thought of both men, though basically Neoplatonic, was original and profound, but we can't go into it in this relatively short book.

By about 1000, the age of invasions was substantially over. The assorted northern invaders had been Christianized, a series of comparatively stable states was spread over Europe, and a relationship of rough interdependence and equality existed between the Pope and the various secular authorities.

Then, during the high Middle Ages, as the next few centuries are called, the Pope became essentially the most powerful leader in Europe. This was to be expected, for the Church controlled royal marriage and divorce, not to mention the pathway to heaven. The Church was the unifying institution of European civilization, and no monarch could act in total defiance of it.

In the growing security and prosperity that followed the Dark Ages, urban centers grew, and intellectual life, centered in the great universities that arose under the auspices of the Church, was stimulated through commercial and military contact with Greek, Arabian, Jewish, and (more indirectly) Indian cultures.

Still, independent or unorthodox thinking was not without its hazards, especially if it laid any foundation for what Church authorities perceived to be a heretical viewpoint. During the medieval Inquisition, those accused of heresy were brought to trial. The trials, however, were secret, and there was no such thing as the right to counsel. One's accusers were not named, and torture was used in service of the truth. An interesting practice was that of torturing not only the accused but those speaking on behalf of the accused. As might be imagined, one was apt to find few witnesses on one's behalf. So it was not unusual for heretics to recant their sins.

Nevertheless, despite all this, the high Middle Ages was a period of growing personal liberty, spreading literacy, and increasing intellectual vigor. In a nearby box we explain the philosophical problem that was most important to thinkers of the time: the problem of universals.

Contact with the Arabian world during the high Middle Ages led to a rekindling of interest among European churchmen in the philosophy of Aristotle. Through the centuries the Muslim world had enjoyed greater access to ancient Greek philosophy than had the Christian, and many Christian thinkers first encountered Aristotle's philosophy through Arabian commentaries on Aristotle and through Latin translations of Arab translations of Greek texts. Because Aristotle's repudiation of Plato's realm of Forms seemed at odds with Christian philosophy, which was Augustinian and Platonic in outlook, some Church thinkers (notably Bonaventura, 1221–1274) thought it necessary to reject Aristotle. Others (notably Albert the Great, 1193–1280) came to regard Aristotle as the greatest of all philosophers and concluded that there must be an underlying accord between Christian principles and Aristotle's philosophy.

The Problem of Universals

The three main philosophical problems from around 1000 to 1200 were these: (1) rationally proving the existence of God, (2) understanding the relationship between reason and faith, and (3) solving the "problem of universals." Herewith, more about (3).

Some words name a single thing—for example, *Ross Perot, Aristotle, Billy the Kid.* Other words are general or "universal" words that apply to several things—for example, *tree, philosopher, horse.* The so-called problem of universals concerns general words.

Pretty clearly, individual things—this tree, that philosopher, this horse—exist out there in the world. Do general things, such as tree, philosopher, horse—and let's just call these **universals**—also exist out there in the world, or do they just exist in the mind? The theory that universals exist outside the mind is known as **real-ism,** and the theory that they don't is called **conceptualism.**

Before you say, "Why would anyone care?" think of this. According to Christianity, the Father, the Son, and the Holy Spirit, three individual things, are the selfsame thing, God. The word *God,* therefore, like the word *horse,* applies to separate individuals and in this respect seems to denote a general thing, a universal.

Or take another example: According to Christianity, when Adam and Eve ate the apple, thereby committing "original sin," the sin tainted *humankind,* and that is why all people need baptism. Humankind, of course, is a general thing, a universal.

Thus the question as to the status of general things is very important from a Christian standpoint. If only individual things exist, as conceptualists maintain, then the three persons of the Trinity ap-parently are three separate individuals. In that case there are three Gods rather than one. If only individual things exist, then only the *individuals* Adam and Eve sinned, and there is no such thing as a general or universal humankind or human nature to be tainted.

Questions about the nature and status of universals are important not merely for their connection with theological issues. Experience itself requires universals, because experience involves *categorizing* particular things, that is, recognizing particular things as this or that *kind* of thing. "Kinds," of course, are universals. A complete theory of experience would therefore require a satisfactory accounting of universals. To date, an entirely satisfactory account has not yet been found, despite the fact that philosophers of all periods have attempted to discover one.

The most important of those who belonged to the second group was **St. Thomas Aquinas** (1225–1274), whose philosophy was deemed by Pope Leo XIII in 1879 to be the official Catholic philosophy. To this day Aquinas's system is taught in Catholic schools as the correct philosophy, and so Aquinas's thought continues to affect living people directly.

Aquinas had access to translations of Aristotle that were directly from the Greek (and not Latin translations of Arab translations), and his knowledge of Aristotle was considerable and profound. In a manner similar to that in which Augustine had mixed Platonic philosophy with Christianity, Aquinas blended Christianity with the philosophy of Aristotle, in effect grafting the principles and distinctions of the Greek philosopher to Christian revealed truth. The result was a complete Christian philosophy, with a theory of knowledge, a metaphysics, ethical and political philosophies, and a philosophy of law. Expect to encounter Aquinas again in this book.

Another way in which Aquinas is important is this. In Aquinas's time a distinction was finally beginning to be made between *philosophy* and *theology*. No person was more concerned with tracing the boundaries of the two fields than was Aquinas. His main idea was that philosophy is based on precepts of reason and theology on truths of revelation held on faith. We shall return to the subject in a later chapter.

As for Aquinas's metaphysics, some of the main points may be summarized as follows. *Change,* Aquinas thought, can be explained using the Aristotelian four-cause theory: the efficient cause is that which produces the change; the material cause is the stuff that changes; the formal cause is the form the stuff takes; and the final cause is what explains why there was a change.

All physical things are composed of matter and form, he said, following Aristotle. Matter, which remains constant throughout a change, is that which a thing is made out of, and form is that which determines what sort of thing it is. By virtue of being separate clumps of matter, these two rocks are different, and by virtue of having the same form, these two rocks are both rocks and thus are the same. Contrary to the Platonic-Augustinian tradition, Aquinas held that the form of a thing cannot exist apart from matter.

But Aquinas went beyond Aristotle to point out that, besides the composition of matter and form in things, there is also a composition of its essence (matter plus form) and its existence. *What* something is (its essence) is not the same as *that* it is (its existence); otherwise, it would always exist, which is contrary to fact. Further, if existing were identical with any one kind of thing, everything existing would be only that one kind; again, contrary to fact. So, Aquinas made a unique contribution to metaphysics by highlighting that existence is the most important actuality in anything, without which even form (essence) cannot be actual.

Moreover, Aquinas also emphasized that nothing could cause its own existence, because it would already need to exist (as cause) before it existed (as effect), which is a contradiction. So, anything that begins to exist is caused to exist by something already existing, and, ultimately, by an Uncaused Cause of Existence, God. Thus, Aquinas went beyond Aristotle's concept of God as Pure Act (because God is changeless, without beginning or end) to an understanding of God as Pure Act of Existence.   *I Am, He Causes to Become*

All living things have a soul, which is indeed the life of a living thing. The *Error* human soul, however, can exist apart from the body, and it is the direct creation of God and not of the individual's parents. Further, it is indivisible (and hence immortal). Finally, it stands in a relationship of mutual interdependency relative to the body. A human being is a *unity* of body and soul, Aquinas taught, for without the soul the body would be formless, and without a body the soul would have no access to knowledge derived from sensation.

That God exists, Aquinas said, is a fact evident to reason unaided by faith. There are, he said, "Five Ways" of proving God's existence; we will be examining

Teleological Explanations

Why do human beings stand upright? Aquinas gave four reasons: (1) Animals use their sense organs for seeking food. Thus, because the sense organs are located chiefly in the face, their faces are turned to the ground. We humans, by contrast, use the senses in the pursuit of truth as well as food, and for this purpose it is better to have the sense organs looking up and about. (2) The brain functions better when it is lifted up above the other parts of the body. (3) If we walked on all fours, our hands would not be available for other purposes. Further, (4) we would have to take hold of food with our mouths, which would require our mouths to protrude and our tongue and lips to be thick and hard, and this would hinder speech.

Now, we mention this not just to amuse you. We want you to note the *kind* of explanation that Aquinas has advanced. Aquinas explains our walking erect in terms of the function or purpose that is served by our doing so—doing so enables us to speak and look out at the world. An explanation of something in terms of its ends, goals, purposes, or functions is known as a **teleological explanation.**

Compare Aquinas's explanation with a modern biological explanation of a human characteristic. According to the latter, chance genetic mutations result in new characteristics in organisms. Those that are not detrimental to the survival of the organisms will be the most influential in the continuing survival of that species of organism and will tend to become characteristics of the species. In this way the characteristics of all species are to be explained as the result of the "natural selection," over the millennia, of comparatively advantageous changes in the gene pool.

Notice that in the modern biological explanation no mention is made of the "purpose" of a characteristic. The explanation looks entirely backward in time and points to those antecedent conditions and events that *produced* or *caused* the characteristic in question (e.g., changes in genes). For this reason it is sometimes called a **causal explanation.** The teleological explanation, by contrast, looks forward in time to the purpose that is served by the characteristic (e.g., by having this characteristic, that type of organism will be able to do such and such).

Is this important? You bet. A teleological explanation implicitly points to an *agency* that determines the purpose served by the characteristics of a species: it points to a designing intelligence, a god. A causal explanation doesn't, although some think that it points toward some original episode of causation.

Further, a switch in emphasis from teleological explanations to causal explanations is a major factor that accompanied and helped make possible the scientific revolution.

Of course, for Aquinas as for Aristotle, a teleological explanation *is* a type of causal explanation. It is an explanation in terms of what Aristotle and Aquinas called a "final" cause.

them in Chapter 12, in case you want to refer to them. Let's just mention here that the proofs are variations on the idea that things must have an ultimate cause, creator, designer, source of being, or source of goodness: namely, God.

Our knowledge of God's *nature,* however, is in terms of what God is *not.* For example, because God is unmoved and unchangeable, God is eternal. Because He is not material and without parts, He is utterly simple. And because He is not a composite, He is not a composite of essence and existence: His essence is His existence, which means that His nature is to be.

St. Thomas Aquinas lived during the zenith hour in the power of the Church and Pope. After 1300 there began a long decline (that continues still) in the importance of the Church as a political institution and of religion as a governing factor in daily life.

Checklist

To help you review, here is a checklist of the key philosophers and concepts of this chapter. The brief descriptive sentences summarize leading ideas. Keep in mind that some of these summary statements represent terrific oversimplifications of complex positions.

Philosophers

- **Plotinus** Held that reality emanates from the One.
- **St. Augustine** Provided Platonic philosophical justification for the Christian belief in a nonmaterial God. Rejected skepticism; diagnosed the cause of error in sense perception.
- **Hypatia** Instructed students in Plato, Aristotle, Plotinus, and Ptolemy and improved the mathematical rigor of Ptolemy's astronomical theories. Stressed the importance of philosophy and mathematics to life.
- **Xenophanes** Said that even if truth were stated, it would not be known.
- **Heraclitus** Said that everything is in flux; you cannot step twice into the same river.
- **Cratylus** Held that because everything is changing, communication is impossible.
- **Gorgias** Said that there is no reality, and if there were, we could not know it, and even if we could, we couldn't communicate our knowledge.
- **Protagoras** Said that man is the measure of all things.
- **Plato** Believed that knowledge is correct belief together with an "account." Said that the proper objects of true knowledge are the Forms.
- **Sextus Empiricus** Most famous total skeptic. Held the position, "I do not know whether knowledge is possible."
- **Pyrrho** Held that every theory can be opposed by an equally valid contradictory theory; we must suspend judgment on all issues.
- **Diogenes Laertius** Third-century Greek biographer whose tales are usually intriguing but sometimes not fully reliable.
- **St. Thomas Aquinas** Blended Christianity with the philosophy of Aristotle; delineated the boundary between philosophy and theology.

Concepts

Neoplatonism   *God indefinable indescribable – not personal apprehended only through mystical experience with the soul.*

creation *ex nihilo*   *out of nothing – Augustine*

Sophists   *debaters + speechwriters*

Academics   *All things are inapprehensible*

62 Pyrrhonists   *we cannot know whether knowledge is possible*

63 *epoche* – *suspension of judgement*

ataraxia – *tranquility unperturbedness*

agoge – *way of living.*

Ten Tropes (modes)   *Knowledge is not possible only relative to self, ea person different perception*
equal argument   only, more, fewer q. than perceived?

principle of noncontradiction   *against skepticism · world cannot exist + not exist at same time*

universal   *general worlds*

realism   *outside the mind*

70 conceptualism   *in mind only*

Look forward teleological explanation   *goal, purpose, function – telos – Gr. end*

Looks backward causal explanation   *(natural cause ie no design) – Scientific revolution*

Questions for Discussion and Review

context
combinations (words
tone, gestures + facial
A.S.L. sign language

1. "Everything is changing, so our words change in their meaning as we speak them. Therefore, true communication is impossible." Evaluate this argument.   *Xenophanes 61*

2. Compare and contrast the views of the Academics and the Pyrrhonists. *62*

There it cannot be known
that : And no evidence
to support this can be known

3. "Nothing can be known." What is a powerful objection to this claim?

4. "I do not know whether knowledge is possible." Critically evaluate this claim.

5. Devise an argument to defend some version of total skepticism.

6. What is creation *ex nihilo?* What are some reasons for thinking that creation *ex nihilo* is impossible?   *the cause cannot be the same as the effect*

ultimate form, ultimate source
of reality, personal God

7. Compare and contrast Plato's The Good, Plotinus's One, and Augustine's God. *53*

8. What connection did Hypatia think philosophy has to mathematics and astronomy?   *perfect shape : circle* *59*

9. Explain the difference between realism and conceptualism. Which theory is the more plausible, and why?   *only individual things exist. Universals are concepts*

10. Can we say only what God is not?   *He cannot be classified*

11. Give a teleological explanation of why polar bears have white fur.

Suggested Further Readings

Julia Annas and Jonathan Barnes, *The Modes of Scepticism: Ancient Texts and Modern Interpretations* (Cambridge: Cambridge University Press, 1985). Reflects the revival of interest in ancient skepticism. Excellent.

Augustine, *Against the Academics,* vol. 3, Sister Mary Patricia Garvey, trans. (Milwaukee: Marquette University Press, 1957). Contains easy-to-understand arguments against skepticism.

Augustine, *Confessions,* John K. Ryan, trans. (Garden City, N.Y.: Image Books, 1962). Much in this isn't purely philosophical, but most of it is interesting.

John Burnet, *Early Greek Philosophy,* 4th ed. (London: Macmillan, originally published in 1930). This is a standard work on early Greek philosophy.

M. T. Clark, ed., *An Aquinas Reader* (New York: Image Books, 1955). Aquinas wrote too much to read it all; a reader like this one may prove more useful.

Lloyd P. Gerson, *Plotinus* (London: Routledge, 1994). A major treatise on the philosophy of Plotinus.

E. Gilson, *History of Christian Philosophy in the Middle Ages* (New York: Random House, 1955). A work by one of the foremost medieval authorities. See also Gilson's *The Christian Philosophy of Saint Augustine,* L. Lynch, trans. (New York: Random House, 1960), and *The Christian Philosophy of St. Thomas Aquinas,* L. Shook, trans. (New York: Random House, 1956).

Philip P. Hallie, ed., *Scepticism, Man, and God: Selections from the Major Writings of Sextus Empiricus* (Middletown, Conn.: Wesleyan University Press, 1964). Clear, readable, authoritative.

Christopher Hookway, *Scepticism* (New York: Routledge, 1990). A review of the historical development of skepticism and its consequences for present-day thought and action.

G. S. Kirk, J. E. Raven, and M. Schofield, *The Presocratic Philosophers: A Critical History with a Selection of Texts,* 2nd ed. (Cambridge: Cambridge University Press, 1983). This is a comprehensive treatment of the pre-Socratics.

Plato, *Theaetetus,* in E. Hamilton and H. Cairns, eds., *The Collected Dialogues of Plato* (New York: Bollingen Foundation, 1961). Plato's classic text on the nature of knowledge.

Waithe, Mary Ellen, "Finding Bits and Pieces of Hypatia," in Linda Lopez McAlister, ed., *Hypatia's Daughters* (Indianapolis: Indiana University Press, 1995).

4 Modern Metaphysics and Epistemology

Every part of the universe is body, and that which is not body is no part of the universe.

—*Thomas Hobbes*

Wood, stone, fire, water, flesh . . . are things perceived by my senses; and things perceived by the senses are immediately perceived; and things immediately perceived are ideas; and ideas cannot exist outside the mind.

—*George Berkeley*

The transitional period between medieval and modern times was the Renaissance (fourteenth through sixteenth centuries). Through its emphasis on worldly experience and reverence for classical culture, the Renaissance helped emancipate Europe from the intellectual authority of the Church. The modern period in history (and philosophy) that followed lasted through the nineteenth century. Its interesting cultural and social developments include, among other things, the rise of nation states, the spread of capitalism and industrialization, the exploration and settlement of the New World, the decline of religion, and the eventual domination of science as the most revered source of knowledge. The last development is the most important to a history of metaphysics and epistemology.

To most educated Westerners today, it is a matter of plain fact that there exists a universe of physical objects related to one another spatiotemporally. These objects are composed, we are inclined to believe, of minute atoms and subatomic particles that interact with one another in mathematically describable ways.

We are also accustomed to think that in addition to the spatiotemporal *physical* universe there exist human (and perhaps other) observers who are able to perceive their corner of the universe and, within certain limits, to understand it. The *understanding*, we are inclined to suppose, and the *minds* in which this understanding exists, are not themselves physical entities, though we also tend to think that understanding and minds depend in some sense on the functioning of physical entities such as the brain and central nervous system. They, the understanding itself

The Scientific Revolution

Science, as you and we too think of it, began with the Scientific Revolution, which itself commenced when Copernicus (1473–1543) broke with long tradition and proposed (mid-sixteenth century) that the earth is not the center of the universe but in fact revolves, with the other planets, around the sun. The essence of the revolution lies in several ideas: (1) it is *important* to understand how the world works; (2) to do that, you have to *examine the world itself* rather than read your Aristotle or consult scripture; (3) a fruitful way of examining the world is through *experimentation*—this is an idea expressed most clearly by Francis Bacon (1561–1626); and (4) the world is a *mechanical system* that can be *described mathematically*—this is an idea expressed most clearly by René Descartes (1596–1650). The details of the mechanistic Cartesian picture of the universe were filled in (to a degree) by the observations and findings of (among others) Tycho Brahe (1546–1601), Johannes Kepler (1571–1630), Galileo (1564–1642), and, most importantly, Sir Isaac Newton (1642–1727), who combined the various discoveries into a unified description of the universe based on the concept of gravitation.

Certain newly invented instruments aided the early scientists in their study of the world, including, most famously, the telescope, the microscope, the vacuum pump, and the mechanical clock. And by no means were the findings of the new science limited to astronomy and the dynamics of moving bodies. There were, for example, William Harvey's (1578–1657) discovery of the circulation of the blood, William Gilbert's (1540–1603) investigations of electricity and magnetism, and the various discoveries of Robert Boyle (1627–1691)—the father of chemistry—concerning gases, metals, combustion, acids and bases, and the nature of colors.

Another important idea that came to be characteristic of the Scientific Revolution was that the fundamental constituents of the natural world are basically corpuscular or atomistic—things are made out of tiny particles. The modern scientists (in effect) declared that Democritus had gotten things right.

and the minds that have it—unlike physical things like brains and atoms and nerve impulses and energy fields—exist in time but not space. They, unlike physical things, are not bound by the laws of physics and are not made up of parts.

Thus, today it is a matter of plain common sense that reality has a dual nature. The world or the universe, we believe, consists of physical objects on one hand, and minds on the other. In a normal living person, mind and matter are intertwined in such a way that what happens to the body can affect the mind, and what happens in the mind can affect the body. The clearest examples of mind-body interaction occur when the mind, through an act of will, causes the body to perform some action or when something that happens to the body triggers a new thought in the mind.

So this *commonsense metaphysics,* as we have been describing it, is dualistic. It supposes that two different kinds of phenomena exist: physical and mental (often called "spiritual"). **Dualism** is essentially the "two worlds view" invented by Plato, incorporated with changes into Christianity by Augustine and others, and transmitted to us in its contemporary form by early modern philosophers.

But, though our commonsense metaphysics is dualistic, it did not have to be that way. In particular, we might have adopted three other metaphysical perspectives:

- **Materialism.** This view holds that only the physical exists. According to this view, so-called mental things are in some sense or other manifestations of an underlying physical reality. (Don't confuse metaphysical materialism with the doctrine that the most important thing is to live comfortably and acquire wealth.)

- **Idealism.** This view holds that only the mental (or "spiritual") exists. According to this view, so-called physical things are in some sense or other manifestations of the mind or of thought. (And don't confuse this type of idealism with the views of the dreamer who places ideals above practical considerations.)

- **Neutralism.** This view holds that what exists is *neither* mental nor physical or, alternatively, is *both* mental and physical. According to this view, the mental and the physical are just different ways of looking at the same things, which in themselves are "neutral."   SPINOZA

Thanks to the legacy of Greek and Christian influences on Western civilization, dualism continued (and continues) to command the assent of common sense. (Read through the alternative positions again. *You* believe in dualism, don't you?) Increasingly, however, the march of science seemed (and seems) philosophically to undermine metaphysical dualism. Thus, given the preeminence of science, the alternatives to dualism have to be considered. *Modern metaphysics is largely an attempt to ascertain the validity of each of the four metaphysical perspectives listed here: dualism, materialism, idealism, and neutralism.*

In what follows we will consider each of these theories as it arose during the modern period of philosophy.

Descartes and Dualism

Many European thinkers of the sixteenth century began to question established precepts and above all to question the accepted authorities as the spokesmen for the truth. In other words, that so-and-so said that P is true was no longer automatically accepted as proof that P is true, no matter who or what so-and-so is. This tendency to question authority effectively set the stage for the Scientific Revolution and modern philosophy, both of which are products of the seventeenth century.

Modern philosophy began with **René Descartes** (1596–1650), mathematician, scientist, and, of course, philosopher. Descartes's importance to Western intellectual history absolutely cannot be overestimated. Others we have mentioned may have equaled him in significance, but none surpassed him. He made important contributions to physiology, psychology, optics, and especially mathematics,

Chronology of Postmedieval History

Here, for easy reference, are the dates of the major periods in postmedieval history mentioned in the text:

The Renaissance: the fourteenth through sixteenth centuries

The Reformation and Counter-Reformation: the sixteenth century

The Scientific Revolution: the seventeenth century (though that revolution still continues)

The Enlightenment or *Age of Reason:* the eighteenth century

The Industrial Revolution: the mid-eighteenth to mid-nineteenth centuries

The Romantic Period: the late nineteenth to very early twentieth centuries

The Age of Technology: the twentieth century

in which he originated the Cartesian coordinates and Cartesian curves. It is thanks to Descartes that students now study analytic geometry; he introduced it to the world.

Descartes was a Catholic, but he also believed there are important truths that cannot be ascertained through the authority of the Church. These include those truths that pertain to the ultimate nature of existing things.

But what, then, he wondered, is to be the *criterion* of truth and knowledge in such matters? What is to be the criterion by which one might separate *certain knowledge* about matters of fact from inferior products such as *mere belief?*

Such questions were not new to philosophy, of course. During the Renaissance, the classical skeptical works, notably those by Sextus, were "rediscovered," published, and taken quite seriously—even contributing to the controversies during the Protestant Reformation about the knowability of religious beliefs. In addition,

PROFILE / René Descartes (1596–1650)

Descartes had the great fortune to be able to transform his inheritance into a comfortable annual income from which he lived. And he did not waste his time. Before he died, he had made important advances in science, mathematics, and philosophy. His work in optics was significant. He originated the Cartesian coordinates and Cartesian curves. Descartes founded analytic geometry and contributed to the understanding of negative roots. He wrote a text in physiology and did work in psychology. His contributions in philosophy are of enormous importance.

As a youth, Descartes attended the Jesuit College at La Fleche and the University of Poitiers. When he was twenty-one, he joined the Dutch army and, two years later, the Bavarian army. His military experience allowed him to be a spectator of the human drama at first hand and granted him free time to think. In 1628, he retired to Holland, where he lived for twenty years in a tolerant country where he was free from religious persecution.

Descartes was a careful philosopher and a cautious person. Although he took great issue with the medievalist thinking of his teachers, he did not make them aware of his reactions. Later, when he heard that the Church had condemned Galileo for his writings, he decided that he would have his works published only one hundred years after his death. He subsequently changed his mind, though he came to wish that he hadn't. For when he did publish some of his ideas, they were bitterly attacked by Protestant theologians; Catholic denunciations came later. This caused Descartes to say that if he had been smarter, he would not have written anything so that he would have had more peace and quiet to think.

Two incidents in Descartes's life are always mentioned in philosophy texts. One is that the insights that underlay his philosophy came to him in dreams after spending a winter day relaxing in an oven in the army in Bavaria. The other is that he accepted an invitation, with some reluctance, to tutor Queen Christina of Sweden in 1649. This was a big mistake, for the cold weather and early hour of his duties literally killed him. We can only speculate what the queen learned from the episode.

Descartes's principal philosophical works: *Discourse on Method* (1637), *Meditations on First Philosophy* (1641), and *Principles of Philosophy* (1644).

---

in the sixteenth century, various new skeptical writings appeared, most importantly by Hervet, Sanches, and Montaigne. The themes of these three writers were similar and reduced mainly to this: Skeptical arguments are unanswerable, and thus the human understanding, unless aided by faith, is restricted to knowledge of appearances, at best. Especially noteworthy in this resurgent skeptical tradition were Pierre Gassendi (1592–1655) and Marin Mersenne (1588–1648), who separately used a variety of skeptical arguments (which we do not have the space to discuss here) to establish the unknowability of the true nature of things. Both believed, however, that a study of the appearances of things could yield information useful for living in this world.

But Descartes, though vitally concerned with skeptical questions as to the possibility of knowledge, was no skeptic. His interest in mathematics strongly affected his philosophical reflections, and it was his more-or-less lifelong intention to formulate a unified science of nature that was as fully certain as arithmetic.

He did, however, employ skepticism as a method of achieving certainty. His idea was simple enough: I will doubt everything that can possibly be doubted, he reasoned, and if anything is left, then it will be absolutely certain. Then I will consider what it is about this certainty (if there is one) that places it beyond doubt, and that will provide me with a *criterion* of truth and knowledge, a yardstick against which I can measure all other purported truths to see if they, too, are beyond doubt.

Skepticism As the Key to Certainty

Let's see how Descartes's *doubting methodology* worked.

To doubt every proposition that he possibly could, Descartes employed two famous conjectures, the **dream conjecture** and the **evil demon conjecture.** For all I know, Descartes said, I might now be dreaming—that's Descartes's dream conjecture. And further, he said, for all I know, some malevolent demon devotes himself to deceiving me at every turn so that I regard as true and certain propositions that are in fact false. That supposition is Descartes's evil demon conjecture.

Yes, these two conjectures are totally bizarre, and Descartes was as aware of that as you are. But that's just the point. What Descartes was looking for was a measure of certainty that escapes even the most incredible and bizarre possibilities of falsehood.

And what he discovered, when he considered everything he thought he knew in the light of one or the other of these two bizarre possibilities, is that he could doubt *absolutely everything—save one indubitable truth:* "I think, therefore I am": ***cogito, ergo sum.*** Remember this phrase, which is from Descartes's *Discourse on Method.*

What Descartes meant is that any attempt to doubt one's existence as a thinking being is impossible because to doubt is to think and to exist. Try for a moment to doubt your own existence, and you'll see what Descartes meant. The self that doubts its own existence must surely exist in order to be able to doubt in the first place.

Augustine, too, had found certain truth in his inability to doubt his own existence, but Descartes went further than this. He examined this one indubitable truth to see what guaranteed its certainty and ascertained that any other proposition that he apprehended with identical "clarity and distinctness" must likewise be immune to doubt. In other words, he had discovered in the certainty of his own existence an essential characteristic or "test" of truth: Anything else that was as clear and distinct as his own existence would also have to be certain.

Descartes's Conjectures

For all I know, I might now be dreaming. This is Descartes's dream conjecture, and it's easy enough to disprove, correct? I just pinch myself. But then again . . . am I just dreaming that I pinched myself? Might not any evidence I have that I am now awake just be dream evidence? Can I really be certain that I won't find myself in a few moments *waking up*, realizing that I have been dreaming? And thus can I really be sure that the things I see around me, this desk and book, these arms and legs, have any existence outside my mind?

Well, you may say, even if I am dreaming, there are still many things I cannot doubt; even if I am dreaming, I can't doubt, for instance, that two and three is five or that a square has four sides.

But then again—and this is where Descartes's evil demon conjecture comes in—of course, it *seems* absolutely certain to me that two and three make five and that a square has four sides. But *some* propositions that have seemed absolutely certain to me have turned out to be false. So how can I be sure that *these* propositions (that

two and three make five and that a square has four sides), or any other proposition that seems certain to me, are not likewise false? For all I know, a deceitful and all-powerful intelligence has so programmed me that I find myself regarding as absolute certainties propositions that in fact aren't true at all.

Descartes thus thought that these two conjectures combined in this way to force him "to avow that there is nothing at all that I formerly believed to be true of which it is impossible to doubt."

Using this **"clear and distinct" criterion,** Descartes was then able to certify as beyond doubt his belief in a God who would not deceive him. And because it was certain that God would not deceive him, Descartes could then also certify as certain his belief that God would not permit him to be deceived in his belief in the existence of the world outside his mind. Thus Descartes ultimately found within the certainty of his own existence the grounds for certainty in the belief in God and the "external world." We will omit the details of this grand deduction, however.

What does all this accomplish? Descartes's doubting methodology is like the axiomatic method in logic and mathematics, in which a theorem whose truth initially seems likely but not *totally* certain is demonstrated to be certain by deriving it from basic axioms by means of rules of inference. Descartes's "axiom" is, in effect, "I think, therefore I am," and his "rule of inference" is clear and distinct perception.

What Descartes accomplished, or what he thought he accomplished, is therefore this: by employing his doubting methodology, he was able to show, at least to his own satisfaction, that many of the things he had previously merely *believed,* such as that God exists and that there is a material world outside his own mind, he now *knew for certain.*

Selection 4.1 is from Descartes's most famous philosophical work, *Meditations on First Philosophy.* It is considered one of the most powerful skeptical arguments ever set forth. The trouble is, the argument is so powerful that it is by no means clear that even Descartes's *cogito, ergo sum* is immune to skeptical doubt. Descartes, of course, thought otherwise, and you may wish to consider the issue yourself.

SELECTION 4.1

*Meditations [I and II] on First Philosophy**   From René Descartes

Reason persuades me that I ought no less carefully to withhold my assent from matters which are not entirely certain and indubitable than from those which appear to me manifestly to be false. . . .

All that up to the present time I have accepted as most true and certain I have learned either from the senses or through the senses; [and], although the senses sometimes deceive us concerning things which are hardly perceptible, or very far away, there are yet many others to be met with as to which we cannot reasonably have any doubt. . . .

For example, there is the fact that I am here, seated by the fire, attired in a dressing gown, having this paper in my hands and other similar matters. And how could I deny that these hands and this body are mine. . . [?]

At the same time I must remember that . . . I am in the habit of sleeping and in my dreams representing to myself the same things. . . . How often has it happened to me that in the night I dreamt that I found myself in this particular place, that I was dressed and seated near the fire, while in reality I was lying undressed in bed! At this moment it does indeed seem to me that it is with eyes awake that I am looking at this paper. . . . But in thinking over this I remind myself that on many occasions I have in sleep been deceived by similar illusions, and in dwelling carefully on this reflection I see . . . that there are no certain indications by which we may clearly distinguish wakefulness from sleep. . . .

At the same time we must at least confess

that . . . whether I am awake or asleep, two and three together always form five, and the square can never have more than four sides, and it does not seem possible that truths so clear and apparent can be suspected of any falsity.

Nevertheless . . . how do I know that I am not deceived every time that I add two and three, or count the sides of a square, or judge of things yet simpler, if anything simpler can be imagined? . . . Possibly God has not desired that I should be thus deceived, for He is said to be supremely good. . . . But let us . . . grant that all that is here said of a God is a fable. . . . I shall then suppose, not that God who is supremely good and the fountain of truth, but some evil genius not less powerful than deceitful, has employed his whole energies in deceiving me; I shall consider that the heavens, the earth, colors, figures, sound, and all other external things are nought but the illusions and dreams of which this genius has availed himself in order to lay traps for my credulity; I shall consider myself as having no hands, no eyes, no flesh, no blood, nor any senses, yet falsely believing myself to possess all these things. . . .

[Yet even if] there is some deceiver or other, very powerful and very cunning, who ever employs his ingenuity in deceiving me[,] then without a doubt I exist also if he deceives me, and let him deceive me as much as he will, he can never cause me to be nothing so long as I think that I am something. So that after having reflected well and carefully examined all things, we must come to the definite conclusion that this proposition: I am, I exist, is necessarily true each time that I pronounce it, or that I mentally conceive it.

---

*Edited slightly for the modern reader.

The "Clear and Distinct" Criterion of Certainty

In Selection 4.1 we saw Descartes finding supposedly certain knowledge in his own existence as a thing that thinks. He then reasoned, as we have explained, as follows:

> I am certain that I am a thing which thinks; but do I not then likewise know what is requisite to render me certain of a truth? Certainly in this first knowledge there is nothing that assures me of its truth, excepting the clear and distinct perception of that which I state, which would not indeed suffice to assure me that what I say is true, if it could ever happen that a thing which I conceived so clearly and distinctly could be false; and accordingly it seems to me that already I can establish as a general rule that all things which I perceive very clearly and very distinctly are true.

In this way, then, Descartes found to his own satisfaction that he could regard as certain knowledge much of what he had initially cast in doubt. All he must do, he reasoned, is ascertain which among his various beliefs he perceives "clearly and distinctly" to be true. Those beliefs he now can regard as absolutely certain. This is the clear and distinct criterion of certainty.

And so Descartes, now finding himself armed with an absolutely reliable criterion of certain knowledge, discovers first that he has certain knowledge that God exists. We shall go over the details of Descartes's proof of God's existence in Chapter 12, but for now let's just let them go. Also Descartes finds that he knows for certain, and that therefore it is the case, that God would not deceive the thinking mind with perceptions of an external world—a world of objects outside the mind—if such did not exist. Thus for Descartes, there are, beyond God, two separate and distinct substances, and reality thus has a dual nature. On the one hand is *material substance*, whose essential attribute is **extension** (occupancy of space), and on the other hand is *mind*, whose essential attribute is **thought.** Because a substance, according to Descartes, "requires nothing other than itself to exist," it follows that

Variations on a Theme

I feel, therefore I exist.

—Thomas Jefferson

I rebel, therefore I am.

—Albert Camus

I ought, therefore I can.

—Immanuel Kant

I want, therefore I am.

—Leo Tolstoy

Sometimes I think: and sometimes I am.

—Paul Valéry

Only the first word of the Cartesian philosophy is true: it was not possible for Descartes to say *cogito, ergo sum*, but only *cogito.*

—Moses Hess

I labor, therefore I am a man.

—Max Stirner

There is, of course, the *cogito ergo sum* principle—perhaps the most famous of all philosophical theories . . . which, incidentally, is fallacious.

—Barrows Dunham

Cogito, ergo sum . . . can only mean, "I think therefore I am a thinker." The truth is, *sum ergo cogito.*

—Miguel de Unamuno

mind and matter are totally independent of each other. Still, he thought that in a living person the mind and the material body interact, the motion of the body being sometimes affected by the mind and the thoughts of the mind being influenced by physical sensations.

This is, of course, familiar stuff. Our commonsense metaphysics is pretty much the dualistic metaphysics of Descartes. Unfortunately, there are unpleasant difficulties in the Cartesian dualistic metaphysics. These difficulties vexed Descartes and haven't yet been plausibly resolved. In Chapter 14 we explain these difficulties in some detail.

To anticipate what is said there, Descartes thought that

1. Material things, including one's own body, are completely subject to physical laws.

But he also thought that

2. The immaterial mind can move one's body.

The difficulty is that if the immaterial mind can do this, then one's body evidently is *not* completely subject to physical laws after all. It seems contradictory to hold both (1) and (2). Do *you* hold both (1) and (2)?

Descartes also found it difficult to understand just how something immaterial *could* affect the movement of something material. He said that the mind interacts with the body through "vital spirits" in the brain, but he recognized that this explanation was quite obscure and almost wholly metaphorical. It was, in short, a dodge.

To date, a satisfactory explanation of this difficulty still has not been found.

Despite these problems, Descartes thought he had succeeded in establishing metaphysical dualism as absolutely certain. He also thought that he had shown

Parallelism

Some of Descartes's followers proposed a solution to the problem of how the immaterial mind interacts with the material body, given that the body is supposed to be subject to physical laws. The solution is called **parallelism.**

The mind, they argued, doesn't *really* cause the body to move. When I will that my hand should move, my act of willing only *appears* to cause my hand to move.

What actually happens is two parallel and coordinated series of events, one a series of mental happenings and the other a series that involves happenings to material things. Thus my act of willing my hand to move doesn't cause my hand to move, but the act of willing and the movement of the hand *coincide*. Hence it *appears* that the willing causes the moving.

Why do these events just happen to coincide? To account for the coinciding of the mental happenings with the physical happenings, Descartes's followers invoked God. God, they said, is the divine coordinator between the series of mental happenings and the series of material happenings. (In a variant of parallelism known as **occasionalism,** when I will my hand to move, that's the occasion on which God causes my hand to move).

This theory of parallelism seems farfetched, true. But perhaps that only illustrates how serious a difficulty it is to suppose both that material things, including one's body, are completely subject to physical laws and that the immaterial mind can move one's body.

The human mind

x

that the mind, because it is not in space and hence does not move, is not in any sense subject to physical laws and therefore is "free." The metaphysical dualism that survives today as mere "common sense," though it originated with Plato and was incorporated into Christianity by Augustine, survives in the form developed by Descartes. Yesterday's philosophy became today's common sense.

Notice Descartes's overall approach to metaphysical issues. Instead of asking "What is the basic stuff?" or "Of what does reality consist?" Descartes took an indirect approach and asked, in effect, "What do I know is the basic stuff?" and "Of what can I be certain about the nature of reality?" What we are saying is that Descartes tried to discover *metaphysical* truth about what *is* through epistemological inquiry about *what can be known.*

We'll call this approach to metaphysical truth the **epistemological detour.** After Descartes and largely because of him, modern philosophy has attached considerable importance to epistemology, and metaphysical inquiry is often conducted via the epistemological detour.

Unfortunately, maybe the least debatable part of Descartes's overall reasoning is the two skeptical arguments (the dream conjecture and the evil demon conjecture) that he advanced at the outset, which seem to make it a live issue whether what passes for knowledge genuinely is knowledge. And thus we find that the philosophers of the seventeenth century after Descartes became divided about the power of reason in overcoming skepticism. Here we refer you to the box later in this chapter entitled "Rationalists and Empiricists."

In Selection 4.2, Descartes explains his view that he is a thinking thing—a mind—that is one and indivisible but "intermingled" at the same time with something entirely different, a body, a thing that is divisible and has parts. You will see how he uses an epistemological approach to these metaphysical issues.

SELECTION 4.2

*Meditations on First Philosophy**   **From René Descartes**

Because I know that all things which I apprehend clearly and distinctly can be created by God as I apprehend them, it suffices that I am able to apprehend one thing apart from another clearly and distinctly in order to be certain that the one is different from the other, since they may be made to exist in separation at least by the omnipotence of God . . . and therefore, just because I know certainly that I exist, and that meanwhile I do not remark that any other thing necessarily pertains to my nature or essence, excepting that I am a thinking thing, I rightly conclude that my essence consists solely in the fact that I am a thinking thing . . . [and as] I possess a distinct idea of body, inasmuch as it is only an extended and unthinking thing, it is certain that this I is entirely and absolutely distinct from my body, and can exist without it. . . .

There is certainly further in me a certain passive faculty of perception, that is, of receiving and recognising the ideas of sensible things, but this would be useless to me, if there were not either in me or in some other thing another active faculty capable of forming and producing these ideas. . . . [A]nd since God is no deceiver, [and since] He has given me . . . a very great inclination to believe that [these ideas] are conveyed to me by corporeal objects, I do not see how He could be defended from the accusation of deceit if these ideas were produced by causes other than corporeal objects. Hence we must

allow that corporeal things exist. . . . [And] we must at least admit that all things which I conceive in them clearly and distinctly, that is to say, all things which, speaking generally, are comprehended in the object of pure mathematics, are truly to be recognised as external objects. . . .

[O]n the sole Ground that God is not a deceiver . . . there is no doubt that in all things which nature teaches me there is some truth contained. . . . But there is nothing which this nature teaches me more expressly than that I have a body which is adversely affected when I feel pain, which has need of food or drink when I experience the feelings of hunger and thirst, and so on; nor can I doubt there being some truth in all this.

Nature also teaches me by these sensations of pain, hunger, thirst, etc., that I am not only lodged in my body as a pilot in a vessel, but that I am very closely united to it, and so to speak so intermingled with it that I seem to compose with it one whole. For if that were not the case, when my body is hurt, I, who am merely a thinking thing, would not feel pain, for I should perceive this wound by the understanding only, just as the sailor perceives by sight when something is damaged in his vessel. . . .

[T]here is a great difference between mind and body, inasmuch as body is by nature always divisible, and the mind is entirely indivisible. For, as a matter of fact, when I consider the mind, that is to say, myself inasmuch as I am

---

*Edited slightly for the modern reader.

only a thinking thing, I cannot distinguish in myself any parts, but apprehend myself to be clearly one and entire; and although the whole mind seems to be united to the whole body, yet if a foot, or an arm, or some other part, is separated from my body, I am aware that nothing has been taken away from my mind. And the faculties of willing, feeling, conceiving, etc., cannot be properly speaking said to be its parts, for it is one and the same mind which employs itself in willing and in feeling and understanding. But it is quite otherwise with corporeal or extended objects, for there is not one of these imaginable by me which my mind cannot easily divide into parts, and which consequently I do not recognise as being divisible. [T]his would be sufficient to teach me that the mind or soul of man is entirely different from the body, if I had not already learned it from other sources.

I further notice that the mind does not receive the impressions from all parts of the body immediately, but only from the brain, or perhaps even from one of its smallest parts, to wit, from that in which the common sense is said to reside.

Hobbes and Materialism   Bodies in motion

Thomas Hobbes (1588–1679) read Descartes's *Meditations* before their publication, and his objections to this work were published by Descartes along with what Descartes took to be a rebuttal. About ten years later, in 1651, Hobbes published his own major work, *Leviathan.*   Contractarian Theory of the State

Hobbes was on close terms with many of the best scientists and mathematicians of the period, including most significantly Galileo, and their discoveries seemed to him to imply clearly that all things are made of material particles and that all change reduces to motion. Accordingly, the basic premise of Hobbes's metaphysics is that *all that exists is bodies in motion,* motion being a continual relinquishing of one place and acquiring of another. Because, according to Hobbes, there are two main types of bodies, physical bodies and political bodies, there are two divisions of philosophy, natural and civil. Here we are concerned with Hobbes's natural philosophy. Later we will examine his "civil," or political, philosophy, which was enormously important.

Now, this business that all that exists is bodies in motion *might* sound plausible, until you consider such things as thoughts or acts of volition or emotion. Can it really be held that *thought* is just matter in motion? That *emotions* are? That *hatred* is? "Yes," said Hobbes.

Perception

Hobbes's strategy was to show that there is a basic mental activity, **perception,** or, as he called it, "sense," from which all other mental phenomena are derived, and that perception itself reduces to matter in motion.

God, Free Will, Immortality

Modern metaphysics is to a large extent a competition among the four metaphysical perspectives mentioned in the text: dualism, materialism, idealism, and neutralism. Three important questions are at stake in this competition:

1. Does an immaterial God exist?
2. Do humans have free will?
3. Is there life after death?

These questions are at stake because materialism, the theory that all that exists is physical, suggests that the answer to each of these questions is "no." Unfortunately for those who would prefer the answer to one or another of these questions to be "yes," materialism seems to be the metaphysics implied by modern science. This is because a scientific understanding of the world does not seem to require a belief in the existence of anything other than matter, broadly construed.

So that is one major reason why modern metaphysics is explosive stuff. Riding on the outcome of the competition among dualism, idealism, neutralism, and materialism is the rationality of believing in an immaterial God, human free will, and existence in the hereafter.

Perception, he maintained, occurs as follows: Motion in the external world causes motion within us. This motion within (which Hobbes called a "phantasm") is experienced by us as an external object (or group of objects) having certain properties. The properties do not *really* exist in the objects, Hobbes said: they are just the way the objects *seem* to us: *"The things that really are in the world outside us are those motions by which these seemings are caused."*

So motion outside us causes motion within us, which is a perception. If the internal motion remains for a while even after the external object is no longer present, it is then *imagination* or *memory*. And *thinking*, he said, is merely a sequence of these perceptions. (There are subtleties in his account of thinking which we won't now bother with.)

Now humans, unlike animals (Hobbes said), are able to form signs or names (words) to designate perceptions, and it is this ability that allows humans to reason. *Reasoning*, in Hobbes's view, is nothing but "adding and subtracting of the consequences of general names." Reasoning occurs, for example, when you see that the consequences of the name "circle" are, among other things, that if a straight line is drawn through the center of a circle, the circle has been divided into two equal parts.

As for *decisions* and other voluntary actions, such as walking or speaking or moving our arms, these are all movements of the body that begin internally as "endeavors," caused by perceptions. When the endeavor is toward something that causes it, this is *desire;* when away from it, it is *aversion*. Love is merely desire, and *hate* merely aversion. We call a thing "good" when it is an object of desire, and "bad" when it is an object of aversion. *Deliberation* is simply an alternation of desires and aversions, and *will* is nothing but the last desire or aversion remaining in a deliberation.

We've left out the finer details of Hobbes's account, but this should show you how Hobbes tried to establish that every aspect of human psychology is a derivative of perception, and that perception itself reduces to matter in motion. (Hobbes speaks for himself on the subject in the next reading selection.)

This theory that all is matter in motion may well strike you as implausible, maybe even ridiculous. Nevertheless, as you will see in Part 5, it expresses in a rudimentary form a view that is quite attractive to many contemporary philosophers and brain scientists, namely, that every mental activity is a brain process of one sort or another. So let us try to focus on the difficulties in this theory that make it seem somewhat implausible.

Difficulties

The most serious difficulty in Hobbes's theory is probably this. All psychological states, according to Hobbes, are derivatives of perception. So if there is anything wrong with his account of perception, there is something wrong with his entire account of mental states.

Now, according to Hobbes, perception is merely a movement of particles within the person, a movement of particles within that is caused by a movement of particles without.

Thus, when I perceive a lawn (for instance), a movement of particles takes place within me, according to Hobbes, that is the perception of a soft, green lawn, and this internal motion of particles is caused by the motion of particles outside me. But here is the difficulty: when I look at the lawn, the internal movement (i.e., the perception) is not *itself* green and soft. Neither, according to Hobbes, is the lawn. So how is it that the internal movement of particles is experienced *as* a soft, green lawn? And, further, *what is it* that *experiences* the internal movement? The internal movement is, after all, just movement. In other words, *how* do the qualities of softness and greenness become apparent, and *to what* do they become apparent?

Later, in Part 5, we will go into this difficulty in more detail, and we will see that it is still a problem even for the most up-to-date versions of materialism.

Let's just say in conclusion that Hobbes's philosophy aroused considerable antagonism—the charge was that Hobbes was an atheist—and in his later years his work had to be printed outside his own country, in Amsterdam. Still, in the long run, and despite the entrenchment of Cartesian dualism in common sense, variations of Hobbes's materialist philosophy were and are accepted by some of the keenest intellects of philosophy and science.

In Selection 4.3, taken from Hobbes's *Leviathan,* remember that by "sense" Hobbes meant what we have been calling "perception."

Leviathan*   From Thomas Hobbes

PART I. OF MAN

Chapter I. Of Sense

Concerning the thoughts of man, I will consider them first singly, and afterwards in sequence, or dependance upon one another. Singly, they are every one a representation or appearance of some quality or other accident of a body without us; which is commonly called an *object*. Which object works on the eyes, ears, and other parts of man's body; and by diversity of working, produces diversity of appearances.

The original of them all is that which we call *sense* (for there is no conception in a man's mind, which was not at first, totally, or by parts, impressed upon the organs of sense). The rest are derived from that original. . . .

The cause of sense is the external body or object, which presses the organ proper to each sense, either directly, as in the taste and touch; or indirectly, as in seeing, hearing, and smelling: which pressure, by the intervention of nerves and other strings and membranes of the body, continues inward to the brain and heart, causing there a resistance or counter-pressure or endeavor of the heart to deliver itself: which endeavor because outward seems to be some matter without. And this seeming or fancy is that which men call *sense;* and consists, to the eye, in a light or figured color; to the ear, in a sound; to the nostril, in an odor; to the tongue and palate, in a savor; and to the rest of the body in heat, cold, hardness, softness, and such other qualities as we discern by feeling. All these sensible qualities are, in the object that causes them, just motions of the matter by which the object presses our organs. Neither in us that are pressed, are they anything else but diverse motions; (for motion produces nothing but motion). . . .

Chapter II. Of Imagination

After the object is removed or the eye shut, we still retain an image of the thing seen, though more obscure than when we see it. And this is what the Latins call *imagination*. . . . Imagination therefore is nothing but decaying sense; and is found in men, and many other living creatures, sleeping as well as waking. . . .

Any object being removed from our eyes, though the impression it made in us remain; yet other objects more present succeeding, and working on us, the imagination of the past is obscured and made weak; as the voice of a man is in the noise of the day. From whence it follows that the longer the time is after the sight or sense of any object, the weaker is the imagination. For the continual change of man's body destroys in time the parts which in sense were moved: So that distance of time and of place have one and the same effect in us. For as at a great distance of place, that which we look at appears dim and without distinction of the smaller parts; and as voices grow weak and inarticulate: so also after great distance of time, our imagination of the past is weak; and we lose (for example) of cities we have seen, many particular streets; and of actions, many particular circumstances. This decaying sense, when we would express the thing itself . . . we call *imagination,* as I said before: But when we would express the decay, and signify that the sense is fading, old, and past, it is called *memory.* So that imagination and memory are but one thing, which for diverse considerations has diverse names.

---

*Edited slightly for the modern reader.

Much memory, or memory of many things, is called *experience*. Again, imagination being only of those things which have been formerly perceived by sense, either all at once or by parts at several times; the former (which is the imagining the whole object as it was presented to the sense) is simple imagination; as when one imagines a man, or horse which he has seen before. The other is compounded; as when from the sight of a man at one time and of a horse at another, we conceive in our mind a Centaur. . . .

Chapter VI. Of the Interior Beginnings of Voluntary Motions; Commonly Called the Passions. And the Speeches by Which They Are Expressed

There are in animals two sorts of motions peculiar to them: One called *vital;* begun in generation, and continued without interruption through their whole life; such as are the course of the blood, the pulse, the breathing, the concoction, nutrition, excretion, etc.; to which motions there needs no help of imagination. The other is animal motion, otherwise called *voluntary motion;* as to go, to speak, to move any of our limbs, in such manner as is first fancied in our minds. . . . Imagination is the first internal beginning of all voluntary motion. These small beginnings of motion within the body of man, before they appear in walking, speaking, striking, and other visible actions, are commonly called *endeavor.*

This endeavor, when it is toward something which causes it, is called *appetite* or *desire;* the latter, being the general name; and the other, often restrained to signify the desire of food, namely hunger and thirst. And when the endeavor is from something, it generally is called *aversion.* . . .

That which men desire they are all said to *love:* and to *hate* those things for which they have aversion. So that desire and love are the same thing; except that by desire we always signify the absence of the object; love, most commonly the presence of the same. So also by aversion we signify absence; and by hate, the presence of the object.

Neutralism: Conway and Spinoza

So, much, then, for Hobbes and materialism. Two philosophers who set forth neutralist metaphysical systems were Anne Conway and Benedictus de Spinoza, who lived at nearly the same time.

Time in the Metaphysics of Anne Conway

The metaphysical system that **Anne Conway** (1631–1679) developed is a monadology: a view that all things are reducible to a single substance that is itself irreducible. (This is roughly what atomic theory was until the discovery of subatomic particles in this century.) It is also a kind of neutralist metaphysics. In Lady Conway's view there is a kind of *continuum* between the most material and the most mental or "spiritual" substances. All created substances ("Creatures," she called them) are *both* mental and physical to some degree or other. Conway also argued

⊓⌿⊔⌿⊔⌿⊔⌿⊔⌿⊔⌿⊔⌿⊔⌿⊔⌿⊓

PROFILE / Anne Finch, The Viscountess Conway (1631–1679)

ike most women of the seventeenth century, Anne Conway, as she is usually called, had no formal education. Her father, who was Speaker of the House of Commons, died a week before Anne was born. But her family remained influential, her half-bother becoming Lord High Chancellor in England. So Anne Finch grew up knowing some of the most important and influential English intellectuals of her time. At home, she somehow managed to learn French, Latin, Hebrew, and Greek. She also studied mathematics and philosophy. She was critical of the work of Descartes (or "Cartes," as he was sometimes called), Hobbes, and Spinoza. And she discussed philosophy with some fairly well-known philosophers who lived in or visited England during her lifetime. The philosophical community was a small one there, and everybody in it seemed to know everybody else. She worked closely with some people known as Cambridge Platonists, including Henry More, Ralph Cudworth (whose daughter, Damaris Cudworth Masham, was also a philosopher and was John Locke's landlady), Joseph Glanvill, George Rust, and Benjamin Whichcote.

Anne Conway suffered from migraine headaches, and that's supposed to account for the unreadable scrawl with which she penciled her book, *The Principles of the Most Ancient and Modern Philosophy*. Depending on which scholar you read, she either wrote it between 1671 and 1674 (according to Marjorie Nicolson) or between 1677 and 1679 (according to Peter Lopston). She died without having a chance to correct or revise it. Her husband was away in Ireland at the time; and Francis Mercury von Helmont, her friend and one of the colleagues with whom she often discussed philosophy and religion, preserved her body in wine until her husband could return for the funeral. (Cheers!)

Von Helmont had Conway's work translated into Latin and published in 1690. Two years later, it was translated back into English by somebody whose initials were J.C. Now, von Helmont was a good friend of Leibniz (see the box coming up shortly), and showed him Conway's book. Scholars who have studied Conway's philosophy consider her to have been a forerunner of Leibniz in many ways.

that all created substances are dependent on God's decision to create them. Moreover, she said that all such Creatures have both an individual essence (what makes one thing different from another) and an essence that is common to all. This essence in common is what later came to be known as *de re* modality. The idea of *de re* essentiality means that a property (in this case, the property of being both mental and physical) must be a property of anything that is created by God; otherwise, it ceases to be what it is. It couldn't exist except that it is necessarily both mental and physical. Everything—persons, animals, plants, inanimate objects (furniture)—is a substance. And everything is partly physical and partly mental, and could not be otherwise.

God, of course, is another matter, Conway believed. God is nonmaterial, nonphysical; God is also all-perfect. Therefore, the one thing God can't do is change his mind about being spiritual. To change his mind and be physical one moment, spiritual the next, and maybe back again, would imply that one state or the other was less than perfect. What possible reason could God have to want to change? What's not to like? Now, that doesn't mean that God *can't* be physical; he just doesn't *want* to be, and never would want to be because that would suggest that he wasn't so perfect before the change. And we all know that if God is anything, he is perfect. God created Christ (making God older than Christ), and Christ, God's first created substance (his first Creature), always had some degree of physical essence and some degree of mental or spiritual essence.

Because God is perfect, Conway held, he is changeless, and therefore exists outside the dimension of time. Conway's concept of time is less technical than but philosophically much like that articulated recently by the great contemporary physicist Stephen Hawking in his book *A Brief History of Time.* Time is the succession of events (Conway called them "motions" and "operations") of created objects (Creatures). Understood this way, time is the measure of changes in things. Because creating (making Creatures) is part of God's primary essence (a necessary property—the way God defines himself, as creator), Conway's God is an eternal creator. The universe is therefore not something that was made at some specific time: it always existed because God always existed and he was always creating. Past and future are all God's present.

SELECTION 4.4

*The Principles of the Most Ancient and Modern Philosophy**

From Anne Conway

Forasmuch as all Creatures are, and do exist simply, or alone from him; because God willed them to be, whose Will is infinitely powerful, and whose Commandment, without any Instrument or Instrumental Cause, is the only Efficient to give Being unto his Creatures. Hence it necessarily follows, seeing the Will of God is Eternal, or from Eternity, that Creation must immediately follow the said Will, without any In-

terposition of Time. And though it cannot be said that Creatures, considered in themselves, are Co-eternal with God, because after this rate Eternity and Time would be confounded together; yet nevertheless the Creatures, and that Will which created them, are so mutually present, and so immediately happen one after another, that nothing can be said to come in between, even as if two Circles should immediately touch each other. Neither can we assign any other Beginning to Creatures, but God him-

---

*Edited slightly for the modern reader.

self and his Eternal Will, which is according to his Eternal Idea or Wisdom. Hence it follows, by Natural Consequence, that Times from the Creation are Infinite, and without all Number, which no created Intellect can conceive. How then can this be Finite or Measured, which had no other beginning but Eternity itself.

But if anyone will say times are Finite, then let us suppose the Measure of them, from the Beginning, to be about 6,000 Years (even as some do think that the whole Age of this World, from the Beginning, is of no greater Extent); or with others (who think that before this World, there was another invisible World, from whence this visible World proceeded) let us suppose the Duration of this world to be 60,000 Years; or any other Number of Years, as great as can be by any Reason conceived. Now I demand whether it could be that the World was created before this time? If they deny it, they limit the Power of God to a certain Number of years; if they affirm it, they allow Time to be before all time, which is a manifest Contradiction.

These things being premised, it will be easy to Answer to that Question, wherewith Numbers have been so exceedingly perplexed: Whether Creation was made or could be made from Eternity or from Everlasting? If by Eternity and Everlasting, they mean an Infinite Number of Times, in this sense Creation was made from Everlasting. But if they mean such an Eternity as God himself hath, so as to say that Creatures are Equal or Co-eternal with God, and to have no beginning of Time, this is false. For both Creatures and Times (which are nothing else but successive Motions and Operations of Created Beings) had a Beginning, which is God or the eternal Will of God. And why should it seem strange to anyone that Times in their whole Collection or Universality may be said to be Infinite, when the least part of Time that can be conceived contains in itself a kind of Infinity? For as there is no Time so great that a greater cannot be conceived, so there is no time so small but there may be a less; for the sixtieth part of a Minute may be divided into sixty other parts, and these again into others, and so ad infinitum.

But the Infiniteness of Times from the beginning of Creation may be likewise demonstrated from the Goodness of God. For God is definitely Good, Loving, and Bountiful; yea, Goodness and Charity itself; an infinite Fountain, and Father of Goodness, Charity, and Bounty. Now how can it be that this Fountain shall not always plentifully flow, and send from itself Living Waters? And shall not this Ocean perpetually abound with its own Efflux to the Production of Creatures, and that with a certain continual Stream? For the Goodness of God in its own proper Nature is Communicative, and Multiplicative, and seeing in him nothing is wanting, neither can anything be added unto him, by reason of his absolute fullness, and transcendent fertility. And also seeing by the same reason he cannot multiply himself, which would be all one, as if we should imagine there were more Gods than one, which is contradictory. Now it necessarily follows that he did give Being to his Creatures from Everlasting, or Times without Number; or else this Communicative Goodness of God, which is his Essential Attribute, would be something Finite, and its Duration consist of a certain Number of Years, than which nothing is more absurd.

It is an Essential Attribute of God, to be a Creator. And so by Consequence God ever was a Creator, and ever will be a Creator, because otherwise he would be changed. And therefore Creatures ever were, and ever will be. But the Eternity of Creatures is nothing else but an Infinity of Times, in which they ever were, and ever will be without end. Neither is this Infiniteness of Times equal to the Infiniteness of God's Eternity because the Eternity of God himself hath no Times in it. Nothing therein can be said to be past, or to come, but the whole is always present: He is indeed in Times; but not comprehended of them. Although the Hebrews seem to speak somewhat different from this . . . yet they do not contradict this Opinion, because they allow an indefinite Duration of Times.

And the reason hereof is manifest: Because Time is nothing else but the successive Motion or Operation of Creatures, if that Motion or Operation should cease, Time would also cease, and the Creatures themselves would cease with Time. Wherefore, such is the Nature of every Creature that it is in Motion, or hath a certain Motion, by means of which it advances forward, and grows to a farther perfection. And seeing that in God there is no successive Motion or Operation to a farther perfection, because he is most absolutely perfect, hence there are not Times in God or his Eternity.

And moreover, because there are no Parts in God, there are also no Times in him; for all Times have their Parts, and are indeed infinitely divisible, as before was said.

Spinoza

About the time Hobbes was having to send his work to Amsterdam for publication, **Benedictus de Spinoza** (1632–1677) was completing his major work, *Ethics*. Hobbes was able to print his work in Amsterdam, but not in England, because Holland, during this period of history, was the most intellectually permissive of all European countries, sort of a seventeenth-century Berkeley, California. It was probably also the only country in which the government would have tolerated Spinoza's opinions, which were considered, like Hobbes's, to be atheistic and repulsive.

Spinoza's *Ethics* consists of some 250 "theorems," each of which he attempted to derive by rigorous deductive logic from a set of eight basic definitions and seven self-evident axioms. Given his axioms and definition of substance (that which depends on nothing else for its conception; i.e., that which is self-subsistent), Spinoza is able to prove that there are no multiple substances, as Descartes thought, but only one infinite substance. Spinoza equated this substance with God, but we must not be misled by his proof of God. Spinoza's "God" is just simply *basic substance:* it is not the personal Judaeo-Christian God; rather it is simply the sum total of everything that is. It is reality, nature. Spinoza was not an atheist. On the contrary, he was a pantheist: God is all.

Because there is only one substance, according to Spinoza, thought and extension are not the attributes of two separate and distinct substances, mind and matter, as Descartes had thought. What they are, in Spinoza's system, are different attributes of the one basic substance—they are alternative ways of conceiving of it.

So a living person, from Spinoza's point of view, is not a composite of two different things. The living person is a single unit or "modification" of substance that can be conceived either as extension or as thought. Your "body" is a unit of substance conceived as extension; your "mind" is the selfsame unit of substance conceived as thought.

Because, according to Spinoza, the infinite substance is infinite in all respects, it necessarily has infinite attributes. Therefore, thought and extension are not the only attributes of substance. They are just the only attributes we know—they are the only ways available to us of characterizing or conceiving substance. They are,

PROFILE / Benedictus de Spinoza (1632–1677)

The gentle Spinoza was among the most ethical men ever to have lived. "As a natural consequence," Bertrand Russell observed, "he was considered, during his lifetime and for a century after his death, a man of appalling wickedness."

Spinoza's family was one of many Jewish families that fled Portugal for Holland to escape the terrors of the Inquisition. His serious nature and love of learning were appreciated by all until he pointed out that the Old Testament and biblical tradition were full of inconsistencies. This produced a venemous wrath in the Jewish community. At first Spinoza was offered an annual pension for concealing his doubts. When this failed, the logical next step was taken: an attempt was made to murder him. He was finally, of course, excommunicated from the synagogue.

For a time, Spinoza lived in the house of his Latin teacher, though he later rented a room in a tiny house in Rhynsburg, now a suburb of Leyden, where he earned a sparse living by grinding glass lenses. He lived a modest and frugal existence and preferred to work on his philosophy than to do anything else.

Spinoza became known despite his quiet and retiring existence, and at one point he was offered a professorship at Heidelberg. He declined the appointment, realizing that there would be restrictions on his academic freedom and fearing that his philosophy might draw sharp reactions in German society. In that suspicion he was probably correct, if the fact that many German professors referred to him as "that wretched monster" is any indication.

Still, after his death, some of the greatest thinkers—including Goethe, Lessing, and Schleiermacher—eventually came to appreciate his depth. Hegel went so far as to say that all subsequent philosophy would be a kind of Spinozism.

Spinoza died when he was forty-four, from tuberculosis. His condition was aggravated by the glass dust that he was forced to breathe in his profession. Today, the society for out-of-work American philosophers is called "The Lensgrinders."

so to speak, the only "languages" in terms of which we can speak and think about reality or substance.

Accordingly, for Spinoza there is no problem in explaining how the mind interacts with the body, for they are one and the same thing. Wondering how the mind and the body interact is like wondering how your last glass of *wine* and your last glass of *vino* could mix with each other. The mind and the body are the same thing, conceptualized from different viewpoints.

In Spinoza's system, there is no personal immortality after death. Further, free will is an illusion; whatever happens is caused by the nature of substance. Material bodies are governed by the laws of physics, and what happens to them is completely determined by what happened before. Because the mental and the material are one and the same, what happens in minds is as inevitable as what happens in bodies. Everything was, is, and will be exactly as it must be.

There is certainly more to Spinoza's philosophy than this, but this is enough for our purposes here. Where Descartes had postulated two separate substances, both Hobbes and Spinoza postulated only one. For Hobbes, however, what exists is only material; a nonmaterial mental realm does not exist. For Spinoza, what exists is both material and mental, depending on how it is conceptualized. Thus, although neither Hobbes nor Spinoza is faced with Descartes's problem of explaining how two realms, the mental and the material, interact, Hobbes is faced with a different problem, that of *explaining away* the mental realm. We are inclined to ask Hobbes just how and why this illusory mental realm seems so clearly to be real when in fact it is not. For Spinoza, the mental realm is real, and there is nothing that he needs to explain away.

Before leaving Spinoza, we should mention that his philosophy is interesting not merely for its content but for its form. Spinoza attempted to geometrize philosophy to an extent unequaled by any other major philosopher.

Maybe you recall that Euclid began his *Elements* with a set of basic definitions and unproved postulates, and from them logically derived a set of geometric theorems. Likewise, as we explained above, Spinoza began with definitions and seemingly self-evident axioms and then proceeded to derive theorems or "propositions," from them.

For example, Spinoza's Proposition III states, "Things which have nothing in common cannot be one the cause of the other." And under that proposition Spinoza gives a proof that refers back to two of his axioms. Thus, giving Spinoza his definitions, and assuming his axioms are beyond doubt and that he made no mistakes in logic, every one of Spinoza's propositions—his *entire* philosophy—is beyond doubt! Spinoza, unlike Descartes, did not take the metaphysical detour by explicitly asking, "What can be known?" But by geometrizing his philosophy, Spinoza attempted to provide a metaphysical system that could be known with certainty to be true.

John Locke; Berkeley and Idealism

Descartes, Hobbes, Conway, and Spinoza all belonged to the lively seventeenth century, the century that produced not only great philosophy but also some of the most important scientific discoveries of all time. The seventeenth century, you may recall from your history books, was also the century of the Thirty Years' War (1618–1648), which was the most brutal European war before this century, and the English Civil War. It also witnessed the Sun King (Louis XIV of France), the opening of Harvard, the founding of Pennsylvania, and the popularization of smoking.

Leibniz

As will be explained in a box coming right up, Descartes, Spinoza, and a third individual, **Gottfried Wilhelm, Baron von Leibniz** (1646–1716), are known as the Continental rationalists. Many recent scholars qualified to make such a judgment think that this third person, Leibniz, was the most brilliant intellect of his age. This judgment is made specifically with the fact in mind that Leibniz was the contemporary of a very bright light, Sir Isaac Newton (1642–1727). Leibniz and Newton, independently of each other, developed the calculus—and at the time there was bitter controversy over who did so first. Leibniz's calculus was published in 1684, a few years before Newton's, but Newton had been slow in publishing his work.

Because Leibniz's philosophy is highly technical and difficult to characterize or summarize in a brief passage, we won't go into it much. Basically, it is a detailed metaphysical system according to which the ultimate constituents of reality are indivisible atoms. But Leibniz's atoms are not indivisible units of matter, for, because matter is extended, a piece of matter no matter how tiny is always further divisible. Instead, Leibniz's atoms are what he called **monads,** which are indivisible units of force or energy or activity. Here Leibniz anticipated by a couple of centuries the views of contemporary physics, according to which material particles are a form of energy. Leibniz, however, believed the monads to be entirely *nonphysical* and often referred to them as "souls,"

though he distinguished them from souls in the ordinary sense.

Don't think Leibniz's philosophy is just haphazard and idle speculation. His entire metaphysical system seems to follow from a few basic and plausible assumptions, or basic principles. One of these principles, for example, the **principle of the identity of indiscernibles,** says that if two beings have exactly the same set of properties then they are identical with one another. Another principle, known as the **principle of sufficient reason,** says that there is a sufficient reason why things are exactly as they are and are not otherwise. Leibniz also used this principle as a proof of God, as we shall see in Chapter 12.

Leibniz's most famous work is the *Monadology.*

dé ré
modality
or
necessity

For an example of idealism, which is the last of the four metaphysical philosophies, we turn to the early eighteenth century and **George Berkeley** (1685–1753).

The eighteenth century, remember, was the Enlightenment. Despite the American and French revolutions, it was marked by comparative peace and stability, an improved standard of living, and an increase in personal freedom. Fewer witches were prosecuted in this century, and the burning of heretics became rare. Religion continued to decline in importance politically, socially, and intellectually. The growth of money through commerce laid the foundations for the Industrial Revolution. In short, all was well. Handel composed *The Messiah.*

It should be very easy to remember Berkeley, whose most important work was done early in the century. Berkeley denied that matter exists. This theory, naturally, convinced many that he was a crackpot. It did not help matters that, in his later years, he came to be rather overly focused on the healthful benefits of tar water, a

PROFILE / Émilie du Châtelet (1707–1749)

One of the important intellectual controversies of the eighteenth century was whether there could be such a thing as action at a distance. On the one hand were the Cartesians (followers of Descartes), who said that, if an object is to move, another object must *come up against it and push it*. On the other hand were the Newtonians (followers of Sir Isaac Newton), who believed in action at a distance—for example, two objects will attract one another through the force of gravity, even though they are separated by space. Cartesians generally viewed the concept of action at a distance,

and the forces postulated to explain such action, as mystical and bizarre.

This controversy was just a minor skirmish in a broader conceptual battle, that between Newtonian empirical physics, which was based on observation and experimentation, and speculative metaphysics, which was grounded to a large extent purely on reason and was represented by the Cartesians and, most importantly, the brilliant Leibniz (see previous box). According to the metaphysicians, even if Newtonian science described *how* the universe operates, it didn't show *why* the universe must operate in that way. Newtonian physics just didn't have the rational grounding or certainty found in the systems of a Descartes or a Liebniz, the metaphysicians felt.

The metaphysical group had other problems with Newtonianism, too, such as how God fit into the Newtonian picture of the universe. If the universe is a vast physical machine, couldn't God change his mind and destroy it—maybe make a different machine? How could there be human free will if the Newtonians were right and humans are just small parts in God's big machine? Do humans have free will, can they do what

they choose, or are they nothing more than bodies, moving in reaction to immaterial forces?

A major player in the disputes between science and metaphysics was **Émilie du Châtelet** (1707–1749). Du Châtelet, a colleague (and lover) of Voltaire, was both a scientist and a philosopher, and her writings were respected by both camps. Her two-volume annotated translation of Newton's *Mathematical Principles of Natural Philosophy* (1759) remains to this day *the* French translation of Newton.

In her three-volume work, *Institutions de Physique* (1740), du Châtelet sought to answer some of the metaphysicians' complaints about Newtonianism. She did this essentially by adapting Leibniz's metaphysical principles (for example, the principle of sufficient reason and the principle of the identity of indiscernibles) to Newtonian science in such a way as to provide, she hoped, a vigorous metaphysical foundation for it, and to allay fears that Newtonianism required abandoning important theological tenets. Although du Châtelet perhaps did not resolve all the problems, it is safe to say that she did as much as anyone to bring to focus exactly what the bones of contention were.

PROFILE / George Berkeley (1685–1753)

Berkeley was born in Ireland and studied at Trinity College, Dublin. He was made a Fellow of the College in 1707. His *Treatise Concerning the Principles of Human Knowledge* (1709) was a great success and gave Berkeley a lasting reputation, though few accepted his theory that nothing exists outside the mind.

Berkeley eventually became Dean of Derry, a post that included a lucrative stipend. But Berkeley gave up the post in what proved to be a futile attempt to establish a college in the Bermudas to convert the Indians in North America. He was made Bishop of Cloyne in 1734.

Berkeley was known for his generosity of heart and mind, and also for his enthusiasm for tar water. He especially liked the fact that tar water did not have the same effects as alcohol. His writings about the healthy benefits of drinking tar water actually caused it to become a fad in English society for a time.

Berkeley's main works, in addition to the one mentioned above, are *Essay Towards a New Theory of Vision* (1709) and *Three Dialogues Between Hylas and Philonous* (1713).

Berkeley, California, was named after Berkeley because of his line of poetry: "Westward the course of empire takes its way."

medicine made from pine tar. Nevertheless, Berkeley's youthful work contained some very powerful arguments.

Berkeley too (like Descartes) took the epistemological detour to metaphysical issues. Now we want to explain why Berkeley's denial of matter was not sheer lunacy.

To understand Berkeley's idealism fully, we have to consider Berkeley's predecessor, **John Locke** (1632–1704). Locke, together with Berkeley and David Hume, are referred to as the British empiricists. In Locke's great epistemological work, *An Essay Concerning Human Understanding,* Locke wished to inquire into the origin, certainty, and extent of human knowledge. Many of his views will almost certainly be shared by most readers of this book, so influential have his views been. Locke's epistemology is indeed so widely accepted that much of it is now thought to be so much common sense. You should be prepared, however. We're going to show you that terrible philosophical difficulties attend Locke's basic position, as commonsensical as it will probably seem. It is precisely these difficulties that led Berkeley to endorse the seemingly crackpot ideas that we mentioned a moment ago. Because of the importance of Locke's philosophy to today's common sense and of Berkeley's criticisms of it, we'll spend a bit more time on Locke and Berkeley than we did on Spinoza or Hobbes.

John Locke and Representative Realism   Empiricist.   dualist.

Profile 307

Locke's fundamental thesis is that all our ideas come from experience. The human mind at birth, he wrote (echoing Aristotle) is essentially a **tabula rasa,** or blank slate. On this blank slate experience makes its imprint. External objects impinge on our senses, which convey into the mind ideas, or, as we might prefer to say today, perceptions, of these objects and their various qualities. In short, sensation furnishes the mind with all its contents. **Nihil in intellectu quod prius non fuerit in sensu**—nothing exists in the mind that wasn't first in the senses. This, of course, is familiar and plausible.

Now these ideas or perceptions of some of the qualities of external objects are accurate copies of qualities that actually reside in the objects, Locke said. This is what he means. Think of a basketball. It has a certain size, shape, and weight, and when we look at and handle the ball, our sensory apparatus provides us with accurate pictures or images or ideas or perceptions of these "primary" qualities, as Locke called them.

The basketball also has the power to produce in us ideas of "secondary" qualities, such as the brown color, the leathery smell, the coolness that we feel when we hold it, and so forth. Are *these* qualities really in the basketball? Well, of course not, you will say. And that's exactly what Locke said. These secondary qualities are not really in the basketball—they are purely subjective and exist in us merely as ideas. In other words, in Locke's view—and we will bet that this is your view as well—if all sentient creatures were removed from the proximity of the basketball, there would not *be* any brownness, leathery odor, or coolness, but only an object of a certain size and shape and weight, composed of minute particles that collectively would smell leathery and feel cool and look brown if any creatures with sense organs then came into existence and held and looked at and sniffed the ball.

This theory that Locke accepted is often called **representative realism.** In a sentence, it is the theory that we perceive objects *indirectly* by means of our "representations" or ideas or perceptions of them, some of which are accurate copies or representations or reflections of the real properties of "external" objects, of objects "outside the mind." This theory is widely held and is probably regarded by most people as self-evident. Open almost any introductory psychology text, and you will behold implicit in its discussion of perception Locke's theory of representative realism.

Now we said a moment ago that terrible philosophical difficulties attend to this very nice, down-to-earth, commonsense theory known as representative realism, and it is time for us to explain ourselves. As justifiable as Locke's theory may seem, it is subject to a powerful objection, stated most eloquently by the Irish bishop and philosopher we mentioned a moment ago, George Berkeley.

Locke's Theory: According to Locke, when we say we are looking at an external object, what we are really doing is attending to the perceptions or "ideas" of the object that are in our mind. Some of these perceptions, like those of a basketball's size and shape, accurately represent qualities that are really in the object itself. Other perceptions, like those of the basketball's color and odor, don't represent anything that is really in the object; the color and shape are just subjective qualities that exist only within us.

George Berkeley   ~IDealism~

If Locke is correct, then we experience sensible things, things like basketballs and garden rakes, *indirectly*—that is, through the intermediary of our ideas or perceptions. But if that's true, Berkeley said, then we cannot know that *any* of our ideas or perceptions accurately represent the qualities of these sensible things. Why can't we know this? Because, Berkeley argued, if Locke is correct, we do not directly experience the basketball (or any other object) *itself*. Instead, what we directly experience is our *perceptions and ideas of the basketball*. And if we do not have direct experience of the basketball itself, then we cannot compare our perceptions or ideas of the basketball with the basketball itself to see if they "accurately represent" the basketball's qualities.

Indeed, given Locke's position, Berkeley said, we cannot really know that a thing like a basketball or a garden rake even *exists*. For according to Locke's theory, it is not the *object* we experience, but rather our perceptions or ideas of it.

This, then, is Berkeley's criticism of Locke's theory. As satisfying as it might seem to common sense, Locke's position is the short road to skepticism. If we accept Locke's theory, then we cannot know that "sensible things," things like basketballs and rakes and even our own hands and feet, actually exist.

Fortunately, Berkeley is an orderly and compelling writer, and we may permit him to set forth his philosophy himself. In Selection 4.5, Berkeley begins by noting that the objects of human knowledge are ideas of various sorts (e.g., ideas of

objection: Primary Qualities verified by 2 or more senses provides sufficient reason

Rationalists and Empiricists

A doctrine that St. Thomas Aquinas (see Chapter 2) accepted and attributed to Aristotle, and that John Locke also accepted, is: *nihil in intellectu quod prius non fuerit in sensu,* that is, there's nothing in the intellect that wasn't first in the senses. Those who accept this doctrine are called **empiricists.** Others, however, known as **rationalists,** hold that the intellect contains important truths that weren't placed there by sensory experience. "Something never comes from nothing," for example, might count as one of these truths, because experience can tell you only that something has never come from nothing so far, not that it can never, ever happen (or so a rationalist might argue). Sometimes rationalists believe in a *theory of innate ideas,* according to which these truths are "innate" to the mind—that is, they are part of the original dispositions of the intellect.

The empiricist is, in effect, a type of modified skeptic—he or she denies that there is any knowledge that doesn't stem from sensory experience. Most rationalists, by contrast, do not deny that *some* knowledge about the world can be obtained through experience. But other rationalists, such as Parmenides (check Chapter 2), deny that experience can deliver up any sort of true knowledge. This type of rationalist is also a type of modified skeptic.

Classical rationalism and empiricism in modern philosophy were mainly a product of the seventeenth and eighteenth centuries. Rationalism is associated most significantly during that time period with Descartes (1596–1650), Spinoza (1632–1677), and Leibniz (1646–1716). These three are often called the *Continental rationalists,* and they are often contrasted with Locke (1632–1704), Berkeley (1685–1753), and Hume (1711–1776), the so-called *British empiricists.* Philosophers from other periods, however, are sometimes classified as rationalists or empiricists depending on whether they emphasized the importance of reason or experience in knowledge of the world. Those earlier philosophers treated in this book who are usually listed as rationalists are, among others, Pythagoras, Parmenides, and Plato. Those who are often listed as empiricists are Aristotle, Epicurus, and Aquinas. Immanuel Kant (1724–1804), discussed in the next chapter, is said to have synthesized rationalism and empiricism because he believed that all knowledge *begins* with experience (a thesis empiricists agree with) but also believed that knowledge is not limited to what has been found in experience (a thesis rationalists agree with). The point is covered in the text.

Modern epistemology, as you will see, has been predominantly empiricist. This is because the Continental rationalists, and later rationalists too, were primarily metaphysicians. That is to say, they were generally less concerned with discussing the possibility of knowledge and related issues than with actually coming to propose some philosophically important theory about reality. The great exception is Descartes, a rationalist who concerned himself explicitly with the possibility of knowledge.

sensation, emotion, memory, imagination, etc.), and that these ideas can only exist in the mind that perceives them. He then observes that there is a contradiction in the "strange opinion" that sensible objects (houses, mountains, rivers, etc.) exist outside the mind.

Berkeley and Atheism

In Berkeley's opinion, the great virtue of his idealist system was that it alone did not invite skepticism about God.

Dualism, he thought, by postulating the existence of objects outside the mind, made these objects unknowable and was just an open invitation to skepticism about their existence. And skepticism about the existence of sensible objects, he thought, would inevitably extend itself to skepticism about their creator, God.

Materialism, he believed, made sensible objects independent of God; and thus it, too, led to skepticism about God.

He thought that his own system, by contrast, made the existence of sensible objects undeniable (they are as undeniably real as are your own ideas). This meant for Berkeley that the existence of the divine mind, in which sensible objects are sustained, was equally undeniable.

SELECTION 4.5

Treatise Concerning the Principles of Human Knowledge (1)

From George Berkeley

It is evident to anyone who takes a survey of the objects of human knowledge, that they are either ideas (1) actually imprinted on the senses, or else such as are (2) perceived by attending to the passions and operations of the mind, or lastly (3) ideas formed by help of memory and imagination, either compounding, dividing, or barely representing those originally perceived in the aforesaid ways. By sight I have the ideas of lights and colors, with their several degrees and variations. By touch I perceive hard and soft, heat and cold, motion and resistance, and of all these more and less either as to quantity or degree. Smelling furnishes me with odors, the palate with tastes, and hearing conveys sounds to the mind in all their variety of tone and composition. And as several of these are observed to accompany each other, they come to be marked by one name, and so to be reputed as one thing. Thus, for example, a certain color, taste, smell, figure, and consistence, having been observed to go together, are accounted one distinct thing, signified by the name "apple." Other collections of ideas constitute a stone, a tree, a book, and the like sensible things. . . .

2. But besides all that endless variety of ideas or objects of knowledge, there is likewise something which knows or perceives them, and exercises divers operations, as willing, imagining, remembering, about them. This perceiving, active being is what I call mind, spirit, soul, or myself. By which words I do not denote any one of my ideas, but a thing entirely distinct from them wherein they exist, or, which is the same thing, whereby they are perceived; for the existence of an idea consists in being perceived.

3. That neither our thoughts, nor passions, nor ideas formed by the imagination, exist without the mind, is what everybody will allow. And it seems no less evident that the various sensations or ideas imprinted on the sense, however

blended or combined together (that is, whatever objects they compose), cannot exist otherwise than in a mind perceiving them. . . .

4. It is indeed an opinion strangely prevailing amongst men, that houses, mountains, rivers, and in a word all sensible objects, have an existence, natural or real, distinct from their being perceived by the understanding. But with how great an assurance and acquiescence soever this principle may be entertained in the world, yet whoever shall find in his heart to call it in question may, if I mistake not, perceive it to in-

volve a manifest contradiction. For what are the forementioned objects but the things we perceive by sense? and what do we perceive besides our own ideas or sensations? and is it not plainly repugnant that any one of these, or any combination of them, should exist unperceived?

5. Light and colors, heat and cold, extension and figures—in a word the things we see and feel—what are they but so many sensations, notions, ideas, or impressions on the sense? And is it possible to separate, even in thought, any of these from perception?

Next, Berkeley sets forth and rejects the Lockian view that our ideas represent to us or copy or resemble the qualities of objects. The main thrust of Berkeley's argument is that whatever considerations suggest that the *secondary qualities* exist only in the mind apply equally to the so-called *primary qualities;* further, secondary and primary qualities are inseparably united and thus both exist only in the mind. In plain English, whatever makes you think that the leathery smell of a basketball is "subjective" or exists "only in the mind" will equally well serve to show that the size and shape of the ball also are subjective and exist only in the mind.

Note especially paragraphs 11, 12, and 14 in Selection 4.6 because they contain one of Berkeley's main arguments for his contention that the qualities you experience when you experience a sensible object are ideas and exist in the mind. The argument is based on the fact that *all* the qualities you perceive—not just the so-called secondary qualities, such as tastes, odors, colors, etc.—are relative to the observer. For instance, the cookie may normally taste sweet to you, but if you have a fever, it may taste sour. This "relativity" of the cookie's taste shows that the cookie's sweetness is in you, does it not? From one angle the *shape* you perceive when you look at a cookie will be round, from another it will be elliptical; and as you move away from it, the *size* you perceive will grow smaller. Indeed, *all* the qualities you perceive are relative to you. Because the cookie cannot itself be both sweet and sour, round and elliptical, large and small, etc., all the qualities you perceive, and not just the so-called secondary qualities, must be ideas in your mind rather than the qualities of something outside your mind.

Simplified to its basics, this line of reasoning involves just two steps. First, the "relative to the observer" argument shows that size, shape, color, and all qualities, just like sweetness, exist only in the mind. Second, sensible objects are nothing more than their various qualities. Conclusion: sensible objects exist only in the mind.

Of course, our inclination is to distinguish the perceived size and shape of a cookie from an unperceived size and shape "that are the cookie's *true* size and shape." But Berkeley argued that size and shape (and the other qualities) are *per-*

ceived qualities. Talking about an unperceived size or shape is nonsense. It's like talking about unfelt pain. And thus sensible objects, because they are nothing more than their qualities, are themselves only ideas and exist only in the mind.

But, you may still insist (in frustration?), surely there really is matter "out there"! *Surely* there are material bodies that have their own size, shape, texture, and the like! Well, Berkeley has already responded to this line of thought: it is contradictory to suppose that size, shape, texture, and so on could exist in unthinking stuff because size, shape, texture, and so on are ideas, and it is contradictory to suppose that ideas could exist in unthinking stuff. If, therefore, the concept of matter is the concept of unthinking stuff that nevertheless can have size, shape, texture, and so on, then the concept of matter is contradictory. Case closed.

SELECTION 4.6

Treatise Concerning the Principles of Human Knowledge (2)

From George Berkeley

8. But, say you, though the ideas themselves do not exist without the mind, yet there may be things like them, whereof they are copies or resemblances, which things exist without the mind in an unthinking substance. I answer, an idea can be like nothing but an idea; a color or figure can be like nothing but another color or figure. . . . Again, I ask whether those supposed originals or external things, of which our ideas are the pictures or representations, be themselves perceivable or no? If they are, then they are ideas and we have gained our point; but if you say they are not, I appeal to anyone whether it be sense to assert a color is like something which is invisible; hard or soft, like something which is intangible; and so of the rest.

9. Some there are who make a distinction betwixt primary and secondary qualities. By the former they mean extension, figure, motion, rest, solidity or impenetrability, and number; by the latter they denote all other sensible qualities, as colors, sounds, tastes, and so forth. The ideas we have of these they acknowledge not to be the resemblances of anything existing without the mind, or unperceived, but they will have our ideas of the primary qualities to be patterns or images of things which exist without the mind, in an unthinking substance which they call matter. By matter, therefore, we are to understand an inert, senseless substance, in which extension, figure, and motion do actually subsist. But it is evident from what we have already shown, that extension, figure, and motion are only ideas existing in the mind, and that an idea can be like nothing but another idea, and that consequently neither they nor their archetypes can exist in an unperceiving substance. Hence, it is plain that the very notion of what is called matter, or corporeal substance, involves a contradiction in it.

10. They who assert that figure, motion, and the rest of the primary or original qualities do exist without the mind in unthinking substances, do at the same time acknowledge that color, sounds, heat, cold, and such-like secondary qualities, do not; which they tell us are sensations existing in the mind alone . . . Now, if it be certain that those original qualities are inseparably united with the other sensible qualities, and not, even in thought, capable of being abstracted from them, it plainly follows that they exist only in the mind. But I desire anyone to

mind classifies + orders external things
compares, qualifies, quantifies

reflect and try whether he can, by any abstraction of thought, conceive the extension and motion of a body without all other sensible qualities. For my own part, I see evidently that it is not in my power to frame an idea of a body extended and moving, but I must withal give it some color or other sensible quality which is acknowledged to exist only in the mind. In short, extension, figure, and motion, abstracted from all other qualities, are inconceivable. Where therefore the other sensible qualities are, there must these be also, to wit, in the mind and nowhere else.

11. Again, great and small, swift and slow, are allowed to exist nowhere without the mind, being entirely relative, and changing as the frame or position of the organs of sense varies. The extension therefore which exists without the mind is neither great nor small, the motion neither swift nor slow, that is, they are nothing at all. . . .

12. That number is entirely the creature of the mind, even though the other qualities be allowed to exist without, will be evident to whoever considers that the same thing bears a different denomination of number as the mind views it with different respects. Thus, the same extension is one, or three, or thirty-six, according as the mind considers it with reference to a yard, a foot, or an inch. Number is so visibly relative, and dependent on men's understanding, that it is strange to think how anyone should give it can absolute existence without the mind. . . .

14. It is said that heat and cold are affections only of the mind, and not at all patterns of real beings, existing in the corporeal substances which excite them, for that the same body which appears cold to one hand seems warm to another. Now, why may we not as well argue that figure and extension are not patterns or resemblances of qualities existing in matter, because to the same eye at different stations, or eyes of a different texture at the same station, they appear various, and cannot therefore be the images of anything settled and determinate without the mind? Again, it is proved that sweetness is not really in the sapid thing, because the thing remaining unaltered the sweetness is changed into bitter, as in case of a fever or otherwise vitiated palate. Is it not as reasonable to say that motion is not without the mind, since if the succession of ideas in the mind become swifter, the motion, it is acknowledged, shall appear slower without any alteration in any external object?

15. In short, let anyone consider those arguments which are thought manifestly to prove that colors and tastes exist only in the mind, and he shall find they may with equal force be brought to prove the same thing of extension, figure, and motion. . . . the arguments foregoing plainly show it to be impossible that any color or extension at all, or other sensible quality whatsoever, should exist in an unthinking subject without the mind, or in truth, that there should be any such thing as an outward object.

And now, in the final selection, Berkeley considers whether the existence of things outside the mind can be proved through reason. He thinks not. He then concludes by saying that he is willing to rest the whole question of whether things exist outside the mind on the results of one very simple test. We invite you to take Berkeley's test. If you can even *conceive* of a sensible thing existing outside the mind, Berkeley says, he will give up his argument.

SELECTION 4.7

Treatise Concerning the Principles of Human Knowledge (3)

From George Berkeley

18. But though it were possible that solid, figured, movable substances may exist without the mind, corresponding to the ideas we have of bodies, yet how is it possible for us to know this? Either we must know it by sense or by reason. As for our senses, by them we have the knowledge only of our sensations, ideas, or those things that are immediately perceived by sense, call them what you will; but they do not inform us that things exist without the mind. . . . It remains therefore that if we have any knowledge at all of external things, it must be by reason, inferring their existence from what is immediately perceived by sense. But what reason can induce us to believe the existence of bodies without the mind, from what we perceive. . . . it is granted on all hands (and what happens in dreams, frenzies, and the like, puts it beyond dispute) that it is possible we might be affected with all the ideas we have now, though there were no bodies existing without, resembling them. Hence, it is evident the supposition of external bodies is not necessary for the producing of our ideas; since it is granted that they are produced sometimes, and might possibly be produced always in the same order we see them in at present, without their concurrence. . . .

20. In short, if there were external bodies, it is impossible we should ever come to know it; and if there were not, we might have the very same reasons to think there were that we have now. Suppose (what no one can deny possible) an intelligence without the help of external bodies, to be affected with the same train of sensations or ideas that you are, imprinted in the same order and with like vividness in his mind. I ask whether that intelligence hath not all the reason to believe the existence of corporeal substances, represented by his ideas, and exciting them in his mind, that you can possibly have for believing the same thing?

22. I am content to put the whole upon this issue: if you can but conceive it possible for one extended movable substance, or, in general, for any one idea, or anything like an idea, to exist otherwise than in a mind perceiving it, I shall readily give up the cause. . . .

23. But, say you, surely there is nothing easier than for me to imagine trees, for instance, in a park, or books existing in a closet, and nobody by to perceive them. I answer, you may so, there is no difficulty in it; but what is all this, I beseech you, more than framing in your mind certain ideas which you call books and trees, and the same time omitting to frame the idea of anyone that may perceive them? But do not you yourself perceive or think of them all the while? . . . When we do our utmost to conceive the existence of external bodies, we are all the while only contemplating our own ideas.

Material Things As Clusters of Ideas

So Berkeley's view is that sensible things, such as tables, chairs, trees, books, frogs, and the like, are not material things that exist outside the mind. Instead, according to Berkeley, so-called material things are in fact groups of ideas and, as such, are

Berkeley's Proofs of God

Berkeley's position is that sensible things cannot exist independent of perception—to be is to be perceived (**esse est percipi**). What, then, happens to this book and desk when everyone leaves the room? What happens to the forest when all the people go away? What, in short, according to Berkeley, happens to sensible things when no one perceives them?

Berkeley's answer is that the perceiving mind of God makes possible the continued existence of sensible things when neither you nor we nor any other people are perceiving them. Because sensible things do not depend on the perception of humans and exist independently of them, Berkeley wrote, "there must be some other mind wherein they exist." This other mind, according to Berkeley, is God.

That sensible things continue to exist when we don't perceive them is thus, for Berkeley, a short and simple proof of God's existence. It is also, perhaps, a proof you have not heard before.

Another, similar proof, in Berkeley's view, can be derived from the fact that we do not ourselves cause our ideas of tables and chairs and mountains and other sensible things. "There is therefore," he reasoned, "some other will or spirit that produces them"—God.

Berkeley was not unaware that his theory that what we call material things are ideas both in God's mind and in our own raises peculiar questions about the relationship between our ideas and minds and the ideas and mind of God. For example, if a mountain is an idea in God's mind and we perceive the mountain, does that mean we perceive or have God's ideas?

perceived directly and exist only within the mind. Because they are ideas, we can no more doubt their existence than we can doubt our own aches and pains (which too, indeed, are ideas).

Berkeley's idealism does not mean, however, that the physical world is a mere dream or that it is imaginary or intangible or ephemeral. Dr. Samuel Johnson believed that he had refuted Berkeley by kicking a stone, evidently thinking that the solidity of the stone was solid disproof of Berkeley. In fact, Johnson succeeded only in hurting his foot and demonstrating that he did not understand Berkeley. A stone is just as hard an object in Berkeley's philosophy as it is to common sense, for the fact that a stone exists only in the mind does not make its hardness disappear.

As for the stones found in dreams, Berkeley distinguished unreal dream stones from real stones just the way you and we do. Stones found in dreams behave in an irregular and chaotic manner—they can float around or change into birds or whatever—compared with those found in waking life. And Berkeley distinguished stones that we conjure up in our imagination from real stones by their lack of vividness and also by the fact that they, unlike real stones, can be brought into existence by an act of our will.

With Berkeley, Hobbes, Descartes, and Spinoza, the four basic metaphysical positions of modern philosophy were set out: either reality is entirely physical (Hobbes) or it is entirely nonphysical or "mental" (Berkeley) or it is an even split (Descartes) or "matter" and "mind" are just alternative ways of looking at one and the same stuff (Spinoza). Take your choice.

Berkeley's Argument Analyzed

Berkeley obviously did not just assert dogmatically, without reason, that sensible things are in fact groups of ideas. He had *arguments* for his view, as set forth in the selections. His main arguments may be analytically summarized as follows:

1. What we experience are sensations or ideas.

2. Among the things we experience are size and shape.

3. Therefore, size and shape are sensations or ideas.

4. Hence it is self-contradictory to say that objects do not have sensations or ideas but do have size and shape. [For size and shape are sensations or ideas.]

5. Hence objects, conceived of as things that don't have sensations or ideas but do have size and shape, cannot exist.

6. Thus, because objects, conceived in this way, cannot exist, they must just *be* clusters of ideas or sensations. To be, Berkeley wrote, is to be perceived: *esse est percipi.*

In this argument, (6) follows from (5), and (5) follows from (4), which follows from (3), which follows from (2) and (1). Because (2) seems indisputable, the entire argument rests on (1).

Can (1) be challenged? Well, try to do so. You might contend (a) that we never experience sensations or ideas. (But is this silly?) Or you might contend (b) that some of the items we experience are sensations or ideas but that others are not. (But then how would we distinguish one from the other?) Or finally, you might contend (c) that although the only things we experience are sensations or ideas, at least some of these *warrant the inference* that external bodies exist. Option (c), of course, is John Locke's representative realism, which leaves it entirely mysterious how our sensations do warrant such an inference, if, according to (c), we experience only sensations, never objects.

If you are not wholly satisfied with any of the options (a), (b), or (c), *or* with Berkeley's argument, you have company, including the next great philosopher after Berkeley, David Hume.

Checklist

To help you review, here is a checklist of the key philosophers and concepts of this chapter. The brief descriptive sentences summarize leading ideas. Keep in mind that some of these summary statements represent terrific oversimplifications of complex positions.

Philosophers

- **René Descartes** "Father" of modern philosophy. Continental rationalist. Dualist; said there are two separate and distinct substances: material substance and mind.

- **Anne Conway** Argued against parts of the philosophies of Descartes, Hobbes, and Spinoza. An essentialist who argued that everything other than God has both physical and mental essences; God is totally mental. A big influence on Leibniz's monadology.

88
- **Thomas Hobbes** The first great modern materialist: held that all that exists is bodies in motion.
- **Benedictus de Spinoza** Neutralist. Continental rationalist. Maintained that thought and extension are attributes of a single substance.
- **Gottfried Wilhelm Leibniz** Continental rationalist. Held that the ultimate constituents of reality are monads, which are nonmaterial, indivisible units of force.
- **Emilie du Châtelet** Adapted Leibniz's metaphysical principles to Newtonian science.
- **John Locke** British empiricist. Held that we perceive objects indirectly by means of our perceptions of them, some of which he believed were accurate copies of the real properties of objects.
- **George Berkeley** British empiricist. Idealist. Denied the existence of material substance; held that sensible objects exist only in the mind.

Concepts

77 dualism   *common sense reality has dual nature physical sh. + minds*

78 materialism   *only the physical exists   Hobbes all that exists is bodies in motion p.88*

   idealism   *only things mental or spiritual exists*

   neutralism   *neither mental or physical or both   Conway, Spinoza*

81 dream conjecture   *Descartes*

   evil demon conjecture   *"*

   cogito, ergo sum   *I think ∴ I am   Descartes*

82 "clear and distinct" criterion   *Descartes*

84 extension as the essential attribute of material substance   *occupancy of space ie brains vs mind*

84 thought as the essential attribute of mind

85 problems of dualism   *mind - brain connection*

86 epistemological detour   *what can be known*

86 parallelism   *Descartes for coincidence movement*

   occasionalism   *God does it*

88 perception   *Hobbes reduces perception to matter in motion*

98 problems of materialism   *explaining away the mental + free will.*

99 Continental rationalists   *Descartes, Spinoza Leibniz.*

99 monad   *indivisible units of force, energy or activity*

99 principle of the identity of indiscernibles   *if same properties then identical*

99 principle of sufficient reason   *There is a sufficient reason why things are exactly as they are*

101 British empiricists   *Locke, Berkeley, Hume*

102 *tabula rasa*   *blank slate - mind at birth*

   Nihil in intellectu quod prius non fuerit in sensu
   nothing in mind that first not was in senses

102 representative realism *Perceive objects indirectly by means / ideas - dualism*

104 theory of innate ideas *truths part of originals disposition g the intellect*

106 primary vs. secondary qualities *dimensional vs sensory*

110 *esse est percipi* *to be is to be perceived.*

Questions for Discussion and Review

1. "Material things, including one's own body, are completely subject to physical laws." "The immaterial mind can move one's body." Are these two claims incompatible? Explain.

2. "Modern science undermines metaphysical dualism." Explain this remark.

3. What is parallelism?

4. Explain how all mental activity reduces to matter in motion, according to Hobbes.

5. "The things that really are in the world outside us are those motions by which these seemings [i.e., objects and their qualities] are caused." Explain and critically evaluate this assertion by Hobbes.

6. What is the relationship of the mind to the body, according to Spinoza?

7. Explain Anne Conway's concept of time and its relationship to her view of God and Creatures.

8. Explain Berkeley's reasons for saying that sensible objects exist only in the mind.

9. Are the qualities of sensible objects (e.g., size, color, taste) all equally "relative" to the observer?

10. Does Berkeley's philosophy make everything into a dream?

11. Why, if all our knowledge comes from experience, is it difficult to maintain that we have knowledge of external objects?

12. *Do* we have knowledge of external objects? Explain.

13. Define or explain dualism, materialism, idealism, and neutralism.

14. Explain and critically evaluate either Descartes's dream conjecture or his evil demon conjecture.

15. "Descartes assumed that there cannot be thinking without an 'I' that does the thinking. Since he wanted to question everything, he should have questioned this assumption." Should we agree with this remark?

16. Explain Berkeley's reasons for maintaining that it is a contradiction to hold that sensible objects exist outside the mind.

17. Is there really a difference between primary and secondary qualities?

18. "We can think. This proves we are not just mere matter." Does it?

19. Is your brain your mind? Explain.

20. Do you see any difficulties with supposing that a nonmaterial mind could make things happen in a brain?

21. Psychokinesis is the mental power by which psychics claim to make changes in the external physical world—to bend spoons, to cause balls to roll, and so on. Is there any difference between using your mind to bend a spoon and using your mind to bend your arm? Explain.

Suggested Further Readings

Margaret Atherton, *Women Philosophers of the Early Modern Period* (Indianapolis: Hackett, 1994). A nice little anthology of excerpts from Princess Elisabeth of Bohemia, Margaret Cavendish, Mary Astell, Damaris Cudworth Masham, Anne Conway, Catharine Trotter Cockburn, and Lady Mary Shepherd.

George Berkeley, *Principles of Human Knowledge/Three Dialogues,* Roger Woolhouse, ed. (New York: Penguin Books, 1988). These are Berkeley's main works. He is so much fun, once you get used to the initial strangeness of his position, that we think it would be a mistake to limit yourself to mere excerpts or "selections."

E. O. Burtt, *The English Philosophers from Bacon to Mill* (New York: Modern Library, 1939). A general book on modern philosophy.

Anne Conway, *The Principles of the Most Ancient and Modern Philosophy* (Cambridge: Cambridge University Press, 1996). At last, an affordable paperback edition of Conway.

John Cottingham, ed., *The Cambridge Companion to Descartes* (New York: Cambridge University Press, 1992). Recent essays on Descartes. Includes a bibliography.

René Descartes, *Philosophical Works,* in two volumes, E. S. Haldane and G. R. T. Ross, trans. (Cambridge: The University Press, 1968). This is what you need to read Descartes.

C. J. Ducasse, *A Critical Examination of the Belief in Life After Death* (Springfield, Ill.: Charles C. Thomas, 1974). The first part of the book contains an excellent elementary discussion of the various theories of mind.

Errol E. Harris, *Spinoza's Philosophy: An Outline* (Atlantic Highlands, N.J.: Humanities Press, 1992). The title says it all.

Nicholas Jolley, ed., *The Cambridge Companion to Leibniz* (New York: Cambridge University Press, 1995). A recent collection of essays on all aspects of Leibniz's philosophy.

S. Lamprecht, ed., *Locke Selections* (New York: Scribners, 1928). If you want to read about Locke's theory of knowledge in more detail, you must turn to his *An Essay Concerning Human Understanding,* in two volumes, A. C. Fraser, ed. (New York: Dover, 1959). This (the Fraser edition) is a heavily annotated work.

Benson Mates, *The Philosophy of Leibniz* (New York: Oxford University Press, 1986). An excellent exposition of the metaphysics of Leibniz.

G. H. R. Parkinson, ed., *Routledge History of Philosophy,* vol. 4, *The Renaissance and Seventeenth Century Rationalism* (London: Routledge, 1994). A collection of fairly readable essays.

Stephen Priest, *The British Empiricists* (London: Penguin Books, 1990). A useful introduction to the British empiricist tradition extending from Hobbes through to Russell and Ayer.

Roger Scruton, *A Short History of Modern Philosophy* (London: Routledge, 1984). From Descartes to Wittgenstein.

J. O. Urmson and A. J. Ayer, *The British Empiricists* (New York: Oxford University Press, 1992). A set of introductory readings on the lives and thoughts of Locke, Berkeley, and Hume.

Mary Ellen Waithe, ed. *A History of Women Philosophers,* vol. 3, *Modern Women Philosophers: 1600–1900* (Dordrecht: Kluwer Academic Press, 1991). Chapters about thirty-one women philosophers of the period.

J. Wild, ed., *Spinoza Selections* (New York: Scribners, 1930). This volume contains enough original material for the introductory student.

F. J. E. Woodbridge, ed., *Hobbes Selections* (New York: Scribners, 1930). Here, too, we think that the selected original material will be sufficient for the introductory student.

5 The Eighteenth and Nineteenth Centuries

The mind has never anything present to it but . . . perceptions, and cannot possibly reach any experience of their connection with [external] objects.

—David Hume

Though all our knowledge begins with experience, it does not follow that it all arises out of experience.

—Immanuel Kant

After Berkeley, the two most important philosophers of the eighteenth century were **David Hume** (1711–1776) and **Immanuel Kant** (1724–1804). Hume and Kant were both very dubious about allowing even the possibility of metaphysical knowledge. Hume, on the one hand, believed that all our knowledge is limited to what we experience, namely, sensory impressions. (Although he wasn't willing to go with Berkeley and say that sensible objects are just clusters of sensory impressions.)

Kant, on the other hand, was slightly more generous about what we can know. We do have knowledge of objects that exist outside the mind, Kant said, but our knowledge is of these objects only *insofar* as they are *experienceable*. About external objects *as they are in themselves* we can have no knowledge, he said.

To be more specific, according to Kant, human reason can discover categories and principles that apply *absolutely and without exception* to experienceable objects. These categories and principles apply absolutely and without exception to experienceable objects because, according to Kant, the mind arranges or orders raw sensation in accordance with them. It is only by being so arranged, he said, that *raw sensation* can qualify as *experience*. If the data of raw sensation were not so organized, they would be mere stimulation and not experience.

In short, according to Kant, the mind *imposes* a certain form and order on experienceable objects. For example, the mind imposes spatiotemporal relationships on the things we experience. But it is beyond our capacities, he said, to know anything about **things-in-themselves,** things as they are apart from and independent of experience. Further, whenever we attempt to apply the concepts that pertain to experienceable objects to things-in-themselves, paradoxes and errors result.

Let's back up and look at each of these two thinkers, Hume and Kant, more closely.

Empiricist
modified Skeptic   **David Hume**

Hume's epistemology, like Berkeley's, is a development of the empiricist thesis that all our ideas come from experience—that is, from sensation or inner feelings. In some passages Hume displays total skepticism, but mostly he appears as a modified skeptic who focuses his attention on certain narrower issues, including, most importantly, the knowledge and nature of the self, causality, induction, God, and the external world. And these issues have tended to dominate epistemological inquiry since Hume's time.

Much of Hume's epistemology rests on four assumptions. To get full value from your reading, you should consider whether you accept them.

1. Thought, knowledge, belief, conception, and judgment each consist in having ideas.

2. All ideas are derived from, and are copies of, *impressions* of sense or inner feelings. (Hume's impressions are what we would call *perceptions*.)

3. Every claim that something exists is a factual claim. (That is, when you claim that something exists, you are expressing what you think is a fact.)

4. Factual claims can be established only by observation or by causal inference from what is observed. (For example, you can tell if an engine is knocking just by listening to it, but to know that it has worn bearings, you have to make an inference as to the cause of the knocking.)

Now, let's consider what these innocent little assumptions entail.

This excludes prayer, revelation, and accumulated evidence in prophesy, internal harmony of script

The Quarter Experiment

Let's begin with (3) and (4). First, go find a quarter and put it in front of you next to this book. You would claim that the quarter exists, correct? This claim, according to principle (4), can be established—that is, proved or justified—only by observation or by inference from what you observe, right?

But what is it you observe? The quarter? Well, no, as a matter of fact that doesn't seem quite right. Look at what you call the quarter. Leave it on your desk, and get up and move around the room a bit, looking at the quarter all the while. Now, then: what you *observe*, as you move about, is a silverish expanse that constantly changes its size and shape as you move. Right now, for example, what you

Scot

PROFILE / David Hume (1711–1776)

David Hume died from cancer at the age of sixty-five. In the face of his own annihilation, he retained his composure and cheerfulness, having achieved the goal of the ancient skeptics, *ataraxia* (unperturbedness). It may be questioned, though, whether his calm good nature resulted from his skepticism, for apparently he exhibited this trait of personality throughout his life.

Born in Edinburgh of a "good family," as he said in his autobiography, Hume was encouraged to study law, but "found insurmountable aversion to everything but the pursuits of philosophy and general learning." Before he was thirty, he published *A Treatise of Human Nature,* one of the most important philosophical works ever written. Yet at the time Hume's *Treatise* "fell dead-born from the press," as he put it, "without reaching such distinction as even to excite a murmur among the zealots." Convinced that the failure of the work was due more to form than content, he recast parts of it anew in *An Enquiry Concerning Human Understanding* and *An Enquiry Concerning the Principles of Morals.* The latter work, in Hume's opinion, was incomparably his best. Hume's last philosophical work, *Dialogues Concerning Natural Religion,* was published posthumously in 1779.

There are differences between Hume's *Treatise* and the *Enquiry,* his two works in epistemology, and philosophers disagree about the merits of each. In any case, during his lifetime Hume's reputation was primarily as a historian rather than as a philosopher. Nevertheless, his impact on subsequent philosophy, especially in Great Britain and other English-speaking countries, and on Kant, was significant.

In the passage that follows, Hume's friend Adam Smith quotes a letter from Hume's physician at the time of Hume's death and then adds a few thoughts of his own.

Dear Sir,
Yesterday, about four o'clock, afternoon, Mr. Hume expired. The near approach of his death became evident in the night between Thursday

observe is probably elliptical in shape. But a *quarter* is not the sort of thing that constantly changes its size and shape, and a quarter is never elliptical (unless someone did something illegal to it). *So what you observe changes its size and shape, but the quarter does not change its size and shape. It follows that what you observe is not the quarter.*

Here you might object. "What I'm seeing is a silver expanse from various distances and angles," you might say.

But in fact, if you consider carefully what you are observing, it is a silverish expanse that changes its size and shape. You do not see a silverish expanse that remains unchanged. What you see does change. Thus, it still follows, because the quarter does not change, that what you see is not the quarter.

and Friday, when his disease became excessive, and soon weakened him so much, that he could no longer rise out of his bed. He continued to the last perfectly sensible, and free from much pain or feelings of distress. He never dropped the smallest expression of impatience; but when he had occasion to speak to the people about him, always did it with affection and tenderness.... When he became very weak, it cost him an effort to speak; and he died in such a happy composure of mind, that nothing could exceed it.

Thus died our most excellent and never to be forgotten friend; concerning whose philosophical opinions men will, no doubt, judge variously ... but concerning whose character and conduct there can scarce be a difference of opinion. His temper, indeed, seemed to be more happily balanced, if I may

be allowed such an expression, than that perhaps of any other man I have ever known. Even in the lowest state of his fortune, his great and necessary frugality never hindered him from exercising, upon proper occasions, acts both of charity and generosity. It was a frugality bounded not upon avarice, but upon the love of independency. The extreme gentleness of his nature never weakened either the firmness of his mind or the steadiness of his resolutions. His constant pleasantry was the genuine effusion of good nature and good humor, tempered with delicacy and modesty, and without even the slightest tincture of malignity, so frequently the disagreeable source of what is called wit in other men. It never was the meaning of his raillery to mortify; and therefore, far from offending, it seldom failed to please and delight, even

those who were frequently the objects of it; there was not perhaps any one of all his great and amiable qualities which contributed more to endear his conversation. And that gayety of temper, so agreeable in society, but which is so often accompanied with frivolous and superficial qualities, was in him certainly attended with the most severe application, the most extensive learning, the greatest depth of thought, and a capacity in every respect the most comprehensive. Upon the whole, I have always considered him, both in his lifetime and since his death, as approaching as nearly to the ideal of a perfectly wise and virtuous man as perhaps the nature of human frailty will permit.

I ever am, dear sir,

Most affectionately yours,
Adam Smith

What is it, then, that you observe? According to Hume, it is your *sense impressions* of the quarter. Thus, if your belief that the quarter exists is to be justified, that belief must be a causal inference from what you observe—that is, from your impressions—to something that is distinct from your impressions and causes them, namely, the quarter. But there is a major problem here: you never experience or are in any way in contact with anything that *is* distinct from your impressions. Thus you never observe a connection between your perceptions and *the quarter!* So how could you possibly establish that the quarter *causes* your impressions? And if you cannot establish that, then, according to Hume, you cannot regard your belief in the existence of the quarter as justified.

objection: memory — previous experience fills in the gaps

A Lot of Destruction

Hume noted that Berkeley's reasons for denying the existence of material substance "admit of no answer, and produce no conviction." The same has in effect been said about much of Hume's own philosophy. The wit Sydney Smith once remarked, "Bishop Berkeley destroyed the world in one volume octavo, and nothing remained after his time but mind—which experienced a similar fate from the hand of Mr. Hume in 1737; so that with all the tendency to destroy there remains nothing left for destruction."

Of course, the same considerations apply to a belief in the existence of any external object whatsoever. Here's Hume expressing these considerations in his own words:

SELECTION 5.1

A Treatise of Human Nature (1)   From David Hume

The only existences, of which we are certain, are perceptions . . . The only conclusion we can draw from the existence of one thing to that of another, is by means of the relation of cause and effect, which shews, that there is a connection betwixt them. . . . But as no things are ever present to the mind but perceptions; it follows that we may observe a conjunction or a relation of cause and effect between different perceptions, but can never observe it between perceptions and objects. 'Tis impossible, therefore, that from the existence of any of the qualities of the former, we can ever form any conclusion concerning the existence of the latter.

Now, go back to innocent assumptions (1) and (2), on page 117. Notice that it follows directly from these two assumptions that there is no knowledge, belief, conception, judgment, thought about, or even idea of external objects (things distinct from our sense impressions of them)! Here again Hume explains:

SELECTION 5.2

A Treatise of Human Nature (2)   From David Hume

Now, since nothing is ever present to the mind but perceptions, and since all ideas are derived from something antecedently present to the mind; it follows, that 'tis impossible for us so much as to conceive or form an idea of anything specifically different from ideas and impressions. Let us fix our attention out of ourselves as much as possible: Let us chase our imagination to the heavens, or to the utmost limits of the universe; we never really advance a step beyond ourselves, nor can conceive any kind of existence, but those perceptions, which have appeared in that narrow compass.

except Bible and Revelation

Hume on the Self

According to Hume, similar careful scrutiny of the notion of the self or mind, supposedly an unchanging nonmaterial substance within us, discloses that we have no knowledge of such a thing. Indeed, we do not really have even an *idea* of the mind, if the mind is defined as an unchanging nonmaterial substance within, Hume holds. For again, our ideas cannot go beyond our sense impressions, and we have no impressions of the mind, except perhaps as a bundle of impressions: *Berkeley*

SELECTION 5.3

A Treatise of Human Nature (3)   **From David Hume**

There are some philosophers, who imagine we are every moment intimately conscious of what we call our Self [or mind]; that we feel its existence and its continuance in existence; and are certain, beyond the evidence of a demonstration, both of its perfect identity and simplicity.... Unluckily all these positive assertions are contrary to that very experience, which is pleaded for them, nor have we any idea of *self*, after the manner it is here explained. For from what impression could this idea be derived? ... It must be some one impression, that gives rise to every real idea. But self or person is not any one impression, but that to which our several impressions and ideas are supposed to have a reference. If any impression gives rise to the idea of self, that impression must continue invariably the same, through the whole course of our lives;

since self is supposed to exist after that manner. But there is no impression constant and invariable.... There is no such idea....

For my part, when I enter most intimately into what I call *myself,* I always stumble on some particular perception or other, of heat or cold, light or shade, love or hatred, pain or pleasure. I never can catch *myself* at any time without a perception, and never can observe any thing but the perception.... The mind is a kind of theatre, where several perceptions successively make their appearance; pass, re-pass, glide away, and mingle in an infinite variety of postures and situations. There is properly no *simplicity* in it at one time, nor *identity* in different.... The comparison of the theatre must not mislead us. They are the successive perceptions only, that constitute the mind.

Hume on Cause and Effect

Because any inference from the existence of one thing to that of another is founded, according to Hume, on the relation of cause and effect, Hume analyzed that relation carefully and discovered that experience reveals no necessary connection between a cause and an effect.

At first, this thesis—that we experience no necessary connection between a cause and its effect—seems straightforwardly false. The car going by *makes* the noise you hear, not so? The impact of the golf club *drives* the ball down the fairway. Disconnecting a spark plug *forces* the engine to idle roughly. The cue ball *moves* the eight ball when it hits it. What could be plainer than that in each case the cause *necessitates* the effect?

Yet by paying careful attention to what he actually experienced in an instance of so-called causation, Hume discovered that he did not experience the cause actually producing the effect. His experience of supposed causation, he discovered, consisted at best in awareness of the nearness in space and successiveness in time of the cause and effect along with recollection of a *constant conjunction* of similar things in past experience. You don't really *see* the cue ball *moving* the eight ball; what you see is just a sequence of events: first, you see the cue ball in motion, then you see it hit the eight ball, and then you see the eight ball in motion. And though you recollect that there is a constant conjunction between a cue ball's hitting another ball and the other ball's starting to move, you do not experience any *necessity* in the other ball's moving. Therefore, Hume wrote, "necessity is something in the mind, not in the objects."

In short, Hume observed that "there is nothing in any object, considered in itself, which can afford us a reason for drawing a conclusion beyond it." "The effect," he wrote, "is totally different from the cause, and consequently can never be discovered in it."

SELECTION 5.4

A Treatise of Human Nature (4)   From David Hume

When I see, for instance a Billiard-ball moving in a straight line towards another; even suppose motion in the second ball should by accident be suggested to me, as the result of their contact or impulse; may I not conceive, that a hundred different events might as well follow from that cause? May not both these balls remain at absolute rest? May not the first ball return in a straight line, or leap off from the second in any line or direction? All these suppositions are consistent and conceivable. Why then should we give preference to one, which is no more consistent or conceivable than the rest? All our reasonings a priori will never be able to show us any foundation for this preference.

Do we see the pin *making* the balloon pop? Hume maintained that all he saw was just (1) the pin coming into spatial contact with the balloon, followed by (2) the balloon popping. He did not see the pin making the balloon pop.

Further, according to Hume, even after we observe a frequent and constant conjunction between a cause and its effect, there is no rational justification for supposing that that conjunction will repeat itself in the future.

Here's an example. You have experienced a constant conjunction between flame and heat. Are you not then rationally justified in supposing that future experience will show a similar conjunction between flame and heat? Can you seriously doubt that this supposition is rationally justified?

Well, Hume's answer is that it is *not* rationally justified. If you say that the next flame you encounter will be accompanied by heat, it is because you suppose that *the future will resemble the past*. Indeed, all reasoning based on present and past experience rests on the supposition that the future will be like the past. But that means, Hume saw in a flash of brilliant insight, that the supposition itself cannot be proved by an appeal to experience. To attempt to prove the supposition by appealing to experience, he observed, "must evidently be going in a circle."

It is hard to exaggerate the significance of this finding, as a moment's thought will show. The fact that all inference from past and present experience rests on an apparently unprovable assumption (that the future will resemble the past) leads to skeptical conclusions even more sweeping than Hume for the most part was willing to countenance. It means, for instance, that much of what we think we know we do not really know. Will food and water nourish you the next time you eat and drink? Will our names be the same this evening as they are now? Will the words in the beginning of this sentence have changed meaning by the time you get to the end of the sentence? Evidently the answers to these questions, while seemingly obvious, *are mere assumptions that we cannot really know.*

Hume As a Total Skeptic

When Hume said that he was ready to reject all belief and reasoning and could look on no opinion even as more probable or likely than another, he was expressing the views of a total skeptic. You should be aware, though, that a true skeptic, Hume said, "will be diffident in his philosophical doubts, as well as of his philosophical conviction." In other words, a true (total) skeptic will doubt his doubts, too.

Perhaps you can now understand why, in the conclusion to Book I of *A Treatise of Human Nature*, Hume reflects that what he has written shows that

> the understanding, when it acts alone, and according to its most general principles, entirely subverts itself, and leaves not the lowest degree of evidence in any proposition, either in philosophy or common life.

Thus, Hume says, he is "ready to reject all belief and reasoning, and can look upon no opinion even as more probable or likely than another." This skepticism is not modified: it is uncompromisingly total.

Now that you have looked at the philosophy of David Hume, you will perhaps see why we have given this book the title it has. If Hume's ideas are correct, then must we not in the end despair as Cratylus did and watch the world from a distance, merely wiggling our fingers?

Immanuel Kant   – Certain Knowledge

It is time now to turn to **Immanuel Kant** (1724–1804). Most scholars regard Kant as one of the most brilliant intellects of all time. Unfortunately, they also consider him one of the most difficult of all philosophers to read. Difficult or not, Kant provided a significant and ingenious response to Hume's skepticism.

In a sentence, Kant believed that certain knowledge does indeed exist and set about to show how this could be possible, given Hume's various arguments that pointed in the opposite direction.

The Ordering Principles of the Mind

Kant agreed with Hume that all knowledge *begins* with experience. But it does not follow, Kant maintained, that knowledge must therefore *arise from* experience. Experience is the occasion for the awakening of the knowing mind, Kant said; but the mind, thus awakened, is not limited in its knowledge to what it has found in experience.

PROFILE / Immanuel Kant (1724–1804)

Kant was one of the first modern philosophers to earn his living as a professor of philosophy. Though he hardly ever left Königsberg, his birthplace, his ideas traveled far, and he is considered by many as the greatest philosopher, ever.

Kant's first works were in natural science and secured for him a substantial reputation before his appointment as professor of logic and metaphysics at Königsberg in 1770. After his appointment, he wrote nothing for ten years as he contemplated the issues that eventually appeared in his most important work, the *Critique of Pure Reason* (1781, 2nd ed. 1787). The actual writing of the book took "four or five months," he said, and was done "with the utmost attention to the contents, but with less concern for the presentation or for making things easy for the reader." Readers universally understand what he meant.

The reaction to the work was primarily one of confusion, and this led Kant to publish a shorter, more accessible version of his major work, entitled *Prolegomena to Any Future Metaphysics* (1783). This is an excellent book with which to begin the study of Kant's epistemology and metaphysics. To fix dates a bit, Kant's *Prolegomena* came out in the same year the American War of Independence ended and, incidentally, the first successful hot-air balloon flight was made.

Two years after publication of the *Prolegomena*, Kant's first major treatise on ethics, the *Foundations for the Metaphysics of Morals*, appeared. A comparatively brief work, it is nevertheless one of the most important books ever written on ethics.

Kant's second and third critiques, the *Critique of Practical Reason* (1788) and *Critique of Judgment* (1790), were concerned with morality and aesthetics, respectively. In addition to the three *Critiques*, the *Prolegomena*, and the *Foundations*, Kant wrote many other lesser works.

In his last years he suffered the indignity of hearing younger German philosophers say that he had not really understood what he had written, an unusually stupid idea that history has long since laid to rest.

Why is the mind not limited to what it has found in experience, according to Kant? Because the constituents of experience must themselves always be ordered and organized in certain ways even to *count* as experience. And it is possible to have knowledge of these underlying principles by means of which the constituents of experience are ordered and organized. Because this knowledge is of the universally applicable preconditions of experience, it is absolutely certain, he held.

An example may help make these difficult thoughts clearer. Suppose we were to suggest to you that someday you might encounter a fire that was not hot or a plant that had no fragrance whatsoever. We imagine that you would discount the

The Copernican Revolution in Philosophy

Kant called his most fundamental epistemological insight the **Copernican revolution in philosophy.** Copernicus (1473–1543) was the modern European credited with the heliocentric theory of planetary motion, according to which the old assumption that the sun and planets circle the earth must be replaced with a new assumption that the earth and other planets circle the sun. Only the new assumption could account for the observed motions of the heavenly bodies, Copernicans maintained.

In a somewhat analogous manner, Kant said that the old assumption that our ideas, to be true, must conform to objects outside the mind must be replaced with a new assumption: that objects outside the mind must conform to that which the mind imposes on them in experiencing them. Only the new assumption could account for our knowledge of certain universally true principles, Kant maintained.

possibility entirely. Still, if we pressed you a bit, you should concede that, well, it's not absolutely *certain* that you would never come across a cool fire or a plant that had absolutely no fragrance, though you would probably regard it as *almost* certain. (Having difficulty imagining the possibility of a cool fire or plants that don't smell at all? Think, for instance, of some strange new synthetic substance burning, say, in alcohol. Or think of a plant developed by genetic engineers to subsist on traces of methane rather than on water and air. Would such a plant have odor? Who knows?)

But suppose we were to suggest to you that someday you might encounter a fire or a plant that was not in *space or time*. Now, this suggestion you would find just plain *absurd*. You would not—indeed you *could* not—take us seriously. Whereas you cannot be *absolutely* certain that sometime in your lifetime you won't encounter a cool fire or a plant that has absolutely no fragrance, you can be absolutely certain that you will *never ever* encounter a fire or plant that will not be in space and time.

Clearly, therefore, a fundamental difference exists between the spatiotemporal qualities of things, on the one hand, and qualities such as their warmth and fragrance, or their heaviness or color or texture, on the other. You know that each event you witness and each object you encounter *must* be experienced in space or in time (or both). But given Hume's principles, you could not absolutely know this, because (remember?) you cannot be certain that future experience will resemble past experience. So something must be wrong with Hume's principles.

Space and time are thus different from other qualities, and their universal applicability to experienced things can only be explained, according to Kant, on the supposition that they are necessary *preconditions* of experience. *To even qualify as experienced, a thing must be experienced as in space or time.*

Let's put it another way. Our certain knowledge that everything we encounter will be experienced in space or time cannot be *derived from* experience, for experience informs us only of the way things have been so far, and not of the way they *must* be. So our knowledge of space and time results from the fact that space and time are the *way* experienced items are experienced: they are the *form* under which experience takes shape. Sensation, we might say, provides the content of perception; space and time provide the form.

Perceptions Must Be Conceptualized and Unified

Now perceptions by themselves are "blind," according to Kant: they must be organized under concepts for genuine experience to occur. In other words, perception of unconceptualized entities is not experience—experience is perception of this *type* of thing—this *car,* this *person,* this *song,* this *piece of lead,* and so on.

To understand what Kant means, just think of an electric door or an auto-focus camera. They are able to process information that comes to them from the external world, but they do not really experience anything, for they do not *recognize* the information that comes to them. They "perceive" a person in front of them, but they do not *experience* a person, for they do not conceptualize what they perceive as a person or *as* anything else.

Further, Kant holds, perceptions, to qualify as experience, must be connected together or *unified* in one consciousness. But conceptualization and unification must conform to certain rules or principles of the understanding, just as perception must conform to spatiotemporal shaping. Thus, for instance, for experience to be possible, things must be apprehended not merely as in space or time but as conforming to cause-and-effect relationships as well; and change must be experienced as the change of a permanent substance whose quantity in nature remains constant.

Let's just take one example of such a principle of the understanding. Every change must have a cause, correct? Now, how can we be sure that *every* change must have a cause? One thing seems clear: if our knowledge of causation were derived solely from observation, then we couldn't be sure that *every* change must have a cause because we cannot be *certain* that future observations will be the same as past observations. So how can we be sure that every change must have a cause? We can have this certainty, Kant answers, because a necessary precondition of our even conceptualizing something as a *change* is that we conceptualize it as *caused.* So the principle that every change must have a cause, just like space and time, is interposed by the mind on the data of experience and thought.

Things in Themselves

In substance, then, this was Kant's response to the challenge put to epistemology by David Hume. Yes, knowledge begins with experience. But no, knowledge does not all arise from experience. Because there are certain underlying principles and categories in terms of which the raw data of sensation must be ordered if these data are even to count as *experience,* we have universally valid knowledge of experience-

except through revelation

Ding-an-sich

Kant drew a distinction between **phenomena,** things as they are as experienced, and **noumena,** things as they are apart from and independent of our experience of them, things as they are "in themselves." **Das Ding-an-sich** is German for "the thing as it is in itself."

Kant maintained that our minds process the raw data of sensation according to certain principles and categories (and philosophers should make it their business to understand and analyze these principles and categories, he thought). For example, according to Kant our minds process the data of sensation in such a way that we perceive a world of *objects* that are related to one another *spatiotemporally* and by *cause* and *effect.* But how the world is in itself—that is, independent of the principles and categories that our minds impose on it as we experience it—is something we cannot know. We cannot know anything about noumena, about *das Ding-an-sich.*

The Absolute Idealists (see text) had no truck with the notion that we can have no knowledge of "the thing in itself." What could there possibly be that the mind could not know as it really is, Hegel asked.

able objects. We thus have certain knowledge that experienceable objects are in space and time, stand in causal relationships with one another, and must otherwise conform to other rules of the understanding. They must so conform, to repeat, because if they did not, they could not qualify as experienced.

So Kant showed that there can be epistemology after Hume.

Now one very important final point must be mentioned about Kant's epistemology. According to Kant, we cannot say that things *as they are in themselves,* as they are independent of experience, must also conform to these principles and rules of the understanding. Concerning the experienceable object we can have certain knowledge, because an object, to be experienced, must conform to these rules and principles. But concerning the other world, the world of the thing-in-itself, *das Ding-an-sich* (as it is said in German), complete skepticism is unavoidable, for Kant. And when rules that apply to the experienced world are applied to a reality-beyond-experience, contradictions and mistakes are the result.

So, relative to the experienceable world, Kant was not a skeptic; but relative to things-in-themselves, he was.

In Selection 5.5 Kant asks, and then answers, the question, "What, then, is time?" *Intuition* is Kant's technical term for *awareness.* An intuition is an awareness. This selection is difficult.

SELECTION 5.5

*Critique of Pure Reason**

From Immanuel Kant

TRANSCENDENTAL AESTHETIC

Section II, Time

§ 4, METAPHYSICAL EXPOSITION OF THE CONCEPT OF TIME

1. Time is not an empirical concept that has been derived from any experience. For neither coexistence nor succession would ever come within our perception, if the representation of time were not presupposed as underlying them *a priori*. . . .

2. Time is a necessary representation that underlies all intuitions. We cannot, in respect of appearances in general, remove time itself, though we can quite well think time as void of appearances. Time is, therefore, given *a priori*. In it alone is actuality of appearances possible at all. Appearances may, one and all, vanish; but time (as the universal condition of their possibility) cannot itself be removed.

3. . . . Time has only one dimension; different times are not simultaneous but successive (just as different spaces are not successive but simultaneous). These principles cannot be derived from experience, for experience would give neither strict universality nor apodeictic certainty. We should only be able to say that common experience teaches us that it is so; not that it must be so. These principles are valid as rules under which alone experiences are possible; and they instruct us in regard to the experiences, not by means of them.

4. Time is not a discursive, or what is called a general concept, but a pure form of sensible intuition. Different times are but parts of one and the same time . . . Moreover, the proposition that different times cannot be simultaneous is not to be derived from a general concept. . . .

§ 6, CONCLUSIONS FROM THESE CONCEPTS

(a) Time is not something which exists of itself, or which inheres in things as an objective determination, and it does not, therefore, remain when abstraction is made of all subjective conditions of its intuition. Were it self-subsistent, it would be something which would be actual and yet not an actual object. Were it a determination or order inhering in things themselves, it could not precede the objects as their condition. . . .

(b) Time is nothing but the form of inner sense, that is, of the intuition of ourselves and of our inner state. It cannot be a determination of outer appearances; it has to do neither with shape nor position, but with the relation of representations in our inner state. . . .

(c) Time is the formal *a priori* condition of all appearances whatsoever. Space, as the pure form of all *outer* intuition, is so far limited; it serves as the *a priori* condition only of outer appearances. But since all representations, whether they have for their objects outer things or not, belong, in themselves, as determinations of the mind, to our inner state; and since this inner state stands under the formal condition of inner intuition, and so belongs to time, time is an *a priori* condition of all appearance whatsoever. It is the immediate condition of inner appearances (of our souls), and thereby the mediate condition of outer appearances. Just as I can say *a priori* that all outer appearances are in space, and are determined *a priori* in conformity with the relations of space, I can also say, from the principle of inner sense, that all appearances whatsoever,

---

*Kant's footnotes omitted.

that is, all objects of the senses, are in time, and necessarily stand in time-relations.

If we abstract from *our* mode of inwardly intuiting ourselves—the mode of intuition in terms of which we likewise take up into our faculty of representation all outer intuitions—and so take objects as they may be in themselves, then time is nothing. It has objective validity only in respect of appearances, these being things which we take *as objects of our senses.* . . .

Time is therefore a purely subjective condition of our (human) intuition (which is always sensible, that is, so far as we are affected by objects), and in itself, apart from the subject, is nothing.

The Nineteenth Century

Kant died in 1804, at the beginning of the nineteenth century. The first part of the nineteenth century was the Romantic era in European arts and letters, which rose up in revolt against the rationalism of the preceding century. This was the period that emphasized adventure and spiritual vision in literature, produced huge and noisy symphonies, and stressed exotic themes in the visual arts. Careful reasoning was out; emotional spontaneity was in.

In philosophy, although Kant's successors didn't exactly repudiate what he had written, they certainly did stand it on its ear. This dramatic response to Kant was German Absolute Idealism, the philosophies of Johann Gottlieb Fichte (1762–1814), Friedrich Wilhelm Joseph von Schelling (1775–1854), and **Georg Wilhelm Friedrich Hegel** (1770–1831).

Kant had argued that the mind imposes certain categories on the objects of experience and that this is what makes it possible to have knowledge of the world of experience. His epistemological thesis, as we have seen, is that we can have knowledge *only* of the world of experience and can have no knowledge of things "as they are in themselves." The Absolute Idealists, however, transformed this epistemological skepticism into metaphysical idealism. What could there be such that the mind could not know it? they asked. If it is not knowable, they reasoned, then it is unthinkable; and if it is unthinkable, why, it just plain isn't. So thought does not merely categorize reality: its categories *are* reality. There cannot be unknowable things-in-themselves, they said, for everything that is, is a product of the knowing mind.

Reality is not, however, the expression of *your* thought or ours or any other particular person's, they said, for neither you nor we nor any other person created the world of independent external things that exist around us. Rather, reality is the expression of *infinite* or *absolute* thought or reason. And when you and we think or philosophize about reality, this is the rational process becoming aware of itself, that is, becoming infinite.

PROFILE / Georg Hegel (1770–1831)

There was a sort of incredible solemnness about Hegel that earned him the nickname "the old man" while he was still a university student at Tübingen, Germany. He was serious about everything he did and was even somber when he drank. In high school he devoted his time to collecting copious notes concerning what he thought were the ultimate questions of life, a sure sign that he would wind up as a philosopher.

Hegel's fellow university student Friedrich Schelling gained a fabulous reputation in philosophy early in life. But for Hegel it was a struggle. After having served as a private tutor, newspaper editor, and director of a high school, he was given a professorship at Heidelberg and then at Berlin, where, finally, he became famous. His lectures, despite his tendency to stop and start and break off in mid-sentence to page furiously through his notes, drew large audiences. His listeners could sense that something deep and important was happening. Hegel was quite handsome and became popular with the society women of Berlin. All this satisfied him enormously.

Not everyone admired Hegel, however. Schopenhauer, another famous philosopher we will mention in a bit, described Hegel as an unimaginative, unintelligent, disgusting, revolting charlatan who ruined the entire generation of intellectuals who followed him. You should bear in mind, though, that poor Schopenhauer attempted to schedule his lectures at Berlin at the same hour as Hegel's—and found himself lecturing to an empty hall.

Hegel's main works are *Phenomenology of Mind* (1807), in which he first presented his metaphysical system, *Science of Logic* (1812–1816), *Encyclopedia of the Philosophical Sciences* (1817), and *Philosophy of Right* (1821).

So, from the perspective of Hegel, the cosmos and its history are the concrete expression of thought. Thus everything that happens and every field of human inquiry are the proper domain of the philosopher, who alone can understand and interpret the true relationship of each aspect of reality to the whole. **Absolute Idealism,** as this philosophy is called, attempted to achieve a complete and unified conception of all reality, a conception that gave meaning to each and every aspect in relationship to the sum total. It was the towering pinnacle of metaphysical speculation, and virtually everything that happened subsequently in metaphysics and epistemology happened in reaction to it, as we are about to see. In a nearby box we explain the main themes of Hegel's philosophy.

The following brief selection will give you the flavor of Absolute Idealism.

Some Main Themes of Hegel

1. Hegel wrote: "Everything depends on grasping the truth not merely as Substance but as Subject as well." This means that what is true, what is real, is not merely that which is thought *of*, but that which *thinks*. Thus what is most real—the Absolute—is thought thinking of itself.

2. Hegel's idealism is different from Berkeley's. For Berkeley, the objective world in fact exists in the minds of individuals. For Hegel, the objective world is an unfolding or expression of infinite thought, and the individual mind is the vehicle of infinite thought reflecting on itself.

3. Reality, the Absolute, for Hegel, is not a group of independent particulars or states of affairs but rather, like a coherent thought system such as mathematics, it is an integrated whole in which each proposition (each state of affairs) is logically connected with all the rest. Thus an *isolated* state of affairs is not wholly real; likewise, a proposition about this or that aspect or feature of reality is only partially true. The only thing that is totally true (or totally real, because these amount to the same thing) is the complete system.

4. According to Hegel, the Absolute, the sum total of reality, is a system of conceptual triads. To formalize Hegel's system somewhat artificially: for proposition or concept A there is a negation, *not-A*; and within the two there is a synthetic unity, or synthesis, *B*. *B*, however, has a negation, *not-B*, and within *B* and *not-B* there is a synthesis, *C*. And so on. Thus, the higher levels of the system are implicit in the lower levels—for example, *C* and *B* are both implicit in A. In this way the entire system of thought and reality that is the Absolute is an integrated whole in which each proposition is logically interconnected with the rest.

Note that for Hegel this triadic structure is not a *method* by means of which we discover truth. Instead, it is the way things are: it is the actual structure of thought. Thus, for example, the most basic or fundamental category or concept is *being*. But being is nothing without *not-being*, which is its opposite. And the synthesis of these opposites is *becoming*; hence the Absolute is becoming. In similar fashion, at each stage of his exposition Hegel posits a *thesis*, to which there belongs an *antithesis*, and the thesis and antithesis are a unity in a higher *synthesis*. The higher levels of the system are always implicit in the lower levels.

The Philosophy of History

From Georg Hegel

The only Thought which Philosophy brings with it to the contemplation of History, is the simple conception of *Reason;* that Reason is the Sovereign of the World; that the history of the world, therefore, presents us with a rational process. This conviction and intuition is a hypothesis in the domain of history as such. In that of Philosophy it is no hypothesis. It is there provided by speculative cognition, that Reason—and this term may here suffice us, without investigation the relation sustained by the Universe to the Divine Being—is *Substance,* as well

Ultimately, therefore, we come to the apex, or highest triad, of Hegel's system: the synthesis of "Idea" and "Nature" in "Spirit." And Idea and Nature are each, in turn, the synthesis of two lower opposing concepts. Thus, Idea is the synthesis of subjectivity (that which thinks) and objectivity (that which is thought of). What Hegel means by "Idea" is self-conscious thought, which is exactly what you would expect to be the synthesis of that which thinks and that which is thought of. "The absolute Idea," Hegel wrote, "alone is being, eternal life, self-knowing truth, and it is all truth."

The antithesis of Idea is Nature. In other words, on the one hand there is self-knowing or self-conscious thought ("Idea"), and on the other there is what we might call the independent world (Nature), the external expression of Idea, or Idea outside itself. (It is in his philosophy of Nature that Hegel attempted to integrate the various concepts of science into his system.)

Nature and Idea, as thesis and antithesis, have their own synthesis. This is the synthesis of the main triad of Hegel's entire system, and is what Hegel called "Spirit." We might translate "Spirit" as "thought knowing itself both as thought and as object" or as "the Idea returning into itself." We didn't say Hegel is easy.

The philosophy of Spirit also has three main subdivisions: subjective spirit and its antithesis objective spirit, with the synthesis as Absolute Spirit. Subjective spirit is the realm of the human mind; objective spirit is the mind in its external manifestation in social institutions. Hegel's analysis of objective spirit contains his social and political philosophy, in which he attempts to display the relationships (always more or less triadic) among such various concepts as property, contract, crime, punishment, right, personality, family, society, and the state.

In the end, therefore, we come to know the part played by every aspect of reality in the whole, and we are led to understand that the highest conception of the Absolute is as Spirit.

So Hegel's system is really a grandiose vision of the history of the universe and the history of human consciousness as a necessary unfolding of infinite reason. It purports to be a complete conceptual framework for each aspect of reality and for every component of human thought and history. This system represents the towering summit of metaphysical speculation.

---

as *Infinite Power;* its own *Infinite Material* underlying all the natural and spiritual life which it originates, as also the *Infinite Form*—that which sets this Material in motion. On the one hand, Reason is the *substance* of the Universe; viz., that by which and in which all reality has its being and subsistence. On the other hand, it is the *Infinite Energy* of the Universe; since Reason is not so powerless as to be incapable of producing anything but a mere ideal, a mere intention—having its place outside reality, nobody knows where; something separate and abstract, in the heads of certain human beings. It is *the Infinite complex of things,* their entire Essence and Truth. It is its own material which it commits to its own Active Energy to work up; not needing, as finite action does, the conditions of an external material of given means from which it may obtain its support, and the objects of its activity. It supplies its own nourishment, and is the object of its own operations. While it is exclusively its own basis of existence, and absolute final aim, it is also the energizing power realizing this aim; developing in it not only the phenomena of the

Empiricist

‿‿‿‿‿‿‿‿‿‿‿‿‿

PROFILE / John Stuart Mill (1806–1873)

Many years ago, one of the authors came across a table of projected IQ scores for various historic "geniuses" in a psychology text. (Who knows how the scores were calculated?) At the top of the list, with some incredible score, was John Stuart Mill.

Mill began reading Greek at three and Latin at eight, and by adolescence had completed an extensive study of Greek and Latin literature, as well as of history, mathematics, and logic. Mill's education was administered by his father, who subjected young John to a rigorous regimen.

At fifteen Mill settled on his lifelong objective, to work for social and political reform, and it is as a reformer and ethical and political philosopher that he is most remembered. Mill championed individual rights and personal freedom, and advocated emancipation of women and proportional representation. His most famous work, *On Liberty* (1859), is thought by many to be the definitive defense of freedom of thought and discussion.

In ethics Mill was a utilitarian, concerning which we will have much to say in Chapter 8. He published *Utilitarianism* in 1863.

Mill's interests also ranged over a broad variety of topics in epistemology, metaphysics, and logic. His *A System of Logic* (1843), which was actually read at the time by the man in the street, represented an empiricist approach to logic, abstraction, psychology, sociology, and morality. Mill's *methods of induction* are still standard fare in university courses in beginning logic.

When Mill was twenty-five, he met Harriet Taylor, a merchant's wife, and this was the beginning of one of the most celebrated love affairs of all time. Twenty years later, and three years after her husband died, Mrs. Taylor married Mill, on whose thought she had a profound influence. *On Liberty* was perhaps jointly written with her, and in any case was dedicated to her.

Harriet Taylor died in 1858. Mill spent his remaining years in Avignon, France, where she had died, to be near her grave.

Mill's *Autobiography*, widely read, appeared in the year of his death. Mill still is the most celebrated English philosopher of his century.

Natural, but also of the Spiritual Universe—the History of the World. That this "Idea" or "Reason" is the *True*, the *Eternal*, the absolutely *powerful* essence; that it reveals itself in the World, and that in that World nothing else is revealed but this and its honor and glory—is the thesis which, as we have said, has been proved in Philosophy, and is here regarded as demonstrated.

If Hegel was the most famous German philosopher of the nineteenth century, **John Stuart Mill** (1806–1873) was perhaps the most widely known British philosopher. The Absolute Idealists, despite their differences with Kant, were greatly under Kant's influence. But Mill was unfazed. He accepted the basic empiricist premise of Locke, Berkeley, and Hume that all ideas and beliefs, and thus, too, all knowledge, derive from sense experience. Further, he tried to provide an account of how we come to know and believe some of the things we do, given this premise.

Mill distinguished between what is directly given to us in perception and what we know on the basis of inference. When we perceive a table, for instance, what is directly given to us is some sensations, but the table is more than just *these* sensations. From these sensations that we are actually having, we infer that if we were to move around a bit, we would experience new and additional sensations. Thus the table consists not only of the actual sensations but also of those sensations that we anticipate having if we were to move around the table, push it, put things on it, etc. The table, in short, Mill says, is a *"permanent possibility of sensation."* Mill's theory, you can see, is a not-too-distant cousin of Berkeley's, according to which tables and other "external objects" are groups or clusters of sensations.

Mill considered whether one could offer a parallel analysis of the mind as a permanent possibility of awareness. But he was not satisfied with this notion, because, in particular, he believed, the mind is sometimes aware of its awareness. He proposed no other analysis of the nature of the mind, however.

It's hard to imagine two more divergent philosophies than those of Hegel and Mill. And so it is that in the twentieth century the philosophy that evolved from nineteenth-century idealism is starkly different from that which grew out of the empiricist tradition of Mill.

Checklist

To help you review, here is a checklist of the key philosophers and concepts of this chapter. The brief descriptive sentences summarize leading ideas. Keep in mind that some of these summary statements represent terrific oversimplifications of complex positions.

Philosophers

- **David Hume** Held there is no metaphysical knowledge; maintained that knowledge is limited to what we experience. Summoned powerful arguments to question our supposed knowledge of the self, causality, God, and the external world.

- **Immanuel Kant** Believed the mind imposes a certain form and order on experienceable objects. Held there can be no knowledge of things "as they are in themselves," independent of experience.

- **Georg Hegel** Premier exponent of Absolute Idealism. Rejected concept of "the thing-in-itself." Held that all reality is the expression of thought or reason.
- **John Stuart Mill** Thoroughgoing empiricist; regarded external objects as permanent possibilities of sensation.

Concepts

122 constant conjunction   *recollection of cause+effect sequence Hume*

123 "The future will resemble the past."   *This is AN assumption*

126 Copernican revolution in philosophy   *objects must conform to mind experience Kant*
Sun around earth or earth around Sun

127 principle that perceptions must be conceptualized and unified to qualify as experience

128 phenomenon/noumenon   *experience / independant of experience Ding an sich*

128 *Ding-an-sich*   *Thing in itself*

131 Absolute Idealism

135 permanent possibility of sensation   *physical object*

Questions for Discussion and Review

1. Do you ever observe anything other than your own perceptions? Explain.
2. Explain Hume's reasons for questioning the idea of the mind/self.
3. "Necessity is something in the mind, not in the objects." Explain what this means and what Hume's reasons were for holding it.
4. Will the future resemble the past? Can you *know* that it will, or must you merely *assume* that it will?
5. If knowledge begins with experience, must it also rise from experience? Explain.
6. Is it possible that we may someday experience an event that is in neither space nor time? If not, why not?
7. Is it possible for extraterrestrial aliens to experience things that are not in space or time?
8. Do infants have experience? Do cats? Fish? Explain.
9. Can we have knowledge of things in themselves? Be sure to clarify what you mean by "things-in-themselves."
10. "Everything depends on grasping the truth not merely as Substance but as Subject as well." Who said this, and what does it mean?   *Hegel 132*

Suggested Further Readings

Frederick C. Beiser, ed., *The Cambridge Companion to Hegel* (New York: Cambridge University Press, 1993). A recent collection of essays.

E. O. Burtt, *The English Philosophers from Bacon to Mill* (New York: Modern Library, 1939). A general book on modern philosophy.

J. N. Findlay, *Hegel, A Re-examination* (New York: Humanities Press, 1970). A readable presentation of Hegel's principal works.

Paul Guyer, ed., *The Cambridge Companion to Kant* (New York: Cambridge University Press, 1992). A recent collection of essays.

G. W. F. Hegel, *The Phenomenology of Mind* (New York: Harper & Row, 1967). Hegel's first major work and a brilliant reinterpretation of Western philosophy through the eyes of an Absolute Idealist. Not light reading, though.

W. T. Jones, *Kant and the Nineteenth Century*, 2nd ed. (New York: Harcourt Brace Jovanovich, 1975). Jones's section on Hegel contains enough original material for the introductory student and explains it all very nicely, too.

Immanuel Kant, *Prolegomena to Any Future Metaphysics*, P. Carus, trans. (Indianapolis: Hackett, 1977). This is Kant's own (relatively) simplified introduction to his thinking about metaphysics and epistemology. If you want to have a look at the *Critique of Pure Reason* itself, the Norman Kemp Smith translation is published by St. Martin's in New York (1965). If you need help with this difficult work, you cannot do better than H. J. Paton's *Kant's Metaphysics of Experience*, in two volumes (London, 1936). Paton's work covers only the first half of the *Critique*, but it explains it, sentence by difficult sentence, in clear English.

J. Loewenberg, ed., *Hegel Selections* (New York: Scribners, 1929). Hegel is very, very difficult.

Stephen Priest, *The British Empiricists* (London: Penguin Books, 1990). A useful introduction to the British empiricist tradition extending from Hobbes through to Russell and Ayer.

Robert C. Solomon and Kathleen M. Higgins, eds., *Routledge History of Philosophy*, vol. 7, *Age of German Idealism* (London: Routledge, 1994). Introductory essays covering from Kant through the first half of the nineteenth century.

6 Now

░░░

It is no truer that "atoms are what they are because we use 'atom' as we do" than that "we use 'atom' as we do because atoms are as they are." Both of these claims . . . are entirely empty.

—Richard Rorty

We have no way of identifying truths except to posit that the statements that are currently rationally accepted (by our lights) are true.

—Hilary Putnam

Absolute Idealism left distinct marks on many facets of Western culture. True, science was indifferent to it, and common sense was more or less stupefied by it. Still, the greatest political movement of the nineteenth and twentieth centuries, Marxism, was to a significant degree an outgrowth of Absolute Idealism. (Bertrand Russell remarked someplace that Marx was nothing more than Hegel mixed with British economic theory.) Nineteenth- and twentieth-century literature, theology, and even art also fell under its spell. The great Romantic composers of the nineteenth century, for example, with their fondness for expanded form, vast orchestras, complex scores, and soaring melodies, searched for the all-encompassing musical statement and in doing so mirrored the efforts of the metaphysicians, whose vast and imposing systems were sources of inspiration to many artists and composers.

As we have said, much of what happened in philosophy after Hegel happened either in continuation of his work or in reaction to it, mostly the latter. On the continent of Europe, the assault on idealism was begun by the nihilistic attacks of Schopenhauer and Nietzsche (**nihilism** is the rejection of values and beliefs) and by the religious anti-idealism of Søren Kierkegaard. Anti-Hegelianism reached its summit in the twentieth century in philosophy known as **existentialism,** according to which life is not only not perfectly rational, it is fundamentally irrational and absurd. We devote all of Chapter 15 to post-Hegelian philosophy on the

European continent. Here we are going to focus on epistemology and metaphysics in the twentieth century in the English-speaking world.

Hegel was ignored at first in England, but then, in the later part of the nineteenth century, neo-Hegelianism became the dominant philosophical school even in that country. But around the turn of the century, there arose a great opposition to Hegelian-type idealism, and this reaction was the point of departure in the early twentieth century for what is known as **analytic philosophy.** Analytic philosophy eventually spread from England to America and the rest of the English-speaking world and to Scandinavia, and was touted by its practitioners as "the proper method of philosophy."

Analytic Philosophy

And so we arrive at the twentieth century, the century of world wars, Einstein, nuclear weapons, television and computers, genetic engineering, space travel, AIDS, the rise and fall of the Soviet Union, racial integration, and Chubby Checker. In art and literature, traditional structures and approaches were cast aside with abandon. Schoenberg and Stravinsky brought the world music that lacked tonality; Cage brought it music that lacked sound. In Europe, existentialist philosophers proclaimed the absurdity of the human predicament. In Russia and China, the followers of Marx declared an end to the then-existing order; still later the followers of the followers declared an end to Marx. Meanwhile, in England and America, philosophers were busy with—what's this? The analysis of language? Sounds deadly. Let's have a closer look.

What Analysis Is

Just what is **analysis,** anyway? Quite simply put, *philosophical analysis resolves complex propositions or concepts into simpler ones.*

Let's take an elementary example. The proposition

"Square circles are nonexistent things"

might be resolved by analysis into the simpler proposition

"No squares are circular."

This second proposition is "simpler" philosophically because it refers only to squares and their lack of circularity, whereas the first proposition refers to two distinct classes of entities, square circles and nonexistent things.

Moreover, the first proposition is very troubling philosophically. It is certainly an intelligible proposition. Hence it would seem that square circles and nonexistent things must (somehow and amazingly) exist in some sense or another. For if

they did not exist, then the proposition would be about nothing and thus would not be intelligible. (It is precisely this reasoning that has led some philosophers to conclude that every object of thought must exist "in some sense," or "subsist.")

So the second sentence contains the same information as the first but does not have the puzzling implications of the first. Not only is it simpler than the second, it is also clearer. Once the first sentence is recast or analyzed in this way, we can accept what the first sentence says without having to concede that square circles and nonexistent things exist "in some sense."

This very simple example of analysis will perhaps help make it clear why many analytic philosophers have regarded analysis as having great importance for the field of metaphysics. Be sure that you understand the example and everything we have said about it before you read any further.

Why Analysis Became Important

To understand better why analysis became so important as a method of philosophy, think back to Kant (Chapter 5). Kant thought that knowledge is possible if we limit our inquiries to things as they are experienceable, because the mind imposes categories on experienceable objects. The Absolute Idealists then expanded on Kant's theory and held that the categories of thought *are* the categories of being.

But this notion, that the categories of thought are the categories of being, is open to a certain amount of abuse and can in fact throw open the doors to the grandiose metaphysical speculation that Kant himself was anxious to combat. And consider this problem: What the categories of thought are to metaphysician A may not be the categories recognized by metaphysician B. So the question arises: How do you determine whose metaphysical system is correct, A's or B's? Granted, if A's system is in some respect self-contradictory, that would be a decisive reason for rejecting it. But even if A's system and B's system are both internally consistent (not self-contradictory), they may still be vastly different. Just how do you determine whose system is correct?

So the situation by the late nineteenth century was this: on the one hand, *science* was making great and striking advances, advances conceded to be genuine by scientists and nonscientists alike. But the situation seemed quite different in *philosophy,* at least in the late stages of Absolute Idealism. Those who worked from within a given metaphysical system could claim that significant headway had been made, but adherents of competing systems were usually of a different opinion about the importance of the touted advances. So to the lay public generally, which could not possibly judge the alternatives or even understand them, the situation in metaphysical philosophy seemed *just awful.* Philosophy, apart from political philosophy and ethics, seems mired in hopeless and verbose speculation. To many scientists and scientifically or mathematically trained philosophers, metaphysics had become a tedious and even repellent mass of trifling verbiage.

One of these scientifically trained individuals was **Bertrand Russell** (1872–1970), a Cambridge mathematician and philosopher. Russell began his philosophical career as a British Hegelian but came to regard Hegel's metaphysics as resting

ANALysis - Key to metaphysical truth

PROFILE / Bertrand Russell (1872–1970)

Bertrand Russell came from a distinguished background. His grandfather, Lord John Russell, was twice prime minister; his godfather was John Stuart Mill, of whom much mention is made in later chapters; and his parents were prominent freethinkers. Because his parents died when he was young, Russell was brought up in the household of Lord Russell. This side of the family was austerely Protestant, and Russell's childhood was solitary and lonely. As a teenager, he had the intuition that God did not exist and found this to be a great relief.

In the fall of 1890, at a time when several other brilliant philosophers were also there, Russell went to Cambridge to study mathematics and philosophy. Many of Russell's important works in philosophy and mathematics were written during his association with Cambridge, first as a student, then as a fellow and lecturer. His association with Cambridge ended in 1916, when he was dismissed for pacifist activities during World War I. He was restored as a fellow at Cambridge, however, in 1944.

Russell was dismayed by the enthusiasm among ordinary people for the war, and his own pacifism created much resentment. After he was dismissed from Cambridge, he was imprisoned for six months for his pacifism; thereafter, he held no academic position again until he began to teach in the United States in 1938.

Russell thought that without a proper education a person is caught in the prison of prejudices that make up common sense. He wanted to create a kind of education that would be not only philosophically sound but also non-threatening, enjoyable, and stimulating. To this end he and his wife, Dora, founded the Beacon Hill School in 1927, which was influential in the founding of similar schools in England and America.

In addition to writing books on education during the period between the wars, Russell wrote extensively on social and political philosophy. His most infamous popular work, *Marriage and Morals* (1929), was very liberal in its attitude toward sexual practices and caused the cancellation of his appointment to City College of New York in 1940. He was taken to court by the mother of a CCNY student, and the court revoked Russell's appointment "for the sake of public health, safety, and morals." Apparently the most damaging part of the evidence against Russell was his recommendation in the book that a child caught masturbating should not be physically punished.

World War II and the Nazi onslaught caused Russell to abandon his pacifism. In 1961, however, he was again imprisoned, this time for activity in demonstrations against nuclear weapons, and in 1967 he organized the so-called war crimes tribunal directed against American activities in Vietnam.

Russell received the Nobel Prize for Literature in 1950, one of many honors bestowed on him. In his autobiography he said that three passions had governed his life: the longing for love, the search for knowledge, and unbearable pity for the suffering of mankind. Throughout his life Russell exhibited intellectual brilliance and extraordinary personal courage.

essentially on a silly verbal confusion and as of no more intrinsic philosophical interest or merit than a pun. When he read what Hegel had to say on the philosophy of mathematics, Russell was horrified, finding it both ignorant and stupid.

To anyone familiar with and sympathetic to nineteenth-century German and British idealistic metaphysics, Russell's opinion of the tradition will seem unduly harsh. But Russell, rightly or wrongly, came to the conclusion that the idealistic metaphysics of his predecessors largely rested on mistakes and confusions—rather like the example described in our opening paragraphs, in which someone concludes from the fact that square circles can be talked about that they exist.

When Russell turned his attention to the philosophy of mathematics, he demonstrated, through the careful use of *analysis,* that mathematical truths could be derived from principles of logic (something that other philosophers had thought was true but had not demonstrated) and that propositions about numbers could be resolved into propositions about classes of classes. The importance of this achievement, of this apparent reduction of number theory to set theory, seemed undeniable to anyone who cared to consider it and was indisputably a stunning intellectual achievement. Russell had in effect shown that there was no more need to credit existence to numbers as something over and above and distinct from classes than there is to credit existence to square circles.

The same method of analysis was then applied by Russell and others to other notorious philosophical problems. The resulting solutions, unlike many so-called solutions of the idealists, seemed definitive to those who considered them. The method of analysis, in short, to those who familiarized themselves with it, seemed to yield substantial and demonstrable results, results very much like those achieved by science. In contrast to what seemed true of the apparently futile disputations of the nineteenth-century metaphysicians, philosophy was perceived at last *to be getting somewhere.*

The Evolution of Analytic Philosophy

Over the first half of the twentieth century, analysis became different things to different people and was used with different purposes in mind. For some, an analysis of an expression was in effect a mere paraphrase that, it was thought, was in some sense less misleading philosophically than the original. **G. E. Moore** (1873–1958), one of the most important early practitioners of analysis, devoted considerable energy to the analysis of some of the beliefs of common sense that earlier philosophers seemed to dispute. Gilbert Ryle (1900–1976) thought the principal business of philosophy was to use techniques of paraphrase to resolve or dissolve traditional philosophical problems, which were asserted largely to rest on "linguistic confusions." Analysis, in this view, was a sort of linguistic therapy for those who were troubled by these traditional problems.

Others, among them Russell, had a larger vision. They thought that analysis was the means by which philosophy could actually disclose the ultimate logical constituents of reality, their interrelations, and their relationship to the world of experience. Russell's student **Ludwig Wittgenstein** (1889–1951) thought the

The World's Shortest Refutation of Skepticism

Suppose someone waved his hand in front of your face and said, "See? Here's a hand, a material object. What more do you want as disproof of skepticism?" That, in effect, was the refutation of skepticism set forth by G. E. Moore (1873–1958), a friend and colleague of Bertrand Russell. It is a sufficient refutation of skepticism, Moore said, simply to point to cases in which we know very well that we are dealing with a material object. He said:

> This, after all, you know, really is a finger: there is no doubt about it: I know it, and you all know it. And I think we may safely challenge any philosopher to bring forward any

argument in favor either of the proposition that we do not know it, or of the proposition that it is not true, which does not at some point, rest upon some premise which is, beyond comparison, less certain than is the proposition which it is designed to attack. The questions whether we do ever know such things as these, and whether there are any material objects, seem to me, therefore, to be questions which there is no need to take seriously: they are questions which it is quite easy to answer, with certainty, in the affirmative.

As an early exponent of philosophical analysis, Moore exerted a

tremendous influence on twentieth-century philosophy (perhaps especially in ethics, as we will see in Chapter 8). He did not advance any particular metaphysical or epistemological theory but was disposed instead to clarify—through analysis—some of the propositions known to common sense. This led him to consider, like Russell, the relationship between sense-data and physical objects. He never was satisfied that he had it figured out.

Many philosophers have not been entirely comfortable with this easygoing refutation of skepticism quoted here. Are you?

---

goal of analysis was to reduce all complex descriptive propositions to their ultimately simple constituent propositions. These latter propositions would consist of "names" in combination, which would represent the ultimate simple constituents of reality.

In the 1920s, Moritz Schlick (1882–1936), a philosopher at the University of Vienna, formed a group known as the **Vienna Circle,** the members of which were much impressed by the work of Russell and Wittgenstein. Calling themselves the **logical positivists,** the group held that philosophy is not a theory but an activity whose business is the logical clarification of thought. The logical positivists proclaimed a **"verifiability criterion of meaning."** According to this criterion, suppose you say something, but nobody knows what observations would verify what you are trying to say. Then you haven't really made a meaningful empirical statement at all. And thus, the logical positivists held, traditional metaphysical utterances are not meaningful empirical statements. Take, for example, Hegel's thesis that reason is the substance of the universe. How could this be verified? Well, it just couldn't. So it isn't a genuine factual proposition; it isn't empirically meaningful.

Moral and value statements, the logical positivists said, are likewise empirically meaningless. They are at best, they held, expressions of emotions, rather than legitimate statements. Philosophy, they said, has as its only useful function the

PROFILE / Ludwig Wittgenstein (1889–1951)

So many discussions of Wittgenstein's philosophy were submitted to philosophy journals in the 1950s and 1960s that for a while some journals declined to accept further manuscripts on his ideas. No other philosopher of this century, save perhaps Bertrand Russell, has had as great an impact on philosophy in Great Britain and in the United States.

Wittgenstein was born in Vienna into a wealthy family and studied to become an engineer. From engineering, his interests led him to pure mathematics and then to the philosophical foundations of mathematics. He soon gave up engineering to study philosophy with Russell at Cambridge in 1912–1913. The following year he studied philosophy alone and in seclusion in Norway, partly because he perceived himself as irritating others by his nervous personality. During World War I he served in the Austrian army; it was in this period that he completed the first of his two major works, the *Tractatus Logico-Philosophicus* (1921).

Wittgenstein's father had left Wittgenstein a large fortune, which after the war Wittgenstein simply handed over to two of his sisters, and he became an elementary school teacher. Next, in 1926, he became a gardener's assistant, perhaps a surprising walk of life for one of the most profound thinkers of all time. He did, however, return to Cambridge in 1929 and there received his doctorate, the *Tractatus*

serving as his dissertation. In 1937, he succeeded G. E. Moore in his chair of philosophy.

During World War II Wittgenstein found himself unable to sit idly by, so he worked for two years as a hospital orderly and for another as an assistant in a medical lab. Time and again Wittgenstein, an heir to a great fortune and a genius, placed himself in the humblest of positions.

In 1944, Wittgenstein resumed his post at Cambridge, but, troubled by what he thought was his harmful effect on students and disturbed by their apparent poor comprehension of his ideas, he resigned in 1947. His second major work, the *Philosophical Investigations,* was published in 1953, two years after his death.

Reportedly, when he became seriously ill in April 1951 and was told by his physician that he was about to die, his response was, simply, "Good." When he died a few days later, his last words were, "Tell them I've had a wonderful life."

analysis of both everyday language and scientific language—it has no legitimate concern with the world apart from language, for that is the concern of scientists.

The Vienna Circle dissolved when the Nazis took control of Austria in the late 1930s, but to this day many people still equate analytic philosophy with logical positivism. This is true despite the fact that nowadays very few philosophers who

The Paradox of Analysis

An analysis of a proposition involves restating the proposition in different words, as you've seen. Thus, for example, you might analyze "Square circles are nonexisting things" as, "Nothing is both square and circular." In other words, according to this analysis: *To say that square circles are nonexisting things is to say that nothing is both square and circular.*

The italicized sentence states the analysis of the proposition "Square circles are nonexisting things." Now think about what the italicized sentence means. If it is true, then the sentence "Square circles are nonexisting things" is

identical with the sentence "Nothing is both square and circular." And if these last two sentences are identical, then you can substitute one for the other whenever either appears, right? So let's make such a substitution in the second half of the italicized sentence. The result is this sentence: *To say that square circles are nonexisting things is to say that square circles are nonexisting things.*

In other words, the first italicized sentence, if true, is identical with the second italicized sentence. But the second italicized sentence is trivial! Hence the first italicized sentence is also trivial.

And that means that our analysis is trivial, because the first italicized sentence expresses our analysis.

This is the **paradox of analysis.** For an analysis of a given proposition to be correct, the proposition and its analysis must be equivalent. But if they are equivalent, then sentences that express the equivalence are mere trivial truisms. In short, analyses are either incorrect or trivial.

G. E. Moore, an analyst for over a half century, professed an inability to resolve this ugly paradox to his satisfaction. Can you resolve it?

refer to themselves as analysts subscribe to the verifiability criterion of meaning or accept many other of the basic assumptions of logical positivism.

In fact, today it's extremely doubtful whether many of those who would call themselves analytic philosophers would even describe analysis as the only proper method of philosophy. Indeed, few would even describe their daily philosophical task as primarily one of analysis. There are other philosophical tasks one might undertake than analysis, and some who would still not hesitate to call themselves analysts have simply lost interest in analysis in favor of these other tasks. Others, like Wittgenstein, for example, have explicitly repudiated analysis as the proper method of philosophy. Wittgenstein's about-face was published in 1953 in his enormously influential *Philosophical Investigations.*

Further, it is now widely held that many philosophically interesting claims and expressions cannot intelligibly be regarded as complexes subject to resolution into simpler and less misleading expressions. Certainly, the intent to recast the meaning of an expression into a less misleading form can be carried out only if its "real" or "true" meaning can be ascertained by the analyst. But concerns have been raised, perhaps most notably by **W. V. O. Quine** (1908–), about whether it is ever possible to say in some absolute, nonrelativistic sense what the meaning of an expression is. And for many expressions it seems inappropriate in the first place to speak of their "meaning." Clearer understanding of many expressions seems to be achieved when we ask how the expression is used or what it is used to do, rather than what it means, unless the latter question is taken as being equivalent to the two former questions, as it often is.

So it has become accepted that there are many useful philosophical methods and techniques other than the analysis of language, and it is pretty widely thought that good, substantial philosophical work is by no means always the result of analysis of some sort. Many of today's analytic philosophers would deny being directly concerned with language (though most are concerned with expressing themselves in clear language). Nor could it be said that all analytic philosophers mean the same thing when they speak of analysis. In its broadest sense, a call for "analysis" today is just simply a call for clarification, and certainly today's analytic philosophers exhibit (or hope they exhibit) a concern for clarity of thought and expression. Most, too, would be inclined to say that at least some opinions expressed by earlier philosophers reflect linguistic confusions if not outright logical errors, but beyond this it is not the case that all analytic philosophers use some common unique method of philosophizing or have the same interests or share an identifiable approach to philosophical problems. In today's world, philosophers are apt to call themselves "analytic" to indicate that they do not have much training or interest in existentialism or phenomenology as much as for any other reason.

So, then, a history of analytic philosophy is, for all intents and purposes, a history of a predominant strain of twentieth-century philosophy in English-speaking countries that has evolved from the philosophical writings and discussions of Russell, Moore, Wittgenstein, and others.

Logical Atomism

Let's back up to consider the metaphysical/epistemological theory of Russell, for it set the stage for most of what followed in analytical metaphysics and epistemology. Russell's metaphysics evolved considerably over the years, but for a major part of his life he subscribed to what is known as **logical atomism.** The world, he believed, is not an all-encompassing Oneness, as Hegelians would have it, but a collection of *atomic facts.*

World is a collection of atomic facts

To say that the world consists ultimately of *facts* is to say that it does not consist just simply of *things,* but of things that have properties and stand in various relations to one another. Your study area, for example, does not just consist of a chair and a desk and a lamp, for these things must stand in a certain relationship to one another if they are to constitute your study area. These things *in their relationship to each other* do not make up just another thing; their being in this relationship is not a thing but a *fact.* Even your desk is not just a *thing;* it is a thing with properties, and that it has the properties it has is a fact. Likewise the world, the universe, reality, does not consist just simply of things, but more precisely of facts.

And the basic or most fundamental facts, Russell believed, are *atomic.* To say

A Parade of Ideas

It used to be that the history of philosophy was largely the history of the philosophies of specific individuals—Plato's philosophy, Aristotle's philosophy, Kant's philosophy, and so forth. But this changed after Russell, Moore, and Wittgenstein. Recent philosophy, especially perhaps philosophy in the analytic tradition, tends to be treated as a history of specific ideas, such as phenomenalism, foundationalism, representationalism, and so on. Historians of recent philosophy often mention specific individuals only to give examples of people who subscribe to the idea at hand. It is the idea, rather than the philosopher, that is most important. You'll notice this shift in perspective in this text, too.

that they are *atomic* is not to relate them to nuclear physics or the scientific atomic theory, but rather to indicate two things: (1) The basic facts are absolutely *simple:* they can be components of more complicated or "molecular" facts, but they are not themselves resolvable into more basic components. (2) Each basic fact is logically independent of every other: any given basic fact could remain exactly the same even if all the other facts were different. For example, even if the world were entirely different, the fact that the top of your desk is rectangular could remain unchanged, assuming that fact is a basic fact.

Russell believed that metaphysical truth is dictated simply by the fact that we can form propositions about the world, some more complex than others. Complex propositions, he thought, must in principle be resolvable into simpler propositions. As an example, the proposition "America elected a Republican to be its president" is resolvable, in principle, into propositions about individual people and their actions, most especially the action of voting. But when people vote, they are really just doing certain things with their bodies. So a proposition about a person voting is resolvable, in principle, into propositions about these doings—about going into an enclosed booth, picking up a pencil, marking a piece of paper, depositing the paper in an envelope, etc. Even a proposition such as "John Smith picked up a yellow pencil" is theoretically resolvable into propositions about John Smith's bodily motions and a piece of wood that has certain properties; and indeed we are still quite far from reaching the end of this theoretical process of resolving complex propositions into more elementary propositions.

Because complex propositions, Russell thought, must in principle be resolvable into simpler propositions by analysis, there must therefore be fundamental and absolutely uncomplex (i.e., simple) propositions that cannot be resolved further. Corresponding to these absolutely simple "atomic" propositions are the fundamental or atomic facts. Because any atomic fact may hold regardless of what is true about the rest of the world, including what we think about it, Hegel was mistaken (Russell said) in believing that the only thing that is true is the Totality. Individual atomic propositions may be true in isolation from all other propositions because the facts they depict are logically unrelated to all other facts.

Wittgenstein's Turnaround

Wittgenstein's philosophy divides into two phases. Both had a great influence on his contemporaries, yet the philosophy of the second phase, that of the *Philosophical Investigations* (1953), is largely a rejection of the central ideas of the first, that of the *Tractatus* (1921). This is an unusual but not a unique occurrence in the history of philosophy, for other philosophers have come to reject their earlier positions.

In both works Wittgenstein was concerned with the relationships between language and the world. The *Tractatus* assumes a single, essential relationship; the *Investigations* denies this assumption.

In the *Tractatus*, Wittgenstein portrays the function of language as that of describing the world and is concerned with making it clear just how language and thought hook onto reality in the first place.

Well, just how does language hook onto reality? According to Wittgenstein, a proposition (or a thought) *pictures* the fact it represents. It can picture it, he said, because both it and the fact share the same *logical form,* a form that can be exhibited by philosophical analysis. All genuine propositions, he held, are reducible to logically elementary propositions, which, he said, are composed of *names* of absolutely simple objects. A combination of these names (i.e., a proposition) pictures a combination of *objects* in the world (i.e., a fact). The *Tractatus* is devoted in large measure to explaining and working out the implications of this *picture theory of meaning* across a range of philosophical topics.

But in the *Investigations*, Wittgenstein casts off completely this picture theory of meaning and the underlying assumption of the *Tractatus* that there is some universal function of language. After all, he notes in the later work, how a picture is *used* determines what it is a picture of—one and the same picture could be a picture of a man holding a guitar, or of how to hold a guitar, or of what a guitar looks like, or of what Bill Jones's fingers look like, and so on. Similarly, what a sentence means is determined by the use to which it is put within a given context or **language game.** Further, says the later Wittgenstein, there is nothing that the various uses of language have in common, and there is certainly no set of ideal elementary propositions to which all other propositions are reducible. In short, according to the later work, the earlier work is completely wrongheaded.

When philosophers ignore the "game" in which language is used—Wittgenstein says in the *Investigations*—when they take language "on a holiday" and try to straitjacket it into conformity with some idealized and preconceived notion of what its essence must be, the result is the unnecessary confusion known as a philosophical problem. From this perspective, the history of philosophy is a catalog of confusions that result from taking language on a holiday.

Now, you may want an example or two of an atomic fact. Just what *is* a basic fact? Are these facts about minds or matter or neutrons or quarks or what? you will ask.

Well, the logical atomists, remember, were *logical* atomists, and this means that not all of those who subscribed to logical atomism were concerned with what *actually are* the atomic facts. Some of them, most famously Ludwig Wittgenstein, were concerned with setting forth what logically must be the basic structure of reality and left it to others to determine the actual content of the universe. Determining the logical structure of reality was enough, no little task in its own right, they thought.

Awareness Without a Subject?

If any single thing seems beyond doubt from a commonsense point of view, it is that sensory awareness requires a subject or "I" or "self" or "mind" that has that awareness. Russell, however, eventually came to think that *only the awareness itself* is present in experience.

The subject, he maintained, is *not* revealed to us by observation, and we only suppose that such a thing exists because it is demanded by language. When you report an experience by saying, "I heard a loud bang," for example, only the bang is given in experience. The "I" part is grammatically convenient, but it is not actually present in the experience. According to Russell,

"If we are to avoid a perfectly gratuitous assumption, we must dispense with the subject as one of the actual ingredients of the world."

Thus Russell came to think that the distinction between the mental and the physical is entirely a matter of the way awarenesses are grouped. In one kind of grouping, an awareness belongs to the physical world and, in another, to the mental world. Take, for example, the sense-data you have when you look at a chair. According to Russell: "If one arranges together all those sense-data that appear to different people at a given moment and are such as we should ordinarily say are appearances of the same physical object, then that class of

sense-data will give you something that belongs to physics, namely, the chair at this moment. On the other hand, if I take all the appearances that the different chairs in this room present to me at this moment, I get something belonging to psychology."

This "neutral monism" was derived from William James, and Russell's conviction that no "I" is given in experience is traceable to David Hume. Consider the matter yourself: Do the data of experience bring you in contact with a subject, or is the subject an inference you make from an assumed premise that consciousness cannot exist without a conscious subject?

As for Russell: he was always somewhat less concerned about what *actually* exists than with what we must *suppose* exists. For all he knew, he said, all the Gods of Olympus exist. But the essential point, he said, is that we have no reason whatsoever to suppose that this is so.

As for what we must suppose exists, Russell changed his mind over the course of his long life. But generally he believed that the bare minimum that must be supposed to exist does *not* include many of the things that "common sense" is inclined to say exist, such as physical objects and atoms and subatomic particles. Russell's view was that what we say and think and believe about such things as these, let's call them the objects of common sense and science, can in theory be expressed in propositions that refer only to *awarenesses* or **sense-data.** His position thus was that philosophically we do not have to believe in the existence of chairs or rocks or planets or atoms, say, as a type of entity that in some sense is more than just sense-data. Here, on the one hand, he said in effect, are the "data" actually given to us in sensation; there, on the other, are the external objects we strongly believe are out there and that science tells us so much about. How do we get from knowledge of our sense-data to knowledge of the objects? What we truly *know,* Russell said, are the data of immediate experience, our sense-data. Therefore, he said, what we *believe* exists (physical objects and scientific entities like atoms and electrons) must be *definable* in terms of sense-data if our belief in physical objects and scientific entities is to be epistemologically secure.

Now this idea, that physical and scientific objects are "definable" in terms of sense-data or, more precisely, the idea that propositions about such objects in theory are expressible in propositions that refer only to sense-data, is known as **phenomenalism.** Let's look at phenomenalism more closely.

Phenomenalism

During the first forty or so years of this century, many philosophers in the analytic tradition were phenomenalists, and the burning issue of epistemology and metaphysics was whether phenomenalism is sound. Why was this issue so important? After all, we are considering a period of time that included two world wars, a global depression, and Buchenwald. What could be so important about phenomenalism?

First, you must remember the seed of uncertainty planted by Descartes at the beginning of the Scientific Revolution and Hume's all-inclusive doubts. Can one really be certain of what passes for knowledge? In particular, can one really know of the continued existence of a realm of objects that exist outside the mind? These questions, from Descartes's time onward, *nagged* many philosophers. To epistemologists, they seemed perhaps the most fundamental of all theoretical questions. As Kant had remarked, it was absolutely scandalous that philosophy had been unable to prove that external, material objects exist.

And phenomenalism seemed *so* plausible as a way of certifying our supposed knowledge of external objects. Think once again of the quarter that we talked about in connection with Hume. At first glance it seems that you could, in a variety of ways, be mistaken when you think that there before you is a quarter. But it is easy to suppose that, even though your belief that you are seeing a *quarter* might be mistaken, you could not possibly be mistaken about your *sense-data*. That is, it is easy to suppose that a proposition that refers to your present sense-data, a proposition like, perhaps, "This seems to me to be a round silverish expanse," is **incorrigible**—that is, *incapable* of being false if you believe that it is true. (After all, could you possibly be mistaken about the way things *seem* to you?) Therefore, if the empirical meaning of a physical-object proposition, a proposition like "There is a quarter," could in fact be captured by an incorrigible sense-data proposition, or set of such propositions, then the nagging skepticism about physical objects would have been answered for once and for all, finally.

So phenomenalism was interesting as a possible way around skepticism about the external world. It was interesting to epistemologists also simply because the precise nature of the *relationship* between, on the one hand, our beliefs about the objects of everyday experience and science (i.e., physical objects and their constituents) and, on the other hand, the sensory information that constitutes the stream of experience, has always been of interest to epistemologists. Phenomenalism is a theory about this relationship.

What I Said Is Nonsense

In *Tractatus Logico-Philosophicus*, Wittgenstein attempted to determine what the basic metaphysical structure of the world must be, given that language, as well as thought about the world, exists. His final conclusion, however, pointed up a possibly serious difficulty in this "linguistic" approach to metaphysics, in which inferences are made to the structure and nature of the world from the manner in which language is said to be related to the world.

That we can represent the world to ourselves in language entailed, according to Wittgenstein, a metaphysics that is very much like Russell's logical atomism, and the bulk of the *Tractatus* boldly set forth this metaphysics with majestic logic. To derive the metaphysics entailed by language's linkage to the world, however, Wittgenstein had to discuss just *how* language links itself to the world, and his discussion of how language represents the world was itself expressed in language. This placed Wittgenstein in the paradoxical situation of having used language to represent how language represents the world. And this, he concluded, could not be done—despite the fact that he had just done it. Language, he said, may be used to represent the world but cannot be used to represent how language represents the world. "What expresses itself in language, we cannot express by means of language."

Thus, Wittgenstein concluded the *Tractatus* with an outrageous paradox: "My propositions serve as elucidations in the following way," he wrote. "Anyone who understands me eventually recognizes them as nonsensical, when he has used them—as steps—to climb up beyond them. (He must, so to speak, throw away the ladder after he has climbed up it.)"

But at bottom, the question of whether phenomenalism is sound just simply is the question whether our supposed knowledge of an external world can be understood in purely sensory terms. It is the question, loosely speaking, of whether "reality" reduces to "appearances." The alternative, that "reality" does not reduce, that it is somehow *inferred* from the appearances, seems to leave the mind uncomfortably severed from the world.

Notice that phenomenalism is also a metaphysical theory: you believe in the existence of physical objects, don't you? And you also believe that these objects are made out of atoms and subatomic particles, just as you learned in high school science, not so? Well, if phenomenalism is correct, your belief in the existence of these things logically does not commit you to believing in anything more than sense-data.

Let us just sum up by saying this: Phenomenalism is what you get when you give content to the purely formal metaphysics of logical atomism, and logical atomism is the metaphysics implied by philosophical analysis. Phenomenalism and philosophical analysis are virtually inseparable.

For these reasons, phenomenalism was of much interest to analytic philosophy even while the world was at war. And the underlying issue of the relationship of appearance to reality has enduring significance. Selection 6.1 will help explain why phenomenalism found initial widespread acceptance.

"Phenomenalism: Its Grounds and Difficulties"   From C. H. Whiteley

49. THE MEANING OF WORDS

When I am teaching a child the meaning of the word "table," I point to the table so that he sees it; I put his hand to it, so that he feels it; that is, I cause him to sense certain sense-data. Surely it is with these sense-data that he thereupon associates the sound "table"; when he sees and feels similar sense-data, he repeats "table." It is by the differences in what they look like and feel like that he distinguishes tables from chairs and apples and half-crowns. It is natural to conclude that when he uses the word "table" or "apple," he is using it to describe what he sees, feels, tastes, etc., rather than to propound some theory about an invisible and intangible material substance.

The word "table" *means* a certain visible squareness and brownness, a certain tangible hardness; i.e., it means a certain type of sense-experience. When I say "There is a table in this room" I am describing the sense-data which I am now sensing, and if I do not sense such sense-data, then, being a truthful person, I do not say that there is a table in the room. If someone else says that there is, I test his statement by looking and feeling, i.e., by finding out whether the appropriate sense-data are available; if they are not, I dismiss his statement as false. If I say "Socrates drank his companions under the table," I am not describing any sense-experiences which I have now, but I am describing sense-experiences which I suppose Socrates and his companions to have had at another time and place.

We cannot, of course, identify "the table" with any one single sense-datum; an experience which was entirely unique and did not recur would not be worth naming. The function of words is not to name everything we see or hear, but to pick out the recurrent patterns in our experience. They identify our present sense-data as being of the same group or type as others which we have sensed before. A word, then, describes, not a single experience, but a group or type of experiences; the word "table" describes all the various sense-data which we normally refer to as appearances or sensations "of" the table. So a material thing is not indeed identical with any sense-datum; but neither is it something different in kind from sense-data. It is a group, or class, or system of sense-data; and nothing but sense-data goes to constitute it. So this doctrine may be expressed by saying that every statement we make about a material thing is equivalent to another statement about sense-data.

50. PHENOMENALISM

This analysis of the notion of a material thing is called Phenomenalism, since it makes of a material thing a group of phenomena, appearances, instead of a transcendent reality distinct from appearances. It is a widespread view, and has been accepted by many philosophers who do not call themselves Idealists and are far from accepting Berkeley's view that the fundamental reality is Mind. The term "idealism" itself, however, though it has shifted in meaning since, does properly denote just this part of Berkeley's theory, that the material world—"the whole choir of heaven and furniture of the earth" says Berkeley—consists of what he calls "ideas" and I have been calling "sense-data." The word in this sense has nothing to do with ideals, and the theory would have been called "ideaism" but for considerations of pronunciation.

Phenomenalism, then, is the doctrine that all statements about material objects can be completely analysed into statements about sense-data. The analysis of any such statement must be very complex; and the value of the "material-object language" is that it enables us to refer in one word, such as "table," to a vast number of sense-data differing very much among themselves. The group of sense-data constituting the table includes all the different views I can obtain at different distances, from different angles, in different lights, no two of them exactly alike, but all of them variations on one central pattern; it includes sense-data of touch, and those of sound (though these last seem somewhat more loosely connected with the main visuo-tactual group); and with other kinds of material things, such as apples, sense-data of taste and smell form important constituents of the thing.

51. ITS ADVANTAGES

This type of theory has certain clear advantages. On the representative theory, the very existence of a material world or of any given material object must always be in principle doubtful. I am directly aware of my sense-data, and so can be certain of their existence and character: but "material objects" are quite different—their existence and character can be known only by an inference, which cannot give the complete certainty which comes from observation. Descartes, for example, accepts this consequence of the theory, and will not allow himself to believe that there is a material world at all, until he has convinced himself that there exists an omnipotent and benevolent God who would never have led him to believe in the material world if it had not been real. But if Descartes really succeeded in keeping up this attitude of doubt for more than a moment, few men have been able to imitate him. We *cannot* believe that the existence of the table is in any way subject to doubt.

The phenomenalist theory, by making the existence of the table *the same thing* as the occurrence of certain sense-data, removes that doubt; for the system of sense-data constituting the table has beyond doubt come under my observation.

The theory not only removes the doubt, but makes it clear why we cannot seriously entertain it. The Plain Man was right after all: material things are seen and touched, are objects of direct awareness, and it is by seeing and touching that we know that they exist, though no material thing is straightforwardly identical with what I am seeing and touching *at this particular moment.*

So, by accepting the phenomenalist analysis, we escape being involved in any reference to an unobservable Matter. We can preserve our empiricism inviolate, and talk about the things we see and hear and smell and touch, and not about other hypothetical things beyond the reach of our observation. Science, the knowledge of nature, on this view becomes the recording, ordering, and forecasting of human experiences. Therein lies its interest for us. If the physical world lay outside our experience, why should we be concerned with it?

The Discrediting of Phenomenalism

Today only a few philosophers would describe themselves as phenomenalists, thanks to the strong adverse criticism of phenomenalism that emerged around the middle of the century. This criticism is complex and technical, generally too much

Private Languages?

'What I mean by 'book' or 'blue' might be entirely different from what you mean by those words, and you and I cannot really understand one another."

This thought, we'll bet, is one that has occurred to you. The empiricist in you may well think that all words ultimately derive their meaning from sense-impressions and that, because one person cannot have another person's sense-impressions, I can't really know what your words mean and vice versa. In short, we all speak **private languages,** right?

Let's pretend you are discussing the issue with a philosopher who is arguing that a private language is an impossibility. You begin with the obvious question.

YOU: And just why is it an impossibility?

PHILOSOPHER: Well, for something to be a word, you have to be able to tell whether you have used it consistently. If you have no way of telling whether you are using some sound to denote the same kind of thing each time you use it, then the sound would just be a noise, not a word.

YOU: So what follows from that?

PHILOSOPHER: Well, if no one else knew what you meant by your words, then *you* couldn't know if you had used them consistently. So then they wouldn't *be* words. They'd just be noises.

YOU: Yes, well, but *why* couldn't I know if I had used a word consistently under those circumstances?

PHILOSOPHER: Because you would only have your own memory to rely on. There would be no independent check for your belief that you used a sound like *book* to apply to the same thing today as you applied it to yesterday. Thus you would, in effect, be using *book* in any way you pleased. And a sound that you use as you please is not a word.

In this little discussion the philosopher is interpreting a sketchy argument against "private languages" laid out in Ludwig Wittgenstein's (1889–1951) *Philosophical Investigations* (published in 1953 and regarded by many as one of the most important philosophical works of this century). As mentioned in the text, phenomenalists were thought to be logically committed to the possibility of private languages. If, as was thought, Wittgenstein had shown a private language to be impossible, then phenomenalism was defective.

The question of whether a private language is impossible is interesting apart from its connection to phenomenalism, for the idea that one person really *doesn't* know what another person means by a given word is an idea that—thanks to the influence of the British empiricists on our thinking—most people find quite plausible, once they think about it. What we tend to believe is that a word stands for an idea, or some other sort of mental entity, that we think is the meaning of the word. And therefore, we think, because a word's meaning is locked up inside the mind, what each of us means by our words is private to each of us.

What Wittgenstein argued is that the whole notion of a "private language," and the theory of meaning on which it rests, is pure bunkum. The meanings of words lie not inside the mind, he said, but in their *uses,* and these uses are governed by rules. As these rules are not our own private rules, other people can check the correctness of our usage of a given word. We don't have private languages, and could not possibly have them, for in such "languages" the correctness of our usage of words is not subject to a public check. In a "private language" the "words" would just be *sounds* that one could use any way one pleased.

Why Phenomenalism Is So Plausible: Jones believes she is looking at a tomato, but if she is a philosopher, she will concede that she might be mistaken. So how can she determine whether her belief is correct? By examining what she sees, surely: by touching, tasting, smelling, and so on. In other words, she confirms (or disconforms) her belief through her senses. Thus, because her belief that she is looking at a tomato is ultimately confirmed or disconfirmed by her sense-data, it is plausible to think that her belief must really just *be* about her sense-data, as phenomenalism maintains.

so to permit discussion of it in any great detail in an introductory textbook. To simplify, however, the main lines of criticism were these:

For one thing, it became generally accepted that there is no set of sense-data, the having of which logically entails that you are experiencing any given physical object. For another, it was unclear that physical-object propositions that mention specific times and places could find their equivalents in propositions that refer only to sense-data. And finally, it was thought that phenomenalists had to believe in the possibility of what is called a **private language,** and it was questioned whether the idea of such a language is coherent (see box).

So much, then, for phenomenalism. The theory sounds good—yes, knowledge of the external world is indeed possible because to experience external objects is just to have sense-data—but alas, this response to skepticism is no longer widely regarded as viable.

Post-Phenomenalist Epistemology and Metaphysics

If you sit back for a second and consider the history of epistemology and metaphysics from Descartes onward, as we have now done, one way of characterizing this history is that it has really just been an extended search for metaphysical truth derived from *incorrigible foundations of knowledge.* (An incorrigible proposition, recall, is one that is incapable of being false if you believe it is true.)

Actually, philosophers from before Socrates to the present have searched incessantly for these incorrigible foundations. They have looked everywhere for an unshakeable bedrock on which the entire structure of knowledge, especially metaphysical knowledge, might be built. Augustine found the bedrock in revealed truth. Descartes thought that he had found it in the certainty of his own existence. Empiricists believed that the foundational bedrock of knowledge must somehow or other lie in immediate sensory experience. Kant found the foundation in principles supplied by the mind in the very act of experiencing the world.

But must a belief really rest on *incorrigible* foundations if it is to qualify as knowledge? More fundamentally, must it even rest on *foundations?* Recently philosophers have begun to question whether knowledge really requires foundations at all. Thus they have begun to question an assumption on which much of traditional epistemology rests.

Foundationalism holds that a belief qualifies as knowledge only if it logically follows from propositions that are incorrigible (incapable of being false if you believe that they are true). For example, take for one last time my belief that this before me is a quarter. According to a foundationalist from the empiricist tradition, I *know* that this before me is a quarter only if my belief that it is absolutely follows from the propositions that describe my present sense-data, because these propositions alone are incorrigible. But, the antifoundationalist argues, why not say that my belief that there is a quarter before me *automatically* qualifies as knowledge, unless there is some definite and special reason to think that it is mistaken?

The question of whether knowledge requires foundations is currently under wide discussion among epistemologists. It is too early to predict what the results of this discussion may be.

Many of those who attack the foundationalist position have been inclined, recently, to endorse what is called **naturalized epistemology.** This is the view that traditional epistemological inquiries should be replaced by psychological inquiries into the processes that are actually involved in the acquisition and revision of beliefs. This view, which in its strongest form amounts to saying that epistemology should be phased out in favor of psychology, is highly controversial. Nevertheless, much recent writing in epistemology has reflected a deep interest in developments in psychology.

Today

In the first half of the century, many philosophers (within the analytic tradition, at any rate) *assumed* that the natural sciences give us (or will eventually give us) the correct account of reality. They assumed, in other words, that natural science—and the commonsense beliefs that incorporate science—is the true metaphysics. And thus the task for philosophy, it was thought, was to *certify* scientific knowledge epistemologically. This was to be done, it was supposed, by "reducing" the propositions of science—propositions about physical objects and their atomic constituents—to propositions that refer to sense-data, i.e., by analyzing the propositions of science in the language of sensory experience. Just as mathematics was shown to

Nonpropositional Foundations

We have proceeded as if the only sort of thing that could qualify as a foundation for knowledge is some type of proposition. But could entities other than propositions serve as well? For example, could my existence *itself*, as distinct from the proposition that I exist, serve as a foundation for knowledge? Could my sense-data *themselves*, as distinct from propositions in which it is asserted that I am having them, serve as the foundations? Doesn't the elliptical silverish expanse that I am now seeing *itself* entail that I am seeing a quarter, and isn't the expanse itself therefore the foundation of my knowledge that I am seeing a quarter?

The difficulty here is that *things* don't entail anything, only propositions do. True, we do say such things as, "His laughter means he is amused," and that sounds as though his laugh, a thing, entails the proposition "He is amused." In fact, though, it is the *proposition* "He is laughing" that entails the proposition "He is amused." His laugh, the thing, *verifies* the proposition "He is laughing" and thus may *show* or *indicate* or *confirm* or *suggest* that he is amused, but it does not entail the proposition "He is amused."

So no *thing* itself could be a foundation for my knowledge because absolutely nothing follows from a thing. Nothing whatsoever follows from the elliptical silver expanse I am now sensing, although from the proposition that I am sensing an elliptical silver expanse the proposition that I am seeing a quarter may follow.

reduce to a foundation of logic, or at any rate to logic and set theory, scientific knowledge was thought to be reducible to an epistemological foundation, namely, the incorrigible knowledge of sense-data.

Eventually, though, as we have seen, philosophers became doubtful that this grand reduction could be carried out even in principle, and likewise many began to question the idea that knowledge requires foundations anyway.

In epistemology in the past couple of decades, as we have just seen, a leading alternative to foundationalism has been naturalized epistemology, which, as we have indicated, is really just the scientific study of the various processes involved in coming to have knowledge—perception, language acquisition, learning, and so forth. Now, in metaphysics during the past few decades, an alternative to the view that physical objects are constructs of sense-data has become widely held. According to this alternative to phenomenalism, physical objects are **theoretical posits,** entities whose existence we in effect hypothesize in order to explain our sensory experience. This nonreductionist view of physical objects as posited entities is also, like naturalized epistemology, associated with the work of W. V. O. Quine.

From a commonsense and scientific standpoint, physical objects are independent of the perceiving and knowing mind, independent in the sense that they are what they are regardless of what the mind thinks about them. The thesis that reality consists of such independent objects is known as **realism.** From a realist perspective, there are two epistemological possibilities: (1) we can know this independent reality; (2) we cannot know it: what is actually true may be different from what is thought to be true. The second view is skepticism, and phenomenalism was thought to be the answer to skepticism. But even if true, phenomenalism would refute skepticism only by denying realism; it would refute skepticism, that is to say, only by denying that objects are independent of the mind, or at least independent of our sense-data. The Quinean view of objects as theoretical posits is consistent with realism; however, it is also consistent with skepticism because (the skeptic would say) theoretical posits may not exist in fact.

Now it would seem that either objects exist outside the mind, or they are some sort of constructs of the mind: it would seem that either realism is true, or some form of idealism is true. But there is another possibility that some philosophers recently have been considering. To understand this third possibility, let's just consider what underlies the realist's conception. What underlies it is the idea that the mind, when it is thinking correctly about the world outside the mind, accurately conceives of this world. Alternatively put, what underlies realism is the idea that true beliefs accurately portray or *represent* reality: what makes them true is the states of affairs to which they "correspond" or that they "mirror" or "depict" or "portray." Let's call this view that beliefs about reality represent reality (either correctly, if they are true, or incorrectly, if they are false) **representationalism.** From the representationalist point of view, your belief counts as knowledge only if it is a true belief, and a belief is true only if it is an accurate representation of the state of affairs that it is about. Representationalism underlay Russell's philosophy, and the *magnus opus* of representationalism was Wittgenstein's *Tractatus Logico-Philosophicus,* commented upon in an earlier box.

But now, it is possible to question the whole premise of representationalism, and that is exactly what several recent analytic philosophers, including most famously **Richard Rorty** (1931–) are doing. **Antirepresentationalism** takes several forms; but basically, it denies that mind or language contains, or is a representation of, reality. According to the "old" picture, the representationalist picture, there is, on the one hand, the mind and its beliefs and, on the other, the world or "reality"; and if our beliefs represent reality *as it really is,* i.e., as it is "in itself" independent of any perspective or point of view, the beliefs are true. Antirepresentationalists, by contrast, dismiss this picture as unintelligible. They find no significance in the notion that beliefs represent reality (or in the notion that they fail to represent reality, if they are false beliefs); and they find no sense in the idea of the world "as it really is," i.e., as it is independent of this or that perspective or viewpoint. According to antirepresentationalists, truth is not a matter of a belief's corresponding to or accurately representing the "actual" state of affairs that obtains outside the mind. When we describe a belief as true, they hold, we are simply praising that belief as having been proven relative to our standards of rationality. And when we say that some belief is "absolutely true," we just mean that its acceptance is so fully justified, given our standards, that we cannot presently imagine how any further justification could even be possible.

Now, this conception of truth seems to imply that different and perhaps even apparently conflicting beliefs could equally well be true—as long as they are fully justified relative to alternative standards of rationality. Perhaps *you,* by contrast, would maintain that although two conflicting beliefs could be *thought* to be true, they could not actually both *be* true. But if you hold this, then it may be because you are a representationalist and think that truth is a matter of a belief's correctly representing reality—reality as it is in itself, independent of any person's or society's perspective. But antirepresentationalists do not understand, or profess not to understand, what this business about a belief's correctly representing the world "as it really is" comes to. They say that nobody can climb outside his or her own perspective, and they say that this talk about the world "as it really is independent of perspective or viewpoint" is just mumbo jumbo.

Many of the themes of Rorty's antirepresentationalism have antecedents in the philosophy of **John Dewey** (1859–1952). Dewey, the American philosopher of this century who is the most famous outside philosophy, is *not* a part of the analytic tradition (though several of his ideas have entered into analytic philosophy through Rorty, Quine, Hillary Putnam, and other contemporary American philosophers). Instead, Dewey is a part of the tradition known as American **pragmatism,** whose brightest lights, if you had to pick three of the "classic" pragmatists, were C. S. Pierce, William James, and John Dewey. To gloss over important differences in the philosophies of pragmatists, we can say that, in general, pragmatists have rejected the idea that there is such a thing as fixed, absolute truth. Instead, they have held that truth is relative to a time and place and purpose and thus is ever changing in the light of new data.

John Dewey's brand of pragmatism is known as **instrumentalism,** according to which, roughly, the forms of human activity, including thought, are instruments used by people to solve practical problems. In Dewey's view, thinking is not a search for "truth" but an activity aimed at solving individual and social problems, a means by which humans strive to achieve a satisfactory relationship with their environment.

From Dewey's perspective, metaphysics, like religious rites and cults, has been a means of "escape from the vicissitudes of existence." Instead of facing the uncertainties of a constantly changing world, metaphysicians have sought security by searching for fixed, universal, and immutable truth.

From Dewey's point of view, nature is experience. This is what he means. Objects are not fixed substances, but individual things ("existences" or "events," he called them) that are imbued with meanings. A piece of paper, for instance, means one thing to a novelist, another to someone who wants to start a fire, still another to an attorney who uses it to draw up a contract, still another to children making paper airplanes, and so on. A piece of paper is an instrument for solving a problem within a given context. What a piece of paper *is* is what it means within the context of some activity or other.

But when he held that an object is what it means within an activity, Dewey did not mean to *equate* the object with the thought about it. That was the mistake made by idealism, in Dewey's view. Idealism equated objects with thought about them and thus left out of the reckoning the particular, individual thing. Objects are not reducible to thought about objects, according to Dewey. Things have an aspect of particularity that idealism entirely neglects, he held.

But this does not mean that Dewey thought that there are fixed, immutable substances or things. The doctrine that "independent" objects exist "out there"

PROFILE / John Dewey (1859–1952)

John Dewey (1859–1952) lived almost a century. He was born before the American Civil War, and he died during the Korean War. His influence on American life was profound.

Dewey was the third of four children in his family. His father owned a grocery business, and then a tobacco business, in Burlington, Vermont, where Dewey was raised. Dewey wasn't considered a brilliant mind as a high school student, but his discovery of philosophy as a junior at the University of Vermont awakened slumbering genius. He received his PhD at Johns Hopkins and taught at Michigan, Minnesota, Chicago, and Columbia. He continued to write, publish, and lecture long after his retirement from Columbia in 1930.

Dewey exerted his greatest influence on society by virtue of his educational theories. He was an effective proponent of progressive education, which opposed formal, authoritarian methods of instruction in favor of having students learn by performing tasks that are related to their own interests. Today educational practice throughout the United States and in many areas across the world generally follows the fundamental postulates of Dewey's educational philosophy, though his belief that the school is the central institution of a democratic society is not always shared by American taxpayers.

A kind, generous, and modest man, Dewey was also an effective social critic and an influential participant in reform movements. He was utterly fearless in advocating democratic causes, even those, like women's suffrage, that were deeply unpopular. Despite having unreconcilable philosophical differences with Bertrand Russell, Dewey was active on Russell's behalf when Russell was denied permission to teach at the City College of New York in 1941 (see the profile on Russell). He was also one of the original founders of the American Civil Liberties Union.

Dewey was not the world's most inspiring public speaker, and one of his students said that you could understand his lectures only by reading your notes afterwards. Maybe the popularity of these lectures of his throughout the world despite the stylistic drawbacks is sound indication of the power of Dewey's ideas.

The bibliography of Dewey's works runs over one hundred fifty pages, and his writings touch on virtually every philosophical subject. All told, he wrote forty books and seven hundred articles. His thought dominated American philosophy throughout the first part of this century. He was and still is America's most famous philosopher.

We certainly can't list all Dewey's works, but among the most famous are *Reconstruction in Philosophy* (1920), *Human Nature and Conduct* (1922), *Experience and Nature* (1925), *The Quest for Certainty* (1929), *Art As Experience* (1934), *Freedom and Culture* (1939), and *Problems of Men* (1946).

outside the mind—realism—is called by Dewey the *"spectator theory of knowledge."* It is no more acceptable to Dewey than is idealism. On the contrary, his view was that, as the uses to which a thing is put change, the thing itself changes. To refer to the earlier example, a piece of paper is *both* (1) a particular item and (2) what is thought about it within the various and forever-changing contexts in which it is used.

Given this metaphysical perspective, from which abstract speculation about so-called eternal truths is mere escapism, it is easy to understand why Dewey was primarily interested in practical problems and actively participated in movements of social, political, and educational reform. He was effective as a social activist, too. Few individuals have had more impact on American educational, judicial, or legislative institutions than did Dewey. The educational system in which you most probably were raised, which emphasized experimentation and practice rather than abstract learning and authoritarian instructional techniques, is the result of his influence.

Richard Rorty, as we said, was much influenced by Dewey: Rorty frequently refers to himself as a "Deweyian" and a "pragmatist." Like Dewey, Rorty recommends just forgetting about trying to discover metaphysical absolutes or attempting "to get in touch with mind-independent and language-independent reality."

The next selection is from Rorty's 1991 book, *Objectivity, Relativism, and Truth.* In it Rorty explains why antirepresentationalism is not really just a newfangled form of idealism. Antirepresentationalism might seem like idealism, you see, because it *seems* to deny that there is any "truth about the way things are" that is independent of what we *believe* to be true about the way things are.

SELECTION 6.2

Objectivity, Relativism, and Truth   **From Richard Rorty**

The antirepresentationalist is quite willing to grant that our language, like our bodies, has been shaped by the environment we live in. Indeed, he or she insists on this point—the point that our minds or our language could not (as the representationalist skeptic fears) be "out of touch with the reality" any more than our bodies could. What he or she denies is that it is explanatorily useful to pick and choose among the contents of our minds or our language and say that this or that item "corresponds to" or "represents" the environment in a way that some other item does not. . . .

Antirepresentationalists . . . see no way of formulating an *independent* test of accuracy of representation—of reference or correspondence to an "antecedently determinate" reality—no test distinct from the success which is supposedly explained by this accuracy. Representationalists offer us no way of deciding whether a certain linguistic item is usefully deployed because it stands in these relations, or whether its utility is due to some factors which have nothing to do with them—as the utility of a fulcrum or a thumb has nothing to do with its "representing" or "corresponding" to the weights lifted, or the objects manipulated, with its aid. . . .

This point that there is no independent test of the accuracy of correspondence is the heart of [Hilary] Putnam's argument that notions like "reference"—semantical notions which relate language to nonlanguage—are internal to our overall view of the world. The representationalists' attempt to explain the success of astrophysics and the failure of astrology is, Putnam thinks, bound to be merely an empty compliment unless we can attain what he calls a God's-eye standpoint—one which has somehow broken out of our language and our beliefs and tested them against something known without their aid. But we have no idea what it would be like to be at that standpoint. As Davidson puts it, "there is no chance that someone can take up a vantage point for comparing conceptual schemes [e.g., the astrologer's and the astrophysicist's] by temporarily shedding his own."[8]

From the standpoint of the representationalist, the fact that notions like representation, reference, and truth are deployed in ways which are internal to a language or a theory is no reason to drop them. The fact that we can never *know* whether a "mature" physical theory, one which seems to leave nothing to be desired, may not be entirely off the mark is, representationalists say, no reason to deprive ourselves of the notion of "being off the mark." To think otherwise, they add, is to be "verificationist," undesirably anthropocentric in the same way in which nineteenth-century idealism was undesirably anthropocentric. It is to fall under the influence of what Thomas Nagel calls "a significant strain of idealism in contemporary philosophy, according to which what there is and how things are cannot go beyond what we could in principle think about."[9] Nagel thinks that to deprive ourselves of such notions as "representation" and "correspondence" would be to stop "trying to climb outside of our own minds, an effort some would regard as insane and that I regard as philosophically fundamental."[10]

Antirepresentationalists do not think such efforts insane, but they do think that the history of philosophy shows them to have been fruitless and undesirable. They think that these efforts generate the sort of pseudoproblems which Wittgenstein hoped to avoid by abandoning the picture which held him captive when he wrote the *Tractatus*. Wittgenstein was not insane when he wrote that book, but he was right when he later described himself as having been buzzing around inside a fly-bottle. His escape from the bottle was not . . . a matter of buzzing off in the direction of transcendental idealism, but rather of refusing any longer to be tempted to answer questions like "Is reality intrinsically determinate, or is its determinacy a result of our activity?" He was not suggesting that we determine the way reality is. He was suggesting that questions which we should have to climb out of our own minds to answer should not be asked. He was suggesting that both realism and idealism share representationalist presuppositions which we would be better off dropping.

---

[8]Donald Davidson, *Inquiries into Truth and Interpretation* (Oxford: Oxford University Press, 1984), p. 185.

[9]Thomas Nagel, *The View from Nowhere* (New York: Oxford University Press, 1986), p. 9.

[10]Ibid., p. 11.

We'll close this survey with a selection by University of Pittsburgh philosopher Nicholas Rescher. Note that the selection is not a reading *in* philosophy but a reading *about* philosophy, in which Rescher considers, among other things, whether contemporary American philosophy exerts influence. The title of the text you are reading emphasizes the *power* of philosophical ideas; yet you will see that Rescher thinks that contemporary American philosophy has little influence beyond the university. It is probably true that *contemporary American* philosophy has little *direct* influence outside academia, though this situation shows some signs of changing. But still, contemporary American philosophy's influence on society, though indirect, has not been insignificant, because what happens in the academy affects what happens beyond its walls.

As one interesting example of this influence, an example that relates to what we've covered in this chapter, Rorty and other American philosophers from the pragmatic and analytic traditions, as well as such Continental philosophers as Jürgen Habermas, Michel Foucault, and Jacques Derrida (all discussed in Chapter 15), have provided a philosophical framework or defense for a kind of *relativism* that has many adherents in American higher education these days, especially in the humanities. This popular academic relativism (to which the philosophers mentioned above may not subscribe in so many words) holds there is no absolute truth and maintains, as a corollary, that the purpose of education therefore cannot be to pass the torch of truth. The university must therefore be, it is thought, just one more instrument for accomplishing social and political objectives. It is held that, in the past, these objectives included the suppression and subjugation and marginalization of women and minorities, and that now education must be used to ensure equality and social justice. These ideas have had a *profound* effect not only on university policies, standards, curriculum, and pedagogy but also on social and political thought beyond the academy, as reflected in current debates on affirmative action, feminism, and multiculturalism.

Other examples of contemporary American philosophy's impact on society include developments in applied ethics (Chapter 8), feminism (Chapter 11), and Cognitive Science (Chapter 14). Nevertheless, Rescher is correct that the impact has been indirect, and mainly via the university. Philosophy's influence on society clearly has not always been indirect (as will become especially obvious when we turn to political philosophy in Part 3), and possibly will not remain so.

SELECTION 6.3

American Philosophy Today and Other Philosophical Studies*

From Nicholas Rescher

Do American philosophers exert influence? Here, of course, the critical question is: Upon whom? First consider: upon *other philosophers*. We have already remarked that the extent to which even "the leading philosophers" manage

*Rescher's footnotes omitted.

to influence others is highly fragmentary—in each case only a small sector of the entire group being involved. Turning now to *the wider society at large,* it must be said that the answer is emphatically negative. American philosophers are not opinion-shapers: they do not have access to the media, to the political establishment, to the "think tanks" that seek to mold public opinion. Insofar as they exert an external influence at all, it is confined to *academics* of other fields. Professors of government may read John Rawls, professors of literature Richard Rorty, professors of linguistics W. V. Quine. But, outside the academy, the writings of such important contemporary American philosophers exert no influence. It was otherwise earlier in the century—in the era of philosophers like William James, John Dewey, and George Santayana—when the writings of individual philosophers set the stage for at least some discussions and debates among a wider public. But it is certainly not so in the America of today. Philosophers (and academics in general) play very little role in the molding of an "informed public opinion" in the U.S.—such work is largely done by publicists, filmmakers, and talk-show hosts. American society today does not reflect the concerns of philosophers but the very reverse is the case—where "relevant" at all, the writings of philosophers reflect the concerns of the society.

Many philosophers are not enthusiastic about this. For American philosophers by and large see themselves, accurately enough, as cultivating one academic specialty in contrast to others— as technicians working in the realm of ideas. And this means that they generally write for an audience of their fellow academics and have little interest in (or prospect of) addressing a wider public of intelligent readers at large. (This is another significant difference between the philosophical situation in North America and in continental Europe.) American philosophy is oriented to academia and academics. By contrast, European—and especially French—philosophy is oriented to the wider culture-complex of an intelligent readership through a concern with currently controverted issues. On this basis "political correctness," which has become a hotbed of controversy on various American campuses, has made comparatively little impact among philosophers—unlike the situation with practitioners of such fields as legal or literary theory.

Outside of rather limited circles, philosophers in America are still expected to give reasons for their contentions, rather than painting those who dissent with the brush of fashionably attuned disapproval—let alone by calling names. The high degree of its technical professionalism has tended to countervail against the pervasive politicization of the field.

The prominence of specialization gives a more professional and technical cast to contemporary American philosophizing in comparison to that of other times and places.... All the same, its increasing specialization has impelled philosophy towards the ivory tower. And so, the most recent years have accordingly seen something of a fall from grace of philosophy in American culture—not that there was ever all that much grace to fall from. For many years, the *Encyclopaedia Britannica* published an annual supplement entitled *19XY Book of the Year,* dealing with the events of the previous year under such rubrics as World Politics, Health, Music, etc. Until the 1977 volume's coverage of the preceding year's developments, a section of philosophy was always included in this annual series. But thereafter, philosophy vanished—without so much as a word of explanation. Seemingly the year of America's bicentennial saw the disappearance of philosophy from the domain of things that interest Americans. At approximately the same time, *Who's Who in America* drastically curtailed its coverage of philosophers (and academics generally). And during this same time period, various vehicles of public opinion—ranging from *Time* magazine to the *New York Times*—voiced laments over the irrelevance of contemporary philosophy to the problems of the human condition and the narcissistic absorption of philosophers in logical and linguistic technicalities that rendered the discipline irrelevant to the problems and interests of nonspecialists. It is remarkable that this outburst of popular alienation from philosophy's ivorytowerishness came at just the time when philosophers in the U.S. were beginning to turn with relish to the problems on the agenda of public policy and personal concern. The flowering of applied ethics (medical ethics, business ethics, environmental ethics, and the like), of virtue ethics (trust, hope, neighborliness, etc.), of social ethics (distributive justice, privacy, individual rights, etc.) and of such philosophical hyphenations as philosophy-and-society—and even philosophy-and-agriculture!—can also be dated from just this period. By one of those ironies not uncommon in the pages of history, philosophy returned to the issues of the day at virtually the very moment when the wider public gave up thinking of the discipline as relevant to its concerns.

The fact is that philosophy has little or no place in American popular (as opposed to *academic*) culture, since at this level people's impetus to global understanding is accommodated—in America, at least—by religion rather than philosophy. Philosophical issues are by nature complicated, and Americans do not relish complications and have a marked preference for answers over questions. The nature of the case is such that philosophers must resort to careful distinctions and saving qualifications. And in this regard Americans do not want to know where the complexities lurk but yearn for the proverbial one-armed experts who do not constantly say "on the other hand." We are a practical people who want efficient solutions (as witness the vast market for self-help books with their dogmatic nostrums).

However, while philosophy nowadays makes virtually no impact on the wider culture of North America, its place in higher education is secure. To be sure, of all undergraduates in American colleges and universities, only about half of one percent *major* in philosophy (compared with nearly three percent for English and over fifteen percent for business and management). But owing to philosophy's role in meeting "distribution requirements" it has secured a prominent place in curriculum of postsecondary education. Unlike the United King-

dom, where post–World War II philosophers held a very technical and narrowly conceived idea of what the job of philosophy is—with the result of effectively assuring the discipline's declining role in the educational system—in America philosophy has managed not only to survive but to thrive in higher education. It has done so in large measure by taking a practicalist and accommodationist turn. American philosophers have been very flexible in bending with the wind. When society demands "relevancy to social concerns" a new specialty of "applied philosophers" springs forth to provide it. When problems of medical ethics or of feminist perspectivism occupy the society, a bevy of eager young philosophical spirits stands ready to leap into the breach.

And so, there is no question that philosophy is alive and well in America today. As long as it maintains its place in collegiate education with at least two or three competent representatives at each of those several thousand institutions that grant baccalaureate degrees, it will continue as an active and productive venture.

It should occasion no surprise that philosophical activity flourishes on the American academic scene in a way that reflects wider social concerns. Of the forty-five thematic sessions on the program of the American Philosophical Association's Eastern Division in 1991, six were devoted to feminist themes and two to issues relating to blacks. This dedication of some fifteen percent of program space to these issues prominent on the agenda of present-day U.S. politics is clearly not accidental, but it does not reflect a comparable prominence of these topics in the current journal literature of the subject, where (as the *Philosopher's Index* entries indicate) the aggregate space occupied by these themes is diminutive. To a cynic, it might seem that American philosophers are seeking to offset the underrepresentation of women and blacks in their ranks by throwing words at the issues involved. (In this regard philosophers are akin to politicians, a consideration that invites second thoughts about Plato's philosopher-kings.)

Sometimes, however, what at first sight looks like a large-scale phenomenon is only the large shadow cast by a smallish object. This seems to be the case with feminist philosophy in North America. At present there are only two journals in the field (*Feminist Studies, Hypatia*) and only two societies (*Society for Analytical Feminism, Society for Women in Philosophy*). As far as philosophy goes, academic feminism, however prominent elsewhere, is at present still no more than a statistically minor blip. (To be sure, the shift from nothing to something is always a big one.)

Insofar as American philosophers collect themselves into biological groupings of (comparatively) substantial size, this conformation is based not on factors of substance (of doctrinal agreement) but on factors of style (of methodological commonality). One major grouping—the "Analysts" as they have come to be called—adopts a scientific model of philosophizing and looks to the sort of detailed investigation by logico-linguistic methods of analysis that was introduced into Anglo-American philosophy in the era of G. E. Moore and Bertrand Russell. The other major affinity grouping—the "Pluralists"—look to continental models of philosophizing through reappraisals of the grand tradition of Western philosophy in the manner prominent in German philosophy in the era from Dilthey to Heidegger. Different culture-heroes are at issue, and different modes of procedure. The one "school" seeks to use the machinery of logic and formal semantics to extract philosophical juice from science and common sense, the other employs the methodology of historical and humanistic studies to extract lessons from the materials of cultural and intellectual history. The upshot is a difference in the substance of philosophizing that roots in a difference in the style of philosophical practice engendered by looking to rather different models of philosophizing. (However, the recent trend towards specialization and the division of labor is just as prominent among the pluralists as among the analysts.) Analysts often as not focus upon doctrines rather than writers. They generally discuss intellectual artifacts in the manner of the introduction, "I take a realist to be someone who endorses the following three theses . . ." where no actual person has ever propounded those theses together in exactly that form. By contrast, the "continental" style of philosophizing addresses the real (or supposedly real) views of identified philosophers—with different writers having somewhat different ideas about membership in the list of canonical authorities, each having a personal register of the good and the wicked.

An interesting—and unexpected—aspect of contemporary American philosophy relates to the fate of "pragmatism." The high priests of this quintessentially American tendency of thought—C. S. Peirce, William James, John Dewey, and C. I. Lewis—while entertaining rather different conceptions of the doctrine at issue, were all agreed on the central point that there is a cogent *standard* for assessing the merit for cognitive products (ideas, theories, methods)—a standard whose basis of validity reaches outside the realm of pure theory into the area of practical application and implementation. For them the ultimate test of our intellectual artifacts lay in seeing them as instrumentalities of effective praxis—in their ability to serve the communal purposes for whose sake and publicity available resources are instituted. But in recent years many philosophers who have laid claim to the label of "pragmatism" have subjected the traditional doctrine to a drastic sea change. Where the classical pragmatists sought in applicative efficacy a test of objective adequacy—an individual-transcending reality principle to offset the vagaries of personal reactions—the pseudo-pragmatists turn their backs on the pursuit of objectivity and impersonality. For traditional pragmatism's communal concern with "what works out *for us* (humans in general)" they have perversely substituted an egocentrism of "what works out *for me* (or *for you*)." The defining object of the pragmatic tradition—the search for objective and impersonal standards—is shattered into a fragmentation of individual impressions in the parochial setting of a limited culture context. We have a total dissolution—that is, destruction—of the classical pragmatic approach that saw the rational validity of intellectual artifacts to reside in the capacity to provide effective guidance in the successful conduct of our extra-theoretical affairs—in matters of prediction, planning, successful intervention in the course of nature, and other such-like aspects of the successful conduct of our practical activities.

The large ongoing response to writers such as Heidegger, Derrida, and their epigones clearly shows that there is more academic hay to be made nowadays by debunking metaphysics and epistemology as traditionally conceived than by practicing them. In this light, one of the striking and paradoxical features of American philosophy today is the widespread assault by a disaffected avant-garde against the discipline as standardly practiced. On many fronts a *fin de siècle* [end-of-the-century] disillusionment with the enterprise is coming to expression and a distaste for actual scholarship is widely manifest among the avant-garde. Some argue—be it on the basis of scepticism or relativism or scientism—that we have entered a "post-philosophical era," where philosophy as traditionally conceived is no longer viable. Others argue on neo-Marxist grounds that interest (not necessarily economic but also cultural or social) is what determines all and that old-style would-be rational philosophy is simply a covering for sexist, racist, or culturalist prejudices. Traditional philosophizing is viewed as mere ideology that should be dismissed as the prejudicial vaporings of dead white males, and the politically correct thing to do is to abandon philosophy as a venture in inappropriate elitism. Other critiques of philosophizing issue from a philosophy-external basis. Followers of the "critical studies" trend of literacy analysis propose to deconstruct philosophical discourse to a point of a variety that renders rational deliberation unrealizable. From the vantage point of such a "postmodernist" disdain for reason, traditional philosophy's commitment to the methodology of reflective analysis and impartial reasonableness continues to earn for it the sort of opposition encountered by Socrates at the very outset of the enterprise. However, the fact that any critical examination of the scope and merits of philosophy will itself form part of the philosophical venture at large—that metaphilosophy is a part of philosophy—continues to assure the discipline with a lively future despite all such critical opposition.

Checklist

To help you review, here is a checklist of the key philosophers and concepts of this chapter. The brief descriptive sentences summarize leading ideas. Keep in mind that some of these summary statements represent terrific oversimplifications of complex positions.

Analytic   ## Philosophers

- **Bertrand Russell** Held that analysis is the key to metaphysical truth. Sought the connection between the "hard" data actually given in experience (sense-data) and supposedly "external," physical (and scientific) objects.

_142_ - **G. E. Moore** Colleague of Russell; influential advocate of the importance of philosophical analysis.

_142-4_ - **Ludwig Wittgenstein** Derived a metaphysics of logical atomism from a consideration of the relationship of language and the world. Advanced the picture theory of meaning, then later rejected it.

- **W. V. O. Quine** American analytic philosopher; questioned whether it is possible to specify the meaning of an expression in an absolute sense. Initial leading advocate of naturalized epistemology.

- **Richard Rorty** Leading American antirepresentationalist. Rejects the idea that truth is a matter of a belief's accurately representing the world as it really is.

- **John Dewey** Instrumentalist; said that thinking is not a search for "truth," but is aimed at solving practical problems. Believed that metaphysics is escapism.

Concepts

_138_ nihilism   _rejection of values & beliefs_

existentialism   _life is irrational + absurd_

_139_ analysis   _simplification_

_143_ Vienna Circle   _mostly Schlick et al. admirers of Russell + Wittgenstein_

—logical positivism   _philo is not theory but logical clarification of thought_

now considered invalid —verifiability criterion of meaning   _unverifiable statements are meaningless ie reason is the substance of Unive or I love you or good vs bad_

_145_ the paradox of analysis   _GE Moore Analysis are either incorrect or trivial_

_146_ logical atomism   _world is a collection of corelated atomic facts_

atomic fact   _Not reducible_

_148_ picture theory of meaning

_148_ language game   _Context_

_149_ sense-data   _Awareness_

_150_ phenomenalism   _objects expressible only as sense data_

_150_ incorrigible   _incapable of being false_

_154_ private language   _impossible - meaningless sounds_

incorrigible foundations of knowledge

foundationalism

naturalized epistemology

theoretical posits

realism

representationalism

antirepresentationalism

pragmatism

instrumentalism

spectator theory of knowledge

Questions for Discussion and Review

1. What does philosophical analysis do? In other words, define philosophical analysis.

2. What is accomplished by the use of philosophical analysis?

3. "Square circles are nonexistent things." "No squares are circles." Which of these two propositions is simpler, philosophically, and why?

4. What is the verifiability criterion of meaning?

5. Explain, in your own words, the paradox of analysis.

6. "The first woman president of the United States is unmarried." Is this sentence true or false or neither? Explain why.   *Neither*

7. What does it mean to say there are "atomic" facts?

8. "If X might exist but we have no reason to suppose that it actually does exist, then as metaphysicians we should not concern ourselves with X." Evaluate this principle.

9. Apply the principle stated in the preceding question by letting X stand for God, ghosts, and space aliens.

10. Explain what phenomenalism is and why so many philosophers accepted it as a sound theory.

11. Can you know that physical objects exist when no one is perceiving them?

12. Explain the logical positivists' reasons for holding that all metaphysics is meaningless.

13. "Everything doubled in size last night." Critically evaluate this remark.

14. "At least in part, a thing is what is thought about it within the various contexts in which it is used." Evaluate this claim.

15. Explain the difference between representationalism and antirepresentationalism.

Suggested Further Readings

A. J. Ayer, *Language, Truth and Logic,* 2nd rev. ed. (New York: Dover, 1946). Stimulating. Ayer explains the basic positivist position in strong language.

A. J. Ayer, *Philosophy in the Twentieth Century* (London: Allen & Unwin, 1984). A partisan yet lucid account of developments in twentieth-century philosophy.

A. J. Ayer, ed., *Logical Positivism* (Glencoe, Ill.: Free Press, 1959). An important anthology that contains essays both sympathetic to and critical of analytic philosophy and positivism, as well as an excellent bibliography.

David Bell and Neal Cooper, eds., *The Analytic Tradition* (Cambridge, Mass.: Basil Black-well, 1990). A series of essays on the nature of analytic philosophy and its place in current debate.

Edwin A. Burtt, *The Metaphysical Foundations of Modern Physical Science: A Historical and Critical Essay* (London: Routledge & Kegan Paul, 1932). Many regard this as the most important philosophical treatise on science.

William Charlton, *The Analytic Ambition* (Cambridge, Mass.: Basil Blackwell, 1991). A basic introduction for beginners to analytic philosophy.

John Dewey, *The Quest for Certainty* (New York: Minton Balch & Company, 1929). One of Dewey's most popular works. Portrays metaphysics as a quest for certainty.

Cora Diamond, *Wittgenstein, Philosophy, and the Mind* (Cambridge, Mass.: Bradford, 1991). Considered by some to be one of the more important recent books on Wittgenstein.

Christopher Hookway, *Skepticism* (New York: Routledge, 1990). A review of the historical development of skepticism and its consequences for present-day thought and action.

John Hospers, *An Introduction to Philosophical Analysis* (Englewood Cliffs, N.J.: Prentice-Hall, 1953). This is what you should read as the next step in acquainting yourself with analytic philosophy.

Hilary Kornblith, *Naturalizing Epistemology,* 2nd ed. (Cambridge, Mass.: Bradford, 1993). An anthology of papers that consider the interaction between psychology and epistemology. Not always easy to read.

Norman Malcolm, "Wittgenstein's Philosophical Investigations," *Philosophical Review* 47 (1956). A reasonably readable explication of important aspects of Wittgenstein's difficult work.

P. K. Moser and A. vander Nat, *Human Knowledge: Classical and Contemporary Approaches* (New York: Oxford University Press, 1987). Excellent anthology of readings, both classical and recent.

John Passmore, *A Hundred Years of Philosophy* (New York: Basic Books, 1967). Excellent, readable general history from Mill on to mid-century.

D. F. Pears, *Bertrand Russell and the British Tradition in Philosophy* (New York: Random House, 1967). Traces the development of Russell's metaphysics from 1905 to 1919.

Hilary Putnam, *Realism and Reason. Philosophical Papers,* vol. 3 (London: Cambridge University Press, 1983). An important work that covers most of the current hot topics in metaphysics and epistemology, by an influential American philosopher. Putnam typically begins his essays in nontechnical language, but also typically can become difficult.

Nicholas Rescher, *American Philosophy Today and Other Philosophical Studies* (Lanham, Md.: Rowman & Littlefield, 1994). A collection of interesting essays on various topics.

George D. Romanos, *Quine and Analytic Philosophy* (Cambridge, Mass.: Bradford, 1983). A good, brief history of analytic philosophy; fine bibliography.

Richard Rorty, *Objectivity, Relativism, and Truth. Philosophical Papers,* vol. 1 (New York: Cambridge University Press, 1991). Explains the antirepresentationalist/representationalist debate in language that will not entirely discourage a beginner in philosophy.

Bertrand Russell, *Autobiography,* 3 vols. (London: George Allen & Unwin, 1967–1969). Candid and highly entertaining.

Bertrand Russell, "The Philosophy of Logical Atomism," in *Logic and Knowledge,* R. C. Marsh, ed. (London: George Allen & Unwin, 1956). Introductory students will find this difficult to read but not impossible.

Barry Stroud, *The Significance of Philosophical Scepticism* (Oxford: Clarendon Press, 1985). Sets forth some of the current issues related to skepticism.

Richard Taylor, *Metaphysics,* 3rd ed. (Englewood Cliffs, N.J.: Prentice-Hall, 1983). An easy introduction to popular metaphysical issues, including the "mind-body problem" and free will.

J. O. Urmson, *Philosophical Analysis* (London: Oxford University Press, 1956). Surveys logical atomism and logical positivism. Not easy reading for introductory students, but detailed and complete.

Geoffrey James Warnock, *English Philosophy Since 1900* (New York: Oxford University Press, 1958). Only covers the first part of the century but is accurate and very easy to read.

Cornel West, *The American Evasion of Philosophy, a Genealogy of Pragmatism* (London: Macmillan, 1989). A critical review of American pragmatism, including such figures as James, Peirce, Dewey, Mills, Quine, and Rawls.

Michael Williams, *Groundless Belief: An Essay on the Possibility of Epistemology* (New Haven: Yale University Press, 1977). Written for philosophers, this book may be tough for the layperson. But it sets forth in clear detail some of the difficulties in foundationalism.

Ludwig Wittgenstein, *Philosophical Investigations,* G. E. M. Anscombe, trans. (Oxford: University Press, 1953). Contains Wittgenstein's attack on private languages, but it is rather bewildering to the layperson (and to the professional philosopher, too). An easy introduction to Wittgenstein's philosophy is George Pitcher's *Wittgenstein, The Philosophical Investigations* (Garden City, N.Y.: Doubleday Anchor, 1966).

Metaphysics and Epistemology: Existence and Knowledge

Summary and Conclusion

Metaphysical speculation was essential to technological mastery of the world, for metaphysics began with those questions that must be asked if there is to be any deeper understanding of the natural order. These are the questions first raised by the pre-Socratics, who sought to comprehend and explain the complex world that we see in terms of a simpler underlying reality. This recognition is required for the full and fruitful development of science and technology.

Also, as we have seen, metaphysics was important to religion, especially the Christian religion. Christianity incorporates many metaphysical elements. Without the Platonic and Neoplatonic interpretations given to it by Augustine, and without the Aristotelian interpretations given to it by Aquinas, Christianity, if it had survived, would have done so in a far different form from that in which it did.

Metaphysical speculation, then, was essential to the emergence of science and was vital to the history of religion. It is scarcely surprising, therefore, that much of what today seems to be common sense is a by-product of metaphysics. For example, today's commonsense dualism, according to which both physical and non-physical things exist, is really nothing more than Cartesian metaphysics. Descartes did not invent this metaphysics out of whole cloth, of course, for his dualism was essentially the two-worlds view of Plato that, with certain changes, had been incorporated into Christianity by Augustine and transmitted down through the ages to Descartes for further refinement and modification.

PART 2

Ethics:
The Moral Order

Ethics Through Hume

7

Happiness, then, is something final and self-sufficient, and is the end of action.

—Aristotle

Morality is not properly the doctrine how we should make ourselves happy, but how we should become worthy of happiness.

—Immanuel Kant

Advice is something you never stop getting, although good, sound advice is perhaps not too common.

Most advice you get—and give—is of a practical nature: "If you want to live longer," someone will say, "you should stop smoking." Or, "If I were you, I'd buy life insurance now while you're young."

But advice is not always intended to be merely practical. Sometimes it is moral advice. Someone—a friend, your minister, a relative—may suggest that you should do something not because it will be in your own best interest to do it, but because doing it is *morally right*. The suggestion expresses a moral judgment.

Ethics is the philosophical study of **moral judgments—value judgments** about what is virtuous or base, just or unjust, morally right or wrong, morally good or bad or evil, morally proper or improper. We say *morally* right and *morally* good and so on because terms like *right* and *good* and *proper* (and their negative correlates *wrong* and *bad* and *improper*) can be used in *nonmoral* value judgments, as when someone speaks of a bad wine or of the right or proper way to throw a pass.

Many questions can be asked about moral judgments, so ethical philosophers discuss quite a wide array of issues. One pretty basic question they ask is: What *is* a moral judgment? In other words, exactly what does it mean to describe something as morally right or wrong, good or evil; what is it to say that one thing ought to be done and another thing ought not be done? Or, they might ask alternatively, what makes a moral judgment a *moral* judgment? How do moral judgments differ from

Ethical Skepticism

Three currently widely accepted doctrines about morals are *skepticism, relativism,* and *subjectivism.* We'll talk about relativism and subjectivism later.

Ethical skepticism is the doctrine that moral knowledge is not possible. According to the skeptic, whether there are moral standards is not knowable, or, alternatively, if there are any moral standards, we cannot know what they are. It ought to be noted that the beliefs that there is no right or wrong and that "everything is permissible" are *not* skeptical beliefs.

The person who says that everything is permissible, or that there is no right or wrong, does claim to have moral knowledge.

Sometimes the Sophists (see text) are viewed as ethical skeptics because even though they demanded rational justification for moral principles, they also seemed to think that rational justification can be devised for alternative and conflicting moral principles. That is, they seemed to think that conflicting moral principles are equally provable, and if they are equally provable, then moral knowledge would not seem obtainable. But the Sophists are also sometimes viewed as believing that you are free to choose whatever standards you want, and this belief seems to imply that there are no absolute moral standards. The two views of the Sophists do not appear entirely compatible because, according to the first, the Sophists were skeptics and, according to the second, they were not. Which interpretation is correct is controversial.

other value judgments, factual assertions, and pieces of practical advice? What distinguishes reasoning about moral issues from reasoning about other things (from reasoning about the structure of matter, say, or about the qualities of good art)? These are some of the questions ethical philosophers ask.

The most important question of ethics, however, is just simply: Which moral judgments are correct? That is, what *is* good and just and the morally right thing to do? What is the "moral law," anyway? This question is important because the answer to it tells us how we should conduct our affairs. Perhaps it is the most important question, not of ethics, but of philosophy. Perhaps it is the most important question, period.

A less obvious question of ethics, though logically more fundamental, is whether there is a moral law in the first place. In other words, do moral obligations even exist? Are there really such things as good and bad, right and wrong? And if there are, what is it that makes one thing right and another wrong? That is, what is the ultimate justification of moral standards?

In what follows we'll examine some of these issues, and related questions, as they have been treated through the history of philosophy.

The Early Greeks

That moral judgments must be supported by reasons is an idea we owe to the **Sophists,** those professional teachers of fifth-century-B.C. Greece, and to **Socrates**

Relativism

Relativism is a popular idea about ethics these days, and many people describe themselves as "relativists."

Now, there are various kinds of relativist doctrines. One very popular doctrine is **descriptive relativism,** according to which the moral standards people subscribe to differ from culture to culture and from society to society.

Descriptive relativism may well be true, though that it is true is not as obvious as it might seem at first glance. For example, suppose one culture approves of abortion and another doesn't. Do they have different moral standards? Perhaps. But perhaps not. They both might accept the standard that it is wrong to kill a *living person* but just differ about whether a fetus counts as a living person. Different practices, in short, do not necessarily entail different standards.

Descriptive relativism, however, is not really an ethical doctrine. It is a *nonprescriptive* and *empirical* doctrine about differences in cultural beliefs and attitudes. A *prescriptive* doctrine is **ethical relativism,** which has two versions. According to **individual relativism,** what is right is what you believe is right: right (and wrong) are relative to the individual's beliefs and standards. According to **cultural relativism,** what is right (as distinguished from what is believed to be right) is what your culture believes is right: right (and wrong) are relative to a culture or society.

Both versions of ethical relativism actually qualify as subjectivist doctrines (see box on subjectivism) because according to both versions, what makes true moral propositions true is the opinions of people: relativists seem committed to holding that there are no "objective" moral truths, truths that hold independently of people's beliefs.

Cultural relativists sometimes say that you should abide by the moral standards of your culture or society. However, the prescription "Abide by the standards of your culture!" seems itself not to be a relativistic pronouncement at all. On the contrary, it seems very absolute and universalistic, because it is presumably supposed to apply to anyone, regardless of his or her culture.

Cultural relativists also sometimes advocate toleration for the morals of other cultures. However, a cultural relativist who advocates toleration would be guilty of inconsistency if his or her culture does not advocate toleration.

(c. 470–399 B.C.). The Sophists, who attacked the traditional moral values of the Greek aristocracy, demanded rational justification for rules of conduct, as did Socrates. Their demands, together with Socrates' skillful deployment of the dialectical method in moral discussions, mark the beginning of philosophical reasoning about moral issues.

Maybe it wasn't inevitable that a time came when someone would insist that moral claims be defended by reasons. When children ask why they should do something their parents think is right, they may be content to receive, and their parents content to give, the simple answer, "Because that is what is done." In some societies, evidently, values are accepted without much question, and demands for justification of moral claims are not issued. In our society it is frequently otherwise, and this is the legacy of the Sophists and Socrates.

It was Socrates especially who championed the use of reason in moral deliberation and with it raised good questions about some still-popular ideas about

Subjectivism

Subjectivism, along with relativism and skepticism (which we already mentioned) is a very popular belief these days. The subjectivist holds that right and wrong, good and bad (i.e., ethical standards in general) depend entirely on the opinions of people: take away people's opinions about right and wrong and good and bad, and right and wrong, good and bad go away.

One currently popular subjectivist belief is that ethical standards are determined by what you yourself believe: what is right is what you believe is right. (This belief is also sometimes called *individual relativism.*) If *you* find this idea plausible (do you?), you should know this: although this idea is accepted by some philosophers and is very popular outside the discipline, many other philosophers regard it as ridiculous.

For one thing, they say, the view entails the presumably absurd notion that an action is neither right nor wrong until *you* have thought about it. This would mean, among other things, that before your birth no acts were either right or wrong and no person was either moral or immoral. The view also entails, the critics say, another absurd notion: If what is right is what you believe is right, then you cannot be mistaken in your moral beliefs. Did you once think that something was right and then later change your mind and come to think that it was wrong? Well, if what is right is what you believe is right, then that thing, whatever it was, *was* right until you changed your mind—and then it *became* wrong. How can your changing your mind turn an act that was right into an act that was wrong? Surely, critics of subjectivism would say, what has changed is not the rightness of the act, but your opinion about its rightness.

morality, such as that good is what pleases, that might makes right, and that happiness comes only to the ruthless.

Socrates was also concerned with the meaning of words that signify moral virtues, words like *justice, piety,* and *courage.* Because a moral term can be correctly applied to various specific acts—many different types of deeds count as courageous deeds, for example—Socrates believed that all acts characterized by a given moral term *must have something in common.* He therefore sought to determine (without notable success, we are sorry to report) what the essential commonality is. Socrates' assumption that a virtue has an essential nature, an essence that may be disclosed through rational inquiry, is still made by many philosophers and is central to several famous ethical theories, including Plato's, as you will shortly see.

Socrates also assumed that any sane person who possessed knowledge of the essence of virtue could not fail to act virtuously. He thus believed that ignoble behavior, if not the result of utter insanity, is always the product of ignorance. This is also a view that Plato shared, and it has its adherents today. .

Plato

So Plato accepted the Socratic idea that all things named by a given term, including any given moral term, share a common essential or "defining" feature. For example, what is common to all things called *chairs* (yes, we know *chair* is not a moral term, but it will illustrate the point) is that feature by virtue of which a thing qualifies as a chair. What is common to all brave deeds is that feature that qualifies them all as brave. This essential or defining characteristic Plato referred to as the **Form** of the things in question; and, for various quite plausible reasons, he regarded this Form as possessing more reality than the particular things that exemplified it. We talked about this in Chapter 2, but let's look into Plato's reasoning again, for this bears closely on Plato's ethics.

For a thing to be a chair, we think you must agree, it must possess that feature that qualifies a thing as a chair. That feature—let us call it *chairness*—is what Plato called the Form. And so, for a thing to qualify as a chair, it must possess chairness. Thus, the Form *chairness* must exist if anything at all is to qualify as a chair. So the Form is more fundamental and "real" than even the chair you're sitting on or any other chair.

Forms, Plato held, are not perceptible to the senses, for what the senses perceive are individual things: particular chairs, particular people, particular brave deeds, and so forth. Through the senses we just don't perceive the Forms. We can't see chairness; and we cannot reach out and grasp bravery or humanity. Thus Forms, he maintained, are known only through reason.

Further, according to Plato, the individual things that we perceive by sense are forever changing. Some things—rocks, for example—change very slowly. Other things, such as people, change a good bit more rapidly. That means that knowledge by sense perception is uncertain and unstable. Not so knowledge of the Forms. Knowledge of the Forms is certain and stable, for the objects known—the Forms—are eternal and unchanging.

Now the various Forms, Plato maintained (and here we'll see what all this has to do with ethics)—the various Forms constitute a *hierarchy* in terms of their inherent value or worth. It's easy enough to understand his point. For example, doesn't the Form *beauty* (i.e., the essence of beautiful things) seem to you to be inherently of more worth than a Form like *wartness* (i.e., the essence of warts)?

At the apex of all Forms, Plato said, is the Form *goodness*, or (as it is often expressed) *the Good*, because it is the Form of highest value. Thus, for Plato, because

a. the Forms define true reality, and because

b. the Form of the Good is the uppermost of all Forms, it follows that

c. individual things are real only insofar as they partake of or exemplify this ultimate Form.

A corollary of (c) is that things are less "real" the less they partake of the Good. Another corollary is that evil is unreal. Make a mental note of this second idea. We will come across it again.

Because the Form of the Good is the source of all value and reality, Plato believed, we must strive to obtain knowledge and understanding of it. This notion seems reasonable enough, surely. Therefore, he maintained, because (remember) Forms can be apprehended only by reason, you and we should govern ourselves by reason. Similarly, the state should be ruled by intellectuals, he said, but more of this in Part 3.

So, to summarize to this point, according to Plato the true reality of individual things consists in the Forms they exemplify, Forms that are apprehended by reason and not by the senses, and the Form highest in value is the Form of the Good. One should therefore strive for knowledge of the Good and hence be ruled by reason.

But now consider this moral edict that Plato has in effect laid down: "Be governed by reason!" Is this not a little too abstract? Does it not fail to enjoin anything *specific* about what the individual should or should not do?

Plato would have answered "no" to both questions. The human soul, he said (a couple of thousand years before Freud proposed an analogous theory), has three different elements: an element consisting of raw appetites, an element consisting of drives (like anger and ambition), and an intellectual element (i.e., an element of thought or reason). For each of these elements there is an excellence or virtue that obtains when reason is in charge of that element, as is the case when you govern yourself by reason. When our *appetites* are ruled by reason, we exhibit the virtue of *temperance;* when our *drives* are governed by reason, we exhibit *courage;* and when the *intellect* itself is governed by reason, we exhibit *wisdom.*

Thus, Plato held, the well-governed person, the person ruled by reason, exhibits the four cardinal virtues of temperance, courage, wisdom, and "justice." How did justice get in the list? Justice is the virtue that obtains when all elements of the soul function as they should in obedience to reason.

So, given Plato's understanding of the soul, the principle "Be governed by reason," which follows from the theory of Forms, dictates that you be temperate, courageous, wise, and "just." And what, in turn, *these* dictates mean more specifically was much discussed by Plato, though we won't go into the details. Further, he said, only by being virtuous—that is, by possessing these four virtues—can you have a *well-ordered soul* and thus have the psychological well-being that is true happiness. In this way Plato connected virtue with happiness, a connection we still acknowledge by saying, "Virtue is its own reward."

But is a well-ordered or "just" or virtuous soul really required for happiness? Plato did not just assert that it is and expect us to close our eyes and blindly swallow the assertion. He knew as well as anyone that exactly the opposite seems to be true: that the people who seem to be the best off often seem to be very unscrupulous. So Plato examined the matter rather carefully, especially in the *Republic.* In that dialogue, Plato has various characters explain and defend the view that the life of the person who cleverly and subtly promotes his own ends at the expense of other people is *preferable* to the life of the virtuous person. Plato (in the person of his Socrates character) does think that this view is mistaken and attempts (at considerable length) to explain what is wrong with it—this attempt actually is the main theme of the *Republic.* Whether he succeeds you may wish to consider for yourself at some point. In any case, a more powerful defense of being *unjust* and *unvirtuous* than the one Plato sets forth (and tries to refute) in the *Republic* has never been devised.

Plato and Divine-Command Ethics

These days a popular idea in Western (and other) societies is that what is morally right and good is determined by divine command, that is, by the edict or decree of God. This is yet another popular idea about morality that Plato examined, and the result of that examination was a question: Is something right or good because the gods (or God) decree that it is, or is it decreed by the gods (or God) as right or good because it is right or good? (If the question interests you, you might wish to read Plato's very short dialogue *Euthyphro*.)

Some critics of "divine-command" theories of ethics argue that Plato's question puts the adherents of these theories in an awkward position. If you say that God decrees that something is good because it *is* good, then you seem to imply that God is not the ultimate authority or the ultimate source of goodness: you seem to imply that there is something beyond God that makes good things good things. But if, on the other hand, you say that something is good because God decrees that it is good, you seem to imply that God's decrees are arbitrary: He could just as well have decreed that that thing was not good.

In short, the question implies—so it is argued—that either God's moral prescriptions are arbitrary or that God is not the ultimate source of goodness.

a God who is Good would not arbitrarily declare Something good if it was not.

Sometimes beginning philosophy students have difficulty seeing how Plato's theories apply to their own lives. Here, though, there seems to be direct applicability. Chances are that from time to time you find yourself in situations in which, apparently, the right or proper or just or virtuous thing to do seems to conflict with the course of action you think would benefit you the most or make you the happiest. In such situations you may not be sure what to do. But now if Plato is right, if you think there is a conflict, you haven't thought these situations through carefully enough. For if he is right, the virtuous course of action is the one most apt to produce your own well-being.

Of course, you may agree with Plato's conclusion, that the virtuous course of action is the one most apt to produce your own well-being, because you believe that God will reward you in an afterlife if you are virtuous here and now and punish you if you aren't. Notice, though, what you are assuming if you accept this belief, namely, that virtuous activity does *not* promote its own reward (i.e., happiness) in *this* life. Plato, though, believed that your well-being in *this* life is best promoted by virtuous activity. *Life is not fair*

Plato's moral philosophy is applicable in other ways. He was also very interested in such popular views (popular both then and now and perhaps forevermore) as that *goodness is the same thing as pleasure*, that *self-control is not the best way to get happiness*, and that *it is better to exploit others than to be exploited by them*. He found, when he considered these ideas carefully, that they are mistaken. So if you are tempted to agree with any of these ideas, we recommend that you read the *Republic* and another famous Platonic dialogue, the *Gorgias*, before arranging your affairs in the belief that they are true. We shall present a brief excerpt from the *Gorgias* in Selection 7.1.

Is the Objective World Value-Neutral?

According to Plato, the Form of the Good is the source of all that is real. It is itself real, of course (according to Plato), and, moreover, has a reality independent of our minds. In other words, it has *objective* reality.

Many people these days are inclined to think of **objective reality**—reality as it exists outside our minds and perceptions—as morally neutral. So far as they've considered the issue at all, they regard values as subjective creations of the mind that the mind superimposes on events and objects, which things are themselves neither good nor bad, right nor wrong. It is very, very likely that this is your view.

Still, *if* it is a fact that the universe "as it is in itself" is value-neutral, this is not a fact that we *discovered* in the same way that we discovered the principles of physics, chemistry, and biology. Rather, it seems to be something we just *believe*. Is this belief more correct than the view of Plato, who thought that what is good does not depend on our opinions but is set by, and is inherent in, a reality external to our minds?

If you think Plato is wrong, how would you establish that?

A Complete Ethical Theory

Plato's moral philosophy is often cited as a *complete* ethical theory.[1] It

- Identifies an *ultimate source of all value* (the Form of the Good).
- Sets forth a *metaphysical justification for accepting this source as ultimate* (the theory of Forms).
- Stipulates a *fundamental moral principle* ("Be governed by reason!").
- Provides a *rationale for accepting the principle as universally binding* (the Form of the Good is the source of all that is real).
- Specifies *how knowledge of the supreme intrinsic good is obtained* (only through reasoning).
- Finally, holds that *obedience to the moral principle is motivated.* For in being governed by reason, you meet the conditions that are necessary and sufficient for the well-being of the soul and thus for true happiness. An additional motivation to accept the governance of reason, according to Plato, is that in doing so, you may obtain knowledge of the Forms. This knowledge is desirable to have because the Forms are unchanging and hence eternal, and that means that when you come to know them, you gain access to immortality.

For these reasons, then, Plato's ethics is said to have provided philosophers with a standard of completeness. Measure your own ethics by this standard.

---

[1] For the concept of a complete ethical theory and this analysis of Plato's ethics as a complete ethical theory, we are indebted to Professor Rollin Workman.

Selection 7.1 is from Plato's *Gorgias*. In it Callicles begins with the frank statement that the best way to live is to allow your desires to get as strong as possible and not to restrain them. Socrates (Plato) then engages Callicles in a brief discussion of this issue and tries to show him that his view leads to the absurd conclusion that the best life would be that of a catamite (someone who keeps young boys around for sexual perversions) or, more generally, the life of a person who does nothing better than continually scratch some terrifically itchy bodily part. Then Socrates examines (and refutes) yet another idea of Callicles, namely, that the good and the pleasant are one and the same.

SELECTION 7.1

Gorgias

From Plato

SOCRATES: The way you pursue your argument, speaking frankly as you do, certainly does you credit, Callicles. For you are now saying clearly what others are thinking but are unwilling to say. I beg you, then, not to relax in any way, so that it may really become clear how we're to live. Tell me: are you saying that if a person is to be the kind of person he should be, he shouldn't restrain his appetites but let them become as large as possible and then should procure their fulfillment from some source or other, and that this is excellence?

CALLICLES: Yes, that's what I'm saying. . . .

SOCRATES: Come then. . . . Consider whether what you're saying about each life, the life of the self-controlled man and that of the undisciplined one, is like this: Suppose there are two men, each of whom has many jars. The jars belonging to one of them are sound and full, one with wine, another with honey, a third with milk, and many others with lots of other things. And suppose that the sources of each of these things are scarce and difficult to come by, procurable only with much toil and trouble. Now the one man, having filled up his jars, doesn't pour anything more into them and gives them no further thought. He can relax over them. As for the other one, he too has resources that can

be procured, though with difficulty, but his containers are leaky and rotten. He's forced to keep on filling them, day and night, or else he suffers extreme pain. Now since each life is the way I describe it, are you saying that the life of the undisciplined man is happier than that of the orderly man? When I say this, do I at all persuade you to concede that the orderly life is better than the undisciplined one, or do I not?

CALLICLES: You do not, Socrates. The man who has filled himself up has no pleasure any more, and when he's been filled up and experiences neither joy nor pain, that's living like a stone, as I was saying just now. Rather, living pleasantly consists in this: having as much as possible flow in.

SOCRATES: Isn't it necessary, then, that if there's a lot flowing in, there should also be a lot going out and that there should be big holes for what's passed out?

CALLICLES: Certainly.

SOCRATES: Now you're talking about the life of a stonecurlew[33] instead of that of a corpse or a stone. Tell me, do you say that there is such a

---

[33]"A bird of messy habits and uncertain identity," Dodds. [In other words, a bird that fouls its nest.]

thing as hunger, and eating when one is hungry?

CALLICLES: Yes, there is.

SOCRATES: And thirst, and drinking when one is thirsty?

CALLICLES: Yes, and also having all other appetites and being able to fill them and enjoy it, and so live happily.

SOCRATES: Very good, my good man! Do carry on the way you've begun, and take care not to be ashamed. And I evidently shouldn't shrink from being ashamed, either. Tell me now first whether a man who has an itch and scratches it and can scratch to his heart's content, scratching his whole life long, can also live happily.

CALLICLES: What nonsense, Socrates. You're a regular crowd pleaser.

SOCRATES: That's just how I shocked Polus and Gorgias and made them be ashamed. *You* certainly won't be shocked, however, or be ashamed, for you're a brave man. Just answer me, please.

CALLICLES: I say that even the man who scratches would have a pleasant life.

SOCRATES: And if a pleasant one, a happy one, too?

CALLICLES: Yes indeed.

SOCRATES: What if he scratches only his head— or what am I to ask you further? See what you'll answer if somebody asked you one after the other every question that comes next. And isn't the climax of this sort of thing, the life of catamites, a frightfully shameful and miserable one? Or will you have the nerve to say that they are happy as long as they have what they need to their hearts' content?

CALLICLES: Aren't you ashamed, Socrates, to bring our discussion to such matters?

SOCRATES: Is it I who bring them there, my splendid fellow, or is it the man who claims, just like that, that those who enjoy themselves, however they may be doing it, are happy, and doesn't discriminate between good kinds of pleasures and bad? Tell me now too whether you say that

the pleasant and the good are the same or whether there is some pleasure that isn't good.

CALLICLES: Well, to keep my argument from being inconsistent if I say that they're different, I say they're the same.

SOCRATES: . . . Tell me: don't you think that those who do well have the opposite experience of those who do badly?

CALLICLES: Yes, I do.

SOCRATES: Now since these experiences are the opposites of each other, isn't it necessary that it's just the same with them as it is with health and disease? For a man isn't both healthy and sick at the same time, I take it, nor does he get rid of both health and disease at the same time.

CALLICLES: What do you mean?

SOCRATES: Take any part of the body you like, for example, and think about it. A man can have a disease of the eyes, can't he, to which we give the name "eye disease"?

CALLICLES: Of course.

SOCRATES: But then surely his eyes aren't also healthy at the same time?

CALLICLES: No, not in any way.

SOCRATES: What if he gets rid of his eye disease? Does he then also get rid of his eyes' health and so in the end he's rid of both at the same time?

CALLICLES: No, not in the least.

SOCRATES: For that, I suppose, is an amazing and unintelligible thing to happen, isn't it?

CALLICLES: Yes, it very much is.

SOCRATES: But he acquires and loses each of them successively, I suppose.

CALLICLES: Yes, I agree.

SOCRATES: Isn't it like this with strength and weakness, too?

CALLICLES: Yes.

SOCRATES: And with speed and slowness?

CALLICLES: Yes, that's right.

SOCRATES: Now does he acquire and get rid of good things and happiness, and their opposites, bad things and misery, successively too?

CALLICLES: No doubt he does.

SOCRATES: So if we find things that a man both gets rid of and keeps at the same time, it's clear that these things wouldn't be what's good and what's bad. Are we agreed on that? Think very carefully about it and tell me.

CALLICLES: Yes, I agree most emphatically.

SOCRATES: Go back, now, to what we've agreed on previously. You mentioned hunger—as a pleasant or a painful thing? I mean the hunger itself.

CALLICLES: As a painful thing. But for a hungry man to eat is pleasant.

SOCRATES: I agree. I understand. But the hunger itself is painful, isn't it?

CALLICLES: So I say.

SOCRATES: And thirst is, too?

CALLICLES: Very much so.

SOCRATES: Am I to ask any further, or do you agree that every deficiency and appetite is painful?

CALLICLES: I do. No need to ask.

SOCRATES: Fair enough. Wouldn't you say that, for a thirsty person, to drink is something pleasant?

CALLICLES: Yes, I would.

SOCRATES: And in the case you speak of, "a thirsty person" means "a person who's in pain," I take it?

CALLICLES: Yes.

SOCRATES: And drinking is a filling of the deficiency, and is a pleasure?

CALLICLES: Yes.

SOCRATES: Now, don't you mean that insofar as a person is drinking, he's feeling enjoyment?

CALLICLES: Very much so.

SOCRATES: Even though he's thirsty?

CALLICLES: Yes, I agree.

SOCRATES: Even though he's in pain?

CALLICLES: Yes.

SOCRATES: Do you observe the result, that when you say that a thirsty person drinks, you're saying that a person who's in pain simultaneously feels enjoyment? Or doesn't this happen simultaneously in the same place, in the soul or in the body as you like? I don't suppose it makes any difference which. Is this so or not?

CALLICLES: It is.

SOCRATES: But you do say that it's impossible for a person who's doing well to be doing badly at the same time.

CALLICLES: Yes, I do.

SOCRATES: Yet you did agree that it's possible for a person in pain to feel enjoyment.

CALLICLES: Apparently.

SOCRATES: So, feeling enjoyment isn't the same as doing well, and being in pain isn't the same as doing badly, and the result is that what's pleasant turns out to be different from what's good.

CALLICLES: I don't know what your clever remarks amount to, Socrates.

SOCRATES: You do know. You're just pretending you don't, Callicles. Go just a bit further ahead.

CALLICLES: Why do you keep up this nonsense?

SOCRATES: So you'll know how wise you are in scolding me. Doesn't each of us stop being thirsty and stop feeling pleasure at the same time as a result of drinking?

CALLICLES: I don't know what you mean.

GORGIAS: Not at all, Callicles! Answer him for our benefit too, so that the discussion may be carried through.

CALLICLES: But Socrates is always like this, Gorgias. He keeps questioning people on matters that are trivial, hardly worthwhile, and refutes them!

GORGIAS: What difference does that make to you? It's none of your business to appraise them, Callicles. You promised Socrates that he could try to refute you in any way he liked.

CALLICLES: Go ahead, then, and ask these trivial, petty questions, since that's what pleases Gorgias.

SOCRATES: You're a happy man, Callicles, in that you've been initiated into the greater mysteries before the lesser. I didn't think it was permitted. So answer where you left off, and tell me whether each of us stops feeling pleasure at the same time as he stops being thirsty.

CALLICLES: That's my view.

SOCRATES: And doesn't he also stop having pleasures at the same time as he stops being hungry or stops having the other appetites?

CALLICLES: That's so.

SOCRATES: Doesn't he then also stop having pains and pleasures at the same time?

CALLICLES: Yes.

SOCRATES: But, he certainly doesn't stop having good things and bad things at the same time, as you agree. Don't you still agree?

CALLICLES: Yes I do. Why?

SOCRATES: Because it turns out that good things are not the same as pleasant ones, and bad things not the same as painful ones. For pleasant and painful things come to a stop simultaneously, whereas good things and bad ones do not, because they are in fact different things. How then could pleasant things be the same as good ones and painful things the same as bad ones?

Aesara, the Lucanian

Aesara, a Greek woman philosopher from Lucania (in southern Italy), probably lived around 350 B.C. Only a fragment of her original work survives.

Aesara claimed that the human soul has three parts: the mind, spiritedness, and desire. The mind analyzes ideas and reaches decisions. Spiritedness is the part of the soul that gives a person the ability to carry out decisions. Desire contains moral emotions such as love. Much of the rest of the fragment explains why her account of the nature and structure of the human soul is correct.

The fragment, which is reprinted below, can be read four different ways. First, read it to get a feel for Aesara's view of the structure of the soul, and why she thinks it pretty much has to be the way she describes it. Second, read it as though it were a sketch of human psychology, with the human *psyche* consisting of the intellect (Aesara's "mind"), the will (Aesara's "spiritedness"), and the positive affective emotions (Aesara's "desire").

Third, take a close look at the opening sentence: "Human nature seems to me to provide a standard of law and justice both for the home and for the city." It's extremely important, and easy to overlook. The role of women in ancient Greek society was to stay at home and raise virtuous, rational offspring, the male versions of which would run the world of government and the marketplace—the world outside the home. As a woman, Aesara was keenly aware that men, even men philosophers, sometimes tended to think that justice applies only to the world outside the home. Do you need two different approaches to moral philosophy: virtue ethics for raising good kids, and theories of justice for the institutions (government and marketplace) through which we deal with people outside our family?

Aesara's answer to that question would be "no." *All* morally significant decisions, whether regarding our families or the state, should reflect the appropriate proportions of reason, love, and will-power. Think about parents disciplining children. *Reason* makes the parents weigh the seriousness of what the child did wrong, along with other factors, including the child's ability to understand the wrongfulness of her act. *Love* motivates the parents to discipline in the first place, and to take into account extenuating circumstances—such as that the child was tired, frightened, or confused when she did something wrong. *Spiritedness* or *will* enables the parent to carry out the unpleasant chore of disciplining and also to refrain from acting out of anger toward the child.

Now, finally, reread the fragment, this time focusing on how the human soul is the model for society. Aesara thought that if you understood the nature of the soul, you could understand how society and, in particular, social justice ought to be. (Plato, too, believed this, as we shall see in Chapter 9.) If law and justice were structured like the human soul, they would be thoughtful. They would take into account all relevant ideas and principles. If they were judgmental, they would reflect the society's shared social judgments about people's obligations and duties. The legal system would contain good laws that deterred lawlessness and served as guidelines for good behavior. On Aesara's account of the structure of the soul as a model for government, it could also be argued that law and justice should be characterized by love. Law should be created to reflect our mutual care, concern, and consideration for others. In the administration of justice, judges should take into account special circumstances under which people might be excused for not obeying the law.

SELECTION 7.2

On Human Nature **From Aesara, Pythagorean of Lucania**

Human nature seems to me to provide a standard of law and justice both for the home and for the city. Through introspection, whoever seeks will make a discovery: law is in us. Justice, which is the orderly arrangement of the soul, is also in us.

The human soul is organized in accordance with its three functions. The mind is that part of the soul which has the capacity for judgment and thoughtfulness. High spirit is that part of the soul which is our capacity for strength, the ability to act. Desire is the part of the soul that includes our capacity for love and kindliness. These parts of the soul are all disposed relative to one another so that the best part is in com-

mand, the most inferior is governed, and the one in between holds a middle place; it both governs and is governed.

God made human nature this way, according to principle. That principle is reflected in both the outline and completion of the human body, because he intended humans alone to become a recipient of law and Justice, and none other of mortal animals.

The human soul is therefore a composite unity of association. Now, a unity of association could not come about from a single thing, nor indeed from several things which are all alike. For it is necessary, since the functions to be performed by the parts of the soul are different, that the parts of the soul also be different. In this sense, the structure of the soul is analogous to the structure of the body. The organs of touch and sight and hearing and taste and smell differ, for these do not all have the same ability to sense the same properties of things.

Nor could the unity come from several dissimilar things assembled together at random. Rather, the unity of the soul derives from the fact that its parts are each formed in accordance with a plan for completion and organization and fitting together of the entire composite whole. Not only is the soul composed from several dissimilar parts, but these parts are fashioned to conform to each other to make the whole, complete soul. In addition these parts of the soul are not arranged haphazardly and at random, but in accordance with rational attention.

What if each part of the soul had an equal share of power and honor, in their control of human action? If all parts were equally able to control human action, even though they were themselves morally unequal (some were inferior, some better, some in between) the association of parts throughout the soul could not have been fitted together. Or, even if they did have an unequal share, but the morally inferior rather than the morally superior had the greater share of power over human action, there would be great folly and disorder in the soul. And what if the morally superior part of the soul had the greater control, and the morally inferior part had the least control, but each of these not in the proper proportion? Then, there could not be

unanimity and friendship and justice throughout the soul, since when each one is arranged in accordance with the suitable proportion, this sort of arrangement I assert to be justice.

And indeed, a certain psychological and moral unanimity and agreement in sentiment accompanies such an arrangement. This sort of arrangement of the parts of the soul would justly be called good order. The good order is due to the better part's ruling and the inferior's being ruled. Such an arrangement of the parts of the soul should add the strength of virtue to the soul. Friendship and love and kindliness, and everything related to them, will sprout from these parts. For closely-inspecting mind persuades, desire loves, and high spirit is filled with strength where it once may have been seething with hatred, it becomes friendly to desire.

Mind having fitted the pleasant together with the painful, mingling also the tense and robust with the slight and relaxed portion of the soul, each part is distributed in accordance with its appropriate and suitable concern for each moral decision to be made. Mind closely inspecting and tracking out things, high spirit adding impetuosity and strength to what is closely inspected, and desire or affection, adapts to the mind, preserving the pleasant as its own and giving up the thoughtful to the thoughtful part of the soul. By virtue of these things the best life for humans seems to me to be whenever the pleasant should be mixed with the earnest, and pleasure with virtue. Mind is able to fit these things to itself, becoming lovely through systematic education and virtue.

Aristotle

The ultimate source of all value for Plato was the Form of the Good, an entity that is distinct from the particular things that populate the natural world, the world we perceive through our senses. This Platonic idea, that all value is grounded in a *nonnatural* source, is an element of Plato's philosophy that is found in many ethical systems and is quite recognizable in Christian ethics. But not every ethical system postulates a nonnatural source of value.

Those systems that do not are called *naturalistic ethical systems.* According to **ethical naturalism,** moral judgments are really judgments of fact about the natural world. Thus Aristotle, for instance, who was the first great ethical naturalist, believed that the good for us is defined by our natural objective.

Now, what would you say is our principal or highest objective by nature? According to Aristotle, it is the attainment of happiness, for it is that alone that we seek for its own sake. And, because the attainment of happiness is naturally our highest objective, it follows that happiness is our highest good.

In what does happiness, our highest good, consist, according to Aristotle? To answer, we must consider man's function, he said. To discover what goodness is for an ax or a chisel or anything whatsoever, we must consider its function, what it actually does. And when we consider what the human animal does, as a *human* animal, we see that, most essentially, it (a) lives and (b) reasons.

Thus happiness consists of two things, Aristotle concluded: *enjoyment (pleasure)* and the *exercise and development of the capacity to reason.* It consists in part of enjoyment because the human being, as a living thing, has biological needs and impulses the satisfaction of which is pleasurable. And it consists in part of developing and exercising the capacity to reason, because only the human being, as distinct from other living things, has that capacity. Because this capacity differentiates humans from other living things, its exercise is stressed by Aristotle as the most important component of happiness. Pleasure alone does not constitute happiness, he insists.

The exercise of our unique and distinctive capacity to reason is termed by Aristotle *virtue*—thus Aristotle's famous phrase that happiness is activity in accordance with virtue. There are two different kinds of virtues. To exercise actively our reasoning abilities, as when we study nature or cogitate about something, is to be *intellectually* virtuous. But we also exercise our rational capacity by moderating our impulses and appetites, and when we do this, we are said by Aristotle to be *morally* virtuous.

The largest part of Aristotle's major ethical work, the *Nicomachean Ethics,* is devoted to analysis of specific moral virtues, which Aristotle held to be the *mean between extremes* (e.g., courage is the mean between fearing everything and fearing nothing). He emphasized as well that virtue is a matter of *habit:* just as an ax that is only occasionally sharp does not fulfill its function well, the human who exercises his rational capacities only occasionally does not fulfill his function, that is, is not virtuous.

Aristotle also had the important insight that a person's pleasures reveal his true moral character. "He who faces danger with pleasure, or, at any rate, without pain, is courageous," he observed, "but he to whom this is painful is a coward." Of course, we might object that he who is willing to face danger *despite* the pain it brings him is the most courageous, but this is a quibble.

So Aristotle's ethics were basically naturalistic: human good is defined by human nature. Plato's were nonnaturalistic: goodness in all its manifestations is

The Good Life

We (the authors, Moore and Bruder) view philosophy as valuable and applicable to real life. But then, we may be biased, because we get paid to philosophize. Nevertheless, here is a case in favor of our view:

As you read about the moral philosophies of Plato, Aristotle, and almost every other thinker covered in Part 2, you might note their concern with the question, *In what does human happiness or well-being or the good life consist?* Maybe this question is not the *central* question of ethics, but it is close to the center. You might say that just about every philosopher we cover in this part of the book offers an alternative answer to this question. The question is also of considerable practical importance—and worth considering *now*. Ultimately, we all die, and sometimes, unfortunately, people die sooner, sometimes much sooner, than they expected. To get a clear focus on this question only to learn that it is too late to do anything about it could be a great tragedy.

Maybe you will find something in this and the next chapter to help you settle on your own answer.

Instrumental and Intrinsic Ends

A distinction of some importance made by Aristotle is that between instrumental ends and intrinsic ends. An **instrumental end** is an act performed as a means to other ends. An **intrinsic end** is an act performed for its own sake.

For example, when we, Bruder and Moore, sat down to write this book, our end was to finish it. But that end was merely instrumental to another end: providing our readers with a better understanding of philosophy.

But now notice that the last goal, the goal of providing our readers with a better understanding of philosophy, is instrumental to a further end, namely, an enlightened society.

Notice, too, that when your teacher grades you and the other students in the class, that act is instrumental to your learning, and that end also is instrumental to an enlightened society.

As a matter of fact, all the activities in the university are aimed at producing an enlightened society. For example, your teacher may recently have received a promotion. Promotions are instrumental to effective teaching in your university, and effective teaching also is instrumental to an enlightened society.

But notice that that end, an enlightened society, is merely instrumental to another end, at least according to Aristotle. For why have an enlightened society? An enlightened society is good, Aristotle would say, because in such a society people will be able to fulfill their natural function as human beings. And therefore, he would say, when we understand what the natural function of people is, then we finally will know what is intrinsically good, good for its own sake. Then we will know what the "Good of Man" is.

defined by the Form of the Good. Despite these differences, Aristotle and Plato would doubtless have agreed to a great extent in their praise and condemnation of the activities of other people. Aristotle, too, deemed the cardinal moral virtues to be courage, temperance, justice, and wisdom, and both he and Plato advocated the intellectual life.

Notice, too, that Plato and Aristotle both conceive of ethics as focusing on good *character traits* of individuals–virtues–rather than on a set of *rules for actions* (such as: treat others as you would have others treat you). In recent years there has been considerable interest among Anglo-American philosophers in this type of ethical theory, which is known as **virtue ethics.** From the point of view of virtue ethics, the fundamental ethical question is not so much, "What ought one do?" but rather, "What kind of person ought one be?"

Nevertheless, despite these similarities, it must be kept in mind that the ultimate source of all moral value—that is, the Good—was for Plato a nonnatural "Form," whereas Aristotle sought to define the good for humans in terms of what the human organism in fact naturally seeks, namely, happiness.

Ever since Aristotle's time, ethical systems have tended to fall into one of two categories: those that find the supreme moral good as something that *transcends* nature, and thus follow the lead of Plato, and those that follow Aristotle by grounding morality *in* human nature.

SELECTION 7.3

The Nicomachean Ethics   **From Aristotle**

Leaving these matters, then, let us return once more to the question, what this good can be of which we are in search.

It seems to be different in different kinds of action and in different arts—one thing in medicine and another in war, and so on. What then is the good in each of these cases? Surely that for the sake of which all else is done. And that in medicine is health, in war is victory, in building is a house—, a different thing in each different case, but always in whatever we do and in whatever we choose, the end. For it is always for the sake of the end that all else is done.

If then there be one end of all that man does, this end will be the realizable good—or these ends, if there be more than one.

Our argument has thus come round by a different path to the same point as before. This point we must try to explain more clearly.

We see that there are many ends. But some of these are chosen only as means, as wealth, flutes,

and the whole class of instruments. And so it is plain that not all ends are final.

But the best of all things must, we conceive, be something final.

If then there be only one final end, this will be what we are seeking,—or if there be more than one, then the most final of them.

Now that which is pursued as an end in itself is more final than that which is pursued as means to something else, and that which is never chosen as means than that which is chosen both as an end in itself and as means, and that is strictly final which is always chosen as an end in itself and never as means.

Happiness seems more than anything else to answer to this description: for we always choose it for itself, and never for the sake of something else: while honour and pleasure and reason, and all virtue or excellence, we choose partly indeed for themselves (for, apart from any result, we should choose each of them), but partly also for the sake of happiness, supposing that they will help to make us happy. But no one chooses happiness for the sake of these things, or as a means to anything at all.

We seem to be led to the same conclusion when we start from the notion of self-sufficiency.

The final good is thought to be self-sufficing. In applying this term we do not regard a man as an individual leading a solitary life, but we also take account of parents, children, wife, and, in short, friends and fellow-citizens generally, since man is naturally a social being. Some limit must indeed be set to this; for if you go on to parents and descendants and friends of friends, you will never come to a stop. But this we will consider further on: for the present we will take self-sufficing to mean what by itself makes life desirable and in want of nothing. And happiness is believed to answer to this description.

And further, happiness is believed to be the most desirable thing in the world, and that not merely as one among other good things: if it were merely one among other good things, it is plain that the addition of the least of other goods must make it more desirable; for the addition becomes a surplus of good, and of two goods the greater is always more desirable.

Thus it seems that happiness is something final and self-sufficing, and is the end of all that man does.

But perhaps the reader thinks that though no one will dispute the statement that happiness is the best thing in the world, yet a still more precise definition of it is needed.

This will best be gained, I think, by asking, What is the function of man? For as the goodness and the excellence of a piper or a sculptor, or the practiser of any art, and generally of those who have any function or business to do, lies in that function, so man's good would seem to lie in his function, if he has one.

But can we suppose that, while a carpenter and a cobbler has a function and a business of his own, man has no business and no function

assigned him by nature? Nay, surely as his several members, eye and hand and foot, plainly have each his own function, so we must suppose that man also has some function over and above all these.

What then is it?

Life evidently he has in common even with the plants, but we want that which is peculiar to him. We must exclude, therefore, the life of mere nutrition and growth.

Next to this comes the life of sense; but this too he plainly shares with horses and cattle and all kinds of animals.

There remains then the life whereby he acts—the life of his rational nature, with its two sides or divisions, one rational as obeying reason, the other rational as having and exercising reason.

But as this expression is ambiguous, we must be understood to mean thereby the life that consists in the exercise of the faculties; for this seems to be more properly entitled to the name.

The function of man, then, is exercise of his vital faculties on one side in obedience to reason, and on the other side with reason.

But what is called the function of a man of any profession and the function of a man who is good in that profession are generically the same, e.g., of a harper and of a good harper; and this holds in all cases without exception, only that in the case of the latter his superior excellence at his work is added, for we say a harper's function is to harp, and a good harper's to harp well.

Man's function then being, as we say, a kind of life—that is to say, exercise of his faculties and action of various kinds with reason—the good man's function is to do well and beautifully.

But the function of anything is done well when it is done in accordance with the proper excellence of that thing.

Putting all this together, then, we find that the good of a man is exercise of his faculties in accordance with excellence or virtue, or, if there be more than one, in accordance with the best and most complete virtue.

But there must also be a full term of years for this exercise; for one swallow or one fine day does not make a spring, nor does one day or any small space of time make a blessed or happy man.

This, then, may be taken as a rough outline of the good.

Epicureanism and Stoicism

In the Greek and Roman period following Aristotle, there were four main "schools" of philosophy, the Epicureans, the Stoics, the Skeptics, and the Neoplatonists. The Neoplatonists were discussed in Chapter 3.

The Skeptics, remember from Chapter 3, denied the possibility of all knowledge, and this denial included moral knowledge. They said that no judgments can be established, and it doesn't matter if the judgments are factual judgments or value judgments. Accordingly, they advocated tolerance toward others, detachment from the concerns of others, and caution in your own actions. Whether the Skeptics were *consistent* in advocating toleration, detachment, and caution while maintaining that no moral judgment can be established you might consider for yourself.

Epicureanism and Stoicism, which mainly concern us in this chapter, were both naturalistic ethical philosophies, and both had a lasting effect on philosophy and ethics. To this day, "taking things philosophically" means responding to disappointments as a Stoic would, and the word *epicure* has its own place in the everyday English found outside the philosophy classroom.

Epicureanism

Epicureanism began with **Epicurus** (341–270 B.C.), flourished in the second and first centuries B.C., spread to Rome, and survived as a school until almost the third century A.D. Though few today would call themselves Epicureans, there is no question that many people still subscribe to some of the central tenets of this philosophy. You may do so yourself. We do.

According to Epicurus, it is natural for us to seek a pleasant life above all other things; it follows, he reasoned (as perhaps you will, too), that we ought to seek a pleasant life above all other things. In this sense Epicurus was a naturalist in ethics.

The pleasant life, Epicurus said, comes to you when your desires are satisfied. And there are three kinds of desires, he maintained:

- Those that are *natural and must be satisfied* for one to have a pleasant life (such as the desire for food and shelter)

- Those that, *though natural, need not necessarily be satisfied* for a pleasant life (including, for example, the desire for sexual gratification)
- Those that are *neither natural nor necessary* to satisfy (such as the desire for wealth or fame)

The pleasant life is best achieved, Epicurus believed, by neglecting the third kind of desire and satisfying only desires of the first kind, though desires of the second kind may also be satisfied, he said, when doing so does not lead to discomfort or pain. It is *never* prudent to try to satisfy unnecessary/unnatural desires, he said, for in the long run trying to do so will produce disappointment, dissatisfaction, discomfort, or poor health. There is, surely, much that is reasonable in this philosophy, even though many people spend a good bit of time and energy in trying to satisfy precisely those desires that, according to Epicurus, are both unnecessary and unnatural.

As is evident, Epicurus favored the pleasant *life* over momentary pleasures and attached great importance to the avoidance of pain as the prime ingredient in the pleasant life. It is one of the great ironies of philosophy that the word *epicure* is often used to denote a person devoted to the indulgence of sensuous pleasures. Epicurus was certainly not an epicure in this sense, for he recommended a life of relaxation, repose, and moderation and avoidance of the pleasures of the flesh and passions. He would not have been fond of lavish vacations or the typical Sunday afternoon tailgate party.

The Stoics

If Epicurus was not exactly an epicure (at least in one meaning of the word), were the Stoics stoical? A stoic is a person who maintains a calm indifference to pain and suffering, and yes, the Stoics were stoical.

The school was founded by **Zeno** (334–262 B.C.), who met his students on the *stoa* (Greek for "porch"). Stoicism spread to Rome and survived as a school until almost the third century A.D. Its most famous adherents, other than Zeno, were **Cleanthes** (303–233 B.C.), **Cicero** (106–43 B.C.), **Epictetus** (A.D. 60–117), **Seneca** (c. 4 B.C.–A.D. 65), and **Marcus Aurelius,** the Roman emperor (A.D. 121–180).

Like the Epicureans, the Stoics believed that it is only natural for a person to seek a pleasant life and that therefore a person ought to seek such a life. But the Stoics were much influenced by the Cynics (see box on Diogenes), who went *out of their way* to find hardship. The Stoics saw that the Cynics, by actively pursuing hardship, acquired the ability to remain untroubled by the pains and disappointments of life. They (the Stoics) thought there was some sense in this. It occurred to them that untroubledness or serenity is a desirable state indeed.

The Stoics, however, more than the Cynics, had a *metaphysical justification* for their ethics. All that occurs, the Stoics believed, occurs in accordance with natural law, which they equated with reason. **Natural law,** they said, is the vital force that activates or (as we might say) energizes all things. It follows that

The Go-for-It Philosophy of Aristippus

At about the time Plato lived in Athens, another Greek, **Aristippus** (435–350 B.C.), who lived in Cyrene, espoused an ethical doctrine quite different from Plato's. Aristippus said our lives should always be dedicated to the acquisition of as many pleasures, preferably as intense as possible, as we can possibly obtain. Even when intense pleasures lead to subsequent pain, they should still be sought, he said, for a life without pleasure or pain would be unredeemingly boring. Pleasures are best obtained, according to Aristippus, when one takes control of a situation and other people and uses them to one's own advantage.

Perhaps you know people who agree with Aristippus.

Cyrenaicism, which is the name of this hedonistic (pleasure-seeking) philosophy, was the historical antecedent of Epicureanism. As you can see from the text, Epicurus's pleasure-oriented philosophy is considerably more moderate than Aristippus's. Epicurus recommended avoiding intense pleasure as producing too much pain and disappointment over the long run.

1. Whatever happens is the inevitable outcome of the logic of the universe.
2. Whatever happens, happens with a reason and therefore is for the best.

So, according to the Stoic philosophy, you can do nothing to alter the course of events because they have been fixed by the law of nature. Do not struggle against the inevitable, they said. Instead, understand that what is happening is for the best, and accept it.

If you're wise, according to the Stoics, you'll approach life as an actor approaches his part. You'll realize that you have no control over the plot or assignment of roles, and therefore you will distance yourself psychologically from all that happens to the character you play. Does the character you play grow ill in the play? Well, you will *act* the part to the best of your ability, but you certainly won't permit yourself to suffer. Do your friends die in the play? Do you die? It is all for the best because it is dictated by the plot.

Now perhaps you are thinking: Well, if I cannot control what happens to me, then how on earth can I control my attitude about what happens? If what happens is inevitable, then what happens to my attitudes is inevitable, too, right? Nevertheless, this was their doctrine: *You can control your attitude. Remain uninvolved emotionally in your fate, and your life will be untroubled.*

The Stoic philosophy also had a political ethic according to which the Stoic had a duty to serve his fellow men and respect their inherent worth as equals under natural law. So the Stoics thought that, although you should seek the untroubled life for yourself, your ethical concerns are not limited to your own welfare. Whether this social component of Stoicism is consistent with a philosophy of emotional noninvolvement, acceptance of the natural order, and seeking tranquility for yourself may be questioned, of course. In fact, whether a philosophy of

Diogenes the Dog

No ethics text would be complete without mention of the fourth-century-B.C. philosopher **Diogenes,** who is famous for having wandered about with a lantern in bright sunlight looking for an honest face.

Diogenes was a disciple of Antisthenes (though it is arguable that it was the other way around), who founded a school of philosophy known as the **Cynics** in Athens just after Socrates died. We mention the Cynics, whose most famous figure was Diogenes, because they were the precursors of the Stoics, who are discussed in the text.

According to the Cynics, who were fiercely individualistic, the wise person avoids even the most basic comforts and seeks total self-reliance by reducing all wants to a minimum and by forgoing any convenience or benefit offered by society. Diogenes, for example, is said to have dressed in rags and lived in an empty tub, and even to have thrown out his drinking cup when he observed a child drinking from his hands. It is reported that Alexander the Great, who admired Diogenes, made his way to the latter and announced that he would fill Diogenes' greatest need. Diogenes replied that he had a great need for Alexander to stop blocking his sunlight.

This answer, by the way, according to legend, moved Alexander to declare that the only person he would like to be if he were not Alexander was Diogenes. Maybe this says more about Alexander than about Diogenes. It certainly says something about Alexander's opinion of his teacher, Aristotle.

Diogenes is also reported to have masturbated in public while observing that it was too bad that hunger could not be relieved in similar fashion merely by rubbing your stomach. His point in part was simply to flout conventions, but it was apparently also to contrast sexual needs with the need for food.

According to another story, Diogenes visited the home of a wealthy man. The man asked Diogenes to avoid spitting on the floor or furnishings because the home was expensively appointed. Diogenes responded by spitting in the man's face, and commented that it was the only worthless thing in the room.

Whether these stories are true or not—and there are many other legends about Diogenes, some of which it wouldn't do for us to repeat—the indifference to material things that they portray was appreciated by the Stoics. Yet even though the Stoics saw the advantages to scaling back needs in the manner of the Cynics, they were not nearly so flamboyant in what they said and did. The Cynics were often willing to do or say something just to shock people.

Incidentally, as the word is most commonly used today, a cynic is one who sneers at sincerity, helpfulness, and other virtuous activity as inspired by ulterior motives. It's clear how the word acquired this meaning, given the contempt the Cynics had for traditional institutions and practices.

self-interest is compatible with concern for the common good is one of the most important questions of ethics, and you know quite well that this is a very live issue even today.

Let's summarize this section: According to the Epicureans, one's ultimate ethical objective is to lead the pleasant life through moderate living. According to the Stoics, the objective is to obtain the serene or untroubled life through acceptance of the rational or natural order of things while remembering that one is obligated to be of service to one's fellow creatures.

Stoicism in particular had an impact on Christian thought, primarily through the philosophy of St. Augustine, to whom we shall turn in a moment.

Selections 7.3 and 7.4 are from, respectively, Epicurus and Epictetus. The latter was among the most famous of all Stoics. He also is unusual among philosophers in that he was sold as a slave when a child but was given an education and later freed, thereafter becoming an influential teacher of philosophy. *Be sure to compare the two selections.* As you might expect from what we have said about Stoicism and Epicureanism, the two philosophies are very similar (even though Epictetus thought he was recommending a way of life quite different from that of the Epicureans).

SELECTION 7.4

"Epicurus to Menoeceus"   **From Epicurus**

The things which I [unceasingly] commend to you, these do and practice, considering them to be the first principles of the good life. . . .

Become accustomed to the belief that death is nothing to us. For all good and evil consists in sensation, but death is deprivation of sensation. And therefore a right understanding that death is nothing to us makes the mortality of life enjoyable, not because it adds to it an infinite span of time, but because it takes away the craving for immortality. For there is nothing terrible in life for the man who has truly comprehended that there is nothing terrible in not living. . . . Death, the most terrifying of ills, is nothing to us, since so long as we exist, death is not with us; but when death comes, then we do not exist. It does not then concern either the living or the dead, since for the former, it is not, and the latter are no more. . . .

We must then bear in mind that the future is neither ours, nor yet wholly not ours, so that we may not altogether expect it as sure to come, nor abandon hope of it, as if it will certainly not come.

We must consider that of desires some are natural, others vain, and of the natural some are necessary and others merely natural; and of the necessary some are necessary for happiness, oth-

ers for the repose of the body, and others for very life. The right understanding of these facts enables us to refer all choices and avoidance to the health of the body and the soul's freedom from disturbance, since this is the aim of the life of blessedness. For it is to obtain this end that we always act, namely, to avoid pain and fear. And when this is once secured for us, all the tempest of the soul is dispersed, since the living creature has not to wander as though in search of something that is missing, and to look for some other thing by which he can fulfill the good of the soul and the good of the body. For it is then that we have need of pleasure, when we feel pain owing to the absence of pleasure; but when we do not feel pain, we no longer need pleasure. And for this cause we call pleasure the beginning and end of the blessed life. For we recognize pleasure as the first good innate in us, and from pleasure we begin every act of choice and avoidance, and to pleasure we return again, using the feeling as the standard by which we judge every good.

And since pleasure is the first good and natural to us, for this very reason we do not choose every pleasure, but sometimes we pass over many pleasures, when greater discomfort accrues to us as the result of them: and similarly we think many pains better than pleasures, since a greater pleasure comes to us when we have endured pains for a long time. Every pleasure then because of its natural kinship to us is good, yet not every pleasure is to be chosen: even as every pain also is an evil, yet not all are always of a nature to be avoided. Yet by a scale of comparison and by the consideration of advantages and disadvantages we must form our judgment on all these matters. For the good on certain occasions we treat as bad, and conversely the bad as good.

And again independence of desire we think a great good—not that we may at all times enjoy but a few things, but that, if we do not possess many, we may enjoy the few in the genuine persuasion that those have the sweetest pleasure in luxury who least need it, and that all that is natural is easy to be obtained, but that which is superfluous is hard. And so plain savours bring us a pleasure equal to a luxurious diet, when all the pain due to want is removed; and bread and water produce the highest pleasure, when one who needs them puts them to his lips. To grow accustomed therefore to simple and not luxurious diet gives us health to the full, and makes a man alert for the needful employments of life, and when after long intervals we approach luxuries disposes us better towards them, and fits us to be fearless of fortune.

When, therefore, we maintain that pleasure is the end, we do not mean the pleasures of profligates and those that consist in sensuality, as is supposed by some who are either ignorant or disagree with us or do not understand, but freedom from pain in the body and from trouble in the mind. For it is not continuous drinkings and revellings, nor the satisfaction of lusts, nor the enjoyment of fish and other luxuries of the wealthy table, which produce a pleasant life, but sober reasoning, searching out the motives for all choice and avoidance, and banishing mere opinions, to which are due the greatest disturbance of the spirit.

Of all this the beginning and the greatest good is prudence. Wherefore prudence is a more precious thing even than philosophy: for from prudence are sprung all the other virtues; and it teaches us that it is not possible to live pleasantly without living prudently and honourably and justly, nor, again, to live a life of prudence, honor and justice without living pleasantly. For the virtues are by nature bound up with the pleasant life, and the pleasant life is inseparable from them. For indeed who, think you, is a better man than he who holds reverent opinions concerning the gods, and is at all times free from fear of death, and has reasoned out the end ordained by nature?

SELECTION 7.5

"The Encheiridion"   **From Epictetus**

1. Some things are under our control, while others are not under our control. Under our control are conception, choice, desire, aversion, and, in a word, everything that is our own doing; not under our control are our body, our property, reputation, office, and in a word, everything that is not our own doing. Furthermore, things under our control are by nature free, un-

hindered, and unimpeded; while the things not under our control are weak, servile, subject to hindrance, and not our own. Remember, therefore, that if what is naturally slavish you think to be free, and what is not your own to be your own, you will be hampered, will grieve, will be in turmoil, and will blame both gods and men; while if you think only what is your own to be your own, and what is not your own to be, as it really is, not your own, then no one will ever be able to exert compulsion upon you, no one will hinder you, you will blame no one, will find fault with no one, will do absolutely nothing against your will, you will have no personal enemy, no one will harm you, for neither is there any harm that can touch you. . . .

Make it, therefore, your study at the very outset to say to every harsh external impression, "You are an external impression and not at all what you appear to be." After that examine it and test it by these rules which you have, the first and most important of which is this: Whether the impression has to do with the things which are under our control, or with those which are not under our control; and, if it has to do with some one of the things not under our control, have ready to hand the answer, "It is nothing to me."

2. Remember that the promise of desire is the attainment of what you desire, that of aversion is not to fall into what is avoided, and that he who fails in his desire is unfortunate, while he who falls into what he would avoid experiences misfortune. If, then, you avoid only what is unnatural among those things which are under your control, you will fall into none of the things which you avoid; but if you try to avoid disease, or death, or poverty, you will experience misfortune. Withdraw, therefore, your aversion from all the matters that are not under our control, and transfer it to what is unnatural among those which are under our control. But for the time being remove utterly your desire; for if you desire some one of the things that are not under our control you are bound to be unfortunate; and, at the same time, not one of the things that are under our control, which it would be excellent for you to desire, is within your grasp. But employ only choice and refusal, and these too but lightly, and with reservations, and without straining. . . .

5. It is not the things themselves that disturb men, but their judgments about these things.

For example, death is nothing dreadful, or else Socrates too would have thought so, but the judgment that death is dreadful, this is the dreadful thing. When, therefore, we are hindered, or disturbed, or grieved, let us never blame anyone but ourselves, that means, our own judgments. It is the part of an uneducated person to blame others where he himself fares ill; to blame himself is the part of one whose education has begun; to blame neither another nor his own self is the part of one whose education is already complete. . . .

8. Do not seek to have everything that happens happen as you wish, but wish for everything to happen as it actually does happen, and your life will be serene. . . .

11. Never say about anything, "I have lost it," but only "I have given it back." Is your child dead? It has been given back. Is your wife dead? She has been given back. "I have had my farm taken away." Very well, this too has been given back. "Yet it was a rascal who took it away." But what concern is it of yours by whose instrumentality the Giver called for its return? So long as He gives it to you, take care of it as of a thing that is not your own, as travellers treat their inn. . . .

15. Remember that you ought to behave in life as you would at a banquet. As something is being passed around it comes to you; stretch out your hand and take a portion of it politely. It passes on; do not detain it. Or it has not come to you yet; do not project your desire to meet it, but wait until it comes in front of you. So act toward children, so toward a wife, so toward office, so toward wealth; and then some day you will be worthy of the banquets of the gods. But if you do not take these things even when they are set before you, but despise them, then you will not only share the banquet of the gods, but share also their rule. For it was by so doing that Diogenes and Heracleitus, and men like them, were deservedly divine and deservedly so called.

16. When you see someone weeping in sorrow, either because a child has gone on a journey, or because he has lost his property, beware that you be not carried away by the impression that the man is in the midst of external ills, but straightway keep before you this thought: "It is not what has happened that distresses this man (for it does not distress another), but his judgment about it." Do not, however, hesitate to sympathize with him so far as words go, and, if occasion offers, even to groan with him; but be careful not to groan also in the centre of your being.

17. Remember that you are an actor in a play, the character of which is determined by the Playwright; if He wishes the play to be short, it is short; if long, it is long; if He wishes you to play the part of a beggar, remember to act even this role adroitly; and so if your role be that of a cripple, an official, or a layman. For this is your business, to play admirably the role assigned you; but the selection of that role is Another's. . . .

20. Bear in mind that it is not the man who reviles or strikes you that insults you, but it is your judgment that these men are insulting you. Therefore, when someone irritates you, be assured that it is your own opinion which has irritated you. And so make it your first endeavour not to be carried away by the external impression; for if once you gain time and delay, you will more easily become master of yourself.

21. Keep before your eyes by day death and exile, and everything that seems terrible, but most of all death; and then you will never have any abject thought, nor will you yearn for anything beyond measure. . . .

33. Lay down for yourself, at the outset, a certain stamp and type of character for yourself, which you are to maintain whether you are by yourself or are meeting with people. And be silent for the most part, or else make only the most necessary remarks, and express these in few words. But rarely, and when occasion requires you to talk, talk indeed, but about no ordinary topics. Do not talk about gladiators, or horse-races, or athletes, or things to eat or drink—topics that arise on all occasions; but above all, do not talk about people, either blaming, or praising, or comparing them. If, then, you can, by your own conversation bring over that of your companions to what is seemly. But if you happen to be left alone in the presence of aliens, keep silence.

Do not laugh much, nor at many things, nor boisterously.

Refuse, if you can, to take an oath at all, but if that is impossible, refuse as far as circumstances allow. . . .

In things that pertain to the body take only as much as your bare need requires, I mean such things as food, drink, clothing, shelter, and household slaves; but cut down everything which is for outward show or luxury.

In your sex-life preserve purity, as far as you can, before marriage, and if you indulge, take only those privileges which are lawful. However, do not make yourself offensive, or censorious, to those who do indulge, and do not make frequent mention of the fact that you do not yourself indulge.

If someone brings you word that So-and-so is speaking ill of you, do not defend yourself against what has been said; but answer: "Yes, indeed, for he did not know the rest of the faults that attach to me; if he had, these would not have been the only ones he mentioned." . . .

41. It is a mark of an ungifted man to spend a great deal of time in what concerns his body, as in much exercise, much eating, much drinking, much evacuating of the bowels, much copulating. But these things are to be done in passing; and let your whole attention be devoted to the mind. . . .

44. The following statements constitute a non-sequitur: "I am richer than you are, therefore I am superior to you"; or, "I am more eloquent than you are, therefore I am superior to you." But the following conclusions are better: "I am

richer than you are, therefore my property is superior to yours"; or "I am more eloquent than you are, therefore my elocution is superior to yours." But you are neither property nor elocution. . . .

46. On no occasion call yourself a philosopher, and do not, for the most part, talk among laymen about your philosophic principles, but do what follows from your own principles.

Christianizing Ethics

Let us next turn to the way the Christian religion shaped the ancient idea of ethics, and the figure most responsible for that transformation.

St. Augustine

The greatness of **St. Augustine** (354–430) lay in this: he helped give Christianity philosophical weight and substance.

Augustine found this philosophical justification for Christianity in the metaphysics of Plato, as reinterpreted by the Neoplatonist Plotinus (204–270). Christianity rests on the belief in a transcendent God, and with the assistance of Platonic metaphysics, St. Augustine was able to make philosophically intelligible to himself the concept of a *transcendent realm,* a realm of being beyond the spatiotemporal universe that contains (or is) the source of all that is real and good. He also saw in Platonic and Neoplatonic doctrines the solution to the *problem of evil.* This problem can be expressed in a very simple question: How could evil have arisen in a world created by a perfectly good God?

One solution to this problem that Augustine considered was that evil is the result of a creative force other than God, a *force of darkness,* so to speak. But isn't there supposed to be just one and only one Creator? That's what Augustine believed, so this solution was not acceptable.

For Plato, remember, the Form of the Good was the source of all reality, and from this principle it follows that all that is real is good. Thus evil, given Plato's principle, *is not real.* This approach to the problem of evil St. Augustine found entirely satisfactory. Because evil is not something, it was not created by God.

This theory of evil is plausible enough as long as you're thinking of certain "physical" evils, like blindness or droughts (though others, like pain, seem as real as can be). Blindness, after all, is the absence of sight, and droughts are the absence of water.

Unfortunately, however, the absence theory does not plausibly explain *moral* evil, the evil that is the wrongdoing of men and women. How did Augustine account for moral evil? His explanation of moral evil was a variation of another idea of Plato's, the idea that a person never knowingly does wrong, that evil actions are the result of ignorance of the good, of misdirected education, so to say. But Augustine added a new twist to this idea. Moral evil, he said, is not exactly a case of misdirected *education* but a case of misdirected *love*. This brings us to the heart of Augustine's ethics.

For Augustine, as for the Stoics, a natural law governs all morality, and human behavior must conform to it. But for Augustine this is not an impersonal rational principle that shapes the destiny of the cosmos. The Augustinian natural law is, rather, the eternal law of God as it is written in the heart of man and woman and is apprehended by them in their conscience; and the eternal law is the "reason and will of God."

Thus the ultimate source of all that is good, for Augustine, is God, and God alone is intrinsically good. Our overriding moral imperative is therefore to love God. The individual virtues are simply different aspects of the love of God.

Augustine didn't mean that you must love *only* God. He meant that while there is nothing wrong with loving things other than God, you must not love them as if they were good in and of themselves: for *only God is intrinsically good*. To love things other than God as if they were inherently good—e.g., to love money or success as if these things were good in and of themselves—is *disordered* love: it is to turn away from God, and moral evil consists in just this disordered love.

Now don't let any of this make you think that Augustine was unconcerned with happiness, for as a matter of fact he did indeed think we should seek happiness. But happiness, he argued, consists in having all you want and wanting no evil. This may seem to be an odd notion at first, but when you think about it, it is by no means absurd. In any event, the only conceivable way to have all you want and to want no evil, Augustine thought, is to make God the supreme object of your love.

So, for Augustine, moral evil arises when man or woman turns away from God. Thus *God* is not the creator of moral evil: it is *we* who create evil through our own free choice. But doesn't it then follow that *we* can create good? No, for God, remember, is the source of all that is good. Thus we can do good only *through* God, Augustine said. Whereas evil is caused by our free acts, goodness is the result of God's grace.

In sum, Augustine borrowed a theme from Plato by maintaining that physical evil can always be explained as the absence of something; and his concept of moral evil as arising from misdirected love can be viewed as a variation of Plato's idea of moral evil as ignorance of the good. In this way Augustine thought he had solved the problem of evil without doing damage to principles of Christian faith.

SELECTION 7.6

"Of the Morals of the Catholic Church"   From St. Augustine

Happiness is the enjoyment of man's chief good. Two conditions of the chief good: **1st, Nothing is better than it; 2d, it cannot be lost against the will.**

How then, according to reason, ought man to live? We all certainly desire to live happily; and there is no human being but assents to this statement almost before it is made. But the title happy cannot, in my opinion, belong either to him who has not what he loves, whatever it may be, or to him who has what he loves if it is hurtful, or to him who does not love what he has, although it is good in perfection. For one who seeks what he cannot obtain suffers torture, and one who has got what is not desirable is cheated, and one who does not seek for what is worth seeking for is diseased. Now in all these cases the mind cannot but be unhappy, and happiness and unhappiness cannot reside at the same time in one man; so in none of these cases can the man be happy. I find, then, a fourth case, where the happy life exists,—when that which is a man's chief good is both loved and possessed. . . .

Man's chief good is not the chief good of the body only, but the chief good of the soul.

Now if we ask what is the chief good of the body, reason obliges us to admit that it is that by means of which the body comes to be in its best state. But of all the things which invigorate the body, there is nothing better or greater than the soul. The chief good of the body, then, is not bodily pleasure, not absence of pain, not strength, not beauty, not swiftness, or whatever else is usually reckoned among the goods of the body, but simply the soul. For all the things mentioned the soul supplies to the body by its presence, and, what is above them all, life. . . .

But if it follows, as it does, that the body which is ruled over by a soul possessed of virtue is ruled both better and more honourably, and is in its greatest perfection in consequence of the perfection of the soul which rightfully governs it, that which gives perfection to the soul will be man's chief good, though we call the body man. For if my coachman, in obedience to me, feeds and drives the horses he has charge of in the most satisfactory manner, himself enjoying the more of my bounty in proportion to his good conduct, can any one deny that the good condition of the horses, as well as that of the coachman, is due to me? So the question seems to me to be not, whether soul and body is man, or the soul only, or body only, but what gives perfection to the soul; for when this is obtained, a man cannot but be either perfect, or at least much better than in the absence of this one thing.

Virtue gives perfection to the soul; the soul obtains virtue by following God; following God is the happy life.

No one will question that virtue gives perfection to the soul. But it is a very proper subject of inquiry whether this virtue can exist by itself or only in the soul. . . . In either case, whether virtue can exist by itself without the soul, or can exist only in the soul, undoubtedly in the pursuit of virtue the soul follows after something. . . .

This something else, then, by following after which the soul becomes possessed of virtue and wisdom, is either a wise man or God. But we have said already that it must be something that we cannot lose against our will. No one can think it necessary to ask whether a wise man, supposing we are content to follow after him, can be taken from us in spite of our unwillingness or our persistence. God then remains, in following after whom we live well, and in reaching whom we live both well and happily.

St. Hildegard of Bingen

Augustine was the last of the great late ancient philosophers. Between the sixth century and the eleventh, Europe went through the Dark Ages, as we discussed in Chapter 3. **Hildegard** (1098–1179) was a light at the end of the tunnel. Her ethical writings typify the beginning of a period in moral philosophy that never really came to a complete end; religious mysticism just went out of fashion with the onslaught of rationalism beginning with Descartes.

Hildegard and other religious mystical philosophers are usually called theologians. But what they have to say is interesting both for moral philosophy, or ethics, and for moral epistemology: theories of the nature of moral knowledge.

For mystical philosophers, experience (albeit a special kind of experience) provided as certain a form of knowledge as pure rational introspection ever could. Their mystical experiences often take the form of visions, and sometimes take the form of ideas, thoughts, and even whole books that seemingly are dictated directly from some divine source during these experiences. Now, we're not going to assess the validity of such claims here; we're just going to reproduce and talk about their contents.

In *Liber Vitae Meritorum,* Hildegard lists thirty-five vices and their opposite virtues. This kind of list of opposites is a traditional format for talking about virtue and vice and dates back to Pythagoras. One vice, *Immoderation* (lack of moderate desires), is opposed to the virtue *Discretion* (keeping things within appropriate bounds). Hildegard describes Immoderation in the following allegory:

> This one is just like a wolf. She is furiously cunning, in hot pursuit of all evils, without distinction. With flexed legs, she crouches, looking in all directions, in such a way that she would devour anything she could snatch. She has a tendency to anything low-grade, following the worst habits of her peculiar mind. She considers every empty, worthless thing.

Now before you jump to conclusions about this medieval Benedictine nun, before you dismiss her views on virtue and vice as narrow and constricted, take a look at her accounts of human sexuality. In these excerpts from her philosophy of medicine in *Causa et Curae* (*Causes and Cures*), she gives the following accounts of what she considered to be healthy male and female sexuality:

> There are some men showing much virility, and they have strong and solid brains. The wind also which is in their loins has two tents to its command, in which it blows as if into a chimney. And these tents surround the stem of all manly powers, and are helpers to it, just like small buildings placed next to a tower which they defend. Therefore, there are two, surrounding the stem, and they strengthen and direct it so that the more brave and allied, they would attract the wind and release it again, just like two bellows which blow into a fire. When likewise they erect the stem in its manliness, they hold it bravely and thus at a later time the stem blossoms into a fruit.

And:

> Pleasure in a woman is compared to the sun which caressingly, gently, and continuously fills the earth with its heat, so that it can bear fruits, since if it would heat the earth more harshly in its constancy, it would hurt the fruits more than it would produce them. And so pleasure in a woman caressingly and gently, but

PROFILE / St. Hildegard of Bingen (1098–1179)

Hildegard was born at the end of the eleventh century in the Rhine River valley in Germany. She was the tenth child and was therefore "tithed" to God; at age seven or eight, she was sent to live with a group of women in a hermitage that eventually became the Benedictine convent of Disibodenberg. Hildegard learned Latin and studied the Bible, and she read the philosophical works of early church fathers including St. Jerome and St. Augustine.

Even as a child, Hildegard experienced mystical visions. By the time Hildegard had been head of the convent at Disibodenberg for three years, God commanded her, during one of these visions, to begin writing them down and to teach others their content. This put Hildegard in a difficult position because women were considered by the church as well as by society to have no religious, theological, or philosophical authority. But the Bishop of Mainz (Germany) was impressed by her writings and convinced Pope Eugene III to consider them. The Pope was convinced that the visions were genuine messages from God and had part of Hildegard's *Scivias* read to the bishops, who had come from all over Europe to attend a conference called the Synod of Trier during the winter of 1147–48.

Hildegard and her little convent were now better known than the adjoining monastery. As Hildegard's fame spread, more and more women flocked to her convent. When the monks at the monastery refused to give the nuns the additional living quarters and library space they needed, Hildegard moved the convent. The monks, who controlled the dowries of the nuns, tried to retain the money and valuables. But Hildegard had some power now and effectively convinced the bishops that the monks were obligated to turn the sizeable dowries over to her. These funds and artifacts were needed to finance the construction of the new convent at Bingen, and to provide support for her nuns. She was a formidable champion for the education of women, which at that time meant establishing convents (she founded two) where ancient copies of philosophical and religious texts were hand-copied by nuns who had been taught to read Latin.

Hildegard was a prolific writer. She wrote books on natural science and on medicine (she is credited with developing the theory that disease can be transmitted by dirty water—resulting in the construction of massive sewage systems in Germany), wrote music (recently released on CD!), and wrote lengthy works of religious philosophy that she had lavishly illustrated with replications of the visions upon which they were based.

She was a very influential thinker and traveled and "preached" the meaning of her visions throughout Germany. She was regularly consulted by a succession of four popes, and her many correspondents included two emperors, a king, and two queens. Hildegard lived to a ripe old age despite a lifetime of recurrent illnesses and the hardships of extended preaching tours.

nevertheless continuously, would have heat so that she can conceive and produce fruit. For when pleasure surges forth in a woman, it is lighter in her than it is in a man.

Clearly, sexual pleasure is not on this nun's list of vices. So, how does the soul recognize virtue and vice? And how does a person choose to follow one rather than the other? Read the following selection from Hildegard, and compare it to the earlier selection from Aesara of Lucania.

SELECTION 7.7

De Operatione Dei   **From Hildegard von Bingen**

Within the soul three powers exist: understanding (*comprehension*) by which the soul grasps heavenly and earthly things through the power of God; insight (*intelligence*) by which the soul has the greatest insight when it recognizes the evil of sin, which the soul then causes to become detestable as a result of repentance; and finally, execution (*motion*) by which the soul moves into itself as it accomplishes holy works according to the example of just persons in their bodies. Understanding and insight work together to promote an active execution on the part of the soul. For if the soul were to grasp more than it had insight for or could undertake, its standard would be incorrect. In this way, the powers of the soul agree with one another and none of them exceeds the other.

The understanding of the soul surrounds the body and all its structures by moving everything in the body to the correct degree toward whatever the flesh demands with respect to our sense of touch and taste, just as a builder correctly measures out a house as the proper abode for humans. Thus the body is moved by the soul, and the soul cannot forget that it needs to incite the body to its various actions. For the soul has an understanding of what the body demands since the body really derives its life from the soul.

And the soul, whose essence is life, lives as a living fire within the body. But the body is a work that has been shaped. And thus the soul does not let itself be kept from being effective in the two ways possible for it: according to the desire of the flesh or according to the longing of the soul.

And these three powers ought to be symmetrical throughout, since the soul does not begin to achieve by spiritualization more than knowledge can grasp or sensation carry out. And thus these powers work in harmony, since none of them exceeds another.

Heloise: Ethics and Philosophy of Love

An important thinker who lived at the same time as Hildegard was the French abbess **Heloise** (1100–1163). Heloise, like Hildegard, was concerned with virtue and vice, although Heloise was especially concerned with a specific virtue.

For Heloise, philosophy was life. If you believed in the truth of a theory of morality, you lived according to its principles. End of story. Heloise's writings on moral philosophy are found in her *Problemata* (*Problems*) and *Epistolae* (*Letters*), all addressed to Abelard (see her Profile). They were written when Heloise was in her thirties.

Heloise's ethics has two primary components. The first component, adapted from the Roman philosopher Cicero, places a high value on the virtue called *disinterested love.* True love for another, whether platonic or sexual, is completely unselfish and asks nothing, Heloise believed. The lover loves the beloved for who the beloved is. A true lover supports the beloved in achieving his goals and realizing his highest moral potential.

In an ideal loving relationship, the beloved has reciprocal feelings for the lover. He loves her for herself, for who she is. He aspires to help her realize her highest moral potential and the fulfillment of her goals. He has no selfish desires.

The other major component of Heloise's moral philosophy concerns the *morality of intent,* which she derived basically from Abelard's own teachings. According to Abelard, the morality of an action depends on the intention the person formed when committing the act. You can do something that is wrong but not be morally responsible or guilty if you didn't intend to do something wrong. Conversely, you can commit a moral wrong simply by intending to do something wrong, even if you fail in your attempt. The morality of an act resides in the intention of the actor. Heloise says in *Epistola 2:* "In a wicked deed, rectitude of action depends not on the effect of the thing but on the affections of the agent, not on what is done but with what dispositions it is done."

These two important features of Heloise's ethics give us an insight into her great personal commitment to living according to her ethics. Heloise argued that by voluntarily marrying Abelard (see her Profile), she would have been the *cause* of Abelard's being barred from final ordination to the priesthood. She did not want to be *morally responsible* for that outcome. She felt that he forced and tricked her into marrying him, and that this was a consequence of her pregnancy, for which she also was not morally responsible.

Abelard's *Historia Calamitatum* (*Story of My Calamities*), as well as Heloise's letters to Abelard, insists that she never agreed to have sex with him: he beat and raped her. She would not accept moral responsibility for the pregnancy because she had no evil intent to seduce him.

But because they actually were married, Abelard could order Heloise to enter a convent. After she did so, Abelard had almost no contact with her. Heloise did not understand why Abelard ignored her letters nor why he ignored the physical and spiritual welfare of her nuns.

Decades later, she read his book and learned about his castration. She put two and two together. She might have loved Abelard in this ideal, disinterested Ciceronian type of love. But it was a one-way street. Although she loved him for himself, and expressed that love by helping him achieve his goals (priesthood and a job as a philosopher at the emerging university), his love for her was purely sexual. After he was no longer able to have sex with her, she realized, Abelard had made her head of her own convent. Heloise had obeyed Abelard (who was both her husband and her religious superior), running the convent and teaching the nuns. All those

Heloise was a French philosopher and poet who received an early education at the Benedictine convent of Argenteuil. By the time she was sixteen years old, she was known as the most learned woman in France. Heloise's uncle Fulbert, who was her guardian and also a canon at Notre Dame, hired an unordained cleric named Pierre Abelard to teach Heloise philosophy.

The traditional literature tends to describe Heloise and Abelard's relationship as one of the great love affairs of all time, right up there with Romeo and Juliet. Now, that is true to a certain extent. Heloise certainly fell in love with her philosophy teacher—but she refused to have sex with him.

Abelard acknowledged that Heloise verbally refused to have sex and physically fought him off. In his words, "I frequently forced your consent (for after all you were the weaker) by threats and blows." Or, as we might say today if he were brought up on charges: on some occasions he beat her and raped her, and on other occasions he threatened to beat her again if she didn't stop resisting.

Heloise became pregnant. Abelard offered to marry her. Heloise refused. As usual, Abelard wouldn't take no for an answer. As her due date came near, he took her to his sister's farm in the country, where she gave birth. They named their son Astrolabe (after an astronomical instrument). Abelard convinced Heloise to marry him so their son wouldn't be a bastard. You see, illegitimate children couldn't be baptized back then, so if Heloise had not married Abelard, she would have been condemning their son to an eternity in limbo.

Now, saving your baby from eternal limbo might well be enough to make you marry someone who, incidentally, had already become an important medieval philosopher. But it's important, if you're going to understand Heloise's moral philosophy, to know about the other sordid details of their personal life. (Unfortunately, there are more.)

When the happy couple returned to Paris (leaving the baby at the farm), they lied to Uncle Fulbert about having gotten married. If the story got out that Abelard was married, Heloise knew, he would not be permitted to continue studying for the priesthood. The Cathedral School of Notre Dame, where Abelard taught, was turning into the University of Paris. It would be the first institution of higher learning in France (the second in Europe) to accept students who were not studying to be priests.

Heloise thought it would be a waste of Abelard's talents for him to miss out on this hot new experiment in education: a university. Worse, Heloise would feel responsible for keeping Abelard from fulfilling his ambitions.

Fulbert, though, was no fool. He figured things out and announced that Abelard had gotten married. Heloise tried to protect Abelard by denying the marriage, so Uncle Fulbert started mistreating Heloise (who was living at his house). To make it appear as if Heloise were not lying, Abelard ordered her to return to the convent and become a nun, which she did. At this point, Uncle Fulbert, who evidently was not given to halfway measures, hired thugs to castrate Abelard. (Heloise, who was in Argenteuil at the convent, didn't hear about this for years.) But now that having sex with Heloise was permanently out of the question, Abelard sought final ordination as a priest. He set up a convent called the Paraclete, and made Heloise its abbess. For decades, she never knew why.

years, Heloise had lived according to the moral theory she thought Abelard shared, loving him unselfishly, for himself.

St. Thomas Aquinas

Augustine fashioned a philosophical framework for Christian thought that was essentially Platonic. He found many Platonic and Neoplatonic themes that could be given a Christian interpretation, and thus is sometimes said to have Christianized Plato. Eight centuries later, **St. Thomas Aquinas** (1225–1274), in a somewhat different sense, Christianized the philosophy of Aristotle. Aquinas's task was perhaps the more difficult of the two, for the philosophy of Aristotle, with its this-worldly approach to things, was less congenial to a Christian interpretation. Thus it is customary to speak of Aquinas as having *reconciled* Aristotelianism with Christianity. In Aquinas's ethical philosophy, this amounted by and large to accepting both Christianity and the philosophy of Aristotle wherever that could be done without absurdity.

Think back for a moment to Aristotle. Aristotle said that the good for each kind of thing is defined with reference to the function or the nature of that kind of thing and is in fact the goal or purpose of that kind of thing. In the case of humans, goodness is happiness. Aquinas agreed. The natural (moral) law, which is God's eternal law as it is applied to man on earth, is apprehended by us in the dictates of our conscience and practical reasoning, which guide us to our natural goal, happiness on earth.

But there is also, according to Aquinas, an eternal, atemporal good—namely, happiness everlasting. The law that directs us to that end is God's divine law, which the Creator reveals to us through His grace.

Thus the **natural law** of Aquinas is the law of reason, which leads us to our natural end insofar as we follow it. The **divine law** is God's gift to us, revealed through His grace. Therefore, according to Aquinas, there are two sets of virtues: the "higher" virtues of faith, love, and hope; and the natural virtues, such as fortitude and prudence, which are achieved when the will, directed by the intellect, moderates our natural drives, impulses, and inclinations. And Aquinas, like Aristotle, thought of the virtues as matters of character or habit—in Aquinas's view, the habit of acting according to the provisions of natural law.

Although Aquinas's ethics are thus a type of virtue-ethics, he does treat the moral goodness of actions. When evaluating an act, and only voluntary acts are subject to moral evaluation, we must consider not only what was done, but also why it was done and the circumstances under which it was done.

Now suppose someone does something, or refrains from doing it, because the person's conscience tells him or her that this would be the morally proper thing to do or refrain from doing. And suppose further that in this case the individual's conscience is mistaken. Yes, an erring conscience is possible, according to Aquinas, despite the fact that it is through conscience that we become aware of natural law. In such a case, if the person acts as he or she honestly thinks is morally right, and the mistake in thinking is due to involuntary ignorance on the person's part, the person hasn't really sinned, according to Aquinas.

Aquinas's ethical system is complete (in the sense explained earlier in this chapter), detailed, and systematic; and it is difficult to convey this in this brief summary. Aquinas treats not only highly general and abstract principles such as the ultimate objective of human existence, the nature of goodness, and the sources of action, but also applies these principles to specific and concrete moral questions. In the brief selection that follows, which is from the *Summa Contra Gentiles*, we find just a small segment of his ethical theory. In this selection Aquinas argues that ultimate human happiness does not consist in wealth, worldly power, health, beauty, or strength, in the sensual pleasures, or in anything else to be found in this life.

SELECTION 7.8

Summa Contra Gentiles   **From Thomas Aquinas**

XVII. THAT ALL THINGS ARE DIRECTED TO ONE END, WHICH IS GOD.

From the foregoing it is clear that all things are directed to one good as their last end.

For if nothing tends to something as its end, except insofar as this is good, it follows that good, as such, is an end. Consequently that which is the supreme good is supremely the end of all. Now there is but one Supreme good, namely God, as their end.

Again. That which is supreme in any genus, is the cause of everything in that genus: thus fire which is supremely hot is the cause of heat in other bodies. Therefore the supreme good, namely God, is the cause of goodness in all things good. Therefore He is the cause of every end being an end: since whatever is an end, is such, insofar as it is good. Now the cause of a thing being such is yet more so. Therefore God is supremely the end of all things. . . .

XXX. THAT MAN'S HAPPINESS DOES NOT CONSIST IN WEALTH.

Hence it is evident that neither is wealth man's supreme good. For wealth is not sought except for the sake of something else: because of itself it brings us no good, but only when we use it, whether for the support of the body, or for some similar purpose. Now the supreme good is sought for its own, and not for another's sake. Therefore wealth is not man's supreme good. . . .

XXXI. THAT HAPPINESS CONSISTS NOT IN WORLDLY POWER.

. . . Man's supreme good cannot be a thing that one can use both well and ill: for the better things are those that we cannot abuse. But one can use one's power both well and ill: for rational powers can be directed to contrary objects. Therefore human power is not man's supreme good. . . .

XXXII. THAT HAPPINESS CONSISTS NOT IN GOODS OF THE BODY.

. . . The soul is better than the body, which neither lives, nor possesses these goods, without the soul. Wherefore the soul's good, such as understanding and the like, is better than the body's good. Therefore the body's good is not man's supreme good. . . .

XXXIII. THAT HUMAN HAPPINESS IS NOT SEATED IN THE SENSES.

. . . Intellect is superior to sense. Therefore the intellect's good is better than the sense's. Consequently man's supreme good is not seated in the senses. . . .

XXXVII. THAT MAN'S ULTIMATE HAPPINESS CONSISTS IN CONTEMPLATING GOD.

Accordingly if man's ultimate happiness consists not in external things, which are called goods of chance; nor in goods of the body; nor in goods of the soul, as regards the sensitive faculty; nor as regards the intellective faculty, in the practice of moral virtue; nor as regards intellectual virtue in those which are concerned about action, namely art and prudence; it remains for us to conclude that man's ultimate happiness consists in the contemplation of the truth.

For this operation alone is proper to man, and none of the other animals communicates with him therein.

Again. This is not directed to anything further as its end: since the contemplation of the truth is sought for its own sake.

Again. By this operation man is united to things above him, by becoming like them: because of all human actions this alone is both in God and in separate substances. Also, by this operation man comes into contact with those higher beings, through knowing them in any way whatever. . . .

Now, it is not possible that man's ultimate happiness consists in contemplation based on the understanding of first principles: for this is most imperfect, as being universal and containing potential knowledge of things. Moreover, it is the beginning and not the end of human study, and comes to us from nature, and not through the study of the truth. Nor does it consist in contemplation based on the sciences that have the lowest things for their object: since happiness must consist in an operation of the intellect in relation to the highest object of intelligence. It follows then that man's ultimate happiness consists in wisdom, based on the consideration of divine things. It is therefore evident by way of induction that man's ultimate happiness consists solely in the contemplation of God. . . .

XLVIII. THAT MAN'S ULTIMATE HAPPINESS IS NOT IN THIS LIFE.

Seeing then that man's ultimate happiness does not consist in that knowledge of God whereby he is known by all or many in a vague kind of opinion, nor again in that knowledge of God whereby he is known in science through demonstration; nor in that knowledge whereby he is known through faith, as we have proved above: and seeing that it is not possible in this life to arrive at a higher knowledge of God in His essence, or at least so that we understand other separate substances, and thus know God through that which is nearest to Him, so to say, as we have proved; and since we must place our ultimate happiness in some kind of knowledge of God, as we have shown; it is impossible for man's happiness to be in this life.

Again. Man's last end is the term of his natural appetite, so that when he has obtained it, he desires nothing more: because if he still has a movement towards something, he has not yet reached an end wherein to be at rest. Now, this cannot happen in this life: since the more man understands, the more is the desire to understand increased in him—this being natural to man—unless perhaps someone there be who understands all things: and in this life this never did nor can happen to anyone that was a mere man; seeing that in this life we are unable to know separate substances which in themselves are most intelligible, as we have proved. Therefore man's ultimate happiness cannot possibly be in this life. . . .

Further. All admit that happiness is a perfect good: else it would not bring rest to the appetite.

Now perfect good is that which is wholly free from any admixture of evil: just as that which is perfectly white is that which is entirely free from any admixture of black. But man cannot be wholly free from evils in his state of life; not only from evils of the body, such as hunger, thirst, heat, cold and the like, but also from evils of the soul. For no one is there who at times is not disturbed by inordinate passions; who sometimes does not go beyond the mean, wherein virtue consists, either in excess or in deficiency; who is not deceived in something or another; or at least ignores what he would wish to know, or feels doubtful about an opinion of which he would like to be certain. Therefore no man is happy in this life.

Hobbes and Hume

We've seen that the naturalism found in Aristotle's ethics and the nonnaturalistic ethics of Plato, with its conception of a transcendental source of ultimate value, flowed in separate streams through the philosophy of the centuries until the time of Aquinas. If it is not quite true to say that Aquinas channeled the waters from each of these two streams into a common bed, it may at least be said that he contrived to have them flow side by side, though in separate channels.

But the next philosopher we wish to discuss, **Thomas Hobbes** (1588–1679), drew exclusively from the Aristotelian channel. This is not surprising, for Hobbes was one of the first philosophers of the modern period in philosophy, a period marked by the emergence of experimental science, in which once again nature itself was an object of study, just as it had been for Aristotle. (You should be aware, nevertheless, that Hobbes, reacting to the Aristotelianism of his Oxford tutors, had harsh things to say about Aristotle.)

Hobbes

Hobbes's metaphysics was a relentless materialism. All that exists, he said, are material things in motion. Immaterial substance does not exist. There is no such thing as the nonphysical soul. Thoughts, emotions, feelings—all are motions of the matter within the brain, caused by moving things outside the brain. Even our reasoning and volition are purely physical processes.

As for values, according to Hobbes the words *good* and *evil* simply denote that which a person desires or hates. And Hobbes, like Aristotle, the Epicureans, the Stoics, and Aquinas, believed that we have a natural "end" or objective toward which all of our activity is directed. Hobbes specified this object of desire as the preservation of our own life. We seek personal survival above all other things, he held.

Now people live under one or another of two basic conditions, Hobbes said: a condition of *war*, in which they can harm each other, or a condition of *peace,* in which they cannot harm each other.

Egoism

There are two types of egoism. First, there is **descriptive egoism,** the doctrine that in all conscious action you seek to promote your self-interest above all else. Then there is **prescriptive egoism,** the doctrine that in all conscious action you *ought* to seek your self-interest above all else. The Epicurean ethical philosophy, for example, was a version of prescriptive egoism.

Often, beginning philosophy students accept descriptive egoism as almost self-evidently true. Many also favor prescriptive egoism as an ethical philosophy. *Of course* we always act to further our own ends! And that's exactly what we *ought* to do, right?

But some philosophers see a difficulty in accepting both prescriptive and descriptive egoism in that it seems *trivial* or *pointless* to tell people they *ought* to do what you think they are *going to do anyway.* That's like advising someone that he or she has a moral obligation to obey the laws of physics, or to remain visible at all times, or to occupy space, they say.

A further comment. If you find yourself subscribing to prescriptive egoism (one ought to seek one's self-interest above all else), as many do, then you should consider this: Does it make sense for you to *advocate* your own egoistic philosophy? If you ought to seek your own self-interest above all else (as prescriptive egoism says), then should you really go round telling others to seek *their* self-interest above all else? Is telling them that in *your* best interests? Might it not be better for your interests to urge others to promote the *common* good?

Notice that Hobbes did not define peace as a condition in which people *do not* harm each other, but as one in which people *cannot* harm each other. This is because Hobbes thought that people are fundamentally so selfish, mean, and stupid that they *will* harm each other unless they are *prevented* from doing so. But because their primary objective—survival—is better achieved under a condition of peace, people should seek peace if they are rational, he said. Fortunately, in Hobbes's opinion, people are possibly just barely rational enough to see that this is so.

But how is a condition of peace supposed to be kept, given the basic brutality, stupidity, and selfishness of the human race? Hobbes thought that a condition of peace could be sustained only if people agree or "contract" among themselves to form a commonwealth by transferring their collective strength to a sovereign power—an individual (or group of individuals) who would *compel* his subjects to honor their commitments and stand by their other agreements and contracts, and thus to live peacefully. Without this third party to keep them in line, people will soon enough return to their original condition, a state of war of each against all.

Now, *justice* and *injustice,* he said, consist entirely in the keeping or breaking of covenants (i.e., agreements). If you keep our agreement, that's just. If you break it, that's unjust. But covenants are empty words, he observed, without this coercive power that can compel people to abide by the terms of the covenant. Thus, justice and injustice, according to Hobbes, really don't even exist until people become smart enough to entrust their power to the sovereign. Justice and morality begin and end with the sovereign, according to Hobbes.

There are difficulties in Hobbes's solution to the problems that arise from the supposed selfishness and brutality of people, but discussion will have to wait until

Chapter 9, when we consider Hobbes's political philosophy. For now what is important is to see that for Hobbes, values (good and evil) are defined by desires, and justice and injustice begin and end with the sovereign.

Given Hobbes's view of good and evil and justice and injustice, it seems surprising at first to find Hobbes affirming the existence of natural laws. For the concept of natural law that we have encountered so far in this chapter is the Stoic concept, which was introduced into Christian philosophy by Augustine and accepted as well by Aquinas. As these earlier philosophers used the concept, the natural law was a moral law; it was a principle of rationality that infused the universe and to which human behavior is morally obliged to conform. For the Christian thinker, of course, the natural law was decreed by God.

But for Hobbes, a natural law is simply a value-neutral principle, discovered by reason, of how best to preserve one's life. Hobbes's laws of nature are therefore nonmoral. When he says, for example, that according to natural law people ought to seek peace, he means only that this is what people ought to do if they want to save their skins.

Hobbes also speaks of **natural right** and affirms that we have a natural right to use all means to defend ourselves. Today we think of a natural right as a moral restriction placed on others in their actions relative to us. For example, when we think of ourselves as having a natural right to life, we mean that others should not act so as to deprive us of our life. But Hobbes meant something rather different when he said that when peace cannot be obtained, we have a natural right to use all means to defend ourselves. He meant that in these conditions we suffer no moral restrictions whatsoever, and each person can use any methods he wishes—including murder—to ensure his own survival.

For Hobbes, therefore, there are natural laws, but these are not moral prescriptions. We have a natural right; but this right does not morally prohibit any activity. Good and evil exist, but these are defined subjectively, in terms of desires and aversions. Justice and injustice likewise are real things, but they are defined as the keeping or breaking of covenants.

Hobbes was important to the history of philosophy for several reasons. In metaphysics, as we have seen, he was the first modern exponent of a thoroughgoing materialism. In political philosophy, which we will get to later, Hobbes is important for his **contractarian** or **contractualist theory** of justice and the state according to which justice and injustice and the state only come to exist when people contract among themselves to transfer their powers to a central agency that forces people to abide by their agreements.

In ethics, Hobbes is important, among other reasons, for his **descriptivism:** he did not attempt to determine how people ought to behave in some absolute sense; rather, he was concerned with describing how they ought to behave *if* they want best to secure their objective. A question Hobbes left for subsequent philosophers, therefore, and one that has not been resolved to this day, is this: If the universe is material, can there really *be* absolute values? Do good and evil, justice and injustice, exist in some *absolute* sense, or must they be regarded, as Hobbes so regarded them, as expressions of desires or the products of human agreements?

Selection 7.9 is from Hobbes's major work, *Leviathan*. A classic in political phi-

Is Altruism Really Egoism?

The story is told of Hobbes that he was asked by a clergyman why he was giving alms to a beggar.

"Is it because Jesus has commanded you to do so?" the latter asked.

"No," came Hobbes's answer.

"Then why?"

"The reason I help the man," said Hobbes, "is that by doing so I end my discomfort at seeing his discomfort."

One moral that might be drawn from the story is that even the most altruistic and benevolent actions can be given an egoistic interpretation. Why did Hobbes help the beggar? To relieve his own discomfort. Why do saints devote their lives to relieving the suffering of others? Because it brings them pleasure to do so. Why did the soldier sacrifice his life to save his comrades? To end the distress he felt at thinking of his friends' dying—or maybe even because it pleased him to think of others praising him after his demise.

In short, because those who act to relieve their own discomfort or to bring pleasure to themselves are acting for their own self-interest, all these seemingly altruistic actions can be interpreted egoistically.

Are you convinced?

Well, if you are, you should know that many philosophers are uncomfortable with this egoistic analysis of altruistic behavior. After all (they argue), it brings the saint pleasure to help others only if the saint is genuinely motivated to help others, right? Thus, if egoism is equated with the doctrine that we are never motivated to help others, it is false. If it is equated with the doctrine that we only act as we are motivated to act, it is true, but not particularly interesting.

losophy, it encompasses as well metaphysics, epistemology, ethics, and psychology and secured for Hobbes a prime-time place in all histories of Western thought.

In Selection 7.9, Hobbes first explains in what good and evil consist. (This part of the selection is a continuation of Selection 4.3, which you read in Part 1.) Then he explains the "natural state" of mankind. This state, according to Hobbes, is a state of war, as explained, in which there is no right or wrong, justice or injustice.

SELECTION 7.9

*Leviathan**

From Thomas Hobbes

OF THE NATURAL CONDITION OF MANKIND AS CONCERNING THEIR FELICITY AND MISERY

Nature has made men so equal, in the faculties of the body, and mind; as that though there be found one man sometimes manifestly stronger in body, or of quicker mind than another; yet when all is reckoned together, the difference between man, and man, is not so considerable, as that one man can thereupon claim to himself any benefit, to which another may not pretend, as well as he. For as to the strength of body, the weakest has strength enough to kill the strongest, either by secret machination, or by confederacy with others, that are in the same danger with himself.

*Edited slightly for the modern reader.

And as to the faculties of the mind . . . I find yet a greater equality amongst men, than that of strength. . . . That which may perhaps make such equality incredible, is but a vain conceit of one's own wisdom, which almost all men think they have in a greater degree, than the vulgar; that is, than all men but themselves, and a few others, whom by fame, or for concurring with themselves, they approve. For such is the nature of men, that howsoever they may acknowledge many others to be more witty, or more eloquent or more learned; yet they will hardly believe there be many so wise as themselves; for they see their own wit at hand, and other men's at a distance. But this proves rather that men are in that point equal, than unequal. For there is not ordinarily a greater sign of the equal distribution of any thing, than that every man is contented with his share.

From this equality of ability, arises equality of hope in the attaining of our ends. And therefore if any two men desire the same thing, which nevertheless they cannot both enjoy, they become enemies; and in the way to their end, which is principally their own conservation, and sometimes their delectation only, endeavour to destroy, or subdue one another. And from hence it comes to pass, that where an invader has no more to fear, than another man's single power; if one plant, sow, build, or possess a convenient seat, others may probably be expected to come prepared with forces united, to dispossess, and deprive him, not only of the fruit of his labour, but also of his life, or liberty. And the invader again is in the like danger of another.

And from this diffidence of one another, there is no way for any man to secure himself, so reasonable, as anticipation; that is, by force, or wiles, to master the persons of all men he can, so long, till he see no other power great enough to endanger him: and this is no more than his own conservation requires, and is generally allowed. . . .

Again, men have no pleasure, but on the contrary a great deal of grief, in keeping company where there is no power able to over-awe them all. For every man looks that his companion should value him, at the same rate he sets upon himself: and upon all signs of contempt, or undervaluing, naturally endeavours, as far as he dares, (which amongst them that have no common power to keep them in quiet, is far enough to make them destroy each other), to extort a greater value from his condemners, by damage; and from others, by the example.

So that in the nature of man, we find three principal causes of quarrel. First, competition; secondly, diffidence; thirdly, glory.

The first, makes men invade for gain; the second, for safety; and the third, for reputation. The first use violence, to make themselves masters of other men's persons, wives, children, and cattle; the second, to defend them; the third for trifles, as a word, a smile, a different opinion, and any other sign of undervalue, either direct in their persons, or by reflection in their kindred, their friends, their nation, their profession, or their name.

Hereby it is manifest, that during the time men live without a common power to keep them all in awe, they are in that condition which is called war; and such a war, as is of every man, against every man. For WAR, consists not in battle only, or the act of fighting; but in a tract of time, wherein the will to contend by battle is sufficiently known: and therefore the notion of *time,* is to be considered in the nature of war; as it is the nature of weather. For as the nature of foul weather, lies not in a shower or two of rain; but in an inclination thereto of many days together; so the nature of war, consists not in actual fighting; but in the known disposition thereto, during all the time there is no assurance to the contrary. All other time is PEACE.

Whatsoever therefore is consequent to a time of war, where every man is enemy to every man; the same is consequent to the time, wherein men live without other security, than what their own strength, and their own invention shall furnish them withal. In such condition, there is no place for industry; because the fruit thereof is uncertain: and consequently no culture of the earth; no navigation, nor use of the commodities that may be imported by sea; no commodious building; no instruments of moving, and removing, such things as require much force; no knowledge of the face of the earth; no account of time; no arts; no letters, no society; and which is worst of all, continual fear, and danger of violent death; and the life of man, solitary, poor, nasty, brutish, and short.

It may seem strange to some man, that has not well weighed these things; that nature should thus dissociate, and render men apt to invade, and destroy one another; and he may therefore, not trusting to this inference, made from the passions, desire perhaps to have the same confirmed by experience. Let him therefore consider with himself, when taking a journey, he arms himself, and seeks to go well accompanied; when going to sleep, he locks his doors; when even in his house he locks his chests; and this when he knows there be laws, and public officers, armed, to revenge all injuries shall be done him; what opinion he has of his fellow-subjects, when he rides armed; of his fellow citizens, when he locks his doors; and of his children, and servants, when he locks his chests. Does he not there as much accuse mankind by his actions, as I do by my words? But neither of us accuse man's nature in it. The desires, and other passions of man, are in themselves no sin. No more are the actions, that proceed from those passions, till they know a law that forbids them: which till laws be made they cannot know: nor can any law be made, till they have agreed upon the person that shall make it. . . .

To this war of every man, against every man, this also is consequent; that nothing can be unjust. The notions of right and wrong, justice and injustice have there no place. Where there is no common power, there is no law: where no law, no injustice. Force, and fraud, are in war the two cardinal virtues. Justice and injustice are none

of the faculties neither of the body, nor mind. If they were, they might be in a man that were alone in the world, as well as his senses, and passions. They are qualities that relate to men in society, not in solitude. It is consequent also to the same condition, that there be no propriety, no dominion, no *mine* and *thine* distinct; but only that to be every man's, that he can get; and for so long, as he can keep it. And thus much for the ill condition, which man by mere nature is actually placed in; though with a possibility to come out of it, consisting partly in the passions, partly in his reason.

The passions that incline men to peace, are fear of death, desire of such things as are necessary to commodious living; and a hope by their industry to obtain them. And reason suggests convenient articles of peace, upon which men may be drawn to agreement. These articles, are they, which otherwise are called the Laws of Nature: whereof I shall speak more particularly, in the two following chapters.

OF THE INTERIOR BEGINNINGS OF VOLUNTARY MOTIONS; COMMONLY CALLED THE PASSIONS. AND THE SPEECHES BY WHICH THEY ARE EXPRESSED.

. . .whatever is the object of any man's appetite or desire, that is what he calls *good;* and the object of his hate and aversion, *evil;* and of his contempt, *vile* and *inconsiderable.* For these words are always used with relation to the person using them, there being nothing simply and absolutely so. Nor is there any common rule of good and evil, to be taken from the nature of objects themselves, but from the person of the man (where there is no commonwealth); or (in a commonwealth), from the person who represents it; or from an arbitrator, whom men disagreeing shall by consent agree to make his sentence their rule.

Hume

Hobbes maintained that the idea of incorporeal or immaterial substance was a contradiction in terms, but he denied being an atheist. Nevertheless, he certainly did not rest his ethics on the authority of the Church. And although most of the major philosophers of the modern period shrank from Hobbes's extreme materialism, they, too—most of them—sought to discover the basic principles of morality elsewhere than in Scripture. Some, such as Locke, though believing that these principles are decreed by God, held, like Hobbes, that they are discoverable—and provable—by reason.

But in the eighteenth century, **David Hume** (1711–1776) argued with some force that moral principles are neither divine edicts nor discoverable by reason. Hume's general position regarding God, as we shall see in Part 4, was that the order in the universe does offer some slight evidence that the universe has or had a creative force remotely analogous to human intelligence. But we certainly cannot affirm anything about the moral qualities of the creator, he held; and we cannot derive guidelines for our own actions from speculating about his (its) nature. Christianity Hume regarded as superstition.

Value Judgments Are Based on Emotion, Not Reason

Hume held likewise that moral judgments are not the "offspring of reason." Scrutinize an act of murder as closely as you can, he said. Do you find anything in the *facts of the case* that reveal that the act is morally wrong? The *facts,* he said, are simply that one person has terminated the life of another in a certain way at a particular time and place. Reasoning can disclose how long it took for death to occur, whether the victim suffered great pain, what the motives of the killer were, as well as the answers to many other factual questions such as these. But it will not show the *moral wrongfulness* of the act. The judgment that an act is immoral, Hume maintained, comes not from reason but from *emotion.* Perhaps this idea has occurred to you as well.

It is the same, Hume believed, with all value judgments. Is the judgment that a portrait is beautiful founded on reason? Of course not. Reason can disclose the chemical composition of the paints and canvas, the monetary value of the work, and many similar factual things. But whether the portrait is beautiful is an issue that cannot be settled by reason.

Thus, for Hume, moral judgments, and all value judgments, are based on emotion. Actions that we find morally praiseworthy or blameworthy create within us feelings of pleasure or displeasure, respectively. Now, obviously, these feelings are different in kind from aesthetic pleasures and pleasures of the palate. Humans clearly have a capacity for moral pleasure as well as for other types of pleasure: we are *morally sensitive creatures.* Behavior that pleases our moral sensibilities elicits our approval and is deemed good, right, just, virtuous, and noble. Behavior that offends our moral sense is deemed bad, wrong, unjust, base, and ignoble.

Cold-Blooded Murder

A fundamental principle of Hume's philosophy is that moral judgments are not the offspring of reason.

A consideration that might possibly favor Hume's thesis is that we tend to think of particularly heinous deeds—execution-style murders, for example—as "cold-blooded" and "heartless," not as "irrational." This is an indication that we view the murderer as lacking in *feeling* rather than as deficient in *reason*.

Is it hard to believe that an absolutely brilliant mind could commit murder? We think not. But is it hard to believe that someone with normal sensibilities could commit murder? We think that it is. These considerations favor Hume's principle.

Character Again

Notice that according to Hume, the act that pleases our moral sensibilities is one that reflects a benevolent *character* on the part of the agent. Hume believed that when we morally praise (or condemn) someone, it is the person's character that we praise (or condemn) primarily: his or her actions we find praiseworthy (or condemnatory) mainly as an indication of character. The idea that we apply moral attributes primarily to a person's *character* and only secondarily or derivatively to his or her *actions* is common to the virtue-ethics tradition of Plato, Aristotle, and Aquinas. In this respect Hume is a part of that tradition.

Benevolence

But just what is it about behavior that elicits our moral approval? *What do virtuous, good, right, and noble acts have in common?* Hume's answer was that the type of act we deem morally praiseworthy is one taken by an agent *out of concern for others.* The act that pleases our moral sensibilities is one that reflects a *benevolent character* on the part of the agent, he said. By "agent," philosophers mean the person who did the act.

Why does benevolence bring pleasure to us when we witness or read about or contemplate it? A cynical answer is that we imagine ourselves as benefiting from the benevolent activity, and imagining this is pleasant. Do you get a warm glow when you read about someone coming to the aid of a fellow person? Well, according to the cynical view that's because you picture yourself on the receiving end of the exchange.

But this cynical theory is really quite unnecessarily complex, said Hume. The reason you get that pleasant feeling when you read about or see someone helping someone else is just simply that you *sympathize* with others. It just plainly upsets a

Me-First Heroes

Hume would say that selfish people, like the character played by Michael Douglas in the movie *Wall Street*, who apparently lack a capacity to sympathize with others, are exceptions to the rule for normal humans. But if this is so, why is it that we make *heroes* out of people like these? How is it that me-first egoism got to be as popular as it seems to be these days?

normal person to see others suffering, and it pleases a normal person to see others happy. True, there are people around who suffer from the emotional equivalent of color blindness and lack the capacity to sympathize with others. But these people aren't the norm. The normal human being is a sympathetic creature, maintained Hume.

This aspect of Hume's moral philosophy may well have some significance for us today. On the one hand, we tend to believe that you should care for others but, on the other hand, that you must also certainly look out for yourself. And we are inclined to think that there is a problem in this because self-concern and other-concern seem mutually exclusive. But if Hume is correct, they are not. Looking out for your own interests includes doing that which brings you pleasure. And if Hume is correct, caring for others will bring you an important kind of pleasure. Indeed, if Hume is correct, when you praise an action as good, it is precisely because it brings you this kind of pleasure.

Hume's idea that goodness consists in traits and actions that promote the welfare of people was appropriated and developed in the nineteenth century by some of the most influential ethical theorists of all time, the utilitarians. There is every possibility that you yourself are a utilitarian; but of utilitarianism, more later.

Can There Be Ethics After Hume?

In sum, then, according to Hume, moral principles are neither divine edicts nor the "offspring of reason." Instead, *a judgment of moral approval is simply an expression of a particular kind of pleasure, a pleasure that we experience when confronted with behavior done out of concern for others.*

Now notice how severe Hume's break with tradition was. Earlier philosophers had asked questions like these: *What actions are virtuous and right and good, and why? What ought we do, and what determines this?* Hume, in contrast, asked questions like these: *What is a moral judgment? What are we doing when we praise something as morally good? What gives rise to our moral opinions? What do all acts considered to be morally praiseworthy have in common?* (This last question, of course, does have a very Socratic flavor.)

The questions asked by preceding philosophers, in short, tend to focus on this issue: What *is* good? Hume's questions, on the other hand, tend to focus on this question: What do we mean by "good"? The first question is a request for *norms—*

that is, for standards or principles of right and wrong. Hume's question, in contrast, is a request for *facts* about what moral judgments are and about what sorts of things are deemed to be good.

It is plain why Hume's inquiries took him away from a consideration of norms or standards. For although other possible ultimate sources of values than God or reason exist, there may not be any as plausible as these two. So it is easy to suppose that, if ethical standards are set neither by God nor by reason, then there just *aren't* any ethical standards apart from those established by people. And if this is true, then you would have to think that there is no *meaning* in the question What is good? beyond what is revealed by considering what people *call* good.

This was, in effect, Hume's position. Neither God nor reason lays down the ethical law. Once you discover what people *mean* by "good," you have found out what *is* good.

As we shall see, Hume's empirical, nonnormative approach to ethics came to dominate contemporary ethical philosophy in English-speaking countries during the first half of the twentieth century.

Nevertheless, for many people today, especially those outside philosophy, the notion that there is nothing left for ethical philosophy beyond the consideration of the meaning of ethical terminology is equivalent to saying that ethics is sterile or dead. They might therefore be inclined to say that, if Hume is correct in maintaining that moral principles are neither divine edicts nor the "offspring of reason," then nothing of much significance is left for ethics.

Can there be ethical philosophy after Hume? In the next chapter we find out.

In Selection 7.10, Hume argues that "morality is not an object of reason." Pay close attention to the last paragraph, in which Hume argues that a proposition about what ought to be the case cannot be deduced from a proposition or set of propositions about what is the case. This famous dictum, that "you can't get an 'ought' from an 'is,'" has been widely discussed in this century, as we will note later.

SELECTION 7.10

A Treatise of Human Nature   **From David Hume**

But to make these general reflexions more clear and convincing, we may illustrate them by some particular instances, wherein this character of moral good or evil is the most universally acknowledged. Of all crimes that human creatures are capable of committing, the most horrid and unnatural is ingratitude, especially when it is committed against parents, and appears in the more flagrant instances of wounds and death.

This is acknowledged by all mankind, philosophers as well as the people, the question only arises among philosophers, whether the guilt or moral deformity of this action be discovered by demonstrative reasoning or be felt by an internal sense, and by means of some sentiment, which the reflection on such an action naturally occasions. This question will soon be decided against the former opinion, if we can show the same relations in other objects, without the notion of any guilt or iniquity attending them. Reason or science is nothing but the comparing of ideas, and the discovery of their relations; and if the same relations have different characters, it must evidently follow, that those characters are not discovered merely by reason. To put the affair, therefore, to this trial, let us choose any inanimate object, such as an oak or elm; and let us suppose, that by the dropping of its seed, it produces a sapling below it, which springing up by degrees, at last overtops and destroys the parent tree: I ask, if in this instance there be wanting any relation, which is discoverable in parricide or ingratitude? Is not the one tree the cause of the other's existence; and the latter the cause of the destruction of the former, in the same manner as when a child murders his parent? It is not sufficient to reply, that a choice or will is wanting. For in the case of parricide, a will does not give rise to any *different* relations, but is only the cause from which the action is derived; and consequently produces the *same* relations, that in the oak or elm arise from some other principles. It is a will or choice, that determines a man to kill his parent; and they are the laws of matter and motion, that determine a sapling to destroy the oak, from which it sprung. Here then the same relations have different causes; but still the relations are the same: And as their discovery is not in both cases attended with a notion of immorality, it follows, that the notion does not arise from such a discovery.

But to choose an instance, still more resembling; I would fain ask any one, why incest in the human species is criminal, and why the very same action, and the same relations in animals have not the smallest moral turpitude and deformity? If it be answered, that this action is innocent in animals, because they have not reason sufficient to discover its turpitude, but that man, being endowed with that faculty, which *ought* to restrain him to his duty, the same action instantly becomes criminal to him; should this be said, I would reply, that this is evidently

arguing in a circle. For before reason can perceive this turpitude, the turpitude must exist; and consequently is independent of the decisions of our reason, and is their object more properly than their affect. According to this system, then, every animal, that has sense, and appetite, and will; that is, every animal must be susceptible of all the same virtues and vices, for which we ascribe praise and blame to human creatures. All the difference is, that our superior reason may serve to discover the vice or virtue, and by that means may augment the blame or praise: But still this discovery supposes a separate being in these moral distinctions, and a being, which depends only on the will and appetite, and which, both in thought and reality, may be distinguished from the reason. Animals are susceptible of the same relations, with respect to each other, as the human species, and therefore would also be susceptible of the same morality, if the essence of morality consisted in these relations. Their want of sufficient degree of reason may hinder them from perceiving the duties and obligations of morality, but can never hinder these duties from existing; since they must antecedently exist, in order to their being perceived. Reason must find them, and can never produce them. This argument deserves to be weighed, as being, in my opinion, entirely decisive.

Nor does this reasoning only prove, that morality consists not in any relations, that are the objects of science; but if examined, will prove with equal certainty, that it consists not in any *matter of fact*, which can be discovered by understanding. This is the *second* part of our argument; and if it can be made evident, we may conclude, that morality is not an object of reason. But can there be any difficulty in proving, that vice and virtue are not matters of fact, whose existence we can infer by reason? Take any action allowed to be vicious: Wilful murder, for instance. Examine it in all lights, and see if you can find that matter of fact, or real existence, which you call *vice*. In whichever way you take it, you find only certain passions, motives, volitions and thoughts. There is no other matter of fact in the case. The vice entirely escapes you, as long as you consider the object. You never can find it, till you turn your reflexion into your own breast, and find a sentiment of disapprobation, which arise in you, towards this action. Here is a matter of fact; but it is the object of feeling, not of reason. It lies in yourself, not in the object. So that when you pronounce any action or character to be vicious, you mean nothing, but that from the constitution of your nature you have a feeling or sentiment of blame from the contemplation of it. Vice and virtue, therefore, may be compared to sounds, colours, heat and cold, which according to modern philosophy, are not qualities in objects, but perceptions in the mind: And this discovery in morals like that other in physics, is to be regarded as a considerable advancement of the speculative sciences; though like that too, it has little or no influence on practice. Nothing can be more real, or concern us more, than our own sentiments of pleasure and uneasiness; and if these be favourable to virtue, and unfavourable to vice, no more can be requisite to the regulation of our conduct and behaviour.

I cannot forbear adding to these reasonings an observation, which may, perhaps, be found of some importance. In every system of morality, which I have hitherto met with, I have always remarked, that the author proceeds for some time in the ordinary way of reasoning, and establishes the being of a God, or makes observations concerning human affairs, when of a sudden I am surprised to find, that instead of the usual copulations of propositions, *is,* and *is not,* I meet with no proposition that is not connected with an *ought,* or an *ought not.* This change is imperceptible, but is, however, of the last consequence. For as this *ought,* or *ought not,* expresses some new relation or affirmation, it is necessary that it should be observed and explained; and at the same time that a reason should be given, for what seems altogether inconceivable, how this new relation can be a deduction from others, which are entirely different from it. But as authors do not commonly use this precaution, I shall presume to recommend it to the readers, and am persuaded, that this small attention would subvert all the vulgar systems of morality, and let us see, that the distinction of vice and virtue is not founded merely on the relations of objects, nor is perceived by reason.

Checklist

To help you review, here is a checklist of the key philosophers and concepts of this chapter. The brief descriptive sentences summarize leading ideas. Keep in mind that some of these summary statements represent oversimplifications of complex positions.

Philosophers

- **Sophists** Professional teachers of fifth-century-B.C. Greece whose attack on traditional moral values marks the beginnings of ethical philosophy.

- **Socrates** Sought to discover the essences of moral virtues and championed the use of reason in moral deliberation.

- **Plato** Also sought the essences of moral virtues; identified these with the unchanging Forms, the highest of which he held to be the Form of the Good, the ultimate source of all value and reality.

- **Aesara of Lucania** Pythagorean philosopher from southern Italy. Held that by introspecting about the nature and structure of the human soul we can identify a standard of personal and public morality.

- **Aristotle** Ethical naturalist; held that moral judgments are judgments of fact about the natural world. Said that happiness is our highest good.

- **Epicurus** An ethical egoist; held that one's highest objective is to lead the pleasant life through moderate living.

- **Aristippus** Held that life should be dedicated to the pursuit of intense pleasure.

- **Zeno** Founder of Stoicism.

- **Cleanthes, Cicero, Seneca,** and **Marcus Aurelius** Famous Stoics.

- **Epictetus** A leading Stoic; held that one's highest objective is to find a serene or untroubled life through acceptance of the rational natural order of things.

- **Diogenes** Most famous Cynic, who taught by shocking example that the wise person reduces all wants and avoids all comforts.

- **Saint Augustine** Used Platonic concepts to solve "the problem of evil"; held moral evil to be misdirected love; identified God as the supreme moral authority and source of all goodness.

- **Hildegard of Bingen** Medieval German mystic philosopher who held that the moral powers of the soul came from its three faculties: understanding, insight, and execution.

- **Heloise** Medieval French philosopher who held that the morality or immorality of an action was determined by the intention with which it was done.

- **Saint Thomas Aquinas** Reconciled Aristotelian ethical naturalism with Christianity.

- **Thomas Hobbes** Held that "good" and "evil" denote what a person desires or hates; maintained that our natural end is preservation of self.

- **David Hume** Held that moral principles are neither divine edicts nor discoverable by reason and that value judgments are based on emotion. Said that the act that pleases our moral sensibilities is one that reflects the agent's benevolent character.

Concepts

ethics

moral judgment

value judgment

ethical skepticism

relativism

descriptive relativism

ethical relativism

individual relativism

cultural relativism

subjectivism

well-ordered soul

divine-command ethics

ultimate source of value

nonnatural source of value

ethical naturalism

mean between extremes

virtue ethics

instrumental vs. intrinsic ends

Epicureans

Stoics

epicure

Cyrenaicism

stoic

natural law

Cynics

misdirected/disordered love

tripartite soul

disinterested love

morality of intent

divine law

descriptive egoism

prescriptive egoism

natural right

contractarian/contractualist theory

descriptivism

altruism

benevolence

getting an "ought" from an "is"

Questions for Discussion and Review

1. Is there some single thing that all morally good actions have in common? Defend your view.

2. "What is right is what you yourself believe is right." Critically evaluate this statement.

3. What is the connection between virtue and happiness, in the philosophy of Plato?

4. Explain how Plato's theory may be regarded as "complete."

5. What is the connection between the structure of the soul, personal morality, and justice, according to Aesara of Lucania?

6. In what does happiness consist, according to Aristotle? When can we be said to be virtuous, according to him?

7. What is the connection between habit and moral character, for Aristotle?

8. Compare and contrast the ethical philosophies of Epicureanism and Stoicism. Which do you think is the superior philosophy, and why?

9. Evaluate Aristippus's philosophy (see box).

10. Is it a sound policy to reduce all wants to a minimum and to achieve utter self-reliance by avoiding all the comforts of society?

11. Can you control your attitude if you cannot control your fate?

12. What is Hildegard's concept of the structure and faculties of the soul? How does it compare to Aesara of Lucania's views on the soul?

13. Explain Heloise's view of the morality of intent and her view of the nature of disinterested love.

14. Explain Augustine's solution to the problem of evil, and determine whether it is sound.

15. Explain and evaluate Aquinas's reasons for believing that ultimate human happiness does not consist in wealth, worldly power, or anything in this life (see Selection 7.6).

16. Do we seek personal survival above all other things?

17. Do we always act selfishly? Explain.

18. Explain and critically evaluate prescriptive egoism.

19. Does it make sense for a (prescriptive) egoist to advocate egoism?

20. Is altruism really disguised egoism?

21. Can reasoning disclose the moral wrongfulness of an act of murder?

22. Is Hume correct in saying that the type of act we deem morally praiseworthy is one done out of concern for others?

23. Is it abnormal not to have sympathy for others? Are selfish people (like the character played by Michael Douglas in *Wall Street*) really admired in today's society?

Suggested Further Readings

Aristotle, *The Nicomachean Ethics*, Martin Ostwald, ed. (Indianapolis: Bobbs-Merrill, 1962).

John Burnet, *Early Greek Philosophy*, 4th ed. (London: Macmillan, originally published in 1930). A standard work on early Greek philosophy.

F. C. Copleston, *Aquinas* (Baltimore: Penguin Books, 1955). See Chapter 5.

Epictetus, *The Handbook of Epictetus*, Nicholas P. White, trans. (Indianapolis: Hackett, 1983). If you enjoyed the Epictetus selection, here's where you can find more.

Epicurus, *The Extant Remains,* C. Bailey, trans. (Oxford: Clarendon Press, 1962). For those who wish to read more from Epicurus.

E. Gilson, *The Christian Philosophy of St. Augustine* (New York: Random House, 1960). See the introduction and Part 2 for relevant material.

J. Gould, *The Development of Plato's Ethics* (London: Cambridge University Press, 1955). Explains the important principles and concepts in Plato's ethics.

E. Hamilton and H. Cairns, eds., *The Collected Dialogues of Plato* (New York: Bollingen Foundation, 1961). This, as we said before, is what you need to acquaint yourself firsthand with Plato's dialogues. Be sure to read *The Republic.* The other dialogues especially relevant to ethics are *Gorgias, Meno,* and *Philebus.*

W. F. R. Hardie, *Aristotle's Ethical Theory* (Oxford: Clarendon Press, 1968). There are several reliable books on Aristotle's ethics. This is one of the most popular.

R. D. Hicks, *Stoic and Epicurean* (New York: Russell and Russell, 1962). See Chapters 3, 4, and 5.

Hildegard of Bingen, *Book of Divine Works,* Matthew Fox, ed. (Santa Fe: Bear & Co., 1987).

Hildegard of Bingen, *Scivias,* Bruce Hozeki, trans. (Santa Fe: Bear & Co., 1986).

J. Kemp, *Ethical Naturalism: Hobbes and Hume* (London: Macmillan, 1970). See Chapters 2 and 3. For original works, try F. J. E. Woodbridge, *Hobbes Selections* and C. W. Hendel, Jr., *Hume Selections,* both published by Scribners in New York.

G. S. Kirk, J. E. Raven, and M. Schofield, *The Presocratic Philosophers: A Critical History with a Selection of Texts,* 2nd ed. (Cambridge: Cambridge University Press, 1983). This is a comprehensive recent treatment of the pre-Socratics.

Betty Radice, trans., *The Letters of Abelard and Heloise* (New York: Penguin Books, 1974).

Waithe, Mary Ellen, *A History of Women Philosophers,* vol. 2, *Medieval, Renaissance, and Enlightenment Women Philosophers: 500–1600* (Dordrecht: Kluwer Academic Publishers, 1989).

8 Ethics After Hume

The moral order is just as much part of the fundamental nature of the universe as is the spatial or numerical structure expressed in the axioms of geometry or arithmetic.

—*W. D. Ross*

Hamlet: *There is nothing either good or bad, but thinking makes it so.*

—*Shakespeare*

In Part 1, we saw that David Hume said some things about what can be known that marked a big turning point in the history of epistemology. And now in Part 2 we see Hume's philosophy pointing out new directions for ethics, too. "Morality," Hume said, "is more properly felt than judged of." Ethical standards are not fixed by reason, he held; further, even if there is a God, he maintained, it is quite impossible for us to gain moral guidance from him.

Loosely speaking, therefore, ethics after Hume seems generally to have had these options: First, it might seek to establish that, despite Hume, morality *can* be grounded on reason or God. This was the option taken by Kant, who favored reason as the ultimate ground of morality. Or second, it might try to find objective sources of moral standards other than reason and God. This is what the utilitarians tried to do. Or third, it might try to determine how one should conduct one's affairs given the absence of objective moral standards. This is a primary concern of contemporary existentialists. Or fourth, it might abandon the search for moral standards altogether and concentrate instead on such factual questions as: What do people believe is good and right? What does it mean to say that something is good or right? How do moral judgments differ from other kinds of judgments? What leads us to praise certain actions as moral and condemn others as immoral? These are some of the issues that have captured the attention of contemporary analytic philosophers.

Let's start with Kant, who survived Hume by twenty-eight years.

Kant

Immanuel Kant (1724–1804) disagreed entirely with Hume's discounting of the possibility that reason can settle whether an act is morally right. In Kant's opinion, reason and reason alone can settle this. Kant's argument, paraphrased and distilled, went like this:

1. *Scientific inquiry can never reveal to us principles that we know hold without exception.* Scientific inquiry is based on experience, and in the final analysis experience can only show how things have been to this point, not how they must be. For example, science reveals to us physical "laws" that hold true of the universe as it is now, but it cannot provide absolutely conclusive guarantees that these laws will forever hold true. (If you have difficulty understanding this point, rereading the section on Kant in Chapter 5 will help.)

2. *Moral principles, however, hold without exception.* For example, if it is wrong to torture helpless animals, then it would be wrong for anyone, at any time, to do so.

    Thus, from these two premises—that moral principles hold without exception and that scientific investigations cannot reveal what holds without exception—it follows that:

3. *Moral principles cannot be revealed through scientific investigation.* Because Kant believed that any principle that holds without exception is knowable only through reason, he maintained that *reason alone can ascertain principles of morality.*

The Supreme Principle of Morality

Further, according to Kant, because a moral rule is something that holds without exception—that is, holds universally—you should act only on principles that could hold universally. For example, if you think you must cheat to pass an exam, then the principle on which you would act (if you were to cheat) would be this: *To obtain a passing grade, it is acceptable to cheat.* But now consider: If this principle were a universal law, then a passing grade would be meaningless, right? And in that case the principle itself would be meaningless. In short, the principle logically could not hold universally, and (this comes to the same thing) it would be irrational for anyone to want it to hold universally.

Now if it would be irrational for you to want the principle on which you act to be a universal law, then that principle is morally improper, and the act should not be done. Thus, for Kant, *the supreme prescription of morality is to act always in such a way that you could, rationally, will the principle on which you act to be a universal law.* In Kant's words: "Act only on that maxim whereby you can at the same time will that it should become a universal law."

Kant, Reason, and Morals

A fundamental principle of Kant's moral philosophy is that reason alone can determine whether an act is morally right.

[margin handwritten note: X need moral guide]

Because, in Kant's view, a universal law would in effect be a sort of law of nature, he offers a second formulation of the categorical imperative: "Act as if the maxim of your action were to become by your will a Universal Law of Nature." In Selection 8.1, Kant will apply this principle to some concrete cases.

Why You Should Do What You Should Do

Now moral principles, Kant observed, may always be expressed in the imperative form: Do not steal! Be kind to others! Further, because moral imperatives must hold without exception, they are different from **hypothetical imperatives,** which state, in effect, that one ought to do something *if* such-and-such an end is desired.

For example, the imperatives "If you wish to be healthy, then live moderately!" and "If you wish to secure your own survival, then surrender your rights to a sovereign power!" are both hypothetical imperatives. Neither is a **moral imperative,** for a moral imperative holds unconditionally or *categorically*. This means that a moral imperative commands obedience for the sake of no other end than its own rightness.

Thus, for Kant, what I should do I should do *because it is right*. Doing something for any other purpose—for the sake of happiness or the welfare of mankind, for example—is not to act morally. It is to act under the command of a hypothetical imperative, which is not unconditional, as a moral imperative must be. According to Kant, you should do your moral duty simply because it is your moral duty. You may well find this position difficult to accept, but we *challenge* you to find a flaw in the reasoning that led Kant to adopt it.

Furthermore, according to Kant, it's not the *effects or consequences* of your act that determine whether your act is good, for these are not totally within your control. What is within your control is the *intent* with which you act. Thus, what determines whether your act is good or bad is the intent with which it is taken: He wrote: "Nothing can possibly be conceived in the world, or even out of it, which can be called good, without qualification, except a good will."

And, because a morally good will is one that acts solely for the sake of doing what is right, it follows, in Kant's opinion, that *there is no moral worth* in, say, helping others because you are sympathetic or inclined to do so. There is moral worth in helping others only because it is right to do so.

Yes, this is an astonishing doctrine, but again we challenge you to find a mistake in Kant's reasoning.

Is It Ever Right to Break a Promise?

According to Kant, if a universal law allowed breach of promise, then there would be no such thing as a promise. Thus the maxim "Break promises!", if it were to become a universal law, would (as Kant says in Selection 8.1) "destroy itself."

But hold on. Suppose I promise to return your car at 4 o'clock. And suppose that shortly before 4 my wife becomes ill and must be rushed to the hospital—and the only transportation available is your car! Should I break my promise to you in order to save my wife's life? And if I did, which maxim would I be acting on, breaking promises or saving lives?

Kant's answer (of course) would be that the maxim I acted on is "Break promises when doing so is required to save a life." And there would apparently be no inconsistency in willing this maxim to be a universal law.

For Kant, then, the maxim "Break your promises!" cannot be universalized. But that doesn't mean that, given his principles, you should never break a promise.

Because to violate the supreme principle of morality, the supreme **categorical imperative,** is to be irrational, rationality may be said to be the source of all value. Hence the rational will alone is deemed inherently good by Kant. Accordingly, Kant offers yet another formulation of the supreme categorical imperative: *Treat rational beings (i.e., humans) in every instance as ends and never just as means!*

That this is an alternative formulation of the same principle may be seen in the fact that if you were to violate the categorical imperative and do something that you could not rationally will to be a law for all, then in effect you would be treating the interests of others as subordinate to your own; that is, you would be treating others as means and not as ends. Kant, it is often said (for obvious reasons), was the first philosopher to provide a *rational basis* for the golden rule found in many religions: Do unto others as you would have them do unto you.

Did Kant provide a viable response to Hume's idea that reason cannot determine whether an act is morally right? You decide.

Selection 8.1 is from Kant's *Foundations of the Metaphysics of Morals.*

SELECTION 8.1

Foundations of the Metaphysics of Morals   From Immanuel Kant

There is, therefore, only one categorical imperative. It is: <u>Act only</u> according to that maxim by which you can at the same time <u>will that it should become a universal law.</u>

Now if all imperatives of duty can be derived from this one imperative as a principle, we can at least show what we understand by the concept of duty and what it means, even though it remains undecided whether that which is called duty is an empty concept or not.

The universality of law according to which effects are produced constitutes what is properly called nature in the most general sense (as to form), i.e., the existence of things so far as it is determined by universal laws. [By analogy], then, the universal imperative of duty can be expressed as follows: Act as though the maxim of your action were by your will to become a universal law of nature.

We shall now enumerate some duties, adopting the usual division of them into duties to ourselves and to others and into perfect and imperfect duties.[10]

suicide

1. A man who is reduced to despair by a series of evils feels a weariness with life but is still in possession of his reason . . . sufficiently to ask whether it would not be contrary to his duty to himself to take his own life. Now he asks whether the maxim of his action could become a universal law of nature. His maxim, however, is: For love of myself, I make it my principle to shorten my life when by a longer duration it threatens more evil than satisfaction. But it is questionable whether this principle of self-love could become a universal law of nature. One immediately sees a contradiction in a system of nature whose law would be to destroy life by the feeling whose special office is to impel the improvement of life. In this case it would not exist as nature; hence that maxim cannot obtain as a law of nature, and thus it wholly contradicts the supreme principle of all duty.

borrow $

2. Another man finds himself forced by need to borrow money. He well knows that he will not be able to repay it, but he also sees that nothing will be loaned him if he does not firmly promise to repay it at a certain time. He desires

to make such a promise, but he has enough conscience to ask himself whether it is not improper and opposed to duty to relieve his distress in such a way. Now, assuming he does decide to do so, the maxim of his action would be as follows: When I believe myself to be in need of money, I will borrow money and promise to repay it, although I know I shall never do so. Now this principle of self-love or of his own benefit may very well be compatible with his whole future welfare, but the question is whether it is right. He changes the pretension of self-love into a universal law and then puts the question: How would it be if my maxim became a universal law? He immediately sees that it could never hold as a universal law of nature and be consistent with itself; rather it must necessarily contradict itself. For the universality of a law which says that anyone who believes himself to be in need could promise what he pleased with the intention of not fulfilling it would make the promise itself and the end to be accomplished by it impossible; no one would believe what was promised to him but would only laugh at any such assertion as vain pretense.

3. A third finds in himself a talent which could, by means of some cultivation, make him in many respects a useful . . . man. But he finds himself in comfortable circumstances and prefers indulgence in pleasure to troubling himself with broadening and improving his fortunate natural gifts. Now, however, let him ask whether his maxim of neglecting his gifts, besides agreeing with his propensity to idle amusement, agrees also with what is called duty. He sees that a system of nature could indeed exist in accordance with such a law, even though man (like the inhabitants of the South Sea Islands) should let his talents rust and resolve to devote his life merely to idleness, indulgence, and propagation—in a word, to pleasure. But he cannot possibly will that this should become a universal law of nature or that it should be implanted in us by a natural instinct. For, as a rational being, he nec-

---

[10]It must be noted here that I reserve the division of duties for a future *Metaphysics of Morals* and that the division here stands as only an arbitrary one (chosen in order to arrange my examples). For the rest, by a perfect duty I here understand a duty which permits no exception in the interest of inclination; thus I have not merely outer but also inner perfect duties. This runs contrary to the usage adopted in the schools, but I am not disposed to defend it here because it is all one to my purpose whether this is conceded or not.

essarily wills that all his faculties should be developed, inasmuch as they are given to him for all sorts of possible purposes.

4. A fourth man, for whom things are going well, sees that others (whom he could help) have to struggle with great hardships, and he asks, "What concern of mine is it? Let each one be as happy as heaven wills, or as he can make himself; I will not take anything from him or even envy him; but to his welfare or to his assistance in time of need I have no desire to contribute." If such a way of thinking were a universal law of nature, certainly the human race could exist, and without doubt even better than in a state where everyone talks of sympathy and good will, or even exerts himself occasionally to practice them while, on the other hand, he cheats when he can and betrays or otherwise violates the rights of man. Now although it is possible that a universal law of nature according to that maxim could exist, it is nevertheless impossible to will that such a principle should hold everywhere as a law of nature. For a will which resolved this would conflict with itself, since instances can often arise in which he would need the love and sympathy of others, and in which he would have robbed himself, by such a law of nature springing from his own will, of all hope of the aid he desires.

The foregoing are a few of the many actual duties, or at least of duties we hold to be actual, whose derivation from the one stated principle is clear. We must be able to will that . . . a maxim of our action become a universal law; this is the canon of the moral estimation of our action generally. Some actions are of such a nature that their maxim cannot even be *thought* as a universal law of nature without contradiction, far from it being possible that one could will that it should be such. In others this internal impossibility is not found, though it is still impossible to *will* that their maxim should be raised to the universality of a law of nature, because such a will would contradict itself. We easily see that the former maxim conflicts with the stricter or narrower (imprescriptible) duty, the latter with broader (meritorious) duty. Thus all duties, so far as the kind of obligation (not the object of their action) is concerned, have been completely exhibited by these examples in their dependence on the one principle.

The Utilitarians

Kant, we have seen, may well have offered a sound refutation of Hume's idea that moral principles are not determined by reason. It is therefore perhaps strange that two of the most celebrated ethical philosophers of the nineteenth century, the Englishmen **Jeremy Bentham** (1748–1832) and **John Stuart Mill** (1806–1873), largely ignored the rationalistic ethics of Kant, Bentham perhaps more so than Mill. Bentham and Mill did not, however, ignore Hume. Instead, they developed further Hume's idea that those traits and actions are virtuous that promote the welfare of people, the "general happiness."

Bentham and Mill were **utilitarians,** which means they believed that *the rightness of an action is identical with the happiness it produces as its consequence.* What's new or exciting about this? Didn't Aristotle and the Epicureans and

Augustine and Aquinas also advocate pursuing happiness? The difference is that according to those earlier philosophers, it is *your own happiness* that you should strive for.

By contrast, when the utilitarians said that the morally best act is the one that produces, compared with all possible alternative acts, the greatest amount of happiness, they meant the greatest amount of happiness *with everyone considered*. But this is ambiguous: should we aim at increasing the *average* happiness or the *total* happiness—even if this would reduce the happiness per person? Usually the utilitarians are interpreted as favoring increasing the average happiness. In any case, they believed that when you are trying to produce happiness, it is not just your own happiness you should aim for, but the happiness of people in general.

It is common to attribute to the utilitarians the view that the right act is the one that produces "the greatest happiness for the greatest number." *That* phrase—the greatest happiness for the greatest number—is unfortunate, because it tells us to maximize two different things. (Just try to plot the greatest happiness for the greatest number as a single line on a graph, with happiness as one variable and number as a second variable!) You can say, "The more people that have a given amount of happiness, the better," and you can say, "The more happiness a given number of people have, the better." But it's not clear what you could mean by saying, "The more happiness the greater number of people have, the better." We'll interpret the utilitarians as favoring the view that the more happiness a given number of people have, the better (i.e., the higher the average happiness, the better). And again, according to this philosophy, your own happiness is *not* more important morally than that of others.

Notice, too, that for the utilitarians, it is the *consequences* of an act that determine its rightness, a position that contrasts strongly with Kant's idea that the moral worth of an act depends on the "will" or motive with which it is taken.

Bentham

Bentham, the earlier of the two utilitarians, equated happiness with pleasure. "Nature," he wrote, "has placed mankind under the governance of two sovereign masters, *pain* and *pleasure*. It is for them alone to point out what we ought to do, as well as determine what we shall do."

The words *ought, right, good,* and the like have meaning only when defined in terms of pleasure, he said. This fact is evident, he argued, in that all other intelligible moral standards either must be interpreted in terms of the pleasure standard or are simply disguised versions of the pleasure standard in the first place.

For example, suppose you maintain that the right act is the one that is preferred by God. Well, said Bentham, unless we know God's preferences—that is, unless we know what, exactly, pleases God—what you maintain is pretty meaningless, isn't it? And the only way "to know what is His pleasure," he said, is by "observing what is our own pleasure and pronouncing it to be His."

Or consider the theory that a moral obligation to obey the law stems from a "social contract" among members of society. That theory, said Bentham, is unnecessarily complicated. For when we have a moral obligation to obey the law, he said,

ᴸᴸᴸᴸᴸᴸᴸᴸᴸᴸᴸᴸᴸᴸ

PROFILE / Jeremy Bentham (1748–1832)

You will find it easy to identify with Jeremy Bentham—if, that is, you studied Latin when you were four, started college when you were twelve, graduated by age fifteen, and finished law school and were admitted to the bar all while you were still a teenager.

Yes, Bentham was a sharp youth. When he was fifteen, he went to hear Sir William Blackstone, the famous English jurist.

Bentham said that he instantly spotted errors in Blackstone's reasoning, especially on natural rights. Bentham came to believe that the whole notion of natural rights, including that found in the American Declaration of Independence, was just "nonsense on stilts." In 1776, he published his first book, *Fragment on Government,* a critique of Blackstone.

For David Hume and Hume's *Treatise on Human Nature,* however, Bentham had more respect, and he claimed that the work made the scales fall from his eyes about ethics. Bentham's own ethical philosophy reflects the great influence of Hume.

Though qualified to do so, Bentham never actually practiced law. He was much more interested in legal and social reform and wrote daily commentaries on English law and society. He advocated a simplified and codified legal system, and worked for prison and education

reform and extension of voting rights. Bentham also published numerous pamphlets on such abuses as jury packing and extortionate legal fees, and his followers, the "Benthamites," were an effective political force that endured after his death.

Bentham was in the habit of not finishing books that he started to write, and the only major philosophical treatise that he published himself is the *Introduction to the Principles of Morals and Legislation* (1789). The title states exactly Bentham's main concern in life: applying sound principles of morality to the law.

If you want to know what Bentham looked like, don't stop with a picture. Bentham's embalmed body, complete with a wax head and dressed just as he liked to, is there for you to see at the University College, London.

that obligation is more simply explained by the fact that obedience to the law would result in more pleasure for more people than disobedience would.

Now Bentham believed that the pain and pleasure an act produces can be evaluated solely with reference to *quantitative* criteria. Which of two or more courses of action you should take should be determined by considering the probable consequences of each possible act with respect to the certainty, intensity, duration, immediacy, and extent (the number of persons affected) of the pleasure or pain it produces, and with respect to the other kinds of sensations it is likely to have as a result over the long run. This "calculus" of pleasure, as it is often called, represents a distinctive feature of Bentham's ethics. Bentham believed that by using these criteria, one could and should calculate which of alternative courses of action

The cartoon points up the foolishness of the notion that we can seek pleasure *by itself*. Such a search has no direction to it. What we seek is food, shelter, companionship, sex, and so forth—we do not, strictly speaking, seek pleasure per se. And if you tried to seek pleasure, you would not know how to go about finding it. Your seeking must always be for something, such as food, that is not *itself* pleasure.

would produce the greatest amount of pleasure and which, therefore, ought morally to be taken.

Through all of this you should be asking: But why ought I seek the *general* happiness and not give higher priority to my own? Bentham's answer was that your own happiness *coincides* with the general happiness: what brings pleasure to you and what brings pleasure to others fortunately go together.

You may wish to consider whether this answer is fully satisfactory.

Here is a selection from Bentham's influential *An Introduction to the Principles of Morals and Legislation*.

SELECTION 8.2

An Introduction to the Principles of Morals and Legislation

From Jeremy Bentham

CHAPTER 1

Of the Principle of Utility

I. Nature has placed mankind under the governance of two sovereign masters, *pain* and *pleasure*. It is for them alone to point out what we ought to do, as well as to determine what we shall do. On the one hand the standard of right and wrong, on the other the chain of causes and effects, are fastened to their throne. They govern us in all we do, in all we say, in all we think: every effort we can make to throw off our subjection, will serve but to demonstrate and confirm it. In words a man may pretend to abjure their empire: but in reality he will remain a subject to it all the while. The *principle of utility* recognizes this subjection, and assumes it for the foundation of that system, the object of which is to rear the fabric of felicity by the hands of reason and of law. Systems which attempt to question it, deal in sounds instead of sense, in caprice instead of reason, in darkness instead of light.

But enough of metaphor and declamation: it is not by such means that moral science is to be improved.

II. The principle of utility is the foundation of the present work: it will be proper therefore at the outset to give an explicit and determinate account of what is meant by it. By the principle of utility is meant that principle which approves or disapproves of every action whatsoever, according to the tendency which it appears to have to augment or diminish the happiness of the party whose interest is in question: or, what is the same thing in other words, to promote or to oppose that happiness. I say of every action whatsoever; and therefore not only of every action of a private individual, but of every measure of government.

III. By utility is meant that property in any object, whereby it tends to produce benefit, advantage, pleasure, good, or happiness, (all this in the present case comes to the same thing) or (what comes again to the same thing) to prevent the happening of mischief, pain, evil, or unhappiness to the party whose interest is considered: if that party be the community in general, then the happiness of the community: if a particular individual, then the happiness of that individual.

IV. The interest of the community is one of the most general expressions that can occur in the phraseology of morals: no wonder that the meaning of it is often lost. When it has a meaning, it is this. The community is a fictitious *body,* composed of individual persons who are considered as constituting as it were its *members.* The interest of the community then is, what?—the sum of the interests of the several members who compose it.

V. It is in vain to talk of the interest of the community, without understanding what is the interest of the individual. A thing is said to promote the interest, or to be for the interest, of an individual, when it tends to add to the sum total of his pleasures: or, what comes to the same thing, to diminish the sum total of his pains.

VI. An action then may be said to be conformable to the principle of utility, or, for shortness sake, to utility, (meaning with respect to the community at large) when the tendency it has to augment the happiness of the community is greater than any it has to diminish it. . . .

X. Of an action that is conformable to the principle of utility one may always say either that it is one that ought to be done, or at least that it is not one that ought not to be done. One may say also, that it is right it should be done; at least that it is not wrong it should be done: that it is a right action; at least that it is not a wrong action. When thus interpreted, the words *ought,* and *right* and *wrong,* and others of the stamp, having a meaning: when otherwise, they have none.

XI. Has the rectitude of this principle been ever formally contested? It should seem that it had, by those who have not known what they have been meaning. Is it susceptible of any direct proof? It should seem not: for that which is used to prove every thing else, cannot itself be proved: a chain of proofs must have their commencement somewhere. To give such proof is as impossible as it is needless.

XII. Not that there is or ever has been that human creature breathing, however stupid or perverse, who has not on many, perhaps on most occasions of his life, deferred to it. By the natural constitution of the human frame, on most occasions of their lives men in general embrace this principle, without thinking of it: if not for the ordering of their own actions, yet for the trying of their own actions, as well as those of other men. There have been, at the same time, not many, perhaps, even of the most intelligent, who have been disposed to embrace it purely and without reserve. There are even few who have not taken some occasion or other to quarrel with it, either on account of their not understanding always how to apply it, or on account of some prejudice or other which they were afraid to examine into, or could not bear to part with. For such is the stuff that man is made of: in principle and in practice, in a right track and in a wrong one, the rarest of all human qualities is consistency.

XIII. When a man attempts to combat the principle of utility, it is with reasons drawn, without his being aware of it, from that very principle itself. His arguments, if they prove any thing, prove not that the principle is *wrong*, but that according to the applications he supposes to be made of it, it *is misapplied*. Is it possible for a man to move the earth? Yes; but he must first find out another earth to stand upon.

Mill

John Stuart Mill, who claimed to have discovered in Bentham's ethical theory what he needed to give purpose to his own life, was also concerned with providing a philosophical justification for the utilitarian doctrine that it is the *general* happiness that one should aim to promote. The justification, according to Mill, lies in the fact that a *moral* principle by its very nature singles out no one for preferential treatment. Thus, Mill wrote, "as between his own happiness and that of others," the utilitarian is required "to be as strictly impartial as a disinterested and benevolent spectator." Compare Mill's justification with that of Bentham, given just before the selection. Mill's justification is sounder, isn't it?

Probably the most important difference between Mill and Bentham is that Mill believed that some pleasures are *inherently better* than others and are to be preferred even over a greater amount of pleasure of an inferior grade.

That some pleasures are better than others can be seen, Mill argued, in the fact that few people would be willing to trade places with an animal or even with a more ignorant person, even if the exchange guaranteed their having the fullest measure of an animal's or an ignoramus's pleasure. Here is what he meant. Would *you* trade places with a pig or a lunkhead? Would you do it even if you knew that as a pig or a lunkhead, you would have more pig or lunkhead pleasures than you now have pleasure as an intelligent human being?

Thus, for Mill, in determining the pleasure for which we should strive, we must consider the *quality* of the pleasure as well as the quantity. Choose the pleasure of the highest quality.

Now this is all very well, but what settles which of two pleasures is of higher quality?

Mill's answer is quite simple: Of two pleasures, if there is one to which most who have experienced both give a decided preference, that is the more desirable pleasure.

Hedonism

Hedonism is the pursuit of plea-sure. Philosophers distinguish be-tween the descriptive doctrine known as **psychological hedo-nism,** according to which the ulti-mate object of a person's desire is always pleasure, and the ethical doctrine known as **ethical hedo-nism,** according to which a per-son ought to seek pleasure over other things. You should remem-ber these doctrines.

The descriptive doctrine may be plausible at first glance, but on closer inspection it appears some-what doubtful. For we do seem to seek things beside pleasure—for example, food, good health, relax-ation, rest, rightness in our ac-tions, success, friends, and many other things, too. As the British moralist and clergyman Bishop Joseph Butler (1692–1752) ob-served, we couldn't seek pleasure at all unless we had desires for something other than pleasure, because pleasure consists in satis-fying these desires. And then too, "the pleasure of virtue," as Irish historian W. E. H. Lecky wrote, "is one which can only be obtained on the express condition of its not being the object sought." In other words, if your motive in acting vir-tuously is to obtain the pleasure that accompanies virtuous acts, then you aren't being virtuous and won't get that pleasure.

As for ethical hedonism, there are two kinds: **egoistic ethical hedonism,** according to which one ought to seek his or her own pleasure over other things, and **universalistic ethical hedo-nism,** otherwise known as utili-tarianism, according to which one ought to seek the greatest plea-sure for the greatest number of people over other things.

One difficulty utilitarians face is in explaining why pleasure for *oth-ers* is something one should seek. One common answer is that only by seeking others' pleasure can you experience a full allotment of pleasure for yourself. But this an-swer seems to assume that one's primary ethical duty is to oneself, after all.

Notice what this answer seems to entail. It seems to entail that the pleasures preferred by the *intellectual* will be found to be of superior quality, for nonintellec-tuals "only know their own side of the question. The other party to the comparison knows both sides."

According to Mill, then, it is not simply the quantity of pleasure an act pro-duces that determines its moral worth; the quality of the pleasure produced must also be taken into account. Mill is thus said to have recognized implicitly (though not in so many words) a factor other than pleasure by which the moral worth of actions should be compared: the factor of quality. In other words, he is said to have proposed, in effect, a standard of moral worth other than pleasure, a standard of "quality" by means of which pleasure itself is to be evaluated. So he sometimes is said not to be a "pure" utilitarian, if a utilitarian is one who believes that the pleasure an act produces is the only standard of good.

It is not unusual, therefore, to find philosophers who think of Bentham's phi-losophy as more consistently utilitarian than Mill's, though everyone refers to both Mill and Bentham as "the" Utilitarians.

There is one other, sort of fuzzy, difference between Bentham and Mill. Ben-tham's utilitarianism is what today is called **act-utilitarianism:** the rightness of

The Paradox of Hedonism

The Paradox of Hedonism

The British moralist **Henry Sidg-wick** (1838–1900) noted the curious fact, which he called the **paradox of hedonism,** that the desire for pleasure, if too predominant, defeats its own aim. Indeed, this seems true: pleasures, if pur-sued too actively, do lose their lus-ter, as noted in the cartoon.

Sidgwick also observed that "the pleasures of thought and study can only be enjoyed in the highest degree by those who have an ardour of curiosity which car-ries the mind temporarily away from self and its sensations." Good point. Can you imagine a great art-work or play or musical master-piece being created by someone who was intent *only* on the plea-sure he got from his work?

an *act* is determined by its effect on the general happiness. Mill also subscribed to act-utilitarianism in some passages, but in other places he seems to have advocated what is called **rule-utilitarianism.** According to this version of utilitarianism, we are to evaluate the moral correctness of an action not with reference to its impact on the general happiness, but with respect to the impact on the general happiness of the *rule* or principle that the action exemplifies.

Take this case, for example: Suppose that by murdering us, Moore and Bruder, you would increase the general happiness (maybe unknown to anyone, we harbor some awful contagious disease). Act-utilitarianism would say that you should mur-der us. But a rule-utilitarian, as Mill in some places seems to be, would say that if society accepted murder as a rule of conduct, ultimately the general happiness would be diminished, so you shouldn't murder us. Rule-utilitarianism is, in a way, much more Kantian than is act-utilitarianism.

Friedrich Nietzsche

Another important nineteenth-century philosopher, one who believed that all previous moral philosophy was tedious and soporific and who had no use at all for the utilitarians, was **Friedrich Nietzsche** (1844–1900). In Nietzsche's view, moralities are social institutions, and basically there are really just two moralities: master morality and slave morality, the morality of the masses. Slave morality—for Nietzsche, epitomized by Christian ethics—emphasizes such virtues as compassion, humility, patience, warmheartedness, and turning the other cheek. Master morality, by contrast, is the morality of the noble individual, who is egoistic, hard, intolerant, but bound by a code of honor to his peers. The noble individual defines harm entirely in terms of what is harmful to himself and despises altruism and humility.

According to Nietzsche, the enhancement of the species is always the result of aristocratic societies, which, he held, are the ultimate justification of human social existence. The primal life force, for Nietzsche, is the will to power, whose essence is the overpowering and suppression of what is alien and weaker, and which finds its highest expression in the nobleman. Slave morality, by contrast, with its emphasis on humility and meekness, is a denial of life. Selection 8.3, from *Beyond Good and Evil*, conveys these themes fairly clearly and may make it clear why attempts often are made to censor Nietzsche from schools and libraries.

SELECTION 8.3

Beyond Good and Evil

From Friedrich Nietzsche

Every enhancement of the type "man" has so far been the work of an aristocratic society—and it will be so again and again—a society that believes in the long ladder of an order of rank and differences in value between man and man, and that needs slavery in some sense or other. . . . Let us admit to ourselves, without trying to be considerate, how every higher culture on earth so far has *begun*. Human beings whose nature was still natural, barbarians in every terrible sense of the word, men of prey who were still in possession of unbroken strength of will and lust for power, hurled themselves upon weaker, more civilized, more peaceful races, perhaps traders or cattle raisers, or upon mellow old cultures whose last vitality was even then flaring up in splendid

fireworks of spirit and corruption. In the beginning, the noble caste was always the barbarian caste: their predominance did not lie mainly in physical strength or in strength of the soul—they were more whole human beings (which also means, at every level, "more whole beasts").

. . . The essential characteristic of a good and healthy aristocracy, however, is that it experiences itself *not* as a function (whether of the monarchy or the commonwealth) but as their *meaning* and highest justification—that it therefore accepts with a good conscience the sacrifice of untold human beings who, *for its* sake, must be reduced and lowered to incomplete human beings, to slaves, to instruments. Their fundamental faith simply has to be that society must *not* exist for society's sake but only as the foundation and scaffolding on which a choice type of being is able to raise itself to its higher task and to a higher state of *being*—comparable to those sun-seeking vines of Java—they called *Sipo Matador*—that so long and so often enclasp an oak tree with their tendrils until eventually, high above it but supported by it, they can unfold their crowns in the open light and display their happiness.

Refraining mutually from injury, violence, and exploitation and placing one's will on a par with that of someone else—this may become, in a certain rough sense, good manners among individuals if the appropriate conditions are present (namely, if these men are actually similar in strength and value standards and belong together in *one* body). But as soon as this principle is extended, and possibly even accepted as the *fundamental principle of society*, it immediately proves to be what it really is—a will to the *denial* of life, a principle of disintegration and decay.

Here we must beware of superficiality and get to the bottom of the matter, resisting all sentimental weakness: life itself is *essentially* appropriation, injury, overpowering of what is alien and weaker; suppression, hardness, imposition of one's own forms, incorporation and at least, at its mildest, exploitation—but why should one always use those words in which a slanderous intent has been imprinted for ages?

Even the body within which individuals treat each other as equals, as suggested before—and this happens in every healthy aristocracy—if it is a living and not a dying body, has to do to other bodies what the individuals within it refrain from doing to each other: it will have to be an incarnate will to power, it will strive to grow, spread, seize, become predominant,—not from any morality or immorality but because it is *living* and because life simply *is* will to power. But there is no point on which the ordinary consciousness of Europeans resists instruction as on this: everywhere people are now raving, even

under scientific disguises, about coming conditions of society in which "the exploitative aspect" will be removed—which sounds to me as if they promised to invent a way of life that would dispense with all organic functions. "Exploitation" does not belong to a corrupt or imperfect and primitive society: it belongs to the *essence* of what lives, as a basic organic function; it is a consequence of the will to power, which is after all the will of life. . . .

Wandering through the many subtler and coarser moralities which have so far been prevalent on earth, or still are prevalent, I found that certain features recurred regularly together and were closely associated—until I finally discovered two basic types and one basic difference.

There are *master morality* and *slave morality*—I add immediately that in all the higher and more mixed cultures there also appear attempts at mediation between these two moralities, and yet more often the interpenetration and mutual misunderstanding of both, and at times they occur directly alongside each other—even in the same human being, with a *single* soul. The moral discrimination of values has originated either among a ruling group whose consciousness of its difference from the ruled group was accompanied by delight—or among the ruled, the slaves and dependents of every degree.

In the first case, when the ruling group determines what is "good," the exalted, proud states of the soul are experienced as conferring distinction and determining the order of rank. The noble human being separates from himself those in whom the opposite of such exalted, proud states finds expression: he despises them. It should be noted immediately that in this first type of morality the opposition of "good" and *"bad"* means approximately the same as "noble" and "contemptible." (The opposition of "good" and *"evil"* has a different origin.) One feels contempt for the cowardly, the anxious, the petty, those intent on narrow utility; also for the suspicious with their unfree glances, those who humble themselves, the doglike people who allow themselves to be maltreated, the begging flatterers, above all the liars; it is part of the fundamental faith of all aristocrats that the common people lie. "We truthful ones"—thus the nobility of ancient Greece referred to itself.

It is obvious that moral designations were everywhere first applied to *human beings* and only later, derivatively, to actions. Therefore it is a gross mistake when historians of morality start from such questions as: why was the compassionate act praised? The noble type of man experiences *itself* as determining values; it does not need approval; it judges, "what is harmful to me is harmful in itself"; it knows itself to be that which first accords honor to things; it is *value-creating*. Everything it knows as part of itself it honors: such a morality is self-glorification. In the foreground there is the feeling of fullness, of power that seeks to overflow, the happiness of high tension, the consciousness of wealth that would give and bestow: the noble human being, too, helps the unfortunate, but not, or almost not, from pity, but prompted more by an urge begotten by excess of power. The noble human being honors himself as one who is powerful, also as one who has power over himself, who knows how to speak and be silent, who delights in being severe and hard with himself and respects all severity and hardness. . . . Noble and courageous human beings who think that way are furthest removed from that morality which finds the distinction of morality precisely in pity, or in acting for others . . . faith in oneself, pride in oneself, a fundamental hostility and irony against "selflessness" belong just as definitely to noble morality as does a slight disdain and caution regarding compassionate feelings and a "warm heart.". . .

A morality of the ruling group, however, is most alien and embarrassing to the present taste in the severity of its principle that one has duties only to one's peers; that against beings of a lower rank, against everything alien, one may behave as one pleases or "as the heart desires," and in any case "beyond good and evil.". . .

It is different with the second type of morality, *slave morality*. Suppose the violated, oppressed, suffering, unfree, who are uncertain of themselves and weary, moralize: what will their moral valuations have in common? Probably, a pessimistic suspicion about the whole condition of man will find expression, perhaps a condemnation of man along with his condition. The slave's eye is not favorable to the virtues of the powerful: he is skeptical and suspicious, *subtly* suspicious, of all the "good" that is honored there—he would like to persuade himself that even their happiness is not genuine. Conversely, those qualities are brought out and flooded with light which serve to ease existence for those who suffer: here pity, the complaisant and obliging hand, the warm heart, patience, industry, humility, and friendliness are honored—for these are the most useful qualities and almost the only means for enduring the pressure of existence. Slave morality is essentially a morality of utility.

Here is the place for the origin of that famous opposition of "good" and "evil": into evil one's feelings project power and dangerousness, a certain terribleness, subtlety, and strength that does not permit contempt to develop. According to slave morality, those who are "evil" thus inspire fear; according to master morality it is precisely those who are "good" that inspire, and wish to inspire, fear, while the "bad" are felt to be contemptible.

The opposition reaches its climax when, as a logical consequence of slave morality, a touch of disdain is associated also with the "good" of this morality—this may be slight and benevolent—because the good human being has to be *undangerous* in the slaves' way of thinking: he is good-natured, easy to deceive, a little stupid perhaps, *un bonhomme* [a "good person"]. Wherever slave morality becomes preponderant, language tends to bring the words "good" and "stupid" closer together.

One last fundamental difference: the longing for *freedom,* the instinct for happiness and the subtleties of the feeling of freedom belong just as necessarily to slave morality and morals as art and enthusiastic reverence and devotion are the regular symptom of an aristocratic way of thinking and evaluating. . . .

A *species* comes to be, a type becomes fixed and strong, through the long fight with essentially constant *unfavorable* conditions. Conversely, we know from the experience of breeders that species accorded superabundant nourishment and quite generally extra protection and care soon tend most strongly toward variations of the type and become rich in marvels and monstrosities (including monstrous vices).

Now look for once at an aristocratic commonwealth—say, an ancient Greek *polis,* or Venice—as an arrangement, whether voluntary or involuntary, for breeding: human beings are together there who are dependent on themselves and want their species to prevail, most often because they *have to* prevail or run the terrible risk of being exterminated. Here that boon, that excess, and that protection which favor variations are lacking; the species needs itself as a species, as something that can prevail and make itself durable by virtue of its very hardness, uniformity, and simplicity of form, in a constant fight with its neighbors or with the oppressed who are rebellious or threaten rebellion. Manifold experience teaches them to which qualities above all they owe the fact that, despite all gods and men, they are still there, that they have always triumphed: these qualities they call virtues, these virtues alone they cultivate. They do this with hardness, indeed they want hardness; ever aristocratic morality is intolerant—in the education of youth, in their arrangements for women, in their marriage customs, in the relations of old and young, in their penal laws (which take into account deviants only)—they consider intolerance itself a virtue, calling it "justice."

In this way a type with few but very strong traits, a species of severe, warlike, prudently taciturn men, closemouthed and closely linked (and as such possessed of the subtlest feeling for the charms and nuances of association), is fixed beyond the changing generations; the continual fight against ever constant *unfavorable* conditions is, as mentioned previously, the cause that fixes and hardens a type.

Eventually, however, a day arrives when conditions become more fortunate and the tremendous tension decreases; perhaps there are no longer any enemies among one's neighbors, and the means of life, even for the enjoyment of life, are superabundant. At one stroke the bond and constraint of the old discipline are torn: it no longer seems necessary, a condition of existence—if it persisted it would only be a form of *luxury,* an archaizing *taste*. Variation, whether as deviation (to something higher, subtler, rarer) or as degeneration and monstrosity, suddenly appears on the scene in the greatest abundance and magnificence; the individual dares to be individual and different.

At these turning points of history we behold beside one another, and often mutually involved and entangled, a splendid, manifold, junglelike growth and upward striving, a kind of *tropical* tempo in the competition to grow, and a tremendous ruin and self-ruination, as the savage egoisms that have turned, almost exploded, against one another wrestle "for sun and light" and can no longer derive any limit, restraint, or consideration from their previous morality. It was this morality itself that dammed up such enormous strength and bent the bow in such a threatening manner; now it is "outlived." The dangerous and uncanny point has been reached where the greater, more manifold, more comprehensive life transcends and *lives beyond* the old morality; the "individual" appears, obliged to give himself laws and to develop his own arts and wiles for self-preservation, self-enhancement, self-redemption.

All sorts of new what-fors and wherewithals;

no shared formulas any longer; misunderstanding allied with disrespect; decay, corruption, and the highest desires gruesomely entangled; the genius of the race overflowing from all cornucopias of good and bad; a calamitous simultaneity of spring and fall, full of new charms and veils that characterize young, still unexhausted, still unwearied corruption. Again danger is there, the mother of morals, great danger, this time transposed into the individual, into the neighbor and friend, into the alley [*sic*], into one's own child, into one's own heart, into the most personal and secret recesses of wish and will: what may the moral philosophers emerging in this age have to preach now?

These acute observers and loiterers discover that the end is approaching fast, that everything around them is corrupted and corrupts, that nothing will stand the day after tomorrow, except *one* type of man, the incurably *mediocre*. The mediocre alone have a chance of continuing their type and propagating—they are the men of the future, the only survivors: "Be like them! Become mediocre!" is now the only morality that still makes sense, that still gets a hearing.

But this morality of mediocrity is hard to preach: after all, it may never admit what it is and what it wants. It must speak of measure and dignity and duty and neighbor love—it will find it difficult *to conceal its irony.*

Early Analytic Ethics

According to Bentham, the rightness of an action is to be *equated* with the amount of pleasure it produces. If this is true, it logically follows that judgments of moral value—judgments that an act is right or ought to be taken or is proper or good—are really judgments of *fact,* judgments about the amount of pleasure the act has as a consequence.

Theories according to which moral judgments are really judgments of fact about the natural world are called *naturalistic* theories, as we've mentioned twice already. Naturalistic theories, you should remember, do not postulate a supernatural or "transcendental" source of value. They're not like Plato's theory, or Augustine's.

Now **G. E. Moore** (1873–1958), with whom contemporary ethical theory of the analytic branch of twentieth-century philosophy is often said to begin, took great issue with all naturalistic ethical theories, as we shall see in a moment. Analytic philosophy, as we have already mentioned, is the tradition of philosophy that came to predominate in the English-speaking world in the twentieth century.

Moore

Moore is regarded as the starting point of contemporary (analytic) ethics because he opened up new issues for consideration and altered the focus of ethical

The Six Biggies

It is fairly common these days to distinguish among six basic types of ethical theory, which we'll set forth here in no particular order:

- First, **divine-command ethics:** What ought I to do? What God ordains I ought to do. Augustine and Aquinas are good examples.

- Second, **consequentialism:** What ought I to do? Whatever has the most desirable consequences. The Epicureans, stoics, and utilitarians are good examples.

- Third, **deontological ethics:** What ought I to do? Whatever it is my moral duty to do (in at least some cases, regardless of consequences). Kant is a good example.

- Fourth, **virtue ethics:** What ought I to do? What the virtuous person would do. (For virtue ethics, the primary question is not, What ought I to do? but What kind of person ought I to be?) Plato and Aristotle are good examples.

- Fifth, **relativism:** What ought I to do? What my culture or society thinks I ought to do. The contemporary American philosopher Gilbert Harman is a good example.

- Sixth, **contractarianism** or **contractualism:** What ought I to do? What the "social contract" calls for me to do. This is the view that moral principles are best constructed through negotiations among impartial, informed, and rational agents. Hobbes and (see Part 3) Rawls and Locke are good examples.

These categories are by no means mutually exclusive. •

discussion. Much of twentieth-century analytic ethics, at least until very recently, treated issues that were raised either by Moore or by philosophers responding to him or to other respondents. Though analytic ethical philosophers discussed many questions that were not directly (or indirectly) considered by Moore, even these questions were raised along tributaries that can be traced back to the main water-way opened by Moore. Some people regret the influence Moore had on ethics. You will have to draw your own conclusions.

Moore believed that the task of the ethical philosopher is to conduct a "general inquiry into what is good." This seems reasonably straightforward and down to earth, surely. And useful. If you know what good or goodness *is* and if you know what things *are* good, then you also know what proper conduct is, right? For the morally right act is the one that produces the greatest amount of good, not so? This, at any rate, is what Moore maintained.

Now good, or goodness, which is the same thing, is a *noncomplex* and *non-natural* property of good things, Moore argued. Goodness is noncomplex in that it cannot be broken down or "analyzed" into simpler constituents. It isn't at all like the property of being alive, for example. A thing's being alive consists in many simpler things, like having a beating heart and a functioning brain (at least for humans and other animals). But a thing's being *good* is rather more like a person's being in pain, at least with respect to the question of complexity. Pain is pain, and that's that. Pain cannot be broken down into simpler constituent parts (though

This idea comes straight from J. S. Mill, who observed that "no instructed person" would consent to become an ignoramus even if he were persuaded that as an ignoramus he would be happier than he presently is. Plato had a similar thing in mind when he said that a person who had found knowledge would rather be the slave of the poorest master than be ignorant.

how we come to have pain can be *explained,* but that is quite a different matter). Good, too, is simple, according to Moore: it is a property that cannot be further analyzed or broken down into simpler constituent parts. Thus good is also *indefinable,* he said; at least you cannot come up with a definition of good that states its constituent parts (because there aren't any). Good is good, and that's that.

Good is also a nonnatural property, Moore stated. This is what he meant. Suppose that you pronounce that something is good. Is what you are saying *equivalent* to saying that it is a certain size or shape or color or is pleasant or worth a lot of money? Of course not. Size, shape, color, pleasantness, and monetary value are all natural properties: they are a part of nature, construed broadly. They can be perceived. But good is not equivalent to these or any other natural properties, or so said Moore. Take something you regard as good, like an act of generosity, for instance. Now list all the natural properties (that is, all the properties that can be apprehended by sense) of this act. Do you find goodness on the list? Not at all. What you find are such items as the duration, location, causes, and consequences of the generous act. The *goodness* of the act is not identical with any of these items. It is something quite different from the act's natural properties.

That goodness does not equate with any natural property is easily seen, Moore argued, in a passage that became one of the most famous in all of twentieth-century ethics. Think of any natural property, like, say, pleasantness. Now, it is certainly reasonable to ask if pleasantness is good. But if pleasantness were *equivalent* to good, then asking "Is pleasantness good?" would be the same as asking "Is good good?", and that is *not* a reasonable question. Because it is legitimate and intelligible to ask of any natural property whether that property is good, it follows that good is not equivalent to any natural property.

You can see that Moore certainly did not agree with the utilitarians, who equated the goodness of an act with the pleasure it produced as a consequence.

Now Moore wanted especially to know which things that are good we can really hope to obtain. His answer? Personal affection and aesthetic enjoyments. Moore wrote: "Personal affection and aesthetic enjoyments include by far the greatest good with which we are acquainted." Note how different this answer is from any that would have been proposed by the other philosophers we have discussed.

But the remarkable thing is that it was not Moore's opinion about what things are good that interested other philosophers. Rather it was Moore's *metaethical* opinions that were most discussed. We'd better explain. *Is* goodness a simple, nonnatural, and indefinable property, as Moore argued? Is it *true,* as Moore asserted, that what makes an act right is that it produces the maximum amount of good? Notice that you can set forth an answer to each of these questions without committing yourself one way or the other about what *actually is* right and wrong, good and bad, or ought and ought not be done. Answers to these questions are thus value neutral. The questions call not for value judgments as answers, but for judgments about the relationships between value judgments and between value judgments and factual judgments.

The philosophical investigation, of a value-neutral sort, into the logical relationships of moral value judgments or into the sources, criteria, meaning, verification, or validation of such judgments (or of theories in which such judgments are proposed) is known as **metaethics.** And it was Moore's metaethical views and not his ethical claims about what actually is good that provoked the most discussion in the professional philosophical literature.

Further, much contemporary (analytic) ethical philosophy, which has grown out of the issues raised by Moore and by those who in turn responded to Moore, has been metaethical. Many people outside the field find this state of affairs just awful. Philosophers should propose theories about what people should do and about what things are good, they believe. But contemporary analytic ethical philosophers have often not attempted to do this, and their opinions on these matters, insofar as they have been given, are not often the subject of much discussion or debate in the professional literature or at professional meetings (though this has been changing during the past twenty or so years).

SELECTION 8.4

Principia Ethica

From G. E. Moore

6. What, then, is good? How is good to be defined? . . . my answer . . . may seem a very disappointing one. If I am asked "What is good?" my answer is that good is good, and that is the end of the matter. Or if I am asked "How is good to be defined?" my answer is that it cannot be defined, and that is all I have to say about it. But disappointing as these answers may appear, they are of the very last importance. To readers who are familiar with philosophic terminology, I can express their importance by saying that they amount to this: That propositions about the

Ethics and Metaethics

Being concerned with what is good or right or just is called **first-order thinking.** But you can also be concerned with thought and talk about what's good and right and just. That's **second-order thinking.**

Metaethics is second-order thinking. The metaethicist doesn't ask: What is good? Instead, he or she asks such questions as: What does it mean to call something good? How are judgments about the goodness of things and the rightness of acts related? How are moral judgments verified or validated? What is a value judgment?

First-order moral thoughts result directly in normative claims— that is, in value judgments, such as "Generosity is good." Metaethical inquiries, by contrast, do not directly yield value judgments. Instead, they yield propositions such as this: "To say that 'generosity is good' is to attribute to generosity a nonnatural property."

Much of contemporary ethics in the analytic tradition has been metaethics.

good are all of them synthetic and never analytic; and that is plainly no trivial matter. And the same thing may be expressed more popularly, by saying that, if I am right, then nobody can foist upon us such an axiom as that "Pleasure is the only good" or that "The good is the desired" on the pretence that is "the very meaning of the word."

7. Let us, then, consider this position. My point is that "good" is a simple notion, just as "yellow" is a simple notion; that, just as you cannot, by any manner of means, explain to any one who does not already know it, what yellow is, so you cannot explain what good is. Definitions of the kind that I was asking for, definitions which describe the real nature of the object or notion denoted by a word, and which do not merely tell us what the word is used to mean, are only possible when the object or notion in question is something complex. You can give a definition of a horse, because a horse has many different properties and qualities, all of which you can enumerate. But when you have enumerated them all, when you have reduced a horse to his simplest terms, then you can no longer define those terms. They are simply something which you think of or perceive, and to any one who cannot think of or perceive them, you

can never, by any definition, make their nature known. . . .

10. "Good," then, if we mean by it that quality which we assert to belong to a thing, when we say that the thing is good, is incapable of any definition, in the most important sense of that word. The most important sense of "definition" is that in which a definition states what are the parts which invariably compose a certain whole; and in this sense "good" has no definition because it is simple and has no parts. It is one of those innumerable objects of thought which are themselves incapable of definition, because they are the ultimate terms by reference to which whatever *is* capable of definition must be defined. That there must be an indefinite number of such terms is obvious, on reflection; since we cannot define anything except by analysis, which, when carried as far as it will go, refers us to something, which is simply different from anything else, and which by that ultimate difference explains the peculiarity of the whole which we are defining: for every whole contains some parts which are common to other wholes also. There is, therefore, no intrinsic difficulty in the contention that "good" denotes a simple and indefinable quality. There are many other instances of such qualities.

Virtue Ethics

Until recently, the normative ethical theories that have been most influential in contemporary moral philosophy are probably those that come from the utilitarians and from Kant. The basic ethical question has been (in some form or other), What ought one do? The answer has been stated in terms of some sort of rule for conduct. But recently, there has been a big resurgence of interest in virtue ethics. To refresh you, virtue ethics is that long tradition of ethics that includes Plato, Aristotle, Aquinas, Nietzsche, and (in certain respects) Hume. It focuses on the character traits of individuals and on the question "What kind of person ought one be?" rather than on rules for actions.

From the standpoint of many of those within this tradition, an ethics of character traits is in some ways more fundamental than an ethics based on rules for action. For instance, a cowardly act seems less commendable morally than a courageous one, even if the cowardly act happens in the case at hand to have better consequences. Whether acts count as moral or immoral seems to depend not just on their consequences, nor even just on the intent with which they are taken on a given occasion, but instead, to a large extent, on the type of character they reflect.

Some of the contemporary philosophers who have helped redirect attention to the virtue ethics tradition are (among others) Philippa Foot, Alasdair MacIntyre, J. L. Mackie, Bernard Mayo, and Martha Nussbaum. An especially widely read recent work is *After Virtue* (1981) by Alasdair MacIntyre.

Consider yellow, for example. We may try to define it, by describing its physical equivalent; we may state what kind of light-vibrations must stimulate the normal eye, in order that we may perceive it. But a moment's reflection is sufficient to show that those light-vibrations are not themselves what we mean by yellow. *They* are not what we perceive. Indeed we should never have been able to discover their existence, unless we had first been struck by the patent difference of quality between the different colours. The most we can be entitled to say of those vibrations is that they are what corresponds in space to the yellow which we actually perceive.

Yet a mistake of this simple kind has commonly been made about "good." It may be true that all things which are good are also something else, just as it is true that all things which are yellow produce a certain kind of vibration in the light. And it is a fact, that Ethics aims at discovering what are those other properties belonging to all things which are good. But far too many philosophers have thought that when they named those other properties they were actually defining good; that these properties, in fact, were simply not "other," but absolutely and entirely the same with goodness. . . .

13. . . . There are, in fact, only two serious alternatives to be considered, in order to establish the conclusion that "good" does denote a simple and indefinable notion. It might possibly denote a complex, as "horse" does; or it might have no meaning at all. Neither of these possibilities has, however, been clearly conceived and seriously maintained, as such, by those who presume to define good; and both may be dismissed by a simple appeal to facts.

(1) The hypothesis that disagreement about the meaning of good is disagreement with regard to the correct analysis of a given whole, may be most plainly seen to be incorrect by consideration of the fact that whatever definition be offered, it may be always asked, with significance, of the complex so defined, whether it is itself good. . . .

(2) And the same consideration is sufficient to dismiss the hypothesis that "good" has no meaning whatsoever. . . . Whoever will attentively consider with himself what is actually before his mind when he asks the question "Is pleasure (or whatever it may be) after all good?" can easily satisfy himself that he is not merely wondering whether pleasure is pleasant. And if he will try this experiment with each suggested definition in succession, he may become expert enough to recognise that in every case he has before his mind a unique object, with regard to the connection of which with any other object, a distinct question may be asked. Every one does in fact understand the question, "Is this good?" When he thinks of it, his state of mind is different from what it would be, were he asked "Is this pleasant, or desired, or approved?" It has a distinct meaning for him.

Ross

In an influential book, *The Right and the Good* (1930), **W. D. Ross** (1877–1970) defined his purpose as "to examine the nature, relations, and implications of three conceptions which appear to be fundamental in ethics—those of 'right,' 'good' in general, and 'morally good.'" Ross's purpose, therefore, was to conduct a metaethical inquiry, and his work was devoted largely to criticism of certain metaethical ideas set forth by G. E. Moore. Let's consider Ross briefly to get the sense of what he, and metaethics generally, was about.

Moore, as we noted, believed that that which alone makes right actions right is that they produce more good than alternative actions do. This seems reasonable enough, doesn't it? If a course of action is right, it must be because it is more productive of good than are alternative courses of action. But Ross disagreed. Certainly, he wrote, it is right and morally obligatory and our duty (these expressions all mean the same, for Ross) to bring into existence as many good things as possible. But the production of maximum good is not the only thing that makes an act right: we have other duties than to bring about good results.

For example, it is your duty to keep promises, Ross said. What makes it right for you to do what you have promised to do is not that your doing it will produce more good, as Moore thought, but simply the fact that you promised to do it.

In short, according to Ross there exist ***prima facie* duties**—things it is our duty to do unless that duty is overridden by some other duty. Our *prima facie* duties include such actions as keeping promises, relieving distress, showing gratitude, improving ourselves, and being truthful. What makes it right to do these things is not that doing so produces the maximum good (though it may have this as a side benefit), but simply that it is right to do them.

According to Ross, our *prima facie* duties are not *absolute* duties—for example, though it is our duty to keep promises, we are justified in breaking a promise to save someone's life—but it *is* at any rate our duty to do them unless other moral considerations take precedence.

And further, according to Ross, that it is right to keep promises, return services rendered, and so forth, is *self-evident*, "just as a mathematical axiom or the validity of a form of inference, is self-evident." "The moral order expressed in these propositions," Ross asserted, "is just as much part of the fundamental nature of the universe . . . as is the spatial or numerical structure expressed in the axioms of geometry or arithmetic."

You should note here the similarity between Ross's views and those of Kant. Kant, too, remember, proposed a duty-based moral philosophy and was also committed to the idea that our moral duty is self-evident. A duty-based moral philosophy, incidentally, is known as a deontological moral philosophy. **Deontological ethics** are usually contrasted with consequentialist ethics and virtue ethics. The box on page 254 explains the differences.

Now Ross recognized not only *prima facie* duties but also *intrinsic goods,* specifically virtue, knowledge, and (with certain limitations) pleasure. We do indeed have a *prima facie* duty to produce as much of these good things as possible, Ross maintained.

But what we wish here to emphasize is that what other philosophers mainly discussed was *not* Ross's thoughts about what things actually are good or about what our duties actually are, but his *metaethical* theories. What was discussed was not any of the duties or ethical norms or standards that he advocated but rather such ideas as that *right is not reducible to good,* that *some true moral propositions are self-evident,* and that *some duties are* "prima facie."

Emotivism and Existentialism

The utilitarians, recall, defined the rightness of an action in terms of the happiness it produces as a consequence. Accordingly, moral judgments, for utilitarians, in effect are a type of *factual judgment,* a judgment about how much happiness some action produces.

Moore and Ross, though denying that the rightness of an act or the goodness of an end can be defined in terms of happiness or any other natural property or thing, and though disagreeing between themselves about the relationship between rightness and goodness, also (like the utilitarians) believed that moral judgments are a type of *factual judgment.* To say that an end is good or that an act is right, for Moore and Ross both, is to state a fact. It is to attribute a property to the thing in question, a "nonnatural" property. Whether a certain type of act possesses the property of rightness and whether a certain end possesses the property of goodness are questions of fact, even though the fact is nonempirical. That it is right to keep a promise, Moore and Ross would agree, is a *fact:* it is *true* that you should keep your promises, and *false* that you should break them.

A radically different view of moral judgments was set forth by the emotivists, a group of analytic philosophers who had read Moore and Ross and disagreed with them both.

Losing Sight of the Big Issues?

Much ethical inquiry in twentieth-century analytic philosophy has been *metaethical* inquiry. This is unfortunate, in the opinion of some people.

Many intellectuals and others expect philosophers to make pronouncements on the "big" issues, such as: What should we strive for? How should we live our lives? What is the fundamental good? What's wrong with the world, anyway? and so on. Some of these individuals view the focus of ana-lytic philosophers on questions of metaethics with disappointment and disdain and believe that meta-ethics contrasts most unfavorably with existentialism, which seems clearly interested in important issues.

Certainly this disappointment in some cases is a product of noncom-prehension, a failure to understand the importance of second-order inquiry to first-order inquiry, of metaethics to ethics. Take Moore's seemingly academic question, whether goodness is a simple, nonnatural, and indefinable prop-erty. The question may perhaps seem trivial and uninteresting, but if Moore's answer is correct, then all who equate goodness with a natural property, as many have done for more than twenty centu-ries, are mistaken in their values.

So metaethics is not com-pletely trivial. In fact, it can be pretty important stuff.

The Emotivists

The **emotivists** maintained that *moral judgments have no factual meaning whatsoever.* Such judgments, according to the emotivists, *are not even genuine propositions.* In their view, the judgment "It is right to keep your promises" is neither true nor false: the utterance is not really a proposition at all.

Thus, according to the emotivists, there is no question about what we are saying if, for example, we state, "Abortion is wrong." For because we are not really asserting a genuine proposition, we are not really *saying* anything at all. The question therefore is only what we are *doing* when we open our mouths and voice an expression like "Abortion is wrong."

And what we are doing, they said, is *expressing our distaste* for abortion and also, sometimes, *encouraging others to feel the same way.* Thus, **C. L. Stevenson** (1908–1979), an influential emotivist, maintained that an ethical judgment like "Abortion is wrong" is a linguistic act by which the speaker expresses his or her attitude toward abortion and seeks to influence the attitude, and in turn the conduct, of the listener.

Can it really be that the rich and varied discourse in which human beings discuss ethical issues amounts to nothing more than expressions of attitude and emotion? Can it really be that the person who maintains, for example, that it is wrong for society not to care for the disadvantaged is merely *expressing distaste* for something? Selection 8.5, by **A. J. Ayer** (1910–1989), is an effective statement of this position.

Language, Truth and Logic

From A. J. Ayer

The fundamental ethical concepts are unanalysable, inasmuch as there is no criterion by which one can test the validity of the judgements in which they occur. . . . We say that the reason why they are unanalysable is that they are mere pseudo-concepts. The presence of an ethical symbol in a proposition adds nothing to its factual content. Thus if I say to someone, "You acted wrongly in stealing that money," I am not stating anything more than if I had simply said, "You stole that money." In adding that this action is wrong I am not making any further statement about it. I am simply evincing my moral disapproval of it. It is as if I had said, "You stole that money," in a peculiar tone of horror, or written it with the addition of some special exclamation marks. The tone, or the exclamation marks, adds nothing to the literal meaning of the sentence. It merely serves to show that the expression of it is attended by certain feelings in the speaker.

If now I generalize my previous statement and say, "Stealing money is wrong," I produce a sentence which has no factual meaning—that is, expresses no proposition which can be either true or false. It is as if I had written "Stealing money!!"—where the shape and thickness of the exclamation marks show, by a suitable convention, that a special sort of moral disapproval is the feeling which is being expressed. It is clear that there is nothing said here which can be true or false. Another man may disagree with me about the wrongness of stealing, in the sense that he may not have the same feelings about stealing as I have, and he may quarrel with me on account of my moral sentiments. But he cannot, strictly speaking, contradict me. For in saying that a certain type of action is right or wrong, I am not making any factual statement,

not even a statement about my own state of mind. I am merely expressing certain moral sentiments. And the man who is ostensibly contradicting me is merely expressing his moral sentiments. So that there is plainly no sense in asking which of us is in the right. For neither of us is asserting a genuine proposition.

What we have just been saying about the symbol "wrong" applies to all normative ethical symbols. Sometimes they occur in sentences which record ordinary empirical facts besides expressing ethical feeling about those facts: sometimes they occur in sentences which simply express ethical feeling about a certain type of action, or situation, without making any statement of fact. But in every case in which one would commonly be said to be making an ethical judgement, the function of the relevant ethical word is purely "emotive." It is used to express feeling about certain objects, but not to make any assertion about them.

It is worth mentioning that ethical terms do not serve only to express feeling. They are calculated also to arouse feeling, and so to stimulate action. Indeed some of them are used in such a way as to give the sentences in which they occur the effect of commands. Thus the sentence "It is your duty to tell the truth" may be regarded both as the expression of a certain sort of ethical feeling about truthfulness and as the expression of the command "Tell the truth." The sentence "You ought to tell the truth" also involves the command "Tell the truth," but here the tone of the command is less emphatic. In the sentence "It is good to tell the truth" the command has become little more than a suggestion. And thus the "meaning" of the word "good," in its ethical usage, is differentiated from that of the word "duty" or the word "ought." In fact we may define the meaning of the various ethical words in terms both of the different feelings they are ordinarily taken to express, and also the different responses which they are calculated to provoke.

We can now see why it is impossible to find a criterion for determining the validity of ethical judgements. It is not because they have an "absolute" validity which is mysteriously independent of ordinary sense-experience, but because they have no objective validity whatsoever. If a sentence makes no statement at all, there is obviously no sense in asking whether what it says is true or false. And we have seen that sentences which simply express moral judgements do not say anything. They are pure expressions of feeling and as such do not come under the category of truth and falsehood. They are unverifiable— because they do not express genuine propositions.

The Existentialists

The emotivist position in essence denies the existence of values, except as mere expressions of likes and dislikes. There is another important group of philosophers who also appear to deny the existence of values and who are therefore at least superficially like the emotivists. These are the **existentialists.**

Existentialism, however, in case you've forgotten what we said in Chapter 1, is an entirely different tradition of philosophy from the analytic tradition of Moore and Ross and Stevenson and Ayer. In a later chapter we provide a close-up of existentialism. Here you must keep in mind that the existentialists, unlike the emotivists, were not reacting to Moore and Ross. There is little evidence that they were even interested in Moore or Ross, or, for that matter, in the emotivists. They were on their own agenda, even though their philosophy superficially resembles that of the emotivists in seeming to deny the existence of values.

Jean-Paul Sartre (1905–1980), perhaps the most famous existentialist, rested his philosophy on the premise that God does not exist: because there is no God, he reasoned, "we do not find before us any values or orders which will justify our conduct." In other words, because there is no God, there is no objective good or evil, right or wrong: as the nineteenth-century Russian novelist Dostoyevsky said, "everything is permissible." And because there is no God, there is no fundamental reason why the world is the way it is and not some other way: the world is therefore irrational and absurd. And because there is no God, we experience ourselves as abandoned and are forlorn. How are we to exist in an absurd world? This is the fundamental human problem for Sartre.

Because values do not exist objectively, we create our own values, Sartre reasoned. We do so, he said, through our choices and decisions, through our actions. But we do so, he said, in *anguish*. Our choices are made in anguish, Sartre thought, for there is nothing objective to guide us, and also because in choosing, one acts as a *lawgiver for all mankind:* to choose a course of action is in effect to say what is right; that is, it is to say what all should do. The awesome responsibility of your choices, in which you in effect act the part of God, is experienced in anguish.

Anguish, thus, for Sartre, comes in the awareness of our freedom to choose in a universe that has no objective values. We may try to *hide* from our responsibility as moral lawgivers, we may try to *escape* anguish, by pretending that we do not impose our values on all people. Or we may try to hide from our responsibility by pretending that we are not free, by pretending that what we choose and do is determined by circumstances or by our heredity. But such pretenses, Sartre said, are a self-deception, the mark of *inauthenticity* and *bad faith*. They are a self-deception, he reasoned, because the very attempt to conceal one's freedom presupposes this freedom exists.

You can now see that the resemblance between Sartre's ethics and the meta-ethics of the emotivists is very superficial indeed. There is an altogether different tone about Sartre's philosophy. It carries a sense of urgency that is entirely lacking in the writings of Ayer and Stevenson. Sartre would never have been content with setting forth some neutral description of the function or meaning of moral expressions. And the emotivists would never have felt comfortable discussing the existential plight of modern humans.

But even more to the point, Sartre's philosophy does not really suppose that there are no values or that "everything is permissible." For Sartre there is something dishonest, something *wrong,* about a way of life in which one seeks to avoid one's responsibility or disguise one's absolute freedom of choice. The notions of inauthenticity and bad faith are clearly pejorative. To act morally, for Sartre, is to act in good faith. Because each person determines his or her own morality, acting in good faith can only mean acting consistently within one's own moral standards.

From an emotivist point of view, therefore, Sartre's moral philosophy is *prescriptive:* it does make value judgments. Therefore, from the emotivist point of view, Sartre's philosophy is merely just one more expression of sentiment.

Selection 8.6 is from Sartre's *Existentialism and Humanism.* (You may wish to turn to Chapter 15 to read more of this essay.) In it Sartre gives a detailed examination of a case in which an important ethical decision must be made by an individual, who must face the decision absolutely alone: no one can help the person choose and no doctrine can guide his way. In that respect he is like all of us, Sartre implies.

Notice how very different the flavor of this piece is from that of the Moore and Ayer selections.

SELECTION 8.6

Existentialism and Humanism   **From Jean-Paul Sartre**

Dostoyevsky has written, "If God did not exist, everything would be allowed." This is the point of departure for existentialism. Indeed, everything is allowed if God does not exist, and con-

sequently man is abandoned, because neither in himself nor beyond himself does he find any possibility of clinging on [to something]. . . . Moreover, if God does not exist, we do not find

Values Without God

In Chapter 7, when we discussed Hume, we noticed how easy it would be to think that if neither God nor reason determines moral standards, then there just would not be any moral standards. But this is by no means certain. Naturalistic ethical theories, for instance, need not assume the existence of God, nor need they assume that reason dictates moral standards. Then, too, there are nonnaturalistic ethical theories, like those of Plato and Moore, that do not require the existence of God and also do not suppose that reason sets the standard on what is right and wrong.

So we should not blithely assume without argument that God is required for there to be ethical standards. Even if we disregard such reason-based ethical theories as that of Kant, there may be other grounds for denying that without God "everything is permissible."

---

before us any values or orders which will justify our conduct. So, we have neither behind us nor before us, in the luminous realm of values, any justifications or excuses. We are alone, without excuses. It is what I will express by saying that man is condemned to be free. Condemned, because he has not created himself, and nevertheless, in other respects [he is] free, because once [he is] cast into the world, he is responsible for everything that he does. . . .

To give you an example which [will] allow [you] to understand abandonment better, I will cite the case of one of my students who came to see me in the following circumstances. His father was on bad terms with his mother, and moreover, was inclined to be a collaborator. His older brother had been killed in the German offensive of 1940, and this young man, with feelings somewhat primitive but generous, wanted to avenge him. His mother lived alone with him, quite distressed by the semi-betrayal of his father and by the death of her eldest son, and found consolation only in him. This young man had the choice, at that time, between leaving for England and enlisting in the Free French Forces—that is to say, to forsake his mother—or to stay near his mother and to help her [to] live. He fully realized that this woman lived only for him and that his disappearance—and perhaps his death—would cast her into despair. He also

realized that, in reality, [and] concretely, each action that he performed with regard to his mother had its surety in the sense that he was helping her to live, whereas each action that he might perform in order to leave and fight was an ambiguous action which could be lost in the sands, to answer no purpose. For example, leaving for England, he might remain indefinitely in a Spanish camp, while passing through Spain; he might arrive in England or in Algiers and be placed in an office to keep records. Consequently, he found himself facing two very different kinds of action: one concrete, immediate, but applying only to one individual; or else an action which applied to a whole [group] infinitely vaster, a national community but which was by that reason ambiguous, and which could be interrupted on the way. And, at the same time, he hesitated between two kinds of ethics. On the one hand, an ethic of sympathy, of individual devotion; and on the other hand a wider ethic but whose effectiveness was more questionable. He had to choose between the two. Who could help him to choose? Christian doctrine? No. Christian doctrine says: "be charitable, love your neighbor, devote yourself to others, choose the hardest way, etc. . . ." But which is the hardest way? Whom must we love as our brother, the soldier or the mother? Which has the greatest utility, the one [which is] definite, to help a definite individual to live? Who can decide it *a priori?* No one. No written ethic can tell him. The Kantian ethic says: "never treat others as [a] means, but as [an] end." Very well; if I remain near [with] my mother I will treat her as an end and not as means, but by this same action, I risk treating those who fight around me as a means; and conversely if I go to rejoin those who are fighting I will treat them as an end, and by this action I risk treating my mother as a means.

If these values are vague, and if they are still too broad for the specific and concrete case that we are considering, it remains for us only to rely on our instincts. This is what this young man tried to do; and when I saw him, he said: "basically, what counts is the sentiment; I ought to choose that which actually pushes me in a certain direction. If I feel that I love my mother enough to sacrifice everything else for her—my desire for vengeance, my desire for action, my desire for adventures—I [will] stay near her. If, on the contrary, I feel that my love for my mother is not sufficient, I [will] leave." But how [do we] judge the weight of a feeling? What constituted the worth of his feeling for his mother? Precisely the fact that he stayed for her. I may say, I love this friend enough to sacrifice such a [a certain] sum of money for him; I can say it, only if I have done it. I may say: I love my mother enough to remain with her, if I have remained with her. I can determine the worth of this affection only if, precisely, I have performed an action which confirms and defines it. Now, as I require this affection to justify my action, I find myself caught in a vicious circle.

Further, Gide has said very well, that a feeling which is acting and a feeling which is real are two nearly indiscernible things: to decide that I love my mother by remaining near her, or to act a part which will make me stay for my mother, is nearly the same thing. In other words, the feeling is constituted by the actions that we perform: I cannot then consult it in order to guide myself according to it. What that means is that I can neither seek for in myself the authentic state which will push me to act, nor demand from an ethic the concepts which will allow me to act. At least, you say, he went to see a professor to ask his advice. But, if you seek advice from a priest, for example, you have chosen this priest, you already knew, after all, more or less, what he was going to advise you. In other words, to choose the adviser is still to commit yourself. The proof of it is what you will say, if you are a Christian: consult a priest. But there are priests who are collaborators, priests who wait for the tide to turn, priests who belong to the resistance. Which [should you] choose? And if the young man chooses a priest who is a member of the resistance, or a priest who is a collaborator, he has already decided [on] the kind of advice he will receive. Thus, in coming to see me, he knew the reply that I was going to make to him, and I had only one reply to make: you are free, choose, that is to say, invent. No general ethic can show you what there is to do; there is no sign in the world. The Catholics will reply: "but there are signs." Let's admit it; it is myself in any case who chooses the meaning that they have.

Contemporary Ethics

Again, it must be stressed that Sartre was not an analytic philosopher. His ethical philosophy should not be construed as in any way a response to Moore or Ross or the emotivists, who came from a radically different tradition of philosophy. Ayer would not have regarded Sartre's moral pronouncements as coming under the categories of truth or falsehood, and perhaps as not being philosophical in the first place.

Until recently, most analytic philosophers did not pay much attention to existentialism. They were much more interested in getting clear on the purpose or function of moral judgments than in finding values in a world thought to be absurd. And though emotivism had strong adherents within analytic philosophy, it seemed to many other analytic philosophers that the emotivist analysis of ethical judgments was essentially incorrect. We think of moral judgments, they pointed out, as things that can be mistaken. But we don't think of expressions of feelings as that way at all. Have a look at these two remarks:

Remark 1: I used to think there was nothing wrong with abortion. How could I have been so mistaken!

Remark 2: I used to feel uncomfortable speaking to large groups of people. How could I have been so mistaken!

The second remark seems peculiar; the first doesn't—but it should, if the judgment that there is nothing wrong with abortion is merely an expression of feeling.

Further, there evidently is such a thing as moral reasoning: we press people to support their moral convictions with arguments. But we don't press people to support their feelings with arguments: what you feel is what you feel, and that seems to be the end of the matter.

One influential suggestion about moral discourse was offered by the British linguistic philosopher **R. M. Hare** (1919–), who suggested that the function of moral discourse is not to express or influence attitudes, but to guide conduct. A moral judgment, he said, is a kind of prescriptive judgment that is "universalizable": when I make a moral judgment, such as "You ought to give Susan back the book you borrowed," I am prescribing a course of conduct, and I intend my prescription to hold not just for you but for anyone else in the same or in relevantly similar circumstances. Given Hare's analysis of moral judgments, it is possible to make sense of the idea that there could be such a thing as reasoning about moral issues, and Hare has explored several important aspects of moral reasoning.

That emotivism misrepresents, or indeed trivializes, moral discourse is now fairly widely accepted by contemporary philosophers.

A further important development in moral theory, along with the rejection of emotivism, is this: Think back to Moore and Ross, and to the emotivists. They all agreed that descriptive statements and value judgments are logically distinct. If you say that (1) Bruder did not do what he promised Moore he would do, you are making a purely descriptive statement. If you say that (2) Bruder did not do what he ought to have done, you are making a value judgment. Most of the philosophers of the first half of this century accepted Hume's opinion that "you cannot deduce an 'ought' from an 'is'" and held that it is a mistake to think that any moral value judgment is logically entailed by any descriptive statement. This mistake was called the *naturalist fallacy*. Thus, for example, it would be committing the naturalist fallacy to suppose that (2) is logically deducible from (1).

But is the naturalist fallacy really a fallacy? The issue is important because if you hold that moral evaluations are logically independent of descriptive premises, it would then seem that you could commend morally any state of affairs you please—and would not logically have to accept as evidence for a moral evaluation the empirical evidence that most people accept as evidence. Eventually, philosophers began to consider this issue carefully—among the first to do so were Oxford's **Phillipa Foot** (1920–) and Berkeley's **John Searle** (1932–)—and now many philosophers do not accept the idea that moral evaluations are logically independent of the descriptive premises on which, in everyday conversation, they are often based. Instead, they maintain there are empirical criteria for ascribing moral predicates to actions, people, and states of affairs.

Now, these two related developments—the rejection of emotivism and the emerging idea that there are empirical criteria for moral evaluations—are important. Here's why. If it is assumed that moral judgments are just expressions of taste and are logically independent of any empirical facts about the world, then why bother discussing concrete moral issues? Given these assumptions, there would seem to be little room for reasoned deliberation in ethical matters. Consequently, as these assumptions were called into question, there was a renewal of interest in concrete ethical issues by moral philosophers. Much discussed in recent years, for example, have been issues of sexual morality, affirmative action, biomedical ethics, business ethics, and the environment.

Further, at the same time emotivism and antinaturalism were being examined, there occurred an independent development in political philosophy, one that also has had a terrific impact on current moral philosophy. This development stems from the work of **John Rawls** (1921–), who set forth a theory of distributive justice—a theory for determining the appropriate distribution of the benefits and burdens of social cooperation. While we will be examining this theory in detail in Part 3, a few brief words are in order here.

Rawls's theory was essentially that the appropriate principles of distributive justice are those that would be agreed upon by rational and self-interested individuals who are ignorant of their own special circumstances. Because these principles are those that would be established by agreement, Rawls's theory is a contractarian theory, as was Hobbes's.

As a result of Rawls's work, there has been widespread discussion of the soundness of **contractarianism** itself, and there has been considerable interest in applying contractarian principles toward the resolution of specific moral issues. Rawls's work, too, therefore served to reinforce the current interest in "real-life" moral issues.

But now a word of caution: that there has been a recent widespread and apparently growing interest in concrete moral questions should not lead you to conclude that metaethics is dead. Indeed, in a nearby box, we list some of the metaethical issues that are currently under discussion. Nevertheless, it is probably fair to say

Current Controversies in Metaethics

Here are some (mainly) metaethical issues currently under discussion. We make no claim as to the completeness of this list.

- What makes a principle a *moral* principle? Can moral principles be about just anything? Or do they have some essential type of content?

- A *morally obligatory act* is one you ought to do, other things being equal. A *supererogatory act* is one that is morally commendable, but beyond the call of duty. Is this a legitimate distinction? Can traditional philosophical theories of ethics accommodate this distinction, if it is legitimate?

- Is ethical truth relative to the ethical beliefs of a society or culture? That is, is ethical relativism true?

- How is the question Why should I be moral? to be understood? Is it a legitimate question?

- Is there a necessary connection between believing that something is morally obligatory and being motivated to choose to do it? (So-called *internalists* assert that there is such a connection; *externalists* deny that there is.)

- What gives a being moral standing?

- Do some beings have a higher moral standing than others?

- How are moral judgments about institutions and other collectives to be understood? Groups are sometimes said to be morally responsible for their actions. Is this responsibility something over and above the responsibility of the individuals in the group?

- Is there a moral difference between doing something that you know will have certain undesirable consequences and doing it with the intention of producing those consequences?

that, as we move toward the end of the twentieth century, many professors of ethics focus their courses on concrete moral dilemmas such as abortion, euthanasia, charity, sexual fidelity, pornography, affirmative action, animal rights, environmental issues, and the other important ethical issues of our times. We want to close this chapter with two examples of this recent literature in **applied ethics,** to give you a feel for the field.

In the first reading, **Judith Jarvis Thomson** (1929–) presents a defense of abortion, a defense that allows that the fetus *is* a human person. We've reprinted those sections of Thomson's paper in which she attacks the view that abortion is impermissible if the mother's life is not at stake, and omitted some of the other sections.

In the final selection, **James Rachels** (1941–) discusses whether it is really true that letting people die of starvation is as bad as killing them (the idea that the two are equally bad is known as the *Equivalence Thesis*). Although Rachels does not, in this selection, try to prove that the two are equally bad, he does try to show that letting people die is considerably worse than we usually think it is.

Environmental Philosophy

Frequently philosophy departments offer courses in environmental ethics, one of the three main areas of applied ethics. The other two are business ethics and biomedical ethics. There is an extensive literature in environmental ethics, but, generally, discussion seems to fall under these two headings:

1. What, if any, are the root *philosophical* causes of ecological crises? Some see ecological problems as primarily due to *shallow* factors including nearsightedness, ignorance, and greed. Others seek a more basic explanation of ecological maladies, and discussion seems to have focused on three possible candidates: Some, deep ecologists, think the fundamental explanation of ecological crises is anthropocentrism, the view that humans are the central value of the universe. Others, known as ecofeminists, think the root problem is patriarchalism, or the oppression and exploitation of women—and nature—as subservient to men. Still others, social ecologists, think the fundamental causes are deep-seated authoritarian social structures based on domination and exploitation by privileged groups. Although there is considerable controversy among these groups, other environmental philosophers view their distinctions as irrelevant to such pressing problems as overconsumption and militarization.

2. What entities have moral standing and intrinsic values? For example, do nonhuman animals have rights or interests? Do plants? Do species? Do biotic communities, ecosystems, wilderness, or the planetary biosphere? And, closely related, what properties or characteristics must a thing have to have moral standing? For example, must it be able to experience sensation? Or must it just be alive? Must it simply have an end, or goal, or good of its own?

Writings on animal rights comprise a large literature in their own right, independent of environmental ethics.

"A Defense of Abortion"[1]

Judith Jarvis Thomson

Most opposition to abortion relies on the premise that the fetus is a human being, a person, from the moment of conception. The premise is argued for, but, as I think, not well. Take, for example, the most common argument. We are asked to notice that the development of a human being from conception through birth into childhood is continuous; then it is said that to draw a line, to choose a point in this development and say "before this point the thing is not a person, after this point it is a person" is to make an arbitrary choice, a choice for which in the nature of things no good reason can be given. It is concluded that the fetus is, or anyway that we had better say it is, a person from the moment of conception. But this conclusion does not follow. Similar things might be said about the development of an acorn into the oak tree, and it does not follow that acorns are oak trees, or that we had better say they are. Argu-

---

[1] I am very much indebted to James Thomson for discussion, criticism, and many helpful suggestions.

ments of this form are sometimes called "slippery slope arguments"—the phrase is perhaps self-explanatory—and it is dismaying that opponents of abortion rely on them so heavily and uncritically.

I am inclined to agree, however, that the prospects for "drawing a line" in the development of the fetus look dim. I am inclined to think also that we shall probably have to agree that the fetus has already become a human person well before birth. Indeed, it comes as a surprise when one first learns how early in its life it begins to acquire human characteristics. By the tenth week, for example, it already has a face, arms and legs, fingers and toes; it has internal organs, and brain activity is detectable.[2] On the other hand, I think that the premise is false, that the fetus is not a person from the moment of conception. A newly fertilized ovum, a newly implanted clump of cells, is no more a person than an acorn is an oak tree. But I shall not discuss any of this. For it seems to me to be of great interest to ask what happens if, for the sake of argument, we allow the premise. How, precisely, are we supposed to get from there to the conclusion that abortion is morally impermissible? Opponents of abortion commonly spend most of their time establishing that the fetus is a person, and hardly any time explaining the step from there to the impermissibility of abortion. Perhaps they think the step too simple and obvious to require much comment. Or perhaps instead they are simply being economical in argument. Many of those who defend abortion rely on the premise that the fetus is not a person, but only a bit of tissue that will become a person at birth; and why pay out more argu-

ments than you have to? Whatever the explanation, I suggest that the step they take is neither easy nor obvious, that it calls for closer examination than it is commonly given, and that when we do give it this closer examination we shall feel inclined to reject it.

I propose, then, that we grant that the fetus is a person from the moment of conception. How does the argument go from here? Something like this, I take it. Every person has a right to life. So the fetus has a right to life. No doubt the mother has a right to decide what shall happen in and to her body; everyone would grant that. But surely a person's right to life is stronger and more stringent than the mother's right to decide what happens in and to her body, and so outweighs it. So the fetus may not be killed; an abortion may not be performed.

It sounds plausible. But now let me ask you to imagine this. You wake up in the morning and find yourself back to back in bed with an unconscious violinist. A famous unconscious violinist. He has been found to have a fatal kidney ailment, and the Society of Music Lovers has canvassed all the available medical records and found that you alone have the right blood type to help. They have therefore kidnapped you, and last night the violinist's circulatory system was plugged into yours, so that your kidneys can be used to extract poisons from his blood as well as your own. The director of the hospital now tells you, "Look, we're sorry the Society of Music Lovers did this to you—we would never have permitted it if we had known. But still, they did it, and the violinist now is plugged into you. To unplug you would be to kill him. But never mind, it's only for nine months. By then he will have recovered from his ailment, and can safely be unplugged from you." Is it morally incumbent on you to accede to this situation? No doubt it would be very nice of you if you did, a great kindness. But do you *have* to accede to it? What if it were not nine months, but nine years? Or longer still? What if the director of the hospital says, "Tough luck, I agree, but you've now

---

[2]Daniel Callahan, *Abortion: Law, Choice and Morality* (New York, 1970), p. 373. This book gives a fascinating survey of the available information on abortion. The Jewish tradition is surveyed in David M. Feldman, *Birth Control in Jewish Law* (New York, 1968), Part 5, the Catholic tradition in John T. Noonan, Jr., "An Almost Absolute Value in History," in *The Morality of Abortion*, ed. John T. Noonan, Jr. (Cambridge, Mass., 1970).

got to stay in bed, with the violinist plugged into you, for the rest of your life. Because remember this. All persons have a right to life, and violinists are persons. Granted you have a right to decide what happens in and to your body, but a person's right to life outweighs your right to decide what happens in and to your body. So you cannot ever be unplugged from him." I imagine you would regard this as outrageous, which suggests that something really is wrong with that plausible-sounding argument I mentioned a moment ago.

In this case, of course, you were kidnapped; you didn't volunteer for the operation that plugged the violinist into your kidneys. Can those who oppose abortion on the ground I mentioned make an exception for a pregnancy due to rape? Certainly. They can say that persons have a right to life only if they didn't come into existence because of rape; or they can say that all persons have a right to life, but that some have less of a right to life than others, in particular, that those who came into existence because of rape have less. But these statements have a rather unpleasant sound. Surely the question of whether you have a right to life at all, or how much of it you have, shouldn't turn on the question of whether or not you are the product of a rape. And in fact the people who oppose abortion on the ground I mentioned do not make this distinction, and hence do not make an exception in case of rape.

Nor do they make an exception for a case in which the mother has to spend the nine months of her pregnancy in bed. They would agree that would be a great pity, and hard on the mother; but all the same, all persons have a right to life, the fetus is a person, and so on. I suspect, in fact, that they would not make an exception for a case in which, miraculously enough, the pregnancy went on for nine years, or even the rest of the mother's life.

Some won't even make an exception for a case in which continuation of the pregnancy is likely to shorten the mother's life; they regard abortion as impermissible even to save the mother's life. Such cases are nowadays very rare, and many opponents of abortion do not accept this extreme view. All the same, it is a good place to begin: a number of points of interest come out in respect to it. . . .

3. Where the mother's life is not at stake, the argument I mentioned at the outset seems to have a much stronger pull. "Everyone has a right to life, so the unborn person has a right to life." And isn't the child's right to life weightier than anything other than the mother's own right to life, which she might put forward as ground for an abortion?

This argument treats the right to life as if it were unproblematic. It is not, and this seems to me to be precisely the source of the mistake.

For we should now, at long last, ask what it comes to, to have a right to life. In some views having a right to life includes having a right to be given at least the bare minimum one needs for continued life. But suppose that what in fact *is* the bare minimum a man needs for continued life is something he has no right at all to be given? If I am sick unto death, and the only thing that will save my life is the touch of Henry Fonda's cool hand on my fevered brow, then all the same, I have no right to be given the touch of Henry Fonda's cool hand on my fevered brow. It would be frightfully nice of him to fly in from the West Coast to provide it. It would be less nice, though no doubt well meant, if my friends flew out to the West Coast and carried Henry Fonda back with them. But I have no right at all against anybody that he should do this for me. Or again, to return to the story I told earlier, the fact that for continued life that violinist needs the continued use of your kidneys does not establish that he has a right to be given the continued use of your kidneys. He certainly has no right against you that *you* should give him continued use of your kidneys. For nobody has any right to use your kidneys unless you give him such a right; and nobody has the right against you that you shall give him this right—if you do allow him to go on using your kidneys, this is a kindness on your part, and not something he can claim from you as his due. Nor has he any right against anybody else that *they* should give him continued use of your kidneys. Certainly he had no right against the Society of Music Lovers that they should plug him into you in the first place. And if you now start to unplug yourself, having learned that you will otherwise have to spend nine years in bed with him, there is nobody in the world who must try to prevent you, in order to see to it that he is given something he has a right to be given.

Some people are rather stricter about the right to life. In their view, it does not include the right to be given anything, but amounts to, and only to, the right not to be killed by anybody. But here a related difficulty arises. If everybody is to refrain from killing that violinist, then everybody must refrain from doing a great many different sorts of things. Everybody must refrain from slitting his throat, everybody must refrain from shooting him—and everybody must refrain from unplugging you from him. But does he have a right against everybody that they shall refrain from unplugging you from him? To refrain from doing this is to allow him to continue to use your kidneys. It could be argued that he has a right against us that *we* should allow him to continue to use your kidneys. That is, while he had no right against us that we should give him the use of your kidneys, it might be argued that he anyway has a right against us that we shall not now intervene and deprive him of the use of your kidneys. I shall come back to third-party interventions later. But certainly the violinist has no right against you that *you* shall allow him to continue to use your kidneys. As I said, if you do allow him to use them, it is a kindness on your part, and not something you owe him.

The difficulty I point to here is not peculiar to the right to life. It reappears in connection with all the other natural rights; and it is some-thing which an adequate account of rights must deal with. For present purposes it is enough just to draw attention to it. But I would stress that I am not arguing that people do not have a right to life—quite to the contrary, it seems to me that the primary control we must place on the acceptability of an account of rights is that it should turn out in that account to be a truth that all persons have a right to life. I am arguing only that having a right to life does not guarantee having either a right to be given the use of or a right to be allowed continued use of another person's body—even if one needs it for life itself. So the right to life will not serve the opponents of abortion in the very simple and clear way in which they seem to have thought it would.

4. There is another way to bring out the difficulty. In the most ordinary sort of case, to deprive someone of what he has a right to is to treat him unjustly. Suppose a boy and his small brother are jointly given a box of chocolates for Christmas. If the older boy takes the box and refuses to give his brother any of the chocolates, he is unjust to him, for the brother has been given a right to half of them. But suppose that, having learned that otherwise it means nine years in bed with that violinist, you unplug yourself from him. You surely are not being unjust to him, for you gave him no right to use your kidneys, and no one else can have given him any such right. But we have to notice that in unplugging yourself, you are killing him; and violinists, like everybody else, have a right to life, and thus in the view we were considering just now, the right not to be killed. So here you do what he supposedly has a right you shall not do, but you do not act unjustly to him in doing it.

The emendation which may be made at this point is this: the right to life consists not in the right not to be killed, but rather in the right not to be killed unjustly. This runs a risk of circularity, but never mind: it would enable us to square the fact that the violinist has a right to life with the fact that you do not act unjustly toward him in unplugging yourself, thereby killing him. For if you do not kill him unjustly, you do not violate his right to life, and so it is no wonder you do him no injustice.

But if this emendation is accepted, the gap in the argument against abortion stares us plainly in the face: it is by no means enough to show that the fetus is a person, and to remind us that all persons have a right to life—we need to be shown also that killing the fetus violates its right to life, i.e., that abortion is unjust killing. And is it?

I suppose we may take it as a datum that in a case of pregnancy due to rape the mother has not given the unborn person a right to the use of her body for food and shelter. Indeed, in what pregnancy could it be supposed that the mother has given the unborn person such a right? It is not as if there were unborn persons drifting about the world, to whom a woman who wants a child says "I invite you in."

But it might be argued that there are other ways one can have acquired a right to the use of another person's body than by having been invited to use it by that person. Suppose a woman voluntarily indulges in intercourse, knowing of the chance it will issue in pregnancy, and then she does become pregnant; is she not in part responsible for the presence, in fact the very existence, of the unborn person inside her? No doubt she did not invite it. But doesn't her partial responsibility for its being there itself give it a right to the use of her body?[7] If so, then her aborting it would be more like the boy's taking away the chocolates, and less like your unplugging yourself from the violinist—doing so would be depriving it of what it does have a right to, and thus would be doing it an injustice.

And then, too, it might be asked whether or not she can kill it even to save her own life: If

she voluntarily called it into existence, how can she now kill it, even in self-defense?

The first thing to be said about this is that it is something new. Opponents of abortion have been so concerned to make out the independence of the fetus, in order to establish that it has a right to life, just as its mother does, that they have tended to overlook the possible support they might gain from making out that the fetus is *dependent* on the mother, in order to establish that she has a special kind of responsibility for it, a responsibility that gives it rights against her which are not possessed by any independent person—such as an ailing violinist who is a stranger to her.

On the other hand, this argument would give the unborn person a right to its mother's body only if her pregnancy resulted from a voluntary act, undertaken in full knowledge of the chance a pregnancy might result from it. It would leave out entirely the unborn person whose existence is due to rape. Pending the availability of some further argument, then, we would be left with the conclusion that unborn persons whose existence is due to rape have no right to the use of their mothers' bodies, and thus that aborting them is not depriving them of anything they have a right to and hence is not unjust killing.

And we should also notice that it is not at all plain that this argument really does go even as far as it purports to. For there are cases and cases, and the details make a difference. If the room is stuffy, and I therefore open a window to air it, and a burglar climbs in, it would be absurd to say, "Ah, now he can stay, she's given him a right to the use of her house—for she is partially responsible for his presence there, having voluntarily done what enabled him to get in, full knowledge that there are such things as burglars, and that burglars burgle." It would be still more absurd to say this if I had had bars installed outside my windows, precisely to prevent burglars from getting in, and a burglar got in only because of a defect in the bars. It remains equally absurd if we imagine it is not a burglar

---

[7] The need for a discussion of this argument was brought home to me by members of the Society for Ethical and Legal Philosophy, to whom this paper was originally presented.

who climbs in, but an innocent person who blunders or falls in. Again, suppose it were like this: people-seeds drift about in the air like pollen, and if you open your windows, one may drift in and take root in your carpets or upholstery. You don't want children, so you fix up your windows with fine mesh screens, the very best you can buy. As can happen, however, and on very, very rare occasions does happen, one of the screens is defective; and a seed drifts in and takes root. Does the person-plant who now develops have a right to the use of your house? Surely not—despite the fact that you voluntarily opened your windows, you knowingly kept carpets and upholstered furniture, and you knew that screens were sometimes defective. Someone may argue that you are responsible for its rooting, that it does have a right to your house, because after all you *could* have lived out your life with bare floors and furniture, or with sealed windows and doors. But this won't do—for by the same token anyone can avoid a pregnancy due to rape by having a hysterectomy, or anyway by never leaving home without a (reliable!) army.

It seems to me that the argument we are looking at can establish at most that there are *some* cases in which the unborn person has a right to the use of its mother's body, and therefore *some* cases in which abortion is unjust killing. There is room for much discussion and argument as to precisely which, if any. But I think we should sidestep this issue and leave it open, for at any rate the argument certainly does not establish that all abortion is unjust killing. . . .

7. Following the lead of the opponents of abortion, I have throughout been speaking of the fetus merely as a person, and what I have been asking is whether or not the argument we began with, which proceeds only from the fetus' being a person, really does establish its conclusion. I have argued that it does not.

But of course there are arguments and arguments, and it may be said that I have simply fastened on the wrong one. It may be said that what is important is not merely the fact that the fetus is a person, but that it is a person for whom the woman has a special kind of responsibility issuing from the fact that she is its mother. And it might be argued that all my analogies are therefore irrelevant—for you do not have that special kind of responsibility for that violinist, Henry Fonda does not have that special kind of responsibility for me. And our attention might be drawn to the fact that men and women both *are* compelled by law to provide support for their children.

I have in effect dealt (briefly) with this argument in section 4 above; but a (still briefer) recapitulation now may be in order. Surely we do not have any such "special responsibility" for a person unless we have assumed it, explicitly or implicitly. If a set of parents do not try to prevent pregnancy, do not obtain an abortion, and then at the time of birth of the child do not put it out for adoption, but rather take it home with them, then they have assumed responsibility for it, they have given it rights, and they cannot *now* withdraw support from it at the cost of its life because they now find it difficult to go on providing for it. But if they have taken all reasonable precautions against having a child, they do not simply by virtue of their biological relationship to the child who comes into existence have a special responsibility for it. They may wish to assume responsibility for it, or they may not wish to. And I am suggesting that if assuming responsibility for it would require large sacrifices, then they may refuse. A Good Samaritan would not refuse—or anyway, a Splendid Samaritan, if the sacrifices that had to be made were enormous. But then so would a Good Samaritan assume responsibility for that violinist; so would Henry Fonda, if he is a Good Samaritan, fly in from the West Coast and assume responsibility for me.

SELECTION 8.8

"Killing and Starving to Death"

From James Rachels

Although we do not know exactly how many people die each year of malnutrition or related health problems, the number is very high, in the millions. By giving money to support famine relief efforts, each of us could save at least some of them. By not giving, we let them die.

Some philosophers have argued that letting people die is not as bad as killing them, because in general our "positive duty" to give aid is weaker than our "negative duty" not to do harm. I maintain the opposite: letting die is just as bad as killing. At first this may seem wildly implausible. When reminded that people are dying of starvation while we spend money on trivial things, we may feel a bit guilty, but certainly we do not feel like murderers. Philippa Foot writes:

> Most of us allow people to die of starvation in India and Africa, and there is surely something wrong with us that we do; it would be nonsense, however, to pretend that it is only in law that we make a distinction between allowing people in the underdeveloped countries to die of starvation and sending them poisoned food. There is worked into our moral system a distinction between what we owe people in the form of aid and what we owe them in the way of noninterference.

No doubt this would be correct if it were intended only as a description of what most people believe. Whether this feature of "our moral system" is rationally defensible is, however, another matter. I shall argue that we are wrong to take comfort in the fact that we *only* let these people die, because our duty not to let them die is equally as strong as our duty not to kill them, which, of course, is very strong indeed.

Obviously, the Equivalence Thesis is not morally neutral, as philosophical claims about ethics often are. It is a radical idea that, if true, would mean that some of our "intuitions" (our prereflective beliefs about what is right and wrong in particular cases) are mistaken and must be rejected. Neither is the view I oppose morally neutral. The idea that killing is worse than letting die is a relatively conservative thesis that would allow those same intuitions to be preserved. However, the Equivalence Thesis should not be dismissed merely because it does not conform to all our prereflective intuitions. Rather than being perceptions of the truth, our "intuitions" might sometimes signify nothing more than our prejudices or selfishness or cultural conditioning. Philosophers often admit that, in theory at least, some intuitions might be unreliable—but usually this possibility is not taken seriously, and conformity to prereflective intuition is used uncritically as a test of the acceptability of moral theory. In what follows I shall argue that many of our intuitions concerning killing and letting die *are* mistaken, and should not be trusted.

I

We think that killing is worse than letting die, not because we overestimate how bad it is to kill, but because we underestimate how bad it is to let die. The following chain of reasoning is intended to show that letting people in foreign countries die of starvation is very much worse than we commonly assume.

Suppose there were a starving child in the room where you are now—hollow-eyed, belly bloated, and so on—and you have a sandwich at your elbow that you don't need. Of course you would be horrified; you would stop reading and give her the sandwich or, better, take her to a hospital. And you would not think this an act of supererogation; you would not expect any special praise for it, and you would expect criticism if you did not do it. Imagine what you would think of someone who simply ignored the child and continued reading, allowing her to die of starvation. Let us call the person who would do this Jack Palance, after the very nice man who plays such vile characters in movies. Jack Palance indifferently watches the starving child die; he cannot be bothered even to hand her the sandwich. There is ample reason for judging him very harshly; without putting too fine a point on it, he shows himself to be a moral monster.

When we allow people in faraway countries to die of starvation, we may think, as Mrs. Foot puts it, that "there is surely something wrong with us." But we most emphatically do not consider ourselves moral monsters. We think this, in spite of the striking similarity between Jack Palance's behavior and our own. He could easily save the child; he does not, and the child dies. We could easily save some of those starving people; we do not, and they die. If we are not monsters, there must be some important difference between him and us. But what is it?

One obvious difference between Jack Palance's position and ours is that the person he lets die is in the same room with him, while the people we let die are mostly far away. Yet the spatial location of the dying people hardly seems a relevant consideration. It is absurd to suppose that being located at a certain map coordinate entitles one to treatment that one would not merit if situated at a different longitude or latitude. Of course, if a dying person's location meant that we *could not* help, that would excuse us. But, since there are efficient famine relief agencies willing to carry our aid to the faraway countries, this excuse is not available. It would be almost as easy for us to send these agencies the price of the sandwich as for Palance to hand the sandwich to the child.

The location of the starving people does make a difference, psychologically, in how we feel. If there were a starving child in the same room with us, we could not avoid realizing, in a vivid and disturbing way, how it is suffering and that it is about to die. Faced with this realization our consciences probably would not allow us to ignore the child. But if the dying are far away, it is easy to think of them only abstractly, or to put them out of our thoughts altogether. This might explain why our conduct would be different if we were in Jack Palance's position, even though, from a moral point of view, the location of the dying is not relevant.

There are other differences between Jack Palance and us, which may seem important, having to do with the sheer numbers of people, both affluent and starving, that surround us. In our fictitious example Jack Palance is one person, confronted by the need of one other person. This makes his position relatively simple. In the real world our position is more complicated, in two ways: first, in that there are millions of people who need feeding, and none of us has the resources to care for all of them; and second, in that for any starving person we *could* help there are millions of other affluent people who could help as easily as we.

On the first point, not much needs to be said. We may feel, in a vague sort of way, that we are not monsters because no one of us could possibly save *all* the starving people—there are just too many of them, and none of us has the resources. This is fair enough, but all that follows is that, individually, none of us is responsible for saving everyone. We may still be responsible for saving someone, or as many as we can. This is so obvious that it hardly bears mentioning, yet it is easy to lose sight of, and philosophers have actually lost sight of it. In his article "Saving Life and Taking Life," Richard Trammell says that one morally important difference between killing and letting die is "dischargeability." By this he means that, while each of us can discharge completely a duty not to kill anyone, no one among us can discharge completely a duty to save everyone who needs it. Again, fair enough: but all that follows is that since we are only bound to save those we can, the class of people we have an obligation to save is much smaller than the class of people we have an obligation not to kill. It does *not* follow that our duty with respect to those we can save is any less stringent. Suppose Jack Palance were to say: "I needn't give this starving child the sandwich because, after all, I can't save everyone in the world who needs it." If this excuse will not work for him, neither will it work for us with respect to the children we could save in India or Africa.

The second point about numbers was that, for any starving person we *could* help, there are millions of other affluent people who could help as easily as we. Some are in an even better position to help since they are richer. But by and large these people are doing nothing. This also helps explain why we do not feel especially guilty for letting people starve. How guilty we feel about something depends, to some extent, on how we compare with those around us. If we were surrounded by people who regularly sacrificed to feed the starving and we did not, we would probably feel ashamed. But because our neighbors do not do any better than we, we are not so ashamed.

But again, this does not imply that we should not feel more guilty or ashamed than we do. A psychological explanation of our feelings is not a moral justification of our conduct. Suppose Jack Palance were only one of twenty people who watched the child die; would that decrease his guilt? Curiously, I think many people assume it would. Many people seem to feel that if twenty people do nothing to prevent a tragedy, each of them is only one-twentieth as guilty as he would have been if he had watched the tragedy alone. It is as though there is only a fixed amount of guilt, which divides. I suggest, rather, that guilt multiplies, so that each passive viewer is fully guilty, if he could have prevented the tragedy but did not. Jack Palance watching the

girl die alone would be a moral monster; but if he calls in a group of his friends to watch with him, he does not diminish his guilt by dividing it among them. Instead, they are all moral monsters. Once the point is made explicit, it seems obvious.

The fact that most other affluent people do nothing to relieve hunger may very well have implications for one's own obligations. But the implication may be that one's own obligations *increase* rather than decrease. Suppose Palance and a friend were faced with two starving children, so that, if each did his "fair share," Palance would only have to feed one of them. But the friend will do nothing. Because he is well-off, Palance could feed both of them. Should he not? What if he fed one and then watched the other die, announcing that he has done *his* duty and that the one who died was his friend's responsibility? This shows the fallacy of supposing that one's duty is only to do one's fair share, where this is determined by what would be sufficient *if* everyone else did likewise.

To summarize: Jack Palance, who refuses to hand a sandwich to a starving child, is a moral monster. But we feel intuitively that we are not so monstrous, even though we also let starving children die when we could feed them almost as easily. If this intuition is correct, there must be some important difference between him and us. But when we examine the most obvious differences between his conduct and ours—the location of the dying, the differences in numbers— we find no real basis for judging ourselves less harshly than we judge him. Perhaps there are some other grounds on which we might distinguish our moral position, with respect to actual starving people, from Jack Palance's position with respect to the child in my story. But I cannot think of what they might be. Therefore, I conclude that if he is a monster, then so are we —or at least, so are we after our *rationalizations* and thoughtlessness have been exposed.

This last qualification is important. We judge people, at least in part, according to whether they can be expected to realize how well or how badly they behave. We judge Palance harshly because the consequences of his indifference are so immediately apparent. By contrast, it requires an unusual effort for us to realize the consequences of our indifference. It is normal behavior for people in the affluent countries not to give to famine relief, or if they do give, to give very little. Decent people may go along with this normal behavior pattern unthinkingly, without realizing, or without comprehending in a clear way just what this means for the starving. Thus, even though those decent people may act monstrously, we do not judge them monsters. There is a curious sense, then, in which moral reflection can transform decent people into indecent ones; for if a person thinks things through, and realizes that he is, morally speaking, in Jack Palance's position, his continued indifference is more blameworthy than before.

The preceding is not intended to prove that letting people die of starvation is as bad as killing them. But it does provide strong evidence that letting die is much worse than we normally assume, and so that letting die is much *closer* to killing than we normally assume. These reflections also go some way towards showing just how fragile and unreliable our intuitions are in this area. They suggest that, if we want to discover the truth, we are better off looking at arguments that do not rely on unexamined intuitions.

Checklist

To help you review, here is a checklist of the key philosophers and concepts of this chapter. The brief descriptive sentences summarize leading ideas. Keep in mind that some of these summary statements represent terrific oversimplifications of complex positions.

Philosophers

- **Immanuel Kant** Held that the supreme prescription of morality is to act always in such a way that you could rationally will the principle on which you act to be a universal law. Believed that what you should do you should do not because it promotes some end but simply because it is right.

- **Jeremy Bentham** A utilitarian; held that the rightness of an action is identical with the pleasure it produces as its consequence and said that pleasure can be evaluated quantitatively.

- **John Stuart Mill** A utilitarian; held that the rightness of an action is identical with the happiness that it produces as its consequence and said that pleasure—a part of happiness—must be measured in terms of quality as well as quantity.

- **Henry Sidgwick** Important British utilitarian philosopher, mentioned here in connection with the paradox of hedonism.

- **Friedrich Nietzsche** Distinguished between slave morality (the morality of the masses) and master morality (the morality of the nobleman). The former represents the denial of life; the latter represents the will to power.

- **G. E. Moore** Most important early figure in contemporary analytic ethics and metaethics. Held that goodness is an undefinable, noncomplex, and nonnatural property of good things. Said that what makes right actions right is that they produce more goodness than alternative actions.

- **W. D. Ross** Held that the production of maximum good is not the only thing that makes an act right; some things are just simply our moral duty to do.
- **C. L. Stevenson** An emotivist; held that ethical judgments are linguistic acts by which we express our own attitudes and seek to influence those of others.
- **A. J. Ayer** Important emotivist; held that ethical judgments are not genuine assertions.
- **Jean-Paul Sartre** An existentialist; held that there are no necessary ethical absolutes and that the fundamental problem of existence is to know how to live, given this fact.
- **R. M. Hare** British analytic philosopher; held that moral judgments are "universalizable" prescriptions whose function is to guide conduct.
- **Phillipa Foot** British philosopher noted for (among other things) examining the dependence of moral evaluations on descriptive or empirical premises.
- **John Searle** American philosopher noted for (among other things) examining the dependence of moral evaluations on descriptive or empirical premises.
- **John Rawls** Important contemporary political philosopher whose theory of justice has been of great interest to moral philosophers.
- **Judith Jarvis Thomson** American philosopher concerned with (among other things) such ethical issues as abortion.
- **James Rachels** American analytic philosopher concerned with (among other things) such ethical issues as the extent of our duty to remedy starvation.

Concepts

Kant's supreme principle of morality

hypothetical imperative

moral imperative

categorical imperative

treating humans as ends and not
    as means

utilitarianism

general happiness

hedonism

psychological hedonism

ethical hedonism

egoistic ethical hedonism

universalistic ethical hedonism

paradox of hedonism

quality vs. quantity of pleasure

master/slave morality

naturalistic ethical theories

noncomplex property

nonnatural property

divine-command ethics

consequentialism

deontological ethics

virtue ethics

relativism

contractarianism/contractualism

first-order thinking

second-order thinking

metaethics

prima facie duty

absolute duty

factual judgment

emotivism

existentialism

prescriptive judgment

naturalist fallacy

supererogatory act

applied ethics

Equivalence Thesis

Questions for Discussion and Review

1. Is it true that moral principles hold without exception? Explain.

2. Is it true that moral principles cannot be revealed through scientific investigation?

3. Suppose you stole something that didn't belong to you. Could you rationally will the principle on which you acted to be a universal law? Explain.

4. Explain the difference between a hypothetical imperative and a categorical imperative.

5. Which is it: Does the nature of an act or its consequences determine whether it is good, or is it the intent with which the act has been taken? Or is it something else altogether?

6. Kant held that there is no moral worth in helping others out of sympathy for them. What reasons are there for holding this view? Are they sound?

7. What does it mean to say that rational beings should be treated as ends and not as means? Give an example of treating another as a means.

8. Is happiness identical with pleasure?

9. Is your own happiness more important morally than that of others? ("It is to me" does not count as an answer.)

10. Was Bentham correct in saying that *ought, right, good,* and the like have meaning only when defined in terms of pleasure?

11. Explain the difference between psychological hedonism and ethical hedonism.

12. Is it true that the ultimate object of a person's desire is always pleasure? Explain.

13. Was Mill correct in saying that some pleasures are inherently better than others?

14. How does Mill propose to establish which of two pleasures is qualitatively better? Can you think of a better way of establishing this?

15. Leslie, who is in the Peace Corps, volunteers to aid starving Ethiopians. She travels to Ethiopia and, risking her own health and safety, works herself nearly to exhaustion for two years, caring for as many people as she can. Meanwhile, her father, Harold, dashes off a huge check for the Ethiopian relief fund. In fact, his check helps more people than Leslie's actions do. But, morally speaking, is Harold more praiseworthy than Leslie? What would Bentham say? Mill? You?

16. Explain the paradox of hedonism.

17. What does it mean to say that good is a nonnatural property? Explain in your own words Moore's reasons for saying that good is not equivalent to any natural property.

18. What does Nietzsche mean when he says life is the will to power?

19. Are moral value judgments merely expressions of taste? Explain.

20. "There cannot be moral values if there is no God." Critically evaluate this assertion.

21. Does the right to life guarantee one the right to use another person's body if the other body is required to sustain one's own life, according to Thomson? Explain why or why not.

22. Is it worse morally to send starving people poisoned food than to let them starve to death? Why?

Suggested Further Readings

A. J. Ayer, *Language, Truth and Logic,* 2nd rev. ed. (New York: Dover, 1946). See Chapter 6 for this important emotivist's treatment of ethics.

J. Bentham, *An Introduction to the Principles of Morals and Legislation* (New York: Methuen, 1982). Bentham's principal work.

Owen Flanagan and Amelie Oksenberg Rorty, eds., *Identity, Character and Morality* (Cambridge, Mass.: MIT Press, 1990). A group of essays relating contemporary ethics to psychology.

Philippa Foot, ed., *Theories of Ethics* (New York: Oxford University Press, 1990). A selection of papers relating to current issues in moral philosophy.

R. M. Hare, *The Language of Morals* (Oxford: Clarendon Press, 1952). An important treatise on the logic of moral discourse.

Immanuel Kant, *Foundations of the Metaphysics of Morals,* R. P. Wolff, ed. (Indianapolis: Bobbs-Merrill, 1959). Contains Kant's most important moral philosophy together with commentary by Kant scholars on assorted problems.

S. Korner, *Kant* (Baltimore: Penguin Books, 1955). See Chapters 6 and 7. A standard work on Kant.

J. S. Mill, *Utilitarianism* (Baltimore: Penguin Books, 1982). A classic. Short and very readable.

G. E. Moore, *Principia Ethica* (New York: Cambridge University Press, 1903). A work of major importance in ethics. Not terribly difficult to read.

W. D. Ross, *The Right and the Good* (London: Oxford University Press, 1930). Clearly written. An important book; good example of metaethics.

W. D. Ross, *Kant's Ethical Theory* (Oxford: Oxford University Press, 1954). Brief; excellent.

J. P. Sartre, *Existentialism and Humanism* (London: Methuen, 1948). The classic shorter treatment of ethics by Sartre.

Samuel Scheffler, ed., *Consequentialism and Its Critics* (New York: Oxford University Press, 1991). Papers by Nozick, Nagel, and others regarding the consequentialist issue.

John Searle, "How to Derive 'Ought' from 'Is'," *Philosophical Review* 73(1964): 43–58. This is technical academic philosophy, but laypersons will find it quite readable.

Henry Sidgwick, *Outlines of the History of Ethics* (Boston: Beacon, 1960) and *The Methods of Ethics* (New York: Dover, 1974). These are classic works in ethics. Many standard ethical concepts, principles, and distinctions originated with Sidgwick, and his treatment of utilitarianism is complete and penetrating.

Peter Singer, ed., *Applied Ethics* (New York: Oxford University Press, 1990). A series of recent papers on diverse issues in applied ethics, such as overpopulation, abortion, and capital punishment.

C. L. Stevenson, *Ethics and Language* (New Haven: Yale University Press, 1944). The most influential emotivist analysis of ethics.

Judith Jarvis Thomson, "A Defense of Abortion," *Philosophy and Public Affairs* 1, no. 1 (1971). This issue of this journal contains many important articles on issues of still-current public interest.

Suzanne Uniacke, *Permissible Killing: The Self-defence Justification of Homicide* (Cambridge: Cambridge University Press, 1994). A good example of a book-length treatment of an interesting issue in applied ethics.

Jeremy Waldron, ed., *Theories of Right* (New York: Oxford University Press, 1990). Recent important essays concerning related topics such as rights, equality, and fairness.

M. Warnock, *Ethics Since 1900* (London: Oxford University Press, 1960). A brief but useful general treatment of analytic ethics in the first half of this century. Chapter 2 is a critical exposition of Moore's ethics. See also her *Existentialist Ethics* (London: Macmillan, 1967) for an introduction to existentialist ethics.

James E. White, *Contemporary Moral Problems,* 2nd ed. (St. Paul: West, 1988). A good anthology of recent literature on contemporary moral issues.

Summary and Conclusion

Ethics, the philosophical study of moral judgments, began with the Sophists and Socrates. But the first complete ethical theory was Plato's, which grounded all ethical values on a nonnatural or "transcendent" source, the Form of the Good. Aristotle's ethics, by contrast, were naturalistic: human good is defined by the highest natural human objective, happiness. Plato also believed that reflecting on the nature and structure of the soul reveals important ethical truths; this view was shared by Aesara of Lucania.

Epicureanism and Stoicism too were naturalistic ethical philosophies. According to the Epicureans, the individual's ultimate ethical goal is to lead the pleasant life through moderate living, and according to the Stoics the goal is to lead a serene or untroubled life through acceptance of your fate.

Augustine, who endeavored to find philosophical justification for Christianity in Platonic metaphysics, interwove Platonic ethical themes with the Christian doctrine that God is the ultimate source of all that is good. Within the nonnaturalistic framework of Augustinian ethics, to love God as the sole intrinsic good is the fundamental ethical imperative. Hildegard of Bingen echoed Platonic themes in holding that the moral powers of the soul come from its three faculties of understanding, insight, and execution. And the medieval French philosopher Heloise emphasized the importance of intention to the morality of an act.

Thomas Aquinas, who is said to have reconciled Aristotelianism with Christianity and who accepted the Aristotelian naturalistic premise that the good for each kind of thing is set by the goal or objective of that kind of thing, thought that there are two sets of virtues. One set, the natural virtues, are those actions that help us achieve our natural objective of happiness on earth; the other set, the higher virtues, direct us to our eternal good, happiness everlasting.

One of the most important contributions of Aquinas to philosophy lies in his use of the Stoic concept of the natural (moral) law. According to Aquinas, the natural law is God's eternal law as it applies to human actions, and it is apprehended by us through conscience and practical reasoning. For Thomas Hobbes, too, there is a natural law, or rather there are natural laws, but these laws he held to be descriptive, nonnormative, rational principles of how best to preserve one's life. According to Hobbes, good and evil are to be defined in terms of desires and aversions, and justice and injustice are to be defined as the keeping or breaking of covenants.

In the eighteenth century David Hume argued that moral principles are not divine prescripts; nor, he said, are they founded on reason. A judgment of moral approval, he held, is in effect an expression of the pleasure we experience when we are presented with an instance of benevolent behavior.

Many of the themes, ideas, and concerns of later ethical philosophers may be found in the philosophy of Hume. Although Immanuel Kant rejected Hume's idea that moral principles are not founded on reason in favor of the opposite view that reason alone can determine what one ought to do, the utilitarians, in the nineteenth century, developed another of Hume's ideas, that goodness consists in behavior and traits that promote the general happiness. The interest in meta-ethics that runs so strongly through twentieth-century analytic philosophy ultimately has its roots in Hume, too, as does the emotivist doctrine that moral value judgments are expressions of likes and dislikes. Even the ethical philosophy of Sartre owes much to Hume, because it rests on the premise that God does not exist: as we shall see in Chapter 12, Hume was a powerful champion of religious skepticism.

G. E. Moore, with whom twentieth-century analytic ethics began, believed that the task of the ethical philosopher is to conduct a general inquiry into what is good. However, though Moore offered his view on what things are good, his meta-ethical opinions were the most influential, especially his opinions that (1) goodness is a simple, nonnatural, and indefinable property; that (2) what makes an act right is that it produces the maximum amount of good; and that (3) whether something is good is a true/false question of nonempirical fact.

This third view of Moore's was vigorously rejected by the emotivists, who held that questions of values are not questions of fact and that moral judgments are not even genuine propositions. The emotivist position in effect denies that there are values, except as expressions of likes and dislikes, and thus is superficially like the existentialist philosophy of Jean-Paul Sartre. But Sartre, though saying "everything is permissible," did not set forth a value-neutral metaethical analysis of the meaning or function of moral judgments, as the emotivists did.

Finally, recent years have seen an increased interest in Anglo-American philosophy, in concrete ethical issues. This interest is linked to developments in metaethics and social/political philosophy.

Let us say this, then, in conclusion. The questions that arise in connection with an introduction to ethical philosophy include some of the most difficult, and yet some of the most important, questions that might be asked. What is the highest human good? Happiness? In what does happiness consist? What is the best means of attaining happiness? What is the relationship between happiness and pleasure? Are some pleasures of a better or higher quality than others? Do people search for things other than their own pleasure or happiness? Should they? How important ethically is the happiness of others compared with one's own happiness? Is the golden rule sound? Why?

Is our ethical first priority even determined by what humans naturally seek? Or is it determined by something else—duty, perhaps, or natural law, or God's wishes? If there is no God, can there be any absolute ethical standards? Are ethical standards determined by one's culture? By one's own opinion? Are moral judgments mere expressions of personal likes and dislikes? What role does reason play in the determination of what is right and good? What is the relationship between what is right and what is good? Are any moral truths self-evident? Is moral knowledge even possible?

These are easy questions not to answer. This is because they are not easy questions to answer. If you want to bring a casual conversation or even a serious discussion to a rapid close, try asking one of them. People really don't know what to say about these issues, or even what to think.

Yet this surely is unfortunate, for making an ethically proper decision about most anything depends on such matters as these. What you have read in this part certainly won't, by itself, give you answers to these questions. But it might make it possible for you to begin to think about them in a systematic way. Knowing something about what important philosophers have thought about these issues may be that big first step toward finding your own sound answers.

In the next part we discuss political philosophy, an area closely related to ethics.

PART 3

Political Philosophy: Justice, Law, and the State

Classical Theory

9

Man, when perfected, is the best of all animals, but, when separated from law and justice, he is the worst of all. . . . Justice is the bond of men in states.

—*Aristotle*

That one human being will desire to render the person and property of another subservient to his pleasures, notwithstanding the pain or loss of pleasure which it may occasion to that individual, is the foundation of government.

—*James Mill*

While the state exists there is no freedom. Where there is freedom, there will be no state.

—*Vladimir I. Lenin*

Ethics, we explained in Part 2, is the philosophical study of moral judgments. But many moral judgments are at the same time political judgments.

Should goods be distributed equally? Or should they be distributed according to need? Or perhaps according to merit, or according to contribution to production, or to existing ownership, or to something else?

Is it justifiable for a government to restrict the liberty of its citizens and, if so, in what measure?

When, if ever, is fine or imprisonment legitimate? And what is the purpose of fine and imprisonment: Punishment? Deterrence? Rehabilitation?

Are there natural rights that all governments must respect? What form of political society or state is best? Should there even be a state?

The answers to these questions are moral judgments of a political variety. Political philosophy considers such issues and the concepts that are involved in them.

More generally, political philosophy seeks to find the best form of political existence. It is concerned with determining the state's right to exist, its ethically legitimate functions and scope, and its proper organization. Political philosophy also seeks to describe and understand the nature of political relationships and political authority, though scholars whose inquiries are focused within the purely descriptive branch of political philosophy now usually call themselves political scientists.

Plato and Aristotle

Let's start with Plato and Aristotle, because they were the first to try to build a political philosophy from the ground up.

Plato

According to Plato's *Republic,* the human soul has three different elements, one consisting of raw appetites, another consisting of drives (such as anger and ambition), and a third consisting of thought or intellect. In the virtuous or "just" person, each of these three elements fulfills its own unique function and does so under the governance of reason. Likewise, according to Plato, in the ideal or "just" state there are also three elements, each of which fulfills its unique function and does so in accordance with the dictates of reason.

The lowest element in the soul—the appetitive element—corresponds in the well-ordered state to the class of *craftsmen.* The soul's drive element corresponds in the state to the class of *police-soldiers,* who are auxiliaries to the *governing class.* This last class, in the well-ordered state, corresponds to the intellectual, rational element of the soul.

The governing class, according to Plato, is comprised of a select few highly educated and profoundly rational individuals, including women so qualified. Though an individual becomes a member of a class by birth, he or she will move to a higher or lower class according to aptitude.

In the healthy state, said Plato, as in the well-ordered soul, the rational element is in control. Thus, for Plato, the ideal state is a class-structured aristocracy ruled by "philosopher-kings."

Unlike the craftsmen, the ruling elite and their auxiliaries, who jointly are the guardians of society, have neither private property nor even private families: property, wives, and children are all possessions held in common. Reproduction among the guardians is arranged always to improve the blood line of their posterity in intelligence, courage, and other qualities apt for leadership. The guardians not only must be trained appropriately for soldiering, but must also be given a rigorous intellectual education that, for the few whose unique abilities allow it, prepares them for advanced work in mathematics, dialectic (that is, the Socratic method; see Chapter 2), and philosophy. These few, at age fifty and after many years of public service, advance to membership in the ruling aristocracy and to leadership of the state. Such is Plato's vision of the ideal political structure.

It is important to be aware that from Plato's perspective the state, like the person, is a *living organism* whose well-being must be sought by its subjects. Although he assumed that the healthy state is best for the individuals in it, Plato believed that the health or well-being of the state is something that is *desirable for its own sake.* And just as a person's health or well-being requires the proper functioning and coordination of the elements of the soul under the overarching rule of reason, the state's health or well-being lies in the proper functioning and coordi-

Plato's Forms of Government

In Book VIII of the *Republic* Plato identified five forms of government. The preferred form, of course, is an *aristocracy*, governed by rational philosopher-kings.

According to Plato, however, even if this ideal state could be achieved, it would in time degenerate into a *timocracy*, in which the ruling class is motivated by love of honor rather than by love for the common good.

A timocracy in turn gives way to a *plutocracy*, which is rule by men who primarily desire riches. Under a plutocracy, society becomes divided between two classes, the rich and the poor, Plato thought.

Nevertheless, this form of government, Plato said, is preferable to the next degeneration, *democracy*, which results because "a society cannot hold wealth in honor and at the same time establish self-control in its citizens." (Perhaps we will eventually see if Plato is correct that a society that honors wealth cannot maintain self-control.) With Plato's democracy, people's impulses are unrestrained, and the result is lack of order and direction. "Mobocracy" is what we would call Plato's "democracy" today.

Tyranny, the last form of government in Plato's classification, results when the democratic mob submits itself to a strongman, each person selfishly figuring to gain from the tyrant's rule and believing that the tyrant will end democracy's evil. In fact, Plato thought, the tyrant will acquire absolute power and enslave his subjects. Further, he, the tyrant, will himself become a slave to his wretched craving for power and self-indulgence.

Plato was not always an optimist.

nation of its elements under the rule of the reasoning elite. The ideal state, according to Plato, is well ordered in this way, and its being well ordered in this way is something that is intrinsically desirable.

We, of course, are more likely to evaluate Plato's prescriptions solely according to what they would do for the general welfare—that is, the welfare of all the citizens or subjects of the state. And so it may occur to you that, if the citizens are satisfied with their class level and do not think that their natural abilities warrant higher placement, then they might well like Plato's form of government. After all, the division of power, responsibility, and labor among classes as envisioned by Plato might maximize (as he thought it would) the productivity of the state; and the unavailability of private property to the ruling elite could conceivably remove acquisitive temptations so that members of the elite would devote their efforts to the public good rather than to personal gain. A state governed by a wise and enlightened aristocracy that seeks the betterment of its citizens might well do much to enhance the public welfare and happiness, even if it sometimes might be difficult for a ruling aristocracy to understand the needs and desires of the populace. In short, you may be disposed to give Plato a passing grade on his state, at least with reference to what it would do for the welfare of its subjects. You would probably not be inclined to think of the state as an organism in its own right whose well-being is something desirable for its own sake.

The Platonic idea of the state as an organism whose well-being is desirable for its own sake has been exploited, as we will see, as justification for the more totalitarian premise that the individual must sacrifice his or her own well-being for that of the state. Plato himself, we add hurriedly, was not advocating tyrannical rule.

In Selection 9.1, from the *Republic,* Plato has just explained that the guardians of society must live together, must not possess private property, and must hold all possessions in common. The question thus arises, Plato thought, of the status of women within the circle of guardians. In this excerpt he gives his views. The main speaker ("I") is "Socrates" (Plato), and he is talking to Plato's two brothers, Glaucon and Adeimantus. Now, please do not be misled: Plato did not argue for women's rights in society generally and does not seem concerned with the roles of women and men outside the ranks of the guardians. The broader issue he is addressing is the need to eliminate private property and interests from within the ruling class. That the "females of the watchdogs" should have the role he describes here is a result of that more fundamental need.

SELECTION 9.1

Republic

From Plato

[Explain, said Glaucon,] how this communion of wives and children among our guardians will be managed, and also about the rearing of the children while still young in the interval between birth and formal schooling which is thought to be the most difficult part of education. Try, then, to tell us what must be the manner of it. . . .

Well, said I . . . our endeavor, I believe, was to establish these men in our discourse as the guardians of a flock?

Yes.

Let us preserve the analogy, then, and assign them a generation and breeding answering to it, and see if it suits us or not.

In what way? he said.

In this. Do we expect the females of watchdogs to join in guarding what the males guard and to hunt with them and share all their pursuits or do we expect the females to stay indoors as being incapacitated by the bearing and the breeding of the whelps while the males toil and have all the care of the flock?

They have all things in common, he replied, except that we treat the females as weaker and the males as stronger.

Is it possible, then, said I, to employ any creature for the same ends as another if you do not assign it the same nurture and education?

It is not possible.

If, then, we are to use the women for the same things as the men, we must also teach them the same things.

Yes.

Now music together with gymnastics was the training we gave the men.

Yes.

Then we must assign these two arts to the women also and the offices of war and employ them in the same way.

It would seem likely from what you say, he replied. . . .

Can it be denied then that there is by nature a great difference between men and women? Surely there is. Is it not fitting, then, that a different function should be appointed for each corresponding to this difference of nature? Certainly. How, then, can you deny that you are mistaken and in contradiction with yourselves when you turn around and affirm that the men and the women ought to do the same thing, though their natures are so far apart? Can you surprise me with an answer to that question?

Not easily on this sudden challenge, he replied.

Come then, consider, said I, if we can find a way out. We did agree that different natures should have differing pursuits and that the natures of men and women differ. . . . We meant, for example, that a man and a woman who have a physician's mind have the same nature. Don't you think so?

I do.

But that a man physician and a man carpenter have different natures?

Certainly, I suppose.

Similarly, then, said I, if it appears that the male and the female sex have distinct qualifications for any arts or pursuits, we shall affirm that they ought to be assigned respectively to each. But if it appears that they differ only in just this respect that the female bears and the male begets, we shall say that no proof has yet been produced that the woman differs from the man for our purposes, but we shall continue to think that our guardians and their wives ought to follow the same pursuits.

And rightly, said he.

Then, is it not the next thing to bid our opponent tell us precisely for what art or pursuit concerned with the conduct of a state the woman's nature differs from the man's? . . . Come then, we shall say to him, answer our question. Was this the basis of your distinction between the man naturally gifted for anything and the one not so gifted—that the one learned easily, the other with difficulty, that the one with slight instruction could discover much for himself in the matter studied, but the other, after much instruction and drill, could not even remember what he had learned, and that the bodily faculties of the one adequately served his mind, while, for the other, the body was a hindrance? Were there any other points than these by which you distinguish the well-endowed man in every subject and the poorly endowed?

No one, said he, will be able to name any others. . . .

Then, [said I,] there is no pursuit of the administrators of a state that belongs to a woman because she is a woman or to a man because he is a man. But the natural capacities are distributed alike among both creatures, and women naturally share in all pursuits and men in all— yet for all the woman is weaker than the man.

Assuredly.

Shall we, then, assign them all to men and nothing to women?

How could we?

We shall rather, I take it, say that one woman has the nature of a physician and another not, and one is by nature musical, and another unmusical?

Surely.

Can we, then, deny that one woman is naturally athletic and warlike and another unwarlike and averse to gymnastics?

I think not.

And again, one a lover, another a hater, of wisdom? And one high-spirited, and the other lacking spirit?

That also is true.

Then it is likewise true that one woman has the qualities of a guardian and another not. Were not these the natural qualities of the men also whom we selected for guardians?

They were.

The women and the men, then, have the same nature in respect to the guardianship of the state, save in so far as the one is weaker, the other stronger.

Apparently.

Women of this kind, then, must be selected to cohabit with men of this kind and to serve with them as guardians since they are capable of it and akin by nature.

By all means.

And to the same natures must we not assign the same pursuits?

The same. . . .

For the production of a female guardian, then, our education will not be one thing for men and another for women, especially since the nature which we hand over to it is the same.

There will be no difference. . . .

All that precedes has for its sequel, [said I,] the following law.

What?

That these women shall all be common to all these men, and that none shall cohabit with any privately, and that the children shall be common, and that no parent shall know its own offspring nor any child its parent. . . . They, having houses and meals in common, and no private possessions of that kind, will dwell together, and being commingled in gymnastics and in all their life and education, will be conducted by innate necessity to sexual union. Is not what I say a necessary consequence?

Not by the necessities of geometry, he said, but by those of love, which are perhaps keener and more potent than the other to persuade and constrain the multitude.

They are, indeed, I said. But next, Glaucon, disorder and promiscuity in these unions or in anything else they do would be an unhallowed thing in a happy state and the rulers will not suffer it.

It would not be right, he said.

Obviously, then, we must arrange marriages, sacramental so far as may be. And the most sacred marriages would be those that were most beneficial.

By all means.

How, then, would the greatest benefit result? Tell me this, Glaucon. I see that you have in your house hunting dogs and a number of pedigreed cocks. Have you ever considered something about their unions and procreations?

What? he said.

In the first place, I said, among these themselves, although they are a select breed, do not some prove better than the rest?

They do.

Do you then breed from all indiscriminately, or are you careful to breed from the best?

From the best.

And, again, do you breed from the youngest or the oldest, or, so far as may be, from those in their prime?

From those in their prime.

And if they are not thus bred, you expect, do you not, that your birds' breed and hounds will greatly degenerate?

I do, he said.

And what of horses and other animals? I said. It is otherwise with them?

It would be strange if it were, said he.

Gracious, said I, dear friend, how imperative, then, is our need of the highest skill in our rulers, if the principle holds also for mankind. . . . The best men must cohabit with the best women in as many cases as possible and the worst with the worst in the fewest, and . . . the offspring of the one must be reared and that of the other not, if the flock is to be as perfect as possible.

Aristotle

Aristotle, too, regarded the state as an organism, as a living being. The state as a living being, he thought, exists for some end, for some purpose. That purpose, he believed, is to promote the good life for humans. Thus, Aristotle offered a standard of evaluation of the state different from Plato's. For Aristotle, a state is good only to the degree to which it enables its citizens themselves to achieve the good life, whereas for Plato a state is good to the extent that it is well ordered.

Aristotle As Political Scientist

We would not wish to imply, by pointing out Aristotle's fondness for observing the world around him, including the political world, that he was a purely neutral describer of political systems. It should be noted, for example, that Aristotle did enunciate principles in terms of which various forms of government can be evaluated. Also, when he listed *monarchy, aristocracy,* and *polity* as proper forms of government and *tyranny, oligarchy,* and *democracy* as their corresponding improper forms, he was not merely describing these forms, as a modern-day political scientist might, but also was evaluating them, as a political philosopher will do.

Nor is Aristotle a historian of political systems. You would have no inkling, from reading Aristotle's *Politics,* that the Greek city-state system of government went out of existence forever during his lifetime.

Aristotle, who had studied the constitutions, or basic political structures, of numerous Greek city- and other states, was a practical thinker. He insisted that the form of the ideal state depends on, and can change with, circumstances. Unlike Plato, Aristotle did not set forth a recipe for the ideal state. A state, he said, can be ruled properly by one person; but it can also be ruled properly by a few people or by many. When a state is properly ruled by one person, he said, it is a *monarchy;* improper rule by one is *tyranny.* Proper rule by the few is *aristocracy;* improper rule, *oligarchy.* Proper rule by the many is a *polity,* and improper rule by them is a *democracy.* Good forms of government tend to degenerate into bad, he thought, as Plato also did. Aristocracies become oligarchies, monarchies become tyrannies, polities become democracies.

Though Aristotle thought that states may be good or bad irrespective of their form, he observed that political societies always have three classes: a lower class of laborers and peasants; a middle class of craftsmen, farmers, and merchants; and an upper class of aristocrats. He further observed that political power rests in one or another of these social classes or is shared by them variously, irrespective of the form of the state.

Aristotle, like Plato, was no egalitarian. (An egalitarian believes that all humans are equal in their social, political, and economic rights and privileges.) But even though Plato's ideal state has no slaves, Aristotle held that some people are by nature suited for slavery, whereas others by nature are suited for freedom. Even freemen are not equals, Aristotle held. Those who, like laborers, do not have the aptitude (or time) to participate in governance should not be citizens. But, he said, beware: the desires of lesser men for equality are the "springs and fountains" of revolution and are to be so recognized by a properly functioning government, which takes precautions to avoid revolt.

In Selection 9.2, Aristotle criticizes Socrates' (Plato's) proposal in the *Republic* that women, children, and property should be the possessions of the entire community (of guardians).

*Politics**   **From Aristotle**

Every state is a community of some kind, and every community is established with a view to some good; for mankind always act in order to obtain that which they think good. But, if all communities aim at some good, the state or political community, which is the highest of all, and which embraces all the rest, aims at good in a greater degree than any other, and at the highest good. . . .

Our purpose is to consider what form of political community is best of all for those who are most able to realize their ideal of life. We must therefore examine not only this but other constitutions, both such as actually exist in well-governed states, and any theoretical forms which are held in esteem. . . .

We will begin with the natural beginning of the subject. Three alternatives are conceivable: The members of a state must either have (1) all things or (2) nothing in common, or (3) some things in common and some not. That they should have nothing in common is clearly impossible, for the constitution is a community, and must at any rate have a common place— one city will be in one place, and the citizens are those who share in that one city. But should a well-ordered state have all things, as far as may be, in common, or some only and not others? For the citizens might conceivably have wives and children and property in common, as Socrates proposes in the *Republic* of Plato. Which is better, our present condition, or the proposed new order of society?

There are many difficulties in the community of women. And the principle on which Socrates rests the necessity of such an institution evidently is not established by his arguments. Further, as a means to the end which he ascribes to the state, the scheme, taken literally, is impracticable, and how we are to interpret it is nowhere precisely stated. I am speaking of the premise from which the argument of Socrates proceeds, 'that the greater the unity of the state the better'. Is it not obvious that a state may at length attain such a degree of unity as to be no longer a state?—since the nature of a state is to be a plurality, and in tending to greater unity, from being a state, it becomes a family, and from being a family, an individual; for the family may be said to be more than the state, and the individual than the family. So that we ought not to attain this greatest unity even if we could, for it would be the destruction of the state. . . .

And there is another objection to the proposal. For that which is common to the greatest number has the least care bestowed upon it. Every one thinks chiefly of his own, hardly at all of the common interest; and only when he is himself concerned as an individual. For besides other considerations, everybody is more inclined to neglect the duty which he expects another to fulfil; as in families many attendants are often less useful than a few. Each citizen will have a thousand sons who will not be his sons individually, but anybody will be equally the son of anybody, and will therefore be neglected by all alike. . . .

Other evils, against which it is not easy for the authors of such a community to guard, will be assaults and homicides, voluntary as well as involuntary, quarrels and slanders, all which are most unholy acts when committed against fathers and mothers and near relations, but not equally unholy when there is no relationship. Moreover, they are much more likely to occur if

_____
*Footnotes have been omitted.

the relationship is unknown, and, when they have occurred, the customary expiations of them cannot be made. Again, how strange it is that Socrates, after having made the children common, should hinder lovers from carnal intercourse only, but should permit love and familiarities between father and son or between brother and brother, than which nothing can be more unseemly, since even without them love of this sort is improper. How strange, too, to forbid intercourse for no other reason than the violence of the pleasure, as though the relationship of father and son or of brothers with one another made no difference.

This community of wives and children seems better suited to the husbandmen than to the guardians, for if they have wives and children in common, they will be bound to one another by weaker ties, as a subject class should be, and they will remain obedient and not rebel. In a word, the result of such a law would be just the opposite of that which good laws ought to have, and the intention of Socrates in making these regulations about women and children would defeat itself. For friendship we believe to be the greatest good of states and the preservative of them against revolutions; neither is there anything which Socrates so greatly lauds as the unity of the state which he and all the world declare to be created by friendship. But the unity which he commends would be like that of the lovers in the *Symposium,* who, as Aristophanes says, desire to grow together in the excess of their affection, and from being two to become one, in which case one or both would certainly perish. Whereas in a state having women and children common, love will be watery; and the father will certainly not say 'my son', or the son 'my father'. As a little sweet wine mingled with a great deal of water is imperceptible in the mixture, so, in this sort of community, the idea of relationship which is based upon these names will be lost; there is no reason why the so-called father should care about the son, or the son about the father, or brothers about one another.

Of the two qualities which chiefly inspire regard and affection—that a thing is your own and that it is your only one—neither can exist in such a state as this.

Again, the transfer of children as soon as they are born from the rank of husbandmen or of artisans to that of guardians, and from the rank of guardians into a lower rank, will be very difficult to arrange; the givers or transferrers cannot but know whom they are giving and transferring, and to whom. And the previously mentioned evils, such as assaults, unlawful loves, homicides, will happen more often amongst those who are transferred to the lower classes, or who have a place assigned to them among the guardians; for they will no longer call the members of the class they have left brothers, and children, and fathers, and mothers, and will not, therefore, be afraid of committing any crimes by reason of consanguinity. Touching the community of wives and children, let this be our conclusion.

Next let us consider what should be our arrangements about property: should the citizens of the perfect state have their possessions in common or not? This question may be discussed separately from the enactments about women and children. Even supposing that the women and children belong to individuals, according to the custom which is at present universal, may there not be an advantage in having and using possessions in common? Three cases are possible: (1) the soil may be appropriated, but the produce may be thrown for consumption into the common stock; and this is the practice of some nations. Or (2), the soil may be common, and may be cultivated in common, but the produce divided among individuals for their private use; this is a form of common property which is said to exist among certain barbarians. Or (3), the soil and the produce may be alike common.

When the husbandmen are not the owners, the case will be different and easier to deal with;

but when they till the ground for themselves the question of ownership will give a world of trouble. If they do not share equally in enjoyments and toils, those who labour much and get little will necessarily complain of those who labour little and receive or consume much. But indeed there is always a difficulty in men living together and having all human relations in common, but especially in their having common property. The partnerships of fellow-travellers are an example to the point; for they generally fall out over everyday matters and quarrel about any trifle which turns up. So with servants: we are most liable to take offense at those with whom we most frequently come into contact in daily life.

These are only some of the disadvantages which attend the community of property; the present arrangement, if improved as it might be by good customs and laws, would be far better, and would have the advantages of both systems. Property should be in a certain sense common, but, as a general rule, private; for, when every one has a distinct interest, men will not complain of one another, and they will make more progress, because every one will be attending to his own business. And yet by reason of goodness, and in respect of use, 'Friends', as the proverb says, 'will have all things common.' Even now there are traces of such a principle, showing that it is not impracticable, but, in well-ordered states, exists already to a certain extent and may be carried further. For, although every man has his own property, some things he will place at the disposal of his friends, while of others he shares the use with them. The Lacedaemonians, for example, use one another's slaves, and horses, and dogs, as if they were their own; and when they lack provisions on a journey, they appropriate what they find in the fields throughout the country. It is clearly better that property should be private, but the use of it common; and the special business of the legislator is to create in men this benevolent disposition. Again, how immeasurably greater is the

pleasure, when a man feels a thing to be his own; for surely the love of self is a feeling implanted by nature and not given in vain, although selfishness is rightly censured; this, however, is not the mere love of self, but the love of self in excess, like the miser's love of money; for all, or almost all, men love money and other such objects in a measure. And further, there is the greatest pleasure in doing a kindness or service to friends or guests or companions, which can only be rendered when a man has private property. These advantages are lost by excessive unification of the state. The exhibition of two virtues, besides, is visibly annihilated in such a state: first, temperance towards women (for it is an honourable action to abstain from another's wife for temperance sake); secondly, liberality in the matter of property. No one, when men have all things in common, will any longer set an example of liberality or do any liberal action; for liberality consists in the use which is made of property.

Such legislation may have a specious appearance of benevolence; men readily listen to it, and are easily induced to believe that in some wonderful manner everybody will become everybody's friend, especially when some one is heard denouncing the evils now existing in states, suits about contracts, convictions for perjury, flatteries of rich men and the like, which are said to arise out of the possession of private property. These evils, however, are due to a very different cause—the wickedness of human nature. Indeed, we see that there is much more quarrelling among those who have all things in common, though there are not many of them when compared with the vast numbers who have private property. . . .

[I]ndeed, Socrates has not said, nor is it easy to decide, what in such a community will be the general form of the state. The citizens who are not guardians are the majority, and about them nothing has been determined: are the husbandmen, too, to have their property in common? Or is each individual to have his own? and are the wives and children to be individual or common? If, like the guardians, they are to have all things in common, in what do they differ from them, or what will they gain by submitting to their government? Or, upon what principle would they submit, unless indeed the governing class adopt the ingenious policy of the Cretans, who give their slaves the same institutions as their own, but forbid them gymnastic exercises and the possession of arms. If, on the other hand, the inferior classes are to be like other cities in respect of marriage and property, what will be the form of the community? Must it not contain two states in one, each hostile to the other? He makes the guardians into a mere occupying garrison, while the husbandmen and artisans and the rest are the real citizens. But if so the suits and quarrels, and all the evils which Socrates affirms to exist in other states, will exist equally among them. He says indeed that, having so good an education, the citizens will not need many laws, for example laws about the city or about the markets; but then he confines his education to the guardians. Again, he makes the husbandmen owners of the property upon condition of their paying a tribute. But in that case they are likely to be much more unmanageable and conceited than the Helots, or Penestae, or slaves in general. And whether community of wives and property be necessary for the lower equally with the higher class or not, and the questions akin to this, what will be the education, form of government, laws of the lower class, Socrates has nowhere determined.

Natural Law Theory and Contractarian Theory

Aristotle, recall from Part 2 on ethics, was an **ethical naturalist.** For answers to questions about what *ought* to be the case, he looked around him (i.e., he turned to "nature") to see what *is* the case. To determine what the purpose of the state ought to be, he considered what the purpose of existing states actually is. Ought all people be equal in freedom? In citizenship? Aristotle's answers to these and other questions of political ethics were grounded on what he observed. In this instance, the apparent natural inequality of people he perceived prompted him to answer negatively.

Because of his naturalism Aristotle is sometimes viewed as the source of natural law political theory. According to this theory, questions of political ethics are to be answered by reference to the so-called natural law, which alone supposedly determines what is right and wrong, good and bad, just and unjust, proper and improper.

As we saw in Chapter 7, however, the first relatively clear concept of natural law per se is probably found not in Aristotle's writings but later, in Stoic philosophy, in which the natural law is conceived as an impersonal principle of reason that governs the cosmos. But the Stoics were not primarily political philosophers. So it is to the celebrated Roman statesman **Cicero** (106–43 B.C.) that one turns for the classic expression of the Stoic concept of natural law as applied to political philosophy:

War!

The philosophical literature on war—its legality, morality (if any), causes, and significance—is pretty expansive, and we just don't have the space to cover it in this book. Many of the major philosophers we discuss have had something to say about it. And the philosophy of war is not an abstract and meaningless subject for after-dinner conversation. At least it certainly wasn't during Vietnam, when differences in perspectives threatened to destroy American society. The powerful anti-war movement of the era was inspired by a set of moral concepts, a moral philosophy of noninterventionism that motivated millions to protest the war.

Two important ethical issues, which were much discussed during the Vietnam era and have subsequently remained so in regard to Nicaragua, Iraq, Somalia, Bosnia, Haiti, and other places, pertain to the *justness* of war: When is a war just? and When is a war being fought justly? The classical theories of when a war is just come from Augustine and, especially, Aquinas. According to Augustine, just wars are those that avenge injuries: a nation or a city should be punished for failing to right a wrong done by its citizens. Aquinas held there are three conditions for a just war: (1) The ruler under whom the war is to be fought must have authority to do so; (2) a just cause is required; and (3) right intention is required: those making the war must intend to achieve some good or avoid some evil.

One fairly widely read recent book that addresses the issue of just war is *Just and Unjust Wars,* by Michael Walzer (whose "communitarian" political philosophy is discussed in Chapter 10). Walzer covered many important sub-issues in this book, including preventive war and preemptive strikes, civil war, noncombatant immunity vs. military necessity, guerilla war, terrorism, the right to neutrality, war crimes, and nuclear deterrence. Here we'll just say a few words about his view on when a war is just, as an example of recent philosophical discussion on the subject.

Walzer maintained that states have rights, including, principally, the right to political sovereignty, territorial integrity, and self-determination. He did not just throw this thesis out, but attempted to *derive* the rights of individual states from the rights of individual people, arguing that states' rights are just the *collective form* of individual rights. Thus states, like people, have duties to one another (as well as to their citizens) and can commit and suffer crimes, just as people can. Any use or imminent threat of military force by one state against the rights of another constitutes criminal aggression and justifies forceful resistance and eventual punishment by either the victim or the international society of states. Further, the use of military force by one state on another can be justified *only* as a response to aggression, and (except for a few unusual cases) not for any other end. For Walzer, democratic governments are not the only ones that possess the right of political sovereignty; so may undemocratic and even tyrannical governments: "Though states are founded for the sake of life and liberty, they cannot be challenged in the name of life and liberty by any other states." This "absolutist" stand for nonintervention and the arguments on which it rests were subject to considerable discussion by Walzer's critics, especially when the Reagan administration made an effort to displace the Sandinista government in Nicaragua. The critics felt that Walzer, despite deriving states' rights from individuals' rights, in fact (and paradoxically) attached more importance to the rights of states than to the rights of individuals. Walzer replied that, although he does think we should *oppose* governments that violate the rights of their citizens, we should do it by making arguments, not by summoning up armies.

Aquinas's Conception of Law

One of Aquinas's most distinctive contributions to political philosophy is his discussion of law. Aquinas distinguished among four kinds of law.

Most fundamental is **eternal law,** which is, in effect, the divine reason of God that rules over all things at all times.

Then there is **divine law,** which is God's gift to man, apprehended by us through revelation rather than through conscience or reason, and which directs us to our *supernatural* goal, eternal happiness.

Natural law is God's eternal law as it applies to man on earth; in effect, it is the fundamental principles of morality, as apprehended by us in our conscience and practical reasoning. Natural law directs us to our *natural* goal, happiness on earth.

Finally, **human law** is the laws and statutes of society that are derived from man's understanding of natural law. A rule or decree of a ruler or government must answer to a higher authority, said Aquinas: it must conform to natural law. Any rule or statute that does not, he said, should not be obeyed: "we ought to obey God rather than men."

Aquinas's conception of law, especially of natural law and human law, bears widely on our own conceptions.

"True law," wrote Cicero,

> is right reason in agreement with Nature; it is of universal application, unchanging and everlasting . . . there will not be different laws at Rome and at Athens; or different laws now and in the future, but one eternal and unchangeable law will be valid for all nations and all times.

In other words, Cicero is proposing that there is only one valid law, the natural law of reason, which holds eternally and universally. This is a bold idea, and to a certain extent we still accept it today.

Augustine and Aquinas

In the thought of **Augustine** (354–430) and **Aquinas** (1225–1274), the natural law as conceived by the Stoics, which according to Cicero was the only valid basis for human law, was *Christianized*. **Natural law** was conceived by these Church philosophers to be the eternal moral law of *God* as it is apprehended by humans through the dictates of their conscience and reason.

With Augustine and Aquinas two vital questions were raised: the relationship of secular law to the natural law of God and, correspondingly, the relationship of state to church. According to both thinkers, the laws of the state must be just, which meant for them that the laws of the state must accord with God's natural law. If secular laws do not accord, they held, they are not truly laws, and there is no legitimate state. For Augustine, the purpose of the state is to take "the power to do hurt" from the wicked; for Aquinas, it is to attend to the common good (which, for Aquinas, meant much more than merely curbing human sinfulness). For both, the church provides for man's spiritual needs, and, though the state does have rights and duties within its own sphere, it is subordinate to the church, just as its laws are subordinate to natural law.

Hobbes

Whereas Augustine, Aquinas, and other Christian thinkers conceived of the natural law as the moral law of God, **Thomas Hobbes** (1588–1679), who was discussed in the section on ethics, construed the natural law as neither the law of God nor moral law. In fact, Hobbes's conception of natural law amounts to discarding the older religious concept.

Hobbes did not speak of *the* natural law in the singular, as did the classical and church philosophers, but of natural laws in the plural. These, for Hobbes, are simply rational principles of prudent action, prescriptions for best preserving your own life. According to Hobbes, who was a naturalist and in this respect resembled Aristotle, there is no higher authority beyond nature that passes judgment on the morality or immorality of human deeds. You obey the laws of nature insofar as you act rationally, and insofar as you don't, you don't live long.

Hobbes's first law of nature is *to seek peace as far as you have any hope of obtaining it, and when you cannot obtain it to use any means you can to defend yourself*. As you can see, this "law" is indeed simply a prescription of rational self-interest.

And it is easy to understand why Hobbes regarded this as the first law of nature. From Hobbes's perspective, the question of how best to prolong one's life was a pressing issue for most people. Historians emphasize the importance of the Scientific Revolution in the seventeenth century, which included the discoveries of Gilbert, Kepler, Galileo, Harvey, Boyle, Huygens, Newton, and others. The seventeenth century, in fact, reads like a *Who's Who* of scientific discoverers. But most seventeenth-century Europeans, plain folk and ruling aristocrats alike, had never even *heard* of these discoveries, and even if they had, they would have considered them uninteresting and irrelevant. That's because this was also a century of political chaos and brutal warfare both in England and on the Continent. The Thirty Years' War, a very ugly spectacle, happened during this century, and most Europeans were somewhat preoccupied with the safety of their skins. For most of them, the question of personal survival was of more than academic interest.

Hobbes's second law is *to be content, for the sake of peace and self-preservation, provided others are also content, with only so much liberty "against other men" as you would allow other men against yourself*. And the third law is *"that men perform their covenants made."* (A covenant is an agreement or contract, a compact.)

But nobody, Hobbes said, is so stupid as to live up to an agreement that turns out not to be in his own best interest. So, if you want people to live by their agreements, you have to make sure that they will *suffer* if they try to break them. This means you have to have some third power to enforce them. "Without the terror of some power to cause them to be observed," Hobbes wrote, covenants are only words.

In light of these considerations, Hobbes concluded, if you apply the "laws of nature" listed here to real-life situations, what they mean is this: For their own welfare, people should transfer both their collective strength and their right to use whatever is necessary to defend themselves to a sovereign power that will use the acquired power to *compel* all citizens to honor their commitments to one another and to live together peacefully. This is the best road to peace and security, according to Hobbes. Without this central power to make them honor their agreements and keep them in line, people live in a "state of nature," a state of unbridled war of each against all, a state of chaos, mistrust, deception, meanness, and violence in which each person stops at nothing to gain the upper hand, and life is "solitary, poor, nasty, brutish, and short."

The central sovereign power to which people will transfer their power and rights, if they are smart enough to see that it is in their own self-interest to do so, is called by Hobbes the **Leviathan.** (A leviathan is a sea monster often symbolizing evil in the Old Testament and Christian literature.) When people transfer their power and rights to the Leviathan, they in effect create a **social contract.** It is this contract that delivers people from the evils of the natural state to civil society and a state of peace.

The social contract is thus an agreement between individuals who, for the sake of peace, are willing to make this absolutely unconditional and irrevocable transfer of right and power to the sovereign or Leviathan.

According to Hobbes, only when people have contracted among themselves and created the Leviathan is there *law* or *justice,* and Hobbes was speaking of civil laws, not natural laws. *Justice* and *injustice* Hobbes defined as the keeping and

Niccolò Machiavelli and Power Politics

One of the most famous political treatises of all time, Machiavelli's *The Prince* (1532), mainly just explains how a prince best may gain and maintain power, and is often regarded as the foundational treatise of modern political science (though be sure to read Selection 9.2 by Aristotle).

Niccolò Machiavelli (1469–1527) didn't mince words. He stated frankly that in the actions of princes the ends justify the means, and that princes who wish to survive had to learn how *not* to be good, and how to be feared as well as loved. If the prince has to choose between the two, being feared or being loved, Machiavelli added, it's much safer for him to

be feared. *The Prince* was a shocker when it was written and is still a shocker today. It established Machiavelli's reputation as a cold-blooded advocate of power politics.

Machiavelli, however, though recognizing the importance of power in politics and having but little belief in the intelligence or rationality of the common run of men, made a distinction between the virtuous leader and the villainous or ignoble one, finding little to admire in the latter type.

Further, his more expansive earlier political work, *Discourses on Livy* (1531), reveals his preference for free republics over monarchies as better means of securing liberty,

order, stability, and the interests of all, though he thought that under the prevailing circumstances the only way to secure order was to establish an absolute power that could curb the excesses of the ambitious and avaricious.

In the Roman republic people had been more devoted to liberty than in his time, he thought, and in general they had been stronger in character and less prone to become prey to evil-minded men. Why had people changed? Christianity, he perceived, in emphasizing humility, meekness, and contempt for worldly objects, had made men feeble and needy of the absolute rule of a prince.

breaking of covenants. Because covenants and laws are meaningless unless there is a Leviathan to enforce them, law and justice can only exist under a Leviathan.

Now the original social covenant or contract that creates the Leviathan is not a contract *between* the Leviathan and its subjects, Hobbes stressed. It is a contract among the subjects themselves. There is not and cannot be any covenant *between* the Leviathan and its subjects. Here's why: because the Leviathan holds all the power, it would be free to break any pledge, promise, agreement, commitment, contract, or covenant that it made. And that means that a covenant between the Leviathan and its subjects would be unenforceable and hence would be empty words.

Therefore, because logically there cannot be any covenant between the Leviathan and its subjects, and because justice is defined by Hobbes as the keeping of a covenant, it is *impossible* for the Hobbesian sovereign or Leviathan to act unjustly toward its subjects. Likewise, the Leviathan's laws—and the Leviathan's laws are the only laws, for they alone can be enforced—cannot be unjust. The Leviathan, according to Hobbes, has the right to lay down any laws it can enforce (although, as we see shortly, it cannot require us to take our own lives), and we are not only

PROFILE / Thomas Hobbes (1588–1679)

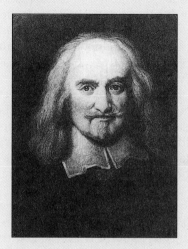

S cientific discovery, geometry, and the violence of civil war and anarchy—these were the major influences on Hobbes's philosophy.

A graduate of Oxford, Hobbes became a tutor in the influential Cavendish family, in which role he was able to meet many of the im-portant intellectual figures of his day, including Gassendi, Galileo, and Bacon. Through his acquain-tance with the work of these and other early scientists, it occurred to him that everything that hap-pens does so as the result of physical matter in motion. This perception became the basis of his entire philosophy, including his metaphysics and political thought.

Amazingly, it was not until his early forties that Hobbes chanced on a copy of Euclid's *Elements*. This work influenced him to think that all knowledge could be derived de-ductively from axioms based on observation. Consequently he de-vised a comprehensive plan, which he never fully completed, to apply the Euclidean deductive method to all questions of physical nature, hu-man nature, and the nature of society.

Hobbes's political philosophy, however, has earned him his greatest fame. The basic themes of his political writings—that man is by nature violent, self-serving, and at war with all other men, and that for their own defense against their natural predaciousness, people must submit to a strong power capable of enforcing peace—are clear reflections of the political turbulence of the times. During Hobbes's lifetime, the Thirty Years' War on the European continent struck down half the population, and in England a state of anarchy followed the Civil War and the rule of Oliver Cromwell. More-over, the plague ravaged England no fewer than four times during Hobbes's long life. Hobbes was no stranger to death, destruction, chaos, and the willingness of men to sacrifice others for their own ends.

physically but also morally obliged to obey them, for only through its laws are we kept from anarchy.

That no covenant exists between the Leviathan and its subjects means that the Leviathan has no legal or moral obligation to them. That it has no legal or moral obligation to its subjects means that they are *gambling* when they agree among themselves unconditionally to transfer all power and rights to it; they are gambling that life under its rule (conditions of "peace") will be better than it would be under the conditions of anarchy that otherwise would obtain. Perhaps a rational sovereign is likely to see that it is not in his own self-interest to destroy or abuse his subjects, but there is always a chance that he won't.

Hobbes, obviously, thought the gamble a wise one. Were people to live without a common power, he wrote, a power "to keep them all in awe," their innate viciousness would preclude the development of any commerce, industry, or culture, and there would be "no knowledge on the face of the earth; no account of time; no arts; no letters; no society." There would only be, he wrote, "continual fear, and danger of violent death." In Hobbes's view, given the alternatives of anarchy and dictatorship (the Leviathan)—and these are the only alternatives—the most reasonable choice is dictatorship, even if it does involve the risk of despotism.

The political establishment of the Leviathan, however, Hobbes made subject to certain minimal safeguards for its subjects. If the Leviathan fails to provide security to its subjects, they may transfer their allegiance to another sovereign. Further, because no one has the right to take his own life, this right is not among those transferred to the Leviathan at the time of the social contract of its subjects. Therefore the Leviathan cannot rightfully compel a subject to take his or her own life, according to Hobbes.

Critics of Hobbes, not too surprisingly, scoff at such "safeguards," because as a practical matter the Leviathan, having been given the collective power of its subjects, is able to do whatever it pleases with its subjects. As John Locke said, with Hobbes you trade the chance of being ravaged by a thousand men acting independently for the chance of suffering the same fate at the hands of one person who has a thousand men at his command.

We have spent some time here on Hobbes. This is because Hobbes, in basing the creation and power of the Leviathan on a social contract, is the first philosopher to enunciate systematically the concept that the state, and with it justice, is created through an agreement or "contract" among the people who comprise the state. This is, of course, a very familiar notion to Americans, because the American Constitution, about which more will be said later, is the social contract that brought the United States into existence.

So Hobbes really did more than reject the principle of natural law as representing God's will and its corollary that the laws of the state, and the state itself, derive their *legitimacy* from their harmony with this divine natural law. According to Hobbes, the legitimacy of the state and its laws derives from an initial consent of those governed (though keep in mind that this consent is "required" by those principles of practical reason that Hobbes refers to as natural laws). With Hobbes begins an important tradition in Western political philosophy, the so-called **contractarian** or **contractualist theory** of justice and the state. We'll encounter other contractarian theories as we proceed, beginning with the philosophy of John Locke.

In Selection 9.3, Hobbes explains two of the laws of nature, as well as the transference of power to the Leviathan. You may also wish to reread Selection 7.9 from Hobbes in Part 2 at this time.

SELECTION 9.3

*Leviathan**

From Thomas Hobbes

CHAPTER XIV. OF THE FIRST AND SECOND NATURAL LAWS, AND OF CONTRACTS

THE RIGHT OF NATURE, which writers commonly called *Jus Naturale,* is the liberty each man has to use his own power as he will himself, for the preservation . . . of his own life; and consequently of doing anything which in his own judgment and reason he shall conceive to be apt.

By LIBERTY is understood, according to the proper significance of the word, the absence of external impediments: which impediments may often take away part of a man's power to do what he would, but cannot hinder him from using the power left him, according as his judgment and reason shall dictate to him.

A LAW OF NATURE (*Lex Naturalis*), is a precept or general rule, found out by reason, by which a man is forbidden to do that which is destructive of his life or takes away the means of preserving the same; and to omit that by which he thinks it may be best preserved. For though they that speak of this subject confound *Jus* and *Lex,* right and law; yet they ought to be distinguished; because right consists in liberty to do or to forbear; whereas law determines and binds to one of them: so that law and right differ as much as obligation and liberty; which in one and the same matter are inconsistent.

And because the condition of man (as has been declared in the preceding chapter) is a condition of war of everyone against everyone; in which case everyone is governed by his own reason; and there is nothing he can make use of, that may not be a help to him, in preserving his

life against his enemies; it follows that in such a condition every man has a right to everything; even to one another's body. And therefore, as long as this natural right of man to everything endures, there can be no security to any man (how strong or wise he is) of living out the time which nature ordinarily allows men to live. And consequently it is a precept or general rule of reason, *that every man ought to endeavor peace, as far as he has hope of obtaining it; and when he cannot obtain it he may seek and use all helps and advantages of war.* The first branch of which rule contains the first and fundamental law of nature; which is *to seek peace and follow it.* The second, the sum of the Right of Nature; which is, *by all means we can, to defend ourselves.*

From this fundamental law of nature, by which men are commanded to endeavor peace, is derived this second law; *that a man be willing, when others are also, as far as for peace, and defense of himself he shall think it necessary, to lay down this right to all things; and be contented with so much liberty against other men, as he would allow other men against himself.* For as long as every man holds this right of doing anything he likes; so long are all men in the condition of war. But if other men will not lay down their right, as well as he; then there is not reason for anyone to divest himself of his: For that would be to expose himself to prey (which no man is bound to) rather than to dispose himself to peace. This is that law of the gospel; *whatsoever you require that others should do to you, that do to them. . . .*

To lay down a man's right to anything, is to divest himself of the liberty of hindering another of the benefit of his own right to the same. For he that renounces or passes away his right, gives not to any other man a right which he had not before; because there is nothing to which

---

*Edited slightly for the modern reader.

every man had not right by nature: but only stands out of his way that he may enjoy his own original right without hindrance from him; not without hindrance from another. So that the effect which reverberates to one man by another man's defect of right, is but so much diminution of impediments to the use of his own right original.

Right is laid aside, either by simply renouncing it; or by transferring it to another. By simply RENOUNCING; when he cares not to whom the benefit thereof reverberates. By TRANSFERRING; when he intends the benefit thereof to some certain person or persons. And when a man has in either manner abandoned or granted away his right; then is he said to be OBLIGED or BOUND not to hinder those to whom such right is granted or abandoned, from the benefit of it: and that he ought, and it is his DUTY, not to make void that voluntary act of his own: and that such hindrance is INJUSTICE and INJURY, as being *sine jure;* the right being before renounced or transferred. . . .

When a man transfers right or renounces it; it is either in consideration of some right reciprocally transferred to himself; or for some good he hopes for. For it is a voluntary act: and of the voluntary acts of every man, the object is good to himself. And therefore there are some rights which no man can be understood by any words or other signs to have abandoned or transferred. As first: a man cannot lay down the right of resisting them that assault him by force to take away his life; because he cannot be understood to aim thereby at good to himself. The same may be said of wounds and chains and imprisonment; both because there is no benefit consequent to such patience; as there is to the patience of suffering another to be wounded or imprisoned: as also because a man cannot tell, when he sees men proceeding against him by violence, when they intend his death or not. And the motive and end for which this renouncing and transferring of right is introduced is nothing else but the security of a man's person, in his life and in the means of so preserving life as not to be weary of it. And therefore if a man by words or other signs seems to rob himself of the end for which those signs were intended; he is not to be understood as if he meant it or that it was his will; but that he was ignorant of how such words and actions were to be interpreted.

The mutual transferring of right, is that which men call CONTRACT. . . .

CHAPTER XVII. OF THE CAUSES, GENERATION, AND DEFINITION OF A COMMONWEALTH

The final cause, end, or design of men (who naturally love liberty and dominion over others) in the introduction of that restraint upon themselves (in which we see them live in commonwealths) is the foresight of their own preservation and of a more contented life; that is to say, of getting themselves out from that miserable condition of war, which is necessarily consequent (as has been shown) to the natural passions of men, when there is no visible power to keep them in awe, and tie them by fear of punishment to the performance of their covenants, and observation of those laws of nature set down in the fourteenth and fifteenth chapters.

For the laws of nature (as justice, equity, modesty, mercy, and, in sum, doing to others as we would be done to) of themselves, without the terror of some power to cause them to be observed, are contrary to our natural passions, that carry us to partiality, pride, revenge, and the like. And covenants, without the sword, are but words, and of no strength to secure a man at all. Therefore notwithstanding the laws of nature (which everyone has then kept, when he has the will to keep them, when he can do it safely) if there be no power erected, or not great enough for our security; every man will, and may lawfully rely on his own strength and art, for caution against all other men. . . .

The only way to erect such a common power as may be able to defend them from the invasion of foreigners and the injuries of one another and thereby to secure them in such a way as that by their own industry, and by the fruits of the earth, they may nourish themselves and live contentedly; is to confer all their power and strength upon one man or upon one assembly of men, that may reduce all their wills, by plurality of voices, unto one will: which is as much as to say, to appoint one man or assembly of men to bear their person. . . .

This is more than consent or concord; it is a real unity of them all in one and the same person, made by covenant of every man with every man, in such manner as if every man should say to every man, I authorize and give up my right of governing myself to this man or to this assembly of men, on this condition that you give up the right to him and authorize all his actions in like manner. This done, the multitude so united in one person, is called a COMMONWEALTH, in Latin, *Civitas*. This is the generation of that great LEVIATHAN, or rather (to speak more reverently) of that mortal God to which we owe under the immortal God our peace and defense. For by this authority, given him by every particular man in the commonwealth, he has the use of so much power and strength conferred on him, that by terror thereof, he is enabled to form the wills of them all, to peace at home, and mutual aid against their enemies abroad. And in him consists the essence of the commonwealth; which (to define it) is *one person, of whose acts a great multitude by mutual covenants one with another have made themselves every one the author, to the end he may use the strength and means of them all, as he shall think expedient, for their peace and common defense.*

And he that carries this person, is called SOVEREIGN, and said to have sovereign power; and everyone besides, his SUBJECT.

The attaining to this sovereign power, is by two ways. One, by natural force; as when a man makes his children submit themselves and their children to his government, as being able to destroy them if they refuse; or by war subdues his enemies to his will, giving them their lives on that condition. The other is when men agree amongst themselves, to submit to some man, or assembly of men, voluntarily on confidence to be protected by him against all others. This latter may be called a political commonwealth, or commonwealth by institution; and the former a commonwealth by acquisition.

```
┌─┐ ┌─┐ ┌─┐ ┌─┐ ┌─┐ ┌─┐ ┌─┐ ┌─┐ ┌─┐ ┌─┐ ┌─┐ ┌─┐ ┌─┐
```
Two Other Contractarian Theorists

Two other contractarian theorists from the modern period were very important to the history of political philosophy. Both influenced American political thought, especially the earlier of the two, John Locke.

Locke

Hobbes lived much of his life during a time of rather unpleasant turmoil, and quite reasonably thought that civil peace should be a primary objective for people. **John Locke** (1632–1704), who was born some forty or so years later, responded in his writing to a threat other than that of anarchy and chaos—namely, the threat posed by a Roman Catholic monarch in Anglican England. To avoid getting lost in the maze known as English history, let's just say that this Catholic monarch, James II, was a blunderer of the first rank who not only suspended laws against fellow Catholics but also did his best to populate higher offices with them. The end result was that English aristocrats invited the Netherlands head of state, the Protestant William of Orange, to take the throne (which, of course, he was only too happy to do). When William landed in England, James was forced to flee to France, and in 1688 the throne was offered jointly to William and his wife, Mary, who, incidentally, was James's daughter.

This switch was known as the Glorious Revolution, and its relationship to Locke's writings was this: Locke wished to define a right to resistance within a theoretical framework that wouldn't at the same time undermine the state's power to govern effectively. Although Locke wrote his *Two Treatises of Government* before the Glorious Revolution, he published them in 1690, and they were regarded as the philosophical justification of the Glorious Revolution.

Locke's treatises, and especially the *Second Treatise,* are essentially an outline of the aims and purposes of the state. They have affected democratic theory at least as much as anything else that has ever been written. At the time of the American Revolution, Locke's political thought was well known to American political leaders and had become considerably incorporated in American popular political thought as well. It had a marked impact on the contents and wording of the Declaration of Independence, the Constitution, and the Bill of Rights and has had a continued substantial impact on American political thought and political institutions to this day. All Americans are directly or indirectly influenced by John Locke.

Locke, unlike Hobbes, believed there is a natural moral law that is more than a set of practical principles for survival. According to Locke, we are all made by God and are his "property." It logically follows that we are obliged to preserve ourselves and, as far as possible, the rest of humankind. Accordingly, except for the sake of just punishment, no person may take away or impair another's "life, liberty, health, limbs or goods," or anything on which these various items may depend.

That no person may destroy or impair another's life, liberty, and property requires, according to Locke, that each person has inalienable *natural rights* and duties. They are inalienable and natural in that their existence is entailed by the fact that we are God's creations.

Locke was considerably less gloomy than was Hobbes in his opinion of people and was not nearly so pessimistic about what they might do to one another in the absence of civil society (i.e., in a hypothetical "state of nature"). Nevertheless, he thought it plainly advantageous to individuals to contract among themselves to establish a state to govern them, because the state, chiefly through its laws, offers the means to protect the right to property and to ensure "the peace, safety, and public good of the people."

Thus Locke, as well as Hobbes, held that the state is created and acquires its legitimacy by an agreement or social compact on the part of its citizens and subjects. For both philosophers the purpose of the social compact is to ensure the

PROFILE / John Locke (1632–1704)

Locke, like Hobbes, was educated at Oxford. Though he became a lecturer there, he turned to the study of medicine, and, as the physician, friend, and advisor of Lord Ashley (who later was the Earl of Shaftesbury and Lord Chancellor of the realm), Locke became an influential man of state.

When Shaftesbury, who was involved in a plot to overthrow King Charles II, was forced to leave England, Locke found himself suspected by the king of disloyalty and went into exile in Holland in 1683. Five years later, when Prince William and Princess Mary of Orange were called to the throne in the Glorious Revolution, Locke returned to England as part of the entourage of the future Queen Mary.

Locke's two most important works, *Two Treatises of Government* and *An Essay Concerning Human Understanding*, were published in 1690, by which time Locke already was a famous philosopher and respected political advisor. In his last years he withdrew from political affairs and devoted himself to religious contemplation and study of the Epistles of St. Paul.

His contributions to epistemology and political theory were of major and lasting significance, and he is recognized as an articulate advocate of natural rights and religious freedom, as well as a strong opponent of the divine right of kings.

Locke's *Two Treatises of Government* were published anonymously. During his life, rumors correctly reported that Locke was the author of these works, but Locke always denied this.

"public good," but for Locke the purpose is also to protect natural rights. For Hobbes, each subject *gives up* his rights to the Leviathan in exchange for, or rather in hopes of obtaining, peace and security. For Locke, the subject *entrusts* his rights to the state for safeguarding.

Locke and the Right to Property

That people have a natural right to property Locke regarded as evident. Because all people are created by God and thus (as explained earlier) have a right to their body (their "limbs"), it follows, Locke reasoned, that they have a right to their body's labor, and thus to whatever things they "mix their labor with." That is, they have a right to those things provided that the things do not already belong to or are not

⌐⌐⌐⌐⌐⌐⌐⌐⌐

PROFILE / Catharine Trotter Cockburn (1679–1749)

Catharine Trotter was an Englishwoman who, with no apparent formal education, learned French, Latin, and Greek and read philosophy. Until very recently, her philosophical writings went unexamined by scholars. We mention her here in connection with Locke.

Trotter was an immensely successful playwright before she turned to writing philosophy. London's Drury Lane is the predecessor of New York's Broadway. When Trotter was a teenager, her first play, *Agnes de Castro*, was produced at Drury Lane. It was so popular that she was immediately able to get hundreds of subscribers to pay money in advance to support the writing of her next play. (The list of her subscribers reads like a *Who's Who* of England.) When she was twenty-one, she had three blockbuster plays on Drury Lane at the same time.

To connect this to Locke, Edward Stillingfleet, the Bishop of Wooster, was a subscriber to Trotter's plays. He was, in addition, a big-time critic of Locke's *Essay on Human Understanding*, especially as to the consequences of it for morality and religion. He thought that Locke's views challenged the authority of divine revelations on the nature of morality and wrote several highly publicized (and unbelievably long) letters condemning Locke. An individual named Thomas Burnet of the Charterhouse anonymously published three sets of "Remarks" in support of Bishop Stillingfleet's criticism of Locke. Everyone ducked these broadsides, even Locke. Nobody would say a word against the powerful Bishop of Wooster.

Then Catharine Trotter anonymously published *A Defence of Mr. Locke's Essay of Human Understanding, Wherein Its Principles, with Reference to Morality, Revealed Religion, and the Immortality of the Soul, Are Considered and Justified: In Answer to Some Remarks on That Essay*. She published her defense of Locke anonymously because she was afraid that a defense of Locke by a woman would further inflame Bishop Stillingfleet (how could a woman claim any religious or moral authority to give an opinion?). However, within six months, Catharine Trotter was identified as the author of the *Defence*, and her plays all closed, in an apparent blacklisting. Locke sought her out, and gave her some books and a large sum of money in gratitude.

Leibniz (see Chapter 4) was working on his own critique of Locke, but put off finishing it until he could read Trotter's *Defence*. Several years after publishing *Defence*, Catharine Trotter married a clergyman named Cockburn (pronounced CO-burn) and continued to publish philosophical pamphlets defending Locke's philosophy from his religious critics until shortly before her death.

needed to sustain someone else, and provided that they do not exceed in amount what can be used before spoiling. Because money is durable, a person may "heap up as much of it" as he can, said Locke.

According to Locke, what's yours is what you mix your labor with (subject to certain provisos mentioned in the text). But here is a problem: Just *what* is the astronaut mixing his labor with?—the entire planet? Or just with what he has walked on? Or maybe just with the sign and the ground in which it is pounded? Also, *whose* labor is involved here, only the astronaut's?

Locke's theory of property implies that, *though all people equally have a right to property, they do not all have a right to equal property,* because how much property a person lawfully has will depend on his ingenuity and industriousness. Yes, Bruder and Moore are equals in the right to acquire property. But no, it doesn't follow that Bruder and Moore have a right to have equal property, in Locke's view. This distinction is important because it can go some way toward justifying an unequal distribution of wealth.

Separation of Power

When people agree to unite themselves in a state, Locke said, they consent to entrust to it the power to make and enforce laws and punish transgressors, and they consent to submit to the will of the majority. The majority must decide for itself what form of government is best—that is, whether it (the majority) will run the government itself or will delegate its ruling power to a select few, or even to one, or will adopt yet some other arrangement. The body to which the power is delegated (or the majority itself if the power is not delegated to anyone) is the *legislative* or lawmaking branch of the government.

Lawmaking is the central function of government, in Locke's opinion, for it is only through law that people are assured of equal, fair, and impartial treatment and are protected from the arbitrary exercise of power by the government.

But, Locke thought, the persons who make the laws should not themselves execute them, and so, he said, the government should have an *executive* branch as well. Further, in addition to the legislative and executive branches of government, there must, he believed, be a *federative* branch with the power to make war and

Tacit Consent

For Locke the legitimacy of the state and its governing of its citizens rests on their prior consent to its existence, authority, and power. Without that prior consent, it is a violation of a person's natural rights for the state to exercise political power over him. Because men are "by nature all free, equal and independent," he wrote, "no one can be . . . subjected to the political power of another without his consent."

It is plain, however, that most people in most states have never explicitly given their consent to be governed by the state. Do you recall ever having given such consent? Can't it therefore be argued that existing states, by having laws and punishing lawbreakers, in effect violate the natural rights of their citizens?

Locke resolves this problem by maintaining that if we accept any of the advantages of citizenship—if, for instance, we own property or rely on the police or travel on a public highway—we have given **tacit consent** to the state to make and enforce laws, and we are obliged to obey these laws. In this way Locke can maintain that states do not violate the natural rights of citizens (and others subject to their authority) by exercise of governmental authority over them even though these individuals have never explicitly expressed their consent to that authority.

peace. Though Locke believed it essential that there be a judiciary to settle disputes and fix the degree of punishment for lawbreakers, the idea that the judiciary should be a separate branch of government was not his but the influential French jurist **Montesquieu's** (1689–1755).

So Locke's political theory also contrasts sharply with Hobbes's in that, for Hobbes, political power is *surrendered* to an *executive authority,* whereas for Locke, political power is *delegated* to the *legislature*. Also, as we have seen, Locke, unlike Hobbes, called for a division of governmental authority.

Because, according to Locke, the power of the government is entrusted to it by the people of the state, the government is the *servant* of the people. Whenever in the view of the people the government acts contrarily to that trust, the people may dismiss their servant. In other words, when this violation of trust is perceived to have happened, rebellion is justified.

It is plain, then, that several basic concepts of the American democratic form of government are found in the political theory of John Locke. These include the ideas that people have natural rights that government cannot infringe on, that the government is the servant of the people and its power is entrusted to it by them, that law rather than force is the basis of the government, that the will of the people is determined by majority vote, and that the government should be divided into separate branches.

In Selection 9.4, Locke sets forth the ends of political society and government.

SELECTION 9.4

Second Treatise of Civil Government

From John Locke

CHAPTER 9: OF THE ENDS OF POLITICAL SOCIETY AND GOVERNMENT

123. If man in the state of Nature be so free as has been said, if he be absolute lord of his own person and possessions, equal to the greatest and subject to nobody, why will he part with his freedom, this empire, and subject himself to the dominion and control of any other power? To which it is obvious to answer, that though in the state of Nature he hath such a right, yet the enjoyment of it is very uncertain and constantly exposed to the invasion of others; for all being kings as much as he, every man his equal, and the greater part no strict observers of equity and justice, the enjoyment of the property he has in this state is very unsafe, very insecure. This makes him willing to quit this condition which, however free, is full of fears and continual dangers; and it is not without reason that he seeks out and is willing to join in society with others who are already united, or have a mind to unite for the mutual preservation of their lives, liberties and estates, which I call by the general name—property.

124. The great and chief end, therefore, of men uniting into commonwealths, and putting themselves under government, is the preservation of their property; to which in the state of Nature there are many things wanting.

Firstly, there wants an established, settled, known law, received and allowed by common consent to be the standard of right and wrong, and the common measure to decide all controversies between them. For though the law of Nature be plain and intelligible to all rational creatures, yet men, being biased by their interest, as well as ignorant for want of study of it,

are not apt to allow of it as a law binding to them in the application of it to their particular cases.

125. Secondly, in the state of Nature there wants a known and indifferent judge, with authority to determine all differences according to the established law. For every one in that state being both judge and executioner of the law of Nature, men being partial to themselves, passion and revenge is very apt to carry them too far, and with too much heat in their own cases, as well as negligence and unconcernedness, make them too remiss in other men's.

126. Thirdly, in the state of Nature there often wants power to back and support the sentence when right, and to give it due execution. They who by any injustice offended will seldom fail where they are able by force to make good their injustice. Such resistance many times makes the punishment dangerous, and frequently destructive to those who attempt it.

127. Thus mankind, notwithstanding all the privileges of the state of Nature, being but in an ill condition while they remain in it are quickly driven into society. Hence it comes to pass, that we seldom find any number of men live any time together in this state. The inconveniencies that they are therein exposed to by the irregular and uncertain exercise of the power every man has of punishing the transgressions of others, make them take sanctuary under the established laws of government, and therein seek the preservation of their property. It is this makes them so willingly give up every one his single power of punishing to be exercised by such alone as shall be appointed to it amongst them, and by such rules as the community, or those authorised by them to that purpose, shall agree on.

And in this we have the original right and rise of both the legislative and executive power as well as of the governments and societies themselves.

128. For in the state of Nature to omit the liberty he has of innocent delights, a man has two powers. The first is to do whatsoever he thinks fit for the preservation of himself and others within the permission of the law of Nature; by which law, common to them all, he and all the rest of mankind are one community, make up one society distinct from all other creatures, and were it not for the corruption and viciousness of degenerate men, there would be no need of any other, no necessity that men should separate from this great and natural community, and associate into lesser combinations. The other power a man has in the state of Nature is the power to punish the crimes committed against that law. Both these he gives up when he joins in a private, if I may so call it, or particular political society, and incorporates into any commonwealth separate from the rest of mankind.

129. The first power—viz., of doing whatsoever he thought fit for the preservation of himself and the rest of mankind, he gives up to be regulated by laws made by the society, so far forth as the preservation of himself and the rest of that society shall require; which laws of the society in many things confine the liberty he had by the law of Nature.

130. Secondly, the power of punishing he wholly gives up, and engages his natural force, which he might before employ in the execution of the law of Nature, by his own single authority, as he thought fit, to assist the executive power of the society as the law thereof shall require. For being now in a new state, wherein he is to enjoy many conveniences from the labour, assistance, and society of others in the same community, as well as protection from its whole strength, he is to part also with as much of his natural liberty, in providing for himself, as the good, prosperity, and safety of the society shall require, which is not only necessary but just, since the other members of the society do the like.

131. But though men when they enter into society give up the equality, liberty, and executive power they had in the state of Nature into the hands of the society, to be so far disposed of by the legislative as the good of the society shall require, yet it being only with an intention in every one the better to preserve himself, his liberty and property (for no rational creature can be supposed to change his condition with an intention to be worse), the power of the society or legislative constituted by them can never be supposed to extend farther than the common good, but is obliged to secure every one's property by providing against those three defects above mentioned that made the state of Nature so unsafe and uneasy. And so, whoever has the legislative or supreme power of any commonwealth, is bound to govern by established standing laws, promulgated and known to the people, and not by extemporary decrees, by indifferent and upright judges, who are to decide controversies by those laws; and to employ the force of the community at home only in the execution of such laws, or abroad to prevent or redress foreign injuries and secure the community from inroads and invasion. And all this to be directed to no other end but the peace, safety, and public good of the people.

Rousseau

According to Hobbes and Locke, people are better off in the properly constituted state than they are or were in the "state of nature." Quite a different point of view was expressed by **Jean-Jacques Rousseau** (1712–1778), at least in his early political writings.

In the state of nature, in which there was neither state nor civilization, people were essentially innocent, good, happy, and healthy, maintained Rousseau in his *Discourse on the Origin and Foundation of the Inequality among Men* (1754). Further, in the state of nature, he said, people enjoyed perfect freedom. But with the advent of private property, this all changed. "The first man who, having enclosed a piece of ground, bethought himself of saying *This is mine,* and found people simple enough to believe him, was the real founder of civil society," which brought with it the destruction of natural liberty and which, "for the advantage of a few ambitious individuals, subjected all mankind to perpetual labor, slavery and wretchedness."

To put this in some sort of perspective, Rousseau wrote this indictment of civilization in 1754. This was fully sixty-seven years after Newton had published his *Principia.* It was two years after Benjamin Franklin, with key and kite, had proved that lightning is electricity. Thirty years earlier, Fahrenheit had devised his thermometer. Bach had been dead four years, and it had been twenty-three years since he had completed the Brandenburg Concertos, a masterpiece of mathematical reasoning expressed in music. This, in short, was the eighteenth century, the Enlightenment, the age of light, the Age of Reason. Civilization was *stuffed* with benefits. Philosophers were (as always) critical, but *this* critical? Civilization a step in retrograde? Rousseau was regarded as insane.

But Rousseau later came to think that, in the proper society, people would surrender their individual liberty for a different and more important *collective* liberty. Through a social compact a people may agree, in effect, to unite into a collective whole, called "the state" or "the sovereign," and through the state or sovereign enact laws reflective of the *general will.* An important point to be aware of here is that, for Rousseau, the state or sovereign is *an entity in its own right,* a "moral person" (as Rousseau says), a nonbiological organism that has its own life and its own *will.* Rousseau's concept of the **general will**—that is, the will of a politically united people, the will of the state—is his most important contribution to political philosophy (see the box).

If you have difficulty conceiving of a state as a person or organic entity, remember that Plato also viewed the state as an organism. Or think of a football team, which can easily be regarded as something "over and beyond" the individual players that make it up, or of a corporation, which the law regards as a person.

The general will, according to Rousseau, defines what is to the common good, and thus determines what is right and wrong and should and should not be done. And the state or sovereign (i.e., the people as a collective agent) expresses this general will by passing laws.

Further, the general will, the will of the people taken collectively, represents the *true* will of each person. Thus, insofar as the individual's actions coincide with the common will, he is acting as he "really" wants to act—and to act as you really want to act is to be free, said Rousseau. Compelling a person to accept the general will by obeying the laws of the state is *forcing him to be free,* Rousseau wrote in a

According to Rousseau, when you force a person to accept the general will, you are forcing him to be free.

famous passage. So we may lose individual or "natural" liberty when we unite to form a collective whole, but we gain this new type of "civil" liberty, "the freedom to obey a law which we prescribe for ourselves." Thus, Rousseau wrote, "it is to law alone that men owe justice and [civil] liberty."

The question arises, of course, Just how do we know what the general will is? Rousseau's answer: If we, the citizens, are enlightened and are not allowed to influence one another, then a majority vote determines what the general will is:

> The general will is found by counting votes. When, therefore, the opinion which is contrary to my own prevails, this proves neither more nor less than that I was mistaken, and that what I thought to be the general will was not so.

Rousseau, however, distinguished between the "will of all" and the general will. The former, Rousseau wrote,

> is indeed but a sum of private wills: but remove from these same wills the pluses and minuses that cancel each other, and then the general will remains as the sum of the differences.

According to Rousseau, it makes no sense to think of either delegating or dividing the general will. Therefore, he calculated, in the state there cannot validly be a division of powers (in contrast to what Locke thought), and, though we may commission some person or persons to administer or enforce the law, these individuals act only as our *deputies*, not as our representatives.

Rousseau maintained that the citizens of the state have the right at any time to terminate the social contract. He also held that they have the right at any time to depose the officials of the state. The implication of the right of the citizenry to terminate the social contract at any time and of their right to remove officials of the state at any time is that the citizenry have a right of revolution and a right to resume anarchy at any time. Thus Rousseau is thought to have provided a philosophical justification for anarchy and revolution.

The General Will

Rousseau's concept of the general will is essentially the same as such familiar concepts as the "sentiment of a nation" and the "aspirations of a people." The idea is that a group of people may *collectively* or *as a group* desire or wish or want something, and that this collective desire, though it may coincide with the desires of the individuals in the group, is a metaphysically distinct entity.

Two questions about the general will, and all similar notions of a collective sentiment, are controversial to this day. First, what is it? Let's suppose, for example, that every member of a group of people believes that the federal deficit should be reduced. We may say, then, that the general will is that the federal deficit should be reduced. But can saying this possibly mean otherwise than simply that every individual in the group believes that it should be reduced? In this instance, that is, the general will seems no different from the wills of all individuals.

Let's suppose now that 60 percent of the group believes that the deficit should be reduced. If we now say that the general will is that the federal deficit should be reduced, can we mean anything other than that 60 percent believes that way? In this instance, then, the general will seems no different from the individual wills of 60 percent.

Suppose, finally, that 50 percent believes in raising taxes to reduce the federal deficit and 50 percent believes in cutting taxes to reduce the federal deficit. If we ignore the differences about how the deficit should be reduced (these, Rousseau might say, are "pluses and minuses that cancel each other") and say that the general will is that the federal deficit should be reduced, do we mean anything other than what we did in the first instance, namely, that everyone believes that it should be reduced?

Thus, if the general will is supposedly something other than the will of all or the will of the majority—which clearly is Rousseau's view because he envisions circumstances in which the majority will and the will of all may actually run counter to the general will—the question is: What is it?

And the second question is: Even granting that a group may have a general will that is distinct from the will of all and the will of the majority, how is one to determine the specific propositions it endorses? Polls and elections disclose the will of all and the will of the majority; what discloses the general will?

Did Rousseau also unwittingly establish a philosophical basis for totalitarianism? Some think that is the case because he said that "the articles of the social contract [reduce] to this single point: the total alienation of each associate, and all his rights, to the whole community." If the community is regarded not just as the sum total of its members but as an entity somehow over and above the individuals in it, an entity with its own life and will that can itself do no wrong and must always be obeyed, then Rousseau's words do have an ominous ring and invoke concepts that are incorporated wholesale in the philosophy of fascism, discussed in the next chapter. (Hitler's claim that the Führer instinctively knows the desires of the Volk and is therefore due absolute obedience is an appeal to the general will.) Also ominous is what Rousseau wrote near the end of *The Social Contract* (1762):

PROFILE / Jean-Jacques Rousseau (1712–1778)

He [Rousseau] is surely the blackest and most atrocious villain, beyond comparison, that now exists in the world; and I am heartily ashamed of anything I ever wrote in his favor.

—David Hume

Rousseau—philosopher, novelist, and composer—loved many women and eventually became paranoid to the point of madness. He was born a watchmaker's son in Geneva. In his early teens he was apprenticed to an engraver but ran away from his master. When he was about sixteen, he met Baroness Louise de Warens, who became his patroness and later his lover. With her he spent most of his time until he was thirty, attempting through wide reading to remedy the deficiencies in his education. In 1742, he went to Paris by himself to make his fortune, which he failed to do, with a new system of musical notation he had invented. There he became a close associate of several important literary figures of the time, including, most significantly, Denis Diderot (editor of the *Encyclopédie,* the crowning jewel of eighteenth-century rationalism). There he also met Thérèse Le Vasseur, an almost illiterate servant girl, who became his common-law wife.

In 1749, Rousseau won first prize in a contest sponsored by the Academy of Dijon for his essay on the question: Has the progress of the sciences and art contributed to the corruption or to the improvement of human conduct? His answer, startling to the sensibilities of the French Enlightenment, was an attack on the corrupting effects of civilization and instantly made him famous. A second essay, *Discourse on the Origin and Foundation of Inequality among Men* (1754), which again portrayed the evils brought to man by civilization, was also highly controversial. Voltaire, to whom Rousseau had sent a copy of the work, thanked him for his "new book against the human race."

At this time Rousseau, disillusioned with Paris, went briefly to Geneva to regain his Genevan citizenship, but he soon returned to Paris and retired to the estate of yet another woman, one Madame d'Epinay. Always emotional, temperamental, suspicious, and unable to maintain constant friendships, however, he suspected his friends —Diderot, Mme. d'Epinay, and others—of conspiring to ruin him. He departed and became the guest of the Duc de Luxembourg, at whose chateau he finished *La Nouvelle Heloise* (1761), written under the influence of his love for (yes!) the sister-in-law of Mme. d'Epinay.

The Social Contract, and his treatise on education, *Emile,* both published the following year, were so offensive to ecclesiastic authorities that Rousseau had to leave Paris. He fled to Neuchatel and then to Bern. Finally, in 1766, he found a haven with David Hume in England. But after a year, Rousseau, who by this time had become deeply paranoid, quarreled with Hume, whom he thought was plotting against him. In fact, Hume had been trying to procure a royal pension for Rousseau. (Hume's last opinion of Rousseau is stated above.)

Rousseau now returned to France, and eventually to Paris, even though he was in danger of arrest. He was left undisturbed, however, and spent his last years copying music, wandering about reading his *Confessions* out loud, and insulting the curious throngs who came to look at him.

Still, few philosophers have had as much impact, either on political philosophy and politics or on education or literature, as Rousseau did.

If any one, after he has publicly subscribed to these dogmas [which dispose a person to love his duties and be a good citizen], shall conduct himself as if he did not believe them, he is to be punished by death.

Selection 9.5 is from *The Social Contract,* which contains Rousseau's mature political philosophy.

---

*The Social Contract**

From Jean-Jacques Rousseau

CHAPTER VI: OF THE SOCIAL CONTRACT

I will suppose that men in the state of nature are arrived at that crisis when the strength of each individual is insufficient to overcome the resistance of the obstacles to his preservation. This primitive state can therefore subsist no longer; and the human race would perish unless it changed its manner of life.

As men cannot create for themselves new forces, but merely unite and direct those which already exist, the only means they can employ for their preservation is to form by aggregation an assemblage of forces that may be able to overcome the resistance, to be put in motion as one body, and to act in concert.

This assemblage of forces must be produced by the concurrence of many; but as the force and the liberty of each man are the chief instruments of his preservation, how can he engage them elsewhere without danger to himself, and without neglecting the care which is due himself? This difficulty, which leads directly to my subject, may be expressed in these words:

"Where shall we find a form of association which will defend and protect with the whole common force the person and the property of each associate, and by which every person, while uniting himself with all, shall obey only himself

and remain as free as before?" Such is the fundamental problem of which the Social Contract gives the solution.

The articles of this contract are so unalterably fixed by the nature of the act that the least modification renders them vain and of no effect; so that they are the same everywhere, and are everywhere tacitly understood and admitted, even though they may never have been formally announced; until, the social compact being violated, each individual is restored to his original rights, and resumes his native liberty, while losing the conventional liberty for which he renounced it.

The articles of the social contract will, when clearly understood, be found reducible to this single point: the total alienation of each associate, and all his rights, to the whole community; for, in the first place as every individual gives himself up entirely, the condition of every person is alike; and being so, it would not be to the interest of any one to render that condition offensive to others.

Nay, more than this, the alienation being made without any reserve, the union is as complete as it can be, and no associate has any further claim to anything: for if any individual retained rights not enjoyed in general by all, as there would be no common superior to decide between him and the public, each person being in some points his own judge, would soon pretend to be so in everything; and thus would the

---

*Rousseau's footnotes have been omitted.

state of nature be continued and the association necessarily become tyrannical or be annihilated.

Finally, each person gives himself to all, and so not to any one individual; and as there is no one associate over whom the same right is not acquired which is ceded to him by others, each gains an equivalent for what he loses, and finds his force increased for preserving that which he possesses.

If, therefore, we exclude from the social compact all that is not essential, we shall find it reduced to the following terms:

Each of us places in common his person and all his power under the supreme direction of the general will; and as one body we all receive each member as an indivisible part of the whole.

From that moment, instead of as many separate persons as there are contracting parties, this act of association produces a moral and collective body, composed of as many members as there are votes in the assembly, which from this act receives its unity, its common self, its life, and its will. This public person, which is thus formed by the union of all other persons, took formerly the name of "city," and now takes that of "republic" or "body politic." It is called by its members "State" when it is passive, "Sovereign" when in activity, and, whenever it is compared with other bodies of a similar kind, it is denominated "power." The associates take collectively the name of "people," and separately, that of "citizens," as participating in the sovereign authority, and of "subjects" because they are subjected to the laws of the State. . . .

CHAPTER VII: OF THE SOVEREIGN

It appears from this formula that the act of association contains a reciprocal engagement between the public and individuals, and that each individual, contracting, as it were, with himself, is engaged under a double character; that is, as a member of the Sovereign engaging with individuals, and as a member of the State engaged

with the Sovereign. But we cannot apply here the maxim of civil right, that no person is bound by any engagement which he makes with himself; for there is a material difference between an obligation to oneself individually, and an obligation to a collective body of which oneself constitutes a part.

It is necessary to observe here that public deliberation, which can bind all the subjects to the Sovereign, in consequence of the double character under which the members of that body appear, cannot, for the opposite reason, bind the Sovereign to itself; and consequently that it is against the nature of the body politic for the sovereign power to impose on itself any law which it cannot break. Being able to consider itself as acting under one character only, it is in the situation of an individual forming a contract with himself; and we see therefore that there neither is nor can be any kind of fundamental law obligatory for the body of the people, not even the social contract itself. But this does not mean that this body could not very well engage itself to others in any manner which would not derogate from the contract; for, with respect to what is external to it, it becomes a simple being, an individual. But the body politic, or the Sovereign, which derives its existence from the sacredness of the contract, can never bind itself, even towards outsiders, in anything that would derogate from the original act, such as alienating any portion of itself, or submitting to another Sovereign. To violate the contract by which it exists would be to annihilate itself; and that which is nothing can produce nothing.

As soon as this multitude is united in one body, you cannot offend one of its members without attacking the body; much less can you offend the body without incurring the resentment of all the members. Thus duty and interest equally oblige the two contracting parties to lend aid to each other; and the same men must endeavour to unite under this double character all the advantages which attend it.

Further, the Sovereign, being formed only of the individuals who compose it, neither has, nor can have, any interest contrary to theirs; consequently, the sovereign power need give no guarantee to its subjects, because it is impossible that the body should seek to injure all its members; and we shall see presently that it can do no injury to any individual in particular. The Sovereign, by its nature, is always everything it ought to be.

But this is not so with the relation of subjects towards the Sovereign, which, notwithstanding the common interest, has nothing to make them responsible for the performance of their engagements if some means is not found of ensuring their fidelity.

In fact, each individual may, as a man, have a private will, dissimilar or contrary to the general will which he has as a citizen. His own private interest may dictate to him very differently from the common interest; his absolute and naturally independent existence may make him regard what he owes to the common cause as a gratuitous contribution, the omission of which would be less injurious to others than the payment would be burdensome to himself; and considering the moral person which constitutes the State as a creature of the imagination, because it is not a man, he may wish to enjoy the rights of a citizen without being disposed to fulfil the duties of a subject. Such an injustice would in its progress cause the ruin of the body politic.

In order, therefore, to prevent the social compact from becoming an empty formula, it tacitly comprehends the engagement, which alone can give effect to the others—that whoever refuses to obey the general will shall be compelled to it by the whole body; this in fact only forces him to be free; for this is the condition which, by giving each citizen to his country, guarantees his absolute personal independence, a condition which gives motion and effect to the political machine. This alone renders all civil engagements justifiable, and without it they would be absurd, tyrannical, and subject to the most enormous abuses.

CHAPTER VIII: OF THE CIVIL STATE

The passing from the state of nature to the civil state produces in man a very remarkable change, by substituting justice for instinct in his conduct, and giving to his actions a moral character which they lacked before. It is then only that the voice of duty succeeds to physical impulse, and a sense of what is right, to the incitements of appetite. Man, who had till then regarded none but himself, perceives that he must act on other principles, and learns to consult his reason before he listens to his inclinations. Although he is deprived in this new state of many advantages which he enjoyed from nature, he gains in return others so great, his faculties so unfold themselves by being exercised, his ideas are so extended, his sentiments so exalted, and his whole mind so enlarged and refined, that if, by abusing his new condition, he did not sometimes degrade it even below that from which he emerged, he ought to bless continually the happy moment that snatched him forever from it, and transformed him from a circumscribed and stupid animal to an intelligent being and a man.

In order to draw a balance between the advantages and disadvantages attending his new situation, let us state them in such a manner that they may be easily compared. Man loses by the social contract his *natural* liberty, and an unlimited right to all which tempts him, and which he can obtain; in return he acquires *civil* liberty, and proprietorship of all he possesses. That we may not be deceived in the value of these compensations, we must distinguish natural liberty, which knows no bounds but the power of the individual, from civil liberty, which is limited by the general will; and between possession, which is only the effect of force or of the right of the first occupant, from property, which must be founded on a positive title. In addition we might add to the other acquisitions of the civil state that of moral liberty, which alone renders a man master of himself; for it is *slavery* to be under the impulse of mere appetite, and *freedom* to obey a law which we prescribe for ourselves. But I have already said too much on this head, and the philosophical sense of the word "liberty" is not at present my subject.

Mary Wollstonecraft

Mary Wollstonecraft (1759–1797) wrote in response both to what she saw around her and to some of the views about women that were being put forward by the philosophers of the time. Her mother and sister were both the victims of domestic violence, which caused her to take issue with the idealized view of marriage being put forth by her culture. As an intellectual, she was familiar with many of the high-minded views of womanhood being perpetuated by her contemporaries. She was particularly annoyed at Rousseau's view of women, because he advocated that women's education should be designed entirely to make them pleasing to men. "To please, to be useful to us, to make us love and esteem them, to educate us when young and take care of us when grown up, to advise, to console us, to render our lives easy and agreeable—these are the duties of women at all times, and what they should be taught in their infancy," reflected Rousseau. Wollstonecraft employed several types of reasoning, both consequentialist and deontological (Remember these concepts? See Chapter 8.), against Rousseau and his allies.

First, she argued that educating women to be the ornaments to, and playthings of, men would have bad consequences for society. How could silly, vain creatures ever be expected to do an adequate job raising a family? They would become "mere propagators of fools."

Second, she argued that raising women to be ornamental would have bad consequences for women. No matter how charming a woman might be, after a few years of daily contact, her husband would ultimately become somewhat bored and distracted. If women have no inner resources to fall back on, Wollstonecraft argued, they will then "grow languid, or become a spring of bitterness," and love will turn to jealousy or vanity.

Third, and perhaps most important, she argued that women were as capable as men of attaining the "masculine" virtues of wisdom and rationality, if only society would allow those virtues to be cultivated. She noted that the "virtues" of women—docility, dependence, and sensitivity—were commonly associated with weakness. She held that there should be no distinction between female excellence and human excellence. Like many intellectuals of the Enlightenment, Wollstone-

PROFILE / Mary Wollstonecraft (1759–1797)

Mary Wollstonecraft's early years were not happy; her father was an unsuccessful gentleman farmer who squandered the family's assets and took out his frustrations on his wife and children. While still quite a young woman, Wollstonecraft struck out on her own to London to become a writer. After some early years of struggle, her work began to gain considerable acceptance among the intelligentsia of London society. She was fairly well known by the time she published "A Vindication of the Rights of Women."

Her personal life was unconventional and tumultuous. An affair with an American led to the birth of her first daughter, Fanny. When Fanny was still very young, Wollstonecraft met William Godwin, the political anarchist. They were quite well matched intellectually and emotionally, and after Wollstonecraft became pregnant, they married. Their life together was cut short, however, when Wollstonecraft died from complications following the delivery of the child. Godwin was devastated at Wollstonecraft's death and wrote a tender book of memoirs about her. This book caused significant public scandal both for Wollstonecraft and for Godwin, since he made no effort to hide the illegitimacy of her first child or the fact that she was pregnant when they married.

Their daughter, Mary Godwin, married Percy Bysshe Shelley and went on to write the novel *Frankenstein*. Mary Shelley had no interest in women's rights and spent considerable energy trying to cover up the unconventionality of her parents' lives. It was not until the end of the nineteeenth century that the scandal associated with Mary Wollstonecraft died down enough to permit later feminists to include her name in their lists of honorable forebears.

craft gave pride of place to rationality and argued that women must have their capacity for reason developed to its fullest extent if they were to become excellent examples of humanity.

In Selection 9.6, Wollstonecraft defends the view that society should abandon its practice of enculturating women to weakness and dependency.

SELECTION 9.6

"A Vindication of the Rights of Woman"   **From Mary Wollstonecraft**

I love man as my fellow; but his sceptre, real, or usurped, extends not to me, unless the reason of an individual demands my homage; and even then the submission is to reason, and not to man. In fact, the conduct of an accountable being must be regulated by the operations of its own reason; or on what foundation rests the throne of God?

It appears to me necessary to dwell on these obvious truths, because females have been insulated, as it were; and, while they have been stripped of the virtues that should clothe humanity, they have been decked with artificial graces that enable them to exercise a short-lived tyranny. Love, in their bosoms, taking the place of every nobler passion, their sole ambition is to be fair, to raise emotion instead of inspiring respect; and this ignoble desire, like the servility in absolute monarchies, destroys all strength of character. Liberty is the mother of virtue, and if women be, by their very constitution, slaves, and not allowed to breathe the sharp invigorating air of freedom, they must ever languish like exotics, and be reckoned beautiful flaws in nature. . . .

But should it be proved that woman is naturally weaker than man, whence does it follow that it is natural for her to labour to become still weaker than nature intended her to be? Arguments of this cast are an insult to common sense, and savour of passion. The *divine right* of husbands, like the divine right of kings, may, it is to be hoped, in this enlightened age, be contested without danger, and though conviction may not silence many boisterous disputants, yet, when any prevailing prejudice is attacked, the wife will consider, and leave the narrow-minded to rail with thoughtless vehemence at innovation.

It is time to effect a revolution in female manners—time to restore to them their lost dignity—and make them, as a part of the human species, labour by reforming themselves to reform the world. It is time to separate unchangeable morals from local manners.

American Constitutional Theory

We also wish to discuss briefly American Constitutional political philosophy because it incorporates several of the concepts and ideas we've been examining. Before the American Constitution, philosophers had theorized about a social compact as the foundation of the state, but there had been only a few instances of written constitutions, and these were of no lasting importance. England was the only great power that had ever had a constitution, lasting a few months in the Cromwell period. Thus, the first significant experience with written constitutions was the American Constitution.

The main trend in American political thought has been embodied in the development of theory pertaining to the Constitution. The trend relates essentially to *natural law* and *natural rights* and to the incorporation in the federal and state constitutions of a *social contract* to establish or control a political state. You now know something about the history of these concepts before the founding of the United States.

Natural Law and Rights in the Declaration of Independence

In 1776, the Declaration of Independence proclaimed the doctrine of natural or divine law and of natural or God-given rights. The Declaration asserted that there are "Laws of Nature and of Nature's God," and the framers appealed "to the Supreme Judge of the World for the rectitude of our intentions." The Declaration also asserted that it is "self-evident" that "all men are created equal, that they are endowed by their Creator with certain unalienable rights, that among these are Life, Liberty and the pursuit of happiness." The framers of the Declaration also stated that "it is the Right of the People to alter or abolish" any form of government, whenever that form of government becomes destructive of "its ends to secure" the unalienable rights with which men are endowed by their creator.

In thus proclaiming the existence of natural or divine law and of natural and God-given rights, the Declaration of Independence incorporated what had become widespread political theory in the colonies by the time of the American Revolution, a theory that was prevalent among those who opposed the British king and parliament. This political theory was rooted in (1) familiarity with the writings of European political theorists, particularly British, and in (2) the constant preaching of the clergy in the colonies, who had been dominant in civil and political as well as in religious matters, that the moral code reflected divine law and should determine civil law and rights.

But as for the philosophically vexing question of *who* should say what natural or divine law ordains and what God-given rights are in particular, it was no longer generally conceded, by the time of the Declaration, that this power belonged primarily in the clergy. Instead, it was recognized that the power lies ultimately in the people and mediately in the legislative branch of government subject (some people thought) to judicial review.

Natural Law and Rights in the U.S. Constitution

The original Constitution itself, before the adoption of the Bill of Rights constituted by the first ten amendments to the Constitution, makes scant allusion to natural law or divine rights. It does so implicitly only in its preamble, in stating its purpose to "establish Justice, insure domestic tranquility, provide for the common defense, promote the General Welfare, and secure the Blessings of Liberty." Although it can plausibly be argued that these purposes are those of natural law and that the "Blessings of Liberty" include natural rights, nevertheless the original Constitution was directed toward establishing law and order and not toward guaranteeing natural rights. Nor is there any explicit reference to divine law or God-given rights in the original.

Ratification of the original Constitution was attained only by assurance that a Bill of Rights would immediately be adopted by amendment, which indeed occurred when the first ten amendments were ratified on December 15, 1791. This Bill of Rights arguably limits the federal government in ways dictated by natural law and arguably guarantees rights in ways dictated by the existence of natural rights. And undoubtedly, the rights explicit (and implicit) in the Bill of Rights were regarded by the framers of the Constitution and by the American people in general as the unalienable rights to which the Declaration of Independence alluded.

Now in *Marbury v. Madison*, decided by the Supreme Court in 1803 under Chief Justice John Marshall, and in Supreme Court cases in its wake, it became firmly established that the Supreme Court has the power under the Constitution to declare void federal and state laws that violate it. Thus, the extent to which what may be called natural law and rights are incorporated in the Constitution is for the Supreme Court to determine.

Under Section 1 of the Fourteenth Amendment, ratified July 9, 1869, most of the limitations on government and guarantees of rights contained in the Bill of Rights became applicable to the states as well as to the federal government. The relationship of the authority of the states to the authority of the federal government has always been a central issue in American Constitutional philosophy.

The Right to Privacy

Today there is much discussion about whether the Constitution protects a right to "privacy." Because it is the Supreme Court that decides such things, the views of potential (and actual) members of the Supreme Court on this important question are of widespread concern to the American people. In 1987, for instance, President Ronald Reagan's nominee to the Supreme Court, Robert H. Bork, was rejected by the U.S. Senate, mainly because of Bork's views on the question of whether there is a constitutional right to privacy. The question is especially controversial because in its landmark decision in *Roe v. Wade* the Supreme Court upheld a woman's right to abortion as included within the right to privacy.

Whether the U.S. Constitution protects a right to privacy is perhaps not a purely philosophical question. But it bears on the larger issue of the legitimate scope and authority of the state, and that issue is a philosophical one.

Selection 9.7 contains part of Mr. Justice Douglas's opinion of the Court in *Griswold v. Connecticut*, 381 US 479, decided June 7, 1965, holding that a Connecticut statute making it criminal to use contraceptives was unconstitutional because it violated the right of privacy. (The dissenting opinion of Messrs. Justices Black and Stewart follows.) The third section of Selection 9.7 is from Mr. Justice Blackmun's opinion of the Court in *Roe v. Wade*, 410 US 113, decided January 22, 1973, finding that the right to privacy includes a woman's right to terminate her pregnancy subject to the power of the state appropriately to regulate that right, and that until the end of the first trimester of pregnancy, the attending physician, in consultation with the woman, is free to determine, without regulation by the state, that in his or her medical judgment the woman's pregnancy should be terminated.

SELECTION 9.7

From Supreme Court Decisions on the Right to Privacy

FROM MR. JUSTICE DOUGLAS'S OPINION OF THE COURT IN *GRISWOLD V. CONNECTICUT*, 381 US 479, DECIDED JUNE 7, 1965.

The foregoing cases suggest that specific guarantees in the Bill of Rights have penumbras, formed by emanations from those guarantees that help give them life and substance. . . . Various guarantees create zones of privacy. The right of associations contained in the penumbra of the First Amendment is one, as we have seen. The Third Amendment in its prohibitions of the quartering of soldiers "in any house" in time of peace without the consent of the owner is another facet of that privacy. The Fourth Amendment explicitly affirms the "right of people to be secure in their persons, houses, papers, and effects, against unreasonable searches and seizures." The Fifth Amendment in its Self-Incrimination Clause enables the citizen to create a zone of privacy which government may not force him to surrender to his detriment. The Ninth Amendment provides: "The Enumerations in the Constitution, of certain rights, shall not be construed to deny or disparage others retained by the people." . . .

We have had many controversies over these penumbral rights of "privacy and repose." . . . These cases bear witness that the right of privacy which presses for recognition here is a legitimate one.

The present case, then, concerns a relationship lying within a zone of privacy created by several fundamental constitutional guarantees. . . . Would we allow the police to search the sacred precincts of marital bedrooms for telltale signs of the use of contraceptives? The very idea is repulsive to the notion of privacy surrounding the marriage relationship.

We deal with a right of privacy older than the Bill of Rights—older than our political parties, older than our school system.

FROM THE DISSENTING OPINION OF MR. JUSTICE BLACK, IN WHICH MR. JUSTICE STEWART JOINED, IN *GRISWOLD V. CONNECTICUT.*

The court talks about a constitutional "right of privacy" as though there is some constitutional provision or provisions forbidding any law ever to be passed which might abridge the "privacy" of individuals. But there is not. There are, of course, guarantees in certain specific constitutional provisions which are designed to protect privacy at certain times and places with respect to certain activities. . . .

One of the most effective ways of diluting or expanding a constitutionally guaranteed right is to substitute for the crucial word or words of a constitutional guarantee another word or words more or less flexible and more or less restricted in meaning. This fact is well illustrated by the use of the term "right to privacy" as a comprehensive substitute for the Fourth Amendment's guaranty against "unreasonable searches and seizures." Privacy is a broad, abstract and ambiguous concept which can easily be shrunken in meaning but which can also, on the other hand, easily be interpreted as a ban against many things other than searches and seizures. . . . I like my privacy as well as the next one, but I am nevertheless compelled to admit that government has a right to invade it unless prohibited by some specific constitutional provision. For these reasons I cannot agree with the Court's judgment and the reasons it gives for holding this Connecticut law unconstitutional.

This brings me to the arguments made by my Brothers Harlan, White and Goldberg [in opinions concurring in the judgment of the Court] for invalidating the Connecticut law. Brothers Harlan and White would invalidate it by the Due Process Clause of the Fourteenth Amendment, but Brother Goldberg, while agreeing with Brother Harlan, relies also on the Ninth Amendment. . . . My disagreement with the Court's opinion . . . is a narrow one, relating to the application of the First Amendment to the facts and circumstances of this particular case. But my disagreement with Brothers Harlan, White and Goldberg is more basic. I think that if properly construed neither the Due Process Clause nor the Ninth Amendment, nor both together, could under any circumstances be a proper basis for invalidating the Connecticut law. . . .

The due process argument which my Brothers Harlan and White adopt here is based, as their opinions indicate, on the premise that this Court is vested with power to invalidate all state laws that it considers to be arbitrary, capricious, unreasonable or oppressive, or this Court's belief that a particular state law under scrutiny has no "rational or justifying" purpose, or is offensive to a "sense of fairness and justice." If these formulas based on "natural justice," or others which mean the same thing, are to prevail, they require judges to determine what is or is not constitutional on the basis of their own appraisal of what laws are unwise or unnecessary. . . .

My brother Goldberg has adopted the recent discovery that the Ninth Amendment as well as the Due Process Clause can be used by this Court as authority to strike down all state legislation which this Court thinks violates "fundamental principles of liberty and justice," or is contrary to the "traditions and conscience of our people." He also states, without proof satisfactory to me, that in making decisions on this basis judges will not consider "their personal and private notions." One may ask how they can avoid considering them. . . . one would certainly have to look far beyond the language of the Ninth Amendment to find that the framers vested in this Court any such awesome veto power over law-making, either by the States or by Congress. . . . The Ninth Amendment was intended to protect against the idea that "by enumerating particular exceptions to the grant of power" to the Federal Government, "those rights which were not singled out, were intended to be assigned into the hands of the General Government [the United States], and were consequently insecure." That Amendment was passed, not to broaden the powers of this Court or any other department of "the General Government," but, as every student of history knows, to assure the people that the Constitution in all its provisions was intended to limit the Federal Government to the powers granted expressly or by necessary implications.

FROM MR. JUSTICE BLACKMUN'S OPINION OF THE COURT IN *ROE V. WADE*, 410 US 113, DECIDED JANUARY 22, 1973.

The Constitution does not explicitly mention any right of privacy. In a line of decisions, however, going back as far as . . . (1891), the Court has recognized that a right of personal privacy, or a guarantee of certain areas or zones of privacy, does exist under the Constitution. In varying contexts, the Court or individual Justices have, indeed, found at least the roots of that right in the First Amendment . . . ; in the Fourth and Fifth Amendments . . . ; in the penumbras of the Bill of Rights . . . ; in the Ninth Amendment . . . ; or in the Fourteenth Amendment.

These decisions make it clear that only personal rights that can be deemed "fundamental" or "implicit in the concept of ordered liberty . . . are included in this guarantee of personal privacy." They also make it clear that the right has some extensions to activities relating to marriage . . . ; procreation . . . ; contraception . . . ; family relationships . . . ; and child rearing and education. . . .

This right of privacy, whether it is founded in the Fourteenth Amendment's concept of personal liberty, as we feel it is, or, as the District Court determines, in the Ninth Amendment's reservations of rights in the people, is broad enough to encompass a woman's decision whether or not to terminate her pregnancy. . . . The Court's decisions recognizing a right of privacy also acknowledge that some state regulation in areas protected by that right is appropriate. . . . The privacy right . . . cannot be said to be absolute. In fact, it is not clear to us that the claim asserted by some amici that one has an unlimited right to do with one's body as one pleases bears a close relationship to the right of privacy previously articulated in the Court's decisions. The Court has refused to recognize an unlimited right of this kind in the past.

Checklist

To help you review, here is a checklist of the key philosophers and concepts of this chapter. The brief descriptive sentences summarize leading ideas. Keep in mind that some of these summary statements represent terrific oversimplifications of complex positions.

Philosophers

- **Plato** Held that the best or "just" state is a class-structured aristocracy ruled by "philosopher-kings."

- **Aristotle** Held that a state is good to the degree to which it enables its citizens to achieve the good life and believed that the form of the ideal state depends on the circumstances.

- **Cicero** Roman statesman who defined the classic Stoic position on natural law: there is only one valid law, the natural law of reason, and it holds universally.

- **St. Augustine and St. Thomas Aquinas** Christianized the concept of natural law; were concerned with the relationship of secular law to natural law and of the state to the church. Aquinas distinguished four kinds of law; this was one of his most important contributions to political philosophy.

- **Thomas Hobbes** Contractarian theorist who held that civil society, civil laws, and justice come into existence when people contract among themselves to transfer their power and rights to a sovereign power who compels people to live in peace and honor their agreements. Hobbes believed the transfer is "commanded" by natural law, which he held to be a set of rational principles for best ensuring self-preservation.

- **Niccolò Machiavelli** Author of *The Prince,* which sets forth the measures by which a prince may best gain and maintain power.

- **John Locke** Held that people have God-given natural rights and that the state is created for the protection of those rights by mutual agreement among its citizens, who entrust their rights to the state for safeguarding.

- **Catharine Trotter Cockburn** Major supporter of Locke against charges of heresy. Showed how Locke's *Essay Concerning Human Understanding* did not undermine the foundation of morality.

- **Charles-Louis de Secondat, baron de Montesquieu** French jurist who held that the judiciary should be a separate branch of government.

- **Jean-Jacques Rousseau** Another contractarian, who held that through a social compact people may agree to unite into a state and through the state to enact laws reflective of the general will. He believed that people neither give up their rights to the state nor entrust them to it, for they *are* the state.

- **Mary Wollstonecraft** Held that males and females should be educated according to the same standards.

Concepts

aristocracy

philosopher-king

timocracy

plutocracy

democracy

tyranny

monarchy

oligarchy

polity

egalitarian

ethical naturalism

natural law political theory

eternal law

divine law

human law

Leviathan

covenant

sovereign

social contract/contractarian theory

justice/injustice in Hobbes's theory

natural rights

tacit consent

division of powers

general will

forcing someone to be free

Bill of Rights

Marbury v. Madison

Roe v. Wade

Griswold v. Connecticut

Questions for Discussion and Review

1. According to Plato, the ideal state consists of three classes. What are they, what are their functions, and how is class membership determined?

2. Is the well-being of the state desirable in its own right, apart from what it contributes to the welfare of its citizens?

3. Evaluate Aristotle's idea that people who do not have the aptitude or time to participate in governance should not be citizens.

4. Explain the four types of law distinguished by Aquinas.

5. In the absence of civil authority, would anyone live up to an agreement that turns out not to be in his or her own best interest?

6. Would it be wise for people, for their own good, to transfer their collective strength to a sovereign power? Explain.

7. Why can't a covenant between the Leviathan and its subjects be made, and why is it impossible for Hobbes's Leviathan to act unjustly toward its subjects?

8. Which is better, in your view, dictatorship or anarchy? Why?

9. Why doesn't the Leviathan have the right to take your life, according to Hobbes?

10. Compare and contrast the purpose of the state and the relationship between it and its subjects for Hobbes, Locke, and Rousseau.

11. What is Locke's argument for saying that each person has inalienable natural rights?

12. Explain the concept of tacit consent.

13. "All people equally have a right to property, but they do not all have a right to equal property." Critically evaluate this claim.

14. Critically evaluate Locke's concept of private property.

15. What is the general will, and how do we know what it is?

16. Can you think of any justification for the principle that people have natural rights other than that proposed by Locke?

17. Do you think people have a natural right to privacy? Explain.

18. Can you think of a sounder justification for abortion rights than the "right to privacy"? Explain.

19. If people have a right to privacy, do children have that right? Do infants? Explain.

20. Would people be better off without any government at all? Explain.

21. For Wollstonecraft, education plays a very significant role in transforming society. Is she right? What evidence is there for your view?

22. Compare and contrast the views of Aquinas and Walzer on when a war is just. Can you think of any wars that Aquinas might consider just that Walzer might not? Explain.

Suggested Further Readings

Julia Annas, *An Introduction to Plato's "Republic"* (Oxford: Clarendon Press, 1981). A systematic introduction to Plato's most important work.

Aristotle, *Politics,* in *The Complete Works of Aristotle,* vol. 2, J. Barnes, ed. (Princeton: Princeton University Press, 1984).

Susan J. Armstrong and Richard G. Botzler, *Environmental Ethics: Divergence and Convergence* (New York: McGraw-Hill, 1993). An anthology of significant articles on environmental ethics, with suggested readings and thoughtful exercises.

E. Barker, *The Political Thought of Plato and Aristotle* (New York: Putnam, 1906). Old but still good.

Cicero, *De re publica,* and *De legibus,* both translated by C. W. Keyes (and both London: Loeb Classical Library, 1928). See Book III of each of these classic works.

E. Gilson, *The Christian Philosophy of St. Thomas Aquinas,* L. Shook, trans. (New York: Random House, 1956). See Part III, Ch. 1, sect. 4 for Aquinas's concept of law.

J. Locke, *The Second Treatise of Government,* Thomas P. Peardon, ed. (Indianapolis: Bobbs-Merrill, 1952). Features a short and critical introduction by the editor.

N. Machiavelli, *The Prince,* C. Detmold, trans. (New York: Airmont, 1965). Required reading for political science students as well as philosophy students.

R. G. Mulgan, *Aristotle's Political Theory* (Oxford: Clarendon Press, 1991). An examination of Aristotle's political theory as a practical, applicable science.

Ellen Frankel Paul, Fred D. Miller, Jr., and Jeffrey Paul, eds., *Property Rights* (Cambridge: Cambridge University Press, 1994). A collection of recent articles on ownership and property rights.

Plato, *Republic,* in *The Collected Dialogues of Plato,* E. Hamilton and H. Cairns, eds. (New York: Bollingen Foundation, 1961). Plato's classic.

J. J. Rousseau, *The Social Contract,* C. Frankel, trans. and ed. (New York: Hafner, 1966). Few political philosophers are easier to read and understand than is Rousseau.

Paul E. Sigmund, *St. Thomas Aquinas on Politics and Ethics* (New York: Norton, 1988). New translations of selections from the *Summa Contra Gentiles* and *Summa Theologica* that include Aquinas's views on government, law, war, property, sexual ethics, the proofs of God, the soul, the purpose of man, and the order of the universe.

Trotter, Catharine, *The Works of Mrs. Catharine Cockburn,* 2 vols., London: Routledge/Thoemmes Press, 1992. Her philosophical writings, plays, poetry, and correspondence.

Mary Ellen Waithe, ed., *A History of Women Philosophers,* vol. 3, *Modern Women Philosophers: 1600–1900* (Dordrecht: Kluwer Academic Press, 1991). Chapters about thirty-one women philosophers of the period.

Michael Walzer, *Just and Unjust Wars: A Moral Argument with Historical Illustrations* (New York: Basic Books, 1977). An influential discussion of the issues.

R. P. Wolff, *In Defense of Anarchism* (New York: Harper & Row, 1970). Also contains critiques of Rousseau and Locke.

Mary Wollstonecraft, "A Vindication of the Rights of Woman," in *The Feminist Papers,* Alice S. Rossi, ed. (New York: Columbia University Press, 1973). Not too hard to read and surprisingly contemporary.

F. J. E. Woodbridge, ed., *Hobbes Selections* (New York: Scribners, 1930). You may also wish to have a look at the complete *Leviathan.* There is a good edition by M. Oakeshott with an introduction by R. S. Peters (New York: Collier, 1962).

10 Contemporary Theory

The passion for freedom of the mind is strong and everlasting, which is fortunate, because so is the passion to squelch it.

—A. M. Rosenthal

The truth, apparent to everyone whose eyes are not blinded by dogmatism, is that men are perhaps weary of liberty. They have had a surfeit of it.

—Benito Mussolini

Classic Liberalism and Marxism

We turn now to the nineteenth century, the century ushered in by Romanticism in art, music, and literature; grandiose metaphysical speculations in philosophy; and (to mention something non-European for a change) the accession of Muhammad Ali (the pasha of Egypt, not the boxer). It was the century that saw spreading industrialization and nationalism, Darwin and Freud, the Suez Canal, civil war in America, the emergence of Italy and Germany as states, and the invention of photography and the automobile. The two major political philosophies were liberalism and Marxism. They still are, for the most part, despite the recent demise of Soviet communism.

Between the development of liberal utilitarianism early in the nineteenth century and Marxism at the end of the century came *utopian* theories: theories about perfect societies. Utopian communities sprang up in Europe and the United States. One thing that competing utopian philosophers like Claude Saint-Simone, Robert Owen, and Charles Fourier did agree on was the social and political equality of women. Anna Wheeler, William Thompson, Harriet Taylor, and John Stuart Mill are some of the libertarian-utilitarians who strongly advocated women's equality.

Harriet Taylor

Harriet Taylor (1807?–1858), like many women philosophers, has been known to the public primarily through her association with a male philosopher; in Taylor's case, the male philosopher was John Stuart Mill. Taylor and Mill shared a long personal and professional intimacy, and each shaped and influenced the ideas of the other. Harriet Taylor was a published author of poetry when she met Mill in 1831. Recently, a draft of an essay on toleration of nonconformity was discovered in Taylor's handwriting. It appears to have been written in 1832. During that year, Mrs. Taylor was a regular contributor of poetry, book reviews, and a literary piece to the radical, utilitarian, and feminist journal *The Monthly Repository.* Later, Mill too became a regular contributor, and eventually Taylor and Mill began writing together. Their writings were always published under Mill's name, partly because a man's name gave the work more legitimacy within a sexist culture, and also because Taylor's husband, John Taylor, was very unhappy with the idea of his wife gaining public notoriety. Nevertheless, from the evidence of their manuscripts and their personal correspondence, it is possible to piece together some idea of which works were primarily Taylor's and which were Mill's.

Taylor was interested both in sweeping transformations of society and in specific legal reforms. One of her greatest concerns was the tendency of English society to stifle individuality, originality, and radical political and religious views. English society, in Taylor's view, was intolerant of opinions that didn't conform to the mainstream. She considered the intolerance of nonconformity to be morally wrong and ultimately dangerous to human progress. Many intellectuals of the era could see that the true liberation of women would require changing the culture down to its roots—which is the literal meaning of the word *radical.* Taylor and Mill, along with Mary Wollstonecraft (discussed in Chapter 9), believed that all differences between men and women (except some difference in physical strength) were socially created. (And actually, they weren't entirely convinced about the physical strength difference being natural, either.) But many activists could also see that certain obvious problems, such as the need for the vote, might make better political targets because they were specific and concrete and had some chance of being achieved. This tack seemed the best to Taylor as well, and her writings focus on the need for women's suffrage and on the necessity for liberalizing marriage and divorce laws.

With regard to the latter subject, Taylor and Mill argued that it would be best for women to be able to support themselves, so that marriage would not be an absolute necessity for them. They argued that everyone would be better off if women had the genuine liberty to decide whether or not they might marry. They further argued that divorce should be permissible because marriage is more or less a lottery; even those who take pains in their selection of a mate are often soon disappointed. And because never-married individuals are of necessity making an uninformed decision, there ought to be a remedy for the mistakes that are likely to be made. If you remember back to Chapter 8, you should not be surprised that all this reasoning was backed up by the view that these policies would result in the greatest happiness for the greatest number.

Taylor also argued vigorously for women's suffrage, a campaign that was being waged in both the United States and England. However, in the following selection Taylor argues that "the opinion of society—majority opinion—is the root of all intolerance." This defense of minority viewpoints and individuality predated by twenty-seven years Mill's stirring statement (*On Liberty*) on the same subject.

Draft of Toleration of Nonconformity   From Harriet Taylor

The root of all intolerance, the spirit of conformity, remains; and not until that is destroyed, will envy, hatred and all uncharitableness, with their attendant hypocrisies, be destroyed too. Whether it would be religious conformity, political conformity, moral conformity or social conformity, the spirit is the same: all kinds agree in this one point, of hostility to individual character. Individual character, if it exists at all, can rarely declare itself openly while there is a standard of conformity raised by the indolent-minded many and guarded by opinion which, though composed individually of the weakest, yet takes up collectively a mass which is not to be resisted with impunity.

What is called the opinion of society is a phantom power, yet as is often the case with phantoms, of more force over the minds of the unthinking than all the flesh and blood arguments which can be brought to bear against it. It is a combination of the many weak, against the few strong; an association of the mentally listless to punish any manifestation of mental independence. The remedy is, to make all strong enough to stand alone; and whoever has once known the pleasure of self dependence, will be in no danger of relapsing into subserviency. Let people once suspect that their leader *is* a phantom, the next step will be, to cease to be led, and each mind guide itself by the light of as much

knowledge as it can acquire for itself by means of unbiased experience.

We have always been an aristocracy-ridden people, which may account for our being so peculiarly a propriety-ridden people. The aim of our life seems to be, not our own happiness, or the happiness of others unless it happens to come in as an accident of our great endeavour to attain some standard of right or duty erected by some or other of the sets into which society is divided like a net—to catch gudgeons.

Who are the people who talk most about doing their duty? Always those who could give no intelligible theory of duty? What are called people of principle, are often the most unprincipled people in the world, if by principle is meant, accordance of the individual's conduct with the individual's self-formed opinion. Grant this to be the definition of principle, then, eccentricity should be prima facie evidence for the existence of principle. So far from this being the case, 'it is odd' therefore it is wrong is the feeling of society; while they whom it distinguishes par excellence as people of principle, are almost invariably the slaves of some dicta or other. They have been taught to think, and accustomed to think, so and so right—others think so and so right—therefore it must be right. This is the logic of the world's good sort of people; and if their right should prove indisputably wrong, they can but plead those good intentions which make a most slippery pavement.

To all such we would say, think for yourself, and act for yourself, but whether you have strength to do either, attempt not to impede, much less to resent the genuine expression of others.

Were the spirit of toleration abroad, the name of toleration would be unknown. The same implies the existence of its opposites. Toleration can not even rank with those strangely named qualities a 'negative virtue'. In order to be conscious that we tolerate, there must remain some vestige of *intolerance:* not to be charitable is to be uncharitable. To tolerate is to abstain from unjust interference. Now, alas, its spirit is not even comprehended by many, the education for its opposite which most of us receive becomes if ever it be attained, a praiseworthy faculty, instead of an unconscious and almost intuitive state. 'Truth must not be spoken at all times' is the vulgar maxim. We would have the Truth, and if possible all the Truth, certainly nothing but the Truth said and acted universally. But we should never lose sight of the important fact that what is truth to one mind is often not truth to another. No human being ever did or ever will comprehend the whole mind of any other human being. It would perhaps not be possible to find two minds accustomed to think for themselves, whose thoughts on any identical subject should take in their expression the same form of words. Who shall say that the very same order of ideas is conveyed to another mind, by those words which to him perfectly represent his thought? It is probable that innumerable shades of variety, modify the conception of every expression of thought. To an honest mind what a lesson of tolerance is included in this knowledge.

There seems to be this great distinction between physical and moral science: that while the degree of perfection which the first has attained is marked by the progressive completeness and exactness of its rules, that of the latter is in the state most favourable to, and most showing healthfulness as it advances beyond all classification except on the widest, and most universal principles. The science of morals should rather be called an art: to do something towards its improvement is in the power of every one, for every one may at least show truly their own page in the volume of human history, and be willing to allow that no two pages of it are alike.

The spirit of Emulation in childhood and of competition in manhood are the sources of selfishness and misery. They are a part of the *conformity* plan, making each person's idea of goodness and happiness a thing of comparison with some received mode of being good and happy. But this is not the proper Creed of Society, for Society abhors individual character. It asks the sacrifice of body, heart and mind. This is the *summary* of its cardinal virtues: would that such virtues were as nearly extinct as the dignitaries who are their namesakes.

At this present time the subject of social morals is in a state of most lamentable neglect. It is a subject so deeply interesting to all, yet so beset by prejudice, that the mere approach to it is difficult, if not dangerous. Yet we firmly believe that many years will not pass before the clearest intellects of the time will expound, and the multitude have wisdom to receive reverently, the exposition of the great moral paradoxes with which Society is hemmed in on all sides. Meanwhile they do something who have courage to declare the evil they see.

Utilitarianism and Natural Rights

Jeremy Bentham, as discussed in Part 2, considered the notion of natural rights nonsense, and utilitarian philosophy in general does not easily accommodate a belief in natural rights. Why? Well, consider a possible natural right—for example, the right to keep what you've honestly earned. If taking from you what you have honestly earned and distributing it to people who are poorer than you are increases the sum total of happiness, utilitarianism apparently requires that we do this, despite your "natural right." Utilitarianism seems to require violating any so-called natural right if doing so increases the total happiness.

Utilitarians often attempt to accommodate our intuitions about natural rights by maintaining that in civilized society more happiness results when what are called natural rights are respected than when they are not. They say that natural rights should, in effect, be regarded as secondary rules of conduct that must be obeyed for the sake of the general happiness. In viewing natural rights as a system of moral rules productive of the general happiness, however, utilitarians do not clearly explain why such rules should not be infringed on or overridden when doing so better promotes the general happiness. It is difficult for utilitarians to provide such an explanation.

Mill

John Stuart Mill (1806–1873), like Locke and Rousseau, was much concerned with liberty. Mill, you'll recall from Part 2, was a utilitarian. He believed that happiness not only is good but also is *the* good, the ultimate end of all action and desire: "Actions are right in proportion as they tend to promote happiness, wrong as they tend to produce the reverse of happiness," he wrote. But remember that utilitarians are not egoists, and Mill believed that it is not one's *own* happiness that one should seek but instead the greatest amount of happiness altogether—that is, the general happiness.

Unlike Rousseau, Mill does not view a community, a society, a people, or a state as an organic entity separate and distinct from the sum of the people in it. When Mill says that one should seek the general happiness, he is not referring to the happiness of the community as some kind of organic whole. For Mill, the general happiness is just the sum total happiness of the individuals in the group.

Now Mill, following Bentham and Hume, and like Rousseau, rejected Locke's theory that people have God-given natural rights. But he maintained that the general happiness requires that all individuals enjoy personal liberty to the fullest extent consistent with the liberties of others. "The only part of the conduct of anyone, for which he is amenable to society, is that which concerns others. In the part which merely concerns himself, his independence is . . . absolute."

Liberalism (from the Latin word for "liberty") is precisely the philosophy articulated by Mill in his treatise *On Liberty*:

> The sole end for which mankind are warranted, individually or collectively, in interfering with the liberty of action of any of their number, is . . . to prevent harm to others. His own good, either physical or moral, is not a sufficient warrant.

Adam Smith

The most important classical liberal economic theorist was **Adam Smith** (1723–1790), a contemporary of David Hume. The basic principle of Smith's economic theory is that in a laissez-faire economy, each individual, in seeking his own gain, is led "by an invisible hand" to promote the common good, though doing so is not his intention. As an exponent of the benefits for everyone of **capitalism** (which is a system of private ownership of property and the means of production and distribution) and a **free market economy** (in which individuals may pursue their own economic interests without governmental restrictions on their freedom), Smith advocated positions that resemble those of some contemporary American conservatives. His *An Inquiry into the Nature and Causes of the Wealth of Nations* (1776) has become a classic in economics.

Mill regarded personal liberty, including freedom of thought and speech, as essential to the general happiness. It is essential, he argued, because truth and the development of the individual's character and abilities are essential to the general happiness, and only if there is personal liberty can truth be ascertained and each individual's capacities developed. It therefore follows that an individual should enjoy unrestrained personal liberty up to the point where his activities may harm others.

Of course, it is a difficult question as to when an action may be said to harm others. Liberalism places the burden of proof on the person who claims that harm to others will be done. That the burden must be so placed is Mill's position.

The best form of government, according to Mill, is that which, among all realistic and practical alternatives, produces the greatest benefit. The form of government best suited to do this, he maintained, is representative democracy. But Mill was especially sensitive to the threat to liberty posed in democracies by the tyranny of public opinion as well as by the suppression by the majority of minority points of view. For this reason he emphasized the importance of safeguards such as proportional representation, universal suffrage, and enforcement of education by the state.

Now promoting the general happiness would seem sometimes to justify (if not explicitly to require) restrictions on personal liberty. Zoning ordinances, antitrust laws, and motorcycle helmet laws, to take modern examples, are, arguably, restrictions of this sort. Mill recognized the dilemma that potentially confronts anyone who wishes both to promote the general happiness and to protect personal liberty. His general position is this: The government should not do anything that could be done more effectively by private individuals themselves; and even if something could be done more effectively by the government, if the government's doing it would deprive individuals of an opportunity for development or education, the government should not do it. In short, Mill was opposed to enlarging the power of the government unnecessarily.

Here, then, is a brief selection from *On Liberty* (1859).

SELECTION 10.2

On Liberty   From John Stuart Mill

CHAPTER 1. INTRODUCTORY

The object of this Essay is to assert one very simple principle, as entitled to govern absolutely the dealings of society with the individual in the way of compulsion and control, whether the means used be physical force in the form of legal penalties or the moral coercion of public opinion. That principle is, that the sole end for which mankind are warranted, individually or collectively, in interfering with the liberty of action of any of their number, is self-protection. That the only purpose for which power can be rightfully exercised over any member of a civilized community, against his will, is to prevent harm to others. His own good, either physical or moral, is not a sufficient warrant. He cannot rightfully be compelled to do or forbear because it will be better for him to do so, because it will make him happier, because, in the opinions of others, to do so would be wise, or even right. There are good reasons for remonstrating with him, or reasoning with him, or persuading him, or entreating him, but not for compelling him, or visiting him with any evil, in case he do otherwise. To justify that, the conduct from which it is desired to deter him must be calculated to produce evil to some one else. The only part of the conduct of any one, for which he is amenable to society, is that which concerns others. In the part which merely concerns himself, his independence is, of right, absolute. Over himself, over his own body and mind, the individual is sovereign.

It is, perhaps, hardly necessary to say that this doctrine is meant to apply only to human beings in the maturity of their faculties. We are not speaking of children, or of young persons below the age which the law may fix as that of manhood or womanhood. Those who are still

in a state to require being taken care of by others, must be protected against their own actions as well as against external injury. For the same reason, we may leave out of consideration those backward states of society in which the race itself may be considered as in its nonage. The early difficulties in the way of spontaneous progress are so great, that there is seldom any choice of means for overcoming them; and a ruler full of the spirit of improvement is warranted in the use of any expedients that will attain an end, perhaps otherwise unattainable. Despotism is a legitimate mode of government in dealing with barbarians, provided the end be their improvement, and the means justified by actually effecting that end. Liberty, as a principle, has no application to any state of things anterior to the time when mankind have become capable of being improved by free and equal discussion. Until then there is nothing for them but implicit obedience to an Akbar or a Charlemagne, if they are so fortunate as to find one. But as soon as mankind have attained the capacity of being guided to their own improvement by conviction or persuasion (a period long since reached in all nations with whom we need here concern ourselves), compulsion, either in the direct form or in that of pains and penalties for noncompliance, is no longer admissible as a means to their own good, and justifiable only for the security of others.

It is proper to state that I forgo any advantage which could be derived to my argument from the idea of abstract right, as a thing independent of utility. I regard utility as the ultimate appeal on all ethical questions; but it must be utility in the largest sense, grounded on the permanent interests of man as a progressive being. Those interests, I contend, authorize the subjection of individual spontaneity to external control, only in respect to those actions of each, which concern the interest of other people. If any one does an act hurtful to others, there is a prima facie case for punishing him, by law, or, where legal penalties are not safely applicable, by general disapprobation. There are also many positive acts for the benefit of others, which he may rightfully be compelled to perform; such as, to give evidence in a court of justice; to bear his fair share in the common defence, or in any other joint work necessary to the interest of the society of which he enjoys the protection; and to perform certain acts of individual beneficence, such as saving a fellow creature's life, or interposing to protect the defenceless against ill-usage, things which whenever it is obviously a man's duty to do, he may rightfully be made responsible to society for not doing. A person may cause evil to others not only by his actions but by his inaction, and in either case he is justly accountable to them for the injury. The latter case, it is true, requires a much more cautious exercise of compulsion than the former. To make any one answerable for doing evil to others, is the rule; to make him answerable for not preventing evil, is comparatively speaking, the exception. Yet there are many cases clear enough and grave enough to justify that exception. In all things which regard the external relations of the individual, he is *de jure* amenable to those whose interests are concerned, and if need be, to society as their protector. There are often good reasons for not holding him to the responsibility; but these reasons must arise from the special expediencies of the case: either because it is a kind of case in which he is on the whole likely to act better, when left to his own discretion, than when controlled in any way in which society have it in their power to control him; or because the attempt to exercise control would produce other evils, greater than those which it would prevent. When such reasons as these preclude the enforcement of responsibil-

ity, the conscience of the agent himself should step into the vacant judgment-seat, and protect those interests of others which have no external protection; judging himself all the more rigidly, because the case does not admit of his being made accountable to the judgment of his fellow-creatures.

But there is a sphere of action in which society, as distinguished from the individual, has, if any, only an indirect interest; comprehending all that portion of a person's life and conduct which affects only himself, or, if it also affects others, only with their free, voluntary, and un-deceived consent and participation. When I say only himself, I mean directly, and in the first instance: for whatever affects himself, may affect others *through* himself; and the objection which may be grounded on this contingency, will receive consideration in the sequel. This, then, is the appropriate region of human liberty. It comprises, first, the inward domain of consciousness, demanding liberty of conscience, in the most comprehensive sense; liberty of thought and feeling; absolute freedom of opinion and sentiment on all subjects, practical or speculative, scientific, moral, or theological. The liberty of expressing and publishing opinions may seem to fall under a different principle, since it belongs to that part of the conduct of an individual which concerns other people; but, being almost of as much importance as the liberty of thought itself, and resting in great part on the same reasons, is practically inseparable from it. Secondly, the principle requires liberty of tastes and pursuits; of framing the plan of our life to suit our own character; of doing as we like, subject to such consequences as may follow; without impediment from our fellow-creatures, so long as what we do does not harm them, even though they should think our conduct foolish, perverse, or wrong. Thirdly, from this liberty of each individual, follows the liberty, within the same limits, of combination among individuals; freedom to unite, for any purpose not involving harm to others: the persons combining being supposed to be of full age, and not forced or deceived.

No society in which these liberties are not, on the whole, respected, is free, whatever may be its form of government; and none is completely free in which they do not exist absolute and unqualified. The only freedom which deserves the name, is that of pursuing our own good in our own way, so long as we do not attempt to deprive others of theirs, or impede their efforts to obtain it. Each is the proper guardian of his own health, whether bodily, or mental and spiritual. Mankind are greater gainers by suffering each other to live as seems good to themselves, than by compelling each to live as seems good to the rest.

From Liberalism to Marxism via Utopianism

Utopians considered themselves to be implementers of Bentham's utilitarian principle: the greatest happiness for the greatest number (see Chapter 8). They envisioned societies in which all members were social equals, where education was reformed to promote the development of "benevolent" or "humanistic" feelings of mutual care and concern, and where property was redistributed to the benefit of all members of society. **Claude Saint-Simone** (1760–1825), an influential French philosopher and social reformer, advocated love for the poor and less powerful members of society, and the redistribution of property and social and political power. **Robert Owen** (1771–1858), an English utopian, supported the formation of voluntary mutual work cooperatives where all shared the production and consumption of necessities and other goods. In France, **Charles Fourier** (1772–1837) promoted the creation of voluntary associations of individuals living and working in harmonious groups where everyone aimed, through voluntary contributions of labor, to contribute to the happiness and well-being of all other members. Model utopian societies sprang up in Europe and the United States, their structures based on varieties and combinations of these utopian socialist philosophies. These utopian movements culminated, in the late nineteenth century, in the most significant utopian philosophy ever implemented: communist socialism.

Anna Wheeler and William Thompson's *Appeal* combines elements of utilitarian and utopian philosophies. For utopians like Saint-Simone, one of government's responsibilities was to help individuals "cultivate their minds," especially to shape the attitudes that people have about others. People should care about others and should take care of those with special needs or special problems. This attitude was called *benevolence*. Utopians like Fourier and Owen were big on the idea that people shouldn't be coerced into working. Societies should help people feel that they are making valuable contributions, doing something important for themselves, their families, and their communities by working. In an ideal society, work should be voluntary, but people would want to work because they would understand that their labor helps make their community a great place to be and ensures that their own needs would also be met.

Yet the largest, most important, most exploited, and only unpaid labor force (slavery was outlawed in Europe before it was illegal here) was women. Wheeler

PROFILE / Anna Doyle Wheeler (1785–1848) and William Thompson (1775–1833)

Anna Doyle Wheeler was an Irish feminist and self-educated philosopher. She became an avid utilitarian and an acquaintance of Jeremy Bentham (1748–1832), who introduced William Thompson to her. Wheeler became closely associated with the utopian and reformist philosophers Claude Saint-Simone, Robert Owen, and Charles Fourier. She was instrumental in promoting exchanges of views between Owenites, Fourierists, and Saint-Simonians. In addition to the *Appeal* (excerpted in Selection 10.3), which was published in 1825, Wheeler published frequent translations of French socialist philosophical writings in the Owenite journal *The Crisis*, numer-ous articles under various pseudonyms, and an 1830 article entitled "Rights of Women" in the *British Co-Operator*.

William Thompson was a political philosopher and economist. A year before writing the *Appeal*, Thompson wrote a work on utilitarianism and economics and, two years following it, wrote a utopian and utilitarian account of labor and capital. Now, although Thompson actually wrote the work we are excerpting here, in a nine-page introductory letter addressed to "Mrs. Wheeler" he says that many of the arguments contained in it are from her prior written work, and from speeches she had given:

I love not literary any more than any other species of piracy: I wish to give every thing to its right owner. Anxious that you should take up the cause of your proscribed sex, and state to the world in writing, in your own name, what you have so often and so well stated in conversation, and under feigned names in such of the periodical publications of the day as would tolerate such a theme. A few only therefore of the following pages are the exclusive produce of your mind and pen, and written with your own hand. The remainder are our joint property, I being your interpreter and the scribe of your sentiments.

and Thompson's *Appeal* responds to part of an article on "Government" in the 1814 *Encyclopedia Britannica Supplement* by James Mill (1773–1836). A close associate of Jeremy Bentham, James Mill was the father of John Stuart Mill. This is what James Mill had to say in the part of his article on government that offended Wheeler and Thompson:

> One thing is pretty clear, that all those individuals whose interests are indisputably included in those of other individuals may be struck off from political rights without inconvenience. In this light may be viewed all children up to a certain age, whose interests are involved in those of their parents. In this light also women may be regarded, the interest of almost all of whom is involved either in that of their fathers, or in that of their husbands.

Mill was referring to the French doctrine called *couverture:* the idea that women's interests are "covered" or taken care of by the men who by law are in charge of them (fathers, husbands, and lacking either, a male relative, even a son or a younger brother). This doctrine provided the basis for denial of legal rights to women. The effect of Mill's inserting this doctrine in his *Encyclopedia Britannica* article on government was to give moral authority to what was still then law and practice.

SELECTION 10.3

The Appeal of One Half of the Human Race, Women, Against the Pretensions of the Other Half, Men, to Restrain Them in Political, and Thence in Civil and Domestic, Slavery

From Anne Doyle Wheeler and William Thompson

Is it then true that, provided the interests of women are involved in those of men, they ought to be excluded from the exercise of political rights? What reason can men give, what reason can any individuals of the human race give, that their happiness should be promoted, which cannot be equally given by any other individuals, by women? We maintain then that it would no more follow that women should, than that men should, be on that account excluded from the exercise of political rights. Now supposing that the interests of men and women were so mysteriously involved in each other, that either party exercising political rights would necessarily promote the civil rights and consequently the happiness of the other equally with their own; as far as civil rights are concerned, this might be a good reason for indifference if the party excluded from political rights as to the possession of them; but it could be no reason at all as to the loss of the second benefit to be derived from the exercise of such political rights. The one party exercising political rights from which the other was excluded could not by any means impart to that other the exercise of the intellectual powers, and that enlargement of sympathy, that interest in the affairs of numbers mixed with our own, which distinguishes the benevolent from the selfish. This vice of character, want of comprehensive views, want of interest in any thing out of themselves or of their own little domestic circle,—the necessary result of the state of barbarous exclusion of domestic imprisonment, in which women have been kept,—can never be cured by the enjoyment by any others than themselves of those opportunities for unfolding their powers, which enlarged social, including political interests, can alone create.

From the casualties of gestation, women are necessarily, at least for a considerable portion of their time, more stationary and confined than men, and more inclined to mere local and personal sympathies. To counteract then this tendency of their physical situation to confined views and feelings, a *greater* necessity than in the case of men, rather than a less, exists, that opportunities should be afforded them for overcoming this tendency to selfishness, and for cultivating the enlarged and benevolent affections. The cultivation of these on a large scale never makes the enjoyment of them less dear on a scale more confined, but clears such enjoyment of its degrading weaknesses, and heightens the sensual, and confined sympathetic, pleasures, by association.

These opportunities for enlargement of character, can never be afforded but by possessing an influence in public affairs, in matters of public interest; for where influence is excluded, interest cannot be felt, influence, not of mere power or command nor of the corruptive class, but influence arising from the exercise of the understanding. How doubly vain therefore is the hollow pretext put forward by the "article," of excluding women from political rights on account of the involving of their interests with those of men! Will enlargement of mind and benevolence tend less to their happiness than to that of men? Will it tend less to the happiness of those with whom they associate? Can these qualities be unfolded in man or woman if opportunities are not given for their development? How but by discussing and influencing the affairs in which numbers, sometimes to the whole extent of all mankind, are concerned, and in which the individual is connected with and merged in the general interest, can such enlargment and such benevolence be produced?

Be consistent, men! Ye stronger half of the race, be at length rational! Three or four thousand years have worn threadbare your vile cloak of hypocrisy. Even women, you poor, weak, contented slaves, at whose impotence of penetration, the result of your vile exclusions you have been accustomed to laugh, begin to see through it and to shudder at the loathsomeness beneath. Be rational human beings, not mere male sexual creatures. Cast aside the ferocious brute of your nature: give up the pleasures of the brute, those of mere lust and command, for the pleasures of the rational being. So shall you enjoy the love of your *equals,* enlightened, benevolent, graceful, like yourselves, founded on an appreciation of your real merits: so shall you be happy. For the intercourse of the *bought* prostitute, or of the *commanded* household slave, you shall have full and equal participation in the compounded and associated pleasures of sense, intellect and benevolence. To the highest enjoyments of which your nature is susceptible, there is no shorter road than the simple road of equal justice.

If therefore a community of rational beings, desirous of promoting equally the happiness of all—and without this desire they are divested of

the noblest attribute of rationality—consisting, as the human race does, of an equal number of men and women, were driven to the absurd necessity of investing all political rights exclusively in the stronger or the weaker portion of the race, instead of investing the best and most intelligent with them, whether stronger or weaker, it would be evidently the interest of the whole to choose the weaker part, women, rather than the stronger part, men, for the exercise of such rights, both as electors and elected.

It is not forgotten that the condition of this second question, was the supposition that the interests of one half the race were absolutely involved in the other, thus taking for granted an equal degree of moral aptitude in the two divisions of the race, for the exercise of political rights. But if from the analysis we have gone through, there is a strong probability that the moral aptitude would be greater on the side of the weaker, it will show more strongly the odiousness of the injustice which, without inquiry, gives to the stronger as a matter of course those exclusive powers, which superior strength necessarily impels any thing short of comprehensive and benevolent wisdom to abuse.

Most certain it unfortunately is, that under the present system of labor and exertion by individual competition, the interests of all are put in such rude opposition to each other, that they render almost impossible the development to any great extent of these kindly feelings of joy in the welfare of others. Till other arrangements of "mutual co-operation" are formed, by means of which personal interests, either for the supply of immediate wants or of all desirable conveniences, instead of being opposed to feelings of benevolence as they now are shall move uniformly in the same direction with them, all, or most all the cheap and delightful pleasures of sympathy and benevolence must be lost to mankind: so difficult is it for the bulk of men to extend their views, in opposition to immediate interest, into the distant consequences of actions in the doubtful future.

Yes, it is only under the system of voluntary associated labor and exertion and equal distribution, that justice can have free scope, that the equal rights of all can prevail, and that women can become in intelligence, virtue and happiness, the equals of men. The general principle of mutual respect and benevolence would be immensely strengthened and diffused by the removal of exclusions.

Marx

According to **Karl Marx** (1818–1883), philosophers have tried only to understand the world, whereas the real point is to change it. Accordingly, Marx viewed his own work not merely as an attempt to understand and interpret the world but as an effort to transform it. In fact, he did not regard his work as philosophy. So it would be wrong for us to view his writings *solely* as efforts accurately to understand or describe the human social and political condition. Marx did not himself present his understanding of social reality as the absolute and final truth. This caution must be kept in mind throughout the following discussion.

Means of Production vs. Productive Relations   For Marx, the ideal society will have no economic classes, no wages, no money, no private property, and no exploitation. Each person will not only be provided a fully adequate material existence but will also be given the opportunity to develop freely and completely all physical and mental faculties. The alienation (estrangement) of the individual from the world around will be minimal.

Furthermore, according to Marx, this type of society will ultimately arise as the result of the historical process. Here's why.

Humans, Marx believed, are social animals with physical needs, needs that are satisfied when we develop the means to satisfy them. These means of producing the satisfaction of needs are called the **means** or **forces of production.** The utilization of any one set of means of production leads to fresh needs and therefore to further means of production. For example, the invention of iron tools (a new means of production) for the cultivation of needed crops leads to still a newer need—for iron—and therewith to the means for satisfying this newer need.

Thus, human history consists of successive stages of development of various means of production.

Furthermore, the utilization of any given means of production, whether it is a simple iron tool or a complex machine, necessarily involves certain social relationships, especially those involving property. These social relationships (or, as we might say, institutions or practices) are called the **productive relations.** Thus, the social relationships (the productive relations) depend on the stage of evolution of the forces of production.

The forces of production at a given stage, however, develop to the point where they come into conflict with the existing social relationships, which are then destroyed and replaced by new social relationships. For example, the need at the end

PROFILE / Karl Marx (1818–1883)

When one of the authors was in high school, his civics teacher, Mr. Benson, listed the most important figures in history as (alphabetically) Einstein, Freud, Jesus, and Marx. (Because Mr. Benson was also the football coach, he included a few others, such as Y. A. Tittle, on the list, but we won't worry about them.)

His Western bias notwithstanding, Mr. Benson was certainly right about the preeminence of these four, especially Jesus and Marx. Of course, the followers of Marx probably outnumber even the followers of Jesus (and by a good margin). Some people, moreover, regard themselves as both Marxists and Christians.

Marx was the son of a Jewish lawyer who converted to Lutheranism despite having descended from generations of rabbis; Marx was thus raised as a Protestant. He studied at Bonn, Berlin, and Jena, first in law and then in philosophy. His PhD at Jena (received when he was only twenty-three) was based on a completely ordinary dissertation on Democritus and Epicurus.

While in Berlin, Marx had come under the sway of Hegelianism and a group of radical Hegelians. But later, strongly influenced by the philosophy of Ludwig Feuerbach, he rejected idealism for materialism and his own theory of history as the outworking of economic factors.

Marx's radical views prevented him from occupying an academic post. In 1842, he became editor of a Cologne newspaper that, during his tenure, became much too radical for the authorities and was suppressed. The twenty-five-year-old Marx then went to Paris, where he mingled with many famous radicals and established another radical periodical. In Paris he also met his future collaborator, Friedrich Engels.

In about one year Marx was expelled from Paris, and from 1845 to 1848 he lived in Brussels. While there, he helped form a worker's union that, together with other similar groups, became known as the Communist League. It was for this organization that he and Engels wrote their famous and stir-ring *Communist Manifesto* (1848). Marx spent a brief period again in Paris and then in Cologne, participating in both the French and German revolutions of 1848. He was, however, expelled once again from both countries. In 1849, Karl Marx went to London and stayed there for the rest of his life.

In London, Marx required financial help from Engels, for, just as some are addicted to gambling, Marx was addicted to reading and writing, and these activities did not produce much of an income. Despite Engels's help and the small amount of money he received for articles he wrote for the New York *Tribune,* he lived in poverty, illness, and—when his children and wife died one by one—immense sadness.

During this period Marx wrote the *Critique of Political Economy* (1859) and, more important, the work destined to become the primary document of international communism, *Capital* (vol. 1, 1867; vols. 2 and 3, edited by Engels, 1885 and 1894). In 1864, he helped create the International Workingmen's Association (the so-called First International), which he later led. The famous clash between Marx and the anarchist Mikhail Bakunin, however, led to its dissolution within about ten years. Marx died in London when he was sixty-five, of pleurisy.

Marxism and Liberalism

"Classical" liberalism and "orthodox" Marxism both drew from the Enlightenment (the eighteenth century, remember) belief that the natural order produces perfection. Both looked forward to a future of ever-increasing human freedom and happiness and placed great faith in human goodness.

To highlight some of the similarities and differences between these philosophies, we'll list ten doctrines that many orthodox Marxists accept, together with comments on how a group of classical liberals might respond to them.

1. *Ideally, society should provide for human beings as much happiness, liberty, opportunity for self-development, and dignity as possible.*

   Liberals would agree to this claim, and who wouldn't? Utilitarian liberals, however, would emphasize the impor-

tance of happiness over the other three values, or would regard the others as a part of happiness.

2. *The only society that can provide these ends is a socialized society—that is, one in which both ownership and production are socialized.*

   Many nineteenth- (and twentieth-) century liberals would not have denied that their ultimate ethical objectives could be achieved within a socialist society, but most would have denied that socialism *alone* could accommodate these objectives. Most also thought that these objectives are more likely to be achieved within a constitutionally based representative democracy with a market economy.

3. *In nonsocialist societies the function of the state is to serve*

and protect the interests of the powerful.

Liberals maintained that in nonsocialist societies it is possible for the state to serve and protect the interests and rights of all its subjects, both strong and weak, even though few states, if any, were thought effectively to have done so.

4. *A group's interests can be protected only through exercise of its power.*

   A common liberal response is that a group's interests can be and are best protected through *law*. Marxists would say in rejoinder that, ever since Locke, the "rule of law" has been slanted toward protecting property and the propertied class.

5. *Human essence is defined historically, and economic factors largely determine history.*

   Liberals also emphasized

of the Middle Ages to supply the new markets in the Far East and the colonies in the New World required new methods of manufacture and commerce, which brought with their development societal changes incompatible with the feudal social structure of the Middle Ages.

The new social relationships then endure until new needs arise and a new stage is reached in the evolution of the forces of production.

This *dialectical process* repeats itself over and over again and is the history of people, economics, and society. To put this another way, *history is the result of productive activity in interplay with social relationships.* According to Marx, this interplay accounts not only for all socio-economic-political situations but also for morality, law, and religion and, to a greater or lesser extent, even philosophy and art.

the importance of economics to social history and evolution but stressed that certain fundamental human characteristics (e.g., having rights, desiring pleasure) are unalterable by history.

6. *The value of a commodity is determined by the amount of labor required for its production.*

    Liberals regarded this thesis as an oversimplification and maintained that many factors affect the value of a commodity.

7. *Capitalist societies necessarily are exploitative of a laboring class.*

    Private ownership, many liberals believed (and still do), is not inherently or necessarily exploitative, though individual capitalists may exploit their workers. Exploitation, they say, may be eliminated through appropriately formulated laws, and a society in which a great

unevenness in the distribution of wealth exists may nevertheless permit equal freedom and opportunity for all.

8. *A capitalist state cannot be reformed for two reasons: (a) It is inherently exploitative. (b) True reforms are not in the interest of the ruling class, which therefore will not permit them. Because such a state cannot be reformed, it must be replaced.*

    Liberals thought (and still think) that through reform many states, including most capitalist states, can gradually be improved. They did not deny the appropriateness of revolutionary overthrow of dictatorships. Contemporary Marxists insist that liberal reforms in the United States are made possible through exploitation of Third World nations.

9. *The redistribution of goods through welfare, taxation, and similar means is mere tokenism serving only to pacify the exploited classes in order to protect the exploiting class from uprising and revolt.*

    Liberals thought (and still think) that measures like these, if they benefit the less well-off, are required by principles of fairness, justice, or utilitarian considerations.

10. *The philosophy of liberalism, with all its talk of fairness and justice, is merely an attempt to rationalize and legitimize capitalist oppression.*

    Liberals regard this as an *argumentum ad hominem* (an attack on them rather than a refutation of their position). Liberal claims must be evaluated on their own merits, they say.

Class Struggle   As already stated, according to Marx the critical social relationships involve property. With the advent of private property, society became divided into basically two classes: those with property and those without.

Hostility between the two classes was, and is, inevitable, Marx said. Those with property, of course, are the dominant class, and government and morality are always the instruments of the dominant class. When the forces of production create conflict with the existing social relationships, class struggle becomes acute; revolution results, and a new dominant class seizes control of the organs of state and imposes its ethic. This dialectical process repeats itself until private property and the division of society into opposed classes disappears.

Capitalism and Its Consequences   In modern capitalist societies, what has happened, according to Marx, is that the means of production are primarily concentrated in large factories and workshops in which a group of individual workers cooperatively produces a product. They collectively "mix their labor with the product," as Locke would say. But the product they mix their labor with is not owned by them. Rather, it is appropriated by the owners of the factories, who thus in effect also own the workers. Out of this circumstance comes the fundamental conflict of capitalist society: *production is socialized, but ownership is not.*

Furthermore, Marx argued, capitalists obviously must sell what their workers produce for more than they pay the workers to make it. The laborers thus produce goods that are worth more than their wages. This exploitation of the workers is inevitable as long as the conflict between socialized means of production and nonsocialized ownership continues. It is a necessary part of the capitalist system and is not a result of wickedness or inhumanity on the part of the capitalist.

There are two further unavoidable consequences of continuing capitalism, in Marx's opinion. First, the longer the capitalist system continues, the smaller and wealthier the possessing class becomes. This is simply the result of the fact that the surplus value of products—that's the value of a product less its "true" cost, which is the cost of the labor put into it—continues to accrue to the capitalists. Further, as smaller capitalists cannot compete, and as a result fail in their enterprise and sink into the ranks of the workers, society's wealth becomes increasingly concentrated: fewer and fewer people control more and more of it.

Alienation   The second consequence of continued capitalism, according to Marx, is the increasing alienation of the workers. The more wealth the workers produce, the poorer they become, relatively speaking, for it is not they who retain this wealth. So the result of increased productivity for the workers is, paradoxically (but inevitably), their *devaluation* in their own eyes and in fact. They have become mere commodities.

In addition, because workers produce through their labor what belongs to others, neither the workers' labor nor the products they make are their own. Both labor and products are as alien things that dominate them. Thus, workers feel at home with themselves only during their leisure time and in eating, drinking, and having sex. Workers' presence at work is not voluntary but imposed and, whenever possible, avoided. Because they have put their lives into what belongs to others, workers are abject, debased, physically exhausted, and overcome with malaise. And, because the relation of people to themselves is first realized and expressed in the relationship between each person and another, workers are alienated from their fellows.

Capitalism Self-Liquidating   The situation Marx describes is, in his view, self-liquidating. The capitalist system of property ownership is incompatible with the socialized conditions of production and ultimately destined to failure. Inevitable overproduction will result in economic crises, a falling rate of profit, and increased

Good Marks for Marx on History

History can be understood in many ways. It can be viewed as the working out of God's divine plan. It can be interpreted as the result of human actions and decisions, especially those of rulers, inventors, revolutionaries, explorers, lawmakers, soldiers, and saints. It can be regarded as the evolution of ideas. But for Marx, as explained in the text, history is to be understood as an interplay of productive forces and social relations—as an interplay, in short, of economic factors. Today the influence of economics on history is widely assumed to be enormous.

exploitation of the working class, which will increasingly become conscious of itself and its own intolerable condition, the inadequacy of capitalism, and the inevitability of history. The revolution of the proletariat (working class), leading to a dictatorship of the proletariat, will follow. In this instance, however, the overturning of the existing social order will eventually result in the classless society just described, for property, as well as the means of production, will have become socialized. The disappearance of classes will mark the end of class struggle and also, therefore, the end of political power, because the sole function of political power is the suppression of one class at the expense of another.

Selection 10.4 is from one of the most famous political documents of all time, the *Communist Manifesto*.

SELECTION 10.4

*Communist Manifesto**

From Karl Marx and Friedrich Engels

I. BOURGEOIS AND PROLETARIANS

The history of all hitherto existing society is the history of class struggles.

Freeman and slave, patrician and plebian, lord and serf, guild-master and journeyman, in a word, oppressor and oppressed, stood in constant opposition to one another, carried on an uninterrupted, now hidden, now open fight, a fight that each time ended either in a revolutionary reconstitution of society at large or in the common ruin of the contending classes.

In the earlier epochs of history we find almost everywhere a complicated arrangement of society into various orders, a manifold gradation of social rank. In ancient Rome we have patricians, knights, plebians, slaves; in the Middle Ages, feudal lords, vassals, guild-masters, journeymen, apprentices, serfs; in almost all of these classes, again, subordinate gradations.

The modern bourgeois society that has sprouted from the ruins of feudal society has not done away with class antagonisms. It has but

---

*The authors' footnotes have been omitted.

Anarchism

> Every man should be his own government, his own law, his own church, a system within himself.
>
> —Josiah Warren

> Our first work must be the annihilation of everything as it now exists.
>
> —Mikhail Bakunin

Anarchists deny that the state is necessary for peace, justice, equality, the optimum development of human capacities, or, indeed, for any other worthwhile thing. In the nineteenth century, anarchism was the main philosophical alternative to liberalism and Marxism.

Pierre Joseph Proudhon (1809–1865), the so-called father of anarchism, was among the first in modern times to call himself an anarchist. Proudhon believed that all authoritarian political institutions hinder human development and should be replaced by social organizations founded on the free and voluntary agreement of individuals, organizations in which no person has power over another. The existence of private property, he argued, creates social inequalities and injustice and gives rise to government; both it and government should be eliminated, though not through violent means. Communists were much influenced by Proudhon's attack on the idea of private property.

The famous Russian anarchist Communists **Mikhail Bakunin** (1814–1876) and **Prince Piotr Kropotkin** (1842–1921) both emphasized the intrinsic goodness of the individual and viewed law and government as the instruments of the privileged classes and the true source of human corruption (both Bakunin and Kropotkin were aristocrats, incidentally).

Kropotkin, much influenced by Charles Darwin, held that humans have a biologically grounded propensity to cooperate that will hold society together even in the absence of government. Bakunin—who, unlike Proudhon and Kropotkin, advocated the violent overthrow of all government—was active in the Communist First International (see the box on Marxism and communism). A clash between Marx and Bakunin, and more generally between Marxist Communists and anarchist Communists concerning the necessity of a transitional dictatorship of the proletariat, led to the demise of that organization.

The slogan "From each according to his means, to each according to his needs" came from the anarchist Communists.

The Inhuman Conditions

According to Marx, humans are different from other animals because only humans can produce the means of satisfying their needs; that is, they can creatively alter the environment for their own purposes. Therefore, to be fully human one must have the freedom to "objectify" oneself through creative interaction with the environment, that is, through creative labor. It follows for Marx that, because under capitalist conditions the product of one's labor is appropriated by another, a laborer does not have this freedom and cannot attain full humanness. Alienation, as discussed in the text, is what results from this unnaturalness in human relationships.

Marxism and Communism

By the end of the nineteenth century most European socialist parties were committed to Marxism, but a split developed between the *revolutionists*, those who believed (as for the most part had Marx) that a violent revolution was necessary to set in place the collective ownership of the means of production and distribution of goods, and the *revisionists* or *evolutionary socialists*, those who thought that these ends could be achieved through peaceful (and piecemeal) reform.

Although evolutionary socialism became strong in Great Britain and survives in the socialist parties of many nations to the present day, the revolutionists gained ascendency in the Second International, the successor to Marx's International Workingmen's Association or the First International (though in deed, as opposed to word, the "revolutionists" were not particularly revolutionary). Under the leadership of Lenin, the revolutionist Bolsheviks came to control the Russian Social Democratic Labor party and seized control of Russia itself in the Revolution of 1917, becoming in 1918 the Communist party of the USSR.

Though the Russian Communists withdrew from the Second International and founded the Third International or Comintern in 1919 in order to gain leadership of the world socialist movement, most European Socialist parties disassociated themselves from the Communists. The term **Communism,** with a capital "C," today denotes the Marxist-Leninist ideology of the parties founded under the banner of the Comintern and is to be distinguished from small-C **communism,** which denotes any form of society in which property or other important goods are held in common by the community.

---

established new classes, new conditions of oppression, new forms of struggle in place of the old ones.

Our epoch, the epoch of the bourgeoisie, possesses, however, this distinctive feature: it has simplified the class antagonisms. Society as a whole is splitting up more and more into two great hostile camps, into two great classes directly facing each other: Bourgeoisie and Proletariat.

From the serfs of the Middle Ages sprang the chartered burghers of the earliest towns. From these burgesses the first elements of the bourgeoisie were developed.

The discovery of America, the rounding of the Cape, opened up fresh ground for the rising bourgeoisie. The East Indian and Chinese markets, the colonization of America, trade with the colonies, the increase in the means of exchange and in commodities generally, gave to commerce, to navigation, to industry, an impulse never before known, and thereby, to the revolutionary element in the tottering feudal society, a rapid development.

The feudal system of industry, under which industrial production was monopolized by closed guilds, now no longer sufficed for the growing wants of the new markets. The manufacturing system took its place. The guildmasters were pushed on one side by the manufacturing middle class; division of labor between the different corporate guilds vanished in the face of division of labor in each single workshop.

Meantime the markets kept ever growing, the demand ever rising. Even manufacture no longer sufficed. Thereupon, steam and machinery revolutionized industrial production. The place of manufacture was taken by the giant,

Modern Industry, the place of the industrial middle class by industrial millionaires—the leaders of whole industrial armies, the modern bourgeois.

Modern industry has established the world market, for which the discovery of America paved the way. This market has given an immense development to commerce, to navigation, to communication by land. This development has, in its turn, reacted on the extension of industry; and in proportion as industry, commerce, navigation, railways extended, in the same proportion the bourgeoisie developed, increased its capital, and pushed into the background every class handed down from the Middle Ages.

We see, therefore, how the modern bourgeoisie is itself the product of a long course of development, of a series of revolutions in the modes of production and of exchange.

Each step in the development of the bourgeoisie was accompanied by a corresponding political advance of that class. An oppressed class under the sway of the feudal nobility, an armed and self-governing association in the medieval commune, here independent urban republic (as in Italy and Germany), there taxable "third estate" of the monarchy (as in France), afterward, in the period of manufacture proper, serving either the semi-feudal or the absolute monarchy as a counterpoise against the nobility, and, in fact, cornerstone of the great monarchies in general, the bourgeoisie has at last, since the establishment of Modern Industry and of the world market, conquered for itself, in the modern representative State, exclusive political sway. The executive of the modern State is but a committee for managing the common affairs of the whole bourgeoisie.

The bourgeoisie, historically, has played a most revolutionary part.

The bourgeoisie, wherever it has got the upper hand, has put an end to all feudal, patriarchal, idyllic relations. It has pitilessly torn asunder the motley feudal ties that bound man to his "natural superiors," and has left remaining no other nexus between man and man than naked self-interest, than callous "cash payment."...

The bourgeoisie cannot exist without constantly revolutionizing the instruments of production, and thereby the relations of production, and with them the whole relations of society....

The need of a constantly expanding market for its products chases the bourgeoisie over the whole surface of the globe. It must nestle everywhere, settle everywhere, establish connections everywhere....

In place of the old wants, satisfied by the production of the country, we find new wants, requiring for their satisfaction the products of distant lands and climes. In place of the old local and national seclusion and self-sufficiency, we have intercourse in every direction, universal interdependence of nations....

The bourgeoisie, by the rapid improvement of all instruments of production, by the immensely facilitated means of communication, draws all, even the most barbarian, nations into civilization. The cheap prices of its commodities are the heavy artillery with which it batters down all Chinese walls, with which it forces the barbarians' intensely obstinate hatred of foreigners to capitulate. It compels all nations, on pain of extinction, to adopt the bourgeois mode of production; it compels them to introduce what it calls civilization into their midst, i.e., to become bourgeois themselves. In a word, it creates a world after its own image.

The bourgeoisie has subjected the country to the rule of the towns. It has created enormous cities, has greatly increased the urban population as compared with the rural, and has thus rescued a considerable part of the population from the idiocy of rural life. Just as it has made the country dependent on the towns, so it has made barbarian and semi-barbarian countries dependent on the civilized ones, nations of peasants on nations of bourgeois, the East on the West.

The bourgeoisie keeps doing away more and more with the scattered state of the population, of the means of production, and of property. It has agglomerated population, centralized means of production, and has concentrated property in a few hands. The necessary consequence of this was political centralization. . . .

The bourgeoisie during its rule of scarce one hundred years has created more massive and more colossal productive forces than have all preceding generations together. Subjection of nature's forces to man, machinery, application of chemistry to industry and agriculture, steam navigation, railways, electric telegraphs, clearing of whole continents for cultivation, canalization of rivers, whole populations conjured out of the ground—what earlier century had even a presentiment that such productive forces slumbered in the lap of social labor?

We see then: the means of production and of exchange, on the foundation of which the bourgeoisie built itself up, were generated in feudal society. At a certain stage in the development of these means of production and of exchange, the conditions under which feudal society produced and exchanged, the feudal organization of agriculture and manufacturing industry, in a word, the feudal relations of property became no longer compatible with the already developed productive forces; they became so many fetters. They had to be burst asunder; they were burst asunder.

Into their place stepped free competition, accompanied by a social and political constitution adapted to it and by the economic and political sway of the bourgeois class.

A similar movement is going on before our own eyes. Modern bourgeois society with its relations of production, of exchange and of property, a society that has conjured up such gigantic means of production and of exchange, is like the sorcerer who is no longer able to control the powers of the nether world whom he has called up by his spells. For many a decade past the history of industry and commerce is but the history of the revolt of modern productive forces against modern conditions of production, against the property relations that are the conditions for the existence of the bourgeoisie and of its rule. It is enough to mention the commercial crises that by their periodical return put on trial, each time more threateningly, the existence of the entire bourgeois society. In these crises a great part not only of the existing products, but also of the previously created productive forces, are periodically destroyed. In these crises there breaks out an epidemic that in all earlier epochs would have seemed an absurdity—the epidemic of over-production. Society suddenly finds itself put back into a state of momentary barbarism; it appears as if a famine, a universal war of devastation had cut off the supply of every means of subsistence; industry and commerce seem to be destroyed; and why? Because there is too much civilization, too much means of subsistence, too much industry, too much commerce. The productive forces at the disposal of society no longer tend to further the development of the conditions of bourgeois property; on the contrary, they have become too powerful for these conditions, by which they are fettered, and as soon as they overcome these fetters, they bring disorder into the whole of bourgeois society, endanger the existence of bourgeois property. The conditions of bourgeois society are too narrow to comprise the wealth created by them. And how does the bourgeoisie get over these crises? On the one hand by enforced destruction of a mass of productive forces; on the other, by the conquest of new markets and by the more thorough exploitation of the old ones. That is to say, by paving the way for more extensive and more destructive crises and by diminishing the means whereby crises are prevented.

The weapons with which the bourgeoisie felled feudalism to the ground are now turned against the bourgeoisie itself.

But not only has the bourgeoisie forged the weapons that bring death to itself; it has also called into existence the men who are to wield those weapons—the modern working class, the proletarians.

A Contemporary Marxist: Marcuse

The thought of Karl Marx has been interpreted, expanded, and amended by his many followers, conspicuously so, of course, by the Communist party. Today Marxism, like Christianity (as Sidney Hook has said), is a *family* of doctrines that is continually being renewed and revived. It is more appropriate to treat the details of the further evolution of Marxism in a text on political history than in this summary overview of political philosophy. Still, because Marxism has been very important in contemporary political philosophy, we shall describe briefly the views of a contemporary Marxist. Later we shall also discuss the philosophy of a contemporary liberal theorist.

In the late 1960s, the most famous philosopher in the United States was **Herbert Marcuse** (1898–1979). This was the era of tumultuous social and political unrest, the era of the New Left, Vietnam protest, "people power," militant black and feminist disaffection, hippies, acid, four-letter words, and Woodstock. Marcuse was in.

Marcuse's reputation on the street arose from his book *One-Dimensional Man* (1964), a Marxist-oriented appraisal of contemporary industrial society. For the New Left the book was a clear statement of deficiencies in American society.

As we have seen, it is a Marxist doctrine (or, at any rate, a doctrine of orthodox Marxists) that a disenfranchised working class is the inevitable instrument of social change. But according to Marcuse, the working class has been *integrated* into advanced capitalist society. Indeed, it has been integrated so well that it "can actually be characterized as a pillar of the establishment," he said. This integration has been effected, he believed, through the overwhelming efficiency of technology in improving the standard of living. Because today's workers share so largely in the comforts of consumer society, they are far less critical of the status quo than if they had been indoctrinated through propaganda or even brainwashed.

In fact, Marcuse said, today's workers don't merely share these comforts: they actually *"recognize themselves* in their commodities." "They find their soul in their automobile, hi-fi set, split-level home, kitchen equipment." Their needs have been determined by what are, in effect, new forms of social control, such as advertising, consumerism, the mass media, and the entertainment industry, all of which produce and enforce conformity in what people desire, think, and do.

Marcuse in Southern California

What may sometimes be the penalty for advocating an unpopular political philosophy is illustrated by the treatment Herbert Marcuse received during his stay in Southern California in the late 1960s.

Marcuse left Germany after Hitler's rise to power and became a U.S. citizen in 1940. He obtained work with the Office of Strategic Services and the State Department and thereafter held positions at Harvard, Columbia, and Brandeis. Later, in 1965, he accepted a postretirement appointment at the University of California, San Diego, where he was a quiet but popular professor. Although he had acquired by then a worldwide reputation among leftists and radicals for his social criticism, in San Diego he was not widely known beyond the campus.

In 1968, however, it was reported in the national media that Marcuse had invited "Red Rudi" Dutschke, a notorious West German student radical, to visit him in San Diego. After this, the local populace quickly informed itself about Marcuse. The outcry against any possible Dutschke visit and against the perceived radicalism of Marcuse in that conservative naval community was vigorous and strident. In thundering editorials the *San Diego Union* denounced Marcuse and called for his ouster. Thirty-two American Legion posts in San Diego County demanded termination of his contract and offered the regents of the University of California the money to buy it out. Marcuse began receiving death threats and hate mail, and his student followers armed themselves with guns to protect him.

When his appointment neared its end in 1969, the question of reappointment arose and attracted nationwide attention. With the strong support of the faculty but in the face of strenuous opposition from the *Union*, the Legion, and other powerful groups, university chancellor John McGill decided to offer Marcuse a one-year contract of reappointment. When the regents of the University of California met to discuss McGill's decision, they had to do so under the protection of the San Francisco Police Department's Tactical Force. Though a substantial number strongly dissented, the majority supported McGill. Marcuse was reappointed.

By the expiration of the reappointment contract Marcuse had passed the age of mandatory retirement. Nevertheless, he was permitted to keep his office and to teach informally.

Thus, according to Marcuse, in the West with its advanced capitalist societies the workers have lost their individual autonomy, their capacity to choose and act for themselves, to refuse and to dissent and to create. Yes, needs are satisfied, but the price the workers pay for satisfaction of need is loss of ability to think for themselves. Further, the perceived needs that are satisfied, in Marcuse's opinion, are *false* needs, needs stimulated artificially by producers to sell new products, needs whose satisfaction promotes insane wastefulness and does not lead to true fulfillment of the individual or release from domination.

Marcuse emphasized that the integration of the working class into the advanced capitalist society by the satisfaction of false needs created by advertising, television, movies, music, and other forms of consumerism does not mean that society has become classless. Despite the fact that their "needs" are satisfied, members of the working class are still in effect slaves, because they remain mere instruments of production that capitalists use for their own purposes. Further, he wrote,

> if the worker and his boss enjoy the same television program and visit the same resorts, if the typist is as attractively made up as the daughter of her employer . . . if they all read the same newspaper, then this assimilation indicates not the disappearance of classes, but the extent to which the needs and satisfactions that serve the preservation of the Establishment are shared by the underlying population.

Thus the working class in advanced capitalist societies, according to Marcuse, has been transformed from a force for radical change into a force for conservatism and the status quo.

The neutralizing of possible sources of radical social change through the integration of the working class into a one-dimensional society is visible everywhere to Marcuse. In the political sphere the one-dimensionalization of society is apparent in the unification of labor and capital against communism in a "welfare and warfare state," in which the cold war and arms race unite all against the Communist threat while simultaneously stimulating the economy through the production of weapons.

Likewise, he said, a one-dimensional quality pervades contemporary art, language, philosophy, science, and all of contemporary culture. Thus, for example, art has lost its power to criticize, challenge, and transcend society and has been integrated as mere entertainment mass-produced in paperbacks, records, and television shows. As such, art now serves to promote conformity in thought, aspiration, and deed. The same is true of philosophy and science, he believed. The elite classes can tolerate free speech simply because such conformity of thought in art, philosophy, science, and politics is present.

Thus, as Marcuse saw it, advanced capitalist society has managed to assimilate and integrate into itself the forces that oppose it and to "defeat or refute all protest in the name of the historical prospects of freedom from toil and domination." Still, at the very end of *One-Dimensional Man* Marcuse acknowledged that there is a slim chance of revolutionary change at the hands of a substratum of the outcasts of society, such as persecuted ethnic minorities and the unemployed and unemployable.

In his later thought, moreover, Marcuse perceived a weakening of the integration of the working classes into society and a growing awareness on the part of workers, students, and the middle class that consumer prosperity has been purchased at too high a price, and that a society without war, exploitation, repression, poverty, or waste is possible. The revolution that will produce this society, Marcuse said—and only through revolution can it be created, he maintained—will be born not of privation but of "disgust at the waste and excess of the so-called consumer society."

We shall see.

Selection 10.5 is from *One-Dimensional Man*.

One-Dimensional Man

From Herbert Marcuse

Does not the threat of an atomic catastrophe which could wipe out the human race also serve to protect the very forces which perpetuate this danger? The efforts to prevent such a catastrophe overshadow the search for its potential causes in contemporary industrial society. These causes remain unidentified, unexposed, unattacked by the public because they recede before the all too obvious threat from without—to the West from the East, to the East from the West. Equally obvious is the need for being prepared, for living on the brink, for facing the challenge. We submit to the peaceful production of the means of destruction, to the perfection of waste, to being educated for a defense which deforms the defenders and that which they defend.

If we attempt to relate the causes of the danger to the way in which society is organized and organizes its members, we are immediately confronted with the fact that advanced industrial society becomes richer, bigger, and better as it perpetuates the danger. The defense structure makes life easier for a greater number of people and extends man's mastery of nature. Under these circumstances, our mass media have little difficulty in selling particular interests as those of all sensible men. The political needs of society become individual needs and aspirations, their satisfaction promotes business and the commonwealth, and the whole appears to be the very embodiment of Reason.

And yet this society is irrational as a whole. Its productivity is destructive of the free development of human needs and faculties, its peace maintained by the constant threat of war, its growth dependent on the repression of the real possibilities for pacifying the struggle for existence—individual, national, and international. This repression, so different from that which characterized the preceding, less developed stages of our society, operates today not from a position of natural and technical immaturity but rather from a position of strength. The capabilities (intellectual and material) of contemporary society are immeasurably greater than ever before—which means that the scope of society's domination over the individual is immeasurably greater than ever before. Our society distinguishes itself by conquering the centrifugal social forces with Technology rather than Terror, on the dual basis of an overwhelming efficiency and an increasing standard of living. . . .

The fact that the vast majority of the population accepts, and is made to accept, this society does not render it less irrational and less reprehensible. The distinction between true and false consciousness, real and immediate interest still is meaningful. But this distinction itself must be validated. Men must come to see it and to find their way from false to true consciousness, from their immediate to their real interest. They can do so only if they live in need of changing their way of life, of denying the positive, of refusing. It is precisely this need which the established society manages to repress to the degree to which it is capable of "delivering the goods" on an increasingly large scale, and using the scientific conquest of nature for the scientific conquest of man.

Fascism

The term *fascist* is sometimes applied today to any totalitarian state that does not pay lip service to Marxism, but it is historically more correct to regard **fascism** as the political philosophy of the Italian government of **Benito Mussolini** (1883–1945). Mussolini was premier of Italy from 1922 to the Allied invasion of Italy in World War II. So regarded, fascism, unlike Marxism, is not a systematic political philosophy, but certain fundamental tenets of fascist thought do distinguish it from other sets of political beliefs.

The first tenet of fascism is that the rights of the state, as distinct from the rights of the individual, are supreme. Liberalism and Marxism both in effect regard the ultimate good as that which benefits individual people, but in fascist thought the ultimate good is that which benefits the state. The fascist state is considered an organic whole, with its own purpose and destiny, to which the interests of the individual are always subservient. Because political activity must redound to the benefit of the state rather than to the individual, the primary virtues for the citizen are service and sacrifice. True liberty, in fascism, consists not in doing what you please, but in accepting the authority of the state.

A corollary of this premise is that the state is morally unlimited by anything exterior to itself in its relationship to its citizens. The state does not exist primarily to protect the rights of its citizens, as is the case in liberal theory; on the contrary, individual citizens exist for the sake of the state. Therefore the state cannot wrong the individual by its actions. (The word *fascist* derives from the Latin *fasces,* a bundle of rods containing an ax with its blade projecting. These were carried by the attendants of the Roman magistrates and symbolized the power of the state to flog or behead any who challenged its decrees.)

A second tenet of fascism is that the destiny and ideals of the state are embodied in its leader, whose authority is, therefore, absolute, but who, in the exercise of his authority, protects the citizenry from mob rule and anarchy. (Mussolini's seizure of power in 1922 was widely condoned by wealthy landowners, industrialists, the military, the Catholic Church, and many workers as well, because he appeared able to protect the social order against anarchy and communism.) The leader governs with the assistance of an elite that embodies the genius of the people and that alone has the intelligence and knowledge to understand the problems that affect the entire nation.

This elitism of fascism contrasts sharply with the egalitarianism of democracy and the rule of the proletariat under communism. (Racism and anti-Semitism, central tenets of Nazism, were not particularly espoused by Italian fascists until it became advisable to do so to please Hitler.)

A third tenet of fascism is that the Darwinian concept of survival of the fittest applies to the state. Because only the fittest state will survive, only the aggressive, self-serving state will win out in the struggle for survival. Imperialism and militarism thus become prominent features of the fascist state. Corollaries of this aggressive nationalism are the rejection of pacifism, disarmament, and "universal embraces" with neighboring nations, along with glorification of the "virtues" of war to maximize human potential for the benefit of the state.

Another tenet of fascism is that the best economic system is that known as the "corporative state," in which the state has unlimited rights to intervene in the economy without owning all property and means of production outright. In Italy, the interests of landowning and monied classes were well protected, and the complaints of workers nullified or silenced, under a system of "corporations." Composed of both capitalists and workers, corporations—one for each branch of business or industry—were permitted, under state leadership, to set policy for that business or industry.

Fascism asserts the power of the state to be opportunistic in its own interest as it pleases. In 1919, Mussolini stated, "We allow ourselves the luxury of being aristocratic and democratic, reactionary and revolutionary, legalistic and illegalistic, according to the circumstances of place, time and environment." Although fascism was never especially democratic, except perhaps within some very small confines, this comment is otherwise true and helps explain why a list of the essential tenets of fascism is so short. The fascists were always prepared to change policies to suit their convenience.

Selection 10.6 contains some so-called fundamental ideas of fascism, as stated by Mussolini.

SELECTION 10.6

Fascism: Doctrines and Institutions   **From Benito Mussolini**

Fascism does not, generally speaking, believe in the possibility or utility of perpetual peace. It therefore discards pacifism as a cloak for cowardly supine renunciation in contra-distinction to self-sacrifice. War alone keys up all human energies to their maximum tension and sets the seal of nobility on those peoples who have the courage to face it. All other tests are substitutes which never place a man face to face with himself before the alternative of life or death. Therefore, all doctrines which postulate peace at all costs are incompatible with Fascism. Equally foreign to the spirit of Fascism, even if accepted as useful in meeting special political situations— are all internationalistic or League superstructures which, as history shows, crumble to the ground whenever the heart of nations is deeply stirred by sentimental, idealistic or practical con-

siderations. Fascism carries this anti-pacifistic attitude into the life of the individual. "I don't care a damn" (*[Non] me ne frego*)—the proud motto of the fighting squads scrawled by a wounded man on his bandages, is not only an act of philosophic stoicism, it sums up a doctrine which is not merely political: it is evidence of a fighting spirit which accepts all risks. . . .

Fascism [is] the resolute negation of the doctrine underlying so-called scientific and Marxian socialism, the doctrine of historic materialism which would explain the history of mankind in terms of the class-struggle and by changes in the processes and instruments of production, to the exclusion of all else.

That the vicissitudes of economic life— discoveries of raw materials, new technical processes, scientific inventions—have their

Twentieth-Century Isms

Liberalism, communism, socialism, capitalism, fascism, conservatism—these ill-defined terms are sometimes thought to denote mutually exclusive alternative forms of government. Actually, they do not stand for parallel alternatives at all.

Classical **liberalism** emphasized the rationality and goodness of humans, individual freedom, representative government, individual property rights, social progress through political reform, and laissez-faire economics, which, by the way, is just the view that the government should not interfere in economic affairs beyond the minimum necessary to maintain peace and property rights. A guiding principle of liberalism was eloquently articulated by Mill: the sole end for which people are warranted in interfering with an individual's liberty is never the individual's own good but rather to prevent harm to others. Contemporary liberals also subscribe to these assorted concepts, except they aren't so wedded to the laissez-faire idea. They are willing to put up with (or even ask for) government involvement in economic affairs when such involvement is perceived to promote equality of opportunity or protect people from exploitation or discrimination or protect the environment, or is done even merely to raise the overall quality of life. Thus, contemporary liberals tend to support social welfare programs paid for through taxation, as well as civil rights, women's rights, gay rights, affirmative action, and environmentalism. But contemporary liberals tend to oppose militarism, imperialism, exploitation of Third World countries, censorship, governmental support of religion, and anti-immigration crusades. American liberals are inclined to interpret the Bill of Rights very, well, liberally.

Conservatism was originally a reaction to the social and political upheaval of the French Revolution. Conservatives, as the word suggests, desire to conserve past social and political traditions and practices as representing the wisdom of a society's experience and are opposed to widespread social reform or experimentation. Even so, **Edmund Burke** (1729–1797), the most eloquent and influential conservative writer of the eigh-

importance, no one denies; but that they suffice to explain human history to the exclusion of other factors is absurd. Fascism believes now and always in sanctity and heroism, that is to say in acts in which no economic motive—remote or immediate—is at work. . . . Fascism also denies the immutable and irreparable character of the class struggle which is the natural outcome of this economic conception of history; above all it denies that the class struggle is the preponderating agent in social transformations. . . .

After socialism, Fascism trains its guns on the whole block of democratic ideologies, and rejects both their premises and their practical applications and implements. Fascism denies that numbers, as such, can be the determining factor in human society; it denies the right of numbers to govern by means of periodical consultations; it asserts the irremediable and fertile and beneficent inequality of men who cannot be levelled by any such mechanical and extrinsic device as universal suffrage. Democratic régimes may be described as those under which the people are, from time to time, deluded into the belief that they exercise sovereignty, while all the time real sovereignty resides in and is exercised by other and sometimes irresponsible and secret forces. Democracy is a kingless régime infested by many kings who are sometimes more exclusive, tyrannical, and destructive than one, even if he be a tyrant. . . .

The key-stone of the Fascist doctrine is its conception of the State, of its essence, its functions, and its aims. For Fascism the State is

teenth century, if not of all time, advocated many liberal and reform causes. Burke considered "society" as a contract among the dead, the living, and those to be born, and each social contract of each state but a clause in the great primeval contract of eternal society.

Contemporary American conservatism is in large measure a defense of private enterprise, laissez-faire economic policies, and a narrow or strict or literal interpretation of the Bill of Rights. Conservatives are reluctant to enlist the power of government, especially its power to tax, to remedy social ills. Critics (liberals, mostly) charge that conservatives give mere lip service to the importance of individual liberty and consider it of lesser importance than a free-market economy. Conservatives respond that individual liberty is best protected by limiting the scope of government, especially in economic matters, and by dispersing its power. In emphasizing both personal freedom and free-market economics and in distrusting centralized power, modern conservatism is similar to nineteenth-century laissez-faire liberalism.

Communists (with a capital C), as explained in an earlier box, accept the social, political, and economic ideology of the Communist party, including the idea that the dictatorship of the proletariat will come about only through revolution; **communism** (small c) is simply a form of economic organization in which the primary goods (usually the means of production and distribution) are held in common by a community. The definitions of **socialism** and communism are essentially the same, and Communists, of course, are advocates of communism.

Capitalism is an economic system in which ownership of the means of production and distribution is maintained primarily by private individuals and corporations. Capitalism, therefore, is an opposite to socialism and communism.

And **fascism,** as you've seen, is the totalitarian political philosophy espoused by the Mussolini government, which emphasized the absolute primacy of the state and leadership by an elite who embody the will and intelligence of the people.

absolute, individuals and groups relative. Individuals and groups are admissable in so far as they come within the State. Instead of directing the game and guiding the material and moral progress of the community, the liberal State restricts its activities to recording results. The Fascist State is wide awake and has a will of its own. For this reason it can be described as "ethical." At the first quinquennial assembly of the régime, in 1929, I said:

The Fascist State is not a night-watchman, solicitous only of the personal safety of the citizens; nor is it organised exclusively for the purpose of guaranteeing a certain degree of material prosperity and relatively peaceful conditions of life; a board of directors would do as much. Neither is it exclusively political, divorced from practical realities and holding itself aloof from the multifarious activities of the citizens and the nation. The State, as conceived and realised by Fascism, is a spiritual and ethical entity for securing the political, juridical, and economic organisation of the nation, an organisation which in its origin and growth is a manifestation of the spirit. The State guarantees the internal and external safety of the country, but it also safeguards and transmits the spirit of the people, elaborated down the ages in its language, its customs, its faith. The State is not only the present, it is also the past and above all the future. Transcending the individual's brief spell of life, the State stands for the immanent conscience of the nation. The forms in which it finds expression change, but the need for it remains. . . .

The Fascist State lays claim to rule in the economic field no less than in others; it makes its action felt throughout the length and breadth of the country by means of its corporative, social, and educational institutions, and all the political, economic, and spiritual forces of the nation, organised in their respective associations, circulate within the State.

A State based on millions of individuals who recognize its authority, feel its action, and are ready to serve its ends is not the tyrannical state of a mediaeval lordling. . . . Far from crushing the individual, the Fascist State multiplies his energies, just as in a regiment a soldier is not diminished but multiplied by the number of his fellow soldiers. . . .

Imperial power, as understood by the Fascist doctrine, is not only territorial, or military, or commercial; it is also spiritual and ethical. An imperial nation, that is to say a nation which directly or indirectly is a leader of others, can exist without the need of conquering a single square mile of territory. Fascism sees in the imperialistic spirit—i.e., in the tendency of nations to expand—a manifestation of their vitality. In the opposite tendency, which would limit their interests to the home country, it sees a symptom of decadence. People who rise or rearise are imperialistic; renunciation is characteristic of dying peoples. The Fascist doctrine is that best suited to the tendencies and feelings of a people which, like the Italian, after lying fallow during centuries of foreign servitude, is now reasserting itself in the world.

But imperialism implies discipline, the coordination of efforts, a deep sense of duty and a spirit of self-sacrifice. This explains many aspects of the practical activity of the régime, and the direction taken by many of the forces of the State, as also the severity which has to be exercised towards those who would oppose this spontaneous and inevitable movement of XXth century Italy by agitating outgrown ideologies of the XIXth century, ideologies rejected wherever great experiments in political and social transformations are being dared.

Never before have the peoples thirsted for authority, direction, order, as they do now.

Two Recent Analytic Political Philosophers

We turn now to the political philosophy of two contemporary American analytic philosophers. Analytic philosophy, as we have mentioned in each part of this book so far, has been the predominant tradition of philosophy in English-speaking countries during the twentieth century. When you read Chapter 15, you will encounter the social/political philosophy of Jürgen Habermas, Michel Foucault, and other Continental philosophers.

A Contemporary Liberal: John Rawls

In the opinion of many, the most important theoretical publication in political philosophy in recent years is *A Theory of Justice* (1971), by **John Rawls** (1921–). Rawls writes from within the liberal tradition, but he had grown dissatisfied with the utilitarianism on which liberalism was often based, yet was also dissatisfied with attempts merely to circumscribe utilitarianism with ad hoc "self-evident" principles about our duties (see the material on W. D. Ross in Chapter 8). Rawls said that in writing *A Theory of Justice* he wanted to "carry to a higher order of abstraction the traditional doctrine of the social contract." The result was a lengthy and systematic attempt to establish, interpret, and illuminate the fundamental principles of justice; to apply them to various central issues in social ethics; to use them for appraising social, political, and economic institutions; and to examine their implications for duty and obligation. We'll focus our discussion on the principles themselves.

The Fundamental Requirements of the Just Society   According to Rawls, because society is typically characterized by a conflict as well as an identity of interests, it must have a set of principles for assigning basic rights and duties and for determining the appropriate distribution of the benefits and burdens of social cooperation. These are the *principles of distributive or social justice.* They specify the kinds of social cooperation that can be entered into and the forms of government that can be established. (It is here that Rawls's theory of justice intersects with traditional philosophical questions about the ethically legitimate functions and organization of the state.) For Rawls, a society (or a state) is not well ordered unless (1) its members know and accept the same principles of social justice, and (2) the basic social institutions generally satisfy and are generally known to satisfy these principles.

If a society is to be well ordered, its members must determine by rational reflection what are to be their principles of justice, says Rawls. If the principles selected are to be reasonable and justifiable, they must be selected through a procedure that is *fair.* (Hence Rawls's book is an elaboration on a 1958 paper he wrote entitled "Justice As Fairness.")

The Veil of Ignorance and the Original Position   Now if the selection of principles of justice is to be fair, the possibility of bias operating in their selection must be removed, correct? Ideally, therefore, in our selection of the principles, none of us should have insider's knowledge. We should all be ignorant of one another's—and our own—wealth, status, abilities, intelligence, inclinations, aspirations, and even beliefs about goodness.

Of course, no group of people ever were or could *really* be in such a state of ignorance. Therefore, says Rawls, we must select the principles *as if* we were behind such a **veil of ignorance.** This is to ensure that nobody is advantaged or disadvantaged in the choice of principles by his or her own unique circumstances.

If from behind a veil of ignorance we were to deliberate on what principles of justice we would adopt, we would be in what Rawls calls the **original position** (or sometimes the *initial situation*). Like Locke and Rousseau's state of nature, the original position is an entirely hypothetical condition: as noted, people never were and never could be in such a condition of ignorance. Rawls's concepts of a veil of ignorance and an original position are intended "simply to make vivid to ourselves the restrictions that it seems reasonable to impose on arguments for principles of

Social Philosophy and Political Philosophy

The focus of some philosophers, like Locke, is mainly on the state—on its justification and on its ethically proper organization and scope and functions. Other philosophers, like Marcuse, focus on society and socioeconomic relationships, what they are and should be. Thus some philosophy texts make a distinction between social philosophy and political philosophy, and they assign some of the philosophers covered here to one category and others to the other category, depending on how the categories are defined. (You can also find books in which each philosopher treated in this chapter is listed as a social philosopher, as well as books that list each as a political philosopher, as we have done here. Very common, too, are texts in which each is treated as a "social-political" philosopher.)

John Rawls, who attempts to ascertain the fundamental principles of social justice—which, according to Rawls, should regulate the basic structure and institutions and political constitution of the state and, hence, derivatively, the laws of the state—is also much discussed in books on philosophy of law.

Feminist philosophy, treated in our next chapter, covers social, political, and ethical concerns, although we are placing it in the part of the book that deals with political philosophy.

justice, and therefore on these principles themselves." Determining our principles of justice by imagining ourselves in the original position simply ensures that we do not tailor our conception of justice to our own case.

In short, according to Rawls, the basic principles of justice are those to which we will agree if we are thinking rationally and in our own self-interest and if we eliminate irrelevant considerations. Because the basic principles of justice are those to which we will agree, Rawls's theory of justice is said to be a *contractarian* theory, as were the theories of Hobbes, Locke, and Rousseau.

The Two Principles of Social Justice   The principles we would select in the original position, if we are thinking rationally and attending to our own self-interest, are two, Rawls says.

The *first*, which takes precedence over the second when questions of priority arise, requires that *each person has an equal right to "the most extensive basic liberty compatible with a similar liberty for others."*

And the *second* requires that *social and economic inequalities be arranged "so that they are both (a) reasonably expected to be to everyone's advantage and (b) attached to positions and offices open to all."*

These two principles, writes Rawls, are a special case of a more general conception of justice to the effect that: *all social goods (e.g., liberty, opportunity, income, etc.) are to be distributed equally unless an unequal distribution is to everyone's advantage.*

We are led to this concept, Rawls writes, when we decide to find a concept of justice that "nullifies the accidents of natural endowment and the contingencies of social circumstances as counters in quest for political and economic advantage."

It follows from these principles, of course, that an unequal distribution of the various assets of society—wealth, for instance—*can* be just, as long as these inequalities are to everyone's benefit. (For example, it may be to everyone's benefit that physicians are paid more than, say, concrete workers.)

It also follows from the priority of the first principle over the second that, contrary to what utilitarian theory seems to require, someone's personal liberty *cannot* be sacrificed for the sake of the common good. Does the pleasure of owning slaves bring more happiness to the slave owners than it brings unhappiness to the slaves? If so, then the total happiness of society may well be greater with slavery than without it. Thus slavery would be to the common good, and utilitarianism would require that it should be instituted. Of course, utilitarians may well maintain that slavery or other restrictions of liberties will *as a matter of fact* diminish the sum total of happiness in a society and for this reason cannot be condoned, but they must nevertheless admit that, *as a matter of principle,* violations of liberty would be justified for the sake of the happiness of the many. According to Rawls's principles, such violations for the sake of the general happiness are not justified.

The Rights of Individuals   Although Rawls does not explicitly discuss the "rights" of individuals as a major topic, his theory obviously can be interpreted as securing such rights (see, for example, Rex Martin's 1985 book, *Rawls and Rights*). Many have believed that without God, talk of rights is pretty much nonsense; Rawls does not discuss God, and it seems plain that he does not need to do so in order to speak meaningfully of a person's rights. Rawls in effect attempts to derive social ethics from a basis in rational self-interest rather than from God, natural law, human nature, utility, or other ground.

Why Should I Accept That?   If Rawls's theory is correct, he has spelled out in plain language the fundamental requirements of the just society. Furthermore, if his theory is correct, these are the requirements that self-interested but rational people would, on reflection, accept.

This means that Rawls's theory provides a strong answer to the person who asks of any provision entailed by one or the other of the two principles just stated, "Why should *I* accept this provision?"

Let's say, for example, that you want to know what is wrong with enslaving another person. The answer is that the wrongfulness of slavery logically follows from the two principles of social justice. But why *should you agree* to those principles? The answer is that you *would* agree to them. Why? Because they are the principles that would be selected by self-interested but rational people playing on a level playing field—one, that is, on which no one has an unfair advantage. They are the principles that would be selected by self-interested but rational people if the procedure through which they were selected was unbiased by anyone having insider's knowledge of his or her or anyone else's unique circumstances. They are, in

Self-Respect

The most important good, according to John Rawls, is self-respect.

Self-respect? Yes.

Self-respect, says Rawls, has two aspects: first, a conviction that one's plans and aspirations are worthwhile, and second, confidence in one's ability to accomplish these objectives.

Without self-respect, therefore, our plans have little or no value to us, and we cannot continue in our endeavors if we are plagued by self-doubt. Thus, self-respect is essential for any activity at all. When we lack it, it seems pointless to do anything, and even if some activity did seem to have a point, we would lack the will to do it. "All desire and activity becomes empty and vain, and we sink into apathy and cynicism."

short, the principles that self-interested but rational people would select if the procedure by which they were selected was a *fair* one.

So, then, the reason you *should* accept that slavery is wrongful is because you *would* accept the principles from which the wrongfulness of slavery logically follows.

Few philosophical works by analytic philosophers have received such widespread attention and acclaim outside the circles of professional philosophers as did Rawls's *A Theory of Justice*. Though uncompromisingly analytical, it dealt with current issues of undeniable importance and interest and did so in the light of recent work in economics and the social sciences. The book was reviewed not merely in philosophical journals but in the professional literature of other disciplines and very widely in the popular press and in magazines of opinion and social commentary. It also became the focal point of numerous conferences, many of them interdisciplinary.

In a very recent work, *Political Liberalism* (1993), Rawls considers more carefully how his conception of justice as fairness can be endorsed by the diverse array of incompatible religious and philosophical doctrines that exist over time in a modern democratic society like ours. To answer this question, he finds that he must characterize justice more narrowly than he did earlier, as a freestanding *political conception* rather than as a *comprehensive value system* (like Christianity) that governs all aspects of one's life, both public and private. Political justice becomes the focus of an overlapping consensus of comprehensive value systems, and thus can still be embraced by all in a pluralistic democratic society. This change in Rawls's theory marks a change in Rawls's own theoretical understanding of justice as fairness. As a practical matter, though, the two principles of justice mentioned earlier still constitute the best conception of political cooperation required for stability in a democratic regime, in Rawls's view.

We'll conclude this discussion with an excerpt from *A Theory of Justice*.

SELECTION 10.7

A Theory of Justice*

From John Rawls

My aim is to present a conception of justice which generalizes and carries to a higher level of abstraction the familiar theory of the social contract as found, say, in Locke, Rousseau, and Kant. In order to do this we are not to think of the original contract as one to enter a particular society or to set up a particular form of government. Rather, the guiding idea is that the principles of justice for the basic structure of society are the object of the original agreement. They are the principles that free and rational persons concerned to further their own interests would accept in an initial position of equality as defining the fundamental terms of their association. These principles are to regulate all further agreements; they specify the kinds of social cooperation that can be entered into and the forms of government that can be established. This way of regarding the principles of justice I shall call justice as fairness.

Thus we are to imagine that those who engage in social cooperation choose together, in one joint act, the principles which are to assign basic rights and duties and to determine the division of social benefits. Men are to decide in advance how they are to regulate their claims against one another and what is to be the foundation charter of their society. Just as each person must decide by rational reflection what constitutes his good, that is, the system of ends which it is rational for him to pursue, so a group of persons must decide once and for all what is to count among them as just and unjust. The choice which rational men would make in this hypothetical situation of equal liberty, assuming for the present that this choice problem has a solution, determines the principles of justice.

In justice as fairness the original position of equality corresponds to the state of nature in the traditional theory of the social contract. This original position is not, of course, thought of as an actual historical state of affairs, much less as a primitive condition of culture. It is understood as a purely hypothetical situation characterized so as to lead to a certain conception of justice. Among the essential features of this situation is that no one knows his place in society, his class position or social status, nor does any one know his fortune in the distribution of natural assets and abilities, his intelligence, strength, and the like. I shall even assume that the parties do not know their conceptions of the good or their special psychological propensities. The principles of justice are chosen behind a veil of ignorance. This ensures that no one is advantaged or disadvantaged in the choice of principles by the outcome of natural chance or the contingency of social circumstances. Since all are similarly situated and no one is able to design principles to favor his particular condition, the principles of justice are the result of a fair agreement or bargain. For given the circumstances of the original position, the symmetry of everyone's relations to each other, this initial situation is fair between individuals as moral persons, that is, as rational beings with their own ends and capable, I shall assume, of a sense of justice. The original position is, one might say, the appropriate initial status quo, and thus the fundamental agreements reached in it are fair. This explains the propriety of the name "justice as fairness": it conveys the idea that the principles of justice are agreed to in an initial situation that is fair. The name does not mean that the concepts of justice and fairness are the same, any more than the phrase "poetry as metaphor" means that the

---

*Rawls's footnotes have been omitted.

concepts of poetry and metaphor are the same.

Justice as fairness begins, as I have said, with one of the most general of all choices which persons might make together, namely, with the choice of the first principles of a conception of justice which is to regulate all subsequent criticism and reform of institutions. Then, having chosen a conception of justice, we can suppose that they are to choose a constitution and a legislature to enact laws, and so on, all in accordance with the principles of justice initially agreed upon. Our social situation is just if it is such that by this sequence of hypothetical agreements we would have contracted into the general system of rules which defines it. . . .

I shall maintain . . . that the persons in the initial situation would choose two rather different principles: the first requires equality in the assignment of basic rights and duties, while the second holds that social and economic inequalities, for example inequalities of wealth and authority, are just only if they result in compensating benefits for everyone, and in particular for the least advantaged members of society. These principles rule out justifying institutions on the grounds that the hardships of some are offset by a greater good in the aggregate. It may

be expedient but it is not just that some should have less in order that others may prosper. But there is no injustice in the greater benefits earned by a few provided that the situation of persons not so fortunate is thereby improved. The intuitive idea is that since everyone's well-being depends upon a scheme of cooperation without which no one could have a satisfactory life, the division of advantages should be such as to draw forth the willing cooperation of everyone taking part in it, including those less well situated. Yet this can be expected only if reasonable terms are proposed. The two principles mentioned seem to be a fair agreement on the basis of which those better endowed, or more fortunate in their social position, neither of which we can be said to deserve, could expect the willing cooperation of others when some workable scheme is a necessary condition of the welfare of all. Once we decide to look for a conception of justice that nullifies the accidents of natural endowment and the contingencies of social circumstance as counters in quest for political and economic advantage, we are led to these principles. They express the result of leaving aside those aspects of the social world that seem arbitrary from a moral point of view.

Robert Nozick's Libertarianism

If any other book by an analytic philosopher attracted as much attention as *A Theory of Justice*, it was *Anarchy, State, and Utopia*, published three years later by **Robert Nozick** (1938–). By this time (thanks largely to Rawls) it was not unusual to find analytic philosophers speaking to "big" issues, and Nozick certainly did that.

The reaction to *Anarchy, State, and Utopia* was more mixed than that to Rawls's book, and, though many reviewers acclaimed it enthusiastically, others condemned it, often vehemently. These negative reactions are easily understandable in view of Nozick's vigorous espousal of principles of political philosophy not very popular with many contemporary liberal political theorists.

The basic question asked in *Anarchy, State, and Utopia* is, simply: Should there even be a political state, and if so, why? Nozick's answer is worked out in elaborate detail through the course of his book, but it consists essentially of three claims:

1. A minimal state, limited to the narrow functions of protection against force, theft, fraud, breach of contracts, and so on, is justified.

2. Any more extensive state will violate persons' rights not to be forced to do certain things, and is unjustified.

3. The minimal state is inspiring as well as right.

To each of these three claims Nozick devotes one part of his book. We won't spend time on his last claim.

A Minimal State Is Justified   The first claim, that a minimal state is justified, will seem so obvious to many as hardly to require lengthy argument. The basic idea accepted by political theorists in the liberal political tradition, from John Locke through Mill and up to and including Rawls, is that the political state, as compared with a state of anarchy or "the state of nature," "advances the good of those taking part of it" (to quote Rawls). But *does* it?

If, as Nozick believes, "individuals have rights, and there are things no person or group may do to them (without violating their rights)," then it may well be true, as anarchists believe, that "any state necessarily violates people's moral rights and hence is intrinsically immoral." In the first part of his book, Nozick considers carefully whether this anarchist belief is true. His conclusion is that it is not. To establish this conclusion, he attempts to show that a minimal state can arise by the mechanism of "an invisible hand" (see box) from a hypothetical state of nature without violating any natural rights. As intuitively plausible as Nozick's conclusion is on its face, his defense of it is controversial, and the issue turns out to be difficult.

Only the "Night-Watchman" State Doesn't Violate Rights   The main claim advanced by Nozick in the second part of his book, and by far the most controversial claim of the work as a whole, is that any state more powerful or extensive than the minimal "night-watchman" state that protects its citizens from force and fraud and like things impinges on the individual's natural rights to his or her holdings and therefore is not legitimate or justifiable. It is further a corollary to this claim that concepts of justice that mandate the distribution of assets in accordance with a formula (e.g., "to each according to his _____") or in accordance with a goal or objective (e.g., to promote the general happiness) always require *re*distributing the goods of society and thus require taking from some individuals the goods that are rightfully theirs. Such concepts of justice are therefore illegitimate, according to Nozick.

Nozick's own concept of justice rests on an idea that comes naturally to many people (at least until they imagine themselves in Rawls's "initial situation" behind a "veil of ignorance" about their own assets and abilities). The idea is that *what's yours is yours*: redistributing your income or goods against your wishes for the sake of the general happiness or to achieve any other objective is unjust. Nozick defends this idea. *A person is entitled to what he or she has rightfully acquired, and justice consists in each person's retaining control over his or her rightful acquisitions.* This is Nozick's "entitlement" concept of social justice.

Invisible-Hand Explanations

Often an action intended for a certain purpose generates unforeseen indirect consequences. According to Adam Smith, people, in intending only their own gain, are "led by an invisible hand to promote an end" that was no part of their intention, namely, the general good.

Nozick, after Adam Smith, calls an **invisible-hand explanation** one that explains the seemingly direct result of what someone has intended or desired to happen as not being brought about by such intentions or desires at all.

For example, it *looks* as if the state is the result of people's desire to live under a common government, and this is indeed what Locke—and many, many others—thought. But Nozick attempts to provide an invisible-hand explanation of the state as the by-product of certain *other* propensities and desires that people would have within a state of nature. Nozick's explanation is intended to show how a minimal state can arise without violating people's rights.

Another famous invisible-hand explanation presents the institution of money as the outcome of people's propensity to exchange their goods for something they perceive to be more generally desired than what they have. Another describes the characteristics and traits of organisms as the result of natural selection rather than God's wishes.

Nozick does not clarify or attempt to defend his entitlement concept of social justice to the extent some critics would like (he basically accepts a refined version of Locke's theory of property acquisition, according to which, you'll remember, what's yours is what you mix your labor with). Instead, he mainly seeks to show that alternative conceptions of social justice, conceptions that ignore what a person is entitled to by virtue of rightful acquisition, are defective. According to Nozick, social justice, that is, justice in the distribution of goods, is not achieved by redistributing these goods in order to achieve some objective but by permitting them to remain in the hands of those who have legitimately acquired them:

> Your being forced to contribute to another's welfare violates your rights, whereas someone else's not providing you with things you need greatly, including things essential to the protection of your rights, does not *itself* violate your rights, even though it avoids making it more difficult for someone else to violate them.

The Rights of Individuals   In the opening sentence of his book Nozick asserts that individuals have rights, and indeed his entire argument rests on that supposition, especially those many aspects that pertain to property rights. Unfortunately, Nozick's theoretical justification of the supposition is very obscure: it has something to do, evidently, with a presumed inviolability of individuals that prohibits their being used as means to ends, and perhaps also with the necessary conditions for allowing them to give meaning to their lives. If Nozick has not made his thought entirely clear in this area, he has set forth very plainly the implications for social theory, as he sees them, of assuming that natural rights exist. In addition, his

Animals and Morality

One interesting side discussion in Nozick's *Anarchy, State, and Utopia* concerns the moral status of animals.

Animals are not mere objects, Nozick says: the same moral constraints apply to what one may do to animals as to what one may do to people. Even a modern utilitarian, who holds that the pleasure, happiness, pain, and suffering that an action produces determine its moral worth, must count animals in moral calculations to the extent they have the capacities for these feelings, Nozick suggests.

Furthermore, he argues, utilitarianism isn't adequate as a moral theory concerning animals (or humans) to begin with. In his view, neither humans nor animals may be used or sacrificed against their will for the benefit of others; that is, neither may be treated as means (to use Kant's terminology) but only as ends. Nozick's argument for this view is a negative argument that challenges a reader to find an acceptable ethical principle that would prohibit the killing or hurting or sacrificing or eating of humans for the sake of other ends that would not equally pertain to animals. Can you think of one?

Here is a good place to mention that the question of animal rights has been widely discussed by contemporary philosophers— and the animal rights movement of recent years, which frequently makes headlines, has received strong theoretical support from several of them. Others do not think that animals have rights in the same sense in which humans have them, and they are not philosophically opposed to medical experimentation involving animals or to eating them. (As far as we know, Nozick has not been an activist in the animal rights movement.)

Taking from the Rich and Giving to the Poor

According to Nozick's view of social justice, taking from the rich without compensation and giving to the poor is never just (assuming the rich didn't become rich through force or fraud, etc.). This would also be Locke's view. According to the strict utilitarian view, by contrast, doing so *is* just if it is to the greater good of the aggregate of people (as would be the case, for example, if through progressive taxation you removed from a rich person's income an amount that he or she would miss but little and used it to prevent ten people from starving). Finally, according to Rawls's view of justice, taking from the rich and giving to the poor is just if it is to the greater good of the aggregate, *provided* it does not compromise anyone's liberty (which, in the case just envisioned, it arguably would not).

work contains many interesting and provocative side discussions, including critical discussions of Marx's theory of exploitation, but we must pass over these.

Selection 10.8, from *Anarchy, State, and Utopia,* is one of these side discussions in which Nozick criticizes the "principle of fairness" defended by John Rawls and philosopher of law Herbert Hart.

Anarchy, State, and Utopia

From Robert Nozick

A principle suggested by Herbert Hart, which (following John Rawls) we shall call the *principle of fairness,* would be of service here if it were adequate. This principle holds that when a number of persons engage in a just, mutually advantageous, cooperative venture according to rules and thus restrain their liberty in ways necessary to yield advantages for all, those who have submitted to these restrictions have a right to similar acquiescence on the part of those who have benefited from their submission. Acceptance of benefits (even when this is not a giving of express or tacit undertaking to cooperate) is enough, according to this principle, to bind one. . . .

The principle of fairness, as we stated it following Hart and Rawls, is objectionable and unacceptable. Suppose some of the people in your neighborhood (there are 364 other adults) have found a public address system and decide to institute a system of public entertainment. They post a list of names, one for each day, yours among them. On his assigned day (one can easily switch days) a person is to run the public address system, play records over it, give news bulletins, tell amusing stories he has heard, and so on. After 138 days on which each person has done his part, your day arrives. Are you obligated to take your turn? You *have* benefited from it, occasionally opening your window to listen, enjoying some music or chuckling at someone's funny story. The other people *have* put themselves out. But must you answer the call when it is your turn to do so? As it stands, surely not. Though you benefit from the arrangement, you may know all along that 364 days of entertainment supplied by others will not be worth your giving up *one* day. You would rather not have any of it and not give up a day than have it all

and spend one of your days at it. Given these preferences, how can it be that you are required to participate when your scheduled time comes? It would be nice to have philosophy readings on the radio to which one could tune in at any time, perhaps late at night when tired. But it may not be nice enough for you to want to give up one whole day of your own as a reader on the program. Whatever you want, can others create an obligation for you to do so by going ahead and starting the program themselves? In this case you can choose to forgo the benefit by not turning on the radio; in other cases the benefits may be unavoidable. If each day a different person on your street sweeps the entire street, must you do so when your time comes? Even if you don't care that much about a clean street? Must you imagine dirt as you traverse the street, so as not to benefit as a free rider? Must you refrain from turning on the radio to hear the philosophy readings? Must you mow your front lawn as often as your neighbors mow theirs?

At the very least one wants to build into the principle of fairness the condition that the benefits to a person from the actions of the others are greater than the costs to him of doing his share. . . .

If the principle of fairness were modified so as to contain this very strong condition, it still would be objectionable. The benefits might only barely be worth the costs to you of doing your share, yet others might benefit from *this* institution much more than you do; they all treasure listening to the public broadcasts. As the person least benefited by the practice, are you obligated to do an equal amount for it? Or perhaps you would prefer that all cooperated in *another* venture, limiting their conduct and making sacrifices for *it*. It is true, *given* that they are not following your plan (and thus limiting what other options are available to you), that the benefits of their venture *are* worth to you the costs of your cooperation. However, you do not wish to cooperate, as part of your plan to focus their attention on your alternative proposal which they have ignored or not given, in your view at least, its proper due. (You want them, for example, to read the Talmud on the radio instead of the philosophy they are reading.) By lending the institution (their institution) the support of your cooperating in it, you will only make it harder to change or alter.

On the face of it, enforcing the principle of fairness is objectionable. You may not decide to give me something, for example a book, and then grab money from me to pay for it, even if I have nothing better to spend the money on. You have, if anything, even less reason to demand payment if your activity that gives me the book also benefits you; suppose that your best way of getting exercise is by throwing books into people's houses, or that some other activity of yours thrusts books into people's houses as an unavoidable side effect. Nor are things changed if your inability to collect money or payments for the books which unavoidably spill over into others' houses makes it inadvisable or too expensive for you to carry on the activity with this side effect. One cannot, whatever one's purposes, just act so as to give people benefits and then demand (or seize) payment. Nor can a group of persons do this. If you may not charge and collect for benefits you bestow without prior agreement, you certainly may not do so for benefits whose bestowal costs you nothing, and most certainly people need not repay you for costless-to-provide benefits which yet *others* provided them. So the fact that we partially are "social products" in that we benefit from current patterns and forms created by the multitudinous actions of a long string of long-forgotten people, forms which include institutions, ways of doing things, and language (whose social nature may involve our current use depending upon Wittgensteinian matching of the speech of others), does not create in us a general floating debt which the current society can collect and use as it will.

Perhaps a modified principle of fairness can be stated which would be free from these and similar difficulties. What seems certain is that any such principle, if possible, would be so complex and involuted that one could not combine it with a special principle legitimating *enforcement* within a state of nature of the obligations that have arisen under it. Hence, even if the principle could be formulated so that it was no longer open to objection, it would not serve to obviate the need for other persons' *consenting* to cooperate and limit their own activities.

Communitarian Critics of Rawls

According to Rawls, in a just society individuals are guaranteed the right to pursue their own ends to the extent that they don't interfere with the right of others to pursue their own ends. Compromising this basic right to individual liberty for the sake of any so-called higher good is not acceptable, in the Rawlsian view, and any such "good" is not really a good thing at all. You could put the point by saying that for Rawls the right to personal liberty is more basic or fundamental than goodness. This is a view widely held by liberals.

However, some recent critics of Rawls say there exists a common good whose attainment has priority over individual liberty. Some of these critics are known as

Political Trends

Recent kaleidoscopic changes in the world's political structure leave us all gasping. Thought the Berlin wall was permanent? It fell overnight. Gorbachev? Gone. The USSR? Finished. The world can no longer be thought of as divided into capitalism and communism. Today's politics displays a wide range of complex movement and forces: nationalism, fascistic defenses of landed privilege, Islamic theocracy, socialism, anticolonialism, anti-imperialism, capitalism, democratic socialism.

Marxism? Well, when Karl Marx developed his theory of revolution, he postulated a dictatorship of the proletariat as a stage of development leading to a classless society. Actual "Communist" governments, perhaps starting with Lenin's leadership, fell a wee bit short of investing actual power in the working class. Privilege and power tended to be concentrated in a minority group, the Communist leadership. Therefore, it makes sense even in the Marxist perspective that the people would also take over power from that oligarchical elite. Whether, however, such yearnings for personal freedom and democratic control of government lead in the direction of a classless society remains to be seen. Certainly in the short run, they have led to outbreaks of sectarianism and extreme nationalism.

The list at the end of the first paragraph of this box mentions *democratic socialism,* a term that denotes a popular political structure, especially in Western Europe, but that many Americans have not yet heard of. Under democratic socialism there is a democratically elected executive and legislature, and there is no state ownership of business, though it permits considerable government intervention in the business sector. Yet this type of system provides guarantees of individual rights and freedom as well as a social safety net for the poor, the old, and the sick, as in Communist political arrangements.

Despite the myriad changes in the world political scene, one trend does appear fairly global: the preference for personal freedom and democratic government.

communitarians, for they hold that this common good is defined by one's society or "community." Important communitarian critics of Rawls include Michael Sandel (*Liberalism and the Limits of Justice,* 1982), Michael Walzer (*Spheres of Justice,* 1983, and *Thick and Thin,* 1994), and Alasdair MacIntyre (most widely known work: *After Virtue,* 1981).

Sandel believes that the community is an intersubjective or collective self because, he argues, self-understanding comprehends more than just an individual human being: it comprehends one's family or tribe or class or nation or people—in short, one's community with its shared ends and common vocabulary and mutual understandings. The Rawlsian principle of equal liberty is subordinate to the good of this social organism for Sandel.

Walzer contrasts "thick" or particularist moral argument, argument that is internal to and framed within this or that specific political association or "culture," and "thin" moral argument, which is abstract and general and philosophical. Political philosophers, according to Walzer, seek an abstract, universal (thin) point of view and are concerned with the appropriate structure of political association in general. But any full account of how social goods ought to be distributed, he says, will be thick; it "will be idiomatic in its language, particularist in its cultural reference, and historically detailed." For Walzer, a society is just if its way of life is faithful to the shared understanding of its members. There "are no eternal or universal principles" that can replace a "local account" of justice. All such principles are abstractions and simplifications that nevertheless still reflect particular cultural viewpoints. (Notice how Walzer's political philosophy echoes some of the relativistic themes discussed in current epistemology and metaphysics—see Chapter 6).

MacIntyre thinks that the Rawlsian idea that individuals should have the freedom to pursue their own various objectives rests on the premise that individuals have their own various "private" goods. But in MacIntyre's view, only a shared vision can make something good: there is something fishy, in MacIntyre's eyes, in the Rawlsian picture of a group of individuals each with his or her own "good." A self, MacIntyre maintains, finds its "moral identity in and through its membership in communities such as those of the family, the neighborhood, the city and the tribe." Human good is thus socially defined for MacIntyre, and the Rawlsian idea of multiple private goods is incoherent. This means, in MacIntyre's view, that the common good takes precedence, ethically speaking, over individual freedom.

The idea of society as an organism in its own right with its own proper "good" is one we encountered in Plato, Aristotle, Rousseau, and Mussolini. There is much current debate in analytic political philosophy among Rawlsian liberals, libertarians, and communitarians. Rawls's 1993 work, mentioned above, is clearly a response to his critics, especially his communitarian critics.

Checklist

To help you review, here is a checklist of the key philosophers and concepts of this chapter. The brief descriptive sentences summarize leading ideas. Keep in mind that some of these summary statements represent terrific oversimplifications of complex positions.

Philosophers

- **Harriet Taylor** Reformist philosopher who advocated the liberation of women and who stressed the importance of political tolerance and individualism.

- **John Stuart Mill** Classical liberal theorist; held that the function of the state is to promote the general happiness (not to safeguard natural rights) and said that a person's liberty may be interfered with only to prevent harm to others.

- **Adam Smith** Classical liberal economic theorist, exponent of capitalism and a laissez-faire economy.

- **Anna Doyle Wheeler** Irish liberal, utilitarian, utopian, feminist philosopher who, with William Thompson, challenged James Mill's views on the utility of granting rights to women.

- **William Thompson** English liberal, utilitarian, utopian, feminist. An economist who argued for women's rights and the rights of workers.
- **Claude Saint-Simone** French utopian philosopher and social reformer who advocated love for the poor and powerless, and the redistribution of property.
- **Robert Owen** English utopian; supported voluntary mutual work cooperatives where all shared the production and consumption of goods.
- **Charles Fourier** French utopian philosopher who promoted voluntary labor to contribute toward the happiness and welfare of members of work cooperatives.
- **Karl Marx** Held that human history is a dialectical interplay between social relationships and economic productive activity that involves class warfare but ultimately leads to an ideal society lacking classes, wages, money, private property, or exploitation.
- **Pierre Joseph Proudhon** Important anarchist; held that all social organizations must be founded on the free and voluntary agreement of individuals.
- **Mikhail Bakunin** and **Prince Piotr Kropotkin** Russian anarchist Communists; held that law and the state are the instruments of the privileged classes. Bakunin advocated the violent overthrow of all government.
- **Herbert Marcuse** Marxist; held that the working class has been transformed from a force for radical change into a force for preserving the status quo because of the satisfaction of false needs created by consumerism and advertising.
- **Benito Mussolini** Italian dictator and leader of the Fascist movement.
- **Edmund Burke** Eighteenth-century conservative political writer.
- **John Rawls** Analytic (liberal) political philosopher; attempted to establish the fundamental principles of distributive justice through consideration of a hypothetical "original position" in which people's choice of principles is not biased by their individual unique circumstances; held that all social goods are to be distributed equally unless an unequal distribution is to everyone's advantage.
- **Robert Nozick** Analytic (libertarian) political philosopher; held that a limited "night-watchman" state is ethically justified but that any more extensive state violates people's rights.

Concepts

general happiness

utilitarianism

liberalism

capitalism

means (forces) of production

productive relations

dialectical process

class struggle

alienation

anarchism

proletariat

bourgeoisie

revolutionists

Communism

Comintern/Third International

communism

false needs

fascism

fasces

corporative state

laissez-faire economics

conservatism

socialism

principles of distributive justice

veil of ignorance

original position

invisible-hand mechanism

night-watchman state

entitlement concept of social justice

communitarians

democratic socialism

Questions for Discussion and Review

1. "The only part of the conduct of anyone, for which he is amenable to society, is that which concerns others. In the part which merely concerns himself, his independence is absolute." Do you agree? Why or why not?

2. What, for utilitarians, are "natural rights"?

3. What did Taylor think was so important about toleration? In what ways did she think English society was intolerant?

4. What is one of the arguments Wheeler and Thompson gave against the view of James Mill that women's interests are "covered" or "included" in those of men?

5. Compare and contrast classical liberalism and orthodox Marxism.

6. What, according to Marx, are the consequences of capitalism, and why are they consequences?

7. Does alienation exist? Defend your answer.

8. Critically discuss Marcuse's theory that the needs satisfied by advanced capitalist societies are to a large extent false needs.

9. Are our needs determined by advertising, consumerism, the mass media, and the entertainment industry?

10. "A revolution will come, born of disgust at the waste and excess of consumer society." Is this very likely? Explain.

11. "The state does not exist primarily to protect the rights of its citizens; citizens exist for the sake of the state." Evaluate this claim.

12. Explain the differences among liberalism, communism, socialism, capitalism, fascism, and conservatism.

13. Is it true that a state is not "well ordered" unless both (a) its members know and accept the same principles of social justice and (b) the basic social institutions generally satisfy and are generally known to satisfy these principles? Does the United States meet these conditions?

14. Do you agree that the principles of justice stated by Rawls are those to which we will agree if we are thinking rationally and in our own self-interest and are not influenced by irrelevant considerations? Explain.

15. Can an unequal distribution of the various assets of society be just? Explain.

16. Would it be right and proper to legalize human slavery if that resulted in an increase in the overall happiness of society? Why or why not?

17. "Any state necessarily violates people's moral rights and hence is intrinsically immoral." Give some reasons for thinking that this is true. Then give some reasons for thinking that it is false.

18. Can you think of an ethical principle that would prohibit the killing, hurting, sacrificing, or eating of humans for the sake of other ends that would not equally pertain to animals?

19. Compare and contrast the concepts of social justice proposed by Rawls and Nozick.

20. Is self-respect the most important good, as Rawls says?

21. In Selection 10.8, Nozick criticizes the "principle of fairness." State that principle and summarize Nozick's reasons for finding it unacceptable.

22. Which do you think is more important, the common good or individual freedom? Why?

Suggested Further Readings

Norman P. Barry, *An Introduction to Modern Political Theory,* 2nd ed. (London: Macmillan, 1991). A review of some of the key issues, in current political parlance.

Alan Brown, *Modern Political Philosophy* (New York: Penguin Books, 1986). A survey of major trends in contemporary political theory, including Rawls, Nozick, and others.

Anthony de Cresigny and Kenneth Minogue, eds., *Contemporary Political Philosophers* (London: Methuen, 1975). An overview of recent political philosophy, including figures not covered in this text.

R. Gettell, *History of American Political Thought* (New York: The Century Co., 1928). Excellent.

R. Gettell, *History of Political Thought* (New York: The Century Co., 1924). The best single-volume history of political theory available.

Jack Lively and Andrew Reeve, eds., *Modern Political Theory from Hobbes to Marx, Key Debates* (New York: Routledge, 1989). Important essays on major political theorists—Hobbes, Locke, Rousseau, Burke, Bentham, Mill, Marx.

Alasdair MacIntyre, *After Virtue: A Study in Moral Theory,* 2nd ed. (London: Duckworth, 1981). Widely known to the general public, this is MacIntyre's most important work.

D. McLellan, *The Thought of Karl Marx* (New York: Macmillan, 1977). Excellent analytic treatment of Marx's philosophy. For an authoritative biography of Marx, see Mc-Lellan's *Marx: His Life and Thought* (New York: Harper & Row, 1973). Finally, for Marx readings, see McLellan's *Selected Writings* (New York: Oxford University Press, 1977).

H. Marcuse, *One-Dimensional Man* (Boston: Beacon Press, 1964). Marcuse's searing indictment of advanced technological societies.

R. Martin, *Rawls and Rights* (Lawrence, Kan.: University Press of Kansas, 1985). Rawls's theory of justice explained, and interpreted in terms of rights.

J. S. Mill, *On Liberty,* E. Rapaport, ed. (Indianapolis: Hackett, 1978). The statement of classic liberalism.

B. Mussolini, *Fascism: Doctrines and Institutions* (New York: Howard Fertig, 1968).

J. Paul, ed., *Reading Nozick: Essays on "Anarchy, State, and Utopia"* (Totowa, N.J.: Rowman & Littlefield, 1981). A collection of essays that explain and criticize Nozick's political philosophy.

Anthony Quinton, ed., *Political Philosophy* (New York: Oxford University Press, 1991). Recent papers on political issues such as sovereignty, democracy, liberty, equality, and the common good.

John Rawls, *A Theory of Justice* (Cambridge: Harvard University Press, 1971). An important work; very clearly written.

John Rawls, *Political Liberalism* (New York: Columbia University Press, 1993). Rawls's most recent book, a series of lectures that makes adjustments in *A Theory of Justice* in the light of criticism of the earlier work.

Michael Sandel, *Liberalism and the Limits of Justice* (Cambridge: Cambridge University Press, 1982). An important work in communitarian political philosophy.

Peter Singer, ed., *In Defense of Animals* (New York: Perennial Library, 1986). Singer is a leading exponent of "animal rights."

R. Stewart, *Readings in Social and Political Philosophy* (Oxford: Oxford University Press, 1986). An excellent anthology of classic and contemporary readings in social and political philosophy.

Harriet Taylor, "Enfranchisement of Women," in *Essays on Sex Equality,* Alice S. Rossi, ed. (Chicago: University of Chicago Press, 1970). Almost all of the writings by Taylor and John Stuart Mill are contained in this volume.

R. Taylor, *Freedom, Anarchy, and the Law: An Introduction to Political Philosophy*, 2nd ed. (Buffalo: Prometheus Books, 1982). A general introduction to political philosophy.

William Thompson (and Anna Wheeler), *Appeal of One Half of the Human Race, Women, Against the Pretensions of the Other Half, Men, to Retain Them in Political, and Thence in Civil and Domestic, Slavery. In Reply to a Paragraph of Mr. Mill's Celebrated "Article on Government."* (New York: Burt Franklin, 1970: reprint of 1825 edition).

Anna Wheeler, "Rights of Women," *British Co-Operator* 1 (1830), pp. 1, 2, 12–15, 33–36.

Michael Walzer, *Spheres of Justice* (New York: Basic Books, 1983). Each society generates its own "sphere of justice."

Michael Walzer, *Thick and Thin, Moral Argument at Home and Abroad* (Notre Dame: University of Notre Dame Press, 1994). An extension and revision of *Spheres of Justice*.

Feminist Philosophy

11

by Ellen Fox

However novel it may appear, I shall venture the assertion, that, until women assume the place in society which good sense and good feeling alike assign to them, human improvement must advance but feebly.

—Frances Wright

In the new society woman will be entirely independent, both socially and economically. She will not be subjected to even a trace of domination and exploitation, but will be free and man's equal, and mistress of her own lot.

—August Bebel

Inferiority is not banal or incidental even when it happens to women.

—Andrea Dworkin

Why are men and women so different? And what can be done to make their lives and circumstances more equal?

These are the questions that have puzzled feminists since the beginning of the modern age. Some of the answers that have been suggested will be outlined in this chapter.

Not every philosopher thought that women and men should be treated equally, of course. Aristotle, for instance, thought that men were natural rulers and women were natural subjects, because women were esssentially defective men. Nor did the list stop with Aristotle; writers from the Middle Ages, the Enlightenment, and right on up through Freud to the present have argued not only that women are different from men, but that they are inferior and should be treated as subordinates. It is an opposition to this view that defines **feminism** and unites all feminists.

Feminist thought is often divided into two "waves"; the first wave, from the late 1700s through the early part of the twentieth century, ended in 1922 with the vote for women. The second wave began in 1949 with the publication of Simone de Beauvoir's *The Second Sex* and is still happening today. In this chapter, we'll concentrate on some of the issues considered in the second wave.

Why Should Women Have a Voice in Government?

The classic answer was provided by Harriet Taylor (1807?–1858), who was discussed in Chapter 10:

Even those who do not look upon a voice in the government as a matter of personal right, nor profess principles which require that it should be extended to all, have usually traditional maxims of political justice with which it is impossible to reconcile the exclusion of all women from the common rights of citizenship. It is an axiom of English freedom that taxation and representation should be coextensive. Even under the laws which give the wife's property to the husband, there are many unmarried women who pay taxes. It is one of the fundamental doctrines of the British Constitution, that all persons should be tried by their peers: yet women, whenever tried, are tried by male judges and a male jury. To foreigners the law accords the privilege of claiming that half the jury should be composed of themselves; not so to women. Apart from maxims of detail, which represent local and national rather than universal ideas; it is an acknowledged dictate of justice to make no degrading distinctions without necessity. In all things the presumption ought to be on the side of equality. A reason must be given why anything should be permitted to one person and interdicted to another. But when that which is interdicted includes nearly everything which those to whom it is permitted most prize, and to be deprived of which they feel to be most insulting; when not only political liberty but personal freedom of action is the prerogative of a caste; when even in the exercise of industry, almost all employments which task the higher faculties in an important field, which lead to distinction, riches, or even pecuniary independence, are fenced round as the exclusive domain of the predominant section, scarcely any doors being left open to the dependent class, except such as all who can enter elsewhere disdainfully pass by; the miserable expediencies which are advanced as excuses for so grossly partial a dispensation, would not be sufficient, even if they were real, to render it other than a flagrant injustice. While, far from being expedient, we are firmly convinced that the division of mankind into two castes, one born to rule over the other, is in this case, as in all cases, an unqualified mischief; a source of perversion and demoralization, both to the favored class and to those at whose expense they are favoured; producing none of the good which it is the custom to ascribe to it, and forming a bar . . . to any really vital improvement, either in the character or in the social condition of the human race.

Simone de Beauvoir

The first wave of feminism did see some dramatic results, including certain changes in the laws regarding women's property rights and, most dramatically, the right to vote, which women finally obtained in 1922. Active theoretical work on feminist issues subsided for a few decades at that point. But the larger social problems did not go away; theorists who had hoped that the right to vote and own property

PROFILE / Simone de Beauvoir (1908–1986)

Simone de Beauvoir graduated from the Sorbonne second in her class, behind only Simone Weil, the Jewish writer and mystic. While at the university, she met Jean-Paul Sartre, Maurice Merleau-Ponty, and many other young intellectuals who would go on to prominence in twentieth-century French letters and politics. Some of these men and women formed the group that Sartre and de Beauvoir would call "The Family"—a collection of writers, actors, and activists who associated for intellectual stimulation and social support for more than sixty years.

De Beauvoir and Sartre formed a partnership while they were in their early twenties. Sartre decided that theirs was an "essential" love which would be most important in their lives—but which did not rule out "contingent" love affairs with other people. Indeed, Sartre went on to develop a reputation as one of France's most compulsive womanizers. De Beauvoir consistently claimed that Sartre's myriad one-night stands did not bother her at all. She herself formed several years-long liaisons with other men, most notably Nelson Algren, the American writer. Algren pressed for marriage, but de Beauvoir was opposed to the institution and unwilling to put anyone before Sartre. De Beauvoir remained active and involved with writing, traveling, and constant political work until close to the end of her life.

would resolve the problem of women's lower social and economic status saw their hopes crumble. Women were still educated differently, still viewed as being primarily ornamental and nurturing, still paid less, and still seen as having a lower fundamental worth than men.

One woman who recognized this problem was the philosopher and novelist **Simone de Beauvoir** (1908–1986). In contrast with earlier writers like Mary Wollstonecraft (Chapter 9) and Harriet Taylor (Chapter 10), who had been steeped in the traditions of empiricism and utilitarianism, de Beauvoir came from the Continental traditions of existentialism and phenomenology. Her approach focused less on the public world of laws, rights, and educational opportunities and more on the cultural mechanisms of oppression that left women in the role of Other to man's Self. She developed this notion of women's essential otherness in her book *The Second Sex*.

And what a book! De Beauvoir undertook a sweeping analysis of all the ideas and forces which conspired to keep women in a subordinate position relative to men. Her examination encompassed Freud, Marx, the evidence of biology, the evidence of history, representative novelists, and what we would call the evidence of sociology. There had not previously been anything like this systematic and sustained analysis of the condition of women; de Beauvoir's work was unique.

But its very scope makes it a difficult book to summarize or outline. De Beauvoir, like some of her existentialist colleagues, was more interested in the fascinating variety of theoretical approaches than in the project of making them—or her own views—completely consistent. Like other existentialists, she borrowed liberally from the insights of psychoanalysis and from Marxian perspectives, but tended to ignore the deterministic conclusions of those approaches. No matter that we may be controlled by our own internal psychodynamics or by the forces of economic history; ultimately, we can always "transcend our own immanence," recreate ourselves anew, and overcome the straitjackets of history and culture. This view, as you can imagine, has important consequences for political action. Suppose you believe that culture shapes individuals and that it is very hard, or impossible, to overcome cultural conditioning. Then if you conclude that the condition of a particular group, such as women, is not what it should be, you should emphasize that society overall should change so that women will be changed. But if you think that the individual can always overcome his or her circumstances, then you might argue that individuals should focus on their own self-transformation. De Beauvoir argued that society should change, but if you are a thoroughgoing existentialist, it is not clear why you should not focus on your own personal transformation to overcome the culture.

What is a woman, de Beauvoir wondered. It cannot be a simple biological category, for there are people who have the relevant biological equipment who are nevertheless excluded from "womanhood." In one of her most famous passages, de Beauvoir argues that "one is not born, but rather becomes, a woman." The category of womanhood is imposed by civilization. And the fundamental social meaning of woman is Other. De Beauvoir held, "No group ever sets itself up as the One without at once setting up the Other over against itself." She argued that people in small towns do this to strangers, natives of one country view natives of another country as Others, and members of one race invariably set up the members of another race as Others. Others are mysterious, and almost by definition need not be treated with the same consideration and respect that the members of one's own group must be accorded. Men set up women as Others, de Beauvoir observed, and because men have the political and social power, women come to see *themselves* as Others. They become alienated from themselves.

One final consequence of de Beauvoir's existentialist perspective is that she does not emphasize freedom of choice to the same extent that the English writers do. Not all choices are okay. From de Beauvoir's perspective, if all you do is stay home and have babies, then you might as well be a brood mare. After all, *all* animals reproduce; there is nothing distinctively human about simple reproduction. Distinctively human activity is the activity of the mind, of culture, and of self-transcendence.

In Selection 11.1, de Beauvoir elaborates on the problems with viewing women as Other and also reveals her existentialist perspective by arguing that women are nothing other than what they make of themselves.

SELECTION 11.1

The Second Sex

From Simone de Beauvoir

Few myths have been more advantageous to the ruling caste than the myth of woman: it justifies all privileges and even authorizes their abuse. Men need not bother themselves with alleviating the pains and the burdens that physiologically are women's lot, since these are "intended by Nature"; men use them as a pretext for increasing the misery of the feminine lot still further, for instance by refusing to grant to woman any right to sexual pleasure, by making her work like a beast of burden.

Of all these myths, none is more firmly anchored in masculine hearts than that of the feminine "mystery." It has numerous advantages. And first of all it permits an easy explanation of all that appears inexplicable; the man who "does not understand" a woman is happy to substitute an objective resistance for a subjective deficiency of mind; instead of admitting his ignorance, he perceives the presence of a "mystery" outside himself: an alibi, indeed that flatters laziness and vanity at once. A heart smitten with love thus avoids many disappointments: if the loved one's behavior is capricious, her remarks stupid, then the mystery serves to excuse it all. . . .

Surely woman is, in a sense, mysterious, "mysterious as all the world," according to Maeterlinck. Each is *subject* only for himself; each can grasp in immanence only himself, alone: from this point of view the other is always a mystery.

To men's eyes the opacity of the self-knowing self, of the *pour-soi*, is denser in the *other* who is feminine; men are unable to penetrate her special experience through any working of sympathy: they are condemned to ignorance of the quality of women's erotic pleasure, the discomfort of menstruation, and the pains of childbirth. The truth is that there is mystery on both sides: as the *other* who is of masculine sex, every man, also, has within him a presence, an inner self impenetrable to woman; she in turn is in ignorance of the male's erotic feeling. But in accordance with the universal rule I have stated, the categories in which men think of the world are established *from their point of view, as absolute*: they misconceive reciprocity, here as everywhere. A mystery for man, woman is considered to be mysterious in essence. . . .

The fact is that [woman] would be quite embarrassed to decide *what* she *is;* but this is not because the hidden truth is too vague to be discerned: it is because in this domain there is no truth. An existent *is* nothing other than what he does; the possible does not extend beyond the real, essence does not precede existence: in pure subjectivity, the human being *is not anything* . . . if one considers a woman in her immanent presence, her inward self, one can say absolutely nothing about her, she falls short of having any qualifications.

The publication of *The Second Sex* in 1949 created a furor, and de Beauvoir was startled at the vitriolic response that many critics had toward her work. But there was no turning back; the ideas were now rolling again, and over the next thirty years there would be a huge resurgence of feminist thought.

PROFILE / Gloria Steinem (1934–)

One of the best-known feminists of the late twentieth century is **Gloria Steinem.** Steinem was born into a working-class family in Toledo, Ohio, in 1934. Her parents were divorced when she was relatively young, and she spent much of her youth and adolescence in relative poverty, caring for her emotionally unstable mother. She graduated from Smith College in 1956 and began her career as a journalist. In the 1960s she became involved in the wom-en's movement and has remained one of feminism's most visible and recognizable activists. Probably her single most important accomplishment was helping to found the original *Ms.* magazine, which brought women's perspective and issues to the attention of main-stream America.

Steinem has written insightfully on many issues, including the differences between male and female college students. Young men, she noted, are often at their most radical and rebellious during their college years. Young women often start out quite conservative in their early twenties and become more radical and politically oriented only later on. Steinem suggests that this difference stems from the divergence in men's and women's lives as they get older.

In college, all students, male and female, are more or less equally poor, have equal living situations in dorms or shared housing, and are generally equally rewarded by their professors for hard work. Thus for many women college students, the feminist bat-tles all seem to be won; men and women are equal. Not until young women get out into the working world and are faced with (for example) the fact that male high school graduates still earn, on average, more than female college graduates, do the differences between men's and women's situations become more apparent. Furthermore, women come to recognize that children are still largely considered the mother's responsibility, so the problems of combining career and mother-hood rest more heavily on them than on men.

Finally, women in their late teens and early twenties are at the peak of their social power: still very sexually desirable, still full of potential as wives and childbear-ers. As women age, however, they lose this social power as their at-tractiveness fades, and this loss can be a very radicalizing experi-ence—particularly when their grey-haired male contemporaries are still being called distinguished, instead of haggard.

The end of the socially turbulent 1960s was a particularly fertile time for femi-nist theory. The five-year period from 1968 to 1973 saw the publication of seve-ral classic feminist texts, including Shulamith Firestone's *The Dialectic of Sex,* Robin Morgan's *Sisterhood Is Powerful,* and Kate Millett's *Sexual Politics.* **Millett's** (1934–) work was inspiring to many writers because she gave a systematic analysis of how women are oppressed by patriarchal institutions. She challenged those who suggested that women actually had lots of power to look at the avenues of power. She ran through the list: industry, the military, technology, academia, science, politics, and finance. How many of these avenues of power had women at the top ranks? There might be women bank tellers, but how many large banks had women presidents, or even vice presidents? How many women were in Congress? How many women were generals? How many women were university presidents—or even tenured professors? Millett directed attention not to personal relationships, but to the structure of society. She also looked at the socialization process and observed that the characteristics systematically encouraged in women—passivity, ignorance, docility, "virtue"—were those which made them convenient subordinates. Millett focused especially on the way the political, sociological, and psychological aspects of male-female relations were interrelated. If you have to take on a certain type of role in society, Millett maintained, it is to your advantage to develop the psychological characteristics that make that role easier. One of Millett's major contributions to the second wave of feminism was to make these links explicit. In Selection 11.2, Millett provides a statement of the thesis of her work.

SELECTION 11.2

Sexual Politics

From Kate Millett

A disinterested examination of our system of sexual relationship must point out that the situation between the sexes now, and throughout history, is a case of that phenomenon Max Weber defined as *herrschaft,* a relationship of dominance and subordinance. What goes largely unexamined, often even unacknowledged (yet is institutionalized nonetheless) in our social order, is the birthright priority whereby males rule females. Through this system a most ingenious form of "interior colonization" has been achieved. It is one which tends moreover to be sturdier than any form of segregation and more rigorous than class stratification, more uniform, certainly more enduring. However muted its present appearance may be, sexual dominion obtains nevertheless as perhaps the most pervasive ideology of our culture and provides its most fundamental concept of power.

This is so because our society, like all other historical civilizations, is a patriarchy. The fact is evident at once if one recalls that the military,

industry, technology, universities, science, political office, and finance—in short, every avenue of power within the society, including the coercive force of the police, is entirely in male hands. . . .

Sexual politics obtains consent through the "socialization" of both sexes to basic patriarchal politics with regard to temperament, role, and status. As to status, a pervasive assent to the prejudice of male superiority guarantees superior status in the male, inferior in the female. The first item, temperament, involves the formation of human personality along stereotyped lines of sex category ("masculine" and "feminine"), based on the needs and values of the dominant group and dictated by what its members cherish in themselves and find convenient in subordinates: aggression, intelligence, force and efficacy in the male; passivity, ignorance, docility, "virtue," and ineffectuality in the female. This is complemented by a second factor, sex role, which decrees a consonant and highly elaborate code of conduct, gesture, and attitude for each sex. In terms of activity, sex role assigns domestic service and attendance upon infants to the female, the rest of human achievement, interest and ambition to the male. . . . Were one to analyze the three categories one might designate status as the political component, role as the sociological, and temperament as the psychological—yet their interdependence is unquestionable and they form a chain.

Androgyny As an Alternative

Suppose you have become convinced that de Beauvoir was right, that people have an unfortunate tendency to set themselves up as Self versus Other, or Us versus Them. One solution that might seem hopeful is to eliminate the differences between groups of people as much as possible so that there would be less reason to feel that the members of a different group were Others. This is the logic of the "melting pot" ideal of race relations. If there were no more distinct races, but rather only one blended race, there would be no more basis for racism.

Well, if there were no obvious differences between the sexes, there would be no more basis for **sexism,** either. There is, of course, no possibility (in the near future) of *completely* eliminating the biological differences between the sexes; our reproductive plumbing will probably remain different. But as almost all feminists have observed, there are really very few other differences between men and women that are not socially constructed. Certainly it seems likely that men's and women's behaviors and interests are formed more by society than by biology. There is plenty of evidence for that claim from anthropology and biology. In some cultures women adorn their bodies, and in some cultures men do. In some cultures men are responsible for the finances, and in other cultures women are. For almost every behavior you can name, there has probably been at least one culture in which it was men's purview and another in which it was women's.

You may think that women are physically weaker than men, and they may be as a general rule, but think how different they might be if they were raised so as to develop their physical strength as a matter of course. After all, look at women athletes. Olympic athlete Jackie Joyner-Kersee and bodybuilder Cory Everson are hardly fragile little flowers. And if you compare women who do manual labor for a living with men who sit behind desks pushing pencils, you will hardly conclude that women are naturally weaker than men. A lot of that strength difference is culturally imposed, just like the more subtle social differences between men and women.

So, many feminists in the late 1960s and early 1970s concluded that perhaps **androgyny** (from *andros*, the Greek word for man, and *gyne*, the Greek word for woman) would be the ideal solution. No more setting up one group as the Other; instead, let's all be one homogeneous group. That way one set of people won't be able to abuse the other set; there will *be* no other set.

An androgynous culture could take several forms. First, you could have a culture in which everyone, girls and boys, was raised exactly the same: given the same education, the same games to play, the same challenges to face, the same rules to follow. You would probably end up with a culture where it wasn't always easy to see right away which people were female and which were male. There would be no sex roles at all; no concept of masculine and feminine. There would only be one standard for everyone.

Or you might have a culture in which there were concepts of masculine and feminine, but they were not always matched directly with males and females. So you could have "feminine" men and "masculine" women. For such a society to work and really be free, there would have to be no social stigma attached to being a "masculine" woman or a "feminine" man. All choices would be equally acceptable. Nobody would think anything about it. A very free world, indeed.

The first possible society, called *monoandrogyny,* is endorsed by **Ann Ferguson** (1938–), a socialist feminist philosopher at the University of Massachusetts–Amherst. Ferguson argues that because men and women are socially unequal, there can be no true love between them. Ideal love is the love between equals. Ferguson also suggests that because of this lack of ideal love, we are all unable to develop fully as human beings. In Selection 11.3, she argues that a truly androgynous society would allow us all to develop fully as human beings.

SELECTION 11.3

"Androgyny as an Ideal for Human Development"

From Ann Ferguson

What would an androgynous personality be like? My model for the ideal androgynous person comes from the concept of human potential developed by Marx in *Economic and Philosophical Manuscripts.* Marx's idea is that human beings have a need (or a potential) for free, creative, productive activity which allows them to control their lives in a situation of cooperation with others. Both men and women need to be equally active and independent; with an equal sense of control over their lives; equal opportunity for creative, productive activity; and a sense of meaningful involvement in the community.

Androgynous women would be just as assertive as men about their own needs in a love relationship: productive activity outside the home, the right to private time, and the freedom to form other intimate personal and sexual relationships. I maintain that being active and assertive—traits now associated with being "masculine"—are positive traits that all people need to develop. Many feminists are suspicious of the idea of self-assertion because it is associated with the traits of aggression and competitiveness. However, there is no inevitability to this connection: it results from the structural features of competitive, hierarchical economic systems, of which our own (monopoly capitalism) is one example. In principle, given the appropriate social structure, there is no reason why a self-assertive person cannot also be nurturant and cooperative.

Androgynous men would be more sensitive and aware of emotions than sex-role stereotyped "masculine" men are today. They would be more concerned with the feelings of all people, including women and children, and aware of conflicts of interests. Being sensitive to human emotions is necessary to an effective care and concern for others. Such sensitivity is now thought of as a "motherly," "feminine," or "maternal" instinct, but in fact it is a role and skill learned by women, and it can equally well be learned by men. . . .

Another important problem with a non-androgynous love relationship is that it limits the development of mutual understanding. In general, it seems true that the more levels people can relate on, the deeper and more intimate their relationship is. The more experiences and activities they share, the greater their companionship and meaning to each other. And this is true for emotional experiences. Without mutual understanding of the complex of emotions involved in an ongoing love relationship, communication and growth on that level are blocked for both people. . . .

As for love relationships, with the elimination of sex roles and the disappearance, in an overpopulated world, of any biological need for sex to be associated with procreation, there would be no reason why such a society could not transcend sexual gender. It would no longer matter what biological sex individuals had. Love relationships, and the sexual relationships developing out of them, would be based on the individual meshing-together of androgynous human beings.

Joyce Trebilcot (1933–), a feminist philosopher at Washington University in St. Louis, argues for the second type of androgynous society discussed earlier. She suggests that we need not eliminate the categories of "masculine" and "feminine." Instead, we should just let individuals choose which type of role they wish to adopt. She calls this type of society *P*, for "polyandrogyny," and contrasts it with hypothetical society *M*, for "monoandrogyny," the type of society Ferguson was arguing for. In this selection Trebilcot argues that society *P* is better than society *M* because *P* allows individuals greater freedom of choice; but she ends by suggesting that if *M* is really the better society, then people will probably eventually freely choose it.

SELECTION 11.4

"Two Forms of Androgynism"

From Joyce Trebilcot

Let us consider, then, which version of androgynism is preferable for a hypothetical future society in which femininity and masculinity are no longer normatively associated with sex.

The major argument in favor of *P* is, of course, that because it stipulates a variety of acceptable gender alternatives it provides greater gender freedom than *M*. Now, freedom is a very high priority value, so arguments for *M* must be strong indeed. Let us consider, then, two arguments used to support *M* over *P*—one psychological, one ethical. . . .

I turn now to [the ethical] argument for *M*, one which claims that androgyny has universal

Liberal Feminism and Radical Feminism

Feminism comes in lots of varieties: socialist, psychoanalytic, postmodern, radical, and liberal. These last two are the kinds you have probably come across the most often when reading the papers and popular magazines. Learning the differences between the two can help you make sense of the next editorial you read on women's issues.

Liberal feminism has its roots in some very traditional American notions: freedom of choice and equality of opportunity. Liberal feminists insist that women can do everything men do if only they are given a fair chance. Liberal feminists do not generally ask whether the things men are doing are really *worth* doing. Nor do they challenge those women who are living out traditional roles. Their focus is on making sure there is freedom and opportunity for those who *don't* want to live out traditional roles. Liberal feminists tend to focus on changing restrictive laws and eliminating formal barriers to women's advancement.

Radical feminists think the problems run very deep, and the solutions must cut deep too. They argue that entrenched social attitudes do as much or more harm than restrictive laws. In order to change social attitudes so women are really taken seriously, they think drastic steps must be taken. In particular, they believe that reducing women to their sexuality is the worst thing the culture does; it fosters rape, violence, and general contempt for women. Thus they target cultural phenomena such as pornography, advertising, and music videos which present women as nothing but sexual toys. Liberal feminists object that protesting these phenomena is too much like censorship, and hence contrary to freedom. Radical feminists reply that until women are safe from violence in the street and in their own homes, they will never truly be free.

---

value. This argument supports *M* not, as the argument from anxiety does, because *M* prescribes some norm or other, but rather because of the content of the norm. The argument holds that both traditional genders include qualities that have human value, qualities that it would be good for everyone to have. Among the elements of femininity, candidates for universal value are openness and responsiveness to needs and feeling, and being gentle, tender, intuitive, sensitive, expressive, considerate, cooperative, compassionate. Masculine qualities appealed to in this connection include being logical, rational, objective, efficient, responsible, independent, courageous. It is claimed, then, that there are some aspects of both genders (not necessarily all or only the ones I have mentioned) which are desirable for everyone, which we should value both in ourselves and in one another. But if there are aspects of femininity and masculinity which are valuable in this way—which are, as we might call them, virtues—they are *human* virtues, and are desirable for everyone. . . . Hence, the argument concludes, the world envisioned by *M*, in which everyone or nearly everyone is both feminine and masculine, is one in which life for everyone is more rewarding than the world advocated by *P*, in which some people are of only one gender; therefore we should undertake to bring about *M*.

The argument claims, then, that both genders embody traits that it would be valuable for everyone to have. But how is this claim to be tested? Let us adopt the view that to say that something is valuable for everyone is, roughly, to say that if everyone were unbiased, well-informed, and thinking and feeling clearly, everyone would, in fact, value it. As things are now, it is difficult or impossible to predict what everyone would value under such conditions.

But there is an alternative. We can seek to establish conditions in which people do make unbiased, informed, etc., choices, and see whether they then value both feminine and masculine traits.

This reminds us, of course, of the program of P. P does not guarantee clear thought and emotional sensitivity, but it does propose an environment in which people are informed about all gender options and are unbiased with respect to them. If, in this context, all or most people, when they are thinking clearly, etc., tend to prefer, for themselves and for others, both feminine and masculine virtues, we will have evidence to support the claim that androgyny has universal value. (In this case, P is likely to change into M.) On the other hand, if "pure" gender is preferred by many, we should be skeptical of the claim that androgyny has universal value. (In this case we should probably seek to preserve P.) It appears, then, that in order to discover whether M is preferable to P, we should seek to bring about P.

Problems with Androgyny As an Ideal

Though the logic behind the push for androgyny seemed reasonable, after a while some feminist theorists began to see that it had some deep conceptual problems. It was all very well to say that there were good feminine qualities and good masculine qualities and that everybody should have some of each; but what if those qualities were really direct opposites? It would then be impossible to combine the two sets of qualities because they would simply cancel each other out. If the ideal for one set of people is to be rational, calm, and silent, and the ideal for the other set is to be emotional and expressive, it is difficult to see how those qualities could all be combined to make one whole, balanced human. Feminist philosopher Mary Daly argued that androgyny as an ideal would not work because it would be like "two distorted halves of a human being stuck together—something like John Wayne and Brigitte Bardot scotch-taped together—as if two distorted 'halves' could make a whole." After all, one cannot expect to combine the concept of "master" and the concept of "slave" and get the concept of a free person. The original concepts are both too warped to be usable. We must completely transcend those original categories and start over from scratch.

More evidence for the view that the categories of "masculine" and "feminine" were too broken ever to be fixed came both from the social sciences and from literature and philosophy. At the beginning of the 1970s, it was often remarked that sex roles inhibited everyone, male and female alike. Men were out of touch with their feelings and were unable to cry or show affection publicly. But soon people began to realize that masculine behavior, though limiting, limited men *into* the positions of power that Kate Millett listed in the selection from *Sexual Politics*. If you are unable to cry and show emotion, by the standards of our culture, that makes you a very good candidate for being a CEO or high-level politician, because

African-American Women and the Economy

Different groups of women see their lives improve at different rates. Though we are making slow progress toward closing the earnings gap between all men and all women, African-American women are still at a significant disadvantage in today's workplace. According to the most recent government data, median income for an African-American woman employed year-round, full-time was $17,389 in 1989—noticeably below the national average. Of all employed African-American women, 33 percent work as retail salespeople, nursing aides, cashiers, cooks, elementary school teachers, janitors, and secretaries. Less than 1 percent are in the category of "skilled labor."

Currently, the most lucrative jobs for women include lawyer; physician; engineer; computer systems analyst; scientist; college professor; manager in marketing, advertising, and public relations; and registered nurse. Only 2.5 percent of total persons in these occupations were African-American, and only 6.6 percent of all women in these fields were African-American women. These numbers are discouraging given that the civil rights movement is about thirty years old now.

we wouldn't want either individual to fall apart emotionally at a crucial moment. Of course, being unemotional isn't a *sufficient* condition for being a CEO, but it is a *necessary* one. Similarly, being ambitious and competitive—traits generally valued in men—limits them from settling down to a nurturant family role; but it also "limits" them into a better economic position. Some people argue that it is a greater benefit to be able to be expressive and nurturing than to be able to earn in the six figures. It certainly isn't bad to be expressive and nurturing, but ask yourself this: would you rather be expressive and emotional while living just above the poverty line? Or would you rather be a little more closed off emotionally and earn a comfortable living? Those are too often the real alternatives that face men and women today.

Marilyn Frye (1941–) argues that the whole system of gender is really one of power. Author of several books on feminism and professor of philosophy at Michigan State University, Frye implies that masculinity is about dominance, and femininity is about subordination. She notes that we go to a great deal of trouble to keep the sexes distinct; even products that have no inherent differences—like shampoos, deodorants, and razor blades—are packaged differently for men and women. Men and women talk, move, and sit differently from each other. In a myriad of unnecessary details, men and women are trained to keep themselves distinct from each other. This whole process contributes to the dominance/subordination dynamic, Frye argues.

For one group to oppress another, Frye reasons, there must be (at least) two distinct groups. The more differences between the members of one group and the members of the other group, the better, because then it will seem more rational to treat the two groups differently. So, Frye argues, those thousands of ways in which artificial differences between women and men are reinforced are all little acts of sexism. It may seem harmless to have men's colognes and women's colognes, Secret

I See by Your Outfit That You Are a Feminist

Ever since feminism first got media attention in the 1960s, there's been lots of fuss over the way women who are feminists dress. Many people criticize feminists for looking sloppy and unfeminine. What do clothes have to do with politics, anyhow?

Actually, most political (as well as social) groups eventually develop a general style of dress that helps them form a sense of community and solidarity. But for feminism, the issue goes deeper. High heels, short skirts, fragile fabrics, and tight-fitting jeans literally hobble women; they keep women more confined and uncomfortable than do the styles men wear. Marilyn Frye comments, "Ladies' clothing is generally restrictive, binding, burdening and frail; it threatens to fall apart and/or to uncover something that is supposed to be covered if you bend, reach, kick, punch, or run." And because physical assault is an all-too-real possibility for most women, being unable to defend yourself is a genuine problem.

British feminist Janet Radcliffe Richards once replied to this line of argument this way: "What feminism really needs is exactly the opposite: women who are very desirable to men, but who will have nothing to do with any man who does not treat them properly." What response do you think Frye might make?

and Mitchum deodorants, and so on; but every time we reinforce the view that men and women are inherently different, we also reinforce the notion that they must inevitably be treated differently. Anything that contributes to the appearance of extreme natural dimorphism also contributes to the practice of male dominance and female subordination.

But there is a double bind here, which particularly harms women. If they are traditionally feminine, then they are participating in social practices that limit them to home and hearth, or to subordinate job positions. But if they act traditionally male, and behave aggressively and competitively, they are often socially "punished," called dykes or ballbreakers, and excluded from the kind of socially approved family life that competitive men freely engage in. So they are damned if they do behave subordinately, and damned if they don't. In Selection 11.5, Frye argues for her thesis that sexism is best defined as the cultural structures that keep men dominant and women subordinate.

SELECTION 11.5

"Sexism"

From Marilyn Frye

The forces which make us mark and announce sexes are among the forces which constitute the oppression of women, and they are central and essential to the maintenance of that system.

Oppression is a system of interrelated barriers and forces which reduce, immobilize and mold people who belong to a certain group, and effect their subordination to another group (individually to individuals of the other group, and as a group, to that group). Such a system could not exist were not the groups, the categories of persons, well defined. Logically, it presupposes that there are two distinct categories. Practically, they must be not only distinct but relatively easily identifiable; the barriers and forces could not be suitably located and applied if there were often much doubt as to which individuals were to be contained and reduced, which were to dominate.

It is extremely costly to subordinate a large group of people simply by applications of material force, as is indicated by the costs of maximum security prisons and of military suppression of nationalist movements. For subordination to be permanent and cost effective, it is necessary to create conditions such that the subordinated group acquiesces to some extent in the subordination. Probably one of the most efficient ways to secure acquiescence is to convince the people that their subordination is inevitable. The mech-

anisms by which the subordinate and dominant categories are defined can contribute greatly to popular belief in the inevitability of the dominance/subordination structure.

For efficient subordination, what's wanted is that the structure not appear to be a cultural artifact kept in place by human decision or custom, but that it appear *natural*—that it appear to be a quite direct consequence of facts about the beast which are beyond the scope of human manipulation or revision. . . .

That we are trained to behave so differently as women and as men, and to behave so differently toward women and toward men, itself contributes mightily to the appearance of extreme natural dimorphism, but also, the *ways* we act as women and as men and the *ways* we act toward women and toward men, mold our bodies and our minds to the shapes of subordination and dominance. We do become what we practice being.

Feminist Topics

Now that you have seen a little bit about the historical development of the answers to the questions we started with—Why are men and women so different? What can be done to make their lives and circumstances more equal?—let's turn to some of the particular topics that contemporary feminists have addressed in the past ten or fifteen years.

Sexism and Language

The ways language has contributed to women's lower social status are quite varied. Many terms in the language which are supposed to be gender-neutral are not; *man,* for example, is supposed to serve double duty, referring both to humanity as a whole and male human beings. Similarly, *he* is the pronoun used both when we know that the person being referred to is male and when we do not know the gender of the individual. This really isn't very logical; either there should be one pronoun to refer to everybody, or there should be three pronouns: male, female, and as-yet-undetermined. Feminist theorists have argued that by making words like *man* and *he* serve both as gender-specific and gender-neutral terms, the net effect is to "erase" women from our conversational landscape. The actual psychology of human beings is such that when we hear *he,* we think "male," even if that is not the speaker's intention. **Janice Moulton,** a philosophy professor at Smith College who writes about philosophy of language (among other things), gives a good example of this tendency to hear *man* and *he* as male even when the original use of the term was gender-neutral. She asks us to consider the familiar syllogism

> All men are mortal.
>
> Socrates is a man.
>
> Therefore, Socrates is mortal.

Now substitute the name "Sophia" for "Socrates". Clearly, "men" in the first line is supposed to be gender-neutral; it is supposed to mean "all members of the human species." Yet when the name Sophia is substituted, the second term of the syllogism seems glaringly false. Thus, Moulton argues, to say we have two meanings for "man," one gender-neutral and one gender-specific, and we can always keep them clear and separate really doesn't hold water. Though we might like to believe there are two clearly differentiated uses of *man* and *he,* in practice we hardly make that distinction at all. This point is all the clearer when we realize that generations of logic teachers have taught that syllogism without ever noticing that it is invalid because the "men" in the first line and the "man" in the second line have different meanings.

Sometimes the causality seems to flow the other way. Many historians and anthropologists have noted that anything associated with women tends to get devalued over time. Occupations associated with women tend to be paid less and have lower status than those associated with men. This holds true across cultures even when the occupation is objectively the same; for instance, in cultures where the women build the homes, that occupation is looked down on, but in our own culture being a contractor is a perfectly respectable thing to do, and often quite well paid.

The same phenomenon holds true of language. Words associated with women come to have lower status and can even degenerate into insults. Many slang expressions and metaphors are evidence of this. These metaphors and slang expressions are taken to be evidence of underlying cultural attitudes toward women. Sometimes words start out with perfectly legitimate, nonderogatory literal meanings and, through their association with women, come to have derogatory and insulting slang meanings. Consider the words *queen, dame, madam, mistress, hussy* (which originally meant *housewife*), or *spinster.* None of the male equivalents of those words has suffered the same kind of devaluation. Through slang, women are also unflatteringly allied to animals, as in *vixen, bitch, pussy, biddy,* and *cow.* And finally, the words we use to describe sexual intercourse are often extremely violent—and the violence is metaphorically directed toward women, not men. The word *fuck* has *strike* as its etymological ancestor; *ream* and *drill* don't require any arcane linguistic background to understand. Language use and attitudes are thought to influence one another; hence, if we make an effort not to use such

Women and Violence

Here are some of the findings of the House of Representatives Select Committee on Children, Youth, and Families:
- In 1984, 2.3 million violent crimes (rape, assault, and robbery) were committed against women over the age of twelve.
- In 1986, 57 percent of violent crimes committed against women were committed by nonstrangers, compared with 37 percent of violent crimes committed against men.
- Seventy-seven percent of the victims of violent crimes committed by relatives are women. Seventy percent of victims of violent crimes committed by strangers are men. Crimes committed by relatives are more likely to involve attacks and injury and are more likely to require medical attention than are crimes committed by strangers.

Of the women in a San Francisco study who were currently or formerly married, 21 percent reported that they were subjected to physical violence by a husband.

One in eight women students reported experiences within the previous twelve months that met legal definitions of rape, according to an extensive three-year survey. Eighty-four percent of college students who were victims of completed rapes knew their assailant, and two-thirds of them were assaulted by a date.

Here are some miscellaneous assertions from the 1994 edition of *A Matter of Fact:*
- Domestic violence accounts for 25 percent of all reported crime in London (Margaret Henry, writing in "Domestic Violence: The Original Vicious Cycle").
- Battering is the single major cause of injury to women—more than auto accidents, muggings, and rape combined ... 25 percent of women who commit suicide are victims of family violence (Congresswoman Constance Morella of Maryland, in the 1993 *Congressional Record*).
- From 22 to 35 percent of women in hospital emergency rooms and from 60 to 70 percent of women in hospital mental health units are there because of symptoms related to ongoing abuse ... 15 to 25 percent of all pregnant women are beaten, and 25 to 45 percent of all battered women are beaten during pregnancy (Congresswoman Constance Morella of Maryland, in the 1993 *Congressional Record*).

violent metaphors, perhaps the attitudes of violence will decrease a little as well. But for the present it seems painfully clear that our language at least partly reflects certain hostile dispositions. In Selection 11.6, **Stephanie Ross** (1949–), who writes on aesthetics, art criticism, and feminism, argues that *screw* is a usefully representative metaphor which tells us more than we want to know about certain cultural attitudes toward women.

SELECTION 11.6

"How Words Hurt: Attitude, Metaphor, and Oppression"

From Stephanie Ross

Return to [the] two examples, "fuck" and "screw." We agree that both these words are insulting and that both are classified as impolite. In addition, I have argued that "fuck" does not offend women because of its etymological ties to "ficken," "fustis," and "buc." Most speakers are unaware of these ties. They find the term offensive because they know it is classed as offensive by their fellow speakers. I believe the offensiveness of "screw" can be explained quite differently, and this is shown even in [Barbara] Lawrence's* summary reference to its "revealing fusion of a mechanical or painful action with an obviously denigrated object." The difference here is that most of us are aware of these aspects of screws. Even if we haven't given much thought to screwing as a method of fastening (as opposed to nailing or gluing) we can immediately acknowledge the correctness of Lawrence's claims. A screw is hard and sharp; wood by contrast is soft and yielding; force is applied to make a screw penetrate wood; a screw can be unscrewed and reused but wood—wherever a screw has been embedded in it—is destroyed forever. Once we marshall these everyday facts about screws and screwing, their ramifications become clear. When the verb *to screw* is used to describe sexual intercourse, it carries with it images of dominance and destruction. The woman's role in intercourse is similar to that of wood destroyed by the screw which enters it. Additional echoes are carried by a fur-

---

*Contemporary feminist writer; author of "Four-Letter Words *Can* Hurt You."

ther use of the verb *to screw* in financial contexts. To screw someone in this sense is to wring her dry, to practice extortion.

Metaphor is the device at work here. The use of the verb *to screw* to describe sexual intercourse invites us to view this latter activity in terms drawn from carpentry and mechanics. As noted above, many facts about screws and screwing are applicable to the new realm as well. And this is just what we should expect of an apt metaphor. But "screwing" is not a fresh, new label for intercourse. This use of the term is accepted, though deemed coarse and impolite. Thus we are dealing here with a dead metaphor—an established use of the word "screw" which has additional depth and resonance because it associates the two realms of sex and mechanics. The central claim I want to make . . . is that metaphors of this sort are our primary vehicles for conveying attitudes. The offensiveness of the verb *to screw* is rooted in the attitude it conveys towards the female role in intercourse, and this attitude can be specified by attending to the details of the metaphor. None of the claims I make are tied to any one theory of metaphor. While there is much debate about the nature of metaphorical truth, the paraphrasability of metaphors, and so on, I shall skirt these issues. I trust that my positive claims about metaphor will apply to any reasonable account of that trope.

Pornography

All along you have been reading passages from feminist writers who suggest, both directly and indirectly, that the relations between men and women are built on the model of domination and subordination. Of course sexuality is one of the important features of the relationships between men and women. It should not surprise you, then, to learn that many feminist critics maintain that our current practices of heterosexual sex are also structured by dominance and subordination. In particular, these critics focus on the issue of pornography. Pornography, they argue, both encapsulates and reinforces all the worst aspects of heterosexual sex. It tends to objectify women; that is, it tends to reduce women to nothing other than their sexuality and suggests that their sexuality is the only important thing about them. To view someone as an object is to treat her as if she had no ends or goals of her own. Thus, they suggest, pornography reinforces certain other problems in the culture, notably rape and sexual harassment. If we grow up in a culture in which women are characteristically viewed as being reducible to their sexuality, it is hard to see why we should not grope them at work or even rape them on dates, since we are not taught to emphasize that women have feelings and plans and purposes—purposes which might not include having sex right that instant. Objectification is always a moral problem because objects are the opposite of persons. Persons must be treated respectfully, but objects have no feelings or ideas; they are there to be used.

But an even more significant (though related) problem with pornography is the rapidly increasing level of violence present even in the so-called "mainstream" magazines and movies; pick up any issue of *Penthouse,* and you will probably be quite surprised to see the number of violent stories and photo spreads. This fact has led some theorists to define pornography as "any use of the media which equates sex and violence." Contemporary women's rights advocates Andrea Dworkin and Catharine MacKinnon's definition of pornography includes reference to "women . . . presented as sexual objects who enjoy pain and humiliation . . . women . . . presented in scenarios of degradation, injury, torture, shown as filthy or inferior, bleeding, bruised, or hurt in a context that makes these conditions sexual." Violence and humiliation are the instruments of oppression and domination. Thus the objection to pornography is that it endorses and reinforces the use of violence and humiliation in the structuring of the relations between the sexes and interferes with true freedom and equality in the relations (sexual and otherwise) between men and women.

In Selection 11.7, **Beverly LaBelle** takes a standard definition of propaganda and argues that pornography is propaganda in the war against women.

SELECTION 11.7

"The Propaganda of Misogyny"   **From Beverly LaBelle**

In his book *Techniques of Persuasion,* J. A. C. Brown lists eight techniques which are universally employed in propaganda campaigns. They are:

1. Use of stereotypes
2. Name substitution
3. Selection
4. Lying
5. Repetition
6. Assertion
7. Pinpointing the enemy
8. Appeal to authority

We will demonstrate that pornography makes extensive use of all of them.

The first technique is the use of *stereotypes* to create a fixed, unfavorable idea of the chosen

Pornography and the Law

The work of University of Michigan law professor Catharine MacKinnon excites tremendous anger in many people, especially those who have not read it. MacKinnon's research extends over a wide variety of topics of interest to feminists; her most well-known work concerns violent pornography: Together with Andrea Dworkin, she authored legislation in Minneapolis and Indianapolis to provide civil remedies for women who could prove they had been injured by pornography. The idea of the legislation was (roughly) to require producers of pornography to meet the kind of strict products liability that manufacturers of cars or hairspray have to meet. The legislation was instantly (misleadingly) branded "censorship," and any reasonable discussion of the merits and demerits of the law was largely swallowed up in the panic generated whenever the word "censorship" is invoked.

scapegoat group. The images of human beings in pornography are blatant examples of stereotyping. Men and women are portrayed as diametrical opposites, as different species, very often as enemies. Women are invariably portrayed as carnal, submissive, promiscuous, whore-victims, perennially and repeatedly subdued and conquered by the eternally worshipped phallus. Their only needed credentials are bare breasts and exposed genitalia. The color of their skin or hair is varied merely to provide an illusion of variety. The personality of the pornographic model is never well developed in any of the X-rated books or films because her mind is completely unimportant. In short, pornography propagates a view of women as nothing but "tits and ass"—silly creatures who exist only to be fucked, sexually used, and forgotten.

The second technique, *name substitution,* helps create a biased reaction to the "victimized" group by referring to them with pejorative terms such as "nigger," "kike," "commie," etc. These terms, invented especially for the group in question, allow people to remove them from the context of "human being" and place them in a sub-human category. Pornography rarely uses anything but derogatory words to describe women and women's sexuality. "Cunt," "scumbag," "twat," "hot tube," "tramp," etc., are just a tiny sampling of the unpleasant terms routinely used in pornography to define women.

Technique number three is *selection,* a process whereby only certain facts are presented to the public. These facts are always those which are favorable to the propagandist and unfavorable to his opponent. Two major forms of *selection* are noticeable in pornography: First, pornographers present only one vision of women's sexuality to their readers and viewers. This vision, contrary to the findings of studies on women's sexuality by Shere Hite and other researchers, portrays women as sexually subservient to men, turned on by every sexual move they make. A good example is the common theme of the rape victim who finds that she "loves it" once she relaxes and allows herself to "enjoy the experience." Real rapes, of course, are physically and emotionally destructive, as most research and many interviews reveal. The second major form of the *selection* technique used by pornographers is in their editorial content. Pornographers (and apologists for pornography) exclusively report the supposedly "good" effects of the pornography and refuse to admit or to print the possible adverse consequences that unrestrained access to such material may engender.

Downright lying is the fourth technique. It requires little explanation to realize that pornography is nothing but a downright lie about women. An example:

"Columbine Cuts Up," a feature in a recent issue of *Chic* magazine, published by Larry Flynt. The photo essay portrays a young blond woman thrusting a large kitchen knife into her vagina. Blood is spurting from the wounds, but the look on her face is one of sexual ecstasy, almost glee. Obviously any real woman who had hurt herself like this would be in severe pain—she would not be smiling.

Repetition is a necessary technique because it helps the public become accustomed to whatever ideas the propagandist is attempting to inculcate. The more a concept is reiterated, the more persuasive and influential it becomes. As Adolf Hitler declared in *Mein Kampf,* only after the simplest ideas are repeated thousands of times will the masses finally remember them. People begin to accept such ideas as the truth because they are pervasive. Slogans and maxims are often used advantageously in this particular technique, e.g., "Heil Hitler," American television advertising jingles, the phrase "all women secretly want to be raped," etc. Pornography is one of the most boringly repetitious types of media. A few seduction plots are endlessly repeated, with minor variations added for spice and stimulation: The old myth that women are inferior and that the male should do whatever he pleases with these easily available "pieces of meat" forms the main theme. . . .

Assertion is similar to the selection technique, but it differs in that it entails not merely pointing out the pertinent idea but also boldly asserting and promoting the idea. Pornography is by its very nature an aggressively assertive philosophy. Its producers proclaim its ideas loudly and forcefully in two main ways. The first is by the inescapable, lurid presence of pornography everywhere in our society (large, gaudy posters on X-rated theaters, and magazines flaunting naked women in drugstores, in corner stores, and even in public buildings where the business of government is carried on). The second is the pornogra-

phers' campaign to silence their opponents by invoking the First Amendment and thereby securing for themselves the right to peddle their anti-women ideas everywhere in the name of free speech.

The seventh technique, *pinpointing the enemy,* is self-explanatory. An enemy or scapegoat is of prime importance in any propaganda campaign because it serves to direct aggression away from the propagandist and to strengthen feelings of solidarity within the group that the propagandist is seeking to influence. Hatred is one of the most powerful unifying emotions, since it permits feelings which are usually suppressed to be brought to the surface and expressed stridently. Women are the enemy in pornography—they are the group to be subdued and vanquished. A good example of this targeting of women is *Hustler* magazine's continued attack on major feminist thinkers in the country. Gloria Steinem, Susan Brownmiller, Shere Hite, and other women have repeatedly been subject to ridicule, name-calling, and slander.

The last technique, *appeal to authority,* is a vital step in proving that the ideas of the propaganda are respectable and intelligent. This approach often incorporates references to the past, testimonials from famous people, and quotations from so-called "experts." Pornography uses all these methods to justify its content. First, there is the underlying assumption that sex as portrayed in pornography is the natural, time-proven way of obtaining satisfaction. "The best propaganda is that which works invisibly, penetrates the whole of life without the public having any knowledge at all of the propagandist initiative," said Joseph Goebbels. Second, famous people are often featured in the more serious articles in soft-core magazines, implicitly expressing their support for the "liberating joys" of pornography. The *Playboy* interview has played a major role in this appeal to authority. . . . Third, psychological and sociological studies describing the beneficial effects of pornography are often quoted as "proof" that such publications are not harmful. Pornography successfully wraps a cloak of respectability around itself via these techniques.

Concealed under its facade of sexually liberating entertainment, pornography propagates the philosophy of male supremacy. It establishes ideologically that women exist solely for the sexual gratification of men. Because such de-humanized ideas about women are so widely accepted, pornography is often not recognized as a system of propaganda designed to exploit and misrepresent the sexual differences between men and women. Beneath the surface of badly written prose and lurid pictures lie millennia of institutionalized female bondage.

Feminist Ethics

Moral theory is another area which has been recently reconceptualized by feminist theory. **Carol Gilligan,** a psychologist specializing in moral development, noticed that many of the studies on children's moral development were actually studies about *boys'* moral development. The original research had been done in boys' schools and universities, and then the research had been assumed to fit the case of little girls and young women as well. Gilligan argued that this was not true; little girls develop differently from little boys, and their moral intuitions and perspectives are different as well. Furthermore, Gilligan argued, little girls who did not fit the mold set by the research on little boys were being judged to be inadequate and immature. Gilligan suggested that much more attention had to be paid to the girls' development and that we should be careful not to think of girls as inadequate or defective just because they are not like little boys. Gilligan argued that when we look at the way girls reason about ethical dilemmas, we will find that they put more emphasis on *care* and on the preservation of personal relationships; issues of abstract justice and rights take a back seat in their moral deliberation. Girls will also put more weight than boys do on knowing all the details of the dilemma before they render any judgment. Context and care for others are central features in women's moral reasoning.

Much of Gilligan's research was grounded in the insights of psychoanalyst **Nancy Chodorow.** Chodorow argued that our contemporary child-rearing practices foster a strong need for connectedness in little girls and for separation and autonomy in little boys. Because mothers are the first people children get attached to and identify with, girls and boys must then go through substantially different processes in establishing their gender identities: the girls can continue to perceive themselves as continuous with their mothers, but the boys must make a shift to adopt the male gender identity.

Little girls and little boys thus learn very different lessons about how to relate to the world and others in it. Girls develop their sense of themselves as women by means of "personal identification" with their mothers. Personal identification consists in "diffuse identification with someone else's general personality, behavioral traits, values, and attitudes." Boys, however, develop their identities by means of "positional identification": "Positional identification, consists, by contrast, in

Shulamith Firestone: Biology and Oppression

Almost all the writers discussed in this chapter take it for granted that women's subordinate status is a social and political problem, not a biological one. Almost all feminists think that the biological differences between men and women, though real, are not in themselves anywhere near sufficient to explain the extremely different social roles men and women play. Conservative thinkers such as Freud, who argued that anatomy is destiny, are routinely dismissed by contemporary feminists and other social philosophers.

One exception to this rule was

Shulamith Firestone. In the early 1970s, she argued that women's childbearing was at the root of their social oppression. Thus she might be categorized as a *biological determinist*. She argued that reproductive technology was the route to women's freedom; developments which liberated women from having to bear and nurse children would free them to participate as equals in the new society.

Firestone was not an unguarded optimist, though. She argued that reproductive technology could be used against women as well as for them. Therefore, it

would be necessary for women to seize control of the new fertility technology to make sure it was put to legitimate uses. Firestone suggested that if babies were born through artificial reproduction, they would be born to both sexes equally and that "the tyranny of the biological family would be broken."

You might not like her suggestions, but can you come up with good reasons for discounting them? Remember that it is important to have good reasons for your views. Try to avoid appeals to simple prejudice.

identification with specific aspects of another's role." In other words, boys learn that to be a man means to be away at work, whereas girls learn that to be a woman means to be just like mommy in her personality, values, etc.

Chodorow argued that this split in gender development has resulted in a great deal of grief for the culture: boys wind up not just isolated and separate but positively misogynous because of their efforts to establish themselves as "not-mom." Girls, on the other hand, often suffer because they do not extricate themselves sufficiently from others in their milieu and wind up unable to distinguish their own needs from those of others and hence are more easily subject to exploitation. Chodorow concluded that these problems could be diminished if men and women took equal responsibility for child rearing and work outside the home, thereby allowing both boys and girls to participate in both positional and personal identification. Presumably, little girls would become more autonomous, and little boys would become more "connected" and less misogynous.

One writer who has picked up on these themes and gone some way toward developing a moral theory in response to them is **Sara Ruddick** (1935–). In Selection 11.8, Ruddick first discusses the concerns and perspectives of mothers in some patriarchal cultures and then discusses how those concerns and perspectives can structure our moral responses to the world. Ruddick calls this approach to the world "maternal thinking."

The Strategy of Separatism

For women, it's not a particularly safe world. In school and the workplace, women are subject to sexual harassment. In her lifetime, a woman has a one in three chance of being raped; she has a one in four chance of being beaten in her own home by a male relative. Just walking down the street can be challenging if you have to walk past a group of construction workers. And, because women still generally only make fifty-nine cents for every dollar a man makes, it's not always all that easy to just walk away from a bad situation.

Suppose that these statistics applied not to women, but to members of some ethnic or racial group. Suppose one in four was beaten by members of the white majority or one in three was raped by the dominant group. Wouldn't it seem to make sense for them to form their own communities, to stay away from a world of such brutality? As Oprah has said many times, "If he hits you, it means he doesn't like you." Many feminists have been angered by the ideology that tells women to stay with people who obviously don't like them—to nurture those people and provide homes for them rather than running for their lives.

Separatism is a strategy for allowing women to take care of themselves and each other. Forming a separate women's community provides warmth and safety for women and allows them to regain their strength and really get to know each other. Why not put your energy into getting to know and to nurture the people who really understand your experiences and who, like you, are brought up to be caring? Who knows. It could ultimately change the world.

SELECTION 11.8

"Maternal Thinking"

From Sara Ruddick

Maternal practice responds to the historical reality of a biological child in a particular social world. The agents of maternal practice, acting in response to the demands of their children, acquire a conceptual scheme—a vocabulary and logic of connections—through which they order and express the facts and values of their practice. In judgments and self-reflection, they refine and concretize this scheme. Intellectual activities are distinguishable but not separable from disciplines of feeling. There is a unity of reflection, judgment, and emotion. This unity I call "maternal thinking." Although I will not digress to argue the point here, it is important that maternal thinking is no more interest-governed, no more emotional, and no more relative to any particular reality (the growing child) than the thinking that arises from scientific, religious, or any other practice.

The demands of children and the interests in meeting those demands are always and only expressed by people in particular cultures and classes of their culture, living in specific geographical, technological, and historical settings. Some features of the mothering experience are invariant and nearly unchangeable; others, though changeable, are nearly universal. It is therefore possible to identify interests that seem to govern maternal practice throughout the species. Yet it is impossible even to begin to specify these interests without importing features specific to the class, ethnic group, and particular sex-gender system in which the interests are realized. In this essay I draw upon my knowledge of the institutions of motherhood in middle-class, white, Protestant, capitalist, patriarchal America, for these have expressed themselves in the heterosexual nuclear family in which I mother and was mothered. Although I have tried to compensate for the limits of my particular social and sexual history, I principally depend upon others to correct my interpretations and translate across cultures.

Children "demand" their lives be preserved and their growth fostered. Their social group "demands" that growth be shaped in a way acceptable to the next generation. Maternal practice is governed by (at least) three interests in satisfying these demands for preservation, growth, and acceptability. Preservation is the most invariant and primary of the three. Because a caretaking mother typically bears her own children, preservation begins when conception is recognized and accepted. Although the form of preservation depends on widely variant beliefs about the fragility and care of the fetus, women have always had a lore in which they recorded their concerns for the baby they "carried." Once born, a child is physically vulnerable for many years. Even when she lives with the father of her child or with other female adults, even when she has money to purchase or finds available supportive health and welfare services, a mother typically considers herself, and is considered by others, to be responsible for the maintenance of the life of her child.

Interest in fostering the physical, emotional, and intellectual growth of her child soon supplements a mother's interest in its preservation. The human child is typically capable of complicated emotional and intellectual development; the human adult is radically different in kind from the child it once was. A woman who mothers may be aided or assaulted by the help and advice of fathers, teachers, doctors, moralists, therapists, and others who have an interest in fostering and shaping the growth of her child. Although rarely given primary credit, a mother typically holds herself, and [is] held by others, responsible for the *malfunction* of the growth process. From early on, certainly by the middle years of childhood, a mother is governed by a third interest: she must shape natural growth in such a way that her child becomes the sort of adult that she can appreciate and others can accept. Mothers will vary enormously, individually and socially, in the traits and lives they will appreciate in their children. Nevertheless, a mother typically takes as the criterion of her success the production of a young adult acceptable to her group. . . .

To a mother, "life" may well seem "terrible, hostile, and quick to pounce on you if you give it a chance." In response, she develops a metaphysical attitude toward "Being as such," an attitude I call "holding," an attitude governed by the priority of keeping over acquiring, of conserving the fragile, of maintaining whatever is at hand and necessary to the child's life. It is an attitude elicited by the work of "world-*protection,* world-*preservation,* world-*repair* . . . the invisible weaving of a frayed and threadbare family life."

The priority of holding over acquiring distinguishes maternal thinking from scientific thinking and from the instrumentalism of technocracy. To be sure, under the pressures of consumerism, holding may become frantic accumulating and storing. More seriously, a parent may feel compelled to preserve her *own* children, whatever befalls other children. The more competitive and hierarchical the society, the more thwarted a mother's individual, autonomous pursuits, the more likely that preservation will become egocentric, frantic, and cruel. Mothers recognize these dangers and fight them.

Holding, preserving mothers have distinctive ways of seeing and being in the world that are worth considering. For example, faced with the fragility of the lives it seeks to preserve, maternal thinking recognizes humility and resilient cheerfulness as virtues of its practice. In doing so it takes issue with popular moralities of assertiveness and much contemporary moral theory.

Humility is a metaphysical attitude one takes toward a world beyond one's control. One might conceive of the world as governed by necessity and change (as I do) or by supernatural forces that cannot be comprehended. In either case, humility implies a profound sense of the limits of one's actions and of the unpredictability of the consequences of one's work. As the philosopher Iris Murdoch puts it: "Every natural thing, including one's own mind, is subject to chance. . . . One might say that chance is a subdivision of death. . . . We cannot dominate the world." Humility that emerges from maternal practices accepts not only the facts of damage and death, but also the facts of the independent and uncontrollable, developing and increasingly separate existences of the lives it seeks to preserve. "Humility is not a peculiar habit of self-effacement, rather like having an inaudible voice, it is selfless respect for reality and one of the most difficult and central of virtues."

If, in the face of danger, disappointment, and unpredictability, mothers are liable to melancholy, they are also aware that a kind of resilient good humor is a virtue. This good humor must not be confused with the cheery denial that is both a liability and, unfortunately, a characteristic of maternal practice. Mothers are tempted to denial simply by the insupportable difficulty of passionately loving a fragile creature in a physically threatening, socially violent, pervasively uncaring and competitive world. Defensive denial is exacerbated as it is officially encouraged, when we must defend against perceptions of our own subordination. Our cheery denials are cruel to our children and demoralizing to ourselves.

Clear-sighted cheerfulness is the virtue of which denial is the degenerative form. It is clear-sighted cheerfulness that Spinoza must have had in mind when he said: "Cheerfulness is always a good thing and never excessive"; it "increases and assists the power of action." Denying cheeriness drains intellectual energy and befuddles the will; the cheerfulness honored in maternal thought increases and assists the power of maternal action.

In a daily way, cheerfulness is a matter-of-fact willingness to continue, to give birth and to accept having given birth, to welcome life despite its conditions. . . .

Because in the dominant society "humility" and "cheerfulness" name virtues of subordinates, and because these virtues have in fact developed in conditions of subordination, it is difficult to credit them and easy to confuse them with the self-effacement and cheery denial that are their degenerative forms. Again and again, in attempting to articulate maternal thought, language is sicklied o'er by the pale cast of sentimentality and thought itself takes on a greeting-card quality. Yet literature shows us many mothers who in their "holding" actions value the humility and resilient good humor I have described. One can meet such mothers, recognize their thought, any day one learns to listen. One can appreciate the effects of their disciplined perseverance in the unnecessarily beautiful artifacts of the culture they created. "I made my quilt to keep my family warm. I made it beautiful so my heart would not break."

Backlash

Susan Faludi's book *Backlash* (1991) drew considerable public attention in the early 1990s. Though most people identify it as a feminist work, it is also an indictment of journalistic ethics. For example, Faludi traces the wide ripples caused by one or two inconclusive studies about women's health and happiness. These stud- ies are grossly distorted by one or two newspapers, and then picked up by television, radio, and maga- zines until the country is saturated with inaccurate and distorted in- formation about women's lives. Nowhere along the line were the facts adequately checked or the conclusions challenged. Faludi also reports the myriad ways the media report half-truths, sensationalize minor, isolated events and portray them as "trends," and generally be- lie their claims to fairness and bal- ance in their reporting. Faludi uses the example of their treatment of women to make her case, but the book leaves the reader wondering how many other topics receive such sloppy and biased treatment.

The Importance of Recognizing Diversity

It is important to recognize that a variety of challenges have been made to feminist theory, some of them from women who are generally sympathetic to some of the claims of feminism. One of the most important of these challenges has come from women of color and women from working-class backgrounds. Feminism has been a very white, middle-class phenomenon; starting back with Mary Wollstonecraft (Chapter 9), most of the women who have dominated feminist thinking have been white and middle-class. Women from different racial and class backgrounds have often felt themselves excluded from the discussion. This is a particularly damaging charge against feminism because the theory emphasizes including the formerly excluded. Women who are not white and middle-class often point out that though they are oppressed as women, that oppression takes different forms when it is seen in context with racial and class oppression. Race, class, and gender are inextricably tied together; a working-class African-American woman will be disadvantaged in different ways from a middle-class white woman. They will both have problems associated with being women, but the problems will be different.

Furthermore, women of color often feel torn between the competing claims of the members of their sex and the members of their ethnic groups. Which form of oppression is more fundamental: racism or sexism? Because women of color are oppressed both as women and as members of a particular racial or ethnic group, they often feel pulled in many directions at once. They are also sometimes inclined to resist both groups because both seem to want them to deny at least one impor- tant feature of their own identities. Feminism has, slowly, begun to try to listen to women from these different social situations and to learn from them how sexism can take many shapes. The theory still has a long way to go. In Selection 11.9, **Maria Lugones** (1944–), a philosophy professor at Carleton College, articulates some of these concerns as they have affected her, a Hispanic woman.

SELECTION 11.9

"Have We Got a Theory for You! Feminist Theory, Cultural Imperialism, and the Demand for 'The Woman's Voice'"

From Maria Lugones and Elizabeth V. Spelman

I think it is necessary to explain why in so many cases when women of color appear in front of white/Anglo women to talk about feminism and women of color, we mainly raise a complaint: the complaint of exclusion, of silencing, of being included in a universe we have not chosen. . . .

I see two related reasons for our complaint-full discourse with white/Anglo women. Both of these reasons plague our world, they contaminate it through and through. It takes some hardening of oneself, some self-acceptance of our own anger to face them, for to face them is to decide that maybe we can change our situation in self-constructive ways and we know full well that the possibilities are minimal. . . .

We and you do not talk the same language. When we talk to you we use your language: the language of your experience and of your theories. We try to use it to communicate our world of experience. But since your language and your theories are inadequate in expressing our experiences, we only succeed in communicating our experience of exclusion. We cannot talk to you in our language because you do not understand it. So the brute facts that we understand your language and that the place where most theorizing about women is taking place is your place, both combine to require that we either use your language and distort our experience not just in the speaking about it, but in the living of it, or that we remain silent. Complaining about the exclusion is a way of remaining silent.

You are ill at ease in our world. You are ill at ease in our world in a very different way than we are ill at ease in yours. You are not of our world and again, you are not of our world in a very different way than we are not of yours. In the intimacy of a personal relationship we appear to you many times to be wholly there, to have broken through or to have dissipated the barriers that separate us because you are Anglo and we are raza. When we let go of the psychic state that I referred to above in the direction of sympathy, we appear to ourselves equally whole in your presence but our intimacy is thoroughly incomplete. When we are in your world many times you remake us in your own image, although sometimes you clearly and explicitly acknowledge that we are not wholly there in our being with you. When we are in your world we ourselves feel the discomfort of having our own being Hispanas disfigured or not understood. And yet, we have had to be in your world and learn its ways. We have to participate in it, make a living in it, live in it, be mistreated in it, be ignored in it, and rarely, be appreciated in it. In learning to do these things or in learning to suffer them or in learning to enjoy what is to be enjoyed or in learning to understand your conception of us, we have had to learn your culture and thus your language and self-conceptions. But there is nothing that necessitates that you understand our world: understand, that is, not as an observer understands things, but as a participant, as someone who has a stake in them understands them. So your being ill at ease in our world lacks the features of our being ill at ease in yours precisely because you can leave and you can always tell yourselves that you will be soon out of there and because the wholeness of your selves is never touched by us, we have no tendency to remake you in our image.

But you theorize about women and we are women, so you understand yourselves to be theorizing about us, and we understand you to be theorizing about us. Yet none of the feminist theories developed so far seems to me to help Hispanas in the articulation of our experience. We have a sense that in using them we are distorting our experiences. Most Hispanas cannot even understand the language that is used in these theories—and only in some cases the reason is that the Hispana cannot understand English. We do not recognize ourselves in these theories. They create in us a schizophrenic split between our concern for ourselves as women and ourselves as Hispanas, one that we do not feel otherwise. . . .

The only motive that makes sense to me for your joining us in this investigation is the motive of friendship, out of friendship. A non-imperialist feminism requires that you make a space for our articulating, interpreting, theorizing and reflecting about the connections among them—a real space must be a non-coerced space—and/or that you follow us into our world out of friendship. I see the "out of friendship" as the only sensical motivation for this following because the task at hand for you is one of extraordinary difficulty. It requires that you be willing to devote a great part of your life to it and that you be willing to suffer alienation and self-disruption. Self-interest has been pro-posed as a possible motive for entering this task. But self-interest does not seem to me to be a realistic motive, since whatever the benefits you may accrue from such a journey, they cannot be concrete enough for you at this time and they may not be worth your while. I do not think that you have any obligation to understand us. You do have an obligation to abandon your imperialism, your universal claims, your reduction of us to your selves simply because they seriously harm us.

I think that the fact that we are so ill at ease with your theorizing in the ways indicated above does indicate that there is something wrong with these theories. But what is it that is wrong? Is it simply that the theories are flawed if meant to be universal but accurate so long as they are confined to your particular group(s)? Is it that the theories are not really flawed but need to be translated? Can they be translated? Is it something about the process of theorizing that is flawed? How do the two reasons for our complaint-full discourse affect the validity of your theories? Where do *we* begin? To what extent are our experience and its articulation affected by our being a colonized people, and thus by your culture, theories and conceptions? Should we theorize in community and thus as part of community life and outside the academy and other intellectual circles? What is the point of making theory? Is theory making a good thing for us to do at this time? When are we making theory and when are we just articulating and/or interpreting our experiences?

Feminist Epistemology

Many feminist writers have argued that the traditional post-positivist empiricist epistemology, which has dominated philosophy in this century, is a limited theoretical approach to human knowing. This mainstream epistemology has tended toward assuming that ideal knowers are disembodied, purely rational, fully informed, and completely objective entities. Although most philosophers admit that no human being ever approximates this ideal knower because real people have bodies, personal histories, points of view, etc., most philosophers are reluctant to let go of that ideal.

Feminist epistemologists have made several challenges. First, they argue, it is troubling that the ideal knower is also rather like the ideal male, who is supposedly more rational, objective, unemotional, etc., than the female. Feminists suggest that this conveniently excludes the knowledge claims of women right off the bat. Lorraine Code, one of today's leading feminist epistemologists, points out that for feminists "the questions continually arise: Whose science—or whose knowledge—has proved? Why has its veneration led Western societies to discount other findings, suppress other forms of experience, deny epistemic status to female . . . wisdom?"

Let us take one example of the way scientific knowledge can be biased. Lila Leibowitz cites a case in which E. O. Wilson, the sociobiologist, argues that mouse lemurs are "essentially solitary" except for certain periods in the mating cycle. It turns out that female mouse lemurs nest together; it is the males who are "essentially solitary," and this behavior is generalized over the entire species. "Dominant" males are those who manage to breed. But why should we suppose them to be dominant just for that simple reason? Perhaps those males are merely the ones the females like best, for some reason known only to the female lemurs. This "evidence" of dominant behavior is then quickly overgeneralized to provide support for Wilson's view that almost all males of almost all species are dominant over females. Scientists are not idealized objective observers. As the Wilson example shows, they import their own prejudices and biases into their observations and theories. Feminist epistemologists ask that this fact about all human beings—male and female—be acknowledged. They point out that knowledge is never gathered in a vacuum. People look for answers to specific questions, even—perhaps especially—in science. Knowledge gathering is always done to serve human purposes, and those purposes shape the kind of knowledge that is gathered.

This is not to say that feminist epistemologists want to denigrate or discount rationality or objectivity. But many are concerned that the rational/emotional, objective/subjective dichotomies are false and misleading. Most emotions are structured by rationality. Suppose, for example, you come across a friend who is obviously extremely angry. You might ask, "What's wrong? What are you angry about?" If the answer is: "Light blue shirts are back in style!" you would probably ask a few more questions since this seems too insignificant to be intensely angry about. Was your friend traumatized by light blue shirts as a child? Was he or she forced to wear them every day? If the answer is "No, I just hate light blue shirts!" you might plausibly conclude that your friend is a little weird. Only emotions based on plausible reasons make sense to most of us. It isn't true that people generally have emotional responses "for no reason at all"; if they do, they are often considered mentally unstable. Reason and emotion are more interconnected than that. Feminist epistemologists generally emphasize that knowledge-gathering is a human project and must be identified as such. Reason, emotion, social class, gender, and other factors play a role in what we can know. Any ideal that rules out the "human factor" in its characterization of knowledge is bound to be wrong and will unjustly privilege the group claiming that true knowledge is only obtainable by people who are just like them and have only their social characteristics.

This small sampling of the history of feminist philosophical theorizing is just an overview. Feminist philosophy is active and growing rapidly.

Checklist

To help you review, here is a checklist of the key philosophers and concepts of this chapter. The brief descriptive sentences that appear with each philosopher summarize one of her leading ideas. Keep in mind that some of these summary statements represent terrific oversimplifications of complex positions.

Philosophers

- **Simone de Beauvoir** Feminist existentialist who extended the discussion of feminism into all areas of intellectual endeavor.
- **Gloria Steinem** Helped found *Ms.* magazine and brought feminist issues to the public's attention.
- **Kate Millett** Contemporary American feminist who argued that patriarchy extends to all areas of life.
- **Ann Ferguson** Argued that we should pursue a monoandrogynous society to ensure that we are all fully human.
- **Joyce Trebilcot** Held that the androgynous society should include as many options as possible, including traditionally male types and traditionally female types.
- **Marilyn Frye** Argued that the concepts of "masculine" and "feminine" are shaped by ideas of dominance and subordination.
- **Stephanie Ross** Suggested that the metaphors we use in ordinary speech can shape the way we think about women.
- **Beverly LaBelle** Argued that there are significant similarities between pornography and war propaganda.
- **Carol Gilligan** Argued that men and women have characteristically different ways of reasoning about moral issues.
- **Nancy Chodorow** Argued that the differences between men and women can be traced to the psychodynamics of the nuclear family.
- **Shulamith Firestone** Argued that new reproductive technologies could free women from oppression.
- **Sara Ruddick** Held that the experience of being a mother influences one's moral perceptions.
- **Maria Lugones** Reminded white/Anglo women that their perspective is not the only "woman's" perspective.

Concepts

feminism

Self/Other

essentialism

patriarchy

sexism

androgyny

monoandrogyny

polyandrogyny

liberal feminism

radical feminism

oppression

sexist language

pornography as a representation
   of male dominance

biological determinism

ethics of care

separatism

maternal thinking

interconnection of race and gender

Questions for Discussion and Review

1. What does de Beauvoir mean by the Self/Other distinction? What examples of this kind of reasoning do you see in politics today (apart from the feminism debates)?

2. What would de Beauvoir say is required of women for them to become fully human? Do you think there should be different pictures of "full humanness" for men and women?

3. Do you think there would be a difference in the world if the "avenues of power" Millett mentions were in the hands of women? What evidence can you give for your view?

4. What is Ferguson's argument for the value of androgyny?

5. Is universal bisexuality a necessary consequence of an androgynous society? Why or why not?

6. How might it be argued that sex roles are more limiting for women than for men?

7. What social purpose is served by having "male" and "female" deodorants, razor blades, etc., according to Frye?

8. What is Frye's definition of oppression?

9. Do all oppressed groups suffer? Are all groups that suffer oppressed?

10. How does sexism influence language use?

11. How much do you think the metaphors we use influence the way we look at the world? What reasons can you give for your view?

12. What is the main feminist criticism of pornography?

13. How are the feminist criticisms of pornography different from the more fundamentalist, right-wing criticisms of pornography on TV or in the papers?

14. There are many interesting feminist analyses of pornography. If you have never actually seen pornography yourself (and many people of college age have not), it can be hard to understand what is being objected to. Here is a suggestion: *If you are over eighteen, get any issue of Penthouse or Hustler off the shelf (you may even find these magazines in your university library). As you flip through the pages, count the number of times you see overt, incontrovertible evidence of hostility or anger toward women. Count the number of times you see women bound or tied. Count the number of derogatory words used for women or women's body parts. Count the number of pictures or stories you read that represent women enjoying pain or force. It can be frustrating to argue about pornography when all you have read is the feminist analysis (or, for that matter, the Larry Flynt–type analysis) without having your own evidence. So get the evidence and then make your own decision.

15. Why do boys and girls develop differently, according to Chodorow?

16. How does maternal practice shape women's moral concerns, according to Ruddick?

17. How can white/Anglo women try to learn about the perspective of women of color? Do you think it is possible for different groups to have true, empathetic understanding of each other?

18. In what ways have you personally benefited from a sexist society? In what ways would you benefit from a non-sexist society?

Suggested Further Readings

Simone de Beauvoir, *The Second Sex,* H. M. Parshley, trans. (New York: Vintage Books, 1974). The book that started the second wave.

Claudia Card, ed., *Feminist Ethics* (Lawrence: University of Kansas Press, 1991).

Nancy Chodorow, *The Reproduction of Mothering: Psychoanalysis and the Sociology of Gender* (Berkeley: University of California Press, 1978).

Nancy Chodorow, *Femininities, Masculinities, Sexualities: Freud and Beyond* (Lexington: University Press of Kentucky, 1994).

Ann Ferguson, "Androgyny As an Ideal for Human Development," in *Feminism and Philosophy,* Mary Vetterling-Braggin, Frederick Elliston, and Jane English, eds. (Totowa, N.J.: Rowman and Littlefield, 1977).

Ann Ferguson, *Blood at the Root: Motherhood, Sexuality, and Male Dominance* (London: Pandora, 1989).

Marilyn Frye, "Sexism," in *The Politics of Reality: Essays in Feminist Theory* (Freedom, Calif.: Crossing Press, 1983). A thorough philosophical analysis of the concept of sexism.

Marilyn Frye, *Willful Virgin* (Freedom, Calif.: Crossing Press, 1992).

Alison Jagger, *Feminist Frameworks* (New York: McGraw-Hill, 1984). A wide variety of feminist essays designed for the student reader.

Alison Jagger, ed., *Living with Contradictions: Controversies in Feminist Social Ethics* (Boulder, Colo.: Westview Press, 1994).

Beverly LaBelle, "The Propaganda of Misogyny," in *Take Back the Night,* Laura Lederer, ed. (New York: William Morrow, 1980). This whole volume covers the subject of pornography and violence against women.

Maria Lugones and Elizabeth V. Spelman, "Have We Got a Theory for You! Feminist Theory, Cultural Imperialism, and the Demand for 'The Woman's Voice,'" in *Women and Values* (Belmont, Calif.: Wadsworth, 1986). A discussion and dialogue between a white/Anglo woman and a Hispanic woman.

Kate Millett, *Sexual Politics* (Garden City, N.Y.: Doubleday, 1970). An in-depth analysis of the workings of patriarchy, with emphasis on examples from literature.

Stephanie Ross, "How Words Hurt: Attitudes, Metaphor and Oppression," in *Sexist Language,* Mary Vetterling-Braggin, ed. (Totowa, N.J.: Littlefield, Adams, 1981). The book as a whole covers many perspectives on the relationship between language and sexism.

Sara Ruddick, "Maternal Thinking," in *Women and Values* (Belmont, Calif.: Wadsworth, 1986). Further discussion of the idea of a woman's moral perspective.

Sara Ruddick, *Maternal Thinking: Toward a Politics of Peace* (New York: Ballantine Books, 1990).

Sean Sayers and Peter Osborne, eds., *Socialism, Feminism, and Philosophy, a "Radical Philosophy" Reader* (New York: Routledge, 1990). An anthology of papers from *Radical Philosophy* on socialist, feminist, and environmental issues.

Elizabeth V. Spelman, *Inessential Woman* (Boston: Beacon Press, 1988).

Joyce Trebilcot, "Two Forms of Androgynism," in *Feminism and Philosophy,* Mary Vetterling-Braggin, Frederick Elliston, and Jane English, eds. (Totowa, N.J.: Rowman and Littlefield, 1977). A more traditionally liberal endorsement of androgyny as freedom of choice.

Joyce Trebilcot, *Dyke Ideas: Process, Politics, and Daily Life* (Albany, N.Y.: SUNY Press, 1994).

Political Philosophy:
Justice, Law, and the State

Summary and Conclusion

To review briefly: Political philosophy began with Plato's *Republic,* in which Plato set forth his vision of the ideal state. Plato conceived the state to be an organism whose health consists in its being well ordered in a manner similar to that in which the human soul, when it is healthy, is well ordered. In the well-ordered state, according to Plato, society is divided into three classes, one of which, an aristocracy of philosopher-kings, rules the state.

Aristotle, in contrast to Plato, thought that the form or structure taken by an ideal state depends on circumstances, though he insisted that a state is praiseworthy only to the extent to which it enables its citizens to achieve the good life. Neither Plato nor Aristotle thought highly of democracies, and neither considered humans to be equal either in ability or in their right to social, political, or economic privileges.

Though Aristotle, because of his naturalism, is often thought of as the father of natural law political theory, the first clear concept of natural law itself—an impersonal principle of reason that governs the universe—is found in the philosophy of the Stoics and was first applied to political philosophy by Roman legal theorists such as Cicero.

Later, the concept of natural law was Christianized in the thought of Augustine and Aquinas and other Christian thinkers. The natural law, they held, is the moral law of God as it is apprehended by people through conscience and reason. No human law that fails to accord with the natural law is valid, they said, and no state whose laws fail to accord is legitimate.

For Hobbes, the natural law is merely a set of rational principles for best preserving one's life. Following these principles, according to Hobbes, would lead people to agree or contract among themselves to transfer their rights and power to a central authority, the Leviathan, that would deliver people from the anarchy of the state of nature by forcing them to honor their commitments and to live peacefully. Hobbes was the first major exponent of social contract theory, the theory that the legitimacy of the state and its laws is derived from an initial consent of its subjects.

Locke and Rousseau also held that the legitimacy of the state and its laws is derived from the consent of its subjects, though Locke, unlike Hobbes, maintained that these subjects delegate (rather than surrender) their power to the legislature (rather than to an executive authority). Locke also emphasized that the will of the people is determined by majority rule and that the government must be divided into separate branches. For Rousseau, the people united into a collective whole that expresses the general will *is* the state, and it is not possible for the people so united either to surrender or to delegate or to divide their power, though they may commission deputies to administer and enforce any laws that they enact.

The two main political philosophies of the nineteenth century were liberalism, as represented most importantly by John Stuart Mill and Harriet Taylor, and Marxism. For Mill and Taylor, the purpose of the state is to promote the happiness of its citizens, a goal that is achieved only when each individual has the fullest freedom, compatible with the freedom of others, to think, speak, act, and otherwise develop his or her own capacities as he or she sees fit. The utopian movements of the period endeavored to implement these values in actual communities.

Marx, too, stressed the importance of individual freedom to develop one's physical and mental abilities, and maintained that the only society in which this is possible is a society in which there is no exploitation: hence, a society with no economic or social classes, no money, wages, or private property. Marx believed that the dialectical interplay between social institutions and the forces of production will result in the overthrow of capitalism by the proletariat and the eventual creation of this classless society. According to the contemporary Marxist Herbert Marcuse, however, in advanced capitalist societies the proletariat has been transformed from a force for radical social change into a pillar of conservatism by insidious new forms of social control found in advertising and consumerism.

For part of the twentieth century, fascism was equal in importance to Marxism and liberalism. Fascism was not a systematic political philosophy, but fascist thinkers were aggressive nationalists who also believed that the interests of the state supersede the interests of its subjects and who emphasized the absolute authority of the leader of the state as one who embodies its ideals and may justifiably use any means to fulfill its destiny.

According to one of the most important liberal philosophers of recent years, John Rawls, the basic social institutions of the well-ordered state, including its constitution, must satisfy the fundamental principles of social justice. These principles, which Rawls states are those that self-interested but rational persons would choose for the role of justice if they were to make the choice in a situation in which irrelevant considerations could not influence their choice, require all social goods to be distributed equally unless an unequal distribution is to everyone's advantage, but also require, unlike utilitarian-based liberal philosophies, that personal liberty never be sacrificed for the common good.

But if personal liberty may never be sacrificed for the common good, can *any* state be morally legitimate? According to Nozick, one and only one type of state, the minimal night-watchman state, can arise without violating any individual rights. Any other state, he argues, requires a redistribution of assets and thus is not morally legitimate.

Feminist thought is divided into two parts; the first part, from the late 1700s through about the first quarter of this century, focused on major legal issues affecting women and ended with the vote for women in 1922. The second part is still going on and tends to be more focused on the personal relationships between men and women. Feminists are united in opposing the notion that women are to be treated as subordinates to men.

A quick check of almost any university library may show more holdings in political philosophy than in all the other areas and fields of philosophy combined. Nevertheless, familiarity with what has been written in this part will be a good first step toward understanding some of the more important basic issues and concepts in political philosophy.

PART 4

Philosophy of Religion: Reason and Faith

Traditional Proofs of God

12

It is morally necessary to assume the existence of God.

   —Immanuel Kant

We ought not to speak about religion to children, if we wish them to possess any.

   —Jean-Jacques Rousseau

What is the difference between a theologian and a philosopher of religion? Let's back up about four steps and get a running start at the question.

If you subscribe to a religion, and the opinion polls say you most likely do, then you also accept certain purely philosophical doctrines. For example, if you believe in a nonmaterial God, then you believe that not all that exists is material, and that means you accept a metaphysics of immaterialism. If you believe that you should love your neighbor because God said you should, then you are taking sides in the debate among ethical philosophers concerning ethical naturalism. You have committed yourself to a stand against naturalism.

Your religious beliefs commit you as well to certain epistemological principles. A lot of people who make no claim to have seen, felt, tasted, smelled, or heard God still say they know that God exists. So they must maintain that humans can have knowledge not gained through sense experience. To maintain this is to take sides in an important epistemological issue, as you know from Part 1.

These and many other metaphysical, ethical, and epistemological points of view and principles are assumed by, and incorporated in, religion; and it is the business of the philosophy of religion to understand and rationally evaluate them.

Of course, *theology,* too, seeks clear understanding and rational evaluation of the doctrines and principles found in religion, including those that are metaphysical, ethical, and epistemological. But for the most part theologians start from premises and assumptions that are themselves religious tenets. The philosopher of

The Metaphysician and the Theologian

An old saying goes that the difference between a metaphysician and a theologian is this: The metaphysician looks in a dark room for a black cat that isn't there. The theologian looks in the same place for the same thing.

And finds it.

religion, in contrast, does not make religious assumptions in trying to understand and evaluate religious beliefs.

The religions of the world differ in their tenets, of course. Therefore, a philosopher of religion usually focuses on the beliefs of a specific religion or religious tradition, and in fact it is the beliefs of the Judaeo-Christian religious tradition that have received the most discussion by Western philosophers. But though philosophers of religion may focus on the beliefs of a specific religion, they will not proceed in their inquiries from the *assumption* that these beliefs are true, though they may in fact accept them as a personal matter.

What are some of the metaphysical, ethical, and epistemological beliefs of the Judaeo-Christian tradition that philosophers have sought to understand and evaluate? Many of these beliefs have to do with *God:* that He exists, that He is good, that He created the universe and is the source of all that is real, that He is a personal deity, that He is a transcendent deity, and so forth. Many have to do with *humans:* that humans were created in the image of God, that they have free will, that they can have knowledge of God's will, that the human soul is immortal, and so on. Others have to do with *features of the universe:* for example, that there are miracles, that there is supernatural reality, that there is pain and suffering (a fact thought to require reconciliation with the belief in a good and all-powerful God). And still others have to do with *language:* that religious language is intelligible and meaningful; that religious utterances are (or are not) factual assertions or are (or are not) metaphorical or analogical; that terminology used in descriptions of God means the same (or does not mean the same) as when it is used in descriptions of other things.

This is a long list of issues. To simplify things, we will concentrate here on the philosophical consideration of the Christian belief in the existence of God. Let's begin with two Christian greats, Saints Anselm and Aquinas.

Two Christian Greats

Our other chapters have started with discussions of ancient Greek philosophers. We could have begun this chapter, too, with the ancient Greeks, for many modern religious beliefs contain ideas that were discussed by, and in some cases originated with, the Greeks. But we've narrowed the focus here to the philosophical consideration of the Judaeo-Christian belief in God's existence, and it is appropriate to begin with the man who was abbot of Bec and later archbishop of Canterbury.

Anselm

St. Anselm (c. 1033–1109) was among the first to evaluate the belief in the Christian God from a purely philosophical perspective, that is, from a perspective that does not make religious assumptions from the outset. Nonetheless, Anselm never entertained the slightest doubt about whether God exists. Further, he made no distinction between philosophy and theology, and he thought it impossible for anyone to reason about God or God's existence without already believing in Him.

Still, Anselm was willing to evaluate *on its own merit and independently of religious assumptions* the idea that God does *not* exist.

The Ontological Argument   This idea, that God does not exist, is attributed in Psalms 14:1 to the "fool," and Anselm thought it plain that anyone who would deny God's existence is *logically* mistaken and is indeed an utter fool. Anselm reasoned that the fool is in a self-contradictory position. The fool, Anselm thought, is in the position of saying *that he can conceive of a being greater than the greatest being conceivable.* This may sound like a new species of doubletalk, so we must consider Anselm's reasoning carefully.

Anselm began with the premise that by "God" is meant "the greatest being conceivable," or, in Anselm's exact words, "a being than which nothing greater can be conceived."

Now the fool who denies that God exists at least *understands* what he denies, said Anselm charitably. Thus God at least exists in the fool's understanding. But, Anselm noted, a being that exists both in the understanding and outside in reality is greater than a being that exists only in the understanding. (That's why people prefer real houses and cars and clothes and vacations to those they just think about.)

But this means, Anselm said, that the fool's position is absurd. For his position is that God exists only in the understanding but not in reality. So the fool's position, according to Anselm, is that "the very being, than which nothing greater can be conceived, is one, than which a greater can be conceived." And yes, this silliness is something like doubletalk; but Anselm's point is that the denial of God's existence leads to this silliness. Hence God exists: to think otherwise is to be reduced to self-contradiction and mumbo jumbo.

This line of argument, according to which it follows from the very *concept* of God that God exists, is known as the **ontological argument.** It represents Anselm's most important contribution to the philosophy of religion. If Anselm's argument is valid, if Anselm did establish that it is self-contradictory to deny that God exists and hence established that God does exist, then he did so without invoking any religious premises or making any religious presuppositions. True, he made in effect an assumption about the *concept* of God, but even a non-Christian

Reductio Proofs

If a claim logically entails something that is absurd, nonsensical, or just plain false, you reject the claim, correct?

For example, if the claim that the butler killed Colonel Mustard in the kitchen means that the butler was in two different places at the same time (because it is known that he was in the library at the time of the murder), then you reject the claim that the butler killed Colonel Mustard in the kitchen.

This type of proof of a claim's denial is known as *reductio ad absurdum:* by demonstrating that a claim reduces to an absurdity or just to something false, you prove the denial of the claim. By showing that claim *C* entails falsehood *F,* you prove *not-C.*

Reductios, as they are called, are encountered frequently in philosophy and in real life. Anselm's ontological argument is a **reductio proof.** Here the claim, *C,* is that

God doesn't exist.

This claim, argued Anselm, entails the falsehood, *F,* that

the very being than which nothing greater can be conceived is one than which a greater can be conceived.

The conclusion of the argument is thus *not-C,* that

God does exist.

[handwritten: The human imagination is capable of conceiving things that are possible but not real.]

or an atheist, he thought, must concede that what is *meant* by "God" is "the greatest being conceivable." Thus, if the argument is valid, even those who are not moved by faith or are otherwise religious must accept its conclusion. Anselm in effect argued that the proposition "God exists" is *self-evident* and can no more be denied than can the proposition "A square has four sides," and anyone who thinks otherwise is either a fool or just doesn't quite grasp the concept of God.

Anselm gave another version of the ontological argument that goes like this: Because God is that than which nothing greater can be conceived, God's nonexistence is inconceivable. For anything whose nonexistence *is* conceivable is not as great as one whose nonexistence is *not* conceivable, and thus is not God.

Are you convinced? Many are not. Many regard the ontological argument in any version as a cute little play on words that proves absolutely nothing.

Gaunilo's Objection   One who found the argument unconvincing was a Benedictine monk from the Abbey of Marmontier, a contemporary of Anselm whose name was **Gaunilo.** One of Gaunilo's objections was to the first version of the argument, which, he argued, could be used to prove ridiculous things. For example, Gaunilo said, consider the most perfect island. Because it would be more perfect for an island to exist both in reality and in the understanding, the most perfect island must exist in reality, if Anselm's line of reasoning is sound. For if this island did not exist in reality, then (according to Anselm's reasoning) any island that did exist in reality would be more perfect than it—that is, would be more perfect than the most perfect island, which is impossible. In other words, Gaunilo used Anselm's reasoning to demonstrate the necessary existence of the most perfect island, implying that any pattern of reasoning that can be used to reach such an idiotic conclusion must obviously be defective.

Anselm, however, believed that his reasoning applied only to God: Because God is that than which a greater cannot be conceived, God's nonexistence is inconceivable; whereas, by contrast, the nonexistence of islands and all others things is conceivable.

As you will see in Selection 12.1, which contains the first version of his ontological argument, Anselm was able to express his thought with elegant simplicity. You may find it a challenge to figure out what, if anything, is wrong with his reasoning.

Don't be confused when Anselm says that God is "something than which nothing greater can be thought." He just means, in plain English, "God is the being with the following characteristic. When you try to think of a greater or higher being, you can't do it." *island could possibly not have existed, a being compared to something which could not possibly not have existed*

SELECTION 12.1

Proslogion   **From St. Anselm**

Lord, who gives understanding to faith give to me as much as you deem suitable, that I may understand that You are as we believe You to be, and that You are what we believe You to be. Now we believe that You are something than which nothing greater can be thought. But perhaps there is no such nature since "the fool hath said in his heart: There is no God"? But surely this very same fool, when he hears what I say: "something than which nothing greater can be thought," understands what he hears, and what he understands is in his mind, even if he does not understand that it exists. For it is one thing for a thing to be in the mind, but something else to understand that a thing exists. For when a painter pre-thinks what is about to be made, he has it in mind but he does not yet understand that it exists because he has not yet made it. But when he has already painted it, he both has it in his mind and also understands that it exists because he has already made it. Hence, even the fool is convinced that something exists in the mind than which nothing greater can be thought, because when he hears this he understands and

whatever is understood is in the mind. But surely that than which a greater cannot be thought cannot exist merely in the mind. For if it exists merely in the mind, it can be thought to exist also in reality which is greater. So if that than which a greater cannot be thought exists merely in the mind, that very same thing than which a greater cannot be thought is something than which a greater can be thought. But surely this cannot be. Hence, without doubt, something than which a greater cannot be thought exists both in the mind and in reality.

Indeed, it exists so truly that it cannot be thought not to be. For something can be thought to exist which cannot be thought not to exist, which is greater than what can be thought not to exist. So, if that than which a greater cannot be thought can be thought not to exist, that very thing than which a greater cannot be thought, is not that than which a greater cannot be thought; which is impossible. So there exists so truly something than which a greater cannot be thought that it cannot be thought not to exist.

You are that very thing, Lord our God.

Assumes that reality is defined by what the human brain can or can not imagine

Aquinas   *Aristotelian empiricist*

About a century and a half after Anselm died, **St. Thomas Aquinas** (c. 1225–1274), whom we've discussed in earlier chapters, interpreted Aristotelian philosophy from a Christian perspective. Aristotle, as we've had occasion to mention before, emphasized the importance to philosophy of direct observation of nature. In keeping with his empiricist, Aristotelian leanings, Aquinas regarded the ontological argument as invalid. You cannot prove that God exists, he said, merely by considering the word *God,* as the ontological argument in effect supposes. For that strategy to work, you would have to presume to know God's essence. The proposition "God exists," he said, unlike "A square has four sides," is not self-evident to us mere mortals. Although you can prove God's existence in several ways, he asserted, you cannot do it just by examining the concept of God. You have to consider what it is about nature that makes it manifest that it requires God as its original cause.

The ways in which the existence of God can be proved are in fact five, according to Aquinas. Although Aquinas's theological and philosophical writings fill many volumes and cover a vast range of topics, he is most famous for his "Five Ways" (but some philosophers—e.g., Richard Swinburne, discussed later—don't regard Aquinas's proofs of God as his best philosophy).

It would be surprising if you were not already familiar with one or another of Aquinas's Five Ways in some version.

The First Way   The *first way* to prove that God exists, according to Aquinas, is to consider the fact that natural things are in motion. As we look around the world and survey moving things, it becomes clear that they didn't put themselves into motion. But if every moving thing were moved by another moving thing, then there would be no first mover; if no first mover exists, there would be no other mover, and nothing would be in motion. Because things are in motion, a first mover must therefore exist that is moved by no other, and this, of course, is God.

We should note here that Aquinas is usually understood as meaning something quite broad by "motion"—something more like *change in general*—and as including under the concept of movement the coming into, and passing out of, existence. Thus, when he says that things don't put themselves into motion, don't suppose that he thought that you can't get up out of your chair and walk across the room. He means that things don't just bring themselves into existence.

The Second Way   Aquinas's *second way* of proving God's existence is very similar to the first. In the world of sensible things, nothing causes itself. But if everything were caused by something else, then there would be no first cause, and if no first cause exists, there would be no first effect. In fact, there would be no second, third, or fourth effect, either: if no first cause exists, there would be no effects, period. So we must admit a first cause, to wit, God.

Note that Aquinas did not say anything in either of the first two proofs about things being moved or caused by *earlier* motions or causes. The various motions

influenced by Albertus Magnus + the Aristotelian

PROFILE / St. Thomas Aquinas (1225–1274)

It is time we gave a little background information on Thomas Aquinas, the Angelic Doctor, one of the most important of Roman Catholic saints.

Aquinas, the son of a count of Aquino, studied for many years with Albertus Magnus (i.e., "Albert the Great"). Albertus, who had the unusual idea that Christian thinkers should be knowledgeable about philosophy and science, wished to make all of Aristotle's writings available in Latin. His fondness for Aristotle was a strong influence on his pupil, Aquinas.

Aquinas eventually received his doctorate from the University of Paris in his late twenties and soon acquired a substantial reputation as a scholar. For ten years in his thirties and early forties he was a professor for the Papal Court and lectured in and about Rome.

Now, the thirteenth century was a time of considerable intellectual controversy between the Platonists and the Aristotelians. Some theologians believed that the teachings of Aristotle could not be harmonized with Christian doctrines. This belief was in part a reaction to Averroes (1126–1198), an absolutely brilliant Arabian philosopher, and his followers, whose philosophy was built entirely around the thought of Aristotle. The Averroist philosophy conflicted with Church doctrine on creation and personal immortality, making Aristotle odious to some Christian theologians.

But Aquinas was no Averroist and defended his own version of Aristotle with inexorable logic. He returned to Paris in 1268 and be- came involved in a famous doctrinal struggle with the Averroists, which he won. Although some factions within the Church voiced strong opposition to his philosophy, opposition that lasted for many years after his death, slowly but surely Aquinas's thinking became the dominant system of Christian thought. He was canonized in 1323 and made a Doctor of the Church in 1567.

Aquinas was a stout fellow, slow and deliberate in manner. He was thus nicknamed the Dumb Ox. But he was a brilliant and forceful thinker, and his writings fill many volumes and cover a vast array of theological and philosophical topics. His most famous works are the *Summa Contra Gentiles* (1258–1260) and the *Summa Theologica* (1267–1273), a systematic theology grounded on philosophical principles. He was, in addition, a most humane and charitable man.

In 1879, Pope Leo XIII declared Aquinas's system to be the official Catholic philosophy.

and causes he is talking about are simultaneous in time. His argument is not the common one you hear that things must be caused by something earlier, which must be caused by something earlier, and so on, and that because this chain of causes cannot go back infinitely, there must be a first cause, God. In Aquinas's opinion, there is no philosophical reason that the chain of causes could not go back infinitely. But there cannot be an infinite series of *simultaneous* causes or movers, he thought.

The Third Way   Aquinas's *third way* is easily the most complicated of the five ways. Many consider it his finest proof, though Aquinas himself seemed to prefer the first.

Many paraphrasings of the third proof are not faithful to what Aquinas actually said, which is essentially this:

In nature some things are such that it is possible for them not to exist. Indeed, everything you can lay your hands on belongs to this "need-not-exist" category: whatever it is, despite the fact that it does exist, it need not have existed.

Now that which need not exist, said Aquinas, at some time did not exist. Therefore if everything belongs to this category, then at one time nothing existed, and then it would have been impossible for anything to have begun to exist—and thus even now nothing would exist. Thus, Aquinas reasoned, not everything is such that it need not exist: "There must exist something the existence of which is *necessary*."

This isn't quite the end of the third proof, however, for Aquinas believed that he had not yet ruled out the possibility that the necessity of this necessary being might be caused by another necessary being, whose necessity might be caused by another, and so on and so on. So, he asserted, "It is impossible to go on to infinity in necessary things which have their necessity caused by another." Conclusion: There must be some necessary being that has its own necessity, and this is God.

We said the third way was complicated.

The Fourth and Fifth Ways   Aquinas's *fourth way* to prove God is to consider the fact that all natural things possess degrees of goodness, truth, nobility, and all other perfections. Therefore, there must be that which is the source of these perfections, namely, pure goodness and truth, and so on, and this is what we call God.

And the *fifth way* or proof of God's existence is predicated on the observation that natural things act for an end or purpose. That is, they function in accordance with a plan or design. Accordingly, an intelligent being exists by which things are directed toward their end, and this intelligent being is God.

Aquinas's first three proofs of God's existence are versions of what today is called the **cosmological argument.** The cosmological argument is actually not one argument but a type of argument. Proponents of arguments of this type think that the existence of *contingent* things, things that could possibly not have existed, points to the existence of a noncontingent or *necessary* being, God, as their ultimate cause, creator, ground, energizer, or source of being. Note the difference between cosmological arguments and ontological arguments, which endeavor to establish the existence of God just by considering His nature or analyzing the concept of God, as we saw attempted by Anselm.

Theology and Philosophy

The distinction we drew at the beginning of this chapter between theology and the philosophy of religion is pretty much the same as the distinction Aquinas drew between theology and philosophy.

According to Aquinas, if your thinking proceeds from principles that are revealed to you in religion and that you accept on religious faith, then your thinking is theological, though he did not often use the word *theology.* If your reasoning proceeds from what is evident in sensory experience, then your thinking is philosophical.

According to Aquinas, some theological truths, truths of revelation, are such that philosophy could never discover them. For example, philosophy cannot establish that the universe had a beginning and is not eternal. And not everything discovered by philosophy is important for salvation. But philosophy and theology, though separate disciplines, are not incompatible, he held; in fact, they complement each other, he thought (in contrast to some other Christian thinkers, who thought that philosophy can lead to religious errors).

From the standpoint of theology, that God exists is a given, a truth that you start out knowing. From the standpoint of philosophy, that God exists is not a given but may be inferred from your experience.

Thus, Aquinas's proofs of God's existence are philosophical proofs. They do not depend for their soundness on any religious principles.

Aquinas's fourth proof, which cites the existence of goodness or good things, is called the **moral argument.** Here again, the term does not refer to just one argument but to a type of argument, and, as we will see, some of the "versions" of the moral argument resemble one another only vaguely.

Arguments like Aquinas's fifth proof, according to which the apparent purposefulness or orderliness of the universe or its parts or structure points to the existence of a divine designer, are called **arguments from design** or **teleological arguments.**

Too much terminology? Then let's summarize all this. The main point is that Anselm and Aquinas between them introduced what have turned out to be the four principal arguments for God's existence. These are:

- the ontological argument *concept*
- the cosmological argument *universal necessity*
- the teleological or design argument *design*
- the moral argument *source of good*

Notice that none of these four arguments rests on any religious assumptions. They should therefore require the assent of every nonreligious person, if they are sound.

To a certain extent, the history of the philosophy of religion is a continuing discussion of various versions and aspects of these four arguments, as we will now learn. Therefore, just to understand each type of argument is already to have a good grasp of the basics of the philosophy of religion.

SELECTION 12.2

Summa Theologica   From St. Thomas Aquinas

The existence of God can be proved in five ways.

The first and more manifest way is the argument from motion. It is certain, and evident to our senses, that in the world some things are in motion. Now whatever is moved is moved by another, for nothing can be moved except it is in potentiality to that towards which it is moved; whereas a thing moves inasmuch as it is in act. For motion is nothing else than the reduction of something from potentiality to actuality. But nothing can be reduced from potentiality to actuality, except by something in a state of actuality. Thus that which is actually hot, as fire, makes wood, which is potentially hot, to be actually hot, and thereby moves and changes it. Now it is not possible that the same thing should be at once in actuality and potentiality in the same respect, but only in different respects. For what is actually hot cannot simultaneously be potentially hot; but it is simultaneously potentially cold. It is therefore impossible that in the same respect and in the same way a thing should be both mover and moved, *i.e.*, that it should move itself. Therefore, whatever is moved must be moved by another. If that by which it is moved be itself moved, then this also must needs be moved by another, and that by another again. But this cannot go on to infinity, because then there would be no first mover, and, consequently, no other mover, seeing that subsequent movers move only inasmuch as they are moved by the first mover; as the staff moves only because it is moved by the hand. Therefore it is necessary to arrive at a first mover, moved by no other; and this everyone understands to be God.

The second way is from the nature of efficient cause. In the world of sensible things we find there is an order of efficient causes. There is no

case known (neither is it, indeed, possible) in which a thing is found to be the efficient cause of itself; for so it would be prior to itself which is impossible. Now in efficient causes it is not possible to go on to infinity, because in all efficient causes following in order, the first is the cause of the intermediate cause, and the intermediate is the cause of the ultimate cause, whether the intermediate cause be several, or one only. Now to take away the cause is to take away the effect. Therefore, if there be no first cause among efficient causes, there will be no ultimate, nor any intermediate, cause. But if in efficient causes it is possible to go on to infinity, there will be no first efficient cause, neither will there be an ultimate effect, nor any intermediate efficient causes; all of which is plainly false. Therefore it is necessary to admit a first efficient cause, to which everyone gives the name of God.

The third way is taken from possibility and necessity, and runs thus. We find in nature things that are possible to be and not to be, since they are found to be generated, and to be corrupted, and consequently, it is possible for them to be and not to be. But it is impossible for these always to exist, for that which can not-be at some time is not. Therefore, if everything can not-be, then at one time there was nothing in existence. Now if this were true, even now there would be nothing in existence, because that which does not exist begins to exist only through something already existing. Therefore, if at one time nothing was in existence, it would have been impossible for anything to have begun to exist; and thus even now nothing would be in existence—which is absurd. Therefore, not all beings are merely possible, but there must exist something the existence of which is necessary. But every necessary thing either has its necessity caused by another, or not. Now it is impossible to go on to infinity in necessary things which have their necessity caused by another, as has been already proved in regard to efficient causes. Therefore we cannot but admit the existence of some being having of itself its own necessity, and not receiving it from another, but rather causing in others their necessity. This all men speak of as God.

moral

The fourth way is taken from the gradation to be found in things. Among beings there are some more and some less good, true, noble, and the like. But *more* and *less* are predicated of different things according as they resemble in their different ways something which is the maximum, as a thing is said to be hotter according as it more nearly resembles that which is hottest; so that there is something which is truest, something best, something noblest, and consequently, something which is most being, for those things that are greatest in truth are great-

est in being. . . . Now the maximum in any genus is the cause of all in that genus, as fire, which is the maximum of heat, is the cause of all hot things, as is said in the same book. Therefore there must also be something which is to all beings the cause of their being, goodness, and every other perfection; and this we call God.

design

The fifth way is taken from the governance of the world. We see that things which lack knowledge, such as natural bodies, act for an end, and this is evident from their acting always, or nearly always, in the same way, so as to obtain the best result. Hence it is plain that they achieve their end, not fortuitously, but designedly. Now whatever lacks knowledge cannot move towards an end, unless it be directed by some being endowed with knowledge and intelligence; as the arrow is directed by the archer. Therefore some intelligent being exists by whom all natural things are directed to their end; and this being we call God.

Mysticism: Gut Philosophy

A radically different approach to God may be found in the writings of **Julian of Norwich** (1342–1414).

We've all had the experience of being unable to explain to someone else our reasons for holding a certain belief or point of view. At times, it seems that there are no "reasons." Parents sometimes are like this. Ask for a reason to justify their decision and they'll say "because, just because." But sometimes no reason is the best reason. Perhaps some kinds of beliefs—about God, about faith, about whom you love—shouldn't have a reason. You believe what you believe because you believe it. That's it. You just know that it's true—you know it in your gut. End of story.

Now, it's one thing to say "I just know it," and it's another to explain *why* we should rely on this "gut" kind of knowledge. Before we go any further, let's be clear: We're not talking about gut instincts or hunches. We're talking about serious beliefs that people hold "just because." When these are beliefs about how we should act or what we should do, it's not unreasonable to ask the people who have these beliefs why they are so sure about them.

Before the development of rationalism in the seventeenth century, back before philosophers decided that reason was the premier tool for acquiring knowledge,

PROFILE / Julian of Norwich (1342–1414?)

Her name was Julian, but sometimes she is called "Juliana." She lived in the English cathedral city of Norwich during a nasty time in history. The Hundred Years War, the Great Schism in the Church, the ruthless suppression by Bishop Despencer of the Peasant's Revolt in Norwich, and the condemnation of John Wycliffe for heresy made the mid-fourteenth century a rough time for folks in Norwich. The fact that the Black Plague hit Norwich when Julian was six, again when she was nineteen, and again when she was twenty-seven didn't exactly make Norwich a fun place to live in. Julian became an anchoress. You see, it was the custom to "anchor" someone to a church. Anchoring was a kind of permanent grounding of a scholarly nun or priest (it was an honor, not a punishment). The lucky person, someone known for saintly behavior and devotion to theology, was walled up alive in a small cell within the outer wall of the church. Food, books, and other items would be passed through a window, and occasionally the anchoress would be allowed to talk through the window to important clergy and nobility. She spent her life there, and when she died would be entombed in a crypt in the church.

Julian wrote two versions (one short and one long) of her *Booke of Showings* (revelations). The short version is a partial description of a series of visions she had in 1373 when she was seriously ill. She became an anchoress soon after that experience. That left her lots of time for study, thought, and religious discussion. Many theologians and philosophers visited her to discuss the "showings" she described in the short version. She spent the next twenty years revising the manuscript, including fuller details and much analysis of what she thought the revelations meant.

Julian was the champion of all humility formula writers. You see, back then, women weren't supposed to claim to have any religious or philosophical authority (or any other kind of authority, for that matter). To avoid criticism for having the crust to act as if she knew something, a woman writer typically began her text with a "humility formula." Here is Julian's as she wrote it:

> Botte god for bede that ȝe schulde saye or take it so that I am a techere, for I meene nouȝt soo, no I mente nevere so; for I am a womann, leued, febille *and* freylle.

Some of Julian's words had special religious and philosophical meanings that her readers would have understood. What she's saying is: "God says don't you act like I'm a teacher. I don't mean to claim to be; and I never meant so. For I am a woman, ordinary ('lewd'), morally weak ('feeble'), and likely to fall from virtue ('frail')." Having disclaimed any authority, Julian went on to write seven hundred pages of philosophy!

Julian's interests are in the nature and certainty of religious knowledge. She held that there were three sources of religious knowledge: natural reason, teachings of religious leaders, and visions given by God. As God gives visions to whomever God chooses, and God loves everyone, in theory everyone is a candidate for mystical revelations. Julian of Norwich lived during the Crusades, when heretics were claiming the Catholic religion was based on false ideas. How can someone tell true religious claims from false ones? Might God make revelations to ordinary people? Julian and many other mystics, including Hildegard of Bingen, St. John of the Cross, and his teacher St. Teresa of Avila (all of whom are known as philosophers), thought so. To claim that only religious leaders have a direct line to God suggests that God has limited ability to communicate. Julian called God "Christ, Our Mother" and "God, our Father." In her mind, God was both male and female, mother and father. God made us and nurtures us through the hard times.

people were willing to allow experience to count as a valid source of knowledge. And for ordinary, day-to-day things, like figuring out what to eat, experience worked pretty well.

But what about knowledge that comes from *mystical* experience? In such experiences, the mystic often is unconscious, appears to be delirious, or seems to be having what we now call an "out-of-body experience." The mystic may be dreaming, awake, or in a trance. He or she may see visions or hear voices. Commonly, those who have such experiences report being told things by God. Sometimes they are told to write down what they experience or to teach others.

Julian of Norwich was one of the greatest mystics of all time. Her analysis of her mystical experiences (which she called "showings") focuses on the nature of personal religious and moral knowledge. She addressed whether it was possible to know God. In part of her analysis, she considers the arguments of a philosopher known variously as Dionysius the Areopagite, pseudo-Dionysius, and St. Denis (also Denys) of France. She agreed with Dionysius that God was above our knowledge. And where Dionysius had tried to chip away at less accurate ideas about God, Julian took an opposite approach. According to Julian, we can know God only partly through revelation; greater knowledge comes through loving God. We could come to love God by loving our own souls (by which most medieval philosophers mean "minds"), our own human nature. And God could reveal to us how to come to know ourselves. She argued that if revelation is the only way to know God, then we should prefer revelation to argument—we should rely on the knowledge about God that comes to us through revelation (even if it comes in a roundabout way by telling us about ourselves and how we can love God).

In this respect, Julian's views agreed with those of Thomas Aquinas (who had recently been made a saint), who believed that visions were the language God uses to convey his meaning. But Julian went farther than Thomas in trying to make relevant to most people the visionary experiences undergone by a very few. Julian felt that ordinary people could learn from visionaries—that people should allow visionary knowledge to act as a kind of psychological antidote to life's sorrow, suffering, and despair. Such knowledge should provide reasons for ordinary people to have hope. Clearly, the plagues, wars, and religious disputes had made many people doubt the existence of a God who loved humans and yet let them suffer so much.

Julian denied that there is any meaningful distinction between the validity of knowledge derived through rationalistic philosophy and the validity of that derived through mystical revelations made directly to our soul. She held indeed that it is mistaken to divorce reason from experience, especially from mystical experience. She also put great importance on the "not showns"—what logically should have been part of the vision but was missing. She believed that God intended her to figure out what *wasn't* being communicated directly: to use insight and instinct (and reason) to piece together the missing parts of the puzzle. In Julian's view, God lives in us and we in God; we are one with God and are nurtured and fed knowledge of God and of ourselves by this divine parent who is *both* mother and father. "God All-Wisdom is our kindly mother." (And Mother knows best.)

SELECTION 12.3

mystical, vague illusory
few truths

*Book of Showings**

From Julian of Norwich

But what I mean is that we stick with God and faithfully trust to be given understanding. This is how God works in us. He opens the eye of our understanding so that we have insight, sometimes more and sometimes less, depending upon how much ability God has given us to deal with what we learn. But this too depends upon our willingness, our readiness to say "yes" to God, to feel him, to be truly willing to be with him with all our heart and soul, and all our might. For that, we have to hate and despise our natural inclinations and tendencies that might let us slip into thinking and doing wrong.

We really ought to enjoy the fact that God lives in our soul; and more, we ought to enjoy that our soul lives in God. Our soul is made by God to be God's place. Our soul lives in God (who was not made). It takes some real insight into yourself to know that God, which made us, lives in our soul. It takes even more understanding to see and know that our soul is something that not only lives in God but which God created to make us what we are.

This was a rich, full, sweet vision: that God's throne is in our soul, because it is God's pleasure to reign in our understanding. He likes us working things out in him. He wants us to be his helpers, giving him all our understanding, learning his laws and keeping them.

Faith is nothing else but a right understanding, with true belief and genuine trust in what we really are: that we are in God and he in us whether we can prove it or not. Faith comes from loving our own souls, from turning on our own light, reason's insight, and by keeping it all together—the way God made us. And when our soul entered our body and our senses began to develop, we had what we needed to live forever.

For I saw, definitely, that what we are is in God, and I also saw that God is in us sensually. The reason God made us sensual is the same reason he made heaven, the city of God. And just as God is always in heaven and heaven exists eternally, God is always in our soul, eternally. Each of us is a city of God.

I saw no difference between what God is and what we are; it's like it's all part of God. And yet, I took it that the stuff we're made of is in God. It's like, God is God and our substance is a part of God, and made by God.

In making us, it's like God knit us. He claimed us as a creation of himself. It's because God claims us that we remain as good as when we were born. By virtue of each precious claiming of each of us, we love him and praise him, and thank him, and enjoy him no end.

And so by making us, God-almighty is our kindly father, and God-all wisdom is our kindly mother. And in the knitting and claiming he is our spouse too, for he says "I love you and you love me, and our love will keep us together."

---

*Adapted for contemporary readers.

Seventeenth-Century Believers

For our purposes here, we can now pass lightly over some three hundred years from the Middle Ages through the Renaissance to the seventeenth century. This is not to suggest that the time was unimportant for the history of religion. Europe had seen a mixture not only of enlightenment and religious revolution, but also of reaction and intolerance; it had brought forth not only printed books and open discussion, but also gunpowder and the stake. Luther had challenged the very foundations of Catholic doctrine, and Protestantism had spread throughout Europe. In England, Henry VIII had forced creation of the Anglican Church so that he could marry young Anne Boleyn, and then, through a liberal use of execution, secured a loyal following. A new disorder had been rung in by the time of Descartes's birth, and before his death modern science was offering its own challenge to the established orthodoxy.

But all this, though of great significance to the history of religion, was only indirectly important to the history of the philosophy of religion. The main point for our purposes is that the seventeenth century was the age of scientific discovery amid intellectual uncertainty and political and religious instability, an age in which past authorities and institutions and truths were questioned and often rejected or discarded.

Descartes

The next major figure in the philosophy of religion after Aquinas was, in fact, **René Descartes** (1596–1650). Descartes, longing for an unshakable intellectual footing, made it his primary business to devise what he thought was a new method for attaining certainty in his turbulent age. When he employed his new method, however, it revealed to him the certain existence of God.

As we saw in Part 1, Descartes's method was to challenge every belief, no matter how plausible it seemed, in order to ascertain which of his beliefs, if any, were absolutely unassailable. Employing this method, Descartes found that he could not doubt his existence as a thing that thinks: *cogito, ergo sum* (I think, therefore I am). He also found that he could not doubt the existence of God, for basically three reasons. These three reasons are Descartes's proofs of God.

Descartes's First Proof   Having established as absolutely certain his own existence as a thinking thing, Descartes found within his mind the idea of God, the idea of an infinite and perfect being. Further, he reasoned, because there must be a cause for his idea, and because there must be as much reality or perfection in the cause of an idea as there is in the content of the idea, and because he himself therefore certainly could not be the cause of the idea, it follows, he concluded, that God exists.

Let's call this Descartes's first proof. It's really quite a simple proof, though Descartes makes it seem somewhat complicated because he has to explain *why* his idea of God could not have arisen from a source other than God, and, of course, it is difficult to do this.

As you can see, Descartes's first proof is sort of a combination ontological-cosmological argument. It's ontological in that the mere idea of God is held by Descartes to entail that God exists. It's cosmological in that the existence of some

Where Did You Get That Idea?

Descartes argued, in what we are calling his first proof, that there must be as much reality in the cause of an idea as there is "objective reality" in the idea. Don't be confused by this terminology. The "objective reality" of an idea is just the idea's content; it's what the idea is an idea *of*. Descartes was simply enunciating a straightforward principle of common sense: that if you have an idea of something—a chair, say—then there must have been something outside the idea that gave the idea this particular content. Even if you have the idea of something imaginary, like a person with a toad's head, common sense still says that this is just a combination of two other ideas, the ideas of a person and of a toad, and that thus there must originally have been things outside those ideas that gave them their specific contents.

contingent thing—Descartes's idea of God—is considered by Descartes to require God as its ultimate cause.

Descartes's Second Proof   Descartes had two other proofs of God's existence. His second proof is only subtly different from the first and is basically this:

1. I exist as a thing that has an idea of God.
2. Everything that exists has a cause that brought it into existence and that sustains it in existence.
3. The only thing adequate to cause and sustain me, a thing that has an idea of God, is God.
4. Therefore God exists.

In this second proof, note, God is invoked by Descartes as the cause of *Descartes*, a being that has the idea of God; whereas in the first proof, God is invoked by Descartes as the cause of Descartes's *idea* of God. In the second proof, Descartes also utilizes the important notion that a thing needs a cause to *conserve* or *sustain* it in existence. We will encounter this idea again.

Descartes's Third Proof   In contrast with the first two, Descartes's third proof is a straightforward and streamlined version of the ontological argument:

1. My conception of God is the conception of a being that possesses all perfections.
2. Existence is a perfection.
3. Therefore I cannot conceive of God as not existing.
4. Therefore God exists.

Now, assuming that this argument successfully gets you to conclusion (3), how about that move from (3) to (4)? Descartes had no difficulty with that move and said simply, "From the fact that I cannot conceive God without existence, it follows that existence is inseparable from Him, and hence that He really exists." He also offered what he thought was a parallel argument to support the move, and it was to this effect: Just as the fact that you cannot conceive of a triangle whose angles do not equal 180° means that a triangle must have angles that equal 180°, the fact that you cannot conceive of God as not existing means that God must exist.

Are you convinced?

Descartes's three proofs may be novel, but certain objections may instantly spring to mind. A common criticism made of the first two proofs is that it seems possible to devise plausible alternative explanations for one's having an idea of God, explanations other than that given by Descartes. As we already said and as you will see from Selection 12.3, Descartes himself anticipates this objection and endeavors to show why the most likely alternative explanations fail. We think you should consider carefully whether Descartes has really eliminated alternative explanations of his idea of God.

The third proof—Descartes's version of the ontological argument—is more difficult to criticize, but about one hundred fifty years later Immanuel Kant formulated what became the classic refutation of ontological arguments. More about this when we turn to Kant.

A different sort of objection to Descartes's proofs is that, given Descartes's method—according to which he vowed not to accept any claim that is in the least bit doubtable—Descartes should not have accepted without question either the principle that he and his ideas must be caused, or the principle that there must be as much perfection and reality in the cause as in the effect. Although Descartes regarded his proofs of God as providing certainty, they seem to rest on principles that many people would think of as less than certain. Yet Descartes seems to accept these principles without hesitation.

Nevertheless, Descartes's proofs are important in the history of our subject, for they raise the important question—at least the first two proofs raise this question—just how *does* a person come to have the idea of an *infinite* being?

In Selection 12.4 Descartes summarizes what we have called his first proof, and then considers and rejects three alternative explanations of how he could come to have the idea of God. If you have difficulty following it, refer back to our summary description of the argument.

SELECTION 12.4

Meditations

From René Descartes

But of my ideas . . . [one] represents a God . . . concerning which we must consider whether it is something which cannot have proceeded from me myself. By the name God I understand a sub-stance, that is infinite [eternal, immutable], independent, all-knowing, all-powerful, and by which I myself and everything else, if anything else does exist, have been created. Now all these characteristics are such that the more diligently I attend to them, the less do they appear capable of proceeding from me alone; hence, from what has been already said, we must conclude that God exists.

For although the idea of substance is within me owing to the fact that I am substance, nevertheless I could not have the idea of an infinite substance—since I am finite—if it had not proceeded from some substance which was veritably infinite.

Nor should I imagine that I do not perceive the infinite by a true idea, but only by the negation of the finite . . . for . . . I see that there is manifestly more reality in infinite substance than in finite. . . .

And we cannot say that this idea of God is perhaps materially false and that consequently I can derive it from nought . . . for . . . as this idea is very clear and distinct and contains within it more objective reality than any other, there can be none which is of itself more true, nor any in which there can be less suspicion of falsehood. . . .

But possibly I am something more than I suppose myself to be, and perhaps all those perfections which I attribute to God are in some way potentially in me . . . [For example,] I am already sensible that my knowledge increases little by little, and I see nothing which can prevent it from increasing more and more into infinitude. . . .

At the same time I recognize that this cannot be. For, in the first place, although it were true that every day my knowledge acquired new degrees of perfection, and that there were in my nature many things potentially which are not yet there actually, nevertheless these excellences do not pertain to [or make the smallest approach to] the idea which I have of God in whom there is nothing merely potential. . . . And further, although my knowledge grows more and more, nevertheless I do not for that reason believe that it can ever be actually infinite, since it can never reach a point so high that it will be unable to attain to any greater increase.

Leibniz

You may recall the name of Gottfried Wilhelm, Baron von Leibniz, or at least the "Leibniz" part, from our discussion in a box in Chapter 4. **Leibniz** (1636–1716) was one of the Continental rationalists of the seventeenth century (Descartes and Spinoza were the other two). He is remembered for developing calculus independently of Newton, and for his metaphysical doctrine of **monads**—the individual nonphysical units of activity that, he said, are the ultimate constituents of reality. Remember also that the Leibnizian metaphysical system is, or so Leibniz believed, derivable logically from a few basic principles, including, perhaps most famously, the **principle of sufficient reason.** According to this principle, there is a sufficient reason why things are exactly as they are and are not otherwise.

The principle of sufficient reason is used by Leibniz as a proof of God. To see how the proof works, consider any occurrence whatsoever—say, the leaves falling from the trees in autumn. According to the principle in question, there must be a sufficient reason for that occurrence. Now a *partial* reason for any occurrence is that something else happened, or is happening, that caused or is causing the occurrence—in our example, the days turning cold. But that happening is only a

The Problem of Evil

Unfortunately, there is a great deal of pain and suffering in the world, not to mention disease, murder, torture, poverty, rape, child abuse, droughts, earthquakes, floods, wars, hijackings, and many other unpleasant things. Now, given that these things exist, it follows either that (1) God cannot do anything about them, which means that God is not all-powerful, or that (2) God does not mind that they exist, which means either that (a) God is not good, or (b) these things are really good things in disguise. One further option is (3) God does not exist.

Assuming that these are the only options—and if you can think of another option, we would like to hear about it—then if you believe that God exists and is good and all-powerful, you will choose option (2b) and say that these things are really good things in disguise. Of course, you might not put it exactly that way: you might say that these things are evil, all right, but the existence of some evil is required for the greater good. But that's saying that these things serve a purpose and to that extent are not *purely* evil.

Theodicy is the defense of God's goodness and omnipotence (all-powerfulness) in view of apparent evil. Many theologians and philosophers have written theodicies. But one of the most important theodicies was that of Leibniz. For Leibniz subscribed to the <u>principle</u> of sufficient reason (see text), and that principle means (according to Leibniz) that God exists. It also means that the reason this world, this state of affairs, exists, and not some other world, some other state of affairs, is that this must be the best of all possible worlds (for otherwise God would not have chosen it for existence). So, according to Leibniz, this is the best or most perfect of all worlds possible, and he is thus especially obligated to explain how apparent evil fits into it.

Leibniz's explanation, briefly, is that, for God to create things other than Himself, the created things logically must be limited and imperfect. Thus, to the extent that creation is imperfect, it is not wholly good, and thus it is "evil."

Further, Leibniz argues, you have to look at the entire painting. You can't pronounce it bad if you look at this or that small part, for if you do that all you will see is a confused mass of colors. Likewise, you have to look at the world from a global perspective and not focus in on this or that unpleasant aspect of it.

Not everyone, of course, will find this explanation of evil satisfactory.

partial reason for the occurrence in question, because it too requires a sufficient reason for happening. Why did the days turn cold?

So it is plain, thought Leibniz, that as long as you seek the sufficient reason for an occurrence from within the sequence of happenings or events, you never get the complete, final, sufficient reason for the occurrence. You only get to some other event, and that event itself needs a reason for having happened. (The days turned cold because of a shift southward in the jet stream. The jet stream shifted southward because of a reduction in solar radiation. The solar radiation was reduced because of changes in the earth's orientation relative to the sun. And so forth.) So, unless there is something *outside* the series of events, some reason for the *entire* series *itself,* there is no sufficient reason for *any* occurrence.

The Best of All Possible Worlds?

The optimism expressed in Leibniz's dictum that this is the best of all possible worlds (see the box "The Problem of Evil") was skewered with dripping sarcasm by Voltaire (1694–1778) in his famous novel *Candide*. Leibniz was of the opinion that one must look at evil from a global perspective, from which unfortunate events might be perceived as a part of a larger fabric that, taken as a whole, is a perfect creation. This notion, in Voltaire's opinion, is meaningless from the standpoint of the individual who suffers a dreadful misfortune, and Voltaire had no difficulty in ridiculing it. If you look at the events of the world with a sober eye, Voltaire suggested, you will see anything but a just, harmonious, and ordered place. What you are more likely to see is injustice, strife, and rampant disorder.

"When death crowns the ills of suffering man, what a fine consolation to be eaten by worms," he wrote. You get the idea.

Therefore, reasoned Leibniz, because there *is* a sufficient reason for every occurrence, it follows that there *is* something outside the series of events that is its own sufficient reason. And this "something outside," of course, is God.

Further, because God is a sufficient reason for God's own existence, God is a *necessary* being, argued Leibniz.

In this way, then, the principle of sufficient reason, coupled with the fact that something has occurred or is occurring, leads straightaway to a necessary being, God—at least according to Leibniz.

This proof is, you can see, yet another cosmological argument, and it is very much like Aquinas's third way. In fact, there is a tendency in the literature to interpret Aquinas's third way in this Leibnizian mode. Further, Leibniz's "argument from sufficient reason" is thought by many to be the soundest cosmological argument, and soundest proof of God of any type, ever put forward. As we will see directly when we turn to David Hume, however, not everyone is impressed with the argument.

Later we will mention that Kant thought that the cosmological argument depends on the ontological argument. Kant thought this, apparently, because Leibniz's version ends up seeming to prove the existence of a necessary being, and it is the concept of God as a necessary being that is the foundation of the ontological argument. But it does seem doubtful that Leibniz's argument *depends* on the ontological argument or in any way *assumes* the existence of a necessary being. Instead, the argument seems to *prove* the existence of a necessary being.

Leibniz thought other proofs of God were sound, including an amended version of Descartes's ontological argument and a couple of others that rest on Leibniz's metaphysics. Leibniz, however, is most noted for the cosmological argument we have explained here, which he presents in Selection 12.5.

[margin handwritten note:] Convergence of cosmological + ontological Argument

SELECTION 12.5

The Monadology   From Gottfried Wilhelm, Baron von Leibniz

36. But there must also be a *sufficient reason* for *contingent truths,* or those of *fact,*—that is, for the sequence of things diffused through the universe of created objects—where the resolution into particular reasons might run into a detail without limits, on account of the immense variety of the things in nature and the division of bodies *ad infinitum.* There is an infinity of figures and of movements, present and past, which enter into the efficient cause of my present writing, and there is an infinity of slight inclinations and dispositions, past and present, of my soul, which enter into the final cause.

37. And as all this *detail* only involves other contingents, anterior or more detailed, each one of which needs a like analysis for its explanation, we make no advance: and the sufficient or final reason must be outside of the sequence or *series* of this detail of contingencies, however infinite it may be.

38. And thus it is that the final reason of things must be found in a necessary substance, in which the detail of changes exists only eminently, as in their source; and this is what we call God.

39. Now this substance, being a sufficient reason of all this detail, which also is linked together throughout, *there is but one God, and this God is sufficient.*

40. We may also conclude that this supreme substance, which is unique, universal and necessary, having nothing outside of itself which is independent of it, and being a pure consequence of possible being, must be incapable of limitations and must contain as much of reality as is possible.

41. Whence it follows that God is absolutely perfect, *perfection* being only the magnitude of positive reality taken in its strictest meaning, setting aside the limits or bounds in things which have them. And where there are no limits, that is, in God, perfection is absolutely infinite.

Hume

Recall now Aquinas's fifth way, a version of the **teleological argument,** which also often is called the **argument from design.** The basic idea of this type of proof of God's existence is that the world and its components act for a purpose and thus exhibit design; therefore the world was created by an intelligent designer. One of the most famous criticisms of the design argument was made by the British empiricist **David Hume** (1711–1776).

Hume was born some sixty years after Descartes died, during a period of European history that saw the very clear emergence of two rivals, science and religion. Between Descartes's *Meditations* and Hume's writings on religion, science had made strong advances, notable especially in 1687 with the publication of Sir Isaac Newton's *Principia Mathematica*. Although Newton himself did not question God's existence, his system seemed to confirm scientifically what Hobbes earlier had concluded philosophically (see Part 1) and what Descartes seemed most to fear: the universe is an aggregate of matter in motion that has no need of, and leaves no room for, God. Hume's case-hardened doubts about religion made blood pressures soar, but by the time he put them in print they were by no means considered capital offenses.

Hume's empiricist epistemological principles (if valid) in fact rule out the possibility of any meaningful ontological argument. But this is complicated business and needn't detain us, because it is Hume's harsh criticisms of the cosmological and especially the teleological arguments that have been most influential in the philosophy of religion. The most important criticism of the ontological argument comes from Kant, anyway.

Hume stated the teleological argument, that is, the argument from design, as follows. You should judge for yourself whether this is a fair statement of that argument, because Hume goes on to criticize it severely, as you will see. Let's just repeat that: Selection 12.6 states the view that Hume proceeds to *attack*.

SELECTION 12.6

Dialogues Concerning Natural Religion   **From David Hume**

Look round the world; contemplate the whole and every part of it: you will find it to be nothing but one great machine, subdivided into an infinite number of lesser machines, which again admit of subdivisions, to a degree beyond what human senses and faculties can trace and explain. All these various machines, and even their most minute parts, are adjusted to each other with an accuracy, which ravishes into admiration all men, who have ever contemplated them. The curious adapting of means to ends, throughout all nature, resembles exactly, though it much exceeds, the productions of human contrivance; of human design, thought, wisdom, and intelligence. Since therefore the effects resemble each other, we are led to infer, by all the rules of analogy, that the causes also resemble; and that the Author of Nature is somewhat similar to the mind of men; though possessed of much larger faculties, proportioned to the grandeur of the work, which he has executed. By this argument *a posteriori*, and by this argument alone, do we prove at once the existence of a Deity, and his similarity to human mind and intelligence.

Now note that in this proof of God, as stated by Hume, the reasoning is from an *effect* (the "world," i.e., the universe) and its parts, to its *cause* (God). Further, the argument is one by *analogy*, in which the effect (the world or universe) is likened to a human contrivance, the cause is likened to a human creator, and the mechanism of creation is likened to human thought and intelligence. Hume's crit-

Miracles

Some Christians regard miracles as evidence of divine action. Hume, however, was highly skeptical of reports of miracles.

A miracle, he reasoned, is a violation of a natural law, such as that water flows downhill or that fire consumes wood. Thus, before it is reasonable to accept a report of a miracle as true, the evidence that supports the report must be even stronger than that which has established the natural law.

Because the evidence that a natural law holds is the uniform experience of humankind, it is almost inconceivable that any report of a miracle could be true. Therefore, before it would be reason-able to accept such a report, it would have to be a miracle in its own right for the report to be false. In fact, the report's being false would have to be a *greater* miracle than the miracle it reports.

"No testimony," wrote Hume, "is sufficient to establish a miracle, unless the testimony be of such a kind, that its falsehood would be more miraculous than the fact that it endeavors to establish."

Thomas Paine once asked which is more likely, that a person would lie or that a river would flow upstream? Hume's point is that before you accept some person's report of a river flowing up-stream, it must be even more un-likely that the person would be mistaken than that a river would indeed flow upstream.

"When anyone tells me, that he saw a dead man restored to life, I immediately consider with myself, whether it be more probable that this person should either deceive or be deceived, or that the fact which he relates should really have happened. I weigh the one miracle against the other; and always reject the greater miracle. If the falsehood of his testimony would be more miraculous than the event which he relates; then, and not till then, can he pretend to command my belief or opinion."

icisms of the proof are mainly related to (1) the appropriateness of these analogies and (2) the legitimacy of this particular instance of effect-to-cause reasoning.

Hume began his criticism by noticing that in an effect-to-cause proof, we can-not attribute to the supposed cause any qualities over and beyond those required for the effect. For example, is the world absolutely perfect? Is it free from every error, mistake, or incoherence? No? Then you cannot say that its cause is absolutely perfect. Does the world reflect infinite wisdom and intelligence? Hume's own opin-ion is that at best the world reflects these qualities to *some degree*. Therefore, though we perhaps can infer that the cause has these qualities to a similar degree, we are unauthorized to attribute to it these qualities in a higher degree; and we certainly are not authorized to attribute to it these qualities in an *infinite* degree.

We also are not authorized to attribute to it *other* qualities, such as pure good-ness or infinite power. The existence of evil and misery, in Hume's opinion, cer-tainly does *not* indicate that the cause of the world is pure goodness coupled with infinite power. His point was not that the existence of pain and misery necessarily means that the creator of the world is *not* good or omnipotent. Rather, his point was just that, given the existence of evil and misery in the world, we cannot legiti-mately try to prove that the creator is all-good and all-powerful *by looking at the world*. To do that is to attribute something other to the cause than is found in the effect.

God's perfect work is not observed in its original state. The altered state is temporary.

Committee Work

The camel, according to the old joke, must have been assembled by a committee, because it looks like a botched job.

Hume suggested that because we don't have any basis for comparison, for all we know the *world* is a botched job that suggests not total perfection on the part of its creator but incompetence and bungling. Further, it doesn't inherently even suggest having had a *single* creator, he wrote—it suggests just as easily that it was put together by a committee of lesser deities.

Free will led to the corruption of a perfect work.

Hume also questioned whether we even *know* how perfect or good the world is. Given the limitations of our position, can we be sure that the world doesn't contain great faults? Are we entitled to say that the world deserves considerable praise? If an ignorant chucklehead pronounces the only poem he has ever heard to be artistically flawless, does his opinion count for much? And isn't our experience with worlds as limited as this ignoramus's experience with poetry? *Poor example*

Further, Hume noted, in the design proof of God, a cause is inferred from a single effect, namely, the world. But, Hume asked, is it legitimate to infer a cause from a *single* effect? If I learn (to take a modern illustration of the point) that a certain weird kind of sound is caused by a new type of electronic instrument, then when I hear that kind of sound again, I can infer that it was caused by a similar instrument. But if it's the first time I hear the sound, I can't say much at all about its cause, save perhaps that it was not made by a trombone or guitar, etc. In other words, if we have experience of only a single instance of the effect, as seems to be the case with the world, then it is not clear "that we could form any conjecture or inference at all concerning its cause." *I flawed Logic* *The world can hardly be considered as a single effect*

Of course, we have had experience with the building of machines and ships and houses and so forth. But can the world really be compared to any of these? Can we pretend to show much similarity between a house and the universe? To speak of the origin of *worlds,* wrote Hume, "it is not sufficient, surely, that we have seen ships and cities arise from human art and contrivance."

Hume laid a great deal of emphasis on the limitedness of our viewpoint. We, who are but a part of the universe, use our intelligence and thought to build cities and machines. And so we suppose that there must be a divine creator who used thought and intelligence to create the universe. But we and our creations are but a tiny aspect of the universe, and human thought and intelligence are just one of hundreds of known principles of activity. Is it legitimate, Hume asked, for us to suppose that the mechanism by which one small aspect of the universe rearranges little bits of wood and steel and dirt is the very same mechanism by which *the entire universe* was originally created? We would be amused by an ignorant peasant supposing that the principles that govern the world economy are the same as those by which he runs his household. Yet we in effect suppose that the principles by which we build our houses and cities are those that govern the creation of the universe!

A Verbal Dispute?

One startling idea proposed by Hume is that the dispute between theists and atheists in certain respects is merely verbal. This is his reasoning:

Theists say that the universe was created by the divine will. But they concede that there is a great and immeasurable difference between the creative activity of the divine mind and mere human thought and its creative activity.

But what do atheists say? They concede that there is some origi-nal or fundamental principle of order in the universe, but they insist that this principle can bear only some remote analogy to everyday creative and generative processes, or to human intelligence.

Thus atheist and theist are very close to saying the same thing!

The main difference between them seems to lie only in this, Hume said: The theist is most impressed by the necessity of there being or having been a fundamental principle of order and genera-tion in the universe, whereas the atheist is most impressed by how wildly different such a principle must be from any creative activity with which we are familiar. But then the more pious the theist, the more he will emphasize the difference between divine intelligence and human intelligence; the more he will insist that the workings of God are incomprehensible to mere mortals. The more pious the theist, in short, the more he will be like the atheist!

Further, even if we can liken the creation of the world to the building of a house or boat, there is this further problem, said Hume: If we survey a ship, we would be tempted to attribute a great deal of ingenuity to its builder, when in fact its builder may be a beef-brained clod who only copied an art that was perfected over the ages by hundreds of people working through a series of trials, mistakes, corrections, and gradual improvements. Can we be sure the world was not the result of a similar process of trial and error and even intermittent bungling, involv-ing a multitude of lesser "creators"?

For that matter, Hume said, is it even proper to liken the world to a ship or watch or machine or other human artifact? Isn't the world arguably as much like a living organism as a machine? And aren't living organisms produced by processes radically different from those by which human artifacts are made?

This, then, is the substance of Hume's complaints about the design argument. Given what seemed to him to be its several difficulties, Hume's own conclusion about the argument, and evidently about God, was just this: There is an apparent order in the universe, and this apparent order provides some slight evidence of a cause or causes bearing some remote analogy to human intelligence. But that's all the evidence warrants, Hume thought. The manifestation of order is no evidence whatsoever for the existence of the God worshipped by people.

As for the cosmological argument, Selection 12.7 will explain Hume's position on the matter. A cosmological argument, in the version Hume examines, says that anything that exists must have a cause (or reason or explanation) that is different from itself; but, because the series of causes cannot go to infinity, there must be a first uncaused cause, God. A variation of the basic argument allows that the causal series can go to infinity but still stands in need of an uncaused cause that causes the whole infinite series. In either case, the uncaused cause cannot *not* exist. Thus, the uncaused cause is a **necessary being.**

Now Selection 12.7 features three characters: Demea, Cleanthes, and Philo. First, Demea states the cosmological argument. Then Cleanthes rips into it. At the end of the piece Philo brings forth an additional consideration against the argument.

SELECTION 12.7

---

*Dialogues Concerning Natural Religion**   **From David Hume**

The argument, replied Demea, which I would insist on is the common one. Whatever exists must have a cause or reason of its existence, it being absolutely impossible for anything to produce itself or be the cause of its own existence. In mounting up, therefore, from effects to causes, we must either go on in tracing an infinite succession, without any ultimate cause at all, or must at least have recourse to some ultimate cause that is *necessarily* existent. Now that the first supposition is absurd may be thus proved. In the infinite chain or succession of causes and effects, each single effect is determined to exist by the power and efficacy of that cause which immediately preceded; but the whole eternal chain or succession, taken together, is not determined or caused by anything, and yet it is evident that it requires a cause or reason, as much as any particular object which begins to exist in time. The question is still reasonable why this particular succession of causes existed from eternity, and not any other succession or no succession at all. If there be no necessarily existent being, any supposition which can be formed is equally possible; nor is there any more absurdity in nothing's having existed from eternity than there is in that succession of causes which constitutes the universe. What was it, then, which

determined *something* to exist rather than *nothing,* and bestowed being on a particular possibility, exclusive of the rest? *External causes,* there are supposed to be none. *Chance* is a word without a meaning. Was it *nothing?* But that can never produce anything. We must, therefore, have recourse to a necessarily existent Being who carries the *reason* of his existence in himself, and who cannot be supposed not to exist, without an express contradiction. There is, consequently, such a Being—that is, there is a Deity.

I shall not leave it to Philo, said Cleanthes, though I know that the stating of objections is his chief delight, to point out the weakness of this metaphysical reasoning. It seems to me so obviously ill-grounded, and at the same time of so little consequence to the cause of true piety and religion, that I shall myself venture to show the fallacy of it.

I shall begin with observing that there is an evident absurdity in pretending to demonstrate a matter of fact, or to prove it by any arguments *a priori.* Nothing is demonstrable unless the contrary implies a contradiction. Nothing that is distinctly conceivable implies a contradiction. Whatever we conceive as existent, we can also conceive as non-existent. There is no being, therefore, whose non-existence implies a contradiction. Consequently there is no being whose existence is demonstrable. I propose this argument as entirely decisive, and am willing to rest the whole controversy upon it.

---

*Hume's footnotes have been omitted.

reality cannot be limited by the human mind

It is pretended that the Deity is a necessarily existent being; and this necessity of his existence is attempted to be explained by asserting that, if we knew his whole essence of nature, we should perceive it to be as impossible for him not to exist, as for twice two not to be four. But it is evident that this can never happen, while our faculties remain the same as at present. It will still be possible for us, at any time, to conceive the non-existence of what we formerly conceived to exist; nor can the mind ever lie under a necessity of supposing any object to remain always in being; in the same manner as we lie under a necessity of always conceiving twice two to be four. The words, therefore, *necessary existence* have no meaning or, which is the same thing, none that is consistent.

But further, why may not the material universe be the necessarily existent Being, according to this pretended explication of necessity? We dare not affirm that we know all the qualities of matter; and, for aught we can determine, it may contain some qualities which, were they known, would make its non-existence appear as great a contradiction as that twice two is five. I find only one argument employed to prove that the material world is not the necessarily existent Being; and this argument is derived from the contingency both of the matter and form of the world. "Any particle of matter," it is said, "may be *conceived* to be annihilated, and any form may be *conceived* to be altered. Such an annihilation or alteration, therefore, is not impossible." But it seems a great partiality not to perceive that the same argument extends equally to the Deity, so far as we have any conception of him, and that the mind can at least imagine him to be non-existent or his attributes to be altered. It must be some unknown, inconceivable qualities which can make his non-existence appear impossible or his attributes unalterable; and no reason can be assigned why these qualities may not belong to matter. As they are altogether unknown and inconceivable, they can never be proved incompatible with it.

Add to this that in tracing an eternal succession of objects it seems absurd to inquire for a general cause or first author. How can anything that exists from eternity have a cause, since that relation implies a priority in time and a beginning of existence?

In such a chain, too, or succession of objects, each part is caused by that which preceded it, and causes that which succeeds it. Where then is the difficulty? But the *whole,* you say, wants a cause. I answer that the uniting of these parts into a whole, like the uniting of several distinct countries into one kingdom, or several distinct members into one body, is performed merely by an arbitrary act of the mind, and has no influence on the nature of things. Did I show you the particular causes of each individual in a collection of twenty particles of matter, I should think it very unreasonable should you afterwards ask me what was the cause of the whole twenty. This is sufficiently explained in explaining the cause of the parts.

Though the reasonings which you have urged, Cleanthes, may well excuse me, said Philo, from starting any further difficulties, yet I cannot forbear insisting still upon another topic. It is observed by arithmeticians that the products of 9 compose always either 9 or some lesser product of 9 if you add together all the characters of which any of the former products is composed. Thus, of 18, 27, 36, which are products of 9, you make 9 by adding 1 to 8, 2 to 7, 3 to 6. Thus 369 is a product also of 9; and if you add 3, 6, and 9, you make 18, a lesser product of 9. To a superficial observer so wonderful a regularity may be admired as the effect either of chance or design; but a skillful algebraist immediately concludes it to be the work of necessity, and demonstrates that it must for ever result from the nature of these numbers. Is it not probable, I ask, that the whole economy of the universe is conducted by a like necessity, though no human algebra can furnish a key which solves the difficulty? And instead of admiring the order of natural beings, may it not happen that, could we penetrate into the intimate nature of bodies, we should clearly see why it was absolutely impossible they could ever admit of any other disposition? So dangerous is it to introduce this idea of necessity into the present question! and so naturally does it afford an inference directly opposite to the religious hypothesis!

Kant

This brings us to **Immanuel Kant** (1724–1804), whose contribution to the philosophy of religion equals in importance his work in epistemology and ethics. When it came to God, Kant was not a doubter. Indeed, he invented one of the most famous moral arguments for God's existence. Nevertheless, Kant's criticisms of traditional proofs of God have seemed to many commentators to be more cogent than his own argument for God. These criticisms are among the most important in the literature.

The Criticisms

According to Kant, there are only three (traditional) ways of proving God's existence, and none of them works.

What's Wrong with the Ontological Proof First, there is the ontological argument. Remember that according to *Anselm's* version of the argument, God is the greatest being conceivable; hence, if you suppose that God does not exist, you are supposing that the greatest being conceivable is not the greatest being conceivable, and that's nonsense. According to *Descartes's* version, God possesses all perfections, and, because existence is a perfection, God exists.

Now we are sure that you will agree that there is something very sneaky about the ontological argument, in any version. It seems intuitively wrong, somehow; yet it is difficult to pin down exactly what the problem is.

Kant provided a criticism that has withstood the test of time, though in recent years there have been challenges to it. What's wrong with the argument, Kant said, is that it assumes that *existence is a "predicate," that is, a characteristic or attribute.* Because Anselm assumed that existence is a characteristic, he could argue that a being that lacked existence lacked an important characteristic and thus could not be the greatest being conceivable. Because Descartes assumed that existence is a characteristic, he could argue that God, who by definition possesses all perfections, necessarily possesses the characteristic of existence.

But existence, said Kant, is not a characteristic at all. Rather, it's a *precondition* of having characteristics. Is there any difference between a warm day and an *existing* warm day? If you state that the potato salad is salty, do you further characterize

[handwritten margin note: Confusing reality with conception]

God and Scripture

Many people (maybe you?) believe in God on the basis of scripture. If you do, it may be because you accept this argument:

> Premise: Scripture states that God exists;
> Conclusion: therefore God exists.

The argument is legitimate if and only if we have sound reason for believing that what scripture states is true. Of course, if we believe in God, then we will say:

> "*Obviously,* what scripture states is true: scripture is God's revealed word."

However, saying this won't convince *doubters* that God exists. They still won't have a reason for believing that what scripture states is true, because they don't believe in God. So, in short, this argument for God works if we assume *in advance* that God exists; but if we already believe in God, we don't need this argument to begin with.

An argument that is superior, *philosophically*, is this:

> Premise: There is no way scripture could contain what it contains unless it was inspired (or dictated) by God;

> Conclusion: therefore God exists.

This argument at least does not require us to assume in advance that God exists in order to establish its premise. For example, we might point to the wisdom and eloquence and power and beauty of scripture, and say that such wisdom and eloquence could not be produced by mere mortals.

In the language of logicians, the second argument does not "beg the question." See the appendix on logic for details on begging the question.

---

the salad if you state that it is salty *and exists?* If you tell the mechanic that your tire is flat, do you further enlighten him if you add that the tire also exists? The answer to all such questions, in Kant's view, is obviously "no." To say of something that it exists is not to characterize it: existence is not a predicate.

So, to apply this lesson first to Descartes: Existence is *not* a perfection or any other kind of characteristic. Certainly, *if* there *is* a being that possesses all perfections, then God exists, for existence is a precondition of something's having any perfections at all. But this fact does not mean that God actually exists.

[margin note, handwritten: Existence is not a perfection not a characteristic]

And, to apply this lesson to Anselm: Existence is not a characteristic, and so it is not one that belongs to greatness. Certainly, *if* the greatest being conceivable exists, then God exists, because God by definition is that being, and something cannot possess any aspect of greatness without existing. But that fact doesn't mean that such a being exists.

If Kant hadn't written another word about God, what he said about the ontological argument would itself have secured his high rank in the philosophy of religion.

What's Wrong with the Cosmological and Teleological Proofs

The second way of proving God's existence, according to Kant, is the cosmological argument, which, he asserts, reduces to this: If something exists, an absolutely necessary being must likewise exist. I, at least, exist. Therefore, an absolutely necessary being exists.

OUR CARS ARE ALL MECHANICALLY SOUND, COME WITH A SIX-MONTH WRITTEN GUARANTEE, AND EXIST.

Kant argued that existence is not a characteristic and that you don't enlarge a description of a thing to say that it exists. Of course, you may wish to assert that something—God, say, or ghosts, or sexism—exists, but that sort of assertion is not really a description, Kant would maintain.

This is certainly a simple and streamlined version of the cosmological argument compared with those set forth by Aquinas and Descartes and Leibniz and Hume. Unfortunately, Kant, who generally did not try to make things easy for his reader, made up for this unusual lapse into simplicity and clarity by submitting the argument to several pages of exceedingly subtle and confusing analysis.

His basic criticisms of the cosmological argument, however, are two: First, the argument really rests on the ontological argument. Kant's explanation of why and how this is so is notoriously obscure, probably unsound, and let's just let it go. Second, and more important anyway, the argument employs a principle (that everything contingent has a cause) that has significance only in the *experienced* world. The argument then uses that principle, Kant maintained, to arrive at a conclusion that goes beyond experience. (Kant, as we tried to make clear in Part 1, believed that causality is a concept applicable only to things-as-experienced. Why Kant held this position is too complicated to repeat here, but his case against the cosmological argument rests on his being correct about causality, which some people are inclined to doubt.)

The third and final way of trying to prove God's existence, according to Kant, is the teleological argument, the argument that cites the purposiveness and harmonious adaptation of nature as proof of the divine designer. Kant's main criticism is that at best the argument proves only an *architect* who works with the matter of the world, and not a creator. A similar line of thinking was found in Hume, as we saw.

what about the design of matter?

Belief in God Rationally Justified   Despite Kant's criticisms of the three traditional proofs for God's existence, Kant believed in God. Further, amazingly to some, he thought this belief to be rationally justified for any moral agent. Here, as almost always, his thinking is complicated, but what he had in mind was this:

Although we do not have theoretical or metaphysical knowledge of God, although we cannot prove or demonstrate that God exists, we must view the world *as if* it were created by God. Why? Because, Kant said, only if we assume the existence of God can we believe that virtue will be rewarded with happiness. Virtue, Kant held, is worthiness to be happy and is the supreme good. But without believing in God, the virtuous individual cannot be certain that the happiness of which he is worthy will in fact be his or that, in general, a person's happiness will be proportionate to his moral worth.

Thus, in Kant's opinion, God's existence cannot be proved but can and must rationally be assumed by a moral agent. That God exists, he said, is a postulate of *practical* reason.

This particular argument for assuming that God exists is another version of the moral argument that we first encountered with Aquinas. In Chapter 13 we will turn to yet a third version of this argument.

In Selection 12.8, taken from the *Critique of Pure Reason* (1781), Kant argues that existence is not a predicate. This will be a good stopping point for this chapter, for the basic arguments and standard objections have now been explained.

SELECTION 12.8

Critique of Pure Reason

From Immanuel Kant

My answer is as follows. There is already a contradiction in introducing the concept of existence—no matter under what title it may be disguised—into the concept of a thing which we profess to be thinking solely in reference to its possibility. . . .

"Being" is obviously not a real predicate; that is, it is not a concept of something which could be added to the concept of a thing. It is merely the positing of a thing, or of certain determinations, as existing in themselves. Logically, it is merely a copula of a judgment. The proposition, "God is omnipotent," contains two concepts, each of which has its object—God and omnipotence. The small word "is" adds no new predicate, but only serves to posit the predicate *in its relation* to the subject. If, now, we take the subject (God) with all its predicates (among which is omnipotence), and say "God is," or "There is

a God," we attach no new predicate to the concept of God, but only posit the subject in itself with all its predicates, and indeed posit it as being an *object* that stands in relation to my *concept*. The content of both must be one and the same; nothing can have been added to the concept, which expresses merely what is possible, by my thinking its object (through the expression "it is") is given absolutely. Otherwise stated, the real contains no more than the merely possible. A hundred real thalers do not contain the least coin more than a hundred possible thalers. For as the latter signify the concept, and the former the object and the positing of the object, should the former contain more than the latter, my concept would not, in that case, express the whole object, and would not therefore be an adequate concept of it. My financial position is, however, affected very differently by a hundred real thalers than it is by the mere concept of them (that is, of their possibility). . . . The conceived hundred thalers are not themselves in the least increased through thus acquiring existence outside my concept.

By whatever and by however many predicates we may think a thing—even if we completely determine it—we do not make the least addition to the thing when we further declare that this thing *is*. Otherwise, it would not be exactly the same thing that exists, but something more than we had thought in the concept; and *man cannot accurately conceive God.*

we could not, therefore, say that the exact object of my concept exists. If we think in a thing every feature of reality except one, the missing reality is not added by my saying that this defective thing exists. On the contrary, it exists with the same defect with which I have thought it, since otherwise what exists would be something different from what I thought. When, therefore, I think a being as the supreme reality, without any defect, the question still remains whether it exists or not. *God should be viewed as a person, not a (definable) thing.*

```
  ⌐_⌐⌐_⌐⌐_⌐⌐_⌐⌐_⌐⌐_⌐⌐_⌐⌐_⌐⌐_⌐⌐_⌐⌐_⌐
```

Checklist

To help you review, here is a checklist of the key philosophers and concepts of this chapter. The brief descriptive sentences summarize leading ideas. Keep in mind that some of these summary statements represent terrific oversimplifications of complex positions.

Philosophers

- **St. Anselm** Author of the ontological argument. *425*
- **Gaunilo** A Benedictine monk, contemporary of Anselm and critic of the ontological argument. *Perfect island   possibly beings cannot be compared with necessary beings* *426*
- **St. Thomas Aquinas** Author of the Five Ways of proving God's existence.
- **Julian of Norwich** English anchoress and mystic. Argued that we are in God and God is in us. We learn about God by learning about ourselves.
- **René Descartes** Offered three proofs of God, including a streamlined version of the ontological argument.
- **Gottfried Wilhelm, Baron von Leibniz** Proposed one of the most effective versions of the cosmological argument.
- **David Hume** Religious skeptic; provided classic criticisms of the teleological and cosmological arguments.
- **Immanuel Kant** Criticized the ontological, cosmological, and teleological proofs of God and thought that God's existence cannot be proved, yet believed that God's existence must be assumed by the rational, moral individual.

Concepts

theology vs. philosophy *423-4*

ontological argument   *Concept can't be* *425*

reductio proof   *reductio ad absurdum   proves denial of claim* *426*
∵ God does not exist
God = greatest
Non-existant god is < existing god ∴ god exists

Assumption of concept of greatness

Aquinas's criticism of the ontological argument   *~ assumes knowledge of the essence of God is possible, empirical necessity is better*

Five Ways   *Cosmological i) 1st move ii) 1st Cause iii) necessary*   *moral iv) source of goodness*   *teleological v) design or goal*

something whose existence is necessary

cosmological argument

moral argument

argument from design/teleological argument

first mover

first efficient cause

something that conserves or sustains something in existence

⟨433⟩ mysticism

revelation as a source of certainty

perfection

monad

principle of sufficient reason

theodicy

problem of evil

best of all possible worlds

argument by analogy

necessary being

456 existence—a predicate?

Questions for Discussion and Review

1. Explain in your own words Anselm's two ontological proofs of God.

2. What is a *reductio* proof? Give an example other than one mentioned in the text.

3. Summarize Gaunilo's objection to Anselm's argument. Evaluate Anselm's response to that objection.

4. State, in your own words, Aquinas's first, second, and third ways. Which of these arguments seems to you the soundest, and why?

5. In your own words, state Julian of Norwich's arguments for knowing that God exists, for knowing what God's nature is, and for knowing what God wants of us.

6. Compare Descartes's version of the ontological argument with one or another of Anselm's. Which version is the soundest, and why?

7. In your own words, state Leibniz's proof of God's existence. Can you find anything wrong with it?

8. Critically evaluate Leibniz's solution to the problem of evil.

9. In your own words, summarize Hume's criticisms of the teleological argument. Are these criticisms sound? Why or why not?

10. Explain Hume's reasoning for remaining skeptical of reports of miracles. Is this reasoning sound?

11. Hume maintained that if you explain the cause of each event in a series by reference to earlier events in the series, there is no sense in then trying to find a single cause for the entire series of events. Is this right? What does it have to do with the question of God's existence?

Suggested Further Readings

Anselm, *Basic Writings*, S. N. Deane, trans. (Lasalle: Open Court, 1974). This work contains Anselm's basic writings, though what we have already given you in this text may well be sufficient for most purposes.

Aquinas, *Basic Writings of Saint Thomas Aquinas*, 2 vols., A. C. Pegis, ed. (New York: Random House, 1945). You have read the Five Ways, but you might also wish to consult the sections of *Summa Theologica* that deal with the nature and attributes of God, and also Part 1, questions 48 and 49, and the first part of Part 2, question 79, for the classical Christian discussion of evil.

D. R. Burrill, ed., *The Cosmological Argument* (Garden City: Doubleday Anchor, 1967). Selected readings on the cosmological arguments, for and against.

A. Flew, *Hume's Philosophy of Belief: A Study of His First Inquiry* (London: Routledge & Kegan Paul, 1961). Contains an analysis of Hume's treatment of the "religious hypothesis."

C. W. Hendel, Jr., *Hume Selections* (New York: Scribners, 1927). See especially pp. 143–282 and 284–401.

Julian of Norwich, *A Book of Showings to the Anchoress Julian of Norwich,* 2 vols., Colledge and Walsh, eds. (Toronto: Pontifical Institute of Medieval Studies, 1978). The early English version. You have to read it aloud to understand it.

Julian of Norwich, *Revelations of Divine Love,* Clifton Wolters, trans. (Harmondsworth, England: Penguin, 1966, 1985). A good, cheap paperback version of "Showings" in modern English.

I. Kant, *Critique of Practical Reason*, L. W. Beck, trans. (New York: Liberal Arts, 1956). See Book II, Chap. II, sect. V.

I. Kant, *Critique of Pure Reason*, N. K. Smith, trans. (New York: St. Martin's, 1965). Check the index under "God." The most important material is in the chapter entitled "The Ideal of Pure Reason."

A. Kenny, *Five Ways: St. Thomas Aquinas's Proofs of God's Existence* (London: Routledge & Kegan Paul, 1969). Good critical discussion of the Five Ways.

G. Leibniz, *Theodicy*, E. M. Huggard, trans., and A. Farrer, ed. (Lasalle: Open Court, 1952).

J. L. Mackie, *The Miracle of Theism: Arguments For and Against the Existence of God* (Oxford: Clarendon Press, 1982). Excellent commentary on all the traditional proofs of God's existence.

R. J. Moore and B. N. Moore, *The Cosmos, God and Philosophy* (New York: Peter Lang, 1988). Contains discussion of modern science on traditional proofs of God.

N. Pike, ed., *God and Evil: Readings on the Theological Problem of Evil* (Englewood Cliffs, N.J.: Prentice-Hall, 1964). A popular anthology on the subject.

A. Plantinga, *The Ontological Argument from St. Anselm to Contemporary Philosophers* (New York: Doubleday Anchor, 1965). Contains relevant articles written mainly by analytic philosophers. Some are very tough.

B. Russell and F. C. Copleston, "The Existence of God: A Debate Between Bertrand Russell and Father F. C. Copleston." This lively debate touches on several lines of proof of God, and Copleston's version of Leibniz's cosmological argument is pretty effectively worded. The debate has been anthologized in many places. See, e.g., E. L. Miller, *Philosophical and Religious Issues: Classical and Contemporary Statements* (Encino, Calif.: Dickenson, 1971).

Mary Ellen Waithe, *A History of Women Philosophers,* vol. 2, *Medieval Women Philosophers, 500–1600.* (Dordrecht, Boston and London: Kluwer Academic Publishers, 1989). Includes an article on Julian of Norwich by Elisabeth Evasdaughter.

13 God in the Age of Science

"God is dead."—Nietzsche

"Nietzsche is dead."—God

   —Graffiti

Religion and science are two high authorities in Western civilization. Unfortunately, they are not always comfortable with each other. Religion understands the world as requiring a deity; science apparently does not. Science portrays the universe as self-sustaining and self-sufficient. God does not figure into the equations of science, and scientists never refer to a nonphysical agency in their professional work. Religion must wager that in some way or another a purely scientific understanding of the world will prove to be incomplete or else be prepared to explain why an intelligent person should adopt the religious perspective.

This tension between science and religion provides the backdrop to the philosophy of religion for the past two centuries, and especially for that aspect of the philosophy of religion on which we are focusing in this text, the philosophical consideration of the Christian belief in God. During the past two centuries, we find philosophers increasingly concerned with whether the age of science leaves room for a belief in God. Some philosophers, you will see, viewed the complexity of the world as revealed by science as a reason *for* believing in God.

Nineteenth-Century Philosophers

Despite the criticism made by Kant and the more sustained barrage leveled at it by Hume, the design argument had (and still has) many defenders. One of these was

BY JOVE, HARGROVE!
WHAT AN UNUSUAL
ROCK!

The speaker seems nutty because he regards something that obviously was made by an intelligent craftsperson as just a rock—something that was created by natural physical processes. From Paley's point of view, it is equally nutty to think that an organ like the eye could be the result of natural physical processes.

the English philosopher **William Paley** (1743–1805), sometimes called ''Pigeon Paley'' during his own day because of his satirical account of some pigeons owning private property.

Paley

Paley had a substantial reputation in the late eighteenth and early nineteenth centuries as a moral philosopher, but he is best remembered now for his clever presentation of the argument from design. Paley is usually thought of as a late eighteenth-century philosopher, but his most important work came out early in the nineteenth century, so we will include him in this discussion.

In *A View of the Evidences of Christianity* (1794), Paley argued against Hume's thesis that reports of miracles are inherently untrustworthy, and in his most famous and important work, *Natural Theology* (1802), he in effect took issue with Hume's attack on the argument from design. We say ''in effect'' because in that book he did not argue against Hume explicitly, as he had in the earlier book; instead, he tendered his own effectively worded version of the argument from design.

In Paley's opinion, you will see, dismissing the argument from design makes no sense whatsoever. Suppose you found a watch lying on the ground somewhere. Would you suppose that it had *just been lying there forever,* like a stone? Obviously not. The watch gives too much evidence of design; it obviously had a maker and was not produced by random forces. But now consider living organisms and their organs. These are things considerably more subtle and intricate in their composition than a mere watch. Are we seriously to suppose that they give no more evidence of intelligent design than a stone? In short, Paley suggests that dismissing the argument from design is a patent absurdity, akin to supposing that watches just happen to come into existence.

As you read Selection 13.1, you may wish to consider whether Paley's version of the argument is subject to Hume's criticism.

SELECTION 13.1

Natural Theology

From William Paley

A WATCH IMPLIES A WATCHMAKER

In crossing a heath, suppose I pitched my foot against a *stone,* and were asked how the stone came to be there; I might possibly answer, that, for anything I knew to the contrary, it had lain there forever: nor would it perhaps be very easy to show the absurdity of this answer. But suppose I had found a *watch* upon the ground, and it would be inquired how the watch happened to be in that place: I should hardly think of the answer which I had given before, that, for anything I knew, the watch might have always been there. Yet why should not this answer serve for the watch as well as for the stone? Why is it not as admissible in the second case, as in the first?

For this reason, and for no other, viz. that, when we come to inspect the watch, we perceive (what we could not discover in the stone) that its several parts are framed and put together for a purpose, e.g., that they are so formed and adjusted as to produce motion, and that motion so regulated as to point out the hour of the day; that if the different parts had been differently shaped from what they are, of a different size from what they are, or placed after any other manner, or in any other order . . . either no motion at all would have been carried on in the machine, or none which would have answered the use that is now served by it. . . . The inference, we think, is inevitable; that the watch must have had a maker; that there must have existed, at sometime, and at some place or other,

an artificer or artificers, who formed it for the purpose which we find it actually to answer; who comprehended its construction, and designed its use.

Nor would it, I apprehend, weaken the conclusion, that we had never seen a watch made. . . .

Neither, secondly, would it invalidate our conclusion, that the watch sometimes went wrong, or that it seldom went exactly right. . . . It is not necessary that a machine be perfect, in order to show with what design it was made: still less necessary, where the only question is, whether it were made with any design at all. . . .

Nor, thirdly, would it bring any uncertainty into the argument, if there were a few parts of the watch, concerning which we could not discover, or had not yet discovered, in what manner they conduced to the general effect. . . .

Nor, fourthly, would any man in his senses think the existence of the watch, with its various machinery, accounted for, by being told that it was one out of possible combinations of material forms. . . .

Nor, fifthly, would it yield to his inquiry more satisfaction to be answered, that there existed in things a principle of order, which had disposed the parts of the watch into their present form and situation. He [cannot] even form to himself an idea of what is meant by a principle or order distinct from the intelligence of the watchmaker.

Sixthly, he would be surprised to hear that the mechanism of the watch was no proof of contrivance, only a motive to induce the mind to think so. . . .

Neither, lastly, would our observer be driven out of his conclusion . . . by being told that he knew nothing at all about the matter. He knows enough for his argument. . . .

EVEN A "SELF-REPRODUCING" WATCH IMPLIES A WATCHMAKER

Suppose, in the next place, that the person who found the watch, should, after sometime, discover, that, in addition to all the properties which he had hitherto observed in it, it possessed the unexpected property of producing, in the course of its movement, another watch like itself (the thing is conceivable), that it contained within it a mechanism, a system of parts, a mould for instance, or a complex adjustment of lathes, files, and other tools, evidently and separately calculated for this purpose; let us inquire, what effect ought such a discovery to have upon his former conclusion. . . .

If it be said, that upon the supposition of one watch being produced from another in the course of that other's movements, and by means of the mechanism within it, we have a cause for the watch in my hand, viz. the watch from which it proceeded: I deny, that for the design, the contrivance, the suitableness of means to an end, the adaptation of instruments to a use we have any cause whatever. It is in vain, therefore, to assign a series of such causes, or to allege that a series may be carried back to infinity; for I do not admit that we have yet any cause at all of the phenomena, still less any series of causes either finite or infinite. Here is contrivance, but no contriver: proofs of design, but no designer.

The conclusion which the *first* examination of the watch . . . suggested, was, that it must have had, for the cause and author of that construction, an artificer, who understood its mechanism, and designed its use. This conclusion is invincible. A *second* examination presents us with a new discovery. The watch is found, in the course of its movement, to produce another watch, similar to itself: and not only so, but we perceive in it a system or organization, separately calculated for that purpose. What effect would this discovery have or ought it to have, upon our former inference? What . . . but to increase, beyond measure, our admiration of the skill which had been employed in the formation of such a machine! Or shall it, instead of this, all at once turn us round to an opposite conclusion, viz. that no art or skill whatever has been concerned in the business, although all other evidences of art and skill remain as they were, and this last and supreme piece of art be now added to the rest? Can this be maintained without absurdity? Yet this is atheism.

This is atheism: for every indication of contrivance, every manifestation of design, which existed in the watch, exists in the works of nature; with the difference, on the side of nature, of being greater and more, and that in a degree which exceeds all computation. I mean, that the contrivances of nature surpass the contrivances of art, in the complexity, subtlety, and curiosity of the mechanism; and still more, if possible, do they go beyond them in number and variety; yet, in a multitude of cases, are not less evidently mechanical, not less evidently contrivances, not less evidently accommodated to their end, or suited to their office, than are the most perfect productions of human ingenuity.

THE EYE AND THE TELESCOPE

I know no better method of introducing so large a subject, than that of comparing a single thing with a single thing; an eye, for example, with a telescope. As far as the examination of the instrument goes, there is precisely the same proof that the eye was made for vision, as there is that the telescope was made for assisting it. They are made upon the same principles; both being adjusted to the laws by which the transmission and reflection of rays of light are regulated. . . . For instance; these laws require, in order to produce the same effect, that the rays of light, in passing from water into the eye, should be refracted by a more convex surface than when it passes out of air into the eye. Accordingly we find, that the eye of a fish, in that part of it called the crystalline lens, is much rounder than the eye of terrestrial animals. What plainer manifestation of design can there be than this difference? What could a mathematical instrument-maker have done more, to show his knowledge of this principle, his application of that knowledge, his suiting of his means to his end . . . [?]

FURTHER EVIDENCE OF DESIGN IN THE EYE

In considering vision as achieved by the means of an image formed at the bottom of the eye, we can never reflect without wonder upon the smallness, yet correctness, of the picture, the subtlety of the touch, the fineness of the lines. A landscape of five or six square leagues is brought into a space of half an inch diameter. . . . A stage-coach travelling at its ordinary speed for half an hour, passes, in the eye, only over one-twelfth of an inch, yet is this change of place in the image distinctly perceived throughout its whole progress. . . .

Besides that conformity to optical principles which its internal constitution displays . . . there is to be seen, in everything belonging to it and about it, an extraordinary degree of care. . . . It is lodged in a strong, deep, bony socket. . . . Within this socket it is embedded in fat, of all animal substances the best adapted both to its repose and motion. It is sheltered by the eyebrows; an arch of hair, which like a thatched penthouse, prevents the sweat and moisture of the forehead from running down into it.

But it is still better protected by its lid. . . . It defends the eye; it wipes it; it closes it in sleep. Are there, in any work of art whatever, purposes more evident than those which this organ fulfills? or an apparatus for executing those purposes more intelligible, more appropriate, or more mechanical? . . .

In order to keep the eye moist and clean . . . a wash is constantly supplied by a secretion for the purpose; and the superfluous brine is conveyed to the nose through a perforation in the bone as large as a goose-quill. When once the fluid has entered the nose, it spreads itself upon the inside of the nostril, and is evaporated by the current of warm air, which, in the course of respiration, is continually passing over it. Can any pipe or outlet for carrying off the waste liquor from a dye-hour or a distillery, be more mechanical than this is? It is easily perceived, that the eye must want moisture: but could the want of the eye generate the gland which produces the tear, or bore the hole by which it is discharged—a hole through a bone? . . .

Were there no example in the world of contrivance, except that of the eye, it would be alone sufficient to suppose the conclusion which we draw from it, as to the necessity of an intelligent Creator. . . . If other parts of nature were inaccessible to our inquiries, or even if other parts of nature presented nothing to our examination but disorder and confusion, the validity of this example would remain the same. If there were but one watch in the world, it would not be less certain that it had a maker. . . . The argument is cumulative, in the fullest sense of that term. The eye proves [divine agency] without the ear; the ear without the eye. The proof in each example is complete; for when the design of the part, and the conduciveness of its structure to that design is shown, the mind may set itself at rest; no future consideration can detract anything from the force of the example.

Newman

Few intellectuals have been as highly esteemed in their own time as **John Henry Newman** (1801–1890) was. Newman, deeply religious from his youth, had been ordained in the Church of England and was made vicar of St. Mary's, Oxford. But in early middle age he revised his views on Roman Catholicism and was received into the Roman Catholic Church, eventually becoming a cardinal and inspiring many other Anglicans to convert as well. Newman was therefore a churchman, but he was also a philosopher.

Newman was much concerned with the differences between formal logic and actual real-life or, as he called it, "concrete" reasoning—and especially with the principles that validate the latter. He came to believe that whenever we concern ourselves with concrete matters of fact, our conclusions may not have the status of logical certainties, but we can nevertheless attain certitude, as a state of mind, about them. In particular, he held, we can achieve certitude in our religious faith.

Now it is by virtue of our experience of *conscience,* according to Newman, that we find certitude about God. Conscience, he said, can be relied on exactly as much as we rely on memory or reason. And feelings of conscience lead us to affirm an intelligent being as their cause, he held. Conscience is a sense of responsibility and duty that points toward something beyond the realm of people, toward a Supreme Governor or Judge whose dictates we are ashamed or fear to violate and whose approval we seek. In short, in the experience of conscience we find ourselves undeniably *answerable* to an intelligence beyond ourselves.

Newman thus endorsed a moral argument for God, but it is rather unlike Kant's moral argument. According to Kant, to assume that one can act morally is to assume that there is justice; it is to assume, that is, that moral uprightness will be rewarded with happiness. And this in turn is to assume the existence of a God who ensures that there is justice. In other words, if what ought to be is, then God exists. The requirements of morality thus lead us to *postulate* God, according to Kant.

But according to Newman, we are simply unable to doubt God's existence, given the experience of conscience. Newman's proof is much more direct, in other words. That God exists is as indisputable as our awareness that we are answerable to Him, and this awareness we find in the dictates of conscience.

Kierkegaard

It is interesting to contrast Cardinal Newman's philosophy with that of the Danish philosopher **Søren Kierkegaard** (1813–1855), who lived about the same time. Neither philosopher thought that you could rationally prove that God exists. But the similarity between the two ends there.

For Kierkegaard, "to exist" is to be engaged in time and history. Because God is an eternal and immutable being, "existence" does not even apply to God. But God as Christ existed, for Kierkegaard. Christ, however, is a paradox that the human intellect cannot comprehend, for in Christ the immutable became changing, the eternal became temporal, and what is beyond history became historical.

In short, Kierkegaard thought that God is beyond the grasp of reason and that the idea that God came to us as a man in the person of Jesus is intellectually absurd. Yet at the same time Kierkegaard's primary mission was to show what it is to be a Christian, and he was himself totally committed to Christianity. How can this be?

First, the notion that we can sit back and weigh objectively the evidence about God's existence pro and contra, that we can conduct an impartial investigation of the issue and arrive at the "truth," is totally rejected by Kierkegaard. He would not have bothered reading this chapter.

In fact, Kierkegaard mocks the whole idea of objective truth. Truth, he said, is subjective. Truth lies not in *what* you believe, but in *how you live.* Truth is passionate commitment.

For example, think of a person who worships the "true" God but does so merely as a matter of routine, without passion or commitment. Compare this person with one who worships a mere idol but does so with the infinite commitment of his soul. In fact, said Kierkegaard, "the one prays in truth to God though he worships an idol; the other prays falsely to the true God, and hence worships in fact an idol."

Second, Kierkegaard rejected completely the Aristotelian idea that the essential attribute of humans is their capacity to reason. For Kierkegaard, the most important attribute of man is not thought but *will.* Man is a being that *makes choices.*

But if truth is not objective, then there are no external principles or criteria that are objectively valid and against which one might judge one's choices. How, then, are we to choose, if there are no objective, rational criteria, and we have only our own judgment to rely on? This problem—the problem of knowing how and what to choose in the absence of objective truth—became, after Kierkegaard, the central problem of existentialism.

Kierkegaard's answer is that we must commit ourselves totally to God. Salvation can be had only through a *leap of faith,* through a nonintellectual, passionate, "infinite" commitment to Christianity. "Faith constitutes a sphere all by itself, and every misunderstanding of Christianity may at once be recognized by its transforming it into a doctrine, transferring it to the sphere of the intellectual."

What Kierkegaard said must not be confused with what earlier Christian thinkers had maintained. Earlier Christian thinkers had said that faith precedes understanding and had held that you must have faith in God before rational thought about Him can begin. But thinkers such as Augustine and Anselm had still looked for, and had fully expected there to be, rational grounds for confirming what they already accepted by faith. Kierkegaard, in contrast, thought that no such rational grounds exist: God is an intellectual absurdity.

Further, he held that rational grounds for believing in God, if there were any, would actually be *incompatible* with having faith. "If I wish to preserve myself in faith I must constantly be intent upon holding fast to the *objective uncertainty* [of God]," he said. The objective uncertainty of God, for Kierkegaard, is thus *essential* to a true faith in Him. Only if there is objective uncertainty, he wrote, can "[I] remain out upon the deep, over seventy thousand fathoms of water, still preserving my faith."

Nietzsche

"God is dead," said Nietzsche. By this infamous remark, **Friedrich Nietzsche** (1844–1900) did not mean that God once existed and now no longer does. He meant that all people with an ounce of intelligence would now perceive that there is no intelligent plan to the universe or rational order in it: they would now understand that there is no reason why things happen one way and not another and that the harmony and order we imagine to exist in the universe is merely pasted on by the human mind.

Nietzsche, however, would have regarded very few people as having this required ounce of intelligence, and he in fact had a way of denigrating everyone in sight. For the mass of people, Nietzsche thought, God certainly is not dead. But these people, in Nietzsche's opinion, are pathetic wretches governed by a world view inculcated by religion, science, and philosophy, a world view that in Nietzsche's opinion makes them feeble losers who are motivated mainly by resentment. They view the world as a rational, law-governed place and adhere to a slave morality that praises the man who serves his fellow creatures with meekness and self-sacrifice.

In Nietzsche's opinion, the negative morality of these pitiful slaves—the mass of humankind, ordinary people—must be reevaluated and replaced by life-affirming values. The new morality will be based on the development of a new kind of human being, whom Nietzsche calls the "overman" or "superman" (*Übermensch*). Such a one not only accepts life in all its facets, including all its pain, but also makes living into an art. Among the forerunners of the overman, Nietzsche cites Alexander the Great and Napoleon. [*German Nationalist philosopher/ early 1800's*]

Nietzsche's thesis that there is no God and its apparent corollary that there are no absolute and necessary criteria of right and wrong were accepted by such twentieth-century existentialist philosophers as Albert Camus and Jean-Paul Sartre. For these thinkers, *the* fundamental problem of philosophy is how to live one's life, given the absence of objectively valid standards by which to evaluate one's choices and decisions.

Nietzsche, Kierkegaard, and some existentialists would all have agreed that the various rational discussions about God's existence to which this chapter is devoted are impotent and meaningless.

The next selection comprises one of the most important passages in which Nietzsche asserts that God is dead and explains what he means.

SELECTION 13.2

*The Gay Science**   **From Friedrich Nietzsche**

The Meaning of Our Cheerfulness. The greatest recent event—that "God is dead," that the belief in the Christian god has become unbelievable—is already beginning to cast its first shadows over Europe. For the few at least, whose eyes—the *suspicion* in whose eyes is strong and subtle enough for this spectacle, some sun seems to have set and some ancient and profound trust has been turned into doubt; to them our old world must appear daily more like evening, more mistrustful, stranger, "older." But in the main one may say: The event itself is far too great, too distant, too remote from the multitude's capacity for comprehension even for the tidings of it to be thought of as having *arrived* as yet. Much less may one suppose that many people know as yet *what* this event really means—and how much must collapse now that this faith has been undermined because it was built upon this faith, propped up by it, grown into it; for example, the whole of our European morality. This long plenitude and sequence of breakdown, destruction, ruin, and cataclysm that is now impending—who could guess enough of it today to be compelled to play the teacher and advance proclaimer of this monstrous logic of terror, the prophet of a gloom and an eclipse of

the sun whose like has probably never yet occurred on earth?

Even we born guessers of riddles who are, as it were, waiting on the mountains, posted between today and tomorrow, stretched in the contradiction between today and tomorrow, we firstlings and premature births of the coming century, to whom the shadows that must soon envelop Europe really *should* have appeared by now—why is it that even we look forward to the approaching gloom without any real sense of involvement and above all without any worry and fear for *ourselves?* Are we perhaps still too much under the impression of the *initial consequences* of this event—and these initial consequences, the consequences for *ourselves,* are quite the opposite of what one might perhaps expect: They are not at all sad and gloomy but rather like a new and scarcely describable kind of light, happiness, relief, exhilaration, encouragement, dawn.

Indeed, we philosophers and "free spirits" feel, when we hear the news that "the old god is dead," as if a new dawn shone on us; our heart overflows with gratitude, amazement, premonitions, expectation. At long last the horizon appears free to us again, even if it should not be bright; at long last our ships may venture out again, venture out to face any danger; all the daring of the lover of knowledge is permitted again; the sea, *our* sea, lies open again; perhaps there has never yet been such an "open sea."—

*Editor's footnotes have been omitted.

James

Paley's main work appeared at the very beginning of the nineteenth century. The next philosopher we consider, **William James,** published his first major work,

The Will to Believe and Other Essays, in 1897, at the end of the century. So James and Paley were really turn-of-the-century philosophers, at different ends of the same century.

One big difference between James's end of the nineteenth century and Paley's beginning of it lay in the marked increase in agnosticism by the year 1900. There is an antagonism between the religious view of the world as a divinely created paradise planned for the sake of human spiritual growth and the supposedly scientific view of the cosmos as a blind churning of material particles in accordance with physical laws. For the past two hundred years the blind-churning view had become more and more congenial to Western intellectuals. Around mid-century, Darwin had explained how the origin of species need not be divine, and Karl Marx had pronounced religion to be the opium of the people. If the power of Hume's and Kant's reasoning did not force philosophers to take seriously their criticisms of the old proofs of God, the spirit of the times did. Before the end of the century, Friedrich Nietzsche, as we have seen, could proclaim that God was dead.

But God wasn't, and isn't, dead for everyone. In fact, the question of God's existence was at the time, and still is, for very many (1) a *live* issue and furthermore (2) a *momentous* one. For William James it is both. It is also, in addition, according to James, (3) *forced,* which means that you cannot suspend judgment in the matter. For James, to profess agnosticism and to pretend to suspend judgment is in fact "backing the field against the religious hypothesis."

Now James argued for deciding this issue (of God's existence) in favor of God. He began his argument, not a simple one, by noting that *"our nonintellectual nature does influence our convictions."* Indeed, usually our convictions are *determined* by our nonintellectual nature, he maintained. Rarely does pure reason settle our opinion. What settles our opinion usually is our wishing and willing and sentimental preferences, our fears and hopes, prejudices and emotions, and even the pressure of our friends. It is our "passional nature" that settles our opinion, he said.

Sometimes we even deliberately will what we believe, James held. Need proof that he is correct? Probably you would prefer not to accept claims that are based on pitifully insufficient evidence (we hope). So when someone asserts something that is based on insufficient evidence, what do you do? You *try not to believe it.* And often you are successful in not accepting the poorly supported claim. When you are, then haven't you in fact *willed* yourself not to accept what the person has asserted? Your will, your desire not to accept unsupported claims, has influenced your beliefs.

Of course, if you are like most of us, you may find yourself accepting what the person says anyway. But if you consider the matter carefully, isn't your acceptance also a case of something other than cold reason influencing your beliefs? You may *hope* that what the person has said is true. You may simply *want* to believe it, *despite* its having been poorly supported. If so, your hope that what has been said is true has simply *overcome* your desire not to accept unsupported claims. So here again your "passional nature" has settled your opinion.

Creation *or* Evolution?

The publication in 1859 of Charles Darwin's *On the Origin of Species by Means of Natural Selection: Or, the Preservation of Favoured Races in the Struggle for Life* (usually referred to as *On the Origin of Species*) provoked responses from within Catholicism and conservative Protestantism. Pope Pius IX in 1870 declared evolution a heresy, and in 1874 Princeton theologian Charles Hodge, a Presbyterian, asked "What is Darwinism?" and answered: "it is atheism."

But another contemporary of Darwin's, American botanist Asa Gray (1810–1888), was not so certain. Gray described himself as "one who is scientifically, and in his own fashion, a Darwinian, philosophically a convinced theist, and religiously an acceptor of the 'creed commonly called the Nicene,' as the exponent of the Christian faith." Gray found room in Darwin's depiction of natural selection for the view that God was the ultimate designer of nature; Hodge himself claimed Darwinism was contrary to the Christian faith only insofar as it denied the existence of purpose in the universe. For Gray, "the issue comes to this: Have the multitudinous forms of living creatures, past and present, been produced by as many special and independent acts of creation at very numerous epochs? Or have they originated under causes as natural as reproduction and birth, and no more so, by the variation and change of preceding into succeeding species? Those who ac-

cept the latter alternative are evolutionists. And . . . their views, although clearly wrong may be genuinely theistic."

Historian George Marsden, writing in 1984, found that twenty years after the publication of *On the Origin of Species*, Bible-believing American Protestant scientists—and even conservative theologians—did not make opposition to any form of evolutionism a necessary test of faith. But such reconciliationist positions began to lose favor in the evangelical community after the Scopes "monkey trial," July 10–21, 1925, in Dayton, Tennessee. Though high school teacher John Scopes was found guilty of teaching evolution in the classroom (and fined $100), defense attorney Clarence Darrow held up to public ridicule the religious views of William Jennings Bryan, the prosecutor.

Revolutionary changes were sweeping American culture: surging immigration meant a breakdown of a common world view—if one ever existed; critical Biblical studies from Germany undermined the perceived authority of the Christian Bible; and a growing secularism in society loosened the ties of science and faith.

There were new currents in philosophy as well. As Marsden summarized: "The fundamentalist outlook preserves essentially Enlightenment and pre-Kantian philosophical categories. Truth is fixed and eternal and something to be discovered either by scientific in-

quiry or by looking at some other reliable source such as the Bible. Much of the rest of modern thought, however, had gradually come to view the human mind as imposing its categories on reality. Perception itself in this view is an interpretive process. Truth, moreover, is relative to the observer and to the community or culture of the inquirer. Speculative theorizing is essential, since human thought in any case involves such imposing of one's constructs on reality."

Contemporary defenders of so-called creation-science, such as Duane Gish and John D. Morris of the Institute for Creation Research (ICR) in El Cajon, California, appear to carry on the Enlightenment tradition. In an article in the January 1992 ICR newsletter, John Morris wrote, "Evolution is not even in a category of things that could ever be a scientific fact! It is a world view about the past—a historical reconstruction. It is a way to interpret scientific data, such as rocks, fossils, and complex living systems which exist in the present. It is a potential answer to the question, 'What happened in the unobserved past to make the present get to be this way?'" Morris finds the evolutionary answer unacceptable; "it embraces strict naturalism, an anti-God philosophy, and results in a denial of the major doctrines of Scripture. . . . If no supernatural agency has been at work throughout history, then creation is dead. But if evolutionists even allow a spark of supernatural design in history, then evolution is dead, for evolution necessarily relies on solely natural processes."

Creation *and* Evolution?

ICR President Henry M. Morris believes that reconciliationist positions are untenable:

- "Theistic evolution" (which maintains that God used evolution as his process of creation) cannot be reconciled with the account of creation in the book of Genesis and the concept of God as loving and all-knowing because it is (1) theologically unsound— evolution requires false starts and inefficiency, and the survival of the fittest is contrary to the working of God's love, (2) Biblically unsound (God created the species), and (3) sociologically harmful (evolution "served Hitler as the rationale for Nazism and Marx as the supposed scientific basis for communism").

- "Progressive creation" (which maintains that the human body evolved but God created the soul) also involves waste in the evolutionary process; if evolution could not provide human beings with souls, why would God use evolution in the first place?

- "The Day-Age theory" (in which the days of creation

mentioned in the first chapter of Genesis are likened to geological ages), according to Henry Morris, contradicts the geological account: "For example, the Bible teaches that the earth existed before the stars, that it was initially covered with water, that fruit trees appeared before fishes, that plant life preceded the sun, that the first animals created were the whales, that birds were made before insects, that man was made before woman...." In addition, given the destruction that geologists say has taken place over the past five billion years or so, how could God have pronounced his creation to be "very good"?

- "The Gap theory" (which places the geologic ages between the first and second verse of the first chapter of Genesis) postulates a cataclysmic event billions of years after God's (first) creation, with a re-creation taking place in the second verse ("and the earth was without form, and void"). But Morris contends that the theory must still face the question of why God would work through evolution and then destroy his creation and re-create it all in a week. Further, the theory makes God the author of evil, using struggle and death to further his purposes in a supposed

primeval world. For Morris, the fossil record was produced not through geologic ages but in the worldwide flood of Noah described in Genesis chapters six through nine.

Scientific Creationism?

Why does ICR describe its position as *scientific* creationism? In an ICR newsletter of July 1980, Henry Morris wrote, "scientific creationism" involves "no reliance on Biblical revelation" and uses "*only scientific* data to support and expound the creation model." The tenets of scientific creationism include the following: "1. The physical universe of space, time, matter and energy has not always existed, but was supernaturally created by a transcendent personal Creator who alone has existed from eternity.... 3. Each of the major kinds of plants and animals was created functionally complete from the beginning and did not evolve from some other kind of organism. Changes in basic kinds since their first creation are limited to 'horizontal' changes (variations) within the kinds, or 'downward' changes (e.g., harmful mutations, extinctions). 4. The first human beings did not evolve from an animal ancestry, but were specifically created in fully human form from the start. Furthermore, the 'spiritual' nature of man (self-image, moral consciousness, abstract reasoning, language, will, religious nature,

(continued)

Creation or Evolution? (continued)

etc.) is itself a supernaturally created entity distinct from mere biological life...."

This example is enough to show that scientific creationism itself is not "science" in the way ICR defines science, for no present-day experiment can determine, for example, if or at what point there was no space, time, matter, or energy. Ultimately, says Duane Gish,

just what happened "back then" is a matter of faith—the faith of either evolutionism or creationism. The directors of ICR believe both "isms" ought to be taught in school. As Henry Morris writes, "Creationists . . . do not propose that the public schools teach six-day creation, the fall of man, and the Noachian flood. They do maintain, however, that they should

teach the evidence for a complex completed creation, the universal principle of decay (in contrast to the evolutionary assumption of increasing organization) and the worldwide evidences of recent catastrophism. All of these are implicit in observable scientific data, and should certainly be included in public education."

Having argued that our nonintellectual nature influences our opinions, James next distinguished between the *two commandments* of rational thinkers. These are

1. To believe the truth
2. To avoid errors

Some individuals, James noted, favor (2) over (1): they would rather avoid errors than find the truth. "Better go without belief forever than believe a falsehood" is the creed dictated to them by their passional nature: better dead than misled.

But favoring (2) over (1) is not James's creed. There are worse things than falling into error, he said. In some cases, he argued, it is best to regard "the chase for truth as paramount, and the avoidance of error as secondary."

Consider moral questions, where you must either act or not act and cannot wait for objective, definitive proof that one choice is right. In such cases, it is not possible to suspend judgment, because *not* to act is itself to make a judgment. In such cases, you make the best decision you can. Furthermore, according to James, it is *legitimate* to do this, even though you have no guarantee that your decision is correct.

And it is the same in religious matters, he said. At least it is the same if religion for you is a live and momentous issue that you cannot resolve through intellect alone. If it is, you cannot escape the issue by remaining skeptical and waiting for more information. To remain skeptical, James said, is tantamount to saying that it is better to yield to the fear of being in error than to yield to the hope that religion is true.

In fact, James argued, when it comes to religion, the other way is better: it is better to yield to the hope that all of it may be true than to give way to the fear of

PROFILE / William James (1842–1910)

ew philosophers have been better writers than William James, whose catchy phrases gave life and succulence to even the driest philosophical subjects. James had a knack for words, and he was able to state complex ideas with easy elegance. This might be expected, because James was the older brother of Henry James, the great American novelist.

The James children were raised by their wealthy and eccentric theologian father in an intellectually stimulating atmosphere that promoted their mental development. The Jameses benefited from diverse educational experiences in several schools both in America and in Europe and were largely free to pursue their own interests and develop their own capacities. They became refined and cosmopolitan.

William James had wide-ranging interests. Though fascinated with science, he decided, at age eighteen, to try to become a painter (not the kind that paints houses). But he was also wise enough to see very soon that his artistic urge exceeded his ability.

So James went off to Harvard and studied science. Then he entered the college's medical school, though he did not intend to practice medicine, and in his late twenties he received his medical degree. A few years later, he joined the Harvard faculty as a lecturer on anatomy and physiology and continued to teach at Harvard until 1907. From 1880 on, he was a member of the Harvard department of philosophy and psychology. You shouldn't think that James got interested in philosophy all of a sudden. He had always been fond of the subject and tended to give a philosophical interpretation to scientific questions.

James suffered from emotional crises until he was able to resolve the question of free will and to answer the compelling arguments for determinism. Around 1870, he found in the ideas of the French philosopher Charles Renouvier philosophical justification for believing in free will, and with it, apparently, the cure to his episodes of emotional paralysis.

In 1890, James published his famous *Principles of Psychology*, thought by many to be his major work. Equally important, from a purely philosophical standpoint, was his *The Will to Believe and Other Essays in Popular Philosophy* (1897). This work is where to find James's solution to the problem of free will, in the essay, "The Dilemma of Determinism." Other important works include *The Varieties of Religious Experience* (1902), *Pragmatism* (1907), *A Pluralistic Universe* (1909), *The Meaning of Truth* (1909), *Some Problems in Philosophy* (1911), and *Essays in Radical Empiricism* (1912).

William James was perhaps the most famous American intellectual of his time. Yet today some philosophers think of him as a lightweight—a popularizer of philosophical issues who failed to make a substantial contribution to technical philosophy (whatever that is). He is thought to bear the same relation to Hume or Kant, say, that Tchaikovsky bears to Mozart or Bach, the philosophical equivalent of the composer who only cranks out pretty melodies. But this is all a mistake. The discerning reader will find in James a great depth of insight.

being in error. If you permit the fear of error to rule you and say to yourself, "Avoid error at any cost!" then you will withhold assent to religious beliefs. Doing so will, of course, *protect* you from being in error—if the religious beliefs are incorrect. But if you withhold your assent to religious beliefs, then you will also *lose the benefits* that come from accepting those beliefs. And it is worse, James thought, to lose the benefits than to gain the protection from erring.

Not the same as Pascal's prudent wager

Further, if the religious beliefs are *true* but the evidence for them is insufficient, then the policy "Avoid error at any cost!" effectively cuts you off from an opportunity to make friends with God. Thus, in James's opinion, the policy "Avoid error at all cost!", when applied to religion, is a policy that keeps you from accepting certain propositions even if those propositions are really true; and that means that it is an *irrational* policy.

In short, even as a rational thinker you will be influenced by your passional nature. Thus you will be led to give way either to the hope that the belief in God, and associated religious beliefs, is true or to the fear that if you accept these beliefs, you will be in error. Because this is the case, it is better to give way to the hope.

Now James stressed that he was *not* saying that you should believe what, as he put it, "you know ain't true." His strategy applies, he said, only to *momentous* and *living* issues that cannot be resolved by the intellect itself. It applies only to issues like God's existence.

This Century

James's reasoning elicited much criticism. Skeptics and believers both took issue with it. Skeptics thought James had elevated wishful thinking to the status of proof, and believers questioned James's implicit assumption that God's existence cannot be established. Still others said that belief grounded in James's way was not the uncompromising and unqualified faith in God demanded by religion. From their perspective, James's belief in God amounted to a gamble (and indeed James seemed to concede this) rather than to true religious acceptance of God.

James, in any event, brings us into our own century, and we shall now consider three twentieth-century discussions of God's existence. The first is a revised and rather sophisticated version of the argument from design.

The second is something like an argument that God does not exist, but in actuality it is an argument that the whole issue is pretty meaningless to begin with.

The third is an extended argument in favor of God that combines elements of the traditional proofs of God.

We will close the chapter by considering the consequences of accepting atheism, according to an important twentieth-century atheistic philosopher of religion.

Pascal's Wager

The French mathematician and philosopher **Blaise Pascal** (1623–1662) is famous, among other reasons, for his wager-argument for God. Either God exists or he does not. By believing that he does exist, you lose nothing if he doesn't and you gain a lot, namely, happiness and eternal life, if he does. So believing that God exists is a prudent wager: you won't lose anything and you might gain much.

James denied that he was offering a version of Pascal's wager in his argument for the existence of God. You may wish to consider whether his denial is warranted.

The Consequences of Belief

James's philosophy was a species of **pragmatism,** according to which, at least in its Jamesian version, the true is "only the expedient in our way of thinking." Confronted with competing views or theories, both of which are more or less equally supportable rationally, you choose the viewpoint that works most beneficially. Instead of inquiring whether God exists, for example, the (Jamesian) pragmatist considers "what definite difference it will make to you and me" if we believe or disbelieve that he does. As can be seen from the text, James argued that the practical benefits of the theistic viewpoint are superior to those of the agnostic or atheistic viewpoint.

Applying the same strategy to the question of whether we have free will, James focused not directly on the question itself but on the outcomes that attend acceptance of the alternative viewpoints. Acceptance of determinism is unworkable, James believed, because it entails never regretting what happens: because what happened had to happen (according to determinism), it is illogical to feel that it should not have happened. Thus acceptance of determinism is inconsistent with the practices of moral beings, who perceive themselves as making genuine choices that can affect the world for better or for worse.

F. R. Tennant's Argument from Design

F. R. Tennant (1866–1957), a Cambridge philosopher of religion, set forth a striking version of the argument from design. His argument, far more subtle than those used by Paley and Hume, takes developments in science, including evolutionary theory, fully into account.

Now at the heart of traditional design-type arguments for God's existence is the fact that organisms and their component parts are amazingly well suited to their environment, and vice versa. The heart, for example, is remarkably well suited to pump blood under just the sort of conditions under which creatures with hearts are found. In this respect the heart is just like a machine that was designed to perform a certain task under certain conditions, and so it is easy to conclude that the heart was designed by a grand designer.

Whole organisms, too, are remarkably well suited to live in their environment; fish, for example, which can swim and breathe in water, are very nicely suited to live in oceans, rivers, and lakes. Thus the fact that fish are so nicely adapted to their environment suggests that they, too, were created with their environment in mind; similar reasoning pertains to any other species of animal.

And looking at things from a slightly different angle, the environment itself seems very well suited for its inhabitants, as if it had been designed for their comfort and development.

In sum, organisms and their parts are adapted to or fit their environment, and vice versa, and this fact gives rise to the argument from design.

Now Tennant thought that the fit between organisms and the physical universe, when considered carefully, exhibits much more subtlety and complexity than traditional design arguments acknowledge.

For one thing, said Tennant, there is the fact that the world is *intelligible*. It is a cosmos and not a chaos. It can be *comprehended*. There is thus a fit between the world and *human thought* that must be considered as evidence of design.

For another, there is the evolutionary process, which operating through natural selection accounts for the adaptation of organisms to their environment. This process is very well suited to produce such adaptation. Further, it exhibits progressiveness. Thus the evolutionary process is *itself* a manifestation of divine purpose. For Tennant, the fact of evolution did not undermine the argument for God; it strengthened that argument.

It must also be considered, he wrote, that the *inorganic* world is remarkably well suited for the emergence and persistence of life. That the basic inorganic conditions could be just the right ones to give rise to life and intelligence and to sustain them is unlikely to have been a chance occurrence, he argued.

For still another thing, the world is not only intelligible to the intellect; it is pleasing and stimulating to the human sense of beauty and proportion. There is a clear fit between the natural order and human aesthetic sensibilities: the world is a bearer of aesthetic value.

And for still another, the world is also suited to foster the intellectual and moral development of humankind. "The whole process of Nature is capable of being regarded as instrumental to the development of intelligent and moral creatures."

Furthermore, according to Tennant, these various instances of fit must be considered not *separately* but *collectively*. So viewed, they make it less reasonable to suppose that existing life, especially human life with its intellectual, moral, and aesthetic aspects, is the result of "cumulative groundless coincidence" (as the blind-churning view mentioned earlier would have it). Tennant thus advances a version of the argument from design that seems fully compatible with such scientific views as the theory of evolution and the idea that life arose from a soup of inorganic chemicals.

The Big Bang

The view now accepted by most scientists is that the universe is an explosion, known as the Big Bang. Unlike other explosions, the Big Bang does not expand outward into space, like a dynamite or bomb explosion, nor does it have a duration in external time, as do all other explosions, because all space and all time are located within it. The beginning of the Big Bang is the beginning of space and time and of matter and energy, and it is, in fact, the beginning of our expanding universe.

The most prevalent view among the qualified experts who have an opinion on the matter is that it is impossible to know what transpired in the Big Bang before 10^{-43} seconds after zero time, when the Big Bang began. But, for various reasons that we need not go into here, most of these experts do apparently believe that there was a zero time, that the universe did have an absolute beginning, that there was a first physical event.

Now the first physical event, assuming that such a thing did take place, either is explainable or it is not. On one hand, it is difficult to believe that the first physical event has no explanation, for that amounts to saying that the entire universe, with its incredible size and complexity, was just a chance occurrence, a piece of good luck. But on the other hand, if the first physical event is explicable, then it would seem that the explanation must refer to some sort of non-physical phenomenon, which certainly could be called "God."

Thus, the Big Bang theory, if true—and there seems to be much reason for supposing that it is true—may well require philosophers to make a hard choice between an unexplainable universe and one explainable only by reference to something nonphysical.

In fact, from Tennant's perspective, a teleological explanation of the world is really a *continuation by extrapolation* of science and is verified in the same sort of way that scientific theories are—namely, it provides the most plausible explanation of the given empirical facts. Tennant did not think that the adaptation of life to the physical world, and vice versa, and the appropriateness of the natural conditions to give rise to life and to biological, intellectual, moral, and aesthetic progress provide a *conclusive demonstration,* as might be found in logic or mathematics, for theism. But he thought that they do offer grounds for *reasonable belief.*

Flew's Simple Central Questions

In the late 1920s, a group of philosophers, mathematicians, and scientists, led by Moritz Schlick, a philosopher at the University of Vienna, set forth a group of ideas known as **logical positivism.** A central tenet of this **Vienna Circle,** and of logical positivism, as we saw in Chapter 6, is the **verifiability principle,** according to which the meaning of a proposition is the experience you would have to have to know that it is true. What does it mean to say, "The sprinkler is on"? Well, to find out if that proposition is true, you'd have to look out the window or go out into the yard or otherwise do some checking. The experience required to do the checking is what the proposition means, according to the verifiability principle.

Is This Atheism?

Logical positivists, who dismissed the utterance "God exists" as meaningless, were usually perceived as denying God's existence. But were they? A person who denies God exists believes God does not exist. But the positivist position was not that God does not exist. It was that the utterance "God exists" is *meaningless*. Equally, they held, the proposition "God does not exist" is meaningless, too. The debate between believers and doubters, they maintained, cannot be settled by sense experience and is therefore stuff and nonsense.

What this principle entails is that a pronouncement that is not verifiable has no factual meaning. Take the remark "The sprinkler stopped working due to fate." What kind of checking would you do to see if this is true? There isn't any kind of experience a person might have that would verify this remark. Therefore, it's factually meaningless, the logical positivists would say.

Of course, some propositions are true by virtue of what their words mean: for example, "You are older than everyone who is younger than you." Such *analytic propositions,* as they are called, are rendered true by definition rather than by experience, according to the logical positivists. But the proposition "The sprinkler stopped working due to fate" isn't like that. It's not an analytic proposition, so it has to be verifiable in experience if it is to have factual meaning. And because it isn't, it doesn't.

So, according to the logical positivists, the good many philosophical assertions from metaphysics, epistemology, and ethics that are neither analytic nor verifiable are factually meaningless. These assertions may perhaps express emotional sentiments, but they are neither true nor false. Rudolph Carnap (1891–1970), one of the most famous members of the Vienna Circle, even declared, "We reject *all* philosophical questions, whether of Metaphysics, Ethics or Epistemology."

The verifiability principle has its difficulties, the most famous of which is that the principle itself isn't verifiable and thus must either be factually meaningless or a mere analytic verbal truth. Perhaps more important, at least to the logical positivists, is that even assuming that the principle is not factually meaningless, what it actually says is unclear. Does it require that a proposition must be *conclusively* verifiable? But in that case universal claims, such as those that state the laws of physics, would be factually meaningless. And if absolute verifiability is not required, to what extent is partial verifiability required?

Today few philosophers would call themselves logical positivists. But most philosophers would still maintain that *empirical* or *factual* propositions must in *some* sense and to *some* extent be verifiable by experience.

So what, then, about such assertions as "God exists" or "God created the world"? These look like factual propositions. But are they in any sense verifiable?

Selection 13.3 is by British philosopher **Antony Flew** (1923–). The influence of positivist thinking on his thought will be very clear to you.

SELECTION 13.3

*"Theology and Falsification"** *[Turned out to be implausible has been rejected]*   **From Antony Flew**

Let us begin with a parable. It is a parable developed from a tale told by John Wisdom in his haunting and revelatory article "Gods." Once upon a time two explorers came upon a clearing in the jungle. In the clearing were growing many flowers and many weeds. One explorer says, "Some gardener must tend this plot." The other disagrees, "There is no gardener." So they pitch their tents and set a watch. No gardener is ever seen. "But perhaps he is an invisible gardener." So they set up a barbed-wire fence. They electrify it. They patrol with bloodhounds. (For they remember how H. G. Wells's "invisible man" could be both smelt and touched though he could not be seen.) But no shrieks ever suggest that some intruder has received a shock. No movements of the wire ever betray an invisible climber. The bloodhounds never give cry. Yet still the Believer is not convinced. "But there is a gardener, invisible, intangible, insensible to electric shocks, a gardener who has no scent and makes no sound, a gardener who comes secretly to look after the garden which he loves." At last the Sceptic despairs, "But what remains of your original assertion? Just how does what you call an invisible, intangible, eternally elusive gardener differ from an imaginary gardener or even from no gardener at all?"

In this parable we can see how what starts as an assertion, that something exists or that there is some analogy between certain complexes of phenomena, may be reduced step by step to an altogether different status, to an expression perhaps of a "picture preference." The Sceptic says there is no gardener. The Believer says there is a gardener (but invisible, etc.). One man talks about sexual behavior. Another man prefers

to talk of Aphrodite (but knows that there is not really a superhuman person additional to, and somehow responsible for, all sexual phenomena). The process of qualification may be checked at any point before the original assertion is completely withdrawn and something of that first assertion will remain (Tautology). Mr. Wells's invisible man could not, admittedly, be seen, but in all other respects he was a man like the rest of us. But though the process of qualification may be, and of course usually is, checked in time, it is not always judiciously so halted. Someone may dissipate his assertion completely without noticing that he has done so. A fine brash hypothesis may thus be killed by inches, the death by a thousand qualifications. *[Needless repetition]*

And in this, it seems to me, lies the peculiar danger, the endemic evil, of theological utterance. Take such utterances as "God has a plan," "God created the world," "God loves us as a father loves his children." They look at first sight very much like assertions, vast cosmological assertions. Of course, this is no sure sign that they either are, or are intended to be, assertions. But let us confine ourselves to the cases where those who utter such sentences intend them to express assertions. (Merely remarking parenthetically that those who intend or interpret such utterances as crypto-commands, expressions of wishes, disguised ejaculations, concealed ethics, or as anything else but assertions, are unlikely to succeed in making them either properly orthodox or practically effective.)

Now to assert that such and such is the case is necessarily equivalent to denying that such and such is not the case. Suppose then that we are in doubt as to what someone who gives vent to an utterance is asserting, or suppose that, more radically, we are sceptical as to whether he

---

*Flew's footnotes have been omitted.

is really asserting anything at all, one way of trying to understand (or perhaps it will be to expose) his utterance is to attempt to find what he would regard as counting against, or as being incompatible with, its truth. For if the utterance is indeed an assertion, it will necessarily be equivalent to a denial of the negation of that assertion. And anything which would count against the assertion, or which would induce the speaker to withdraw it and to admit that it had been mistaken, must be part of (or the whole of) the meaning of the negation of that assertion. And to know the meaning of the negation of an assertion is, as near as makes no matter, to know the meaning of that assertion. And if there is nothing which a putative assertion denies then there is nothing which it asserts either: and so it is not really an assertion. When the Sceptic in the parable asked the Believer, "Just how does what you call an invisible, intangible, eternally elusive gardener differ from an imaginary gardener or even from no gardener at all?" he was suggesting that the Believer's earlier statement had been so eroded by qualification that it was no longer an assertion at all.

Now it often seems to people who are not religious as if there was no conceivable event or series of events the occurrence of which would be admitted by sophisticated religious people to be a sufficient reason for conceding "There wasn't a God after all" or "God does not really love us then." Someone tells us that God loves us as a father loves his children. We are reassured. But then we see a child dying of inoperable cancer of the throat. His earthly father is driven frantic in his efforts to help, but his Heavenly Father reveals no obvious sign of concern. Some qualification is made—God's love is "not a merely human love" or it is "an inscrutable love," perhaps—and we realize that such sufferings are quite compatible with the truth of the assertion that "God loves us as a father (but, of course . . .)." We are reassured again. But then perhaps we ask: what is this assurance of God's (appropriately qualified) love worth, what is this apparent guarantee really a guarantee against? Just what would have to happen not merely (morally and wrongly) to tempt but also (logically and rightly) to entitle us to say "God does not love us" or even "God does not exist"? I therefore put to the succeeding symposiasts the simple central questions: "What would have to occur or to have occurred to constitute for you a disproof of the love of, or of the existence of, God?"

Swinburne's Probabilist Argument

A lengthy argument for the existence of God that has attracted considerable recent interest is one by **Richard Swinburne** (1934–), professor of philosophy at the University of Keele, in *The Existence of God* (1979, revised 1991). The entire book is in fact an extended single argument for God's existence.

Swinburne concedes that the main traditional proofs of God do not establish God's existence with certainty. Most of what Swinburne views as the main proofs are variations of the proofs we've talked about in this chapter—that is, the cosmological, teleological, and moral proofs. His list includes some others, too, that we haven't mentioned, including one based on "history and miracles" and another based on the experiences of God many people seem to have had. Swinburne carefully presents his versions of these several proofs and then evaluates them.

Proofs of God Are "Personal Explanations"   Now all these proofs are alike in that each is an *explanation:* each cites specific features of the world that need explaining, and each then provides the needed explanation by referring to God. Thus, to evaluate these arguments, Swinburne examines at length the general criteria by which explanations may be evaluated. He includes in his examination both scientific explanations and "personal explanations," which are given when we explain something as resulting from the intentional actions of a rational agent. The main traditional proofs of God are all personal explanations in Swinburne's sense.

Ordinarily, these proofs are considered in isolation from one another, according to Swinburne. This, he insists, is improper. In fact, he maintains, the various arguments back each other up and are interrelated in such a manner that collectively they show that it is "more probable than not" that there is a God who made and sustains people and the universe. Thus, Swinburne's proof of God's existence is in actuality a complicated interweaving of some of the traditional proofs, after he has "knocked them into clear shape" (as he puts it).

The Evidence for God's Existence   Let's get to the essentials. The evidence for God's existence, according to Swinburne, and here we condense what he says, is this: a universe exists in which there is great order, in that (e.g.) physical things obey the same principles and have identical properties throughout a vast region of space and time; and in which there are conscious beings. This category of things includes people, who are agents of limited power and knowledge but who have the ability to grow in these capacities; who can marvel at the order in nature and can worship God; who are subject to desires, many of which are biologically useful but some of which are not; who are therefore subject to temptations; who are able to choose whether or not to act rightly and can develop, or fail to develop, a morally good character; who are interdependent and capable of increasing each other's power, knowledge, freedom, and happiness; and who, because they are subject to birth and death, know responsibility to distant generations. The world is also providential in permitting people to satisfy their needs; and though it contains suffering, this evil may be increased or diminished by human activity and "is necessary if men are to have knowledge of the evil consequences of possible actions." And finally, within this world there have been prophets and wise men who encouraged all people to worship God, and there is some slight evidence of miraculous occurrences having happened in religious contexts.

The preceding paragraph, which focuses on certain key features of the world, describes, as we said, the *evidence* for God's existence. Each feature of the world mentioned there, says Swinburne, adds to the probability that there is God. But merely *adding to the probability* that something is so, he says, doesn't automatically show that *it is probable* that it is so. You *add to the probability* that you will die of heart disease if you smoke and drink; but even if you do, it still isn't *probable* that you will die that way. So what Swinburne wants to know is this: Does this evidence show that it is *probable* that there is a God? Does it show that the God hypothesis is probable?

Evaluating Explanatory Hypotheses   When we consider how probable an explanatory hypothesis is in the light of the evidence in its favor, we must consider several things, Swinburne notes. First, we must consider whether the hypothesis would enable us to *predict* that evidence.

Here's a simple example of the principle: Suppose, knowing that our car won't start, we hypothesize that our battery is dead. This hypothesis is not unsound, because it would lead us to *expect* that the car wouldn't start. In other words, if we had supposed that the battery was dead, we would have predicted that the car wouldn't start. Our hypothesis would have enabled us to *predict* the evidence for it.

When we evaluate a hypothesis, then, we must consider its *predictive power.*

But we must consider something else as well when we are trying to ascertain the probability of a hypothesis. Before we can accept the dead-battery hypothesis, we have to consider whether other possible conditions would make the car not start, and how likely it is that one of them exists. If the dead-battery hypothesis is to be accepted, then the *prior probability* that the car wouldn't start even if the battery were good would have to be low. If, for instance, the spark plugs aren't working, then there would be a high probability that the car wouldn't start even if the battery were good. Knowing that the spark plugs aren't working obviously would give us reservations about the dead-battery hypothesis.

So we have to consider not only the predictive power of a hypothesis, but also the prior probability that what we are viewing as evidence would have existed even if the hypothesis is false.

But we must also consider how *complicated* the hypothesis is. Here is the car, and it won't start. One explanatory hypothesis is that the battery is dead. Another explanatory hypothesis is that the car won't start because the dog wasn't fed: the dog went out looking for food under the car and caused a wire to the starter to short out. But this dog hypothesis is altogether too complicated. The first hypothesis about the dead battery is shorter, simpler, better.

So the more complicated the hypothesis is, the lower its intrinsic probability.

Let's now apply these three principles to the hypothesis that God exists. We must consider:

1. The *predictive power* of the hypothesis: whether that hypothesis would warrant the prediction that the universe would be as just described, with order and people and so on. We must also consider:

2. The *prior probability* of the universe as just described: how likely it is that the universe would be that way even if God didn't exist. And we must consider:

3. The *complexity* of the hypothesis.

Evaluating the God Hypothesis   In regard to the first principle, Swinburne thinks that the supposition that God exists does *not* warrant a very secure prediction that the universe would be as it is. We leave out the details of his argument, but his thesis is that, given God, the universe might well be as described above, but it certainly isn't necessary that it would be that way.

Error

God's Foreknowledge and Free Will

false assumption

God supposedly knows everything, no? So, whatever you did, he knew before you did it that you would do it. Did you sleep late this morning? God knew that you would.

And that means that you couldn't have *not* slept late this morning, because God knew that you would sleep late. And if you couldn't have not slept late, then in what sense did you sleep late of your own free will? See the problem? It seems that the view that God knows everything conflicts with the idea that you have free will.

This problem is sometimes dismissed by beginning philosophy students as "merely verbal" or as "easily solved." If this is true, it will come as news to the heavyweight philosophers and theologians who have grappled with it, including Paul, Augustine, Luther, Calvin, and others. It is because they saw the logical implications of crediting God with omniscience (all-knowingness) that Calvinists (followers of the great sixteenth-century Protestant theologian John Calvin), for example, believed that God must preordain who will be saved and who will be damned.

erroneous religious beliefs

In regard to the second principle, however, Swinburne argues that it is even less likely that the universe would be as described if God didn't exist.

And in regard to the third principle, the explanation of the world as caused by God is extremely uncomplicated, Swinburne argues. His reason for saying that this hypothesis is simple rather than complicated is this: God is hypothesized to be unlimited in his powers. Now, if that which explains the universe had any limitations, those limitations would themselves have to be explained. Because God doesn't have limitations, the God explanation is a simple one.

When we put all this together, what we find, he says, is that the probability that God exists, given the way the universe is, is neither 1 (certain) nor 0 (impossible). It's not a certain hypothesis because it does not have much predictive power. On the other hand, the prior probability of the universe happening by itself is very low, and the God hypothesis is very uncomplicated. Thus the hypothesis is not a 0, either.

No Scientific Explanation of the Universe Is Possible   But even though the hypothesis that God exists is not certain—Swinburne then argues—it does nevertheless provide the only possible explanation of the universe as just described. Why? There can be no scientific explanation of the universe, he says, because science can only explain how one state of the universe is brought about by a past state; it cannot explain why the basic laws of physics are what they are and are not different. And the possibility that the universe has no explanation at all Swinburne discounts on the grounds of the universe's immense complexity.

Who Needs Reasons for Believing in God?

For a belief to be rational, must we have supporting evidence for its truth? Maybe not, if the belief is a "basic belief," a belief that is not inferred from evidence or from other beliefs but rather itself provides the rational foundation from which other beliefs are derived. For example, it seems rational to believe that there is an external world, that the past existed, and that other people have minds. Yet do we believe these things on the basis of evidence? On the contrary (it might be argued), we accept these beliefs just straight out and

without evidence. Further, it is because we accept these things that we can even talk of evidence and rational inference in the first place. For example, unless we assume there was a past, the "evidence" we have that the car *now* has a flat because it ran over a nail doesn't make any sense—because without a past, there was no past for the car to have done anything.

Contemporary analytic philosopher **Alvin Plantinga** (1932–) has argued that the theist may accept the belief in God as a "basic belief," a belief that it is rational to

hold without supporting evidence and that is foundational for the entire system of the theist's beliefs. Rationally speaking, the theist has the right, Plantinga suggests, to *start from* belief in God. The belief need not be an *end product* of justification and inference.

Interested? An easy-to-read essay by Plantinga entitled "Advice to Christian Philosophers" may be found in the journal *Faith and Philosophy*, vol. 1, no. 3 (July 1984), pp. 253–271.

The Testimony of Witnesses   Now, as a final consideration, many witnesses have testified to having had apparent experience of God, Swinburne says. This testimony, from so many individuals, makes the existence of God probable, *provided*, he says, there is no reason for thinking God's existence is very improbable. Because, according to what he's just shown, there is no such reasoning, Swinburne's final conclusion is that, yes, the combined evidence makes the hypothesis that God exists "more probable than not."

So that's Swinburne's argument. You have to work to follow it, but the basic idea is not difficult to grasp. Certain features of the world give evidence of God as a probable explanation for their existence, if you consider what is really involved in an explanation's probability.

By focusing on Swinburne's overall argument, we have glossed over what to many reviewers is most original and exciting in Swinburne's approach, namely, his use of the technical apparatus of probability and confirmation theory. If you are interested, you have only to read his book.

Selection 13.4 is from a chapter called "The Argument from Providence" in Swinburne's book. Think of someone you loved very dearly who died, perhaps before his or her time. In your grief, did you perhaps wonder why this person had to die? Did you wonder what possible purpose his or death served? Did you perhaps reject death as a great evil? Probably everyone wonders, at some time or other, why

IF YOU ARE REAL, GOD, WHY DID YOU LET THE REPUBLICANS WIN THE ELECTION?

This, of course, is a variation of the problem of evil (see box in Chapter 12) from a Democrat's viewpoint.

death has to be. Religious persons, of course, often turn toward God when a loved one dies, in the belief that God will restore the person in the hereafter. But many others find they must dismiss the notion of a "hereafter" as a fairy tale. For them, death is oblivion. And because they cannot believe that a good God would require all to die, they stop believing in God. In this selection, Swinburne argues that a *false* God has reason to make us mortal, and that there is some probability that he would make a world of mortal beings. In effect Swinburne is arguing that our mortality can be seen as a *good*. True, he stops short of stating explicitly that death *as oblivion* is a good, but it seems clear that his argument has that implication.

SELECTION 13.4

The Existence of God

From Richard Swinburne

Birth is fine, but what about death? Does a God have reason to make a world in which either by natural causes or by the action of agents, there is death? I believe that he does have a number of reasons to make mortal agents. The first is that if all agents are immortal, there is a certain harm (of a qualitatively different kind to other harms) which agents cannot do either to themselves or to others—they cannot deprive of existence. However much I may hate you or myself, I am stuck with you and me. And in this vital respect humanly free agents would not share the creative power of God. In refusing them this power, a God would refuse to trust his creatures in a crucial respect. To let a man have a gun is always a mark of profound trust. Secondly, a world without death is a world without the possibility of supreme self-sacrifice and courage in the face of absolute disaster. The ultimate sacrifice is the sacrifice of oneself, and that would not be possible in a world without death. ("Greater love hath no man than this, that a man lay down his life for his friends.") Supreme generosity would be impossible. So too would cheerfulness and patience in the face of absolute disaster. For in a world without death the alternatives would always involve continuance of life and presumably too the possibility that others would rescue one from one's misfortunes. There would be no absolute disaster to be faced with cheerfulness and patience.

Thirdly, a world with natural death would be a world in which an agent's own contribution would have a seriousness about it because it would be irreversible by the agent. If I spent all my seventy years doing harm, there is no time left for me to undo it. But if I live for ever, then whatever harm I do, I can always undo it. It is good that what people do should matter, and their actions matter more if they have only a limited time in which to reverse them. Fourthly, a world with birth but without natural death would be a world in which the young would never have a free hand. They would always be inhibited by the experience and influence of the aged.

The greatest value of death however seems to me to lie in a fifth consideration which is in a way opposite to my second one. I wrote earlier of the great value which lies in agents having the power to harm each other. Only agents who can do this have real power. Yet it may seem, despite the arguments which I gave earlier, unfair that creatures should be too much subject to other agents. Clearly for the sake of the potential sufferer, there must be a limit to the suffering which an agent can inflict on another. It would, I believe that we would all judge, be mor-

ally wrong for a very powerful being to give *limitless* power to one agent to hurt another. Giving to agents the power to kill is giving vast power of a qualitatively different kind from other power; but it involves the end of experience. It is very different from a power to produce endless suffering. Clearly the parent analogy suggests that it would be morally wrong to give limitless power to cause suffering. A parent, believing that an elder son ought to have responsibility, may give him power for good or ill over the younger son. But a good parent will intervene eventually if the younger son suffers too much—for the sake of the younger son. A God who did not put a limit to the amount of suffering which a creature can suffer (for any good cause, including that of the responsibility of agents) would not be a good God. There need to be limits to the intensity of suffering and to the period of suffering. A natural death after a certain small finite number of years provides the limit to the period of suffering. It is a boundary to the power of an agent over another agent. For death removes agents from that society of interdependent agents in which it is good that they should play their part. True, a God could make a temporal limit to the harm which agents could do to each other without removing them from each other's society. But that would involve agents being in mutual relation with each other while being immunized from each other's power for good or ill—and that arrangement has its own disadvantages in that the deep mutual interdependence of creatures would not hold there.

I could conclude that God would have reason to make what I shall call a World–IV. In a World–IV agents are born and die and during their life give birth, partly through their own choice, to other agents. They can make a difference to the world; but there is endless scope for improvement to it, and each generation can only forward or retard its well-being a little. Agents can make each other happy or unhappy, and can increase or decrease each other's power, knowledge, and freedom. Thereby they can affect the happiness and morality of generations distant in time. Our world is clearly a World–IV. A God has reason for making such a world.

In it there is the possibility of agents damaging each other over a number of generations until they fall badly down the ladder of ascent to divinity. Such a fall is described in a pictorial form in Genesis 3. Many modern commentators seem to me to have missed the point of this story. The point is not just that we are in a mess (of course we are), but that many of us are in a mess which is not largely of our making but which is due to others, our ancestors (and that is of course also fairly evidently so). Many, perhaps all, of the tragic situations—the hatreds and the violence—in the world today result largely from the choices of generations long past—Ireland, South Africa, the Iron Curtain, and so on. And those bad choices of centuries ago themselves were partly facilitated by bad choices of centuries before that, and so on until we reach back close to the early morally conscious choices of man.

But also in a World–IV there is the possibility of man's gradual ascent up the evolutionary scale, of man gradually developing his moral and religious awareness, and of each generation handing on to the next some new facet of that awareness. Man may grow in understanding moral truths and in applying them to the care of the less fortunate; he may grow in sensitivity to aesthetic beauty and in the creation and appreciation of works of art; in the acquisition of scientific knowledge and in its application to the betterment of the human condition and to the exploration and comprehension of the universe.

Although a God would have reason to make a World–IV, such a world is obviously a very unsatisfactory one in the crucial respect that lives capable of flourishing happily for years to come, if not for ever, are cut short, deprived of future experiences and choices. God would have reason to intervene in the process to preserve in existence in some other part of this world agents who cease to exist in our part (and of course Christian theism claims that he has so intervened). But if the advantages of a world with death are to remain, the mutual interdependence in this world must cease after a finite period (to give a limit to the suffering allowed herein) and the future existence must in no way be foreknown for certain by agents (else there would be no opportunity in our part of the world for choices of great seriousness). If God did intervene in this way, our part of the world would still be, as far as appears to its inhabitants, much like a World–IV.

Is Atheism Dangerous to Your Moral Health?

One of the important current side discussions relative to the question of God's existence is whether a belief in absolute right and wrong makes sense in the absence of belief in God. That it doesn't make sense can't blithely be assumed without argument, as pointed out in Chapter 8; the issue itself falls somewhere between ethics and the philosophy of religion. A related concern is whether acceptance of atheism would, as a matter of fact, have the effect of undermining morals. What differences it might make to morality if people did not associate their morality with religious belief has been discussed, among others, by Oxford philosopher **J. L. Mackie** (1917–1981). The following selection from his 1982 book, *The Miracle of*

Theism, although it does not present his views completely, does make it clear that, in Mackie's opinion, there are at least no more dangers in a distinctively nonreligious morality than in a distinctively religious morality.

Mackie, we should mention, is a noted atheist. In the book cited above, Mackie examined all the arguments we have talked about here, including those proposed by Swinburne, and others besides, and concluded that "the balance of probabilities comes out strongly against the existence of a god." Reports of miracles and other apparent experiences of God are not good evidence of God, he argued, because there are superior naturalistic explanations for these things. (A *naturalistic explanation* is one that depends on no theistic or other supernaturalist assumptions.) He also argued that, given that the natural world permits life to evolve, there are "no additional improbabilities in the circumstance of conscious beings coming to exist and possessing moral values."

Theists will protest, of course, that there are improbabilities involved in the natural world's permitting life to evolve in the first place, and this issue has indeed been the subject of much recent popular discussion. Mackie argued that *that* improbability is not lessened by supposing there is a God—and that there *is* a God is itself improbable. We will not go into the details of the argument. We can see, though, that, although Mackie's argument (like Swinburne's) is given in the language of probability, it is really a version of the common-sense idea that we do not give an ultimate explanation of the universe by invoking God—unless we are able to provide an explanation of God.

[handwritten margin note: evolutionary assumptions flawed probability arguments]

SELECTION 13.5

The Miracle of Theism*

From J. L. Mackie

It is widely supposed that Christian morality is particularly admirable. Here it is important to distinguish between the original moral teachings of Jesus, so far as we can determine them, and later developments in the Christian tradition. Richard Robinson has examined the synoptic gospels (Matthew, Mark, and Luke) as the best evidence for Jesus' own teaching, and he finds in them five major precepts: "love God, believe in me, love man, be pure in heart, be humble." The reasons given for these precepts are "a plain matter of promises and threats": they are "that the kingdom of heaven is at

hand," and that "those who obey these precepts will be rewarded in heaven, while those who disobey will have weeping and gnashing of teeth." Robinson notes that "Certain ideals that are prominent elsewhere are rather conspicuously absent from the synoptic gospels." These include beauty, truth, knowledge, and reason. . . .

The later tradition of Christian ethics has tended to add to Jesus' teaching some deplorable elements, such as hostility to sex, and many more admirable ones, such as concern with justice and the other requirements for the flourishing of human life in society, and ideals of beauty, truth, knowledge, and (up to a point) reason. But it has in general retained the concern with salvation and an afterlife, and the

---

*Mackie's footnotes have been omitted.

God Is Coming, and She Is Pissed

So says the bumper sticker.

We speak of God as "He," and there is no doubt that most people who believe in God think of God as, in some sense or another, a male.

But in what sense is God a male? Certainly not in the sense that he possesses male genetic or anatomic features. And it seems doubtful that the qualities we attribute to him are uniquely male. For example, God, it is said, is knowing, loving, caring. But these are not uniquely male characteristics.

Even the qualities associated with God when he is viewed as like an earthly king or emperor are not uniquely male qualities. Yes, all kings are males. But queens too can and have functioned as beneficent, just, powerful, and wise rulers. And the concept of God as the creator of the heavens and earth—that concept seems to call to mind nonhuman properties as much as anything else.

So our custom of speaking of God in the masculine voice is largely honorific. We honor God by speaking and thinking of him as a male: God is the best there is; therefore God is not female or neuter.

But if we think we honor God by referring to him as "He," then that fact implies that we think there is something inferior about not being a male. If God is defined as male, everything outside maleness is automatically inferior. For this reason various feminist philosophers have been more than casually interested in the question "Why is God thought to be a male?"—and in the possible harmful social consequences of our internalized ideas about God's gender.

view that disbelief, or even doubt, or criticism of belief, is sinful, with the resulting tendencies to the persecution of opponents—including, of course, the adherents of rival Christian sects and rival religions—the discouragement of discussion, hostility (even now in some places) to the teaching of well-confirmed scientific truths, like the theory of evolution, and the propagation of contrary errors, and the intellectual dishonesty of trying to suppress one's own well-founded doubts. Many people are shocked at the way in which the Unification Church ("the Moonies") entraps converts and enslaves their minds and emotions; but the same methods have been and are used by many more orthodox sects. Religion has, indeed, a remarkable ability to give vices the air of virtues, providing a sanctified outlet for some of the nastiest human motives. It is fashionable to ascribe the horrors of Nazism to an atheistic nationalism; but in fact the attitudes to the Jews which it expressed had long been established within the Christian tradition in Germany and elsewhere (sanctioned, for example, by Luther's writings), and the Old Testament itself reports many atrocities as having been not merely approved but positively demanded by God and his spokesmen. And while, following Robinson, I have spoken here particularly of Christian ethics, it is only too obvious that Islamic fundamentalism displays today, more clearly than Christianity has done recently, the worst aspects of religious morality. We do not need to go back in history to illustrate the dictum of Lucretius: *Tantum religio potuit suadere malorum* (So great are the evils that religion could prompt!). By contrast, there is a long tradition of an essentially humanist morality, from Epicurus to John Stuart Mill and modern writers, including Richard Robinson himself, centered on the conditions for the flourishing of human life and stressing intellectual honesty, tolerance, free inquiry, and individual rights.

There are, then, some marked dangers in a distinctively religious morality. . . .

But are there no corresponding dangers in a distinctively non-religious morality? Admittedly, there are. . . .

An alleged weakness, not of non-religious moralities in general, but specifically of moralities explained and understood in the naturalistic way outlined above, is that different groups of people can develop different moral views, which will produce conflict when these groups are in contact with one another, and that there is, on this basis, no clear way of resolving such conflicts. This is true. But it is not a *distinctive* weakness of the naturalistic approach. Absolutist and objectivist moralities, including ones with religious attachments, also differ from one another, and there is no clear way of resolving their conflicts either. That each party *believes* that some one morality is objectively right is no guarantee that they will be able to agree on what it is. Indeed, conflicts between rival absolutists were likely to be less resolvable than conflicts between those who understood morality in a naturalistic way, for the latter can more easily appreciate the merits of compromises and adjustment, or of finding, for the areas of contact, a *ius gentium,* a common core of principles on which they can agree. . . .

Checklist

To help you review, here is a checklist of the key philosophers and concepts of this chapter. The brief descriptive sentences summarize leading ideas. Keep in mind that some of these summary statements represent terrific oversimplifications of complex positions.

Philosophers

459 • **William Paley** Concocted one of the most effective pre-Darwin design arguments. *watch, eye*

463 • **John Henry Newman** Famous nineteenth-century religious thinker; held that God's existence is evidenced by the experience of conscience.

463-4 • **Søren Kierkegaard** Held that God is beyond reason's grasp, that truth is subjective, and that salvation can be attained only through a leap of faith to Christianity. *absolute rational proof would be incompatible with faith*

465 • **Friedrich Nietzsche** Believed that the masses are ruled by a slave morality inculcated by religion, science, and philosophy. His statement "God is dead" meant that there is no rational order, not that people don't believe in God.

467 • **William James** Held that it is rationally justifiable to yield to your hope that a God exists.

473 • **Blaise Pascal** Seventeenth-century French mathematician whose "wager" was that it is prudent to bet that God exists.

475 • **F. R. Tennant** Twentieth-century religious thinker who proposed a subtle version of the design argument that takes into account contemporary science and evolutionary theory. *organisms suited to environment suited to organism*

476 • **Antony Flew** Contemporary analytic philosopher; argued that talk about God is unverifiable and hence meaningless. *imaginary gardener*

479 • **Richard Swinburne** Contemporary analytic religious thinker; believed that
     God is an inductively sound explanatory hypothesis. *Cosmological teleological, moral + rel. experience*

482 • **Alvin Plantinga** Contemporary analytical philosopher of religion. Noted for
     his analysis of the ontological proof and for the concept of a basic belief. *that God exists*

485-6 • **J. L. Mackie** Contemporary analytic critic of theism. *would atheism undermine Morals*
     improbability of God

Concepts

460 Paley's watch

464 leap of faith *nonintellectual, passionate, infinite*

465 "God is dead" *no plan or rational order in universe*

"   overman *accepts all facets of life good, bad, pain...*

467 live, momentous, and forced issues *consequences, no indecision possible*

470 James's "two commandments" of rationality *believe truth, avoid error*

469 scientific creationism *beginning, separate species, nature of man created, faith*

473 Pascal's wager

"   pragmatism *practical benefits of belief*

     logical positivism *verifiable by experience*

456 Vienna Circle *experience only*

     verifiability principle

475 Big Bang → *space time + matter* *1st event*

479 personal explanation *events explained by intentional actions of a rational agent*

480 explanatory hypothesis : *could hypothesis → predict evidence*

480 predictive power *if G then the universe*

     prior probability *the universe ∴ G*

     complexity *not complex*

481 God's foreknowledge vs. free will *Absolute foreknowledge excludes free will*

482 basic belief *Plantinga*

487 God's gender?

486 naturalistic explanation

Questions for Discussion and Review

1. Explain and critically evaluate Paley's design argument. Is it crazy to think that an
   organ like the eye is anything other than strong evidence of God?

2. Does the world/universe—or something or another in it—give evidence of divine
   design? Explain.

3. Does the theory of evolution undermine the design argument?

4. Is Newman correct in thinking that the existence of God is given to us in the
   experience of conscience? Explain.

5. Explain James's argument for God. Is it a version of Pascal's wager? Is it sound? Why?

6. Is James correct in saying that you cannot really suspend judgment about God's existence?

7. Is the question of God's existence live and momentous, as James says?

8. Is it rare for people to decide things on the basis of reasoned argument? Is it possible for them to do so?

9. Which is "better," to doubt everything that is less than certain or highly probable, or to believe falsehoods?

10. "It is impossible for normal people to believe that free will does not exist. Therefore it does exist." Evaluate this remark. "It is impossible for normal people to believe that free will does not exist. Therefore it is reasonable to believe that it does exist." Evaluate this remark.

11. "Most people believe in God; therefore God must exist." Evaluate this claim.

12. Is the fact that the world is intelligible evidence of divine design?

13. "He died because God called on him." "The sprinkler stopped working due to fate." Are these claims equally meaningless? Explain. Is the claim "God exists" verifiable or falsifiable? Are any (other) claims made about God verifiable?

14. Assuming that there is scientific evidence that the universe had an absolute beginning, does that evidence also prove the existence of God? Explain.

15. Is the belief that the proposition "God exists" is meaningless a form of atheism?

16. "The features of the world add to the probability that God exists, but do not automatically make it probable that God exists." Explain this remark.

17. Can you logically believe both that God knows everything and that there is free will? Explain the difficulty.

18. How valid as proof of God's existence are purported eye-witness reports of miracles?

19. "Even assuming that the existence of God explains why there is a world, what explains why there is a God?" Does this question contain a valid criticism of the cosmological proof of God? Is Mackie correct in saying that the explanation of the universe as caused by God doesn't advance our understanding of why there is a universe?

20. Would universal acceptance of atheism be morally disastrous for society?

21. In what sense is it legitimate rationally to think of God as male?

Suggested Further Readings

A. Flew and A. MacIntyre, eds., *New Essays in Philosophical Theology* (New York: Macmillan, 1984). A popular anthology covering a range of topics. For a follow-up to the article by Flew (Selection 13.3), see the pieces in this anthology by R. Hare and B. Mitchell entitled "Theology and Falsification."

J. Hick, "Theology and Verification," In *Theology Today*, vol. 17, no. 1 (April 1960). A response to verificationist attacks on religious language.

W. James, *The Will to Believe and Other Essays in Popular Philosophy,* Frederick H. Burk-hardt, ed. (Cambridge: Harvard University Press, 1979). James is among the most pleasurable of philosophers to read.

W. T. Jones, *A History of Western Philosophy,* 2nd ed., vol. 6 (New York: Harcourt Brace Jovanovich, 1975). See Chapter 6 for a good discussion of Kierkegaard and Nietzsche.

W. Kaufmann, *Nietzsche* (New York: Meridian, 1956). A good introduction to Nietzsche's philosophy.

J. L. Mackie, *The Miracle of Theism: Arguments For and Against the Existence of God* (Oxford: Clarendon Press, 1982). Excellent commentary on all the traditional and recent proofs (and other discussions) of God's existence.

Basil Mitchell, ed., *The Philosophy of Religion* (New York: Oxford University Press, 1991). A collection of recent papers on various themes connected with God and religious belief.

R. J. Moore and B. N. Moore, *The Cosmos, God and Philosophy* (New York: Peter Lang, 1988).

Thomas V. Morris, ed., *The Concept of God* (New York: Oxford University Press, 1987). Recent writings on the existence and nature of God.

J. H. Newman, *A Grammar of Assent,* C. F. Harrold, ed. (New York: Longmans, Green and Co., 1947). Newman's most important book.

W. Paley, *Natural Theology: Selections,* Frederick Ferré, ed. (Indianapolis: Bobbs-Merrill, 1963). There is more to Paley than his famous stone and watch analogy, as the reader of this book will discover.

Alvin Plantinga, "Advice to Christian Philosophers," *Faith and Philosophy,* vol. 1, no. 3 (July, 1984), pp. 253–271. Plantinga sets forth the idea that a belief in God may be a "basic belief."

I. Ramsey, *Religious Language* (New York: Macmillan, 1963). A discussion of the questions surrounding the meaning of religious language.

Richard Swinburne, *The Existence of God* (New York: Oxford University Press, 1991). This new edition contains a response to the criticisms of J. L. Mackie and considers the evidential force of recent scientific discoveries.

F. R. Tennant, *Philosophical Theology,* vol. 2 (New York: Cambridge University Press, 1928).

J. Thompson, *Kierkegaard* (Garden City, N.Y.: Doubleday, 1972). A collection of essays on Kierkegaard that were selected "so as to give the reader some sense of the shape and direction of recent Kierkegaardian criticism."

Philosophy of Religion: Reason and Faith

Summary and Conclusion

Let's just take stock of all this. Anselm, with whose philosophy we began this part, thought it follows from the very concept of God that God exists. This was the ontological argument.

The ontological argument was rejected by Aquinas, who said you can prove God's existence only by considering God's work, that is, by considering the world we perceive around us. Aquinas laid out five ways in which God can be inferred to exist from the evidence presented to us by the world. Three of these are forms of what is called the cosmological argument, according to which God may be deduced as the first cause or ultimate explanation of the world. Another of Aquinas's proofs was a version of the teleological argument, which reasons from the appearance of design in the world around us to the existence of God as its designer. And the remaining proof infers God from the existence of goodness; this is a type of moral argument for God's existence.

A different kind of proof of God came from the anchoress Julian of Norwich, who emphasized the importance of her mystical visions as a legitimate source of religious knowledge.

Descartes thought that once you consider the matter closely, you will see that the existence of your own idea of God proves that God exists. He also found a version of the ontological argument compelling. Leibniz argued that there must always be an explanation of why things are exactly as they are and are not otherwise, and this simple fact entails absolutely that there exists a necessary being, God.

With Hume and Kant we saw the other side of the coin, for both attacked the teleological and cosmological arguments as unsound. Kant also raised a fundamental objection to the ontological argument, though he nevertheless believed that the belief in God is rationally justified for any moral agent.

William Paley, we saw, ignored Hume's and Kant's criticisms of the design argument and published a version of the design argument that has remained popular to this day. Somewhat later, John Henry Newman, who was concerned with real-life or "concrete" reasoning, believed that in the experience of conscience we can attain certitude that God exists. Søren Kierkegaard and Friedrich Nietzsche, on the other hand, dismissed so-called rational discussion of God's existence as a waste of time.

William James approached the issue from a different perspective. Does God exist? Well, said James, if you are like I am in finding that the unaided intellect just does not settle whether God does or does not exist, and if you consider what attaches to believing in God on the one hand and disbelieving in him on the other, then you shall find it makes good sense to believe in God.

In the twentieth century, we found F. R. Tennant proposing yet another version of the design argument. Tennant's careful and complex rendering of the argument emphasized the richness, subtlety, and beauty of the fit between human beings and their physical environment and, unlike Paley's, took into account the theory of evolution. Another complex argument for God was proposed in recent years by Richard Swinburne: the argument draws on probability theory to reach the final conclusion that, when all the evidence that bears on the matter one way or the other is duly considered, the hypothesis that God exists is more probable than not.

But again on the other side of the coin, in this century A. N. Flew suggested that assertions about God are in fact meaningless, and J. L. Mackie criticized the hypothesis that God exists as improbable and unenlightening. Suffice it to say that the jury is still out on God, at least among professional philosophers.

Now not terribly long ago a student of one of the authors told him that the section on philosophy of religion in his introductory course had significantly affected her life. "How so?" he asked. "Did the course change your opinion about God?"

The student said, no, she had believed in God before the course, and still believed in God. But she now felt that there was a *rational justification* for believing in God. That discovery, she said, was very important to her. It had made her comfortable with her belief. It had given moorings to her faith.

Of course, her experience might have had a different outcome. She might have concluded that there really is no rational support for a belief in God. Many people who read in the philosophy of religion have come to that conclusion, after all. Coming to that conclusion, we suspect, would have been equally momentous to this student.

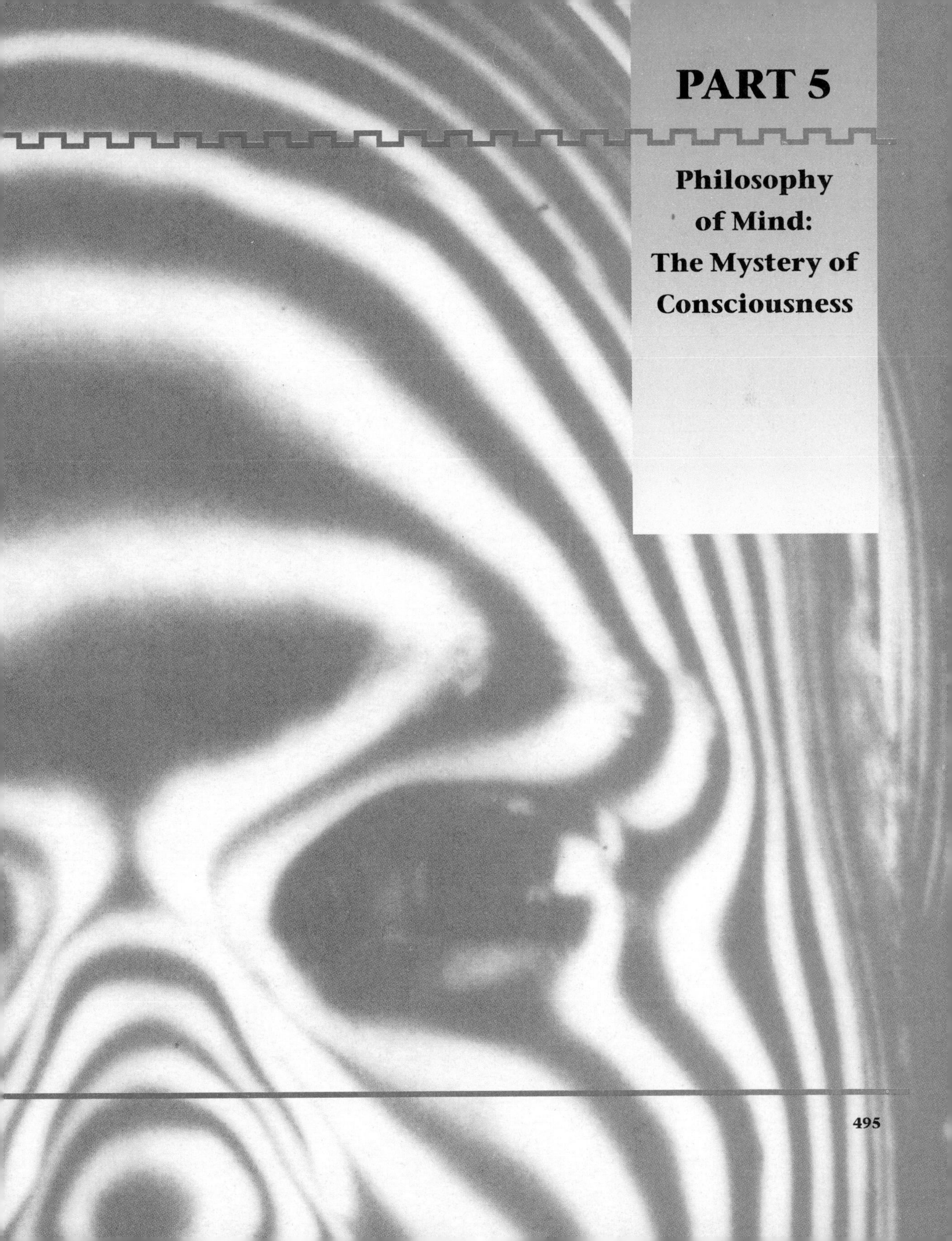

PART 5

Philosophy of Mind: The Mystery of Consciousness

Philosophy of Mind

14

I am, I exist; that is certain.

—René Descartes

[The self, the "I"] is introduced, not because observation reveals it, but because it is linguistically convenient and apparently demanded by grammar. Nominal entities of this sort may or may not exist, but there is no good ground for supposing that they do.

—Bertrand Russell

The philosophy of mind is a vast area of analytic philosophy that deals not with a single problem but with a host of interrelated issues and concerns. These issues and concerns have become so numerous, complicated, and involved that many philosophers now treat the philosophy of mind as a separate major philosophical area in its own right, like epistemology and the philosophy of religion. What follows is only a brief overview.

The **philosophy of mind** is concerned primarily with the nature of consciousness, mental states (or psychological states, these being the same), and the mind. The approach usually taken (as you might expect from what we've said about analytic philosophy) is to look at everyday psychological vocabulary—with its reference to mental states of various sorts, including beliefs, desires, fears, suspicions, hopes, ideas, preferences, choices, thoughts, motives, urges, and so forth—and ask what this psychological vocabulary means or how it is to be analyzed. In recent years these inquiries have broadened to encompass the research and findings of psychologists, neuroscientists, computer scientists, linguists, artificial intelligence researchers, and other specialists. The philosophy of mind is no longer the preserve of the professional philosopher.

A good approach to this large subject is to ask whether the mind is physical (material), nonphysical, or both, or neither?

Let's begin by noting that many—perhaps most—members of Western societies take the position that a person has a nonmaterial mind or soul or spirit

Abstract and Meaningless Philosophy?

Please note that the question "Is the mind physical, nonphysical, both, or neither?" is not some abstract and remote theoretical query. The fundamental metaphysical problem of whether reality is physical or nonphysical or both (or neither) can be resolved only after this important subquestion about the mind has been answered.

Further, the assumption of human free will may rest largely on the premise that humans have a nonphysical mind, a mind that is not subject to the apparently deterministic principles that govern physical things. Also, the possibility of life after death of the body seems to depend on the mind's not being a purely physical thing. Peo-

ple find something extremely distasteful in the idea that the human mind is mere matter, for many believe that blind matter, matter unrelieved and unelevated by a spiritual dimension, is of necessity lacking in the intelligence and incorporeality that is one with God.

The question is important.

associated with his or her physical body. *You* may well take this position. And, as you may recall from Part 1 on metaphysics, this position is known as **dualism.** Let's take a closer look at it.

Dualism

According to the dualist, every existing thing (except for abstract items, e.g., geometric points, numbers, and brotherhood) is either *physical* (or material, these terms being used interchangeably here) or *nonphysical* (or immaterial or incorporeal, these terms also being interchangeable).

Physical things possess physical properties (like density, velocity, charge, temperature, mass, and, most fundamentally, spatial occupancy), and nonphysical things possess nonphysical properties. These latter properties are difficult to specify, though dualists would say that only nonphysical entities can have conscious states or exercise volition. Both physical and nonphysical things can have neutral properties. For example, physical and nonphysical things both have temporal properties, both may be numerous, belong to groups, and so forth.

A human being, according to the dualist, has (or is) both a physical body and a nonphysical mind (or soul or spirit). Further, according to the dualist, a person's nonphysical and physical components are *interactive:* if someone comes along and gives you a *shove,* you may well become angry. In other words, the shoving of your physical body causes anger to arise in your nonphysical mind. Or—to run things in reverse—when you decide to do something, your body normally follows through; that is, your nonphysical mind causes your physical body to walk or run or speak or whatever it is you want your body to do.

Popular Reasons for Believing That We Are Not Purely Physical Things

Why believe that a human being is not a thing purely physical (material, corporeal)? Here are some *popular* reasons.

- What's the difference between people and physical objects? People, but not physical objects, have feelings, emotions, thoughts, and beliefs and can do things purely physical things cannot. Seems people must have something that purely physical things lack, something nonphysical.

- People have free will, which they wouldn't have if their minds were mere physical things.

- People are artistically (and otherwise) creative and have aesthetic sensibility—impossibilities for mere blind physical things.

- People can sometimes override the constraints of physics. An example is overcoming a terminal disease through the exertion of will. Even leaving aside such questionable things as extrasensory perception, out-of-body travel, and walking on burning coals, people often demonstrate the power of mind over matter.

- People can have *knowledge*. Purely physical things can't. Therefore people are not themselves totally physical.

- It is possible to doubt the existence of any given physical thing, as **René Descartes** made clear. But it is not possible to doubt the existence of your own mind (as Descartes also made clear). Therefore your mind is not a physical thing.

- Beliefs and thoughts have properties that physical things by definition cannot have.

Beliefs, for instance, are true or false. Physical things are not. So beliefs and thoughts are not physical. Conversely, physical things have properties that beliefs and thoughts cannot have, properties like location, density, temperature, and so forth. The same conclusion follows.

- I have knowledge of my mental states, but it is not gained through observation. Physical things, on the other hand, I find out about only through observation. So physical things and my mind states are essentially different.

Further considerations possibly supportive of dualism are mentioned in the text. Can you think of any others yourself?

(Most analytic philosophers, incidentally, would dispute many or all these reasons.)

Actually, a dualist doesn't have to believe that the immaterial mind and the material body interact, but most dualists do, so when we talk about dualism here, we mean **interactionist dualism.**

Now to the extent that many people have ever thought about it, it seems pretty nearly self-evident that a human being has a nonphysical component of some sort, be it called a mind, soul, spirit, or something else. Do you believe this? Then you are in good company (see box "Popular Reasons for Believing . . ."). But you should be aware that there are reasons to suppose otherwise (see box "Reasons for Doubting . . ."). The difficulties in dualism have led many analytic philosophers to doubt whether dualism is a viable theory at all, and they have cast about for more attractive alternatives.

rejecting Dualism

Reasons for Doubting That the Mind Is Nonphysical

- First is the *characterization problem.* An immaterial mind and its states tend always to be characterized negatively, e.g., as not being divisible, as not being in space, as not being tangible, and so forth. A thing characterized only negatively is difficult to distinguish from nothingness.

- Second is the *individuation problem.* Two people cannot share a single mind. So let us consider what would account for this fact. If the mind were a *physical* thing like a brain, what would account for it is that a physical thing like a brain cannot be in two separate locations at the same time. But if the mind is nonphysical, then the fact that one mind cannot be shared by two people seems just inexplicable.

- Third is the *emergence problem.* If minds are immaterial, then at some stage in the evolution of human beings immaterial minds first made their appearance. But the selection of a point in the evolutionary history of humans at which minds first emerged could never be determined, even in principle. Further, for the immaterial mind to have emerged, it must have had some advantage in regard to the survival of the species. To account for the survival of the human species, however, it is not necessary to postulate the existence of an immaterial mind: the development of the brain and nervous system is sufficient for this purpose.

- Fourth is the *dependency problem.* There is an apparent dependency of mental states on brain states. For example, that my thoughts or beliefs or any of my mental states might change without something changing within my brain is unimaginable. Again, the effects of physical injury, alcohol, narcotics, psychotropic chemicals, and nerve-tissue degeneration on consciousness—via their effects on the brain—are obvious. Further, specific cognitive failings have been tied to damage of specific areas of the brain. In addition, learning is known to be accompanied by physical and chemical changes within the brain, changes without which it apparently would not occur. And other evidence of apparent dependency of mind processes on brain processes

Four Nondualist Theories of Mind

Let's now consider four nondualist analytic philosophies of the mind and mental states, in rough chronological order, beginning with the theory called neutral monism. Then we will close the chapter with a brief look at some of the issues that are now current in physicalist discussions of the mind.

Theory 1: Neutral Monism

Recall that for **Bertrand Russell** (Chapter 6), analysis meant resolving a complex proposition into simpler propositions, propositions that do not make reference to unnecessary or questionable categories of things. Indeed, for Russell, the process of

is abundant. The simplest explanation of this dependency is that the affected mental processes and the physical brain processes with which they are associated are in reality not two things but one.

- Fifth is the *no-necessity problem*. Brain scientists don't find it necessary to postulate the existence of the mind to explain and account for what happens in the brain. There is, in short, no necessity to postulate the existence of immaterial causes to account for what happens in the brain, contrary to what we would expect if an immaterial mind were involved in human thought and behavior.

- Sixth is the *interaction problem*. If an immaterial mind is involved in human thought and behavior, then it must interact with the brain, as explained already. But it is difficult even to conceptualize how such interaction could occur. An immaterial mind could not push, pull, tug on, spin, or divide physical things within the brain, for pushing, pulling, and the like are physical activities. Nor, for the same reason, could it pulverize, energize, electrify, or magnetize things within the brain. In other words, how an immaterial mind could exert an influence on the brain is most unclear, because such exertion would, apparently, have to be nonphysical, and the idea of nonphysical exertion or activation is most unclear.

- Last is the *understanding problem*. If mental states are nonphysical things separate and distinct from the brain and body, then no one could know what someone else's mental states are really like or what expressions referring to another's mental states really mean. But this is absurd: we *can* know what each other's mental states are like and what others mean by expressions that refer to their mental states. So mental states are not nonphysical things separate and distinct from the brain and body; they must have a physical component or dimension, which makes them physical.

None of these objections to dualism is thought to be decisive. But collectively they are thought to have much force in showing that it is (1) unnecessary and (2) unduly perplexing to suppose that a human being has a nonphysical mind or mental states.

analysis is itself the proper method by which the metaphysician determines which categories of things are necessary to assume in the first place. Thus, as we've seen, propositions about numbers can be resolved into propositions about classes, according to Russell. We could express the same point by saying that, for Russell, numbers are *reducible* to classes.

Russell believed that other metaphysically important reductions could be achieved through analysis. In particular, he held that such entities of physics as points, instants, and particles—indeed, physical objects in general—are reducible to sense-data. He also maintained that minds are likewise reducible to sense-data, and this is the point of interest here.

What does it mean to say that one kind of thing is "reducible" to another kind of thing, and why on earth would anyone think it important to make such reductions in the first place?

⎍⎍⎍⎍⎍⎍⎍⎍⎍⎍

PROFILE / Luisa Maria Oliva Sabuco de Nantes Barerra

Descartes speculated that the mind interacts with the body in the pineal gland. Sixty or so years before Descartes, **Oliva Sabuco de Nantes** (1562–?) proposed that, as the properties of the mind (or "soul," as she called it) are not physical properties, they cannot be physically located in some specific spot. Thus, she reasoned, the connection between body and soul occurs *throughout* the brain. The brain and the rest of the body "serve the soul like house servants serve the house," she maintained. She argued that a person is a microcosm (a miniature version) of the world, and this discloses that, in the same way as God activates, rules, and governs the world, the soul governs the "affects, movements, and actions of humans."

It is worth mentioning that Sabuco also believed that the intimate connection between soul and brain means there is a close relationship between psychological and physical health and between morality and medicine. For example, as soon as a negative emotion like *sorrow* begins to affect our body, she said, we must control it before it becomes unmanageable *despair*. Virtuous passions promote good health, she said; immoral passions cause sickness and disease. As an illustration, she cited excessive sexual activity, which causes (she believed) excessive loss of an essential brain fluid, resulting in brainstem dehydration and the insanity found in advanced cases of syphilis and gonorrhea. There exists, she reasoned, a natural, medical basis for moral sanctions against sexual promiscuity. (It's pretty easy to think of a modern illustration of this thesis.)

Sabuco, born in Alcaraz, Spain, published her important book, *New Philosophy of Human Nature,* when she was only twenty-five years old. This was at the tail end of the Spanish Inquisition—not the most congenial of times for objective scholarship—and Sabuco was taking something of a risk as a woman writer of philosophy. Nevertheless, she was highly knowledgeable about ancient and medieval thinkers, and her book was cleared by the Church with only a few changes. It became quite influential and was published several times during her lifetime and in every century after her death.

Certainly Sabuco did not solve the problem of mind-body interaction, but she anticipated by several hundred years today's holistic medicine with its emphasis on the intimate connection between mental and physical well-being.

To reduce something, a physical object, for example, to something else, sense-data, for example, is (as we've noted) to replace a sentence about the physical object by a set of sentences about sense-data, a set of sentences that means the same thing as the original sentence. Thus, the sentence "I am eating an apple" theoretically might be replaced by a set of sentences that refers to a certain set of sense-data of taste, smell, touch, and sight (those sense-data that you have when you eat an apple). To replace the original sentence in this way would be to "reduce" the apple to sense-data.

What is gained by this procedure? The reduction reveals that what we think we know when we say, "I am eating an apple," can be expressed without even men-

"Nothing-But" Philosophy

Philosophical analysis, as explained in the text, seeks to replace complex propositions or concepts with others thought to be in some important sense simpler. Propositions about one kind of thing—numbers, for example—are thus resolved by analysis into propositions about a more basic or "simpler" type of entity, classes of classes.

Accordingly, analytic philosophy is sometimes castigated and belittled as a philosophy of "nothing-buts" (Herbert Feigl's phrase): minds are nothing but brains; physical objects are nothing but sense-data; numbers are nothing but classes of classes; Xs are nothing but Ys.

As explained in the text, however, depending on what the Xs and Ys are, it can be metaphysically and epistemologically significant if statements about Xs can be replaced by statements about Ys. So, it would be inappropriate to discount the significance of analytic philosophy on the grounds that it is "merely" a philosophy of nothing-buts.

tioning apples; it can be expressed without assuming the existence of anything beyond our sense-data. In short, *the analysis reveals that our belief in the existence of the apple we are eating is in fact a belief in the existence of nothing beyond sense-data.* The reduction *simplifies* our metaphysics; it shortens the list of entities that we are obliged to credit with existence. The reduction thus has metaphysical significance.

The reduction also has epistemological significance. As we saw in Part 1, skeptics have powerful arguments for saying that you really don't know that physical objects exist. But it's harder for them to argue that you don't know that your sense-data exist. By reducing apples to sense-data, we place our belief in the existence of apples on a much surer epistemological footing.

Russell eventually thought that minds, too (just like apples and other physical objects), could be reduced to (i.e., analyzed in terms of) sense-data. In other words, what I say about my mind could, at least in theory, be expressed by sentences that refer only to sense-data. Thus, according to Russell, my body (which, like an apple, is a physical object) and my mind are both reducible to the same kind of thing, sense-data.

This doctrine, that mind and matter are both reducible to the same kind of thing, which is itself neither mental nor material, is called **neutral monism.** *Monism* means "one-ism." Neutral monism is therefore a rejection of dualism, which is "two-ism." **Materialism** (the doctrine that reality is ultimately physical or "material") and **idealism** (the doctrine that reality is ultimately nonphysical or "ideal" mind-stuff) are types of monism, too.

Yes, a theory like Russell's, that minds and bodies *both* are reducible to sense-data, could be (and sometimes is) viewed as a kind of idealism. But Russell held that sense-data are neither mental nor physical, for the very good reason that they are what mental things and physical things both reduce to. For this reason, he held

Ockham's Razor

If you don't have a *reason* to believe in something, just don't. This principle is a variation of **Ockham's razor,** named after the English philosopher William of Ockham (c. 1285–c. 1349). Ockham said, translating loosely, "If you can fully explain something by making fewer assumptions, it's stupid to explain it by making more," meaning that given competing adequate explanations of something, the theory that is the most economical—makes the fewest assumptions or posits the fewest theoretical entities—is preferable. Thus, for example, if you can adequately explain what happens in the brain without postulating immaterial causes (the soul, the mind, spirit, etc.), don't endorse an explanation that postulates such causes. (As you can see, the no-necessity problem—see earlier box—is just Ockham's razor.) Philosophers of mind and philosophers in general all accept Ockham's razor. (They just disagree, from time to time, on which explanations are truly *adequate*.)

Sense-Data Not Mental?

For there to be a sensation, something must do the sensing, a receptor of some sort. Thus, many people, equating this receptor with the mind, will think it contradictory of Russell, Ayer, and othersto regard sense-data as nonmental.

The term **sense-data,** however, at least as used by these philosophers, and as misleading as that use may be, denotes simply the *contents* of what we see, hear, feel, taste, and so on.

To take the sense-data of sight, for an example: as you look at this book, the contents of your visual field—the various colors and shapes that you see—in and of themselves are neutral as between mind and matter. Whether you regard them as physical things (e.g., as the surfaces of physical objects) or as mental things (e.g., as "images" produced within your mind by the action of external objects on your sensory organs) depends on your *interpretation* of them. Before any interpretation, or as they are considered independently of interpretation, they are "neutral"; that is, they are just there. At any rate, so say neutral monists (and phenomenologists—see Chapter 15).

that sense-data are *neutral* as between mind and matter; hence this philosophy is known as *neutral* monism. The American philosopher **William James** and the British analytic philosopher **A. J. Ayer,** who was a member of the Vienna Circle mentioned in Chapter 6, were also, at one point or another during their careers, neutral monists. So was **Spinoza** (Chapter 4).

Selection 14.1 is a nontechnical exposition of this neutral monist position excerpted from Russell's *The Philosophy of Logical Atomism.*

SELECTION 14.1

The Philosophy of Logical Atomism   From Bertrand Russell

You all know the American theory of neutral monism, which derives really from William James and is also suggested in the work of Mach, but in a rather less developed form. The theory of neutral monism maintains that the distinction between the mental and the physical is entirely an affair of arrangement, that the actual material arranged is exactly the same in the case of the mental as it is in the case of the physical, but they differ merely in the fact that when you take the thing as belonging in the same context with certain other things, it will belong to psychology, while when you take it in a certain other context with other things, it will belong to physics, and the difference is as to what you consider to be its context, just the same sort of difference as there is between arranging the people in London alphabetically or geographically. So, according to William James, the actual material of the world can be arranged in two different ways, one of which gives you physics and the other psychology. It is just like rows or columns: in an arrangement of rows and columns, you can take an item as either a member of a certain row or a member of a certain column; the item is the same in the two cases, but its context is different.

If you will allow me a little undue simplicity I can go on to say rather more about neutral monism, but you must understand that I am talking more simply than I ought to do because there is not time to put in all the shadings and qualifications. I was talking a moment ago about the appearances that a chair presents. If we take any one of these chairs, we can all look at it, and it presents a different appearance to each of us. Taken all together, taking all the different appearances that that chair is presenting to all of us at this moment, you get something that belongs to physics. So that, if one takes sense-data and arranges together all those sense-data that appear to different people at a given moment and are such as we should ordinarily say are appearances of the same physical object, then that class of sense-data will give you something that belongs to physics, namely, the chair at this moment. On the other hand, if instead of taking all the appearances that that chair presents to all of us at this moment, I take all the appearances that the different chairs in this room present to me at this moment, I get quite another group of particulars. All the different appearances that different chairs present to me now will give you something belonging to psychology, because that will give you my experiences at the present moment. Broadly speaking, according to what one may take as an expansion of William James, that should be the definition of the difference between physics and psychology.

We commonly assume that there is a phenomenon which we call seeing the chair, but what I call my seeing the chair according to neutral monism is merely the existence of a certain particular, namely the particular which is the sense-datum of that chair at that moment. And I and the chair are both logical fictions, both being in fact a series of classes of particulars, of which one will be that particular which we call my seeing the chair. That actual appearance that the chair is presenting to me now is a member of me and a member of the chair, I and the chair being logical fictions. . . . There is no simple entity that you can point to and say: this entity is physical and not mental. . . .

I ought to proceed to tell you that I have discovered whether neutral monism is true or not, because otherwise you may not believe that logic is any use in the matter. But I do not profess to know whether it is true or not. I feel more and more inclined to think that it may be true. I feel more and more that the difficulties that oc- cur in regard to it are all of the sort that may be solved by ingenuity. But nevertheless there *are* a number of difficulties; there are a number of problems, some of which I have spoken about in the course of these lectures.

Theory 2: Behaviorism

Another influential analyst concerned with the philosophy of mind was **Gilbert Ryle** (1900–1976), who, in *The Concept of Mind* (1949), one of the most widely read books of twentieth-century analytic philosophy, argued for what we will call the behaviorist analysis of the mind.

Before we begin, however, *caution:* the word *behaviorism* is notoriously am- biguous. **Behaviorism** in one sense is a *methodological principle of psychology,* according to which fruitful psychological investigation confines itself to such psy- chological phenomena as can be behaviorally defined. *Philosophical behaviorism* is the doctrine we'll now explain that we are attributing to Ryle. Ryle denied being a behaviorist, incidentally. Still, *The Concept of Mind* is regarded as one of the most powerful expositions of (philosophical) behaviorism ever written. (Hereafter, when we refer to behaviorism, we'll mean *philosophical* behaviorism.)

According to Ryle, when we refer to someone's mental states (and this someone might be oneself), when we refer, for example, to a person's beliefs or thoughts or wishes, we are *not,* contrary to what is ordinarily supposed, referring to the imma- terial states of a nonphysical mind. There is indeed no such thing as a nonphysical mind. There is, Ryle says, *no ghost within the machine.* A person is only a compli- cated—a very highly complicated—physical organism, one capable of doing the amazing sorts of things that people are capable of doing. When we attribute a so- called mental state to a person, we are in fact attributing to him or her a *propensity* or *disposition* to act or behave in a certain way.

For example, when you attribute to your friend the belief that it is going to rain, it might *seem* that you view her as having or possessing a nonphysical thing of some sort, termed a *belief*—a nonphysical, intangible, and unobservable entity that exists within her mind. But in fact, argues Ryle, to say that someone believes it is going to rain is merely to attribute to her a propensity or disposition to do things like close the windows and cover the barbecue and say things like "It's going to rain" and not to do certain other sorts of things like wash the car and hang out the sheets.

It is likewise when we credit someone with a thought or an idea. Thoughts and ideas, like beliefs, are not nonmaterial things, says Ryle. They are not even *things* at all. To be sure, "thought," "idea," and "belief" are words for things, that is, *thing- words.* But these thing-words are (to borrow an expression Ryle used in a different context) *systematically misleading.* Because they are thing-words, they mislead or

THAT JEROME CERTAINLY HAS A BIG EGO. I WONDER WHERE HE KEEPS IT WHEN HE'S ASLEEP.

Although "ego" is a thing-word, when we say that someone has a big ego, we do not really mean that there is a thing, a big ego, that he or she keeps around someplace. We just mean that the person has a tendency or a disposition to do such things as brag, talk excessively about himself, never admit mistakes, and so forth.

tempt us into thinking that there must be things for which they stand. And because there seem to be no physical things for which they stand, we are tempted to conclude that they stand for nonphysical things.

In fact, however, when we say that someone has a specific thought, all we can really be doing is attributing to him or her a propensity to say or do certain things, a propensity to behave in certain ways. It's rather like what we mean when we say that someone has mechanical knowledge. "Mechanical knowledge" is a thing-word, too. But we really don't think that someone who has mechanical knowledge possesses a *thing* that's out there in the tool box alongside the screwdriver and adjustable crescent; nor do we think that mechanical knowledge is a ghostly non-physical thing that is hidden away in the person's "mind." When we say that someone has mechanical knowledge, all we mean is that he or she is able, and apt, to do certain things in certain situations.

In short, references to someone's beliefs, ideas, thoughts, knowledge, motives, and to other mental "things" must be analyzed or understood as references to the ways the person is apt to behave given certain conditions.

Might not Ryle strengthen his case by providing an *actual analysis* of a mental-state expression, a translation into behavioral language of a simple mental-state proposition like "She believes it is time to go home"? Indeed Ryle could *not* strengthen his case in this way, for it is not his position that such translations can be made. According to behaviorists, there is no definite and finite list of behaviors and behavioral propensities that we are attributing to someone when we say, "She believes it is time to go home." Instead, we are referring in an *oblique and loose way* to an indefinite and open set of behaviors and behavioral tendencies.

This, then, is **philosophical behaviorism:**

Gilbert
Ryle

- There is no such thing as a nonphysical mind.
- Mental-state thing-words do not really denote things at all. A statement in which such words appear is a kind of loose shorthand reference to behaviors (including verbal behaviors) and behavioral propensities.
- Statements about a person's mental states cannot actually be translated into some set of statements about the person's behavior and behavioral propensities, because the sets of behaviors and behavioral propensities to which they in fact refer are indefinite and open and depend on the situations in which the person happens to be.

Thus, behaviorism, too, is a kind of monism, a materialistic kind of monism. And as a monistic theory it escapes one dilemma faced by a dualist, noted in the earlier box "Reasons for Doubting . . .": the dilemma of how two such different things as nonphysical minds and physical bodies can have an effect on each other.

It also nicely accounts for another problem facing dualism, namely, explaining why it is that brain- and neuroscientists just never do have to postulate the existence of nonphysical mental states to explain the causes and origin of our behavior. The reason they never have to postulate such things, according to the behaviorist, is because there *aren't* such things.

SELECTION 14.2

"Which Should Not Be Set in General Terms"

From Gilbert Ryle

The story is told of some peasants who were terrified at the sight of their first railway-train. Their pastor therefore gave them a lecture explaining how a steam-engine works. One of the peasants then said, "Yes, pastor, we quite understand what you say about the steam-engine. But there is really a horse inside, isn't there?" So used were they to horse-drawn carts that they could not take in the idea that some vehicles propel themselves.

We might invent a sequel. The peasants examined the engine and peeped into every crevice of it. They then said, "Certainly we cannot see, feel, or hear a horse there. We are foiled. But we know there is a horse there, so it must be a ghost-horse which, like the fairies, hides from mortal eyes."

The pastor objected, "But, after all, horses themselves are made of moving parts, just as the steam-engine is made of moving parts. You know what their muscles, joints, and blood-vessels do. So why is there a mystery in the self-propulsion of a steam-engine, if there is none in that of a horse? What do you think makes the horse's hooves go to and fro?" After a pause a peasant replied, "What makes the horse's hooves go is four extra little ghost-horses inside."

Poor simple-minded peasants! Yet just such a story has been the official theory of the mind for the last three very scientific centuries. Several, though not all, of the scientists in this series have automatically posed their problem in this very way. I think that Lord Samuel still accepts

Behaviorism, Pro and Con

Behaviorism makes plain how it is that we could come to understand and use expressions that refer to mental phenomena. These expressions do not refer to private, behind-the-scenes states and episodes within an immaterial mind but rather to publicly witnessable behavior and behavior tendencies.

Nevertheless, the philosophical literature is filled with objections to behaviorism, including the following:

1. Even if some behavioral dispositions could be correlated with a particular mental state, say, experiencing sorrow, it seems more plausible to view that state—the sorrow—as the *cause* of the behavior than to *equate it* with the behavior. We say a person is crying because he is saddened. We don't say or think his crying (among other behaviors) *is* his sadness.

2. Consider two people with their motor nerves severed, one of whom has also had his pain fibers cut. Because they would both have the same behavioral dispositions, according to the behaviorist either both would feel pain or neither would feel pain. Neither alternative is plausible.

3. To believe in behaviorism, you in effect have to believe people are anaesthetized, for only someone who is anaesthetized could think that mental images or sensations of pain are no more than behavioral dispositions.

4. What about paralysis? A paralyzed person can certainly have mental states—even though he or she would not have any particular behavioral dispositions.

As always, these objections are not definitive, and philosophers have devised ways, usually somewhat complicated, of meeting them. You should evaluate them for yourself.

---

the whole story, and that Professor Ayer would like to reject it, but does not see how to do so. For the general terms in which the scientists have set their problem of mind and body, we philosophers have been chiefly to blame, though we have been obsessed, not by the rustic idea of horses, but by the newer idea of mechanical contrivances. The legend that we have told and sold runs like this. A person consists of two theatres, one bodily and one non-bodily. In his Theatre A go on the incidents which we can explore by eye and instrument. But a person also incorporates a second theatre, Theatre B. Here there go on incidents which are totally unlike, though synchronized with those that go on in Theatre A. These Theatre B episodes are changes in the states, not of bits of flesh, but of something called "consciousness," which occupies no space. Only the proprietor of Theatre B has first-hand knowledge of what goes on in it. It is a secret theatre. The experimentalist tries to open its doors, but it has no doors. He tries to peep through its windows, but it has no windows. He is foiled.

We tend nowadays to treat it as obvious that a person, unlike a newt, lives the two lives, life A and life B, each completely unlike, though mysteriously geared to the other. Ingrained hypotheses do feel obvious, however redundant they may be. The peasants in my story correctly thought that a steam-engine was hugely different from a cart and automatically but incorrectly explained the difference by postulating a ghost-horse inside. So most of us, correctly thinking that there are huge differences between a clock and a person, automatically but incorrectly explain these differences by postulating an extra set of ghost-works inside. We correctly say that people are not like clocks, since people meditate, calculate, and invent things; they make plans, dream dreams, and shirk their obligations; they get angry, feel depressed, scan the heavens, and have likes and dislikes; they work, play, and idle; they are sane, crazy, or imbecile; they are skilful at some things and bunglers at others. Where we go wrong is in explaining these familiar actions and conditions as the operations of a secondary set of secret works.

Everybody knows quite well when to describe someone as acting absent-mindedly or with heed, as babbling deliriously or reasoning coherently, as feeling angry but not showing it, as wanting one thing but pretending to want another, as being ambitious, patriotic, or miserly. We often get our accounts and estimates of other people and of ourselves wrong; but we more often get them right. We did not need to learn the legend of the two theatres before we were able to talk sense about people and to deal effectively with them. Nor has this fairly new-fangled legend helped us to do it better.

When we read novels, biographies, and reminiscences, we do not find the chapters partitioned into Section A, covering the hero's "bodily" doings, and Section B, covering his "mental" doings. We find unpartitioned accounts of what he did and thought and felt, of what he said to others and to himself, of the mountains he tried to climb and the problems he tried to solve. Should an examiner mark the paper written by the candidate's hand but refuse to assess the candidate's wits? Theorists themselves, when actually describing people, sensibly forget Theatre A and Theatre B. Sir Charles Sherrington paid a well-deserved compliment to Professor Adrian, but he did not pay one cool compliment to Professor Adrian A and another warmer compliment to Professor Adrian B.

In saying that a person is not to be described as a mind coupled with a body I am not saying, with some truculent thinkers, that people are just machines. Nor are engines just wagons or live bodies just corpses. What is wrong with the story of the two theatres is not that it reports differences which are not there but that it misrepresents differences which are there. It is a story with the right characters but the wrong plot. It is an attempt to explain a genuine difference—or rather a galaxy of differences—but its effect, like that of the peasants' theory, is merely to reduplicate the thing to be explained. It says, "The difference between a machine like a human body on the one hand and a human being on the other, is that in a human being, besides the organs which we do see, there is a counterpart set of organs which we do not see; besides the causes and effects which we can witness, there is a counterpart series of causes and effects which we cannot witness." So now we ask, "But what explains the differences between what goes on in the Theatre B of a sane man and what goes on in that of a lunatic? A third theatre, Theatre C?"

No, what prevents us from examining Theatre B is not that it has no doors or windows, but that there is no such theatre. What prevented the peasants from finding the horse, was not that it was a ghost-horse, but that there was no horse. None the less, the engine *was* different from a wagon and ordinary people *are* different not only from machines, but also from animals, imbeciles, infants, and corpses. They also differ in countless important ways from one another. I have not begun to show how we should grade these differences. I have only shown how we should not grade them.

One last word. In ordinary life (save when we want to sound knowing) we seldom use the noun "mind" or the adjective "mental" at all. What we do is talk of people, of people calculating, conjuring, hoping, resolving, tasting, bluffing, fretting, and so on. Nor, in ordinary life, do we talk of "matter" or of things being "material." What we do is to talk of steel, granite, and water; of wood, moss, and grain; of flesh, bone, and sinew. The umbrella-titles "mind" and "matter" obliterate the very differences that ought to interest us. Theorists should drop both these words. "Mind" and "matter" are echoes from the hustings of philosophy, and prejudice the solutions of all problems posed in terms of them.

BEHAVIORISM

The general trend of this book [*The Concept of Mind*] will undoubtedly, and harmlessly, be stigmatised as "behaviourist." So it is pertinent to say something about Behaviourism. Behaviourism was, in the beginning, a theory about the proper methods of scientific psychology. It held that the example of the other progressive sciences ought to be followed, as it had not previously been followed, by psychologists; their theories should be based upon repeatable and publicly checkable observations and experiments. But the reputed deliverances of consciousness and introspection are not publicly checkable. Only people's overt behaviour can be observed by several witnesses, measured and mechanically recorded. The early adherents of this methodological programme seem to have been in two minds whether to assert that the data of consciousness and introspection were myths, or to assert merely that they were insusceptible of scientific examination. It was not clear whether they were espousing a not very sophisticated mechanistic doctrine, like that of Hobbes and Gassendi, or whether they were still cleaving to the Cartesian para-mechanical theory, but restricting their research procedures to those that we have inherited from Galileo; whether, for example, they held that thinking just consists in making certain complex noises and movements or whether they held that though these movements and noises were connected with "inner life" processes, the movements and noises alone were laboratory phenomena.

However, it does not matter whether the early Behaviourists accepted a mechanist or a para-mechanist theory. They were in error in either case. The important thing is that the practice of describing specifically human doings according to the recommended methodology quickly made it apparent to psychologists how shadowy were the supposed "inner-life" occurrences which the Behaviourists were at first reproached for ignoring or denying. Psychological theories which made no mention of the deliverances of "inner perception" were at first likened to *Hamlet* without the Prince of Denmark. But the extruded hero soon came to seem so bloodless and spineless a being that even the opponents of these theories began to feel shy of imposing heavy theoretical burdens upon his spectral shoulders.

Novelists, dramatists and biographers had always been satisfied to exhibit people's motives, thoughts, perturbations and habits by describing their doings, sayings, and imaginings, their grimaces, gestures and tones of voice. In concentrating on what Jane Austen concentrated on, psychologists began to find that these were, after all, the stuff and not the mere trappings of their subjects. They have, of course, continued to suffer unnecessary qualms of anxiety, lest this diversion of psychology from the task of describing the ghostly might not commit it to tasks of describing the merely mechanical. But the influence of the bogey of mechanism has for a century been dwindling because, among other reasons, during this period the biological sciences have established their title of "sciences." The Newtonian system is no longer the sole paradigm of natural science. Man need not be degraded to a machine by being denied to be a ghost in a machine. He might, after all, be a sort of animal, namely, a higher mammal. There has yet to be ventured the hazardous leap to the hypothesis that perhaps he is a man.

Theory 3: Identity Theory

The third of the four nondualistic analytic philosophies of the mind is **identity theory.** According to identity theory, so-called mental phenomena are all physical phenomena within the brain and central nervous system. A thought, for example, according to identity theory, is in fact some sort of occurrence within the brain/nervous system, though we do not yet know enough about the brain or central nervous system to stipulate which particular occurrence it is.

Notice that the identity theorist does not say merely that thinking (or any other mental occurrence) is *correlated* with or *involves* a neural process of some sort. The claim is rather that thinking *is* a neural process. Just as light *is* electromagnetic radiation (and is not just "involved in" or "correlated with" electromagnetic radiation), and just as heat *is* movement of molecules, thinking and all other mental phenomena, according to identity theory, *are* physical states and happenings within the brain and central nervous system.

Beginning philosophy students sometimes have a difficult time distinguishing behaviorism from identity theory, usually, we think, for two reasons.

First, behaviorism and identity theory are both physicalistic (materialist) theories in the sense that, according to both, you and we and all other people are completely physical organisms: neither theory countenances the existence of the nonmaterial or nonphysical soul, spirit, or mind; and neither theory thinks that mental-state thing-words denote nonmaterial or nonphysical things.

Second, few theorists are *pure* behaviorists or identity theorists. Most philosophers who call themselves identity theorists do in fact accept a behavioristic analysis of at least some assertions about mental states, and most behaviorists do likewise accept identity theory with respect to some mental states.

But the two theories really should not be confused. *Identity theory* holds that mind-states are brain-states, that when we speak of a person's beliefs, thoughts, hopes, ideas, and the like, we are in fact referring to events and processes and states within his or her brain and nervous system. *Philosophical behaviorism* holds that when we use our everyday psychological vocabulary to describe someone, we are really just talking in a shorthand way about his or her behavioral propensities.

Of course, all three of the theories discussed so far have points of intersection. As already noted, the behaviorist and identity theorist both accept the premise that a human being is an entirely physical organism. Further, if Russell is correct and propositions about physical things can in principle be resolved into (more complicated but philosophically more basic) propositions about sense-data, then propositions about behavior and propositions about brain/nervous system states both also can in principle be resolved into propositions about sense-data. Thus both the behaviorist and the identity theorist could accept neutral monism, if they were willing to accept Russell's thesis that physicalist propositions are reducible to sense-data propositions. (In fact, for the reasons explained in Chapter 6, most behaviorists and identity theorists would probably not be inclined to accept this condition.)

In Selection 14.3 Australian philosopher **J. J. C. Smart** (1920–) explains a version of identity theory and then considers some objections to it.

behaviorist – identity overlap

differences

The Soul

We hope it is clear that physicalist (materialist) theories, including behaviorism, identity theory, and functionalism (yet to be explained), all deny that human beings have a soul. Whatever else the soul is conceived as being, whether it is conceived of as identical with or separate from the mind, it at least is thought to be a nonphysical (immaterial) something embodied in a person, and physicalist (material- ist) theories all maintain that only physical things exist. You cannot believe that we are *just* physical organisms *and* that we also have souls.

SELECTION 14.3

"Sensations and Brain Processes"

From J. J. C. Smart

It seems to me that science is increasingly giving us a viewpoint whereby organisms are able to be seen as physico-chemical mechanisms: it seems that even the behavior of man himself will one day be explicable in mechanistic terms. There does seem to be, so far as science is concerned, nothing in the world but increasingly complex arrangements of physical constituents. All ex- cept for one place: in consciousness. That is, for a full description of what is going on in a man you would have to mention not only the phy- sical processes in his tissue, glands, nervous system, and so forth, but also his states of con- sciousness: his visual, auditory, and tactual sen- sations, his aches and pains. That these should be *correlated* with brain processes does not help, for to say that they are *correlated* is to say that they are something "over and above." You can- not correlate something with itself. You corre- late footprints with burglars, but not Bill Sikes the burglar with Bill Sikes the burglar. So sensa- tions, states of consciousness, do seem to be the one sort of thing left outside the physicalist pic- ture, and for various reasons I just cannot be- lieve that this can be so. That everything should be explicable in terms of physics (together of course with descriptions of the ways in which the parts are put together—roughly, biology is to physics as radio-engineering is to electro- magnetism) except the occurrence of sensations seems to me to be frankly unbelievable. . . .

Why should not sensations just be brain processes of a certain sort? There are, of course, well-known (as well as lesser-known) philo- sophical objections to the view that reports of sensations are reports of brain-processes, but I shall try to argue that these arguments are by no means as cogent as is commonly thought to be the case.

Let me first try to state more accurately the thesis that sensations are brain processes. It is not the thesis that, for example, "after-image" or "ache" means the same as "brain process of sort X" (where "X" is replaced by a description of a certain sort of brain process). It is that, in so far as "after-image" or "ache" is a report of a process, it is a report of a process that *happens to be* a brain process. It follows that the thesis does not claim that sensation statements can be *translated* into statements about brain processes. Nor does it claim that the logic of a sensation statement is the same as that of a brain-process statement. All it claims is that in so far as a sensation statement is a report of something, that something is in fact a brain process. Sensations are nothing over and above brain processes. Nations are nothing "over and above" citizens, but this does not prevent the logic of nation statements being very different from the logic of citizen statements, nor does it insure the translatability of nation statements into citizen statements. . . .

Remarks on identity. When I say that a sensation is a brain process or that lightning is an electric discharge, I am using "is" in the sense of strict identity. (Just as in the—in this case necessary—proposition "7 is identical with the smallest prime number greater than 5.". . .

I shall now discuss various possible objections to the view that the processes reported in sensation statements are in fact processes in the brain. Most of us have met some of these objections in our first year as philosophy students. All the more reason to take a good look at them. Others of the objections will be more recondite and subtle.

Objection 1. Any illiterate peasant can talk perfectly well about his after-images, or how things look or feel to him, or about his aches and pains, and yet he may know nothing whatever about neurophysiology. . . .

Reply. You might as well say that a nation of slug-abeds, who never saw the morning star or knew of its existence, or who had never thought of the expression "the Morning Star," but who used the expression "the Evening Star" perfectly well, could not use this expression to refer to the same entity as we refer to (and describe as) "the Morning Star.". . .

Consider lightning. Modern physical science tells us that lightning is a certain kind of electrical discharge due to ionization of clouds of water-vapor in the atmosphere. This, it is now believed, is what the true nature of lightning is. Note that there are not two things: a flash of lightning and an electrical discharge. There is one thing, a flash of lightning, which is described scientifically as an electrical discharge to the earth from a cloud of ionized water-molecules. . . .

In short, the reply to Objection 1 is that there can be contingent statements of the form "A is identical with B," and a person may well know that something is an A without knowing that it is a B. An illiterate peasant might well be able to talk about his sensations without knowing about his brain processes, just as he can talk about lightning though he knows nothing of electricity.

Objection 2. It is only a contingent fact (if it is a fact) that when we have a certain kind of sensation there is a certain kind of process in our brain. Indeed it is possible, though perhaps in the highest degree unlikely, that our present physiological theories will be as out of date as the ancient theory connecting mental processes with goings on in the heart. It follows that when we report a sensation we are not reporting a brain-process.

Reply. The objection certainly proves that when we say "I have an after-image" we cannot *mean* something of the form "I have such and such a brain-process." But this does not show that what we report (having an after-image) is not *in fact* a brain process. . . .

Now how do I get over the objection that a sensation can be identified with a brain process only if it has some phenomenal property, not possessed by brain processes, whereby one-half of the identification may be, so to speak, pinned down?

My suggestion is as follows. When a person says, "I see a yellowish-orange after-image," he is saying something like this: *"There is something going on which is like what is going on when* I have my eyes open, am awake, and there is an orange illuminated in good light in front of me, that is, when I really see an orange.". . .

Objection 4. The after-image is not in physical space. The brain-process is. So the after-image is not a brain-process.

Reply. This is an *ignoratio elenchi.* I am not arguing that the after-image is a brain-process, but that the experience of having an after-image is a brain-process. It is the *experience* which is reported in the introspective report. Similarly, if it is objected that the after-image is yellowy-orange but that a surgeon looking into your brain would see nothing yellowy-orange, my reply is that it is the experience of seeing yellowy-orange that is being described, and this experience is not a yellowy-orange something. So to say that a brain-process cannot be yellowy-orange is not to say that a brain-process cannot in fact be the experience of having a yellowy-orange after-image. . . .

Objection 5. It would make sense to say of a molecular movement in the brain that it is swift or slow, straight or circular, but it makes no sense to say this of the experience of seeing something yellow.

Reply. So far we have not given sense to talk of experiences as swift or slow, straight or circular. But I am not claiming that "experience" and "brain-process" mean the same or even that they have the same logic. "Somebody" and "the doctor" do not have the same logic, but this does not lead us to suppose that talking about somebody telephoning is talking about some-

one over and above, say, the doctor. . . .

Objection 6. Sensations are private, brain processes are *public.* If I sincerely say, "I see a yellowish-orange after-image" and I am not making a verbal mistake, then I cannot be wrong. But I can be wrong about a brain-process. The scientist looking into my brain might be having an illusion. Moreover, it makes sense to say that two or more people are observing the same brain-process but not that two or more people are reporting the same inner experience.

Reply. This shows that the language of introspective reports has a different logic from the language of material processes. It is obvious that until the brain-process theory is much improved and widely accepted there will be no *criteria* for saying "Smith has an experience of such-and-such a sort" *except* Smith's introspective reports. So we have adopted a rule of language that (normally) what Smith says goes.

Objection 7. I can imagine myself turned to stone and yet having images, aches, pains, and so on.

Reply. . . . I can imagine that the Evening Star is not the Morning Star. But it is. All the objection shows is that "experience" and "brain-process" do not have the same meaning. It does not show that an experience is not in fact a brain process.

Difficulties

There are important difficulties within each of these three nondualistic theories. The *neutral monist* idea that mental-state statements and physicalist statements can both be resolved into sense-data statements is vulnerable to the objections to phenomenalism, discussed in Chapter 6. No "private language" Subject to public check

The *behaviorist* thesis, on the other hand, the thesis that mental-state statements are really disguised references to behavioral propensities, may seem plausible enough for *some* mental-state statements. For example, it doesn't sound terribly unreasonable to maintain that, when we attribute to someone *insane jealousy,* or credit him or her with having *an understanding of computers,* we are in fact saying something about the sorts of things he or she is apt and able to do (and say). But think for a moment about *mental images*. For example, picture in your mind Robert Redford. Is it really plausible to regard a statement like "I can picture Redford's face very clearly" as a remark about your behavioral propensities? Or consider *specific thoughts*. Can it seriously be supposed that the statement "I am thinking about my new Honda" is really a shorthand for a series of behavioral propensities? Doesn't it seem much more plausible to view mental images and specific thoughts as *brain/ nervous-system events* of some sort and to regard statements about them not as references to behavioral propensities but as unscientific language for certain neuro-physiological phenomena?

There also are theoretical difficulties involved in the third theory, *identity theory*, as will become clear in our next selection, from philosopher **Paul Churchland** (1942–).

Nevertheless, despite these difficulties, though some analytic philosophers remain dualists, most are physicalists; that is, most would deny that a living human being has a nonphysical component and most would deny that mental-state thing-words designate nonphysical states. For them the question is not whether physicalism is true but which version of physicalism is true.

In Selection 14.4 two *apparent* difficulties in identity theory are presented and rejected by Paul Churchland. The objections are similar to, but not exactly the same as, those discussed by J. J. C. Smart in Selection 14.3.

SELECTION 14.4

"Arguments Against the Identity Theory"   **From Paul Churchland**

It may be urged that one's brain states are more than merely not (yet) known by introspection: they are not know*able* by introspection under any circumstances. Thus,

1. My mental states are knowable by intro-spection.

2. My brain states are *not* knowable by intro-spection. Therefore, by Leibniz' Law [If *x* is identical with *y*, then *x* and *y* have the same properties],

3. My mental states are not identical with my brain states.

. . . Now the materialist is in a position to insist

that the argument contains a false premise—premise (2). For if mental states are indeed brain states, then it is really brain states we have been introspecting all along, though without fully appreciating what they are. And if we can learn to think of and recognize those states under mentalistic descriptions, as we all have, then we can certainly learn to think of and recognize them under their more penetrating neurophysiological descriptions. At the very least, premise (2) simply begs the question against the identity theorist. The mistake is amply illustrated in the following parallel argument:

1. Temperature is knowable by feeling.

2. Mean molecular kinetic energy is *not* knowable by feeling. Therefore, by Leibniz' Law,

3. Temperature is not identical with mean molecular kinetic energy.

This identity, at least, is long established, and this argument is certainly unsound: premise (2) is false. Just as one can learn to feel that the summer air is about 70° F, or 21° C, so one can learn to feel that the mean KE of its molecules is about 6.2×10^{-21} joules, for whether we realize it or not, that is what our discriminatory mechanisms are keyed to. Perhaps our brain states are similarly accessible. . . .

Consider now a final argument, again based on the introspectible qualities of our sensations. Imagine a future neuroscientist who comes to know everything there is to know about the physical structure and activity of the brain and its visual system, of its actual and possible states. If for some reason she has never actually had a sensation-of-red (because of color blindness, say, or an unusual environment), then there will remain something she does *not* know about certain sensations: *what it is like to have a sensation-of-red.* Therefore, complete knowledge of the physical facts of visual perception and its related brain activity still leaves something out. Accordingly, materialism cannot give an adequate account of all mental phenomena, and the identity theory must be false.

The identity theorist can reply that this argument exploits an unwitting equivocation on the term "know." Concerning our neuroscientist's utopian knowledge of the brain, "knows" means something like "has mastered the relevant set of neuroscientific propositions." Concerning her (missing) knowledge of what it is like to have a sensation-of-red, "knows" means something like "has a prelinguistic representation of redness in her mechanisms for noninferential discrimination." It is true that one might have the former without the latter, but the materialist is not committed to the idea that having knowledge in the former sense automatically constitutes having knowledge in the second sense. The identity theorist can admit a duality, or even a plurality, of different *types of knowledge* without thereby committing himself to a duality in *types of things known.* The difference between a person who knows all about the visual cortex but has never enjoyed the sensation-of-red, and a person who knows no neuroscience but knows well the sensation-of-red, may reside not in *what* is respectively known by each (brain states by the former, nonphysical *qualia* by the latter), but rather in the different *type,* or *medium,* or *level* of representation each has of exactly the same thing: brain states.

In sum, there are pretty clearly more ways of "having knowledge" than just having mastered a set of sentences, and the materialist can freely admit that one has "knowledge" of one's sensations in a way that is independent of the neuroscience one may have learned. Animals, including humans, presumably have a prelinguistic mode of sensory representation. This does not mean that sensations are beyond the reach of physical science. *It just means that the brain uses more modes and media of representation than the mere storage of sentences.* All the identity theorist needs to claim is that those other modes of representation will also yield to neuroscientific explanation.

The identity theory has proved to be very resilient in the face of these predominantly antimaterialist objections. But further objections, rooted in competing forms of materialism, constitute a much more serious threat.

Theory 4: Functionalism

Now we will consider the last of the four nondualist theories of mind, functionalism, and then, to close the chapter, say something about current issues in the philosophy of mind.

Physicalist philosophers do not believe that people have nonphysical minds, and they deny that mental-state thing-words stand for states or processes of a nonphysical variety. But many physicalists question the identity theory, according to which each distinct mental state or process equates with one and only one brain state or process. It is possible, these physicalists say, that the selfsame psychological (mental) state could be correctly ascribed to quite different physiological systems.

For example, there may be beings in a far distant galaxy whose brains and nervous systems are radically different from our own but who nevertheless have thoughts and beliefs and desires and motives and other mental states. This certainly is not a terribly far-fetched possibility. Now if there are such beings, it's quite possible that when they believe something, what goes on in their "brains" and "nervous systems" may not be the same thing at all as what goes on in ours when we believe something. (They might not even have what we would call brains!)

For that matter, the belief process in a brain-damaged *human* may not be quite the same as in a normal human. And some day, thinking robots may be created (at least physicalists must admit that this is theoretically possible) with "brains" made out of silicon and plastic. Though these robots will think, in all probability somewhat different physical processes will be involved when they do than are involved when we think.

In the light of such examples as these it seems unwise to say, as identity theory does, that each distinct mental phenomenon equates with one and only one brain/nervous-system phenomenon. It seems sounder philosophically to say that a given mental state is identical with *some* brain/nervous-system phenomenon *or other*.

This is what so-called functionalists say. According to **functionalism** a mental state is defined by its *function*. For example, you may believe it is going to rain. If you do, your belief will have been caused by certain sensory stimuli in conjunction with other beliefs that you have, and it (your belief that it is going to rain) will in turn have an effect on your behavior and other beliefs. In short, the belief will interact with your other mental states (including sensations) and your behavior in a way that is unique to just that belief. To play just that causal role it does play in this network of relationships is the *function* of that belief.

Thus, according to the functionalist, *any* physical process (regardless of what type of organism or physical system it occurs in) that has that precise function *is* that belief.

For the functionalist, therefore, a mental state is analogous to a mousetrap or a garage door opener or a word processor or anything else that is *defined by its function*. Mousetraps (or garage door openers or word processors) are not defined by what they are made of or how they are put together. Mousetraps may actually be made of *most anything* and put together in indefinitely many ways. Hence they are not defined by what they are made of or how they are assembled but by their

The Big Issues

Although the views of some philosophers, perhaps especially Russell, Wittgenstein, Ryle, and Ayer, have been enormously influential within analytic philosophy, it is probably true to say that the course of analytic philosophy has been determined primarily by the journal articles published by the large "rank and file" of professional philosophers. These papers are undeniably technical, are directed at other professionals within the field, and usually deal with a fairly limited aspect of a larger problem. Articles and books that deal in wholesale fashion with large issues (e.g., What is the mind? Is there knowledge? What is the meaning of life? What is the ideal state? What is truth?) are comparatively rare. For this reason, and perhaps for others, the work of analytic philosophers strikes outsiders as narrow, theoretical, irrelevant, inaccessible, and tedious. The work of twentieth-century mathematicians is doubtlessly equally incomprehensible to laypersons, but the public's expectations are different for philosophers.

functions, that is, by what they do. Anything that has the function of a mousetrap, no matter how it is assembled and out of what it is made, is a mousetrap. The same holds true for garage door openers and word processors, and, according to the functionalist, the same holds for beliefs, thoughts, ideas, and other mental states and processes. Beliefs and the like, functionalists say, are defined by their *function*—the role they play in affecting behavior and in affecting and being affected by other mental states.

Therefore, according to the functionalist, beliefs and other mental phenomena must be analyzed functionally, *not reductively*. You can't *reduce* talk about mousetraps to talk about what they are made of. If someone were to ask what a mousetrap *is*, you would explain what a mousetrap *does*, what its unique function is. Beliefs and other mental phenomena, according to the functionalist, are likewise to be explained in terms of their unique functions—the specific roles they play relative to sensory data and other mental states and to behavioral output.

Thus, says the functionalist, though it is true that nothing nonphysical happens to you when you have a belief, that doesn't mean that we could somehow "translate" statements about your beliefs into statements about neurological processes. And conversely, the fact that we cannot translate talk about your beliefs into talk about neurological processes doesn't mean that beliefs are nonphysical.

So you can see that functionalism explains nicely why psychology—whether of the commonsense ("folk") or the scientific variety—has resisted reduction to neurology. It has been resistant not because psychological states are nonphysical but because they are functional. Functionalism is therefore thought to provide a conceptual framework for psychological research that, on one hand, does not commit the researcher to murky and questionable dualistic metaphysical notions and, on the other, also does not commit the researcher to the implausible idea that psychology, just like chemistry, "reduces" to physics.

Theories of Mind

Note: Noninteractionist dualism, according to which a person's nonphysical and physical components do not interact causally with one another, and idealism, according to which only mind (thought) exists, have not generally been regarded as serious options by analytic philosophers.

A brief comment seems in order here. It has been the fond thought of many a philosopher that anything that happens could, in principle, be expressed in the language of physics. Let's call this thought **straightforward reductivist physicalism** or, for short, **physicalist reductivism.** The thought is this: just as chemistry is really just a matter of physics—that is, is reducible to physics—biology and neurophysiology are reducible to chemistry and physics, and hence ultimately are reducible just to physics. Further (according to physicalist reductivism, because psychology is really just a matter of neurophysiology, ultimately it, too, reduces to physics. Sociology and the other social sciences (according to physicalist reductivism) likewise ultimately reduce to the psychology of groups and hence, ultimately, they too reduce to physics. And hence, if the Grand Reduction of physics itself to a single force and/or particle is achieved, as some physicists apparently believe it will be, everything from human thoughts and political elections to interactions of leptons and quarks will be reduced to and explained by a single physical factor (the physical version, perhaps, of God). If functionalism is correct, however, though everything that happens may indeed be physical, a thoroughgoing reduction of *everything* to physics is most unlikely.

Neutral monism, behaviorism, identity theory, and functionalism, then, are four nondualist theories of mind that have been developed by analytic philosophers in this century. As we said earlier, these days perhaps most analytic philosophers of mind (not to mention cognitive psychologists and artificial intelligence researchers) accept some physicalist theory of the mind (usually functionalism). Nevertheless, they are aware of several philosophical problems that physicalist theories encounter, as we see in the final section of this chapter.

Current Issues in Physicalist Philosophies of Mind

So, as we just said, most contemporary analytic philosophers who study the philosophy of mind tend to accept some sort of physicalism, according to which a human being is an entirely physical organism that has no nonphysical, nonmaterial components or features.

But physicalist theories are not without their difficulties, and we shall now briefly list the most important of these. Contemporary work in analytical philosophy that is concerned with the mind is usually related to one or another of these issues. If you believe in the soul or free will or life after death, you may find physicalism unpleasant; in any case, the issue seems important.

Final Authority Problem

Through introspection you gain knowledge of your own conscious states. It also seems that you are the *final authority* on what these states are. If you think that something looks brown to you, then you would be startled if we tried to tell you that it looks blue to you. If you say you are thinking of hiking in the mountains, it would be peculiar for us to say, "Oh, no, in fact you are thinking of the Panama Canal Treaty."

It would be odd for us to say these things because everyone appreciates that only oneself is the final authority on one's own conscious states. Provided others think you can speak English, that you are honestly reporting your states, and that you haven't made a slip of the tongue, they would not consider correcting you. The notion that someone else might speak with equal authority about your conscious states seems not only false, but nuts.

But if conscious states are physical processes (as per identity theory), or are functional states of some physical system or other (as per functionalism), or are behavioral dispositions (as per behaviorism), then it would seem that, at least in principle, others could speak as authoritatively about your conscious states as you can. Whether (and in what sense) one truly is the final authority on his or her own conscious states, and how, if he or she is the final authority, physicalistic theories can accommodate that fact, are issues of current controversy.

Intentionality and Related Issues

Thinking, it seems, is not merely a process, for thinking is always about something. Thinking has content or an object that is thought about. Let's consider an example. Take two thoughts, let's say one about *Santa Claus* and the other about *the tooth fairy*. How are these two thoughts different?

Well, they differ from one another by virtue of their *objects,* namely, Santa Claus and the tooth fairy. Thoughts are thus said to have the property of **intentionality,** which is merely a way of saying that they "point to" or "contain" an object beyond themselves. This kind of intentionality has nothing to do with doing something deliberately, by the way.

According to some philosophers, *intentionality is the mark of mental phenomena.* Desires, beliefs, ideas, plans, doubts, imaginings—many (if not all) mental things are characterized by their objects. You don't just desire, you desire *something,* and one desire differs from the next because of its object. The same holds true for beliefs and the rest. A good bit of work is currently being done by philosophers of mind in grappling with whether and how a purely physical system can have intentional states.   *intentions of the heart, pain, disappointment, grief*

Notice, too, that the objects that apparently characterize and define beliefs, desires, and the like may be completely *imaginary*. Consider the two thoughts just mentioned. How is it that nonexistent things, Santa Claus and the tooth fairy, can distinguish two thoughts from one another and from other mental states? The problem seems especially troublesome for physicalists.

Another way to approach the problem of intentionality is to note that thoughts, desires, beliefs, and the like are *propositional attitudes,* which is a philosopher's way of saying that to have a thought or desire or belief is to hold some proposition to be true. For example, when you think about Santa Claus, in fact your thought in large measure consists of the propositions you are thinking, such as that Santa Claus wears a red suit, that he has a white beard, or whatever it is that you are thinking. How is it, then, that a purely physical system can have states that are propositional—that is, true or false?

Look at it this way. A computer can cause sentences to be printed on a sheet of paper or flashed on a video screen in response to electric signals that are typed in on a keyboard. Inside the computer all that is going on is electrical processes of one sort or other. The signals, sentences, and processes are all physical things, flashes of light or bits of ink or bursts of electricity. These physical things can become true or false propositions to us, but are they true or false to the computer? What do you think?

If you are uncomfortable saying that they are true or false to the computer, then you can appreciate the problem presented to physicalists by the propositional nature of mental states. For, according to the physicalist, when a person is thinking, all that is going on internally is electrochemical processes of some sort. These processes are not the same processes as go on in a computer, but they, like those in the computer, are entirely physical (or so says the physicalist). How can these supposedly purely physical things be propositional? You can see that this is a problem.

A related issue is this. Through thought the world is *represented* to us. Thus, two questions arise. The first question has to do with the representing. How does a purely physical thing, whether it is ink marks, electrical impulses, flashes of light, bioelectric signals, neurological processes, or any other physical thing, come to *represent* anything? And the second question has to do with the "us." Surely, representations do not understand themselves: to be representations, they must be understood *by* a consciousness, by an "us" that is *distinct* from the representations. Assuming that neurological processes do have representational capabilities, how do they become understood, and what is it that understands them?

(*Historical note:* Harvard philosopher **Hilary Putnam** [1926–], who was the originator of the term *functionalism* as denoting a theory of the mind, has recently especially emphasized the difficulties posed for functionalist theories by intentionality. The difficulties he has stressed are not exactly the difficulties we have mentioned, however, and are too technical to discuss here, except to say: The basic problem, according to Putnam, is that, although functionalism correctly rejects the

Brentano and Intentionality

To say that conscious states are "intentional" just means that they have objects (you don't just imagine, you imagine *something*; you don't just hope, you hope *for something*). The thesis that conscious states are intentional is attributed to the German philosopher and psychologist **Franz Brentano** (1838–1917).

The objects of conscious states, Brentano noted, have "intentional inexistence," which means that they (the objects) need not exist. For instance, you can think about someone even if that person no longer exists and even if such a person never did exist. Thus, *thinking* about someone seems to be quite fundamentally different from, say, *helping* someone, because you can't help someone unless he or she exists.

That conscious states are intentional was a fundamental tenet of Brentano's "descriptive psychology," which, in the hands of his student Edmund Husserl, evolved into phenomenology (which is discussed in the next chapter). Husserl asserted that if it weren't for Brentano's thesis of the intentionality of conscious states, phenomenology could not have come into being.

Contemporary *analytic philosophers* are endeavoring to understand how, if humans are purely physical entities, their conscious states could be intentional. The *phenomenologists'* interest in intentionality is entirely different, as will become clear in the next chapter. Phenomenology is not especially concerned with the issue of whether a physical system could have intentional states.

"species-chauvinist" idea that intentional states correspond one by one to human neurochemical states, it assumes, incorrectly, that each human intentional state corresponds one by one to some human neurochemical state.)

The Irreducibility of Conscious Experience

Let's move on to one more issue of concern for contemporary philosophy of mind. Can people who are blind from birth know what it is like to see? No, you say? Well, couldn't we explain it to them? No again?

This seems correct. It seems that we could *not* explain, to a person who had never had sight, what sight, as a conscious experience, is. Any explanation would be incomplete. Likewise any *physical* explanation would be incomplete. It just could not convey what sight is as a *subjective experience*. A blind person *could* understand any physical explanation of sight we might come up with, but he or she still would not know what sight is; so it seems that a physical explanation of sight just cannot capture all there is to visual experience.

This problem is not peculiar to sight. In a famous essay, "What Is It Like to Be a Bat?" Thomas Nagel raised this problem in general terms. If a bat could speak, it still could not explain to us what it is like to experience the world through sonar. If we could communicate with creatures from other galaxies who had no sense of smell or taste, we would not be able to explain to them what smell and taste are as conscious experiences. If a person has never felt pain or depression or frustration, it is futile to try to explain to him or her what these things are like. Even poets cannot do it. They can *express* depression (let us say); they can *evoke* depression (get us to feel depressed); but they cannot *explain what depression is* in such a way that someone who has never experienced depression would then know what it is. In short, there's just something irreducible about conscious experience, something that can't be captured by any set of words, and physicalist explanations of consciousness seem especially inappropriate for the task. Consciousness is subjective; physicalist explanations are all objective. Until physicalist theories can somehow account for the irreducibly subjective nature of conscious states, these theories will be incomplete.

In sum, the final authority problem, the problem of intentionality, and the problem of the irreducibility of subjectivity are all currently unresolved issues in the philosophy of mind. All three issues are especially perplexing from a physicalist perspective.

On the other hand, maybe philosophers are making too much of all this and imagining difficulties where there are none. One who thinks this is **John Searle** (1932–). It seems appropriate to end this chapter with an excerpt from a famous article by Searle, in which he argues that the mind-body problem is really much simpler than philosophers have made it out to be.

Minds, Brains, and Science

From John Searle

I want to plunge right into what many philosophers think of as the hardest problem of all: What is the relation of our minds to the rest of the universe? This, I am sure you will recognize, is the traditional mind-body or mind-brain problem. In its contemporary version it usually takes the form: how does the mind relate to the brain?

I believe that the mind-body problem has a rather simple solution, one that is consistent both with what we know about neurophysiology and with our commonsense conception of the nature of mental states—pains, beliefs, desires, and so on. But before presenting that solution, I want to ask why the mind-body problem seems so intractable. . . .

There are four features of mental phenomena which have made them seem impossible to fit into our "scientific" conception of the world as made up of material things. . . .

The most important of these features is consciousness. I, at the moment of writing this, and you, at the moment of reading it, are both conscious. It is just a plain fact about the world that it contains such conscious mental states and events, but it is hard to see how mere physical systems could have consciousness. How could such a thing occur? How, for example, could this grey and white gook inside my skull be conscious? . . .

The second intractable feature of the mind is what philosophers and psychologists call "intentionality," the feature by which our mental states are directed at, or about, or refer to, or are of objects and states of affairs in the world other than themselves. . . . Now the question about intentionality is much like the question about consciousness. How can this stuff inside my head be *about* anything? How can it *refer* to anything? . . .

The third feature of the mind that seems difficult to accommodate within a scientific conception of reality is the subjectivity of mental states. This subjectivity is marked by such facts as that I can feel my pains, and you can't. I see the world from my point of view; you see it from your point of view. I am aware of myself and my internal mental states, as quite distinct from the selves and mental states of other people. . . .

Finally, there is a fourth problem, the problem of mental causation. We all suppose, as part of common sense, that our thoughts and feelings make a real difference to the way we behave, that they actually have some *causal* effect on the physical world. I decide, for example, to raise my arm and—lo and behold—my arm goes up. But if your thoughts and feelings are truly mental, how can they affect anything physical? . . . These four features, consciousness, intentionality, subjectivity, and mental causation, are what make the mind-body problem seem so difficult. . . .

The first thesis I want to advance toward "solving the mind-body problem" is this:

Mental phenomena, all mental phenomena
whether conscious or unconscious, visual
or auditory, pains, tickles, itches, thoughts,
indeed, all of our mental life, are caused by
processes going on in the brain. . . .

To our first claim . . . we need to add a second claim:

Pains and other mental phenomena just are
features of the brain (and perhaps the rest of
the central nervous system).

One of the primary aims of this chapter is to show how *both* of these propositions can be true together. . . . To do this, I will turn away from the relations between mind and brain for a moment to observe some other sorts of causal relationships in nature.

A common distinction in physics is between micro- and macro-properties of systems—the small and large scales. Consider, for example, the desk at which I am now sitting, or the glass of water in front of me. Each object is composed of micro-particles. The micro-particles have features at the level of molecules and atoms as well as at the deeper level of sub-atomic particles. But each object also has certain properties such as the solidity of the table, the liquidity of the water, and the transparency of the glass, which are surface or global features of the physical systems. Many such surface or global properties can be causally explained by the behavior of elements at the micro-level. For example, the solidity of the table in front of me is explained by the lattice structure occupied by the molecules of which the table is composed. Similarly, the liquidity of the water is explained by the nature of the interactions between the H_2O molecules. Those macro-features are causally explained by the behavior of elements at the micro-level.

I want to suggest that this provides a perfectly ordinary model for explaining the puzzling relationships between the mind and the brain. In the case of liquidity, solidity, and transparency, we have no difficulty at all in supposing that the surface features are *caused by* the behavior of elements at the micro-level, and at the same time we accept that the surface phenomena *just are* features of the very systems in question. I think the clearest way of stating this point is to say that the surface feature is both *caused by* the behavior of micro-elements, and at the same time is *realised in* the system that is made up of the micro-elements. There is a cause and effect relationship, but at the same time the surface features are just higher level features of the very system whose behavior at the micro-level causes those features. . . .

If we apply these lessons to the study of the mind, it seems to me that there is no difficulty in accounting for the relations of the mind to the brain in terms of the brain's functioning to cause mental states. Just as the liquidity of the water is caused by the behavior of elements at the micro-level, and yet at the same time it is a feature realised in the system of micro-elements, so in exactly that sense of "caused by" and "realised in" mental phenomena are caused by processes going on in the brain at the neuronal or modular level, and at the same time they are realised in the very system that consists of neu-rons. . . . Nothing is more common in nature than for surface features of a phenomenon to be both caused by and realised in a micro-structure, and those are exactly the relationships that are exhibited by the relation of mind to brain.

Checklist

To help you review, here is a checklist of the key philosophers and concepts of this chapter. The brief descriptive sentences summarize leading ideas. Keep in mind that some of these summary statements represent terrific oversimplifications of complex positions.

Philosophers

- **Luisa Maria Oliva Sabuco de Nantes Barrera** Held that the soul occurs throughout the brain. Stressed the connection between psychological and physical health and between morality and medicine.
- **William of Ockham** Medieval English philosopher most famous for the principle known as Ockham's razor. *explain using the fewest assumptions*
- **René Descartes** Interactionist dualist.
- **Bertrand Russell** Neutral monist (at one point in his life).
- **Benedictus de Spinoza, A. J. Ayer,** and **William James** Other neutral monists.
- **Gilbert Ryle** Held that when we talk about a person's psychological states, we are referring not to the immaterial states of a nonphysical mind but to the person's behavioral dispositions.
- **J. J. C. Smart** Identity theorist.
- **Paul Churchland** Contemporary physicalist philosopher of mind.
- **Hilary Putnam** Coined the term *functionalism,* but now rejects the theory.
- **Franz Brentano** Held that conscious states have intentional inexistence.
- **John Searle** Held that the mind is a "surface feature" of the brain.

Concepts

494 dualism

499 interactionist dualism

500 characterization problem

individuation problem

emergence problem

dependency problem

501 no-necessity problem

interaction problem

understanding problem

503 neutral monism *"One-ism" mind+ matter are reducible to same thing which is n. mental nor material Bertrand Russel*

philosophical reduction *sense Data*

504 Ockham's razor *explain using the fewest assumptions*

materialism *physical*

idealism *non physical*

504 sense-data *contents of what we see here, feel, taste*

507 philosophical behaviorism *propensity or disposition to Act in a certain way*

512 identity theory *mind-states are brain-states identical to simply Nervous systems processes ie that it will rain*

518 functionalism *Function of belief in in Affecting behaviour + other beliefs ∴ Physical process is that belief. simply triggered by sensory stimuli*

520 straightforward reductivist physicalism/physicalist reductivism *to a single force or particle*

521 final authority problem

521 intentionality *thoughts point to or contain an object beyond themselves*

523 intentional inexistence *thinking of things that no longer exist or never did exist.*

523-4 irreducibility of conscious experience *subjective (everyone) cannot be expressed in words (objective)*

Questions for Discussion and Review

1. Present some reasons for believing that a human being is not a purely physical thing.

2. If humans are purely physical things, can they have free will? Explain.

3. Does the fact that a person can have knowledge of nonmaterial things, such as the truths of mathematics, demonstrate that humans are not purely physical?

4. Assuming that it is possible to doubt the existence of physical things but not your own mental states, does that show that your mental states are not physical things?

5. "Beliefs are true or false; physical things are not. So beliefs are not physical things." Evaluate this argument.

6. "My mental states are knowable by introspection, but my brain states are not; therefore my mental states are not brain states." Evaluate this argument.

7. Can a mind be characterized only "negatively," that is, as not divisible, as not existing in space, and so on?

8. Explain and try to resolve, in favor of dualism, either the emergence problem or the individuation problem.

9. Explain and try to resolve, in favor of dualism, the dependency problem, the understanding problem, or the no-necessity problem.

10. Explain and try to resolve, in favor of dualism, the interaction problem.

11. Explain philosophical reduction. What is the connection between reduction and analysis?

12. What are sense-data, and are they physical, mental, or what?

13. What is philosophical behaviorism? Make clear in your explanation what a "disposition" is.

14. Do all thing-words refer to things?

15. Must the behaviorist say that actors feigning pain must actually be in pain?

16. Explain the difference between identity theory and behaviorism.

17. Do mental states reduce to brain states, according to the functionalist? Explain. Do functionalists believe that the mind and mental states are nonphysical?

18. "A brain scientist could never tell from looking at my brain what I am thinking. Therefore my thoughts are not brain states." Discuss this argument.

19. What does it mean to say, "Intentionality is the mark of the mental"?

20. When all is said and done, which of the theories of mind discussed in this chapter do you think is the soundest, and why?

Suggested Further Readings

David Armstrong, *A Materialist Theory of the Mind* (London: Routledge and Kegan Paul, 1968). An important statement of a materialist position.

N. Block, *Readings in Philosophy of Psychology* (Cambridge, Mass.: Harvard University Press, 1980). A good collection of (not always easy-to-read) essays in the philosophy of mind.

C. D. Broad, *The Mind and Its Place in Nature* (New York: The Humanities Press, 1951). You won't find a better introduction to the subject, though it was originally written in 1925.

Keith Campbell, *Body and Mind* (London: Macmillan, 1970). This slender volume clearly sets forth the basic positions on this subject.

Paul M. Churchland, *Matter and Consciousness* (Cambridge, Mass.: Bradford, 1984). Excellent critical introduction to philosophy of mind. Slightly more difficult than Campbell.

Paul M. Churchland, *The Engine of Reason, The Seat of the Soul* (Cambridge, Mass.: Bradford, 1995). Covers the ongoing research of the neurobiological and connectionist communities and probes the social and ethical parameters of recent experimentation in consciousness.

Daniel Dennett, *Brainstorms* (Montgomery, Vt.: Bradford Books, 1978). A widely read collection that contains sometimes difficult, but always well-written and entertaining essays on the mind and psychology.

Daniel Dennett, *Consciousness Explained* (New York: Little, Brown, 1991). An important recent philosophical examination of consciousness. A fine piece of writing, the book can be understood by nonphilosophers.

Thomas Nagel, "What Is It Like to Be a Lot?" in *Mortal Questions* (Cambridge: Cambridge University Press, 1979). A famous essay that explains the irreducibility of conscious experiences.

Hilary Putnam, *Representation and Reality* (Cambridge, Mass.: M.I.T. Press, 1988). The most important current controversies in the philosophy of mind are all carefully examined. Mostly very readable.

Howard Robinson, ed., *Objections to Physicalism* (New York: Oxford University Press, 1993). A collection of papers, mostly nontechnical, but not introductory.

Bertrand Russell, *The Analysis of Mind* (London: George Allen & Unwin, 1921). From Russell's "neutral monist" phase.

Gilbert Ryle, *The Concept of Mind* (New York: Barnes and Noble, 1949). An important work, very readable.

John Searle, *Minds, Brains, and Science* (Cambridge: Harvard University Press, 1984). This short book raised hackles throughout cognitive science. Read it and find out why. The argument is very easy to follow.

John Searle, *The Rediscovery of the Mind* (Cambridge, Mass.: Bradford, 1992). A readable attack by Searle on current theories of mind.

Peter Smith and O. R. Jones, *The Philosophy of Mind* (Cambridge: Cambridge University Press, 1986). Another introductory text on this subject, with a fairly good bibliography.

Philosophy of Mind:
The Mystery of Consciousness

Summary and Conclusion

The main focus of analytic philosophers who have been concerned with the mind has been to find a proper understanding, or "analysis," if you will, of everyday discourse about the mind and its states. By "proper" is meant (roughly) one that is consistent, intelligible, and unconfused; one that is consonant with our scientific knowledge of the brain and human behavior and psychology (and with the findings of computer science and artificial intelligence research as well); and one that is not too at odds with our commonsense opinions about human psychology.

The overall objective might alternatively be described as one of seeking to delineate the interconnections between "folk psychology"—our "common-sense" understanding of the mind and its states and processes—and what brain science and psychology (and computer science and artificial intelligence research) tell us about consciousness, intelligence, and the internal causes of human behavior.

Beginning students sometimes wonder, *why not just get on with it* and study the mind and its states directly, and forget trying to understand mere *talk* about the mind? The answer to this question is as follows. If the concepts of the mind and mental phenomena were like the concepts of the sun and the brain and the Rocky Mountains, you could do that. You already know what objects you must study if you wish to study the sun, the brain, or the Rocky Mountains. But there is no similar understanding yet of just what the mind and its states are. You don't yet quite know just what you must undertake to examine if you wish to examine the mind or its states. By seeking to clarify the concept of mind, analytic philosophers of the mind strive to produce this understanding. Thus, their objective might also be described as trying to provide understanding of what the mind and its states are, no small task.

What we've written here is intended to give you some comprehension of one important set of issues addressed by analytic philosophers (as well as some understanding of an analytic approach to philosophy). In the next part we turn to Continental philosophy, the other main tradition in twentieth-century Western philosophy.

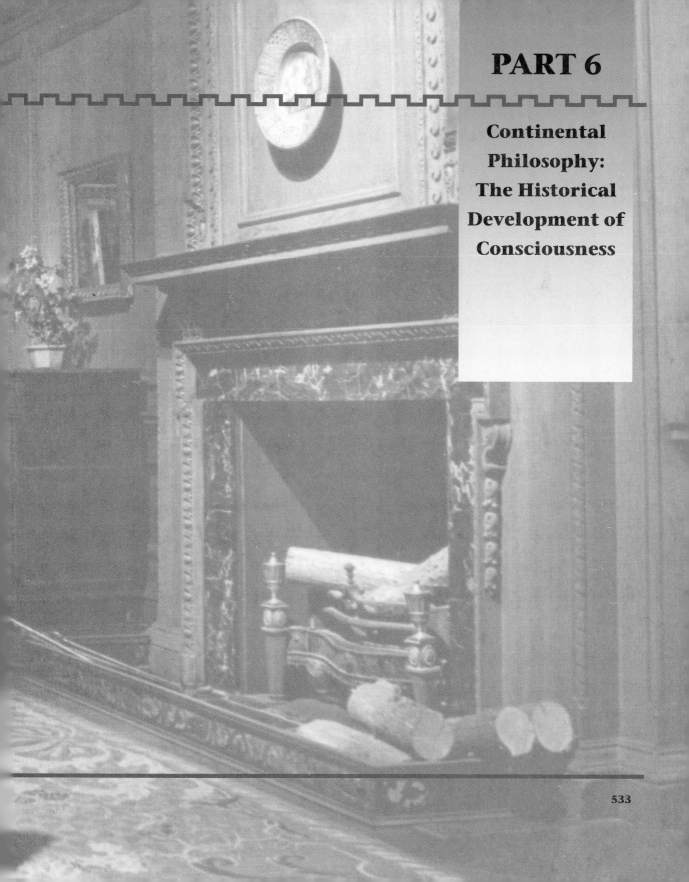

PART 6

Continental Philosophy: The Historical Development of Consciousness

The Continental Philosophers

15

The existentialist says at once that man is anguish.

—Jean-Paul Sartre

Although analytic philosophy has been the predominant tradition of philosophy in English-speaking countries during most of the twentieth century, other movements from Continental Europe have been increasingly influential. Identifiable "schools" of philosophical thought remain, and scholars continue to work within a given tradition, but some contemporary philosophy shows a noticeably interdisciplinary approach. In this chapter we'll outline several European approaches to philosophy, most notably those of existentialism, phenomenology, and critical theory, and show their interdisciplinary nature. Then we'll give an example or two of how **Continental philosophy** is influencing a contemporary debate over the very nature (and possible accomplishments) of philosophy itself.

Both existentialism and phenomenology have their roots in the nineteenth century; many of their themes can be traced back to Socrates and even to the pre-Socratics. And each has influenced the other to such an extent that two of the most famous and influential Continental European philosophers of this century, **Martin Heidegger** (1889–1976) and **Jean-Paul Sartre** (1905–1980), are important figures in both movements, though Heidegger is primarily a phenomenologist and Sartre, primarily an existentialist. Critical theory traces its roots to the so-called Frankfurt school in Germany in the 1920s and 1930s, which attempted to develop Marxism (see Chapter 10) as an interpretive tool applied to social and philosophical thought. Herbert Marcuse (1898–1979) in the United States (see Chapter 10) and

Jürgen Habermas (1929–) in Germany are two of the most influential and creative critical theorists.

The focus and concerns of Continental philosophy, especially those of existentialism and phenomenology, are markedly different from those of analytic philosophy—so much so that beginning students are amazed to learn that analytic philosophers and Continental philosophers both call themselves philosophers. It amazes some philosophers, too. It's not just that analytic philosophers and Continental philosophers come up with different answers; they don't even ask the same questions.

Existentialism

Many of the themes of **existentialism** had already been introduced by those brooding thinkers of the nineteenth century, **Søren Kierkegaard** (1813–1855) and **Friedrich Nietzsche** (1844–1900), two of the most important forerunners of existentialism. Both men had a strong distaste for the optimistic idealism of Hegel and for metaphysical systems in general. Such philosophy, they thought, ignored the human predicament. For both Kierkegaard and Nietzsche, the universe, including its human inhabitants, is seldom rational, and philosophical systems that seek to make everything seem rational are just futile attempts to overcome pessimism and despair. This point of view will become clearer as we proceed.

For Kierkegaard, existence in this earthly realm must lead a sensitive person to despair. Despair, Kierkegaard held, is the inevitable result of the individual's having to confront momentous concrete ethical and religious dilemmas *as an individual*. It is the result of the individual's having to make, *for himself and alone,* choices of lasting significance.

According to Kierkegaard, despair is the *sickness-unto-death* and is the central philosophical problem. Is there anything in this world or outside it to which the individual can cling to keep from being swept away by the dark tides of despair? This, for Kierkegaard, is the fundamental question. His eventual conclusion was that nothing earthly can save a person from despair. Only a subjective commitment to the infinite and to God, not based on abstract intellectualizing or theoretical reasoning, can grant relief.

Kierkegaard emphasized the theme of the irrationality of the world in opposition to Hegel's belief in its utter rationality. The earth, Kierkegaard thought, is a place of suffering, fear, and *dread*. Of these three, dread, according to Kierkegaard, is the worst because it has *no identifiable object or specifiable cause*. Dread renders us almost helpless to resist it. Kierkegaard regarded the idea that philosophy should be concerned with general or ideal "truths" and abstract metaphysical principles with disdain. Philosophy must speak to the anguished existence of the individual who lives in an irrational world and who must make important decisions in that world.

PROFILE / Søren Kierkegaard (1813–1855)

Søren Kierkegaard, Danish philosopher and religious thinker, was virtually unknown outside Denmark until the twentieth century. Ultimately, however, his thought had a profound impact on existentialist philosophy and Protestant theology.

Kierkegaard's life was outwardly unexciting. He attended the universities of Copenhagen and Berlin and was much influenced by German culture, though he made polemical attacks on Hegel, whose metaphysics he re-

garded as totally inapplicable to the individual.

As for his inward life, Kierkegaard professed himself to have been, since childhood, "under the sway of a prodigious melancholy," and his grim outlook was made even gloomier by the confession of his father—himself no carefree spirit—that he had sinned and had even cursed God. Finding himself without moorings, Kierkegaard regarded dread and despair as the central problems of his life, and he learned that he could escape their grasp only through a passionate commitment of faith to God and the infinite.

Although Kierkegaard became engaged to marry, he found it necessary to break off the engagement, apparently because God occupied the "first place" in his life, though his own writing about the subject is murky. The episode, at any rate, was so momentous that even the sketchiest biography of Kierkegaard is obliged to mention the woman's name: Regine Olsen. The agony of choosing between God and Regine, a choice Kierkegaard felt he had to make, affected him profoundly.

Kierkegaard defined three

types of life: the aesthetic, the ethical, and the religious. These correspond to what English philosophy professor Ray Billington has called the life of the observer, the life of the follower, and the life of the initiator. The "aesthetic" life is dominated by impulse, emotions, and sensual pleasures and does not truly involve making choices. The "ethical" life does involve making choices, but those who live this life make choices on the basis of some kind of moral code, which they in effect fall back on as a sort of crutch. But at a higher and much more difficult plane, that of the "religious," the individual realizes that he must decide all issues for himself. He faces the agony of having to rely on his own judgment while never knowing whether his judgment is correct. The despair one faces at this level is overcome only by a "leap of faith," that total and infinite commitment to God.

Some of Kierkegaard's most important philosophical works, *Either/Or* (1843), *Philosophical Fragments* (1844), and *The Concluding Unscientific Postscript* (1846), were published under pseudonyms.

If Kierkegaard found Hegel's philosophy of absolute reason unpalatable, **Arthur Schopenhauer** (1788–1860), who must be mentioned in prelude to Nietzsche, found it beneath contempt. For Schopenhauer, Hegel's "reason" was an

Dostoyevsky's *Notes from the Underground*

In his 1864 novel, *Notes from the Underground*, **Fyodor Dostoyevsky** (1821–1881) told how an imperfect society can waste the lives of its best members. The "underground man" lives in a society that prefers and rewards mediocrity. Hence his intelligence, sensitivity, and strength of character are neither needed nor wanted. He is condemned to watch second-rate compatriots surpass him and achieve success while his own superior talents languish unused. He is left with a life of bitterness, hopelessness, and shame. His sole pleasure consists in acts of spite and revenge, more imaginary than real. A passage:

"I was ashamed," he said; "I got to the point of feeling a sort of secret abnormal, despicable enjoyment in returning home to my corner on some disgusting Petersburg night, acutely conscious that that day I had committed a loathesome action again, that what was done could never be undone, and secretly, inwardly gnawing, gnawing at myself for it, tearing and consuming myself till the last of the bitterness turned into a sort of sweetness and at last into positive real enjoyment!

"I insist upon that . . . the enjoyment was just from the too intense consciousness of one's own degradation; it was from feeling oneself that one had reached the last barrier, that it was horrible, but that it could not be otherwise; that there was no escape for you: that you could never become a different man."

Dostoyevsky said in *The Brothers Karamazov* (1879–1880) that "the world stands on absurdities." It is just possible (is it not?) that a sense of uselessness is the most humiliating absurdity one can encounter.

exercise in philistine self-deception; his attempt to paint the world in rational terms, a part of a larger conspiracy. The sciences and humanities have all been mustered, he believed, to picture the universe as reasonable, governed by law, and under the mastery of the rational human intellect. Reality, he maintained, is very different.

Specifically, human beings are for Schopenhauer rarely rational in their actions. On the contrary, they are blindly driven by their wills in pursuit of selfish desires. Reason is invoked after the fact as a way of rationalizing what has been done from impulse, he held. Schopenhauer's world is peopled with vicious little men who commit atrocities in pursuit of trifling objects. It is a world in which no one can be trusted, and security requires sleeping with a loaded pistol underneath the pillow. Their willfulness makes humans a violent part of a grotesque scenario that has neither sense nor reason, in Schopenhauer's view.

Nietzsche further developed Schopenhauer's astringent critique of the blind optimism of rationalist idealists. According to Nietzsche, Western society had become increasingly decadent. People had come to lead lives largely devoid of joy or grandeur. They were enslaved by a morality that says "no" to life and to all that affirms it. They had become part of a herd, part of a mass that is only too willing to do what it is told. The herd animal, he held, is cowardly, reactionary, fearful, desultory, and vengeful. The mediocrity of Western civilization, he believed, was a reflection of these qualities. Nietzsche was under no illusions about the fate of the

PROFILE / Friedrich Wilhelm Nietzsche (1844–1900)

After studying at the universities of Bonn and Leipzig, Nietzsche, whose genius was evident from the beginning, was appointed associate professor of classical philology at the University of Basel at the unheard-of young age of twenty-four without even having written a doctoral thesis. Within two years he had become a full professor. In 1879, however, he was forced by ill health to resign his chair, and by 1889, he, like his father earlier, had become irretrievably insane. Nietzsche's insanity, however, may have been caused by medication.

Two of the principal intellectual influences on Nietzsche's life were the writings of Schopenhauer and the music of Richard Wagner, which Nietzsche compared to hashish in its ability to relieve mental pressure. For a period Nietzsche and Wagner—one of the century's most brilliant philosophers and one of its most brilliant composers—were friends, though this friendship did not last.

Nietzsche's writings have been enormously influential in Continental philosophy. Nietzsche saw himself as an active nihilist whose role was to tear down the old "slave morality" of Christian civilization. He looked to the "overman" whose "will to power" would set him beyond conventional standards of morality, a line of thought that later was seized upon, misinterpreted, and misused by defenders of Nazism.

Nietzsche's widespread popularity outside philosophical circles owes much to the power of thought expressed in numerous infamous quotations. "Which is it," Nietzsche asked in one of these, "is man one of God's blunders or is God one of man's?"

Nietzsche, like Kierkegaard, was the son of a Lutheran minister. His father died of insanity when Nietzsche was four, and Nietzsche was raised until he was fourteen in a household of women, consisting of his mother, sister, grandmother, and two maiden aunts.

mass of mankind: only the rare and isolated individual is likely to escape a trivial life and pathetic fate, he maintained.

These writers gave signal that the smug self-satisfaction of nineteenth-century European philosophy—and culture—camouflaged emptiness and decadence. Their concern for the situation of the individual person; their disdain for abstract, remote, and (in their view) meaningless systems of thought; their denial of the rationality of the world and the people within it; their awareness of a vacuity, triviality, and pettiness within human existence; their efforts to find a reason for not despairing entirely—these themes spread rapidly into *belles lettres* (literature) as a whole in the late nineteenth and early twentieth centuries.

Sigmund Freud, for example, regarded the human being as a sexual animal from birth, one moved by drives that are unconscious and irrational and over which there is little intelligent control. Art movements like Dadaism, Surrealism, and Expressionism expressed disenchantment with the established life of the bourgeoisie and its culture and values and sought to break out of the straightjacket of worn-out ideas and safe lifestyles. A sense that life is meaningless and empty, that the individual is alone and isolated and unable to communicate with others except on the most trivial of levels, permeated the thinking of the intellectuals and *literati* of the time and has persisted in art, literature, and philosophy.

In *The Bald Soprano* (1950), to take one example, **Eugène Ionesco** (1912–1994), a playwright in the dramatic tradition known as the *theater of the absurd,* had two strangers meeting at a dinner party and entering into a conversation. Slowly they discover that they had sat in the same train compartment five weeks earlier, live in the same city and house, and both have a daughter with one red eye and one white eye. Ultimately, to their delight, they discover that they are husband and wife.

The inability of humans to communicate with one another was a principal theme of the Irish playwright **Samuel Beckett** (1906–1989), in whose influential play *Waiting for Godot* (1953) the two principal characters wait in a desertlike environment for someone to arrive who will tell them what to do. They talk only to pass the time, not because they have anything to say. They seem often to be talking at the same time on entirely different subjects without either one noticing. And it doesn't matter, for it doesn't interrupt the emptiness of the words.

Another powerful depiction of the inability of people to reach one another can be found in the films of the Swedish director **Ingmar Bergman** (1918–). In film after film, Bergman delineated the silence that exists between husband and wife, son and father, sister and sister. He further showed how the frustration and loneliness of the inner being lead to deep feelings of anger, resentment, and desire for revenge. Much time and energy is expended by Bergman's isolated characters in carefully hiding these feelings from themselves and others. Our separation and estrangement from others, Bergman implied, leave our lives tragically and intolerably unfulfilled. A more recent example of separation and isolation can be found in the 1993 Merchant/Ivory film of Ishiguro Kazuo's novel *The Remains of the Day,* in which actor Anthony Hopkins's character is unable even to understand, let alone to express or fulfill, his love and profound longing for a younger woman (played by Emma Thompson).

Another theme present in twentieth-century literature pertains to the horror of coping in an absurd world—a world in which there is no apparent reason why things happen one way and not another. The characters in the stories and novels of **Franz Kafka** (1883–1924), a Czech whose mother tongue and language in which he wrote was German (a fact itself suggestive of human dislocation), invariably find themselves thrust into a situation they do not comprehend but in which they must nevertheless act and be judged for their actions. Nor are they certain that the situation in which they find themselves is not one of their own making. Kafka's parable "The Metamorphosis," for example, tells of an ordinary salesman who supports his sister and aging parents. One day the salesman awakens at home to find that his body has been changed into a giant insect. He does not know why this has happened, and he will die without finding out. At first he is treated com-

"The Death of Ivan Ilyich"

Leo Tolstoy (1828–1910) provides a powerful and moving example of the meaninglessness and futility of life in the story "The Death of Ivan Ilyich" (1884).

Ivan Ilyich had led what he thought was a successful, busy, ambitious life. But then he learns that, though still in the prime of life, he has an incurable disease and will soon die. Quite naturally, he begins to look more closely at his life.

He notices that his wife and family members are really only concerned about the inheritance, and that his fellow workers have already begun jockeying to replace him. He sees that no one really cares about him or has any genuine sympathy for his situation. In short, his whole life seems to be a meaningless game. He finds that he cannot understand the insincerity and cruelty of others, including his own family. He also cannot understand God's cruelty and His absence in time of need. Above all, he cannot understand why he is so *alone*, abandoned to suffer and die. Has he done something deserving of such punishment? "'I am not guilty,' he exclaims, but he is not certain it is so."

"Life," wrote Tolstoy, "a series of increasing sufferings, flies further and further towards its end—the most terrible suffering." One of the implications of the story is that only when an individual faces the horror and suffering in life will he or she begin to understand its meaning—or lack of it.

The Trial

In Kafka's novel *The Trial* (1925), a man is arrested, convicted, and executed without ever being able to find out what crime he is supposed to have committed. Nor is he conscious of having committed any crime. Yet such is his sense of self-doubt that he is never sure he doesn't deserve to be condemned.

That we can feel responsible—or even *be* responsible—for the situations in which we find ourselves (and the causes of which we certainly do not understand) is another existentialist theme that focuses on the tragic aspects of human existence.

passionately by the other family members, on whom he is of course dependent, but soon they resent his not supporting them and eventually come to regard him as a nuisance as well as an unwelcome family secret. At one point, pieces of fruit thrown by a frustrated and irate sister become embedded in his body and grow infected. Slowly but inevitably, the metamorphosized man loses heart and dies. Kafka presumably thought the story represented to some extent the fate of all human beings.

The themes we have been alluding to here, which began to surface in the nineteenth century and were developed throughout our own century (and give little indication of dying out today), are among the main themes of **existentialism.** The most important existentialist philosophers, about whom we shall say more later, only achieved worldwide recognition and notoriety just after World

War II. But the ideas essential to existentialism were shared by many artists, novelists, poets, dramatists, and theologians much before that time.

Specifically, these main themes of existentialism (or at any rate some of them) may be listed as follows:

- Traditional and academic philosophy is sterile and remote from the concerns of real life.

- Philosophy must focus on the individual in his or her confrontation with the world.

- The world as found is irrational (or in any event, beyond total comprehending or accurate conceptualizing through philosophy).

- The world also is absurd, in the sense that no ultimate explanation can be given for why it is the way it is.

- Senselessness, emptiness, triviality, separation, and inability to communicate pervade human existence, giving birth to anxiety, dread, self-doubt, and despair.

- The individual confronts, as the most important fact of human existence, the necessity to choose how he or she is to live within this absurd and irrational world.

As will be seen, the existentialists do not guarantee that this *existential predicament* can be solved. What they do say is that without utter honesty in confronting the assorted problems of human existence, life can only deteriorate; that without struggling doggedly with them, the individual will find no meaning or value in life.

SELECTION 15.1

Thus Spoke Zarathustra {style="inline"}

From Friedrich Nietzsche

THE LAST MAN

And thus spoke Zarathustra to the people: . . .

"Alas, the time is coming when man will no longer give birth to a star. Alas, the time of the most despicable man is coming, he that is no longer able to despise himself. Behold, I show you the *last man*.

"'What is love? What is creation? What is longing? What is a star?' Thus asks the last man, and he blinks.

"The earth has become small, and on it hops the last man, who makes everything small. His race is as ineradicable as the flea-beetle; the last man lives longest.

"'We have invented happiness,' say the last men, and they blink. They have left the regions where it was hard to live, for one needs warmth. One still loves his neighbor and rubs against him, for one needs warmth.

"Becoming sick and harboring suspicion are sinful to them: one proceeds carefully. A fool, whoever still stumbles over stones or human beings! A little poison now and then: that makes for agreeable dreams. And much poison in the end, for an agreeable death.

"One still works, for work is a form of entertainment. But one is careful, lest the entertainment be too harrowing. One no longer becomes poor or rich: both require too much exertion. Who still wants to rule? Who obey? Both require too much exertion.

"No shepherd and one herd! Everybody wants the same, everybody is the same: whoever feels different goes voluntarily to a madhouse.

"'Formerly all the world was mad,' say the most refined, and they blink.

"One is clever and knows everything that has ever happened: so there is no end of derision. One still quarrels, but one is soon reconciled—else it might spoil the digestion.

"One has one's little pleasure for the day, and one's little pleasure for the night: but one has regard for health.

"'We have invented happiness,' say the last men, and they blink."

Two Existentialists

Existentialism as a philosophical movement was something of a direct reaction to perceived social ills and was created by artists and writers as much as by philosophers per se. So it isn't remarkable that two of the greatest existentialist philosophers, Albert Camus and Jean-Paul Sartre, wrote drama, novels, and political tracts as well as philosophical works. Both also thought it important to disseminate their ideas into society as a whole in the hope of having some direct influence. Both were involved in the French Resistance during World War II against the terror of German fascism. Both thought—despite their belief in the absurdity of life—that responsible social action is as necessary as is an understanding of the sociopolitical forces at work in the world.

Camus and Sartre are by no means the only existentialist philosophers. Other famous existentialists include Gabriel Marcel and Simone de Beauvoir in France, Karl Jaspers in Switzerland, Martin Heidegger in Germany, Miguel de Unamuno and José Ortega y Gasset in Spain, and Nicola Abbagnano in Italy. But Camus and Sartre are especially representative of the movement, and we will focus on them. Camus, we might note, was reluctant to be classified as an existentialist because that lumped him together with Sartre, with whom Camus quarreled.

Albert Camus

Albert Camus (1913–1960) grew up in poverty in Algeria and fought in the French Resistance against the Nazis. He saw much suffering, waste, and death even before the war; and, perhaps not surprisingly, the principal philosophical question, for him, was: *Is there any reason not to commit suicide?* Camus believed that this question arises when a person stops deceiving himself and begins seeing the world without pregiven illusions.

Many people, Camus believed, live their whole lives and die without ever seeing things as they really are. More specifically, instead of seeing the "tragic nature of life," they waste their lives in "stupid self-confidence." That is, although they in fact spend their lives in or near despair in an absurd world that continually frustrates true human needs, they mask the fact with a forced optimism. And the more "profitable" such false optimism is, the more entrenched it becomes. In Camus's view, for many of us self-deception has become a dominant mode of being. This implies as well that often we are strangers to ourselves and to our own inability to meet our fundamental needs.

What are these basic needs? According to Camus, there are two: the need for clarity or understanding and the need for social warmth and contact. Unfortunately, however, we live in an absurd world, a world in which these basic human needs are unmet. On one hand, the need for clear understanding of the world founders on the "opaqueness and density of the world"; indeed, it founders on the very fact that the world is absurd and consequently provides no sufficient reason for why things happen one way and not another.

The second essential need, the need for human warmth and contact, also remains unfulfilled, Camus thought. Humans in this violent age tend to remain strangers to one another (as well as to themselves); they live solitary existences in which relationships are matters of convention rather than of mutual sharing and understanding. The absurdity of life in frustrating essential human needs means that hoped-for happiness often turns to misery and despair—even though many hide this tragedy from themselves behind a façade of baseless hopes.

Camus likened life to the fate of Sisyphus in the myth of the same name. Sisyphus had provoked the wrath of the gods and was condemned to roll a huge stone up a hill, only to see it roll back down again. This repeated itself forever. Human beings, according to Camus, are similarly condemned to lives of "futile and hopeless labor," without reasonable hope of fulfilling their true needs. No matter how hard we try to live a just and meaningful existence, it is unlikely that our efforts will lead to lasting results.

In this context it may easily be understood why Camus considered the question of suicide to be a primary philosophical issue. *Why indeed* should one wish to continue living under such circumstances as Camus has depicted? Nevertheless, Camus regarded suicide as unacceptable. Suicide, he thought, is a kind of weak-minded acquiescence to an unjust destiny. Camus believed, perhaps paradoxically, that by struggling against the Sisyphusian fate to the end, by rebelling against the absurdity and tragedy of life, it is possible to give life meaning and value. His position indeed is that *only* through this struggle with an absurd world can the individual achieve fulfillment, solidarity with others, and "a brief love of this earth."

Increasingly Camus focused his concern on the grotesque inhumanity and hideous cruelty of a world torn asunder by war and Nazism. Civilization, he thought, certainly with some justification, is suffering from a "plague" of epidemic proportions, a plague that kills many and sickens all. In such an unjust world one finds oneself committing violent acts *merely to survive*. Camus viewed the world as,

PROFILE / Albert Camus (1913–1960)

Camus was born in Mondovi, Algeria, on November 7, 1913. His French father was a farmworker and his Spanish mother, a maid. His father died in the war soon after Camus's birth, forcing Camus's mother to move into the impoverished quarter of Algiers at the end of the Casbah. Camus later considered the poverty in which he grew up the great source of his deepest insights. His Spanish pride and intensity as well as his intellectual acumen were noticed by a teacher, Louis Germain, who made sure that Camus could attend a first-rate high school, one normally accessible only to the rich.

Camus was athletic and played goalie for the Racing Universitaire. After one game he left the playing field in a sweat, which developed into a cold and then into tuberculosis. This meant that he would not be able to become a teacher after he passed his state examination in philosophy. Instead, he turned to journalism, working at first for the *Algeria Republican*. By the age of twenty he was already married and separated, and had both joined and quit the Communist Party. He had also formed his own theater group, l'Équipe.

Camus was eventually thrown out of Algeria for writing articles concerning the poverty and backwardness in its provincial areas. During World War II, he was the lead article writer for the Resistance newspaper *Combat*. After the war, he wrote his major works, and also maintained his involvement with theater groups. In 1957, he received the Nobel Prize for Literature. He was killed in an automobile accident in 1960.

Camus was a straightforward, unpretentious person who always had time for his friends, for actors, and for young people starting out. Many looked upon him as a kind of big brother. He was proud to be a human being and dedicated himself to the love and enjoyment of this world. He believed that the secret of the art of living lies in the sun, the sea, and a youthful heart.

Life Is Absurd

One of Camus's principal theses is that life as we find it is absurd. The notion of absurdity implies that there is no ultimate reason that things are the way they are. It also implies that life is unjust and frustrates human needs. Most important, perhaps, that the world is absurd seems to mean, for Camus, that it provides no absolute or necessary basis of value.

That we must make choices and decide how to act in a valueless and absurd world is often called the "existential predicament."

Camus on Life

It is from the clash between our desire for complete explanation and the essential opacity of the world that the absurd is born.

[The Gods] had thought with some reason that there is no more dreadful punishment than futile and hopeless labor.

I draw from the absurd three consequences, which are my revolt, my freedom, and my passion. . . . I transform into a rule of life what was an invitation to death—and I refuse suicide.

He who despairs of events is a coward, but he who hopes for the human lot is a fool.

Truth is mysterious, elusive, always to be conquered. Liberty is dangerous, as hard to live with, as it is elating. We must march towards these goals painfully but resolutely, certain in advance of our feelings on so long a road.

We are still waiting, and I am waiting, for a group of all those who refuse to be dogs and are resolved to pay the price that must be paid so that man can be something more than a dog.

The true rebel chooses the present over the future, the fate of humanity for the delusion of power. He gives us an example of the only original

rule of life today, "to learn to live and to die, and, in order to be a man, to refuse to be a god."

In all circumstances of his life, the writer can recapture the feelings of a living community that will justify him. But only if he accepts as completely as possible the two truths that constitute the nobility of his calling: the service of truth and the service of freedom.

in effect, sponsoring on ongoing competition in murder, as a place in which it is difficult to raise a finger without killing somebody. Capital punishment, he thought, is just one example of how the "decent citizen" is reduced to the level of a murderer. And in outright warfare the morality of violence exceeds control and comes into the open.

Camus wrote that "one cannot always live on murders and violence." By living out the values of the lowest animals, the individual is delivered up to the merciless power of despair and cynicism. Camus loathed the "absolute cynicism" of modern society that, he implied, drove humans to desperation and prevented them "from taking responsibility for their own life."

Thus, Camus came increasingly to insist that each individual must spend life fighting the plague—that is, the degeneracy of the world. Each must resist the temptations offered by cunning and violence; what is called for, he thought, is a "revolt" against the existing "order." Perhaps as a way of fighting the plague, Camus's thinking after the war became increasingly concerned with social and political issues. This represents a shift from his early works, which are focused much more strictly on the concerns of the individual.

But Camus thought that the revolt against a revolting world must be "measured" and limited. What Camus means is made clearer in his play *Caligula* (1944),

The Just

In his play *The Just* (1950), Camus expresses approval of a Russian terrorist who murders the Grand Duke and then insists on paying for his deed with his own life, the point being that there can be no justification for taking another's life. Camus is sometimes described as a "courageous humanist." His emphasis on the necessity of brave and unceasing struggle against violence and inhumanity discloses an implicit faith that human goodness ultimately will reign victorious.

in which the Roman emperor Caligula is presented as an example of a man who discovers the implicit cruelty and viciousness of human existence. In order not to fall victim to this evil, Caligula revolts against it in an unmeasured way, through his own acts of cruelty and viciousness. Such an unmeasured reaction was unacceptable to Camus; it meant becoming more bestial than the other beasts. In short, for Camus, the violence of the world does not excuse or justify violence in response.

Thus, the best that is possible for the individual, Camus implied, is a measured revolt wherein he or she spends life resisting violence and injustice. The effort, he maintained, must be predicated on the assumption that "any mutilation of mankind is irrevocable." The individual must fight for justice and liberty and against all forms of tyranny: "Let us die resisting," he wrote. Yet we must have no illusions or false optimism about the possible results of our action. For it may well be that nothing will improve: in an absurd world nothing is guaranteed.

Selection 15.2 is from Camus's 1955 essay, "The Myth of Sisyphus."

SELECTION 15.2

"The Myth of Sisyphus"   **From Albert Camus**

ABSURDITY AND SUICIDE

There is but one truly serious philosophical problem and that is suicide. Judging whether life is or is not worth living amounts to answering the fundamental question of philosophy. All the rest—whether or not the world has three dimensions, whether the mind has nine or twelve categories—comes afterwards. These are games; one must first answer. And if it is true, as Nietzsche claims, that a philosopher, to deserve our respect, must preach by example,

you can appreciate the importance of that reply, for it will precede the definitive act. These are facts the heart can feel; yet they call for careful study before they become clear to the intellect.

If I ask myself how to judge that this question is more urgent than that, I reply that one judges by the actions it entails. I have never seen anyone die for the ontological argument. Galileo, who held a scientific truth of great importance, abjured it with the greatest ease as soon as it endangered his life. In a certain sense, he did right.[1] That truth was not worth the stake. Whether the earth or the sun revolves around the other is a matter of profound indifference. To tell the truth, it is a futile question. On the other hand, I see many people die because they judge that life is not worth living. I see others paradoxically getting killed for the ideas or illusions that give them a reason for living (what is called a reason for living is also an excellent reason for dying). I therefore conclude that the meaning of life is the most urgent of questions. How to answer it? On all essential problems (I mean thereby those that run the risk of leading to death or those that intensify the passion of living) there are probably but two methods of thought: the method of La Palisse and the method of Don Quixote. Solely the balance between evidence and lyricism can allow us to achieve simultaneously emotion and lucidity. In a subject at once so humble and so heavy with emotion, the learned and classical dialectic must yield, one can see, to a more modest attitude of mind deriving at one and the same time from common sense and understanding.

Suicide has never been dealt with except as a social phenomenon. On the contrary, we are concerned here, at the outset, with the relationship between individual thought and suicide. An act like this is prepared within the silence of the heart, as is a great work of art. The man himself is ignorant of it. One evening he pulls the trigger or jumps. Of an apartment-building manager who had killed himself I was told that he had lost his daughter five years before, that he had changed greatly since, and that that experience had "undermined" him. A more exact word cannot be imagined. Beginning to think is beginning to be undermined. Society has but little connection with such beginnings. The worm is in man's heart. That is where it must be sought. One must follow and understand this

fatal game that leads from lucidity in the face of existence to flight from light.

There are many causes for a suicide, and generally the most obvious ones were not the most powerful. Rarely is suicide committed (yet the hypothesis is not excluded) through reflection. What sets off the crisis is almost always unverifiable. Newspapers often speak of "personal sorrows" or of "incurable illness." These explanations are plausible. But one would have to know whether a friend of the desperate man had not that very day addressed him indifferently. He is the guilty one. For that is enough to precipitate all the rancors and all the boredom still in suspension.[2]

But if it is hard to fix the precise instant, the subtle step when the mind opted for death, it is easier to deduce from the act itself the consequences it implies. In a sense, and as in melodrama, killing yourself amounts to confessing. It is confessing that life is too much for you or that you do not understand it. Let's not go too far in such analogies, however, but rather return to everyday words. It is merely confessing that that "is not worth the trouble." Living, naturally, is never easy. You continue making the gestures commanded by existence for many reasons, the first of which is habit. Dying voluntarily implies that you have recognized, even instinctively, the ridiculous character of that habit, the absence of any profound reason for living, the insane character of that daily agitation, and the uselessness of suffering.

What, then, is that incalculable feeling that deprives the mind of the sleep necessary to life? A world that can be explained even with bad reasons is a familiar world. But, on the other hand, in a universe suddenly divested of illusions and lights, man feels an alien, a stranger.

---

[1] From the point of view of the relative value of truth. On the other hand, from the point of view of virile behavior, this scholar's fragility may well make us smile.

[2] Let us not miss this opportunity to point out the relative character of this essay. Suicide may indeed be related to much more honorable considerations—for example, the political suicides of protest, as they were called, during the Chinese revolution.

His exile is without remedy since he is deprived of the memory of a lost home or the hope of a promised land. This divorce between man and his life, the actor and his setting, is properly the feeling of absurdity. All healthy men having thought of their own suicide, it can be seen, without further explanation, that there is a direct connection between this feeling and the longing for death.

The subject of this essay is precisely this relationship between the absurd and suicide, the exact degree to which suicide is a solution to the absurd. The principle can be established that for a man who does not cheat, what he believes to be true must determine his action. Belief in the absurdity of existence must then dictate his conduct. It is legitimate to wonder, clearly and without false pathos, whether a conclusion of this importance requires forsaking as rapidly as possible an incomprehensible condition. I am speaking, of course, of men inclined to be in harmony with themselves.

Stated clearly, this problem may seem both simple and insoluble. But it is wrongly assumed that simple questions involve answers that are no less simple and that evidence implies evidence. *A priori* and reversing the terms of the problem just as one does or does not kill oneself, it seems that there are but two philosophical solutions, either yes or no. This would be too easy. But allowance must be made for those who, without concluding, continue questioning. Here I am only slightly indulging in irony: this is the majority. I notice also that those who answer "no" act as if they thought "yes." As a matter of fact, if I accept the Nietzschean criterion, they think "yes" in one way or another. On the other hand, it often happens that those who commit suicide were assured of the meaning of life. These contradictions are constant. It may even be said that they have never been so keen as on this point where, on the contrary, logic seems so desirable. It is a commonplace to compare philosophical theories and the behavior of those who profess them. But it must be

said that of the thinkers who refused a meaning to life none except Kirilov who belongs to literature, Peregrinos who is born of legend,[3] and Jules Lequier who belongs to hypothesis, admitted his logic to the point of refusing that life. Schopenhauer is often cited, as a fit subject for laughter, because he praised suicide while seated at a well-set table. This is no subject for joking. That way of not taking the tragic seriously is not so grievous, but it helps to judge a man.

In the face of such contradictions and obscurities must we conclude that there is no relationship between the opinion one has about life and the act one commits to leave it? Let us not exaggerate in this direction. In a man's attachment to life there is something stronger than all the ills in the world. The body's judgment is as good as the mind's, and the body shrinks from annihilation. We get into the habit of living before acquiring the habit of thinking. In that race which daily hastens us toward death, the body maintains its irreparable lead. In short, the essence of that contradiction lies in what I shall call the act of eluding because it is both less and more than diversion in the Pascalian sense. Eluding is the invariable game. The typical act of eluding the fatal evasion that constitutes the third theme of this essay is hope. Hope of another life one must "deserve" or trickery of those who live not for life itself but for some great idea that will transcend it, refine it, give it a meaning, and betray it.

Thus everything contributes to spreading confusion. Hitherto, and it has not been wasted effort, people have played on words and pretended to believe that refusing to grant a meaning to life necessarily leads to declaring that it is not worth living. In truth, there is no necessary common measure between these two judgments. One merely has to refuse to be misled by

---

[3]I have heard of an emulator of Peregrinos, a post-war writer who, after having finished his first book, committed suicide to attract attention to his work. Attention was in fact attracted, but the book was judged no good.

the confusions, divorces, and inconsistencies previously pointed out. One must brush everything aside and go straight to the real problem. One kills oneself because life is not worth living, that is certainly a truth—yet an unfruitful one because it is a truism. But does that insult to existence, that flat denial in which it is plunged come from the fact that it has no meaning? Does its absurdity require one to escape it through hope or suicide—this is what must be clarified, hunted down, and elucidated while brushing aside all the rest. Does the Absurd dictate death? This problem must be given priority over others, outside all methods of thought and all exercises of the disinterested mind. Shades of meaning, contradictions, the psychology that an "objective" mind can always introduce into all problems have no place in this pursuit and this passion. It calls simply for an unjust—in other words, logical—thought. That is not easy. It is always easy to be logical. It is almost impossible to be logical to the bitter end. Men who die by their own hand consequently follow to its conclusion their emotional inclination. Reflection on suicide gives me an opportunity to raise the only problem to interest me: is there a logic to the point of death? I cannot know unless I pursue, without reckless passion, in the sole light of evidence, the reasoning of which I am here suggesting the source. This is what I call an absurd reasoning. Many have begun it. I do not yet know whether or not they kept to it.

When Karl Jaspers, revealing the impossibility of constituting the world as a unity, exclaims: "This limitation leads me to myself, where I can no longer withdraw behind an objective point of view that I am merely representing, where neither I myself nor the existence of others can any longer become an object for me," he is evoking after many others those waterless deserts where thought reaches its confines. After many others, yes indeed, but how eager they were to get out of them! At that last crossroad where thought hesitates, many men have arrived and even some of the humblest. They then abdicated what was most precious to them, their life. Others, princes of the mind, abdicated likewise, but they initiated the suicide of their thought in its purest revolt. The real effort is to stay there, rather, in so far as that is possible, and to examine closely the odd vegetation of those distant regions. Tenacity and acumen are privileged spectators of this inhuman show in which absurdity, hope, and death carry on their dialogue. The mind can then analyze the figures of that elementary yet subtle dance before illustrating them and reliving them itself.

Jean-Paul Sartre

Albert Camus was agnostic, maintaining that he did not know whether or not there is a God. **Jean-Paul Sartre** (1905–1980) was atheistic. Man, Sartre said, is *abandoned,* by which "we mean that God does not exist." And according to Sartre, the abandonment of man—that is, the nonexistence of God—has drastic philosophical implications. Basically, there are four.

First, because there is no God, there is no maker of man and no such thing as a divine conception of man in accordance with which man was created. This means, Sartre thought, that there is no such thing as a human nature that is common to all humans; no such thing as a specific essence that defines what it is to be human. Past philosophers had maintained that each thing in existence has a definite, specific essence; Aristotle, for example, believed that the essence of being human was being rational. But for Sartre, the person must produce his or her own essence, because no God created human beings in accordance with a divine concept. Thus, in the case of man, Sartre wrote, "existence precedes essence," by which he meant very simply that you are what you make of yourself. You are what *you* make of yourself.

The second implication of the nonexistence of God is this. Because there is no God, there is no ultimate reason why anything has happened or why things are the way they are and not some other way. This means that the individual in effect has been *thrown* into existence without any real reason for being. But this does not mean that the individual is like a rock or a flea, which also (because there is no God) have no ultimate reason or explanation. Rocks and fleas, Sartre would say, only have what he calls "being-in-itself" (in French, *être-en-soi*), or mere existence. But a *human being,* according to Sartre, not only exists, that is, has being-in-itself, but also has "being-for-itself" (*être-pour-soi*), which means that a human being, unlike an inanimate object or vegetable, is a self-aware or conscious subject that creates its own future. We will return to this point momentarily.

Third, because there is no God and hence no divine plan that determines what must happen, "there is no determinism." Thus, "man is free," Sartre wrote; "man is freedom"; in fact, he is *condemned* to be free. Nothing forces us to do what we do. Thus, he said, "we are alone, without excuses," by which he means simply that we cannot excuse our actions by saying that we were forced by circumstances or moved by passion or otherwise determined to do what we did.

Fourth, because there is no God, there is no objective standard of values: "It is very troubling that God does not exist," Sartre wrote, "for with him disappears every possibility of finding values . . . there can no longer be any good a priori." Consequently, because a Godless world has no objective values, we must establish or invent our own values.

Consider briefly what these various consequences of our "abandonment" entail. That we find ourselves in this world without a God-given "human nature" or "essence"; that we are active, conscious, and self-aware subjects; that we are totally free and unconstrained (and unexcused) by any form of determinism; and that we must create our own values—these facts mean that each individual has an awesome responsibility, according to Sartre:

First of all, we are responsible for what we are. "Abandonment implies that we ourselves choose our being," he wrote. Second, we must *invent* our own values. And third and finally, because, according to Sartre, "nothing can be good for us without [also] being [good] for all," in inventing our own values we also function as *universal legislators* of right and wrong, good and evil. In choosing for ourselves, we choose for all. "Thus," he wrote, "our responsibility is much greater than we had supposed it, for it involves all mankind."

This responsibility for oneself and thus for all humankind, Sartre thought, we experience as anguish, and it is clear why he maintained that this is so: our responsibility is total and profound, and *absolutely inescapable.* You might perhaps object that many people, perhaps even most, certainly do not seem to be particularly anxious, let alone anguished. It is true, Sartre admitted, that many people are not

Is Sartre Only for Atheists?

If God does exist, then technically speaking we are not "abandoned." But some of the main problems that arise from abandonment seem also to arise merely if we cannot *know* whether God exists. For if we do not know whether God exists, then we do not know whether there is any ultimate reason why things happen the way they do, and we do not know whether those values we believe are grounded in God really do have objective validity.

In fact, even if we do know that God exists and also know that values are grounded in God, we still may not know *which* values are grounded in God: we may still not know what the absolute criteria and standards of right and wrong are. And even if we know what the standards and criteria are, just what they *mean* will still be a matter for subjective interpretation. And so the human dilemma that results may be very much the same as if there were no God.

Nonatheists should not dismiss Sartre too hastily.

PROFILE / Jean-Paul Sartre (1905–1980)

Jean-Paul Sartre studied philosophy at the École Normale Superieure. He also studied the philosophies of Husserl and Heidegger, and spent one year in Berlin. While still a graduate student, he met Simone de Beauvoir, who later played a key role in the early phases of the women's liberation movement, especially with her famous book, *The Second Sex* (1948). Their friendship and mutual support lasted until Sartre's death, though in the opinion of historian Paul Johnson, "in the annals of literature, there are few worse cases of a man exploiting a woman." (Sartre never wrote anything about their relationship.)

During World War II, Sartre served in the French army, became a German prisoner of war, escaped, and worked in the Resistance movement. Throughout his life he supported political causes and movements, including the French Communist party. In 1951, he tried unsuccessfully to found a new political party, radically leftist but non-Communist in orientation.

In 1964, Sartre declined the Nobel Prize in Literature.

When Sartre died, fifty thousand people marched behind his coffin through the streets of Paris.

consciously or visibly anxious. But this merely is because they are hiding or fleeing from their responsibility: they act and live in self-deception, inauthenticity, and **"bad faith."** Further, he said, they are ill at ease with their conscience, for "even when it conceals itself, anguish appears."

It is not difficult to understand why one might seek to avoid shouldering one's responsibility to oneself and thus to others, for as Sartre depicted it, this responsibility is overwhelming. But in Sartre's view something else also contributes to the difficulty of this task: one does not know *what* to choose because the world is experienced as absurd. It is experienced as absurd, Sartre maintains, because, since God does not exist, it lacks necessity—it lacks an ultimate rhyme or reason for being this way and not that way. It (the world) therefore is experienced as fundamentally senseless, unreasonable, illogical, and, therefore, nauseating. It calls forth both revulsion and boredom. It is "perfectly gratuitous" (*gratuité parfaite*) and often just simply too much (*de trop*).

Nevertheless, according to Sartre, it is only through acceptance of our responsibility that we may live in **authenticity.** To be responsible, to live authentically, means intentionally to make choices about one's life and one's future. These choices are made most efficaciously, Sartre maintained, by becoming "engaged" in the world and by selecting a *fundamental project.* A life gains wholeness and purpose through adoption of such a fundamental project, for this project can mobilize and direct all one's life energies and permit one to make spontaneous choices. Through this project, in short, the individual creates a world that does not yet exist and thus gives meaning to his or her life.

So Sartre's metaphysics (or antimetaphysics), which stood opposed to the belief in God, determinism, necessity, and the objectivity of values, in effect leaves the human individual in what may plausibly be called an absurd situation. There is nothing that one must do; there is nothing that must be done. To find meaning in life, the individual must create his or her world and its values by making authentic choices. These choices first take the form of intentions directed toward future events. Then they become actions of an engaged being in a world of people, a political (and politically troubled) world. The choices that we make are made by us for all humankind and are, therefore, in this limited sense "absolute" ethical principles. Although we initially find ourselves in an absurd world not of our choosing, we can remake that world through our choices and actions, and we must do so, as difficult as that may be.

This exposition of Sartre's thought focuses on his understanding of what might be called the existential predicament. His thinking evolved over time, and he became increasingly concerned—like Camus—with social and political issues. These interests and his fascination with Marxist philosophy led to a modification of his existentialist stance, but we can do no more in this book than mention this. We have also not dealt with his epistemology, his aesthetics, or his views on psychoanalysis.

Sartre and Kant on Ethics

"I choose myself perpetually," Sartre wrote. By this he meant that we each are in a continual process of constructing ourselves and our values or ethics. And, as discussed in the text, Sartre believed that when a person determines something to be right for him or herself, he or she is also determining it to be good for all.

This universalization of individual choices is reminiscent of Immanuel Kant's supreme precept of morality, the categorical imperative, according to which you must only act in such a way that the principle on which you act could be a universal law. Kant, however, as we saw in Part 2, grounded the categorical imperative and hence all morality in reason, which he thought determines *a priori* what is right and wrong. Sartre, however, maintains that there is no *a priori* moral law and that Kant's formal law is inadequate as a guide for concrete action in everyday life. It is rather what a person does that in fact determines his morality. "In choosing myself, I choose man," Sartre said.

It is perhaps arguable, however, that *this* principle ("in choosing myself, I choose man") is for Sartre a universal principle underlying morality.

Sartre on Life

Human life begins on the other side of despair.

Man's freedom is to say no, and this means that he is the being by whom nothingness comes into being.

Thus, there is no human nature, because there is no God to have a conception of it. Man simply is.... Man is nothing else but that which he makes of himself. That is the first principle of existentialism.

Nothing will be changed if God does not exist; we will rediscover the same norms of honesty, progress, and humanity.

To live "authentically" we must be conscious of our freedom to choose and be concerned with the effect our choice will have on all men.

The existentialist does not believe in the power of passion. He will never think that a noble passion is a devastating torrent which leads man to [do] certain actions, and which, consequently, is an excuse. He thinks that man is responsible for his passion.

SELECTION 15.3

Existentialism and Humanism

From Jean-Paul Sartre

What is this that we call existentialism? . . . Actually it is the least shocking doctrine, and the most austere; it is intended strictly for techni-

cians, and philosophers. However, it can easily be defined. What makes the matter complicated is that there are two kinds of existentialists: the

Sartre and Heidegger

In the early 1930s, Sartre studied for a short time in Germany and was deeply influenced by Martin Heidegger. Sartre attributed the concept of abandonment (treated in the text) to Heidegger, and, like Heidegger, Sartre was concerned with the concepts of bad faith, authenticity, a life's project, and others.

Still, in decisive ways, Sartrian and Heideggerian philosophies are dissimilar. Heidegger, on one hand, never did abandon his belief in Being as the basic principle of philosophy, whereas for Sartre individual existence was of paramount importance. Sartre believed that, as a consequence of the nonexistence of God, nothing about Being is necessary; Heidegger, on the other hand, believed that Being is abso-lutely necessary. Politically, Sartre considered himself a Marxist and accepted much of the Marxist view of historical events; Heidegger, in comparison, was not in any sense sympathetic to the Marxist world view.

On balance, the philosophies of Sartre and Heidegger are quite different, despite the superficial resemblances.

You Are What You Do

According to Sartre, you create yourself through your choices, as we have explained in the text. But be aware that for Sartre these self-creating choices are not found in mere "philosophical" abstractions or speculations. The choices that count, for Sartre, are those that issue forth in actions. "There is reality only in action," he wrote—"man is nothing other than the whole of his actions."

This means that, according to Sartre, no hidden self or true you lies behind your deeds. If, for example, in your actions you are impatient and unforgiving, it is a fiction for you to think, "Well, if others could see into my heart they would know that in reality I am patient and understanding." If you are cowardly in your deeds, you deceive yourself if you believe that "in truth" or "deep, down inside" you are courageous. If you have not written great poetry, then it is an illusion for you to believe that you nevertheless have the soul of a great poet.

It is easy to see why Sartre believed that his doctrine horrified many people. Many people think of their behavior as but poorly reflecting their true character, which they believe is in some way superior to the character that displays itself in their actions. Those who think this deceive themselves, according to Sartre.

---

first who are Christian, and among whom I will include Jaspers and Gabriel Marcel, of the Catholic faith; and also, the atheistic existentialists among whom we must include Heidegger, and also the French existentialists, and myself. What they have in common is simply the fact that they think that existence precedes essence, or, if you wish, that we must start from subjectivity. . . .

. . . What does it mean here that existence precedes essence? It means that man exists first, experiences himself, springs up in the world, and that he defines himself afterwards. If man, as the existentialist conceives him, is not definable, it is because he is nothing at first. He will only be [something] afterwards, and he will be as he will have made himself. So, there is no human nature, since there is no God to think it.

Man simply is, not only as he conceives himself, but as he determines himself, and as he conceives himself after existing, as he determines himself after this impulse toward existence; man is nothing other than what he makes himself. This is the first principle of existentialism. It is also what we call subjectivity. . . . Man is at first a project which lives subjectively, instead of being a moss, a decaying thing, or a cauliflower; nothing exists prior to this project; nothing is intelligible in the heavens, and man will at first be what he has planned to be. Not what he may wish to be. . . . If existence really precedes essence, man is responsible for what he is. Thus, the first step of existentialism is to show every man [to be] in control of what he is and to make him assume total responsibility for his existence. And, when we say that man is responsible for himself, we do not [only] mean that man is responsible for his precise individuality, but that he is responsible for all men. . . . When we say that man determines himself, we understand that each of us chooses himself, but by that we mean also that in choosing himself he chooses all men. Indeed, there is not one of our actions which, in creating the man we wish to be, does not [also] create at the same time an image of the man we think we ought to be. To choose to be this or that, is to affirm at the same time the value of what we choose, for we can never choose evil; what we choose is always the good, and nothing can be good for us without [also] being [good] for all. . . .

This enables us to understand what some rather lofty words, like anguish, abandonment, despair mean. As you will see, it is quite simple. First, what do we mean by anguish? The existentialist readily declares that man is [in] anguish. That means this: the man who commits himself and who realizes that it is not only himself that he chooses, but [that] he is also a lawgiver choosing at the same time [for] all mankind, would not know how to escape the feeling of his total and profound responsibility. Certainly, many men are not anxious; but we claim that they are hiding their anguish, that they are flee-

ing from it; certainly, many men believe [that] in acting [they] commit only themselves, and when one says to them: "what if everyone acted like that?" they shrug their shoulders and reply: "everyone does not act like that." But really, one should always ask himself: "what would happen if everyone did the same?" and we cannot escape this troubling thought except by a kind of bad faith. The man who lies and who excuses himself by declaring: "everyone does not act like that," is someone who is ill at ease with his conscience, because the act of lying implies a universal value attributed to the lie. Even when it conceals itself, anguish appears. . . .

And when we speak of abandonment, an expression dear to Heidegger, we mean only that God does not exist, and that we must draw out the consequences of this to the very end. . . . The existentialist, on the contrary, thinks that it is very troubling that God does not exist, for with him disappears every possibility of finding values in an intelligible heaven; there can no longer be any good a priori, since there is no infinite and perfect consciousness to think it; it is not written anywhere that the good exists, that we must be honest, that we must not lie, since precisely we exist in a context where there are only men. Dostoyevsky has written, "If God did not exist, everything would be allowed." This is the point of departure for existentialism. Indeed, everything is allowed if God does not exist, and consequently man is abandoned, because neither in himself nor beyond himself does he find any possibility of clinging on [to something]. At the start, he finds no excuses. If, indeed, existence precedes essence, we will never be able to give an explanation by reference to a human nature [which is] given and fixed; in other words, there is no determinism, man is free, man is freedom. Moreover, if God does not exist, we do not find before us any values or orders which will justify our conduct. So, we have neither behind us nor before us, in the luminous realm of values, any justifications or excuses. We are alone, without excuses. It is what I will express by saying that man is condemned to be free. Condemned, because he has not created himself, and nevertheless, in other respects [he is] free, because once [he is] cast into the world, he is responsible for everything that he does. . . .

Abandonment implies that we ourselves choose our being. Abandonment goes with anguish. As for despair, this expression has a very simple meaning. It means that we will restrict ourselves to a reliance upon that which depends on our will, or on the set of the probabilities which make our action possible. . . . From the moment when the possibilities that I am considering are not strictly involved by my action, I must take no further interest in them, because no God, no design can adjust the world and its possibilities to my will. . . . Quietism is the attitude of men who say: "others can do what I cannot do." The doctrine that I am presenting to you is exactly opposite to quietism, since it claims: "there is reality only in action." It goes further [than this] besides, since it adds: "man is nothing other than his project, he exists only in so far as he realizes himself, thus he is nothing other than the whole of his actions, nothing other than his life." According to this, we can understand why our doctrine horrifies a good many men. Because often they have only one way of enduring their misery. It is to think: "circumstances have been against me, I was worth much more than what I have been; to be sure, I have not had a great love, or a great friendship, but it is because I have not met a man or a woman who was worthy of it. I have not written very good books because I have not had the leisure to do it. I have not had children to whom

 critique

to devote myself because I did not find a person with whom I could have made my life. [There] remains, then, in me, unused and wholly feasible a multitude of dispositions, inclinations, possibilities which give me a worth that the simple set of my actions does not allow [one] to infer." Now, in reality, for the existentialist there is no love other than that which is made, there is no possibility of love other than that which manifests itself in a love; there is no genius other than that which expresses itself in works of art. The genius of Proust is the totality of Proust's works; the genius of Racine is the set of his tragedies, beyond that there is nothing. Why [should we] attribute to Racine the possibility of writing a new tragedy, since precisely he did not write it? In his life a man commits himself, draws his own figure, and beyond this figure there is nothing. Obviously, this thought may seem harsh to someone who has not had a successful life. But, on the other hand, it prepares men to understand that only reality counts, that the dreams, the expectations, the hopes allow [us] only to define a man as [a] disappointed dream, as miscarried hopes, as useless expectations; that is to say that that defines them negatively and not positively. However, when we say "you are nothing other than your life," that does not imply that the artist will be judged only by his art-works, for a thousand other things also contribute to define him. What we mean is that man is nothing other than a set of undertakings, that he is the sum, the organization, the whole of the relations which make up these undertakings.

Phenomenology

Phenomenology, much more than existentialism, has been a product of philosophers rather than of artists and writers. But like existentialism, phenomenology has had enormous impact outside philosophical circles. It has been especially influential in theology, the social and political sciences, and psychology and psychoanalysis. Phenomenology is a movement of thinkers who have a variety of interests and points of view; phenomenology itself finds its antecedents in Kant and Hegel (though the movement regarded itself as anything but Hegelian). Kant, in the *Critique of Pure Reason,* argued that all objective knowledge is based on phenomena, the data received in sensory experience. In Hegel's *Phenomenology of Mind,* beings are treated as phenomena or objects for a consciousness.

These phenomena, as you may recall from Chapter 5, are, according to Kant, immediately organized by the understanding through *a priori* certain categories and the intuited forms of space and time. All knowing, Kant said, is limited to phenomena and does not extend to things in themselves. Many Kantian ideas recur in the phenomenological movement, and the influence of Descartes and Plato will also be evident.

The first great phenomenologist, **Edmund Husserl** (1859–1938), attempted to rekindle Europeans' waning faith in the possibility of rational certainty. He proposed to establish a new scientific foundation for human knowing, a **universal phenomenology of consciousness,** a phenomenology that is the same for every consciousness and can be made as well into an absolutely certain science. He rejected what he felt were the dualistic assumptions of the natural sciences, which studied the subject or independent mind with the same methods used to study the physical or objective world "outside" the mind. But such methods, Husserl thought, meant that there could be no knowledge of the self independent of supposed knowledge of the physical world.

Accordingly, Husserl developed **transcendental phenomenology,** whose purpose it was to investigate phenomena (see box) without making any assumptions or judgments about the world. To investigate phenomena in this way is to "bracket" or "exclude" one's presuppositions about the existence or nature of an "external" or "physical" or "objective" world. This process Husserl called the **phenomenological reduction.** Its purpose was to examine the meanings produced by pure impersonal consciousness, to describe the human "life-world" in terms of those essences (which all human beings share) of the intended objects of consciousness. (Recall that Brentano, discussed in Chapter 14, suggested that consciousness is always consciousness *of* something; there is no bare consciousness without an intended object.) Husserl's call to "return to the things themselves" (that is, phenomena), he believed, opens up for scrutiny a realm of being that escapes the uncertainty and conditional status of the empirical world.

Martin Heidegger

Martin Heidegger (1889–1976) was stimulated by Husserl's *Logical Investigations* (1900) and especially by Husserl's call to return to the things themselves. Heidegger, too, was convinced that it is necessary to look at things with fresh eyes, unshrouded by the prejudices of the present and past. He, too, wanted rigorously to ground the truth of things in a deeper source. But for Heidegger, this source is

Phenomena

It is difficult to convey precisely what is meant by **phenomena**. It may help, however, to consider the age-old distinction between the way something appears and the way it is. A penny as it appears to you, for instance, is thought to be distinct from the way "it really is." (For example, it may appear elliptical, even though "it really is" round.) Now, from Husserl's point of view, this distinction (between "appearance" and "reality") is the scientific/dualistic distinction between the subjective (the way the penny appears) and the objective (the

way it really is). Science, of course, is supposedly concerned with the way things "really are," that is, with the "objective penny." Husserl wished to concern himself with the subjective penny, that is, with the penny-as-appearance or penny-as-experience. It is this "apparent" or "subjective" penny that is an example of a "phenomenon."

However, it is somewhat misleading to refer to this phenomenal object, the subjective penny, as an *appearance.* To refer to it in this way is to presuppose that it is the appearance *of* something (the

"real" penny) and thus is to assume that there are things out there "in the objective world" beyond the appearances. In short, to refer to the subjective penny as an "appearance" is to assume the scientific/dualistic perspective, which we must not do if we are to perform the phenomenological reduction. We must concentrate on phenomena themselves and not think of them as appearances or representations of a world beyond them. It is the stream of conscious experience—the phenomena—that Husserl is interested in.

Is This Idealism?

Husserl's phenomenological realm is somewhat reminiscent of Plato's realm of Ideas, and some critics thought Husserl's philosophy represented a falling back into traditional idealistic metaphysics, in which, in effect, being is reduced to thought.

Can phenomenology escape the charge that it reduces being to thought? This is the question that Husserl's student, Martin Heidegger, answered negatively. Thus Heidegger, as shall be seen, sought to reestablish the primacy of being over thought. For Heidegger,

thought does not create being, as he interpreted Husserl as implying; rather, being makes thought possible.

not phenomena, as it was for Husserl, or anything subjective at all. On the contrary, for Heidegger the ultimate source is *Being itself.*

Although Being is continuously manifesting itself in things, according to Heidegger, Being itself has been forgotten. Humans have been caught up in their own ideas. Being has been reduced to a world of "objects" that are manipulated and dominated by human "subjects" through a series of man-made logics. Logic is equated with truth when in fact, according to Heidegger, it is only a means to control and use things after human designs; that is, logic is logistics.

⌐_⌐_⌐_⌐_⌐_⌐_

PROFILE / Martin Heidegger (1889–1976)

Heidegger was born in the small town of Messkirch near the Black Forest of Germany. Originally he went to the University of Freiburg to study theology, but he soon after began studying philosophy. Heidegger studied Husserl's philosophy closely and became personally acquainted with Husserl after the latter took a chair in Freiburg in 1916.

Almost from the beginning Heidegger stood out—not merely because of his countrified mode of dress, but also because of his profound thought. Over the years Heidegger grew increasingly critical of Husserl's philosophy, and, though he was named to Husserl's chair in philosophy at Freiburg in 1928, their friendship came to an end.

Although Heidegger did not teach formally after World War II, he remained in Freiburg until his death. His works are in the process of being published—in eighty volumes.

Loved nature – hated technology.

Heidegger believed that it is both arrogant and destructive to assume that humans are the masters of nature, or to follow Protagoras's dictum that man is the measure of all things. This assumption of the absolute power of humanity was for Heidegger the real cause of the cultural destitution and social dissolution within the twentieth century. Heidegger thought that we live in an intellectually impoverished (*dürftig*) time, and that it is likely to become worse until we abandon our presumptuousness and return to the wisdom inherent in Being itself. The return must involve *listening* to Being instead of toying with things arbitrarily.

According to Heidegger, we are basically ignorant about the thing that matters most: the true nature of Being. Our lives are a kind of Socratic search for this lost and unknown source of all things. Consciousness of the priority of Being would mean a new beginning for philosophy as well as for Western civilization, he held.

Heidegger, therefore, initially sought to establish a fundamental ontology or a scientific study of Being as the root of all meaning and necessity in things. This effort broadened out later and became a quest for an even more direct approach to Being itself. Early on—as, for example, in his first major work, *Being and Time* (1927)—Heidegger's ideas still contained much that is Husserlian and Kantian in approach. He still sought true knowledge in *a priori* structures found in the human mind. It is only in his later thinking—after he had what he called a fundamental "turning about"—that he sought to uncover Being directly, beyond the *a priori* categories or structures of human perception and thought. He did so without assurance that any absolute certainty about Being itself is even possible.

Heidegger and the Nazis

Initially Heidegger was quite taken with the National Socialist (Nazi) party in post–World War I Germany and apparently remained a party member until the end of World War II. This was rather a prestigious gain for the Nazis, es-pecially when Heidegger was made rector of the University of Frei-burg. During Heidegger's brief term as rector (he withdrew after ten months), he made speeches and was otherwise active in sup-port of Hitler and his movement. After the war, Heidegger did not speak out to condemn Nazi atroc-ities. There is controversy as to what his true sentiments were, however.

It is usually with reference to his earlier work that Heidegger is sometimes called an existentialist. Heidegger himself resisted this appellation. Yet he was very much influenced by Kierkegaard and Nietzsche, and the concern expressed in his early works with such existentialist themes as fear, dread, meaninglessness, inau-thenticity, and death is very evident.

At the heart of *Being and Time,* for example, is the notion of *Sinn* (sense, mean-ing), the absence of which in life is said to be the problem of human existence. For Heidegger, the human being is *"thrown into the world"* and soon experiences both fear and dread when confronted with forces beyond his understanding. The better part of human life, he maintains, needs to be used in *"headbreaking,"* that is, in attempting to discover what the appearances mean—what they suggest and hide.

Further, humans are *"beings-in-the-world,"* which means that they can be open only to what is within the horizons of their world. They exist and are conscious within a world with other beings, but the meaning of human relationships is at first but dimly perceived and poorly understood. As a consequence of their lack of insight and understanding, many humans live ungenuine and inauthentic lives. They do not make adequate or appropriate choices for themselves because they do not understand who they are or what they are confronting. And although they may experience unease living in a world beyond their comprehension, they make too little effort to extend their comprehension. They suffer from a kind of "primi-tive" being which Heidegger refers to as *everydayness.* They fail to fulfill their real potential. Thus Heidegger invoked the concept of everydayness to explain why human beings continue to lead unthinking lives.

Another typical existential theme connected by Heidegger with an everyday existence is an inauthentic mode of communication, namely, *chatter.* Speech is reduced to a meaningless flood of words that camouflages fear, prevents under-standing, and precludes any meaningful communication. Nothing truly meaning-ful is ever said or allowed to be said.

An authentic existence can be found, according to Heidegger, only if one can understand oneself as a totality. And seeing oneself as a whole can happen only by

Lost Lives

Examples of lives lost to the inertia of everydayness are common in twentieth-century literature. One might think, for example, of Eugene O'Neill's *Long Day's Journey* *into Night* (1956) or Tennessee Williams's *The Glass Menagerie* (1945) or Arthur Miller's *Death of a Salesman* (1949). These plays show how lives can be wasted, with the tragic loss only experienced near the end, if at all. As Kierkegaard suggests, the greatest loss is to have died and not to have noticed.

facing the hard fact that one is mortal. We are, Heidegger said, *"beings-unto-death."* By facing death, we can see and delineate the limits of our being. We begin to see the limited amount of time yet available and begin to realize it must not be wasted.

The innermost nature of the human being, according to Heidegger, is caring—a concern for beings in the world. This caring takes place over time. And thinking must be timely as well. Thus, for Heidegger, we are essentially *temporal* beings.

According to Heidegger, the temporality of human thinking is *"ecstatic,"* that is, it is intentionally directed toward the future, which means simply that humans think and act toward an anticipated future. The most effective way of embracing one's future, he thought, is by throwing oneself open into Being. This project (*Entwurf*) opens the person to the fundamental truth of Being that has been forgotten. Therefore, the individual who has been thrown into the world finds his or her ground and truth in the openness and lighting of the truth of Being itself.

As noted earlier, Heidegger thought that the cultural and intellectual poverty of the twentieth century is a direct result of the pervasive assumption that the value of things is solely determined by human intelligence and human will (the assumption that man is the measure of all things). This assumption or metaphysical stance, he thought, has led not merely to individual loneliness, alienation, and unfulfillment, but to social destructiveness as well. For Heidegger, this metaphysical point of view, which he perceived as entrenched in Western civilization since Plato, assumed the superiority of Ideas over any physical reality existing "outside" the mind. In Heidegger's opinion, Nietzsche's "will-to-power," where the will becomes the absolute determiner of the value of things and of oneself, represented the philosophical culmination of this Platonic metaphysics.

Poetry   According to the later Heidegger, instead of imposing our thought on things, we must be *gelassen. Gelassenheit,* for Heidegger, means thinking in a quiet, nonimpositional way so that one can *catch a glimpse* of Being as it shows itself. Thought, he believed (in contrast with others in the phenomenological tradition), cannot impose itself on Being because Being makes thought possible. What is required, therefore, he said (in contrast with the existentialists), is a new kind of thinking in which humans look to Being itself for enlightenment and not merely to themselves. This kind of thinking occurs, according to Heidegger, in the best *poetry.* And some poets, such as Hölderlin, can serve as examples of this kind of

Poetry and Philosophy

In his later years Heidegger not only avoided the word *metaphysics* to describe the philosophy of Being but even tended not to use the word *philosophy*. He thought a new kind of "thinking" was needed, one that might focus again on the light of Being. One kind of thinking, in his view, was particularly apt for this task, namely, poetic thinking. Poetry, according to Heidegger, has a unique access to what has not yet been spoken and has not yet even been thought. Poetry can bring humans back into an awareness of their source, namely, Being itself.

Heidegger wrote tracts on many poets, including Hölderlin, Rilke, Trakl, and others. But he also wrote poems that suggest how the poet might bring a glimmer of light to the darkness within existence. For example:

> When the early morning light quietly grows above the mountains....
> The world's darkening never reaches to the light of Being.
> We are too late for the gods and too early for Being. Being's poem, just begun, is man.
> To head toward a star—this only.
> To think is to confine yourself to a single thought that one day stands still like a star in the world's sky.

But to enter into the abyss of Being, for Heidegger, is a difficult, long, and solitary undertaking. It requires patience and large-mindedness, and courage, too. He wrote:

> All our heart's courage is the echoing response to the first call of Being which gathers our thinking into the play of the world.

It is the poet, for Heidegger, who ventures out into the unknown, in order to find the "unique thought" that will bring the necessary light for the coming time.

Heidegger and Lao Tzu

Especially later in his life, Heidegger grew interested in Eastern philosophy and especially the philosophy of Lao Tzu (see Chapter 16). Perhaps Heidegger's new way of thinking—listening to Being—represents a coming together of Eastern and Western philosophizing. Certainly there are common currents and themes. Both believed that "nature is not human-hearted" (Lao Tzu) and that what is called human "knowledge" is mostly ignorance. Both felt that "those who care will be cared for" (Lao Tzu). What is necessary, according to both, is to take nature [Being] as a "guide." And it is as Lao Tzu suggested: "In the clarity of a still and open mind, the truth will be revealed."

thinking. Poetic thinking can uncover the as-yet unseen, unthought, and unspoken. Therefore, he said, systematic philosophy with its grandiose and willful schemes, with its mind-body and other dualist splits, with its metaphysics and metaphysical traditions, must give way to this more original kind of thinking. Through this deeper way of thinking, he said, we may at long last rediscover the depth of what has been forgotten—Being itself.

Selection 15.4 illustrates Heidegger's concern with the habitable world and with language. He would reverse the description of a human being as one who imposes his will on things to one who builds connections with the world around him by dwelling simply. Additionally, Heidegger wants to shift the focus in the study of language from one that is human-centered (and language is seen as the servant of the human mind) to one that is language-centered (and a realization that what it means to be an individual human being is in large part due to the speaking of language itself). Later in this chapter we will see how important Continental philosophers consider language to be in shaping the human world we all inhabit.

SELECTION 15.4

"Building Dwelling Thinking" and "Language"   From Martin Heidegger

We attain to dwelling, so it seems, only by means of building. The latter, building, has the former, dwelling, as its goal. . . . Dwelling and building are related as end and means. However, as long as this is all we have in mind, we take dwelling and building as two separate activities, an idea that has something correct in it. Yet at the same time by the means-end schema we block our view of the essential relations. For building is not merely a means and a way toward dwelling—to build is in itself already to dwell. Who tells us this? Who gives us a standard at all by which we can take the measure of the nature of dwelling and building?

It is language that tells us about the nature of a thing, provided that we respect language's own nature. In the meantime, to be sure, there rages round the earth an unbridled yet clever talking, writing, and broadcasting of spoken words. Man acts as though *he* were the shaper and master of language, while in fact *language* remains the master of man. Perhaps it is before all else man's subversion of *this* relation of dominance that drives his nature into alienation. . . .

What, then, does *Bauen*, building, *mean?* The Old English and High German word for building, *buan,* means to dwell. This signifies: to remain, to stay in a place. The real meaning of

the verb *bauen,* namely, to dwell, has been lost to us.

When we speak of dwelling we usually think of an activity that man performs alongside many other activities. We work here and dwell there. . . .

But if we listen to what language says in the word *bauen* we hear three things:

1. Building is really dwelling.
2. Dwelling is the manner in which mortals are on the earth.
3. Building as dwelling unfolds into the build-ing that cultivates growing things and the building that erects buildings. . . .

We do not dwell because we have built, but we build and have built because we dwell, that is, because we are *dwellers.* But in what does the nature of dwelling consist? Let us listen once more to what language says to us. The Old Saxon *wuon,* the Gothic *wunian,* like the old word *bauen,* mean to remain, to stay in a place. But the Gothic *wunian* says more distinctly how this remaining is experienced. *Wunian* means: to be at peace, to be brought to peace, to remain in peace. The word for peace, *Friede,* means the free, *das Frye,* and *fry* means: preserved from harm and danger, preserved from something, safeguarded. To free really means to spare. The sparing itself consists not only in the fact that we do not harm the one whom we spare. Real sparing is something *positive* and takes place when we leave something beforehand in its own nature, when we return it specifically to its being, when we "free" it in the real sense of the word into a preserve of peace. To dwell, to be set at peace, means to remain at peace within the free, the preserve, the free sphere that safeguards each thing in its nature. *The fundamental character of dwelling is this sparing and preserving.* It pervades dwelling in its whole range. That range reveals itself to us as soon as we reflect that human being consists in dwelling and, indeed, dwelling in the sense of the stay of mortals on the earth. . . .

Mortals dwell in that they save the earth. . . . To save really means to set something free into its own presencing. To save the earth is more than to exploit it or even wear it out. Saving the earth does not master the earth and does not subjugate it, which is merely one stop from spoliation.

To reflect on language means—to reach the speaking of language in such a way that this speaking takes place as that which grants an abode for the being of mortals. . . .

Language speaks as the peal of stillness. Stillness stills by the carrying out, the bearing and enduring, of world and things in their presence. . . .

The peal of stillness is not anything human. But on the contrary, the human is indeed in its nature given to speech—it is linguistic. The word "linguistic" as it is here used means: having taken place out of the speaking of language. What has thus taken place, human being, has been brought into its own by language, so that it remains given over or appropriated to the nature of language, the peal of stillness. Such an appropriating takes place in that the very *nature,* the *presencing,* of language *needs and uses* the speaking of mortals in order to sound as the peal of stillness for the hearing of mortals. . . .

If attention is fastened exclusively on human speech, if human speech is taken simply to be the voicing of the inner man, if speech so conceived is regarded as language itself, then the nature of language can never appear as anything but an expression and an activity of man. But human speech, as the speech of mortals, is not self-subsistent. The speech of mortals rests in its relation to the speaking of language. . . .

Language speaks.

Man speaks in that he responds to language. This responding is a hearing. It hears because it listens to the command of stillness.

An Era of Suspicion

"My experiences," wrote Friedrich Nietzsche in his posthumously published confessional called *Ecce Homo,* "entitle me to be quite generally suspicious of the so-called 'selfless' drives, of all 'neighbor love' that is ready to give advice and go into action." In the last third of the twentieth century diverse Continental voices have been raised against what they see as suspicious assumptions about the meaning of right and wrong, the nature of language, and the very possibility of human self-understanding. Some Continental philosophers have been suspicious about Western metaphysical systems that they claim lead to the manipulation of nature or that set up a certain ethnic or cultural perspective as absolute truth. Some voices have raised suspicions about the common assumption that language in some way represents external reality. Still others claim to find deep ideological biases in even the most "neutral" philosophical observations.

Philosopher and sociologist **Jürgen Habermas** (1929–) has challenged the legitimacy of some of the rational principles assumed by the human sciences. French philosopher **Michel Foucault** (1926–1984) explored the deeply ingrained social power systems that shape how social institutions deal with the sexuality of their members and with those who are sick, or criminal, or insane. **Jacques Derrida** (1930–) developed the technique of deconstruction in literary and philosophical criticism to show, he said, that language meanings cannot be "tied down" and that as a result claims that certain passages express the "truth" become suspicious indeed. Finally, American philosopher **Richard Rorty** (1931–), deeply influenced by Continental philosophy and the American pragmatism of **William James** (1842–1910) and **John Dewey** (1859–1952), proposed a new task for philosophy. Because the discipline could never find "the truth," it must be used in the service of human beings to extend one's horizons, one's possibilities.

Jürgen Habermas

Habermas, a professor at the University of Frankfurt, is one of many thinkers influenced by the critical approach of the Frankfurt School (see box). In this context "critical" does not necessarily mean "negative," but rather "reflective" or "thoughtful." This goes far beyond the reflection a physicist might bring to the results of a failed experiment ("What went wrong? Is there a hidden variable I have not accounted for? Is my theory faulty?"). The kind of reflection critical theory emphasizes is reflection on the very assumptions of science or philosophy. For instance, empirical science approaches the world with a view to finding lawlike regularities in the things it examines; the measure of knowledge thus becomes the predictive power of the experimental method. Underlying the practice of empirical science is the assumption that its findings are independent of the observer (or, if not, then the presence of the observer can be corrected for). When the experimental method is used on the human being, it is no surprise that what emerges is a picture of a thing (a human thing) which also follows lawlike regularities and for which more or less sophisticated predictions can be made.

The tendency in modern technocratic society, Habermas says, is for this description of experimental science to become definitional of all knowledge. Though logical positivism has been sharply criticized (see Chapter 6), its influence is still felt in the normal, ongoing scientific enterprise. But Habermas points out that "positivistic science" is only one way of looking at the world, and it is no surprise that such a perspective would claim to find "objective facts" that would make it possible for human beings to exert control over nature. Yet such a perspective, says Habermas, is inappropriate for the investigation of mutually shared meanings we experience in the everyday human world in which we live out our lives. Positivistic

Philosophical Anthropology

When he was a tender undergraduate, one of the authors traveled to the University of Tübingen in Germany, to study. He signed up for a course called "Philosophishe Anthropologie." He had no idea what the course might be about, but he could at least translate its name, which is the main reason he signed up for it. It was the first course in philosophy he had ever taken.

On the first day of class, he sat in the middle of a huge lecture hall—more German students were in that one class than were in all the courses in philosophy he took after that, back in America, combined. The Herr Professor walked to the lectern, shuffled through some notes, ripped off his glasses and sucked on them like a pipe, and gazed heavenward for several minutes, deep in thought. "Was," he asked the ceiling, "ist der Mensch?"—What is man? This struck your author as a fairly interesting question—at least to get things started—and he waited for the answer.

What is man? What is a human being? This is the fundamental question of philosophical anthropology, which, along with beer, is important in German universities.

The term *anthropology* goes back to the Greeks and has been used ever since to denote the study of humans (*anthropos*) and their society. Early Church fathers used the term to distinguish the study of humans from the study of God; over the centuries—and especially during the sixteenth to eighteenth centuries—anthropology became increasingly divorced from theology, metaphysics, and the natural sciences. Kant, for example, held that to be worldly wise, we must go beyond the natural sciences and acquire an extensive knowledge of human nature through biographies, histories, travel books, plays, and so forth. For Kant, such an anthropology, though not a science, provided a practical study of what a free and self-determined human being is.

In the nineteenth century, German romantics ("romantic" here doesn't mean "lover"; it denotes a member of the important nineteenth-century movement that emphasized imagination and emotions in literature and art) sought a vision of the total human being. Hegel, however, distinguished between anthropology, which considers humans as they are *potentially*, and philosophy of history, which considers humans as they are *actually*. The Hegelian attack on anthropology and its lack of historical grounding has been carried on by selected German philosophers up to the present, where we find it lingering in Martin Heidegger and the Frankfurt School of social philosophy, both mentioned in this chapter. Today, "philosophical anthropology," as the philosophical study of human nature and existence is called, is moving away from the philosophy of history and seeks to establish itself as an independent discipline. It includes semiotics and structuralism, discussed in another box.

Was ist der Mensch? Unfortunately, the professor's answer lasted the entire semester. Unfortunately, too, your author didn't understand the answer. In fact, that single question, Was ist der Mensch, was the *only* thing your author understood in the entire course; for his knowledge of German was none too good. (Later, when he read an English translation of the professor's lectures, he found he still didn't understand the answer.)

science treats human beings as objective things; what is needed is an approach to knowledge that treats the human being as a subject, one not isolated from other subjects, but, on the contrary, interacting with them. This interaction takes place in a domain that allows the sharing of intersubjective experiences and that provides contexts of history, art, literature, and language itself that enable us to understand one another. (Imagine a visitor who begins putting asphalt in his mouth after you suggest, "Let's eat up the street." He doesn't understand that you mean that fast food restaurant a block away, but it's likely he will learn fast.)

This "practical" interest each of us has in understanding one another Habermas says is the realm of a science he calls historical/hermeneutical. (**Hermeneutics** deals with the principles of interpretation—of the Bible, of other texts, and of the language of human interactions.) He emphasizes that in this "practical" science, the individual cannot be treated as an objective unit; on the contrary, my human identity is to a greater or lesser extent the creation of human language and of the society into which I am born. Through this society and language, I gain a "preunderstanding" of others in my quest for mutual self-understanding; that is, I cannot understand myself if I cannot understand the words and actions of others. The very meanings of those words and actions give me a context for making sense of myself in the human world. (It might be helpful to recall Wittgenstein's idea, discussed in Chapter 6, that a "private language" would be impossible.)

But for Habermas there is a second kind of knowledge that is also inappropriate for the positivistic sciences. Habermas calls this "emancipatory knowledge," and it is the concern of **critical theory.** It is the work of critical theory to make explicit the controlling ideology of a political or social order. "Ideology" misrepresents and distorts the truth about the existence and use of arbitrary power throughout a society. The roots of ideology go deep into the heart of what a society takes to be knowledge. For example, a social order may be blind to its own fundamental belief that the method of positivistic science, which reduces the human being to the status of a thing for purposes of study, is the surest road to truth. In the realm of the practical, such a reductionistic ideology can be seen, say, in the treatment of a poem as a single object, independent of the society that produced it, to be studied just for itself alone. (Habermas would agree with Marx that ideology produces reification; that is, reification takes human acts or properties, objectifies them, and then treats them as independent of the human world. In a capitalist society, for example, money is the reification of human labor and is in the end used against the laborer. But Habermas is critical of Marx's own reduction of human art and literature—Marx called them the "superstructure"—to the "base" of strict materialism. Thus Habermas's own critical theorizing is Marxian—in the critical spirit of Marx—but not Marxist.)

For Habermas, critical theory can bring a kind of freedom or emancipation from the chains of ideology as those who practice the method come to reflect on their own most deeply held assumptions and come to see that they are false. Ultimately, such emancipation would change society and the way human beings communicate one with another. Habermas proposed a theory of communicative competence in which what he called "the ideal speech situation" supplies the basis for rational (that is, nonideological) communication. The ideal speech situation, in which persons are free to speak their minds and listen to reason without fear of being blocked, is a norm of language itself, he said, and is presupposed in every discourse. The person who lies, for example, does so with the assumption that there is such a thing as speaking the truth (otherwise the concept of a lie would be

LANG. Note   Sincerity
                    Powerful

Frankfurt School

The Institute for Social Research was founded in 1923, affiliated with the University of Frankfurt, and, after exile in New York during the Nazi era, returned to Frankfurt in 1949. Those associated with the school were loosely united in the task of developing from Marxism a critical theory approach to art and the human sciences that would, on one hand, reject crude materialist determinism as an ideology and, on the other hand, reject positivism and any possibility of a value-free social science. Those associated with the school include Herbert Marcuse, Theodor Adorno (1903–1969), and Jürgen Habermas.

meaningless). In a paper published in 1970, Habermas declared that "[i]nsofar as we master the means for the construction of an ideal speech situation, we can conceive the ideas of truth, freedom, and justice, which interpret each other— although of course only as ideas. On the strength of communicative competence alone, however, . . . we are quite unable to realize the ideal speech situation; we can only anticipate it." Recent work by Habermas has focused on the rise of counter-cultural groups, feminism, and various liberation movements and whether they constitute the beginnings of the kind of free society he envisions.

In Selection 15.5, Habermas characterizes modern "technocratic consciousness."

SELECTION 15.5

On Society and Politics: A Reader   **From Jürgen Habermas**

Technocratic consciousness reflects not the sundering of an ethical situation but the repression of "ethics" as such as a category of life. The common, positivist way of thinking renders inert the frame of reference of interaction in ordinary language, in which domination and ideology both arise under conditions of distorted communication and can be reflectively detected and broken down. The depoliticization of the mass of the population, which is legitimated through technocratic consciousness, is at the same time men's self-objectification in categories equally of both purposive-rational action and adaptive behavior. The reified models of the sciences migrate into the sociocultural lifeworld and gain objective power over the latter's self-understanding. The ideological nucleus of this consciousness is *the elimination of the distinction between the practical and the technical*. It reflects, but does not objectively account for, the new constellation of a disempowered institutional framework and systems of purposive-rational action that have taken on a life of their own.

The new ideology consequently violates an interest grounded in one of the . . . fundamental conditions of our cultural existence: in language, or more precisely, in the form of socialization and individuation determined by communication in ordinary language. This interest extends to the maintenance of intersubjectivity of mutual understanding as well as to the creation of communication without domination. Technocratic consciousness makes this practical interest disappear behind the interest in the expansion of our power of technical control. Thus the reflection that the new ideology calls for must penetrate beyond the level of particular historical class interests to disclose the fundamental interests of mankind as such, engaged in the process of self-constitution.

Michel Foucault
Knowledge is power
was a sadomasochist

Foucault is intensely suspicious of philosophic or scientific truth claims, especially claims by the human sciences (such as psychology and sociology) to have discovered something true—that is, objectively true—about the human being. At first, Foucault thought of himself as an archaeologist, digging through historical strata to lay bare the discourses that shaped societies (and shape our own). "Discourse" here is a word that describes how people talk, the shape they give to the multitude of interactions within a society, and how they act as a result. It is Foucault's point that a study of such discourse reveals not the steady march of science in its smashing of superstition (that image itself is a kind of superstition) but rather the substitution of one invented reality for another, neither more nor less "true."

For example, the old view of disease as an outside "evil power" that attempted to kill the body was replaced in the late eighteenth century by the discourse of professionalized medicine, in which disease was spoken of as internal to the body. The proper role of medicine was not to cast out invading evil spirits but physically to cut out diseased flesh. But the "success" of such surgery has come at the price of turning ourselves into mere objects in need of fixing up. Medical technology can sustain the human body for a long time if in our discourse it is seen as some complex machine; but the image of a machine, which permeates our thinking, effectively reduces the human being to a mere mechanism, an object. The meaning (or lack of meaning) this image gives to human existence is not truer than the ancient view, just other. The dominant view of death (or of insanity, or criminality) is part of a discourse that—lo and behold!—finds (that is, creates) a never-ending parade of sick people, the insane, the criminal.

In his archaeological period, Foucault's work seemed to owe something to the structuralist movement in France (see box), though he would disavow any connection. Foucault claimed to have found in his archaeological method a series of discontinuous "created realities" or "epistemes" that serve in each era as the ground of the true and the false. But since these epistemes are a social given, there can be no appeal to any absolute truth of things (unless "absolute truth" is part of the particular episteme; but that would mean such a concept is merely a construct of social discourse and not "absolute" at all). Though the nature of the epistemes cannot be spelled out here, suffice it to say that Foucault's program is decidedly anti-Hegelian. Where Hegel saw the working out of history as the Absolute Reason becoming self-conscious, Foucault saw history as a series of discontinuities, one following the next but with no hint of true progress.

Michel Foucault

Foucault told a group of American philosophers in Berkeley, California, in April of 1983 that when Jürgen Habermas had visited him in Paris, Foucault "was quite struck by his observation of the extent to which the problem of Heidegger and of the political implications of Heidegger's thought was quite a pressing and important one for him." Habermas interpreted Heidegger as a German neoconservative and Heidegger's Nazism as somehow connected with Heidegger's own philosophical positions. Foucault told the interviewers that he believed there was "a very tenuous 'analytic' link between a philosophical conception and the concrete political attitude of someone who is appealing to it; the 'best' theories do not constitute a very effective protection against disastrous political choices." But,

Foucault added, "I don't conclude from this that one may say just anything within the order of theory, but, on the contrary, that a demanding, prudent, 'experimental' attitude is necessary; at every moment, step by step, one must confront what one is thinking and saying with what one is doing, with what one is." Before he died on June 25, 1984, of toxoplasmosis-produced lesions on the brain as a result of AIDS, Foucault was engaged during most of his academic career in a project that attempted to chart the power relations by which societies exclude, lock up, or institutionalize the insane, the prisoner, the homosexual—those persons society defines as "other." Unlike Habermas, Foucault denied that societies could ever free themselves from such exclusionary forces; no "ideal speech sit-

uation" was possible. Foucault himself was something of a scandal to "polite" French society. One biographer writes of the philosopher's sadomasochistic erotic practices, his appearance in public wearing leather clothes, his open affection for men, and his fondness of the gay bathhouses of San Francisco. Born in Poitiers, France, on October 15, 1926, Foucault was the firstborn son of a surgeon. He was a professor of the Collège de France from 1970. Foucault's major works include *Madness and Civilization* (English translation 1965); *The Birth of the Clinic: An Archaeology of Medical Perception* (1973); *Discipline and Punish: The Birth of the Prison* (1977); *The Order of Things: An Archaeology of the Human Sciences* (1970); and *The History of Sexuality* (3 volumes, English translation 1978–1986).

Yet Foucault's own project was brought into question by the implications of the archaeological method. It assumes a kind of objectivity on the part of the researcher and his "findings," but such objectivity, Foucault came to believe, was mere illusion. After all, if Foucault was himself working from within a particular episteme, no objective history of other epistemes would even be possible. Rather than abandon his relativistic stance, Foucault abandoned archaeology. Instead, beginning in the 1970s, he devoted himself to what Friedrich Nietzsche had earlier called "genealogy."

For Foucault, genealogy did not commit one to a universal theory or to a particular view of the human subject. The emphasis in genealogy was not knowledge (as it had been in archaeology) but power. In his later books Foucault was less concerned with the language-worlds created by various societies than with the "micropractices" of the body within a given society. This is not simply the physical body, but the lived body, an embodied consciousness. For example, one of the features of the embodied person is ability to dominate others; therefore it is possible to trace the development (the genealogy) of various laws against assault. A court sets up its own rules and acts on them and calls it justice; the practice of the court is just what justice is, but justice is really an illusion for a reordering of power relationships. Genealogy doesn't provide any theories to explain what is going on; it simply evokes the small practices and social habits that constitute you and us, illuminating how such practices express the working of the power of the body. Genealogy is not prescriptive, but descriptive.

In Selection 15.6, Foucault takes up the often voiced characterization of modern bourgeois society as sexually repressed and in need of psychoanalytic liberation. Why else the endless talk shows with their parade of experts on sex? But Foucault suggests that the power of the body is being expressed in the very methods designed to prevent and treat sexual "perversity." Why else the endless "confessions" about sex on those same talk shows?

SELECTION 15.6

The History of Sexuality

From Michel Foucault

The medicalization of the sexually peculiar was both the effect and the instrument of this [power]. Embedded in bodies, becoming deeply characteristic of individuals, the oddities of sex relied on a technology of health and pathology. And conversely, since sexuality was a medical and a medicalizable object, one had to try and detect it—as a lesion, a dysfunction, or a symptom—in the depths of the organism, or on the surface of the skin, or among all the signs of behavior. The power which thus took charge of sexuality set about contacting bodies, caressing them with its eyes, intensifying areas, electrifying surfaces, dramatizing troubled moments. It wrapped the sexual body in its embrace. There was undoubtedly an increase in effectiveness and an extension of the domain controlled; but also a sensualization of power and a gain of pleasure. This produced a twofold effect: an impetus was given to power through its very exercise; an emotion rewarded the overseeing control and carried it further; the intensity of the confession renewed the questioner's curiosity; the pleasure discovered fed back to the power that encircled it. . . .

The medical examination, the psychiatric investigation, the pedagogical report, and family controls may have the overall and apparent objective of saying no to all wayward or unproductive sexualities, but the fact is that they function as mechanisms with a double impetus: pleasure and power. The pleasure that comes of exercising a power that questions, monitors, watches, spies, searches out, palpates, brings to light; and on the other hand, the pleasure that kindles at having to evade this power, flee from it, fool it, or travesty it. The power that lets itself be invaded by the pleasure it is pursuing; and opposite it, power asserting itself in the pleasure of showing off, scandalizing, or resisting. Capture and seduction, confrontation and mutual reinforcement: parents and children, adults and adolescents, educators and students, doctors and patients, the psychiatrist with his hysteric and his perverts, all have played this game continually since the nineteenth century. These attractions, these evasions, these circular incitements have traced around bodies and sexes, not boundaries not to be crossed, but *perpetual spirals of power and pleasure*. . . .

We must therefore abandon the hypothesis that modern industrial societies ushered in an age of increased sexual repression. . . . It is said that no society has been more prudish; never have the agencies of power taken such care to feign ignorance of the thing they prohibited, as if they were determined to have nothing to do with it. But it is the opposite that has become apparent, at least after a general review of the facts: never have there existed more centers of power; never more attention manifested and verbalized; never more circular contacts and linkages; never more sites where the intensity of pleasures and the persistency of power catch hold, only to spread elsewhere.

Richard Rorty

American philosopher **Richard Rorty** (1931–) is suspicious of the traditional claims of philosophy itself to have the methods best suited to finding "truth." He has adopted the way of American pragmatism exemplified by William James and John Dewey (see Chapter 6) and has applied it to the role of literature in society. The "best" literature, he says, can open to its readers new possibilities for constructing a meaningful life. Some philosophical writing falls into this category (Rorty offers the example of Derrida), but philosophy has no corner in helping a person extend the possibilities of life. Rorty would characterize himself as a liberal ironist, adhering to the tradition of political liberalism in the public square (which offers us the freedom to pursue private projects) and irony in the private sphere (in which our "absolute" values are human constructs and in which we must live with meanings we have ourselves created).

In the last few years, Rorty has sought to combine American liberalism with Continental literature and philosophy, and to do so through the medium of pragmatism. Heidegger, he says, was a brilliant thinker, but chance events played a great role in Heidegger's personal choices and commitments. If it had been otherwise, Heidegger might have come to the United States before investing in Nazi ideology and might thus have lived a wholly honorable life. As it was, says Rorty, Heidegger was "a coward, a liar and the greatest philosopher of the century." What is important now is that Heidegger can function as an example: "What binds early to late Heidegger," writes Rorty, "is the hope of finding a vocabulary which will keep him authentic—one which will block any attempt to affiliate oneself with a higher power, . . . to escape from time into eternity. . . . He wants a self-consuming and continually self-renewing final vocabulary. . . . Reading Heidegger has become one of the experiences with which we have to come to terms, to redescribe and make mesh with the rest of our experiences, in order to succeed in our own projects of self-creation. But Heidegger has no general public utility." That is, says Rorty, Heidegger fails as a public philosopher because in part he succumbs to a tendency to claim that those words that are meaningful to him ought to be meaningful to others. But in the private sphere, Heidegger offers an example of a philosophy professor who quested after authenticity—an example that Rorty, for one, can take to heart.

Structuralism vs. Deconstruction

Structuralism is a methodology that seeks to find the underlying rules and conventions governing large social systems such as language or cultural mythology. It hearkens back to Swiss linguist **Ferdinand de Saussure** (1857–1913), who emphasized the study of the language system itself (*langue*) rather than particular speech (*parole*). Saussure was concerned with the "deep structures" of language common to all speakers. He saw linguistics as the study of signs, which he defined as a combination of the signifier (the physical thing that signifies) and the signified (that which is signified). A sentence is a sequence of signs the meaning of which depends not only on the order of the signs ("I can go" vs. "Can I go?") but on the contrast of each sign with other signs in the language that are not present. Thus, the "I" in "I can go" contrasts with other possible subjects: she, he, you, and so on. It is the relationship between the "I" and these other signs not present that give the "I" its meaning because our understanding of "I" takes place with the linguistic system and its interrelationships as background. How the "I" differs from other subjects gives the sign its meaning. Notice here that the emphasis Saussure makes is on the internal linguistic system and its infrastructure; it is of little concern

to him whether a given sentence expresses something true about the outside world.

French anthropologist **Claude Lévi-Strauss** (1908–) adapted Saussure's methods and applied them to his ethnographic research. Lévi-Strauss was interested in finding the underlying structures of thought in the myths of nonindustrial societies and in human communities generally. Characteristic of Lévi-Strauss's structuralist approach, as shown, for example, in *The Savage Mind* (1962; English translation 1966), is the search for a group of rules or "laws" that account for the social complexities of even so-called "primitive" cultures. Cultures (and literary works) were seen as systems of signs the meaning of which could be found in the particular relationships of signs with other signs in the system itself. The implication is that the individual person is very much a construct of the underlying, impersonal rules of the system.

The analysis of sign systems of various types, from advertising slogans to animal communication, is now called semiotics (from the Greek word *semeion,* meaning "sign"); most of the structuralist methodology fits within this "science of signs." But is such a science really possible? That is, are meanings within language or cultural

systems stable enough to provide a definitive interpretation of texts or rituals arising from those systems? In the late 1960s, French philosopher and literary theorist **Jacques Derrida** (1930–) said the answers were "no." He maintained that no such stable meanings were possible and that no definitive meaning of a text could ever be established. In fact, the very notion of a "definitive meaning" implied certain unproven (and unprovable) assumptions about texts and language.

Derrida's "deconstructive" method is to lay bare those assumptions about language, to "question" the text about possible multiple meanings, and in so doing to show what he calls "the free play of signifiers." By this Derrida means that the writer of a word "privileges" that word for a moment; this "privileging" becomes the medium for the play of the signifier—*différence*—rather than any background of a fixed linguistic system (which, according to Derrida, does not exist). This is reminiscent of the Heraclitean tradition that "you can't step into the same river twice"; only now it means "you can't step into the same language twice." Because meaning can occur only as experience, our experiences are constantly overriding ("overwriting") the dictionary definitions of words, effacing those definitions, which in turn are also in flux. A printed dictionary gives the false impression that language has stable meanings, whereas those meanings are continuously "at play" and changing. The use of a word not only goes beyond the dictionary definition but also "effaces" those forces at work that act just beyond the horizon of consciousness. These "forces" are no more available to us than Kant's *Ding-an-sich* or "things in themselves" (see Chapter 5). From the perspective of of deconstruction, then, there are no extralinguistic connections available to anchor meanings within language.

The use of a word at one moment implies at least a slightly different background context than the use of the word at another time, and thus a difference in meaning. But precisely what this difference is can never be pinned down because even to ask a question about a change in meaning is to change a meaning. Derrida put it this way in a speech in 1966 at Johns Hopkins University in Baltimore, Maryland: "The concept of centered structure is in fact the concept of a play based on a fundamental ground, a play constituted on the basis of a fundamental immobility and a reassuring certitude, which is itself beyond the reach of play. And on the basis of

this certitude anxiety can be mastered, for anxiety is invariably the result of a certain mode of being implicated in the game, of being caught by the game, of being as it were at stake in the game from the outset." But now, says Derrida, there has come (in deconstruction) a rupture of the metaphysical center (whether it be Plato's unchanging Forms or some other metaphysical conception that has no "play," no give). "This [rupture] was the moment when language invaded the universal problematic, the moment when, in the absence of a center or origin, everything became discourse . . . that is to say, a system in which the central signified, the original or transcendental signified, is never absolutely present outside a system of differences. The absence of the transcendental signified extends the domain and the play of signification infinitely."*

Derrida's comments recall Saussure's system of "differences," but Derrida takes Saussure's observation to its logical extreme: because all things intelligible to human beings must pass through their language systems in order to be understood, they inevitably become "texts." Thus the meaning of, say, the transcendental Forms can be found only through an exploration of the continual play of signifiers as Plato is interpreted

and interpreted again. No ultimate meaning can be found—what Plato really meant, what a Form really is—because, if all human understanding comes through textuality, there is no ultimate meaning to be found.

Thus Derrida is suspicious of any claim to final interpretation (he calls such claims absolutely ridiculous). He wants to break down the binary thinking of the structuralists (and others), who tend to privilege the first term in each dyad: male/female, white/black, mind/body, master/slave, and so on. Derrida suggests that the first term has significance only in relation to, and only because of, the second term. That is, a master can be a master only if there are slaves; the existence of the master is dependent on the existence of the slave. Derrida's method seeks to bring to the foreground the less privileged terms and thus the implicit assumptions embedded within language systems.

Derrida's books include *Of Grammatology* (1967; English translation 1976) and *Writing and Difference* (1967; English translation 1978).

---

*Jacques Derrida, "Structure, Sign and Play," in *Writing and Difference* (Chicago: University of Chicago Press, 1978), pp. 279, 280.

Some of Rorty's works include *Philosophy and the Mirror of Nature* (1979), *Consequences of Pragmatism* (1982), and *Contingency, Irony, and Solidarity* (1989).

In Selection 15.7, Rorty characterizes the pragmatic program in a speech delivered to a meeting of the American Philosophical Association in 1976.

Consequences of Pragmatism

From Richard Rorty

Pragmatism is the doctrine that there are no constraints on inquiry save conversational ones— no wholesale constraints derived from the nature of the objects, or of the mind, or of language, but only those retail constraints provided by the remarks of our fellow-inquirers. . . . The pragmatist tells us that it is useless to hope that objects will constrain us to believe the truth about them, if only they are approached with an unclouded mental eye, or a rigorous method, or a perspicuous language. He wants us to give up the notion that God, or evolution, or some other underwriter of our present world-picture, has programmed us as machines for accurate verbal picturing, and that philosophy brings self-knowledge by letting us read our own program. The only sense in which we are constrained to truth is that . . . we can make no sense of the notion that the view which can survive all objections might be false. But objections—conversational constraints—cannot be anticipated. There is no method for knowing *when* one has reached the truth, or when one is closer than before.

I prefer this . . . way of characterizing pragmatism because it seems to me to focus on a fundamental choice which confronts the reflective mind: that between accepting the contingent character of starting-points, and attempting to evade that contingency. To accept the contingency of starting-points is to accept our inheritance from, and our conversation with, our fellow-humans as our only source of guidance. To attempt to evade this contingency is to hope to become a properly programmed machine. This was the hope which Plato thought might be fulfilled at the top of the divided line [in the *Republic*], when we passed beyond hypotheses [to contemplate the eternal Forms]. Christians have hoped it might be attained by becoming attuned to the voice of God in the heart, and Cartesians [followers of Descartes's metaphysical method] that it might be fulfilled by emptying the mind and seeking the indubitable. Since Kant, philosophers have hoped that it might be fulfilled by finding the a priori structure of any possible inquiry, or language, or form of social life. If we give up this hope, we shall lose what Nietzsche called "metaphysical comfort," but we may gain a renewed sense of community. Our identification with our community—our society, our political tradition, our intellectual heritage—is heightened when we see this community as ours rather than nature's, shaped rather than found, one among many which men have made. In the end, the pragmatists tell us, what matters is our loyalty to other human beings clinging together against the dark, not our hope of getting things right. James, in arguing against realists and idealists that "the trail of the human serpent is over all," was reminding us that our glory is in our participation in fallible and transitory human projects, not in our obedience to permanent nonhuman constraints.

Checklist

To help you review, here is a checklist of the key philosophers and concepts of this chapter. The brief descriptive sentences summarize leading ideas. Keep in mind that some of these summary statements represent terrific oversimplifications of complex positions.

Philosophers

- **Arthur Schopenhauer** Emphasized the irrationality of the universe and the people within it; regarded Hegelian metaphysics as deluded and beneath contempt.

- **Søren Kierkegaard** Nineteenth-century philosopher who rejected the Hegelian idea of a rational universe and anticipated some of the themes of existentialism.

- **Friedrich Nietzsche** Also reacted strongly against Hegelian idealism; anticipated important themes of existentialism.

- **Fyodor Dostoyevsky, Leo Tolstoy, Franz Kafka, Eugène Ionesco, Samuel Beckett,** and **Ingmar Bergman** Nineteenth- and twentieth-century writers and a filmmaker who depicted the emptiness, meaninglessness, triviality, and loneliness of existence, the self-doubt and anxiety of the individual, as well as the inability of humans to communicate with one another and their profound need to choose how to live within an irrational world.

- **Albert Camus** French existentialist writer; emphasized the absurdity of the world and the inability of the individual to meet genuine human needs within it.

- **Jean-Paul Sartre** French existentialist writer; emphasized the significance of abandonment and its implications.

- **Edmund Husserl** First great phenomenologist.

- **Martin Heidegger** Emphasized the importance of returning to Being itself independent of the mental categories we assign to it.

- **Jürgen Habermas** One of the major German contributors to critical theory.

- **Michel Foucault** French philosopher who provided a critique of conventional social attitudes regarding madness and sexuality.

- **Ferdinand de Saussure** Swiss thinker who laid the foundations for modern linguistics.

- **Claude Lévi-Strauss** French anthropologist who adapted and applied Saussure's structuralist approach to ethnographic research.

- **Jacques Derrida** Influential French deconstructionist.

- **Richard Rorty** American philosopher who interprets Continental philosophy through a pragmatic perspective.

Concepts

Continental philosophy

existentialism

existential predicament

abandonment

"existence precedes essence"

"condemned to be free"

bad faith

authenticity

fundamental project

"I choose myself perpetually"

"in choosing myself, I choose man"

phenomenology

phenomena

universal phenomenology of consciousness

transcendental phenomenology

phenomenological reduction

Sinn

"thrown into the world"

everydayness

chatter

being-unto-death

Gelassenheit

critical theory

ideal speech situation

epistemes   created realities

570-1   "archaeology" and "genealogy"   Language research

Desconstruction   expose Assumptions about language

574   "free play of signifiers"   personal word usage : temporary 'privileged' word

Questions for Discussion and Review

1. Discuss the extent to which we are responsible for the situations in which we find ourselves. Does responsibility begin at birth or at what other time?

2. Discuss the extent to which we are responsible for the situations in which others find themselves. If we cannot hold others to blame for our troubles, does it make sense for us to hold ourselves to blame for theirs?

3. Can humans communicate with one another? (Do not assume that communicating is the same as talking.) Are people ever really *not* strangers? Explain.

4. If there is no objective right and wrong, good and bad, then how should we determine how to live?

5. Suppose you set a goal for yourself and then achieve it. What do you do then—set other goals and achieve them? Why?

6. Are any goals inherently better than others? Why?

7. What is "bad faith," and how do we recognize whether we have it?

8. Discuss in what sense suicide is the "principal philosophical question."

9. What does it mean to say that we live in an absurd world? *Do* we live in an absurd world?

10. Explain the myth of Sisyphus. Discuss the extent to which this situation is an accurate depiction of life.

11. What does it mean to say that we are abandoned?

12. What does it mean to say that existence precedes essence?

13. Does a belief in God rescue us from the existential predicament?

14. What does Sartre mean by saying that we are condemned to be free? What does he mean by saying, "I choose myself perpetually"? And what does he mean by saying, "In choosing myself, I choose man"?

15. Was Heidegger an idealist? Explain.

16. Do you think it is true that most humans live inauthentic lives?

17. Is most human conversation really "chatter"? Is most of *your* conversation really chatter?

18. Can having a "fundamental project" save us from a "lost life"? Explain.

19. Is it possible to detect one's own ideological biases?

20. What attitudes do we harbor today concerning madness and sexuality?

21. Do human beings use language, or does language "use" human beings? Discuss.

22. Must a technocratic society also be a dehumanizing society?

Suggested Further Readings

Samuel Beckett, *Waiting for Godot* (New York: Grove, 1954). In its way, this play is the ultimate expression of the predicaments faced by human beings in an absurd world.

Roy Boyne, *Foucault and Derrida, the Other Side of Reason* (Boston: Unwin Hyman, 1990). An accessible review of the contrasting viewpoints of Derrida and Foucault.

Albert Camus, *Myth of Sisyphus and Other Essays* (New York: Random House, 1959). Camus's thematic rendering of the absurdity of the world and possible reactions to it.

Fyodor Dostoyevsky, *Notes from the Underground* with *The Grand Inquisitor* (New York: E. P. Dutton, 1960). A presentation of life's suffering, irrationality, and absurdity, themes that were to become hallmarks of existentialism in the next century.

Hubert L. Dreyfus, *Being-in-the-World: A Commentary on Heidegger's "Being and Time," Division 1* (Cambridge, Mass.: Bradford, 1990). A famous commentary on Heidegger's difficult and most famous work.

Michael Hammond, Jane Howarth, and Russell Keat, *Understanding Phenomenology* (Cambridge, Mass.: Basil Blackwell, 1991). An introduction to phenomenology via the thought of Husserl, Sartre, and Merleau-Ponty.

Martin Heidegger, *Basic Writings* (New York: Harper & Row, 1977). A sampling of Heidegger's writings from his earlier and later periods of thought, covering his most important themes.

David Couzens Hoy, ed., *Foucault: A Critical Reader* (Cambridge, Mass.: Basil Blackwell, 1991). Critical essays on Foucault by leading contemporary figures such as Rorty and Habermas.

Edmund Husserl, *Ideas Pertaining to a Pure Phenomenology and to a Phenomenological Philosophy,* in Edmund Husserl, *Collected Works,* F. Kersten, trans. (The Hague: Martinus Nijoff Publishers, 1982). An introduction to Husserl's transcendental phenomenology.

Franz Kafka, *The Metamorphosis, The Penal Colony, and Other Stories* (New York: Schocken, 1988). A good collection of Kafka's stories.

Peggy Kamuf, ed., *A Derrida Reader, Between the Blinds* (New York: Harvester Wheatsheaf, 1991). A representative collection of Derrida's writings.

Richard Kearney, ed., *Routledge History of Philosophy,* vol. 8, *Twentieth Century Continental Philosophy* (London: Routledge, 1994). An excellent overview of Continental philosophy. Contains a useful timeline.

Søren Kierkegaard, *Fear and Trembling* (New York: Penguin, 1986). An excellent introduction to some of the themes developed later by the existentialists.

John Lecte, *Fifty Key Contemporary Thinkers* (London: Routledge, 1994). Covers Continental philosophers from structuralism to postmodernity, as well as other thinkers.

Stephen T. Leonard, *Critical Theory in Political Practice* (Princeton, N.J.: Princeton University Press, 1990). An attempt to evaluate critical social theory in terms of its practical application. Thinkers criticized include Marx, Habermas, and Foucault.

David McLellan, *Ideology* (Milton Keynes: Open University Press, 1989). A discussion of the nature of ideology and its development within Marxist and non-Marxist traditions.

Friedrich Nietzsche, *A Nietzsche Reader,* R. J. Hollingdale, trans. (New York: Penguin, 1978). A good contemporary translation of selections that provide a broad overview of Nietzsche's concerns.

Paul Rabinow, ed., *The Foucault Reader* (New York: Penguin Books, 1991). A good introduction to one of the seminal thinkers of our time.

Jean-Paul Sartre, *Being and Nothingness,* Hazel Barnes, trans. (London: Routledge, 1969). Sartre's most important work in philosophy. Not light reading.

Jean-Paul Sartre, *Existentialism and Humanism* (London: Methuen, 1987). A clear, nontechnical depiction of some of the principal concepts of existentialism, including essence, existence, freedom, and responsibility.

Arthur Schopenhauer, *Essays and Aphorisms,* R. J. Hollingdale, trans. (New York: Penguin, 1973). A nice introduction to the psychological insights of Schopenhauer.

Hugh J. Silverman, ed., *Derrida and Deconstruction* (New York: Routledge, 1989). A compilation of essays studying Derrida's interpretation of philosophers from Plato to Foucault and including Freud, Heidegger, and Sartre.

Rolf Wiggershaus, *The Frankfurt School,* Michael Robertson, trans. (Cambridge, Mass.: Bradford, 1994). A massive book on the history and accomplishments of the Frankfurt school.

Continental Philosophy: The Historical Development of Consciousness

Summary and Conclusion

We've seen that many themes of existentialism and phenomenology were introduced in the nineteenth century and before. Both movements originated in part in response, as did analytic philosophy, to the rationalistic idealistic metaphysics of that century. In addition, existentialism and phenomenology both arose in reaction to a perceived crisis in nineteenth- and twentieth-century European society, a crisis whose manifestations ranged from individual despair and disorientation to widespread catastrophic social violence and inhumanity. But whereas existentialists saw this crisis as in part the result of an excessive belief in the rationality of the world, transcendental phenomenologists like Husserl attributed it to undue anti-rationalism and a forgetting of ancient thinkers like Plato.

Existentialists like Camus and Sartre, we have seen, were concerned, primarily, with the problems of coping in an absurd world; phenomenologists like Husserl, in contrast, sought certainty in the vast realm of human subjectivity. Heidegger, who in his early work subjected human existence to phenomenological analysis, treated such existentialist themes as the temporality of humans and our relationship to death and concerned himself especially with the inauthenticity of much of modern existence. But Heidegger had a grander project—to reopen the quest for Being. It is only by regaining an understanding of Being that humans may recover an authentic mode of existence, he believed. Heidegger thought that if human thinking can be refocused on Being, the consequence will be a new starting point for Western civilization as well as for philosophy.

Later developments in Continental philosophy, in the diverse work of Habermas, Foucault, and Derrida, have emphasized how language has shaped human consciousness and human existence.

The Path of Right Living

┌─┐ ┌─┐ ┌─┐ ┌─┐ ┌─┐ ┌─┐ ┌─┐ ┌─┐ ┌─┐ ┌─┐ ┌─┐ ┌─┐ ┌─┐ ┌─┐ ┌─┐ ┌─┐

16

The tree that brushes the heavens
grew from the tiniest sprout.
The most elegant pagoda, nine stories high,
rose from a small pile of earth.
The journey of a thousand miles
began with but a single step.

—*Lao Tzu*

Is there really a point in studying Eastern thinkers, some of whom lived more than two thousand years ago? Can they possibly have anything to say to us?

The answer is yes, for the foreign enlightens the domestic in more than wine and cheeses. As the German poet Hölderlin suggested, we can never understand our home until we have left it. The philosophy of another civilization provides a new vantage point from which to view our own thought; it offers us a different perspective, one from which we may reconsider and reevaluate what is important to us in our own philosophy. Besides, it is a potential source of fresh ideas and new concepts.

The study of ancient Eastern philosophers is, of course, more than a journey in distance. It is a travel back in time to periods in the history of thought that have left messages of perhaps telling importance to us today. For many of the Westerners who have studied it, the philosophy of ancient Eastern thinkers has offered secure guidance to the full and contented life.

In this chapter we will consider the three main philosophies of China: **Confucianism, Taoism,** and **Buddhism.** Buddhism, as will be seen, originated in India. In addition, we will discuss Hinduism, Japanese Zen Buddhism, and the philosophy of the samurai, another traditional Japanese way of thought. No effort will be made to present the history of these important traditions or to trace their evolution over the centuries. Our intent is merely to introduce the philosophy of their original or most important thinkers.

Confucianism

Three great systems of thought dominate Chinese civilization: Confucianism, Taoism, and Buddhism. The most dominant is the one founded by **Confucius** (551–479 B.C.).

Confucius

Confucius loved learning, and by age fifteen he had committed his life to a diligent study of the ancient wise men. In addition, he sought a better way and order of doing things. Learning and knowledge, Confucius believed, must be practical. They must transform life for the better. The result of his own learning was a system of moral, political, and social precepts bound together by what is best called a philosophy of nature and by a faith in the perfectibility of the human character.

That the human person is perfectible was a central tenet of Confucius's thinking. The human person, Confucius believed, is not always good but can become better. Betterment, he thought, comes through learning and service to others. No one begins with wisdom, but with diligence and determined study, wisdom can be acquired; and once acquired, wisdom becomes an instrument for perfecting oneself, the family, and society. Even nature itself, Confucius believed, cannot resist the power of wisdom: "It is man that can make the Way great," he said, "and not the Way that can make man great."

The Way, as here mentioned by Confucius, is a key concept in his philosophy. For Confucius, as for the Taoists, whom we discuss later, **the Way** or **Tao** (*tao* means "path" or "way" in English) is basically the path taken by natural events. Confucius uses the word *Way* or *Tao* often and in different senses. There is a way of the good man, a way of music, a way of proper government, and a cosmological way. Confucius even speaks of "my *tao*." Although interpreters are not in total agreement about this, it would seem that the Tao, for Confucius, is not a fixed and eternal transcendental principle that stands outside and above events and determines them. Rather, it is affected in no small part by human thought and human action. "It is man that can make the Way great." One can study the practices of the wise ancients to learn how to make the Way great in one's own time. Essentially, this means knowing how best to regulate your life. Confucius set forth ideals of human behavior based on his understanding of the Way. He believed that once you have achieved a knowledge of the Tao or Way of things, you cannot die in vain.

For Confucius, everything "thrives according to its nature." One way in which heaven works, he thought, is through the principle of the *Mean,* which provides a standard of measure for all things. Human behavior should avoid extremes and seek moderation. In the philosophy of Confucius, when things function in accordance with this principle of the Mean, they stand in a relationship of mutual dependence. In other words, the principle essentially requires reciprocal cooperation among things—between people and between people and nature. And when the

PROFILE / Confucius (551–479 B.C.)

Confucius, or, in Chinese, K'ung Fu Tzu (K'ung the Great Master), was born "without rank in humble circumstances" in the small Chinese kingdom of Lu. Information about his life is scanty and is derived chiefly from the *Analects,* a collection of his sayings assembled by his disciples. Because of his father's death, he had to work at an early age to help support his mother. He was largely self-taught, and his hunger for learning was insatiable. With the exception of a brief period in which he served as prime minister of Lu, he did not have many opportunities to put his principles about statecraft into practice.

Confucius's ideas have influenced Chinese and Asian ways of life like those of no other philosopher, although their impact has varied from period to period. From the third to the seventh century, Confucianism was eclipsed by other philosophies, but under the T'ang dynasty (618–907) it became the state religion. Neoconfucianism (which incorporated both a more developed metaphysics and Taoist and Buddhist principles) emerged during the Sung dynasty (960–1279) and was the predominant stream of Chinese philosophy until its decline in the twentieth century, which was especially rapid after the Communist revolution in 1949. This was, in part, a consequence of the difference between Chinese communism and the more traditional world views. But it was also a side effect of the change in the system of state civil service examinations, which had formerly been based on the Chinese classic texts, including Confucius.

principle is followed, things flourish and nourish one another without conflict or injury.

Confucius formulated this principle of reciprocity in a general way as it applied to human affairs by saying, "Do not do to others what you would not want them to do to you." Thus likewise, according to Confucius, "A virtuous man wishing to establish himself seeks also to establish others, and wishing to enlighten himself, seeks also to enlighten others." Just as nature is built on a principle of reciprocal cooperation rather than strife, so reciprocal cooperation must reign in human affairs, he believed.

Another key concept in Confucius's thought is that of the *sage* or superior man. The sage represents, in effect, an ethical ideal to which humans should aspire. To achieve the status of sage, Confucius believed, requires having intimate knowledge both of change and of the order of things; it requires, more specifically, having a correct understanding both of human relationships and the workings of nature. A

Confucius's Humanism

The switch in Chinese thought from concern for the deity to concern for human effort and excellence began hundreds of years before Confucius was born. Nonetheless, it was Confucius who made humanity (*jen*) a cornerstone of Chinese philosophy. "The measure of man," he said, "is man."

The nature and duties of the human being must be studied diligently and cultivated, he insisted, and humanity is to be loved.

To help others, Confucius said, one must first establish one's own humane character, which is done by imitating models of superior men from the past. Once the individual has a character that contains nothing contrary to humanity, he can rely on his humanity in all his actions. Through humanistic thinking and acting, according to Confucius, the superior man makes the Way (Tao) great.

correct understanding, according to Confucius, involves, among other things, setting right in thought or *rectifying* what is distorted or confused, and especially involves the correct use or *rectification* of names. (This meant knowing, for example, when it is legitimate to accord someone a title or rank.) The sage or superior person, according to Confucius, puts this correct understanding into action and seeks the mutual cooperation that enables others to fulfill their own destiny.

According to Confucius, the sage's actions are superior to those of other men because his model of behavior is superior. Specifically, he patterns his behavior on the great men of the past. In addition, he constantly learns from his own personal experience. (Confucius said that if he were able to study change for fifty years, he would finally be free of mistakes.) Wisdom requires constant learning, and constant learning allows the superior man better to know the measure of things and to perform his duty accordingly.

Thus, the sage, in the philosophy of Confucius, not only thinks correctly, but also lives correctly. Indeed, according to Confucius, for the sage no discrepancy exists between thought (or speech) and action. The sage does not think (or say) one thing and do a different thing: he matches word with deed.

Further, according to Confucius, the superior man is an altruist who provides impartial and equitable service to others. He is kind and benevolent; he does not repay evil with evil but rather with uprightness. His concern is with reform, not revenge. And his virtuous behavior is a matter of habit that holds even in the direst crisis. For this reason, Confucius believed, the sage can be counted on at all times. His fairness makes him a figure of trust to all, including the rulers of state.

Now the rulers of the Chinese states of Confucius's time did not entrust their affairs to superior men; nor did the rulers themselves merit this title. Instead, these states were dominated by military regimes that ruled by force and were constantly at war with one another, and whose subjects lived in a state of dread. In the opinion of Confucius, the ignoble policies of such inferior rulers were based on four root evils: greed, aggressiveness, pride, and resentment, which singly or together cause a ruler to rationalize and to excuse the most odious behavior on his part. Further,

Confucius: Insights on Life

At fifteen, I began to be seriously interested in study; at thirty, I had formed my character; at forty, doubts ceased; at fifty, I understood the laws of Heaven; at sixty, nothing that I heard disturbed me; at seventy, I could do as my heart desired without breaking the moral law.

I never take a walk in the company of three persons without finding that one of them has something to teach me.

The superior man is distressed by his want of ability; he is not distressed by men's not knowing him.

The superior man understands righteousness; the inferior man understands profit.

What you do not want done to yourself, do not do to others.

A man who is strong, resolute, simple, and slow to speak is near to humanity.

The way of the superior man is threefold, but I have not been able to attain it. The man of wisdom has no perplexities; the man of humanity has no worry; the man of courage has no fear.

according to Confucius, a ruler is invariably the model for the behavior of his subjects, and as a consequence societies ruled by vicious men are themselves vicious societies.

By contrast, a state so fortunate as to be ruled by a superior man, Confucius believed, will be peaceful, secure, and prosperous. Because the superior man is governed by the principle of the Mean, as a ruler he will be unswervingly just and impartial and will seek to establish a fair distribution of wealth, which in turn will promote security and peace. And because his behavior will be emulated by his subjects, he will rule through virtuous example rather than by force of arms. Further, because he is conscientious in his service to all, he will act without fear or sadness.

Confucius's philosophy touched not only on the state and the individual, but also on the family. In fact, for Confucius, the well-ordered family is a model for the well-ordered state and ultimately the world as a whole. The family, Confucius believed, should, like the state, be patriarchal and authoritarian.

Thus, the proper functioning of the family depends on the obedience of the subordinate members and the responsible governance of the parents (and ultimately the father) in accordance with the principle of the Mean and on the fundamental virtues of filial piety and brotherly respect. Together, these two virtues, according to Confucius, allow an optimal functioning of the five primary human relationships generally: those between ruler and subject, between parent and child, between elder and younger brother, between husband and wife, and between one friend and another. In the well-ordered family, because relationships are clearly defined, life will be stable and will provide the means for all members of the family to develop their capacities to the fullest extent.

Confucius on Government

To govern means to make right. If you lead the people uprightly, who will dare not to be upright? Employ the upright and put aside all the crooked; in this way the crooked can be made to be upright. Go before the people with your example, and spare yourself not in their affairs. He who exercises government by means of his virtue may be compared with the polar star, which keeps its place, and all the stars turn toward it.

According to the nature of man, government is the greatest thing for him. There is good government when those who are near are made happy and when those who are afar are attracted.

Remember this, my children: oppressive government is more terrible than tigers. A ruler has only to be careful of what he likes and dislikes. What the ruler likes, his ministers will practice; and what superiors do, their inferiors will follow.

Guide the people with government measures and control or regulate them by the threat of punishment, and the people will try to keep out of jail but will have no sense of honor or shame.

Guide the people by virtue and control and regulate them by respect, and the people will have a sense of honor and respect.

Do not enter a tottering state nor stay in a chaotic one.

When the Way prevails in the empire, then show yourself; when it does not prevail, then hide.

Tzu-kung asked about government. Confucius said, "Sufficient food, sufficient armament, and sufficient confidence of the people." Tzu-kung said, "Forced to give up one of these, which would you abandon first?" Confucius said, "I would abandon armament." Tzu-kung said, "Forced to give up one of the remaining two, which would you abandon first?" Confucius said, "I would abandon food. There have been deaths from time immemorial, but no state can exist without the confidence of the people."

Confucius's Worldliness

Confucius limited his investigation and concern to this changing world: his philosophy was this-worldly and not other-worldly. When he was asked by Ke Loo about serving the spirits of the dead, he answered: "While you are not able to serve men, how can you serve their spirits?" And he said: "We don't know about life; how can we know about death?" It is in this world that the human being must live and with other people that he must associate, Confucius emphasized.

Nevertheless, Confucius understood the importance of religious ritual for the state and was fastidious in carrying out its mandates. To achieve a proper balance in this regard is the mark of a superior man, he said: "Devote yourself earnestly to the duties due to men, and respect spiritual beings but keep them at a distance. This may be called wisdom."

Confucius's ideal of the superior man, who is wise, humane, honest, and just and whose actions spring from morality and not greed or pride; his urging of a society built not on force or military power but on justice and fairness; his belief in the inherent worth, perfectibility, and goodness of humankind; and his overall concern for humanity and human relationships all represented a strong and influential new vision in Chinese thought.

Mencius

The work of the great Confucian philosopher **Mencius** (371–289 B.C.) is regarded as second only to that of Confucius himself. Mencius, like Confucius, was very saddened by the quality of life during his time. He spoke of princes who were deaf and blind to the terrible events about them that "boom like thunder and flash like lightning." Nevertheless, a central tenet of his thought, as with Confucius, was that human beings are basically good.

According to Mencius, the natural goodness of humans had become perverted by circumstances. Still, he said, each person has the potential for becoming perfect: doing so is a matter of recovering his lost mind and forgotten heart; it is a matter of thinking and feeling *naturally*, a matter of following intuition and conscience.

Mencius never lost his optimism about the possibility of human betterment. For him, if anything is tended properly, it will grow and thrive. Therefore, human beings should nourish the noble or superior part of themselves, so that it will come to predominate. Each person, however, will decide for himself whether he will transform his life for the better.

For the person who has chosen to seek it, the way to self-betterment, the way to a noble existence and the upright life, according to Mencius, can be found only within oneself. Conscience, for Mencius, is "the mind that cannot bear suffering [on the part of others]." The pathway to the upright life, however, must include *self*-suffering and difficulty, he said. "When Heaven is about to confer a great office on any man," he said, "it first exercises his mind with suffering, and his sinews and bones with toil. It exposes his body to hunger and subjects him to extreme poverty. It confounds his undertakings. By all these methods, it stimulates his mind, hardens his nature, and supplies his incompetencies."

Difficulty and suffering, according to Mencius, are to be considered privileges and opportunities to develop independence, excellence, mental alertness, freedom from fear, and quietude of spirit. He goes so far as to imply that prudence and the other virtues are hardly possible for those who have not suffered deeply.

In the process of perfecting one's own life, Mencius said, one is put in a position of benefiting one's family and, through teaching and leadership, society as a whole. Indeed, true happiness, he said, does not consist in ruling an empire merely for the sake of power, the desire for which is the driving ambition of the inferior mind, the mind that, like that of an animal, contains no notion of what is great or honorable. True happiness consists in seeing one's parents and family alive and free from anxiety and in helping one's society. Further, he maintained, whoever is happy in this way is happy in another way, for he need never feel shame for his actions.

Mencius

Mencius, or Meng-tzu, was born in what is now the Shantung province of China. He purportedly was taught by Confucius's grandson. Like Confucius, he lived in a time of political turmoil; he spent forty years traveling and teaching. His works became part of the "Four Classics" of ancient China and are based on his belief in the original goodness of human nature. These quotations reveal some of his insights.

The great end of learning is nothing else but to seek for the lost mind.

To preserve one's mental and physical constitution and *nourish one's nature* is the way to serve Heaven.

If you let people follow their feelings (original nature), they will be able to do good. This is what is meant by saying that human nature is good. If man does evil, it is not the fault of his natural endowment.

Humanity, righteousness, propriety, and wisdom are not drilled into us from outside. We originally have them with us. Only we do not think [to find them]. Therefore, it is said, "Seek and you will find it, neglect and you will lose it."

With proper nourishment and care, everything grows, whereas without proper nourishment and care, everything decays.

Those who follow the greater qualities in their nature become great men and those who follow the smaller qualities in their nature become small men.

That whereby man differs from the lower animals is small. The mass of the people cast it away, while the superior men preserve it.

The disease of men is this— that they neglect their own fields and go weed the fields of others.

Thus it may be said that what they require from others is great, while what they lay upon themselves is light.

Thus it may be seen that Mencius, too, like Confucius, was concerned not only with the person but also with the state. Disorder in a state, he believed, is often caused by a ruler who takes no notice of conditions within his own state, a ruler who—again like an animal—is indifferent to all but his own selfish interests and petty ambitions. This indifference and selfishness is a form of blindness, maintained Mencius, and a state governed without vision, he said, inevitably falls into ruin and death.

Further, according to Mencius, the subjects of the state ruled by the inferior person follow the example of their leader and also become like beasts set to devour each other. In this thought Mencius echoed Confucius. But, unlike Confucius, Mencius held that killing such a monarch is not murder, for the establishment of a humane government is not possible under such an individual.

The good ruler, Mencius maintained, is benevolent toward his subjects as a father is toward his children and will seek to establish a good order and a just regime. He displays, in addition to benevolence, three other primary virtues or attributes: righteousness, propriety, and knowledge. Further, the good ruler is mild in manner and governs with mind and heart rather than with the strong arm. Because of his mild manner, he encounters no enemies; and because he is humane

Mencius on Virtuous Activity

It is said that the superior man has two things in which he delights, and to be ruler over the empire is not one of them.

That the father and mother are both alive and that the condition of his brothers affords no cause for anxiety, this is one delight.

That when looking up he has no occasion for shame before Heaven, and below he has no occasion to blush before men—this is the second delight.

In the view of a superior man as to the ways by which men seek for riches, honors, gain, and advancement, there are few of their wives who would not be ashamed and weep together on account of them.

Men must be decided on what they will not do, and then they are able to act with vigor on what they ought.

If on self-examination I find that I am not upright, shall I not be in fear even of a poor man in loose garments of hair cloth?

If on self-examination I find that I am upright, neither thousands nor tens of thousands will stand in my path.

I have not heard of one's principles being dependent for their manifestation on other men.

Benevolence is man's mind and righteousness is man's path.

How lamentable it is to neglect the path and not pursue it, to lose the mind and not know to seek it again.

Benevolence subdues its opposite just as water subdues fire.

Those, however, who nowadays practice benevolence do it as if with one cup of water they could save a whole wagon load of fuel which was on fire, and, when the flames were not extinguished, were to say that water cannot subdue fire. This conduct greatly encourages those who are not benevolent.

Mencius and Thomas Hobbes on Human Nature

Mencius was quite aware that, by and large, people in his time were violent, self-serving, inclined to stop short of the mark in everything they attempted, and successful only in bringing premature death on themselves. But for Mencius, this evil came on people because circumstances had not allowed them to cultivate their inherent nobility and to search out within themselves love, wisdom, virtue, a sense of duty, and self-perfection. Human nature, according to Mencius, is inherently good, and this goodness can be actualized if people would develop their potentiality—as would happen under a just and humane regime.

Among the many Western philosophers who have also viewed people as selfish and violent, Thomas Hobbes (1588–1679) is probably the most famous. In the state of nature, Hobbes wrote, the life of man is "solitary, poor, nasty, brutish, and short." But Hobbes, unlike Mencius, attributed the ugly ways of humankind to human nature. So Hobbes believed that only through force wielded by an absolute sovereign can humans be prevented from devouring one another: *Homo lupus homini,* said Hobbes, quoting the Roman poet Plautus (c. 254–184 B.C.): *Man is the wolf of man.* Mencius, in contrast, believed that a wise ruler will successfully call forth the goodness inherent in human nature through mild and benevolent leadership.

Whether their malevolent actions mean that human beings, although essentially good by nature, exist in a fallen state or whether they indicate that human nature is essentially bad is a question that has not been resolved. Perhaps it is not resolvable.

Mencius on Government

If a man should love others and the emotion is not returned, let him turn inward and examine his own benevolence.

If a man is trying to rule others, and his government is unsuccessful, let him turn inward and examine his wisdom.

If he treats others politely and they do not return the politeness, let him turn inward and examine his own feelings of respect.

Only the benevolent ought to be in high stations. When a man destitute of benevolence is in a high station, he thereby disseminates his wickedness among all below him.

Virtue alone is not sufficient for the exercise of government; laws alone cannot carry themselves into practice.

[In a state] the people are the most important; the spirits of the land (guardians of territory) are the next; the ruler is of slight importance. Therefore to gain [the hearts of] the peasantry is the way to become emperor.

Killing a bad monarch is not murder.

If a ruler regards his ministers as hands and feet, then his ministers will regard him as their heart and mind. If the ruler regards his ministers as dogs and horses, his ministers will regard him as any other man. If a ruler regards his ministers as dirt and grass, his ministers will regard him as a bandit and an enemy.

To say that one cannot abide by humanity and follow righteousness is to throw oneself away. Humanity is the peaceful abode of man and righteousness is his straight path.

All men have the mind which cannot bear [to see the suffering of] others.... When a government that cannot bear to see the suffering of the people is conducted from a mind that cannot bear to see the suffering of others, the government of the empire will be as easy as making something go round in the palm.

Humanity, righteousness, loyalty, faithfulness, and the love of the good without getting tired of it constitute the nobility of Heaven, and to be a grand official, a great official, and a high official—this constitutes the nobility of man.

and his subjects accordingly have confidence in his goodness, he will have only little opposition.

In short, this superior ruler, who has himself suffered on the path to betterment, acquires the mind that cannot bear the suffering of others, and, because it is humane and just, his governance is the foundation of all present and future good within the state.

Thus Mencius's philosophy exhibits the humanistic concerns and faith in human goodness and perfectibility that characterize Confucian philosophy in general. Both Mencius and Confucius were aware, however, that in practice humans are often self-seeking and that their potential for goodness must be cultivated or nurtured. As may be seen in the boxes, Mencius offers much advice and sets forth many telling maxims that, in effect, constitute a method for cultivating the better part of human nature.

Hsün Tzu

Another important Confucian philosopher, who blended Taoism with Confucianism and added his own, rather more pessimistic conception of human nature, was **Hsün Tzu** (298–238 B.C.). He was rationalistic and realistic in his approach, believing that the hierarchical order of society was established by the following of unchanging moral principles. If moral practices, laws, and the rules of propriety were followed, then order, peace, and prosperity would inevitably be the result. If they were not followed, disorder and disaster would result.

Hsün Tzu's view of the basic nature of human beings is what makes him strikingly dissimilar to other major Confucian thinkers. He did not agree with Mencius that human beings are originally good and therefore naturally inclined to goodness. Hsün Tzu believed that human beings are basically bad but that they are impelled to compensate for and overcome this defectiveness, this badness, through education and moral training. Fortunately, the human being is perfectible. Through a study of past and present sages, a human being may develop a

moral understanding based on the ultimate virtues of humanity and righteousness.

For Hsün Tzu, the state, like the individual, can lose itself in seeking profit. The result is strife, violence, lewdness, and rebellion. Such an inferior state must be reconstructed through moral principles, which must come to be embodied in the person of the ruler. Hsün Tzu's thought was the official creed during the Han period (c. 206–220), and it has continued to have an important influence on Asian societies to the present.

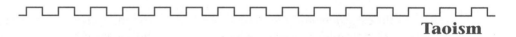

Taoism

Taoism, another great system of Chinese thought, derives chiefly from **Lao Tzu** (c. seventh–sixth century B.C.) and his chief follower, **Chuang Tzu** (c. fourth century B.C.). We will look at these two in turn.

Lao Tzu

In an oft-reported meeting between Confucius and Lao Tzu, Confucius expressed his admiration for the depth of Lao Tzu's thought. Lao Tzu, in turn, is said to have expressed doubts about the heroes of the past whom Confucius had chosen as models of behavior. Lao Tzu also tried to convince Confucius of the hopelessness of the latter's attempts to improve society by direct action.

This little story nicely indicates an essential difference between Confucius and Lao Tzu and between Confucianism and Taoism. Confucius sought to become an advisor to a ruler and directly to change society for the better, using heroes of the past as models. Lao Tzu's vision of things and strategy for change are very different, as will be seen. And within the Taoist tradition, one strain of thought even uses Lao Tzu's ideas as a means cunningly to obtain and retain power (the military and

Lao Tzu

Almost nothing is known of Lao Tzu's life because he spent it trying to remain unknown and nameless. He is thought to have been born in the late seventh or early sixth century B.C. and to have worked in the archives at Loyang (present-day Hunan province). Confucius is thought to have visited the older man during one of his journeys, as noted in the text. These quotations reveal some of Lao Tzu's insights on the Tao or Way.

The Tao that can be told of is not the eternal Tao;
The name that can be named is not the eternal name.
The Nameless is the origin of Heaven and Earth.

Can you understand all and penetrate all without taking any action?
To produce and to rear them,
To produce, but not to take possession of them,
To act, but not to rely on one's own ability,
To lead them, but not to master them—
This is called profound and secret virtue.

Reversion is the action of Tao.
Weakness is the function of Tao.
All things in the world come from being.
And being comes from non-being.

Tao produced the One.
The One produced the two.
The two produced the three.
And the three produced the ten thousand things.

To know that you do not know is the best.
To pretend to know when you do not know is a disease.

The sage desires to have no desire . . . and returns to what the multitude has missed (Tao).
Thus he supports all things in their natural state, but does not take any action.

A good traveler leaves no track or trace.

political strategies of Sun Tzu—see box on the martial arts—might be mentioned as an example). Our way of looking at Lao Tzu's ideas is thus not the only possible one, and there are also a variety of different ways of interpreting his thought within the long Taoist tradition.

Lao Tzu's view of humankind is in at least one respect like that of the Greek philosopher Socrates. Both thought that even the wisest of humans is still quite ignorant. And to act on that ignorance under the pretense that it is knowledge, both held, is folly that leads not to progress and betterment within the individual and society but to the opposite effect. It is especially here that Taoists like Lao Tzu and Chuang Tzu found Confucius wanting. They thought that he sought to impose solutions without knowledge or understanding.

According to Lao Tzu, what is needed is not interference with the world but humble understanding of the way it functions, namely, understanding of the Tao. Humans cannot force "change" on the world without injuring themselves. All arbitrary interventions using "models" of the past simply lead to further disorder. The sage, he maintained, is the one who knows enough to do nothing: instead of intervening, he simply follows the patterns of the universe, of the ineffable Tao that gives order and substance to all things.

Now the Tao, for Lao Tzu, is one, natural, and eternal. It gives rise to the expansive forces (*yang*) in the universe, and it gives rise to the contractive forces (*yin*).

The Tao, Logos, and God

Ancient Chinese and Western philosophy show a striking similarity in their identification of the first principle (beginning) of all being and truth. In ancient Chinese philosophy this first principle is the eternal Tao, the source of all necessity, meaning, order, and existence, the Way the universe functions. Yet the Tao itself, according to Taoism, remains hidden, its nature ineffable. Any attempt to define the Tao or even to describe it in words must fail. According to Lao Tzu, it is the sign of the truly wise man that he will not even try to name it. He only seeks to submit to it and follow it humbly.

In ancient Greek philosophy a like notion was posited as the root of all things. Heraclitus (c. 535–c. 475 B.C.) named it *logos* and regarded it as the source of all order, lawfulness, and justice. There is no consensus on how *logos* should be translated into English, and dictionaries provide many different meanings for the term, including "reason," "proportion," "word," and others.

Logos, as Heraclitus sees it, is almost entirely unknown by earthly mortals—in part, because nature loves to hide. Humans, Heraclitus thought, see the world in terms of opposites and as full of strife. But the deeper reality is the logos, the unity of opposites in which all is one. Seeing this deeper reality is reserved only for the gods and for those few humans who can escape conventional modes of understanding, according to Heraclitus.

The concept of God as it evolved in traditional Christian philosophy is a variation of Heraclitus's notion of logos as developed by Plato and Aristotle and reinterpreted by St. Augustine, St. Thomas Aquinas, and others. In fact, the "Word" that was "in the beginning" in *Genesis* was *logos* in the Greek text. (*Genesis* may not have been originally composed in Greek, of course.)

The Tao is like an empty bowl that holds and yields the vital energy (*ch'i*) in all things. It is also the *means* by which things come to be, take shape, and reach fulfillment. In contrast to Confucius, who believed that the Tao can be improved on (remember Confucius's remark that "it is man that can make the Way great"), Lao Tzu believed that the Tao cannot be improved on, for it *is* the natural order of things.

According to Lao Tzu, the wise person, the sage, cultivates tranquility and equilibrium in his life in order to recognize the Tao. He comes to recognize that the enduring foundation of life is peace, not strife. The harshest storm, the sage understands, can last only a short while. He frees himself of selfish desires and turns his attention to the deep-rooted Tao, where all is one; and by doing so, he acquires the secrets of both the quiet and the long-lasting life.

By following the Tao, Lao Tzu held, the behavior of the sage is natural and free, for he harbors no unfit desires and no unnatural expectations. He simply does what is appropriate in the present circumstances. Like water, he accepts the lowest places with contentment and without resistance. He deems valuable what others consider worthless and have discarded. And, because he is selfless, he seeks to care for all things and to benefit them rather than use them for his own ends.

The sage's way, maintained Lao Tzu, is modest, slow, and cautious. Again like water, the sage is soft rather than hard, and (like water), while appearing to do

Lao Tzu on Virtuous Activity

Good words shall gain you honor in the marketplace, but good deeds shall gain you friends among men.

There is no guilt greater than to sanction unbridled ambition.
No calamity greater than to be dissatisfied with one's own lot.
No fault greater than to wish continually of receiving.

With the faithful I would keep faith; with the unfaithful I would also keep faith, in order that they may become faithful.

The ability to perceive the significance of the small things of the world is the secret of clear-sightedness; the guarding of what is soft and vulnerable is the secret of strength.

The superior man hoards nothing. The more he uses for the benefit of others, the more he possesses himself. The more he gives to his fellow men, the more he has of his own.

The superior man is skillful in dealing with men, and so does not cast away anyone from his doorway.

The superior man prizes three things. The first is gentleness, the second is frugality, the third is humility. By being gentle he can be bold; by being frugal he can be liberal, and by being humble he becomes a leader among men.

The superior man anticipates tasks that are difficult while they are still easy, and does

things that would become great while they are small. Therefore, the superior man, while he never does what is great, is able on that account to accomplish the greatest of things.

The superior man diminishes his actions and diminishes them again until he arrives at doing nothing on purpose.

Having arrived at this point of non-action, there is nothing that he does not do.

He who keeps his mouth open and spends his breath in the continual promotion of his affairs will never, in all his life, experience safety.

nothing, he achieves lasting effects. To others, the results seem mysteriously produced, for they are produced without apparent effort. The sage is merely following the flow and letting events unfold themselves at their proper time and in their own way. Further, in doing so, he seeks to remain hidden, and he takes no credit for what is achieved, for, as said before, he seeks neither possession nor domination. This absence of selfish desire is his secret virtue.

Lao Tzu believed that all enduring change is brought about by weakness, not by strength; by submission, not by intervention. Like an infant, the sage conserves his vital force and progresses gradually day by day. His strength lies in his softness and flexibility. As he lives in accord with the Tao, he is preserved from harm.

Lao Tzu extended his philosophy of nonstriving to the political sphere. He recognized the disadvantages of coercion: the use of force brings retaliation, and mutual hostility quickly escalates to the detriment of both sides. As coercion and the use of force arise from greed, he advocated a political strategy of nonacquisitiveness, in which weapons are regarded as instruments of destruction and wars are to be fought only when absolutely necessary and then only with regret.

Lao Tzu and the Martial Arts

As mentioned in the text, Lao Tzu was against the use of force unless absolutely necessary. His secret for living was to *yield* whenever possible. Far more could be achieved by withdrawing than by attacking or competing. He wrote:

> The strategists have a saying...
> I dare not be a host,
> but rather a guest;
> I dare not advance an inch,
> But rather retreat a foot.

Taoist philosophy was extended to military and political strategy by, among others, the sixth-century-B.C. general **Sun Tzu**, whose *The Art of War,* a treatise on tactics, logistics, and espionage, has strongly influenced many Chinese leaders to the present day (including Mao Tse-tung). Taoism is also the essential philosophy of the most sophisticated of the martial arts, for example, tai chi ch'uan. For Lao Tzu, the soft and supple always conquers the hard and rigid.

The wise ruler, Lao Tzu believed, understands that violence is a last resort and knows that it can often be avoided by anticipation, by reconciling potential enemies and resolving difficulties when they first arise. It is because such a ruler sidesteps problems by anticipation that his success is unfathomable to others. And because he recognizes that there is no safety in the use of force, he remains calm and unhurried in dealing with any problems that cannot be avoided. His preference is to yield rather than to attack. Gentleness brings him eventual victory with apparently no effort. His strategy is "not to advance an inch but rather to retreat a foot." Slowly he wins over the enemy without the use of weapons. And the gain is lasting because it is achieved without the destructiveness of war and therefore without the long memories of resentment.

To achieve peace and stability, the sage ruler has no wish to dominate or exploit others, Lao Tzu believed. Rather, the wise ruler encourages openness and broadmindedness. Cognizant of the sometimes violent ways of the world, he is cautious and reserved. The very essence of his method lies in not requiting injury with injury, a practice that leads only into the endless cycle of revenge. He responds to injury with kindness. He remains faithful even to the unfaithful. In this way, he gradually and effortlessly turns people from that lower nature that tends to dominate in times of war and strife, away from aggressive ambition to thoughtfulness and the search for modest goals.

A kingdom, according to Lao Tzu, cannot be preserved by force or cunning. Further, he said, too much government only means confusion. Too many laws create disorder rather than preventing it. Too much activity upsets the balance within a state, just as it does in the life of the individual. The wise ruler does only what is absolutely necessary; because his heart is calm and nonacquisitive, his subjects are not excited to hysteria either by fear or avarice. The state achieves a stability in which all things come to completion in accordance with the Way.

In sum, according to Lao Tzu, the way of life recommended by the Tao is one of simplicity, tranquility, weakness, unselfishness, patience, and, above all, non-

Lao Tzu on Government

It is the way of Heaven to take from those who have too much and give to those who have too little. But the way of man is not so. He takes away from those who have too little, to add to his own superabundance.

He who assists the ruler with Tao does not dominate the world with force.
The use of force usually brings requital.
Wherever armies are stationed, briers and thorns grow . . .
Whatever is contrary to Tao will soon perish.

Weapons are the instruments of evil, not the instruments of a good ruler.

When he uses them unavoidably, he regards calm restraint as the best principle. Even when he is victorious, he does not regard it as praiseworthy.
For to praise victory is to delight in the slaughter of men.

Tao invariably takes no action, and yet there is nothing left undone.

If kings and barons can keep it, all things will transform spontaneously.
If, after transformation, they should desire to be active,
I would restrain them with simplicity, which has no name.

Simplicity, which has no name, is free of desires.
Being free of desires, it is tranquil.
And the world will be at peace of its own accord.

Violent and fierce people do not die a natural death.
I shall make this the father [basis or starting point] of my teaching.

Govern the state with correctness.
Operate the army with surprise tactics.
Administer the empire by engaging in no activity.

striving or nonaction—allowing the world to follow its natural course. This way of life is its own reward, for Lao Tzu. Thus he, like Confucius, was concerned with this world, the world of living people; he, like Confucius, was concerned with the human condition and not with otherworldly or supernatural subjects. Unlike Confucius, he did not believe that the Way can be improved on; and therefore, unlike Confucius, he did not think the wise ruler would seek to impose his way of thinking on the state.

Today's reader may well think Lao Tzu's philosophy naive or idealistic. But Lao Tzu was only too aware that a path of quiet nonstriving was one that few, if any, had chosen or would choose to tread. He made it quite clear that he did not expect rule by force to die out soon or quickly to be replaced by a policy of noninterference. He only drew up what he thought would be a superior way of living for any who might wish to consider his opinion in the matter.

Chuang Tzu

Chuang Tzu (c. fourth century B.C.), the most important Taoist next to Lao Tzu, was a contemporary of Mencius—though he and Mencius were not familiar with

Chuang Tzu

Chuang Tzu was born in the fourth century B.C. in the kingdom of Meng, which borders the present-day Shantung. He had a wife, was poor, and worked for an office connected with the city of Tsi Yuan. Little else is known about him except that he enjoyed differing with the followers of Confucius. He was not interested in holding public office because doing so, he feared, might disturb his peace of mind. A few of his insights emerge in these quotations:

> The mind of a perfect man is like a mirror. It grasps nothing. It expects nothing. It reflects but does not hold. Therefore, the perfect man can act without effort.
>
> Proof that a man is holding fast

to the beginning lies in the fact of his fearlessness.

> The still mind discovers the beautiful patterns in the universe.
>
> Flow with whatever may happen and let your mind be free: Stay centered by accepting whatever you are doing. This is the ultimate.
>
> Only the intelligent know how to identify all things as one. Therefore he does not use [his own judgment] but abides in the common [principle]. The common means the useful and the useful means identification. Identification means being at ease with oneself. When one is at ease with himself, one is near Tao. This is to let [nature] take its own course.

> Heaven and earth are one attribute; the ten thousand things [infinite things] are one horse.
>
> When "this" or "that" have no opposites, there is the very axis of Tao.
>
> He who knows the activities of Nature lives according to Nature.... How do we know that what I call Nature is not really man and what I call man is not really Nature?
>
> Your master happened to come because it was his time, and he happened to leave because things follow along. If you are content with the time and willing to follow along, then grief and joy have no way to enter in.

one another's philosophy. As might be expected, Chuang Tzu's philosophy is quite similar to Lao Tzu's, as you will see.

Chuang Tzu perceived that many people live their lives as "slaves of power and riches." Chained by ambition and greed, they are unable to rest and are in constant friction with the world around them. They often feel trapped and do not know how to change their situation. They seem blind to what is happening and why it is happening. Their lives are driven and hectic, and they are in constant warfare with an indifferent world, a world that does not acquiesce to their desires.

But the world has its own wisdom, Chuang Tzu believed, as did Lao Tzu before him, and things come to fruition only at their proper time. Nature cannot be forced or hurried, because nature, Chuang Tzu believed, unfolds according to the Tao: a tree's fruit must be picked only when it is ripe, not before and not after. If people choose to impose their will on the world, the result is strife, disquietude, and disruption.

Chuang Tzu also believed, as did Lao Tzu, that there is no need for people to force things for the sake of ambition or in the pursuit of profit, or, indeed, for any

Cook Ting

Chuang Tzu gave this story of Cook Ting as an illustration of the secret of the sage—to follow the Way of things, responding to them appropriately and never with force.

Cook Ting was cutting up an ox for Lord Wenhui. At every touch of his hand, every heave of his shoulder, every move of his feet, every thrust of his knee—zip! zoop! He slithered the knife along with a zing, and all was in perfect rhythm, as though he were performing the dance of the Mulberry Grove or keeping time to the Ching-shou music.

"Ah, this is marvelous!" said Lord Wen-hui. "Imagine skill reaching such heights!"

Cook Ting laid down his knife and replied, "What I care about is the Way, which goes beyond skill. When I first began cutting up oxen, all I could see was the ox itself. After three years I no longer saw the whole ox. And now—now I go at it by spirit and don't look with my eyes. Perception and understanding have come to a stop and spirit moves where it wants. I go along with the natural makeup, strike in the big hollows, guide the knife through the big openings, and follow things as they are. So I never touch the smallest ligament or tendon, much less a main joint.

"A good cook changes his knife once a year—because he cuts. A mediocre cook changes his knife once a month—because he hacks. I've had this knife of mine for nineteen years and I've cut up thousands of oxen with it, and yet the blade is as good as though it had just come from the grindstone. There are spaces between the joints, and the blade of the knife has really no thickness. If you insert what has no thickness into such spaces, then there's plenty of room—more than enough for the blade to play about it. That's why after nineteen years the blade of my knife is still as good as when it first came from the grindstone.

"However, whenever I come to a complicated place, I size up the difficulties, tell myself to watch out and be careful, keep my eyes on what I'm doing, work very slowly, and move the knife with the greatest subtlety, until—flop! the whole thing comes apart like a clod of earth crumbling to the ground. I stand there holding the knife and look all around me, completely satisfied and reluctant to move on, and then I wipe off the knife and put it away."

"Excellent!" said Lord Wen-hui. "I have heard the words of Cook Ting and learned how to care for life!"

Cook Ting does not wear himself out by trying to force things. This would mean unnecessary friction. Like water, he seeks the empty places. When things become knotted, he only slows down and proceeds carefully. Even then, there is no need for friction or confrontation. Cook Ting's task is done by following rather than disturbing the order of things. By anticipating problems, he solves them before they become major. Total satisfaction is his reward.

other objective. Because it is the Tao, and not the person, that determines what is possible and what will happen, the wise individual accepts the course of events as it unfolds, with neither hope nor regret, for the Tao brings all things to fulfillment in due time. Thus for Chuang Tzu, as for Lao Tzu, the secret of the sage—the key to freedom from fear and stress—is simply to follow the Way of things, responding to them appropriately and dwelling in nonaction. The sage is a mirror: he seeks to be utterly clear about what is before him, but he has no wish to change things.

As was true for Lao Tzu, Chuang Tzu applied his principles to statecraft, though he placed somewhat less emphasis on political affairs than did Lao Tzu. The sage ruler, Chuang Tzu believed, first gains knowledge of himself and of his subjects—gains knowledge of his and their nature and destiny—then effortlessly "goes along with what is right for things." He permits nothing to disturb either his own inner harmony or the harmony within the state. Like a tiger trainer, who anticipates the wildness of his charges, he knows how to deal with the violence of others before it arises, thus minimizing the need for force. In his fearless adherence to the Way, he remains free from selfish designs and preset goals. Because he puts forth no special effort, his success is unfathomable to others. This philosophy is, of course, quite similar to that espoused by Lao Tzu. (And Chuang Tzu, like Lao Tzu before him, was quite aware that rulership in accordance with these principles would be a rare occurrence.)

Chuang Tzu, it is perhaps well to add, is famous for his principle of the "equality of things," according to which opposites—life and death, beauty and ugliness, and all the rest—are in fact equal as a single entity within the Tao. Thus, he reasoned, the wise individual, the sage, does not distinguish between himself and the world, and thus finds oneness with Tao.

Chuang Tzu's philosophy is also distinctive for the emphasis he placed on the danger of usefulness. Useful trees, like fruit and nut trees, he explained, are constantly cut back, kept small, and soon stripped of their fruit. Only "useless" trees live out their full term of life unhindered and unsavaged—but then it is only these useless trees that are able to provide shade and beauty. Likewise, Chuang Tzu reasoned, the sage avoids becoming too useful, if he is to fulfill his destiny. These and other nuggets of Chuang Tzu's philosophy are set forth in the nearby boxes.

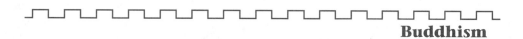

Buddhism

The third great traditional movement in Chinese philosophy is Buddhism, which arose in India in the person of a prince, Siddhartha Gautama, later known as **Buddha** (563-483 B.C.). As may be inferred from the date and place of its beginning, Buddhism was originally free of any influence from Confucian or Taoist thought. This eventually changed, as will be seen, when Buddhism was exported to China. Originally, Buddhism essentially was a philosophical response to what might be called the problem of suffering—and suffering is here to be understood in the broad sense as including not merely outright pain and misery but also sorrow, disappointment, frustration, discontent, disaffection, pessimism, and the sense of unfulfillment that so often grows with the passing of the years.

Buddha

When he was twenty-nine, Buddha, tortured by the suffering he saw around him, abandoned a life of luxury as well as a wife and son to discover why it is that

Chuang Tzu on Virtuous Activity

Chuang Tzu was fishing in the river Phu when the king of Khu sent two high officers to him with the message, "I wish to trouble you with the charge of all within my territories."

Chuang Tzu kept holding his rod without looking around and said, "I have heard that in Khu there is a magnificent tortoise shell, the wearer of which died three thousand years ago, and which the king keeps in his ancestral temple. Was it better for the tortoise to die, and leave its shell to be thus honored? Or would it have been better for it to live, and drag its tail after it over the mud?"

The two officers replied, "It would have been better for it to live and drag its tail through the mud."

"Go your way," said Chuang Tzu. "I will keep on dragging my tail after me through the mud."

Public spirited, and with nothing of the partisan; easy and compliant, without any selfish tendencies; following in the wake of others, without a double mind; not easily distracted because of any anxious thoughts; not scheming in the exercise of one's wisdom; not choosing between parties, but going along with all— all such courses are the path to true enlightenment.

Vacuity, tranquility, mellowness, quietness, and taking no action are the roots of all things.... These are the virtue of rulers and emperors when they manage things above. If one assumes office with them [scholars] to pacify the world, his achievements will be great...and the empire will become unified. In tranquility he becomes a sage, and in activity he becomes a king. He takes no action and is honored. He is simple and plain and none in the world can compete with him in excellence. For such a one understands this virtue of Heaven and Earth. He is called the great foundation and the great source of all being and is in harmony with nature. One who is in accord with the world is in harmony with men. To be in harmony with men means human happiness, and to be in harmony with Nature means the happiness of Nature.

suffering exists and what its cure must be. After six years of wandering and meditation, he found enlightenment.

Buddha's answer to the problem of suffering was contained in his doctrine of the **Four Noble Truths:** (1) There is suffering; (2) suffering has specific and identifiable causes; (3) suffering can be ended; (4) the way to end suffering is through enlightened living, as expressed in the **Eightfold Path** (coming up right away).

Suffering is in part the result, according to Buddha, of the transience and hence uncertainty of the world: indeed, all human problems are rooted in the fact of change and the uncertainty, anxiety, and fear that it causes. Suffering is also in part the result of karma. **Karma** is the doctrine that one's point of departure in this life is determined by one's decisions and deeds in past lives, and that decisions and deeds in this life determine one's beginning points in future incarnations.

But the most immediate causes of human suffering, according to Buddha, are ignorance, which closes the door to enlightenment, and selfish craving, which enslaves an individual to his desires and passions. The individual who is ruled by his desires cannot possibly be happy in an ever-changing, uncertain world, especially because what happens is so much beyond one's control. For even when life goes as is hoped for, there is no guarantee that it will continue that way, and inevitably anxiety and fear overwhelm temporary satisfaction.

According to Buddha, through meditation and self-abnegation, selfish craving can be stilled and ignorance overcome. The result of doing so is a cessation of suffering in **nirvana,** a permanent state of supreme enlightenment and serenity that brings the continuing cycle of reincarnation to an end for the individual.

But Buddha held that attainment of nirvana requires more than merely not clinging to selfish desires. It requires understanding that what is ordinarily thought of as one's body and one's consciousness are not real, are not the true Self. This understanding, this totally nonegoistic perspective, is itself freedom from egoistic thoughts and desires and brings with it as well freedom from all fear and anxiety. By rejecting the fetters of egoistic craving, the individual overcomes the false self and releases himself into "the unsurpassed state of security . . . and utter peace" that is nirvana.

The way to the cessation of suffering is the Eightfold Path. In effect, the Eightfold Path sets forth the means of proper living:

1. *Right View,* which implies having adequate knowledge about those things that make human life sick and unwholesome—ignorance, selfish craving and grasping, and so on.

2. *Right Aim,* which requires overcoming selfish passions and desires by an effort of will and thus having no resentment, envy, or reason to harm another person.

3. *Right Speech,* which means refraining from lies, deceptions, harmful gossip, idle chatter or speculation about others, and so on.

4. *Right Action,* which means not responding to improper desires and cravings, including those that are sexual; and above all means not taking a human life. Right Action also includes doing good deeds (described by Buddha as the "treasure" of the wise).

5. *Right Living,* which requires obtaining one's livelihood through proper means and living one's life free from selfish cravings and graspings.

6. *Right Effort,* which means struggling against immoral and corrupt conditions.

7. *Right Mindfulness,* which is the source of Right Effort. Right Mindfulness implies having a duty to attain enlightenment and to understand the nature and effects of selfish craving. The right-minded person, according to Buddha, has no sense of attachment toward body, feelings, perceptions, activities, and thought, and naturally controls all covetous longings and desires. Right mindfulness likewise means to develop the noble principles of life, especially the six just listed. It develops a pure mind and a clear memory, which are necessary if our every action, no matter how seemingly trivial, is to be imbued with "mindfulness." It brings all human activities under conscious control and thoughtfulness.

PROFILE / Siddhartha Gautama Buddha (563–483 B.C.)

Siddhartha Gautama, the Buddha, was born in northeastern India. His father was a wealthy king or clan chieftain, Shuddhodana by name; through his mother, Maya, he was related to the Shakya tribe of Nepal. The family enjoyed a luxurious lifestyle and the father sought to keep Siddhartha sheltered from the dust and trouble of the outside world. The young Siddhartha was athletic, handsome, and highly intelligent. He was married at the age of sixteen to Yasodhara, who eventually gave birth to a son, Rahula.

One day on a visit to the city of Kapilavastu, Siddhartha became deeply disturbed by the sight of suffering in its various guises. First, he encountered an old man whose body showed the ravages of the years. Next he saw a man in the throes of a virulent disease. Finally, he passed a funeral with its corpse and attendant mourners, meeting the problem of death on one hand and anguish on the other. His last experience of that eventful day was to behold a monk deep in meditation. All these sights had a profound effect on Siddhartha, and the problem of suffering became the central focus of his thoughts. At the age of twenty-nine, he slipped away from his family during the night and entered the forest to seek a solution to the conundrum of suffering, shaving his head and taking on the raiments of poverty.

Early on in his quest, Siddhartha studied under at least two Hindu ascetics. From them he learned a form of yoga, as well as the arts of breathing and motionless meditation. Later Siddhartha joined a small band of ascetics who begged for a living. Like them, Siddhartha performed many acts of self-abnegation and self-renunciation. He grew extremely thin from excessive fasting and one day fell unconscious from his attempts to control his senses. When he awoke, he was fed milk and gruel. From that moment, it was clear to Siddhartha that ascetic practices, in and of themselves, do not lead to enlightenment.

Siddhartha dwelt in the forest for about six years. Thereafter he is thought to have sought a *middle way* between sensual indulgence and ascetic self-denial, striving for enlightenment through concentrating his mind in deep meditation. Siddhartha achieved enlightenment one day while meditating under a fig tree near the present-day town of Gaya in northeastern India. He continued to meditate for seven days. Henceforth this tree was known as the bodhi tree—the tree of enlightenment.

For almost fifty years, Siddhartha, now the Buddha or Enlightened One, went about teaching the way of dealing with suffering. He founded a group or order, to which his wife and son ultimately belonged. Before he died, his philosophy had already found a large following. For Western readers, perhaps the most affecting account of the life of Buddha is presented by Hermann Hesse in his novel *Siddhartha*.

Buddhism and the West

The parallel concern of Buddhists and Stoics (see Chapter 7) with the problem of suffering is intriguing, but it is difficult to say whether there was any reciprocal influence between Buddhism and the philosophies of ancient Greece and Rome. The first major modern Western philosopher to be influenced in a significant way by Buddhist thought was Arthur Schopenhauer (1788–1860). Schopenhauer believed that human life is basically not rational and that humans are driven by blind and insatiable will. Only by overcoming one's ego and desires can a state of calm bliss be achieved, according to Schopenhauer.

After Schopenhauer, Buddhist and other Asian ideas have increasingly come to the West, mostly via Indian and Japanese gurus, monks, and martial artists. Many of these ideas are now entering the mainstream of popular culture.

Eastern Philosophy and Eastern Religion

Eastern philosophy and Eastern religions are closely intertwined. Both Confucianism and Taoism took on the trappings of religion, with priests, rituals, and moral codes. Some forms of Taoism also were influenced by Chinese popular religions and superstitions. Today in Taiwan, for example, there are six levels of Taoism, including two kinds of Taoist priests, the red and the black. Only the highest level reflects the Taoist philosophy in its purest form, free from religious and superstitious add-ons.

Buddhism in China was influenced not only by Confucianism and Taoism, but by popular religions as well. In India, a similar interaction took place among the ancient Buddhist writings and various religious belief systems and practices.

8. *Right Contemplation,* which is the ultimate concentration of mind, integrates the aforementioned principles in dealing with all aspects of life. It is the liberating consciousness that frees the mind from the bonds of our cravings, inclinations, and desires. Any personal consciousness is replaced by an "invisible, infinite, all-penetrating consciousness" that brings lasting peace. It is pure cognition, free from any selfishness. This way to liberation is achieved by the utter annihilation of craving and therefore ultimately of suffering. Buddha emphasizes that this way is achieved slowly. Deliverance is attained step by step by constant effort in building an unshakeable concentration. Right concentration is uninterrupted, blissful thoughtfulness that purifies deeds, words, and thoughts.

As can be seen, the first two stages on the Eightfold Path have to do with the initial mental outlook of the individual; the next four specify appropriate behavior; and the last two pertain to the higher mental and spiritual qualities involved in a total disattachment from self.

Islamic Philosophy

Muslim philosophy arose around the eighth century, a time when Western Europe was experiencing its Middle Ages. From the beginning, it took into account theological considerations such as the person of Mohammed, the Koran, and the schools of theology; but these were not the only sources of influence. Neoplatonism and Aristotle played important roles in shaping both the problems faced and their proposed solutions. Many translations from the Greek were made during the ninth century.

Among the concerns of the early Islamic philosophers were the nature of God (Allah), the hierarchy of creation, the nature of the human being and his place within the universe, as well as the relationship between theology and philosophy. **Al-Kindi** (d. after 870) developed the idea of God as an absolute and transcendent being, which was in accord with certain Muslim ideas of the time. His definition of God took elements from both Aristotle and the Neoplatonists. He developed a cosmology based on the Neoplatonist idea of emanation, where everything evolves out of God and in some way participates in God. Al-Kindi also added the Muslim notion that God created the first being out of nothing by force of will.

Al-Fārābī (875–950) further elaborated on the notion of God in terms of Plotinus's notion of the One and also the notion that everything emanates out of the One. He added Aristotle's notion of God as the first cause of everything. Al-Fārābī looked to the prophet-philosopher to gain the philosophical illumination that would be of profound meaning to his society.

Avicenna (Abū Ali ibn-Sīnā, 980–1037) produced the best known medieval system of thought. He envisioned God as a Necessary Being who emanated the contingent, temporal world out of himself. Everything was dependent on God, and the ultimate goal of human activity was a prophetic mind that attains an intuitive knowledge of God and his creation. For Avicenna, there was a parallelism between philosophy and theology. During this time, philosophy, and especially the mystical identification of a thinker with God, were occasionally considered a threat to Muslim orthodoxy. For example, **Al-Ghazālī** (1058–1111) in his *Incoherence of the Philosophers* attacked Avicenna. Among other things, he criticized Avicenna's notion of the eternity of the world as well as the lower status given to the religious law as

Two additional concepts traditionally believed to have been introduced by Gautama Buddha became important for later Buddhism. The first, Gautama Buddha identifies in his *Sayings* as "clinging to existence" (*upadana*). This clinging is an extreme form of egoistic craving or desire and must be "destroyed" if the human being is ever to reach a state of peace and imperturbability. This clinging can take different forms—a clinging to the body and its worldly pleasure (*kāmûpādāna*), a clinging to views (*ditthûpādāna*), a clinging to rules and rituals (*sīlabbatûpādāna*), and a clinging to ego beliefs (*attavādûpadāna*). It is necessary to cultivate nonclinging or nonattachment, but in such a way that there is not clinging to nonclinging.

The other important concept is silence (*moneyya*). Gautama Buddha sat and meditated under the bodhi tree to reach enlightenment. Such enlightenment requires going beyond the verbiage and logics of discursive reasoning. In the *Sayings,* Gautama Buddha is thought to have spoken of three kinds of silence: the silence of body, the silence of mind, and the silence of word. Only the person who is silent in

a mere symbol of higher truths to be accessed through intuition.

The antagonism between mystical philosophy and Muslim orthodoxy represents an ongoing problem. **Averroës** (1126–1198), for example, was interpreted as holding a theory of two separate truths, the truth of religion and the truth of philosophy. Averroës, who taught the idea of eternal creation, was trying to extricate Aristotle's thought from both Neoplatonic and Islamic derivations.

Perhaps what is most intriguing to modern-day Western thought is the development of Sufism. Sufism represents a mystical, theosophical, and ascetic strain of Muslim belief that seeks union with God (Allah). **Sadr al-Dīn als Shīrazī** (1571–1640), later known as Mulla Sadrā, sought a monistic return to the First Principle of Be-

ing. Sufism, perhaps to a greater degree than orthodox Islamic belief, was influenced by the mystical tendencies of Neoplatonism and gnosticism. There was a seeking after a direct communion with the Absolute Being, who likewise represented Absolute Beauty. Through ascetic practices and concentrated inwardness, a human being might experience a sudden illumination and a sense of ecstatic union with God (Allah). This intuition might reveal to the person his utter nothingness, on the one hand, as well as his pantheistic immanence in God, on the other. It is hardly surprising that a number of Sufis during the medieval period were executed for the blasphemy of identifying themselves with God. This ongoing difficulty was to some degree mollified by Al-Ghazālī, who brought Sufism closer to orthodox Muslim belief

by playing down the pantheistic elements of Sufism.

There have been four main periods of Sufism: the first period (c. 750–1050), the second period (c. 1050–1450), the modern period (c. 1450–1850), and the contemporary period (1850 to the present). There are about one hundred Sufi orders in the world today with several million adherents. The movement has produced a number of great mystical poets; **Kabir** (1435–1518) from Benares, India, is one of the best known in the West thanks to Robert Bly's translations. The Sufi literature, Sufi poetry, and the whirling dervishes have continued to influence the West's own contemporary pantheistic and mystical traditions.

all three ways can be said to be free of taint. It is not surprising, then, that silent meditation becomes a critical way to enlightenment in later developments of Buddhism.

Buddha believed that he had found the cause of suffering in the world and a way of escaping it as well. He set forth a strategy for eliminating unnecessary fear and specified a way of living that is calming for the person but that also allows the person to be of service to others. Buddha did not believe in a divine creator or in divine salvation; thus, in his thinking, the problem of suffering is one that humans must cope with themselves.

Buddhism was purportedly brought to China by the Indian monk Bodhidharma about A.D. 520. There it gradually mixed with Taoism, Confucianism, and other influences and underwent a rather marked transformation. This change is quite noticeable in what is now called Ch'an or Chinese Zen Buddhism, to which we next turn.

Zen and Ch'an

Zen Buddhism, as the text explains, is one of the Buddhist sects of Japan and China. (Buddhism, it may be recalled, originated in India.) *Zen* is Japanese and *Ch'an* is Chinese, and both words derive from the Sanskrit word for meditation, *dhyana*. When Buddhism first came to China, it emphasized the importance of meditation, rather than any particular scripture or doctrine, as the key to ultimate reality.

Although the heading for this section is "Zen Buddhism," we discuss both the Chinese and Japanese traditions, Zen and Ch'an. It should be noted that other forms of Buddhism developed as well, but the Zen tradition is the one that has awakened the most philosophical interest in the West.

Zen Buddhism

The growth of Ch'an Buddhism (Chinese Zen Buddhism) was slow at first, and it always was numerically one of the smaller sects. But over the centuries this sect spread throughout China and into neighboring countries like Japan and Korea. In our century it has taken root in the United States and Europe. Its current spread in the West seems to indicate that Ch'an Buddhism responds to a need in a highly complex, technological world.

Buddhism in China and Japan has a long and rich history. Here it will only be possible to look briefly at a few of its most original and profound thinkers, the sixth patriarch of Chinese Zen, **Hui Neng** (638–713), **Murasaki Shikibu** (970–1031), and **Dogen Zenji** (1200–1253) of the Japanese Soto tradition. The philosophies of these thinkers complement one another and give an overall perspective on basic elements in the Zen Buddhist tradition.

Hui Neng

Hui Neng (638–713) lost his father in childhood and had to sell firewood to keep his mother and himself alive. He was illiterate.

One day, while delivering firewood to a shop, Hui Neng heard the chanting of the Buddhist *Diamond Sutra* (perhaps the most important scripture of Chinese Buddhism, in which Buddha strips his student Subhuti of his coarse views and allows him to see the fundamental oneness of all things and the immutability of perceived phenomena). Hui Neng immediately grasped the deep truth latent in its words. But not until some time later did a gift of money enable him to confirm his perception of truth by seeking out Master Hung-jen, the fifth Chinese patriarch of Ch'an Buddhism, at Huang-mei Mountain in Hupei.

During the first meeting with the fifth patriarch, Hui Neng did not hesitate to manifest the unshakeable strength of his vision, and he was accordingly accepted

Hui Neng's Poem of Enlightenment

Hui Neng's spontaneous poem in answer to the request by the fifth patriarch of Ch'an Buddhism revealed immediately that he saw the fundamental nature of truth:

Fundamentally no bodhi-tree exists

Nor the frame of a mirror bright.
Since all is voidness from the beginning
Where can the dust alight?

Hui Neng intimates here that the ultimate reality or truth is beyond all conceptualization, as explained in the text.

in the Huang-mei monastery. For eight months, however, he worked in the kitchen without even entering the main temple.

At this time, the fifth patriarch was seeking a successor and asked the monks to write a poem showing the depth of their insight into truth. Only the person who has a direct intuition into the truth achieves peace of mind, the Ch'an Buddhists believed, and they also thought that each person must discover this truth for himself. That all is ultimately one was a basic precept of the fifth patriarch. This one reality was thought to be our true self-nature and was held to be immanent within human beings from the beginning. To see this ever-present truth exactly as it is would require going beyond the usual way of thinking, which breaks down ultimate being into distinct entities and classifies and relates them, so that they are understood only in terms of the categories to which they belong and their relationships to one another. Hence poetry rather than a normal form of discourse would be required to express insight into this truth, for normal forms of thought and language can express neither the uniqueness of the individual entity nor the underlying oneness of all things. Perhaps you are reminded here of Heidegger, discussed in the previous chapter.

Shen-hsui, the senior monk at the monastery, was the only one who dared to write the requested poem, and the other monks doubted their ability to surpass him in depth of understanding. His contribution, however, according to tradition, only showed that he had not seen the ultimate truth and had not escaped the confines of normal thought. Hui Neng, though illiterate, is said immediately to have sensed the inadequacy of the vision conveyed by this poem when he overheard it being recited by another monk and to have composed a reply to the poem on the spot. Hui Neng's response, recorded by another monk, may be found in a nearby box.

The monks, it is said, were astounded by the words of this twenty-three-year-old illiterate, who had not yet even been admitted into the meditation hall. The fifth patriarch was moved as well and immediately recognized in Hui Neng his successor. Perceiving the possibility of jealousy and anger among the monks, he is said to have had Hui Neng come to him in the middle of the night to receive the

Hui Neng

As mentioned in the text, Hui Neng sought out the fifth patriarch of Ch'an Buddhism, Master Hung-jen, who eventually confirmed Hui Neng's insight into the truth and appointed him his successor. On meeting the fifth patriarch, Hui Neng is said to have said: "I confess to Your Reverence that I feel wisdom constantly springing from my own heart and mind. So long as I do not stray from my nature, I carry within me the field of bliss."

Other interesting quotations of Hui Neng as to life and truth are as follows:

How could I expect that the self-nature is in and of itself so pure and quiet! How could I expect that the self-nature is in and of itself unborn and undying! How could I expect that the self-nature is in and of itself self-sufficient, with nothing lacking in it! How could I expect that the self-nature is in and of itself immutable and imperturbable! How could I expect that the self-nature is capable of giving birth to all dharmas [laws]!

The *Bodhi* or Wisdom, which constitutes our self-nature, is pure from the beginning. We need only use our mind to perceive it directly to attain Buddhahood.

One Reality is all Reality.

Our original nature is Buddha, and apart from this nature there is no other Buddha. Within, keep the mind in perfect harmony with the self-nature; without, respect all other men. This is surrender to and reliance on one's self.

Light and darkness are two different things in the eyes of the ordinary people. But the wise and understanding ones possess as penetrating insight that there can be no duality in the self-nature. The Non-dual nature is the Real Nature... both its [the Real Nature's] essence and its manifestations are in the absolute state of suchness. Eternal and unchanging, we call it the Tao.

robe and bowl symbolic of his new status as sixth patriarch and to learn the wisdom of the *Diamond Sutra*. According to tradition, Hung-jen, the fifth patriarch, convinced that the truth of the *Buddha-Dharma* (ultimate reality) would ultimately prevail through Hui Neng, instructed Hui Neng to leave the monastery immediately and to remain in hiding until he was ready to teach.

What is the ultimate Dharma (reality/truth/law)? Hui Neng gave it a number of different titles: the Self-Nature, the Buddha-Dharma, the Real Nature, and the eternal and unchanging Tao (note the Taoist influence implicit in the last name). All things, he said, are in reality one: there are no "things." Human thought and understanding, to make sense of a totality that cannot be grasped at once, impose categories, contrasts, and distinctions on reality (including thirty-six basic pairs of contrasts or opposites, such as light and darkness, yin and yang, birth and death, good and bad, and so on). But in truth there is only one thing, the Real Nature, and, as it is in itself, it exists prior to any distinctions or categorizations; it is (so to speak) beyond good and evil, permanence and impermanence, content and form. It is an absolute state of "suchness" that neither comes nor goes, neither increases nor decreases, neither is born nor dies. It is exactly as it is: it is reality and truth.

According to Hui Neng, though this ultimate reality or truth is in principle accessible to all, it remains hidden to many of us because we are focused on false attachments and selfish interests: in short, we lack a balanced, objective outlook. And, as a result of this imbalance in our perspective, our efforts too are one sided in pursuit of our goals. Hui Neng made it his purpose to free humans from selfish, one-sided visions of reality. His recommendation was for a state of "no-thought" or "mindlessness," in which the mind does not impose itself on the truth but remains open and spontaneous—a mirror reflecting the wisdom inherent in reality, one that reflects but does not impede the flow of events.

To deepen one's spirit, he said, is to live in harmony with the true or "self-nature" of all things. When the mind is right, it thinks without bias or partiality and is thus considerate of the needs of each and every thing.

The blend of Taoist, Confucian, and Buddhist precepts is thus very much in evidence in Hui Neng's thought.

Stirring Up the Melting Pot of Eastern Philosophy

At this point we depart from China for Japan, where Zen was introduced from China. As we have seen, under Hui Neng, Zen emerged as a distinct and separate Buddhist sect that combined elements of Indian Buddhist and Chinese thought. When it traveled to Japan, the sect was influenced by Japanese culture as well.

Medieval Japan was like the USA of the Orient: a real melting pot of philosophical and religious views. For men, the mixture of oriental philosophies probably was good enough, but its effect on women was rather less fortunate. If there were a recipe for medieval Japanese philosophy, it would read as follows:

> 1 cup Shinto animism
> 4 Buddhist Noble Truths
> 1 *yin*
> 1 *yang*
> 1 handful Confucian virtues
> 1 Mahayana Buddhist doctrine of the void
>
> Mix all ingredients well, apply liberally to everyone. Prepares men for salvation. Prepares women for reincarnation as men.

By the late ninth century, Japanese culture reflected an unequal mixture of Shinto, Confucianism, Taoism, and Zen Buddhism (and its Mahayana branch, and *its* branches, Tendai and Shigon). Why was this recipe so unfortunate for women? See the section on **Murasaki Shikibu,** following. What are these ingredients? You already are familiar with most of them, other than Shinto and Mahayana.

Shinto, an ancient native religion of Japan, related humans to the *kami*, or gods of nature, that created the universe. People were said to be just another part of the physical universe. The Japanese language didn't even have a word for nature as something distinct from humans. People were regarded as "thinking reeds" completely identified with and part of the natural and divine universe. Such a view is called *animism.*

People's duties were derived through their blood relationships. You were connected to the gods of nature through your ancestor's clan and through the divine

```
 ┌─┐ ┌─┐ ┌─┐ ┌─┐ ┌─┐ ┌─┐ ┌─┐ ┌─┐
─┘ └─┘ └─┘ └─┘ └─┘ └─┘ └─┘ └─┘ └─
```

PROFILE / Murasaki Shikibu (970–1031)

Murasaki Shikibu, or Lady Murasaki, as she is sometimes called, is an important Japanese, Shinto Buddhist, feminist philosopher. Murasaki Shikibu is almost certainly not her real name, however. She was given the nickname "Murasaki" because the real author strongly resembled a character by that name in the book she wrote. Murasaki came from a literary family of the Fujiwara clan. In Japan at that time, it was forbidden for women to study Chinese characters (the original written form of Japanese language). Murasaki learned young how to read Chinese characters by hanging around when her brother was being tutored. She eventually entered court service in the entourage of the teenaged empress Joto-Mon'in Shoshi, to whom Murasaki secretly taught Chinese. Learning how to read gave Murasaki access to the forbidden literatures of religion and philosophy.

In addition to some poetry, Murasaki left two works: a diary, *Murasaki Shikibu Nikki,* and an epic philosophical novel, *Genji Monogatari.* Despite the fact that it was written centuries before the invention of the printing press, once it was printed, *Tale of Genji* (as it is also known) never went out of print. It has been translated into more than thirty languages. Murasaki's primary philosophical interest was with the moral status of women under Japanese Buddhist ethics.

clan of the *Mikado,* who was both national high priest and head of state. The Japanese word for government, *matsuri-goto,* means "things pertaining to worship." So there was no conceptual difference between religion, ethics, and government. And there was no conceptual difference between people and other natural objects.

Mahayana Buddhism was just a twist on Zen. It was introduced into Japan in the late 6th century, when Japan lost its territory in Korea, and its ally, the Paekche Kingdom, suffered military defeat. Many Korean war refugees, most of them Buddhists, fled to Japan, where their religion gained acceptance among Japanese diplomats and aristocrats. Prince Shotoku (his name means "sovereign moral authority") made it the official religion of Japan, incorporating it into Shinto. Shinto connected you to your historical, anthropological past; Mahayana Buddhism connected you to the present and to the future eternity. It incorporated the Confucian virtues of filial piety, veneration of ancestors, duties based on rank and position, honesty, and so forth. (Taoism, too, fit in nicely, with its views about the oneness of humans and nature, spiritual freedom, and peace—not to mention *yin/yang* emphasis on orderliness and balance.)

Mahayana saw humanity unified through spiritual enlightenment, in the worship of one god, who, as luck would have it, turned out to be the *Mikado,* the greatest earthly *kami.* This was the form of Buddhism adopted by Japanese aristocracy. The higher up the sociopolitical aristocracy you were, the closer you were to god—and thus the theory did not displace aristocrats.

This brings us to Murasaki.

Murasaki

Murasaki Shikibu (970–1031) lived at the height of the Mahayana Buddhist influence in Japan. And while all Japanese shared this philosophical heritage, not all shared social and political equality.

The Tendai sect of Mahayana Buddhism held that the closer you were to the *Mikado,* the greater was your potential for moral excellence and for admission to the Western Paradise (heaven). But in Buddhism, women generally were considered to be of lesser moral worth than men. Women could achieve salvation, or reach the psychological state of *nirvana* that would prepare them to enter the Western Paradise, but only after reincarnation as a male.

The fact that you were a woman was evidence that in a past life you had been a male who was now making up for a past life lacking in virtue. In the Buddhist doctrine of reincarnation, a good woman can hope at best for reincarnation as a man. After a lifetime as a virtuous man, it would be possible to achieve salvation and enter heaven. Women, no matter their virtue, could not hope for salvation, as Murasaki says:

> But then someone with as much to atone for as myself may not qualify for salvation; there are so many things that serve to remind one of the transgressions of a former existence. Ah, the wretchedness of it all!

Murasaki's women characters illustrated just how hopeless life was for Japanese women, especially those who thought about things like self-identity, morality, free will and determinism, predestination and salvation. Judging from the popularity of her very long book and the fact that it was initially circulated a chapter at a time among aristocratic women (obviously, many had learned how to read Chinese characters on the sly), lots of Japanese women did care about these philosophical issues.

Murasaki kept the basic recipe we gave above in the melting-pot section. But she changed the directions and added a few ingredients. Here's Murasaki's version of the recipe:

> 1 cup Shinto animism
> 4 Buddhist Noble Truths
> 1 *yin*
> 1 *yang*
> 1 handful Confucian virtues
> 1 Mahayana Buddhist doctrine of the void
> 1 lifetime of spiritual enlightenment

> Mix all ingredients well with a strong, feminist hand. Contemplate for a lifetime with as much detachment from wordly distractions as possible. (Become a nun if you can.) Use as an antidote to determinist, misogynist elements of Tendai. With lifelong use, women may achieve salvation.

Murasaki's version of the recipe added the importance of spiritual enlightenment and contemplation. She also emphasized the virtues of simplicity and detachment from wordly possessions.

Zen Buddhism in Japan

There are two major forms of Zen Buddhism in contemporary Japan: Rinzai Zen and Soto Zen. Over the centuries, each has mutually influenced the other. The difference between the two has more to do with method than with doctrine. Both seek enlightenment apart from the scriptures.

Rinzai Zen, named after the famous Zen monk Rinzai (785–867) seeks sudden enlightenment, as preached by Hui Neng. To achieve the *satori* or enlightenment experience, *koans* are often used in addition to sitting in meditation (*zazen*). *Koans* are illogical, even nonsensical, puzzles that are designed to break the stranglehold of conceptual thought so that the absolute, indivisible truth or reality may be suddenly and utterly seen or intuited. Among the most famous of all *koans* is, "What is the sound of one hand clapping?"

The Soto Zen tradition places less emphasis on sudden enlightenment and tends not to use *koans*. As exemplified by Dogen, enlightenment is to be found slowly through *zazen* (meditation) and also by performing all daily duties in the same state of awareness as when sitting in *zazen*. This tradition recognizes no single moment of *satori*, for enlightenment is believed to be possible in all moments.

In sharp contrast to the views of women present in Buddhism and reflected in Japanese culture, Murasaki's female characters struggled with the problem that in Japanese culture and Buddhist religion women existed only as predestined, natural objects.

Murasaki's main character, Ukifune (which means "loose boat," "loose woman," or "person with no direction and uncertain destination"—you get the idea), becomes so depressed following a rape that she attempts to commit suicide; but she is saved by a monk, against the advice of other monks who think she should be allowed to drown.

Everyone, especially other women, has told Ukifune that she can't do anything about the rape and its social consequences; it's just her fate. There is no hope for her other than to become a prostitute. Ukifune rages against the double injustice: First, she is just an object to a man who forcibly rapes her; second, she is punished socially for having been wronged. Rather than accept her fate, she challenges her destiny through suicide, hoping for reincarnation as a man.

But her rescue, although also attributed by the monk to fate, leads her to a path of religious contemplation. Ultimately, she becomes a nun—but not an ordinary nun performing public service. Ukifune spends her life contemplating life's meaning and seeking enlightenment. Ultimately, a lifetime of contemplation will reveal to her that she can control her destiny through self-knowledge.

Murasaki's women characters struggle to become free, responsible moral agents, who assert that they have natural rights. They also assume moral responsibilities to others. Although Murasaki rejected mainstream Buddhism's view of women, her philosophy represents a minority Buddhist view that women are moral agents who, instead of blaming fate, can assume moral responsibility for their actions. Murasaki held that women should challenge their *karma* (destiny) and take control of their own lives by engaging in what were then forbidden, illegal activities such as reading the *sutras* (secret doctrines and sacred teachings) of the great Buddhist monks.

Murasaki's personal decision to become a nun and to read the *sutras* was the product of a wager that was worthy of Pascal (see Chapter 13):

> The time too is ripe. If I get much older my eyesight will surely weaken to the point that I shall be unable to read the sutras, and my spirits will fail. It may seem that I am merely going through the motions of being a true believer, but I assure you that I can think of little else at the present moment.

By understanding and living according to what Murasaki argued was the true meaning of Buddhism, women could achieve a state of contemplation that is compatible with reaching *nirvana*. Under Murasaki's philosophy, women need not be content to wait until they have been reincarnated as males to begin the difficult and long process of philosophical enlightenment. They can begin that process in this life by living, as do men, according to the teachings of Shinto Buddhism.

Dogen

By age fourteen, Dogen was already a monk. He eventually became dissatisfied with the decadent state of Tendai Buddhism, which, being egalitarian and anti-elitist in nature, adopted many popular rituals like chanting the name of Amitabba Buddha. Dogen therefore sought out a Tendai monk, Eisei, who had twice traveled to China to study Ch'an Buddhism. Eisei died soon after the encounter with Dogen, but Dogen continued his studies for nine years under Eisei's successor, Myozen. Afterward, Dogen went to China himself to deepen his studies, and eventually he came under the tutelage of Ju-Ching, at T'ien T'ung Shan monastery. After five years, he returned to Japan in 1227.

Dogen continued to teach and write in monasteries in and around the old capital city of Kyoto until 1243. During this time, he came increasingly in conflict with the predominant Tendai tradition and eventually withdrew into the mountains to establish the Eikei monastery. To this day, Eikeiji is the principal monastery of the Soto branch of Japanese Zen Buddhism.

Many of life's numerous problems, Dogen realized, are not easily solvable. There is, for example, the problem of the impermanence of life. Life passes like the rush of a spring stream, flowing on, day after day, and then it is gone. Dogen, therefore, urged humans not to waste a single second. Time must be utilized in a worthy pursuit, a single objective that merits an all-out effort. The life goal must be nothing small, selfish, or narrow-minded. It must be chosen from a broad perspective and with an eye to benefiting others as well as oneself. Dogen's philosophy is, in essence, a prescription for an unwasted or noble life, a life of happiness here and now.

It is difficult, of course, Dogen realized, to choose how to live, and equally difficult, if not more so, to carry out that choice. One lives in an uncertain and hurried world, and "our minds go racing about like horses running wild in the

Dogen

Dogen, a Zen monk since early youth who traveled to China for further studies, gained a reputation as a strict teacher. His writings have had a profound influence up to the present day. Many of his works have been translated into English and have played an important part in the growth of Zen Buddhism. The following are his prescriptions for virtuous activity.

To plow deep but plant shallow is the way to a natural disaster. When you help yourself and harm others, how could there be no consequences?

Everyone has the nature of Buddha; do not foolishly demean yourself.

Even worldly people, rather than study many things at once without really becoming accomplished in any of them, should just do one thing well and study enough to be able to do it even in the presence of others.

While simply having the appearance of an ordinary person of the world, one who goes on harmonizing the inner mind is a genuine aspirant to the Way. Therefore as an Ancient said, "Inside empty, outside accords." What this means is to have no selfish thought in the inner mind, while the outer appearance goes along with others.

Emperor Wen of Sui said, "Secretly cultivate virtue, await fulfillment."... If one just cultivates the work of the Way, the virtues of the Way will appear outwardly of their own accord.

To practice the appropriate activity and maintain bearing means to abandon selfish clinging.... The essential meaning of this is to have no greed or desire.

Students of the Way, do not think of waiting for a later day to practice the Way. Without letting this day and this moment pass by, just work from day to day, moment to moment.

It is written (in the *Vinaya*),

"What is praised as pure in character is called good; what is scorned as impure in character is called bad." It is also said, "That which would incur pain is called bad; that which should bring about happiness is called good."

In this way should one carefully discriminate; seeing real good, one should practice it, and seeing real evil, one should shun it.

Jade becomes a vessel by carving and polishing. A man becomes humane by cultivation and polish. What gem has highlights to begin with? What person is clever at the outset? You must carve and polish, train and cultivate them. Humble yourselves and do not relax your study of the Way.

There is a saying of Confucius: "You can't be apart from the Way for even a second. If you think you are apart from it, that's not the Way." He also said, "As the sages have no self, everything is themselves."

fields, while our emotions remain unmanageable like monkeys swinging in the trees." The rapidity of life and the uncertainty of its course make people's lives full of torment and confusion. They do not understand its nature or how best to manage themselves.

Moreover, according to Dogen, the mind overwhelmed by a world not understood seeks safety in selfish and self-protective acts. Life is perceived as a succession of real and suspected dangers, and it is viewed in stark contrasts of good and bad, right and wrong, black and white. This perception of the world is what Dogen called the "Lesser Vehicle," and it arises out of ignorance and fear. The ignorant, fearful mind constructs a list of things deemed bad and to be avoided, and anger and resentment are felt toward perceived sources of danger. The individual caught in a dark and threatening world he does not understand finds little rest or peace, and doing violence to himself or others is a frequent consequence of his entrapment.

This state of malcontent, according to Dogen, in which the world is perceived in terms of stark and fearful divisions, remains with the individual until he or she achieves clarification about the true nature of things. But everyone, Dogen said, has the nature of Buddha. Everyone can see the truth and live calmly and peacefully in its presence. It is simply necessary to abandon the selfish and narrow perspective in favor of the broad and unbiased view, in which the mind is expanded beyond the limitations of divisive categories like good/bad and desirable/undesirable; in which greed gives way to generosity, self-serving to other-serving. It is necessary to see things as the ancient sages did, from the perspective of the universe or "Buddha-Dharma" or "universal Self." To do this is to practice the Great Way.

Understanding from this broad perspective, Dogen thought, also involves acceptance—going along with things, following the Way. This, he said, is the wisdom of emptiness—allowing things to be, without exercising any preference or desire whatsoever. The similarity to the philosophy of Chuang Tzu is evident.

How does one acquire this perspective of the universal Self? For Dogen, the answer is practice—seeking to help others without reward or praise, caring for others as a parent would. If one makes a continuous effort to do all things with a parental mind and without seeking profit or praise, then one's life will be suffused with the attitude of a "Joyful Mind," in which life takes on a buoyancy and lightness that cannot be diminished by any external event.

Thus Dogen endeavored to set forth a way to achieve permanent joy in *this* life, a way of living that enables the human to achieve a majestic dignity, uncompromisable nobility of character, and peace. "No one or anything could ever make merit decay in any way," he said. In his precepts, Dogen continued the tradition begun by Chuang Tzu, Lao Tzu, and Hui Neng. Life does involve suffering, pain, and transience. But despite the presence of these and of evil, too, life, if lived according to the Tao, should be a joyful and fulfilling event. Dogen urged, "Rejoice in your birth in the world." If one does not escape the fears and insecurities of the small self, life is a torment. But if one lives as would the Magnanimous Mind, then one is living out the truth of the Way itself—the Way of the Buddha-Dharma.

Hinduism

No chapter on Eastern philosophy would be complete without at least a brief look at Hinduism. **Hinduism,** from the Urdu word for India, *Hind,* is the Western term for the religious beliefs and practices of the majority of the Indian people.

Ommmmm

During the 1960s Indian philosophy, or what passed for it, became popular in the American youth culture, thanks in part to the Beatles' interest in it and in the music of the Indian sitar master Ravi Shankar. In San Francisco and New York and Madison, Wisconsin, it was common to see hippies chanting, "ommmm," "ommmm," "ommmm" in an effort to induce a mystical state of higher consciousness.

What is "ommm"? It's the sound of the letters A, U, and M, which are the symbols in Hindu writings for the three ordinary states of consciousness: waking experience, dreaming sleep, and deep sleep. There is in addition, according to Hinduism, a fourth state (in Vedanta philosophy, *moksa*), one of higher awareness, which is described in the *Mandukya Upanishad* as "the coming to peaceful rest of all differentiated existence." *Yoga* is the general term for the spiritual disciplines in Hinduism and Buddhism that aim at the attainment of this higher state. It is also the name of one of the six orthodox systems of Hindu philosophy (see text).

The origins of Hinduism stretch back into the unknown past. Unlike other religions, it had no founder, and there is no single religious body to judge orthodoxy. In fact, Hinduism does not even contain a unified set of doctrines—or, to the extent it does, they are given diversified interpretations. All this makes it difficult to talk about Hinduism in a limited space. Speaking of Hinduism as a single belief system is something like speaking of philosophy in the same way. It is best to view it as a spiritual attitude that gives rise to a wide range of religious and philosophical beliefs and practices. These range from the worship of village and forest deities, which often take zoomorphic forms, to sophisticated metaphysical theories.

Common to all forms of Hinduism, however, is acceptance of the authority of the Vedic scriptures as the basis for understanding the true hidden nature of things. The *Vedas* are the most ancient religious texts of Hinduism—indeed, they are the oldest religious texts in an Indo-European language. The *Veda* was the literature of the Aryans, who invaded northwest India around 1500 B.C. Many, if not most, Hindu writings are commentaries on the Vedic scriptures.

In terms of popular religion, three contemporary movements might be mentioned. *Saivism* worships Siva as the supreme being and source of the universe; *Saktism* worships Sakti, the female part of the universe, and wife of Siva. *Vaisnavism* worships the personal god Vishnu. Buddha, according to orthodox Hindus, was an incarnation (*avatar*) of Vishnu.

The basis of Hindu *philosophy* is the belief that reality is absolutely one, that there is only one ultimate reality-being-consciousness. Six classical philosophical schools or traditions, however, interpret this reality variously: these six "insights," as they are called, are *Nyāya, Vaiśesika, Sāmkhya, Yoga, Mīmāmsā,* and *Vedānta*. All are designed to lead the searcher to a knowledge of the Absolute and the liberation of the soul. Vedanta is the best known in the West (*Vedanta* means "the end of the Veda").

Philosophically, the most important Vedic scripture is the last book, the *Upanishads.* The *Upanishads,* which date from about the eighth to the fifth centuries B.C., are the inspiration for the six systems of philosophy just mentioned. The *Upanishads* are best known for the theories of *brahman* (the ultimate cosmic principle or reality) and *atman* (the inner self), and the identification of *brahman* with *atman.* There are four great sayings (*mahavakya*) of the *Upanishads,* which are all ways of saying that *brahman* and *atman* are one:

1. Consciousness is *brahman.*
2. That art thou.
3. The self is *brahman.*
4. I am *brahman.*

Now, *brahman* is considered the ultimate reality or principle and the source and sustainer of all things, including people and gods. It is absolute and eternal spirit—the supreme consciousness, the One, the One-and-only-One. A lower manifestation of *brahman*—namely, *brahma*—may be thought of as an individual deity or personal god, but *brahman* itself is without attributes or qualities. This absolute remains the hidden, unknown, ultimate mystery.

Atman, on the other hand, is the self, the soul, the principle of individual life. Ultimately, however, the individual must come to a realization, through meditation and contemplation, that *brahman* and *atman* are the same thing—*brahman-atman.* With the realization of this absolute oneness of all things comes recognition of the relative nonreality of the world and of the individual ego. The identification of *brahman* and *atman* is sometimes spoken of by commentators as a pantheism, but it goes beyond the claim that all things are God. In Hinduism, the gods are parts or symbolic personifications of the absolute principle, *brahman.*

Further, the identification of *brahman* and *atman* has been subject to various interpretations over the centuries. It has been looked on both as transcendent and as an immanent. Samkara, who is thought to have lived between A.D. 788 and 820 (though these dates are controversial) and who gave the most rigorous interpretation of the *Upanishads,* was a pure monist who thought that all things are one—only the ultimate principle exists, and all else is an illusion. But another way of looking at the ultimate principle or reality was introduced by Rāmānuja (b. A.D. 1027). He believed in the ultimate principle, but he also believed that souls are real and that the world is not merely an illusion. For a time, at least, the souls and the world must be separate from the ultimate principle in order to be of service to it, he held.

Yet a third way of interpreting the underlying ultimate reality is represented by the outright dualism of Madhva (1199–1278), who believed that, although the ultimate principle is the cause of the world, the soul still has a separate and independent existence of its own. You can see that Hindu philosophy in fact admits a variety of viewpoints.

Much of the wisdom of Hinduism in all times lies in its sages. This certainly holds true for this century, whose wise men include Rabīndranāth Tagore (1861–

1941), Aurobindo Ghose (1872–1950), and Mohandas K. Gandhi (1869–1948). Tagore won the Nobel Prize in 1913 for his poetry, in which he expressed the human quest for freedom and the divine. Aurobindo, who was educated in the West, sought political freedom for India. After being accused of terrorism and violence, he withdrew from political life altogether and developed a theory of spiritual evolution according to which the individual through self-effort can rise to ever higher states of spiritual consciousness.

Gandhi, of course, is known everywhere for his use of nonviolence to help attain political freedom for India and for striving to instill a sense of self-respect in all human beings (he called the lowest caste, the "untouchables," the children of God). Through the example of his simple life and teachings, Gandhi tried to make the traditional values of Hinduism available to all.

The Philosophy of the Samurai (c. 1100–1900)

Japan's warrior class, the **samurai,** were also the ruling class for long periods of time. Their wisdom was transmitted in the form of martial precepts, the earliest dating to the twelfth century or earlier. These precepts were handed down the generations within the class, and they were often used to train the samurai and to teach them the art of ***bushido,*** that is, the art of being a samurai warrior.

The literature of the samurai tradition has influenced all areas of Japanese thought and behavior. Westerners who have wished to understand the basis of the Japanese economic "miracle" since World War II have looked to such samurai classics as Miyamoto Musashi's *A Book of Five Rings* and Yamamoto Tsunetomo's *Hagakure.* Also influential in determining the samurai world view were the Chinese classical views, including the writings of Confucius, Lao Tzu, and Sun Tzu as well as the *I Ching* or *Book of Changes.* **Miyamoto Musashi** (1584–1645) was one of Japan's greatest swordsmen and military strategists. His ideas teach martial strategy, but they seem to lend themselves equally well to business methods and to life generally. **Yamamoto Tsunetomo** (1659–1719) served only a short time as a retainer before his master died. Thereafter, he withdrew from the world and lived as a recluse studying Zen Buddhism. During the final years of his life, his thoughts on the essence of the samurai way of life were written down and preserved. The ideals of the samurai tradition have endured and still determine to no small extent the life and thought of modern-day Japan.

The world view expressed in Tsunetomo's *Hagakure* will be familiar to readers of the material on Dogen. Human life at best Tsunetomo sees as "a short affair." No time may be squandered without regret and loss. Yet brevity is not what makes life so difficult and painful; this effect comes rather from life's uncertainty. Humans exist in a world of constant and unpredictable change.

When these changes are not anticipated, the result is often disastrous. Therefore, a samurai must train himself to be ready at all times for anything that may

The Ancient Philosophies Today

Early in its history, Taoism had a relatively strong influence on rulers in China. But as Confucianism replaced it as the dominant value system within society, beginning with the T'ang dynasty (618–906), it increasingly focused on religious functions, an area in which it eventually had to compete with Buddhism. More and more, Taoism came to encompass magic, soothsaying, and incantations for healing and for warding off evil spirits. To this day, Taoist priests perform ceremonies at funerals and on other important occasions. Reportedly, Taoist hermits are still living out the highest forms of Taoist practice in the mountains of China.

As Confucianism established itself as the dominant moral and political philosophy, the Confucian classics became the basis of civil service examination, and in this way Confucianism became even further embedded into Chinese thinking. Between the eleventh and eighteenth centuries, there was a significant Neoconfucian movement, one of whose major figures was Wang Yang-ming (1472–1529).

Confucianism received a severe blow from the Communist revolution in 1949, and Mao Tsetung made it a repeated target for ridicule. This does not mean that Mao was not himself influenced by Confucius both in his style of writing and of ruling, nor does it mean that Mao was loathe to use Confucianism to his own ends—for example, in transferring the individual's family allegiance to state allegiance. In any case, after Mao, Confucian thought is again making itself apparent.

Chinese Buddhism developed a number of different schools from the fourth to the ninth centuries. Ch'an Buddhism was especially powerful and innovative during the seventh to ninth centuries. Chinese Buddhist temples have provided religious services for the people from that time even until the present day. Further, the influence of Ch'an Buddhism spread to Japan, where Zen Buddhism and other forms of Buddhism have endured until the present. Currently Zen Buddhism especially enjoys growing popularity in the United States and the West generally.

happen. He must train to anticipate all eventualities and deal with them before they become a problem. A samurai precept is, "Win beforehand."

According to Tsunetomo, not only the uncertainty of events is problematic. Human beings themselves are often flawed, ignorant, selfish, and unreasonable. Accordingly, the samurai must learn to be self-reliant. He cannot and does not depend on others acting properly. He knows that human beings will not always act either reasonably or justly. He is prepared for treachery and cowardice and awaits their arrival. Only by practicing alertness and bravery can a samurai avoid wasting his life.

Because of the uncertainty of the world and the unreliability of the human character, the samurai must learn the arts of war as well as the arts of peace. Human beings, like states, must be able to defend themselves. Kuroda Nagamasa (1568–1623), known as a great military strategist, wrote: "The arts of peace and the arts of war are like the wheels of a cart which, lacking one, will have difficulty in standing."

The samurai strives to realize Confucius's notion of the complete man, who is both scholar and warrior. Life requires constant training and learning. Without learning, a person would be ignorant of what is necessary; without hard training, he would be unable to carry the necessary actions into effect quickly and efficiently. The samurai works hard to know where his duty lies and to carry it out "unflinchingly." To do this, he hardens himself to suffering. He welcomes death if it comes in pursuit of duty. He learns to abhor luxury and considerations of money in order not to be attached to them or to life generally.

An important part of the samurai's study is past traditions, particularly the Confucian and other classical Chinese philosophies, and Zen Buddhism. These determine and shape *bushi* (see the box on governance) and are in turn unified and synthesized by *bushi* into a single, effective way of life.

The Influence of Confucius

As mentioned, the model of the perfect samurai closely shadows the Confucian idea of the complete man. He is a scholar warrior, literate yet deeply knowledgeable about practical affairs. He knows that life involves change and that survival depends on understanding the inner workings of change. Though a few samurai teachers emphasized the art of war and the ways of increasing courage, more usual is the view of the *Hagakure*. Here the samurai is called on to develop his knowledge of whatever might be useful, "querying every item night and day." Above all, he must understand the Confucian principle of the Mean: more than merely the middle way between two extremes, the Mean is the universal standard that determines what is right and appropriate. The wise samurai reads the sayings of the ancients as the best way to find out what the Mean recommends and how best to follow it.

For Confucius, the three basic and interrelated qualities to be pursued are humanity, wisdom, and courage. According to the samurai tradition, these virtues allow those who have them to enjoy a useful life of service as well as a life free from anxiety and fear.

As Confucius also prescribed, the samurai should be filial, making every effort to respect and honor his parents; he should be polite, discreet in manners and conduct, proper in dress and speech, and upright and sincere. He must not lie. There is the story, for example, of the samurai who refused to take an oath because the word of the samurai is more certain than any oath.

In historical Japan, those who possessed these qualities exhibited enormous dignity. The samurai's dignity displayed itself in every action and in every word. His solemn behavior and resoluteness frequently struck fear in the ordinary observer. The samurai code sought to create a character that was flawless in behavior and taut in spirit.

Another samurai virtue had its roots in the philosophy of Confucius: the samurai was to be economical, and, as noted, avoid luxury. He was to save what he could, but only with an eye to using it on campaign when it was needed.

Because of his virtues, the samurai could be expected to establish and maintain an ordered state in the midst of the most chaotic times. His own steady and unshakeable behavior would then serve as a model to be trusted and followed by all others. This, of course, is a Confucian theme.

Courage and Poetry

Samurai warriors often sought to discipline their spirit and free themselves from fear by training with Buddhist masters. At various times, samurai and Zen monks both used poetry, especially short forms of poetry like *haiku*, to test the strength and validity of their insight into truth. At a critical moment, just before death, for example, a trainee was expected spontaneously to write a poem that revealed his perfect freedom under all circumstances, as well as the depth of his insight. He was expected to remain calm, clear-headed, and imperturbable even at the point of a sword. There are stories of captured warriors being spared death if they were sufficiently intrepid and their poem manifested deep wisdom.

The greatest of all the Japanese *haiku* writers was **Basho** (1644–1694). He was deeply involved with Zen, and his death poem is regarded as profound:

> Stick on a journey,
> Yet over withered fields
> Dreams wander on.

Dogen also gives an example of the genre:

> Scarecrow in the hillock
> Paddyfield
> How unaware! How useful!

Here are two more poems considered to reveal the deep insight and spontaneous expression of the truly free individual:

> Coming and going, life and
>   death:
> A thousand hamlets, a million
>   houses.
> Don't you get the point?
> Moon in the water, blossom in
>   the sky.
> —Gizan (1802–1878)

> Fifty-four years I've entered
>   [taught]
> Horses, donkeys, saving
>   limitless beings.
> Now farewell, farewell!
> And don't forget—apply
>   yourselves.
> —Jisso (1851–1904)

The Magnificent Seven

One of the most popular Hollywood movies of all time was the 1960 John Sturges Western, *The Magnificent Seven,* a story about seven gunslingers hired by a Mexican village as protection against a band of cutthroat bandits who preyed on the helpless villagers. Unknown to many American audiences at the time, the film was a remake of Akira Kurosawa's *The Seven Samurai* (1954), which at one point had been titled "The Magnificent Seven" for release in the United States. Kurosawa's story about a sixteenth-century Japanese village that hires professional warriors to protect them depicts the martial skill, humaneness, and strict sense of justice and honor of the samurai, whose virtues enable them to confront adversity unflinchingly and victoriously. Sturges's movie helped focus attention in America on Kurosawa's film, which in turn led to much interest in the United States in the samurai tradition.

Governance by the Warrior

According to William Scott Wilson's *Ideals of the Samurai*, the word *bushi* (samurai warrior) is first recorded in an early history of Japan, one dated A.D. 797. These educated warriors served at the time in close attendance to the nobility. The weakness of civil government, however, led to the practice of clans and private estates developing their own armies and to increasing involvement by samurai in government. The warrior class eventually replaced the court aristocracy, and the late twelfth century marked the beginning of warrior-class rule, which lasted seven hundred years.

The Influence of Zen Buddhism

It is slightly ironic that members of the warrior class in Japan went to Zen monks for training, for Zen monks dedicated their lives to saving all living beings. Kamakura, a Zen center, which dates back as far as the thirteenth century, was especially noted for training samurai warriors. Perhaps the most famous instance of this relationship was the influence of the Zen monk Takuan (1573–1645) on two of Japan's greatest swordsmen and strategists, Miyamoto Musashi and **Yagyu Munenori** (1571–1646). All three men produced classic works that were used in the training of samurai.

The samurai, recall, were warriors who trained themselves to be ready at any moment to fight to the death. The ability to fight, of course, is frequently hampered by fear; for fear, if it does not paralyze a fighter completely, may well prevent the lightning-fast response that may be the difference between winning and losing. Though samurai engaged in ceaseless martial arts training, a state of fearlessness sometimes escaped even the best of them. Some samurai, therefore, sought out Zen masters in order to free themselves of their own fear.

Fear, according to the Zen Buddhist, arises from an excessive attachment or clinging to things and to life generally, a perspective of possessiveness from which anything and everything is viewed as a threat. The remedy to fear—the samurai learned from the Zen masters—is to free oneself from attachments and personal preferences, to rid oneself of the desire to possess anything, including life itself. The samurai was taught to overcome himself, so to speak—to free himself from all thoughts of gain or loss. He was taught to accept what happens without joy or sadness, without complaint, and even without resignation. This hard lesson was thought to require constant meditation on death, so that the warrior was ready to "die completely without hesitation or regret."

In this way Zen training sought to rid the samurai of the self-imposed paralysis of fear. Both the Zen and the samurai traditions shared the same ideal: to attain *an unobstructed state of instant, untainted response*. For the samurai this state of mind was the key to total preparedness.

The samurai tradition therefore emphasized that through a vigorous training of the body and the mind the individual can perfect his character to respond im-

Samurai Insights (from Yamamoto Tsunetomo, *The Hagakure*)

Everything in this world is a marionette show.

[The samurai] remains undistracted twenty-four hours a day.

A samurai's word is harder than metal.

The Way of the samurai is in desperateness. Ten or more men cannot kill such a man.

With an intense, fresh, and undelaying spirit, one will make his judgment within the space of seven breaths. It is a matter of being determined and having the spirit to break right through to the other side.

If one will do things for the benefit of others and meet even those whom he has met often before in a first-time manner, he will have no bad relationships.

A samurai's obstinacy should be excessive.

It is natural that one cannot understand deep and hidden things. Those things that are easily understood are rather shallow.

Courage is gritting one's

teeth . . . and pushing ahead, paying no attention to the circumstances.

There is nothing other than the single purpose of the present moment.

I never knew about winning . . . but only about not being behind in a situation.

There is nothing that one should suppose cannot be done.

One must be resolved in advance.

Human life is a short affair. It is better to live doing the things that you like.

If one will rectify his mistakes, their traces will soon disappear.

At a glance, every individual's own measure of dignity is manifested just as it is.

One cannot accomplish things simply with cleverness.

By being impatient, matters are damaged and great works cannot be done. If one considers something not to be a matter of time, it will be done surprisingly quickly.

A man's life should be as toilsome as possible.

People become imbued with the idea that the world has come to an end and no longer put forth any effort. This is a shame. There is no fault in the times.

When I face the enemy, of course it is like being in the dark. But if at that time I tranquilize my mind, it becomes like a night lit by a pale moon. If I begin my attack from that point, I feel as though I will not be wounded.

It is the highest sort of victory to teach your opponent something that will be to his benefit.

Win first, fight later.

There is nothing so painful as regret.

Money is a thing that will be there when asked for. A good man is not so easily found.

Meditation on inevitable death should be performed daily. . . . It is to consider oneself as dead beforehand.

mediately to any situation. Such training can create a resolute single-mindedness, in which the present moment is all there is and the present action alone is real, that is both efficient and powerful.

The ultimate goal of both Zen Buddhist and samurai training is the state of *mushin,* that is, the state of no mind, no thought. This is a state of awareness beyond calculation in which one moves "no-mindedly" in the here and now, doing exactly what is appropriate without any hesitation. This mind is the "secret" of the great swordsmen like Musashi and Yagyu Munenori.

The samurai tradition, together with Confucianism and Zen Buddhism, provided the Japanese with a noble ideal of character, a context in which the efficiency of Japanese society, and much of what is good and successful in Japan, may perhaps be understood. Certainly the vision of the noble person who trains all his life to be of benefit to others seems a fulfillment of the ideal of humanity put forward by Confucius, Zen, and the samurai. On the other hand, the chauvinist nationalism of the Japanese in World War II, the unquestioning obedience to authority, and the glorification of death may also perhaps be explained by reference to these same influences. It is interesting to speculate what these traditions might have yielded, what their effect on Japanese society might have been, if they had been stripped of their authoritarian and excessively militaristic qualities.

Checklist

To help you review, here is a checklist of the key philosophers and concepts of this chapter. The brief descriptive sentences summarize leading ideas. Keep in mind that some of these summary statements represent terrific oversimplifications of complex positions.

Philosophers

- **Confucius** Founder of the most dominant system of Chinese thought; emphasized the perfectibility of people as well as their ability to affect things for the better.

- **Mencius** Confucian thinker second in importance to Confucius.

- **Hsün Tzu** Confucian philosopher who set forth a blend of Confucianism and Taoism.

- **Lao Tzu** Founder of Taoism; held that the Tao is ineffable and beyond our ability to alter; emphasized the importance of effortless nonstriving.

- **Chuang Tzu** Most important Taoist after Lao Tzu; stressed the equality of opposites and the danger of usefulness.

- **Sun Tzu** Sixth-century B.C. Taoist philosopher and general; applied Taoist philosophy to military strategy.

- **Siddhartha Gautama Buddha** Indian prince, founder of Buddhism. Sought the causes of and cures for human suffering.

- **Hui Neng** Sixth patriarch of Chinese Zen; emphasized the oneness of all things.

- **Murasaki Shikibu** Influential Japanese Mahayana Buddhist philosopher of the late tenth and early eleventh centuries. Held that women were responsible moral agents who were capable of enlightenment and could influence their destinies, reach *nirvana,* and achieve salvation.

- **Dogen Zenji** Japanese Zen monk; stressed the importance of acquiring the perspective of the universal Self, given the impermanence of life.

- **Miyamoto Musashi, Yamamoto Tsunetomo, Yagyu Munenori** Samurai writers who helped record and preserve samurai ideals of preparedness; indifference to pain, death, and material possessions; wisdom; and courage.

- **Basho** Greatest Japanese haiku writer.

- **Al-Kindi (Ya'qūb ibn-Ishāq al-Kindi)** Ninth-century Islamic thinker; used Greek ideas to define God as an absolute and transcendent being.

- **Al-Fārābī** Ninth-century Islamic philosopher; posited the philosopher-prophet as the one providing the necessary illumination for his society.

- **Avicenna (Abū 'Ali ibn-Sīnā)** Tenth-century Islamic thinker; felt that there is a parallelism between philosophy and theology.

- **Al-Ghazālī (Abū Hamid al-Ghazālī)** Late-eleventh-century and early-twelfth-century Islamic philosopher; attacked Avicenna regarding the eternity of the world and the reduction of religious law to a mere symbol of higher truths.

- **Averroës** Twelfth-century Islamic thinker; was thought of as holding two separate truths, that of religion and that of philosophy.

- **Sadr al-Dīn als Shīrazī** Late-sixteenth- and early-seventeenth-century thinker; influenced by the mystical tendencies in neoplatonism, he sought a return to the first principle of being.

- **Kabir** Late-fifteenth- and early-sixteenth-century Indian poet, considered one of the great mystical poets in the tradition of Sufism.

Concepts

Confucianism

Way/Tao

Mean

sage

rectification

Analects

jen

Taoism

yin/yang

soft and supple

Buddhism

Four Noble Truths

Eightfold Path

karma

nirvana

Sufism

Ch'an Buddhism

Zen Buddhism

dhyana

dharma

kami

reincarnation

Rinzai Zen

Soto Zen

satori

koan

zazen

Hinduism

Veda

Upanishads

Vishnu

brahman

atman

samurai

bushido

haiku

mushin

"win beforehand"

Questions for Discussion and Review

1. Do you agree with Confucius's belief in the goodness and perfectibility of humans? Give reasons.

2. What is the Tao?

3. Compare and contrast the philosophies of Confucius and Lao Tzu. Take sides, and determine whose prescriptions are soundest and why.

4. Evaluate Mencius's idea that difficulty and suffering are opportunities to develop independence and peace of mind.

5. Do the subjects of the state adopt the ethical standards of their leaders? Or is it the other way around?

6. "Benevolence subdues its opposite just as water subdues fire." Evaluate this claim.

7. Are Lao Tzu's prescriptions for behavior realistic and practical? Explain.

8. Are power and riches chains, or are they the keys to freedom and happiness?

9. Do you believe in reincarnation? Why?

10. What is the sound of one hand clapping? Is this an intelligible question?

11. Comment on Hui Neng's poem of enlightenment (see box).

12. How did Mahayana Buddhism reinforce sexism and elitism?

13. Why would suicide help a woman achieve salvation under Mahayana Buddhism?

14. How did Murasaki Shikibu's philosophy challenge Buddhist doctrines of *karma,* enlightenment, and salvation?

15. How important is it to have a life goal?

16. Is it possible for a person completely to abandon selfish desires?

17. How important is it to be self-reliant? Is total self-reliance possible?

18. Should the complete person be both wise and brave? If you wished to improve your wisdom or free yourself from fear, what would you do? How would you know if you had succeeded?

Suggested Further Readings

John Blofield, *The Secret and Sublime* (New York: E. P. Dutton, 1973). A very readable presentation of the philosophy of Taoism, popular Taoism, Taoist mysticism, and the relationship of Taoism and yogic practices.

Brian Carr, ed., *Companion Encyclopedia of Asian Philosophy* (London: Routledge), 1995.

Wing-tsit Chan, *A Source Book in Chinese Philosophy* (Princeton: Princeton University Press, 1963). First-rate anthology of Chinese philosophical writings placed in historical and philosophical context.

Diane Collinson and Robert Wilkinson, *Thirty-Five Oriental Philosophers* (New York: Routledge, 1994). A comprehensive overview of Eastern philosophy.

Confucius, *The Analects,* D. C. Lau, trans. (New York: Penguin, 1979). A good, inexpensive, and readily available collection of Confucius's philosophical insights.

Dogen and Kosho Uchiyama, *Refining Your Life,* Thomas Wright, trans. (New York: Weatherhill, 1983). Dogen in this short treatise on Zen cooking provides an extraordinary method of performing any activity well and of living life as a whole.

Aislee T. Embree, ed., *The Hindu Tradition* (New York: Vintage Books, 1972). Readings that review the development of Hindu thought from the beginnings to the present.

D. C. Lau, trans., *Mencius* (Hammondsworth, England: Penguin, 1970). A highly readable translation of Mencius's writings.

Trevor Leggett, *Zen and the Ways* (Rutland, Vt.: Charles E. Tuttle, 1987). Shows how the meditative calmness taught in Zen can be applied to the ways of the martial arts and of life generally.

Murasaki Shikibu, *Tale of Genji/Genji Monogatari.* Many, many editions available at most public libraries.

Miyamoto Musashi, *A Book of Five Rings,* Victor Harris, trans. (New York: Bantam, 1982). Written by the most famous swordsman and samurai, this is the great book of Japanese strategy. It is a guide for making decisions and acting decisively in even the worst of times.

Sarvepalli Radhakrishnan and Charles A. Moore, *A Source Book in Indian Philosophy* (Princeton: Princeton University Press, 1957). A splendid historical selection of philosophical writings with background information.

D. Howard Smith, *Confucius and Confucianism* (London: Paladin, 1973). Places the teachings of Confucius in historical context and treats the interaction of Confucianism with Taoism and Buddhism.

Yamamoto Tsunetomo, *Hagakure* (Tokyo: Kodansha International, 1979). The seventeenth-century classic that encapsulates the ethics, strategies, and world view of the samurai class. Enlightening in itself, the *Hagakure* can also be used to understand contemporary Japanese ways of thinking.

Chuang Tzu, *The Complete Works,* Burton Watson, trans. (New York: Columbia University Press, 1968). A highly regarded translation of Chuang Tzu that is said to retain the wit of the philosopher himself.

Lao Tzu, *Tao Te Ching* (New York: Penguin, 1973). A good and inexpensive translation of a classic.

Waithe, Mary Ellen, *A History of Women Philosophers,* Vol. 2, *Medieval Women Philosophers, 500–1600* (Dordrecht, Boston and London: Kluwer Academic Publishers, 1989). Includes a chapter by Waithe on Murasaki Shikibu.

Post-Colonial Thought

17

by Gregory Tropea

. . . the true criterion of leadership is spiritual. Men are attracted by spirit. By power, men are forced. Love is engendered by spirit. By power, anxieties are created.

—*Malcolm X (el-Hajj Malik el-Shabazz)*

I cannot understand what indigenous theory there might be that can ignore the reality of nineteenth-century history.

—*Gayatri Chakravorty Spivak*

In this chapter we survey post-colonial thought in Africa, the Americas, and Asia. Post-colonial thought is an essentially modern phenomenon. Growing out of group experiences of colonialist domination on every populated continent, it is shaping new work in ethics, metaphysics, epistemology, political philosophy, and every other subdiscipline of philosophy. Some well-known post-colonial thinkers include Mahatma Gandhi, Martin Luther King, Jr., Fidel Castro, Malcolm X, and Desmond Tutu.

These and other post-colonial thinkers have brought traditional and radical ideas together in a uniquely modern synthesis that opens up new possibilities of practical engagement for philosophy. Whether reflecting through a history of slavery, systematic marginalization, or overt repression, post-colonial thinkers do their work in a time which they perceive to be overshadowed by deep cultural traumas that have occurred in the histories of their respective peoples. Such traumas the world over have left indigenous traditions self-consciously compromised and needful of imaginative reconstruction from within. Post-colonial thought addresses this need by taking up problems of cultural dissolution and challenges to the coherence of previously unquestioned worldviews just as any modern way of thinking must. As is true of modern thought generally, post-colonial thought does not advocate an uncritical acceptance of the notion of progress; indeed, post-colonial thought problematizes the phenomenon of progress along the same lines as recent Continental philosophy.

The essential modernity of all expressions of post-colonial thought is a unifying factor that overcomes the undeniable differences among the philosophical endeavors of various cultural groups. It means also that while the claims, arguments, and explanations of post-colonial philosophy exhibit a distinctive constellation of common features, the shared modern methodology of post-colonial thinkers also places them in a close *generic* relationship to each other. Some of those same features also serve to relate post-colonial thinkers to many of the contemporary philosophers discussed in other chapters. Realization of this connection has occurred only recently in the history of ideas. Interestingly, the nature of the relationship between post-colonial and other modern philosophers has itself become a topic of conversation in post-colonial philosophy.

One of the issues in this conversation is the question of what shall count as a warranted claim. This is important because philosophers tend to be especially careful to avoid claims that cannot be rigorously justified. Although modern culture has for the most part standardized on the scientific method as the preferred way to obtain and validate knowledge, no such agreement exists among the traditional societies that are evolving into post-colonial cultures. From a modernist perspective, in which the efficacy of scientific technology is unquestioned, alternative ways of thinking can look quaint or whimsical. Assuming the universal seriousness of human attempts to understand self and world, however, this dismissive sort of judgment risks missing an important philosophical point: any way of knowing is intimately bound up with one's metaphysical understanding of the nature of the world and existence in it. Thus, a challenge to what one knows and how one knows is not necessarily *just* addressing the issue of whether a claim about an alleged fact is true, but can also be construed as a challenge to one's deepest beliefs. This is a point of no small significance for post-colonial thought, which deals in part with the effects of precisely such challenges. The epistemological problem first arises with the impressive achievements of the science and technology of the colonizing or oppressing forces. Claims supported by this technology possess a certain power, but when credibility in one area is presumed to generalize to other areas, unwarranted propositions result. For example, when Western science is pressed into service to address some specific problem in a nontechnological culture, there exists also the possibility that it may serve as the basis for inferences that undermine religion in that culture. Post-colonial thinkers have argued for metaphysical and epistemological versions of the legal notion of severability, the idea that if one part of an agreement cannot be fulfilled, the other parts remain in force. If followed, this advice would have the effect of preserving at least some subset of the indigenous conceptions that had evolved over thousands of years into an agreed traditional consensus.

The streams of wisdom and understanding that converge in post-colonial thought are diverse, and many influences are hard to fix historically. In traditions with an ancient written literature, of course, texts that can be dated with a degree of certainty provide historians with a convenient way to mark the beginning of a thread of philosophy in some distant time or place. Indeed, it has been standard practice for historians of ideas to claim that philosophy began with the earliest writings on philosophical themes in Asian and European texts that we know to be thousands of years old. However, commencing with the critical study of non-Western languages in the nineteenth century, some European thinkers began to rethink the conceptual restriction of philosophy to the kinds of things that showed up in written texts. In one case, results from the discipline of hermeneutics suggested that the Dravidians of India could represent an ancient, preliterate tradition of philosophy, traces of which were detected by analysis of metaphysical shifts in the writings of the Aryans, who invaded Dravidian territory in the second millennium BC. This is an interesting case for post-colonial studies because it arguably illustrates the significant philosophical influence of a conquered people on an invading group and suggests that other such cases may be found. It also directs our attention to the possibility of an oral tradition of philosophy, which has been a marginal concept or even an outright categorical impossibility in the minds of some theorists.

In the post-colonial world, there is no agreement on how to integrate indigenous tradition into a modern philosophical project. There is agreement, however, on the centrality of a good liberal education. Then the question arises as to what the purpose or purposes of education might be. In the economically constrained circumstances of the Third World, it has been common for people to insist that education should be narrowly vocational and practical. But philosophy is not optional, argue the majority of post-colonial thinkers who write on the topic, because it is the best way to keep emerging nations conscious and aware of the implications of their decisions. The issue for these philosophers is not whether resources should be devoted to the teaching of philosophy, then, but rather what sort of philosophy is appropriate for their countries. Without an indigenous philosophical literature in many cases, philosophy in these nations needs to be invented almost from the ground up. Even in those countries with extensive philosophical literatures, however, revaluations of key concepts have led to the introduction of radically new ways of thinking that seek to recast entire traditional vocabularies.

Post-colonial thinkers have long since realized that direct appeals for justice, reasonable as they might be, are not sufficiently compelling to bring about change. This is why raising consciousness through philosophy has become such an important undertaking. It is one thing to affirm that justice is a social good and yet another to have an idea of what justice might be, what conditions might be prerequisite to it, and how the best intentions may be subverted by subtly conflicting ideological claims. Detailed analysis of these sorts of issues occurs frequently as post-colonial thought pursues the ideal of sustainable social justice.

Because the post-colonial style of analysis is closely tied to concrete historical conditions, the writing of history itself has become an issue for philosophical investigation. Historiography, which takes the writing of history as a matter to be studied and analyzed, typically begins with a preconception of causation in history, an overarching idea of why events happen as they do. Having such a preconception directs the search for facts and guides the selection of what is meaningful from the mass of data. Thus, individual elements can be assembled into a story with a definite logic and a point of view. Recognizing that there are no bare facts apart from a conceptual framework and that those who would report those facts would not have a "God's-eye view" to reveal them even if the possibility of perfectly simple atoms of truth existed, many post-colonial thinkers who take up the task of understanding history begin by making the choice of a conceptual framework within which the writing of history can have sense and purpose. As nineteenth-century positivism fades from influence, a principled perspectivism has become an accepted part of post-colonial writing. In the twentieth century, some flavor of Marxism has been the overwhelming theoretical choice among Third World writers even as Marxism has been overwhelmingly rejected by First World writers.

Among the topics most intensively developed in post-colonial studies of history and justice has been the matter of domination. This theme has been known to extend beyond quick intuitive understanding since Hegel's discussion early in the nineteenth century of master-slave dynamics, in which the powerlessness of the slave was shown to entail numerous unavoidable consequences for the master. As the post-colonial program began to require an analysis of justice that satisfied both experiential and critical needs, the nature of the links between the subjective apprehensions of the people and the systemic conditions under which they live began to come into view. For many thinkers, the international market system was the major force for injustice through a form of domination that reduces everything to a dollar value. This analysis is not unique to post-colonial thinkers, of course, but is shared in greater or lesser part with a number of modern philosophers outside the Third World.

Historical Background

In the premodern world, geographical and linguistic barriers ensured that most of humanity's ideas and techniques would originate and initially develop in relative isolation within their own particular cultures. The result: even now we often find distinctly different mythologies and ethical norms in groups whose territories border on each other. Although modern communications greatly facilitate the spread of ideas, we should recall that in the ancient world, such activities as trade, conquest, or itinerant teaching only rarely expanded the geographical distribution of any concept.

Occasionally, research turns up multiple instances of a concept arising apparently independently in several different, isolated places. Some examples are kinship concepts, ethical categories of right and wrong, certain logical relationships, and the psychological concept of the other. More typically in philosophy and religion, though, apparent similarities among concepts, worldviews, and schools of thought that arise independently in multiple cultures have only a coincidental, superficial relationship to each other; even so, it has not been unusual for those who detect resonances of their own views in other cultures to claim a common grounding in human universals. From anthropology we learn to be very careful in making comparisons of concepts across cultures or historical periods.

Oral Philosophy

The search for wisdom and understanding occurs everywhere, but it must begin somewhere. Before any direct statement of abstract principles or any intentional construction of a rational system of thought comes the telling of stories of desire, of bravery, of ancestors, of trickery, of the unseen, and of all else that is important to people. In these narratives, which are often highly ambiguous, the world's cultures and subcultures have developed their unique visions and voices over thousands of years. As thoroughly as in literate cultures, oral traditions have transmitted complex value systems and their rationales. Exclusively oral traditions were fairly common until the middle of the twentieth century, but are fast either disappearing entirely or being supplemented with literacy. Thus, we are among the last generations that will be able to find the origins of philosophy right before our eyes in living oral traditions. Nigerian philosopher Olu Sodipo observes in this connection that "even if it is true that an idea or attitude needs to be reflective and critical in order to deserve being called philosophical, it does not follow that any idea or attitude that is not expressed in writing is *ipso facto* unphilosophical." Although continuing indigenous written traditions of philosophy exist only in the lineages of the Asian civilizations following China's lead and in the Indo-European civilizations ranging chronologically across northern Africa, India, Europe, and the European cultures of the New World, all cultures possess continuous oral and folk traditions.

Connections

The connections between post-colonial philosophy and what occurs elsewhere in the field of philosophy are many and substantial. Post-colonial thought includes critical analysis and ethical reasoning that address philosophy's concern for significance of insight and methodological sophistication, but it does so in a way that remains mindful of the lived world of marginalized and oppressed populations. Students of philosophy who have acquainted themselves with Hegel's world-historical grasp of his own work will see why this nineteenth-century German thinker—whose politics were anything but post-colonial—is a seminal influence in post-colonial thinking, especially with regard to its pronounced consciousness of historical context. This perspective is exactly what Nietzsche's methodological critiques argued for. We're not saying that post-colonial thought is Hegelian or Nietzschean, but rather and more generally that many themes and problems of academic philosophy in First World contexts also have identifiable influences and expressions in post-colonial thought.

With the advent of post-colonial consciousness, though, true cross-cultural commonality has become a much more frequent occurrence than ever before. Now, the development of similar viewpoints in the work of thinkers in several different modern cultures has become less likely to be a matter of mere coincidence and more likely to derive from participation in those common social/cultural realities that began to emerge in the fifteenth century, when the Spanish and

Portuguese shifted from thinking locally to thinking globally. This development in imperial thinking led the Iberian powers to pursue a comparatively simple strategy of colonization based on extracting traditionally valuable metals and other commodities from the areas under their control and taking them back to the mother country.

The Latin American pattern of colonialism was not precisely replicated in other colonial experiments. A different profile occurred when the British realized that their colonies could serve not only as sources of raw materials, exotic produce, and precious minerals, but also as markets for manufactured goods. This changed everything. To support trade in manufactured goods, British colonies in the eighteenth century needed to be fully functioning economic entities. This plan determined that the social tone of eighteenth-century British colonies on the North American continent would be set by an unambiguously economic agenda that quickly supplanted the religious concerns that dominated in the seventeenth century. To a certain degree, the influences that shaped the self-understandings of the colonists worked similarly on native Americans. The indigenous inhabitants of areas colonized by the British seem to have acquired their sense of Old World values less through religious missions than through trade and territorial expansion, though missionary activity certainly did occur on a significant scale. The colonial pattern of relationship between whites and Indians of North America, which was based primarily on economic exploitation, continued after the American colonies won their independence. According to most histories, colonialism came to an end in the United States with the surrender of the British at Yorktown, but from an Indian perspective, nothing of the sort occurred.

Thus, colonial activity went beyond simple extraction of wealth to become linked to technological development for some imperial powers. At varying levels of integration, colonized peoples joined the world money economy whether they wanted to or not, and had to face all the cultural changes that such a development implies. Among the most dramatic effects of these policies was the impoverishment of rural India, which most analysts attribute directly to British mercantilism. There, centuries-old patterns of labor and exchange vanished within a few decades, creating not only economic hardship, but social dislocation as well. In Southeast Asia and some other areas where money economies could be sustained among the colonized population, the French instituted a colonial model that was midway between the Spanish strategy of simple transfer of valuable materials and the British strategy of constructing a dynamic trading system that had a reasonable chance of providing comparatively stable returns over the long term. Whatever the model, colonization entailed not only the violent physical subjugation of indigenous peoples, but also the introduction of the colonizers' values and beliefs into traditional societies around the world. The reduction of existence to financial equivalences is a continuing theme in post-colonial metaphysical critiques.

During the intense colonial activity of the eighteenth and nineteenth centuries and the first part of the twentieth, then, huge populations were participating directly or indirectly in some sort of militarily enforced experience of cultural contrast. Whether one was on the winning or the losing side, these events occurred on

Colonialism and the Church

From the very beginning of colonial activity in the fifteenth century, heated debate occurred within the Roman Catholic Church about the motives and methods involved in the introduction of European cultural norms and religion to indigenous populations. With the subjection of native peoples to European colonial masters whose well-known cruelties actually differed from indigenous imperialistic practices only a little, some clergy became concerned about associa-tions that would be made between these methods and Christianity's metaphysical and ethical teachings. Indeed, half a millennium later, many native groups, in the American West especially, still make a connection between colonial coercion and mission Christianity. The encounter of native peoples with Christianity cannot be categorized in purely negative terms, however, because in virtually all former colonies, active indigenous Christian communities of varying size and demographics exist. Of special note, Latin American thinkers have taken the religious consequences of colonialism as a key issue and are actively debating the ambiguous legacy of Europe's highest ideals and most violent behaviors. The religious turbulence initiated by colonial adventurism has evolved into a dynamic set of spiritual and philosophical challenges on several continents.

such a scale and with such intensity that reflective interpretation on all sides was virtually inevitable. The depth of this interpretation was not uniform by present standards, however. Some thinkers in the West, such as England's Herbert Spencer, pleased large followings in their own countries by celebrating successful military adventures as evidence of the natural superiority of the victorious imperial nation. Others, whose peoples had endured colonial domination, inclined to more critical efforts to come to terms with their experience. These latter reflections, which consciously situate themselves within a history of subjugation and revolutionary impulses, constitute the substance of post-colonial philosophy. In the colonial and former colonial powers, post-colonial thought has often been marginalized, summarily dismissed, or even totally ignored. Just the opposite has been the case among subjugated and formerly subjugated populations, however, for whom the analyses and calls to action of post-colonial thinkers have resonated powerfully, providing ethical and metaphysical understandings that ring true to lived experience. Frequently, post-colonial thinkers have become social and political leaders in their respective countries; the roster includes Mahatma Gandhi in India, Sun Yat-sen in China, Léopold Senghor in Senegal, Ho Chi Minh in Vietnam, Kwame Nkrumah in Ghana, Paulin Hountondji in Benin, Vaclav Havel in the Czech Republic, and numerous others.

Post-colonial philosophy is a diverse genre, but its voices share an intentionally substantial engagement with the historical realities of Third World peoples or those who have been systematically excluded from power in their societies. For these populations, the shared experience of domination has helped to structure a general revolutionary consciousness which often resists not only the values and conceptualizations of the colonizers, but the very methods of interpretation and decision of the oppressive culture. This critical commonality may be obscured at first glance by the variety of expression in post-colonial thought, a range of beliefs that includes advocacy of both violence and nonviolence, capitalism and utopian socialism, absolute standards and anarchic relativism, to touch on only a few of the categories. Further, post-colonial thinkers within their respective traditions frequently disagree among themselves in their valuations of events and situations; if one ever needed proof that radically different conclusions could be inferred from very similar historical facts, post-colonial philosophy would provide it.

In no small measure, though, post-colonial thought constitutes a distinctive category of endeavor because it consciously traces back to the ineluctable dislocations that ensued from encounters with conquerors whose imperialism aimed at nearly total domination. Although the invaders asserted both physical and philosophical superiority, their ideas have received at best a mixed reception in the lands they once controlled. Given the available historical and anthropological information, it seems most reasonable to believe that the commonalities of post-colonial thought around the world are not so much due to the conceptual similarities of the specific ideas introduced by different groups of colonizers as to the similarities among experiences of invasion and foreign domination. This is not a trivial claim in the analysis of post-colonial thought, for it locates post-colonial thought as a defining event in the history of subjugated peoples, rather than as a minor footnote in the intellectual history of colonizing powers. Post-colonial thought includes articulations of value systems and critical analyses that challenge the adequacy of the colonizers' understandings at every turn; this is partly reaction to the past and partly creation of the future through imagination of new ways of being and thinking.

Africa

Among the peoples of Africa and from there into the Western hemisphere, diverse languages and traditions have constructed richly variant worlds of thought and experience, each developing its own ways of speaking of the good, the true, and the real. In the philosophies of African cultures, as in the other major geographical groupings in world philosophy, one finds that certain themes tend to recur, while at the same time no single worldview or school of thought enjoys general acceptance. Very few universal claims apply accurately across the many expressions of the philosophical impulse in African cultures and their offshoots beyond Africa. Taken together, this impulse has come to be known as **Pan-African philosophy,** a term with a range of meanings in the late twentieth century. Understood in this inclusive sense, Pan-African philosophy reveals itself to be many philosophies in both content and method, all united by a geographical reference point. The first step in appreciating Pan-African philosophy as a cross-cultural phenomenon is to survey its realization in Africa itself.

Understanding Post-Colonial Thought

Post-colonial thought can be deceptively difficult to understand because metaphysical, epistemological, and stylistic assumptions shared by the writer and the intended audience may not be obvious to someone from outside that particular culture. In contrast to the emphasis on defensible universals and timeless principles found in most traditional philosophical essays, post-colonial writing usually includes an explicit sense of its occurrence in a concrete historical situation. This awareness of the circumstances of philosophical production, which is never far from the surface of the post-colonial text, can be somewhat disorienting to a reader accustomed to the stylistic conventions of academic philosophy. If one wants to understand the nuances of post-colonial thought, there is no substitute for background knowledge of the thinker's historical context. As is true of philosophy generally, post-colonial threads have developed their own specialized vocabularies. Perhaps more so than other areas of philosophy, post-colonial discourse includes technical terms drawn from existing general vocabulary that have become rich in emotive force.

By the way, this is a good place to note that this chapter's selections have been sequenced so that the earlier readings and introductory notes often provide background information for one or more selections that follow.

The study of African philosophy in the twentieth century presents some unique opportunities because of the sharp contrasts that occur in its truly multicultural milieu. Existing virtually side by side with contributions to international conversations on technical issues in semantics or the impact of technology on society are statements of ancient tribal memories and understandings transmitted by oral tradition. Of special significance, the centuries-long encounter of African cultures with powerful influences from outside Africa has inspired efforts in African and African-American communities to preserve and extend originally African intellectual and spiritual resources.

The many tensions and tragedies of colonialism and its aftermath constitute the complex origin of African post-colonial philosophy. In Africa, reconciliation of tradition and modernity is emerging as an increasingly important concern for the present generation of philosophers. Charting new directions in the last half of the twentieth century, they have often constructed their discourse purposefully to contribute to a distinctively African articulation of history of ideas and critical analysis. One point of agreement among most twentieth-century Pan-African philosophers is that both antecedent and contemporary energies must be taken up into thinking; with very few exceptions, neither pure traditionalism nor pure modernism is accepted as an adequate style of response to the issues that African philosophers and their societies face.

After centuries of contact between African and non-African cultures, it is difficult to isolate a set of purely traditional African philosophical positions today. Even employing complex strategies of textual analysis, this may be an impossible task, for in spite of the well-documented resistance of traditional cultures to new ideas, the transcultural movement of ideas has been the rule in the development of philosophy around the world. Some analysts maintain that when intellectual boundary-lines have been drawn in the past by non-Africans, they have been constructed to minimize the achievements of African cultures and transfer them elsewhere. In no small measure as a result of African critiques, the entire boundary-drawing enterprise—once commonplace in the history of ideas—has become seriously suspect. So now, when Africanists point out the high probability that Egyptian concepts figure prominently in the thinking of such European figures as Pythagoras and Plato, for example, they also serve to remind their readers of the broader point that, over the centuries, thinkers have always appropriated and re-worked the ideas of others, regardless of whatever cultural boundaries might exist. They also obviously make the point that Africa is to be viewed as a source of a share of those ideas.

We recall in this connection that the division between Mediterranean Africa and sub-Saharan Africa, so obvious today, seems to have been much less distinct before the comparatively recent desertification of huge areas in the northern part of the continent, so contact among the peoples of Africa did not entail overcoming quite the same geographical barriers in earlier times as now. Similarly, the distinction between Africa and Europe, more pronounced today than the north-south split in Africa itself, was not a very prominent consideration to the peoples of the ancient world who settled the coast of the Mediterranean and whose sense of place was more strongly defined by their shared relation to the sea than by the modern world-geographical categorization of continents. Given these facts, the most promising preliminary question to guide an inquiry into Pan-African philosophy, then, is not what a purely African philosophy precisely is, but *how philosophy has been done* in Africa and in the places outside Africa where Africans have resettled, whether voluntarily or by force. With this sensibility, African philosophy in the twentieth century comes into view as a modern development in thinking even as some of its exponents retrieve the most ancient traditional concepts extant on the continent where humanity originated.

Parts of Africa's oral traditions have been transcribed by missionaries, anthropologists, and linguists from both African and non-African cultures. Along the way, mistaken interpretations and intentional editorializations have corrupted the oral texts, which have then been quoted and passed on. Because the disputed readings are often those of non-Africans, an increasingly important issue within African studies has been the need to distinguish the ideas which indigenous peoples themselves take to constitute African traditions from the interpretations ventured speculatively or inferentially by those who have studied those traditions from an outside perspective. In more than a few cases historically, the original voices of African thought have been nearly lost in the overlays of analysis and interpretation. In one sense, philosophical activity cares less about what has been true in the past than about what is true in the present, but for post-colonial thought as an enterprise that is reconstructive in addition to being critical and constructive, the accuracy of accounts of traditional thinking is an issue.

Nearly as important as the issue of factual accuracy in representing African thought is a comparatively recent awareness in Pan-African philosophy that Africans must take the lead in defining their place in world philosophy, not only as interpreters of African traditions, but as interpreters of all that African thinkers choose to include as worthy of philosophical reflection. This is the post-colonial decision as African philosophers have defined it. Thus, African philosophy in the twentieth century intends to include not only reflection on specifically African issues, but also African participation in the conversations of analytic and Continental philosophy, producing work on formal logic, existentialism, idealism, and so on. Although such a delineation of the endeavors of Pan-African philosophers might seem self-evident as a description of philosophy generally, this has not been so historically. One need not search too deeply to find prejudiced assertions by well-known thinkers that Africans have nothing to contribute to philosophy. In the post-colonial era, a considerable amount of work has gone into simply establishing the possibility that African voices will be heard at all in the worldwide discourse of philosophy.

In this chapter, African post-colonial thought is set in a context which includes two other major textual categories. The first is oral and traditional philosophy and the second is modern African philosophy, which includes post-colonial work. Within the first category, it is impossible to separate philosophy sharply from religion, much as in Asian thought. As well, it is difficult to separate philosophy from story and from history, as in explicitly self-identified Jewish and Christian philosophy. Some commentators argue that the material in this category does not belong in a discussion of philosophy at all, but in a study of post-colonial philosophy, there are good reasons to make this inclusion. First, any philosophical development in a culture occurs within a history of ideas; even a rudimentary acquaintance with that history helps provide perspective for the understanding of current thinking. Also, and perhaps more important, post-colonial philosophy frequently draws on the traditional sensibilities of a culture as points of departure for critical reflection. Third, given our claim that post-colonial thought should be categorized as occurring in the histories of peoples seeking to deal with the effects of colonialism, it is important to recognize the genetic relationship of contemporary understandings to ideas that preceded them.

We should recognize, though, that the very idea of oral philosophy—especially relevant to a study of African thought—remains contested among modern African philosophers and others around the world. Nonetheless, it remains true that these thinkers are heirs to traditions that have transmitted philosophically relevant ideas orally up to the present day, and have done so in utterances as long as epic narratives and as brief as a single contextualized word. Philosophers may disagree whether the teachings and cultural information transmitted by oral traditions should count as proper philosophy, but virtually all are willing to accept the claim that any occurrence of the themes of philosophy has a place in the history of philosophy. We begin our topical look at African philosophy with the echoes of archaic thought that are still to be found in traditional worldviews.

The second important textual category in African philosophy is modern academic and political philosophy. This includes work that creates, interprets, and supplements the texts that one might study in a philosophy curriculum in any university in the world. Although most of the writings excerpted in this chapter were intentionally created as philosophical texts, this intention is not by any means essential to post-colonial thought, which occurs in political speeches, songs, commemoration addresses, and other venues. The spectrum of subjects that engage African philosophers—ranging from austere treatments of abstractions of mathematical logic to the high passion of radical ideology that is at once theoretical and practical—is as broad as anywhere else in the world.

Oral and Traditional Philosophy

Person   Physically, the distinction between self and other appears to be given in the biology of organisms. In virtually all cultures of the world, this distinction appears to have psychological and philosophical reality as well. That such a distinction seems to exist across species lines certainly does not mean, however, that different organisms possess uniform or even logically compatible senses of their own individuality. The same holds true for cultures. From our knowledge of human beings, at least, the sense of what it means to be a human being is something that must be created as much as discovered. One way philosophers have approached the matter of individuality has been to develop the notion of "person."

What a person is cannot be adequately determined simply by observation or experiment. It is, rather, a metaphysical question, that is, a question whose answer is more a matter of decision about the general nature or being of something than of empirical knowledge about it. In other words, the idea of "person," which can seem so self-evident, is more an invention of human beings than an inherent fact of nature. As such, the notion of "person" might be expected to vary greatly from culture to culture, and indeed it does. In the following selection, Richard C. Onwuanibe describes how this metaphysical issue of personhood is construed among the Ibo, a comparatively large cultural group in what is now Nigeria.

SELECTION 17.1

"The Human Person and Immortality in Ibo (African) Metaphysics"

From Richard C. Onwuanibe

THE HUMAN PERSON

The traditional African philosophy of the human person is more existential and practical than theoretical. It is based on the conviction that the metaphysical sphere is not abstractly divorced from concrete experience; for the physical and metaphysical are aspects of reality, and the transition from the one to the other is natural. In this regard, some writers have made derogatory remarks to the effect that Africans have no speculative bent; but this misrepresentation stems from ignorance of the true nature of their philosophical thinking. The Ibos are not total materialists in their fundamental views of reality, especially with regard to the human person as it can be argued from their view of soul (*mkpuru obi*) and presence.

An essential aspect or source of the human person is the soul (*mkpuru obi*), spirit (*mmuo*). The philosophical problem here is whether these are identifiable with the body. These primitive notions which are embedded in Ibo language and other African languages are not identified with the body, though related to it.

How is it that in virtually every language of the world, not only African languages, people say, "I have a body," "This is my body" or "This body is mine," and not "I am this body,"—meaning by this, "I am totally this body"? It is absurd to identify oneself totally with one's body, for example, to say "I am totally identified with this body"; for one is *prima facie* aware that one is more than one's (this) body. One might object to the nonidentifiability of oneself totally with one's body by saying that when somebody pushes one, one could react by saying, "Don't push me." It seems that here one is identifying oneself with one's body which is pushed. However, within one's consciousness, this does not mean total identification of oneself with one's body but an identification of a relation of one's body to oneself. The seemingly complete identification of the expression, "Don't push me," is due to the vagueness of ordinary language. The possessive case phenomenologically and linguistically indicates that there is more to one than one's body.

The Ibo notions of soul (*mkpuru obi*) and spirit (*mmuo*), as essential aspects of man, bear out the transcendence of the human person from the metaphysical point of view. When one says "*O meturu m na mmuo*" (It touches my spirit), one is acknowledging that what has happened, or is at stake, touches the deepest part of oneself. We shall see later how this aspect of man is the vehicle of immortality. By maintaining the irreducibility of this core of the human person to materialistic basis, the Ibos subscribe to a view of transcendence in their metaphysic of the human person. It can be argued that materialist or physicalist views are not adequate for a total conception of man; for man's aspira-tions, values and relative achievements in the arts and sciences do not make full sense when discussed only from the backdrop of materialism and physicalism.

Another pointer to the Ibo view of the transcendence of the human person in view of immortality is *presence*. The Ibo conception of the human person involves the notion of presence. High regard for the human person in terms of presence is displayed in everyday living in warm greetings. It is offensive not to be greeted. In Heideggerian terminology, man in-the-world is not merely ready-to-hand, that is, functionalized. Man's existence (*dasein*) transcends the level of a role to be played or used. In Ibo metaphysics, living is a form of participation in which a fundamental distinction is made between the ontological and the ontic, between humans and animals. To be said to be an animal is to be depersonalized. The distinction between humans and animals is shown in corresponding attitudes: for one does not greet animals even if they are highly regarded pets. Not to be greeted among the Ibos can be construed as a form of depersonalization. When one looks at you, one may see you as an object or a subject. Looked at as an object by another in terms of Sartre's notion of "gaze", you lose the transcendence of subjectivity. In Buber's terminology, the relation here is an I-It relation; but what the Ibos mean in greeting another person is an I-Thou relation. The greeting is genuine, and you can feel its authenticity through the concomitant smile of the one who greets you. A foreigner from the western world will be surprised at the shower of warm greetings he or she will receive when staying in an Ibo community, and at the loud and warm conversations that go on among passengers in public vehicles. This is a contrast to the silence one often experiences among passengers in public vehicles in the western world. An American alone taking a bus from Cleveland to Washington D.C. will enter the bus, go straight to his seat, take up a paper to read, and most probably will not greet any fellow passengers.

He or she is lonely in the midst of a crowd of passengers. He or she is not really a "fellow passenger" for fellowship at its lowest level of meaning of communication is absent; and others in this case are not present. Silence or lack of communication constitutes an acute problem of alienation in the western world today. Where there appears to be communication it is mostly object-oriented rather than subject-oriented. . . .

True personhood, as pure subject, is not something that can be analyzed into anything. Hence, for example, Kant could not get at himself as object of awareness; nor could Hume find his "self" either. Personhood is a manifestation or presence even through a body, but never identifiable with it. Since "person" is primitive, the inability to analyze person (qua subject or soul) is not an argument for its non-existence but for its "transcendence" or "no-thingness" ("Thou"). In Ibo greetings, the "Thou" is manifest and emphasized. Nobody greets a body but "what" is manifest through the body.

In Ibo philosophical reflection, the self deriving from the soul and spirit indicates the personhood. To talk of human person makes sense only when to be human includes not only the physical aspects but also the transcendental aspect. Here the transcendental aspect includes the mental to a certain extent, the spiritual aspirations and values of man.

In this context, it is worthwhile to note that the essential greatness of a culture consists of the commitment to personhood and to all that it stands for, viz., in terms of human rights, human aspirations and development; and conversely, a decline in the consideration of personhood is symptomatic of a decline of a culture. Periods of high culture, philosophical options included, give expression to the transcendence of the human person, for culture is not essentially materialistic. In Ibo culture the transcendence or subjectivity of the human person finds expression in egalitarian spirit. On the contrary, a culture which emphasizes materialistic attainments can achieve mechanical perfections without adequate idea of personhood.

While, on the one hand, what is empirical and objective carries a sense of clarity and comprehensibility, on the other hand, the subjective sphere is fraught with a certain opaqueness, incomprehensibility and mystery because the subjective domain cannot be totally subsumed under the categories of reason. Human existence is metaproblematic because it is not totally discoverable, and consequently, it allows for philosophical faith, which is not a denial of reason but a recognition of its limits, and an option for the domain of transcendence which goes beyond death and includes immortality.

Good and Evil   Among the perennial problems in philosophy is that of good and evil. Although what counts as good or evil has varied greatly from place to place and from time to time, the basic concepts of "good" and "evil" seem to be cultural universals. Even so, it is one thing to have a general sense of good and evil and yet another to have a way of determining whether novel actions fit into one category or the other. Elsewhere in this book, discussions of the ethical theories of Kant, Mill, Rawls, and others have demonstrated that this decision can be made by assessing conformity of an action with a specific set of rules or avoidance of breaking taboos, by considering the intentions that motivate an action, by evaluating the consequences of an action, and so on. All traditions make choices in this regard as well, although the choice may be mostly determined by a traditional mythology rather than by the autonomous reasoning or judgment of an individual. Some commentators have claimed that this distinction is crucial, that it is the dividing line between unthought habits of mind or culture, on the one hand, and true philosophy, on the other. This judgment itself, though, is a case in point of the kind of problem critical thought identifies—in this instance, whether to privilege individual thought processes over those of a group. In the selection that follows, it is clear that a philosophical position exists, but it is the evolutionary product of group thinking over a period of generations rather than the achievement of a single person.

Ghanian writer **Kwame Gyekye** has looked closely at one traditional African belief system. Since its publication in 1987, Gyekye's discussion of Akan thought has become widely regarded as one of the definitive descriptions of a traditional African worldview. Gyekye is one of the first writers to produce a careful, generally phenomenological documentation of traditional beliefs with a native's access to the subjectivity of the group being studied. The belief system of the Akan tribe of Ghana is the subject of this selection.

SELECTION 17.2

An Essay on African Philosophical Thought: The Akan Conceptual Scheme

From Kwame Gyekye

8.1.1. THE CONCEPTS OF GOOD AND EVIL

I shall begin with the Akan moral concepts of good (or goodness: *papa*) and evil (*bōne*), which are fundamental in the moral thought and practice of any culture. In Akan thought goodness is not defined by reference to religious beliefs or supernatural beings. What is morally good is not that which is commanded by God or any spiritual being; what is right is not that which is pleasing to a spiritual being or in accordance with the will of such being. In the course of my field research none of my discussants referred to Onyame (God) or other spiritual entities in response to the questions What is good? What is evil? None of them held that an action was good or evil because Onyame had said so. On the contrary, the views that emerge in discussions of these questions reveal an undoubted conviction of a nonsupernaturalistic—a humanistic—origin of morality. Such views provide insight into the Akan conception of the criterion of moral value.

In Akan moral thought the sole criterion of goodness is the welfare or well-being of the community. Thus, in the course of my field research, the response I had to the question, "What do the Akan people mean by 'good' (or, goodness)?" invariably included a list of goods, that is, a list of deeds, habits, and patterns of behavior considered by the society as worthwhile because of their consequences for human well-being. The list of such good invariably included: kindness (generosity: *ayamyie*), faithfulness (honesty, truthfulness: *nokwaredi*), compassion (*mmōbrōhunu*), hospitality (*ahōhoyē, adōe*), that which brings peace, happiness, dignity, and respect (*nea ede asomdwee, ahomeka, anuonyam ne abuo ba*), and so on. The good comprehends all the above, which is to say that the good (*papa*) is explained in terms of the qualities of things (actions, behavioral patterns). Generosity, hospitality, justice are considered (kinds of) good. Generosity is a good thing, but it is not identical with goodness. Goodness (or the good), then, is considered in Akan moral thinking as a concept comprehending a number of acts, states, and patterns of behavior that exemplify certain characteristics.

On what grounds are some acts (etc.) considered good? The answer is simply that each of them is supposed (expected or known) to bring about or lead to social well-being. Within the framework of Akan social and humanistic ethics, what is morally good is generally that which promotes social welfare, solidarity, and harmony in human relationships. Moral value in the Akan system is determined in terms of its consequences for mankind and society. "Good" is thus used of actions that promote human interest. The good is identical with the welfare of the society, which is expected to include the welfare of the individual. This appears to be the meaning or definition of "good" in Akan ethics. It is clear that this definition does not at all refer to the will or commands of God. That which is good is decreed not by a supernatural being as such, but by human beings within the framework of their experiences in living in society. So that even though an Akan maxim says

> I am doing the *good* (thing) so that my way to
> the world of spirits might not be blocked,
> (*mereye papa na ankosi me nsaman kwan*)

what constitutes the good is determined not by spiritual beings but by human beings.

Just as the good is that action or pattern of behavior which conduces to well-being and social harmony, so the evil (*bōne;* that is, moral evil) is that which is considered detrimental to the well-being of humanity and society. The Akan concept of evil, like that of good, is definable entirely in terms of the needs of society. Thus, even though one often hears people say "God does not like evil" (*Onyame mpē bonē*), yet what constitutes evil is determined by the members of the community, not by Onyame.

Akan ethics recognizes two categories of evil, *bōne* and *musuo,* although *bōne* is the usual word for evil. The first category, *bōne,* which I shall call "ordinary," includes such evils as theft, adultery, lying, backbiting (*kōkōnsa*), and so on. The other category of evil, *musuo,* I shall call "extraordinary." As described by a group of discussants, "*musuo* is an evil which is great and which brings suffering (*ōhaw, ahokyerē:* disaster, misfortune) to the whole community, not just to the doer alone." Another discussant also stated that "the consequences of committing *musuo* affect the whole community." *Musuo* was also defined as an "uncommon evil" (*bōne a wōntaa nhu*), and as an "indelible evil" (*ade a woye a wompepa da*), "remembered and referred to by people even many years after the death of the doer." Thus, *musuo* is generally considered to be a great, extraordinary moral evil; it is viewed by the community with particular abhorrence and revulsion because its commission is believed not only to bring shame to the whole community, but also, in the minds of many ordinary people, to invite the wrath of the supernatural powers.

The category of *musuo* includes such acts as suicide, incest, having sexual intercourse in the bush, rape, murder, stealing things dedicated to the deities or ancestral spirits, etc. Moral evils that are *musuo* are also considered as taboos (*akyiwade:* abominations, prohibitions), a taboo being, to most people, an act that is forbidden or proscribed just because it is supposedly hateful to some supernatural being. That *musuo* are classifiable as taboos was in fact the view of some discussants: "*musuo* is something we abominate" (*musuo ye ade a yekyi*); "*musuo* is a taboo" (*akyiwade*). Now, it is remarkable that the same evils considered as taboos by Bishop Sarpong, such as murder, sexual intercourse with a woman impregnated by another man, suicide, incest, words of abuse against the chief, and stealing from among the properties of a deity are all *musuo.* This gives the impression that the category of extraordinary moral evils (*musuo*) is coextensive with the category of taboos (*akyiwade*). But in reality this is not so. The *musuo* are indeed taboos, but from this we can only infer that some taboos are *musuo;* since *musuo* are moral evils, such taboos (as are *musuo*) are also moral evils. It seems to me that extraordinary moral evils (which include both *musuo* and moral taboos) are the kinds of moral evil that are *never* to be committed under any circumstances. This view is based on the force of the word *kyi,* to abhor, hate, from which *akyiwade* (hateful things, taboos) derives. Henceforth, I shall simply use the expression "moral taboos" to cover both *musuo* and *akyiwade.* . . .

How would the traditional Akan thinker explain the origin and role of taboos in Akan morality? In connection with taboo, Bishop Sarpong observed: "If one were to ask the Ashanti why he keeps these taboos, he will probably not be able to give the reasons I have propounded. All he is likely to assert is that they existed from time immemorial, that the ancestors want him to observe them." Bishop Sarpong is right as far as the ordinary Akan is concerned; but the wise persons (*anyansafo*) among them would be able to furnish the underlying reasons for considering such acts as moral evils of a high order. Their statements quoted above indicate clearly that they believe that committing a taboo act affects the welfare of the whole community. Moral taboos are thus explained by reference to their social function and purpose. Communal well-being, then, appears to be the principal reason for the proscription of the category of moral evils referred to as moral taboos (*musuo* and *akyiwade*). The following explanation given by Bishop Sarpong for tabooing sexual intercourse in the bush is in line with the thinking of the Akan thinkers:

> Those who indulge in it expose themselves to the risk of being bitten by venomous creatures like the snake, the scorpion, and the spider. (It should be borne in mind that Ashanti is a forested region with dangerous creatures whose bites may easily be fatal.) Let a mishap of this nature take place and there is every likelihood that misapprehensions are conceived about the conjugal act itself. That this would be detrimental to the human species is too obvious to emphasize.

In the view of Akan thinkers, the real, underlying reason for regarding sexual intercourse in the bush as a great moral evil and thus for tabooing it is not that it is hated by the earth goddess (*Asase Yaa*), but that it has undesirable social consequences. Their position is plainly that the acts classified as moral taboos were so regarded simply because of the *gravity* of their consequences for human society, not because those acts were hateful to any supernatural beings.

Academic and Political Philosophy

Method One of the hallmarks of philosophy's search for wisdom and understanding has been the development of methodical reasoning. By examination of assumptions, provable deductions, precise definitions, and other techniques of critical thinking, philosophers have been able to refine theories, discover implications, produce careful descriptions and analyses, and correct errors. Post-colonial analysts have noted on many occasions that colonialist thinking, informed as it has been by elements of Western philosophy, has frequently been deficient in both discipline and benevolence. These failures of rigor and ethics have led some post-colonial thinkers to conclude that methodical thinking itself is an affliction. Most, however, have demonstrated that the traditional tools of philosophy can be used profitably in the post-colonial project. For them, it is clear that methodical thinking is a skill and not a birthright, even though they were repeatedly subjected to such documents as a 1950s UN-funded study which concluded that North Africans were biologically incapable of the sorts of higher mental activity that came naturally to Europeans. Realizing that the existence of bad science and bad logic does not invalidate science and logic generally, these thinkers have argued that a grasp of method is essential for the further philosophical development that is needed for Africa to define its place in the modern world. In the following selection, Lansana Keita, a pragmatist who avoids ideological argument and advocates analytic rationality, explains Africa's stake in the development of methodological sophistication.

SELECTION 17.3

"Contemporary African Philosophy"   **From Lansana Keita**

An examination of the thought systems of the technologically advanced societies demonstrates that the educational instruction of those members of society necessary for its functioning has been taken over by disciplines that may be regarded as the intellectual descendants of philosophy: the natural sciences and the social sciences. Philosophy proper is relegated, for the most part, to the history of ideas, mainly in the form of textual analyses of the original writings of philosophers, to studies in the methodology of the special sciences, to the analysis of concepts and terms and to subjective reflections on the human condition. Yet the important point to recognize is that modern Western society does not look to philosophy for solutions to technological and social problems. Philosophical debates, if they are of any importance at all, are carried on within the special disciplines themselves, but for purposes and orientations peculiar to given social and political contexts.

It would be an error, therefore, for the philosopher in the African context to assume that philosophy as it is practiced in the Western world should serve as a model for the practice of philosophy. A useful approach, it seems, would be to regard philosophical activity as engaging in theoretical analysis of issues and ideas of practical concern. But in modern society it is the social and natural sciences that discuss ideas and issues relevant to practical concerns. Thus the practice of philosophy in the African context should be concerned first with the analysis of the methodology and content of the social sciences (i.e., history, economics, anthropology, political science, etc.), for it is the methodology of research of a given discipline that determines the orientation of research in that discipline and the kinds of solutions to problems ultimately proposed. Furthermore, analysis of the methodology of the sciences of human behavior would be constantly alert to the notion that the modes and objects of human thought are potentially value-laden. And this is indeed the case with the existent research programs in African universities, inherited as they are from the colonial period.

In this connection, it would also be incumbent on the African philosophers to raise questions concerning the epistemological basis for the analysis of human behavior in terms of the special disciplines. In other words, is it possible, for example, to fully understand people as economic beings without paying attention to the total sociological person? Or can one fully understand political institutions without regard for the study of history, etc? These theoretical questions are of practical concern in matters relating to the formulation of university curricula, and critically important for the training of an adequate work force. In these critical times, the African philosopher's contributions to African development in the areas of economic theory, political theory, historiography, anthropology, and the other sciences of human behavior should be of significance. For by the very nature of the enterprise, most of which consists of critical analysis, the philosopher is less paradigm-bound than colleagues in the social sciences, more inclined to see how the particular fits into the universal—to see the whole picture. As an historical note, it is no accident that Marx, one of the great theoreticians of the social sciences, was trained in philosophy.

Again, the practice of philosophy in the African context should be strongly concerned with the study of the methodology and applications of the natural sciences and their relationships to the social sciences. And the point to be recognized is that despite the evident universality of the methodology of the natural sciences, it is still instructive to recognize that the pursuit of empirical science is not just simply a matter of performing experiments: the methodology of scientific research is founded on a number of important theoretical assumptions which, if recognized by the researcher, could lead to investigative approaches that are more creative, hence potentially more fruitful. In this regard, it is instructive to consider the importance of the theoretical analysis of the foundations of empirical science as a possible encouragement for research. The role of theoretical analysis in this context, as a possible aid to the development of scientific research in Africa, is evident. Economic development and technological development usually proceed simultaneously.

Yet the above discussion and proposals require some comment about the modes whereby such ideas may be implemented. It has been argued above that the history of ideas in Europe may be understood as being partially determined by the material and psychological needs of that society. It follows, therefore, that there are no commanding reasons why the structure and orientation of knowledge in African society should correspond exactly to those of exmetropolitan Europe. In this connection, and in the light of what has been discussed, a review of the academic status of philosophy in African universities is in order.

It would be useful, for example, if the methodological issue concerning the different disciplines was discussed from within the context of the disciplines themselves. Thus the philosophy of the social sciences would be pursued from within the confines of the various social sciences. The same requirement holds for theoretical discussions on the natural sciences. One might also consider the hypothesis that discussions of the methodological issues in the special areas of knowledge could be more competently carried out by those who have had extensive training in the relevant disciplines. Given the above, I recommend that further research in theoretical and methodological issues beyond the most advanced degree hitherto granted in African universities should be required in order to generate adequate competence in the area of philosophical analysis. Thus the researcher concerned to examine theoretical issues in, say, applied physics would be trained to the level of physicists practicing in that area and beyond. Philosophers concerned to examine the theory and content of traditional African thought would have had training in linguistics and cognate disciplines. I assume that the results of this remodeling of the received systems of instruction in the African context would do much to shape modern modes of inquiry to fit African realities and to encourage creativity in research.

Although a number of issues have been discussed above, this essay's main purpose is to discuss a possible methodology for a modern

African philosophy. It is generally agreed that there is some sensed intellectual discomfort at the idea of philosophy in contemporary Africa being a replica of philosophy as practiced in the ex-metropolis. The genesis of the concepts of "traditional African philosophy" and "philosophic sagacity" derives from this issue. But I argued above that there are questions as to how traditional African philosophy and philosophic sagacity fit into the new scheme of things in contemporary Africa. I believe that intellectual effort in the African context should be strongly geared to the training of personnel in modern techniques of natural and social scientific inquiry, appropriate for application in the ongoing transformation of society. Clearly, those beliefs and theoretical ideas characterizing traditional African thought systems which are proven vital for contemporary development should be nurtured and incorporated into the social philosophies and technological orientation of modern Africa. In this context research into traditional African thought systems has an important role to play.

But if the pursuit of research in traditional African thought is to serve the narrow purpose of proving to others that "Africans knew how to think consistently before colonial times," and that "African world-views were not inherently irrational," then it is difficult to see how this debate could be of any great moment in the current transformations taking place in African society. Purely academic debates among minorities of university scholars can perhaps be afforded in the universities of the Euro-American world, but there is some doubt as to the viability of similar kinds of debates in African universities.

A cursory study of any African language demonstrates that consistency and coherence of expression should be taken for granted. How else could there be intralinguistic communication within a given society, unless consistency and coherence were assumed on the part of its members? It seems to me that the old colonial ideology that dichotomized the worlds of Europe and Africa as those of reason and unreason is obsolete. The problem of Africa today is that of adapting modern techniques and modes of knowing to societies being transformed from those in which the most important factors of production were human beings themselves, to those in which the machine constitutes the major factor of production. Of course, the traditional beliefs concomitant with the traditional society are giving way to new beliefs. And the important question arises as to what should be the nature of the new beliefs.

A study of the historical development of European and Asian societies demonstrates that important ideological debates and subsequent transformations of social orders and accompanying modes of thought were witnessed in Europe and those parts of Asia now in the age of modern technology. Research will also show that a similar function is demanded of those who, in the African context, engage in intellectual pursuits.

The Nature of Philosophy   A series of articles breaking with past practice and proposing a rigorous program for the future of African philosophy has brought Paulin Hountondji to the forefront of post-colonial thought in the late twentieth century. Hountondji, whose career includes service as Minister of Education in his native Benin, brings techniques of French critical theory to bear on the question of the integrity of African philosophy, focusing especially on the task of deconstructing texts which, in his analysis, perpetuate a colonial mentality. He has been most concerned to dismantle what he sees as the destructive influence of two connected positions in the African intellectual milieu—namely, **ethnophilosophy** and the advocacy of the concept of negritude. Hountondji's claim is that both of these positions work against African interests by perpetuating related falsehoods. The problem with ethnophilosophy, which seeks to describe traditional beliefs, is that its practitioners violate the experience of those they describe by abstracting ideas from their practical contexts. Ethnophilosophy's first offense, then, is that it imposes external categorizations on those it studies. Its second offense is more historical in that its practitioners have often justified their work in terms of its usefulness to those who would control African consciousness by the judicious manipulation of symbols and concepts. A critical view of ethnophilosophy sees that Africans who buy into the ethnophilosophic story, which does contain an element of fact, are prone to mistake these facts for truth and thus acquiesce to control strategies they would otherwise resist. The same problem afflicts the adherents of the negritude position, says Hountondji, when they valorize African soul and relinquish African intellect. Not only is this a bad trade, he claims, but it is also built on an ideological illusion which serves the purposes of the colonizing forces. The remedy Houndondji prescribes at this juncture in history is a sustained critical examination of the task of a post-colonial philosophy and, to avoid unconscious perpetuation of conservative traditionalist or colonialist assumptions, a renunciation of most notions of cultural pluralism.

SELECTION 17.4

"Philosophy and Its Revolutions"   **From Paulin Hountondji**

I should like to demonstrate three things: First, that philosophy is not a system but a history, essentially an open process, a restless, unfinished quest, not closed knowledge; second, that this history does not move forward by continuous evolution but by leaps and bounds, by successive revolutions, and consequently follows not a linear path but what one might call a dialectical one—in other words, that its profile is not continuous but discontinuous; third, after this rough sketch of a theory of theoretical development, of a theory of theoretical history, of a theory of philosophy seen as a discontinuous theoretical history, that African philosophy may today be going through its first decisive mutation, the outcome of which depends on us alone, on the courage and lucidity we show in bringing it to its conclusion.

PHILOSOPHY AS HISTORY

First, then, philosophy is a history, not a system. I do not consider here the word 'system' in its weak sense of 'methodical knowledge'. If we took it in that sense, it is obvious that philosophy would indeed be a system, simply meaning that one does not philosophize without some method and prior knowledge, that philosophy requires a rather special conceptual ability on the part of the practitioner, that there is a terminology, a vocabulary, a conceptual apparatus bequeathed by philosophical tradition which we can never do without but must, on the contrary, use with profit if we want to be authentic philosophers. It goes without saying that philosophical reflection in this sense inevitably includes a *systematic* aspect, which is both methodical and constantly related to an existing theoretical tradition which may either confirm or confute it, and that no philosophers can evade the rigours of this discipline if they really want to philosophize and not just (in Plato's words) 'tell stories'. In this sense it seems obvious to me that African philosophers, like any others, need have no qualms about philosophizing, methodically and rigorously, in and through the conceptual heritage labelled 'philosophy.' African physicists are not generally ashamed to use the concepts which are proper to their discipline. Likewise, the African philosophers must not shirk the technicalities of philosophical language. We shall never create an authentic African philosophy, a genuine philosophy, genuinely African (that's what I mean by the term 'authentic'), if we skirt round the existing philosophical tradition. It is not by skirting round, and still less by ignoring, the international philosophical heritage that we shall really philosophize, but by absorbing it in order to transcend it.

In this sense, but only in this sense, it seems to me evident that philosophy, whether we like it or not, is a system involving a special method of inquiry.

But in another sense, the strong sense of the word 'system'—that is to say, a set of propositions regarded as definitive, a set of ultimate truths, the be-all and end-all of all thought— philosophy *is not* a system. For philosophy never stops; its very existence lies in the to and fro of free discussion, without which there is no philosophy. It is not a closed system but a history, a debate that goes on from generation to generation, in which every thinker, every author, engages in total responsibility: I know that I am responsible for what I say, for the theories I put forward. I am 'responsible' for them in the literal sense of the word, because I must always be prepared to 'answer' for them; I must be ready to justify them, to attest to their validity. It is as an individual that I take part in this debate, and in doing so I take part in the gradual unveiling of a truth that is not *mine* but everyone's, the outcome of the confrontation of all individual thoughts which constitutes an unending collective search.

The contention that philosophy is a history and not a system means, among other things, that no philosophical doctrine can be regarded as *the Truth*. It follows in a sense that there is no absolute truth in philosophy, or rather, that in this context the absolute is contained in the relative of an infinite, open-ended process. In other words, truth cannot be a set of definitive, untranscendable propositions but rather the process by which we look for propositions more adequate than others. In a way, then, truth is the very act of looking for truth, of enunciating propositions and trying to justify and found them.

Ideology and Truth   In every society that has produced philosophers, people have questioned what need there is for philosophy. Because philosophizing does not grow food, defend the state, or produce useful artifacts, the motivation for this question is clear enough, especially in societies struggling to meet basic needs. In remarks outside the following selection, **Kwasi Wiredu,** one of modern Africa's most prominent philosophers, endeavored to show that there are practical benefits of philosophical activity and that these benefits are worth working to attain, perhaps especially when a society is facing difficult conditions. Wiredu's sympathies lie with analytic philosophy, the school of thought which has dominated professional philosophy in the English-speaking world. As an analytic philosopher,

Wiredu's chief concerns are clarity of expression and justifiable inference. Having established the probability that philosophy offers certain practical benefits to Africa, Wiredu deepens his analysis to address one of the perennial issues of philosophy: truth. Wiredu's position should be understood against the backdrop of traditional realism, the epistemological view that one's perceptions can correspond faithfully to the way things are in the world and—here is what separates traditional realism from scientific realism—that one's metaphysical and ethical conceptions can be the correct ones according to standards that are independent of anyone's personal views.

SELECTION 17.5

Philosophy and an African Culture   **From Kwasi Wiredu**

Consider the problem of the choice (or discovery) of a social and political system. There is at the present time in Africa a vocal and perhaps widespread belief in the desirability and effectiveness of ideology in national life. This on the face of it is an invitation to the philosopher, for it appears to indicate that people are anxious to listen to him. An ideology is, in the best sense of this highly ambiguous word, a set of ideas about what form the good society should take, and any such set of ideas needs a basis in first principles, which is where philosophy enters. But, on account of the ambiguity in the meaning of the word 'ideology', a preliminary clarification is necessary when considering this matter.

It turns out that frequently the call for ideology is a cryptically expressed call for a particular ideology, namely, socialism. This, however, is not what gives rise to problems, for, of course, there is nothing wrong with advocating socialism. The fact is that usually such calls for ideology are a demand for a ready made set of ideas meant to be adopted by governments as the *exclusive* basis for the political organisation of society. In this sense an ideology is a set of dogmas to be imposed by the government, with force if necessary. This sense is, of course, not openly avowed, and can only be gathered from circumstantial evidence. In Ghana in the early sixties,

for example, this is what ideology amounted to in actual practice, notwithstanding the official praise for humanism. It would be hard to forget the atmosphere of intellectual strangulation in Ghana in those days when it was taken almost to be subversion to express publicly any doubts about dialectical materialism. But I must not digress. The immediate reason for calling attention to this other meaning of 'ideology' is to point out that much of the current controversy on the question of ideology in Africa today is at cross-purposes. It may reasonably be presumed that those, at any rate some of those, who would have no truck with 'ideology', interpret the term in the second sense. Meanwhile, because of the existence of the first sense, the proponents of ideology can point to the absurdity of the suggestion that society can be expected to move in the right direction without people having any coherent idea as to its ideal destiny. The point, however, is that to oppose ideology in the second sense is not necessarily to deny it in the first sense.

In this matter the philosopher's role is not just to clarify the semantics of ideological talk; he must positively oppose the emergence in Africa of ideology in the second, I would say degenerate, sense. Let us, for the time being, understand the word 'ideology' in just this degenerate sense. Then, it seems to me to be the case not only that ideology is the negation of philosophy, but also that it is a bar to development. . . . development does not mean merely the acquisition of sophisticated technology with its associated material benefits; it means also the securing of such conditions as shall permit the self-realisation of men as rational beings. I am tempted to re-echo here the question as to what it would profit a man if he were to gain all the world and lose his soul.

One way in which a man can lose his soul is by being prevented from trying to think for himself, or, even more terribly, by being rendered unable to think for himself. In Africa nowadays people have learnt all sorts of euphemisms for anti-humanism. Where they may say that we need an ideology to mobilise the population for rapid development they are likely to mean in actual fact that they want to force their pet preconceptions down the throats of their countrymen in order, among other things, that their actions might seem to have the support of the 'masses'. The essential anti-humanism of this kind of procedure is more easily masked by the circumstance that forms of speech are apt to make personal opinions look like independent realities. While likely to be ashamed to be seen to be forcing others to accept their own opinions, people are perfectly able to do just this with a sense of righteousness when these opinions are recommended not merely as their own but as the Truth. If some people through pigheadedness, obtuseness, or pure wilfulness are not immediately ready to embrace the things that are true and good especially in matters affecting a whole nation, may it not seem legitimate to apply some pressure?

I cannot forbear to relate in this connection a conversation I once had with a friend who obviously had a sense of mission, many years ago when we were both studying abroad. He was a citizen of one of our sister West African countries where the authorities were not very particular about such things as putting a political opponent on trial before putting him in jail. He had finished his training and was returning to his country with one ambition: to win political power and set things right. In our parting conversation he assured me that when he got into power, as he thought he inevitably would, he would never detain his opponents without trial. Everybody, he said, would be absolutely free to organise or join whatever party they pleased without the fear of arbitrary arrest and detention. But he set one small condition: Unlike the evil-minded politicians, he would summarily detain only people whose actions were really incompatible with the good of his dear country. It had apparently not occurred to him that it was just conceivable that the evil politicians had been detaining only those people whose actions struck *them* as really incompatible with the good of their own country. The impression has since grown on me that this kind of illogicality is one of the most fundamental causes of inhumanity in Africa as, of course, elsewhere.

Truth is personal, and so, even more obviously, are goodness and beauty. Or, not to seem to be begging philosophical questions, I will put it in this way: Let truth, beauty and goodness—I have used small letters but whoever is given to talking of the Eternal Verities is welcome to capitals—let this trinity be of whatever metaphysical nature they may be, still that something is true, good or beautiful is a personal affirmation. If I punish another for not adhering to the true, the good, the beautiful, the penalty he pays is a result of his not adopting *my* opinions, attitudes and preferences. I have previously defined ideology, in what I called the best sense of the word, as a set of ideas as to what the good society should be like; a more naked characterisation is that an ideology is a set of personal opinions and preferences in the matter of alternative social arrangements. I venture the psychological observation that anybody who grasps this and keeps it steadfastly in mind is unlikely to feel entitled forcibly to impose his ideology on others.

Let me quickly note the standard objection to suggestions like those just put forward. Such views, it would be said, amount to subjectivism and the degrading of truth, goodness and beauty. I have always been intrigued by this kind of response, for it creates the following paradox: Tell a person that in practice truth, say, is nothing more than opinion, and he is instantly scandalised. He will not stand for any attempt to render truth worthless. But try, in the first place, to suggest to him that his opinion on some important matter is worthless and he will be equally outraged, for his opinion is, of course, precious. Which seems to suggest that in the affair of defining truth, wisdom comes in trying to eat your cake and have it.

Historiography   It is often said that history is written by the winners. For post-colonial consciousness, steeped in awareness of the vast differences between the stories told by the colonizers and the stories told by the colonized, history is most certainly not a simple matter. Writing in the early and mid-twentieth century, W. E. B. Du Bois argued that African-Americans needed a long period of intense concentration on their history to come to terms with the enormity of the events that had led them to their present situation. Prominent among the concerns of post-colonial historians is a need to write history in such a way that a people's grasp of continuity with its past will help reveal its concrete situation in the present and its direction into the future. As always in the writing of history, in the post-colonial context the task of selecting and organizing information entails the exercise of judgment. Distinguished Tanzanian historian Arnold Temu and Nigerian historian Bonaventure Swai argue that judgment must be guided by consciously constructed and philosophically justified theory, for the only alternative is an unconscious theory propped up by the shoddiest unexamined philosophy. The following selection presents methodological points they maintain must be examined before one begins to write history.

SELECTION 17.6

Historians and Africanist History: A Critique

From Arnold Temu and
Bonaventure Swai

The point to be made immediately is that the production of knowledge is a social process to be understood in the context of society, which is historically determined. Under capitalism, as well as its role in serving the purposes of capital, knowledge is intended to legitimize a particular historical course. Thus in the case of African history, colonial historiography denied African societies their past so as to legitimize the process of 'colonial enlightenment'. Postcolonial Africanist historiography, on the other hand, sought to resurrect the precapitalist African past with a view, however, not to elucidating but obfuscating the real impact of that 'colonial enlightenment', as well as the ongoing imperialist context of postcolonial African social formations.

African postcolonial historiography did not go beyond exposing the chauvinistic content of colonial historiography.

THE FALLACY OF OBJECTIVISM

Like world history the term, African history, has been used widely and at times wantonly. But what is African history? Perhaps the answer to such a question is too obvious to be considered seriously by the learned and erudite. The common view is that African history is the study of the African past or its remains as well as the results of such scholarly investigation. An historian of African history is therefore concerned with remains of the African past, from which he can collect facts to be ascertained in the course of reconstructing history, so as to show it as it really was. Facts are past events made by men in the form of such things as social, political and economic institutions. The duty of an historian is to get the facts right and to present them with strict and clinical objectivity. This historical method of collecting and assessing facts is called objective empiricism.

Rigorous use of the empirical method to study the past was established in the nineteenth century by such prominent professional scholars as Ranke. Nowadays Ranke is mostly remembered for having introduced into the professional study of history the 'cult of facts and documents'. He saw the limits of writing history as determined by the availability of documents from which facts could be extracted, and the historian's detachment (objectivism), which would guarantee that history is written objectively. 'The virtue of a thing, Plato tells us in the *Republic,* is that state or condition which enables it to perform its proper function well. The virtue of a knife is its sharpness, the virtue of a racehorse its fleetness of foot.' So, too, the cardinal virtue of detachment is an excellence which enables an historian to fulfil his professional function properly and efficiently. Detachment, neutrality, impartiality, or objectivism is considered an important precondition in the

historian's craft. Commitment, on the other hand, signifies delinquency, a failure of professional rigour, since it tends to invite a confusion between facts and values. Detachment is acquired by suppressing one's subjectivity. Such a mental posture enables an historian to acquire an 'Olympian view' of historical events, considered crucial in the production of objective knowledge.

But, as one revolutionary historian observed, 'Nobody has yet clearly explained what this impartiality consists of'. . . . Thus it can be argued that 'this was mediated by that, and that was assimilated into the other, and all this went on in a world of discourse as congenial as the reading rooms in which we consult old periodicals.' But events take place in situations of actual social confrontation: there is a 'river of fire' in the real world of historical events. . . .

Two seminal points stand out about the empirical method as it applies to professional history: it believes that an historian is capable of becoming objective by suppressing the subjective element within him, and that his subject can also be treated objectively given the rise of the modern society. It has been argued that the professionalization of history is inextricably linked with the rise of the 'modern society', whether this is understood as the industrial system or its political institutions. According to Toynbee, the subjugation of 'the ancient kingdom of thought' to scientific thought which is critical as well as positivistic, and its application to the physical world, constitute the industrial system. Scientific thought also found its way into the 'continent of human history', where it was applied. 'Historical thought', therefore, is among the 'foreign realms in which the prestige of the Industrial system has asserted itself; and herein a mental domain which has had a far longer history than our Western Society and which is concerned not with things but with people'.

In modern society, as opposed to traditional societies, 'real history', 'the learned monograph or article resting upon original research', the collection and establishment of facts considered as 'the indestructible atoms of the past', is possible. Besides collecting the indestructible atoms of the past, an historian is supposed to add them one to another and so help construct a solid element of true history. The learned monographs and articles would, in turn, be added to each other and so enable the writing of 'a definitive, universal history in some remote future'. 'The gathering of materials bearing upon minute local events', 'the collection of MSS and the registry of their small variations, the patient drudgery in archives of state and municipalities, all the microscopic research that is carried on by armies of toiling students', all the monographs on various obscure subjects 'serve as chapters in a single historical work', universal history. This, however, cannot be fulfilled by one mind. Rather, it will be the result of the efforts of myriads of individuals. . . .

By the beginning of the twentieth century, and especially after the First World War, historians were openly admitting that what they were writing was not the absolute truth, but a selection of it. Much of the selection, too, was 'refracted' through their own minds. It was also realized that what was regarded as a passive and neutral mind was in actual fact very much influenced by the prevailing climate of opinion.

Nineteenth-century confidence in professional history has given way to pessimism; so much so that even facts are now doubted. The ideology of academia which was previously stated so confidently is no more. History now seems to be nothing more than what a professional chooses to tell his audience. Call it objectivity, subjectivity or what you will, historical facts as well as history itself are now regarded as a creation of the historian; they do not exist outside his own mind. . . .

THE MATERIAL BASIS OF ACADEMIA

Perhaps this 'radical' change in thinking about their craft by professional historians is symptomatic of the dynamism inherent in the writing of history. It could also be that, however weird, the various views and interpretations produced in the course of writing history belong, in the final analysis (it might be added), to the totality of human knowledge. Such change might underline the reason for rewriting history every generation or so. But it seems to others, that change *per se* is not crucial; rather the quality of change is more important. It may be that topics of research are determined not by individual choice, but by the prevailing historical conditions under which the choice is made. To know the nature of such historical conditions is of paramount importance because they are not neutral. The problem of objectivity in history should be discussed within such a context.

Violence   The publication in 1961 of *The Wretched of the Earth* by **Frantz Fanon** (1925–1961) was a seismic event in the history of post-colonial thought. Uncompromising in its indictment of the use of physical and psychological-conceptual violence in the history of colonial domination, the book set the agenda for a generation of theorists on several continents. Fanon argued that all colonial activity was violent invasion, whether accompanied by heavy bloodshed or not. From this position, he argued further that violent incursions must be met with a physically violent response that radically replaces the social structure of a decolonized area and destroys the outside settlers' capacity for aggression. In his own view, Fanon is proposing not only a political strategy to restore the integrity of the Third World, but a psychological one as well. Trained in psychiatry, Fanon maintained this focus as he articulated his belief that the psychological wounds of the colonized would be remedied in the catharsis of violence that occurs in the same movement that brings about physical liberation. His understanding of how a revolution can maintain itself by preserving the stake of the common people in national life has proved enormously influential in the Third World, though difficulties of putting theory into practice have sometimes been cited as evidence that Fanon's ideas are impractical. That there have been crude implementations of Fanon's ideas, however, does not argue definitively against either his analyses or the mitigation strategies he proposed.

SELECTION 17.7

The Wretched of the Earth   **From Frantz Fanon**

CONCERNING VIOLENCE

National liberation, national renaissance, the restoration of nationhood to the people, commonwealth: whatever may be the headings used or the new formulas introduced, decolonization is always a violent phenomenon. At whatever level we study it—relationships between individuals, new names for sports clubs, the human admixture at cocktail parties, in the police, on the directing boards of national or private banks—decolonization is quite simply the replacing of a certain "species" of men by another "species" of men. Without any period of transition, there is a total, complete, and absolute substitution. It is true that we could equally well stress the rise of a new nation, the setting up of a new state, its diplomatic relations, and its economic and political trends. But we have precisely chosen to speak of that kind of *tabula rasa* which characterizes at the outset all decolonization. Its unusual importance is that it constitutes, from the very first day, the minimum demands of the colonized. To tell the truth, the proof of success lies in a whole social structure being changed from the bottom up. The extraordinary importance of this change is that it is willed, called for, demanded. The need for this change exists in its crude state, impetuous and compelling, in the consciousness and in the lives of the men and women who are colonized. But the possibility of this change is equally experienced in the form of a terrifying future in the consciousness of another "species" of men and women: the colonizers.

Decolonization, which sets out to change the order of the world, is, obviously, a program of complete disorder. But it cannot come as a result of magical practices, nor of a natural shock, nor of a friendly understanding. Decolonization, as we know, is a historical process: that is to say that it cannot be understood, it cannot become intelligible nor clear to itself except in the exact measure that we can discern the movements which give it historical form and content. Decolonization is the meeting of two forces, opposed to each other by their very nature, which in fact owe their originality to that sort of substantification which results from and is nourished by the situation in the colonies. Their first encounter was marked by violence and their existence together—that is to say the exploitation of the native by the settler—was carried on by dint of a great array of bayonets and cannons. The settler and the native are old acquaintances. In fact, the settler is right when he speaks of knowing "them" well. For it is the settler who has brought the native into existence and who perpetuates his existence. The settler owes the fact of his very existence, that is to say, his property, to the colonial system.

Decolonization never takes place unnoticed, for it influences individuals and modifies them fundamentally. It transforms spectators crushed with their inessentiality into privileged actors, with the grandiose glare of history's floodlights upon them. It brings a natural rhythm into existence, introduced by new men, and with it a new language and a new humanity. Decolonization is the veritable creation of new men. But this creation owes nothing of its legitimacy to any supernatural power; the "thing" which has been colonized becomes man during the same process by which it frees itself.

In decolonization, there is therefore the need of a complete calling in question of the colonial situation. If we wish to describe it precisely, we might find it in the well-known words: "The last shall be first and the first last." Decolonization is the putting into practice of this sentence. That is why, if we try to describe it, all decolonization is successful.

The naked truth of decolonization evokes for us the searing bullets and bloodstained knives which emanate from it. For if the last shall be first, this will only come to pass after a murderous and decisive struggle between the two protagonists. That affirmed intention to place the last at the head of things, and to make them climb at a pace (too quickly, some say) the well-known steps which characterize an organized society, can only triumph if we use all means to turn the scale, including, of course, that of violence.

You do not turn any society, however primitive it may be, upside down with such a program if you have not decided from the very beginning, that is to say from the actual formulation of that program, to overcome all the obstacles that you will come across in so doing. The native who decides to put the program into practice, and to become its moving force, is ready for violence at all times. From birth it is clear to him that this narrow world, strewn with prohibitions, can only be called in question by absolute violence. . . .

The colonial world is a world cut in two. The dividing line, the frontiers are shown by barracks and police stations. In the colonies it is the policeman and the soldier who are the official, instituted go-betweens, the spokesmen of the settler and his rule of oppression. In capitalist societies the educational system, whether lay or clerical, the structure of moral reflexes handed down from father to son, the exemplary honesty of workers who are given a medal after fifty years of good and loyal service, and the affection which springs from harmonious relations and good behavior—all these aesthetic expressions of respect for the established order serve to create around the exploited person an atmosphere of submission and of inhibition which lightens the task of policing considerably. In the capitalist countries a multitude of moral teachers, counselors and "bewilderers" separate the exploited from those in power. In the colonial countries, on the contrary, the policeman and the soldier, by their immediate presence and their frequent and direct action maintain contact with the native and advise him by means of rifle butts and napalm not to budge. It is obvious here that the agents of government speak the language of pure force. The intermediary does not lighten the oppression, nor seek to hide the domination; he shows them up and puts them into practice with the clear conscience of an upholder of the peace; yet he is the bringer of violence into the home and into the mind of the native. . . .

The violence which has ruled over the ordering of the colonial world, which has ceaselessly drummed the rhythm for the destruction of native social forms and broken up without reserve the systems of reference of the economy, the customs of dress and external life, that same violence will be claimed and taken over by the native at the moment when, deciding to embody history in his own person, he surges into the forbidden quarters. To wreck the colonial world is henceforward a mental picture of action which is very clear, very easy to understand and which may be assumed by each one of the individuals which constitute the colonized people. To break up the colonial world does not mean that after the frontiers have been abolished lines of communication will be set up between the two zones. The destruction of the colonial world is no more and no less than the abolition of one zone, its burial in the depths of the earth or its expulsion from the country.

Historiography   Poet, philosopher, and president of his native Senegal, **Léopold Sédar Senghor** almost single-handedly determined the issues and methods of philosophy in francophone Africa in the mid-twentieth century. From his studies in France, Senghor acquired an intimate acquaintance with the thoughtways of Continental philosophy. This background, demonstrated in close readings of the texts he considered foundational, also clearly informs his political writings, in which Senghor's erudition establishes a discipline far removed from the colorful rhetorical assertions that often take the place of thinking in the lives of nations. Senghor's hope was that Africans would find a way to adapt socialist theory to the needs of their post-colonial societies. Adaptation was necessary, in his view, because European ways and values were inadequate to the depth and richness of African understandings of life. To this end, he attempted to create a methodology that would work for Africans.

His doctrine of negritude, a concept that remains widely misunderstood to this day, sought to outline a distinctively African epistemology to explain the claim that there was an African way of knowing which was different from the European. Senghor's own method was phenomenological, that is, aiming to be dispassionately descriptive, but his claim that African cultures evaluate metaphors differently from European ones was widely treated as a simple opinion. In the following selection, Senghor addresses a general audience on some matters of principle.

SELECTION 17.8

On African Socialism   **From Léopold Sédar Senghor**

Let us then consider the Negro African as he faces the object to be known, as he faces the Other: God, man, animal, tree or pebble, natural or social phenomenon. In contrast to the classic European, the Negro African does not draw a line between himself and the object; he does not hold it at a distance, nor does he merely look at it and analyze it. After holding it at a distance, after scanning it without analyzing it, he takes it vibrant in his hands, careful not to kill or fix it. He touches it, feels it, *smells* it. The Negro African is like one of those Third Day Worms,* a pure field of sensations. Subjectively, at the tips of his sensory organs, his insect antennas, he discovered the Other. Immediately he is moved,

---

*An allusion to the Age of Reptiles. [Trans.]

going centrifugally from subject to object on the waves of the Other. This is more than a simple metaphor; contemporary physics has discovered universal energy under matter: waves and radiations. Thus the Negro African *sympathizes,** abandons his personality to become identified with the Other, dies to be reborn in the Other. He does not assimilate; he is assimilated. He lives a common life with the Other; he lives in a symbiosis. To use Paul Claudel's expression, he "knows† the Other." Subject and object are dialectically face to face in the very act of knowledge. It is a long caress in the night, an embrace of joined bodies, the act of love. "I want you to feel me," says a voter who wants you to know him well. "I think, therefore I am," Descartes writes. The observation has already been made that one always thinks something, and the logician's conjunction "therefore" is unnecessary. The Negro African could say, "I feel, I dance the Other; I am." To dance is to discover and to re-create, especially when it is a dance of love. In any event, it is the best way to know. Just as knowledge is at once discovery and creation— I mean, re-creation and recreation, after the model of God.

Young people have criticized me for reducing Negro-African knowledge to pure emotion, for denying that there is an African "reason" or African techniques. This is the hub of the problem; I should like to explain my thought once again.

---

*In the French text, *sym-pathise,* literally, "feels with." [Trans.]

†Here again the word is separated, *con-nait,* literally, "is born with." [Trans.]

See Arthur Koestler, *The Lotus and the Robot* (New York: The Macmillan Co., 1961) p. 43:

> The traditional Eastern way of looking at things is to deny that there *are* things independently from the act of looking. The objects of consciousness cannot be separated from the conscious subject; observer and observed are a single, indivisible, fluid reality, as they are at the dawn of consciousness in the child, and in the cultures dominated by magic. The external world has no existence in its own right; it is a function of the senses; but that function exists only in so far as it is registered by consciousness, and consequently has no existence in its own right.

Obviously, there is a European civilization and a Negro-African civilization. Anyone who has not explained their differences and the reasons for them has explained nothing and has left the problem untouched.

Thus, I explain myself. However paradoxical it may seem, the vital force of the Negro African, his surrender to the object, is animated by reason. Let us understand each other clearly; it is not the *reasoning-eye* of Europe, it is the *reason of the touch,* better still, the *reasoning-embrace,* the sympathetic reason, more closely related to the Greek *logos* than to the Latin *ratio.* For *logos,* before Aristotle, meant both reason and the word. At any rate, Negro-African speech does not mold the object into rigid categories and concepts without touching it; it polishes things and restores their original color, with their texture, sound, and perfume; it perforates them with its luminous rays to reach the essential surreality in its innate humidity—it would be more accurate to speak of subreality. European reasoning is analytical, discursive by utilization; Negro-African reasoning is intuitive by participation.

Young people in Black Africa are wrong to develop a complex and to believe the latter inferior to the former. "The most beautiful emotion that we can experience," wrote the great scientist Einstein, "is mystic emotion. It is the germ of all art and all true science." To return to Negro-African speech, I refer you to two significant articles. The first, "Ethnologie de la parole," is by Maurice Leenhardt, the second, "Introduction à l'étude de la musique africaine," is by Geneviève Calame-Griaule and Blaise Calame. Leenhardt studies the New Caledonians, who are blacks; he contends that the New Caledonian meaning of the *word* is related to that of Negro Africans; the Calame article confirms this. For him, therefore, the black word, "uttered under the shock of *emotion*" (my italics) surpasses that emotion. Coinciding with the real, it is not only an expression of knowledge, but knowledge itself, ready for action, already action. "The word," he concludes, "is thought, speech, action." Now

PROFILE / Desmond Tutu (1931–)

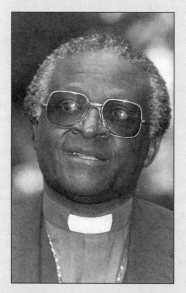

Desmond Tutu became prominent as a fighter against police brutality in South Africa in objecting to the massacre of children during the Soweto uprising. He pleaded with then President Vorster to dismantle apartheid for the future of the children. He also gave an impassioned speech at the gravesite of Steve Biko, a leader of the Black Consciousness movement who was murdered on September 12, 1977. Tutu became Secretary of the South African Council of Churches in 1978 and a leader in the fight against apartheid in South Africa. He called the South African government the most evil since the Nazis.

Apartheid for Tutu was "intrinsically evil" and had to be dismantled. He believed that no one could be neutral in this matter. "You are either on the side of the oppressed or on the side of the oppressor." To be fully free, Tutu believed, all must have freedom. He continually risked imprisonment traveling the world and condemning the brutal injustice of the apartheid system.

Tutu's method of fighting for liberation was through nonviolent action, a strategy with parallels to that of Martin Luther King, Jr. This was initially also the method of the African National Congress and Nelson Mandela. However, the strategy of that organization changed in 1961 after the introduction of the stringent Security Laws, which were seen to interpret nonviolent resistance as weakness. The new method was to use force to resist force. Nelson Mandela immediately began to organize the armed resistance, was captured in 1962, and remained in prison until 1990. The question of the efficacy and necessity of armed resistance versus "nonviolent" resistance remains one of the central issues confronting the contemporary world. Archbishop Desmond Tutu was a vice-chairman of a group on "Christianity and the Social Order" at the 1988 Lambeth Conference, which adopted a resolution on South Africa stating that it "understands those who, after exhausting all other ways, choose the way of armed struggle as the only way to justice, whilst drawing attention to the dangers and injustices possible in such action itself."

Underlying the philosophy of Desmond Tutu is the concept of humaneness. Everyone must have the freedom to become fully human; apartheid prevented this both for whites and for blacks, he argued. "I lay great stress on humaneness and being truly human. In our African understanding, part of Ubantu—being human—is the rare gift of sharing. . . . Blacks are beginning to lose this wonderful attribute, because we are being inveigled by the excessive individualism of the West. I loathe Capitalism because it gives far too great play to our inherent selfishness."

you will understand why, in my definition of Negro-African knowledge, I rejected abstract analysis on the European pattern, why I preferred to use analogous imagery, the metaphor, to make you *feel* the object of my speech. The metaphor, a symbolic short-cut in its sensitive, sensual qualities, is the method par excellence of Negro-African speech.

Today, it is also, quite often, the style of European speech. . . . So, our young people should not repudiate the Negro-African method of knowledge since, once again, it is the latest form of the European method. *Participation* and *communion* . . . are the very words that ethnologists specializing in the study of Negro-African civilizations have used for decades.

The Good Life   The question of what constitutes the good life is one of the oldest in philosophy. It assumes particular poignancy when the conditions of life are as difficult as they have been under colonial rule. Among the most painful realizations of post-colonial thinkers is the fact that colonialist regulations that provide a comparatively small economic or political benefit to the ruling class may cause a great deal of suffering among the colonized population. Over time, the consciousness of the people may become distorted through sustained brutalization, and traditional values and virtues may fall into obscurity. Countering the tendency to give in to baser motivations, especially once independence has been achieved, requires constant vigilance and personal discipline. In addressing this issue, some recommend socialism, some recommend democracy, some recommend religion. All, however, unite in recommending justice.

Archbishop **Desmond Tutu** (1931–) is widely credited with helping to maintain civility and and minimize bloodshed as one of the architects of South Africa's revolutionary transition to representative democracy from an authoritarian regime characterized by apartheid's rigidly enforced subjugation of the mostly impoverished black majority. Speaking out frequently against economic exploitation, official brutality, and broad application of the death penalty, Archbishop Tutu not only helped focus the eyes of the world on injustice in his country, he also articulated basic principles to guide his fellow citizens in what he saw as the inevitable shift to black control of the levers of power. In the following selection from a 1979 article, Tutu succinctly addresses the perennial philosophical problem of the nature of the good life.

SELECTION 17.9

"My Vision for South Africa"

From Desmond Tutu

From an article dated 25 March 1979.

We should all have the freedom to become fully human. That is basic to my understanding of society—that God created us without any coercion, freely for freedom. Responsibility is a nonsense except in the context of freedom—freedom to accept or reject alternative options, freedom to obey or disobey. God, who alone has the perfect right to be a totalitarian, has such a tremendous respect for our freedom to be human, that he would much rather see us go freely to hell than compel us to go to heaven.

According to the Bible, a human being can be a human being only because he belongs to a community. A person is a person through other persons, as we say in our African idiom. And so separation of persons because of biological accidents is reprehensible and blasphemous. A person is entitled to a stable community life, and the first of these communities is the family. A stable family life would be of paramount importance in my South Africa.

There would be freedom of association, of thought and of expression. This would involve freedom of movement as well. One would be free to go wherever one wanted, to associate with whomsoever one wished. As adult humans we would not be subject to draconian censorship laws. We can surely decide for ourselves what we want to read, what films to view and what views to have. We must not be frog-marched into puritanism.

Because we are created in the image of God one of our attributes is creativity. South Africa is starved of the great things many of her children can create and do, because of artificial barriers, and the refusal to let people develop to their fullest potential. When one has been overseas and seen for example the Black Alvin Ailey dance group, which performed modern ballet to standing room only crowds at Covent Garden, then one weeps for how South Africa has allowed herself to be cheated of such performances by her own inhabitants. How many potentially outstanding people are being denied the opportunity to get on?

When I think of the splendid young people I have met, who despite some horrendous experiences at the hands of the system, have emerged quite unscathed with bitterness, and who have a tremendous humanity and compassion, then I weep because we are so wantonly wasteful of human resources. We need a course on human ecology.

I lay great stress on humaneness and being truly human. In our African understanding, part of Ubantu—being human—is the rare gift of sharing. This concept of sharing is exemplified at African feasts even to this day, when people eat together from a common dish, rather than from individual dishes. That means a meal is indeed to have communion with one's fellows. Blacks are beginning to lose this wonderful attribute, because we are being inveigled by the excessive individualism of the West. I loathe Capitalism because it gives far too great play to our inherent selfishness. We are told to be highly competitive, and our children start learning the attitudes of the rat-race quite early. They mustn't just do well at school—they must sweep the floor with their rivals. That's how you get on. We give prizes to such persons, not so far as I know to those who know how best to get on with others, or those who can coax the best out of others. We must delight in our ulcers, the symbols of our success.

So I would look for a socio-economic system that placed the emphasis on sharing and giving, rather than on self-aggrandisement and getting. Capitalism is exploitative and I can't stand that. We need to engage the resources that each person has. My vision includes a society that is more compassionate and caring, in which 'superfluous appendages' [*the government's way of describing families of black workers*] are unthinkable, where young and old are made to feel wanted, and that they belong and are not resented. It is a distorted community that trundles its aged off into soulless institutions. We need their accumulated wisdom and experience. They are splendid for helping the younger to feel cared for; certainly that has been the experience in the extended family.

I believe too that in a future South Africa we must be supportive of the family. The nuclear family is not geared to stand all the strains placed on it by modern day pressures. There are things we can survive better in a group than singly. I know there are pressures in the extended family, but I need to be persuaded that these are greater than those presently haunting the nuclear family.

Basically I long and work for a South Africa that is more open and more just; where people count and where they will have equal access to the good things of life, with equal opportunity to live, work, and learn. I long for a South Africa where there will be equal and untrammelled access to the courts of the land, where detention without trial will be a thing of the hoary past, where bannings and other such arbitrary acts will no longer be even so much as mentioned, and where the rule of law will hold sway in the fullest sense. In addition, all adults will participate fully in political decision making, and in other decisions which affect their lives. Consequently they will have the vote and be eligible for election to all public offices. This South Africa will have integrity of territory with a common citizenship, and all the rights and privileges that go with such a citizenship, belonging to all its inhabitants.

The Americas

The history of colonialism and subjugation of native peoples in the Americas properly begins even before the arrival of Europeans in the fifteenth century. On both continents of the Western hemisphere, native Americans from the Toltecs to the Onondagas engaged in vigorous campaigns of empire-building. With the coming of the Europeans, however, imperial ambitions in the Americas were pursued from a position of technological superiority that the colonized could not match and with a sustained, single-minded acquisitiveness outside the experience of most tribes. Just as the numerically superior Dacians of Eastern Europe could not withstand the organized onslaught of Roman legions, so the Indians of the Americas were confronted by forces whose methods and ultimate objectives were utterly foreign to anything they had imagined in their mythology. Montezuma's destruction by a handful of Spaniards is just the most dramatic instance of a story line that played itself out numerous times on both continents of the Western hemisphere and is still very much an issue in the rain forests of South America.

With a few exceptions, especially in what is now Latin America, the evidence preserved in Indian oral histories suggests that even cataclysmic dislocations in the natural world could be grasped within the Indians' existing mythological and conceptual schemes. The usual events in the life of a warrior or a warrior's victim could similarly be accommodated. Upon the coming of the Europeans, however, history turned inscrutable for native Americans and has largely remained a sequence of unwelcome surprises. Buffeted by centuries of broken agreements and militarily enforced control strategies, the Indian nations have tried to maintain their integrity by negotiation, by violent resistance, by legal process, and by plumbing the depths of their religious and philosophical traditions. By all accounts, these strategies have met with mixed success at best; in worst cases, whole tribes have disappeared. With first-person accounts of genocidal aggression still part of the experience of many Indians, the post-colonial philosophical response has only begun to enter the literature.

While the African diaspora has resulted in the establishment of populations of African descent in many areas of the world, only in the United States has there developed on a large scale a distinctive and continuous thread of critical and normative philosophy growing out of the transplanted group's unfolding historical-cultural experience. Thinking on these things has developed into a multifaceted effort to come to grips with the everyday realities of African-American life, in which racial factors figure in some issues for virtually all writers and in virtually all issues for some of them. As occurs in the case of traditional thought, there are some who argue that this material does not belong in a discussion of philosophy at all; but given the problematics of post-colonial thought, drawing more inclusive category boundaries for the field of philosophy makes good sense, and for the same reasons. Some conventional conceptions of philosophy are challenged in this categorization, for unlike most academic philosophy, African-American post-colonial thinking occurs not only in self-identified philosophical texts, but also in story and song—wherever propositions are presented and explicitly considered or justified. For most post-colonial thinkers, allowing the possibility of departures from the stylistic norms of philosophy is a strength, not a disqualification; the subtextual message is that any occasion may open up a space for philosophical reflection.

In Latin America, the colonial order established in the fifteenth and sixteenth centuries did not evolve uniformly in all areas. Spain did not relinquish Cuba until the end of the nineteenth century, and Britain still maintains a tiny foothold on the Falkland Islands. After independence, most nations of Central and South America continued to be controlled by small, wealthy elites supporting dictatorial regimes. These regimes tended to attract the support of positivistic thinkers whose methods and metaphysics reinforced authoritarian views, though there was great variation from country to country. In this regard, Latin America philosophy roughly paralleled that of Western Europe. Beginning early in the twentieth century, however, positivism's influence began to decline in Latin America as in Europe, but for somewhat different reasons. Positivism's close identification in some places with discredited political factions was one factor, as was the vitality of French and German philosophy after the turn of the century. The introduction of Marxism to Latin America, which occurred mostly outside the traditional academic circles, provided the first serious challenge to the hegemony of Roman Catholic metaphysics. It also solidified the still-vital commitment of Latin American thinkers to a discourse that was attentive to the problematics of practical engagement. Strongly influenced by intellectual advances made in Europe and, to a lesser extent, the United States, Latin American thinkers nonetheless avoided the style of European and American philosophizing. By the middle of the twentieth century, a major part of Latin American philosophical discourse had taken on a heavily religious cast;

interestingly, this move, which would have been avoided by most philosophers in Europe and North America, has been almost uniformly celebrated among post-colonial thinkers.

This fact points up a little-recognized commonality among the expressions of post-colonial thought: in virtually all cases except those in which Marxist materialism has been consciously adopted, the line between religion and philosophy seems very hard to draw. Whether the religion is the Christianity of Latin America, the pantheisms and myriad mythologies of Africa and the Americas, or the Hinduism of India, religiously metaphysical claims regularly serve as points of departure or elements of the presuppositional structures of post-colonial texts. In their own terms, this does not make them any less philosophical; instead, it is viewed as a technique to engage the whole person in the act of thinking and interpretation. As a larger methodological consideration, post-colonial thinkers contend, this mode of engagement seeks to overcome the kind of personal alienation that made colonialist brutality thinkable in the first place and that perpetuates its effects to this day.

American Indian Thought

For as long as the thoughts of American Indians have been recorded, the views and ideas of these peoples have integrally included philosophical and religious elements. Appreciation of the larger moral and spiritual contexts of thought and action is an essential element of post-colonial thought; American Indian thinkers have been unwavering in their insistence that thinking must properly appreciate the conditions of life.

Philosophy of Religion

In traditional societies, the structures and rhythms of life are defined by myths and stories that endure through the generations. Religion, in these cultures, consists of the mostly unquestioned acceptance of the truth of the stories and dedicated adherence to the norms and prescriptions they transmit. The disruption of tradition by invasion, oppression, and enforced removal from native lands presents problems for traditional religion, not only because specific claims are challenged or specific rituals cannot be performed, but because the nature of reality itself—long self-evident to traditional consciousness—is brought into question. This is the point at which philosophy of religion must enter the thinking of a people. Once religion itself becomes an issue, as it does when a society's integrity is compromised, then a new role for religion in the culture must be imagined. Because traditional religion has defined the culture since time immemorial, it is too important to forsake. Because traditional religion is fractured, however, it cannot repair itself. One of the tasks of philosophy of religion in a post-colonial context is to make the recovery of religion possible.

Perhaps the most influential Indian writer of nonfiction in late twentieth-century America, **Vine Deloria, Jr.** (1933–), has undertaken this task with particular care. A practicing lawyer with formal training in theology and a record of years

PROFILE / Vine Deloria, Jr. (1933–)

For Vine Deloria, Jr., a member of the Standing Rock Sioux, Indian tribal ways are not just matters of nostalgic yearning but live possibilities for the future of North America. Turning these possibilities into reality has defined the career of this eclectic thinker, who is considered by many to be the leading spokesperson for American Indians in the late twentieth century.

Deloria had already achieved some prominence as Executive Director of the National Congress of American Indians in the mid-sixties, but with the publication of *Custer Died for Your Sins: An Indian Manifesto* in 1969, he achieved broad recognition in academic and social-activist circles. Although his polemical writings have been criticized by some within the Indian movement as excessively rhetorical, Deloria's credentials as a thinker of substance are guaranteed by his diverse publications and sustained personal involvement in the practical issues that face Indians in particular and Americans generally. He has focused his legal training toward becoming one of America's leading experts on treaties, serving for a time as Chair of the Institute for Development of Indian Law. As well, his discussions of religious and spiritual issues are highly regarded by theologians and scholars of religion. Some of his other writings include *The Metaphysics of Modern Existence* (1979) and *We Talk, You Listen: New Tribes, New Turf* (1970). At this writing, he is a member of the political science faculty of the University of Arizona.

As a post-colonial thinker, Vine Deloria, Jr., pursues a path shared by many. Specifically, he begins with the situation of American Indians, but analyzes the problems they face as part of a larger problem that includes them and the European culture that has acted with deviousness and genocidal malice for hundreds of years. The root issue is not money or power, in Deloria's view, but a kind of spiritual poverty. His recent work has included research into the Indian religion and legends he believes offer a vision of a sustainable future. Thus, he draws on indigenous spiritual resources as the corrective to the truncated understanding of humanity and nature often promoted by technological civilization.

of advocacy for native Americans, Deloria brings traditional values to bear on modern problems. Moreover, he clearly rejects the strategy of strengthening his people by affirming every belief and behavior exhibited in the native culture. Deloria's purpose is not limited to a narrowly ethnic agenda. He sees in modern civilization, especially that of the culturally Christian heirs of European traditions, a danger to human well-being that can be addressed by reconsidering Indian ways. This means for Deloria not only adoption of ecologically sound practices, but also a reorientation of our understanding of life itself.

SELECTION 17.10

God Is Red

From Vine Deloria, Jr.

In our present situation, we therefore, face a most difficult question of meaning. Ecologists project a world crisis of severe intensity within our lifetime, whereas the religious mythologies projecting the existence and eventual salvation of another world had better be correct in their beliefs. It is becoming increasingly apparent that we shall not have the benefits of this world for much longer. The imminent and expected destruction of the life cycle of world ecology can be prevented by a radical shift in outlook from our present naive conception of this world as a testing ground to a more mature view of the universe as a comprehensive matrix of life forms. Making this shift in viewpoint is essentially religious, not economic or political. . . .

Many thoughtful and useful systems of belief of ancient peoples have been simply rejected *a priori* by Western thinkers in the religious sphere. This attitude has intruded into Western science and then emerged as criteria by which the world of our experience is judged, condemned, and too often sentenced to death. Many people, for example, have developed astrological systems by which they have charted the nature of relationships between the lives of men and the movement of the planets and stars. Given that modern science now views the universe as an extremely sophisticated electromagnetic complex, the contentions of astrologers as to the influence of the heavens on individual propensities to behave in certain ways may not be as superstitious as it would at first appear. Yet astrology is rejected out of hand by many followers of Western religious thinking, because it conflicts with the philosophical problem of free will. . . .

A number of religions have concentrated on the development of beliefs covering the spirits

of places; the relationship of man to animal, bird, and reptile forms of life; and the nature of religious healing. Again these beliefs have been rejected on dogmatic grounds, not because they were not suitable for the communities which held them as beliefs. The usual answer given to questions about the nature of religion is highly unsatisfactory. Other religions have been given credibility to the extent to which they conformed or paralleled certain Christian doctrines. To the extent to which they varied or were in direct opposition to Christian doctrines, they have been regarded as false and sometimes as deliberate attempts on the part of the Christian devil to mislead people. . . .

We cannot conclude that other peoples spent centuries in a state of delusion simply because their experiences of God were so different than those of Western peoples. That their experiences could not be either described accurately by Westerners or understood in Western categories of thought does not make them false. The least we can do is to understand that it is in the nature of religion to exert a profound influence within societies and groups and sustain the community or national group over a period of time. Having retreated even that much, the Western world must be prepared to analyze religion as a phenomenon that does not necessarily explain the unanswered questions posed by the philosophical mind, but which may, in itself, cause such questions to occur to all manner of men in a great variety of situations. . . .

The major step to be taken to understand religion today is to understand the nature of religion as it occurs in specific places. There is a reason why shrines exist over and above the piety of the uneducated religious person who has visions while tending sheep. Mount Sinai, for example, has been a holy mountain for a considerable length of time, thus indicating that it has a religious existence over and above any temporary belief held by particular people. If this concept is true then economics cannot and should not be the sole determinant of land use.

Unless the sacred places are discovered and protected and used as religious places, there is no possibility of a nation ever coming to grips with the land itself. Without this basic relationship, national psychic stability is impossible.

Personal Identity   In most of the world's philosophies, the notion of person is never discussed in isolation from other beings and a general understanding of the world. The questions of who one is and what one does, the first being metaphysical and the second being ethical, can be explored in reflective discourse but, for many cultures, can only be decided by the living of a life. Within a traditional framework, the experience of a people over time may often be represented in continuations of mythic stories or in alternative plot branchings that give insight into how the tradition meets the major dilemmas of life. When traditions break down, however, the problems that force these kinds of decisions reassert themselves. In the following selection, Joseph Bruchac presents a glimpse of some of the issues surrounding the construction of the person. Author of more than twenty books of poetry, fiction, and retellings of American Indian folk tales, Bruchac is also an American Book Award winner. Space does not permit inclusion of the entire essay, but it is worth noting that it contains autobiographical recollections reaching back to childhood and a poem, as well as discussions of ideas as in the excerpt here. This is an important point about how philosophy occurs among native Americans and others whose traditions have been until recently primarily oral. In reading the texts that come out of these traditions, one must be attentive to the fact that many of the arguments they present are enthymemic, that is, they contain unstated propositions; in traditional societies, one is expected to be able to fill in the unstated elements and draw the proper conclusions. That style seems to persist in the discourse of many cultures even after traditions have become fragmented, formally posing a challenge to reconstruct culture so as to make shared understanding possible again.

SELECTION 17.11

"Walking Between the Worlds"

From Joseph Bruchac

It is sometimes hard to explain to people just what it is that you see when you look at these worlds with something like a native eye. Even the words you speak may seem simple and clear but have another meaning. When you say

"drum," do you see something to be played in a band or something, *some thing,* to be made by an elementary school student in a crafts class in a "Native American" unit? Or do you see a living creation, and does the word *drum,* in whatever language it is spoken, mean to you the heartbeat of Earth? When you say the word *dog,* is it a word that just means an animal or a word that is an insult? Or does it refer to one of the animal people, an honorable being, even a relative? The animals, you see, are seen as ancestors, and when native people speak of the time when animals could talk, they are speaking in the present tense. How vastly different are the views of European and Native American with regard to our animal brothers and sisters can be seen when we talk about "hunting and fishing for sport." I was in Chicago to speak on Native American publishing at the American Library Association Meeting. On the panel with me was Paul DeMain, an enrolled member of the Oneida nation, the editor of the Wisconsin native newspaper *News from Indian Country.* Much has been written recently about the opposition (violent, at times) of white sportfishing groups to the native people spearing fish, an exercise of their treaty rights (given to them in exchange for giving up the entire northern half of the state). Paul spoke of the importance of people understanding that there are different ways to see the same thing. "In our traditions," he said, "it's sacrilegious to pull a fish from the water, tear its mouth with a hook, damage the layer of protective slime on its body by taking it in your hand, and then throw it back in. To us, that is not sport. If we hunted or fished, we had good reason to do so and we did it to provide for our people. But five hundred years ago, sport in Europe was the king's army chasing a fox through the forests, while our people here on this continent were playing lacrosse and ball games which were the ancestors of football and hockey, basketball, baseball, and soccer."

The simple truth is, as Paul DeMain said, that sport to Europeans often means the killing of nonhuman beings which want no part in that sport and are given no choice, while team sports, groups of men and women playing together in agreed-upon competition, is characteristic of the native people of the Americas. The new idea of team sports (like the basic principles of democracy which the Founding Fathers borrowed from the Iroquois League) has been so wholeheartedly absorbed by white culture that there is hardly any awareness of its Native American roots. It is hard to communicate with people when they do not understand your language, though they think it is their own. And to really appreciate the writings of contemporary native people, it is also necessary to have some understanding of the living cultures that shape their thoughts and language—which is why Paul DeMain spoke of sports and fishing as part of a discussion of native publishing.

We are now in the seventh generation of native people since the coming of the Europeans five centuries ago. That period of five centuries, hard as it has been for native people, is not seen by Indians as a long time. It is still commonly said by the Iroquois and other native people that we must make our decisions not just with tomorrow's result in mind but thinking of how it will affect seven generations to come. In one of the stories of the time of Creation, there were two brothers. One was good-minded and cared for life on Earth. The other was hard-hearted, like flint. Good Mind and Flint fought each other, and when Good Mind won, the hard-hearted brother was cast out—but not out of the minds of human beings. All of us have within us those two sides. We must recognize this in order to choose the side of Good Mind, to give good thoughts strength. So, as I speak of walking between the worlds, there is also that balance to keep in mind, that balance between the human power to destroy and the human ability to preserve.

African-American Thought

Social Justice   Decades after his assassination, the call for justice articulated in the writings of **Martin Luther King, Jr.** (1929–1968) remains the single most powerful determinant in the American civil rights movement. King's basic message was a simple one, stated memorably in the oft-quoted dedication to *Why We Can't Wait:* "To my children . . . for whom I dream that one day soon they will no longer be judged by the color of their skin but by the content of their character." How to turn vision into reality was, for King, not just a matter of the mass organizational strategies for which he is often remembered, but of personal responsibility. King was strongly influenced by the example and the writings of Mahatma Gandhi in both setting his agenda and deciding on the appropriate methods to achieve it. Like Gandhi, King did not separate the two, nor did he minimize the difficulties of this comprehensive project. It is no coincidence that King's background was religious, for as other thinkers in the post-colonial world found, commonly held religious sensibilities can provide a point of departure for ethical reasoning from a strong set of broadly accepted premises. In the following selection, King affirms his perception that right behavior leads to right consequences.

SELECTION 17.12

"The Sword That Heals"   **From Martin Luther King, Jr.**

The argument that nonviolence is a coward's refuge lost its force as its heroic and often perilous acts uttered their wordless but convincing rebuttal in Montgomery, in the sit-ins, on the freedom rides, and finally in Birmingham.

There is a powerful motivation when a suppressed people enlist in an army that marches under the banner of nonviolence. A nonviolent army has a magnificent universal quality. To join an army that trains its adherents in the methods of violence, you must be of a certain age. But in Birmingham, some of the most valued foot soldiers were youngsters ranging from elementary pupils to teen-age high school and college students. For acceptance in the armies that maim and kill, one must be physically sound, possessed of straight limbs and accurate vision. But in Birmingham, the lame and the halt and the crippled could and did join up. Al Hibbler, the sightless singer, would never have

been accepted in the United States Army or the army of any other nation, but he held a commanding position in our ranks.

In armies of violence, there is a caste of rank. In Birmingham, outside of the few generals and lieutenants who necessarily directed and coordinated operations, the regiments of the demonstrators marched in democratic phalanx. Doctors marched with window cleaners. Lawyers demonstrated with laundresses. Ph.D.'s and no-D's were treated with perfect equality by the registrars of the nonviolence movement.

As the broadcasting profession will confirm, no shows are so successful as those which allow for audience participation. In order to be somebody, people must feel themselves part of something. In the nonviolent army, there is room for everyone who wants to join up. There is no color distinction. There is no examination, no pledge, except that, as a soldier in the armies of

PROFILE / Martin Luther King, Jr. (1929–1968)

Martin Luther King, Jr., was America's most famous civil rights leader. He helped end racial segregation by organizing nonviolent resistance to unjust law.

The son of the pastor of the Ebenezer Baptist Church in Atlanta, Georgia, King was ordained in 1947, and in 1954 became the minister of a Baptist church in Montgomery, Alabama. He re-

ceived his PhD in 1955 from Boston University. In 1955 he led the boycott by Montgomery blacks against the segregated city bus lines; this landmark civil rights battle ended in 1956 with the desegregation of the city buses. King's passive resistance philosophy had won its first major victory, and King was catapulted to national prominence.

King organized the Southern Christian Leadership Conference, through which he fought for civil rights in the South and throughout the nation. Though he always advocated and used nonviolent methods, he was arrested and imprisoned many times and was, allegedly, the victim of a vendetta by FBI director J. Edgar Hoover.

In 1963 King organized the March on Washington. This, the largest demonstration in U.S. history, brought more than 200,000 people to the nation's capital. In

1964 King was awarded the Nobel Peace Prize.

By the mid-1960s, King's methods were being challenged by more militant civil rights leaders like H. Rap Brown ("Violence is as American as apple pie") and groups like the Student Nonviolent Coordinating Committee and the Black Panthers. At the same time, King's fight for justice was expanding; he became critical of the Vietnam War and concerned with poverty in general.

King was organizing a Poor People's March on Washington in 1968 when he made a side trip to Memphis, Tennessee, to support striking sanitation workers. There, standing on the balcony of a motel, he was slain by an assassin's bullet. James Earl Ray was convicted of the murder.

Martin Luther King, Jr., was a philosopher who made a difference.

violence is expected to inspect his carbine and keep it clean, nonviolent soldiers are called upon to examine and burnish their greatest weapons—their heart, their conscience, their courage and their sense of justice.

Nonviolent resistance paralyzed and confused the power structures against which it was directed. The brutality with which officials would have quelled the black individual became impotent when it could not be pursued with stealth and remain unobserved. It was caught—

as a fugitive from a penitentiary is often caught—in gigantic circling spotlights. It was imprisoned in a luminous glare revealing the naked truth to the whole world. It is true that some demonstrators suffered violence, and that a few paid the extreme penalty of death. They were the martyrs of last summer who laid down their lives to put an end to the brutalizing of thousands who had been beaten and bruised and killed in dark streets and back rooms of sheriffs' offices, day in and day out, in hundreds of summers past.

Black Power

In the 1960s, with Stokely Carmichael at the lead, the ideology of Black Power emerged as the high-profile response of some African-Americans to the perception that a hundred years after Lincoln's Emancipation Proclamation, a pervasive reality of race-based inequalities still existed. The basic premise of the Black Power movement was that although African-Americans might achieve cultural recognition and even economic security, true well-being required meaningful political power as well. Black Power advocates faced resistance not only from those outside their ethnic group, but from those within as well. Renouncing the program of gradual improvement and assimilation identified with Booker T. Washington as unworkable, Black Power sought rapid transition to African-American leadership wherever possible by use of racially conscious voting. Black Power ideology encompassed a wide range of beliefs, from the relatively uncontroversial theory about the meaning of elections to the African-American population to proposals for a separate state. The positions of individuals within the movement evolved as well, with no consensus emerging.

The striking thing about the nonviolent crusade of 1963 was that so few felt the sting of bullets or the clubbing of billies and nightsticks. Looking back, it becomes obvious that the oppressors were restrained not only because the world was looking but also because, standing before them, were hundreds, sometimes thousands, of Negroes who for the first time dared to look back at a white man, eye to eye. Whether through a decision to exercise wise restraint or the operation of a guilty conscience, many a hand was stayed on a police club and many a fire hose was restrained from vomiting forth its pressure. That the Revolution was a comparatively bloodless one is explained by the fact that the Negro did not merely give lip service to nonviolence. The tactics the movement utilized, and that guided far-flung actions in cities dotted across the map, discouraged violence because one side would not resort to it and the other was so often immobilized by confusion, uncertainty and disunity.

Nonviolence had tremendous psychological importance to the Negro. He had to win and to vindicate his dignity in order to merit and enjoy his self-esteem. He had to let white men know that the picture of him as a clown—irresponsible, resigned and believing in his own inferiority—was a stereotype with no validity. This method was grasped by the Negro masses because it embodied the dignity of struggle, of moral conviction and self-sacrifice. The Negro was able to face his adversary, to concede to him a physical advantage and to defeat him because the superior force of the oppressor had become powerless.

To measure what this meant to the Negro may not be easy. But I am convinced that the courage and discipline with which Negro thousands accepted nonviolence healed the internal wounds of Negro millions who did not themselves march in the streets or sit in the jails of the South. One need not participate directly in order to be involved. For Negroes all over this nation, to identify with the movement, to have pride in those who were the principals, and to give moral, financial or spiritual support were to restore to them some of the pride and honor which had been stripped from them over the centuries.

Sexuality   In the late twentieth century, beginning in France and the United States, the feminist movement pursued a thorough revaluation of the traditional themes and methods of philosophy. Feminism is sometimes caricatured as a movement of political reaction, but from a feminist perspective, this constitutes a rather transparent strategy to undermine the philosophical authenticity of feminist thinking. Within philosophical feminism, several schools of thought have emerged, each with its own profile of insights and emphases. In the African-American community, awareness of the successes of the civil rights movement and the rise of feminism in the white middle class combined with first-hand knowledge of a mostly unwritten history of the particular difficulties of black women, including a high incidence of domestic violence, to produce a variant of feminism that is especially sensitive to the social-ethical problematics of marginalization. In the view of **bell hooks** (c. 1955–), whose writings range from general-audience essays in popular magazines to highly nuanced discourse most appreciated by academically trained minds, it is important to make some distinctions within the feminist movement. Claims hooks, the feminism of the founders of the movement, at least in the United States, centered on careerism, a specifically middle-class concern. As such, it was liable to be co-opted by the existing power structure to perpetuate a culture of competition and individualism, which she analyzes to be antithetical to the best, inclusive impulses of feminism. The problems of the more thoroughly disenfranchised require a more radical rethinking, hooks and others have argued.

SELECTION 17.13

Feminist Theory: From Margin to Center   **From bell hooks**

Sexual norms as they are currently socially constructed have always privileged active sexual expression over sexual desire. To act sexually is deemed natural, normal—to not act, unnatural, abnormal. Such thinking corresponds with sexist role patterning. Men are socialized to act sexually, women to not act (or to simply react to male sexual advances). Women's liberationists' insistence that women should be sexually active as a gesture of liberation helped free female sexuality from the restraints imposed upon it by repressive double standards, but it did not remove the stigma attached to sexual inactivity. Until that stigma is removed, women and men will not feel free to participate in sexual activity when they desire. They will continue to respond to coercion, either the sexist coercion that pushes young men to act sexually to prove their "masculinity" (i.e., their heterosexuality) or the sexual coercion that compels young women to respond to such advances to prove their "femininity" (i.e., their willingness to be heterosexual sex objects). The removal of the social stigma attached to sexual inactivity would amount to a change in sexual norms. It would have many positive implications for women and men, especially teenagers who are at this historical moment most likely to be victimized by sexist sexual norms. . . .

. . . Within the feminist movement lesbian women have worked hardest to call attention to the struggle to end heterosexist oppression. Lesbians have been on both sides of the larger sexual liberation debate. They have shown many

PROFILE / bell hooks (Gloria Watkins) (c. 1955–)

Acknowledged as one of the most provocative essayists in America today, bell hooks has devoted special attention to the suppression of the voices of black women. Writing under the name of her unlettered great-grand-mother to symbolize this very problem, hooks often takes up controversial themes that other writers avoid by design or over-sight. Her mordant analyses typi-cally begin by calling attention to something that has been missed or covered over. Her interruptions of the conventional flow of cul-tural conversation have discom-fited nearly every sort of reader in one way or another, and hooks does not spare herself as she searches for the examples that will inspire, edify, and (even) entertain. Among the thorniest issues she has raised is that of class distinc-tions in the construction of Amer-ican feminism; specifically, hooks has argued that a feminism which emphasizes the concerns of white, middle-class women with career plans does not do justice to minor-ity women, many of whom must contend regularly with a very dif-ferent set of economic realities.

At this writing, bell hooks is on the faculty of the Department of Afro-American Studies at Yale. She is the author of nine books and numerous articles, including *Ain't I a Woman: Black Women and Femi-nism* (1981), *Feminist Theory: From Margin to Center* (1984), *Breaking Bread: Insurgent Black Intellectual Life* (with Cornel West; 1991), and *Black Looks: Race and Representa-tion* (1992). Her earlier writings are strongly flavored with Marxist ideology, but ideology seems to be less a concern for hooks than is finding ways to think and act inclu-sively. Thus, she advocates con-sensus decision making—and the redistribution of power that is im-plied by adoption of that way of thinking. Moreover, she valorizes the authentically collective action and liberation from repressive hi-erarchy that consensus can lead to. Adopting this set of values ad-dresses the problem of the out-sider, whose concerns are often submerged in the strong currents of majority views. The writing of bell hooks attacks domination that is sometimes obvious and some-times hidden. She does not stop at critique, but instead ventures pro-posals that promise not only to benefit a narrow constituency, but to create a more just society generally.

heterosexual women that their prejudices against lesbians support and perpetuate com-pulsory heterosexuality. They have also shown women that we can find emotional and mutual sexual fulfillment in relationships with one an-other. Some lesbians have suggested that ho-mosexuality may be the most direct expression of pro-sex politics, since it is unconnected to procreation. Feminist movement to end female sexual oppression is linked to lesbian liberation. The struggle to end prejudice, exploitation, and oppression of lesbians and gay men is a crucial feminist agenda. It is a necessary component of the movement to end female sexual oppression.

Affirming lesbianism, women of varied sexual preferences resist the perpetuation of compulsory heterosexuality.

Throughout feminist movement, there has been a tendency to make the struggle to end sexual oppression a competition: heterosexuality versus lesbianism. Early in the movement, attempts to exclude and silence lesbians were justified through the specter of a "lavender menace." Later, lesbianism was presented as a choice that would eliminate the need to deal with issues of heterosexual conflict or as the most politically correct choice for a feminist woman. Even though many feminists acknowledge that fighting sexual oppression, particularly male domination of women, is not the same as man-hating, within feminist gatherings and organizations intense anti-male sentiments are sometimes expressed by heterosexual women and lesbians alike, and women who are not lesbians, who may or may not be in relationships with men feel that they are not "real" feminists. This is especially true of women who may support feminism but who do not publicly support lesbian rights. It is often forgotten that we are all in the process of developing radical political consciousness, that it is a "process," and that it defeats efforts to build solidarity to condemn or judge women politically incorrect when they do not immediately support all the issues we deem relevant. . . .

Feminist activists must take care that our legitimate critiques of heterosexism are not attacks on heterosexual *practice*. As feminists, we must confront those women who do in fact believe that women with heterosexual preferences are either traitors or likely to be anti-lesbian. Condemnation of heterosexual practice has led women who desire sexual relationships with men to feel they cannot participate in feminist movement. They have gotten the message that to be "truly" feminist is not to be heterosexual. . . .

Just as feminist movement to end sexual oppression should create a social climate in which lesbians and gay men are no longer oppressed, a climate in which their sexual choices are affirmed, it should also create a climate in which heterosexual practice is freed from the constraints of heterosexism and can also be affirmed. One of the practical reasons for doing this is the recognition that the advancement of feminism as a political movement depends on the involvement of masses of women, a vast majority of whom are heterosexual. As long as feminist women (be they celibate, lesbian, heterosexual, etc.) condemn male sexuality, and by extension women who are involved sexually with men, feminist movement is undermined. . . .

A feminist movement that aims to eliminate sexist oppression, and in that context sexual oppression, cannot ignore or dismiss the choice women make to be heterosexual. Despite heterosexism, many women have acknowledged and accepted that they do not have to be heterosexual (that there are other options) and have chosen to be exclusively or primarily heterosexual. Their choices should be respected. By choosing they exercise sexual freedom. Their choices may not, as those who oppose them suggest, be influenced by heterosexual privilege. Most heterosexual privilege is diminished when compared to the degree of exploitation and oppression a woman is likely to encounter in most heterosexual relationships. There are exceptions. Many women choose to be heterosexual because they enjoy genital contact with individual men. Feminist movement has enriched and added new dimensions to lesbian sexuality and there is no reason it cannot do the same for heterosexuality. Women with heterosexual preferences need to know that feminism is a political movement that does not negate their choices even as it offers a framework to challenge and oppose male sexual exploitation of women.

There are some feminists (and I am one) who believe that feminist movement to end sexual oppression will not change destructive sexual norms if individuals are taught that they must choose between competing sexualities (the most obvious being heterosexuality and homo-sexuality) and conform to the expectations of the chosen norm. Sexual desire has varied and multiple dimensions and is rarely as "exclusive" as any norm would suggest. A liberatory sexual-ity would not teach women to see their bodies as accessible to all men, or to all women for that matter. It would favor instead a sexuality that is open or closed based on the nature of individual interaction. Implicit in the idea of sexual pref-erence is the assumption that anyone of the pre-ferred sex can seek access to one's body. This is a concept that promotes objectification. In a het-erosexual context it makes everyone, especially women, into sex objects. Given the power dif-ferential created by sexist politics, women are likely to be approached by any man since all men are taught to assume they should have ac-cess to the bodies of all women. Sexuality would be transformed if the codes and labels that strip sexual desire of its specificity and particularity were abandoned.

Theory of Literature   The writing of Charles Johnson embodies the con-vergence of two threads in the history of philosophy, the Continental and the post-colonial. This mix makes for challenging reading as Johnson draws on episte-mology, literature studies, and phenomenology to state his case. Among his points: experience is more complex than we commonly believe, which places the engaged author in a problematic position. Johnson assumes literature may include philo-sophical theses. Indeed, from the neoclassical period in early eighteenth-century Europe to the present, philosophers have presented their ideas in drama and nar-rative, as well as in traditional monographs. As well, post-colonial writers in Africa, India, the United States, and elsewhere have often sought to include literary art as a medium of philosophical reflection. This is one of the phenomena Johnson, an award-winning writer who infuses his own creative work with the methods and insights of formal philosophy, wants to understand more deeply. As a theorist of literature, he not only draws on multiple intellectual and cultural sources but also consults his own experience to forge a uniquely informed synthesis that sets a rigorously high standard for this mode of thinking. The following selection chal-lenges the reader's conceptions of literature both through its range of ideas and through the implications of its premises.

SELECTION 17.14

"Being and Fiction"

From Charles Johnson

Because no experience is "raw." None is *given* to us meaningful, or as meaning only one thing.

Seldom, if ever, is an isolated event or "expe-rience" significant by itself or worthy of fic-tional treatment. No, its value lies in its relation to other events. Or, as E. M. Forster puts it, "to events arranged in time sequence." In *Aspects of the Novel*, a series of lectures that has deservedly been in print for over half a century, this is his minimalistic definition of story—lunch follows breakfast and precedes dinner, or using his own example, "The king died, and then the queen died." Even so spare an account of the *eidos*, or essence, of every story is freighted with judgment, for it presents the story (which in this form can also be a newspaper article, a joke, or history) as a temporal being, an organization of before-and-after, or, in Aristotelian terms, structured with a "beginning, middle, and end." Are those structures of events in the world? Well, yes, but only to the extent that they are structures of you and me. Temporality describes *our* being, how *we* see. Even that, of course, is too sketchy. We perceive in the present only, remember the past, and project ourselves into the future, a constant flip-flopping about of mind that Edmund Husserl analyzes in *The Phenomenology of Internal Time-Consciousness* and that Richard Wright adroitly exploits to generate tension in *Native Son*—that is, half the things that make Bigger's heart wham and push the novel along are his imagined scenarios of capture and death, his habit of preliving scenes of racial torment. Though skeletal, this orderly description of the story plunges us into a pattern that says a great deal more about Western esthetic logic than, say, cultures (or modes of consciousness) less linear than our own. And by the time Forster proceeds to define "plot" by use of the example "The king died, and then the queen died of grief," we as readers have rushed boldly into the forest of hermeneutic philosophy. Here, with the introduction of causation (died of grief), events have *glue* between them, connectedness, an immaterial linkage between matter and mind, objective occurrence and subjective response: the soul and the world are one. Plot, if this traditional definition is credible, is an act of faith.

And whatever else it may be dramatically, each plot—how events happen and why—is also an *argument*. To plot well is to say, "This is how the world works," that if you place *this* person A in *this* situation B, the result will be event

C. If plot is anything, it is a vehicle of reason. Or, if you prefer, high speculation on why things turn out as they do. If some writers find plot to be a difficult problem to solve, I would wager it is because they also find it difficult to engage in the ballet of argumentation, and also because they are not familiar with the many forms that reason or reasoning can assume. It is this basic, genuinely exploratory element in creative writing that leads some phenomenologists such as Maurice Merleau-Ponty to conclude that philosophy and fiction—both disciplines of language—are about, at bottom, the same business. Merleau-Ponty, of course, goes farther than that, making it clear in *Sense and Non-Sense* that our lives are inherently metaphysical insofar as each moment of perception, each blink of the eye, involves the activity of interpretation; perception is an *act*, and this observation puts the lie to that ancient stupidity that says the processes of philosophy and fiction are two different enterprises—they are sister disciplines, I would say, and unless a critic realizes this, his position is simply untenable. More specific to this point of the sisterhood of fiction and philosophy is the article "Phenomenological Variations and Artistic Discovery" in philosopher Don Ihde's *Existential Technics*, where he persuasively argues that the method known as "phenomenological (fantasy) variations" performed on the phenomenon in order to exhibit its full range of meaning or profiles (*Abschattung*) is a systematic form of discovery already present in the arts. The arts, he says, are "latently 'phenomenological' in their primary use of variations." Ihde lays out these forms of variations as follows: figure-ground reversals, juxtapositions of context, the isolation of dominant and recessive characteristics, transformations of perspectives, and even deconstruction as devices used to shock and to cause disjuncture, thereby freeing perception from the familiar. To this I would add another shared technique: namely, "phenomenological description" itself, the manner in which we use words, particularly in prose that is charged or poetic or surrealistic, to fling the reader of fiction toward revelation and unsealed vision.

Afrocentrism   Afrocentrism, a school of thought primarily focused on investigating the heritage and influence of African cultures, came to prominence with the work of Chaikh Anta Diop. Diop, an Africanist, brought his acknowledged expertise in ancient Egyptian history and culture to bear in arguing for a set of theses that ran counter to ancient history as told by Europeans. Diop's history claimed among other things that black Africa was the origin of Egyptian civilization and that Europeans who were not purely Nordic traced their ancestry back to Africa. The matter remains hotly contested among historians at this writing. Whether Diop's case prevails in whole or in part is a matter for archaeologists and historians to decide, but whatever the eventual verdict, Diop has inspired a school of cultural interpretation that is pursuing a revaluation of virtually all things African. Afrocentric thinkers hold to a range of not necessarily compatible positions, but something of a mainstream constellation of ideas has been articulated by **Molefi Kete Asante** (1942–) in numerous publications. The selection that follows, from one of the major statements of Afrocentrism, illustrates how the Afrocentric school of thought approaches the problem of philosophically consistent elaboration of a position.

SELECTION 17.15

"Defining Afrocentric Discourse"

From Molefi Kete Asante

I suggest three fundamental Afrocentric themes of transcendent discourse: (1) human relations, (2) humans' relationship to the supernatural, and (3) humans' relationships to their own being. In any culture and under any conceivable circumstances, these would be the areas of discourse that occur to me. To posit these three general themes is to try to diffuse some of the specific issues that occur as "universals" in contemporary analyses. Almost all knowledge has cultural relevance and must be examined for its particular focus. Cultural differences do exist and must be explained by perspective in any discussion of themes. Take the Ebonics example in language, "Got no money," or the fact that guilt and innocence elicit different responses in

whites and blacks. There needs to be more cultural data to give us something like a literary and oratory file. . . .

Certain Afrocentric assumptions are necessary when we approach the discussion of African American discourse, both in its theory and its criticism. First, we assume that the objective of such discourse, in the large, is the successful presentation of one of the three principal themes, often within the context of resistance to oppression, liberation from stereotypes, and action in anticipation of reaction. Secondly, we assume that the discourse conforms to certain elementary materials of our corpus of culture; this would suggest stylistic and argumentative features as well. Thirdly, we assume that the discourse is directed principally towards either a black, a non-black, or a mixed audience. Furthermore, we assume that the discourse will have certain adjustment features to various audiences.

Since so much of African American discourse, in the sense of people speaking and writing, occurs within a Eurocentric context, it is necessary to isolate those aspects of a critical theory, derived from the condition, that are applicable to discourse. The assumptions serve as emblematic stools upon which to rest the critical case. You cannot rightly call any African American discourse, merely because it is uttered by a black person, *Afrocentric*. In fact, donning the *agbada* of a critic, I believe that much so-called "black discourse" is essentially white or Eurocentric discourse by black people. A black person's writing does not make the writing Afrocentric, no more than living in Africa makes a person Afrocentric. . . .

Speaking about black issues does not make a discourse Afrocentric. Perhaps there is a cruel hoax being played out in the context of our Western experience. We are often victims of assumptions that support the established value systems and critical theories with little regard to our own profound historical experiences. Among those experiences are the achievements of transcendence against great odds; furthermore, rhythm has been the way to that connection with the cosmic. A truly Afrocentric rhetoric must oppose the negation in Western culture; it is combative, antagonistic, and wholly committed to the propagation of a more humanistic vision of the world. Its foundation is necessarily the slave narrative. Its rhythms are harmonious, discordant only to those who have refused to accept either the truth of themselves or the possibility of other frames of reference. Afrocentric rhetoric, while it is in opposition to the negative in Western culture, allows other cultures to co-exist, and in that particular aspect is substantially different from Western rhetoric. It is neither imperialistic nor oppressive. Therein lies its invigorating power. While

beauty is artifactual for the Western world, it is dynamic in the Afrocentric sense. Expression itself can be beautiful to the Afrocentric critic. Thus rhetoric is a transforming power, a mythic discourse in the midst of a plethora of symbols.

Furthermore, it does not secure its efficacy or originality in the same manner as Western discourse, perhaps because it does not force the same separations as Eurocentric lines of argument. Foucault points out that "the reason-madness nexus constitutes for western culture one of the dimensions of its originality." In effect, Foucault says, from Bosch to Shakespeare to Nietzsche and the Western poets and musicians of the nineteenth and twentieth centuries, the threads of madness exist in the cultural fabric. This is not the case with Afrocentric approaches to knowledge and knowing. A more circular system of thought is implied in Afrocentric rhetoric, one with numerous elements united in a grand movement towards freedom of the mind, the irrepressible will to harmony. . . .

The *etic* and *emic* debate constitutes one way of viewing the challenge I have set. Etic approaches to criticism are those methods that are from *outside* the discourse perspective, whereas the emic approach, which views the perspective from within, is criticism derived from *within* the same culture as the discourse. What is proposed here is an emic criticism, derived from the culture, capable of speaking to the discourse in the language of the culture.

Albert Murray insists that it is necessary to see all statements as counterstatements, inasmuch as blacks in the United States possess a natural, historical, different view of reality than whites. This calls into being the need for emic criticism, an internal understanding without the fault of Eurocentric social sciences, which assures a peculiar universality of European views. Murray contends that "the one place U.S. negroes [sic] have always found themselves most rigidly segregated is not in the inner sanctum of the is-white family but in the insistent categories of behavioral science surveys, studies,

PROFILE / Cornel West (1953–)

There are some very deep questions confronting American culture, asserts Cornel West, and they cannot be addressed effectively if the society continues to think in conventional ways. Indeed, conventional thinking is precisely the barrier to a better quality of life. Lecturing and publishing frequently, West seeks to help chart the direction of genuinely beneficial change as he prophetically urges creation of a more compassionate society. Bringing about the necessary social reforms, he claims, requires changes in the way individuals live their lives, especially in the degree to which self-understanding develops. By living the examined life—here West sounds a perennial theme in the history of philosophy—one may progressively overcome the strictures of habit and prejudice. Now, says West, it is time to transcend the limits of Eurocentrism, multiculturalism, and all the other "isms" that keep people from perceiving the realities of life. This is not just a matter of intellectual clarity for West, but a challenge to a deeply personal commitment.

Always involved in the church throughout a career that has included appointments at Union Theological Seminary, Princeton University, and now as Professor of Afro-American Studies and Philosophy of Religion at Harvard University, West has consistently articulated philosophical positions that cannot be separated from religious insight. His major writings range topically from work in the critical history of ideas, represented by *The American Evasion of Philosophy: A Genealogy of Pragmatism* (1989) to the kind of personal statement represented by *Race Matters* (1993), excerpted here. In the realm of post-colonial thought, Cornel West occupies a position in the methodological mainstream by virtue of his explicit rootedness in social-historical experience, his use of religious tradition as a reference for thinking, and his critical analysis of current conditions and their causal antecedents.

and statistics." Without sensitivity to the intellectual and cultural elements of others, the white social scientist has often proceeded as if what is correct for whites is correct for everybody.

In African philosophy there is a commitment to harmony that some might call spirituality. It is the manifest essence of a search for resolution of cultural and human problems. This essence may be present in poetry, music, or dance. Duke Ellington, Martin Luther King Jr., and Malcolm X all possessed it. In spoken discourse, it is possible to choose spirituality, word power, and call-and-response as the principal constituents of a culture-sensitive African-base critical method. Yet it seems to me that a proper understanding of spirituality leads us to the conclusion that the discourse of the preacher is of the same genre as that in the good blues musician. The so-called culture-sensitive African-base approach begins to answer these questions better than the neo-Aristotelian, phenomenological, structuralism, or post-structuralism approach to criticism because it admits the possibility of other views. It is one more evidence that African intellectuals question the basis of Western rhetoric as applied to African discourse. . . .

However, Afrocentricity is not merely cultural sensitivity. To be culturally sensitive, one may remain grounded in one's own particular plot of history and mythology. The Eurocentricist may be culturally sensitive to the Wolof custom of leavetaking without ever modifying the central ground. An Afrocentricist may express cultural sensitivity to the Malay greeting behavior. Cultural sensitivity should be valued and practiced, but that does not constitute a cohesive critical direction for a body of discourse. This is why the attempt to define the scope of the concept *Afrocentricity* is important for the development of a more robust theoretical discussion.

Nihilism   Nihilism—seeing all things and possibilities as worthless and dead—is not just a matter of depressed mood, but a value system that essentially denies life. The problem of nihilism is philosophically complex. It has a long history in East and West and has faced Western thinkers squarely since Nietzsche revived it over a century ago. In Nietzsche's analysis, nihilism in European society arose out of a refusal to abandon caution and grasp one's own destiny, wherever it might lead. In the modern world, nihilism is not just an affliction of Europeans.

Taking up the problem of nihilism in the selection that follows is **Cornel West** (1953–). Professor of Afro-American Studies and the Philosophy of Religion at Harvard University, West is among the most influential thinkers exploring the theological and philosophical vectors of social activism in the closing years of the twentieth century. Although West's philosophical writings have dealt with a variety of issues, essays in which he combines trenchant analysis with positive recommendations for future action command his widest readership. This excerpt from one of his essays provides a glimpse of West's approach to a long-standing philosophical issue while also illustrating this important contemporary scholar's style.

SELECTION 17.16

"Nihilism in Black America"

From Cornel West

The proper starting point for the crucial debate about the prospects for black America is an examination of the nihilism that increasingly pervades black communities. *Nihilism is to be understood here not as a philosophic doctrine that there are no rational grounds for legitimate standards or authority; it is, far more, the lived experience of coping with a life of horrifying meaninglessness, hopelessness, and (most important) lovelessness.*

The frightening result is a numbing detachment from others and a self-destructive disposition toward the world. Life without meaning, hope, and love breeds a coldhearted, mean-spirited outlook that destroys both the individual and others.

Nihilism is not new in black America. The first African encounter with the New World was an encounter with a distinctive form of the

Liberation Theology

Post-colonial thought in Latin America is closely connected with Christian social activism. Seeking to show how adherence to Christian principles can lead to a better life, theologians of liberation have become especially well known for their work in ethics. Epistemology has also been an important concern, however, because it offers methodological resources with which to address prevailing prejudices. Theologians of liberation, as other post-colonial thinkers do, lay great emphasis on knowledge derived from experience as the first line of defense against illusion. One reason post-colonial thinkers so often privilege experience is that, for generations, religiously inspired other-worldly hopes and a quasi-medieval hierarchical understanding of society preached by conservative clergy functioned to disarm revolutionary sentiments that might arise among the large numbers of peasants. These sorts of claims may have been spiritually beneficial, say thinkers who are inclined to give the Church the benefit of the doubt, but they did not lead to sufficient nurturing of the people. Moving beyond the straightforward social gospel school of preaching that was popular among North American Christians seeking a just society, liberation theology has not only delivered the homiletic message of social change through Christian love, but has also developed a complex critical-theoretical infrastructure grounded in Continental philosophy.

Absurd. The initial black struggle against degradation and devaluation in the enslaved circumstances of the New World was, in part, a struggle against nihilism. In fact, the major enemy of black survival in America has been and is neither oppression nor exploitation but rather the nihilistic threat—that is, loss of hope and absence of meaning. For as long as hope remains and meaning is preserved, the possibility of overcoming oppression stays alive. The self-fulfilling prophecy of the nihilistic threat is that without hope there can be no future, that without meaning there can be no struggle.

The genius of our black foremothers and forefathers was to create powerful buffers to ward off the nihilistic threat, to equip black folk with cultural armor to beat back the demons of hopelessness, meaninglessness, and lovelessness. These buffers consisted of cultural structures of meaning and feeling that created and sustained communities; this armor constituted ways of life and struggle that embodied values of service and sacrifice, love and care, discipline and excellence. In other words, traditions for black surviving and thriving under usually adverse New World conditions were major barriers against the nihilistic threat. These traditions consist primarily of black religious and civic institutions that sustained familial and communal networks of support. If cultures are, in part, what human beings create (out of antecedent fragments of other cultures) in order to convince themselves not to commit suicide, then black foremothers and forefathers are to be applauded. In fact, until the early seventies black Americans had the lowest suicide rate in the United States. But now young black people lead the nation in the rate of increase in suicides. . . .

Black people have always been in America's wilderness in search of a promised land. Yet many black folk now reside in a jungle ruled by a cutthroat market morality devoid of any faith in deliverance or hope for freedom. Contrary to the superficial claims of conservative behaviorists, these jungles are not primarily the result of pathological behavior. Rather, this behavior is the tragic response of a people bereft of resources in confronting the workings of U.S. capitalist society. Saying this is not the same as asserting that individual black people are not responsible for their actions—black murderers and rapists should go to jail. But it must be recognized that the nihilistic threat contributes to criminal behavior. It is a threat that feeds on poverty and shattered cultural institutions and grows more powerful as the armors to ward against it are weakened. . . .

Only recently has this nihilistic threat—and its ugly inhumane outlook and actions—surfaced in the larger American society. And its appearance surely reveals one of the many instances of cultural decay in a declining empire.

What is to be done about this nihilistic threat? Is there really any hope, given our shattered civil society, market-driven corporate enterprises, and white supremacism? If one begins with the threat of concrete nihilism, then one must talk about some kind of *politics of conversion*. New models of collective black leadership must promote a version of this politics. Like alcoholism and drug addiction, nihilism is a disease of the soul. It can never be completely cured, and there is always the possibility of relapse. But there is always a chance for conversion—a chance for people to believe that there is hope for the future and a meaning to struggle. This chance rests neither on an agreement about what justice consists of nor on an analysis of how racism, sexism, or class subordination operate. Such arguments and analyses are indispensable. But a politics of conversion requires more. Nihilism is not overcome by arguments or analyses; it is tamed by love and care. Any disease of the soul must be conquered by a turning of one's soul. This turning is done through one's own affirmation of one's worth—an affirmation fueled by the concern of others. A love ethic must be at the center of a politics of conversion.

A love ethic has nothing to do with sentimental feelings or tribal connections. Rather it is a last attempt at generating a sense of agency among a downtrodden people. . . .

Like liberal structuralists, the advocates of a politics of conversion never lose sight of the structural conditions that shape the sufferings and lives of people. Yet, unlike liberal structuralism, the politics of conversion meets the nihilistic threat head-on. Like conservative behaviorism, the politics of conversion openly confronts the self-destructive and inhumane actions of black people. Unlike conservative behaviorists, the politics of conversion situates these actions within inhumane circumstances (but does not thereby exonerate them). The politics of conversion shuns the limelight—a limelight that solicits status seekers and ingratiates egomaniacs. Instead, it stays on the ground among the toiling everyday people, ushering forth humble freedom fighters—both followers and leaders—who have the audacity to take the nihilistic threat by the neck and turn back its deadly assaults.

Latin American Thought

Post-colonial Latin American thinkers work in a context that is at once strongly influenced by European philosophy and powerfully motivated to move out from under the shadow of European domination. One feature that importantly distinguishes Latin American thought from most European philosophy is the sustained effort to explore the relevance of philosophy to problems of social justice. The concerns of Latin American philosophy encompass the full range of the philosophical spectrum, but its activity in post-colonial thought has concentrated on analysis of Marxist theses.

Ontology   Ontology is the branch of philosophy that concerns itself with the question of being. In the twentieth century, ontology was revived by the work of Martin Heidegger and Jean-Paul Sartre after centuries of dormancy. While there is always a danger that orthodoxy will stifle thinking whenever the work of a philosopher is widely acknowledged, recent writings of Latin American philosophers demonstrate the possibility of interpreting Heidegger's work in ways that probably were not anticipated by either the politically conservative German philosopher or the politically progressive French philosopher. Consider the essay by Argentinian philosopher **Carlos Astrada** (1894–1970) excerpted here. In it, Astrada takes Heidegger's thinking as evidence of the collapse of the bourgeois mentality that determined much of the course of colonial activity. Though Latin America's colonial pattern was more feudal than bourgeois, most historians agree that bourgeois influences from North America have played a great role in perpetuating unequal distributions of wealth inherited from colonial times. Post-colonial reality has brought with it the realization that surprises can overtake whole civilizations, including the awareness that long-standing patterns of wealth and poverty are not necessarily permanent fixtures in a society. Recent history, unfolding at the pace of technological change, plants doubts about the stability of existence. It should not be surprising, then, that a school of philosophy, existentialism, should arise which sees the fundamental fact of existence as becoming. For post-colonial thinkers, it is not surprising either that the wealthy would project the instability of their own power structures onto the existence of humanity itself. Astrada's essay demonstrates that works of existentialist ontology can be read as political-economic texts.

SELECTION 17.17

"Existentialism and the Crisis of Philosophy"   **From Carlos Astrada**

TOWARD A NEW IMAGE OF MAN

The rationalist concept of man is dogmatically constructed on the peripheries of concrete humanity, of individual historic man, and of vital reality. Over against this rationalist concept, a real, living image of man is being raised, an image with blood and viscera, with earthly fluids and air to breathe.

A new image of man, man conceived according to other necessities and purposes, necessarily presupposes a new social order, a new hierarchical order of values to which the historical sensitivity of the age gives allegiance. The concept of man of rationalist humanism with its parallel postulate of progressivism is embedded in all the instances and sectors wherein it was able to gain preeminence, but even now, it is dead, though still hauled around on a declining verbal rather than mental plane on which are placed all the survivors of individual liberalism and its residual doctrinaire expressions.

This type of man, purely rational, antihistorical, and anonymous, is a ghostlike entity that eludes reality and struggles along a retreating front against the great events the future is preparing. It cannot be ignored, however, that this image of man has reigned for almost three centuries in the cultural and political life of the West, having shown that in the past it was an efficient reagent in the multiple aspects of this life. However, for the past three decades, this image of man is in obvious decline. It is barely a vanishing shadow that those adrift in the historical present vainly attempt to seize.

The completed man, conceptually constructed by rationalist humanism, that is to say, the isolated, completed, purely ideal man, without roots in a specific soil, with no vital ties to a nationality, with no connections to an instinctive and emotional repertoire of historically conditioned preferences—such a man does not exist. Neither is there an essential equality of all men based solely on universal reason as a constant and unalterable factor that would act independently in the psycho-vital, historical reality of national communities, classes, and racial constellations.

Having surpassed it, we are also far beyond the pseudoantinomy of *individualism* and *collectivism*. Our age no longer knows the individual as a social atom nor over against him the collectivity, considered as an aggregation of such atoms and billed as the leading actor of social and political history. It does recognize, however, opposing classes whose struggle, undoubtedly, is the crux of the economic-social process. There is also a growing awareness of the concrete historical man, the man who, without turning loose the bonds and surroundings in which he is implicated, stands out as a personal, psycho-vital unit, who affirms and gives life to his humanity as a function of his real goals, which are immanent in his particular becoming.

THE EXTINCTION OF MODERN MAN

The unbalanced society of our age, especially the capitalist and mercantile commanders who

are the possessors of political power, attempt in vain to live off the remains of the rationalist idea of man embodied in so-called "modern man," an image already in a state of dessication. These commanders are the crusty bark oppressing and retarding the buds of a new idea of man of great historical significance that have been germinating rapidly in the deeper levels of contemporary life. Suppressed forces that are emotionally and historically articulated by a generation destined to place its seal on the future give added thrust and life to this idea of man with which the coming generation will impose a new *ethos,* affirming a particular political will and instituting also a different scale of evaluation for the culture, economy, and society.

Modern man is a cadaver that senescent human groups, adrift in the storm of these days, attempt vainly to galvanize, appealing to slogans and incantations that no longer have meaning. In a letter to Dilthey,* Count Yorck von Wartenburg said: "Modern man, the man who began with the Renaissance and has endured until our time, is ready to be buried."

This type man, the man of individualistic liberalism, the ultimate, valedictory expression of "modern man," imbued with vestiges of the rationalist ideals of the nineteenth century is the corpse to be buried. The present age is responsible for carrying out this task so the new man can cover the whole surface of history and thus affirm and give full meaning to the spiritual and political orders now germinating.

History has no compassion for values in decline nor for human types that are repositories of endangered sensibilities and ideals, inanimate modules of a destiny that has made its rounds and can no longer swell history with new hope or give it new impetus. History takes into its flow only the vital ascending force, the *ethos* in which a new message for men is given

---

*Wilhem Dilthey (1833–1911) was a German philosopher noted for his work in textual analysis and the history of ideas.

form, the promise of accomplishment that is the incentive for renewed effort. History—the matrix of all possibilities—yields itself only to those generations capable of engendering the fullness of a new age, that is, to that type of man capable of implanting an ascending meaning in history and of proposing to it new and valuable goals. . . .

SAMENESS, OTHERNESS, AND *HUMANITAS*

To be sure, there is a realm of ends, norms, and values structured on an objective plane that transcends individual consciousness. One may also conceive and accept the effectiveness of an objective spirit as a structured whole that has emerged from the historical process, but this process is a far cry from being the domain of pure contingency and subjective irrationality. For it is precisely man's ability to establish an objective realm of the spirit that permits him, in each moment of his becoming, to be himself, to apprehend his own self-sameness.

While man aspires to fulfill himself in his being, to affirm himself in his humanity, to feel identical with himself in each moment of temporal transition, the personal identity to which he aspires leads him to postulate time, a transcendence in the sense of otherness, as a guarantee of his identity and as the goal of his efforts. Stating this problem as a function of the finite-infinite, historicity-eternity antinomy, Kierkegaard tells us that man in his sameness, in his desired self-existence, always finds something, the Absolute, before which he is his own self-sameness.

While the sameness of man lives and exists, in the proper sense of these terms, through his becoming this sameness is bound to a concrete self-consciousness that, because it is expressed in temporality, is also becoming and thus never crystallizes, since there is no crystallizing in the existing man. This concrete self-consciousness gathers man into the lived experience of its own identity, anchored to the temporal structures of existence. This is because man, in everything (ideals, values, objective norms of life) toward which he transcends and projects himself from his concrete historicity—which is the ineradicable moment of his being, of his being made in time—in all this transcending, man searches only for himself, he attempts only to seal his identity in the midst of mutations and change, shaping it into a consistent and stable image of himself, into an idea of his "humanitas."

He now strives toward a new actualization of his being, a new image of himself. He aspires to actualize and conceive himself in all his immanent possibilities, to integrate himself with his potentialities, to reencounter himself, at last, in the full concretion of his essential humanity.

Magnetizing its thrust, which is historically conditioned and limited, the ideal of the *full man*—as proposed by Max Scheler—is lifted up as the goal that at the same time that it transcends pure becoming, receives from it its meaning, which is latent, to the degree it is *existential,* in the immanence of the temporal structure. Although "this full-man, in an absolute sense, is far from us, . . . a relatively whole-man, a maximum of full humanity, is accessible to each age."

For the concrete, existing man, this ideal of the whole-man as a goal and model is an index of transcendence, a mediating synthesis of all objective structures. These structures represent *the other,* not in the sense of the naturalist idea of being or of an absolute conceived as a personal God, but of an *other* that, as a transcending instance toward which what is human is projected, permits man in each moment and stage of his temporal passing to know his concrete sameness. It is the apparently fixed limit that as an ideal point of reference hovers above historical becoming. Ultimately, however, existence activates and gives meaning to historical becoming, for existence historically determines and actualizes the humanity in man.

Metaphysics of the Human   For as long as we have been keeping records of our thoughts, human beings have sought a reliably firm foundation upon which to base ideas about ourselves, our laws, our destiny, and so on. Many promises of a final answer have been made, but outside of religious faith—a category of claims that arguably has its own distinct rules of discourse—no claims of foundational insight have stood the tests of time and philosophical investigation. In the sensibilities of post-colonial thinkers, though, the moral and metaphysical claims of the ruling elites of past and present demand constant vigilance and persistent critique. Marx called these dangerous claims ideology, meaning in his vocabulary a kind of self-interested delusion which infected the bourgeoisie and which they half-cynically, half-unconsciously passed on to the proletariat. Marx believed that the proletariat would eventually realize as he had that ideological claims were without necessity or merit, and could, therefore, be contradicted. But, contends Peruvian philosopher **Francisco Miró Quesada** (1918–) with the pragmatism that has become a trademark of recent Latin philosophy, contradicting the claims of one group with the claims of an alternative theory of reality does not solve the problem. Instead, it creates conflict, and conflict creates suffering. Quesada continues on to argue that humanity itself must be reimagined. His argument, reproduced in part in the excerpt that follows, consists of two main parts: first, a critique of the truth claims of theories, which concludes that theories cannot reliably deliver the truth, and second, a consequentialist argument centered on the suffering caused by people who take theories too seriously. The eventual proposal is to divide the human race into those who are willing to exploit people and those who are willing to defend them from exploitation.

"Man Without Theory"

From Francisco Miró Quesada

The history of humanity is an impressive succession of complicated, yet false theories that man has woven around himself. Along the millennial pathway of history, theories lay semidestroyed and rusted like military equipment left behind by an army in retreat. Each great theoretical crisis, each great change, each new development marks the shift from one culture to another, from one age to another. In earlier days men were not sufficiently aware of what was happening, although they were aware that something was happening and expectantly waited the new. At times their desires were implemented in a conscious, more or less rapid manner. At other times, however, the restructuring process lasted centuries. Intuitively men grasped the significance of the situation, but the mechanism for restructuring was not grasped for two reasons: the lack of historical consciousness, that is, awareness of the relationship between their world view and historic era, and the lack of understanding of what a theory is. In the nineteenth century a great movement began that culminated in our day and overcame both limitations. For this reason, in the present, in this modern, troubled atomic era, the era of the machine and technology, we are aware nevertheless of what is really happening. We have a clear understanding that history is a succession of ways of conceiving the world and man, of ways considered absolute by men of different ages but that today are no more than vague shadows, difficult to understand. Our civilization, therefore, is the most philosophical of all, because none has had as clear an awareness of its limitation and relativity. In truth, our age is characteristically an age of search, of disorientation, and of acute consciousness of its negative traits. Contemporary man is one who experiences in his own flesh the failure of a great theory concerning himself: European rationalism, in all its facets, from the liberalism of "laissez faire" to Nazism and Marxism. Ortega has said of our age that it is an "age of disillusioned living," but to be more precise we should say, "an age of disillusioned theorizing." Scheler begins one of his books, perhaps his best, with the celebrated phrase, "Never has man been such an enigma to himself."

Given this situation the inevitable question is "What shall we do?" The depth of the question does permit a dogmatic answer. Indeed, perhaps this essay should end here. However, to be human means to try unceasingly to overcome every "non plus ultra" and since we do not wish to deny our human condition, we have no alternative but to forge ahead. Yet, before continuing we wish to emphasize that what follows is no more than the point of view of a particular individual who, along with all other individuals in this age, is faced with an immense problem that by its very nature transcends any purely individual response.

The first thought that might come to mind, and perhaps a majority already favors it, is to commit our efforts to the reconstruction of the old theory, making it more comprehensive and adapting it to the demands of our modern circumstance. Or, should this not be possible, to elaborate a new theory that may or may not be related to the old or to earlier theories, but would constitute an organic system, capable of providing answers to the most pressing questions and have the scope and flexibility necessary to permit men of our day to work with the total range of their problems. In actual experience, the normal or spontaneous attitude always develops a theory. So we, although disillusioned by theories, in seeing ourselves in a bind, think of amplifying or creating theories, like men of other ages. In this day, however, there is a difference: men of previous ages were not aware of the relativity or limits of their theories, nor of the horrible dangers implicit in creating a complicated theory concerning man from which unforeseeable and mortal consequences were derived. Furthermore, they did not suspect that their theories ran the same risks as all preceding theories. Therefore they created under illusion, but in faith, and so their theories had "vital force" and served to resolve human problems since men believed in them and were convinced that all previous ages had been in error whereas they were in the truth. In this day, however, we are not convinced our position is unique, true, or definitive. Indeed, we know that whatever we do, our theory about man will suffer the same end as the others.

Yet, instead of searching for a new theory and instinctively following the destiny of Sisyphus, what if we assume a completely different attitude? Instead of inventing a new and dangerous theory, why not simply give up formulating theories about ourselves? Now this proposal may well produce a scandal and for two good reasons. First, because man is so accustomed to formulating theories about himself, to taking for granted that he knows what he is, to feeling himself at the helm of a world of structures and hierarchies, to renounce theory leaves him with the impression that he is giving up the possibility of finding solutions, that he is spineless and morally decadent, that he has given up the struggle for good and against evil. Second, because it is believed, more for theoretical than practical considerations, that no matter what man does he is condemned to theorize and that he can give up everything except formulating a complete concept of the world, of things, and of himself. It is believed that man needs theory to live, that without it he flounders and does not know what to hold on to, he is a lost soul on a ship without a rudder. For, although he may deny theory, implicitly he is always constructing a system of concepts for clarifying the meaning of his life.

To be sure, this second argument is much more powerful than the first. Its strength, however, lies in its inclusive breadth, for its detailed analysis of situations is slipshod. For example, if one analyzes all the elements constituting the world within which man includes himself, one sees there are various dimensions. One dimension is the surrounding world. This dimension, naturally, is undeniable. If man does not possess a well-formulated theory concerning the surrounding world he is not even able to walk down the street. The simple act of dodging an automobile indicates the possession of a rather clear concept of the principles of causality and the laws of dynamics. Further, our cultural crisis is not a crisis in knowledge of the natural world. The cosmic world, our surrounding environment, is known with increasingly greater certainty and vigor. It is perhaps the only part of our general vision of the world that at present follows a linear evolution. We have reached such a comprehension of what physical theory is, that the elaboration of that type theory is carried out in the awareness that in time it will be surpassed, and that it will be necessary to amplify it to include new facts. For this reason, it is possible that the nuclear emphasis of the old theory may be preserved intact and that it may be possible to consider it as a special case of a new theory. Some might believe that this procedure is applicable to the theory about the nature of man. However, given the complexity of all anthropological theory, this is not possible. Physical as well as mathematical theories are very simple, since they are based on broad abstractive processes. Therefore, this approach is not adequate for anthropological theory. But if

we do not make use of it, we encounter the earlier objection, namely, that every theory concerning the surrounding world presupposes an integrated theory of the human being. And here we come to the crux of the issue. For, if this affirmation is true, then we will never be able to free ourselves from a theory concerning ourselves and we will always return to that monotonous, well-beaten path. This, however, we believe to be false, because even though it is undeniable that every theory concerning the cosmos presupposes a theory concerning man, it does not presuppose necessarily that the theory of the cosmos is complete. In order to grant validity to a theory about the cosmos, we must presuppose certain epistemological postulates, certain beliefs concerning the structure and organization of our consciousness, but in no way does such a theory necessarily include hypotheses about the moral life or destiny of man. The most to be said is that from these epistemological presuppositions, one can derive many consequences as to the possibilities of knowing the world in general and even ourselves and that these consequences may be positive or negative in some or in many aspects. However, this does not invalidate our point of view because what we are specifically trying to do is place brackets around our cognitive faculties insofar as these are applied to ourselves.

However, man is so accustomed to living on the theoretical level that he does not conceive the possibility of refraining from decisions about his own nature and fundamental relationships with the surrounding world. Thus he always finds arguments that justify his use of theories. In the present case, those who deny the possibility of avoiding theory about man adduce that this avoidance is impossible because determining one's orientation in the world without language is impossible. To establish interhuman communication, whatever it may be, is impossible without speech, but speech is in itself a theory. The philosophical analysis of language shows unequivocally that every expressive system acquires its ultimate meaning from theoretical presuppositions about the nature of the world and of man. Thus the very possibility of language implies the immersion of the human being in a complete theory concerning himself, a theory that refers not only to his objective relationship with the environing world, but also to his norms of action and destiny. Philological analysis of the most trivial words reveals, in a surprising way at times, the immense background of cosmological, metaphysical, and ethical theory upon which all possible language rests. The argument, then, would seem to be de-

finitive: man cannot live without an orientation in the world and to seek an orientation in the world requires a specific theory concerning the physical structure of the cosmos. This theory, however, cannot be elaborated without language, but language is the great, universal theory, the expression of what in the ultimate, collective, anonymous, and therefore inevitable sense man believes about the world and himself. Thus, it is impossible to live as a human being without presupposing certain theoretical axioms concerning our nature and our destiny.

Gender Issues   The most recent phase of feminism began in 1959 as a movement of middle-class European and American women. Analysis of the early rhetoric of the movement suggests an underlying assumption among that generation of feminists that all women shared common concerns. It was not long, however, before women in more traditional societies began to assert that the universal claims of most feminist literature did not speak well to the conditions of marginalized peoples. From both unreformed colonial and post-colonial perspectives, a certain myopia afflicted mainstream feminism.

Two major expansions of feminist intentionality have been suggested from outside the mainstream. The first calls for more attention to issues of class. In this connection, the argument is made that commonalities based in shared gender become functionally irrelevant when class-based exploitation determines not only woman-to-woman relationships, but also the circumstances of domestic relationships. A woman living in grinding poverty has few resources with which to overcome traditional strictures and inequities, Third World writers observe. The second major modification of feminist discourse suggested by several post-colonial writers was the abandonment of a black-white racial dichotomy. Because the majority of the women in the world are neither Euro-American white nor are they black, the reasoning goes, feminists who fall into a black-white polarization not only exclude a large ethnic segment, but, more ominously, they exclude a wide range of situations from analysis. Without analysis of diverse circumstances, the understanding of women's issues is truncated, and consciously constructed corrections are unlikely to be forthcoming. Sonia Saldívar-Hull addresses these problems in the following selection.

SELECTION 17.19

"Feminism on the Border: From Gender Politics to Geopolitics"

From Sonia Saldívar-Hull

Is it possible for Chicanas to consider ourselves part of this "sisterhood" called feminism? Can we assume that our specific interests and problems will be taken care of by our Marxist compañeros? In her essay, "Feminism, Marxism, Method, and the State," Catherine MacKinnon decrees that "[s]exuality is to feminism what work is to marxism: that which is most one's own yet most taken away" (1982, 515). Mac-Kinnon argues that while we can draw parallels between Marxist and feminist methodologies, we must remember not to conflate these two "theories of power and its distribution" (1982, 516), that one theory must not be subsumed into the other. . . .

But to the Chicana, a woman with a specific history under racial and sexual and class exploitation, it is essential that we further problematize the feminist/Marxist discussion by adding the complication of race and ethnicity. Our feminist sisters and Marxist compañeros/as urge us to take care of gender and class issues first and race will naturally take care of itself. Even MacKinnon, as thorough as she is, constantly watching that she herself does not recreate a monolithic "woman," uses footnotes to qualify the difference between the white woman's and the black woman's situations. . . .

My project . . . does insist, however, that our white feminist "sisters" recognize their own blind spots. When MacKinnon uses the black woman as her sign for all dispossessed women, we see the extent to which Chicanas, Asian-American, Native American, or Puerto Rican women, for example, have been rendered invisible in a discourse whose explicit agenda is to expose ideological erasure. Chicana readings of color *blindness* instead of color consciousness

in "politically correct" feminist essays indicate the extent to which the issues of race and ethnicity are ignored in feminist and Marxist theories. . . .

As Chicanas making our works public—publishing in marginalized journals and small, underfinanced presses and taking part in conferences and workshops—we realize that the "sisterhood" called feminism professes an ideology that at times comes dangerously close to the phallocentric ideologies of the white male power structure against which feminists struggle. In her essay, "Ethnicity, Ideology, and Academia," Rosaura Sánchez reminds us of the ideological strategies that the dominant culture manipulates in order to mystify "the relation between minority cultures and the dominant culture" (1987, 80). She points out that U.S. cultural imperialism extends beyond the geopolitical borders of the country, "but being affected, influenced, and exploited by a culture is one thing and sharing fully in that culture is another" (1987, 81). If we extend the analogy to feminism and the totalizing concept of sisterhood, we begin to understand how the specific interests of Anglo-American and other European feminists tend to erase the existence of Chicana, Puerto Rican, Native American, Asian-American, and other Third World feminisms. Indeed, feminism affects and influences Chicana writers and critics, but feminism as practiced by women of the hegemonic culture oppresses and exploits the Chicana in both subtle and obvious ways.

When white feminists begin to categorize the different types of feminisms, we in turn can begin to trace the muting of issues of race and ethnicity under other feminist priorities. Elaine

Showalter in *A Literature of Their Own* charts the "stages" of writing by women into the categories of "feminine, feminist, and female" (1977, 13). She first establishes that *all* "literary subcultures, such as black, Jewish, Canadian, Anglo-Indian, or even American," go through phases of imitation, internalization, protest, and finally self-discovery (1977, 13). In addition to the misrepresentation of what "literary subcultures" write, Showalter creates an ethnocentric, Eurocentric, middle-class history of women's writing. . . .

In our search for a feminist critical discourse that adequately takes into account our position as women under multiple oppressions we must turn to our own "organic intellectuals." But because our work has been ignored by the men and women in charge of the modes of cultural production, we must be innovative in our search. Hegemony has so constructed the idea of method and theory that often we cannot recognize anything that is different from what the dominant discourse constructs. We have to look in nontraditional places for our theories: in the prefaces to anthologies, in the interstices of autobiographies, in our cultural artifacts, our *cuentos,* and if we are fortunate to have access to a good library, in the essays published in marginalized journals not widely distributed by the dominant institutions. . . .

In the same way that we must break with traditional (hegemonic) concepts of genre to read Chicana feminist theory, working-class women of color in other Third World countries articulate their feminisms in nontraditional ways and forms. The Chicana feminist acknowledges the often vast historical, class, racial, and ethnic differences among women living on the border, but the nature of hegemony practiced by the united powers of patriarchy, capitalism, imperialism, and white supremacy promotes an illusion of an irreconcilable split between feminists confined within national borders. We must examine and question the First versus Third World dichotomy before we accept the opposition as an inevitable fissure that separates women politically committed in different ways from any common cause.

In her testimony, *Let Me Speak* (1978), Bolivian activist Domitila Barrios de Chungara acknowledges the separation between "First" and "Third" World feminists: "Our Position is not like the feminists' position. We think our liberation consists primarily in our country being freed forever from the yoke of imperialism and we want a worker like us to be in power and that the laws, education, everything, be controlled by this person. Then, yes, we'll have better conditions for reaching a complete liberation, including a liberation as women" (Barrios 1978, 41). Her statement, however, is problematized by her occasion for speaking. As a participant at the UN-sponsored International Year of the Woman Conference held in Mexico City in 1975, Barrios witnessed co-optation of "feminism" by governments which use women and women's issues to promote their own political agendas. Barrios observed Imelda Marcos, Princess Ashraf Pahlevi, and Jihan Sadat as some of the conference's "official" Third World representatives. We begin to reformulate the dichotomy when we no longer choose to see these representatives as "Third World feminists," but as agents of their respective governments: agents of patriarchy, capitalism, and imperialism. Suddenly the First World/Third World dichotomy emerges as the arena where the split between the ruling class and the working class, between those in power and the disenfranchised, is exposed.

REFERENCES

Barrios de Chungara, Domitila. 1978. *Let Me Speak! Testimony of Domitila, a Woman of the Bolivian Mines*. With Moema Viezzer. New York: Monthly Review Press.

MacKinnon, Catherine. 1982. "Feminism, Marxism, Method and the State: An Agenda for Theory." *Signs 7*, no. 3:515–44.

Sánchez, Rosaura. 1987. "Ethnicity, Ideology and Academia." *The Americas Review* 15, no. I:80–88.

Showalter, Elaine. 1977. *A Literature of Their Own: British Women Novelists from Brontë to Lessing*. Princeton: Princeton University Press.

South Asia

The history of European colonial rule in Asia began in the early sixteenth century and continues to this day. It included such developments as British domination of large areas of India and other parts of South Asia; French control of Vietnam, Cambodia, and Laos; the partitioning of Ch'ing China by multiple Western colonial powers; and much more. Although the vast inland deserts of Asia and the rugged Deccan plateau of India remained mostly outside the grip of invading powers, most of Asia's population centers experienced alien invasion at one time or another. The reactions of indigenous peoples to these events ranged from the pacifism of Gandhi to murderous secret societies from Afghanistan to China, with the Vietnam war marking the bloody culmination of the era of highly confrontational violence. According to the majority of contemporary analysts, colonialism has been economically and socially destructive in the former colonies. A few, however, claim that the legacy of specifically Northern European colonialism has been positive in terms of modern political infrastructure and value systems that facilitate success in a technological world. These sorts of determinations are hard to make at a distance, but one thing is certain: the formerly colonized peoples of Asia have documented their own ideas of what counts as good at great length over thousands of years. Post-colonial thought in Asia draws sustenance from these cultural wellsprings.

Unlike the cultures of sub-Saharan Africa, the nations of Asia have traditions of written philosophy that stretch back more than three millennia, longer than in the West by more than a thousand years. The ancient Vedas of India and the Chinese classics anchor their respective cultures with unmistakable gravity, testifying to resources beyond the grasp of any colonizing power. The shock of colonialism to Asia was deep, but not so comprehensive for these cultures that their philosophers have felt impelled to the kind of sustained reflection and cultural reconstruction that has been so prominent in Africa. Certainly colonialism wrecked the economy of the Indian countryside and changed China's self-image forever, but the effect on the discourse of Indian and Chinese philosophy seems to have been a relatively small dislocation. This does not mean that no serious reflection occurred, only that Asian cultures already had so much internally generated philosophical momentum that outside influences, even outside influences with the intellectual resources of the West, could not effect a significant change of course. Instead, outside ideas and techniques, from British aesthetics to Marxist political-historiographical philosophy, were appropriated and reworked to conform to indigenous values.

From another angle, Asian thinkers in the colonial era could acknowledge Western technological superiority without the least impulse to generalize military and industrial might to philosophical capability. On the contrary, they frequently regarded Western thought as crude, simplistic, or just wrong-headed. Even so, the Western presence was hard to ignore. It prompted thoughtful efforts not only to develop an appropriate sense of history, but also to project an appropriate relationship with the foreigners. The result included such disparate expressions as the highly reflective Young India school of thought in the waning years of the British Empire and the cynically manipulative, sloganeering rhetoric of Chairman Mao.

Our focus in these pages will be on India, which endured about two centuries of economic despoilment at the hands of the mercantilist-capitalist forces of Britain. It cannot be argued that the leaders of the independence movement relied on indigenous values to develop their notions of economic justice, for India had traditionally established rigid class lines that effectively excluded large numbers of people from the possibility of economic well-being. Ironically, the introduction of British values into India created the conceptual resources that Indians would use to remake their society—after figuring out how to expel the British. While Gandhi looked to India's own traditions primarily in his quest for the contours of a future just society, the majority of members of the dominant Congress party believed with Jawaharlal Nehru, independent India's first prime minister, that the road to modernization also necessitated adoption of modern political-economic thinking.

The independence movement's greatest influence was certainly Gandhi, but many of its leading thinkers also set great store in the writings of modern socialists, including Marx. Drawing on Hindu psychology, which views grudging obedience to rules as a very serious problem, Nehru and his followers sought to avoid the imposition of socialism on a populace that was in part unwilling to engage in this transformation of Indian society. Though most of the early leaders of the Indian resistance to the British were convinced that socialism was the surest path to peace and justice, they also saw that domination of the minority by the majority, always possible in a democracy, had to be avoided. These thinkers consciously renounced the use of a colonialist style of coercion to achieve a post-colonial objective.

The topics taken up by Asian post-colonial thought are similar to those considered elsewhere in the world. As well, thinkers in the countries of Asia draw on indigenous thought forms to develop their inferences and expositions. Asian writers are the most likely of the post-colonial thinkers surveyed in this chapter to couch their discussions in terms of the abstract principles and linear inferences typical of Western philosophy. This stylistic similarity is not a borrowing from Western thought, however, but a continuation of local traditions of discourse.

Satyagraha

Satyagraha, a concept closely identified with the social and political thinking of **Mohandas (Mahatma) Gandhi** (1869–1948), has been translated as "clinging to truth." This definition immediately raises the question of the nature of truth. In traditional Indian philosophy, this issue had already received a great amount of attention. Thousands of years before Husserl's phenomenological method called for clearing the perceptions of prejudices, Indian philosophers were insisting on

PROFILE / Mohandas Gandhi (1869–1948)

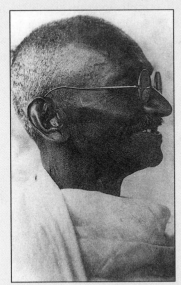

Mohandas Gandhi was the world's leading exponent of the strategy of passive resistance— the attempt to change unjust laws through nonviolent civil disobedience to them. This philosophy, which Gandhi used successfully time after time to produce legal and political change, was the inspi-

ration and guiding light for protest movements throughout the world and was adopted by many American civil rights leaders, including Martin Luther King, Jr. Gandhi's life, like King's, was ended by an assassin—a Hindu fanatic upset by Gandhi's concern for Muslims.

Gandhi began his political activism not in India but in South Africa, where he was a successful lawyer and leader in the Indian community. While there, he gave up a Western mode of life and began living according to Hindu ideals of self-denial. It was there in South Africa, in 1907, that he organized his first campaign of civil disobedience, and this *satyagraha,* as it is called, was so successful that the South African government agreed to alleviate anti-Indian discrimination.

In 1915 Gandhi returned to India a famous man. There he used satyagrahas to advance numerous democratic reforms. He became known as Mahatma, or "great

soul," and his influence was so considerable that he could exact concessions from the British government of India by merely threatening to fast to death. Not only was he the spiritual leader of the Indian people, he was also a major political figure. He was the leader of the Indian National Congress and was a principal participant in the post–World War II conferences that led to India's independence and the creation of a separate Muslim state, Pakistan (although he opposed the partition). When there was violence between Muslims and Hindus, Gandhi used his influence to help control it, often resorting to fasts and prayer meetings. It was during one such prayer meeting that he was assassinated.

Gandhi altered the courses of nations; his extraordinary power came not through guns but through his ability to bring out the best in people by setting the highest standards for his own life.

the same thing and developing a yoga, or discipline, to facilitate it. The discipline needed in the search for truth was not simply a matter of acquiring the tools of scientific investigation; one also had to practice such virtues as giving, nonattachment, and non-injury to develop mental purity. Without adjusting one's way of life to this task, they argued, truth would remain an empty abstraction no matter how much knowledge one accumulated. Gandhi is a part of this tradition in his adoption of its rigorous demands for personal integrity and cultivation.

Gandhi is also a modern figure, however, a student not only of the classical texts of India but also of Thoreau and Tolstoy. Seeking what was best in his tradition, he repudiated the claims of human inequality by circumstances of birth that underlay the caste system. Declaring freedom from ancient caste laws marked Gandhi as a modern figure despite his notable adherence to ancient ascetic forms. Gandhi's uncompromising concern for the welfare of the people of India and his courage in the struggle for independence from Britain established him as a political leader. His devotion to Hindu ideals and the simple life he lived made him a spiritual leader. Hailed as a saint in his own time and acknowledged as one of the most influential thinkers of the modern age, Gandhi insisted that his way was open to any who would simply decide to follow it.

SELECTION 17.20

"Satyagraha"   **From Mohandas K. Gandhi**

3: SATYAGRAHA

For the past thirty years I have been preaching and practising Satyagraha. The principles of Satyagraha, as I know it today, constitute a gradual evolution.

Satyagraha differs from Passive Resistance as the North Pole from the South. The latter has been conceived as a weapon of the weak and does not exclude the use of physical force or violence for the purpose of gaining one's end, whereas the former has been conceived as a weapon of the strongest and excludes the use of violence in any shape or form.

The term *Satyagraha* was coined by me in South Africa to express the force that the Indians there used for full eight years and it was coined in order to distinguish it from the movement then going on in the United Kingdom and South Africa under the name of Passive Resistance.

Its root meaning is holding on to truth, hence truth-force. I have also called it Love-force or Soul-force. In the application of Satyagraha I discovered in the earliest stages that pursuit of truth did not admit of violence being inflicted on one's opponent but that he must be weaned from error by patience and sympathy. For what appears to be truth to the one may appear to be error to the other. And patience means self-suffering. So the doctrine came to mean vindication of truth not by infliction of suffering on the opponent but on one's self.

But on the political field the struggle on behalf of the people mostly consists in opposing error in the shape of unjust laws. When you have failed to bring the error home to the law-giver by way of petitions and the like, the only remedy open to you, if you do not wish to submit to error, is to compel him by physical force to yield to you or by suffering in your own person by inviting the penalty for the breach of the law. Hence Satyagraha largely appears to the public as Civil Disobedience or Civil Resistance. It is civil in the sense that it is not criminal.

The lawbreaker breaks the law surreptitiously and tries to avoid the penalty, not so the civil resister. He ever obeys the laws of the State to which he belongs, not out of fear of the sanctions but because he considers them to be good for the welfare of society. But there come occasions, generally rare, when he considers certain laws to be so unjust as to render obedience to them a dishonour. He then openly and civilly breaks them and quietly suffers the penalty for their breach. And in order to register his protest against the action of the law givers, it is open to him to withdraw his co-operation from the State by disobeying such other laws whose breach does not involve moral turpitude.

In my opinion, the beauty and efficacy of Satyagraha are so great and the doctrine so simple that it can be preached even to children. It was preached by me to thousands of men, women and children commonly called indentured Indians with excellent results. . . .

7: THE THEORY AND PRACTICE OF SATYAGRAHA

Carried out to its utmost limit, Satyagraha is independent of pecuniary or other material assistance; certainly, even in its elementary form, of physical force or violence. Indeed, violence is the negation of this great spiritual force, which can only be cultivated or wielded by those who will entirely eschew violence. It is a force that may be used by individuals as well as by communities. It may be used as well in political as in domestic affairs. Its universal applicability is a demonstration of its permanence and invincibility. It can be used alike by men, women and children. It is totally untrue to say that it is a force to be used only by the weak so long as they are not capable of meeting violence by violence. This superstition arises from the incompleteness of the English expression, *passive resistance*. It is impossible for those who consider themselves to be weak to apply this force. Only those who realize that there is something in man which is superior to the brute nature in him and that the latter always yields to it, can effectively be Satyagrahis. This force is to violence, and, therefore, to all tyranny, all injustice, what light is to darkness. In politics, its use is based upon the immutable maxim, that government of the people is possible only so long as they consent either consciously or unconsciously to be governed. We did not want to be governed by the Asiatic Act of 1907 of the Transvaal, and it had to go before this mighty force. Two courses were open to us: to use violence when we were called upon to submit to the Act, or to suffer the penalties prescribed under the Act, and thus to draw out and exhibit the force of the soul within us for a period long enough to appeal to the sympathetic chord in the governors or the law-makers. We have taken long to achieve what we set about striving for. That was because our Satyagraha was not of the most complete type. All Satyagrahis do not understand the full value of the force, nor have we men who always from conviction refrain from violence. The use of this force requires the adoption of poverty, in the sense that we must be indifferent whether we have the wherewithal to feed or clothe ourselves. During the past struggle, all Satyagrahis, if any at all, were not prepared to go that length. Some again were only Satyagrahis so called. They came without any conviction, often with mixed motives, less often with impure motives. Some even, whilst engaged in the struggle, would gladly have resorted to violence but for most vigilant supervision. Thus it was that the struggle became prolonged; for the exercise of the purest soul-force, in its perfect form, brings about instantaneous relief. For this exercise, prolonged training of the individual soul is an absolute necessity, so that a perfect Satyagrahi has to be almost, if not entirely, a perfect man. We cannot all suddenly become such men, but if my proposition is correct—as I know it to be correct—the greater the spirit of Satyagraha in us, the better men will we become. Its use, therefore, is, I think, indisputable, and it is a force, which, if it became universal, would revolutionize social ideals and do away with despotisms and the ever-growing militarism under which the nations of the West are groaning and are being almost crushed to death, and which fairly promises to overwhelm even the nations of the East. If the past struggle has produced even a few Indians who would dedicate themselves to the task of becoming Satyagrahis as nearly perfect as possible, they would not only have served themselves in the truest sense of the term, they would also have served humanity at large. Thus viewed, Satyagraha is the noblest and best education. It should come, not after the ordinary education in letters, of children, but it should precede it. It will not be denied, that a child, before it begins to write its alphabet and to gain worldly knowledge, should know what the soul is, what truth is, what love is, what powers are latent in the soul. It should be an essential of real education that a child should learn, that in the struggle of life, it can easily conquer hate by love, untruth by truth, violence by self-suffering.

Metaphysics

To this day, it is common for Indian thinkers to hold the view that India's role in the international community consists at least partly in promoting a spiritual understanding of the human race and the issues of the times. This orientation is not new to India, but there is novelty in the relatively recent need to adapt this thought to the problematics of colonialism and then modernity. Once other cultures entered the Indian sphere of consciousness, they were evaluated to see not only how they met the standards of indigenous tradition, but also what they might contribute to the evolution of Hinduism, which has always absorbed new ideas from outside and recast them as needed to fit them into the Hindu framework.

Around the turn of the twentieth century, while India was still a colony of Britain, **Rabindranath Tagore** (1861–1941) developed his sense of a possible modern Indian consciousness in poetry and essays. His approach to the issues of modernity was not a grand strategy, but a path of individual cultivation. For Tagore, a realistic consciousness of the challenges and opportunities of the time can come only if the true nature of human beings is acknowledged and actions are carried out accordingly. Indian tradition provides a guide to the complexities of human nature and the behaviors needed for a harmonious and enlightening life. The needed learning is not something that can be acquired once and then stored away for future reference, but something that must be examined and extended throughout one's life. In this way of thinking, human beings must devote themselves to living the examined life. Tagore's thoughts are intended to remind us of this most central theme in the history of world philosophy.

SELECTION 17.21

Towards Universal Man

From Rabindranath Tagore

The flesh is impure, the world is vanity, and stern renunciation is the way to salvation—that was the ideal of spiritual life held forth in medieval Europe. Modern Europe, however, considers it unwholesome to admit an everlasting feud between the human world of natural desires and social aims on one hand and the spiritual life with its aspirations and discipline on the other. According to her, we enfeeble the moral purpose of our existence if we put too much stress on the

PROFILE / Rabindranath Tagore (1861–1941)

Modern India's best-known poet was also in the vanguard of post-colonial thought. Rabindranath Tagore was not simply an advocate for an interest group, but a thinker who saw that philos-ophy and action must be unified in the life of the individual. Thus, his political claims were intentionally grounded in the traditions of Indian spirituality. As we have noted, post-colonial thought often makes use of traditional ideas and values in its critiques of the structures and methods of domination. It also tends to begin with concrete social situations; for Tagore, this translated into heartfelt advocacy of social reform as a task for Indians themselves, regardless of British policy. Tagore was himself inspired by the beauty and manifold possibilities of life, and he sought to share his vision as an artist through both the written word and the painted image.

Born to an upper-class family in Calcutta, Tagore's opportunities were broad, including a brief period of study in England. In later life, as he established a worldwide reputation, he traveled to Europe, the United States, and Japan. He began writing for periodicals while still very young and acquired a life-long interest in education as a great hope for the betterment of the human condition. In 1901 he established a school in his native Bengal to put his ideas into practice. He continued to write and, in 1913, was awarded the Nobel Prize for Literature. He promptly devoted the proceeds to his school. Knighted in 1915, Tagore resigned the title in 1919 in protest against the harshly repressive tactics employed by the British in maintaining their empire in India. Among his many works are *One Hundred Poems of Kabir* (1915), *Nationalism* (1917), *The Home and the World* (1919), *Broken Ties* (1925), and *The Religion of Man* (1931).

illusoriness of this world. To drop down dead in the race-course of life, while running at full speed—that is acclaimed as the most glorious death.

Europe, it is true, has gained a certain strength by pinning her faith onto the world, by refusing to dwell on its evanescence and condemning the preoccupation with death as morbid. Her children are trained up in the struggle which, as science says, is for the survival of the fittest. That, Europe seems to think, is the whole meaning of life. But then, whatever the practical value of such a philosophy of living, the fact remains that our connection with the world is far from permanent.

Nature, for its own biological purposes, has created in us a strong faith in life by keeping us unmindful of death. Nevertheless, not only does our physical existence end, but all that it had built up goes to pieces at the peak of achievement. The greatest prosperity dissolves into emptiness; the mightiest empire is overtaken by stupor amidst the flicker of its festive lights. We may be weary of this truism, but it is true none the less. Therefore, all our actions have to be judged according to their harmony with life's background, the background which is death.

And yet it is equally true that, though all our mortal relationships must end, we cannot ignore them while they last. If we behave as if they do not exist, merely because they will not persist, they will all the same exact their dues, with a great deal over by way of penalty. We cannot claim exemption from payment of fare because the railway train has not the permanence of the dwelling house. Trying to ignore bonds that are real even if temporary, only strengthens and prolongs the bondage.

That is why the spirit of attachment and that of detachment have to be reconciled in harmony, and then only will they lead us to fulfilment. Attachment is the force drawing us to truth in its finite aspect, the aspect of what is, while detachment leads us to freedom in the infinity of truth which is the ideal aspect. In the act of walking, attachment is in the step that the foot takes when it touches the earth; detachment is in the movement of the other foot when it raises itself. The harmony of bondage and freedom is the dance of creation. According to the symbolism of Indian thought, Shiva, the male principle of Truth, represents freedom of the spirit, while Shivani, the female principle, represents the bonds of the material. In their union dwells perfection.

In order to reconcile these opposites, we must come to a true understanding of man; that is, we must not reduce him to the requirements of any particular duty. To look on trees only as firewood, is not to know the tree in its entirety; and to look on man merely as the protector of his country or the producer of its wealth, is to reduce him to soldier or merchant or diplomat, to make his efficiency the measure of his manhood. Such a narrow view is hurtful; those whom we seek to invest with glory are in fact degraded.

How India once looked on man as greater than any purpose he could serve, is revealed in an ancient Sanskrit couplet which may be translated thus:

> For the family, sacrifice the individual;
> For the community, the family;
> For the country, the community;
> For the soul, all the world.

A question will be asked: "What is this soul?" Let us first try to answer a much simpler question: "What is life?" Certainly life is not merely the facts of living that are evident to us, the breathing, digesting and various other functions of the body; not even the principle of unity which comprehends them. In a mysterious manner it holds within itself a future which continually reaches out from the envelopment of the present, dealing with unforeseen circumstances, experimenting with new variations. If dead materials choke the path of its ever-unfolding future, then life becomes a traitor that betrays its trust.

The soul is our spiritual life and it contains our infinity within it. It has an impulse that urges our consciousness to break through the dimly lighted walls of animal life where our turbulent passions fight to gain mastery in a narrow enclosure. Though, like animals, man is dominated by his self, he has an instinct that struggles against it, like the rebel life within a seed that breaks through the dark prison, bringing out its flag of freedom to the realm of light. Our sages in the East have always maintained that self-emancipation is the highest form of freedom for man, since it is his fulfilment in the heart of the Eternal, and not merely a reward won through some process of what is called salvation. . . .

Renounce we must, and through renunciation gain—that is the truth of the inner world. The flower must shed its petals for the sake of fruition, the fruit must drop off for the rebirth of the tree. The child leaves the refuge of the womb in order to achieve further growth of body and mind; next, he has to leave the self-centered security of a narrow world to enter a fuller life which has varied relations with the multitude; lastly comes the decline of the body, and enriched with experience man should now leave the narrower life for the universal life, to which he must dedicate his accumulated wisdom on the one hand and on the other, enter into relationship with the Life Eternal; so that, when finally the decaying body has come to the very end of its tether, the soul views its breaking away quite simply and without regret, in the expectation of its own rebirth into the infinite.

From individual body to community, from community to universe, from universe to Infinity—this is the soul's normal progress.

Checklist

To help you review, here is a checklist of the key philosophers and concepts of this chapter. The brief descriptive sentences summarize leading ideas. Keep in mind that some of these summary statements represent terrific oversimplifications of complex positions.

- **Kwame Gyekye** Ghanian philosopher whose phenomenological account of traditional Akan thoughtways has contributed importantly to development of an African history of ideas.
- **Kwasi Wiredu** Leading contemporary African philosopher, generally analytic in his approach; best known for his work to define the conditions of an indigenous African philosophy.
- **Frantz Fanon** Radical anticolonialist thinker; born in the Caribbean, studied in France, then joined Algerian rebels; best known for including violence as a desirable recourse for subjugated peoples.
- **Léopold Sédar Senghor** President of Senegal, poet, and philosopher who formulated the concept of negritude, which asserts an essential uniqueness in African cultures that explains certain historical phenomena and determines an African way of understanding.
- **Desmond Tutu** South African Anglican bishop who provided significant spiritual and moral leadership in the successful struggle against apartheid.
- **Vine Deloria, Jr.** American Indian leader and widely published interpreter of Indian experience; active in advocacy organizations, where he combines pragmatism with traditional spiritual values.
- **Martin Luther King, Jr.** Leader of African-American drive for equal civil rights; his nonviolent methods were influenced by the teachings of Mahatma Gandhi and were embraced by a majority of his constituents
- **bell hooks** African-American essayist whose analyses have helped shape feminist consciousness; noted for insights about the interests and sensibilities of marginalized ethnic groups.
- **Molefi Kete Asante** Professor of African and African-American Studies at Temple University; long associated with Afrocentrist thought.
- **Cornel West** African-American scholar active in fields of theology and philosophy; best known for his analysis of depth dimensions of racial issues.

- **Carlos Astrada** Argentinian philosopher whose early work in existential phenomenology transitioned into a deeply felt commitment to Marxist politics.
- **Francisco Miró Quesada** Peruvian philosopher with degrees in mathematics, philosophy, and law; noted for his work in theory of knowledge and political theory, which avoids metaphysical solutions to problems.
- **Mohandas (Mahatma) Gandhi** The twentieth century's greatest theorist of nonviolence and architect of India's independence from Great Britain.
- **Rabindranath Tagore** Indian poet and essayist, winner of 1913 Nobel Prize for literature; united a sense of Indian tradition with a vision of how India might adapt to the changing conditions of the modern world.

Concepts

Note: Many of the terms listed below have a variety of meanings, but the authors of the readings use them in specific ways that you should be able to discuss.

person

moral taboo

traditional religion

methodology

ethnophilosophy

negritude

philosophy as history

narrative as philosophy

dance as a way of knowing

ideology

capitalism

object empiricism

decolonization

intuitive reasoning

freedom

nonviolence

liberation

oppression

Afrocentric discourse

nihilism

rationalist idea of man

theory

satyagraha

Questions for Discussion and Review

1. Is a person only a body? Can you think of two alternative understandings of what is essential to a person?

2. Does one need to appeal to a supernaturally determined standard to demonstrate that an act is good, or at least permissible? Why or why not?

3. Should philosophy concern itself with practical matters?

4. What difference would it make for people in various disciplines to study epistemology along with their particular subjects?

5. Is it reasonable for a philosopher to hold to a particular ideology? On the other hand, is it possible for anyone not to have an ideology?

6. Should philosophy be done the same way in all cultures?

7. Is truth simply a matter of personal belief? Why does the answer to this question matter at all?

8. If Country A invades Country B, do the inhabitants of Country B have the right (or even the responsibility) to harass or kill any citizen of Country A they encounter?

9. If you believed that establishing an American colonial government in some country in South America would benefit the native peoples and help save the rain forests, would you have a responsibility to support colonialism under those circumstances?

10. What does Senghor mean by the phrase "sympathetic reason"?

11. Can a set of explained but otherwise unargued claims about life count as philosophy? Why or why not?

12. Is it possible for a religion to be right for one geographical location and wrong for another?

13. It is sometimes said that people who live in different cultures live in different worlds. What philosophical issues arise when people from "different worlds" find themselves in the same physical space?

14. Why would a physically stronger adversary refrain from destroying a nonviolent opponent? Try to avoid purely strategic considerations; instead, specifically address philosophical issues such as personal identity (or being), ethics, political philosophy, etc.

15. Must a true feminist be anti-male? Should the definition of a "true feminist" be very broad or very restrictive?

16. Can there be experience without interpretation?

17. What might it mean to me if I were to learn that many people speak of me in categories that I would not use to speak of myself?

18. What is nihilism? Is it a philosophical problem or is it a philosophical position? Can you construct arguments for and against nihilism?

19. Is there such a thing as a fixed human nature? Or does human nature change with historical circumstances?

20. Can people live without theories and principles? If you say "yes," then what determines what one does at any moment? If you say "no," then what is the proper role of theories and abstract principles in the conduct of daily life?

21. Should people who believe in political organization as a way for their group to increase its power participate in empowering members of their group with whom they have serious disagreements? For example, should middle-class "Anglo" feminists, most of whom believe in the right to abortion, help to empower Chicanas, many of whom probably do not believe in such a right?

22. Can religious claims be the basis of a philosophical position?

23. Could traditional modes of spirituality be an important or even essential element in overcoming colonialist reductionism that persists in a culture even after a people has regained its autonomy? Or should traditional ways of thinking be avoided in post-colonial reconstruction because following them opened up the people to conquest from the outside in the first place?

Suggested Further Readings

Aurobindo Ghose (Sri Aurobindo), *The Essential Aurobindo,* Robert A. McDermott, ed. (New York: Schocken Books, 1973). Selected writings of a thinker whose career began with radical political activism and concluded as a worldwide spiritual mission.

John A. A. Ayoade, "Time in Yoruba Thought," in *African Philosophy: An Introduction,* Richard A. Wright, ed. (Washington, D.C.: University Press of America, 1984). Analysis of assumptions and implications relevant to Yoruba metaphysics.

James Baldwin, *No Name in the Street* (New York: Dial Press, 1972). Analysis of social and philosophical issues in late twentieth-century America from an African-American perspective.

P. O. Bodunrin, ed., *Philosophy in Africa* (Ile-Ife, Nigeria: University of Ife Press, 1985). Collection of readings on various aspects of African philosophy.

Stokeley Carmichael and Charles V. Hamilton, *Black Power: The Politics of Liberation in America* (New York: Vintage Books, 1967). Provides an analysis of antecedent conditions of the Black Power movement and outlines essential tenets of this ideology.

Fidel Castro, *History Will Absolve Me,* Robert Taber, trans. (New York: Lyle Stuart, 1961). The full text of Castro's defense at his 1953 trial for conspiracy and armed insurrection.

Chaikh Anta Diop, *The African Origin of Civilization,* Mercer Cook, ed. and trans. (Westport, Conn.: Lawrence Hill & Co., 1974). The most thorough argument to date for the claim that a great portion of European thought traces back to black Africa.

W. E. B. Du Bois, *The Souls of Black Folk* (Millwood, N.Y.: Kraus-Thomson Organization, 1973). Groundbreaking social analysis from early in the twentieth century that has become a classic.

Ralph Ellison, *Invisible Man* (New York: Random House, 1947). National Book Award–winning novel rich in ideology and argumentation relevant to post-colonial issues.

Gustavo Gutierrez, *Liberation and Change* (Atlanta, Ga.: John Knox Press, 1977). A leading liberation theologian explains what sorts of spiritual and intellectual changes are needed to translate the desire for social justice into reality.

Kwame Gyekye, "Akan Concept of a Person," in *African Philosophy,* Richard Wright, ed. (Lanham, Md.: University Press of America, 1984). A widely respected voice in African philosophy uses analytic and comparative methods to explain a key metaphysical category.

J. Newton Hill, "African Sculpture," in *Africa from the Point of View of American Negro Scholars* (New York: American Society of African Culture, 1963). Focused on examples of sculpture in a single collection, this essay includes valuable insights into African aesthetics.

Paulin J. Hountondji, *African Philosophy* (Bloomington: Indiana University Press, 1983). Represents the position that African philosophy should be intentionally situated as an element of a worldwide philosophical conversation.

Hu Shih, *The Chinese Renaissance* (Chicago: University of Chicago Press, 1934). Influential work in China and the West concerning China's transition from an isolated empire vulnerable to Western colonial incursion into a modern state integrated into world culture.

Miguel Jorrín and John D. Martz, *Latin American Political Thought and Ideology* (Chapel Hill: University of North Carolina Press, 1970). Fleshes out the intellectual context of Latin American post-colonial thought.

Lacinay Keita, "The African Philosophical Tradition," in *African Philosophy,* Richard Wright, ed. (Lanham, Md.: University Press of America, 1984). Sketches connections of African thought with European and Islamic philosophical traditions from ancient to modern times.

Joseph R. Levenson, *Liang Ch'i-ch'ao and the Mind of Modern China* (Berkeley: University of California Press, 1953). Through the example of a turn-of-the-century writer, explains how Chinese thinkers moved beyond the false dilemma of adherence to tradition versus acceptance of Western technological values.

Mao Tse-tung, *Selected Works* (New York: International Publishing, 1954). Mao's early thinking on social and political issues is presented without coloration from the Cultural Revolution of his last decades.

John S. Mbiti, *African Religions and Philosophy* (London: Heinemann, 1988). General survey of African thought encompassing both traditional and more recent perspectives.

Jawaharlal Nehru, *India's Freedom* (New York: Barnes & Noble, 1962). Selections from the writings of the first prime minister of independent India, who was Gandhi's closest disciple.

Kwame Nkrumah, *Revolutionary Path* (New York: International Publishers, 1973). A collection of essays in which the former president of Ghana explains and justifies his plans for a Pan-African socialist program.

Arturo Andrés Roig, *The Actual Function of Philosophy,* C. Schofield, trans., excerpted in Jorge J. E. Gracia, ed., *Latin American Philosophy in the Twentieth Century* (Buffalo,

N.Y.: Prometheus, 1986). Recent critical appraisal of major threads in twentieth-century Latin philosophy.

Tsenay Serequeberhan, *African Philosophy: The Essential Readings* (New York: Paragon House, 1991). General readings in modern African thought.

Gayatri Chakravorty Spivak, *The Post-Colonial Critic: Interviews, Strategies, Dialogues,* Sarah Harasym, ed. (New York: Routledge, Chapman, and Hall, 1990). Uses concepts from recent political and literature theory to enhance understanding of ethnic and gender issues in post-colonial thought.

Placide Tempels, *Bantu Philosophy* (Paris: Présence Africaine, 1969). Controversial groundbreaking attempt to situate the ideas of an African people typologically in the history of ideas.

Arnold Temu and Bonaventure Swai, *Historians and Africanist History: A Critique* (London: Zed Press, 1981). Detailed exposition of theoretical and critical issues in the construction of post-colonial historiography.

UNESCO, *Teaching and Research in Philosophy: Africa* (Paris: United Nations Scientific and Cultural Organization, 1984). A collection of essays surveying the organization and content of philosophy instruction in Africa and arguing for future emphases and directions.

Kwasi Wiredu, *Philosophy and an African Culture* (New York: Cambridge University Press, 1980). Discussion of traditional philosophical problems from an analytic perspective.

Malcolm X, *The Autobiography of Malcolm X* (New York: Balantyne, 1964). Traces the development of a thinker who demonstrates the dynamic nature of critical consciousness through an account of his life from childhood up to his assassination.

Eastern and Post-Colonial Philosophy

Summary and Conclusion

The three principal systems of Chinese philosophical thought are Confucianism, Taoism, and Buddhism.

Confucius and Mencius, the two most important Confucian thinkers, were practical, socially minded philosophers who placed great emphasis on the perfectibility and innate goodness of human beings and on human ability to affect the Tao, or Way of things, for the better.

Lao Tzu and Chuang Tzu, the principal Taoists, regarded the Tao as ineffable and beyond man's ability to alter, and believed that the superior person reveals wisdom through understanding and effortless nonstriving.

Buddhism, which originated in India, set forth an Eightfold Path for coping with suffering; and, in China, where it is known as Ch'an, it was modified with Taoist and Confucian elements and emphasized the oneness and indivisibility of ultimate being. Zen, or Japanese Buddhism, evolved from Chinese Ch'an Buddhism; Dogen, of the Soto branch of Zen, stressed the importance of acquiring the perspective of the universal Self as a means of attaining enlightenment and enduring joy.

The samurai philosophy exhibited marked Confucian and Zen Buddhist influences; it was Confucian especially in the importance it attached to practical wisdom as a counterbalance to proficiency as a warrior, and it showed the influence of Zen in the emphasis it placed on a universal perspective and the containment of selfishness as the antidote to fear.

Hinduism is the term that embraces the religious beliefs and practices of the majority of the Indian people. Common to all forms of Hinduism is acceptance of the authority of the Vedic scriptures. The last of these scriptures, the *Upanishads,* are the most important philosophically and are best known for identifying *atman* with *brahman,* though this identification is subject to various interpretations.

Post-colonial philosophy is a modern-era innovation in the history of ideas. With roots in both the practical difficulties of subjugated peoples and the discipline of the academy, it emphasizes thoughtful attention to the conditions of life. Intentionally constructed to subvert the ideologies of imperialist and dominating powers, post-colonial philosophy includes work in ethics, epistemology, metaphysics, and all the other traditional categories of philosophical endeavor. Virtually all of the world's cultures have given rise to post-colonial texts as the problems of domination have become more widely understood.

In addition to its insistence on linking theory and practice, post-colonial thought seeks to accomplish a wide range of tasks. Some thinkers concentrate on revealing the metaphysical decisions that lie behind common beliefs and practices. Others employ phenomenological method and ideological critique to analyze cultural identity. Still others articulate constructive visions of the good, tell the stories of the history of ideas, and link tradition to modernity. By extending the boundaries of the field and by making rich connections between philosophy and practical concerns, post-colonial thought contributes importantly to creative work in twentieth-century philosophy.

APPENDIX 1 Logic

There is only one way to prove a proposition, and that is by means of an **argument.**

Example of an argument:

1. Pain and suffering are real.
2. If pain and suffering are real, then God does not exist.
3. Therefore, God does not exist.

In this argument, propositions (1) and (2) are used in an effort to prove (3). They—propositions (1) and (2)—provide the reasons for accepting (3) and are known as the *premises* of the argument. Proposition (3) is the *conclusion* of the argument.

Outside logic texts, arguments are not usually stated so "formally." What you are more likely to encounter is something like this, which is exactly the same argument stated more casually.

Pain and suffering are real, so there is no God.

When the argument is stated this way, the arguer thinks premise (2) is so obvious that he or she is not even bothering to state it. This is still the same argument as given earlier, however.

Logic is concerned with arguments: their types and structures; the relationships among the propositions within them; the basic assumptions and principles governing those relationships; the extent to which mathematics, science, and ordinary thought exemplify those relationships; and other related matters. Most especially, logic is concerned with whether the premises of a given argument warrant acceptance of the conclusion.

Twentieth-century logic is a vast and technical discipline, and we are going to beg your forgiveness for not going into it in this book. What we want to do here is simply give you a useful introduction to the subject, one that focuses on some of the types of arguments you will encounter in this book and in real life.

Deductive and Inductive Arguments

It is *impossible* for the conclusions of some arguments to be false if their premises are true. If your argument is *supposed* to be like that, it is a **deductive argument.** And if indeed it *is* impossible for your conclusion to be false if the premises are true, then your argument is a *valid* deductive argument. And finally, if the premises of your valid deductive argument *really* are true, then your argument is sound. The example above is a valid deductive argument. Whether it is sound (i.e., whether the premises are in fact true) we will leave up to you.

If, on the other hand, your argument is only supposed to show that it is *improbable* that the conclusion is false if the premises are true, then it is an **inductive argument.** Inductive arguments are neither valid nor invalid nor sound; they are just *strong* or *weak*, depending on just how probable the conclusion is, given the premises.

Example of an inductive argument:

Sixty percent of those surveyed in the Gallup Poll believe in God, so sixty percent of all Americans favor a tax increase.

In this example, the premise (the proposition about the Gallup Poll) is intended to show that the conclusion is probable, not that it could not possibly be false.

Common Types of Deductive Arguments

Here are the two most common valid types or "patterns" of deductive arguments.

Valid deductive pattern 1: (p and q stand for propositions)

If *p* then *q*.
p.
Therefore *q*.

Example:

If pain and suffering are rare, then God is good. They are rare. Therefore, God is good.

Valid deductive pattern 2:

If *p* then *q*.
Not-q.
Therefore, *not-p*.

Example:

If God is all-good, then pain and suffering are rare. So, because they aren't, God is not all-good.

Now here are two invalid patterns of deductive arguments that are sometimes mistakenly viewed as valid.

Invalid deductive pattern 1:

If *p* then *q*.
q.
Therefore, *p*.

Example:

If God is all-good, then pain and suffering are rare. That proves that God is good, because pain and suffering are rare.

Invalid deductive pattern 2:

If *p* then *q*.
p isn't true.
Therefore, *q* isn't true.

Example:

If pain and suffering are rare, then God exists. That shows that God doesn't exist, because pain and suffering are not rare.

The four patterns just given are the most frequently used patterns of deductive argument. Two other patterns of deductive argument are common, however.

One is called **reductio ad absurdum,** or, sometimes, just the **reductio proof** (see Chapter 12 for one example). The principle here is that if some proposition *p* "reduces to" or entails some other proposition that is absurd, nonsensical, or just patently false, then *not-p* must hold true. Here are two examples:

Examples of reductio proof:

1. God is not self-caused, because if He were, then He would have to exist before Himself, which is absurd.

2. If there truly is a good and all-powerful God, then pain and suffering must serve His purpose, and that means they actually are good things. But that's ridiculous, because it means that it's a good thing that Uncle Charlie's terminal cancer is causing him so much agony. So I don't agree that there is a good and all-powerful God.

Schematically, these two *reductio* proofs look like this:

1. *p,* because if *not-p,* then *q,* which is absurd.
2. *p.*
If *p* holds, then so does absurd result *q.*
Therefore *not-p.*

As you can see, *reductio* proofs are closely related to valid pattern 2, noted earlier. As you can also see, the *reductio* pattern of argument is persuasive only if the result touted as absurd truly is absurd. Actually, a *reductio* proof is valid in the technical sense defined only if the allegedly absurd result cannot possibly be true.

And finally, the other commonly encountered valid pattern is **"begging the question."** But watch out for this pattern! Begging the question is what you get if your premises assume the very conclusion they are supposed to prove. So even though begging the question is technically valid, it is worthless as proof. Anyone who disputes your conclusion won't accept your premises, if your premises assume the very point at issue.

Here's the standard example:

Example of begging the question:

It says in the Bible that God exists. Because the Bible is the revealed word of God, what it says is true. Therefore God exists.

And here's another example, even less subtle:

God is unlimited. This follows immediately from the fact that God has no limits.

Schematically, question-begging arguments ultimately amount to this:

p.
Therefore, *p.*

The vast majority of deductive arguments you encounter in this book, and in philosophy outside this book, are instances of one or another of these six patterns.

Common Types of Inductive Arguments

The two most common types of inductive arguments are inductive generalizations and analogical arguments.

In the premises of an **inductive generalization,** something is said to be characteristic of a *sample* of a class of things, and the conclusion is that the same thing is characteristic of *all* (or most) of the class. Schematically, it looks like this:

A certain percentage or portion of a sample of class C has characteristic F.

Therefore, about the same percentage or portion of the entire class C has characteristic F.

Examples of inductive generalizations:

1. Thirty percent of a sample of seniors at Hollow University are atheists, so about thirty percent of all the seniors at Hollow University are atheists.

2. A majority of Americans surveyed by ABC believe God answers their prayers, so it is clear that a majority of Americans are not atheists.

3. All events so far experienced have been caused; therefore all events, period, are caused.

Again, inductive generalizations are not just simply "valid" or "invalid." Instead, they are to varying degrees strong or weak, depending on just how probable the conclusion is, given the premise or premises. And how probable the conclusion is, given the premise or premises, depends mainly on the extent to which the sample of class C is truly *representative* of the entire class C.

In an **analogical argument,** the fact that two or more things are alike in certain respects is given as reason for believing that they are alike in further respects.

Example of an analogical argument:

The human eye in certain obvious ways resembles an autofocus camera.

Therefore, because an autofocus camera is the product of intelligent design, the human eye is the product of intelligent design, i.e., God.

Analogical arguments are also strong or weak in varying degrees, depending on how alike the items in the analogy are.

These, then, are the most common basic types of argument.

APPENDIX 2 Truth

About any belief (statement, assertion, proposition, claim, etc.) we may ask two different questions:

Nature 1. What is it for this belief to be true, assuming that it is?

Justification 2. What are the standards or criteria by means of which it may be determined whether this belief is true?

Yes, other questions might be asked of the belief, but it is in answer to these questions that so-called philosophical theories of truth have been proposed.

Recent practice is to regard question (2) as a request for a theory of *justification*. Only the first question is a query about the *nature* of truth.

Principal Philosophical Theories of Truth

In this appendix, then, we will discuss answers to the question: What is it for a belief to be true? Further, we'll limit the discussion to empirical beliefs—those known to be true or false only by observation.

Here, then, are the leading "theories of truth."

Correspondence Theory

According to the **correspondence theory of truth,** a belief is true if and only if it corresponds to its object—that is, to what it is a belief about.

If this theory strikes you as correct, then you should be aware of the notorious difficulties it encounters.

First, what *is* a belief about? To what, exactly, does a true belief correspond? I believe my stapler is on my desk. Does my belief correspond only to the stapler and to the desk, or does it correspond to the *fact* that my stapler is on my desk? Surely the latter, you say? But then, what is a fact? Do facts exist on the side of the objects—that is, along with the stapler and desk—or are they a contribution to reality made by the mind—that is, do they exist on the side of the belief? To date, there is no generally accepted account of the nature of facts or of what true beliefs correspond to.

A second difficulty: To what do negative beliefs, and general beliefs, and compound beliefs, and beliefs about future and past events, and about mythical entities, and about probabilities correspond, if they are true? To what do beliefs expressed as subjunctive conditional propositions ("If such-and-such were the case, then . . .") correspond, if they are true?

And what about false beliefs? Well, we might say that they *fail* to correspond. But there are many different false beliefs. Does one failure of correspondence differ from another failure of correspondence?

A third difficulty in the correspondence theory: What, exactly, is *correspondence?* In one sense of the term *correspond,* to say that a belief corresponds to reality just is to say that it is true (it's because the word carries this sense that the correspondence theory seems so intuitively plausible). But in that sense of *correspond,* we do not clarify or elucidate the concept of truth by saying that a true belief corresponds to reality: we do not make clear in what way or just how a true belief hooks on to reality. After all, a belief is not very much like a fact, if that's what a true belief corresponds to. So just *how* does a true belief correspond to a fact? By picturing it? By mirroring it? By copying it? Or what?

And here is one more problem: The correspondence theory seems to presuppose the existence of a reality external to one's mind, a realm to which one's beliefs may or may not correspond. Common sense may have no difficulty with this presupposition, but philosophy does. Its validity has been debated throughout the history of philosophy and has been subject to recent vigorous attack.

Coherence Theory

According to the **coherence theory of truth,** an empirical belief is true if and only if it *coheres* with a system of other beliefs, which together form a comprehensive account of reality.

What is meant by "coheres"? Well, that's one of the big problems in the theory: Just what is it for a system of beliefs to cohere?

Although it may not be possible to clarify fully this idea of coherence, we think you can get some idea of the thinking behind the coherence theory if you consider a false arithmetical proposition, such as "$2 + 3 + 3 = 57\frac{1}{4}$."

What makes this proposition false? Well, it just doesn't cohere with the rest of arithmetic. It doesn't fit into the system.

According to the coherence theory, the truth of even empirical propositions, propositions about the world, must be analyzed along similar lines.

Still, this analogy does not help very much. Coherent beliefs must, of course, be logically consistent, and beyond this they must be connected by some sort of relationships of mutual implication. But what sort is not very clear.

Nevertheless, before you reject the coherence theory, consider this: With the coherence theory we have only two things to explain, beliefs and coherence. With the correspondence theory we have three things to explain: beliefs, correspondence, and facts.

There are other problems associated with the coherence theory, however. To run through the most notorious:

1. Might there not be more than one internally coherent system of beliefs? (Indeed, might not virtually every belief belong to some system or other?) How does one select from among alternative systems?

2. What's to guarantee the truth of the *whole system* of beliefs?

3. Because, according to the coherence theory, the internal coherence of the system of beliefs constitutes the truth of the system and its member beliefs, it must be asked: What connects the entire system of beliefs, or any belief within it, to external reality, if indeed there is an external reality?

4. Doesn't the theory require that we know *everything* that is true before we can know *anything* that is true? *No . puzzle*

Other Theories

Frequently a third major theory of truth is mentioned in philosophy texts, the so-called **pragmatic theory of truth,** worked out in various forms by the "classic" American pragmatists C. S. Peirce (1839–1914), William James (1842–1910), and John Dewey (1859–1952) and by contemporary American pragmatists including notably Richard Rorty (1931–). Some of the views as to truth held by contemporary analytic philosophers such as Hilary Putnam and Donald Davidson are closely related.

According to Peirce, "The opinion which is fated to be ultimately agreed to by all who investigate, is what we mean by the truth." James and Dewey, though having their differences about truth, seemed both to offer theories of justification, that is, theories concerning when it is appropriate or justified to assert a claim as true. In scientific affairs, James maintained, the truth of a belief is established by experimental verification; metaphysical and theological beliefs, in contrast, are to be deemed true if they provide the individual with "vital benefits." For Dewey, a belief is something like a map; when you have determined that it helps you find your way out of the woods and safely to home, you may regard your belief map as true.

For Rorty, whose views on the subject have been quite influential in recent years, truth isn't something that needs a "theory" to begin with. According to the correspondence theory, truth is to be explained in terms of a relation between beliefs and the world; according to the coherence theory, it is to be explained in terms of a relation among beliefs. According to the Rortian view, there really isn't anything about truth to be explained. "True" is just a form of praise we use for a belief that currently is considered so solidly established that we do not think that anything further is required to justify our accepting it. Rorty attaches no significance to the idea of the world "as it really is" independent of the perspective from which it is conceived. Thus he is especially critical of the correspondence theory of truth, according to which a belief is true when it corresponds to the world "as it really is."

Very similar to some of the ideas about truth found in the literature of pragmatism is what is called the **performative theory of truth,** associated with Oxford philosopher P. F. Strawson (1919–). According to this theory, to assert that a proposition is true is really to emphasize or endorse or concede or confirm the proposition itself rather than to attribute a property to it. Because the word *true* is a linguistic device used to emphasize or agree with a claim, there is no point in searching for the nature of truth, proponents of this theory hold.

The concept of truth is basic, and the question What is it for a belief to be true? seems straightforward enough. Nevertheless, no answer has been universally accepted by philosophers. A comprehensive recent survey of all the theories of truth, by Richard L. Kirkham, is titled *Theories of Truth: A Critical Introduction* (Cambridge, Mass.: Bradford, 1992).

APPENDIX 3 Knowledge

Epistemology, as we stated in Part 1, is concerned primarily with two questions: What is knowledge? and Is knowledge possible? Part 1 was devoted mainly to the second issue.

So a word here about the first question.

What, then, *is* knowledge?

There is evidently a difference between knowing *how to do something*—knowing how to tune up a car, for example, or how to speak German—and knowing *that something is true*—knowing that it is time for a tune-up, say, or that the German word for "window" is *Fenster.* Epistemologists usually are concerned with understanding "knowing that." They wish to determine what it is to know that something is true.

What is it to know that something is true? What is it to know, for instance, that you are alive right now and that you are reading this book? Is it merely to believe these things? Or is knowledge something beyond or different from belief? Does knowledge differ from mere information, from the data stored in computers or books, for example? Does it include what is remembered—that, for example, you had toast and jelly, or whatever, for breakfast?

Plato was the first philosopher carefully to consider the question What is knowledge? His most extensive treatment of the matter is found in the *Theaetetus,* a dialogue devoted almost entirely to the question.

In this dialogue it first is suggested that knowledge may be equated with sense perception. This idea sounds plausible. After all, it might seem that to see a candle burning would be to know a candle is burning; to hear Socrates talking would be to know that he is talking; to feel pain would be to know you are in pain; and so forth. In addition, sensory experience seems quite beyond doubt, just as knowledge apparently is.

Nevertheless, Plato rejected the suggestion. If you come to know that something is true, he argued, you can retain your knowledge even after you are no longer in sensory contact with the thing about which you have knowledge. And besides, he pointed out, whereas sense perception only provides information within this or that sensory channel, knowledge reaches across sensory channels. When I eat a strawberry, my taste informs me of its sweetness, and my eyes inform me of its redness, but my knowledge brings together the redness and the sweetness. So knowledge seems to involve some sort of integrative activity on the part of the mind that goes beyond sense perception.

Plato then considered the idea that knowledge is correct thinking or true belief. But he rejected this idea because true belief may be based on hearsay evidence or just a lucky guess.

He then concluded that knowledge consists of "correct belief together with an account." Unfortunately, he was unable to clarify this concept of an "account," either to his own or to anyone else's satisfaction.

Most philosophers who considered the matter after Plato thought that he was on the right track in the *Theaetetus* to maintain that knowledge is true belief together with an account. Most contemporary philosophers, however, would not put things just that way. Instead, they would say this: For you to know that something is true—say, that Socrates is dead—means that three conditions must hold, namely:

1. You must believe that Socrates is dead.

2. Your belief that Socrates is dead must be true.

3. Your belief that Socrates is dead must be *justified:* it must be based on evidence, grounds, or reasons that warrant that belief.

As can be seen, "justification" is just the modern word for what Plato called an "account."

Unfortunately, there is a big difficulty in this justified-true-belief (JTB) analysis of knowledge. For it seems possible to imagine situations in which a person meets the three conditions stated and yet does not have knowledge. For instance, suppose that you believe that your car won't start. Suppose further that you believe this for the excellent reason that you removed the battery. Suppose finally that your car indeed won't start. This is a case of justified true belief. Is it a case of knowledge?

Ordinarily, perhaps it is. But imagine that while your back was turned, two things happened. First, unknown to you, someone put a brand-new battery in the car. And second, when she did it, she accidentally severed the connection between the battery and the starter. The result? Your justified true belief that the car won't start doesn't qualify as knowledge. So the JTB analysis of knowledge seems defective.

Around thirty years ago, examples of this sort to the justified-true-belief analysis of knowledge were noted by Edmund Gettier, and soon philosophy journals were flooded with articles proposing modifications to the JTB theory in the light of Gettier-type counterexamples. According to one modification, for example, proposed by Alvin I. Goldman, a belief is justified to the extent required for knowledge if and only if it is *caused* by the facts that make it true.

Thus, for instance, in the example just given, I am not justified in believing that the car won't start because the facts that caused my belief are not the facts that made that belief true.

Unfortunately, there are counterexamples that defeat that modification, and similar stories can be told for other modifications that have been proposed.

Perhaps the underlying problem is this: Possibly, for a belief to be justified to the extent required for knowledge, it must be inferred from other beliefs that are themselves known to be true. Thus, to use the example, we might say that you weren't justified in believing that the car wouldn't start. You weren't justified, because you inferred that belief from the proposition that the car didn't have a battery and you didn't really know that proposition was true.

But if everything that is known must be inferred from something else that is known, then how could knowledge ever have gotten started? This requirement for justification seems to lead to skepticism.

Perhaps, then, we should maintain that some beliefs, to be justified, don't have to be *inferred* from other beliefs; in other words, perhaps some beliefs are just plain *self-justifying*.

Unfortunately, independent epistemological inquiry raises difficulties with the idea that any beliefs are self-justifying, as we saw in Part 1.

Another alternative might be to say that some beliefs, to be justified, don't have to be inferred from beliefs *known* to be true. But if that is so, then we can know something on the basis of something else that is not known, and that seems curious.

So there are problems with all three alternatives.

The real problem, of course, is that the concept of justification is really not very clear. In fact, it isn't much clearer than Plato's concept of an account. Knowledge seems to be justified true belief, but it isn't very clear what the justification part involves. Current epistemological inquiry into the nature of knowledge is focused on this problem.

APPENDIX 4 Pronunciation Guide to Names

Aesara ai-SAH-ruh
Al-Farabi el-fuh-RAHB-ee
Al-Ghazali el-guh-ZAHL-ee
Al-Kindi el-KIN-dee
Anaxagoras an-ak-SAG-uh-rus
Anaximander a-NAK-suh-MAN-der
Anaximenes a-NAK-suh-MEN-eez
Anselm, St. AN-selm
Aquinas, St. Thomas (see Thomas Aquinas, St.)
Aristippus air-uh-STIPP-us
Aristotle AIR-uh-STAH-tul
Asante, Molefi Kete uh-SAN-tay
Astrada, Carlos uh-STRAH-duh
Augustine, St. AW-guh-steen or uh-GUST-un
Aurelius, Marcus aw-RAIL-i-us
Averroës ah-VAIR-oh-eez
Avicenna av-uh-SEN-uh
Ayer, A. J. air
Bakunin, Mikhail ba-KOO-nin
Basho bah-sho
Beauvoir, Simone de bow-VWAHR
Beckett, Samuel BECK-et
Bentham, Jeremy BEN-thum
Bergman, Ingmar BURG-mun
Berkeley, George BAR-klee
Bingen, Hildegard von BING-un
Brentano, Franz bren-TAH-no
Bruchac, Joseph BROO-shak
Buddha, Siddhartha Gautama BOO-duh, sid-HAR-tuh GO-tuh-muh
Burke, Edmund burk
Camus, Albert kAh-MOO
Châtelet, Emilie du SHA-ta-lay

Chodorow, Nancy CHO-duh-row
Chuang, Tzu CHWANG-tsuh
Churchland, Paul CHURCH-lund
Cicero SIS-uh-ro
Cleanthes clee-AN-theez
Cockburn, Catherine Trotter KO-burn
Confucius kun-FYOO-shus
Conway, Anne Finch KAHN-way
Cratylus KRA-tuh-lus
Deloria, Vine, Jr. duh-LOR-ee-uh
Derrida, Jacques day-ree-DAH
Descartes, René day-KART
Dewey, John DOO-ee
Diogenes Laertiús die-AH-juh-neez/lay-EWR-she-us
Dogen DOE-gen
Dostoyevsky, Fyodor dohs-tuh-YEF-skee
Empedocles em-PED-uh-kleez
Epictetus ep-ik-TEET-us
Epicurus ep-uh-KYUR-us
Fanon, Frantz fuh-NOHN
Ferguson, Ann FER-guh-sun
Firestone, Shulamith FIRE-stone
Flew, Antony floo
Foucault, Michel foo-KO
Fourier, Charles foor-YAY
Frye, Marilyn fry
Gandhi, Mahatma GAHN-dee
Gaunilo GO-nee-low
Gilligan, Carol GILL-uh-gun
Gorgias GOR-jee-us
Gyekye, Kwame JYEH-chay
Habermas, Jürgen HAHB-ur-mahs

725

Hare, R.H. hair
Hegel, Georg Wilhelm Friedrich
  HAY-gul
Heidegger, Martin HY-duh-ger
Heloise HELL-oh-eez
Heraclitus hayr-uh-KLITE-us
Hobbes, Thomas hahbz
Hountondji, Paulin J. hoon-TON-jee
Hsün Tzu SHWIN-tsuh
Hui Neng HWAY-nung
Hume, David hyoom
Husserl, Edmund HOO-surl
Hypatia hy-PAY-sha
Ionesco, Eugéne ee-uh-NES-ko
James, William jaymz
Johnson, Charles JAHN-sun
Kabir, Ezekiel kuh-BEER
Kafka, Franz KAHF-kuh
Kant, Immanuel kahnt
Keita, Lansana KAY-tuh
Kierkegaard, Søren KEER-kuh-gore
King, Martin Luther Jr. king
Kropotkin, Piotr krah-POT-kin
LaBelle, Beverly luh-BELL
Lao Tzu LAO-tsuh
Leibniz, Gottfried Wilhem LIBE-nits
Lévi-Strauss, Claude LAY-vee-
  STROWSS
Locke, John lahk
Lugones, Maria lu-GO-nayz
Machiavelli, Niccolò mak-yah-VEL-ee
Mackie, J. L. MACK-ee
Marcuse, Herbert mar-KOO-zeh
Marx, Karl marks
Mencius MEN-shus
Mill, John Stuart mill
Miyamoto, Musashi mee-yuh-moh-
  toh, mu-sah-shee
Montesquieu, Charles-Louis de
  Secondat, baron de MAHN-tes-kyu
Moore, G. E. more
Murasaki, Shikibu MOO-ruh-sah-kee,
  shih-kih-boo
Mussolini, Benito moo-suh-LEE-nee
Newman, John Henry NEW-man
Nietzsche, Friedrich NEE-cheh
Norwich, Julian of NOR-wich
Nozick, Robert NO-zik

Onwuanibe, Richard C. on-wan-EE-bay
Owen, Robert O-win
Paley, William PAY-lee
Parmenides par-MEN-uh-deez
Pascal, Blaise pahs-KAHL
Perictione II puh-rik-TYE-oh-nee
Plantinga, Alvin PLAN-tin-guh
Plato PLAY-toe
Plotinus pluh-TIE-nus
Protagoras pro-TAG-uh-rus
Proudhon, Pierre Joseph prew-DOHn)
Putnam, Hilary PUHT-nuhm
Pyrrho PEER-row
Pythagoras puh-THAG-uh-rus
Quesada, Francisco Miró keh-SAH-duh
Quine, W. V. O. kwyne
Rachels, James RAY-chels
Rawls, John rawlz
Rorty, Richard ROAR-tee
Ross, Stephanie rawss
Ross, W. D. rawss
Rousseau, Jean-Jacques roo-SO
Russell, Bertrand RUS-ul
Ryle, Gilbert rile
Sabuco de Nantes Barrera, Maria
  Luisa Oliva sah-BOO-ko
Saint-Simon, Claude san-SEE-mon
Saldívar-Hull, Sonia sal-DEE-bar-hul
Sartre, Jean-Paul sartr
Saussure, Ferdinand de so-SIWR
Schopenhauer, Arthur SHOW-
  pun-owur
Searle, John surl
Seneca SEN-uh-kuh
Senghor, Léopold Sédar SENG-oh
Sextus Empiricus SEX-tus
  em-PEER-uh-kus
Smart, J. J. C. smart
Smith, Adam smith
Socrates SOK-ruh-teez
Spinoza, Benedictus de spin-O-zuh
St. Anselm (see Anselm)
St. Augustine (see Augustine)
St. Thomas Aquinas (see Thomas
  Aquinas)
Steinem, Gloria STY-num
Stevenson, C. L. STEE-ven-sun
Sun Tzu SWUN-tsuh

Swai, Bonaventure swai
Swinburne, Richard SWIN-burn
Tagore, Rabindranath tuh-GORE
Taylor, Harriet TAY-lur
Temu, Arnold TEH-moo
Tennant, F. R. TEN-unt
Thales THAY-leez
Theano thee-AHN-o
Thompson, William TOMP-son
Thomson, Judith Jarvis TOM-son
Tolstoy, Leo TOL-stoy
Tutu, Desmond too-too
West, Cornel west

Wheeler, Anna Doyle WHEE-lur
Wiredu, Kwasi wih-RAY-du
Wittgenstein, Ludwig
    VITT-gen-shtyne
Wollstonecraft, Mary WOLL-stone-
    kraft
Xenophanes zeh-NAF-uh-neez
Yagyu, Munenori yah-gyu, mu-neh-
    noh-ree
Yamamoto, Tsunetomo yah-muh-
    moh-toh, tsu-neh-toh-moh
Zeno ZEE-no

Glossary

Absolute, the   That which is unconditioned and uncaused by anything else. It is frequently thought of as God, perfect and solitary, self-caused eternal being that is the source or essence of all that exists but that is itself beyond the possibility of conceptualization or definition.

Absolute Idealism   The early-nineteenth-century school of philosophy that maintained that being is the transcendental unfolding or expression of thought or reason.

Academics   Philosophers of the third and second centuries B.C. in what had been Plato's Academy. They had the reputation of maintaining that all things are inapprehensible.

act-utilitarianism   A form of utilitarianism (subscribed to by Bentham) in which the rightness of an act is determined by its effect on the general happiness.

aesthetics   The philosophical study of art and of value judgments about art and of beauty in general.

agoge   Way of living.

analogical argument   An argument that attributes to one thing a characteristic found in a similar thing or things.

analysis   Resolving a complex proposition or concept into simpler ones in order to gain better understanding of the original proposition or concept. *Analysis* comes from a Greek word meaning to "unloosen" or "untie."

analytic philosophy   The predominant twentieth-century philosophical tradition in English-speaking countries. Analytic philosophy has its roots in British empiricism and holds that analysis is the proper method of philosophy.

anarchism   A utopian political theory that seeks to eliminate all authority and state rule in favor of a society based on voluntary cooperation and free association of individuals and groups.

ancient philosophy   Sixth century B.C. through, approximately, the third century A.D.

androgyny   Having both male and female characteristics; unisex.

antirepresentationalism   A philosophy that denies that the mind or language contains or is a representation of reality.

applied ethics   Moral theory applied to specific contemporary moral issues, such as abortion, affirmative action, pornography, capital punishment, etc.

***a priori* principle**   A proposition whose truth we do not need to know through sensory experience and that no conceivable experience could serve to refute.

argument   A series of propositions, one of which is supposedly supported by the others.

argument from design   A proof for the existence of God based on the idea that the universe and its parts give evidence of purpose or design and therefore require a divine designer.

ataraxia   The goal of unperturbedness and tranquility of mind that was considered the highest good by ancient thinkers such as the Skeptics.

Atomism   The ancient Greek philosophy that holds that all things are composed of simple, indivisible minute particles.

authenticity   A way of understanding the essential nature of the human being by seeing it as a totality.

bad faith   In the philosophy of Jean-Paul Sartre, essentially self-deception or lying to one-self, especially when this takes the form of blaming circumstances for one's fate and not seizing the freedom to realize oneself in action.

begging the question   An argument begs the question if its premises assume the point at issue as a preexisting given.

behaviorism   The methodological principle in psychology according to which meaning-ful psychological inquiry confines itself to psychological phenomena that can be behavior-ally defined; also, the theory in philosophy that when we talk about a person's mental states, we are referring in fact to the person's disposition to behave in certain ways.

Buddhism   A philosophical tradition, founded by Gautama Siddhartha Buddha in the fifth century B.C., that took on various forms as a religion and spread throughout Asia. Buddhism attempts to help the individual conquer the suffering and mutability of human existence through the elimination of desire and ego and attainment of the state of nirvana.

bushido   The way or ethic of the samurai warrior, based on service and demanding rigorous training, usually both in the military and literary arts.

capitalism   An economic system in which ownership of the means of production and distribution is maintained mostly by private individuals and corporations.

categorical imperative   Immanuel Kant's formulation of a moral law that holds uncon-ditionally, i.e., categorically. In its most common formulation, states that you are to act in such a way that you could desire the principle on which you act to be a universal law.

causal explanation   An explanation of the cause or causes of an event.

"clear and distinct" criterion   René Descartes's criterion of truth, according to which that, and only that, which is perceived as clearly and distinctly as the fact of one's own existence is certain.

cogito, ergo sum   "I think, therefore I am." The single indubitable truth on which Des-cartes's epistemology is based.

cognitivist   One who believes that knowledge is possible.

coherence theory of truth   The theory that an empirical belief is true if and only if it "coheres" with a body of propositions that collectively form a comprehensive account of reality.

Communism   The ideology of the Communist party.

communism   An economic system in which goods are owned in common and are available to all as needed.

communitarian   One who holds that there is a common good defined by one's society, the attainment of which has priority over individual liberty.

conceptualism   The theory that universals are concepts and exist only in the mind.

Confucianism   A philosophical tradition that began with Confucius in the sixth century B.C. and continues to the present day. Confucianism is a practical philosophy that hopes to establish a better world order by means of the moral perfection of the individual.

consequentialism   Ethical theories that evaluate actions by their consequences.

conservatism   A political philosophy based on respect for established institutions and traditions and that favors preservation of the status quo over social experimentation.

contemporary philosophy   Twentieth-century philosophy.

Continental philosophy   The philosophical traditions of continental Europe; includes phenomenology, existentialism, hermeneutics, deconstruction, and critical theory.

contractarianism   *See* **contractualism.**

contractarian theory   The political theory according to which a legitimate state exists only by virtue of an agreement or "contract" among the subjects of the state.

contractualism   Ethical theories according to which right and wrong are established by a societal agreement or social contract.

Copernican revolution in philosophy   A new perspective in epistemology, introduced by Immanuel Kant, according to which the objects of experience must conform in certain respects to our knowledge of them.

correspondence theory of truth   The theory that a belief is true if and only if it corresponds to its object.

cosmological argument   An argument for the existence of God according to which the universe and its parts can be neither accidental nor self-caused and must ultimately have been brought into existence by God.

critical theory   A philosophical method that seeks to provide a radical critique of knowledge by taking into account the situation and interests involved.

cultural relativism   The theory that what is right (and wrong) is what your culture believes is right (and wrong).

Cynicism   A school of philosophy founded around the fifth century B.C., probably by Antisthenes or Diogenes. The Cynics sought to lead lives of total simplicity and naturalness by rejecting all comforts and conveniences of society.

Cyrenaicism   The philosophy of Aristippus and others who lived in Cyrene about Plato's time; it emphasized seeking a life of as many intense pleasures as possible.

deductive argument   An argument whose premises are intended to provide absolutely conclusive reasons for accepting the conclusion.

deontological ethics   Ethical theories according to which what I ought to do is whatever it is my moral duty to do.

descriptive egoism   The doctrine that maintains that in conscious action a person always seeks self-interest above all else.

descriptive relativism   The doctrine that the moral standards people subscribe to differ from culture to culture and from society to society.

descriptivism   A philosophy that seeks to describe the moral principles that people accept rather than prescribing the principles they should accept; alternatively, a philosophy that seeks to determine what people ought to do if they wish to achieve a certain end.

determinism   The doctrine that a person could not have acted otherwise than as she or he did act.

Ding-an-sich   German for "thing-in-itself": a thing as it is independent of any consciousness of it.

divine-command ethics   Ethical theory according to which what is morally right and good is determined by divine command.

divine law   In the philosophy of Thomas Aquinas, God's gift to humankind, apprehended through revelation, that directs us to our supernatural goal, eternal happiness.

dream conjecture   The conjecture, used by Descartes, that all experience may be dream experience.

dualism   Two-ism; the doctrine that existing things belong to one or another but not both of two distinct categories of things, usually deemed to be physical and nonphysical or spiritual.

efficient cause   One of Aristotle's four kinds of causes—specifically, the agency that initiates a change, the "doer" of an action.

egoism   The doctrine that in conscious action one seeks (or ought to seek) self-interest above all else.

egoistic ethical hedonism   The theory that one ought to seek one's own pleasure above all else.

Eightfold Path   The way or practice recommended in Buddhism that includes: Right View, Right Aim, Right Speech, Right Action, Right Living, Right Effort, Right Mindfulness, and Right Contemplation.

emotivism   The theory that moral (and other) value judgments are expressions of emotions, attitudes, and feelings.

empiricism   The philosophy that all knowledge originates in sensory experience.

Epicureanism   The philosophy of followers of Epicurus, who believed that personal pleasure is the highest good but advocated renouncing momentary pleasures in favor of more lasting ones.

epicureanism   The practices of an epicure, one who has sensitive and discriminating tastes in food or wine.

epistemological detour   The attempt to utilize epistemological inquiry to arrive at meta-physical truths.

epistemology   The branch of philosophy concerned primarily with the nature and possibility of knowledge.

epoche   The suspension of judgment concerning the truth or falsity of a proposition. Edmund Husserl's *epoche* is the suspension of judgment regarding the being or nonbeing of the physical world and its objects, which he thought would open the way to a sighting of pure consciousness itself.

Equivalence Thesis   The idea that letting people die of starvation is as bad as killing them.

Esse est percipi   Latin for "to be is to be perceived," a doctrine that George Berkeley made the basis of his philosophy: Only that which is perceived exists. Berkeley held, however, that the minds that do the perceiving also exist.

eternal law   In the philosophy of Thomas Aquinas, the divine reason of God that rules over all things at all times.

ethical hedonism   The doctrine that you ought to seek pleasure over all else.

ethical naturalism   The belief that moral value judgments are really judgments of fact about the natural world.

ethical relativism   The theory that there are no absolute and universally valid moral standards and values and that therefore the moral standards and values that apply to you are merely those that are accepted by your society.

ethical skepticism   The doctrine that moral knowledge is not possible.

ethics   The branch of philosophy that considers the nature, criteria, sources, logic, and validity of moral value judgments.

ethnophilosophy   A systematically descriptive method of investigating the philosophical concepts that are important in a culture, especially a culture which is primarily transmitted through unwritten stories, rituals, and statements of belief.

evil demon conjecture   The conjecture used by Descartes that states: For all I know, an all-powerful "god" or demon has manipulated me so that all I take as true is in fact false.

existentialism   A tradition of twentieth-century philosophy having its roots in the nineteenth century but coming to flower in Europe after World War II. Of central concern is the question of how the individual is to find an authentic existence in this world, in which there is no ultimate reason why things happen one way and not another.

ex nihilo   Latin for "out of nothing."

extension   A property by which a thing occupies space; according to Descartes, the essential attribute of mind.

external relations   To believe that relations are external is to believe that a thing's relations to other things are not a part of the essence or nature of the related things.

fascism   The totalitarian political philosophy of the Mussolini government in Italy, which stressed the primacy of the state and leadership by an elite who embody the will and intelligence of the people. The term is sometimes more generally used for any totalitarian movement.

feminism   Movement in support of the view that men and women should have equal social value and status.

final cause   One of Aristotle's four kinds of causes—specifically, the ultimate purpose for which something happens.

first-order thinking   Thinking about a subject directly; contrasted with second-order thinking, which is thinking about discourse on the subject.

Form   In Plato's philosophy, that which is denoted by a general word, a word (such as "good") that applies to more than a single thing.

formal cause   For Aristotle, the form of a thing; that which answers the question "What is the thing?"

foundationalism   The doctrine that a belief qualifies as knowledge only if it logically follows from propositions that are incorrigible (incapable of being false if you believe that they are true).

Four Noble Truths   Buddha's answer to the central problem of life: (1) There is suffering; (2) suffering has specific and identifiable causes; (3) suffering can be ended; (4) the way to end suffering is through enlightened living, as expressed in the Eightfold Path.

free market economy   An economic system built around the belief that supply and demand, competition, and a free play of market forces best serve the interests of society and the common good.

functionalism   The doctrine that what a thing is must be understood and analyzed not by what it is made of but by its function. For example, anything that functions as a mousetrap is a mousetrap, regardless of what it is made of or how it looks or is assembled.

general will   In the philosophy of Jean-Jacques Rousseau, the will of a politically united people, the will of a state.

hedonism   The pursuit of pleasure.

Hellenistic age   The period of Macedonian domination of the Greek-speaking world, from around 335 B.C. to about 30 B.C.

hermeneutics   Interpretive understanding that seeks systematically to access the essence of things.

Hinduism   The Western word for the religious beliefs and practices of the majority of the people of India.

human law   In the philosophy of Thomas Aquinas, the laws and statutes of society that are derived from our understanding of natural law.

hypothetical imperative   An imperative that states what you ought to do if a certain end is desired.

Idea *See* **Form.**

idealism   The doctrine that only what is mental (thought, consciousness, perception) exists and that so-called physical things are manifestations of mind or thought.

identity theory   The theory that mental states and events are brain states and events.

incorrigibility   The property of a proposition that cannot be false if you believe it to be true.

individual relativism   The theory that what is right (and wrong) is what you believe is right (and wrong).

inductive argument   An argument whose premises are intended to provide reasons for accepting the conclusion as probable.

inductive generalization   An argument that attributes a characteristic of a sample of a group to all or most members of the group.

instrumental end   Something that is desirable as a means to an end, but is not desirable for its own sake.

instrumentalism   A theory held by John Dewey, among others, that ideas, judgments, and propositions are not merely true or false; rather, they are tools to understand experience and solve problems.

intentionality   The characteristic of consciousness that defines it as consciousness *of* something: it always points to or contains an object beyond itself.

interactionist dualism   The theory that the physical body and the nonphysical mind interact with each other.

intrinsic end   Something that is desirable for its own sake and not merely as a means to an end.

invisible-hand explanation   An explanation of a phenomenon as an unforeseen indirect consequence of action taken for some other purpose.

karma   The idea that your point of departure in life is determined by your decisions and deeds in earlier lives.

language game   The context in which an utterance is made, which determines the purposes served by the utterance and hence its meaning. Wittgenstein believed that philosophical problems are due to ignoring the "game" in which certain concepts are used.

Leviathan   The coiled snake or dragon in the Book of Job in the Bible. In the philosophy of Thomas Hobbes, "that mortal God, to which we owe our peace and defense"; that is, the state (or its sovereign) created by social contract.

liberalism   A political philosophy whose basic tenet is that each individual should have the maximum freedom consistent with the freedom of others.

libertarian   Someone who believes in free will; alternatively, someone who upholds the principles of liberty of thought and action.

logic   The study of the methods, principles, and criteria of correct reasoning.

logical atomism The metaphysical theory that the world does not consist of things but of facts, that is, things having certain properties and standing in certain relationships to one another. The ultimate facts are atomic in that they are logically independent of one another and are unresolvable into simpler facts; likewise, an empirically correct description of the world will consist ultimately of logically independent and unanalyzable atomic propositions that correspond to the atomic facts.

logical construction Xs are logical constructions out of Ys if statements about Xs could be replaced without loss of meaning by statements about Ys. For example, you could (theoretically) replace statements about the "average taxpayer" with statements about real-life, flesh-and-blood taxpayers; therefore, the average taxpayer is a logical construction out of real-life taxpayers.

logical positivism The philosophy of the Vienna Circle, according to which any purported statement of fact, if not a verbal truism, is meaningless unless certain conceivable observations would serve to confirm or deny it.

Marxism The socialist philosophy of Karl Marx, Friedrich Engels, and their followers that postulates the labor theory of value, the dialectical interplay of social institutions, class struggle, and dictatorship of the proletariat leading to a classless society.

material cause For Aristotle, the matter or stuff out of which something is made.

materialism The theory that only physical entities exist, and that so-called mental things are manifestations of an underlying physical reality.

means (forces) of production In Marxism, the means of producing the satisfaction of needs.

medieval philosophy Fourth through sixteenth centuries, approximately.

metaethics The philosophical investigation of the sources, criteria, meaning, verification, validation, and logical interrelationships of moral value judgments.

metaphysics The branch of philosophy that studies the nature and fundamental features of being.

modern philosophy Fifteenth through nineteenth centuries, approximately.

modified skeptic A skeptic who does not doubt that at least some things are known, but denies or suspends judgment on the possibility of knowledge about some particular subject.

monad From the Greek word meaning "unit." Pythagoras used the word to denote the first number of a series, and Gottfried Wilhelm von Leibniz used it to denote the unextended, simple, soullike basic elements of the universe.

monism One-ism; the philosophy that there is only one ultimate substance or type of thing. Materialism and idealism are both monistic theories.

moral argument for the existence of God The argument that maintains that morality, to be more than merely relative and contingent, must come from and be guaranteed by a supreme being, God.

moral imperative Distinguished by Kant from a hypothetical imperative, which holds conditionally (e.g., "If you desire health, then eat well!"), a moral imperative holds unconditionally (e.g., "Do your duty!").

moral judgment   A value judgment about what is morally right or wrong, good or bad, proper or improper.

naturalism   The doctrine that the universe is all there is and that physical laws are adequate to explain all its features.

naturalized epistemology   The view that the important epistemological problems are those that can be resolved by psychological investigation of the processes involved in acquiring and revising beliefs.

natural law   In the Stoic philosophy, a principle of rationality that infuses the universe, to which human behavior ought to conform; in the philosophy of Thomas Aquinas, God's eternal law as it applies to humans on earth and dictates the fundamental principles of morality; in ordinary English, a law of physical science.

natural right   A right thought to belong by nature to all human beings at all times and in all circumstances.

necessary being   A being whose nonexistence is impossible.

Neoplatonism   A further development of Platonic philosophy under the influence of Aristotelian and Pythagorean philosophy and Christian mysticism; it flourished between the third and sixth centuries. Neoplatonism stressed a mystical intuition of the highest One or God, a transcendent source of all being.

neutralism   The theory that existing things are neither mental nor physical; alternatively, the theory that each existing thing is both mental and physical.

neutral monism   The theory that mind and matter are reducible to or are manifestations of the same kind of thing, which itself is neither mental nor material.

nihil in intellectu quod prius non fuerit in sensu   Nothing is in the intellect that was not first in the senses; an epistemological principle formulated by Thomas Aquinas as an extrapolation of Aristotle's thinking.

nihilism   The rejection of values and beliefs.

nirvana   In Buddhism, the highest good; the extinction of will and of the accompanying ego, greed, anger, delusion, and clinging to existence. Achievement of nirvana means being freed from all future rebirths.

normative   Of, relating to, or prescribing norms or standards.

noumena   In the philosophy of Immanuel Kant, things as they are in themselves independent of all possible experience of them.

nous   A Greek word variously translated as "thinking," "mind," "reason," "spirit," and "intellect."

objective reality   The reality possessed by anything whose existence or characteristics do not depend on our consciousness of them.

objectivism   The theory that the universe and the things in it do not depend on our consciousness of them for their existence or characteristics.

occasionalism   A variant of parallelism according to which an act of willing your body to do something is the occasion for God to cause your body to do it.

Ockham's razor   The principle that, if you can fully explain something by making fewer assumptions, it's pointless to explain it by making more.

ontological argument   The argument that God's existence is entailed by the definition or concept of God.

original position   John Rawls's name for a hypothetical condition in which rational and unbiased individuals select the principles of social justice that govern a well-ordered society.

Pan-African philosophy   a cultural categorization of philosophical activity which includes the work of African thinkers and thinkers of African descent wherever they are located.

paradox of analysis   The problem that an analysis of a proposition must apparently either be incorrect or trivial.

paradox of hedonism   Henry Sidgwick's term for the fact that the desire for pleasure, if it is too strong, defeats its own aim.

parallelism   The doctrine that there are two parallel and coordinated series of events, one mental and the other physical, and that apparent causal interaction between the mind and the body is to be explained as a manifestation of the correlation between the two series.

perception   A modern word for what Thomas Hobbes called "sense," the basic mental activity from which all other mental phenomena are derived.

performative theory of truth   In the philosophy of P. F. Strawson, the theory that to assert that a proposition is true is to endorse it rather than to attribute a property to it.

phenomena   Things as they appear to us or, alternatively, the appearances themselves; in the philosophy of Immanuel Kant, objects as experienced and hence as organized and unified by the categories of the understanding and the forms of space and time.

phenomenalism   The theory that we only know phenomena; in analytic philosophy, the theory that propositions referring to physical objects can, in principle, be expressed in propositions referring only to sense-data.

phenomenological reduction   A method of putting aside the ordinary attitude toward the world and its objects in order to see the objects of pure consciousness through intuition.

phenomenology   A tradition of twentieth-century Continental philosophy based on the phenomenological method, which seeks rigorous knowledge not of things-in-themselves but rather of the structures of consciousness and of things as they appear to consciousness.

philosophical behaviorism   *See* **behaviorism.**

philosophy of mind   That area of analytic philosophy concerned with the nature of consciousness, mental states, the mind, and the proper analysis of everyday psychological vocabulary.

physicalism   Materialism.

physicalist reductivism   *See* **straightforward reductivist physicalism.**

political philosophy   The philosophical study of the state, its justification, and its ethically proper organization.

pragmatic theory of truth   In the philosophy of C. S. Peirce, a species of correspondence theory; in the philosophies of John Dewey and William James, a theory of justification, according to which (roughly) a belief may be accepted as true if it "works."

pragmatism   Philosophies that hold that the meaning of concepts lies in the difference they make to conduct and that the function of thought is to guide action.

prescriptive egoism   The doctrine that in all conscious action you ought to seek your self-interest above all else.

pre-Socratic philosophers   Greek philosophers who lived before Socrates.

***prima facie* duty**   In the philosophy of W. D. Ross, something it is your moral duty to do unless it is overridden by a higher moral duty.

principle of noncontradiction   The principle that a proposition and its contradictory cannot *both* be true and one or the other *must* be true.

principle of reason   An *a priori* principle.

principle of sufficient reason   The principle that there is a sufficient reason why things are exactly as they are and are not otherwise.

principle of the identity of indiscernibles   The principle according to which, if entity X and entity Y have exactly the same set of properties, then X = Y.

private language   In the philosophy of Ludwig Wittgenstein, a language that can be understood by only a single individual.

productive relations   In Marxism, social institutions and practices.

psychological hedonism   The theory that pleasure is the object of a person's desire.

Pyrrhonism   A school of philosophical skepticism initiated by Pyrrho of Elis (c. 360–270 B.C.) whose members advocated suspending judgment on all issues.

rationalism   The epistemological theory that reason is either the sole or primary source of knowledge; in practice, most rationalists maintain merely that at least some truths are not known solely on the basis of sensory experience.

realism   The theory that universals exist outside the mind. Also the theory that the real world is independent of the mind.

reduction   Another word for analysis.

***reductio* proof**   Proving a proposition by showing that its nonacceptance would involve an absurdity.

relativism   *See* **descriptive relativism** and **ethical relativism.**

representationalism   The doctrine that true beliefs are accurate representations of the state of affairs they are about.

representative realism   The theory that we perceive objects indirectly by means of representations (ideas, perceptions) of them.

rule-utilitarianism   A form of utilitarianism (subscribed to by Mill) in which the rightness of an act is determined by the impact on the general happiness of the rule or principle the action exemplifies.

samurai   The warrior aristocracy of Japan.

second-order thinking   *See* **first-order thinking.**

sense-data   That which you are immediately aware of in sensory experience; the contents of awareness.

sexism   Attitudes and social practices that foster rigid roles based on gender and which tend to work to the detriment of women.

skeptic   One who questions or suspends judgment on the possibility of knowledge.

Skepticism   A school of philosophy that emerged in the Hellenistic and Roman periods after Plato; included the Academics and the Pyrrhonists.

skepticism   The doctrine that true knowledge is uncertain or impossible.

social contract   An agreement among individuals forming an organized society or between the community and the ruler that defines the rights and duties of each.

socialism   The theory that communal ownership of land, capital, and the means of production is the best way of serving the common good.

social philosophy   The philosophical study of society and its institutions; concerned especially with determining the features of the ideal or best society.

Stoicism   The ethical philosophy of the ancient Greek Stoics, who emphasized the serene or untroubled life as the highest good and thought it best reached through acceptance of the natural order of things.

stoicism   The practice of a stoic, one who is indifferent to pleasure and pain.

straightforward reductivist physicalism   The theory that all true propositions can, in principle, be expressed in the language of physics.

subjectivism   In ethics, the doctrine that what is right is determined by what people believe is right; elsewhere, the theory that limits knowledge to conscious states.

tabula rasa   Latin for "blank tablet"; also, John Locke's metaphor for the condition of the mind prior to the imprint of sensory experience.

tacit consent   An implied rather than explicit consent, as, for example, when you consent to the laws of your state by continuing to live in it.

Tao   In Chinese philosophy, the Way: the ultimate and eternal principle of unity, meaning, and harmony in the universe.

Taoism   One of the great philosophical traditions in China, according to which the individual will find peace and tranquility through quietly following the Tao.

teleological argument   *See* **argument from design.**

teleological explanation   An explanation of a thing in terms of its ends, goals, purposes, or functions.

Ten Tropes   A collection of ten arguments by the Skeptics against the possibility of knowledge.

theoretical posits   Entities whose existence we hypothesize in order to explain our sensory experience.

thing-in-itself   English for *Ding-an-sich:* a thing as it is independent of any consciousness of it.

Third Man argument   Aristotle's criticism of Plato's Theory of Forms, according to which there must be a third thing that ties together a Form with the particular things that exemplify it.

thought   According to Descartes, the essential attribute of mind.

total skeptic   One who maintains nothing can be known or, alternatively, suspends judgment in all matters.

transcendental phenomenology   An epistemological method that seeks the certainty of a pure consciousness of objects in the transcendental ego.

universal   That which is denoted by a general word, a word (such as "chair") that applies to more than a single thing.

universalistic ethical hedonism   The doctrine that one ought to seek, over everything else, the greatest pleasure for the greatest number of people.

universal phenomenology of consciousness   Attempts made by Hegel and Husserl to devise a pure science of knowing.

utilitarianism   The doctrine that the rightness of an action is identical with the happiness it produces as its consequence.

value judgment   A proposition that explicitly or implicitly assigns a value to something.

veil of ignorance   In Indian philosophy, the perspective from which the world is viewed as a multiplicity of things; also, John Rawls's metaphor for the conditions under which rational individuals are to select the principles of justice that govern the well-ordered society.

verifiability criterion (theory) of meaning   The dictum that a sentence must express something verifiable if it is to express an empirically meaningful statement.

verifiability principle   *See* **verifiability criterion of meaning.**

Vienna Circle   A group of philosophers and scientists centered at the University of Vienna in the 1920s and 1930s who espoused logical positivism.

virtue ethics   Ethical theories according to which what I ought to do is what the virtuous person would do. For virtue ethics, the primary question is, What kind of person ought I to be?

Way, the   *See* **Tao.**

Zen Buddhism   A form of Buddhism that reached its zenith in China and later developed in Japan, Korea, and the West. Its name (Chinese *Ch'an,* Japanese *Zen*) derives from the Sanskrit *dhyana* (meditation). In early China, the central tenet of Zen Buddhism was meditation rather than adherence to a particular scripture.

Credits

Photo and Illustration Credits

Cartoons: Kevin Opstedal. **Pages 22–23** © The Royal Photographic Society, Bath, England. **Page 41** © The Bettmann Archive. **Page 43** Pen and ink drawing by Nina Rosenstand. **Pages 45, 55, 58, 80** © The Bettmann Archive. **Page 93** Detail from *Young Woman with a Letter,* Samuel van Hoogstraeten (1627–1678), from the collection of Mauritshuis, The Hague, The Netherlands. Reproduced in Peter Lopston, ed., *The Principles of the Most Ancient and Modern Philosophy,* by Anne Conway. The Hague: Martinus Nijhoff, 1982. **Pages 97, 100, 101, 118, 125, 131, 134, 141** © The Bettmann Archive. **Page 144** Courtesy of the Master and Fellows of Trinity College, Cambridge. **Page 160** © The Bettmann Archive. **Pages 174–175** © Erich Lessing/ Art Resource. **Page 207** Reprinted from *Hildegard of Bingen's Book of Divine Works,* edited by Matthew Fox, illustrations by Angela Werneke, copyright 1987 Bear & Co., Santa Fe, NM. **Pages 210, 237** © The Bettmann Archive. **Pages 282–283** © Hiroyuki Matsumoto/Tony Stone Images. **Pages 301, 307** © The Bettmann Archive. **Page 308** © National Portrait Gallery, Archive Engravings Collection; Neg. no. 47398. **Pages 316, 321, 345** © The Bettmann Archive. **Pages 383, 386** © UPI/The Bettmann Archive. **Pages 420–421** Laura Gilpin, *Storm from La Bajada Hill,* New Mexico, 1946, gelatin silver print, P1979. 95.96. Copyright 1981. Laura Gilpin Collection. Amon Carter Museum, Fort Worth, Texas. **Pages 429,** **471** © The Bettmann Archive. **Pages 494–495** Ralph Morse, Life Magazine, © 1954 Time Inc. **Pages 532–533** © Jerry Uelsmann. **Pages 537, 539** © The Bettmann Archive. **Pages 545, 552** © UPI/The Bettmann Archive. **Page 560** © The Bettmann Archive. **Pages 584–585** © Tony Stone Images. **Pages 589, 608** © The Bettmann Archive. **Page 666** © UPI/The Bettmann Archive. **Page 672** Courtesy the University of Colorado, Boulder. **Page 677** © UPI/ The Bettmann Archive. **Page 680** © Donna Dietrich. **Page 686** © Stephen Shames/Matrix. **Pages 701, 705** © UPI/The Bettmann Archive.

Text Credits

Page 66 Reprinted by permission of the publishers and the Loeb Classical Library from *Sextus Empiricus: Outlines of Pyrrhonism,* Vol. 1, translated by R. G. Bury, Cambridge, Mass.: Harvard University Press, 1933. **Pages 83, 87, 439** Excerpts from René Descartes, *The Philosophical Works of Descartes,* E. S. Haldane and G. R. T. Ross, trans. Copyright 1968 Cambridge University Press. Reprinted with the permission of Cambridge University Press. **Pages 129, 453** Copyright © 1969 by St. Martin's Press, Inc. From *Immanuel Kant's Critique of Pure Reason,* translated by Norman Kemp Smith. Reprinted by permission of St. Martin's Press, Inc. **Page 152** From C. H. Whiteley, *An Introduction to Metaphysics,* Methuen & Co., Ltd., London, 1950. Reprinted by permission of Methuen & Co., Ltd. **Page 161** From *Objectivity, Rel-* *ativism and Truth* by Richard Rorty. Copyright © 1990 Richard Rorty. Reprinted with the permission of Cambridge University Press. **Page 163** From *The Review of Metaphysics,* vol. 46, pp. 717–45. Reprinted with permission. **Page 199** *Epicurus: The Extant Remains,* trans. Cyril Bailey (1926). Reprinted by permission of Oxford University Press. **Page 200** Reprinted by permission of the publishers and the Loeb Classical Library from *Epictetus: The Discourses,* Vol. II, translated by W. A. Oldfather, Cambridge, Mass.: Harvard University Press, 1925. **Page 204** From Augustine, *The Works of Aurelius Augustine,* ed. M. Dods, by permission of T. and T. Clark Ltd., Edinburgh. **Page 212** From Aquinas's *Summa Contra Gentiles,* published by Benziger Publishing Company, 1928. **Page 233** From *Kant: Foundations of the Metaphysics of Morals,* 2e, trans. Lewis White Beck, pp. 39–42. Reprinted by permission of Prentice Hall, Upper Saddle River, New Jersey. **Page 243** From *Beyond Good and Evil* by Friedrich Nietzsche, trans. by Walter Kaufmann. Copyright © 1966 by Random House, Inc. Reprinted by permission of Random House, Inc. **Page 250** From George E. Moore's *Principia Ethica.* Copyright Cambridge University Press. Reprinted with the permission of Cambridge University Press. **Page 256** Reprinted from *Language, Truth and Logic,* by A. J. Ayer, Dover Publications. Reprinted by permission. **Pages 258, 554** From *Existentialism and Humanism* by Jean-Paul Sartre. Deanna Stein McMahon, trans. Les Editions Nagel and Methuen & Co.

Index

	1000	1400	1450	1500	1550	1600	1650

Part 1
Metaphysics and Epistemology

—— St. Thomas Aquinas (1225–1274)
—— Julian of Norwich (1342–1414)
Oliva Sabuco de Nantes (b. 1562) •
Anne Finch Conway (1631–1679) ——
Re

Part 2
Ethics

—— Hildegard von Bingen (1098–1179)
—— Heloise (1100/1–1163)
—— St. Thomas Aquinas (1225–1274)

Part 3
Political Philosophy

—— St. Thomas Aquinas (1225–1274)
Niccolò Machiavelli (1469–1527) Catharine Trotter Cockburn (1
Thomas Hobbes (1588–1679) ——
Charles Louis de Secondat, Baron Montesqui

Part 4
Philosophy of Religion

—— St. Anselm (c. 1033–1109)
—— St. Thomas Aquinas (1225–1274)
• Gaunilo (eleventh century)
—— Julian of Norwich (1342–1414)
Re

Part 5
Philosophy of Mind

Oliva Sabuco de Nantes (b. 1562) •
Re

Part 6
Continental Philosophy

Part 7
Eastern and Post-Colonial Philosophy

—— Murasaki Shikibu (970–1031)
—— Avicenna (980–1037)
—— Al-Ghazālī (1058–1111)
—— Averroës (1126–1198)
—— Dogen Zenji (1200–1253)
Sadr al-
Yagy
Miyar

• Al-Kindi (d. after 870)
—— Al Fārābī (875–950)

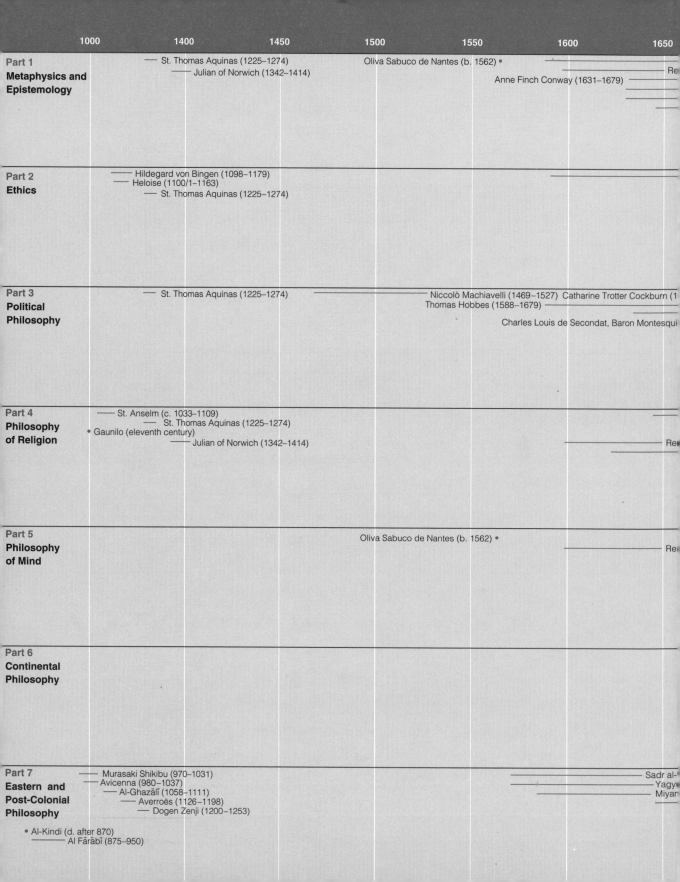